THE BLACKWELL ENCYCLOPAEDIA OF
ANGLO-SAXON
ENGLAND

Edited by
MICHAEL LAPIDGE,
JOHN BLAIR, SIMON KEYNES and DONALD SCRAGG

BLACKWELL
Publishers

© 1999, 2001 by Blackwell Publishing Ltd
'Animal Husbandry' © 1999, 2001 by Sebastian Payne

BLACKWELL PUBLISHING
350 Main Street, Malden, MA 02148-5020, USA
9600 Garsington Road, Oxford OX4 2DQ, UK
550 Swanston Street, Carlton, Victoria 3053, Australia

First published 1999
First published in paperback 2001

5   2005

Library of Congress Cataloging-in-Publication Data

The Blackwell encyclopaedia of Anglo-Saxon England / edited by Michael
  Lapidge; with John Blair, Simon Keynes, and Donald Scragg.
       p.cm.
  Includes bibliographical references.
  ISBN 0-631-15565-1 (hardbound: alk. paper) ISBN 0-631-22492-0 (pbk)
    1. Great Britain—History—Anglo–Saxon period, 449–1066—
Encyclopedias.   2. England—Civilization—To 1066—Encyclopedias.
  I. Lapidge, Michael.
  DA152.B58   1998
  942.01—dc21   98–20814
                                                                    CIP

ISBN-13: 978-0-631-15565-2 (hardbound: alk. paper) ISBN-13: 978-0-631-22492-1 (pbk)

A catalogue record for this title is available from the British Library.

Set in 9 on 10.5 pt Ehrhardt
by Intype London Ltd
Printed and bound in the United Kingdom
by TJ International, Padstow, Cornwall

The publisher's policy is to use permanent paper from mills that operate a sustainable
forestry policy, and which has been manufactured from pulp processed using acid-
free and elementary chlorine-free practices. Furthermore, the publisher ensures that
the text paper and cover board used have met acceptable environmental accreditation
standards.

For further information on
Blackwell Publishing, visit our website:
www.blackwellpublishing.com

CONTENTS

ILLUSTRATIONS

Plates

Maps

Figures

LIST OF CONTRIBUTORS

Richard Abels, United States Naval Academy, Annapolis, Maryland

Grenville Astill, University of Reading

Mark Atherton, Regents Park College, Oxford

Richard N. Bailey, University of Newcastle

Peter S. Baker, University of Virginia

Debby Banham, Newnham College, Cambridge

Julia Barrow, University of Nottingham

Martha Bayless, University of Oregon

Alex Bayliss, University College, London

Paul Bibire, University of Cambridge

Martin Biddle, Hertford College, Oxford

Carole Biggam, University of Glasgow

M. A. S. Blackburn, The Fitzwilliam Museum, Cambridge

John Blair, The Queen's College, Oxford

C. J. Bond, Walton-in-Gordano (Somerset)

Martin Brett, Robinson College, Cambridge

Mark Brisbane, University of Bournemouth

Nicholas Brooks, University of Birmingham

Kevin Brown, English Heritage, Bristol

Michelle P. Brown, The British Library, London

Esther Cameron, Institute of Archaeology, Oxford

Laurence Cameron, University of Halifax

James P. Carley, York University, Toronto

Martin Carver, University of York

Mary Clayton, University College, Dublin

Simon Esmonde Cleary, University of Birmingham

Elizabeth Coatsworth, Manchester Metropolitan University

Julie Coleman, University of Leicester

H. E. J. Cowdrey, St Edmund Hall, Oxford

Barrie Cox, University of Nottingham

Rosemary Cramp, University of Durham

Sally Crawford, University of Birmingham

John Crook, Winchester

C. R. E. Cubitt, University of York

Maria Amalia D'Aronco, University of Udine

R. J. Darrah, Hodnet (Shropshire)

Robert DiNapoli, University of Birmingham

Tania M. Dickinson, University of York

Nicole Guenther Discenza, University of Notre Dame

Daniel Donoghue, Harvard University

Rosamond Faith, Finstock (Oxon.)

Dora Faraci, University of Aquila

Gillian Fellows-Jensen, University of Copenhagen

Sarah Foot, University of Sheffield

Paul Fouracre, Goldsmiths College, London

P. J. Fowler, University of Newcastle

Allen J. Frantzen, Loyola University

Richard Gameson, University of Kent

George Garnett, St Hugh's College, Oxford

Mary Garrison, University of Utrecht

Richard Gem, Cathedrals Commission, London

Helen Gittos, The Queen's College, Oxford

Malcolm Godden, Pembroke College, Oxford

Diana E. Greenway, Institute of Historical Research, London

Mechthild Gretsch, University of Munich

Michael Gullick, The Red Gull Press

R. A. Hall, York Archaeological Trust

Thomas N. Hall, University of Illinois at Chicago

Helena Hamerow, University of Oxford

Paul Antony Hayward, Jesus College, Oxford

Isabel Henderson, Newnham College, Cambridge

T. A. Heslop, University of East Anglia

John Higgitt, University of Edinburgh

N. J. Higham, University of Manchester

Joyce Hill, University of Leeds

Terry Hoad, St Peter's College, Oxford

Philip Holdsworth, Archaeology Section, Cumbria County Council, Kendal

Stephanie Hollis, University of Auckland

Carole Hough, University of Glasgow

Gillian Hutchinson, National Maritime Museum, Greenwich

George Jack, University of St Andrews

Rohini Jayatilaka, Pembroke College, Oxford

Joy Jenkyns, St Edmund Hall, Oxford

S. E. Kelly, Portsmouth

Alan Kennedy, University of Sydney

Simon Keynes, Trinity College, Cambridge

Birthe Kjølbye-Biddle, Oxford

Anne L. Klinck, University of New Brunswick

Lucia Kornexl, University of Munich

Michael Lapidge, Clare College, Cambridge

Vivien Law, Trinity College, Cambridge

Graeme Lawson, Corpus Christi College, Cambridge

M. K. Lawson, St Paul's School, London

Patrizia Lendinara, University of Palermo

R. M. Liuzza, Tulane University

R. C. Love, Robinson College, Cambridge

K. A. Lowe, University of Glasgow

Peter J. Lucas, University College, Dublin

Niels Lund, University of Copenhagen

Arthur MacGregor, The Ashmolean Museum, Oxford

Patrick McGurk, Birkbeck College, London

Helen McKee, Oxford

Keith Manchester, Bradford

Richard Marsden, University of Leeds

Audrey Meaney, Cambridge

Sean Miller, Fitzwilliam Museum, Cambridge

Bruce Mitchell, St Edmund Hall, Oxford

Marco Mostert, University of Utrecht

Janet Nelson, King's College, London

Máire Ní Mhaonaigh, St John's College, Cambridge

William Noel, Walters Art Gallery, Baltimore

Katherine O'Brien O'Keeffe, University of Notre Dame

Éamonn Ó Carragáin, University College, Cork

Andy Orchard, Emmanuel College, Cambridge

Gale R. Owen-Crocker, University of Manchester

O. J. Padel, Peterhouse, Cambridge

R. I. Page, Corpus Christi College, Cambridge

David Park, Courtauld Institute of Art, London

David Parsons, University of Leicester

Sebastian Payne, Ancient Monuments Laboratory, London

David A. E. Pelteret, University of Toronto

Richard W. Pfaff, University of North Carolina at Chapel Hill

Kathryn Powell, University of Notre Dame

David Pratt, Emmanuel College, Cambridge

Phillip Pulsiano, Villanova University

Oliver Rackham, Corpus Christi College, Cambridge

Philip Rahtz, University of York

Susan Rankin, Emmanuel College, Cambridge

Christine Rauer, Corpus Christi College, Oxford

Barbara C. Raw, Oxford

Roger E. Ray, University of Toledo

Paul G. Remley, University of Washington

Charlotte A. Roberts, University of Bradford

Jane Roberts, King's College, London

David Rollason, University of Durham

Susan Rosser, University of Manchester

Donald Scragg, University of Manchester

Richard Sharpe, Wadham College, Oxford

Alice Sheppard, Cornell University

Jeremy J. Smith, University of Glasgow

Pauline Stafford, University of Huddersfield

Wesley M. Stevens, University of Winnipeg

Matthew Stiff, Oxford

Alan Thacker, Victoria History of the Counties of England, London

Rodney M. Thomson, University of Tasmania

David E. Thornton, Bilkent University, Ankara

Elaine M. Treharne, University of Leicester

Elisabeth van Houts, Emmanuel College, Cambridge

Alan Vince, City of Lincoln Archaeology Unit, Lincoln

Keith Wade, Bury St Edmunds

Lorna Watts, Harome (Yorks.)

Leslie Webster, The British Museum, London

Jonathan Wilcox, University of Iowa

Ann Williams, Wanstead, London

Tom Williamson, University of East Anglia

D. R. Wilson, University of Keele

Ian Wood, University of Leeds

Patrick Wormald, Christ Church, Oxford

Margaret Worthington, University of Manchester

Charles D. Wright, University of Illinois at Urbana-Champaign

B. A. E. Yorke, King Alfred's College, Winchester

S. M. Youngs, The British Museum, London

PREFACE

The past generation has seen enormous advances in all aspects of Anglo-Saxon studies. Archaeology has brought to light hundreds of sites and thousands upon thousands of artifacts (including countless coins, which often provide indispensable evidence for dating) and revolutionary new techniques have evolved to assist the analysis of this unfathomable wealth of evidence; architectural historians have identified innumerable new buildings, secular and ecclesiastical; refinements in palaeographical method have made it possible for the first time to identify, list and date all the manuscripts likely to have been written or owned in Anglo-Saxon England; historians have developed and perfected new skills in analysing the surviving documentary evidence; many new Anglo-Latin authors and texts have been discovered; and even the relatively stable corpus of literature in Old English has undergone waves of reassessment as new critical approaches gain ascendancy. The burgeoning of knowledge – and *ipso facto* the vitality of the subject – are witnessed by that fact that each year some 1,000 publications are recorded in the annual bibliography, covering all aspects of the subject, which is printed in *Anglo-Saxon England*. The time has long passed when any professional scholar, let alone layman, could expect to control the whole of the field of Anglo-Saxon studies; and so vast is the secondary literature in any particular field that hardly anyone is in a position to keep up with it. Growing specialization in individual fields has meant that it is increasingly difficult to find even basic bibliographical orientation in ancillary disciplines.

The need for a single handbook which would provide such orientation has long been felt. Some fifteen years ago, Blackwell Publishers took steps to address the need by establishing an editorial committee under the direction of R. I. Page, with the aim of producing a single-volume companion to all aspects of Anglo-Saxon studies. The editorial board consisted (at various times) of R. I. Page as general editor, together with Catherine Hills, Christine Fell, Simon Keynes, Malcolm Godden, Fred Robinson and myself. Many hours' work went into devising a list of head-words, drawing up guidelines for contributors, drafting specimen entries, and commissioning articles from specialists. Although many invitations were sent out to contributors in 1984–5, and although a number of contributions was received, the project faltered, perhaps because of its comprehensive scope, perhaps because the editors had underestimated the amount of energy which would be required to see it to completion.

A number of years later, on the occasion of the ISAS meeting in Oxford (July 1993), I happened to find myself in conversation with John Davey (then chief editor of Blackwell Publishers, and one of the initiators of the original conception of a companion to Anglo-Saxon studies). We reiterated our mutual conviction that the conception of the single-volume companion was an excellent one, and lamented that it had been abandoned. After some discussion I agreed to try to resuscitate the project, on the condition that a new editorial team could be appointed, which would have the single-minded determination necessary to see the project through to completion.

That the book stands complete is due to the determination and dedication of my three co-editors: John Blair, Simon Keynes and Donald Scragg. It would be difficult to find three more energetic and dedicated scholars anywhere in the field of Anglo-Saxon studies. Although I have borne the responsibility for the general administration, in other respects the burden of editorial responsibility has been quadripartite, and the exhilaration of working together has been rewarding for all of us. We have had excellent support from Blackwell's: in particular from John Davey, Tessa Harvey, Sarah Howlett and Thelma Gilbert. We gratefully acknowledge our debt to the original editorial team: without their groundwork, the project would have been even more time-consuming than it has been. Lastly, we are grateful to all of the 150 contributors for their patience in dealing with our requests for clarification and revision: their unhesitating willingness to participate in a project of this kind is another sign of the vitality of the subject. We all – contributors and editors – want the book to serve the purpose for which it was conceived: that of providing orientation and guidance in ancillary disciplines within the field as a whole. We could not expect that an expert (say) on Anglo-Latin will find revolutionary new insights in the articles pertaining to Gildas or the *Historia Brittonum*; the more important criterion is whether an archaeologist might find helpful bibliographical orientation in these articles, and whether the expert in Anglo-Latin will be stimulated by articles on less familiar matters – agriculture, for example, or codicology, mining, surgery, or whatever. Taken as a whole, the book provides eloquent testimony to the range and interest of Anglo-Saxon studies today, and as editors we hope that it will maintain and stimulate the interdisciplinary approach which has invigorated the field for the past generation.

MICHAEL LAPIDGE
(for the Editors)
January 1998

The editors and publishers wish to acknowledge that the article on 'Music' was co-authored by Graeme Lawson and Susan Rankin. The full attribution was mistakenly excluded from the first impression of this volume.

LIST OF ABBREVIATIONS

AB	*Analecta Bollandiana.*
Acta SS.	*Acta Sanctorum*, ed. J. Bolland *et al.* (Antwerp and Brussels, 1643–).
Æthelwold	*Bishop Æthelwold: His Career and Influence*, ed. B. Yorke (Woodbridge, 1988).
AJ	*Antiquaries Journal.*
Alexander, *Insular MSS*	J.J.G. Alexander, *Insular Manuscripts, 6th to the 9th Century* (London, 1978).
Alfred the Great	*Alfred the Great. Asser's Life of King Alfred and other Contemporary Sources*, trans. S. Keynes and M. Lapidge (Harmondsworth, 1983).
ANS	*Anglo-Norman Studies.*
ASC	*The Anglo-Saxon Chronicle*, ed. C. Plummer, *Two of the Saxon Chronicles Parallel*, 2 vols. (Oxford, 1892–9); trans. D. Whitelock *et al.*, *The Anglo-Saxon Chronicle: a Revised Translation* (London, 1961).
ASE	*Anglo-Saxon England.*
ASPR	The Anglo-Saxon Poetic Records, ed. G. P. Krapp and E. V. K. Dobbie, 6 vols. (New York, 1931–42).
ASSAH	*Anglo-Saxon Studies in Archaeology and History.*
BAR	British Archaeological Reports.
Bassett, *Origins*	*The Origins of Anglo-Saxon Kingdoms*, ed. S. Bassett (London, 1989).
Bately FS	*Alfred the Wise. Studies in Honour of Janet Bately on the Occasion of her sixty-fifth Birthday*, ed. J. Roberts *et al.* (Cambridge, 1997).
BCS	W. de G. Birch, *Cartularium Saxonicum*, 3 vols. plus index (London, 1885–99).
BEC	*Bibliothèque de l'École des Chartes.*
BHL	*Bibliotheca Hagiographica Latina*, 2 vols. (Brussels, 1899–1901), with *Supplementum* by H. Fros (Brussels, 1986).
Blair, *AS Oxon*	J. Blair, *Anglo-Saxon Oxfordshire* (Stroud, 1994).
Blair and Sharpe, *Past. Care*	*Pastoral Care before the Parish*, ed. J. Blair and R. Sharpe (Leicester, 1992).
BL	London, British Library.
BLJ	*British Library Journal.*
BN	Paris, Bibliothèque Nationale.
Bolton, *ALL*	W.F. Bolton, *A History of Anglo-Latin Literature* i. *597–740* (Princeton, NJ, 1967).
Brooks, *Canterbury*	N. Brooks, *The Early History of the Church of Canterbury* (Leicester, 1984).
Butler and Morris, *AS Church*	L. A. S. Butler and R. K. Morris (ed.), *The Anglo-Saxon Church: Papers on History, Architecture and Archaeology in Honour of Dr H.M. Taylor* (London, 1986).
CamComp	*The Cambridge Companion to Old English Literature*, ed. M. Godden and M. Lapidge (Cambridge, 1991).

Campbell, *Essays*	J. Campbell, *Essays in Anglo-Saxon History* (London, 1986).
CASSS	Corpus of Anglo-Saxon Stone Sculpture.
CCCC	Corpus Christi College, Cambridge.
CCSL	Corpus Christianorum, Series Latina.
CHELang	Cambridge History of the English Language.
CLA	*Codices Latini Antiquiores*, ed. E.A. Lowe, 11 vols. and supp. (Oxford, 1934–71; 2nd ed. of vol. ii, 1972).
Clemoes FS	*Learning and Literature in Anglo-Saxon England. Studies presented to Peter Clemoes*, ed. M. Lapidge and H. Gneuss (Cambridge, 1985).
CMCS	*Cambridge* [later: *Cambrian*] *Medieval Celtic Studies*.
Councils & Synods	*Councils & Synods with other Documents relating to the English Church* I. *AD 871–1204*, ed. D. Whitelock, M. Brett and C. N. L. Brooke, 2 vols. (Oxford, 1981).
CSASE	Cambridge Studies in Anglo-Saxon England.
Cuthbert	*St Cuthbert, his Cult and his Community to AD 1200*, ed. G. Bonner, D. Rollason and C. Stancliffe (Woodbridge, 1989).
DACL	*Dictionnaire d'archéologie chrétienne et de liturgie*, ed. F. Cabrol and H. Leclercq, 15 vols. in 30 (Paris, 1907–53).
DHGE	*Dictionnaire d'histoire et de géographie ecclésiastiques*, ed. A. Baudrillart (Paris, 1912–).
Dornier, *MS*	A. Dornier (ed.), *Mercian Studies* (Leicester, 1977).
Dumville, *Britons*	D. N. Dumville, *Britons and Anglo-Saxons in the Early Middle Ages* (Aldershot, 1993).
Dumville, *Histories*	D. N. Dumville, *Histories and Pseudo-histories of the Insular Middle Ages* (Aldershot, 1990).
Dumville, *Wessex*	D. N. Dumville, *Wessex and England from Alfred to Edgar* (Woodbridge, 1992).
Dunstan	*St Dunstan, his Life, Times and Cult*, ed. N. Ramsay, M. Sparks and T. Tatton-Brown (Woodbridge, 1992).
EEMF	Early English Manuscripts in Facsimile.
EETS	Early English Text Society.
—, os	—, original series.
—, ss	—, supplementary series.
EHD i	D. Whitelock, *English Historical Documents* i. *c.500–1042*, 2nd ed. (London, 1979).
EHD ii	D.C. Douglas, *English Historical Documents* ii. *1042–1189*, 2nd ed. (London, 1981).
EHR	*English Historical Review*.
ELN	*English Language Notes*.
EME	*Early Medieval Europe*.
ES	*English Studies*.
Fernie, *Architecture*	E. Fernie, *The Architecture of the Anglo-Saxons* (London, 1983).
Frank – Cameron	*A Plan for the Dictionary of Old English*, ed. R. Frank and A. Cameron (Toronto, 1973).
Freeman, *NC*	E. A. Freeman, *History of the Norman Conquest*, 6 vols. (Oxford, 1867–79).

LIST OF ABBREVIATIONS

Golden Age of AS Art	*The Golden Age of Anglo-Saxon Art*, ed. J. Backhouse, D. H. Turner and L. Webster (London, 1984).
Gneuss FS	*Words, Texts and Manuscripts. Studies in Anglo-Saxon Culture presented to Helmut Gneuss*, ed. M. Korhammer (Cambridge, 1992).
H&S, *Councils*	*Councils and Ecclesiastical Documents relating to Great Britain and Ireland*, ed. A. W. Haddan and W. Stubbs, 3 vols. (Oxford, 1869–78).
Hart, *Danelaw*	C. Hart, *The Danelaw* (London, 1992).
Haslam, *Towns*	J. Haslam, *Anglo-Saxon Towns in Southern England* (Chichester, 1984).
HBS	Henry Bradshaw Society Publications.
HE	*Historia ecclesiastica.*
Hill, *Atlas*	D. Hill, *An Atlas of Anglo-Saxon England* (Oxford, 1981).
Hill and Rumble, *The Defence of Wessex*	D. Hill and A. R. Rumble (ed.), *The Defence of Wessex: the Burghal Hidage and Anglo-Saxon Fortifications* (Manchester, 1996).
HSJ	*Haskins Society Journal.*
JBAA	*Journal of the British Archaeological Association.*
JBS	*Journal of British Studies.*
JEGP	*Journal of English and Germanic Philology.*
JEH	*Journal of Ecclesiastical History.*
JMH	*Journal of Medieval History.*
JTS	*Journal of Theological Studies.*
JW	John of Worcester, *Chronica chronicarum*, ed. R. R. Darlington and P. McGurk (OMT, 1995–).
JWCI	*Journal of the Warburg and Courtauld Institutes.*
Ker, *Catalogue*	N. R. Ker, *Catalogue of Manuscripts containing Anglo-Saxon* (Oxford, 1957).
Kirby, *Kings*	D. P. Kirby, *The Earliest English Kings* (London, 1991).
Lapidge, *ALL* i	M. Lapidge, *Anglo-Latin Literature 600–899* (London, 1996).
Lapidge, *ALL* ii	M. Lapidge, *Anglo-Latin Literature 900–1066* (London, 1993).
Liebermann, *Gesetze*	F. Liebermann, *Die Gesetze der Angelsachsen*, 3 vols. (Halle, 1903–16).
Loyn, *Governance*	H. R. Loyn, *The Governance of Anglo-Saxon England 500–1087* (London, 1984).
LSE	*Leeds Studies in English.*
MÆ	*Medium Ævum.*
MArch	*Medieval Archaeology.*
Making of England	*The Making of England. Anglo-Saxon Art and Culture* AD *600–900*, ed. L. Webster and J. Backhouse (London, 1991).
Memorials, ed. Stubbs	*Memorials of St Dunstan*, ed. W. Stubbs, RS (London, 1874).
MGH	Monumenta Germaniae Historica.
—, AA	—, Auctores Antiquissimi.
—, Epist.	—, Epistolae (in quarto).
—, ES	—, Epistolae Selectae.
—, PLAC	—, Poetae Latini Aevi Carolini.
—, SS	—, Scriptores (in folio).
MidH	*Midland History.*

MLN	*Modern Language Notes.*
MP	*Modern Philology.*
MS	*Mediaeval Studies.*
NA	*Neues Archiv.*
Nelson, *Politics*	J. L. Nelson, *Politics and Ritual in Early Medieval Europe* (London, 1986).
NH	*Northern History.*
NM	*Neuphilologische Mitteilungen.*
OE	Old English.
OEN	*Old English Newsletter.*
Ohlgren	T. H. Ohlgren, *Insular and Anglo-Saxon Illuminated Manuscripts: an Iconographic Catalogue c. AD 625 to 1100* (Binghamton, NY, 1986).
OMT	Oxford Medieval Texts.
Oswald of Worcester	*St Oswald of Worcester: Life and Influence*, ed. N. Brooks and C. Cubitt (London, 1996).
P&P	*Past & Present.*
PBA	*Proceedings of the British Academy.*
PL	Patrologia Latina, ed. J.-P. Migne, 221 vols. (Paris, 1844–64).
Plummer, *VBOH*	*Venerabilis Baedae Opera Historica*, ed. C. Plummer, 2 vols. (Oxford, 1896).
PMLA	*Publications of the Modern Language Association of America.*
RB	*Revue Bénédictine.*
RES	*Review of English Studies.*
RS	Rolls Series.
Rumble, *Cnut*	*The Reign of Cnut, King of England, Denmark and Norway*, ed. A. R. Rumble (London, 1994).
S	P. H. Sawyer, *Anglo-Saxon Charters. An Annotated List and Bibliography* (London, 1968) [cited by document no.].
Sawyer FS	*People and Places in Northern Europe 500–1600. Essays in Honour of Peter Hayes Sawyer*, ed. I. Wood and N. Lund (Woodbridge, 1991).
Settimane	*Settimane di studio del Centro italiano di studi sull'alto medioevo.*
Sharpe, *Handlist*	R. Sharpe, *A Handlist of the Latin Writers of Great Britain and Ireland before 1540* (Turnhout, 1997).
SM	*Studi medievali.*
SN	*Studia Neophilologica.*
SP	*Studies in Philology.*
Stafford, *Unification*	P. Stafford, *Unification and Conquest. A Political and Social History of England in the Tenth and Eleventh Centuries* (London, 1989).
Stenton, *ASE*	F. Stenton, *Anglo-Saxon England*, 3rd ed. (Oxford, 1971).
Taylor and Taylor, *AS Arch*	H. M. and J. Taylor, *Anglo-Saxon Architecture*, 3 vols. (Cambridge, 1965–78).
TCBS	*Transactions of the Cambridge Bibliographical Society.*
Temple, *AS MSS*	E. Temple, *Anglo-Saxon Manuscripts, 900–1066* (London, 1976).
TRHS	*Transactions of the Royal Historical Society.*
VCH	*Victoria County History* (London, 1900–75; Oxford, 1976–).
Verfasserlexikon	*Die deutsche Literatur des Mittelalters: Verfasserlexikon*, 2nd ed. by K. Ruh *et al.* (Berlin and New York, 1977–).

LIST OF ABBREVIATIONS

Whitelock, *Bede to Alfred*	D. Whitelock, *From Bede to Alfred: Studies in Early Anglo-Saxon Literature and History* (London, 1980).
Whitelock, *History*	D. Whitelock, *History, Law and Literature in 10th–11th Century England* (London, 1981).
WHR	*Welsh Historical Review.*
Wilson, *Archaeology*	D. M. Wilson (ed.), *The Archaeology of Anglo-Saxon England* (London, 1976).
WMalm, *GP*	William of Malmesbury, *Gesta pontificum*, ed. N. E. S. A. Hamilton, RS (London, 1870).
WMalm, *GR*	William of Malmesbury, *Gesta regum*, ed. R. A. B. Mynors, M. Winterbottom and R. M. Thomson (OMT, 1998).
YES	*Yearbook of English Studies.*
Yorke, *Kingdoms*	B. Yorke, *Kings and Kingdoms of Early Anglo-Saxon England* (London, 1990).
Yorke, *Wessex*	B. Yorke, *Wessex in the Early Middle Ages* (London, 1995).
ZCP	*Zeitschrift für celtische Philologie.*

An asterisk (*) preceding a word indicates a relevant article elsewhere in the *Encyclopedia* under that (or a closely similar) heading.

THE ENCYCLOPAEDIA ENTRIES TO

The Blackwell Encyclopaedia of Anglo-Saxon England

A

ABBO OF FLEURY (d. 1004) was one of the great scholars of tenth-century Europe, who spent two years (985–7) at the abbey of *Ramsey, and exerted considerable influence on English learning, both through books and disciplines which he brought with him, and through students whom he trained at Ramsey, notably *Byrhtferth. Abbo was born in the vicinity of Orleans; the precise date of his birth is unknown (c.945–50), but he is known to have studied at Paris, Rheims and Orleans, as a result of which he became a many-sided scholar, expert in subjects of both the trivium and the quadrivium, and has left writings on *computus, logic, *grammar, and *canon law, as well as historical and hagiographical works. Together with Gerbert of Aurillac, with whom he studied at Rheims, he was one of the first scholars in Europe to know the treatises of logic of Boethius and to have composed a comprehensive treatment of syllogisms.

In 985, having been unsuccessful in an attempt to obtain the abbacy of *Fleury, Abbo consented to come to England to teach at Ramsey Abbey. He regarded his time spent in England as an exile, and, according to the *Vita S. Abbonis* by his hagiographer Aimoin (*BHL* 3), became fat from drinking English beer; but a short poem on Ramsey which is preserved in Byrhtferth's *Vita S. Oswaldi* shows that Abbo was not wholly impervious to the charms of the fenland. During his stay at Ramsey he taught the computus to his English pupils, and the impact of this teaching is reflected in Byrhtferth's own computistical writings. It was also probably at Ramsey that he composed his *Passio S. Eadmundi* (*BHL* 2392), an account of the murder of King *Edmund of East Anglia by the Danes in 869. Other compositions which date to his stay in England include a small corpus of *acrostic poems. While in England he visited *Dunstan and *Oswald, as well as influential secular persons such as King *Æthelred.

When the abbacy of Fleury became vacant in 987, Abbo returned to take up the position, and was abbot of Fleury from 988 until his death. After returning to Fleury he composed his *Quaestiones grammaticales*, a detailed treatise on the scansion of Latin verse, at the request of his former students at

Ramsey. He remained in close touch with colleagues in England, and was asked by the abbot of St Augustine's, Canterbury, to convert the *Vita S. Dunstani* by the unknown cleric B. into hexameters, but he died before he was able to undertake this task. Abbo was murdered by insurgent monks during an inspection of the abbey of La Réole on 13 November 1004.

Sharpe, *Handlist*, 1; PL cxxxix.417–578; A. Van de Vyver, 'Les oeuvres inédites d'Abbon de Fleury', *RB* 47 (1935), 125–69; A. Guerreau-Jalabert, *Abbo Floriacensis: Quaestiones Grammaticales* (Paris, 1982); *Abbonis Floriacensis Opera Inedita: Syllogismorum cathegoricorum et hypotheticorum enodatio*, ed. A. Van de Vyver (Bruges, 1966); M. Winterbottom, ed., *Three Lives of English Saints* (Toronto, 1972), pp. 67–87 [*Passio S. Eadmundi*]; R. B. Thomson, 'Two Astronomical Tractates of Abbo of Fleury', in *The Light of Nature. Essays presented to A. C. Crombie* (Dordrecht, 1985), pp. 113–33; G. R. Evans and A. M. Peden, 'Natural Science and the Liberal Arts in Abbo of Fleury's Commentary on the Calculus of Victorius of Aquitaine', *Viator* 16 (1985), 109–27; M. Mostert, 'Le séjour d'Abbon de Fleury à Ramsey', *Bibliothèque de l'Ecole des Chartes* 144 (1986), 199–208; *idem, The Political Theology of Abbo of Fleury* (Hilversum, 1987); E.-M. Engelen, *Zeit, Zahl und Bild. Studien zur Verbindung von Philosophie und Wissenschaft bei Abbo von Fleury* (Berlin and New York, 1993); S. Gwara, 'Three Acrostic Poems by Abbo of Fleury', *The Journal of Medieval Latin* 2 (1992), 203–35; A. Gransden, 'Abbo of Fleury's *Passio S. Eadmundi*', *RB* 105 (1995), 20–78; M. Lapidge and P. S. Baker, 'More Acrostic Verse by Abbo of Fleury', *The Journal of Medieval Latin* 7 (1997), 1–32.

MARCO MOSTERT

ABINGDON (Berks.), an Iron Age valley-fort and small Roman town in the upper Thames, was probably re-used for a double monastic community in the late seventh or eighth century. The name (*Æbban dūn*, 'Æbbe's hill') originally described high ground three miles away; a late legend that the minster itself was re-located possibly explains the shift of the name. Early charters hitherto ascribed to it are now thought to relate to the minster of Bradfield (Berks.), of which Abingdon may, however, have been a dependency under an eponymous abbess Æbbe. A late legend that the female community was at *Helnestoue*, the area around St Helen's church in a corner of

3

the Iron Age rampart, is supported by the discovery there of an eighth-century cruciform pin.

The minster declined, and was annexed, possibly by Alfred's reign, to the West Saxon crown. In 954 King *Eadred gave it to *Æthelwold, who re-founded it as a reformed abbey and built up its estates. Æthelwold's church lay apart from *Helnestoue*, though still within the Iron Age fort; a later description suggests that it was a rotunda based on the Aachen chapel, and its magnificent furnishings included precious objects made by Æthelwold himself. The abbey remained rich and successful, and stimulated the growth of a small town around it: *Domesday Book mentions 'ten merchants dwelling before the gate of the church'.

T. Allen, 'Abingdon', *Current Archaeology* 121 (1990), 24–7; F. M. Stenton, *The Early History of the Abbey of Abingdon* (Reading, 1913); M. Gelling, 'The Hill of Abingdon', *Oxoniensia* 22 (1957), 54–62; M. Biddle, G. Lambrick and J. N. L. Myres, 'The Early History of Abingdon, Berkshire, and its Abbey', *MArch* 12 (1968), 26–69; A. Thacker, 'Æthelwold and Abingdon', *Æthelwold*, pp. 43–64; Blair, *AS Oxon*, pp. 64–5, 113–14; *Charters of Abingdon Abbey*, ed. S. E. Kelly, Anglo-Saxon Charters 7-8 (Oxford, 2000).

JOHN BLAIR

ABLAUT: *see* Sound Changes

ACCA (d. 740), bishop of *Hexham from 709 until he was deposed in 732. Acca was a disciple of both Bishop *Bosa and Bishop *Wilfrid and was an intimate friend of *Bede, who composed a number of exegetical treatises at Acca's prompting and dedicated several of them to him. Acca supplied Bede with the materials in *HE* iii.13 and iv.13; he also supplied material on Wilfrid to *Stephen of Ripon for use in his *Vita S. Wilfridi*, which is similarly dedicated to Acca. Of Acca's own writings nothing survives except for part of a letter to Bede preserved in the prologue to Bede's *Commentarius in Lucam*. The reasons for his deposition from the bishopric of Hexham are unknown, but were presumably politically motivated.

Sharpe, *Handlist*, 2; Bede, *HE* v.20; *Bedae Venerabilis Opera Exegetica III*, ed. D. Hurst, CCSL cxx (Turnhout, 1960), 5–10; Bolton, *ALL*, pp. 202–4.

MICHAEL LAPIDGE

ACROSTICS are a form of (Greek or Latin) verse in which, in simplest form, the individual letters of the first line of the poem also supply the first letters (hence *acros*, the 'point', and *stichos*, 'verse') of each successive line of the poem, so that the poem will have as many lines as there are individual letters in its first line. More complex acrostic verses may also include a mesostich and/or telestich (in which the median and/or final letters of the verses also spell out a legend). The earliest surviving Greek acrostic poem, having the legend ΙΗΣΟΥΣ ΧΡΕΙΣΤΟΣ ΘΕΟΥ ΥΙΟΣ ΣΩΤΗΡ ('Jesus Christ, Son of God, Saviour': the first letters here spell out ΙΧΘΥΣ, the Greek word for 'fish', and a widespread early Christian symbol of Christ), was quoted in Latin translation by *Aldhelm, and was possibly translated by him as well (an illustration of the Greek learning which was available at *Theodore's school at *Canterbury, where Aldhelm was trained). Aldhelm composed acrostic verses as prefaces to his *Enigmata* and *Carmen de virginitate*, and one of his imitators, *Tatwine, used a forty-letter acrostic structure to link together all the forty poems which constitute his *Enigmata*; another imitator, *Boniface, composed twenty poems on the virtues and vices in acrostic form. Aldhelm thus established a model for later Anglo-Latin poets, and in the tenth century, both *Dunstan and *Abbo of Fleury composed complex acrostic verses. A particularly complex form of acrostic, the 'carmen figuratum', in which not only the initial, median and final verses bear legends, but other legends woven into the poem create various shapes and forms, was pioneered in Latin by the Late Latin poet Porphyrius (fl. *c.*325), a copy of whose poems is mentioned in a letter from Bishop *Milred of Worcester to *Lul on the occasion of Boniface's martyrdom (754); one of the greatest practitioners of *carmina figurata* in the Middle Ages was Hrabanus Maurus (d. 856), lavish copies of whose poems were copied in Anglo-Saxon England (e.g. in Cambridge, Trinity College, B.16.3).

DACL i.356–72; MGH, AA xv.97–9, 350–2 [Aldhelm], ES i.245 [Milred]; CCSL cxxxiii.167–208 [Tatwine]; 283–343 [Boniface]; Lapidge, *ALL* ii.147–9 [Dunstan]; S. Gwara, 'Three Acrostic Poems by Abbo of Fleury', *The Journal of Medieval Latin* 2 (1992), 203–35; M. Lapidge and P. S. Baker, 'More Acrostic Verse by Abbo of Fleury', *The Journal of Medieval Latin* 7 (1997), 1–32.

MICHAEL LAPIDGE

ADELARD of Utrecht (fl. s. xi^med), a German scholar with a reputation for skill in *medicine who was one of the twelve canons that constituted the community of secular clerics at *Harold Godwineson's foundation at Waltham (Essex). Adelard was responsible for instituting at Waltham the rules and observances of the Lotharingian church and, although he left no writings, is a representative of the influence of continental, especially

Lotharingian, scholars in England during the reign of *Edward the Confessor.

The Waltham Chronicle, ed. L. Watkiss and M. Chibnall (OMT, 1994); Freeman, *NC* ii.442, 584–5; *Vita Haroldi*, ed. W. de G. Birch (London, 1885), pp. 17–19.

MICHAEL LAPIDGE

ADOMNÁN (d. 704), ninth abbot of *Iona, was famous in his own time as the author of 'the Law of Innocents', promulgated to protect women and children from involvement in warfare. He is now best known as the author of the Life of St *Columba. The two were distant kinsmen, both belonging to Cenél Conaill, the lineage which in their time provided the kings of the Northern Uí Néill. We meet him first as a monk of Iona in the time of Abbot Failbe (669–79), another distant kinsman. Adomnán was chosen as his successor, ninth abbot of Iona and the seventh to come from the saint's lineage. In 685 the Northumbrian king *Ecgfrith was defeated and killed in battle against the *Picts in eastern Scotland, and his elder half-brother *Aldfrith inherited the crown. Aldfrith, the son of King *Oswiu, was born before 634 during his father's exile among the Irish. He was a scholar and a friend of Adomnán, and it appears that he may have been in Iona when Ecgfrith was killed. Within the year Adomnán acted as ambassador for the Southern Uí Néill king, visiting King Aldfrith in Northumbria and seeking the return of Irish captives held by the late King Ecgfrith. He visited *Northumbria a second time, in 687 or 688, when he spent some time with Abbot *Ceolfrith at *Jarrow. It is possible that Adomnán and King Aldfrith may have hoped for a return of the Iona community to *Lindisfarne, from where they had withdrawn in 664 because of controversy over the date of *Easter. During these visits he was persuaded that Roman practice over the date of Easter should prevail, and Bede tells us that he was instrumental in spreading this view in northern Ireland, though he was unable to convert the seniors of his own community. In 692 Adomnán made a visitation of the monasteries of his community in Ireland, and in 697 the 'Law of Innocents', also known as the 'Law of Adomnán', was adopted at a major synod of the rulers and clergy of Ireland held at Birr. His *Life of St Columba* is a fundamental source for Irish monastic life in the seventh century. His only other extant work of scholarship was a book *De locis sanctis*, based on the experiences in the Holy Land and in Constantinople of a Frankish traveller named Arculf; Adomnán's work was the main source of Bede's more popular work on the same subject. Bede as a child may have met Adomnán and would surely have heard about him from Ceolfrith. He described the Irish abbot as 'a good and wise man with an excellent knowledge of the scriptures' and as 'a champion of peace and unity'.

Sharpe, *Handlist*, 49; Bede, *HE* v.15–17; *Adomnán's Life of Columba*, ed. and trans. A. O. and M. O. Anderson, 2nd ed. rev. M. O. Anderson (OMT, 1991); *Adomnán of Iona: Life of St Columba*, trans. R. Sharpe (Harmondsworth, 1995); *Adomnán's De Locis Sanctis*, ed. D. Meehan (Dublin, 1958); J. M. Picard, 'The Purpose of Adomnán's *Vita Columbae*', *Peritia* 1 (1982), 160–77; A. D. S. MacDonald, 'Aspects of the Monastery and Monastic Life in Adomnán's Life of Columba', *Peritia* 3 (1984), 271–302.

RICHARD SHARPE

ADRIAN AND RITHEUS: see *Solomon and Saturn*, Prose.

ADVENT LYRICS. The *Advent Lyrics* (also called *Advent*, *Christ I* and *Christ A*) are twelve short poems which begin the *Exeter Book, formerly seen collectively as the opening 439 lines of *Christ. The group, assumed now to be the work of a single anonymous poet, begins imperfectly because of the loss of a leaf, and it is thought that perhaps three more poems may have preceded these. Each of the poems is based upon an antiphon, the 'O' antiphons (or choric responses, invocations involving biblical quotations) sung in the *liturgy during Advent and at Christmas, and each begins with the Old English equivalent, *Eala*. The poet, surely a religious, shows considerable familiarity with patristic writings, and uses the antiphons merely as a starting-point for each of his poems. They are elaborate constructs, each self-standing, but building into an extended narrative sequence in which the thought is complex, and the language and imagery appropriate to it. The seventh antiphon, which consists largely of a dialogue between Mary and Joseph, is regarded as especially fine.

ASPR iii.3–15; *The Advent Lyrics of the Exeter Book*, ed. J. J. Campbell (Princeton, NJ, 1959); R. B. Burlin, *The Old English Advent: a Typological Commentary* (New Haven, CT, 1968); S. Rankin, 'The Liturgical Background of the Old English Advent Lyrics: a Reappraisal', in Clemoes FS, pp. 317–40; P. Clemoes, *Interactions of Thought and Language in Old English Poetry*, CSASE 12 (Cambridge, 1995), 371–80.

DONALD SCRAGG

ADVENTUS SAXONUM (also known as the 'Adventus Anglorum'). The first arrival of Germanic invaders or settlers in Britain, supposed in historical tradition to be an event which took place towards the middle of the fifth century; in effect, however, the first recorded non-event in English history (cf. Anglo-Saxon *settlement). The notion of the 'Adventus Saxonum' originated in *Gildas's need to present the arrival of Germanic peoples in Britain as a sudden and dramatic event, which in accordance with his polemical ends could be interpreted as a manifestation of divine punishment for the sins of the British. It was adopted from Gildas by *Bede, who located it during the joint reigns of the emperors Marcian and Valentinian (449–56), and thus gave it a measure of historical respectability; see *HE* i.15, i.23, ii.14, and v.23. It was adopted in turn by the compiler of the *Anglo-Saxon Chronicle*, in the late ninth century, and placed in the annal for 449; and in this form it was taken over by the Anglo-Norman chroniclers, and so entered the mainstream of historical tradition. The 'Adventus Saxonum' endures to this day in the Library of Congress Cataloguing-in-Publication Data, which defines the Anglo-Saxon period as extending from 449 to 1066.

P. Sims-Williams, 'The Settlement of England in Bede and the *Chronicle*', *ASE* 12 (1983), 1–41; N. Higham, *The English Conquest: Gildas and Britain in the Fifth Century* (Manchester, 1994).

SIMON KEYNES

ÆDILUULF (fl. 803–21), Anglo-Latin poet and author of a poem of 819 hexameter lines entitled *Carmen de abbatibus* concerning the abbots and monks of an unidentified monastery in *Northumbria which was subservient to the church of *Lindisfarne (the poem is dedicated to Ecgberht, bishop of Lindisfarne, 803–21). Nothing is known of Ædiluulf save what can be gleaned from his poem, but the diction of the verse shows clearly that his technique of composition was informed by (and possibly learned at) the school of *Alcuin at *York, which may imply that the monastery in question was at Crayke, some twelve miles north of York and a dependency of Lindisfarne. The poem contains much of interest in its descriptions of the accomplishments of the various monks and abbots, and for its descriptions of various *visions (some of them involving interesting architectural detail).

Sharpe, *Handlist*, 69; MGH, PLAC i.582–604; A. Campbell, ed., *Æthelwulf De Abbatibus* (Oxford, 1967); H. J. Kamphausen, *Traum und Vision in der lateinischen Poesie der Karolingerzeit* (Bern, 1975), pp. 86–114; H. M. Taylor, 'The Architectural Interest of Æthelwulf's *De Abbatibus* ', *ASE* 3 (1974), 163–74; M. Lapidge, 'Aediluulf and the School of York', in *Lateinische Kultur im VIII. Jahrhundert. Traube-Gedenkschrift*, ed. A.

Lehner and W. Berschin (St Ottilien, 1990), pp. 161–78, repr. in Lapidge, *ALL* i.381–98.

MICHAEL LAPIDGE

ÆLBERHT, archbishop of York (767–78), known principally to history as the mentor of *Alcuin, who inherited Ælberht's vast library and who commemorated his beloved teacher at length in his poem on the bishops, kings and saints of *York. On Alcuin's evidence, Ælberht established a curriculum in the *school at York which, in its range, was without parallel in Europe at that time, in its concern not only with *grammar, rhetoric and *computus, but with *astronomy, geometry, arithmetic – and, to judge from the books he bequeathed to Alcuin – logic. According to Alcuin he made one trip to *Rome (presumably to collect his *pallium). An exchange of letters between one 'Koaena' (which may be a nickname of Ælberht) and *Lull survives as part of the Bonifatian correspondence.

Sharpe, *Handlist*, 65; MGH, PLAC i.200–7, ES i.261–2 (nos. 124–5); P. Godman, ed., *Alcuin: the Bishops, Kings, and Saints of York* (OMT, 1982); M. Lapidge, 'Surviving Booklists from Anglo-Saxon England', Clemoes FS, pp. 33–89, esp. 45–9.

MICHAEL LAPIDGE

ÆLFFLÆD of Whitby (d. 713), was the sister of King *Aldfrith of Northumbria and spent most of her life as a nun at *Whitby, from the time of Abbess *Hild, whom she succeeded as abbess in 680. From that time Ælfflæd ruled Whitby jointly with her mother, *Eanflæd. She was the confidante of both *Cuthbert and *Wilfrid, and is described by *Stephen of Ripon in his *Vita S. Wilfridi* as 'always the source of consolation for the entire kingdom, and the best of advisers'. Of her writings a brief letter of introduction addressed to an abbess of Pfalzel (near Trier) is preserved among the corpus of Bonifatian correspondence. The anonymous *Vita S. Gregorii* was written at Whitby while she was abbess.

Sharpe, *Handlist*, 51; Bede, *HE* iii.24, iv.24; Stephen of Ripon, *Vita S. Wilfridi*, cc. 43, 59, 60; MGH, ES i.3–4 (no. 8); Bolton, *ALL*, pp. 199–200; P. Hunter Blair, 'Whitby as a Centre of Learning in the Seventh Century', Clemoes FS, pp. 3–32.

MICHAEL LAPIDGE

ÆLFHEAH I, bishop of Winchester (934–51), was possibly a monk (his nickname 'the Bald' may refer to a tonsure), in which case he was in some sense a forerunner of the monastic revival which took place in later tenth-century *Winchester under the impetus of Bishop *Æthelwold.

Ælfheah is known to have consecrated both *Dunstan and Æthelwold; he was buried in the choir of the Old Minster, Winchester.

Wulfstan of Winchester, *Vita S. Æthelwoldi*, c. 8 (ed. M. Lapidge and M. Winterbottom (OMT, 1991), pp. 12–13); WMalm, *GP*, pp. 164–5.

MICHAEL LAPIDGE

ÆLFHEAH (Alphege), St, archbishop of *Canterbury (1006–12). Initially a monk at *Deerhurst (Glos.), and perhaps for a while at *Glastonbury, Ælfheah moved to *Bath in the early 960s and became abbot there soon afterwards. He was appointed bishop of *Winchester in October 984, in succession to *Æthelwold, and held that office until 1006. At Winchester Ælfheah was able to bring to completion a vast programme of building works at the Old Minster initiated by his predecessor, including eastern porticus and a crypt, a tower and a huge organ, all of which are described in detail by *Wulfstan of Winchester in a poem dedicated to Ælfheah (the *Narratio metrica de S. Swithuno*). Ælfheah was translated to Canterbury on 16 November 1006, in succession to Archbishop Ælfric (995–1005). As bishop of Winchester, Ælfheah may have been instrumental, in the early 990s, in persuading King *Æthelred to mend the errors of his ways; and as archbishop of Canterbury he would have been required to take a lead in the face of Danish invasions on an unprecedented scale. In September 1011 Canterbury was besieged by Thorkell's army, and Ælfheah was captured. In the words of a contemporary chronicler, 'He was then a captive who had been head of the English people and of Christendom' (*ASC*, MSS. CDE, s.a. 1011). The Danes kept Ælfheah in captivity for the next seven months, probably at Greenwich on the south bank of the Thames. Ealdorman *Eadric 'and all the chief councillors of England' made a large payment of tribute to the Danes soon after Easter (13 April) in 1012; but Ælfheah refused to make any payment on his own account, or to allow himself to be ransomed. In a drunken stupor the enraged Danes brought Ælfheah to their assembly at Greenwich, on Saturday 19 April, and put him to death: 'They pelted him with bones and with ox-heads, and one of them [named Thrum] struck him on the head with the back of an axe, so that he sank down with the blow, and his holy blood fell on the ground, and thus he sent his holy soul to God's kingdom' (*ASC*). On the next morning Ælfheah's body was taken upriver to *London, and buried in St Paul's. The German chronicler Thietmar of Merseburg provides a fuller and in

certain respects a rather different account of Ælfheah's martyrdom, on the authority of a certain Sewald (*EHD* i, no. 27); we are told, for example, that Earl Thorkell tried to intervene on the archbishop's behalf, without success. In 1023 King *Cnut authorised a public display of veneration for the martyred archbishop: on 8 June Ælfheah's body was raised from its tomb in St Paul's, taken first across the river to Southwark, thence to *Rochester, and so to Canterbury, where it arrived on 11 June and was reburied on 15 June (*ASC*, MS. D). It may be that in the manner of his death Ælfheah had become a symbol of English resistance to the Danes, and that Cnut was concerned to move the focal point of his cult from London to Canterbury, where it might not be so highly charged; or it may be that Cnut, having recently come to terms with Earl Thorkell in Denmark, was able to countenance the promotion of a cult in a way which might help to reconcile the English to his rule. The tale of Ælfheah's martyrdom in 1012, and especially of his translation to Canterbury in 1023, was re-told in the late eleventh century by Osbern, monk of Christ Church, Canterbury. The cult of St Alphege prospered, but was presently eclipsed by that of St Thomas.

Brooks, *Canterbury*, pp. 278–81, 283–5; M. K. Lawson, *Cnut: the Danes in England in the Early Eleventh Century* (London, 1993), pp. 140–2, 180–2. For Osbern's *Passio S. Ælfegi* (*BHL* 2518) and *Translatio S. Ælfegi* (*BHL* 2519), see A. R. Rumble with R. Morris, 'Textual Appendix', *Cnut*, ed. Rumble, pp. 283–315.

SIMON KEYNES

ÆLFHELM of Ely (fl. 946–55), cleric of the church of *Ely in the reign of King *Eadred, and author of an account of the miracles of St *Æthelthryth which has not survived, but which was used as a source and is quoted *in extenso* in the late twelfth-century *Liber Eliensis* (i.43–9).

Liber Eliensis, ed. E. O. Blake (London, 1962), pp. xxxii, 57–61.

MICHAEL LAPIDGE

ÆLFRIC BATA (fl. s. xi[1]), a student of the more famous *Ælfric of Cerne, is known only as the author of Latin scholastic *colloquies. Nothing is known of his life (evidence that he might have been involved in a dispute with Canterbury over land is late and of uncertain relevance), and the significance of his epithet or cognomen, Bata, is unknown as well. From his pen we have two works: the *Colloquia*, an extensive classroom colloquy which throws fascinating light on students' life in a monastic school (and includes extensive quotation from the Old Testament wisdom books, which were presumably required classroom reading), and the *Colloquia difficiliora*, a similar but shorter work which contains much difficult vocabulary, much of it drawn from *Aldhelm. He also produced a redaction of Ælfric's better-known *Colloquium*, although the precise extent of his redactorial activity cannot be determined.

Sharpe, *Handlist*, 54; *Early Scholastic Colloquies*, ed. W. H. Stevenson (Oxford, 1929), pp. 27–74; *Latin Colloquies from pre-Conquest Britain*, ed. S. Gwara (Toronto, 1996); P. Lendinara, 'Il *Colloquio* di Ælfric e il *Colloquio* di Ælfric Bata', in *Feor ond Neah*, ed. P. Lendinara and L. Melazzo (Palermo, 1983), pp. 173–249; D. Porter, 'The Latin Syllabus in Anglo-Saxon Monastic Schools', *Neophilologus* 78 (1994), 1–20; S. Gwara and D. Porter, *Anglo-Saxon Conversations: the Colloquies of Ælfric Bata* (Woodbridge, 1997).

MICHAEL LAPIDGE

ÆLFRIC OF EYNSHAM (*c.*950–*c.*1010) was one of the most learned scholars of late Anglo-Saxon England and a prolific and elegant writer of vernacular prose whose works were widely read in his own time and later played an important part in Reformation controversy. He was educated under Bishop *Æthelwold in the monastic school at Winchester, and after becoming a monk and priest was sent around 987 to the abbey of Cerne Abbas, newly founded (or refounded) by the *thegn Æthelmær, son of Ealdorman *Æthelweard. In 1005 Æthelmær refounded the abbey of *Eynsham and Ælfric became the first abbot. Internal allusions suggest that he had travelled in the north of England and in Italy, and that he may have been taught by *Dunstan as well as by Æthelwold.

His earliest known works are the *Sermones Catholici* produced 990–5, comprising two series of forty *homilies on the Gospels, the saints and doctrinal themes. The prefaces and incidental notes show that he anticipated readers as well as listeners, including learned laity and clergy. The project was evidently encouraged by Sigeric, archbishop of *Canterbury, and by Ealdorman Æthelweard, and the homilies were widely circulated: some thirty manuscripts drawing on the collection are still extant, ranging from the late tenth century to the early thirteenth. Over the next decade or so Ælfric built on this project, revising the collection, adding about forty new homilies and organising them into different collections. The original impetus for his work, which Ælfric identified in his first preface, was the coming reign of Antichrist and the consequent need for orthodox teaching in the vernacular to replace erroneous teachings which were circulating widely in England. While the idea of the approaching millennium came to figure less in his writings as time went by, to be replaced in part by the new crisis posed by the *Vikings, the importance of knowledge and orthodoxy remained central. He made extensive use of Augustine, *Gregory the Great, Jerome, *Bede, and the Carolingians Haymo and Smaragdus (as well as a range of anonymous saints' lives), and frequently cited them as authorities; but although he presented his work as translation it was rather a process of selection, adaptation and independent argument. His homilies mostly take the form of either close interpretation of the Bible, often using allegory, or narratives of saints, but in the process they discuss a range of topics such as fatalism and free will, auguries, the Trinity, the resurrection of the body, the origin of the soul, clerical marriage, medicinal magic and the belief in the devil as a creator.

These two collections were closely followed by a third devoted mainly to the lives and passions of saints. The collection was made at the request of Ealdorman Æthelweard and his son Æthelmær and was apparently designed for reading rather than preaching. The choice of subjects and appended discussions show a particular interest in such topics as the doctrine of the just war, royal and military saints, the history of English monasticism, the problem of the Vikings, the interpretation of dreams, the careers and fates of Old Testament kings, and the gods of classical and Danish paganism. About the same time (*c.*998) Ælfric produced a *grammar of Latin, written in English and partially designed to explain the vernacular too, a Latin *colloquy on trades and occupations, and the first of a succession of Old Testament translations and paraphrases, written in part for the use of the more learned laity: these were subsequently combined with the work of another translator to produce an illustrated copy of the Hexateuch. His role as an authority on church practice and *canon law is evident in the pastoral letters commissioned from him by *Wulfsige, bishop of *Sherborne, and *Wulfstan, bishop of *Worcester and archbishop of *York, for circulation to their clergy; and his importance as an adviser to the king and his counsellors is suggested by a text, perhaps part of a letter, in which he cites the biblical and classical precedents for a king delegating leadership of the army to others.

As a scholar, Ælfric was the leading product of the tenth-century monastic reform, reflecting that movement's characteristic concerns with learning and monastic ideals and also its close relations with the leading laity. His works were in great demand and copied and read for the next two centuries and more, but often heavily adapted and selected by others. As a writer Ælfric perfected a form of Old English which has become the model for modern analysis of the language, and the manuscripts testify to his care in the use of grammar and vocabulary. He was a conscious stylist, but explicitly rejected the obscure vocabulary and convoluted syntax which was fashionable in contemporary Anglo-Latin writings and even in the vernacular, and created instead an elegant and balanced prose using simpler vocabulary and structures. In his later writings he developed a style of writing modelled in part on verse, using rhythm and *alliteration and occasional poetic language, though in a form that remained firmly prose and preserved the balance and lucidity of the earlier style. He left a few works in Latin and was a very competent Latinist, but chose to devote his energies almost entirely to writing in English.

Sharpe, *Handlist*, 53; Frank–Cameron, 1.4–1.9 (pp. 76–88); L. M. Reinsma, *Ælfric: an Annotated Bibliography* (New York, 1987); *Ælfric's Prefaces*, ed. J. Wilcox (Durham, 1994); *Ælfric's Catholic Homilies: the First Series*, ed. P. Clemoes, EETS ss 17 (Oxford, 1997); *Ælfric's Catholic Homilies: the Second Series*, ed. M. Godden, EETS ss 5 (London, 1979); *Homilies of Ælfric: a Supplementary Collection*, ed. J. C. Pope, EETS os 259–60 (London, 1967–8); *Ælfrics Grammatik und Glossar*, ed. J. Zupitza, rev. H. Gneuss (Berlin, 1966); C. A. Jones, *Ælfric's Letter to the Monks of Eynsham*, CSASE 24 (Cambridge, 1998); M. Lapidge and M. Winterbottom, *Wulfstan of Winchester: Life of St Æthelwold* (OMT, 1991), pp. 70–80 [*Vita S. Æthelwoldi*]; *Ælfric's De temporibus anni*, ed. H. Henel, EETS os 213 (London, 1942); *Die Hirtenbriefe Ælfrics*, ed. B. Fehr rev. P. Clemoes (Darmstadt, 1966); *Ælfric's First Series of Catholic Homilies: British Museum Royal 7.C.XII*, EEMF 13 (Copenhagen, 1966); G. E. MacLean, 'Ælfric's Version of Alcuini Interrogationes Sigeuulfi in Genesim', *Anglia* 6 (1883), 425–73, 7 (1884), 1–59; M. McC. Gatch, *Preaching and Theology in Anglo-Saxon England: Ælfric and Wulfstan* (Toronto, 1977); L. Grundy, *Books and Grace: Ælfric's Theology* (London, 1991); *The Cerne Abbey Millennium Lectures*, ed. K. Barker (Cerne Abbas, 1988); *The Old English Homily and its Backgrounds*, ed. P. E. Szarmach and B. F. Huppe (Albany, NY, 1978); *Holy Men and Holy Women: Old English Prose Saints' Lives and their Contexts*, ed. P. E. Szarmach (Albany, NY, 1996).

M. R. GODDEN

ÆLFTHRYTH, queen (b. probably before 944, d. 17 November, 999 × 1001), was the daughter of Ordgar, a powerful noble of south-west England, and of a royally-descended mother. She was married twice, first to Æthelwold, ealdorman of *East Anglia, son of *Æthelstan Half-king; and in 964 to King *Edgar, by whom she had two sons, Edmund and *Æthelred. Ælfthryth was the first tenth-century queen to be certainly crowned and anointed as queen in 973, an emphasis on her status which was important to the claims of her two sons. She was to attract a colourful historical reputation, beginning with accusations of her complicity in the murder of her stepson, King *Edward the Martyr. Most of the stories can be dismissed as later stereotyped elaboration, gathering around the memory of a politically active and important woman. But her involvement in Edward's death is possible; court and family politics bred such action, and he was murdered by Ælfthryth's own followers as he arrived to visit her and his young brother Æthelred at Corfe. Her landed possessions as queen in the north-east-midlands and East Anglia made her an integral part of the extension of West Saxon control. Although important at Edgar's court, her greatest power came during the minority of her son, Æthelred II. His majority ended this, though she remained dowager *queen, eclipsing her son's first wife and rearing the heirs to the throne. The monastic reformers at Edgar's court gave her responsibility for *nunneries, and she exercised control over several, including Wherwell, where she lived in retirement and died.

C. Fell, *Edward, King and Martyr* (Leeds, 1971); C. Hart, 'Two Queens of England', *Ampleforth Journal* 82 (1977), 10–15, 54; M. A. Meyer, 'Women and the Tenth Century English Monastic Reform', *RB* 87 (1977), 34–61; S. Keynes, *The Diplomas of King Æthelred the Unready, 978–1016* (Cambridge, 1980); P. A. Stafford, 'The King's Wife in Wessex', *P & P* 91 (1981), 3–27; J. Nelson, 'The Second English Ordo', in Nelson, *Politics*, pp. 361–74; M. A. Meyer, 'The Queen's "Demesne" in Later Anglo-Saxon England', *The Culture of Christendom*, ed. M. A. Meyer (London, 1993), pp. 75–113; P. A. Stafford, 'The Portrayal of Royal Women in England, Mid-Tenth to Mid-Twelfth Centuries', *Medieval Queenship*, ed. J. Parsons (Stroud, 1994), pp. 143–67; idem, *Queen Emma and Queen Edith: Queenship and Women's Power in Eleventh-Century England* (Oxford, 1997).

PAULINE STAFFORD

ÆLFWINE, PRAYERBOOK OF. Ælfwine was a monk, dean and subsequently abbot of the New Minster, *Winchester (1031–57); his 'Prayerbook' (preserved in London, BL, Cotton Titus D.xxvi + xxvii) is a personal handbook in tiny format containing a liturgical calendar (to which have been added numerous obits, principally of the royal family, prominent churchmen and *eald-ormen, against years from 978–1023), computistical and prognostic materials, a copy of the *De temporibus anni* of *Ælfric, a collectar and three special liturgical Offices, and miscellaneous texts (some in Old English). The 'Prayerbook' was written by two scribes, Ælfwine himself (while he was still dean), and another named Ælfsige, probably between 1023 and 1031.

Temple, *AS MSS*, pp. 94–5 (no. 77); Ker, *Catalogue*, pp. 264–6 (no. 202); *Ælfwine's Prayerbook*, ed. B. Günzel, HBS 108 (London, 1993); *The Liber Vitae of the New Minster and Hyde Abbey Winchester*, ed. S. Keynes, EEMF 26 (Copenhagen, 1996), 68, 111–23.

MICHAEL LAPIDGE

AERIAL RECONNAISSANCE, or the study of features on the ground by observation from the air, is both a means of discovering new archaeological sites and an aid to their interpretation. Archaeological remains, when only slight or poorly preserved, will often appear confused and unintelligible to a visitor on the ground; yet when seen from the air (or recorded on an air-photograph), the same remains can display a coherent plan that is full of meaning. This is even more true for those sites where all the surface traces have been levelled by ploughing and the only signs of their buried remnants are given by corresponding differences in the seasonal growth of crops. There is only one way to get an adequate view of the resulting 'crop-marks' and that is to look at them from above: the marks then trace out (with variable degrees of clarity and completeness) a plan of the underlying features, by which they can be recognised and at least partly understood. This method of research can be applied to archaeological sites of all kinds, given a favourable combination of soil, crop and weather, but only the more substantial features can normally be expected to show up (see pl. 1).

In Anglo-Saxon England the main contribution of aerial reconnaissance has been made in relation to sites in three categories.

Some inhumation *cemeteries of the pagan period are marked by low circular mounds, typically 5–8 m in diameter and no more than 0.6 m high. Few such cemeteries survive intact; when they are ploughed, crop-marks may show the full extent of the cemetery for the first time, by revealing the position of flat graves in addition to those previously beneath mounds. Each grave is shown by a mark about 2 m long, while those that had mounds are also enclosed by the circular mark of a narrow surrounding ditch, usually interrupted

at some point for an entrance. Burial-mounds of this kind are a distinctively early Saxon feature. Cemeteries without mounds are more difficult to identify without excavation or documentary evidence, since their appearance on air-photographs differs little from that of inhumation cemeteries of Roman or medieval date. A clue may nevertheless be given by their siting in relation to known settlements. Thus, crop-marks of the *Bernician royal site at Sprouston include an extensive inhumation cemetery, presumably contemporary with some part of its history. The east-west alignment of the graves, although not necessarily Christian, has prompted some to see a possible connexion with the conversion of Northumbria by *Paulinus, but this can be no more than speculation.

The feature that identifies a *royal site is the presence of at least one great hall 15–30 m long, associated with a complex of other *timber buildings such as lesser halls, stores and workshops. At least seven such sites have been recognised on air-photographs from the crop-marks of their buildings, which in one instance even included a small grandstand, perhaps for public oratory. Three of the sites were found within 20 km of each other in Bernicia: at Milfield (Northumb.), at Sprouston (just across the modern Scottish border, but still south of the Tweed), and at *Yeavering (Northumb.). Another lies near Atcham (Salop.), while a fifth is in *Wessex near *Malmesbury (Wilts.). These five have in common the presence of a particular type of hall, with annexes at each end, which at Yeavering was dated by excavation around the beginnning of the seventh century. Simple rectangular plans were also common, and these were the only sort to feature at the two other sites: Drayton (Berks.), and Hatton Rock near Stratford-upon-Avon (Warwicks.).

Minor buildings on royal sites are like those in less important *settlements elsewhere. Fortunately, the two commonest types have plans that identify them as being of Saxon date, even if known only from crop-marks. Rectangular halls with opposed entrances at the centres of their long sides are normally 8–12 m long. They are most easily detected on air-photographs when their wall-posts have been set in a continuous foundation-trench. The walls sometimes bow outwards slightly to the entrances, and these may be emphasized by the presence of large post-pits at either side of the opening. Groups of timber buildings including one or more halls of this type have been recognised on air-photographs in various contexts – both adjacent to an existing village and at a distance from it on the parish boundary. Another kind of

Pl. 1 Aerial photograph of crop marks showing cemetery.

settlement widely found in southern England is composed largely of huts with sunken floors. The huts can occur in considerable numbers (213 were excavated at *Mucking). They appear on air-photographs as rectangles of solid tone, 2–6 m long and of nearly square proportions, often with rounded ends (larger houses with sunken floors also occur, but are not limited to Anglo-Saxon contexts, being also found in some Roman villas). D. Benson and D. Miles, 'Crop Marks near the Sutton Courtenay Saxon Site', *Antiquity* 48 (1974), 223–6 [Drayton]; P. Rahtz, 'A Possible Saxon Palace near Stratford-upon-Avon', *Antiquity* 44 (1970), 137–43; J. K. S. St Joseph, 'Air Reconnaissance: Recent Results, 35', *Antiquity* 48 (1974), 213–15 [Eastry]; idem, 'Air Reconnaissance: Recent Results, 39', *Antiquity* 49 (1975), 293–5 [Atcham]; idem, 'Sprouston, Roxburghshire: an Anglo-Saxon Settlement Discovered by Air-Reconnaissance', *ASE* 10 (1982), 191–9; D. R. Wilson, *Air Photo Interpretation for Archaeologists* (London, 1982).

D. R. WILSON

ÆTHELBALD, king of the Mercians (716–57). When cast into exile during the reign of Ceolred,

king of the Mercians (709–16), Æthelbald joined the steady stream of people who came to seek solace from *Guthlac in his hollowed-out burial mound at Crowland in the fens. No doubt he was pleased to hear prophecies of his future prosperity as ruler of his people (*Felix, *Vita S. Guthlaci*, cc. 40, 49, 52), and gratified when the prophecies were fulfilled; for since the story originated in the 730s (or thereabouts), it has some authority as contemporary testimony. Æthelbald became king of the Mercians in 716, and soon began to extend his authority over the sprawling assortment of Anglian peoples in midland England. The political equilibrium which had prevailed south of the Humber in the late seventh and early eighth centuries was broken, in effect, by the death of Wihtred, king of *Kent, in 725, and by the departure of *Ine, king of *Wessex, to *Rome in 726. Æthelbald seems to have been able to take advantage of their going, and rose to great prominence during the next five or ten years. When *Bede had occasion to name the bishops holding office in

11

731 – in Kent, *Essex, *East Anglia, Wessex and *Mercia, as well as among 'the people who dwell west of the river Severn' (i.e. the *Magonsætan*) and among the *Hwicce, and also in *Lindsey and *Sussex – he remarked: 'all these kingdoms (*prouinciae*) and the other southern kingdoms which reach right up to the Humber, together with their various kings, are subject to Æthelbald, king of the Mercians' (*HE* v.23). It is not certain how clear was the view from Jarrow; and the view from Worcester was not necessarily much clearer. In the famous *charter recording the king's grant of land at Ismere, Worcs., to Ealdorman Cyneberht, in 736 (S 89: *EHD* i, no. 67), Æthelbald is styled 'king not only of the Mercians but also of all the provinces which are called by the general name "South English"'. 'South English', in this context, could refer to the southern as opposed to the northern Angles, as opposed to *all* the people living south of the river Humber; but the designation of Æthelbald in the witness-list as 'king of Britain' puts him clearly enough in a special class (cf. *Bretwalda).

Much depends on the general impression created by Bede, Felix, and the draftsman of the Ismere charter, but there need be little doubt that Æthelbald's political and economic interests extended way beyond his own kingdom of the Mercians. He seems sooner or later to have assumed control over the *metropolis* of *London, presumably at the expense of the rulers of the East Saxons; for he was able to profit from the tolls due on ships visiting London (described by Bede as 'an emporium of many peoples who come to it by land and sea' [*HE* ii.3]), and it appears that he made friends or repaid favours by remitting the toll on *ships belonging to certain parties, including the abbess of *Minster-in-Thanet, and the bishops of *Rochester, London, and *Worcester. An act which would appear to represent Æthelbald's seizure of control in Somerset took place in 733 (*ASC*), which might suggest that Bede had overestimated the extent of Æthelbald's power in 731. There is no reason, however, to assume that Æthelbald's control of Wessex was sustained thereafter for any length of time. He met resistance from Cuthred, king of the West Saxons (740–56); and since he is known to have controlled the monasteries at *Bath (on the Avon) and at Cookham (on the Thames), it may well be that he posed a serious threat in border territories. In 740 Æthelbald 'treacherously devastated part of Northumbria' (*HE Continuatio*), taking full advantage of the fact that the king of the Northumbrians was occupied at the time fighting the *Picts; and

a note in the 'Book of Llandaff' suggests that he was also active in securing his south-west border with Wales. One of Æthelbald's last recorded acts was to grant an estate in north-east Wiltshire to Abbot Eanberht [of ?Malmesbury] (S 96); the charter was attested by Cynewulf, king of the West Saxons (757–86), which suggests how complex was the political situation in this area at this time.

The appointment of Cuthbert, formerly bishop of Hereford, as archbishop of Canterbury (740–60), is conceivably a reflection of Æthelbald's influence in Kent; and the fact that it was Cuthbert who put into effect the king's grant of Cookham to Christ Church, Canterbury (S 1258: *EHD* i, no. 79), points in the same direction. Certainly they made a good pair. The most striking indication of Æthelbald's dominating position among his contemporaries, and of the nature of his rule, is given in the letters sent by Boniface and his fellow-bishops, in 746–7, to Archbishop Cuthbert, and to King Æthelbald himself (*EHD* i, no. 177), urging both to set their respective houses in order. In a council convened at *Clofesho* in 747, Cuthbert instituted various important reforms; and in a council held at Gumley, Leics., in 749, Æthelbald granted privileges to the churches in his (Mercian) realm (S 92). It would appear that both of Boniface's letters, together with the canons of the Council of *Clofesho* and the text of Æthelbald's charter, and an expurgated version of Pope *Gregory's *Regula pastoralis*, were circulated in association with each other as part of a concerted programme of reform promoted by the archbishop and the king, represented by the surviving fragments of BL, Cotton Otho A. i.

King Æthelbald was responsible for embellishing the shrine of St Guthlac at Crowland (Felix, *Vita S. Guthlaci*, c. 51), and was later credited with the foundation and endowment of the abbey itself (see Orderic, *HE* iv [ed. Chibnall, ii.338–40], and the twelfth-century 'Guthlac Roll' [BL Harley Roll Y. 6]). Little is known of the fortunes of the abbey in the later eighth and ninth centuries, but it may well have become a place of special importance in the Mercian world. Æthelbald was killed at Seckington, near Tamworth, by members of his own bodyguard (*HE Continuatio*, s.a. 757), and was buried at *Repton, in Derbyshire. It is a pleasant thought that he may be the mounted warrior depicted on the 'Repton Stone', bearing a shield, wielding a sword, and sporting a fine moustache. Æthelbald's power as a Mercian overlord was rebuilt and extended after his death by his successor, King *Offa (757–96).

Stenton, *ASE*, pp. 202–6; P. Wormald, 'The Age of Bede

and Æthelbald', *The Anglo-Saxons*, ed. J. Campbell (Oxford, 1982), pp. 70–100; Yorke, *Kingdoms*, pp. 111–17; Kirby, *Kings*, pp. 129–36; S. E. Kelly, 'Trading Privileges from Eighth-Century England', *EME* 1 (1992), 3–27; *Making of England*, pp. 193–253; *Charters of St Augustine's Abbey, Canterbury, and Minster-in-Thanet*, ed. S. E. Kelly, Anglo-Saxon Charters 4 (Oxford, 1995), nos. 49–51; S. Keynes, 'England, 700–900', *The New Cambridge Medieval History*, II: *c.700–c.900*, ed. R. McKitterick (Cambridge, 1995), pp. 18–42; S. Keynes, 'The Reconstruction of a Burnt Cottonian Manuscript: the Case of Cotton MS. Otho A. I', *BLJ* 22 (1996), 113–160.

SIMON KEYNES

ÆTHELBERHT, king of Kent (d. 616), was the first Anglo-Saxon ruler to convert to Christianity. The date at which he became king is uncertain; it may have been as early as 560 or as late as *c*.590. He was a member of the Kentish royal dynasty, traditionally founded by *Hengest in the fifth century, and he succeeded his father Eormenric. Æthelberht came to hold a very powerful and influential position; he was one of a small number of kings who are said to have ruled over all the English kingdoms lying south of the river Humber (*HE* ii.5; cf. *Bretwalda). At some point before 581 Æthelberht married a Christian wife, Bertha, who was a *Frank and the daughter of a former king of Paris. He himself remained pagan, but he allowed Bertha to practise her religion without interference. In 597 a Christian mission, sent from Rome by Pope *Gregory the Great and led by *Augustine, arrived on the Isle of Thanet in Æthelberht's kingdom. The king received the missionaries with initial reserve, insisting on a meeting in the open air to nullify any magic spells that they might cast, but he was won over by their preaching and offered them hospitality in his capital city at *Canterbury (*HE* i.25). Soon afterwards he himself accepted Christian baptism, and with his support the Roman mission enjoyed great success in Kent and in the neighbouring kingdom of *Essex, then ruled by Æthelberht's nephew Sæberht and subject to his influence (*HE* i.26, ii.2, ii.3). Within a few years of the arrival of the missionaries, perhaps in 602–3, the king and his counsellors established a code of *laws for the Kentish people, which was partly designed to integrate the fledgling Church and its property within the existing legal system. The lawcode was written in *Old English, and was presumably prepared with the help of Augustine (since the English had no tradition of using writing); this must have been one of the first documents ever written down in the English vernacular (*HE* ii.5).

The king collaborated with Augustine in renovating an ancient building in Canterbury which was to become Christ Church cathedral, the seat of the archbishops of Canterbury, and he himself is credited with building and endowing St Andrew's church in *Rochester and St Paul's church in *London. Another project in which he was deeply involved was the construction of a monastery dedicated to SS Peter and Paul on the eastern outskirts of Canterbury, which was to develop into the famous St Augustine's Abbey; the abbey-church was designed as a mausoleum for the kings of Kent and the archbishops of Canterbury (*HE* i.33, ii.3). Æthelberht died on 24 February 616 and was buried in the mausoleum, alongside Bertha who had pre-deceased him (*HE* ii.5). In the later medieval period he came to be regarded as a saint.

Brooks, *Canterbury*, pp. 5–14; N. Brooks, 'The Creation and Early Structure of the Kingdom of Kent', in Bassett, *Origins*, pp. 55–74; *The Charters of St Augustine's Abbey, Canterbury, and Minster-in-Thanet*, ed. S. E. Kelly, Anglo-Saxon Charters 4 (Oxford, 1995).

S. E. KELLY

ÆTHELBERHT, ST, king of *East Anglia, was assassinated on the orders of King *Offa of *Mercia in 794. This much is made explicit by the *Anglo-Saxon Chronicle* (s.a. 792 [794]), while numismatic evidence confirms his status as the official ruler of East Anglia. Why and how he came to be venerated as a martyred 'innocent' in a cult centred upon Hereford cathedral, on the other side of Mercia, is much less clear. Though far from its natural constituency and impaired by the absence of relics – purportedly stolen by the Welsh when they sacked the cathedral in 1055 – a cult flourished, inspiring no less than three saints' lives.

M. R. James, 'Two Lives of St Ethelbert, King and Martyr', *EHR* 32 (1917), 214–44; A. T. Thacker, 'Kings, Saints and Monasteries in Pre-Viking Mercia', *MidH* 10 (1985), 1–25, at 16–18.

PAUL ANTONY HAYWARD

ÆTHELFLAED, 'LADY OF THE MERCIANS': *see* Æthelred, 'Lord of the Mercians'

ÆTHELING is used poetically for 'a good and noble man', and is applied in Old English verse to Christ, prophets, saints, and other heroes. In historical texts, ætheling and its Latin equivalents *filius regis* and *clito(n)* mean 'prince of the royal house'. In the eighth century, an Oswald is called ætheling apparently because his great-great-grandfather was king of the West Saxons (*ASC* s.a. 728); the definitions are much narrower in the ninth century and later. Edgar the Ætheling is so called because of his grandfather, King *Edmund Ironside, but most æthelings in this later period are sons or brothers of reigning kings. From the ninth century to the early eleventh, æthelings often witness the king's *charters as members of the royal family; after the Danish conquest in 1016, the surviving English æthelings were in exile on the Continent. *Edward the Confessor and Alfred, sons of *Æthelred the Unready, stayed in Normandy, whence Alfred returned to his death in 1036 and Edward returned to joint kingship of England in 1041. Edmund and Edward the Exile, sons of Edmund Ironside, travelled more widely until Edward and his son Edgar returned home in 1057.

Details of the trappings of æthelings only appear in the late tenth and eleventh centuries: charters mention officials assigned to the æthelings (S 1454 notes a *discthegn*; S 1422 notes a larger train of a *discthegn*, two *cnihtas*, and perhaps two priests), and estates set aside for the use of æthelings (S 937). The place-names *Æthelinga-ig* (Athelney, Somerset) and *Æthelinga-dene* (Dean, Sussex) refer to lands associated with æthelings: Dean was perhaps where Queen *Ælfthryth brought up her grandchildren, sons of King Æthelred. In the early eleventh century æthelings first appear in *law codes (II Cnut, *Norðleoda Laga*, *Grið*), where they are granted a special legal status, equivalent to archbishops and second only to the king.

D. Dumville, 'The Ætheling: a Study in Anglo-Saxon Constitutional History', *ASE* 8 (1979), 1–33; S. Keynes, 'The Crowland Psalter and the Sons of King Edmund Ironside', *Bodleian Library Record* 11 (1985), 359–70; idem, 'The Æthelings in Normandy', *ANS* 13 (1990), 173–205.

SEAN MILLER

ÆTHELRED, 'Lord of the Mercians' (d. 911), and Æthelflæd, 'Lady of the Mercians' (d. 918). Æthelred followed King Ceolwulf (874–9) as ruler of the Mercians. He appears to have submitted to the overlordship of King *Alfred in the early 880s; and it was probably during this period that he oppressed the rulers of the southern Welsh in ways which induced them to turn to Alfred for protection (Asser, c. 80). In 886 he was entrusted by Alfred with the control of the borough of *London. It was at about this time, or shortly before, that 'English' Mercia was subsumed into the newly-conceived 'Kingdom of the *Anglo-Saxons'. Æthelred married Alfred's daughter, Æthelflæd, and is named as a beneficiary in the king's *will. After the death of King Alfred in

899, Æthelred and Æthelflæd continued to hold power in English Mercia, acknowledging the overlordship of *Edward the Elder, king of the Anglo-Saxons (899–924), and co-operating closely with Edward in campaigns against the Scandinavian intruders. They were empowered to issue charters; but the 'Mercian' coinage of the early tenth century was struck in Edward's name. When Æthelred died, in 911, Edward succeeded to London and *Oxford 'and to all the lands which belonged to them', but Æthelflæd succeeded to her husband's position as ruler of the Mercians. When Æthelflæd died, in 918, Edward assumed direct control of English Mercia, depriving Ælfwynn, their daughter, of any power and taking her into Wessex. Æthelred and Æthelflæd were viewed in certain quarters as 'king' and 'queen', and some may even have hoped that Ælfwynn would succeed them as ruler of the Mercians; no doubt they found the political reality hard to accept. Æthelred and Æthelflæd were instrumental in the foundation and endowment of the 'New Minster' (St Oswald's), *Gloucester, where both were buried.

Stenton, *ASE*, pp. 324–30; F. T. Wainwright, 'Æthelflæd, Lady of the Mercians', *Scandinavian England*, ed. H. P. R. Finberg (Chichester, 1975), pp. 305–24; S. Keynes, 'King Alfred and the Mercians', *Kings, Currency and Alliances: the History and Coinage of Southern England in the Ninth Century*, ed. M. A. S. Blackburn and D. N. Dumville (Woodbridge, 1998), pp. 1–45, at 19–34.

SIMON KEYNES

ÆTHELRED AND ÆTHELBERHT, SS, were two princes of the royal house of *Kent who were murdered during the reign of (and perhaps at the instigation of) Ecgberht, king of Kent (664–73); in expiation of the murder, Ecgberht founded the church of *Minster-in-Thanet. For reasons that are irrecoverable, their relics were preserved at Wakering (Essex), and from there they were translated to *Ramsey by Bishop *Oswald and Ealdorman Æthelwine (hence before 992, when both these men died). The earliest account of the murdered princes is the *passio* by *Byrhtferth of Ramsey (*BHL* 2643), which forms cc. 1–10 of his *Historia regum*; later versions of the legend are recorded by *Goscelin (*BHL* 5960) and *William of Malmesbury.

Symeonis Monachi Opera Omnia, ed. T. Arnold, 2 vols., RS (London, 1882–5), ii.1–13; WMalm, *GR* ii.209; M. Lapidge, 'Byrhtferth of Ramsey and the Early Sections of the *Historia Regum* attributed to Symeon of Durham', *ASE* 10 (1981), 97–122, repr. in Lapidge, *ALL* ii.317–42; D. Rollason, *The Mildrith Legend. A Study in Early*

Medieval Hagiography in England (Leicester, 1982), esp. pp. 15–21, 89–104.

MICHAEL LAPIDGE

ÆTHELRED THE UNREADY (d. 23 April 1016), son of *Edgar and *Ælfthryth, was king of the English (978–1016) after his half-brother *Edward the Martyr. Æthelred's epithet 'Unready' is a very late coinage, probably twelfth century. Its first certain appearance is in the early thirteenth century, as 'Unrad', a play on the literal translation of Æthelred's name, 'noble counsel', and *un-ræd*, meaning 'no counsel' or 'ill-advised counsel'. As he himself admits in 993 that advisers were able to take advantage of his ignorance, and as he supported the treacherous *Eadric Streona after 1006, the charge that he was sometimes a poor judge of advisers seems well-deserved.

The facts that Æthelred was forced into exile in Normandy in 1013–14 by the Dane *Swein Forkbeard, and that by the end of 1016 Swein's son *Cnut was king of England, demonstrate that Æthelred was not equal to the task of keeping the *Vikings out of England. This may have more to do with the strength of the Vikings than with Æthelred's alleged incompetence. Æthelred ruled for thirty-eight years and had to deal with the Viking threat for over three decades; so perhaps it is no wonder that there were major problems in the last decade of his reign. It is clear from the continuation of Edgar's reform of the coinage and the institution of *heregeld* in 1012 that the machinery of government worked well throughout Æthelred's reign. But the best-known narrative sources were written towards the end of the reign when things looked very grim, and Æthelred's reputation has suffered in consequence. The *Anglo-Saxon Chronicle* for the whole reign was written after Æthelred's death, and was perhaps designed to explain the eventual conquest. The one contemporary annal that does survive (for 1001) is certainly less doom-laden than the later chronicle. Likewise *Wulfstan's *Sermo Lupi ad Anglos*, that great catalogue of things rotten in England, is a reflection of the state of things in 1014, not the whole reign.

The internal politics of Æthelred's reign can be divided into four periods. The first period dates from Æthelred's accession in 978 to 984. These were Æthelred's teenage years, and he was probably carefully guided by Bishop *Æthelwold and Ælfthryth. Æthelwold died in 984, and in that same year Ælfthryth ceased witnessing her son's charters. In the second period, 984 to 993, Æthelred was led astray by greedy counsellors into seizing church lands and redistributing them to his nobles, as he repentantly explains in a charter of 993 (S 876). The third period, from 993 to 1006, was marked by the return of Ælfthryth and seems to be a much more stable period for English internal affairs, though Viking attacks continued. Such a stable period helps to explain the flowering of literature (works by *Ælfric, *Byrhtferth, *Wulfstan of Winchester), manuscripts, and other artwork datable to the turn of the century. The fourth period, from 1006 to 1016, was marked by an upheaval of the king's council in 1006 and the growing prominence thereafter of the notorious turncoat Eadric Streona, who became the king's chief counsellor.

The Viking attacks during Æthelred's reign can also be divided into four phases. The first phase, 980 to 991, saw the resumption of Viking activity in England after a twenty-five year absence, though with mainly local effects. The second phase, 991 to 1005, involved much heavier Viking attacks, and could be seen as the effects of a single large Viking army on English territory from its arrival with ninety-three ships in 991 until the famine of 1005 forced it to return to Denmark. It was this army that fought Byrhtnoth at the *Battle of Maldon, and received tribute in 991 (£10,000), 994 (£16,000), and 1002 (£24,000). The third phase, from 1006 to 1012, saw two major invasions. The first, in 1006, was only stopped by a massive payment of tribute in 1007 (£36,000). In 1008 Æthelred ordered that a huge English fleet be built, but feuds involving Eadric's kin limited its usefulness, and it did not prevent the arrival in 1009 of another immense Viking army led by Thorkell the Tall. This army ravaged much of southern England, and only stopped after the payment of tribute of £48,000 in 1012. The fourth phase, from 1013 to 1016, again saw two major invasions, both of which culminated in the conquest of England, by Swein in 1013 and Cnut in 1016.

Æthelred was twice married, and all his sons bear the names of earlier English kings. With his first wife, Ælfgifu, he had six sons (Æthelstan, Ecgberht, King *Edmund Ironside, Eadred, Eadwig, Edgar), and perhaps five daughters. In 1002 Æthelred married *Emma, sister of Richard II, duke of Normandy, and they had three children, King *Edward the Confessor, Alfred the ætheling, and Godgifu.

Ethelred the Unready: Papers from the Millenary Conference, ed. D. Hill (Oxford, 1978); S. Keynes, *The Diplomas of King Æthelred 'the Unready' 978–1016: a Study in Their Use as Historical Evidence* (Cambridge, 1980);

idem, 'A Tale of Two Kings: Alfred the Great and Æthelred the Unready', *TRHS* 5th ser. 36 (1986), 195–217; idem, 'The Vikings in England, 790–1016', *The Oxford Illustrated History of the Vikings*, ed. P. Sawyer (Oxford, 1997), pp. 48–82

SEAN MILLER

ÆTHELSTAN, king of the Anglo-Saxons (924/ 5–27), and king of the English (927–39), succeeded in 924 or 925, in uncertain circumstances. His father, *Edward the Elder, died in July 924. Edward's son and Æthelstan's half-brother Ælfweard succeeded, but died within a month. If Æthelstan had become king immediately after that, he might have ruled from August 924, but he was not crowned king until September 925, over a year later. Contemporary sources do not explain this, but *William of Malmesbury is full of details: he notes that Æthelstan was raised at the Mercian court, and that there was a plot to have him blinded at *Winchester. Civil war between Mercians and West Saxons, with Mercians favouring Æthelstan and West Saxons favouring Ælfweard's brother Eadwine, is certainly one possible explanation of Æthelstan's delayed coronation. The 'disturbance in the kingdom' that drove Eadwine to his death in a storm at sea in 933 may have been another sign of this tension; Æthelstan's lack of known heirs, which led to the succession of his half-brother Edmund in 939, may have been a deliberate concession to end the conflict.

Æthelstan's external affairs are more clearly recorded. He had a treaty with Sihtric of York in 926, but after Sihtric's death the alliance collapsed, and Æthelstan invaded Northumbria to assert his control. In July 927, at a meeting at Eamont (near Penrith), he received the submission of the Northumbrians and the Scots, the Welsh and the Strathclyde Britons. The northerners had previously submitted to Edward, but Æthelstan was the first southern king to exercise real control over Northumbria. However, his supremacy did not go unchallenged. Æthelstan led his army into Scotland in 934, and in 937 the Scots allied with the Norse and invaded England, to be roundly defeated at the *Battle of *Brunanburh*. The Old English poem celebrating that victory is perhaps the best-known product of Æthelstan's reign.

*Charters and *law-codes throw much light on the working of royal government during Æthelstan's reign. The charters issued from 928 to 934/ 5 are the work of a single individual, arguably a royal scribe (see *chancery, royal). From 931 they accord the king titles which claim not only kingship of the English but lordship over all of Albion

or Britannia. A similar development is seen in Æthelstan's coins, which bear the motto 'king of the whole of Britain'. The fact that various Welsh and Scottish sub-kings appear in the witness-lists adds substance to this boast. The charters also note the day and place of issue, which means that the king's itinerary can be traced more accurately than that of any other early king. Seven lawcodes survive from Æthelstan's reign. Four are official royal productions, including two general proclamations of laws from the king, one issued at Grately, another issued at Exeter in response to continuing violations of the Grately code. Of the three remaining codes, one is a report back to the king from his officials in Kent on how the Grately code would be implemented and supplemented.

Foreign scholars and dignitaries flocked to the English court. *Asser notes that scholars from various lands had come to the court of King *Alfred the Great, and one of Alfred's daughters had married a count of Flanders; but Æthelstan had more continental contacts than any of his predecessors. At least four of his half-sisters were married into continental noble families, including the royal families of Francia (Eadgifu to King Charles the Simple) and *Germany (Edith to Emperor Otto I), as well as the family that would supplant the rulers of Francia (Eadhild to Duke Hugh). When Charles was captured by his enemies, Eadgifu brought his son and heir Louis to be fostered in England until the Franks sued for his return in 936. Also fostered at Æthelstan's court were Alan of Brittany and Hakon, son of King Harald of Norway. Visiting scholars included Germans, Irish, Franks, Bretons, Italians, and even the Icelander Egill Skallagrímsson; perhaps the most distinguished was *Israel the Grammarian. Æthelstan was known to be a keen collector of holy relics: some came from the Continent as gifts, and others were gathered by his agents. Æthelstan was also renowned for his generosity in giving relics, books, and other treasures to religious houses throughout England. He died on 27 October 939, and was buried at *Malmesbury.

M. Lapidge, 'Some Latin Poems as Evidence for the Reign of Athelstan' (1979), *ALL* ii. 49–86; idem, 'Israel the Grammarian in Anglo-Saxon England', *ALL* ii. 87–104; C. Brett, 'A Breton in England in the Reign of King Æthelstan: a Letter in British Library MS. Cotton Tiberius A.xv', in *France and Britain in the Early Middle Ages*, ed. D. Dumville and G. Jondorf (Woodbridge 1991), pp. 43–70; M. Wood, 'The Making of King Aethelstan's Empire: an English Charlemagne?', *Ideal and Reality in Frankish and Anglo-Saxon Society*, ed. P. Wormald (Oxford, 1983), pp. 250–72; S. Keynes, 'King

Athelstan's Books', Clemoes FS, pp. 143–201; idem, 'Royal Government and the Written Word in Late Anglo-Saxon England', *The Uses of Literacy in Early Medieval Europe*, ed. R. McKitterick (Cambridge, 1990), pp. 226–57, esp. 235–41; Dumville, *Wessex*, pp. 141–71.

SEAN MILLER

ÆTHELSTAN ÆTHELING (d. 25 June 1014) was the eldest son of King *Æthelred the Unready, by his first wife Ælfgifu. Æthelstan makes an early appearance among the witnesses to his father's charters in 993 (S 876), when he would have been a young boy. He was probably being brought up at this stage by his grandmother, Queen *Ælfthryth, perhaps on her estate at *Æthelingadene* (Dean, in west Sussex); he also refers in his will to his foster-mother, Ælfswith. Æthelstan continued to attest charters in the later 990s and 1000s, invariably ahead of his brothers; his last appearance is in a charter dated 1013. It is not known what became of him and of his surviving younger brothers (Edmund and Eadwig) during the reign of King *Swein Forkbeard (1013–14): one can but assume that he lay low somewhere in England, and that on his father's return from exile in Normandy, in the spring of 1014, he resumed his accustomed position as the king's prospective successor. It seems, however, that Æthelstan became ill during the summer of 1014, and sought his father's permission to draw up his *will. Two copies of the will (S 1503) survive in single-sheet form, both from the archives of Christ Church, *Canterbury; one of them, written by two scribes, is the upper part of a *chirograph. Two copies of the will were also preserved at the Old Minster, *Winchester; one of them was the lower part of a chirograph. The second copies of the will, in each archive, may have been produced as part of the process of its publication. It emerges from the will that Æthelstan held land in at least ten counties of south-eastern England, and took special interest not only in the religious houses at Winchester and Canterbury, but also at *Shaftesbury and *Ely. A noteworthy feature is the great care taken in disposing of his personal possessions, including no fewer than eleven swords (one of which had belonged to King *Offa), a coat of mail (which had been lent to Morcar), two shields, a drinking-horn, a silver-coated trumpet, and a string of fine horses. Æthelstan's friends and associates included *Godwine (probably the person of that name who later became an earl), and Siferth (one of the leading thegns in eastern England, and a prominent figure at his father's court); he also had a mass-priest (Ælfwine), a *disc-thegn* (Ælfmær), a

sword-polisher, and a staghuntsman. Æthelstan's obit on 25 June (in a year not specified) was recorded at Christ Church, Canterbury (BL Arundel 68, 32r), and, independently, at the Old Minster, Winchester (BL Add. 29436, 73r). Æthelstan had received his father's permission 'on the Friday after the feast of Midsummer [24 June]': in 1013 the Friday in question was 26 June; in 1014 it was 25 June; and in 1015 it was 1 July. So it would appear that Æthelstan received permission to make his will on 25 June 1014, and died later on the same day; he was buried at the Old Minster, Winchester. Æthelstan's death would have projected his brother, *Edmund Ironside, into prominence as the prospective successor; and it was in 1015 that Edmund took a stand against the regime personified by his ailing father, but controlled by *Eadric Streona.

Anglo-Saxon Wills, ed. D. Whitelock (Cambridge, 1930), pp. 56–63 (no. 20), and *EHD* i, no. 129; M. Brown, *Anglo-Saxon Manuscripts* (London, 1991), pp. 42–3 [facsimile of the will]; S. Keynes, 'Queen Emma and the *Encomium Emmae Reginae*', *Encomium Emmae Reginae*, ed. A. Campbell, Camden Classic Reprints 4 (Cambridge, 1998), xiii–lxxxvii, at xxi n. 1; N. J. Higham, *The Death of Anglo-Saxon England* (Stroud, 1997), pp. 44–7, 56–9.

SIMON KEYNES

ÆTHELSTAN HALF-KING (d. after 957) was ealdorman of *East Anglia (932–57), then a monk of *Glastonbury. The byname 'Half-King' appears in *Byrhtferth's *Vita S. Oswaldi*. His province was the whole eastern Danelaw, and from 943 to 957 he was the chief *ealdorman. His brothers were also ealdormen: Æthelwold in the south-east (940–6) and Eadric in Wessex (942–9). For a while, therefore, the three brothers controlled over half the country, inviting comparison with *Godwine's family in the eleventh century. Æthelstan was King *Edgar's foster-father, and his retirement coincides neatly with the division of the kingdom in 957, when Edgar became king of the Mercians. *Glastonbury, where he was buried, remembered Æthelstan as a benefactor; his son Æthelwine, co-founder of *Ramsey and himself chief ealdorman (983–92), was a prominent supporter of the monastic reform movement.

C. Hart, 'Athelstan "Half King" and his Family', in his *The Danelaw* (London, 1992), pp. 569–604

SEAN MILLER

ÆTHELSTAN PSALTER, a diminutive copy of the Gallican psalter (with canticles) which possibly served as a personal *prayerbook; it was written at an unidentified centre in Northern Francia in

17

the earlier ninth century, but was in England by the beginning of the tenth, when leaves containing an illustrated Latin *metrical calendar were added at the beginning of the manuscript (3r–20v); at a later point, in the second quarter of the tenth century, a series of psalter collects and various Greek prayers (litany, Pater Noster, Creed) were added at the end (178r–200v). The manuscript is now London, BL, Cotton Galba A.xviii. There is various evidence to suggest that the manuscript at one time belonged to King *Æthelstan (924–39), and that the Greek prayers were added in connection with the presence at Æthelstan's court of the Breton scholar known as *Israel the Grammarian.

Temple, *AS MSS*, pp. 36–7 (no. 5); S. Keynes, 'King Athelstan's Books', Clemoes FS, pp. 143–201, at 193–6; idem, 'Anglo-Saxon Entries in the "Liber Vitae" of Brescia', Bately FS, pp. 99–119, at 117–19; Dumville, *Wessex*, pp. 74–7, 87–8; P. McGurk, 'The Metrical Calendar of Hampson: a New Edition', *AB* 104 (1986), 79–125; M. Lapidge, 'Israel the Grammarian in Anglo-Saxon England', *ALL* ii.87–104; R. Deshman, 'The Galba Psalter: Pictures, Texts and Context in an Early Medieval Prayerbook', *ASE* 26 (1997), 109–38.

MICHAEL LAPIDGE

ÆTHELTHRYTH (= Etheldreda, Audrey; d. 679), queen, and abbess, was the daughter of Anna, king of *East Anglia. In about 652 she was given in marriage to Tondberht, ealdorman of the South Gyrwas; on his death (c.655) she retired to *Ely, but in 660 was again married, to Ecgfrith, king of Northumbria, who was only fifteen years old. She apparently remained a virgin throughout both of these marriages; indeed, when Ecgfrith finally insisted that their union be consummated, Æthelthryth, assisted by *Wilfrid, bishop of Northumbria, left her husband and became a nun at *Coldingham, under her aunt Æbbe. In 673 she returned south and founded a double monastery at Ely. She remained there as abbess, living a life of austerity, until her death, of a neck-tumour, which she regarded as divine punishment for the wearing of necklaces in her youth. She was succeeded by her sister *Sexburg. Seventeen years after her burial at Ely, Æthelthryth's body was found to be incorrupt; she was translated in 695, and her shrine became a popular place of pilgrimage. Bede was deeply impressed by Æthelthryth and included a poem in praise of her in his *Historia ecclesiastica* (iv.20). In the mid-tenth century *Ælfhelm composed a Latin Life of the saint which is lost except for excerpts in the *Liber Eliensis* (i. 43–9). A prose Life and a verse Life of Æthelthryth (by Gregory of Ely) were composed

in Latin in the early twelfth century; these add little to Bede's account of the saint's life, but include detailed accounts of the later translations and miracles at Ely. Feast day: 23 June; translation: 17 October.

Bede, *HE* iv.19–20, ed. B. Colgrave and R. A. B. Mynors, *Bede's Ecclesiastical History of the English People* (OMT, 1969), pp. 392–401; E. O. Blake, ed., *Liber Eliensis*, Camden Third Series 92 (London, 1962).

R. C. LOVE

ÆTHELWEARD (d. c.998), great-great-grandson of King Æthelred I, was *ealdorman 'of the western provinces' (presumably Devon, Somerset, and Dorset) in the late tenth century, the author of a Latin translation of the *Anglo-Saxon Chronicle*, and a literary patron of *Ælfric. He attested charters as ealdorman from the mid-970s, and was accorded the primacy among the ealdormen from 993; he took a leading part in negotiations with Olaf Tryggvason in 994, and presumably died soon after his last appearance as a witness in 998.

After 975, and probably before 983, Æthelweard produced a Latin translation of the *Anglo-Saxon Chronicle*, including material not found in surviving English versions. The work was dedicated to his cousin Matilda, abbess of Essen (in *Germany), herself a great-great-granddaughter of King *Alfred. In his prologue, Æthelweard charged Matilda to send him information about the family's continental affairs: the *Anglo-Saxon Chronicle* entry for 982, which included the death of the German Duke Otto, a great-grandson of King *Edward the Elder, was probably Æthelweard's rendering of news from Matilda. Æthelweard's Latin style was deplored by *William of Malmesbury, but is not untypical of its time. Æthelweard was also instrumental in encouraging Ælfric to translate Latin religious texts into Old English, as acknowledged in prefaces to Ælfric's translations of *Genesis* and *Lives of Saints*. Æthelweard was followed in this respect by his son Æthelmær, who refounded *Eynsham Abbey in the early eleventh century (S 911), and who was ealdorman in the south-west in the closing years of Æthelred's reign.

Sharpe, *Handlist*, 67; L. Whitbread, 'Æthelweard and the Anglo-Saxon Chronicle', *EHR* 74 (1959), 577–89; *The Chronicle of Æthelweard*, ed. A. Campbell (London, 1962); M. Winterbottom, 'The Style of Æthelweard', *MÆ* 36 (1967), 109–18; E. van Houts, 'Women and the Writing of History in the Early Middle Ages', *EME* 1 (1992), 53–68; *Ælfric's Prefaces*, ed. J. Wilcox (Durham, 1994).

SEAN MILLER

ÆTHELWOLD, abbot of *Abingdon (c.954–63) and bishop of *Winchester (963–84), a scholar of considerable learning and one of the principal proponents of the reform of Benedictine *monasticism in late tenth-century England. The place and precise date of his birth are unknown (in Wessex, presumably, during the years 904×909); during his adolescence he was a member of the royal household of King *Æthelstan; he was ordained a priest and monk by *Ælfheah, bishop of Winchester (934–51) sometime before 939, and following the death of Æthelstan he retired to *Glastonbury with his colleague *Dunstan, where he spent more than a decade in intensive study of texts such as the psalter, *Aldhelm, and the *Benedictine Rule. He was appointed abbot of the delapidated monastery of *Abingdon by King *Eadred in c.954, and he took with him from Glastonbury several followers (Osgar, Foldbriht and Frithegar) who were later to accompany him to Winchester; while at Abingdon he significantly increased the abbey's endowment and rebuilt and rededicated the church there. In 963 he was appointed bishop of Winchester by King *Edgar, to whom he had once served as tutor, and with the king's support was able to expel from the Old Minster the secular canons and replace them with Benedictine monks from Abingdon. He ruled Winchester vigorously for twenty-one years, taking a leading role in King Edgar's *witan, promoting the interests of Benedictine monks throughout the realm, and initiating a vast programme of reconstruction and refurbishment at the Old Minster; he also greatly increased the prestige of the Old Minster by his translation of the relics of St *Swithun on 15 July 971. Æthelwold survived at least one attempt to poison him, and although he suffered bodily infirmities affecting his stomach and legs, he lived into ripe old age and died on 1 August 984.

Æthelwold was one of the leading scholars and teachers of his age. It has recently been demonstrated that the Old English psalter gloss in the 'Royal Psalter' (London, BL, Royal 2.B.V) is his composition, as is the corpus of glosses to Aldhelm's prose De virginitate preserved inter alia in Brussels, Bibliothèque Royale, 1650. Of his known writings, he translated at the request of King Edgar and Queen *Ælfthryth the Regula S. Benedicti into English (the OE tract known as 'King Edgar's Establishment of Monasteries' was also composed by Æthelwold, almost certainly to serve as a preface to the Benedictine Rule); and the Latin customary known as the *Regularis Concordia, which was issued after the council of Winchester in 973 and which served as the norm for reformed Benedictine monasticism in England, is his composition as well. His Old English prose (in the translation of the Benedictine Rule) is a model of clarity and accuracy, whereas his Latin, particularly in the preface to the Regularis Concordia, is a flamboyant example of the 'hermeneutic' style which was practised by Latin authors in tenth-century England. Among his pupils he numbered *Ælfric, whose Old English prose matches that of his master in clarity, and *Wulfstan, sometime precentor (cantor) at the Old Minster, who was one of the most prolific Latin authors of pre-Conquest England. After his death, the cult of St Æthelwold was initiated at Winchester by Wulfstan, who composed the first Vita S. Æthelwoldi (Ælfric's vita of the saint is an abbreviation of Wulfstan's); it spread to a few other centres with Winchester connections, but was not widely observed in England. Feast days: 1 August (deposition); 10 September (translation).

Sharpe, Handlist, 68; Die angelsächsischen Prosabearbeitungen der Benediktinerregel, ed. A. Schröer, rev. H. Gneuss (Darmstadt, 1964); Regularis Concordia, ed. T. Symons (London, 1953); Councils & Synods i.142–54 ['King Edgar's Establishment of Monasteries']; Wulfstan of Winchester: the Life of St Æthelwold, ed. M. Lapidge and M. Winterbottom (OMT, 1991); Æthelwold, ed. Yorke; M. Gretsch, Die Regula Sancti Benedicti in England (Munich, 1973); idem, 'Æthelwold's Translation of the Regula Sancti Benedicti and its Latin Exemplar', ASE 3 (1974), 125–51; idem, 'The Benedictine Rule in Old English: a Document of Bishop Æthelwold's Reform Politics', Gneuss FS, pp. 131–58; idem, The Intellectual Foundations of the English Benedictine Reform Movement, CSASE 25 (Cambridge, 1998); L. Kornexl, Die Regularis Concoria und ihre altenglische Interlinearversion (Munich, 1993).

MICHAEL LAPIDGE

ÆTHELWOLD, BENEDICTIONAL OF. The Benedictional of Æthelwold (BL, Add. 49598) was written for Bishop *Æthelwold of Winchester, probably in the period 971–84. Benedictionals contain the episcopal blessings pronounced during high mass, immediately before the communion itself. As a class of book, they are very rare – the texts normally occur as part of pontificals – and Æthelwold's benedictional is the most opulent example of the genre. Its text is unusually full, combining blessings from the 'Gregorian' and 'Gallican' traditions alongside additional English material, and was probably compiled at Winchester in Æthelwold's day. The manuscript is written in a spacious, rounded, early English Caroline minuscule (the touchstone for the so-called 'Style I' of the script), golden Square capitals and Uncials being used as display scripts. The scribe was a certain *Godeman (possibly to be identified with the Godeman whom Æthelwold appointed abbot of Thorney). The volume is lavishly decorated: there is a prefatory cycle of figures representing the choirs of heaven, while the most important feasts in the body of the book are introduced by a full page framed miniature (showing the person or event commemorated) facing an incipit page within a matching frame. While the compositions are comparatively simple, the iconography is rich, including novel features such as the earliest western representations of the Dormition of the Virgin, and the Crowned Magi. The figural style is stolid, but the paintings are animated by agitated draperies and rich swirling colours which complement the lavish foliate frames: the overall effect is highly decorative. The most important sources for decoration, style and iconography were Carolingian (notably the Metz and Franco-Saxon schools), though debts to Byzantine and earlier Anglo-Saxon art are also apparent. Nevertheless, the choice of subject matter, details of the iconography and the general aesthetic were distinctive *'Winchester school' creations. Text, script and decoration all reflect the simultaneous embracing and adaptation of continental traditions that were the hallmarks of Æthelwold's Winchester; while the intertwining of the spiritual and the political in the iconography echoes the nature of the monastic reform he fostered.

G. F. Warner and H. A. Wilson, *The Benedictional of St Æthelwold* (Oxford, 1910); F. Wormald, *The Benedictional of St Ethelwold* (London, 1959); A. Prescott, 'The Text of the Benedictional of St Æthelwold' in *Æthelwold*, pp. 119–47; R. Deshman, *The Benedictional of Æthelwold* (Princeton, NJ, 1995).

RICHARD GAMESON

ÆTHELWULF, king of *Wessex (839–58), had the distinction of being succeeded by four of his sons, the youngest of whom was King *Alfred. His fifth and eldest son Æthelstan (who predeceased him) became king of the south-eastern provinces when Æthelwulf succeeded his father *Ecgberht as king of Wessex. Æthelwulf had to contend with increasingly severe attacks from *Vikings and won a notable victory in 851. In 855 Æthelwulf made a pilgrimage to *Rome and returned in 856 with a new wife, Judith, daughter of the Frankish king Charles the Bald. His eldest surviving son Æthelbald, who had been entrusted with control of Wessex in his absence, rebelled

and Æthelwulf was obliged to end his reign ruling only part of his former kingdom.

Stenton, *ASE*, pp. 244–5; Kirby, *Kings*, pp. 193–204.

B. A. E. YORKE

ÆTHELWULF, POET: *see* Ædiluulf

ÆTHILWALD the poet was a student of *Aldhelm (who died in 709 or 710), presumably at Malmesbury, and evidently proved a worthy disciple: his only surviving prose work, a letter to his teacher, is clearly composed in imitation of Aldhelm's idiosyncratic and highly ornate *Latin prose style, while all that survives of his verse are four Latin poems in rhythmical *octosyllables, a form which Aldhelm himself employed to great effect. Two of these octosyllabic poems are referred to by Æthilwald in his letter, to which they were apparently appended along with a third poem (now lost) seemingly composed in *Latin metre in some form of hexameters; it would appear from the somewhat insecure syntax of the extant poems that they were sent to Aldhelm as much for correction as for commendation. Æthilwald went much further than Aldhelm in his use of *alliteration in his octosyllables, and at times consciously adopts the idiosyncratic alliterative patterning of vernacular Old English verse. Apart from a poem in praise of Aldhelm and a prayer to God, Æthilwald's remaining two octosyllabic compositions are addressed to one Wihtfrith (presumably the same person to whom Aldhelm also wrote a letter), and an otherwise unknown Offa. Æthilwald has also been suggested as a possible author of the so-called *Liber monstrorum, although the evidence is decidedly thin.

Sharpe, *Handlist*, 66; 'Carmina rhythmica II–V' and 'Epistulae VII and XI', in *Aldhelmi Opera*, ed. R. Ehwald, MGH AA xv. 528–37, 495–7, 499–500; M. Lapidge and M. Herren, *Aldhelm: the Prose Works* (Cambridge, 1979), pp. 147–8, 164–6, 168; A. Orchard, *The Poetic Art of Aldhelm*, CSASE 8 (Cambridge, 1994), 21–7, 60–7.

ANDY ORCHARD

ÆTHILWALD, bishop of *Lindisfarne (c.731–737 or 740), who had previously been abbot of *Melrose and a student of St *Cuthbert (d. 687). He had a reputation for modest piety, and is known to have supplied anecdotes concerning St Cuthbert to the anonymous Lindisfarne author of the *Vita S. Cuthberti* (iv.4); according to Symeon of Durham, he also commissioned a stone cross in memory of Cuthbert. According to a tenth-century notice by *Aldred, Æthilwald also commissioned a lavish binding for the *Lindisfarne Gospels. He is possibly the author or compiler of an *Ympnarius Edilwaldi* recorded in a sixteenth-century booklist at Fulda, which is now lost but may have been the source of the hymns of *Bede printed by Georg Cassander in 1556. Æthilwald may also have been the addressee of an *acrostic poem preserved in the ninth-century *Book of Cerne.

Bede, *HE* v.12; *Two Lives of St Cuthbert*, ed. B. Colgrave (Cambridge, 1940), pp. 116, 254; *Symeonis Monachi Opera Omnia*, ed. T. Arnold, 2 vols., RS (London, 1882–5), i.39; Lapidge, *ALL* i.325–6; D. N. Dumville, 'Liturgical Drama and Panegyric Responsory from the Eighth Century? A Re-examination of the Origin and Contents of the Ninth-Century Section of the Book of Cerne', *JTS* ns 23 (1972), 374–406.

MICHAEL LAPIDGE

AGILBERT (fl. *c.*650–*c.*680) was from a leading Frankish family, certainly connected with the family of St Audoin (St Ouen), and probably with the royal Merovingian family itself. He was the second bishop of the West Saxons and, later, bishop of Paris. Agilbert's career serves to emphasise the strong links between the Frankish and the English ruling elites in the mid seventh century. His very name was the Frankish form of Æthelberht, which may suggest that he had some family relationship with the Kentish royal house, and it was at this time, according to *Bede (*HE* iii.8), that Earcongota, daughter of Eanbald king of Kent, and several other Anglo-Saxon princesses joined Frankish monasteries, perhaps through the agency of Agilbert himself.

According to Bede (*HE* iii.7), sometime after Cenwealh had been restored as leader of the West Saxons in 646, Agilbert arrived in *Wessex. He was a 'Gaul', or Frank, who was already a bishop when he arrived, having been ordained in Francia, presumably without a see. Prior to his arrival in England he had been studying in Ireland. Cenwealh invited Agilbert to stay amongst the West Saxons as their bishop, in the see established by *Birinus at *Dorchester-on-Thames. This position Agilbert held 'for some years' until Cenwealh tired of his 'barbarous speech', which presumably means that the bishop never properly mastered the language of his hosts. The West Saxon kingdom was then divided into two sees, one being given to Bishop Wine. Agilbert, we are told, was deeply offended and left the kingdom. He then seems to have headed north to the court of the Northumbrian kings *Oswiu and Alhfrith, for *Stephen's *Life of St Wilfrid* says that Agilbert ordained *Wilfrid priest at *Ripon at the king's command. This happened in 663 or 664. In 664 Agilbert appeared alongside Wilfrid and with his priest Agatho at the Synod of *Whitby where he championed the Romanist cause. It was, however, Wilfrid who spoke 'in his own tongue' for their side in the dispute, which again hints at Agilbert's poor command of English. Shortly after the synod, Agilbert is seen back in Francia where, along with eleven other bishops, he took part in Wilfrid's consecration as bishop at Compiègne (*Life of St Wilfrid*, c. 12). This also took place in 664. Although Bede refers to Agilbert in this context as bishop of Paris, he cannot have been appointed to that city until 666 or 667, for there is a charter of that date attested by Importunus his predecessor as bishop there. By 668, however, Agilbert must have become bishop since in that year he entertained *Theodore in Paris as the latter made his way from *Rome to *Canterbury to take up the archbishopric.

Agilbert's fortunes in England seem to have been governed by the tide of Mercian expansion, rather than to have been the result of his inability to speak English properly. He left southern England at around the time the Mercians acquired control of the area to the south of the Thames Valley, but at a later point (*c.*670), when Mercian influence in Wessex was on the wane, Cenwealh invited him back to become bishop of Winchester. Now bishop of Paris, Agilbert declined the offer and sent his nephew *Leuthere in his place. He died sometime between 679 and 690, and he was buried in the crypt which he had built at the double monastery of Jouarre, over which his sister Theodechild had presided as abbess.

P. Fouracre and R. Gerberding, *Late Merovingian France. History and Hagiography 640–720* (Manchester, 1996); J. Guerot, 'Les origines et le premier siècle de l'abbaye', in Y. Chaussy *et al.* (ed.), *L'Abbaye Royale de Notre-Dame de Jouarre* (Paris, 1961); W. Levison, *England and the Continent in the Eighth Century* (Oxford, 1946); A. Lohaus, *Die Merowinger und England* (Munich, 1974); I. Wood, *The Merovingian Kingdoms 450–751* (London, 1994).

P. FOURACRE

AGRICULTURE was the economic basis of Anglo-Saxon England: most people gained their livelihood, directly or indirectly, from the activity of farming and its products. Society as a whole was essentially agrarian. The evidence for this basis is, however, fragmentary as well as diverse: it derives from documents and manuscript illustrations; from the present landscape, including its place-names; and from archaeological and related investigations (see also *field systems).

The principal documentary sources are contemporary *laws, biographies and land *charters. Of the first, the laws of King *Ine (688–726), for example, set out to regulate many of the practical matters which arise when many individuals are seeking to wrest their living from the same area of land; thus the laws refer to cornland and fences, meadows and pasture, straying animals and the felling of trees. The general impression is of an agriculture effectively, even expansively, exploiting a range of resources in the Wessex landscape. Later codes tend to follow Ine's pattern of attempted regulation. Works such as *Felix's *Life of St Guthlac* and *Asser's *Life of King Alfred* contain topographical descriptions. Charters contain much detail pertaining to specific areas of land, including headlands and *woodland in working agrarian landscapes, mainly in Southumbria in the tenth and eleventh centuries. Manuscript illustrations include agrarian scenes, though few originate before *c.*1100.

Research in the later twentieth century has significantly modified both long-established views of the topic and the significance of some of the 'classic' pieces of evidence. That Anglo-Saxons brought with them proper ploughs and the 'open field' system were ideas abandoned in the 1960s. Nor is it now necessary to believe that Anglo-Saxon agriculture presents 'a general picture of uniformity' throughout England; while excavated archaeological evidence of cultivation in ridges from Gwithian, Cornwall, and Hen Domen near Montgomery, precisely because it continues to be rare rather than typical, has seen its significance overwhelmed by the implications of widespread landscape survey elsewhere.

Anglo-Saxon agriculture developed in a landscape already long-farmed and consequently littered with the cultural and environmental debris of its predecessors. The land charters clearly show that, at least later in the period, the inhabitants of the time were aware of this: they referred to old tracks, burial mounds and lynchets of fields we know were prehistoric, to roads which we know as Roman, and to heathen burial places. Most of the mechanical technology of the Roman period had lapsed by the mid-sixth century, yet it seems highly likely that much of the agriculture being practised in England by indigenous communities at the time of the settlement was at least on a par in technological terms with the husbandry of later pre-Roman Britain. That of the immigrants was probably similar. With it they found space to farm in a mosaic of well-farmed and derelict areas. Later, the impression is of a land with much tree-cover, probably most of it regenerated and managed rather than wild-wood.

Archaeology has been very successful in demonstrating the existence and nature of agrarian settlements, especially those of the sixth–eighth centuries, usually long-abandoned and characterised by many timber buildings. In places such as *Raunds (Northants.), West Heslerton and Wharram Percy (N. Yorks.), and the Middle Thames valley, excavation coupled with fieldwork has glimpsed the landscape context, and even social and tenurial links, within which early-mid Anglo-Saxon agriculture may well have operated. More widely, without settlement excavation, landscape study has successfully argued for the existence of complex *estate and tenurial arrangements providing the framework within which the routine of farming was carried out. Hints of pre-Anglo-Saxon origins for some elements of that framework have been noted throughout the country, for example in Kent, Wiltshire and Northumberland.

Though specifically agrarian evidence remains sparse archaeologically for the earlier part of the period in particular, botanical studies of excavated plant remains, pioneered largely from urban deposits like *Winchester, *Hamwic* and *Gloucester, have now become significant in rural contexts. The main cultivars and aspects of cropping practices are emerging within an agriculture characterised by regional diversity. By the eighth century, in a pattern of what can perhaps be seen as a distinctively Anglo-Saxon crop husbandry compared to late-Roman times, einkorn (*T. aestivum*), rye (*Secale cereale*), barley (*Hordeum vulgare*) and oats (*Avena sativa*) were becoming the main cereals in England, supplemented by peas and beans, with different emphases between these components from region to region. With einkorn and rye apparently favoured in place of the traditional wheats, emmer and spelt, nothing in the palaeo-botanical evidence indicates any major, long term improvement in cereal farming in the period. Information about yields which might qualify such a generalisation is non-existent.

Agricultural implements are not well-attested in contemporary sources, though a recently-discovered hoard of carpentry tools from Flixborough, Lincs., of tenth-century date, also contains an iron hoe-sheath and a bill-hook. Archaeologically, given the amount of relevant excavation now accomplished, the absence of unequivocal evidence of a plough from Anglo-Saxon contexts before the tenth century is almost certainly significant. Indeed, on the rare occasions when cultivating implements have been suggested, as at *Sutton Hoo and *York, they are ards. Since land-cultivation was undoubtedly the basis of Anglo-Saxon agriculture, it seems most likely that the tilling implement in use until at least the tenth century was most probably a wooden ard without iron fittings. Such was almost certainly of bow-and/or crook type, familiar in the arable fields of the first half of the first millennium AD and earlier.

The existence before the Conquest of a fully-fledged plough as illustrated in medieval sources such as the Luttrell Psalter is not validated by such evidence, though a plough with mouldboard might conceivably have developed late in the period. If so, no firm evidence links it with Viking introduction or development, and a few ostensibly late Saxon iron shares could have fitted on to ards and are not in themselves proof of a framed, wheeled or mouldboard plough. The Gwithian evidence of plough-marks and a turned furrow belonged to a pre-West Saxon context and is most likely to have occurred so far to the west precisely because it emanated from a different cultural context altogether, reminding us that the cultural reservoir in the post-Roman Celtic West may not have been confined to the religious and linguistic tradition. The *Bayeux Tapestry itself illustrates an ard, not a plough, *un araire* not *une charrue*. Farm-carts and most other farming implements – mainly rakes, forks and spades – are also likely to have been entirely or mainly of wood throughout the period.

Probably at no time was the situation static. The emergence of towns from the eighth century would have significantly affected certain areas, particularly estates with urban centres; the growth of powerful estates, especially regal and ecclesiastical ones, and a probable rise in population in the later half of the period also imply agricultural change. The fundamental change in agrarian settlement pattern from the eighth century onwards, and possible technological improvements in such things as drainage, iron smelting, farming implements and harness, hint at a quiet rather than dramatic dynamism of an agriculture operating within a framework of non-synchronous regional diversity. It managed to maintain and develop an increasingly English countryside basically in good heart over 600 critical years in the emergence of a distinctive Insular society.

The Agrarian History of England and Wales I.2: A.D. 43–1042, ed. H. P. R. Finberg, and *II: 1042–1350*, ed. H. E. Hallam (Cambridge 1972–88); P. J. Fowler, 'Farming in the Anglo-Saxon Landscape; an Archaeologist's Review', *ASE* 9 (1982) 263–80; idem, 'Farming in Early Medieval England: some Fields for Thought', in *The Anglo-Saxons from the Migration Period to the Eighth Century; an Ethnographic Perspective*, ed. J. Hines (Woodbridge, 1997), pp. 245–61; *Environment and Economy in Anglo-Saxon England: a Review of Recent Work on the Environmental Archaeology of Rural and Urban Anglo-Saxon Settlements in England* (York, 1994).

P. J. FOWLER

AIDAN (d. 651), saint and bishop of *Lindisfarne, was an Irishman, a monk of *Iona, who was chosen in 635 to answer King *Oswald's request for a bishop through whose teaching and ministry his people might learn the doctrine of the faith and receive the sacraments. He was consecrated in Iona. In *Northumbria he lived a life of personal austerity but remained moderate in his expectations of others. Among twelve English boys whom Aidan at the start of his ministry raised up to serve the church, Bede names only *Eata, abbot of *Melrose, who became the first English bishop of Lindisfarne. Aidan often stayed on royal *estates, preaching to people living nearby. Bede adds that King Oswald himself acted as interpreter for his *ealdormen and *thegns, for the king had a perfect knowledge of Irish. He used also to retire for solitary prayer to Farne Island, near the king's seat at Bamburgh. After Oswald's death in 642 Aidan remained close to King *Oswiu, also an Irish-speaker, but Bede tells of the special warmth which existed between Aidan and Oswiu's rival, Oswine, king of *Deira, emphasising that Aidan lived only eleven days after Oswine was murdered on Oswiu's instructions. He died on an estate of Oswiu on 31 August 651 and was buried in the cemetery at Lindisfarne; at a later date his bones were moved into a newly enlarged church to a grave at the south side of the altar. When the last Irish bishop of Lindisfarne withdrew to Iona, he is said to have taken with him some of Aidan's bones. In the eleventh century *Glastonbury claimed to possess relics of St Aidan.
Bede, *HE* iii. 3, 5, 14–17, 26.

RICHARD SHARPE

ALBINUS (d. 733 or 734), abbot of the monastery of SS Peter and Paul (later St Augustine's) in *Canterbury, who in 709 or 710 succeeded Abbot *Hadrian and remained abbot of the house until his death. He was a former student of both *Theodore and Hadrian at Canterbury, and was a scholar with a considerable reputation for learning (Bede calls him *doctissimus*) in both Greek and Latin. None of his writings survive. In the preface to his *Historia ecclesiastica*, *Bede warmly acknowledges the help of Albinus, and in fact a separate prefatory letter to Bede's work, addressed to Albinus, is preserved in early printed editions of the *Historia ecclesiastica*.

Bede, *HE* praef., v.20; *HE*, ed. Plummer, *VBOH*, p. clxxix.

MICHAEL LAPIDGE

ALCUIN OF YORK (*c.*735–19 May 804; alias Albinus, Alchuuine, Alcuinus), Anglo-Saxon deacon, scholar, and teacher from *York who later became one of Charlemagne's chief advisers and finished his career as abbot of Tours. A man of prodigious learning and a prolific writer, Alcuin is often regarded as the architect of the Carolingian Renaissance; he was characterised by Einhard as 'a man most learned in every field'. Through his writings, his personality, and his role as a teacher he exerted a decisive influence on European literary and ecclesiastical culture. His extant works include texts of elementary instruction in orthography, *grammar, rhetoric, dialectic, *astronomy and perhaps mathematics; biblical *exegesis, theology, basic religious instruction and saints' lives; also prayers and votive masses. In addition over 270 letters survive by Alcuin as well as a substantial corpus of verse in a wide range of genres.

Born in Northumbria, perhaps in the 730s, Alcuin was raised and educated by the religious community at York Minster from an early age. Beyond his kinship with *Willibrord and his family's ownership of a church at Spurn Point, nothing is known of Alcuin's biological family. At York Minster, Alcuin was taught by *Ecgberht, archbishop of York (d. 766) and by *Ælberht. He accompanied Ælberht on trips to the Continent and, on his retirement succeeded him as teacher. He also inherited his precious collection of books, a portion of which he eventually had transported to the Continent.

After Ælberht's death in 780, Alcuin was sent to Rome to collect the pallium for Ælberht's successor, Eanbald I. On his way back, in 781, he met Charlemagne in Parma. Although Alcuin had then written none of the works for which he is known, Charlemagne recognised his talents and invited Alcuin to join his court which, since the arrival of scholars from the Lombard kingdom (conquered in 774), had begun its development as an international centre of learning. Alcuin is believed to have taken up residence at court in 781 or 782, but there is no firm evidence for this date. Alcuin remained with the Carolingian Court until 794, the date of his elevation to the abbacy of Tours; thereafter, when old age and increasing infirmity prevented his attendance at court gatherings, he

remained in close touch with Charlemagne by letter. Alcuin's letters and poems from the court years offer a lively picture of intimacy with the royal family, and friendship, intellectual exchange and rivalry with fellow scholars. The nicknames that Alcuin devised for his students and colleagues illustrate the warmth and *familiaritas* of his circle.

At court, Alcuin served as teacher to the royal family (including Charlemagne himself). There and subsequently at Tours, he reintroduced texts which had been unstudied for centuries, including works of Boethius, Priscian's *Institutiones*, and the treatise *De decem categoriis*, of signal importance for the history of logic and speculative thought. His renown as a teacher ensured that pupils were sent from distant centres to study with him, with the result that he trained most of the high-ranking continental churchmen of the following generation.

Alcuin's influence beyond the classroom was no less significant. He helped to draft important statements of royal policy, including the *Admonitio generalis* and *De litteris colendis*. Alcuin also wrote energetically against the Adoptionist heresy and contributed in some way to the debate about the image controversy. He left his mark on the liturgy too, although the precise extent of his activity is still debated. He introduced votive masses and the singing of the creed during Mass to the Continent; he encouraged the observance of All Saints' Day and compiled a lectionary and perhaps a homiliary, although he should probably no longer be credited with the revision of the Gregorian Sacramentary. At Charlemagne's request, Alcuin produced an emended text of the Bible and during and after his abbacy, Tours became an important centre for the production of bibles.

Although he did not use the new Caroline minuscule script himself, Alcuin insisted on new standards of accuracy and clarity in the scriptorium. He brought the same concern for clarity to the pronunciation of Latin. As a native speaker of English, Alcuin would have learnt a Latin free of vulgarisms typical of the latinity of the Latin/Romance-speaking areas of the Continent. Alcuin's imposition of a reformed system of pronunciation (in which every syllable was articulated) may ultimately have contributed to the emerging gulf between Latin and the Romance vernaculars.

Alcuin's career in Francia was interrupted by two return visits to England. In 786, Alcuin accompanied the legatine mission and perhaps helped to draft some of the chapters of the legatine council (see *councils, ecclesiastical). Alcuin was in England again in 790 × 793 when he was delegated to negotiate between Charlemagne and *Offa. During that interval, and after his return when he learned of the *Viking attack on *Lindisfarne, Alcuin was much troubled by the disorder and violence of English affairs and expressed his concern in numerous letters of admonition to his English associates. This concern was one factor in Alcuin's decision to finish his career on the Continent. However, he maintained contact with English correspondents in Northumbria, Mercia and Kent and students from England went abroad to study with him.

Alcuin's writings survive in numerous manuscripts scattered across Europe. Even during his lifetime, his letters were assiduously copied by contemporaries. Due to subsequent losses and destruction, the English tradition of Alcuin's writings is difficult to trace. *Wulfstan the Homilist had access to Alcuin's letters and Alcuin's De virtutibus et vitiis circulated in an Old English translation. Alcuin's letters and his poem on 'The Bishops, Kings and Saints of York' offer essential contemporary testimony for English affairs during the otherwise poorly documented interval between the death of Bede and the beginning of the Anglo-Saxon Chronicle as a contemporary source (in the last quarter of the ninth century). No writings by Alcuin in Old English survive and it is doubtful if any existed. Sentiments and expressions in his verse occasionally evince some resemblance to Old English poetry, but the apparent similarities can usually be credited to a shared biblical and patristic heritage. His prose style is straightforward, in the tradition of Bede rather than *Aldhelm. His verse owes much to the example of Venantius Fortunatus.

Sharpe, Handlist, 87; D. Schaller, Verfasserlexikon i.241–53; PL c–ci; MGH, PLAC i.160–351; MGH, Epistolae iv. 1–493; Alcuino: De Orthographia, ed. S. Bruni (Florence, 1997); W. S. Howell, The Rhetoric of Alcuin & Charlemagne (Princeton, NJ, 1941); Alcuin: the Bishops, Kings and Saints of York, ed. P. Godman (OMT, 1982); S. Allott, Alcuin of York: his Life and Letters (York, 1974); E. Dümmler, 'Zur Lebensgeschichte Alchvins', Neues Archiv 18 (1892–3), 51–70; D. Bullough, 'Alcuin and the Kingdom of Heaven: Liturgy, Theology and the Carolingian Age', in Carolingian Essays, ed. U.-R. Blumenthal (Washington, DC, 1983), pp. 1–69; idem, 'Albuinus deliciosus Karoli regis: Alcuin of York and the Shaping of the Early Carolingian Court', in Institutionen, Kultur und Gesellschaft im Mittelalter: Festschrift für Josef Fleckenstein, ed. L. Fenske, W. Rösener and T. Zotz (Sigmaringen, 1984), pp. 73–92; J. Fleckenstein, 'Alcuin im Kreis der Hofgelehrten Karls des Grossen', in Science in Western and Eastern Civilization in Carolingian Times, ed. P. L. Butzer and D. Lohrmann (Basel, 1993), pp. 3–22.

MARY GARRISON

ALDFRITH, king of *Northumbria (686–705), illegitimate son of King *Oswiu (642–70) by an Irish mother, as a result of which he spoke Irish fluently. During the reign of Ecgfrith (670–85) he spent time in exile in Ireland, perhaps at *Iona, where through his studies he acquired a reputation for great learning (Bede calls him a uir undecumque doctissimus). At Iona he had perhaps known (and studied with?) *Adomnán, who subsequently came to Northumbria to redeem Irish captives and presented Aldfrith with a copy of his work De locis sanctis. On another occasion, he is said to have purchased a codex cosmographiorum for the substantial price of eight *hides and given it to the monastery of *Wearmouth-Jarrow. He was married at some point to *Cuthburg, a sister of King *Ine of Wessex and eventual abbess of Wimborne; through her he was also related in some way to *Aldhelm, who stood as sponsor at his baptism and who dedicated to Aldfrith his massive Epistola ad Acircium.

Bede, HE iv.26, v.15, v.19; Historia abbatum, c. 15; Stenton, ASE, pp. 88–90; D. N. Dumville, 'Two Troublesome Abbots', Celtica 21 (1990), 146–52; N. J. Higham, The Kingdom of Northumbria AD 350–1100 (Stroud, 1993), pp. 140–1.

MICHAEL LAPIDGE

ALDHELM (d. 709 or 710), abbot of *Malmesbury and bishop of *Sherborne (from 705), a scholar of immense learning and the earliest native Anglo-Saxon to have left a corpus of Latin writing. The date of Aldhelm's birth is unknown (c.640?), but he was evidently descended from Wessex nobility, and had connections with the royal court. The details of his early education are similarly unknown; what is certain is that he studied at the school of *Canterbury, from 670 onwards, under the supervision of Archbishop *Theodore and Abbot *Hadrian (part of a letter from Aldhelm to Hadrian is preserved by *William of Malmesbury), and this schooling had a profound effect on his scholarly orientation. He left Canterbury to become abbot of Malmesbury at a date unknown; although William of Malmesbury gives the date of appointment as 675, no charter witnessed by Aldhelm as abbot carries a date earlier than 680, and there is some possibility, therefore, that Aldhelm may have spent as much as a decade studying in Canterbury (the longer the period in question, the more explicable becomes the vast range of his learning). As abbot of Malmesbury, Aldhelm increased the abbey's endowment and built several churches there, one dedicated to SS Peter and Paul (the dedication of which is commemorated in his own *titulus on the church, *Carmen ecclesiasticum* i), and another to the Virgin Mary (perhaps the church commemorated in his *Carmen ecclesiasticum* ii). It was also at this time that Aldhelm composed a lengthy letter (his *Ep.* iv) to Geraint, king of *Domnonia*, setting out the correct principles of the Roman method of calculating Easter. When the West Saxon diocese was divided in 706, Aldhelm became the first bishop of its western part, with its episcopal see in Sherborne. According to William of Malmesbury he built a church at Sherborne (which no longer exists); it was possibly during the period of his bishopric that he built churches at *Bradford-on-Avon (Wilts.) and *Wareham (Dorset). Although Bede reports that Aldhelm 'presided vigorously' over his diocese, nothing further is known of this activity.

Aldhelm's literary achievements are much better known, thanks to the large corpus of his writing which has survived, which includes: a group of *tituli* for churches and altars (the so-called *Carmina ecclesiastica*); a collection of one hundred metrical *enigmata; a prose treatise *De virginitate* and a corresponding metrical version of the same, consisting of some 2,900 hexameters; a poem in rhythmical octosyllables describing a journey through Cornwall and Devon; a lengthy *Epistola ad Acircium* consisting of a treatise on the arithmological significance of the number seven and of treatises on metre (*De metris*) and scansion (*De pedum regulis*); and a small corpus of letters. Of these, the *Carmina ecclesiastica* consist of the aforementioned *tituli* for churches of SS Peter and Paul and the Virgin Mary, as well as for an unidentified church built by a daughter of King Centwine (676–85) named Bugga (no. iii), and for a series of altars dedicated to the apostles, including Matthias (nos. iv–v). These *tituli* circulated widely and frequently served as models for inscriptional verse by later Anglo-Latin poets. The collection of 100 *enigmata* is ostensibly modelled on a similar, earlier collection by the anonymous Late Latin poet who calls himself 'Symposius'; but whereas the riddles of Symposius are three-line trifles built on plays of words, Aldhelm attempted in his *enigmata* ('mysteries') to evoke the life-forces of gestation, birth and death which animate the universe; the imaginative conception in these poems exercised a powerful influence on later Anglo-Latin authors of *enigmata*, such as *Boniface, *Tatwine and Eusebius, as well as on the anonymous poets of the OE *riddles. The *enigmata* were inserted by Aldhelm into his massive *Epistola ad Acircium* (a letter or treatise addressed to *Aldfrith, king of Northumbria)

ostensibly to illustrate the properties of metre explained by Aldhelm in the two metrical treatises included in the same work (of these, *De metris* provides discussion of the various kinds of metrical feet and the construction of the hexameter, whereas *De pedum regulis* is a metrical *gradus* for non-Latin speakers in which Aldhelm provides long lists of words constituting the various metrical feet, such as spondees, iambs, trochees, etc.). The prose *De virginitate* was addressed to Abbess *Hildelith and her community of nuns at Barking; it consists of some chapters of theoretical discussion on virginity (drawn from Ambrose, Augustine and Jerome) illustrated by a long catalogue of examples of male virgins, beginning with Old Testament patriarchs, John the Baptist, apostles, fathers of the Church, martyrs and confessors (including Martin, Antony and Benedict), followed by a sequence of female martyrs (including Cecilia, Agatha, Agnes, etc.); it concludes with an exhortation to modest dress (drawn from an earlier treatise on the subject by Cyprian). The flamboyant style of Aldhelm's prose, consisting of excessively long sentences built up of synonymous phrases often linked by alliteration and adorned by a dazzling variety of unusual grecisms, archaisms and words drawn from glossaries, also exerted a profound influence on later Anglo-Latin authors, and was ardently imitated by *Boniface, *Æthelwold, *Byrhtferth and the draftsmen of the charters of King *Æthelstan. The *Carmen de virginitate* is a contrafactum to the prose: it closely follows the structure of the prose work, but Aldhelm added various new virgins, and heightened the diction so that virginity itself is pictured as a vigorously aggressive virtue. As in the case of the prose work, the diction of the *Carmen* was often imitated by later Anglo-Latin poets, including Boniface, *Bede, *Alcuin and *Wulfstan of Winchester. Finally, the rhythmical form of the brief octosyllabic poem concerning a journey originating in Cornwall and culminating in the description of a mighty storm at an unidentified church in Devon or Dorset (Wareham?), also influenced later poets, notably Aldhelm's own student *Æthilwald. It is fair to say that, in the realm of diction – both prose and verse – Aldhelm was the most influential Anglo-Latin author.

Aldhelm reportedly died at Doulting (Somerset) and was buried at Malmesbury. His deposition is commemorated on 25 May in Anglo-Saxon liturgical calendars. From the tenth century onwards his cult was celebrated at Malmesbury, and is reflected in two post-Conquest *vitae*: those by Faricius of Abingdon and by William of Malmesbury (whose account of Aldhelm occupies the whole of bk v of his *Gesta pontificum*).

Sharpe, *Handlist*, 89; *Aldhelmi Opera*, ed. R. Ehwald, MGH, AA 15 (Berlin, 1919); M. Lapidge and M. Herren, *Aldhelm: the Prose Works* (Cambridge, 1979); M. Lapidge and J. L. Rosier, *Aldhelm: the Poetic Works* (Cambridge, 1985); WMalm, *GP*, pp. 330–443; M. Winterbottom, 'Aldhelm's Prose Style and its Origins', *ASE* 6 (1977), 39–76; S. Gwara, 'Manuscripts of Aldhelm's "Prosa de Virginitate" and the Rise of Hermeneutic Literacy in Tenth-Century England', *Studi medievali* 3rd ser. 35 (1994), 101–59; M. Lapidge, 'Aldhelm's Latin Poetry and Old English Verse', *ALL* i.247–69; A. Orchard, *The Poetic Art of Aldhelm*, CSASE 8 (Cambridge, 1994); idem, 'After Aldhelm: the Teaching and Transmission of the Anglo-Latin Hexameter', *The Journal of Medieval Latin* 2 (1992), 96–133; M. L. Cameron, 'Aldhelm as Naturalist', *Peritia* 4 (1985), 117–33.

MICHAEL LAPIDGE

ALDRED. A *colophon in the *Lindisfarne Gospels names 'Aldred, unworthy and most miserable priest' as the writer of the English interlinear gloss to the Latin text. This Aldred has been shown to be the same man as the 'Aldred, provost' who is named in Durham, Cathedral Library, A.IV.19 (the 'Durham Ritual') as having added four Latin collects to that work, and who also wrote the English interlinear gloss to the main text in it. Aldred probably wrote the Lindisfarne Gospels gloss between *c*.950 and 970, while a priest of the community of Chester-le-Street, and that to the Durham Ritual *c*.970 (being by then provost). The two glosses are of great importance for the study of late Old English *Dialects.

N. R. Ker, 'Aldred the Scribe', *Essays and Studies* 28 (1943 for 1942), 7–12; 'The Anglo-Saxon Gloss', ed. A. S. C. Ross and E. G. Stanley, in *Codex Lindisfarnensis*, ed. T. D. Kendrick *et al.*, 2 vols. (Olten and Lausanne, 1960), ii. 25–33; *The Durham Ritual*, ed. T. J. Brown *et al.*, EEMF 16 (Copenhagen, 1969); W. J. P. Boyd, *Aldred's Marginalia* (Exeter, 1975).

T. HOAD

ALEXANDER THE GREAT, LETTER TO ARISTOTLE. The *Letter of Alexander to Aristotle* is one of a number of late Anglo-Saxon prose fictions that demonstrate an interest in the East. A single copy exists in the *Beowulf* manuscript, 107r–131v, written in the hand of the first scribe of *Beowulf*. The work is the earliest vernacular translation of the Latin *Epistola Alexandri ad Aristotelem*. The date suggested for the translation varies from the late ninth to the late tenth century.

The *Letter* presents itself as an epistle written by Alexander the Great to his tutor, Aristotle. In it, Alexander offers a first-hand account of his campaigns in India and his encounters with a number of monstrous creatures, from flying mice and fish-eating men to two-headed snakes as big around as columns. The Old English translation is by no means a literal rendering of the Latin, but instead focuses the narrative more clearly on Alexander rather than on his adventures. While an Anglo-Saxon interest in Alexander may seem unlikely, he also figures in the Old English *Orosius, the *Marvels of the East, and *Widsith.

Three Old English Prose Texts in MS. Cotton Vitellius A.xv, ed. S. Rypins, EETS os 161 (London, 1924); G. Cary, *The Medieval Alexander*, ed. D. J. A. Ross (Cambridge, 1956); A. Orchard, *Pride and Prodigies: Studies in the Monsters of the* Beowulf-*Manuscript* (Cambridge, 1995), pp. 116–39, 204–53.

KATHRYN POWELL

ALFRED, king of Wessex (871–99), successfully withstood *Viking attempts to capture his kingdom and ended his reign as 'king of the Anglo-Saxons', the dominant ruler in England. Alfred came to the throne, following the death of his brother Æthelred, in a year in which nine major engagements were fought with the Great Army of the Vikings. A temporary peace was made at the end of the year, but at the beginning of 878 Alfred narrowly escaped capture in a surprise attack on his residence at Chippenham. He fled to the Somerset marshes and it was there (according to later apocryphal tradition) that he burnt the cakes and was comforted by a visit from St *Cuthbert. He rallied the West Saxons and won a decisive victory at Edington (Wilts). The Viking leader *Guthrum agreed to be baptised with Alfred as his sponsor and withdrew permanently from Wessex. Alfred then set about ensuring that his kingdom was better protected from further Viking attacks. He extended the system of burghal defences and established permanent garrisons within them; the details of the arrangements are recorded in the *Burghal Hidage. The army was reorganised so that only half the force was on duty at any one time, and with Frisian help he commissioned ships to a new design. An aggressive policy was adopted against Vikings settled in southern England which also allowed Alfred to extend his power beyond the borders of the Wessex he had inherited. In 886 Alfred 'occupied' London which had been under Viking control, and, in the words of the *Anglo-Saxon Chronicle, 'all the English people that were not under subjection to the Danes submitted to him'. A celebratory coinage was issued, but control of the city, which had previously been a Mercian possession, was entrusted to his son-in-law Æthelred, the ruler of western Mercia. The value of Alfred's reforms and alliances were made clear between 892 and 896 when an invading Viking army was kept on the move by the West Saxons and Mercians working together and was ultimately frustrated in its aims.

Alfred not only physically protected his people, he also sought their moral and religious regeneration, as can be seen in his law-code which is placed in the tradition of Old Testament legislation. In this he was undoubtedly influenced by ideals of Christian kingship developed during the Carolingian Renaissance. Two Frankish scholars, *Grimbald of Saint-Bertin and *John the Old Saxon, joined others from Mercia, and the king's biographer *Asser from St David's, to aid Alfred in the revival of Christian learning. Asser writes of the personal piety of Alfred. The king founded a nunnery at *Shaftesbury for one of his daughters and a monastery at Athelney where he had retreated in 878. But the greatest testimony to Alfred's commitment are the Old English translations he made of four major Latin works with the aid of his scholarly advisers (see *Alfredian texts). The four works, which are linked by distinctive features of style and vocabulary, are the *Regula pastoralis* of *Gregory the Great, the *De consolatione Philosophiae* by Boethius, St Augustine's *Soliloquia* and the first fifty Psalms. In addition Alfred commissioned from other scholars translations of Gregory's *Dialogi*, *Orosius's *Historiae adversus paganos* and, probably, Bede's *Historia ecclesiastica*. It is likely that Alfred was also directly involved in the commissioning of the *Anglo-Saxon Chronicle* and of his own biography by Asser. Others were intended to benefit as Alfred had done from studying such works. His Preface to his translation of the *Regula pastoralis* makes it clear that he expected the bishops to take its precepts to heart and make sure that their priests did so too. *Ealdormen and other royal officials were required to study or risk losing their offices. Alfred was no doubt aware that the respect for kings as God's representatives on earth, which Christian teaching encouraged, was very much to his own advantage.

Alfred may have been more aware than many Anglo-Saxon rulers of his responsibilities as a Christian king, but he did not neglect the traditional expectations of a Germanic ruler either. The *Alfred Jewel is testimony to the high standards of craftmanship in works commissioned by the king, and Asser praises the king's generosity.

Generous gifts required a good income, and Alfred took good care of the sources of revenue available to him. Burhs could also function as sites where trade could take place under the supervision and taxation of royal officials. The *coinage was reformed, with two major periods of re-coinage in *c.*875 and *c.*880, and new *mints opened up. Asser reveals that Alfred could act harshly if he needed to, and his *law-code is concerned to extend the effectiveness of royal control and lordship. A certain ruthlessness can be seen in the manoeuvres, revealed in his *will, to ensure that his son *Edward, rather than one of his nephews, succeeded on his death. Nor did personal piety prevent Alfred from replenishing the royal coffers through the annexation of former church lands, actions which earned him a rebuke from Pope John VII. Such policies were the hallmarks of a powerful king who could command respect, and not only the English outside Wessex, but also Welsh kings and even Vikings were eager to seek his protection. In this way Alfred provided the springboard for his successors of the tenth century to become kings of England. Alfred died on 26 October 899, and was buried in *Winchester.

J. M. Wallace-Hadrill, *Early Germanic Kingship in England and on the Continent* (Oxford, 1971); Whitelock, *Bede to Alfred*; Keynes and Lapidge, *Alfred the Great*; J. Nelson, ' "A King across the Sea": Alfred in Continental Perspective', *TRHS* 5th ser. 36 (1986), 45–68; J. R. Maddicott, 'Trade, Industry and the Wealth of King Alfred', *P&P* 123 (1989), 3–51; Dumville, *Wessex*; Bately FS; R. Abels, *Alfred the Great* (London, 1998).

B. A. E. YORKE

ALFRED JEWEL. This remarkable object consists of an enamelled figural plaque set beneath a polished rock-crystal, the whole framed in goldwork terminating in a grotesque animal-head socket (see pl. 2). It was found in 1693 four miles from Athelney (Somerset), and is the most elaborate of four (known so far) prestige fittings which probably served as the handles of manuscript pointers. Its modern name derives from the openwork inscription in Old English around the crystal setting. This records that '+ Alfred ordered me to be made' and is taken by most scholars to refer to King *Alfred (871–99); though not conclusive, this is a very plausible attribution on historical, stylistic and linguistic grounds.

As long ago as 1709, Thomas Hearne suggested that this enigmatic object might be the handle of one of the *æstels* which Alfred ordered to be sent out to every diocese in his kingdom, accompanying copies of his translation of *Gregory the Great's *Regula pastoralis*; each *æstel* was worth 50

Pl. 2 The Alfred Jewel.

mancuses, a considerable sum, equivalent to a half-pound weight of gold. The word's context and etymology suggest that it signifies a pointer used in formal readings and teaching from manuscripts. The sumptuous nature of the Jewel suggests a courtly origin, while its narrow socket, which it shares with the three other related fittings, is more suited to holding a slender ivory or wooden rod than the more substantial shaft of a sceptre or staff of office. A suggestion that they may have been fittings on a crown is equally implausible on practical and representational grounds.

The identification of the Jewel with one of Alfred's *æstels* is supported by the iconography of the enamelled half-length figure which dominates the object. The meaning of this figure, with its prominent eyes and floriate sceptres, has attracted much speculation; the two most convin-cing readings identify it as the personification of Sight, or of the Wisdom of God. Both would be very appropriate to its supposed function as an instrument associated with the reading and teaching of holy texts. The use of rock crystal, traditionally a symbol of purity and of light, may also be significant here.

The three related fittings, the Minster Lovell Jewel and two others found in recent years, are all much less ambitious in scope and scale, but all share some features – blue glass or enamel, filigree or rock crystal – seen on the Alfred Jewel, as well as the distinctive small socket. Perhaps significantly, all have been found within Alfred's kingdom of *Wessex; but caution argues against associating all of these directly with Alfred's particular initiative in distributing the *Pastoral Care*, since manuscript pointers certainly existed before and after his reign.

E. Bakka, 'The Alfred Jewel and Sight', *AJ* 46 (1966), 277–82; D. A. Hinton, *A Catalogue of the Anglo-Saxon Ornamental Metalwork 700–1100 in the Department of Antiquities, Ashmolean Museum* (Oxford, 1974), pp. 29–48; D. R. Howlett, 'The Iconography of the Alfred Jewel', *Oxoniensia* 39 (1974), 49–52; idem, 'Alfred's Æstel', *English Philological Studies* 14 (1975), 65–74; *Alfred the Great*, pp. 203–6; R. L. Collins, 'King Alfred's Æstel Reconsidered', *Leeds Studies in English*, n.s. 16 (1985) 37–58; *The Making of England*, pp. 282–3.

LESLIE WEBSTER

ALFREDIAN TEXTS are those Old English texts associated with the reign of King *Alfred the Great of Wessex (871–99), sponsor of the first programme of translation from Latin into Old English. The king translated four works himself, while at least two others (the *Dialogi*, translated by *Werferth, bishop of Worcester; and *Orosius) were translated under his patronage. Two more anonymous translations (the OE *Martyrology and the OE Bede) may have benefited from the king's sponsorship, and some scholars link the *Anglo-Saxon Chronicle* to him as well.

The Old English rendering of *Gregory the Great's *Regula pastoralis*, called the *Pastoral Care*, is the best-known and probably the first of Alfred's own translations. While the dates and chronology of Alfred's works are uncertain, the *Pastoral Care* is usually assigned to the early 890s. A letter prefacing the text, addressed by Alfred to his bishops, contrasts the former greatness of England with its recent decline and proposes a programme of education and translation to recover the people's lost wealth and wisdom. The letter asks each bishop to arrange instruction in reading English for 'all free young men' with means and opportunity while Alfred and his helpers translate 'those works which are most necessary for all men to know'. The translation itself remains fairly close to its Latin source, although the Old English text has more secular colouring than the Latin; the translation frequently addresses a 'ruler' or 'teacher' instead of the 'bishop' instructed by the Latin text. Both the Latin and the Old English texts treat the proper regulation of the conduct of the leader and how that leader should tend to the spiritual needs of his subjects.

Alfred's translations of Boethius's *De consolatione Philosophiae* into the Old English *Boethius* and Augustine's *Soliloquia* into the Old English *Soliloquies* apparently followed his work on the *Pastoral Care*. Both translations sometimes diverge from their source texts, occasionally radically. The *Boethius* explores most of the same issues as the Latin text: the goal of all created things; the nature of Fortune; the distinction between worldly and true goods; the problem of evil; and the question of human free will. Yet Alfred has removed or shortened passages, especially those dealing with eternity and free will, and added other passages, particularly ones commenting upon rulers' responsibilities to their subjects. The *Boethius* also employs formal logic and philosophy less than its source text and relies more on arguments based on authority and analogy; moreover, it is explicitly Christian, unlike the Latin text. The *Soliloquies* not only diverge several times from the source text, but include an additional book based on patristic sources, including Augustine's *De videndo deo* (*Ep.* cxlvii), several works of Gregory the Great, Boethius's *De consolatione* (which Alfred apparently translated simultaneously or slightly earlier), and Jerome's Vulgate translation of the Bible and his *Commentary on Luke*. The direction of all three books, however, is still determined by the fundamental question asked by Augustine's *Soliloquia*: is the human soul immortal?

Alfred probably also translated the first fifty Psalms into Old English prose in the form in which they are preserved in the Paris Psalter. Although his name is not attached to the manuscript and the place of this work in the chronology of Alfred's translations is uncertain, both stylistic and external evidence points to the king. The translation is fairly close to the source text, like the *Pastoral Care*, but not word-for-word; some passages have been slightly expanded to gloss the text.

While the Alfredian translations display a variety of translational strategies, ranging from almost word-for-word translation to the use of additional sources and the introduction of original phrases and ideas, two major themes recur in all the Alfredian texts: issues of leadership and responsibility for others, and the relation of the individual to God and the care of the soul. The translations also demonstrated that Old English could handle complex forms and ideas previously confined to Latin, thereby asserting the sophistication of Anglo-Saxon language and culture.

J. Bately, 'Old English Prose before and during the Reign of Alfred', *ASE* 17 (1988), 93–138 [includes references to editions of the primary texts]; A. J. Frantzen, *King Alfred* (Boston, 1986); Keynes and Lapidge, *Alfred the Great*; Whitelock, *Bede to Alfred* ['The Prose of Alfred's Reign', 'William of Malmesbury on the Works of King Alfred', and 'The Genuine Asser'].

NICOLE GUENTHER DISCENZA

ALLITERATION, the echoing of the initial sounds of words, is perhaps the most distinctive stylistic feature of Anglo-Saxon literature, and is found widely in both Latin and Old English, in prose and especially in verse, where it has a primary structural function. Its roots are ancient, and undoubtedly derive from the prehistoric period: *Germanic languages in their earliest stages generally carried the main stress on the initial syllables of words, and alliteration (the intentional ornamentation of those initial stressed syllables) is attested widely in the earliest written records not only of Old English, but of other related languages, such as *Old Norse. Many early Old English texts, including *laws and *genealogies, exhibit alliterative ornamentation in their phrasing, and many Anglo-Latin authors employed alliteration far more extensively than previous Latin writers had done. Such a preference for alliteration especially in Anglo-Latin verse reflects its fundamental structural importance in Old English poetry, although many poets (notably *Cynewulf) also used extra alliteration for ornamental purposes. Presumably because of its aural and memorial impact, alliteration, often combined with rhythmical effects, is also very prominent in much Old English *preaching; *Ælfric developed a highly rhetorical style based on balanced alliteration loosely resembling what is found in Old English verse, while *Wulfstan preferred to pepper his prose with highly alliterative 'purple passages'.

D. L. Hoover, 'Evidence for Primacy of Alliteration in Old English Metre', *ASE* 14 (1985), 75–96; A. Orchard, 'Artful Alliteration in Anglo-Saxon Song and Story', *Anglia* 113 (1995), 429–63.

ANDY ORCHARD

ALMS (OE *ælmesse*). Forms of payment made to churches, and to agencies of the church, for the support of charitable causes in ways which might serve the purposes of those assuming responsibility for making the payments in the first place. The distinction recognised in the tenth century between tithes, church-scot, *Romfeoh*, plough-alms and soul-scot (e.g. I Edm., ch. 2, and II Edg., chs. 1–5) represents the product of a process of development which probably originated in the seventh century. King *Offa promised to send 365 mancuses each year to the pope, 'for the support of the poor and the provision of lights' (*EHD* i, no. 205); a coin of King Offa, inscribed 'S. Petrus' and found in northern Italy, was recorded in the nineteenth century but is now lost. King *Æthelwulf ordered that 300 mancuses should be taken to Rome each year, for similar purposes (Asser, c. 16). In 883 King *Alfred made a payment of alms to *Rome, as a way of gaining God's help against the Vikings, during the pontificate of Marinus I (882–4); a chronicler made a point of recording later payments of the 'alms of King Alfred and the West Saxons' to Rome (*ASC*, s.a. 887–90); and special coins, inscribed 'Aelfred rex Saxonum' and 'Elimo[sina]' (alms), appear to have been minted for the purpose, probably at *Exeter or *Winchester. It is not known how these early payments were raised, or how the burden was shared among the people; but by the middle of the tenth century alms-giving was a duty incumbent upon all Christian men, and payment was enforced with the full panoply of royal law. The payment known as *Romfeoh* developed into the form of taxation known as 'Peter's Pence', levied at the rate of a penny per household payable each year by St Peter's Day (1 August). The prompt and proper payment of church-dues, tithes, and alms, is a theme which runs through the legislation drawn up on behalf of *Æthelred and *Cnut by Archbishop *Wulfstan II of York, 'so that God Almighty may have mercy upon us and grant us victory over our enemies' (VII Atr. ch. 8, perhaps with intended reference to the symbolism of the 'Agnus Dei' pennies minted in 1009).

Anglo-Saxon Coins, ed. R. H. M. Dolley (London, 1961), pp. 44–6, 77–8; H. Loyn, 'Peter's Pence' (1984), repr. in his *Society and Peoples: Studies in the History of England and Wales, c.600–1200* (London, 1992), pp. 241–58; J. Graham-Campbell and E. Okasha, 'A Pair of Inscribed Anglo-Saxon Hooked Tags from the Rome (Forum) 1883 Hoard', *ASE* 20 (1991), 221–9.

SIMON KEYNES

ALPHABET. Most vernacular manuscripts are written in Insular minuscule, developed from Insular half-uncial, although late in the tenth century scribes began writing Latin in Caroline minuscule (see *script). The Anglo-Saxon alphabet was based on the Roman alphabet, and so included the ligature *æ* but lacked *j* and *v*; *q* and *z* were used only in foreign names. As it was adapted to meet the demands of the Old English sound system, a variety of *d* with a cross-stroke through the ascender, ð (known since the nineteenth century as eth) represented the sounds for which we use *th*, while two *runes were incorporated, þ (thorn), interchangeable with eth, and *p* (wynn) for *w*. See also *spelling and pronunciation.

Ker, *Catalogue*, pp. xxv–xxxiii; A. Campbell, *Old English Grammar* (Oxford, 1959), ch. 1.

DONALD SCRAGG

AMIATINUS, CODEX. The third of three massive Vulgate pandects (single-volume Bibles) made at *Monkwearmouth-Jarrow under the direction of Abbot *Ceolfrith. Now in the Biblioteca Laurenziana in Florence (as MS. Amiatino 1), it is the oldest extant complete Latin Bible. The text was copied mostly from good Italian exemplars and was consulted during the Sixtine revision of the Vulgate (1587–90). The volume's 1030 leaves measure 505 × 340 mm and it is 250 mm thick in its present nineteenth-century binding. The first quire contains ancillary material, including the 'Ezra miniature', apparently copied from the *Codex grandior*, an Old Latin Bible formerly in the possession of Cassiodorus at Vivarium, Italy, but brought to Northumbria c.679. Destined for presentation to Pope Gregory II at St Peter's in Rome, Amiatinus left England in 716 with Ceolfrith and 80 monks in attendance, but the abbot died on the way. It appears to have reached Rome but by the end of the ninth century was at the monastery of San Salvatore at Monte Amiata in the Central Apennines. Here Ceolfrith's original dedication was altered, thereby disguising the Bible's English origin. It was taken to Florence shortly after the dissolution of San Salvatore in 1782.

CLA iii.299; Alexander, *Insular MSS*, no. 7; R. L. S. Bruce-Mitford, 'The Art of the Codex Amiatinus', Jarrow Lecture 1967 (Jarrow, [1968]); P. Meyvaert, 'Bede, Cassiodorus, and the Codex Amiatinus', *Speculum* 71 (1996), 827–83; R. Marsden, *The Text of the Old Testament in Anglo-Saxon England*, CSASE 15 (Cambridge, 1995), chs. 3–5.

RICHARD MARSDEN

AMULETS. An amulet is something kept (worn, carried or put in position, for example, in a house) for good luck, or against disease, the Evil Eye or the like. The *penitential of Archbishop *Theodore probably provides the earliest documentary evidence for Anglo-Saxon amulets since it allowed 'stones and herbs' to someone 'afflicted by an evil spirit'. *Bede related that early Christians, when suffering from the plague, resorted to amulets (*philacteria* or *ligaturas*), and in *Alcuin's time some amulets already contained Christian ingredients. *Ælfric (quoting 'Augustine') wrote that it was permissible to take herbs as *medicine, but not to bind them on oneself, except on the sore; however, the *medical literature has several references to herbs, and rather fewer to parts of animals, worn as pendants to aid healing (see also *charms and *magic). Brief texts (often using foreign letter forms or garbled language) could themselves act as amulets, when written directly onto the patient's skin, or on vellum and hung around the neck.

For the illiterate pagan period the best evidence for amulets comes from the *cemeteries, particularly from feminine inhumation burials. Claws and bones of birds such as eagles, and teeth of such mammals as wolves, often pierced for suspension and worn with beads on a necklace (though visually unattractive), were probably amulets, since in many cultures such objects symbolise the strength of the creature from which they came. Pendants shaped like miniature buckets might likewise symbolise the woman's part in the social and ritual role of alcohol. Ornamental beads could also have been amulets; for example, Pliny ascribed some virtues to amber – frequent in sixth-century burials – and some early preachers condemned it as superstitious. Other artifacts, like the so-called 'Hercules clubs' (also found in *Germany), fit into a general typology which begins with objects associated with a hero or deity. Some rare coin-shaped gold pendants known as bracteates (mostly imported from Scandinavia) are ornamented with mythological scenes. Fossils, however, were not worn, but kept in bags or boxes, or held in the hand (for example, an echinoid found in a woman's grave at Westgarth, *Bury St Edmunds), or kept within houses like the porospherae at West Stow, Suffolk.

Other possible amulets are found mainly in burials with seventh-century grave goods: for example, little models of spears and tools, worn on long chatelaine chains; and circular silver pendants in the shape of model shields. Cowry shells, whose amuletic character is known from many cultures, were imported from the Middle East; and pendants which may have been children's teething amulets were made from the strong teeth of beavers. In the later Christian period pendant crosses may usually have replaced the varieties of earlier amulets.

A. L. Meaney, *Anglo-Saxon Amulets and Curing Stones*, BAR Brit. ser. 96 (1981); T. M. Dickinson, 'An Anglo-Saxon "Cunning Woman" from Bidford-on-Avon', in M. Carver, ed., *In Search of Cult* (Woodbridge, 1993), pp. 45–54.

AUDREY MEANEY

ANDREAS. The first poem in the *Vercelli Book is an anonymous life of St Andrew, based on a lost version of the apocryphal Latin *Acta Andreae et Matthiae apud Anthropophagos*. (An earlier view that the immediate source is Greek is now largely discounted.) Andrew, sent by God to rescue Matthew from the cannibalistic Mermedonians, survives a storm at sea, captivity and Christ-like torments, to convert the citizens and travel home triumphant. The anonymous author uses lively and vigorous heroic language extensively, with the apostles in the first section described in military terminology, the heroic diction continuing in references throughout the poem to the 'loyalty' which the 'thegn' Andrew displays towards his Lord. Similarities to *Beowulf, from the opening line *Hwæt we gefrunan on fyrndagum*, convinced many older critics that *Andreas* was consciously based upon it, but it is more likely that both poets drew upon a common poetic stock. A prose account of Andrew, one of the Blickling Homilies, again tells the story of his dealings with the Mermedonians and testifies to Anglo-Saxon interest in the tale, but *Ælfric's account of the saint concentrates on his martyrdom and ignores the apocryphon.

ASPR ii. 3–51; *Andreas and the Fates of the Apostles*, ed. K. R. Brooks (Oxford, 1961); E. B. Irving, Jr, 'A Reading of *Andreas*: the Poem as Poem', *ASE* 12 (1983), 215–37; P. Clemoes, *Interactions of Thought and Language in Old English Poetry*, CSASE 12 (Cambridge, 1995), 249–72.

DONALD SCRAGG

ANGELCYNN: *see* English People

ANGLIAN DIALECT: *see* Dialects

ANGLO-NORMAN (IN PRE-CONQUEST TEXTS). A difficulty attendant upon distinguishing French words in Old English is their similarity with *loan-words which are very freely borrowed from Latin. Among the few certain French words recorded in English texts dating from before the Norman Conquest are *pride* and *sot*. But others, recorded only after the Conquest, presumably entered the spoken language earlier since otherwise they would not have been intelligible in the vernacular contexts in which they are found. The *Anglo-Saxon Chronicle has a number of loans in post-Conquest entries: *castle, prison, service*, and other texts have *capon, bacon* and the verb *serve*.

M. S. Serjeantson, *A History of Foreign Words in English* (London, 1935); A. Campbell, *Old English Grammar* (Oxford, 1959), §567.

DONALD SCRAGG

ANGLO-SAXON ART, CHRONOLOGY.

Although very few works of art are closely dated, sufficient numbers are broadly datable through archaeological or historical context, or (in the case of manuscripts) on palaeographical grounds, to clarify the general outlines of stylistic and ornamental development. Nevertheless, most works can only be assigned to a wide time-band via the imprecise tools of stylistic comparison and typology; and the dating of many individual pieces, especially stone *sculpture, remains problematic.

The earliest Anglo-Saxon art, as it survives, is largely confined to objects of personal adornment, like brooches, buckles and wrist-clasps. Such items, whatever their quality, were invariably decorated, some of them outstandingly. Characteristic of the fifth century is the 'Quoit brooch style' (with motifs based on crouching animals) which is represented most splendidly on the silver quoit brooch from Sarre, Kent. While the origins of this style are disputed – it has been seen as an offshoot of provincial Roman art, as Frankish, or (more plausibly) Jutish – the two main subsequent types of decoration (Salin's Styles I and II) are unequivocally linked to the wider Germanic world. Salin's Style I, which was almost certainly imported from Scandinavia, was current in England from the late fifth century, continuing throughout the sixth, and (in the midlands) into the seventh. Used, for instance, on many Square-headed brooches, it is characterised by chip-carved patterns based on animals and masks. Style II ornament, which gradually superseded it (especially in the south-east), being employed from the second half of the sixth century into the seventh, is dominated by serpentine beasts with interlacing bodies. It is well represented on Kentish triangular buckles.

By the later sixth century the best works from the south-east are distinguished by greater use of expensive materials, above all gold and garnets, reflecting the growing prosperity of a more organised society which had greater access to imported precious materials. The point is underlined by the finer Kentish composite disc brooches, and, in particular, by the buckle from the *Taplow burial and the *jewellery from that at *Sutton Hoo, interments of *c.*600 and *c.*625 respectively. While the possible symbolism of the decorative elements like interlace and beast forms that were used in these early works remains obscure, it is clear that such objects were the products of a society that invested its modest surpluses in personal display, which fostered craftsmen and jewellers of a high standard, and in which the possession of a fine brooch or buckle was a valuable status symbol – in death as much as in life.

The coming of Christianity revolutionised the visual arts as well as other aspects of society – although the change during the seventh century from burial with grave goods to burial without them undoubtedly over-emphasises the phenomenon. Not only were many new models now available, but art also had to fulfil new functions; moreover, whereas pagan art favoured abstraction, Christianity required legible figural *iconography. The interface between the Christian and pagan traditions is occasionally apparent in seventh-century works. Examples include the Crundale buckle (a rich Kentish triangular buckle decorated with garnet-filled cloisons and Style II animal ornament, which is dominated by the Christian symbol of a fish) and the Canterbury pendant (essentially a Kentish disc brooch adapted to pendant form, whose design revolves around a cross).

In addition to fostering such re-applications of traditional *metalworking skills, the imported faith stimulated work in new media – stone sculpture and manuscript *illumination. Henceforth, Germanic motifs, such as interlace and animal ornament along with Celtic spiral patterns, are juxtaposed with Christian imagery and Mediterranean decoration, notably vine-scroll. The balance between these elements varied from one location to the next according to its cultural contacts. In general, works from the south are more restrained in their use of Insular ornament than are those from Northumbria – a notable exception being *Monkwearmouth-Jarrow, whose classicising works such as the Codex *Amiatinus reflect the foundation's direct connections with *Rome and Gaul.

Though specifically Christian art was probably produced as soon as the faith was established in a given location, the oldest surviving approximately datable works come from the end of the seventh century. The jamb of the doorway at Wearmouth, carved with a pair of lacertine beasts, probably dates from the 680s; the golden, garnet-adorned pectoral cross of St *Cuthbert was presumably made before 687; while the wooden coffin of the same saint (incised with Christ and the evangelist symbols, the Virgin and Child, archangels and apostles), the *Lindisfarne Gospels, and the Codex Amiatinus all date from c.700. The fact that these works are all from *Northumbria might be held to reflect the particular strength of the church in that kingdom during the second half of the century.

The full flowering of Christian art is generally associated with the eighth century, to which are assigned most of the grand decorated manuscripts and sculptures, along with 'secular' works which bear comparable ornament, like the Witham pins and the Coppergate helmet. Despite a few markers such as the 'St Petersburg Bede' (probably soon after 746) and, perhaps, the Codex Aureus (for which a mid-eighth-century date is likely on circumstantial grounds), there are precious few absolute dates here: the accepted chronology relies on inference, assumption and scholarly tradition. The flourishing of sculpture in *Mercia, for instance (best exemplified by the friezes at *Breedon-on-the-Hill, Leics.), is believed to have occurred slightly later than in Northumbria and is dated to the second half of the eighth century – ultimately because this corresponds to the rise of the kingdom's political power. Similarly, more naturalistic work both in Mercia and Northumbria (e.g. the Breedon angel from the former, and the Easby and Rothbury crosses from the latter) is assigned to the early ninth century on the grounds that it represents a response to Carolingian art.

How far these traditions continued into the ninth century is debatable, but undoubtedly they varied according to region: continuity is most obvious in the south and the west. Some fine decorated southern books, above all the Bible fragment, London, BL, Royal 1. E. VI, can be securely assigned to the earlier ninth century, owing to the similarity of their script to that of charters from that period; while the Book of *Cerne is probably datable on internal grounds to 818 × 830. Furthermore, certain decorated motifs used in these manuscripts, such as hunched, triangular beasts, also appear on objects from the Trewhiddle hoard (buried in the 870s) and on the rings which bear the names of King *Æthelwulf (d. 858) and Queen Æthelswith (d. 888/9), which are the centre of a small corpus of fine ninth-century metalwork.

Yet despite some demonstrable continuity in the south, it is indisputable that the *Viking invasions and settlement represented a watershed in England's artistic tradition. The ravages removed or destroyed much Anglo-Saxon art, while the settlement introduced new Scandinavian craftsmen and patrons. The result was to accentuate the pre-existing distinction between the art of the north and that of the south. In the tenth and eleventh centuries, the Viking dominated areas were characterised by stone sculpture in which the Anglo-Saxon tradition of cross shafts took on new forms, and a distinctive Anglo-Scandinavian monument, the *'hogback' tomb, was produced. The ring-headed cross type of Celtic ancestry was now favoured; some shafts, such as those at Sockburn, Co. Durham, and Middleton, Yorks., featured depictions of warriors; while others, such as that at *Gosforth, included scenes from Scandinavian mythology.

The decorative motifs used on these northern carvings (as on items of personal adornment or everyday use) echo Scandinavian styles. The chronology of ornament types in Scandinavia thus provides approximate termini post quos for their deployment in England. The Borre style (characterised by ribbon-plait) was current in Norway from the mid-ninth century to the end of the tenth. The Jellinge style (based on a swirling ribbon-like animal), which in England is largely confined to Yorkshire and Teeside, appeared in Denmark at the end of the ninth century. Overtly Viking works are comparatively rare in the south; but those that do occur (such as the grave marker from St Paul's, London, and the brooch from Pitney, Somerset) are decorated in the Ringerike or Urnes styles, which were current in Scandinavia from the late tenth century to the late eleventh, and from the early eleventh to the twelfth respectively. The former (an adaptation of Anglo-Saxon and Ottonian foliage) is characterised by a foliate scroll with tendrilly shoots, the latter by stylised quadrupeds and ribbon-like snakes. Such items are reasonably associated with the reigns of the Danish kings in the eleventh century.

The expansion of the house of *Wessex and, subsequently, the monastic reform movement appear to have been the catalysts for the rebirth of art in southern England from the end of the ninth century. Here artists responded primarily to Carolingian art, foliage supplanting interlace as the preferred decorative motif. Key early works are the *Alfred Jewel (probably pre-899), which has fleshy leaves engraved on the back plate; and the stole and maniples of Bishop Frithestan of Winchester (c.909 × 916), which are ornamented with acanthus leaves, alongside figures that bear the stamp of Byzantine art.

The surviving evidence highlights *Winchester and *Canterbury as the leading centres of manuscript art in the second half of the tenth century: they developed colourful paintings with lavish foliate borders, and coloured line drawings respectively. Two key datable Winchester works, the New Minster Charter (966) and the *Benedictional of St Æthelwold (971 × 984), provide a firm framework for the development of its style. By the early eleventh century, these two traditions had intermeshed – as the Canterbury psalter in London, BL, Arundel 155 (datable 1012 × 1023) reveals – and had spread to other centres. Though manuscripts dominate the corpus, sufficient architectural sculpture, ivory carving and metalwork survives to show that the same styles were current in secular art, and became widespread in the south at parochial level. The wealth of England in the later tenth and eleventh century is clearly reflected in the lavish use of gold in manuscript art as well as for vessels, textiles and statues (now known only from descriptions). Widely admired, southern English art was highly influential in Normandy, France and *Flanders from c.1000. Indeed, keen to possess it, the Normans seem to have appropriated it in large quantities in the wake of the Conquest. The *Bayeux Tapestry, probably designed by a Canterbury artist for Odo of Bayeux, is arguably the swansong of Anglo-Saxon art.

Surveying nearly 600 years of continuous change, three common strands stand out: first, a love of lavish colour, allied to a taste for rich materials; secondly, an interplay between abstract ornament and representational subject matter; and thirdly, a continuing interrelationship with Ireland, Scandinavia, the Continent, and *Byzantium. Art reflects more clearly than any other single source how far England was linked to its neighbours, not divided from them, by the sea.

B. M. Ager, 'The Smaller Variants of the Anglo-Saxon Quoit Brooch', *ASSAH* 4 (1985), 1–58; M. Pinder, 'Anglo-Saxon Garnet Cloisonné Composite Disc Brooches', *Journal of the British Archaeological Society* 148 (1995), 6–28; G. Speake, *Anglo-Saxon Animal Art and its Germanic Background* (Oxford, 1980); D. M. Wilson, *Anglo-Saxon Ornamental Metalwork 700–1100 in the British Museum* (London, 1964); idem, *Anglo-Saxon Art* (London, 1984); *Making of England; The Golden Age of AS Art*; R. G. Gameson, *The Role of Art in the Late Anglo-Saxon Church* (Oxford, 1995); R. Cramp *et al.*, CASSS.

RICHARD GAMESON

ANGLO-SAXON CHRONICLE. The 'Anglo-Saxon Chronicle' is a term of convenience applied by modern scholars to a composite set of annals which provides the basis for the greater part of our knowledge of Anglo-Saxon history. The understanding of the *Chronicle* as a literary text is, however, a matter of great complexity. The original compilation is the so-called 'common stock', probably put together in the late ninth century at the court of King *Alfred the Great. The earliest material was drawn from a variety of written sources, including *Bede's *Historia ecclesiastica*, supplemented by *annals bearing on Kentish, South Saxon, Mercian, and above all West Saxon history; but with the notable exception of the annal for 757 (which narrates the story of King Cynewulf), the annals do not pick up momentum until they begin to tell of the Danish invasions from the late eighth century onwards. It is essentially the broad vision of an 'English' history, with its roots in Roman Britain and resolving itself in King Alfred's heroic struggle against the Danes, which commends the view that the common stock was compiled by scholars who moved in court circles and was in that sense a court (as opposed to a 'private') production; and since the *Chronicle* was compiled in the early 890s, when the survival of the English people was still threatened by Viking invasion, it was perhaps the chronicler's purpose to create an image of the past which might help to draw people together in resistance to the common enemy.

There is reason to believe that the *Chronicle* was made available for copying and circulation in 892; and the multiplication of copies ensured that the work would be continued thereafter under a variety of different circumstances, and as a result of a variety of different initiatives. It is important, therefore, to emphasise that the *Chronicle*, as we have it, is by no means a uniform or homogeneous work. Anyone who had access to a copy (ecclesiastic or layman) might have been moved to add as little as a single annal on a parochial event or as much as a whole block of annals on a sequence of greater events; and it would then be a matter of chance whether this information found its way into the line of transmission which determined the contents of the manuscripts which happen to survive. Moreover, the chroniclers were neither objective nor necessarily authoritative, and simply recorded events from their different points of view. The first continuation of the common stock, which may have originated close to the king, represents the literary genre at its best (annals for 893–6). A second continuation covers the early stages of *Edward the Elder's campaign against the Danes (annals for 897–914), and a third picks up with coverage of the later stages (annals for

35

915–20, in MS. A); both sets of annals are determinedly 'Edwardian' in their view of events, and must be compared with the 'Mercian Register' (a separate set of annals for 902–24, in MSS. BCD). The coverage of the fifty years from *c*.925 to *c*.975 lacks the quality or continuity which might be considered commensurate with the singular interest of this period in every other respect, attested (for example) by the *charters and *law-codes which survive in good quantity for the same period; but at least we should note that the chroniclers were moved on certain occasions to break into verse (Battle of *Brunanburh, 937; Redemption of the Five Boroughs, 942; Coronation of Edgar, 973; Death of Edgar, 975). The annals describing events during the reign of King *Æthelred the Unready represent another high point (*ASC*, MSS. CDE, s.a. 983–1022), notable for the personal instrusion of the anonymous chronicler in the sorry tale that he had to tell, but not necessarily good history; comparison with MS. A, s.a. 1001, is salutary. And while the coverage for the reign of *Cnut is disappointing, matters improve from 1035, when domestic politics breaks surface as a theme suitable for treatment in a record of this kind. The accounts of the events of the following thirty years or so, in MSS. C, D, and E, share much common ground, but have a special interest in so far as the material has on occasion been 'edited' in accordance with one or other of the political positions available.

*Asser, who wrote his *Vita Ælfredi regis* in 893, was first in the long line of those who have used the *Chronicle* to provide a framework for their own historical enterprises. Another was *Æthelweard, ealdorman of the Western Provinces (d. *c*.998), who translated the *Chronicle* from English into Latin, probably in the 980s. The 'Northern Recension' of the *Chronicle* (which lies behind MSS. DEF) was produced probably at *York in the early eleventh century, and involved the augmentation of a copy of the common stock with much additional material, including two sets of earlier northern annals. Each of the three main Anglo-Norman historians – *John of Worcester, *William of Malmesbury, and *Henry of Huntingdon – had a copy of the *Chronicle*, using and adapting the information in his own distinctive way; a fourth, working at Bury St Edmunds, had a copy held by some to have been textually closer to the original compilation than any of the copies which survive. Some later medieval historians used the *Chronicle*, and others took their material from those who had used it before them; in this way, the *Chronicle* has long been central to the mainstream of English historical tradition.

The reliability of any part of the *Chronicle* as a record of events cannot be taken for granted, but the information which it contains can sometimes be tested by reference to independent sources (charters, annals entered in the margins of Easter Tables, or obits registered in ecclesiastical calendars), or checked scientifically (in the case of records of lunar and solar eclipses), or compared with observations made elsewhere (in the case of records of comets, plagues, and other kinds of natural phenomena), and is generally found to be accurate. The detached manner of reporting should not, however, be mistaken for objectivity: a great deal can be concealed behind its seemingly straightforward statements (and, indeed, behind its omissions).

Manuscripts of the *Anglo-Saxon Chronicle*: see Ker, *Catalogue*, nos. 39 (MS. A ['The Parker Chronicle']), 188 (MS. B), 191 (MS. C), 192 (MS. D), 346 (MS. E ['The Peterborough Chronicle']), 148 (MS. F), 180 (MS. G), and 150 (MS. H). Editions and translations: *MS A*, ed. J. Bately, The Anglo-Saxon Chronicle: a Collaborative Edition 3 (Cambridge, 1986); *The Anglo-Saxon Chronicle: a Revised Translation*, ed. D. Whitelock (London, 1961); M. Swanton, *The Anglo-Saxon Chronicle* (London, 1996). General discussion: Keynes and Lapidge, *Alfred the Great*, pp. 39–41, 275–81; J. Bately, *The Anglo-Saxon Chronicle: Texts and Textual Relationships*, Reading Medieval Studies, Monograph 3 (Reading, 1991). Anglo-Norman chroniclers: see separate entries, and *The Annals of St Neots with Vita Prima Sancti Neoti*, ed. D. Dumville and M. Lapidge, The Anglo-Saxon Chronicle: a Collaborative Edition 17 (Cambridge, 1985), esp. pp. xxxi–xxxix.

SIMON KEYNES

ANGLO-SAXONISM. The perception of the history and culture of Anglo-Saxon England at different times from the sixteenth century to the present day, developing in response to contemporary purposes or fashions, and the representation of these perceptions in word and image; or, a vast subject about which a book has yet to be written. If Anglo-Saxon England provided food for religious thought in the late sixteenth century, and material for political ideology in the seventeenth and eighteenth centuries, it came thereafter to provide more harmless inspiration for craftsmen, poets, artists, composers, novelists, and film-makers. Richard Verstegan's *Restitution of Decayed Intelligence in Antiquities* (1605), on the Germanic origins of the English people, was the source for a remarkable series of near life-size sculptures representing the pagan deities made in the 1720s by J. M. Rysbrack (1694–1770), for display in a 'Saxon Temple' devised for the gardens at Stowe (Bucks.); sadly, the sculptures are now dispersed. It was the case, however, that there was more mileage in political history. The received view of the period, largely determined by the Anglo-Norman historians writing in the first half of the twelfth century and by their successors in the thirteenth century, was refined in the seventeenth century by John Speed's *Historie of Great Britaine* (1611) and by John Milton's *History of Britain* (1670), and popularised in the eighteenth century by a succession of voluminous 'Histories of England'. A few of these histories, like Paul Rapin-Thoyras's *History of England* (1726–31), and David Hume's *History of England* (1754–63), were of considerable merit; but others were not, and made up for the deficiency with copious illustrations of selected events. As art, the illustrations may verge on the ephemeral; but it is interesting to see what themes were chosen, how they were treated, and whether they had any impact on later work. Engravings by Charles Grignion, and others, of drawings by Samuel Wale (1721–86), depicting various events (or pseudo-events) in Anglo-Saxon history, appeared in a succession of popular histories published in the 1760s and 1770s; and they were joined by another series of illustrations by Messrs Hamilton and Edwards, published in the 1770s and 1780s. The respectability of 'history painting' was elevated to a higher plane by artists eager to exploit increasingly familiar themes as their own way of giving expression to the developing historical consciousness of the nation. Prominent among them was Benjamin West (1738–1820), who from origins in Pennsylvania rose to become Historical Painter to King George III. West's 'Alfred the Great divides his Loaf with a Pilgrim' was painted for the show at the Royal Academy in 1779, and presented soon afterwards to the Worshipful Company of Stationers; it was then copied by Josiah Boydell, and engraved by William Sharp (1782). Sir David Wilkie (1785–1841) produced his striking vision of 'Alfred Reprimanded by the Neatherd's Wife' in response to a private commission in 1806; the painting was engraved by James Mitchell in 1828. The paintings were complemented, of course, by works of other kinds, ranging from interminable poems on Alfred the Great to Wordsworth's 'Ecclesiastical Sonnets' (one of which concerns 'The pious Alfred, King to Justice dear! Lord of the harp and liberating spear'). From these roots (and others) sprang the high Victorian perception of the Anglo-Saxon age.

Alfred continued to move the creative spirit, as the embodiment of virtue and valour, and as the personification of the nation's view of itself; and under these circumstances the myth became a legend. Henry Taylor's historical drama *Edwin the Fair* (1842), which focused on events during the reign of King *Eadwig, is representative of the many other themes which were found suitable for treatment. Among painters we encounter G. F. Watts (1817–1904), who produced his monumental 'Alfred inciting the English to resist the Danes' in 1847, for the competition to decorate the new Houses of Parliament (where it still hangs), and Daniel Maclise (1806–70), who chose to depict yet another Alfredian theme ('King Alfred in the Camp of the Danes') for the show at the Royal Academy in 1852, and who worked in the evenings on a series of forty-two drawings depicting the Norman Conquest, engraved and published in 1866. The more scholarly reconstruction of the Anglo-Saxon past, which can be traced back to its roots in the work of Matthew *Parker and his circle, and in the papers read at meetings of the Elizabethan 'College of Antiquaries', was extended in the late seventeenth and early eighteenth centuries by the prodigious labours of George *Hickes and Humfrey *Wanley. It was then brought before a wider audience with Sharon *Turner's *History of the Anglo-Saxons* (1799–1805), followed by the various works of John Mitchell *Kemble in the 1830s and 1840s. It is, nonetheless, the illustrated histories, the poems, and the paintings which in combination did so much to shape the received view of Anglo-Saxon England; and while they remain of considerable interest in their own right, it could be said that historians have been trying to break free, ever since, from their pervasive influence.

A. G. Temple, *England's History as Pictured by Famous Painters* (London, 1896–7); T. S. R. Boase, 'Macklin and Bowyer', *JWCI* 26 (1963), 148–77, at 169–76 [illustrated histories]; *Daniel Maclise 1806–1870* (London, 1972); J. Sunderland, 'Mortimer, Pine and some Political Aspects of English History Painting', *Burlington Magazine* 116 (1974), 317–26; R. Strong, *And when did you last see your father? The Victorian Painter and British History* (London, 1978), also published as *Recreating the Past: British History and the Victorian Painter* (New York, 1978), esp. pp. 114–18, 155–7 [paintings with historical themes from Anglo-Saxon England, exhibited at the Royal Academy 1769–1904]; E. G. Stanley, 'The Glorification of Alfred King of Wessex [1678–1851]', *Poetica* [Tokyo] 12 (1981), 103–33.

SIMON KEYNES

ANGLO-SAXONS, KINGDOM OF THE. A

contemporary term for the political order transitional between the kingdom of the West Saxons and the kingdom of the English. The term 'Anglo-Saxon' appears to have originated on the Continent in the eighth century, to distinguish some part or all of the Germanic inhabitants of Britain from the 'Angles' and '(Old) Saxons' who remained on the Continent. The term was, however, adopted at the court of King *Alfred the Great in a different, overtly political, sense, to express the combination or amalgamation of 'Anglian' and 'Saxon' peoples, and thereby to denote the distinctive political order established under Alfred's leadership in the early 880s. The term was arguably far more significant in political terms than the concept of the *'English People' (gens Anglorum), which had been freely employed by Pope *Gregory in the late sixth century, which was given wider currency by *Bede, and which became familiar in the ninth century in the form of its vernacular equivalent, *Angelcynn. On this basis, it is King Alfred, not Gregory or Bede, who should be accorded the credit for devising the label which encapsulated and expressed the driving political vision of the day; and on the same basis it is King *Æthelstan who can take all due credit for reformulating the vision in a way of his own. The Alfredian 'kingdom of the Anglo-Saxons' is the political order implicit on the 'English' side of the border in the treaty between Alfred and Guthrum (c.880), and perhaps established more formally at *London in 886; it is the political order reflected in the king's law-code, and represented by the royal styles in several of the king's charters (e.g. 'king of the Anglo-Saxons', and 'king of the Angles and Saxons'); it is the political order which lies behind the portrayal of the king in *Asser's Life of King Alfred (893); and it is the political order which appears to lie behind the conception of kingship in the 'Second' *coronation order, and perhaps in the location of coronations in the tenth century at *Kingston-upon-Thames. *Edward the Elder succeeded Alfred as 'king of the Anglo-Saxons' (though like his father he also retained his more natural identity as 'king of the West Saxons'), and during his reign the frontier of the kingdom was extended northwards to the river Humber; see Map 11. The enlarged kingdom was taken over by Æthelstan in 924/925, who was initially designated 'king of the Anglo-Saxons' or 'king of the Anglo-Saxons and of the Danes'. In 927 Æthelstan succeeded to the kingdom of the Northumbrians, which gave him control of the kingdom of York and also, it seems, of the land extending beyond the Tees northwards to the Tyne

and the Tweed. The 'kingdom of the Anglo-Saxons' was thus superseded by the 'kingdom of the English', which itself was for some time a kingdom in the making. The 'kingdom of the English' was also reformulated in the tenth century as the 'kingdom of the whole of Britain', at once harking back to an older ideological story (cf. *Bretwalda), and no less premature.

W. Levison, England and the Continent in the Eighth Century (Oxford, 1946), p. 92, n. 1 [on the term 'Anglo-Saxon']; R. H. C. Davis, 'Alfred and Guthrum's Frontier' (1982), in his From Alfred the Great to Stephen (London, 1991), pp. 47–54, and Dumville, Wessex, pp. 1–27 [on the Alfred-Guthrum boundary]; J. Campbell, 'The United Kingdom of England: the Anglo-Saxon Achievement', Uniting the Kingdom? The Making of British History, ed. A. Grant and K. J. Stringer (London, 1995), pp. 31–47; S. Keynes, 'King Alfred and the Mercians', Kings, Currency and Alliances: the History and Coinage of Southern England in the Ninth Century, ed. M. A. S. Blackburn and D. N. Dumville (Woodbridge, 1998), pp. 1–45, at 34–9 [on the 'kingdom of the Anglo-Saxons']; idem, 'England, 900–1016', The New Cambridge Medieval History, III: c. 900–1024, ed. T. Reuter (Cambridge, 1999), pp. 456-84.

SIMON KEYNES

ANIMAL HUSBANDRY, the management of domestic animals, was essential to the economy of Anglo-Saxon England to an extent that is hard for us to grasp nowadays. Domestic animals were important as a source of food – meat, milk, cheese and butter – and a wide range of materials such as wool, leather, tallow (for lighting), bone and horn; and were even more important for transport and for the cultivation of fields, and for dung to fertilise the fields. Animals, and especially cattle, were also important as a measure of wealth and a medium of exchange, especially in the earlier Anglo-Saxon period.

Despite this, documentary sources tell us relatively little about Anglo-Saxon animal husbandry. *Domesday Book, at the end of the period, is of limited value as it ignores animals apart from plough teams which are used in parts of the country as a measure of arable land. Little Domesday, and similar more detailed surveys, list demesne holdings of cattle (other than plough teams), horses, pigs, sheep and goats, but ignore what were probably much larger numbers of animals owned by villans, and cover only limited parts of the country. Otherwise there are stray references in earlier documents which are primarily concerned with other topics, including mention in the Anglo-Saxon Chronicle of losses of animals from disease or raiding, and a small number of Anglo-Saxon *charters and *wills. Valuable information is increasingly being provided by the scientific study of animal bones from archaeological excavations, but this is limited in what it can tell us and by the relatively small number of sites for which information is at present available; in some areas (especially those with more acid soils), few bones survive.

Cattle, sheep and pigs were, as in Roman Britain and later medieval England, the commonest and economically most important farm animals. They were relatively small and lightly built in comparison with modern stock. Cattle stood between 100 and 130 cm high at the shoulder and probably weighed no more than 150–250 kg; sheep stood between 50 and 70 cm at the shoulder. Pigs were very small by modern standards; they were probably like the pigs shown in later medieval manuscripts, which are small, dark and hairy, with prick ears, long legs and short bodies. There were probably no distinct breeds of farm animals in the modern sense, but stock would have varied from place to place and area to area. Similarities between Romano-British and Anglo-Saxon animal bone assemblages suggest continuity in stock and animal husbandry rather than abrupt change or the large-scale import of new blood.

As *Domesday indicates, the main importance of cattle was for labour, and particularly for ploughing: cultivated land is measured by plough teams, and the numbers of other cattle recorded in Little Domesday are relatively small. The preponderance of bones of older beasts among the cattle bones from Anglo-Saxon sites confirms that meat and milk were of secondary importance. Sheep were multipurpose animals, kept for milk, meat, manure and wool. Sheep bones tend to be commoner in late Saxon sites than in early and middle Saxon sites, and documentary references suggest that wool production was of increasing importance in the later Saxon period, both trends foreshadowing the economic importance of the later medieval wool and textile industries. Pigs were an important source of meat and fat; they were slower to fatten than modern pigs and were usually killed in their second or third year. They would generally have been herded rather than kept in sties, scratching a living from middens, waste and pasture land most of the year and fattened on acorns and beech mast in the autumn. Pig bones are notably common at Wicken Bonhunt, a high-status early Saxon site in Essex, and tend to be scarcer from later sites, possibly declining as *woodland was cleared.

Stock was usually well cared for; there is no evidence from Saxon animal bones of common or chronic malnutrition or other health problems, and farmers would have been well aware that healthy and well-fed animals are more profitable. Winter feed is likely to have been in short supply, and there was probably some autumn slaughter of surplus animals when they were still in good condition; however, the relatively low proportion of animals killed in their first year suggests that this was not a major problem. But bad years and epidemics caused disastrous losses from time to time: there are records of an epidemic causing heavy losses of cattle in 810, and epidemics killing many cattle and people in 896–7, 986–7 and 1000–1.

Other domestic animals were less common. Horses were used for riding and as pack-animals; they normally stood between 12 and 14 hands high (120–40 cm at the shoulder), and would have looked more like large ponies than small horses. Donkeys and mules were rare. Goats were much less common than sheep and were probably kept mainly for milk. Dogs were used mainly as guards, for herding and for hunting; they varied considerably, and different types were probably recognised and kept for different purposes, as in later medieval England, but would not have been as standardised as modern breeds. Cats were kept to control mice; in the tenth-century (Welsh) *Laws of Hywel Dda* the penalty for killing a cat which guards a king's barn is appropriately measured in wheat. Chickens were kept for eggs as well as for meat; they were almost as small as modern bantams. Geese were also commonly kept and valued particularly for goose-grease and for down. J. Clutton-Brock, 'The Animal Resources', in Wilson, *Archaeology*, pp. 373–92; R. Welldon Finn, *An Introduction to Domesday Book* (London, 1963); J. Rackham, *Environment and Economy in Anglo-Saxon England*, CBA Research Report 89 (York, 1994); R. Trow-Smith, *A History of British Livestock Husbandry to 1700* (London, 1957), pp. 43–65.

SEBASTIAN PAYNE

ANNALS refer to entries made annually – in theory at least – and retrospectively to record significant events which occurred during the past year. It is thought that the original framework for annals during the early medieval period was paschal tables, which were set out in columns for periods of nineteen, eighty-four or 532 years (depending on time and place); in such a layout it would be easy to record, say, an obit or the outcome of a battle in the margin alongside the relevant year (a clear example is found in London, BL, Cotton Caligula A. xv, fols. 133–7). When the marginal entries were recopied on their own, various degrees of elaboration became possible, leading to the creation of narrative entries of various length. The *Anglo-Saxon Chronicle*, for example, consists mostly of annal-type entries which have been elaborated to a greater or lesser degree. Various sets of annals survive from Anglo-Saxon England: the annals for 731–4 added to the Moore manuscript of Bede's *HE*; the annals 732–66 which occur in certain manuscripts of Bede's *HE*; the so-called 'York Annals' or 'First Set of Northern Annals' for 732–802 preserved in *Byrhtferth's *Historia regum*, as well as the 'Second Set of Northern Annals' preserved by Symeon of Durham. Annal collections are also a crucial source both for Welsh history (the *Annales Cambriae*) and Irish history (many collections are extant, notably the 'Annals of Ulster', the 'Annals of Innisfallen' and the 'Annals of Tigernach').

F. Liebermann, *Ungedruckte anglonormannische Geschichtsquellen* (Strasbourg, 1879), p. 3; *Bede's Ecclesiastical History of the English People*, ed. B. Colgrave and R. A. B. Mynors (OMT, 1969), pp. 572 [annals 731–4], 572–6 [annals 732–66)]; *Symeonis Monachi Opera Omnia*, ed. T. Arnold, 2 vols., RS (London, 1882–5), ii.30–66 ['York Annals'], ii. 119–28 ['Second Set of Northern Annals']; R. L. Poole, *Chronicles and Annals: a Brief Outline of their Origin and Growth* (Oxford, 1926); G. N. Garmonsway, *The Anglo-Saxon Chronicle* (London, 1954).

MICHAEL LAPIDGE

ANTIPHONARY: *see* Liturgical Books

ANTIQUARIES. The role of individual antiquaries in the preservation of manuscripts from the pre-Conquest period is crucial because of political, cultural and technological developments in the first half of the sixteenth century. When Henry VIII came to the throne, England was a model daughter of the Church, the printing press still a novelty and English humanism in its infancy. By the time he died, the English church was fully independent, the London print trade flourishing, and the study of classics an essential part of the school and university curriculum.

The 1530s constitute the key decade. As early as 1527 Henry had decided that his marriage to Catherine of Aragon was invalid in the eyes of God and set about obtaining a divorce in the face of ecclesiastical opposition. His dissatisfaction with the papacy and desire for independence increased over the next years; in 1533 he proclaimed England an Empire, thus throwing off the yoke of Rome. Soon afterwards, he began dissolving the monasteries and transferring their financial resources to the Court of Augmentations;

in 1540 when Waltham fell the process was complete. In order to justify his break with tradition, however, Henry had first to turn to precisely those repositories of learning with which he would soon dispense. Many of the issues raised in both his 'Great Matters' were legal ones and law by nature depends on precedent. As part of his divorce campaign he sent agents to search monastic archives and bring back relevant texts to his royal libraries (and at least one annotated list, that from Lincolnshire, survives). Utilising these resources, the 1533 Act in Restraint of Appeals based itself very firmly on 'divers sundry old authentic histories and chronicles'. It is no coincidence either that England's first self-proclaimed 'antiquarius', John *Leland, began to appear in the records at this time and that his commission 'to peruse and dylygentlye to searche all the lybraryes of monasterees and colegies of thys youre noble realme' dates from 1533. The accounts of Leland's first library tours survive in his so-called *Collectanea* and show the influence both of Henry's political agenda and Leland's own more general concerns. A product of St Paul's School, Leland had spent the late 1520s in Paris where he had become fascinated by philology and textual edition. He witnessed the growth of the library of Francis I and modelled himself on its humanist librarians. Like many of the French and German humanists whom he emulated he was an ardent nationalist and wanted to retrieve the history of his own nation through the publication of the works of its earliest authors. His records of the contents of the English monastic libraries stand as preliminary notes to his own grander enterprises as well as useful reference tools for those involved in defining Henrician policy.

By 1536, when Leland petitioned Thomas Cromwell for a renewal of his commission, the state of the monasteries had become more precarious and he henceforth turned his energies towards collecting rather than cataloguing. By his own accounts he retrieved many ancient manuscripts for Henry and he stated that Henry himself reorganised palace libraries at Hampton Court, Greenwich, and Westminster for the reception of monastic strays. Leland's own optimistic assurances about the success of his mission, however, do not altogether tally either with the statements of his contemporaries or with the evidence of the royal library itself. Although much more polemical than Leland, much more rigid in his views of what should or should not be retrieved, his compeer and fellow collector, John *Bale, deeply lamented the wholesale destruction of valuable records during the period of the dissolution and pleaded if not for a central depot then at least for the establishment of just 'one solempne lybrary' in every shire in England. In its surviving form, the actual collection put together by Leland is a disappointing one and there are relatively few books from the pre-Conquest period and almost none in Old English. In terms of Anglo–Saxon manuscripts, then, the achievements of Leland's less 'vainglorious' contemporary, Robert *Talbot, are much more impressive. On the other hand, it is hard to know what precisely got into the collection Leland was establishing, since after Henry's death the new royal librarian Bartholomew Traheron oversaw the weeding out of many manuscripts (some of which turned up in the collections of strategically placed individuals such as Sir Thomas Pope). It is quite possible, therefore, that many monastic manuscripts, whose first known post-dissolution provenances are in the collections of the second generation of antiquaries, may have originally been rescued by Leland.

Of the first generation of English antiquaries – Leland, Bale, Sir John Prise and Talbot in particular – only Leland had royal support, and this gave him some sense of a coherent mission with the potential of a successful resolution. He had, as well, seen most of the major collections of England and Wales and had been able to decide on what was worth saving, what not. Although never completed, his *De uiris illustribus* (later published as *Commentarii de scriptoribus Britannicis*) represented for him a faithful account of England's past. Bale's access to books, on the other hand, was much more limited and his library a private one, subject to the vagaries of fate and the malice of his enemies. What characterises the antiquarian movement after Leland's descent into madness, beginning with Bale's commentary on Leland's New Year's Gift of 1546, is a sense of urgency, a concern about fragmentation and loss. These individuals had no way of knowing what might have already disappeared and they were well aware that much more might soon go, manuscripts (as Bale pointed out) being ignominiously found 'in stacyoners and bokebynders store howses, some in grosers, sope sellers, taylers, and other occupyers shoppes, some in shyppes ready to be carryed over the sea into Flaunders to be solde'. The antiquaries' collective sense of transience manifests itself most strongly in a desire to consolidate, to find some sort of permanent institution to replace the dissolved monasteries. As early as 1557 John Dee, himself a considerable collector, made a 'Supplication to Queen Mary for the Recovery

and Preservation of Ancient Writers and Monuments'. Eleven years later, observing that: 'if this opportunity be not taken in our time, it will not so well be done hereafter', Matthew *Parker persuaded the Privy Council to give him the right to demand books (ostensibly on loan) from less wellplaced collectors and antiquaries. In Elizabeth's reign individuals associated with the Society of Antiquaries also had this goal in mind and around 1602 there was a proposal to set up an 'Academye for the studye of Antiquity and History', the centrepiece of which was to be its library.

In fact all the great national library schemes foundered (Parker gave the bulk of his manuscripts to a Cambridge college) and it was the work of well-to-do private collectors which consolidated the efforts of the early antiquaries, some of whom seem to have preserved manuscripts in concealment. From the perspective of Anglo–Saxon studies the most important of the collectors were Matthew Parker and Sir Robert *Cotton. Parker had a clearly articulated agenda and his collection was built up to promote his vision of the *Ecclesia Anglicana*. For him, pre-Conquest manuscripts provided crucial historical precedents for his ecclesiastical policies and he made printed editions of several of the texts he collected so that they could be known more widely. In his enterprise his principal assistant was his chaplain and Latin secretary John Joscelyn, who put together his own collection of ancient manuscripts and who also examined Old English manuscripts *in situ* at *Exeter and *Worcester. In the mid 1560s Joscelyn also drew up a list of Anglo–Saxon manuscripts and another list of writers on medieval English history. Parker's bequest of his library to Corpus Christi College gave it an institutional status: he further attempted to maintain its integrity by the imposition of strict penalties for loss.

Sir Robert Cotton began collecting thirteen years after Parker's death, and his collection was much more diffuse. He obtained manuscripts from earlier antiquaries – Thomas Allen, Robert Bowyer, Lord Burghley, William Camden, Henry Ellzing, Joseph Holland, Joscelyn, Lord Lumley and Samuel Ward, for example, provided manuscripts containing Old English – and made several complex exchanges with the royal librarian Patrick Young. Like Parker he saw his collection as a useful ecclesiastical and political tool and he hoped that it would become a national archive; to this end he was one of the proposers of the abortive 'Academye'. Ultimately, Cotton's own motives in assembling such a vast private library came under suspicion and at the end of his life he was denied free access to it. Although the term 'antiquarius' had fallen into disrepute by Cotton's time, the very act of debarring shows a general recognition in the tempestuous years of Charles I's reign of the potential of ancient manuscripts for propaganda and manipulation of government policy.

E. N. Adams, *Old English Scholarship in England from 1566–1800* (New Haven, CT, 1917); M. Aston, 'English Ruins and English History: the Dissolution and the Sense of the Past', *JWCI* 36 (1973), 231–55; J. P. Carley, 'John Leland and the Contents of the English Pre-Dissolution Libraries: Lincolnshire', *TCBS* 9 (1989), 330–57; T. D. Kendrick, *British Antiquity* (London, 1950); Ker, *Catalogue*; J. M. Levine, *Humanism and History. Origins of Modern English Historiography* (Ithaca and London, 1987); M. McKisack, *Medieval History in the Tudor Age* (Oxford, 1971); S. G. Mendyk, *'Speculum Britanniae'. Regional Study, Antiquarianism, and Science in Britain to 1700* (Toronto, 1989); A. Momigliano, 'Ancient History and the Antiquarian', *JCWI* 13 (1950), 285–315; T. Ross, 'Dissolution and the Making of the English Literary Canon: the Catalogues of Leland and Bale', *Renaissance and Reformation* 15 (1991), 57–80; C. E. Wright, 'The Dispersal of the Monastic Libraries and the Beginnings of Anglo-Saxon Studies' *TCBS* 1 (1951), 208–37; idem, 'The Elizabethan Society of Antiquaries and the Formation of the Cottonian Library', in *The English Library Before 1700*, ed. F. Wormald and C. E. Wright (London, 1958), pp. 176–212.

JAMES P. CARLEY

APOCRYPHA, BIBLICAL, IN OLD ENGLISH, include a large number of early Christian and medieval texts which attempt to supplement biblical narratives but which were never accepted as part of the Bible. (This category does not include deuterocanonical texts such as Judith, Tobit, or Ecclesiasticus which were incorporated into the Septuagint and Vulgate and were universally assumed to possess full biblical authority in the early Middle Ages.) During the tenth and eleventh centuries English scholars translated and adapted a wide variety of apocryphal texts, including the *Gospel of Nicodemus*, an account of Christ's trial before Pilate and descent into hell which survives in three Old English translations, the earliest of which is probably the first in any European vernacular. Two of these Old English versions are accompanied by translations of a second apocryphon, the *Vengeance of the Saviour*, which relates the destruction of Jerusalem by Titus and Vespasian and the veneration of Christ's image by St Veronica. The Old English *Jamnes and Mambres*, a pseudepigraphon concerning the two magicians who confronted Moses at Pharaoh's court, is the only medieval vernacular version of this text in existence. Of seminal

importance for the development of Insular eschatology is the *Vision of St Paul*, a Latin version of the Greek *Apocalypse of Paul* which tells of St Paul's tour of hell and heaven and which functioned in Anglo-Saxon England as a virtual manual for the fate of the soul after death (see also *visions). A partial Old English translation was made in the mid-eleventh century. Five Old English translations are extant of the *Apocalypse of Thomas*, a vivid description of the cataclysmic events that will precede the end of the world. Particularly well represented are the overlapping categories of Infancy Gospels and Marian apocrypha. The *Gospel of Pseudo-Matthew*, an eighth- or ninth-century compilation of narratives about the births and childhoods of Mary and Christ, provided the main source for two Old English sermons and an entry in the OE *Martyrology. Two versions of the *De transitu Mariae*, an account of the death and bodily assumption of the *Virgin, were adapted for use in Old English sermons. Anglo-Saxon manuscripts also contain Latin versions of two other Infancy Gospels, the *Protevangelium of James* and *De nativitate Mariae*.

Although wary of apocryphal texts that promoted heterodox teaching,*Ælfric made frequent use of apocryphal acts of the apostles in composing his homilies and saints' lives. Thus his *Life of St Thomas* (*Lives of Saints*, no. 36) translates portions of the originally Syriac *Passion of Thomas*, and his homily on Philip and James (*Catholic Homilies* ii. 17) is based on the *Passion of Philip*. Ælfric likewise translated excerpts from apocryphal passions of Andrew, Bartholomew, James the Greater, John, Mark, Matthew, Peter and Paul, and Simon and Jude. In addition, the poem *Andreas paraphrases a lost Latin redaction of the apocryphal *Acts of Andrew and Matthew*, which was separately translated twice into Old English prose. Other texts typically classed as apocrypha were also translated into Old English, including the *Sunday Letter, the *Revelation of Ezra*, and the *Letters of Abgar and Jesus*.

The Old English Vision of St Paul, ed. A. diP. Healey, Speculum Anniversary Monographs 2 (Cambridge, MA, 1978); A. diP. Healey, 'Anglo-Saxon Use of the Apocryphal Gospel', in *The Anglo-Saxons: Synthesis and Achievement*, ed. J. D. Woods and D. A. E. Pelteret (Waterloo, Ontario, 1985), pp. 93–104; F. M. Biggs *et al.*, 'Apocrypha', in *Sources of Anglo-Saxon Literary Culture: A Trial Version*, ed. F. M. Biggs *et al.*, Medieval & Renaissance Texts & Studies 74 (Binghamton, NY, 1990), 22–70; *Two Old English Apocrypha and Their Manuscript Source: 'The Gospel of Nichodemus' and 'The*

Avenging of the Saviour', ed. J. E. Cross *et al.*, CSASE 19 (Cambridge, 1996).

T. N. HALL

APOLLONIUS OF TYRE is the earliest surviving example of the romance genre in English and the only example in Old English. The prose fiction is a translation of the Latin *Historia Apollonii regis Tyri*, which itself may have been translated from Greek. The Old English version survives only in Cambridge, Corpus Christi College 201, a manuscript consisting of two codices joined in the sixteenth century. *Apollonius* appears in the first codex, which can be dated to the mid-eleventh century and which also contains a large collection of *Wulfstan the Homilist's works copied in the same hand. *Apollonius of Tyre* tells of a nobleman's exile from Tyre, his marriage to a king's daughter, and a series of shipwrecks after which he is reunited with his family and his kingdom. The Old English translation follows the Latin closely, except in omitting a lengthy episode from the middle of the story. Nonetheless, the translator does make changes that lend the story an Anglo-Saxon character. For example, Apollonius is referred to as an *ealdorman and romance is downplayed in comparison with the Latin tale. The story remained popular in England throughout the Middle Ages and was a source for Gower's *Confessio Amantis* and Shakespeare's *Pericles*.

The Old English Apollonius of Tyre, ed. P. Goolden (Oxford, 1958); A. Riedinger, 'The Englishing of Arcestrate: Women in *Apollonius of Tyre*', in *New Readings on Women in Old English Literature*, ed. H. Damico and A. Hennessey Olsen (Bloomington, IN, 1990), pp. 292–306; E. Archibald, *Apollonius of Tyre: Medieval and Renaissance Themes and Variations* (Cambridge, 1991).

KATHRYN POWELL

ARCHITECTURAL STONE SCULPTURE

survives almost entirely in churches, most commonly in the forms of imposts, string courses, friezes, wall-panels and the frames of openings.

The earliest sculpture is associated with a group of seventh-century Northumbrian churches at the monasteries of *Ripon, *Hexham, and *Monkwearmouth-Jarrow. Monkwearmouth had a highly decorated entrance porch: the jambs carved with Insular ribbon animals, the frieze above with naturalistic animals, as at Hexham, and in the gable a large-scale standing figure. Rectangular and chamfered imposts, decorated with fine geometric interlace, occur here and at Ripon, but a revival of Roman taste is also apparent at these sites and in the balustrade and petalled ornament on imposts,

friezes, and panels, at Jarrow, Hexham, and Simonburn (Northumberland). At Jarrow, uniquely, plant-scroll ornament occurs not only on panels from the church and on crosses, but on panels and a decorated column from a domestic building.

From the eighth century, openings elaborately surrounded with plant-scrolls survive at Britford (Wilts.), Lastingham and Ledsham (Yorks.), but the outstanding collection of sculpture is to be found at *Breedon on the Hill (Leics.). The fine and distinctive cutting as well as the *iconography of the friezes, with lively birds, animals, and human figures, betray a foreign and eastern influence, whilst the panels of human figures, some of which are paralleled at Fletton and Peterborough, have a grace and naturalism comparable to Carolingian ivories.

The most elaborate external sculpture surviving in the next generation is be found at Barnack church (Northants.), where there is on the western tower a window frame with paired birds in high relief, a *sundial decorated with acanthus, and, on each face, large panels, *c.*1.68m high, carved with tree-scrolls topped by large birds. In addition there is a projecting beast-head above a window. Such projecting heads, others of which occur at *Escomb and *Deerhurst churches, can be paralleled in Near Eastern churches, where also there is the enrichment of openings by surrounding ornament, and of façades by the lavish application of inorganic panels and friezes. It is possible that eastern influences were early transmitted to Anglo-Saxon England via Gaul, and then became widely accepted; certainly the forms which existed in the seventh century continue throughout the period, although ornament changes.

It is nevertheless remarkable that, despite a few early attempts to copy Roman capitals and columns at *Reculver, Hexham, and Monkwearmouth, and the isolated ninth-century capitals from *Canterbury, there is nothing before the eleventh century to match the numerous capitals, of various levels of competence, which also occur contemporaneously in Italy and France. There is however a marked increase in scale in later sculpture, as has been demonstrated from the excavated fragments from *Gloucester and *Winchester, and can be seen in the large roods, for example at *Bradford-on-Avon, *Breamore, Romsey and Langford.

Traces of paint have been identified on architectural sculpture from the seventh century onwards, so that it seems likely that it was usually polychrome.

CASSS; R. N. Bailey, *England's Earliest Sculptors*, Publications of the Dictionary of Old English 5 (Toronto, 1996); *Early Medieval Wall Painting and Painted Sculpture in England*, ed. S. Cather, D. Park and P. Williamson, BAR Brit. Ser. 216 (Oxford, 1990); E. Coatsworth, 'Late pre-Conquest Sculptures with the Crucifixion South of the Humber', in *Æthelwold*, pp. 161–93; R. Cramp, 'The Furnishing and Sculptural Decoration of Anglo-Saxon Churches', in Butler and Morris, *AS Church*, pp. 101–4; idem, *Studies in Anglo-Saxon Sculpture* (London, 1992); C. M. Heighway, 'Excavations at Gloucester. Fifth Interim Report: St Oswald's Priory, 1977–8', *AJ* 60 (1980), 207–26; Taylor and Taylor, *AS Arch*; H. M. and J. Taylor, 'Architectural Sculpture in Pre-Norman England', *JBAA* 3rd ser. 29 (1966), 3–51; F. H. Thompson, ed., *Studies in Medieval Sculpture*, Society of Antiquaries, Occasional Papers (London, 1983).

ROSEMARY CRAMP

ARCHITECTURE, ECCLESIASTICAL. The building of churches in Anglo-Saxon England essentially began with *Augustine of Canterbury in Kent following 597; for this he probably imported workmen from Frankish Gaul. The cathedral and abbey in *Canterbury, together with churches in Kent at *Minster in Sheppey (c.664) and *Reculver (669), and in Essex at Bradwell-on-Sea (653 × 664), define the earliest type in southeast England. A simple nave without aisles provided the setting for the main altar; east of this a chancel arch separated off the apse for use by the clergy. Flanking the apse and east end of the nave were side chambers or *porticus* serving as sacristies; further *porticus* might continue along the nave to provide for burials and other purposes. In Wessex a comparable building is the Old Minster in *Winchester (c.648).

In *Northumbria the early development of Christianity was influenced by the Irish mission from Iona to *Lindisfarne (633), important churches being built in timber. Masonry churches became prominent from the late seventh century with the foundations of *Wilfrid at *Ripon and *Hexham, and of *Benedict Biscop at *Monkwearmouth-Jarrow. These buildings had long naves and small rectangular chancels; *porticus* sometimes surrounded the naves. Elaborate crypts are a feature of Wilfrid's buildings. The best preserved early Northumbrian church is *Escomb.

From the mid-eighth century to the mid-tenth there is no good historical narrative of church history, but a number of important buildings survive. One group comprises the first evidenced aisled churches: *Brixworth (mid or late eighth century?), *Wareham, St Mary's (c.800?), and *Cirencester (early or mid ninth century?); also the rebuilding of *Canterbury cathedral (probably by *Wulfred in c.808–13). These buildings may be compared with aisled churches in the Carolingian empire. Other lesser churches may be dated to the late eighth and early ninth centuries on the basis of their elaborate sculptured decoration: Britford (Wilts.), Edenham (Lincs.) and Ledsham (W. Yorks.) are examples and show the continuation of simple naves with side *porticus*.

The church of *Deerhurst (fig. 5) may be dated in substantial part to the ninth century on the basis of its sculptures; to it may be related the apse of *Wing. Significant parts of *Repton are dated archaeologically prior to 873; its crypt (pl. 15) was perhaps similar to that of St Oswald's in Gloucester (c.880×918). Together these four buildings are indicators of major church design in ninth-century *Mercia. The tower of Barnack (near Peterborough) takes the picture forward to the West Saxon reconquest in the early tenth century. These buildings suggest that during the ninth century several of the decorative features that were to be characteristic of Late Anglo-Saxon architecture were already developed, such as narrow raised bands of stone ('pilaster strips') to surround archways and to articulate wall surfaces. In plan, however, the churches remained essentially conservative.

The monastic revival of the second half of the tenth century again provides a narrative background for church history and the construction of buildings, but only a few documented buildings actually survive or have been excavated, for example: the abbeys of *Glastonbury; Winchester, Old Minster; Romsey; Cholsey; and Peterborough. To these may plausibly be added the chapel of *Barton on Humber, which has links with *Æthelwold. *Byrhtferth's Life of St *Oswald describes his church at *Ramsey (969×991) as a cruciform building with central and western towers; comparisons may be made with the surviving churches of *Breamore and St Mary de Castro at Dover (c.1000). Also of c.1000 may be the chapel of St Laurence at *Bradford-on-Avon (pl. 4).

The majority of churches that have been described as Anglo-Saxon fall into the period between the late tenth century and the early twelfth; but seldom is precise dating possible. During this period many settlements were first provided with stone churches, but timber also continued to be used, as at Greensted (datable c.1063×1108 by dendrochronology). Characteristics of this body of buildings have been analysed by authors such as Taylor.

On the Continent during the eleventh century was developed a group of inter-related Romanesque styles, associated with the rebuilding of many churches on a grand scale, made possible by a general advance in architectural technology and masoncraft. The first fully Romanesque church in England was *Edward the Confessor's abbey of *Westminster (c.1050s and following), while the main development of the style only followed the Norman Conquest. However, at Stow (Lincs.) the crossing piers of the early 1050s are clearly 'proto-Romanesque'. A more decorative interpretation of Romanesque in lesser churches can be dated only somewhere between the mid and late eleventh century, e.g. Hadstock (Essex), Clayton and Sompting (Sussex); this style continued towards the end of the century as at Milborne Port (Somerset). At St Augustine's Abbey in Canterbury c.1048–61 Abbot Wulfric aimed to retain the earlier churches while linking them with an octagonal rotunda: but the concept was still essentially pre-Romanesque.

Anglo-Saxon churches of all periods would have been embellished with a range of arts: *sculpture, *wall-painting, *glass, *tiles, *metalwork, *woodwork and *textiles. They provided a setting for the *liturgy and associated *music, for the *shrines of saints and *pilgrimage.

G. Baldwin Brown, *Anglo-Saxon Architecture*, 2nd ed. (Edinburgh, 1925); A. W. Clapham, *English Romanesque Architecture*, 2 vols. (Oxford, 1930–4); Taylor and Taylor, *AS Arch*; Fernie, *Architecture*; W. Rodwell, *Archaeology of the English Church* (London, 1981); Butler and Morris, *AS Church*; J. Blair, ed., *Minsters and Parish Churches: the Local Church in Transition, 950–1200*, Oxford University Committee for Archaeology, Monograph 17 (1988); R. D. H. Gem, 'L'architecture pré-romane et romane en Angleterre', *Bulletin monumental* 142 (1984), 233–72; idem, 'Tenth-century Architecture in England', *Settimane* 38 (1991), 803–36; idem, 'Architecture of the Anglo-Saxon Church, 735 to 870: from Archbishop Ecgberht to Archbishop Ceolnoth', *JBAA* 146 (1993), 29–66.

RICHARD GEM

ARCHITECTURE, SECULAR: *see* Forts and Fortifications; Mills; Royal Sites; Timber Building

ARMES PRYDEIN, 'The Prophecy of Britain', a tenth-century Welsh poem in the fourteenth-century Book of Taliesin. The poem (199 lines) consists of an exhortation to the Welsh to unite and expel the English, here called *Lloegrwys* 'the people of *Lloegr* (England)', from Britain; a promise that they will be aided by other non-English peoples (including the 'men of Dublin', the Irish, the Cornish, the Bretons and the men of Strathclyde); and a prediction that, with St David's help, the English will be forced to return overseas to their homeland, leaving the island to the victors. It is notable that the predicted leaders of the Welsh are Cynan and Cadwaladr (not *Arthur). Probably composed in south Wales, the poem has been linked with King *Æthelstan's exaction of tribute from the Welsh (it refers disparagingly to the 'king's stewards' and their taxes), and more particularly with the coalition of British and Norse at the *Battle of *Brunanburh*. The hope of Breton involvement does not chime well with Æthelstan's reign, but the poet probably drew upon a legendary Welsh convention of a pan-Brittonic alliance under Cynan and Cadwaladr. A date later in the tenth century (perhaps recalling the alliance of *Brunanburh*) may be equally appropriate.

Armes Prydein. The Prophecy of Britain, ed. I. Williams, transl. R. Bromwich (Dublin, 1972); D. N. Dumville, 'Brittany and "Armes Prydein Vawr"' [1983], in his *Britons and Saxons in the Early Middle Ages* (Aldershot, 1993), ch. XVI.

O. J. PADEL

ARMS AND ARMOUR. The evidence derives from three types of source, which are unevenly distributed chronologically and raise contrasting problems of interpretation. First, the archaeolog-

Pl. 3 The Coppergate Helmet.

ical record comprises grave goods from 'pagan Anglo-Saxon cemeteries' of the fifth to the seventh centuries and swords of the Viking age deposited in English rivers. It remains problematic how accurately and how fully the items that were chosen for deposit may represent those that were in actual use. Secondly, the written sources range in date from the eighth to the eleventh century. Poetry (especially *Beowulf, *Brunanburh and *Maldon) provides valuable descriptions of combat, but must be used cautiously in view of its uncertain dating and the imagination involved in its composition. *Law-codes and *wills provide some brief and factual evidence for tenth- and eleventh-century military equipment of the nobles. Thirdly, artistic representations of armed warriors are occasionally found in sculpture, more commonly in manuscript illustrations (especially of biblical or psalter scenes) and most notably in the detailed embroidered representation of the battle of *Hastings in the *Bayeux Tapestry. The value of such evidence, however, depends upon understanding its provenance and the artist's conventions.

Defensive Armour

(a) Helmets. Only four helmets from the Anglo-Saxon period survive: from the *Sutton Hoo ship-burial, from Coppergate in *York, and from rich barrow burials at Benty Grange (Derbyshire) and a recently discovered site in Northamptonshire. They all date from the seventh or early eighth centuries and are richly decorated with Germanic animal and interlace ornament, with silver-wire inlay and with bronze or tinned panels. But their segmental form, their crests, cheek-guards and flaps or mail protecting the neck all derive from late-Roman parade helmets. Parallels with helmets from Vendel and Valsgärde suggest that the Sutton Hoo helmet may have been made by Swedish armourers; others have Frankish links. The newly discovered and the Benty Grange helmets are both surmounted by boars; Benty Grange also has a nose-guard decorated with a silver cross. More explicitly Christian is the Coppergate helmet, adorned with transverse brass mouldings inscribed with pious Latin invocations (see pl. 3).

These helmets were high-status objects, perhaps suitable for early Anglo-Saxon king-making rituals (later ordines substitute a crown). Despite several references to helmets (and boar-helmets) in Beowulf, Anglo-Saxon warriors may normally have worn headgear of boiled leather, rather than iron helmets. Certainly the *heriots ('war-gear') of Anglo-Saxon nobles, detailed in their wills, routinely include helmets only from the first decade of the eleventh century, thus coinciding with

*Æthelred II's order for the manufacture of helmets and byrnies in 1008. By 1066, however, the Bayeux Tapestry shows helmets to be standard equipment in the Anglo-Saxon army.

(b) Byrnies. Mail body-armour is even rarer in pagan Anglo-Saxon cemeteries than are helmets, being found only at Sutton Hoo and (possibly) at Benty Grange. The 'byrnie' or shirt of mail, though part of the gear of Beowulf's noble companions, plays no role in the account of heroic English defence in the Battle of Maldon and is listed in heriots only from the early eleventh century. By 1066 byrnies, like helmets, were standard equipment; the Bayeux Tapestry and a frieze fragment from *Winchester cathedral suggest that they were worn closely gathered around the arm and leg – a protection devised for infantry warfare.

(c) Shields. The round shield – normally comprising a flat wooden board with a central hole for the hand-grip protected by an iron boss – was the commonest item of defensive equipment throughout the early Middle Ages. Bosses of conical or elongated form are common in pagan burials, but since the wood has perished, we cannot confirm whether limewood construction was regular, as the term lind as a poetic synonym for shield suggests. The Bayeux Tapestry shows some round and convex shields in use at Hastings, but the vast majority of the English shields depicted are long and kite-shaped, like those of the Normans. A characteristic feature of English battle tactics, both at Maldon and at Hastings, was the use of shields by densely-packed foot-soldiers to form a 'shield-wall'.

Offensive weapons

(a) Spears. The spear (whose possession, with a shield, was a sign of free status) is the commonest weapon found in male burials in pagan Anglo-Saxon cemeteries. The iron spearheads vary enormously in size and form, from the elongated and sometimes barbed 'angons' intended to penetrate and burst mail armour, to the more common leaf-shaped varieties, suitable both for piercing and for lateral cutting blows. Where residues of wood have survived attached to the socket, they prove that the poles were of ash, as the use of the term æsc in poetry would suggest. Though important as a throwing weapon in hunting and in battle, the primary function of the spear was to keep the enemy at a distance, beyond the reach of sword blows.

(b) Axes. The axe was a standard woodman's tool, readily adaptable for warfare, both in its single-handed (chopping) and its double-handed (tree-felling) forms. Light throwing axes – traditionally identified as *franciscae*, the distinctive weapon of the Franks – are found in pagan Anglo-Saxon burials. The two-handed battle-axe, later to be identified as the characteristic weapon of the Scandinavian and English troops of the Varangian guard, is shown in use in the Bayeux Tapestry, both as a ceremonial object and in the battle.

(c) Swords. The sword was the most prized offensive weapon, associated in law with aristocratic status. In pagan Anglo-Saxon cemeteries swords are mainly found in the richer male burials and are outnumbered by spears by more than 20:1. In order to produce long blades (*c.*90–5 cm) with edges hardened to retain their sharpness, early medieval smiths had first to devise elaborate 'pattern-welding' techniques and then, from the ninth century, to improve their furnace technology. As elite weapons and ceremonial objects, some swords had their hilts and scabbards elaborately ornamented with gold or with silver and niello. Anglo-Saxon poetry has a rich tradition of sword imagery and references to swords as heirlooms, as prestigious gifts or trophies of war abound; gold-adorned swords also feature in the wills of leading late Anglo-Saxon *ealdormen. By the time of Hastings, however, the sword had become part of the standard equipment of the well-armed English soldier.

(d) Bows. In early medieval warfare (and perhaps even in hunting) the bow was an implement of the unfree. Occasional arrowheads in pagan burials, a reference in the *Battle of Maldon* to bows being 'busy' and a single English archer shown on the Bayeux Tapestry do little to enhance the role of the archer.

(e) Knives. As a standard tool in general use the knife (*seax*) in warfare developed into a single-edged dagger (known by Gregory of Tours as the *scramasax*) or into fine single-edged swords, with blades up to 80 cm in length which are occasionally found in pagan burials or deposited in rivers. Some *seaxes* have elaborately decorated and inscribed blades, suggesting ceremonial use.

H. R. Ellis Davidson, *The Sword in Anglo-Saxon England* (Oxford, 1962); M. J. Swanton, *The Spearheads of the Anglo-Saxon Settlements* (Royal Archaeological Institute, 1973); idem, *A Corpus of Pagan Anglo-Saxon Spear-Types*, BAR Brit. ser. 7 (1974); N. P. Brooks, 'Weapons and Armour' in *The Battle of Maldon AD 991*, ed. D. Scragg (Oxford, 1991), pp. 208–19; T. Dickinson and H. Härke, 'Early Anglo-Saxon Shields', *Archaeologia* 101 (1992), 1–94.

N. P. BROOKS

ARMY. The term *fyrd* is used both in *law-codes and in the *Anglo-Saxon Chronicle* to connote a royal military expedition. *Here also seems to have meant 'army', but was mainly used to describe invading forces, especially *Viking armies. Given the prevalence of war in the history of Anglo-Saxon England and its prominence in the literature of the period, it is remarkable how little evidence has survived concerning the composition and organisation of English armies before the Norman Conquest. Anglo-Saxon kings, with the notable exception of *Alfred the Great, did not maintain standing armies. The royal armies of pre-Viking England were essentially royal war bands composed of a king's noble retainers and their own followers. The core of the army was the royal household, which was supplemented by levies of free landowners who looked to the king as their personal lord. Local forces were raised and led by royal reeves and *ealdormen. The armies of seventh-century England were probably small in size, numbering in the hundreds or, at most, the low thousands. An often cited law issued by King *Ine of Wessex (688–726) defines an army (*here*) as any force exceeding thirty-five men (ch. 13 § 1).

As a consequence of his wars against the Vikings, King Alfred (871–99) reorganised the military forces of *Wessex. By 893 he had established a standing army. He divided those eligible for service into two rotating groups, so that half would always be in the field and half at home protecting the localities. Alfred's mobile field force was designed to be used in conjunction with a system of *fortifications that dotted Wessex with thirty garrisoned *burhs*. In the 890s perhaps one out of every five free men in Wessex was serving either in a garrison or in the king's army. These military reforms, which also included constructing a small *navy, proved effective in campaigns against Viking invaders in 892–6, and were used by Alfred's son *Edward the Elder (899–924), his daughter, Æthelflæd, 'Lady of the Mercians', and his grandsons to conquer the *Danelaw. By the reign of *Æthelred the Unready (978–1016), however, royal armies had reverted to being *ad hoc* forces raised upon the command of the king or an ealdorman. Their ineffectiveness led Æthelred to supplement them with Scandinavian mercenary troops led by Thorkell the Tall. The Danish conquest of England led to the introduction of *housecarls, a closely-knit organisation of professional warriors who served in the king's household, but they may not have differed as much from earlier royal military households as formerly believed. The military administration of late Anglo-Saxon England was quite sophisticated. By 1066 the *fyrd* was raised on the basis of the assessed value of landed estates. According to a customal in the Berkshire folios of *Domesday Book, one soldier was to be sent on expedition from every five hides of land; he was to serve at his own expense for sixty days. Although this rule could not have prevailed over all of England, since some shires were assessed in carucates rather than hides, it is likely that a similar principle was in general use in 1066. It has been suggested that in late Anglo-Saxon England all able bodied free men were obliged to fight for home defence (the 'great fyrd'), while only a select number were obliged to serve on expeditions (the 'select fyrd'), but the evidence for the existence of a 'great fyrd' as an institution is not strong. The army was organised territorially, by shire and hundred, and contained smaller units defined by loyalty to a common lord. Leadership rested upon the king's greater officials, the earls, bishops, stallers, and sheriffs. The rank and file of the late Anglo-Saxon army was probably composed largely of sokemen and others from the 'peasant elite'. Royal lordship continued to play a crucial role in the organisation of the *fyrd*. For king's *thegns, the tenurial obligation did not so much supersede as reinforce and define more exactly their personal duty. In a sense, the Anglo-Saxon army never ceased to be a royal war band.

H. M. Chadwick, *The Origin of the English Nation* (Cambridge, 1907); C. W. Hollister, *Anglo-Saxon Military Institutions* (Oxford, 1962); M. Powicke, *Military Obligation in Medieval England* (Oxford, 1962), pp. 1–25; E. John, *Orbis Britanniae* (Leicester, 1966), pp. 128–53; N. Hooper, 'Anglo-Saxon Warfare on the Eve of the Conquest: A Brief Survey', *ANS* 1 (1979), 84–93; N. Brooks, 'England in the Ninth Century: The Crucible of Defeat', *TRHS*, 5th ser., 29 (1979), 1–20; N. Hooper, 'The Housecarls in England in the Eleventh Century', *ANS* 7 (1985), 161–76; R. Abels, *Lordship and Military Obligation in Anglo-Saxon England* (Berkeley, CA, 1988).

RICHARD ABELS

ARTHUR, legendary war-leader, is first mentioned in the (ninth-century) *Historia Brittonum*, both as leader of the British resistance against the Germanic invaders in the fifth or sixth century and as the central figure in local wonder-tales of the Welsh borders. The context of Arthur as war-leader is the English settlement led by *Hengest and opposed by Vortigern, more immediately the descent of the Kentish kings from Hengest's son Octha. 'Then Arthur fought against them in those days with the kings of the British, but he was war-leader' (*sed ipse erat dux bellorum*). The twelve battles attributed to him, at nine different sites (four at one site), cannot be identified, for lack of any further context; but there have been many attempts. The best discussion is that of Jackson. The sites include *Cat Coit Celidon* 'the battle of the Caledonian Forest', presumably in Scotland, and the battle of Mount Badon, generally supposed to have been in southern England, and named earlier by *Gildas but without any mention of Arthur. The list is likely to represent the accumulation of legend around a figure who, whether originally legendary or historical, had come to be portrayed as the leader of British resistance. However, it is notable that *Armes Prydein*, in the tenth century, made no mention of Arthur but named other heroes who should lead the anti-English forces.

Another early text which mentions Arthur is the Welsh Annals. The two entries are concerned with his part in the battle of Badon and his death, along with *Medraut* (the later Mordred), in the battle of Camlann, not mentioned in the *Historia Brittonum*. These entries could date from any time between the eighth century (when the Annals were probably first compiled) and *c*.1100 (the date of their earliest manuscript), and that concerning Badon has an indirect relationship to the text of the *Historia Brittonum* (a text of which occurs in the same manuscript); but they have little or no historical value for the sixth century.

Of Arthur's two aspects in the *Historia Brittonum*, later writers, notably Geoffrey of Monmouth in his *History of the Kings of Britain* (*c*.1138), emphasised the war-leader rather than the figure of local wonder-tales. Geoffrey's popularity ensured that this was the aspect which became well-known internationally. However, the local legends continued in Wales, *Cornwall, Brittany and elsewhere, seemingly little affected by the international literary industry.

L. Alcock, *Arthur's Britain* (Harmondsworth, 1973); T. Charles-Edwards, 'The Arthur of History', *The Arthur of the Welsh*, ed. R. Bromwich *et al.* (Cardiff, 1991), pp. 15–32; D. N. Dumville, 'Sub-Roman Britain: History and Legend', *History* ns 62 (1977), 173–92; K. Jackson, 'Once again Arthur's Battles', *Modern Philology* 43 (1945–6), 44–57; idem, 'Arthur's Battle of Breguoin', *Antiquity* 23 (1949), 48–9; idem, 'The Site of Mount Badon', *Journal of Celtic Studies* 2 (1953–8), 152–5; J. Morris, *The Age of Arthur* (London, 1973); O. J. Padel, 'The Nature of Arthur', *CMCS* 27 (1994), 1–31.

O. J. PADEL

ASSER (d. 908/9), author of the *Vita Ælfredi regis Angul Saxonum* (*Life of Alfred, King of the Anglo-Saxons*). Asser was a native of Wales and was brought up, tonsured and ordained at the monastery of St David's in the kingdom of Dyfed. There is some possibility that he was actually bishop of St David's. He was summoned from Wales by King *Alfred, whom he met for the first time at Dean in Sussex, probably in 885. After some negotiation Asser agreed to spend six months in every year with Alfred in Wessex and the remaining six months with his community at St David's; it is doubtful whether he adhered rigidly to this arrangement and likely that he came to spend more and more of his time in Wessex. On Christmas Eve (?)886, Alfred gave Asser the two monasteries at Congresbury and Banwell in Somerset (now Avon), and a few years later the king gave him charge of the monastery of *Exeter with all its jurisdiction in *Wessex and *Cornwall; he may have acted as a suffragan bishop at *Exeter within the diocese of *Sherborne. According to his own account Asser was closely involved in the process by which Alfred learnt to read Latin, and he participated fully in Alfred's programme for the revival of learning in England. He helped the king translate Pope *Gregory the Great's *Regula pastoralis* into English, and *William of Malmesbury records that he also helped in the translation of Boethius's *Consolation of Philosophy*. Asser was made bishop of Sherborne some time between 892 and 900, and he died in 908 or 909.

Asser's *Life of King Alfred* was written in 893. The narrative content of the *Life* is based on the *Anglo-Saxon Chronicle* (annals 851–87), to which Asser added from his own knowledge many valuable details of the king's upbringing, personality, family, and rulership. The *Life* is written in the florid Latin cultivated by many Insular Latin authors of the early Middle Ages (see *prose style, Latin); of particular interest is the Frankish element in Asser's vocabulary, which may reflect the influence of *Grimbald, another of King Alfred's literary helpers. A quotation from Einhard's *Vita Caroli* (*Life of Charlemagne*), in the *Life of King Alfred*, ch. 73, indicates that Asser was conscious of Einhard's work as a literary model. Among the other Latin works with which Asser appears to have been familiar are *Aldhelm's prose *De virginitate*, *Bede's *Historia ecclesiastica*, the anonymous *Vita Alcuini*, and the *Historia Brittonum*. He also shows familiarity with the 'Old Latin' (Vetus Latina) translation of the Bible, with the works of Pope Gregory the Great and St Augustine of Hippo, and with the poetry of Vergil and Caelius Sedulius. Though dedicated to the king himself it would appear that the work was intended primarily for a Welsh readership. By the time of writing all the Welsh rulers had submitted to King Alfred, and it was probably Asser's intention to give his friends in Wales some idea of the character and achievements of their new overlord, in a way which might help them to identify with the king's noble cause. The *Life* also contains disparaging remarks about the English in general, and about the Mercians in particular, which might not have been well received by a readership at Alfred's court but which would have been perfectly welcome in Wales.

The authenticity of the *Life of King Alfred* has often been called into question. It should be emphasised, therefore, that there is nothing in the text which is fatal to the authenticity of the work, and that it contains detailed points of information which can be substantiated by independent and contemporary evidence (to which a forger is not likely to have had access). When Asser stands on his own, he tells stories which are calculated to achieve a particular effect, and which might well involve an element of hyperbole, exaggeration, and distortion. This is no more, however, than we should expect of a work of this nature; and while it is necessarily a matter of judgement, the genuine Asser seems in every respect to capture the genuine Alfred of the late ninth century.

The only manuscript of Asser's *Life of King Alfred* known to have survived into modern times was written *c*.1000 at an unknown place presumably in southern England. It passed into the hands of Sir Robert *Cotton (1571–1631), in whose library it was designated Otho A. xii; alas, the manuscript was destroyed by fire in 1731. The text can be reconstructed from two sixteenth-century transcripts of the Cottonian manuscript (Cambridge, Corpus Christi College 100, and BL Cotton Otho A. xii*) and from the editions published by Matthew *Parker (1574) and Francis Wise (1722). Extensive extracts from the *Life of King Alfred* occur in the historical miscellany compiled by *Byrhtferth of Ramsey in the late tenth or early eleventh century (later incorporated in the *Historia Regum* of *Symeon of Durham), in the chronicle compiled by *John of Worcester in the 1120s, and in the so-called *Annals of St Neots*, compiled at Bury St Edmunds in the second quarter of the twelfth century. It is possible that Byrhtferth and John used the Cotton manuscript itself; the compiler of the *Annals of St Neots* seems to have used a different manuscript with some better readings. This evidence suggests that the *Life of King Alfred* had a fairly limited circulation as a separate work. That it was not better known (in the sense of more widely copied) before the Conquest may reflect the relatively belated development of the cult of King Alfred, or it may indicate that for whatever reason the *Life* had not been made formally available for copying and distribution.

Sharpe, *Handlist*, 134; *Asser's Life of King Alfred*, ed. W. H. Stevenson (Oxford, 1904), reissued with contr. by D. Whitelock (Oxford, 1959); D. Whitelock, *The Genuine Asser*, Stenton Lecture 1967 (Reading, 1968); D. P. Kirby, 'Asser and his Life of King Alfred', *Studia Celtica* 6 (1971), 12–35; S. Keynes and M. Lapidge, *Alfred the Great: Asser's 'Life of King Alfred', and other Contemporary Sources* (Harmondsworth, 1983), 2nd ed. (forthcoming); J. Campbell, 'Asser's *Life of Alfred*', *The Inheritance of Historiography 350–900*, ed. C. Holdsworth and T. P. Wiseman (Exeter, 1986), pp. 115–35; A. P. Smyth, *Alfred the Great* (Oxford, 1995), with M. Lapidge, in *The Times Higher Education Supplement*, 8 Mar. 1996, p. 20, and S. Keynes, 'On the Authenticity of Asser's *Life of King Alfred*', *JEH* 47 (1996), 529–51; A. Scharer, 'The Writing of History at King Alfred's Court', *EME* 5 (1996), 177–206; D. R. Howlett, *British Books in Biblical Style* (Dublin, 1997), pp. 365–445; S. Keynes, 'King Alfred and the Mercians', *Kings, Currency and Alliances: History and Coinage of Southern England in the Ninth Century*, ed. M. A. S. Blackburn and D. N. Dumville (Woodbridge, 1998), pp. 1–45, at 41–4.

SIMON KEYNES

ASTRONOMY. 'There is a crowd of calculators who are able to continue the Easter cycles and keep the sequences of sun, moon, month and week in the same order as before', according to *Ceolfrith, abbot of Wearmouth-Jarrow in AD 706 (Bede, *HE* v. 21). Therefore they must have known how sun and moon move relative to the stars, the celestial poles, and the terrestrial horizons. Many literary sources, drawings, and tables show that they did this in terms of spherical models of the heavens and of the earth. For analysis of stellar phenomena, Anglo-Saxon scholars described and used the Hellenistic five-zone model of the heavens with tropics of Cancer and Capricorn, two arctic circles, and two poles of the globe. This model could also display the ecliptic path of the sun at its extremes which defined the tropics, or at its equinoxes: twice each year in spring and autumn there would be a day when the sun was above the horizon for twelve hours and below it for the same number of hours. On such a day the sun's course would correspond with the celestial equator. Between the tropics was the Zodiac which provided a standard of reference for locating bright stars, constellations, planets, comets, colures, and milky way. The Zodiac was divided for this purpose into thirteen parts of width (*latitudo*) and twelve equal divisions of length (*longitudo*). Longitudinal divisions were each named for its brightest constellation and called signa: Aries with Libra

opposite, Pisces matched with Virgo, Aquarius with Leo, Capricorn with Cancer, Sagittarius with Gemini, Scorpio with Taurus. Illustrations accompanying such works are often dismissed today as mere astrology, though they do have basic astronomical uses. In the dark of night, only half of the Zodiac or six signa could be seen at one time, while the other six were opposite and out of sight, measuring the other side of the heavens. Anglo-Saxon masters recognised some possible correspondences of human disposition with weather conditions, the heat of the sun, or the influence of moon, especially if full; after *Bede had explained the tides, the moon's force on the seas was not in doubt. Until the twelfth century, however, they did not teach judicial astrology and looked with disfavour on casting horoscopes, prognostications, or use of astrological schemata to seek medical cures.

Planets were known to have varied paths through eight parts of zodiacal latitude above the ecliptic and five parts below; drawings of these upper (northern) and lower (southern) parts of that extensive space were modified by draftsmen to appear as six parts above and six below the middle line. The moon's path went to the extremes of the Zodiac, and the course of Venus surpassed those limits. The sun's path was not necessarily a perfect circle; rather, it was said to vary by one degree north and one degree south from the ecliptic in a wavy line. The different colours of wandering stars assisted in identifying them.

Apses and perigees of planetary orbits were known, that is, their farthest distances from the earth, as well as their nearest. Apparent pauses and reversals in the courses of Mercury, Venus, and Mars were explained often in terms of circular paths eccentric to the earth and rarely in terms of secondary epicycles. Hipparchan and Ptolemaic ideas were not taught in Anglo-Saxon schools, and thus the orbits of planets were not assumed to be earth-centred. New ideas about planetary orbits were introduced by *Abbo of Fleury in 985–7, and in the eleventh century a manuscript was received from Limoges at a school in Wales which explained eccentric orbits of planets and exhibited drawings of the orbits of Mercury and Venus centring on the Sun.

The different periods of planetary orbits through zodiacal longitude were reported by Bede (*De natura rerum*, c. 13) and other masters according to Hellenistic estimates: Saturn (30 years), Jupiter (12 years), Mars (2 years), and Sun ($365\frac{1}{4}$ days); periods of Venus and Mercury were usually given in varying numbers of days, more and less, relative to the sun. This probably means that some observations were done. The theory of solar and lunar eclipses was explained particularly well.

Three systems were used to locate a planet along the longitude of a zodiacal sign: for solar movement position was expressed on five parts of a sign; for lunar movement, there were four parts; but for Mercury and the other planets a sign was divided into thirty parts. In order to track the course of the sun, Bede suggested dividing a sign into three parts of ten. The use of thirty parts of each sign was soon extended to lunar and solar cycles, or 360 degrees. For latitudinal position there were two systems: six parts above, six below the theoretical ecliptic; or parts equivalent with those 360 used for longitude, that is, degrees. For example, Mercury could vary within the Zodiac as much as 22 *partes* from the Sun, Venus up to 46 *partes* or degrees.

In practice the zonal model of the heavens was often drawn on parchment as a rota with straight lines respresenting curved orbits or circular demarcations; those were also projected onto the rota to represent the spherical earth in several ways. The zonal model allowed for two methods of estimating position on the earth. The shadow of a stick cast by the Sun on the meridian at solstice formed a triangle whose ratio of height to length always corresponded with any position on the round earth which was the same distance from the equator or from the north pole. That ratio was always more or less than other known ratios to the north or to the south of that position. At times of equinox the shadow of a stick cast by the Sun could serve the same purpose but on a different scale of ratios. Both systems were explained by Bede and later scholars; tables of such data are found in Latin manuscripts from Anglo-Saxon schools, sometimes in the format of rotas. With either system, one could use the zonal rota of the heavens to travel on the earth without fear of getting lost or of not finding one's way home.

The zonal model also allowed Bede to use a *horologium in terra* for careful observations of the sun, moon, and stars. He could place a stick upright and sight the sun at meridian in order to determine on the ground exact directions of true North and true South. On the north/south line, one could construct right angles for determining directions of East and West. By *horologium* Bede did not mean *sundial, as once thought, for he used the same instrument during hours of darkness to observe the stars and the North Pole. During the Anglo-Saxon period the Pole did not

correspond with any star but was the geometrical point at the centre of stars revolving in circles around it. Use of the *horologium* must not have allowed for precision enough to determine the current equinox which in AD 725 was perhaps 17/18 March (rather than 21 March, as Bede supposed), but it did allow one to exclude any claim that equinox was a week later on 25 March. It seems that his calendar was also two days late. Bede's observations of the moon and those of his students allowed him to apply the regularity of an average synodical month of 29 days and twelve hours to some phenomena and the regularity of an average sidereal month of 28 days and eight hours to other phenomena. The former was good for computistical tables of Easter reckoning, while the latter was more useful for planetary positions on the zodiacal scale.

Although *Aldhelm created a table for tracking planets through the Zodiac, it was based upon the *computus lunar cycles of 29 days, 12 hours, that is, coordinated with regular appearances of new moon on the horizon; and it soon ceased to be useful. On the other hand Bede created a *pagina regularum* for the same purpose based upon the position of stars in the Zodiac, for which the lunar cycle was 28 days, 8 hours; it was relatively more precise, but not enough. Bede doubted validity of his own A-P tables for long-term observations of planetary orbits and encouraged others to produce a better system. No one could do so until new intruments and better data were introduced into England by Walter of Malvern and Petrus Alphonsus in the eleventh century.

The zonal model and the *horologium in terra* also allowed Anglo-Saxon scholars to base their time calculations on 24 parts of the day of equinox. Equinoctial hours were used in monastic schools throughout the year, rather than the twelfth part of daylight which varied from season to season. It should not be supposed that in practice, equinoctial hours could be observed with great precision. But the numerous masters and students trained in computus would certainly be asked to advise priors, abbots, and bishops about schedules for organising work, times of prayer, and special celebrations; when they were elected to offices responsible for such matters, they would surely not want unequal hours of a simple sundial in place of regular, equinoctial hours day and night, so far as possible. Astronomy would assist their sense of the times.

W. M. Stevens, *Bede's Scientific Achievement*, Jarrow Lecture 1985, repr. in his *Cycles of Time and Scientific Learning in Medieval Europe* (Aldershot, 1995), no. II;

idem, 'Scientific Instruction in Early Insular Schools', repr. in *Cycles of Time*, no. IV; idem, 'Sidereal Time in Anglo-Saxon England', repr. in *Cycles of Time*, no. V.

WESLEY M. STEVENS

AUGUSTINE, first archbishop of *Canterbury (597–604×609) and in effect the 'apostle of the English'. A Roman monk who was prior of the monastery of St Andrew (on the Coelian Hill) and who was chosen by Pope *Gregory to Great to lead a mission to convert the pagan English to Christianity. Our knowledge of this mission derives almost wholly from *Bede, *HE* (i.23–33, ii.2–3), who reports that Augustine and forty Roman monks left Rome in 595 or 596, made their way slowly through Gaul, and arrived in England (probably) in spring 597. They were received hospitably by King *Æthelberht of Kent (whose wife Bertha, a Frankish princess, was already a Christian) at a meeting on Thanet, who with his retainers listened sympathetically to Augustine's Christian message and then granted lodging in Canterbury (and subsequently the church of St Martin) and freedom to preach in his country. In due course King Æthelberht himself was converted, and by the end of 597 Gregory could write that Augustine had baptised more than 10,000 converts to the faith. It had been Gregory's plan to divide the country into two ecclesiastical provinces, with archiepiscopal sees at *York and *London, but in the event Augustine and his see remained in Canterbury. By 604 Augustine was able to consecrate two more Roman missionaries to English sees: *Justus to the bishopric of *Rochester, and *Mellitus to London, so that by the time of his death (on 26 May in an unknown year between 604 and 609) the ecclesiastical organisation was in place, and was able to grow from there. In the first instance the missionaries brought books and ecclesiastical furniture (including relics and vestments) to England from Rome – one such book still survives as the 'St Augustine's Gospels', now Cambridge, Corpus Christi College 286 – but one of their principal tasks will have been to establish schools for the training of native English clergy. The existence of these early schools must be inferred, but there is some evidence of Augustine's own scholarly attainment in the form of replies sent by Gregory to written questions raised by Augustine on the conduct of the mission (the *Libellus responsionum*, written in 601 and preserved in Bede, *HE* i.27) and possibly in two anonymous sermons preserved in a manuscript from Mainz.

Bede, *HE* i.23–33, ii.2–3; Sharpe, *Handlist*, 137; A. J. Mason, *The Mission of St Augustine to England* (Cambridge, 1897); Brooks, *Canterbury*, pp. 3–14; R. Meens, 'A Background to Augustine's Mission to Anglo-Saxon England', *ASE* 23 (1994), 5–17; *English Heritage Book of St Augustine's Abbey Canterbury*, ed. R. Gem (London, 1997); *CLA* ii.126; F. Wormald, 'The Miniatures in the Gospels of St Augustine: Cambridge, Corpus Christi College MS 286', in his *Collected Writings* I, ed. J. J. G. Alexander, T. J. Brown and J. Gibbs (London, 1984), pp. 13–35; P. Meyvaert, 'Le libellus responsionum à Augustin de Cantorbéry: une oeuvre authentique de saint Grégoire le Grand', *Grégoire le Grand*, ed. J. Fontaine et al. (Paris, 1986), pp. 543–50; P. Chaplais, 'Who Introduced Charters into England? The Case for Augustine', in *Prisca Munimenta*, ed. F. Ranger (London, 1973), pp. 88–107; L. Machielsen, 'Fragments patristiques non-identifiés du ms Vat. Pal. 577', *Sacris Eruditi* 12 (1961), 488–539.

MICHAEL LAPIDGE

AZARIAS: *see Daniel*

B

BAKEWELL (Derbs.) must already have been an important minster when *Edward the Elder fortified it in 920. The church, which controlled a huge parish into the late Middle Ages, contains an extraordinary accumulation of Anglo-Saxon and later monumental sculpture, of which the earliest items include rich late eighth- and ninth-century crosses and sarcophagi. It well illustrates the continuity, even in the *Danelaw, of major religious centres across the *Viking period.

C. R. Hart, *The North Derbyshire Archaeological Survey* (Chesterfield, 1981), pp. 118–21; R. Cramp, 'Schools of Mercian Sculpture', in Dornier, *MS*, pp. 191–233.

JOHN BLAIR

BALD: *see* Medical Literature and Medicine

BALE, JOHN (1495–1563), was a committed evangelical and also a collector of monastic manuscripts, of which he had 'great plenty', most acquired soon after the dissolution of the monasteries. Bishop of Ossory (Kilkenny) in Edward's reign, he was forced to abandon his library when he fled to the Continent in 1553. Bale published two bibliographical works – the *Illustrium maioris Britannie Scriptorum . . . Summarium* (1548) and the *Scriptorum illustrium maioris Britannie . . . Catalogus* (1557/59) – neither of which is altogether reliable in its account of individual authors and their works, but which together constitute an important early essay in the history of Anglo-Latin literature. Much more useful for bibliographers is his so-called *Index Britanniae Scriptorum*: based on first-hand evidence and listing source documents for each entry, this was a private notebook compiled for the most part between 1548 and 1552. In the second volume of the *Catalogus* Bale included a list of the manuscripts left behind in Ireland, many of which have been identified among surviving books.

Index Britanniae Scriptorum. John Bale's Index of British and Other Writers, ed. R. L. Poole and M. Bateson, with an introduction by C. Brett and J. P. Carley (Cambridge, 1990); P. Happé, *John Bale* (New York, 1996); H. R. Luard, 'A Letter from Bishop Bale to Archbishop Parker', *Cambridge Antiquarian Communications* 3 (1865–79), 157–73; H. McCusker, 'Books and Manuscripts Formerly in the Possession of John Bale', *The Library*, 4th ser. 16 (1935), 144–65; W. O'Sullivan, 'The Irish "Remnaunt" of John Bale's Manuscripts', in *New Science Out of Old Books*, ed. R. Beadle and A. J. Piper (Aldershot, 1995), pp. 374–87.

JAMES P. CARLEY

BARBERINI GOSPELS (Vatican City, Biblioteca Apostolica Vaticana, Barb. lat. 570), a Latin gospelbook, of the 'English' textual family, whose origins remain obscure. It was written by four scribes, two of whom appear to be of Northumbrian background and one Mercian. A *colophon reads 'Ora pro uuigbaldo'; a tentative association with Bishop Hygbald of Lindisfarne has not won general acceptance. It exhibits affinities with the Southumbrian 'Tiberius' group of manuscripts, such as the Book of Cerne, and with Northumbrian art. York has been suggested as a possible home, reinforced by artistic similarities with the Maeseyck Gospels. Stylistic parallels suggest a late eighth-century date. The elegant bearded evangelist portraits, canon tables, and elements of the incipit pages are indebted to Italo-Byzantine art. The Biblioteca Barberini was mainly founded by Francesco Barberini (1597–1679) and entered the Vatican in 1902.

CLA i.63; Alexander, *Insular MSS*, no. 36; M. P. Brown, *The Book of Cerne* (London and Toronto, 1996).

MICHELLE P. BROWN

BARKING (Essex) was a nunnery founded by *Eorcenwald, bishop of London, for his sister Æthelburg (cf. *Chertsey). *Bede, who says that she 'established an excellent form of monastic rule and discipline' there, preserves miracle stories from a lost *libellus*. These show that the minster contained segregated female and male communities, both ruled by the abbess; that it was built on a cramped site, and contained a church dedicated to St Mary and a large building in which the nuns slept; and that infant boys were lodged and educated in the nuns' quarters. Æthelburg was succeeded as abbess by *Hildelith (d. after 716), to whom *Aldhelm dedicated his prose treatise on virginity. Recent excavations have found timber buildings, evidence of weaving and glass-working, and a range of objects including gold thread, pins, manicure sets, styli and coins: evidence of Barking's rich material culture under Hildelith. In later tradition Barking was sacked by the *Vikings, but the glass-furnace was apparently operating in the early tenth century, and 'St Mary's foundation at Barking' received a bequest in 946 × c.951. King *Edgar re-founded it as a Benedictine nunnery, with St Wulfhild (whom according to *Goscelin he had tried to seduce) as first abbess.

Bede, *HE* iv.6–10; C. R. Hart, *The Early Charters of Eastern England* (Leicester, 1966), pp. 117–45; *Aldhelm: the Prose Works*, trans. M. Lapidge and M. Herren (Cambridge, 1979), pp. 51–2; K. MacGowan, 'Barking Abbey', *Current Archaeology* 149 (1996), 172–8; *Making of England*, pp. 88–94; D. Whitelock, *Anglo-Saxon Wills* (Cambridge, 1930), no. 2.

JOHN BLAIR

BARTON-UPON-HUMBER church (Lincs.) retains its late tenth-century tower-nave, with elaborate stripwork decoration (compare *Earls Barton), and the contemporary west *porticus*. Excavations in 1978–81, which found the chancel and an earlier cemetery underlying the church, also recovered rare evidence for liturgical arrangements, including a font-base in the west *porticus* and the fittings around the altar. The preserved late Anglo-Saxon timber coffins are unique discoveries. The church seems to have been built on the western edge of a large ditched enclosure, perhaps a noble residence.

W. Rodwell and K. Rodwell, 'St Peter's Church, Barton-upon-Humber', *AJ* 62 (1982), 283–315.

JOHN BLAIR

BATH (Somerset) was the Roman town of *Aquae Sulis*. Its hot springs, at the heart of the massive Roman temple and bath complex within their walled precinct, must have ensured that it remained a celebrated place throughout the fifth to seventh centuries. There are traces of sub-Roman occupation, and the 'hot streams' mentioned in *The *Ruin*, in the context of crumbling 'work of giants', were probably at Bath. It was one of the three 'chesters' which, according to the *Anglo-Saxon Chronicle* for '577', the Gewisse captured from the British at the battle of Dyrham. In 675 the sub-king Osric granted land for founding a nunnery at Bath to the abbess Berta. This name is Frankish, as is that of another nun, Folcburg: Bath was evidently one of the many early nunneries founded under Gallic influence. It probably contained aligned churches of St Peter and St Mary, the latter built within the Roman temple courtyard just north of the main hot bath (fig. 15).

By 758 Bath had apparently become an all-male community, and in the late 770s it was annexed by *Offa. Now it was a royal proprietary monastery, a fact underlined by the charter which King Ecgfrith issued 'in the celebrated monastery' at Bath in 796. At just this time Charlemagne was building his palace at the hot springs of Aachen, and the Mercian kings' choice of Bath for residential purposes suggests a Carolingian-inspired *Romanitas*. The same Roman and imperial connotations must explain why *Edgar's coronation as 'emperor of Britain' in 973 took place there. Meanwhile the *town had been re-fortified, and is listed in the *Burghal Hidage with an assessment of 1,000 hides. *Alfred minted coins there, and the street-plan is probably late ninth- or tenth-century. Bath was a *mint continuously from Edgar's reign, and appears in *Domesday Book with perhaps 192 burgesses. The minster received royal grants in the 930s and 950s. In 944 a group of monks from Saint-Bertin in *Flanders were settled at St Peter's by King *Edmund; over a century later, after the Norman Conquest, the then abbot of St Peter's, one Sæwold, returned with the community to Saint-Vaast in Arras (Flanders). Bath was reformed in the early 960s as a Benedictine abbey with St *Ælfheah as its first abbot.

B. Cunliffe, 'Saxon Bath', in Haslam, *Towns*, pp. 345–58; H. Edwards, *The Charters of the Early West Saxon Kingdom* (Oxford, 1988), pp. 209–27; P. Sims-Williams, *Religion and Literature in Western England, 600–800*, CSASE 3 (Cambridge, 1990), 204–9; W. Rodwell, 'Churches in the Landscape', *Studies in Late Anglo-Saxon Settlement*, ed. M. Faull (Oxford, 1984), pp. 7–8; Hill and Rumble, *The Defence of Wessex*, pp. 190–2.

JOHN BLAIR

BATTLE OF BRUNANBURH. The Battle of *Brunanburh* is the longest, and, most critics would agree, the best of the poems recorded in versions A B C and D of the *Anglo-Saxon Chronicle*, where it is the sole entry for 937, when the battle was fought. The poem relates how *Æthelstan and his brother *Edmund with an army of West Saxons and Mercians defeated a combined force of *Vikings (led by Anlaf or Olaf, Viking king of Dublin), Strathclyde Welsh and Scots. Æthelstan's victory was the culmination of his attempts to control the whole of Britain, and to keep Northumbria out of Viking hands. The poem structurally is a simple panegyric or praise-song of the victorious English, a tissue of conventional images from *heroic poetry, but the verse is handled competently. Events are seen solely from the English point of view, with Olaf fleeing with the remnant of the host to Dublin and Constantine, king of Scots, leaving his son dead on the battlefield. The site of the battle has not been established with certainty (see Campbell) but the earliest records of Bromborough, Wirral, Cheshire (see Dodgson) strongly support its case. The alternative of Burnswork, Dumfriesshire, is now thought less likely.

ASPR vi.16–20; *The Battle of Brunanburh*, ed. A. Campbell (London, 1938); J. McN. Dodgson, *The Place-Names of Cheshire* IV, English Place-Name Society 47 (Cambridge, 1972), 237–40; B. J. Muir, *Leoð: Six Old English Poems: A Handbook* (New York, 1989).

DONALD SCRAGG

BATTLE OF FINNSBURH. *The Battle of Finnsburh*, part of an Old English poem first printed in *Hickes' *Thesaurus* in 1705 from a subsequently lost single-folio manuscript fragment, describes the beginning of an attack which we can identify from extra-textual information as being by Finn's men (Frisians) on the hall occupied by the Danish Hnæf and his company whilst visiting Finn's wife Hildeburh, Hnæf's sister. The viewpoint is that of the Danes. The story is alluded to in *Widsith* and is exploited in *Beowulf* (lines 1063–1159). *Finnsburh* was probably a lay of about 200–300 lines; it is relatively swiftly-moving and seems to delight in the action of battle, by contrast with the episode in *Beowulf*, which is elegiac and preoccupied with moral tensions in a feuding society. Dating is particularly difficult because there is no manuscript and Hickes' text contains obvious errors, although there are nonetheless indications of a late date in lexis, inflexions and alliteration. Hickes' exemplar, which he claims to have found in a 'semi-Saxon' manuscript in Lambeth Palace Library, probably as a loose leaf, could well have been from an eleventh-century copy, but on the grounds of subject-matter the poem's composition is often assumed to be contemporary with *Beowulf*. The fragment is an important witness of the vernacular tradition of *heroic poetry and is commonly included in editions of *Beowulf* as a complementary text.

ASPR vi.3–4; *The Finnsburh Fragment and Episode*, ed. D. K. Fry (London, 1974); *Old English Minor Heroic Poems*, ed. J. Hill (Durham, 1983; rev. ed. 1994).

JOYCE HILL

BATTLE OF MALDON. Amongst the long series of *Viking raids during the reign of *Æthelred the Unready, perhaps the best known encounter is a battle fought between an English army under the command of Byrhtnoth, *ealdorman of *Essex, and a large naval force which had, according to the *Anglo-Saxon Chronicle*, sacked *Ipswich and then sailed up the river Blackwater to Maldon in Essex. Although there is

some discrepancy between the date given for the battle in different versions of the *Chronicle* (993 in the A-version, 991 in CDEF), the earlier date is generally accepted as the true one. Byrhtnoth died in the battle, and his obit is recorded in monastic calendars, enabling us to date it more precisely as occurring on either the 10th (Ely) or the 11th (Winchester) of August. The battle is important in that, according to the *Chronicle*, thereafter the English paid *Danegeld. But the real reason for the general familiarity of the battle is that an account of it survives in 325 lines of alliterative verse in Old English. The poem, universally entitled since the nineteenth century as *The Battle of Maldon*, has been frequently anthologised and translated. It survives by extraordinary good fortune. When first identified, it was found written on three bifolia, folded into a booklet of six pages, but the poem is fragmentary at the beginning and the end, and further leaves must once have existed both before and after the surviving text. The early history of the three bifolia is lost (they may have been used as part of a medieval binding), and the first that is known is when they were catalogued, in 1621, as part of a composite manuscript in the *Cotton collection, shelf-mark Otho A.xii. The manuscript was badly burned in the fire of 1731 and nothing of the poem remains. Shortly before this, David Casley, deputy keeper of the library, had made a line-by-line transcription of the text, and modern editions are based on his copy (which, until 1985, was assumed to have been made by John Elphinston, to whom it was ascribed by Thomas Hearne, who first published the text in 1726).

The fragment opens with Byrhtnoth arraying his forces along the river Blackwater (called *Pante* in the poem), with the Vikings waiting on the opposite bank. A Danish messenger asks for tribute in return for peace, but this is scornfully refused. As the tide recedes, it becomes apparent that the Vikings can attack only across a narrow causeway which the English easily defend. Consequently the invaders, using what the poet calls 'guile', ask for leave to cross the ford unopposed, and Byrhtnoth allows them, again in the poet's words, 'too much land'. This is because of his *ofermod*, literally 'pride', but glossed by critics across a spectrum ranging from 'arrogance' to 'high courage and a sense of fair play'. But there can be no doubt that 'too much land' is condemnatory, nor that Byrhtnoth's character is subsequently re-established, both by his own actions and by those of his followers who remain loyal to him.

The rest of the fragment describes the battle. There is little indication of strategy on either side, but individual encounters alternate with scenes of general confusion, noise and slaughter. Throughout there is a great sense of realism in the portrayal of the English characters, which has given rise to the assumption of first-hand reporting. But it should be remembered that the account is a poem, and artifice is everywhere. Images of loyalty, the theme of the poem, abound, to be contrasted with disloyalty. Early in the battle Byrhtnoth is killed, and his retainer Godric who witnesses the fact leaps on his horse and leaves the field. Many of the English assume that the fugitive is Byrhtnoth, and they too run away, and the last third of the poem is concerned with the brave words and actions of those who fight on in a vain attempt to avenge their lord. Consequently, much of this part of the poem, with its open references to the bonds of loyalty expected of members of the *comitatus, is seen as the last and fullest exposition in Old English of the Germanic heroic spirit.

ASPR vi.7–16; *The Battle of Maldon*, ed. E. V. Gordon (London, 1937); *The Battle of Maldon*, ed. D. G. Scragg (Manchester, 1981); H. L. Rogers, 'The Battle of Maldon: David Casley's Transcript', *Notes and Queries* n.s. 32 (1985), 147–55; *The Battle of Maldon AD 991*, ed. D. G. Scragg (Oxford, 1991); *The Battle of Maldon: Fiction and Fact*, ed. J. Cooper (London, 1993).

DONALD SCRAGG

BAYEUX TAPESTRY. The Bayeux Tapestry depicts the events of *Edward the Confessor's reign which led to the Norman conquest of England in 1066 and the battle of *Hastings in which, on 14 October, Duke William of Normandy defeated King *Harold Godwinson of England, who died in the battle. The Tapestry lacks its final scene or scenes through damage. Strictly speaking an embroidery rather than a tapestry, it was worked upon a strip of linen which varies between 45.7 and 53.6 centimetres in height; as it survives, it is some 68.38 m long. The material comprises eight constituent pieces of differing lengths. There is no certain reference to its existence or history before a Bayeux cathedral inventory of 1476. But the prominence which it accords to Bishop Odo of Bayeux, the half-brother of the Norman duke, points to its close association with him; many historians favour a date for its design and execution between *c.*1075 and Odo's imprisonment by William in 1082. The English form of some of the letters and proper names in the captions which accompany its scenes creates a virtual certainty

that it was embroidered in England rather than Normandy; similarities between certain of the scenes and manuscript illuminations associated with St Augustine's abbey at Canterbury, in Odo's earldom of Kent, point to an origin in southeastern England. For the whole length of the Tapestry, which is embroidered in lively colours that are remarkably well preserved from fading although there has been some restoration, a central narrative which is brilliantly designed to maintain dramatic continuity and movement is flanked by upper and lower borders. While the borders often serve only to provide animation and vitality, the lower, in particular, may sometimes be interpreted as offering comment upon, or amplification of, the central narrative. From beginning to end, the Tapestry calls for a close study of its highly significant details and for interpretation which at many points remains a matter of lively debate. It is a highly propagandist document which, while it provides invaluable evidence for eleventh-century life, especially social and military, and for the political context of the Norman conquest, should be approached less as a source of assured information than as a pointer to the judgements on men and events that those who designed it were concerned to propagate.

The narrative falls into three portions of unequal length. The first concentrates upon Harold. It opens with Edward the Confessor in royal state as he instructs Harold about a journey to Normandy. Misfortune delivers Harold into captivity by Duke William's vassal, Count Guy of Ponthieu, who disarms him and takes him to the duke. Harold serves the duke well during a campaign in Brittany; William thereafter bestows arms upon him and, in a culminating scene, Harold takes a solemn oath to William. Throughout in the main narrative, Harold is ostensibly a noble and heroic figure. But subliminal doubts are cast: comment in the borders seems to harp on the theme that appearances are deceptive – in particular, references to Aesop's fables with their prudential moral to guard against deceit; a generous William restores to Harold the arms of which Guy of Ponthieu stripped him and which the observer knows that Harold will turn against William at Hastings; likewise, Harold takes an oath to William which will be the basis of his perjury. A condensed second portion foreshortens the events of 1066 so that Harold's return to England, hunchbacked as a man of shame, leads up to the Confessor's deathbed, to Harold's taking of the crown, and to his displaying his regality – only to be warned by the comet of its imminent collapse;

ghostly invasion ships in the border foreshadow the avenging of his perjury. Thirdly and at length, the Tapestry turns to Duke William's preparation of ships for the invasion, to the battle of Hastings, and to Harold's death, perhaps shown twice in scenes that show an arrow striking his eye and a Norman knight hacking his thigh with a sword. Like Shakespeare in *Henry V*, the Tapestry displays war in all its glories and miseries. The final surviving scene is of the victorious Normans pursuing the fleeing English. It can only be a matter of conjecture that the Tapestry may have ended with William's royal coronation at Christmas 1066, thus matching the earlier scenes of Edward the Confessor and Harold in their regality.

The Bayeux Tapestry: a Comprehensive Survey, ed. F. M. Stenton, 2nd ed. (London, 1965); *The Bayeux Tapestry: the Complete Tapestry in Colour*, ed. D. M. Wilson (London, 1985); *The Study of the Bayeux Tapestry*, ed. R. Gameson (Woodbridge, 1997).

H. E. J. COWDREY

BEASTS OF BATTLE. The beasts of battle typescene appears frequently in Old English poetic battle descriptions (Griffith gives a comprehensive list). Typically, the raven, the eagle and the wolf rejoice in anticipation of the feast which the onset of battle will provide for them, although in *Exodus* there is no battle, in *Genesis* and The *Battle of Maldon* the enemy are the wolves, and in *Beowulf* the conversation of raven and eagle about their feast in the past tense brings home the sense of doom surrounding an impending battle.

F. P. Magoun, 'The Theme of the Beasts of Battle in Anglo-Saxon Poetry', *NM* 56 (1955), 81–90; A. Bonjour, '*Beowulf* and the Beasts of Battle', *PMLA* 72 (1957), 563–73; M. S. Griffith, 'Convention and Originality in the Old English "Beasts of Battle" Typescene', *ASE* 22 (1993), 179–99.

DONALD SCRAGG

BEDE (*c.*673–735) was the most learned, voluminous, and influential Latin writer of Anglo-Saxon England. To his best known work, the *Historia ecclesiastica gentis Anglorum* (*HE*), he appended a short autobiography, written within perhaps a year of his death; it tells us virtually all that we know about his life. Born in the region of modern Newcastle-upon-Tyne, he lived there from boyhood onward, except for rare and short trips away, as a monk of the twin monastery *Monkwearmouth-Jarrow. The abbey followed a mixed rule, with important Benedictine ingredients, and answered to the bishop of *Hexham. The range and quality of his writings reflect a fine

education in *grammar, biblical *exegesis, *chant, and *computus. The documentable sources of his books are evidence that the founder of the abbey, *Benedict Biscop, built a remarkable library from his repeated continental travels. Bede read widely in Latin Christian literature, especially in the works of the four great Latin Fathers (Ambrose, Augustine, Jerome, *Gregory); he knew a few Greek biblical manuscripts and several pagan writings, including all the works of Vergil. At the canonical ages Bede was ordained deacon and then priest. In a stimulating environment of books and art, Bede was mainly the devout *eruditus*, ever 'learning, teaching, and writing', as he says in his autobiography.

Just afterwards in the *HE*, Bede lists his works. The bibliography is a few items short, includes two books which survive only in fragments, but perhaps only one title which is now lost. Bede's extant Latin writings exceed thirty, if one counts his collected homilies and letters as a total of two volumes. A pupil named Cuthbert claims that as Bede lay dying he translated into Old English a part of the Gospel of John, but there is no other trace of anything that Bede may have written in the vernacular, save perhaps the poem known as *Bede's Death Song. His works survive in an enormous body of manuscripts, copied in worthy numbers in every century from the eighth to the fifteenth, mainly on the Continent, especially in Germany and France. Not many of his books can be dated to the year. The furious output in the last decade of his life gives credibility to Cuthbert's report that Bede was still writing on his deathbed. Bede lists his works not in chronological order but by subject matter and genre.

He gives pride of place to his writings on the Bible, about two-thirds of the surviving *oeuvre*. They include fifty homilies, gathered in two books of twenty-five each, and a treatise on biblical geography. Except for two devoted to questions, the rest are verse-by-verse commentaries. Bede expounded at least a substantial selection from every division of the Roman canon, including the Apocrypha. Like all his books, the biblical writings are eclectic, pastoral, and catholic. They draw together disparate sources, above all extracts from the four Latin Fathers. Yet the resulting mosaics are Bede's own instructional achievement, not mere scissors-and-paste. Though most at ease when expounding the literal sense, he often preferred allegorical exegesis to give milk not meat to his readers, many of whom were barely literate. Indeed it was the anticipated audience, not Bede's own tastes, which set the intellectual level of the commentaries. They embody an unremitting papal and patristic devotion, for the major goal of Bede's career was to cause his Insular compatriots to see themselves in the international world of Roman tradition. None the less his exegesis owed an important debt to Celtic Ireland, especially its outpost in *Iona. However derivative his biblical studies often were, he all but pioneered the exposition of the Acts of the Apostles, which he read in both Latin and Greek. He had only a passive knowledge of Hebrew, though he was a notorious champion of Jerome's translation of the Old Testament from the original language. Exegesis was, as Bede says, his lifework. He wrought so well in the field that he no doubt discouraged subsequent Anglo-Saxon writers from seriously entering it. It was certainly the biblical commentaries which caused medieval luminaries like *Alcuin, Abelard, and Dante to put Bede among the fathers of the church.

Bede mentions next a book of five letters, and two of these, both addressed to Bishop *Acca of Hexham, a major supporter of his biblical studies, are examples of what might be called familiar exegesis. The remaining three have to do with computus. In one of these Bede responds to a charge of heresy with a rather fine piece of Latin vituperation directed against his accusers, unnamed millennialists in the household of Bishop *Wilfrid of Hexham. This may not have been his only polemical work. Cuthbert reports that among Bede's last literary efforts was a (now lost) book of 'exceptions' to the *Liber rotarum* of Isidore of Seville. The five letters have survived separately. They do not include his most important extant letter, the magisterial assessment of the state of English faith sent to Bishop *Ecgberht of York in the autumn of 734, nor the letter to *Albinus of Canterbury written at about the same time to accompany a copy of the *HE*. Several of Bede's works begin with dedicatory letters.

Then Bede comes to his product in the genre *historia*, which in the Greco-Latin tradition included any narrative work, prose or poetry, whose subject matter was real or at least plausible events. First among them he mentions several lives of saints, one of which, a corrected translation of a Greek life of St Anastasius, has recently been identified. The others have long been attested in surviving manuscripts. The most famous are the separate verse and prose lives of the Northumbrian hero *Cuthbert, about whom Bede also wrote in the *HE*. After the hagiographical *vitae* Bede places the *Historia abbatum*, an affecting account of his abbey down to the first acts of *Hwaetberht.

Written to replace an anonymous hagiographical *vita*, it was the first of the monastic local histories, a historical sub-genre which flourished in the twelfth century. This same century also produced the majority of the surviving manuscripts of the work.

The *HE* follows. It remains in more than 130 complete English and continental manuscripts, two of them copied in *Northumbria within years of Bede's death, one of these (St Petersburg, Public Library, Lat. Q. v. I. 18) almost certainly at Monkwearmouth-Jarrow. Translated into English in the time of King *Alfred and copied in record numbers in the twelfth century, the *HE* had been printed three times by 1507. That Bede attached his bio-bibliography to it reflects his confidence that among all his works this one would have a special future. The narrative surmounts its scattered, mostly Northumbrian, and mainly oral sources to provide at least an artful account of England from the end of the Roman occupation down to 731. Other evidence of this story allows us to alter or augment Bede's narrative in but few details. The title he no doubt chose to evoke a distinguished Late Roman predecessor, the *Historia ecclesiastica* of Eusebius of Caesarea, which Bede had read closely in the Latin translation of Rufinus. Yet his theme came not from Eusebius but from the Acts of the Apostles, a book which Bede expounded twice, the second time while he was probably at work also on the *HE*. Like Luke, Bede narrated the triumph of catholic faith over mixed customs among a new people of God destined to preach the Gospel abroad. If biblical study was preparatory to the writing of the narrative, so too was Bede's work as a hagiographer and a chronographer. And though Vergil may have been the only classical narrator known at firsthand to Bede, his text nonetheless has a number of classical affinities. There is a splendid Latinity which includes locutions more characteristic of (say) Livy or Cicero than of Gregory the Great or the Vulgate. In the Graeco-Roman rhetorical tradition, Bede wrote history primarily for effect, to improve the conduct of his readers. His preferred method was the rhetorical *exemplum*. Other features of the narrative – an elegant preface, the rhetorical set piece on the geography of Britain, the deliberative oratory which elevates the account of the Synod of *Whitby – reflect self-conscious classical scholarship. Last in the list of his historical works Bede puts the *Martyrologium*. Adding brief historical information to the anniversaries, Bede redefined the genre for a tradition of medieval imitators. We have this work only in a text reconstructed from interpolated versions.

In his bibliography Bede then goes on to two books of verses, one of hymns and another of epigrams, both of which survive to us only in fragments. He is thought to have written in addition a poem entitled *De die iudicii*. His most widely read verses were the metrical life of St Cuthbert and the long poem on virginity dedicated to St *Æthelthryth included in the *HE*. Bede was a competent Latin poet, praised among others by Alcuin. His bibliography ends with a group of textbooks. Written from available books of Pliny's *Historia naturalis*, the *De natura rerum* is about Christian cosmology, hexameral exegesis, and computus. Bede wrote two other volumes strictly on chronology, the later of which, *De temporum ratione*, quickly swept the field and held it for centuries. This book, together with the *HE*, assured the victory of the *annus domini* in European historical thought, and the chronicle attached to it became almost canonical among medieval world chroniclers. Bede's three literary treatises – *De orthographia*, *De arte metrica*, and *De schematibus et tropis* – appropriated Late Roman grammar to claustral instruction and would be in continual use all over Europe for three hundred years.

Sharpe, *Handlist*, 152; CCSL cxviii–cxxiii; Plummer, *VBOH*; *Bede's Ecclesiastical History of the English People*, ed. B. Colgrave and R. A. B. Mynors (OMT, 1969); *Bede, his Life, Times and Writings*, ed. A. H. Thompson (Oxford, 1935); M. L. W. Laistner and H. H. King, *A Hand-List of Bede Manuscripts* (Ithaca, NY, 1943); P. Hunter Blair, *The World of Bede*. rev. ed. (Cambridge, 1990); *Famulus Christi*, ed. G. Bonner (London, 1976); A. C. Dionisotti, 'On Bede, Grammars and Greek', *RB* 92 (1982), 11–41; Campbell, *Essays*, pp. 1–120; G. H. Brown, *Bede the Venerable* (Boston, 1987); *Bede and His World: The Jarrow Lectures 1958–93*, pref. M. Lapidge, 2 vols. (Aldershot, 1994); P. Meyvaert, 'Bede's *Capitula lectionum* for the Old and New Testaments', *RB* 105 (1995), 348–80; M. Gorman, 'Wigbod and the *lectiones* on the Hexateuch attributed to Bede in Paris lat. 2342', *RB* 105 (1995), 310–47, esp. 343–7 [annotated list of Bede's writings]; Lapidge, *ALL* i.313–79.

ROGER RAY

BEDE'S DEATH SONG. The only vernacular composition by *Bede to survive is a five-line poem composed on his death-bed, noted by Wilberct who happened to be in the room transcribing Bede's translation of St John's Gospel, and recorded by Cuthbert who quotes it in his letter to Cuthwin. The song, which simply notes that no man can know how his soul may be judged after death, has the dubious distinction of being

the most frequently attested Old English poem, some forty-five copies having been identified, the earliest being in the original Northumbrian *dialect in continental manuscripts, many later ones being in a *West Saxon dialect in English manuscripts.

ASPR vi.107–8; *Three Northumbrian Poems*, ed. A. H. Smith (London, 1933).

DONALD SCRAGG

BELLS AND BELLRINGING. Small handbells, and bells which could be placed around the necks of animals, are known from a few pagan Anglo-Saxon contexts. Such bells, usually constructed of two iron sheets bent and rivetted to form a truncated wedge, were often preserved as saints' relics in the Celtic world; over fifty survive in Ireland, some with elaborate covers.

With the establishment of English Christianity large bells were introduced from the Continent, where they are known from *c*.600. Bede mentions a bell at *Whitby in 680, when Begu heard the death-knell of Abbess *Hild, and Archbishop *Ecgberht commanded every priest to sound the bells of his church at the proper hours. Casting-pits and mould-fragments have been found in tenth-century contexts at *Gloucester (St Oswald's) and *Winchester (Old Minster), the former with an inscription in relief. Patronage associated with the tenth-century monastic reform must have stimulated bell production, and *Regularis Concordia* includes rules for ringing the canonical hours. By the Conquest both the death-knell and lych-bells following the coffin were well-established, and are shown in the funeral scene on the *Bayeux Tapestry.

During the later period there are many references to gifts of bells to churches. Abbot Thurcytel presented a great bell to Crowland Abbey in about 960; Archbishop *Ealdred gave two bells to Southwell minster in 1063, as did King *Cnut to Winchester in 1035. It seems that a typical manor-house would have had a bell by *c*.1000, when 'a church, a kitchen, a bell and a fortress-gate' are listed as expected possessions of an aspirant *thegn.

The surviving late Anglo-Saxon bell-towers and louvres also indicate the importance of large bells in churches, for example at Barnack and *Earls Barton (Northants.). Bells were also hung in turrets, as shown in an illustration in the *Benedictional of St *Æthelwold, although the earliest securely dated surviving examples are Norman. The earliest English bells with dates on them are thirteenth century, but several survive which are typologically earlier; those at Hanford (Dorset) and Hardham (Sussex) are perhaps the most likely to be eleventh century.

Golden Age of AS Art, p. 138; M. Biddle, *Object and Economy in Medieval Winchester* (Oxford, 1990), pp. 102–24; G. P. E. Elphick, *The Craft of the Bellfounder* (Chichester, 1988); Fernie, *Architecture*; E. Morris, *Tintinnabula* (London, 1959); M. Stokes, *Early Christian Art in Ireland* (London, 1887); H. B. Walters, *Church Bells of England* (Oxford, 1912).

ALEX BAYLISS

BENEDICT BISCOP (d. 689), sometime abbot of SS Peter and Paul (later St Augustine's), *Canterbury, and founder and first abbot of *Monkwearmouth-Jarrow. His life is known to us principally from Bede's *Historia abbatum* (cc. 1–13). He was the scion of a noble Northumbrian family (his secular name was Biscop Baducing), and spent the early years of his life as a layman in the household of King *Oswiu (642–70). In 652 or 653, however, he decided to travel to *Rome; in *Kent he joined forces with his younger colleague *Wilfrid, who harboured similar ambitions, and the two set off together on what was to be the first of five trips by Biscop to Rome. Following his second visit to Rome in *c.* 664, Biscop became a monk at Lérins (*c.*666), taking on the name Benedict, and spent two years there studying monastic observance. He returned to Rome, his visit coinciding with the presence there of Wigheard (667), archbishop-elect of Canterbury. Wigheard died of the plague in Rome, and in his stead Pope Vitalian consecrated *Theodore, and Benedict was deputed to accompany Theodore to England. They left Rome on 27 May 668 and arrived in Canterbury almost precisely a year later; Benedict temporarily assumed the abbacy of the monastery of SS Peter and Paul, pending the arrival of Theodore's companion *Hadrian in 670. The following year (671–2) Benedict went again to Rome, this time to acquire books for a monastic foundation; when he returned to *Northumbria – for the first time in nearly ten years – he was given land at Monkwearmouth by King Ecgfrith (670–85) for a monastery, probably in 673 or 674, and was joined there by *Ceolfrith, who was eventually to succeed him as abbot. With the help of imported Frankish stonemasons and glaziers, the church was completed in 675 or 676, whereupon Benedict and Ceolfrith set off for Rome, and once again brought back books as well as pictures to adorn the church at Monkwearmouth; they also brought with them John, the precentor of St Peter's in Rome (who had come to England in 679 as a papal emissary)

to teach their Northumbrian monks the rules of liturgical chant. The success of St Peter's in Wearmouth encouraged King Ecgfrith to endow a second monastery, and Jarrow was established in 681 or 682, with Ceolfrith as its abbot. A few years later, in 685, Benedict made his final journey to Rome, and once again brought back books and treasures. It was largely through Benedict's efforts that Monkwearmouth-Jarrow acquired the substantial library which was to sustain the scholarship of *Bede.

Bede, *HE* iv.18, v.19; *Historia abbatum*, cc. 1–13 (Plummer, *VBOH*, i.364–77); Bolton, *ALL*, pp. 62–6; P. Hunter Blair, *The World of Bede* (London, 1970), pp. 155–83; P. Wormald, 'Bede and Benedict Biscop', in *Famulus Christi*, ed. Bonner, pp. 141–69.

MICHAEL LAPIDGE

BENEDICTINE REFORM: *see* Benedictine Rule, OE; Monasticism; *Regularis Concordia*

BENEDICTINE RULE, OE. The *Regula S. Benedicti* is one of the great texts of western spirituality and the principal text for the Benedictine reform in late-tenth-century England. Its Old English translation, the 'Benedictine Rule', is the only prose rendering of this work to have survived in any European vernacular from the early Middle Ages. The authorship of the Old English Rule is ascribed to *Æthelwold, bishop of Winchester (963–84), in an early-twelfth-century Latin source (the *Libellus Æthelwoldi*), based on a late-tenth century account (now lost) in the vernacular concerning the endowments of *Ely, one of Æthelwold's principal foundations. A date for the translation cannot be established with certainty, but historical and stylistic grounds suggest composition in the 940s or 950s; it would hence have been available from the earliest stages of the reform onwards. The Rule is preserved in some five manuscripts and one substantial fragment (minor fragments are found in two further manuscripts); of these manuscripts, one is of tenth-century date (Oxford, Corpus Christi College 197, s. x³/₄, of unknown origin). The text was (moderately) revised and modernised in the course of its transmission, as is revealed by three (eleventh-century) manuscripts. An adaptation to early Middle English, the so-called 'Winteney Version', is preserved in one manuscript (s. xiii^in). In four of the Anglo-Saxon manuscripts, the Latin and English text of the *Regula* alternate chapter by chapter, in one the Latin text precedes the English version, and one contains the English translation only. Thus the textual transmission indicates that the

Rule and the Latin original were intended to be studied side by side. In some of the manuscripts, the Latin and Old English text bear unmistakable traces (such as feminine pronouns) of having been derived from exemplars intended for the use in nunneries (the 'Winteney Version' preserves such a 'feminine' recension), and there are reasons to think that, in addition to the translation of St Benedict's text (intended for monks), Æthelwold himself prepared a version for nuns. For his translation he based himself on the *textus receptus* recension of the *Regula*, that is on the version then in use in the reformed monasteries on the Continent, but not previously in England. Æthelwold's orientation towards continental monasticism is further reflected by the recourse he made in his translation to the early-ninth-century commentary (the *Expositio in Regulam S. Benedicti*) by Smaragdus, abbot of Saint-Mihiel, who belongs in the ambit of the Carolingian reforms instituted by the Emperor Louis the Pious (814–40) and Benedict of Aniane, his chief ecclesiastical adviser. Similarly, it has been shown that the (Latin and English) text of ch. 62 which apparently replaced the text of the *Regula* in the version for nuns, draws heavily on the rule for canonesses as laid down in the 'Institutiones Aquisgranenses', promulgated in the train of the synods held at Aachen in 816/17. The Old English Rule is a fairly accurate and idiomatic translation revealing Æthelwold as a proficient Latinist and a powerful author of English prose. He supplemented his translation by a lengthy preface in English (preserved in one manuscript and usually referred to as 'Edgar's Establishment of Monasteries') which relates the history of the conversion of the English, the origin and progress of the English Benedictine reform and which includes an apologia for translations into the vernacular. A continuous interlinear gloss to the *Regula* survives in one manuscript (London, BL, Cotton Tiberius A. iii, 118r–163v, s. xi^med from Christ Church, Canterbury). It is independent of the prose translation, but lexical evidence strongly suggests an origin in the orbit of Æthelwold's school at Winchester.

A. Schröer, ed., *Die angelsächsischen Prosabearbeitungen der Benediktinerregel*, 2nd ed. with a supplement by H. Gneuss (Darmstadt, 1964; 1st ed. 1885–8); A. Schröer, ed., *Die Winteney-Version der Regula S. Benedicti*, repr. with a supplement by M. Gretsch (Tübingen, 1978; orig. publ. 1888); *Councils & Synods* i.142–54 [Æthelwold's preface]; H. Logemann, ed., *The Rule of S. Benet. Latin and Anglo-Saxon Interlinear Version*, EETS os 90 (London, 1888); M. Gretsch, *Die Regula Sancti Benedicti in England und ihre altenglische Übersetzung* (Munich, 1973); idem, 'Æthelwold's Translation of the *Regula*

Sancti Benedicti and its Latin Exemplar', *ASE* 3 (1974), 125–51; idem, 'The Benedictine Rule in Old English: a Document of Bishop Æthelwold's Reform Politics', in FS Gneuss, pp. 131–58; D. Whitelock, 'The Authorship of the Account of King Edgar's Establishment of Monasteries', in *Philological Essays: Studies in Old and Middle English Language and Literature in Honour of Herbert Dean Meritt*, ed. J. L. Rosier (The Hague, 1973), pp. 124–36; W. Hofstetter, *Winchester und der spätaltenglische Sprachgebrauch* (Munich, 1987), pp. 117–23.

MECHTHILD GRETSCH

BENEDICTIONAL: *see* Liturgical Books

BEORHTGYTH was one of the *missionaries who followed *Boniface as a nun to *Germany; although only three (and perhaps only two) of her letters survive, all addressed to her brother Baltheard back in England, her writings, which include two poems in Latin *octosyllables, are among the most poignant and heartfelt relics of the period, amply attesting to the isolation and even despair felt by the early missionaries. Beorhtgyth and her mother, Cynehild, who was the aunt of *Lull, Boniface's successor as archbishop of Mainz, had both gone, presumably at Boniface's request, to teach in Thuringia, and after their mother's death Beorhtgyth writes to her brother and asks him in increasingly heart-rending tones to visit her; no reply survives.

S. *Bonifatii et Lullii Epistolae*, ed. M. Tangl, MGH ES 1 (Berlin, 1916), nos. 143, 147, 148; P. Dronke, *Women Writers of the Middle Ages* (Cambridge, 1984), pp. 30–3; C. Fell, 'Some Implications of the Boniface Correspondence', in *New Readings on Women in Old English Literature*, ed. H. Damico and A. H. Olsen (Bloomington, IN, 1990), pp. 29–43.

ANDY ORCHARD

BEORNSTAN, a bishop of Winchester who during his brief tenure of the see (931–4) acquired a great reputation for holiness; according to *William of Malmesbury, he used to wander about cemeteries at night praying for the souls of the departed. In the late tenth century, according to *Wulfstan of Winchester, his remains were translated to a shrine in the choir of the rebuilt Old Minster, probably at the instigation of Bishop *Æthelwold, and he was commemorated in liturgical calendars from Winchester (feast day: 4 November).

WMalm, *GP*, pp. 163–4; Wulfstan of Winchester, *Narratio metrica de S. Swithuno*, Epistola specialis, lines 269–70.

MICHAEL LAPIDGE

BEOWULF, 3182 lines in length, is the major

surviving *heroic poem in Old English. Though certainly of Anglo-Saxon composition, the work is set in Scandinavia and is chiefly concerned with three Scandinavian peoples: the Geats (of whom Beowulf becomes king, and whose realm was in the southern part of what is now Sweden), the Danes, and the Swedes. The main narrative of the poem falls into two distinct parts, the first of which (lines 1–2199) recounts Beowulf's defeat of the monster Grendel and of Grendel's avenging mother, deeds accomplished to aid the Danish king, Hrothgar, while Beowulf was a young man. The second part (lines 2200–3182) narrates events many years later, when the aged Beowulf overcame a fire-breathing dragon that had been ravaging his people; but Beowulf was mortally wounded, and the poem ends with his funeral. In addition to these major narrative elements concerning battles against monsters, *Beowulf* includes much other material drawn from Germanic history and legend, often treated in an allusive or fragmentary way, and frequently paralleled in Scandinavian and other sources. Some elements in the narrative of *Beowulf* can be shown to be based on events which took place in the earlier part of the sixth century; but in the shaping of the poem its historical constituents have been blended with others of a legendary or fictional kind, including in all probability the figure of Beowulf himself.

The date of composition of *Beowulf* is uncertain and has been much disputed; but although the dates that have been proposed range from the later seventh century to the early eleventh, the likelihood is that it was composed in the eighth century or the earlier part of the ninth. The provenance of the poem is uncertain, though there is some linguistic evidence suggesting that it derives from an Anglian kingdom. It is clear that there was a degree of historical distance between the world depicted in the poem and that of the poet and his audience, most importantly because the figures within the poem, though showing piety towards God, are portrayed as following pagan practices, whereas the poet and his audience were Christians; indeed the poet draws on biblical narrative to explain the ancestry of Grendel, who is said to be descended from Cain, and he evidently expected his audience to understand references to biblical events such as the slaying of Abel and the Flood.

The first modern edition of the poem, by G. J. *Thorkelin, was published in 1815, and since then *Beowulf* has been the most intensively studied work in Old English. Some nineteenth-century scholars advanced mythological interpretations of

the poem, the monsters, for instance, being seen as symbols of elemental forces, and Beowulf as a deity of some sort or a figure of civilisation itself. In the twentieth century much greater weight has been placed on the Christian culture within which *Beowulf* must have been composed, though this has led to divergent interpretations: allegorical readings have been advanced, Beowulf being understood by some as a figure of Christ but by others as symbolic of fallen man; and it has been held that the Christian poet would have seen the pagan figures of his poem as almost certainly damned. Other critics have rejected such interpretations, arguing that the poem is primarily a celebration of the heroic ideals of which Beowulf himself is the supreme exemplar.

In his command of metrical form and the resources of style the *Beowulf*-poet shows exceptional gifts. His metrical usage conforms to extremely precise constraints, and his style is distinguished particularly by its richness in the use of compound words and by its control of syntactic form. In these respects, as in the power and range of its narrative, *Beowulf* is a work of outstanding accomplishment.

ASPR iv.3–98; *Beowulf and The Fight at Finnsburg*, ed. F. Klaeber, 3rd ed. (Boston, 1950); D. Whitelock, *The Audience of 'Beowulf'* (Oxford, 1951); A. G. Brodeur, *The Art of 'Beowulf'* (Berkeley and Los Angeles, 1959); E. B. Irving, Jr, *A Reading of 'Beowulf'* (New Haven, CT, 1968); M. E. Goldsmith, *The Mode and Meaning of 'Beowulf'* (London, 1970); *The Dating of Beowulf*, ed. C. Chase (Toronto, 1981); J. D. Niles, *'Beowulf': the Poem and its Tradition* (Cambridge, MA, 1983); F. C. Robinson, *'Beowulf' and the Appositive Style* (Knoxville, TN, 1985); G. Clark, *Beowulf* (Boston, 1990); *Interpretations of 'Beowulf': a Critical Anthology*, ed. R. D. Fulk (Bloomington and Indianapolis, IN, 1991); C. B. Kendall, *The Metrical Grammar of 'Beowulf'*, CSASE 5 (Cambridge, 1991); *A Beowulf Handbook*, ed. R. E. Bjork and J. D. Niles (Exeter, 1997).

GEORGE JACK

BEOWULF MANUSCRIPT. The manuscript which contains the sole extant copy of **Beowulf*, BL, Cotton Vitellius A.xv, is composite, probably put together by Sir Robert *Cotton. It contains material in a mid-twelfth-century hand (fols. 4–93), including the only surviving copy of King *Alfred's rendering of Augustine's *Soliloquia*, coupled with a manuscript in two hands of a much earlier date (fols. 94–209; earlier commentators, including Klaeber in his edition of *Beowulf*, use a different foliation which depends on the inclusion of extra leaves in the twelfth-century manuscript). It is this second, earlier manuscript which is generally called the *Beowulf* manuscript, also known as the Nowell codex from the name Laurence *Nowell which appears at the head of its first leaf. Critics have argued about the precise date of the manuscript, Ker opting for late in the tenth century or early in the eleventh, Dumville narrowing this to the second half of Æthelred's reign (*c*.997 to 1016), and Kiernan pressing the case for a date after the accession of *Cnut. The second hand is much rougher in appearance than the first and of a somewhat earlier character (the first is influenced by Caroline minuscule).

The *Beowulf* manuscript now contains five items, two incomplete. It opens with three vernacular prose pieces, a life of St Christopher, lacking the first third (leaves are missing at the beginning of the manuscript), the *Marvels of the East*, illustrated by coloured drawings in what Sisam calls 'childish draughtsmanship', and the *Letter of Alexander to Aristotle*. These are followed by *Beowulf*, during the copying of which the second hand takes over at line 4 of 175v (text line 1939). The poem ends on the last leaf of a quire, after which more leaves are missing before the last item, the poem *Judith, a poem in numbered sections which begins in mid-sentence with the last fourteen lines of section IX. Since Nowell's signature is at the head of the first surviving leaf (of Christopher), it follows that the manuscript was defective at the beginning in the sixteenth century. The conclusion of *Judith* has been added at the foot of the last surviving leaf in a hand of Cotton's day, and it is reasonable to assume that Cotton was responsible for removing the last leaf or leaves. The defective opening of *Judith* means that the poem may not always have followed *Beowulf*, either immediately or at all. The poor state of the last leaf of *Beowulf* may point to the poem once having ended the volume. Sisam has argued, on the basis of some distinctive spellings, that Christopher and *Judith* were added to an earlier nucleus of the other three pieces during the course of transmission. If this were so, then *Judith* may once have been at the beginning of the book with Christopher. But the linguistic evidence is far from conclusive. Ker and Malone disagree on the collation, the former assuming that the first two quires are eights, the latter that they are a ten and a six, and against the traditional view that *Beowulf* begins partway through a quire, Kiernan maintains that it opens a new one. The problem stems from the fact that the manuscript was damaged in the Cotton fire and the leaves are now mounted separately within nineteenth-century paper frames. The fire singed the margins, and

the frames cover many letters which have only been recovered recently by electronic photography. Although there has been much critical discussion of the organisation of the manuscript, there has been little advance on Sisam's view of it as 'a collection in verse and prose of marvellous stories', first put forward in 1934. Orchard, the latest to tackle the question, sees it as a coherent collection, linked by theme and subject matter.

In a highly controversial book, Kiernan argues that *Beowulf* was once contained in a separate codex, perhaps joined to the other items in Vitellius A.xv only in the sixteenth century. Even more controversially, he has used the fact that fol. 179 recto, written by the second scribe, is a palimpsest as evidence that it was copied by the author of the poem, who was revising his material in the course of copying.

ASPR iv.3–98; K. Sisam, *Studies in the History of Old English Literature* (Oxford, 1953); *The Nowell Codex: British Museum Cotton Vitellius A. XV, Second MS*, ed. K. Malone, EEMF 12 (Copenhagen, 1963); K. S. Kiernan, *Beowulf and the Beowulf Manuscript* (New Brunswick, NJ, 1984); D. N. Dumville, 'Beowulf Come Lately. Some Notes on the Palaeography of the Nowell Codex', *Archiv* 225 (1988), 49–63; A. Orchard, *Pride and Prodigies: Studies in the Monsters of the Beowulf-Manuscript* (Cambridge, 1995).

DONALD SCRAGG

BERHTWALD, abbot of *Reculver and archbishop of *Canterbury (692 [consecrated 693]–731), who is described by *Bede as a man with a deep knowledge of the Scriptures, well versed in ecclesiastical and monastic doctrine. In spite of the long tenancy of his archbishopric, no writings by Berhtwald survive, but he was the addressee of a surviving 'letter-close' from Waldhere, bishop of London (704–9), and is commemorated in a metrical epitaph which may have been engraved in the choir of the church of Canterbury where he was buried.

Sharpe, *Handlist*, 160; Bede, *HE* v.8, 19, 23; Bolton, *ALL*, pp. 200–1; P. Chaplais, 'The Letter from Bishop Wealdhere of London to Archbishop Brihtwold of Canterbury: the Earliest Original "Letter Close" Extant in the West', in *Medieval Scribes, Manuscripts & Libraries: Essays presented to N. R. Ker*, ed. M. B. Parkes and A. G. Watson (London, 1978), pp. 3–23; *EHD* i.792–3 (no. 164); Lapidge, *ALL* i.369–70 [epitaph].

MICHAEL LAPIDGE

BERNICIA, an English kingdom north of the Tyne. The name is British in origin and may derive from a tribe displaced by English settlers. *Bede names King Ida (547–59) as founder of the Bernician dynasty. Between the late sixth and

63

seventh century the kingdom expanded west and north into British territory. It dominated relations with its southern neighbour, *Deira, except for the period of King *Edwin's reign (616–33). Bernicia retained its own rulers after the Scandinavian take-over of York in 867, and its last known ruler, Aldred, was reigning in 927. See also *Northumbria.

D. Dumville, 'The Origins of Northumbria: Some Aspects of the British Background', in Bassett, *Origins*, pp. 213–22.

PHILIP HOLDSWORTH

BESTIARIES: *see Physiologus*

BEWCASTLE (Cumb.) is famous for its imposing early Northumbrian stone *sculpture. Standing 4.4 m high, the now-headless cross carries three figural panels on its principal west face. The upper two, closely comparable to scenes at *Ruthwell, show John the Baptist and Christ in Majesty. A lengthy, but now worn, runic inscription separates these two scenes from an arched panel below containing a cloaked falconer; though often interpreted as an unorthodox depiction of John the Evangelist this is more likely to be a portrait of the deceased in whose honour, according to the inscription, the cross was erected. On the east side there is a full-length panel of inhabited vine-scroll whilst the south and north faces carry smaller panels with interlace, vine-scrolls (one incorporating a sundial) and chequer ornament. Parallels between the figural ornament and vine-scrolls of Ruthwell and Bewcastle suggest that they are roughly contemporary in date, and a variety of art-historical, liturgical, epigraphic and historical arguments combine to place both carvings in the early eighth century – probably in the period *c.*725–50.

R. N. Bailey and R. J. Cramp, *Cumberland, Westmorland and Lancashire North of the Sands*, CASSS 2 (Oxford, 1988), 19–22, 61–72; É. Ó. Carragáin, 'A Liturgical Interpretation of the Bewcastle Cross', in *Medieval Literature and Antiquities: Studies in Honour of Basil Cottle*, ed. M. Stokes and T. Burton (Cambridge, 1987), pp. 15–42.

RICHARD N. BAILEY

BIBLE. The Bible of the Anglo-Saxons was the Latin Vulgate, as revised extensively by Jerome with reference to the Hebrew and Greek originals. Certainly manuscripts transmitting earlier 'Old Latin' versions were in use in Northumbria alongside the Vulgate during the seventh century (by *Bede, for instance, who consulted Greek versions also), and indeed Monkwearmouth-Jarrow pos-

sessed a Bible in an Old Latin version brought from Italy *c.*679 (the *Codex grandior*). However, the Old Latin scriptural citations found in the works of Anglo-Saxon writers can in general be attributed to the influence of their patristic sources or of conservative liturgical versions (including the canticles). Good Vulgate manuscripts imported directly from Italy provided most of the exemplars used for the surge of new biblical manuscripts copied in *Northumbria (and to a lesser extent in the south) late in the seventh century and in the early deacdes of the eighth. It is convenient to talk of an 'Italo–Insular' textual tradition at this time, although in fact it encompassed much diversity. In the Gospels, the influence of Ireland remained strong and produced a characteristic 'Hiberno-Northumbrian' textual tradition. The poor textual and calligraphic quality of some manuscripts of the later eighth century signals the virtual cessation of copying during the ninth. When biblical manuscripts were again being produced in the second half of the tenth century, mainly in the south, new textual traditions were in use. They derived from recently imported exemplars produced on the Continent in the wake of the great Carolingian textual reforms associated primarily, but not exclusively, with Theodulf of Orléans and *Alcuin. Textual diversity is again evident, and even among the relatively numerous gospelbooks, clear lines of transmission are hard to establish. Lack of textual uniformity seems to have caused no problems for the Anglo-Saxons. The move towards standardisation which was to be so characteristic of the later medieval period, under the influence of the Schoolmen, had hardly begun. Indeed variant readings from different textual traditions provided biblical commentators with extra means of illuminating their allegorical interpretations of Scripture, as the works of Bede in the early eighth century and *Ælfric at the close of the tenth show.

The Bible known to the Anglo-Saxons included several of the 'deuterocanonical' Old Testament books not found in the Hebrew Bible and disdained by Jerome: namely, Wisdom, Sirach (or Ecclesiasticus), Judith, Tobit, and I–II Maccabees. Eventually given official sanction by the Council of Trent, they were relegated to the Apochrypha by Protestants at the Reformation. These books were popular with the Anglo-Saxons. Bede wrote a commentary on Tobit (in Latin) and Ælfric produced homiletic paraphrases of Judith and Maccabees in Old English.

The earliest biblical manuscripts used in Anglo-Saxon England were imported, and volumes arriving with, or in the wake of, *Augustine's mission to *Kent in 597 were among the first; an extant Italian gospelbook (Cambridge, Corpus Christi College 286) may be one of these. The north probably received its earliest manuscripts from Ireland, but in the later seventh century considerable numbers arrived direct from Italy and provided the exemplars from which subsequent copies were made. Some of these then went to the Continent with the Anglo-Saxon *missionaries. Complete Bibles were a rarity in Anglo-Saxon England, especially in the earlier period, and the three celebrated pandects produced at Monkwearmouth-Jarrow around the end of the seventh century, including the extant Codex *Amiatinus, were exceptional. More usually, Scripture circulated in separate collections of books. Smaller in format than complete Bibles, they were both more portable and cheaper to make. Among such part-Bibles the gospelbook, a basic requirement for every monastic church, dominated, but there is manuscript evidence also for volumes of New Testament epistles, Old Testament prophets, and the Pentateuch (perhaps as part of a Heptateuch), and a collection of five wisdom books is extant (the 'Egerton' codex). These remnants illustrate an important point: sumptuous volumes made for special purposes attracted attention and were more likely to survive, but workaday volumes, poorly bound and sometimes badly written were more common. Library booklists prove that part-Bibles of all sorts continued to be used until the end of the Anglo-Saxon period, though none except gospelbooks survives. By the early eleventh century, however, complete Bibles seem to have become relatively more common. Only one survives complete, the late tenth-century Royal 1. E. VII + VIII, in two volumes, but there are fragments of three others.

Although there was never a complete Old English Bible, a tradition of rendering portions of scripture into the vernacular for teaching purposes went back at least to Bede, and word-for-word interlinear glosses of Latin psalters (such as the *'Vespasian Psalter') and gospelbooks (such as the *'Lindisfarne Gospels') are known from the ninth century onwards. During the second half of the tenth century the four Gospels were put into continuous Old English prose; and early in the eleventh, translations of Genesis, much of Exodus, and parts of Leviticus, Numbers, Deuteronomy and Joshua were collected from several sources to make a compilation whose most notable extant manuscript version, lavishly illustrated, is known as the 'Old English Hexateuch'. Its version of the first half of Genesis was based on one made by

Ælfric, who nevertheless attached a preface in which he voiced his unease about exposing unlearned people to the bare narrative of Scripture. He noted also both the theoretical desirability of rendering the sacred words of scripture literally, word for word, and the practical impossibility of doing so, if the result was to be intelligible to speakers of a syntactically different language. The influence of the Bible, above all the Old Testament, on the vernacular literature of the Anglo-Saxons was profound, and one result was the composition of poetical Old English versions of parts of *Genesis, *Exodus, *Daniel and *Judith.

R. Marsden, ' "Ask What I Am Called": The Anglo-Saxons and their Bibles', in *The Bible as Book*, ed. J. Sharpe and K. Van Kampen (London, 1998), pp. 145–76; idem, *The Text of the Old Testament in Anglo-Saxon England*, CSASE 15 (Cambridge, 1995); R. Loewe, 'The Medieval History of the Latin Vulgate', in *Cambridge History of the Bible* 2, ed. G. W. H. Lampe (Cambridge, 1969), pp. 102–54; P. Hunter Blair, *The World of Bede*, rev. ed. (Cambridge, 1990), chs. 20–1; P. McGurk, *Latin Gospel Books from AD 400 to AD 800*, Les publications de Scriptorium 5 (1961); idem, 'Text', in *The York Gospels*, ed. N. Barker (London, 1986), pp. 43–63; R. Gameson, 'The Royal 1. B. vii Gospels and English Book Production in the Seventh and Eighth Centuries', in his *The Early Medieval Bible: its Production, Decoration and Use*, Cambridge Studies in Palaeography and Codicology 2 (Cambridge, 1994), 24–52 and pls. 2.1–4.

RICHARD MARSDEN

BIBLE, ILLUSTRATIONS. Most Anglo-Saxon representations of biblical events (as opposed to author portraits and symbolic representations) occur in non-biblical manuscripts. Only three Anglo-Saxon Bibles contain illustrations. The late seventh-century Codex *Amiatinus (Florence, Biblioteca Medicea Laurenziana, Amiatinus 1) includes a portrait of the scribe Ezra and a representation of Christ enthroned among the evangelists, together with a diagrammatic representation of the Tabernacle in the Temple at Jerusalem and roundels with symbols of the three persons of the Trinity. An eighth-century Bible from Canterbury, now represented only by the gospels (London, BL, Royal 1. E. VI), originally contained full-page paintings of the *Agnus Dei* surrounded by the evangelist symbols, and representations of the baptism of Christ and the annunciation to Zechariah. A tenth-century Bible, also from Canterbury (London, BL, Royal 1. E. VII), includes a diagrammatic representation of the creation added to the manuscript in the mid-eleventh century. Some gospelbooks include representations of the crucifixion (Durham, Cathedral Library, A. II. 17; New York, Pierpont Morgan Library, 709 and 869), and the late tenth-century Boulogne Gospels (Boulogne, Bibliothèque municipale, 11) includes pictures of the annunciation, visitation and nativity, placed before the opening of St Matthew's gospel, and a representation of the annunciation to Zechariah in the initial to the gospel of Luke. There are, however, no fully-illustrated gospelbooks similar to those from Ottonian Germany apart from the fragments of one gospellectionary (Malibu, California, J. Paul Getty Museum, 9).

The biblical text which was most extensively illustrated in the Anglo-Saxon period was the Psalter. Representations of David accompanied by his musicians, playing the harp, fighting Goliath or rescuing the lamb from the lion are common (*Vespasian Psalter, in London, BL, Cotton Vespasian A.i; Cotton Tiberius C.vi), as are a small number of gospel scenes, included to draw attention to the prophetic nature of the text (*Æthelstan Psalter, now London, BL, Cotton Galba A.xviii; Vatican City, Biblioteca Apostolica Vaticana, Regin. lat. 12). The mid-eleventh-century Tiberius Psalter (BL, Cotton Tiberius C.vi) is prefaced by depictions of New Testament scenes from the temptation of Christ to the descent of the Holy Spirit at Pentecost, which were probably intended as a focus for meditation. The early eleventh-century *Harley Psalter (BL, Harley 603), on the other hand, is decorated with composite scenes which illustrate the individual phrases of the psalms and which may have served as mnemonics for the text.

The most extensive sets of pictures of biblical events from the Anglo-Saxon period occur in two vernacular versions of parts of the Old Testament (Oxford, Bodleian Library, Junius 11; London, BL, Cotton Claudius B.iv), in a ninth-century manuscript of Caelius Sedulius's *Carmen paschale* copied from an eighth-century Anglo-Saxon exemplar (Antwerp, Museum Plantin-Moretus, M. 17.4) and in two liturgical manuscripts: the Benedictional of *Æthelwold (London, BL, Add. 49598) and the Sacramentary of Robert of Jumièges (Rouen, Bibliothèque municipale, Y. 6). The two Old Testament manuscripts, which may have been produced for wealthy laymen or women, are illustrated throughout by narrative drawings and paintings, often in the form of strip cartoons, which provide a translation of the written text into pictorial form. The pictures in the Sedulius manuscript include four scenes from the stories of Abraham and Isaac, Jonah and Daniel, and twelve gospel scenes, beginning with the adoration of the magi and the massacre of the Innocents and ending with Christ's command to Peter to feed his sheep. Whereas in these three manuscripts pictures and text are closely related, the paintings in the two liturgical manuscripts draw attention to the commemorative function of the liturgy, reminding the viewer of the way in which the liturgy makes biblical events present. The Sacramentary of Robert of Jumièges includes paintings of the ascension and of Pentecost, together with three small narrative sequences. The first shows Christ's birth, the angels with the shepherds and the flight into Egypt; the second is concerned with the story of Herod and the magi; the third consists of four scenes from the story of the passion (the betrayal, the crucifixion, the deposition and the women at the tomb). These paintings are straightforward representations of biblical events. The paintings in the Benedictional of Æthelwold, on the other hand, interpret events, showing Mary reading a book at the annunciation to remind viewers of the fulfilment of Isaiah's prophecy, and angels holding crowns and sceptres at the baptism to symbolise Christ's royal status.

Alexander, *Insular MSS*; R. Deshman, *The Benedictional of Æthelwold*, Studies in Manuscript Illumination 9 (Princeton, NJ, 1995); C. R. Dodwell and P. Clemoes, ed., *The Old English Illustrated Hexateuch (British Museum Cotton Claudius B. iv)*, EEMF 18 (1974); I. Gollancz, ed., *The Cædmon Manuscript of Anglo-Saxon Biblical Poetry, Junius XI in the Bodleian Library* (Oxford, 1927); T. H. Ohlgren, *Anglo-Saxon Textual Illustration. Photographs of Sixteen Manuscripts with Descriptions and Index* (Kalamazoo, MI, 1992); Temple, *AS MSS*; H. A. Wilson, ed., *The Missal of Robert of Jumièges*, HBS 11 (1896); F. Wormald, 'An English Eleventh-Century Psalter with Pictures, British Library, Cotton MS Tiberius C. vi', in *Collected Writings 1: Studies in Medieval Art from the Sixth to the Twelfth Centuries*, ed. J. J. G. Alexander, T. J. Brown and J. Gibbs (Oxford, 1984), pp. 123–37.

BARBARA C. RAW

BIBLICAL TRANSLATION: POEMS. Various poems rendering passages of the Latin Bible into the *Old English language constitute some of the more remarkable products of the Anglo-Saxon Christian communities, especially when it is recalled that no systematic translation of the whole Bible into English would be undertaken before the fourteenth-century efforts of John Wyclif (d. 1384) and his followers and that the use of translations of Latin biblical texts recited in the liturgy remained controversial into the twentieth century. The officials of the Anglo-Saxon churches, by contrast, seem to have embraced the use of vernacular texts, even popular poems, for the promotion of scriptural knowledge from the earliest times. Around the year 600, Pope *Gregory the Great authorised *Augustine of Canterbury to make use of virtually any non-Roman Christian practice in furthering the spread of the new religion among the Anglo-Saxons. In the eighth century, *Bede, *Boniface, *Alcuin and the canonists of the Council of *Clofesho all offer specific recommendations concerning the use of the vernacular in the edification of the faithful. Although these authorities do not all mention specifically the translation of the Bible, in later centuries the practices encouraged by their admonitions culminated in the promotions of the literary use of Old English undertaken by *Alfred, king of Wessex, who, according to *William of Malmesbury, himself began (but never completed) an English translation of the Psalms toward the end of the ninth century, and in the groundbreaking (if incomplete) translations of biblical prose carried out by *Ælfric in the wake of the tenth-century Benedictine reform. To turn to the surviving monuments of Old English poetry, if the term 'biblical translation' is reserved for determinedly literalistic renditions from the Scriptures reflecting minimal artistic intervention on the part of their translators, the most outstanding example of such faithful versification occurs in the voluminous metrical treatment of Psalms LI–CL preserved in the so-called Paris Psalter (Paris, Bibliothèque Nationale, lat. 8824). Brief examples of similarly literalistic translation include independent Old English metrical treatments of Psalms XVII, LI and XC–XCV, various fragments related to the versification in the Paris Psalter, and close renditions of biblically derived liturgical texts, such as the Lord's Prayer, might also be cited in this connection. The term 'biblical verse' is often applied to compositions which maintain reasonable fidelity to biblical narratives while evincing their own distinctive poetical identities. Exemplary in this regard are the main part of *Genesis (known as Genesis A) and *Daniel, both in the *Junius manuscript; Azarias, a fragment related to Daniel; and *Judith, rendering the apocryphal book whose canonicity was accepted in Anglo-Saxon England. Also frequently classed as biblical verse are the comparatively free adaptations of biblical episodes found in the Junius *Exodus and in the Old Saxon-based interpolation into the Junius Genesis known as Genesis B. There is, moreover, an amorphous body of poetry that might well be associated with Old English biblical verse despite its debt to miscellaneous extrabiblical traditions, most notably those deriving from apocryphal, patristic and homiletic sources: *Christ and Satan; The *Advent Lyrics; *Christ III; *Descent into Hell; *Cynewulf's Fates of the Apostles; Judgement Day I and Pharaoh (both in the Exeter Book); Judgement Day II (in Cambridge, Corpus Christi College 201); and a copy of the lengthy Old Saxon poem celebrating the life of Christ (known as the Heliand), preserved in a later tenth-century manuscript produced at an English centre (now BL, Cotton Caligula A. vii, fols. 11–176).

C. W. Kennedy and C. R. Morey, The 'Cædmon Poems' Translated into English Prose (London, 1916); G. Shepherd, 'Scriptural Poetry', Continuations and Beginnings, ed. E. G. Stanley (London, 1966), pp. 1–36; D. C. Fowler, 'Old English Translations and Paraphrases', The Bible in Early English Literature (London, 1977), pp. 79–124; S. B. Greenfield and D. G. Calder, 'Old Testament Narrative Poetry', A New Critical History of Old English Literature (New York, 1986), pp. 206–26; M. Godden and B. C. Raw, 'Biblical Literature', CamComp, pp. 206–42; P. G. Remley, Old English Biblical Verse, CSASE 16 (Cambridge, 1996).

PAUL G. REMLEY

BIRINUS, ST (d. 650), founder and first bishop of the West Saxon see, with its centre at *Dorchester-on-Thames (Oxon.), came as a missionary to south-west England in about 634. He converted and baptised Cynegils, king of the West Saxons. The earliest source for this is *Bede's Historia ecclesiastica (iii.7). Little is known of Birinus's origins – apparently N. Italian – or of his ministry; the eleventh-century Vita S. Birini (BHL 1361), written at Winchester, is highly conventional hagiography, attributing commonplace biblical-style miracles to the saint. Birinus was buried at Dorchester, but when in 648 the centre of the West Saxon see was transferred to Winchester, under Bishop *Hædddi (676–705), his relics were translated likewise. As a satellite of the cult of the more famous St *Swithun, veneration to Birinus, never very widespread, persisted at Winchester throughout the Middle Ages (feast: December 3; translation: September 4).

Bede, HE iii.7, iv.12, ed. B. Colgrave and R. A. B. Mynors, Bede's Ecclesiastical History of the English People (Oxford, 1969), pp. 232–5, 369; R. C. Love, ed. and trans., Three Eleventh-Century Anglo-Latin Saints' Lives (OMT, 1996), pp. xlix–lxxxviii, 1–47.

R. C. LOVE

BLICKLING HOMILIES: see Homilies

BOETHIUS: see Alfredian Texts

BOISIL (d. c.660 or 661), prior of *Melrose in

the time of Abbot *Eata, Boisil was described by *Bede as a priest of great virtue, endowed with a spirit of prophecy; it was from him that the young *Cuthbert learned the Scriptures and the performance of good works. Bede's *Vita S. Cuthberti* contains a moving account of Boisil's death from the plague, and of his dying prophecy that Cuthbert would be made a bishop (c. 8). After his death, Boisil was commemorated by a stone shrine now preserved in fragmentary form at Jedburgh, whence it was moved from Melrose, and memory of his name is also preserved in the place-name of St Boswells (Roxburghshire). His relics were translated to Durham in 1020.

Bede, *HE* iv.27–8, v.9; *Two Lives of St Cuthbert*, ed. B. Colgrave (Cambridge, 1940), pp. 170–2, 180–4; C. A. Ralegh Radford, 'Two Scottish Shrines: Jedburgh and St Andrews', *Archaeological Journal* 112 (1955), 43–60.

MICHAEL LAPIDGE

BONE AND IVORY CARVING. The Anglo-Saxons were expert carvers, and adept at using whatever suitable media they had to hand; all kinds of bone, antler and ivory are therefore included under this head (see also *bone working). Almost nothing survives of artistic quality from the early Anglo-Saxon period, where the majority of the evidence comes from burials. The decorated objects which survive from the fifth and sixth centuries are chiefly practical items such as combs, spindle whorls and knife handles, with simple incised decoration; though an early seventh-century bone knife handle from Fishergate, *York, and an antler plaque from *Hamwic* both with elaborate animal ornament, suggest that a more sophisticated tradition existed alongside. However, while our knowledge of ivory carving in this period must be distorted by the poor survival of organic material in burials, and the selective nature of the grave accompaniments, it seems likely that the development of elaborate carving in ivory and similar media is associated with the intellectual and artistic expansion which was a product of the introduction of Christianity and the new access to the cultural traditions of the classical world which accompanied this.

While a tradition of secular carving certainly runs throughout the period, as accomplished decoration on later Saxon seal-dies, strap-ends, knife-handles, spoons and so on shows, the finest carving is primarily associated with objects of ecclesiastical or scholarly function. By the eighth century, Anglo-Saxon craftsmen were producing works of considerable iconographic complexity and intellectual ambition, as the *Franks Casket, itself an idiosyncratic Insular version of a late antique ivory reliquary, shows. This famous piece may have been produced in or for a courtly context, but its learned content clearly indicates an ecclesiastical mind – or hand – at work. Equally sophisticated is the elegant house-shaped reliquary known as the *Gandersheim Casket, with its brilliantly executed teeming menagerie of creatures. The range of carving in the eighth century is hinted at by other fragmentary pieces – the writing tablet leaf from Blythburgh, Suffolk, and the delicately ornamented panel from a book-cover from Larling, Norfolk. The excellence of eighth-century Anglo-Saxon ivory carving is also indicated by its visible influence on certain continental pre-Carolingian ivories, such as the Genoels Elderen book-cover panels. The documented activities of Anglo-Saxon churchmen abroad at this period were clearly accompanied by the movement of Insular books and artefacts, and indeed, craftsmen.

By contrast, virtually no carving survives that can be ascribed to the ninth century, a period disrupted by *Viking invasions, and for much of its course marked by ecclesiastical stagnation; these facts are doubtless connected. But the reforms of *Alfred's reign brought fresh impetus to the intellectual and artistic life of the church, and where ivory carving is concerned, in a very practical way. All the ambitious Anglo-Saxon carvings of the eighth century are of whale bone – for the obvious reason that this was the only available medium capable of being cut into large panels suitable for use in reliquaries, book covers and so on. Some elephant ivory reached England in the sixth century, but its use seems to have been confined to the making of circular bag-handles, cut transversely from the tusk. However, this source petered out by the seventh century, and the dearth is confirmed by the fact that elsewhere in northern Europe, eighth-century ivory carvers were reduced to recutting late antique ivories. However, the opening up of the North Atlantic through Viking trading activity brought a new substance, walrus ivory, into the repertoire. The famous account given to King Alfred by the Viking traveller, *Ohthere, tells how he sailed to the White Sea in search of walruses, for their hide and their fine tusks, some of which he presented to the king. It is no surprise that this novel luxury commodity henceforth dominated the production of fine ivory carving.

This access to a new ivory source coincided with the tenth-century Anglo-Saxon Benedictine reform movement's huge new demand for devotional carvings, and it is from the tenth and early eleventh century that some of the finest examples of Anglo-Saxon ivory carving survive. The distinctive influence of various Carolingian schools infuses the art of the Reform movement, which is usually, though somewhat misleadingly, referred to as the *Winchester style. The expressive power of this style, with its fluttering draperies and emotive gestures, familiar from manuscripts such as the Benedictional of St *Æthelwold, is eloquently reflected in the numerous ivory carvings produced for church use and private devotion during this period. These include masterpieces of the genre, such as the British Museum's Baptism of Christ, the Winchester angels panel, and the moving figures of the Virgin and St John from a crucifix group, now at Saint-Omer. But alongside this powerful tradition of figural art ran a parallel and continuing tradition of animal and plant motifs, as the splendid London pencase demonstrates. Increased Scandinavian influences apparent in the eleventh century as a consequence of Danish rule have an equal part to play in ivory carving, particularly where secular objects are concerned. At the time of the Conquest, Anglo-Saxon ivory carving had developed a complex and highly sophisticated tradition, the influence of which was to continue reverberating in the art of the Romanesque.

A. Goldschmidt, *Die Elfenbeinskulpturen aus der Zeit der karolingischen und sächsischen Kaiser, VII–XI. Jahrhundert*, 2 vols. (Berlin, 1914–18); idem, *Die Elfenbeinskulpturen aus der romanischen Zeit XI–XIII. Jahrhundert*, vol. III (Berlin, 1923); J. Beckwith, *Ivory Carvings in Early Medieval England* (London, 1972); P. Williamson, *Medieval Ivory Carvings* (London, 1982); *Golden Age of AS Art*; D. M. Wilson, *Anglo-Saxon Art* (London, 1984); *Making of England*.

LESLIE WEBSTER

BONE WORKING, in contrast to certain other craft activities such as pottery-making, shows no very marked discontinuity between the late Roman and early Anglo-Saxon periods: some types enter the bone worker's repertoire, others disappear; many continue with only minor stylistic changes. The principal casualties in the fifth century were no doubt those producers who had developed a measure of settled existence supplying the needs of towns and the military. Those whose trade was geared to the scattered rural populations were better placed to survive; their mode of operation – largely itinerant – served them well enough until the early medieval revival of urbanism once again provided the prospect of a settled existence.

Combs form the single most characteristic product of this industry. They are almost invariably of composite construction, a method of manufacture that has been shown to be based on an appreciation of the mechanical properties of the raw material. The fact that the majority of composite combs are made of antler shows a further degree of sensitivity to the raw material, for antler has been shown to be mechanically superior to skeletal bone. It also gives an insight into what must have been a perennial feature of the bone-worker's lot – the need to ensure a steady supply of raw materials. This was probably achieved largely through trade or exchange with local populations. Although styles changed, composite combs remained in use throughout the Anglo-Saxon period.

The degree of skill and the rather specialised tool-kit required in the production of combs leaves little doubt as to the professional status of their manufacturers (although the question of whether they were engaged full-time in this activity remains problematic). Other items in their repertoire may have included some of the more carefully made items in bone and antler that occur throughout the Anglo-Saxon period, including pins, dice, playing pieces, and handles. Many communities well accustomed to relying on their own resourcefulness would, however, have been self-reliant in more utilitarian items. This would apply to simple craft tools such as spindles, beaters and whorls used in the production of yarns and *textiles, and for stamps used to impress simple designs on *pottery. Almost anyone would have been capable of producing for personal use a bone whistle or a pair of skates – items which require little preparation once an appropriate bone has been chosen. A third set of circumstances under which objects of bone were produced must be envisaged: into this category fall certain luxury products which were evidently produced by consummate craftsmen whose skills were not necessarily limited to working in a single material (see *bone and ivory carving).

A. MacGregor, *Bone, Antler, Ivory and Horn: the Technology of Skeletal Materials since the Roman Period* (Beckenham, 1984).

ARTHUR MACGREGOR

BONIFACE (*c*.675–754), best known of the *missionaries to *Germany, was, alongside *Alcuin, perhaps the Anglo-Saxon who had the widest and longest-lasting influence on the Continent. Named Wynfrith at his birth in *Wessex (perhaps at Crediton), and apparently educated at 'Nhutschelle' (probably Nursling in Hampshire), he first travelled to *Frisia in 716 in the footsteps of *Wilfrid and Willibrord, but returned to England unsuccessful thanks to the hostility of the heathen chief Radbod in Frisia. Following a trip to *Rome in 718–19 he was given (along with the new name Boniface) the task of preaching to the heathens by Pope Gregory II, a mission he prosecuted with vigour, being ordained bishop (without a fixed see) in 722. In an act of high drama, he caused to be felled the sacred oak of the heathens at Geismar, and went on to participate in the founding of monasteries at Fritzlar, Fulda, Herzfeld, Holzkirchen, Karlburg, Ochsenfurt, and Tauberbischofsheim, receiving the *pallium* of archbishop from Pope Gregory III in 732, and eventually setting up from his own base at Mainz, with bishoprics at Salzburg, Eichstätt, Regensburg, and Passau. Ever keen to press still further north, Boniface and a band of fifty-two followers were attacked and martyred at Dokkum in the Netherlands in 754. He had been succeeded as archbishop of Mainz (within his own lifetime) by his disciple *Lull, himself educated at *Malmesbury, and *Willibald, a compatriot, produced a biography of him which owes less to history than to *hagiography.

Among the few of Boniface's extant writings which date from the period before he left England are two brief treatises on *grammar and Latin *metre respectively (*Ars grammatica* and *Ars metrica*), together with a handful of letters (notably one to *Eadburg, abbess at Thanet, describing a *vision of heaven and hell by a monk at Wenlock), and some rhythmical Latin verse in *octosyllables. The later writings of Boniface include a cycle of twenty *enigmata (ten on virtues, ten on vices) and a copious correspondence. In his metrical verse Boniface is sometimes little more than a slavish imitator of *Aldhelm, and indeed seems rather less scrupulous about the finer points of Latin metre, although in his choice of abstract subject-matter in his *Enigmata* he clearly differs from his predecessor. But it is in his *letters (*Epistolae*) where the subtlety and vigour of his Latin style are most demonstrable. Once again a clear debt to Aldhelm is apparent in almost every letter, together with an intimate knowledge of scripture, and a love of balanced syntax, *alliteration, and wordplay. Boniface's command of Latin *prose style is evident not only from the explicit requests of some of his correspondents (such as *Leofgyth) that he correct their own efforts, but from the clarity and structure of his writing, particularly in the letters written on the Continent, when the sometimes stifling influence of Aldhelm had begun to diminish. Although much of his correspondence is with popes, archbishops, and kings, perhaps the most affecting of his letters are those to his own followers and supporters, where a distinctively compassionate and lighter tone is found. Boniface seems at his most relaxed in his letters to various religious women, five of whom wrote extant letters to him, alongside which the works of other women, such as *Beorhtgyth, are preserved; it is in the Bonifatian correspondence that some of the earliest and clearest evidence for the education of Anglo-Saxon *women is to be found. The personal picture of Boniface that these and similar letters afford is an attractive one; moreover, it is possible that Boniface's own handwriting can be identified in three extant manuscripts, and that a clever and difficult metrical poem on St John in one of them should therefore be considered an autograph copy.

Sharpe, *Handlist*, 166; *Ars grammatica*, ed. G. Gebauer and B. Löfstedt, CCSL 133B (Turnhout, 1980), 1–99; *Ars metrica*, ed. G. Gebauer and B. Löfstedt, CCSL 133B (Turnhout, 1980), 109–13; *Enigmata Bonifatii*, ed. F. Glorie, CCSL 133 (Turnhout, 1968), 273–343; *S. Bonifatii et Lullii Epistolae*, ed. M. Tangl, MGH ES 1 (Berlin, 1916); E. Kylie, trans., *The English Correspondence of Saint Boniface* (London, 1911); E. Emerton, trans., *The Letters of Saint Boniface* (New York, 1940); C. Fell, 'Some Implications of the Boniface Correspondence', in *New Readings on Women in Old English Literature*, ed. H. Damico and A. H. Olsen (Bloomington, IN, 1990), pp. 29–43; M. Lapidge, 'Autographs of Insular Latin Authors of the Early Middle Ages', in *Gli Autografi Medievali*, ed. P. Chiesa and L. Pinelli (Spoleto, 1994), pp. 103–36, at 108–15; M. B. Parkes, 'The Handwriting of St Boniface: a Reassessment of the Problems', *Beiträge zur Geschichte der deutschen Sprache und Literatur* 48 (1976), 161–79; T. Reuter, ed., *The Greatest Englishman: Essays on St Boniface and the Church at Crediton* (Exeter, 1980); U. Schaefer, 'Two Women in Need of a Friend: a Comparison of The Wife's Lament and Eangyth's Letter to Boniface', in *Germanic Dialects: Linguistic and Philological Investigations*, ed. B. Brogyanyi and T. Krömmelbein (Amsterdam and Philadelphia, 1986), pp. 491–524.

ANDY ORCHARD

BOOKBINDINGS. Very few bookbindings made in Anglo-Saxon England have survived. There is enough evidence to suggest that none of those which have survived have any peculiarly Anglo-Saxon characteristics but in their fundamental features can be grouped with contemporary continental bookbindings. However, there is no such thing as a typical or characteristic 'early bookbinding'. Different kinds of manuscripts would have been bound using different techniques and materials depending on their intended use and life. (A collection of *homilies intended for private reading would not have been bound in the same way as a lavishly decorated *gospelbook intended for display in a church.) Even among the surviving Anglo-Saxon bookbindings, mostly from what can be termed 'library books' and therefore from only one kind of book, there is considerable diversity in the technical and structural details. Variety and ingenuity appear to be the principal characteristics of early bookbindings from all over Europe.

Various Anglo-Saxon bookbindings have survived more or less intact, several of which have been the subject of individual studies, and the wooden boards from a larger number have survived, reused by later binders. The pioneer survey of Pollard in 1975, which discussed twenty-one bookbindings, remains useful, although several more bookbindings have been identified subsequently. Its descriptions and observations have now been almost entirely superseded by Clarkson, whose work demonstrates that wide experience and specialised knowledge is vital in the interpretation and understanding of the surviving evidence.

The single most important bookbinding is that of the *Stonyhurst Gospel of St John. Its decorated covers are not likely to have been unusual in their conception and execution. However, the nature of the manuscript itself, and the absence of almost any other bookbindings contemporary with it from anywhere in Europe, means that its structural and decorative features are difficult to place in a wider context.

The study of bookbindings is concerned with four aspects of the objects. First, the materials and techniques employed in linking together the quires of a manuscript (sewing structure). Secondly, the means by which the sewn quires were joined to what is described as the cover or covers (board attachment). Thirdly, the materials and techniques with and by which covers were manufactured and finished. Fourthly, the treatment applied to the exterior of a binding, which might range from the minimal to the elaborate (as in treasure bindings covered with metalwork and precious stones). The last aspect has been frequently (and mistakenly) regarded as a study unrelated to the study of the structures, techniques and materials of bookbindings. Only one Anglo-Saxon bookbinding has extensive decoration using metal, twenty-two silver mounts, on a manuscript taken to Europe by or for *Boniface.

Bookbindings are of particular concern to book conservators in understanding the quality of materials, the nature and interaction of materials and techniques, and the development and variety of bookbinding structures. Too few more or less complete bookbindings have survived for scholars to be able to use much binding evidence to help place and date manuscripts and centres of book production. An increased sensitivity and knowledge of sewing structures ought to prove useful as so many pre-Conquest manuscripts have been rebound and manuscripts of different dates, origins and provenances bound together during the medieval period and later.

D. M. Wilson, 'An Anglo-Saxon Bookbinding at Fulda (Codex Bonifatianus 1)', *AJ* 41 (1961), 199–217; R. Powell and P. Waters, 'Technical Description of the Binding' in T. J. Brown, *The Stonyhurst Gospel* (Oxford, 1969), pp. 45–55; G. Pollard, 'Some Anglo-Saxon Bookbindings', *The Book Collector* 24 (1975), 130–59; B. C. Raw, 'The Construction of Oxford, Bodleian Library, Junius 11', *ASE* 13 (1984), 187–207; R. Stevick, 'The St Cuthbert Gospel Binding and Insular Design', *Artibus et Historiae* 8 (1987), 9–19; J. Morrish Tunberg, 'Binding', in J. E. Cross and J. Morrish Tunberg, *The Copenhagen Wulfstan Collection. Copenhagen Kongelige Bibliotek Gl. Kgl. Sam. 1595*, EEMF 25 (Copenhagen, 1993), 50–8; C. Clarkson, 'Further Studies in Anglo-Saxon and Norman Bookbinding: Board Attachment Methods Re-examined', in *Roger Powell: The Compleat Binder*, ed. J. L. Sharpe, Bibliologia 14 (Turnhout, 1996), 154–214; J. A. Szirmai, 'The Archeology of Bookbinding and Book Restoration', *Quærendo* 26 (1996), 144–64; idem, *The Archeology of Medieval Bookbinding* (forthcoming).

MICHAEL GULLICK

BOOKLAND: *see* Land tenure; Manors and manorial lordship

BOOK-PRODUCTION: *see* Scriptorium

BOROUGH: *see* Burghal Hidage; Five Boroughs

BOSA (d. 706), sometime bishop of York who had been trained at *Whitby under Abbess *Hild (he was one of five Whitby alumni who attained to bishoprics). He was consecrated bishop of *Deira (with his see at York) in 678 after *Wilfrid had been expelled from this see by King Ecgfrith and the vast Northumbrian diocese divided; but when Wilfrid was restored to his see in 686, Bosa was expelled in turn, only to be restored in 691 or 692 when Wilfrid was expelled yet again, this time by King *Aldfrith. *Bede described Bosa as a man of great holiness and humility; it was Bosa who trained Bede's friend and colleague *Acca.

Bede, *HE* iv.12, 23, v.3, 20.

MICHAEL LAPIDGE

BOSHAM (Sussex) is a minster sited on a peninsula above a broad tidal inlet. *Bede calls it a 'very small' monastery housing an Irish monk called Dicuil with five or six brethren when St *Wilfrid was converting the South Saxon aristocracy (in the 680s), but says that 'none of the natives cared to follow their way of life or listen to their preaching'. This is rare evidence for an Irish monastic presence in southern England, and given its later status Bosham may have been more important than Bede's dismissive tone implies. It is not, however, mentioned again until *Edward the Confessor's reign, when the vast minster estate was divided between Earl *Godwine and royal chaplains; the *Bayeux Tapestry depicts King *Harold riding to the church and feasting in an adjoining house. *Domesday Book shows that Bosham, with a surviving endowment of 147 hides, was probably the richest unreformed minster left in England. The nave and storied west *porticus* are late Anglo-Saxon.

Bede, *HE* iv.13; R. D. H. Gem, 'Holy Trinity Church, Bosham', *Archaeological Journal* 142 (1985), 32–6; J. Blair, 'St Cuthman, Steyning and Bosham', *Sussex Archaeological Collections* 135 (1997), 173–92.

JOHN BLAIR

BOSWORTH, JOSEPH (1789–1876), clergyman, grammarian, lexicographer, Rawlinson Professor of Anglo-Saxon at Oxford (1858–76); founded the professorship of Anglo-Saxon at Cambridge in 1867 on the proceeds of his many successful books, which included a Latin syntax (1821) and Anglo-Saxon grammar (1826), as well as writings on Dutch language and Scandinavian literature. Apart from a translation (1855) and subsequently an edition (1858) of the Old English Orosius, Bosworth's major contribution to scholarship was *A Dictionary of the Anglo-Saxon Language* (1838), which grew in size and scope in subsequent editions (see *dictionaries).

J. Bosworth, *A Compendious Grammar of the Primitive English or Anglo-Saxon Language* (London, 1826); idem, *A Dictionary of the Anglo-Saxon Language* (London, 1838); idem, *Latin Construing; or, Rules for Translating Latin into English*, 5th ed. (London, 1850); *King Alfred's Anglo-Saxon Version of the Compendious History of the World by Orosius*, ed. J. Bosworth (London, 1858).

MARK ATHERTON

BOSWORTH PSALTER: *see* Hymns

BOTWULF, ST (d. 680), founder, in 654, of the monastery of *Icanho* (Iken) in the Fens, was of unspecified Anglo-Saxon origin. He is believed, in company with his brother Adulf, to have travelled to northern France to enter an unidentified monastic community, and subsequently returned to England to establish his own community on the basis of the discipline he had learned abroad. The source for this is the eleventh-century *Vita S. Botulphi* (*BHL* 1248) by *Folcard, acting abbot of Thorney (1069–85), a text which in combining hagiographical commonplaces with dubious historical data conveys the impression that Folcard was able to discover little information about Botwulf at Thorney. In another text, *Translatio SS. Thorneiensium*, Folcard describes the translation of Botwulf's relics from *Icanho* to Thorney Abbey by *Æthelwold, bishop of Winchester. Feast: 17 June.

Acta SS., Iun., iii.402–3; C. Clark, 'Notes on a Life of three Thorney Saints Thancred, Torhtred and Tova', *Proceedings of the Cambridge Antiquarian Society* 69 (1979), 45–52; S. E. West, N. Scarfe and R. Cramp, 'St Botulph and the Coming of East Anglian Christianity', *Proceedings of the Suffolk Institute of Archaeology and Natural History* 35 (1984), 279–301.

R. C. LOVE

BRADFORD-ON-AVON (Wilts.), thought by *William of Malmesbury to have had a church built by *Aldhelm (d. 709), retains an exceptionally lavish and finely-detailed small church of the early eleventh century. It comprised nave, chancel and north and south *porticus* (the last now missing); a frieze of flat blind arcading runs around the exterior. The interior, which retains its tall, narrow openings and has the remains of a large crucifix flanked by angels on the east wall of the nave, conveys the atmosphere of Anglo-Saxon religious space better, perhaps, than any other surviving building (see pl. 4).

Taylor and Taylor, *AS Arch* iii.86–9; Fernie, *Architecture*, pp. 147–50.

JOHN BLAIR

BRANDON (Suffolk) is the site of a high-status eighth-century settlement on an island in the fens. It contained a probable church, two cemeteries, a dense cluster of rectangular timber buildings and a cloth-processing industrial area, and there was a timber-revetted waterfront. The site is notable for the range and quality of small-finds – silver-gilt pins, writing styli, imported luxury *pottery and *glass and a gold plaque with an Evangelist's symbol – which suggest that it should be interpreted as a small but high-status monastery.

R. D. Carr, A. Tester and P. Murphy, 'The Middle-Saxon Settlement at Staunch Meadow, Brandon', *Antiquity* 62 (1988), 371–7; *Making of England*, pp. 81–8.

JOHN BLAIR

Pl. 4 Bradford-on-Avon church.

BREAKING: *see* Sound Change

BREAMORE (Hants.) retains the best example still standing of a late Anglo-Saxon church of below monastic but above village status. The low crossing-tower, with a nave of equal width to the west and a narrower chancel and *porticus* on the other three sides, exemplifies a type which was standard for minor minsters but is elsewhere only known from fragments. There was also a western chamber (now demolished), which may originally have housed the fine but mutilated late Anglo-Saxon rood-group. The Old English inscription over the south *porticus* arch, 'Here is made manifest the covenant to you', refers to Gen. IX.8–17 and probably represents the rainbow arc.

Taylor and Taylor, *AS Arch* i.94–6; W. Rodwell and E. C. Rouse, 'The Anglo-Saxon Rood and Other Features in the South Porch of St Mary's Church, Breamore, Hants.', *AJ* 64 (1984), 298–325; R. and F. Gameson, 'The Anglo-Saxon Inscription at St Mary's Church, Breamore, Hampshire', *ASSAH* 6 (1993), 1–10.

JOHN BLAIR

BREEDON-ON-THE-HILL (Leics.), one of the great minsters of central *Mercia, stands in an Iron Age fort on a commanding hill. In the 680s the nobleman Frithuric gave land for founding it to the community of *Medeshamstede* (Peterborough), which appointed Hædde, one of its own priests and later bishop of *Lichfield, as first abbot. The foundation *charter (unfortunately corrupt) is exceptional in stipulating pastoral care among the local people. That Breedon became a major cultural centre is suggested by the fact that *Tatwine, archbishop of *Canterbury 731–4 and described by Bede as 'renowned for his devotion and wisdom and excellently instructed in the Scriptures', had been a priest there. Furthermore, the church still contains its spectacular collection of carved friezes and panels, dating from *c*.800 and influenced by antique and Byzantine models, which are among the supreme artistic products of Mercia at its height. In 848 the community was released from royal hospitality services in return for land and treasure, and a grant to the bishop for the church of Breedon in 967 shows that the old minster was in some sense still functioning.

A. Dornier, 'The Anglo-Saxon Monastery at Breedon-on-the-Hill', in Dornier, *MS*, pp. 155–68; S. Keynes, *The Councils of Clofesho*, Vaughan Paper 38 (Leicester, 1994), 37–40; R. Cramp, 'Schools of Mercian Sculpture', in Dornier, *MS*, pp. 191–231; R. H. I. Jewell, 'The Anglo-Saxon Friezes at Breedon-on-the-Hill', *Archaeologia* 108 (1986), 95–115.

JOHN BLAIR

BRETWALDA or *BRYTENWALDA*. A word (probably signifying 'ruler of Britain') applied by a West Saxon chronicler in the late ninth century to *Ecgberht, king of the West Saxons (802–39). In recording Ecgberht's conquest of the kingdom of the Mercians and 'everything south of the Humber', the chronicler described him as 'the eighth king who was Bretwalda' (*ASC*, s.a. 829), adding his name to the list of seven kings whom Bede had credited with *imperium* or rule over the same area (*HE* ii.5). Bede's list is best understood as the product of personal reflection on his part. It is likely, in the same way, that the chronicler's use of the term 'Bretwalda' did not represent Ecgberht's succession to a recognised office, with powers and responsibilities particular to itself, but rather a flight of fancy, important to the chronicler but of no real importance in the unfolding course of political development; cf. *heptarchy. The term belongs in the context of the aspirations to rulership throughout Britain which had been entertained on behalf of certain seventh-century Northumbrian kings, and on behalf of certain eighth-century Mercian kings, and which were entertained again on behalf of several of Ecgberht's successors, including *Alfred, *Æthelstan, and *Edgar. As such, it is a useful reminder of the continued significance of 'Britain', as a unifying principle, throughout the Anglo-Saxon period, subsuming all the inhabitants of the island and harking back to the Roman past (cf. Bede, *HE* i.1).

D. P. Kirby, *The Making of Early England* (London, 1967), pp. 54–5; P. Wormald, 'Bede, the *Bretwaldas* and the Origin of the *Gens Anglorum*', *Ideal and Reality in Frankish and Anglo-Saxon Society*, ed. P. Wormald *et al.* (Oxford, 1983), pp. 99–129; Yorke, *Kings and Kingdoms*, pp. 157–62; Kirby, *Earliest English Kings*, pp. 14–20; S. Keynes, 'Rædwald the Bretwalda', *Voyage to the Other World: the Legacy of Sutton Hoo*, ed. C. B. Kendall and P. S. Wells (Minneapolis, MI, 1992), pp. 103–23; N. J. Higham, *An English Empire: Bede and the Early Anglo-Saxon Kings* (Manchester, 1995).

SIMON KEYNES

BRIDGES are often mentioned in OE place-names and *charter-boundaries, and may have been increasingly important for internal communications as political organisation and the economy grew from the seventh century onwards. The public duty to maintain bridges is reserved (as one of the 'three common burdens': see *Trinoda necessitas*) in Mercian charters from the 740s and Kentish ones from the 790s, and became standard practice during the ninth century. Given the survival (or revival) of so many Roman *roads, the maintenance or rebuilding of Roman bridges over major rivers must often have been essential. The best-known case of this is at *Rochester, where the stone piers of the Roman bridge survived: an eleventh-century text records the detailed hidage-based obligations, imposed on manors in the lathe of Aylesford, to provide the massive beams which spanned from pier to pier and the planks of the carriageway above. All-timber bridges of trestle form were technically possible and are likely to have been used for other major crossings, as possibly at *Oxford. Late sources show that assessed communal liabilities for maintaining important bridges survived down to the thirteenth century (e.g. *London and Cambridge) or even later (e.g. Huntingdon and Nottingham).

Late Anglo-Saxon England must have contained innumerable smaller river- and stream-crossings. The extant charter-bounds include eleven instances of 'stone bridge' and twenty-four of 'stone ford', terms which may describe the same sort of structure: a causeway of rubble or rammed earth exposed in dry seasons but otherwise submerged. In *The *Battle of Maldon* the causeway linking Northey Island to the mainland is called both *bricg* and *ford*; at Ducklington (Oxon.) a feature described in bounds of 958 as *stan ford*, and again in 969 as *stan bricge*, has been identified by excavation as a rubble-paved ford. 'Plank bridge' also occurs in charter-bounds.

N. P. Brooks, 'Church, Crown and Community: Public Work and Seigneurial Responsibilities at Rochester Bridge', *Warriors and Churchmen in the High Middle Ages*, ed. T. Reuter (London, 1992), pp. 1–20; idem, 'Rochester Bridge, AD 43–1381', *Traffic and Politics*, ed. N. Yates and J. M. Gibson (Woodbridge, 1994), pp. 1–40; J. Blair and A. Millard, 'An Anglo-Saxon Landmark Rediscovered: the *Stan Ford/ Stan Bricge* of the Ducklington and Witney Charters', *Oxoniensia* 57 (1992), 342–8.

JOHN BLAIR

BRIXWORTH, NORTHAMPTONSHIRE, ALL SAINTS' CHURCH. The twelfth-century chronicle of Hugo Candidus claims that a monastery was founded at Brixworth some time after AD 675. As at *Breedon-on-the-Hill, Leicester-

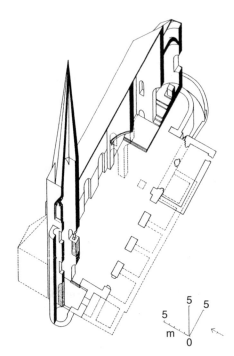

Fig. 1 Brixworth: Anglo-Saxon phase (broken line) in relation to present church.

shire, 675 × 691, monks from *Medeshamstede* (Peterborough) probably formed the nucleus of the initial community. The later history of the church implies high status: the Domesday manor was royal and the king subsequently granted the church to the cathedral at Sarum as a prebend. The church evidently ceased to be monastic during the Anglo-Saxon period. In the grounds of the present vicarage excavation in 1972 revealed the remains of a V-shaped ditch, interpreted as the *vallum monasterii*, and lay burials from a cemetery extending across the former vicarage garden.

The surviving church building retains much of the fabric of a substantial Anglo-Saxon church, consisting of a nave with north and south arcades of four arches with semi-circular heads of one or two flush orders of thin brick (Roman reused); to the east a square choir with a narrower apse of seven panels externally (all but two reconstructed in the nineteenth century), surrounded by a ring-crypt; west of the nave a square tower of two Anglo-Saxon phases, with a stilted-semicircular stair turret, contemporary with the second phase, attached to its west face. Additions to the fabric after the Norman Conquest are a late twelfth-century south door, the Lady or Verdun Chapel of *c.*1300 south of the choir and the belfry stage of

the tower surmounted by a spire (fourteenth-century); medieval additions removed in the 1865–6 restoration included a south porch of *c.*1190–1220, a long rectangular chancel which had replaced the pre-Conquest apse, and several multiple-light traceried windows.

In its initial phase, possibly late eighth/early ninth century, the nave was flanked by three ranges, each of five *porticus*, attested by various archaeological investigations, most recently in 1981–2. Those to the north and south overlapped the choir by one bay; the northeast *porticus* had a door in its east wall. The west range had chambers of varying size, the central of which survives as the lowest stage of the tower. The main entrance at this phase was through a major arch in the west wall of this chamber, later blocked by the addition of the turret along with the upper stages of the tower, probably in the eleventh century. In the course of this rebuilding the floor levels in the central compartment were changed; a round-headed doorway above the entrance door to the nave was blocked, but is still visible in the fabric, and its head was cut by a new triple-arched opening between tower and nave at first-floor level. Access to the upper level was by the turret stair, constructed in Roman fashion as a helical barrel vault of tufa rubble. The remaining *porticus* were demolished at an unknown date, but not later than *c.*1200.

The church is remarkable for its wide variety of building stone, some of it drawn from far afield. In both pre-Conquest phases much of the stone was reused from earlier buildings, and some of it is fire-damaged.

Taylor and Taylor, *AS Arch* i.108–14; D. Parsons, 'Barrel-vaulted Staircases in England and on the Continent, with special reference to Brixworth Church, Northamptonshire', *Zeitschrift für Archäologie des Mittelalters* 6 (1978), 129–47; D. S. Sutherland and D. Parsons, 'The Petrological Contribution to the Survey of All Saints' Church, Brixworth, Northamptonshire: an Interim Account', *JBAA* 137 (1984), 45–64; M. Audouy *et al.*, 'Excavations at the Church of All Saints, Brixworth, Northamptonshire (1981–82)', *JBAA* 137 (1984), 1–44; D. S. Sutherland, 'Burnt Stone in a Saxon Church', in *Stone: Quarrying and Building in England, AD 43–1525*, ed. D. Parsons (Chichester, 1990), pp. 102–13; D. Parsons, 'Brixworth, Northamptonshire', in *Dictionary of Art*, ed. J. Turner (London, 1996), iv.829–30.

DAVID PARSONS

BROOCHES: *see* Jewellery

BUILDING MATERIALS AND TECHNIQUES: *see* Timber Building

BURGHAL HIDAGE. A document listing the burhs (or *fortifications) which formed part of a defensive network across southern England, indicating how many hides of land 'belonged' to each. The basic requirement was that one pole of 'wall' (i.e. a defensive length of 5½ yards) had to be manned by four men, and, on the principle that one man would be provided from one hide of land, the number of hides allocated to each burh would suffice to ensure that the defences at each place were adequately manned and maintained. The provision of fortress-work of one kind or another was one of the services which had long been extracted by royal authority from the holders of land in Anglo-Saxon England (cf. *Trinoda necessitas), and is made explicit in charters from the mid eighth century onwards. In the years following his victory over the Danes at the battle of Edington (878), and the departure of another *Viking army from Fulham to the Continent (880), King *Alfred had embarked upon the construction of a network of fortifications which was probably more burdensome on the people than any defensive programme undertaken before (cf. *Asser, ch. 91); it bears comparison in certain respects with the defensive measures undertaken by Carolingian kings, notably Charles the Bald, and there can be little doubt that the fortifications played a significant part in the successful defence of Alfred's kingdom when the Vikings returned to England in 892. The fortifications continued to serve their purpose in the first quarter of the tenth century, and the network expanded further thereafter; while some of the burhs fell into disuse, others developed into prosperous towns. The Burghal Hidage thus represents the network at a particular stage in its unfolding history. It is generally supposed that the document dates from the period after 914 (given the inclusion of Buckingham), and might reasonably be associated with the preparations for *Edward the Elder's major offensive against the Danes in 917; but it must be admitted that this argument depends on certain assumptions which may not be tenable, and that the document might just as well reflect a position in the 880s, with the network conceived within the political context of the 'Kingdom of the *Anglo-Saxons'. The figures in the Burghal Hidage afford a precise indication of the length of the defensive works at each burh, and the calculated length will be found to correspond closely to the actual length of the defences measured on the ground (see Hill, *Atlas*, fig. 149). The document is shown on this basis to be the work of a central authority, and as such is presumed to be a product of royal administration.

Anglo-Saxon Charters, ed. A. J. Robertson, 2nd ed. (Cambridge, 1956), pp. 246–9, 494–6; Keynes and Lapidge, *Alfred the Great*, pp. 24–5, 193–4, 339–41; *The Defence of Wessex: the Burghal Hidage and Anglo-Saxon Fortifications*, ed. D. Hill and A. R. Rumble (Manchester, 1996).

SIMON KEYNES

BURGHARD or **BURCHARD** (d. 754), an Anglo-Saxon missionary and colleague of St *Boniface, probably of Southumbrian origin, who became bishop of Würzburg in 743. Little is known of his episcopacy, but his name is associated with a *gospelbook known as the 'Burghard Gospels' (now Würzburg, Universitätsbibliothek, M. p. th. f. 68), an uncial manuscript of sixth-century Italian origin to which were added various leaves in Northumbrian uncial characteristic of *Monkwearmouth-Jarrow (s. vii/viii). The manuscript was subsequently taken to the Continent, perhaps by Burghard; it is significant for the fact that it preserves a series of pericope-markings from the church of Naples, which arguably derive from a lost gospelbook brought from Naples to England by Abbot *Hadrian.

MGH, ES i.94–5; *CLA* ix.1423a–b; G. Morin, 'Les notes liturgiques de l'évangile de Burchard', *RB* 10 (1893), 113–26; idem, 'Liturgie et basiliques de Rome au milieu du VIIe siècle d'après les listes d'évangiles de Würzburg', *RB* 28 (1911), 296–330; B. Bischoff and M. Lapidge, *Biblical Commentaries from the Canterbury School of Theodore and Hadrian*, CSASE 10 (Cambridge, 1994), 157–60.

MICHAEL LAPIDGE

BURIAL: *see* Cemeteries, Furnished; Cemeteries, Unfurnished

BURY ST EDMUNDS (Suffolk) (*Bedricesweord*), possibly an early minster, was identified in late tradition as the burial-place of King Sigeberht (d. *c.*636). In *c.*900–20 the relics of the royal martyr *Edmund were brought there and became the centre of a major cult, promoted in a *Life* by *Abbo of Fleury. Through the tenth century the minster housed a community of secular clerks; *Cnut re-founded this in 1020 as a Benedictine abbey, and new churches were built including a rotunda housing Edmund's body. Meanwhile at the abbey gates a town was growing up, greatly enlarged and re-planned by Abbot Baldwin (1065–97), *Edward the Confessor's physician.

P. Warner, *The Origins of Suffolk* (Manchester, 1996); S. J. Ridyard, *The Royal Saints of Anglo-Saxon England* (Cambridge, 1988), pp. 211–33; R. Gem, 'A Recession in English Architecture during the Early Eleventh Century', *JBAA*, 3rd ser. 38 (1975), 28–49, at 35–7; R. Gem and L. Keen, 'Late Anglo-Saxon Finds from the Site of St Edmund's Abbey', *Proceedings of the Suffolk Institute of Archaeology and History* 35 (1981), 1–30; M. D. Lobel, *The Borough of St Edmund's* (Oxford, 1935).

JOHN BLAIR

BY-NAMES are characterising names added to, or occasionally substituted for, forenames. The forename was normally an adequate means of distinguishing one person from another. Where necessary, however, a person could be distinguished by the addition to the forename of a patronymic or metronymic, e.g. *Eadwine Ecgferthes sunu* and *Wulfric Wulfrune sunu*, of a title or occupational term, e.g. *Leofwine ealdorman* and *Eadric stiresman* 'steersman', of a locational phrase, e.g. *Æthelric æt Boccinge*, or of a by-name describing appearance, character or behaviour, e.g. *Beorhtric se calwa* 'the bald', *Tofi pruda* 'the proud', *Godwine peningfæder* 'the miser'. Occasionally a by-name was substituted for the forename, as when the seventh-century Æthelburg, wife of King *Edwin of Northumbria, was alternatively called *Tate* 'the merry'.

By-names tended to be informal, not to say offensive, and they occur comparatively rarely in written records. Scribes were not unduly worried about the possibility of confusion between individuals bearing the same name. The witnesses to an eleventh-century will, for example, include *Ordger and other Ordger*.

Many Anglo-Saxon by-names are recorded for the first time in *Domesday Book of 1086 or in Middle English sources. One of the earliest sources to record the use of by-names is Bede's *Historia ecclesiastica* with its account of the two English missionary priests called *Hewald who were martyred in about 700 (*HE* v.10). Bede says that because of the different colour of their hair one was called *Niger Heuuald* and the other *Albus Heuuald*. Adjectives occur frequently as by-names and adjectives of colour referring to hair are among the commonest of these. There is *Wulfsige se blaca* 'the black', also referred to as *Wulfsige maurus* 'the moor', *Wulfhun se blaca*, and *Æthelwine niger*. Several men bear the by-name *se reada* or *rufus* 'red' and there was a *Wulfgar se gyldena* 'the golden'. Other adjectival by-names recorded are *langa* 'tall', *greata* 'stout', *litla* 'little', *calwa* and *bleriga* both 'bald', *leofa* 'beloved', *hoga* 'prudent' and *syfra* 'sober'.

Appellatives occurring as by-names fall into three categories. Firstly there are the personal appellatives, standing as it were in apposition to the forename. The tenth-century witness *Eadric papa* was not, of course, pope and his by-name probably referred to his pontificating manner. The name of the traitor *Eadric streona* 'the acquisitor' probably reflects the fact that his loyalty was for sale. Two of the legatees named in a will dated 1014, *Æthelweard stamera* and *Godwine dref(e)la*, are bluntly distinguished as 'the stammerer' and 'the driveller'. The second category is the zoological one. *Ælfric mus* 'mouse' was an eleventh-century Cambridgeshire peasant. *Ælfric puttoc* 'kite' became archbishop of York in 1023. *Eadric pur* 'bittern' was a *thegn of *Edward the Confessor. *Leofric snipa* 'snipe' and *Ælfric stari* 'starling' were Suffolk peasants in 1066, while *Leofwine draca* 'dragon' had property in *Winchester then. The third category refers to some bodily feature. *Wulfric spot* made his will at the beginning of the eleventh century. His by-name is most likely to refer to a facial blemish but it might have been used of a dumpy person. Bearers of even less flattering by-names are the eleventh-century *Godric gupe* 'buttock' and *Leofwine bealluc* 'bollock'.

A small category of by-names consists of derivative formations which did not have an independent existence as words in the English language. Many of the derivative names would seem to be based on Germanic stems associated with swelling or roundedness, e.g. *Wulfstan ucca* (*uk-), *Beorhtmær bubba* (*bub(b)-).

There is little trace in the Anglo-Saxon period of the Bluebeard- or Shakespeare-types of by-name. There are a few instances of compound nouns functioning as by-names but these are not of the Bluebeard-type. In the case of the tenth-century *Eadwulf yvelcild* 'evil child', for example, the by-name stands as it were in apposition to the forename, where the Bluebeard-type names would seem to have been linked to the forename by an imaginary 'who has'. Several of the Domesday under-tenants bear by-names of this type: *Aluredus taddebelloc* 'toad bollock', *Aluricus fulebiert* 'foul beard', *Alestanus braders* 'broad arse', *God' clenehand* 'clean hand' and *Borewoldus horloc* 'grey lock'. Domesday Book is also one of the earliest sources to record imperatival Shakespeare-type names: *Godwinus clawecunte* 'claw cunt', *God' cunnebried* 'test bread', *Aluricus stikestac* 'stab stag'. Although some of the Bluebeard- and Shakespeare-type names are simply translations into English of by-names and surnames brought over by the Normans, most of them probably developed in Anglo-Saxon England.

C. Clark, 'Onomastics: 7.2 Anthroponymy', CHELang, i.456–71; O. von Feilitzen, 'The Personal Names and Bynames of the Winton Domesday', *Winchester in the Early Middle Ages*, ed. M. Biddle, Winchester Studies 1 (Oxford, 1976), 143–229; G. Tengvik, *Old English Bynames* (Uppsala, 1938).

GILLIAN FELLOWS-JENSON

BYRHTFERTH (*c.*970–*c.*1020), monk of *Ramsey and one of the most prolific authors – in both Latin and Old English – of his age. Very little is known of his life, but it would seem likely that he was given as an oblate to Ramsey, and was at Ramsey as a student when the great scholar *Abbo of Fleury spent two years there (985–7) instructing the Ramsey monks in such subjects as *computus and *metrics and composing his *Passio S. Eadmundi*. Byrhtferth followed the example of his master in these various disciplines. Byrhtferth's earliest composition, dating probably from the years 988–96, appears to be a Latin *Computus* consisting of arithmetical tables, formulas and rules for calculating the movable feasts (principally Easter) of the Christian year. Byrhtferth took over many of these tables from Abbo's *Computus*, but also added various items of his own composition. When complete, Byrhtferth's *Computus* formed part of what might be called a 'computistical miscellany', consisting of a preface (called *Epilogus* by Byrhtferth), followed by the *Computus* proper, then *Bede's scientific treatises *De temporum ratione* and *De natura rerum*, and the computistical treatise by Helperic of Auxerre. A later copy of Byrhtferth's 'computistical miscellany' is preserved in Oxford, St John's College 17 (Thorney, AD 1110–11). Various marginal glosses which accompany the texts of Bede in this manuscript are probably by Byrhtferth (one of them significantly contains a calculation of the *annus praesens* = AD 993). In any event Byrhtferth also assembled an anthology of patristic quotations designed to explicate Bede's *De temporum ratione* and *De natura rerum*; this anthology, known as the 'Brideferti glossae', was printed at Basel in 1563 as part of an edition of Bede's *opera omnia* by Johannes Herwagen. The manuscript used by Herwagen has since been lost, but the 'Brideferti glossae', as he called them, are an impressive witness to the breadth of Byrhtferth's reading, and have interesting links both with the marginal glosses to Bede's works in St John's 17, and with the introductory *Enchiridion* or 'handbook' which Byrhtferth composed to accompany his Latin *Computus*. The *Enchiridion*, on which Byrhtferth was working in 1011 (as may be deduced from a calculation contained in that

work) is essentially a commentary, in Latin and English, on his *Computus*, and must be read alongside that work; however, in characteristic fashion, Byrhtferth also included long digressions on various scholarly matters, such as metrical scansion, rhetorical terminology, weights and measures, and arithmology (part iv of the *Enchiridion* consists of a self-contained Latin treatise on the significance of numbers from one to 1000).

Byrhtferth's study of *computus led him, as it had led Bede three hundred years earlier, to the study of chronography and the writing of history. We have from Byrhtferth's pen a work entitled *Historia regum* (which is not preserved intact, but as incorporated into a work of the same name by the early twelfth-century historian *Symeon of Durham). Byrhtferth's *Historia regum* treats English history from the earliest kingdoms down to the death of King *Alfred, and is drawn from various earlier texts, including a *passio* of SS *Æthelred and Æthelberht (a composition by Byrhtferth himself), Bede's *De die iudicii*, *Historia abbatum* and *Historia ecclesiastica*, a set of *annals known as the 'York Annals' covering the years 732–802, and the *Vita Ælfredi* of *Asser.

Byrhtferth was also an active hagiographer. In addition to his previously mentioned *Passio SS Æthelredi et Æthelberhti*, Byrhtferth composed *vitae* of *Oswald (d. 992), bishop of Worcester and archbishop of York, and of *Ecgwine, an early eighth-century bishop of Worcester and the founder of Evesham. Byrhtferth's *Vita S. Oswaldi* is one of the longest surviving Anglo-Latin saints' lives; although it contains valuable information not found elsewhere concerning Oswald and his uncle *Oda, archbishop of Canterbury (941–58), Byrhtferth's intention was to depict Oswald as an icon of Benedictine monasticism. His *Vita S. Ecgwini* is a work of somewhat different character, inasmuch as Byrhtferth had virtually no historical information concerning Ecgwine beyond a (spurious) foundation charter; the work is accordingly teased out with pedantic allegorical and arithmological digressions of various kinds.

In spite of his occasional pedantry, Byrhtferth was one of the most learned scholars of the late Anglo-Saxon period. He quotes from a wide range of reading, including the poets (both classical and Christian) and many church fathers. His favourite author appears to have been *Aldhelm, whose flamboyant prose style had an unfortunate influence on Byrhtferth, who was able to imitate the verbosity, but not the clear structure, of Aldhelm's sentences.

Sharpe, *Handlist*, 174; *Byrhtferth's Enchiridion*, ed. P. S.

Baker and M. Lapidge, EETS ss 15 (London, 1995); *Symeonis Monachi Opera Omnia*, ed. T. Arnold, 2 vols, RS (London, 1882–5), ii.3–91 [Byrhtferth's *Historia regum*]; *The Historians of the Church of York and its Archbishops*, ed. J. Raine, 3 vols, RS (London, 1879–94), i.399–475 [*Vita S. Oswaldi*]; *Vita quorundum Anglo-Saxonum*, ed. [sic] J. A. Giles (London, 1854), pp. 349–96 [*Vita S. Ecgwini*]; *Byrhtferth of Ramsey: the Lives of Oswald and Ecgwine*, ed. M. Lapidge (OMT, forthcoming); P. S. Baker, 'The Old English Canon of Byrhtferth of Ramsey', *Speculum* 55 (1980), 22–37; idem, 'Byrhtferth's *Enchiridion* and the Computus in Oxford, St John's College 17', *ASE* 10 (1982), 123–42; M. Lapidge, 'Byrhtferth and the *Vita S. Ecgwini*', *MS* 41 (1979), 331–53 (repr. in Lapidge, *ALL* ii.293–315); idem, 'Byrhtferth of Ramsey and the Early Sections of the *Historia regum* attributed to Symeon of Durham', *ASE* 10 (1982), 97–122 (repr. in Lapidge, *ALL* ii.317–42); idem, 'Byrhtferth at Work', *Words and Works: Studies in Medieval English Language and Literature in Honour of Fred C. Robinson*, ed. P. S. Baker and N. Howe (Toronto, 1998), pp. 25–43; M. Gorman, 'The Glosses on Bede's *De temporum ratione* attributed to Byrhtferth of Ramsey', *ASE* 25 (1996), 209–32.

MICHAEL LAPIDGE

BYZANTIUM is the name given to the eastern, largely Greek-speaking, part of the Roman empire, from the founding of Constantinople in 325 (and especially from the effective division of the empire into western/Latin-speaking and eastern/Greek-speaking under Honorius in 395) until the fall of Constantinople to the Turks in 1453. In the early centuries the Byzantine empire included most of the eastern Mediterranean littoral: Libya and Egypt in North Africa, Palestine and Syria, Cilicia and Anatolia (modern Turkey), Armenia, the Black Sea littoral, Thrace, Macedonia and Greece; with the explosion of Islam in the early seventh century, North Africa, Palestine and Syria were lost to the empire. There were sporadic, but significant, contacts between the Byzantine empire and Anglo-Saxon England. These contacts may have begun very early: the *Sutton Hoo burial yielded a silver bowl bearing the stamp of the eastern Emperor Anastasius (491–518) and two ceremonial spoons bearing inscriptions in Greek. One of the most significant early contacts was the advent in England of Archbishop *Theodore, who was born in Tarsus in Cilicia in 602, was trained in Antioch and Edessa (both in Syria), and spent some time in Constantinople, following lectures at the university in law, medicine and rhetoric. Theodore brought to England a vast knowledge of Greek patristic literature, some of which is reflected in the biblical commentaries from his school at *Canterbury; he also imported certain liturgical practices from Antioch, such as the form of prayer known as the litany of the saints, which had a wide diffusion first in England, then in Ireland and Carolingian Europe, as well as the cults of various Byzantine saints, notably St Anastasius. He created an Anglo-Latin metrical form, the trochaic *octosyllable, on the basis of a widespread Greek metrical form, the anacreontic. His colleague *Hadrian was from Greek-speaking North Africa, probably Libya Cyrenaica, but his direct influence on Anglo-Saxon culture is less easily defined. It is tempting to associate the presence in England of a sixth- or seventh-century Byzantine *censer found near Glastonbury with the advent of Theodore and Hadrian, but proof positive is lacking. Evidence from later periods is less compelling, but sporadic contact between England and the Byzantine East continued. Bald's *Leechbook* contains a medical recipe which is claimed to have been sent to King *Alfred by the patriarch of Jerusalem, Helias (c.879–907). In the eleventh century a number of English pilgrims went to Jerusalem and (probably) Constantinople, including Swein son of *Godwine, Bishop *Ealdred, Wythman, sometime abbot of *Ramsey (c.1020), a lady named Leofgyth (S 1029), and Ulf and his wife in 1066–8. According to Eadmer's *Vita S. Dunstani*, Æthelwine, a monk of Christ Church, Canterbury, visited Constantinople c.1055 and brought back a splendid pall for *Dunstan's shrine. In 1090, a monk of the same house, one Joseph, visited Constantinople in the attempt to obtain relics of St Andrew for *Rochester. It was probably one of these English visitors who produced the description of Constantinople which is preserved in Oxford, Bodleian Library, Digby 112 (s. xii[in]). And it was in the immediately post-Conquest period that various Englishmen served in the Varangian regiment of the imperial (Byzantine) guard.

C. Mango, *Byzantium: the Empire of the New Rome* (London, 1980); *The Oxford Dictionary of Byzantium*, ed. A. P. Kazhdan, 3 vols. (Oxford, 1991); B. Bischoff and M. Lapidge, *Biblical Commentaries from the Canterbury School of Theodore and Hadrian*, CSASE 10 (Cambridge, 1994); *Archbishop Theodore*, ed. M. Lapidge, CSASE 11 (Cambridge, 1995); *Alfred the Great*, p. 270, n. 220; R. S. Lopez, 'Le problème des relations anglo-byzantines du septième au dixième siècle', *Byzantion* 18 (1948), 139–62; A. A. Vasiliev, 'The Opening Stage of the Anglo-Saxon Immigration to Byzantium in the Eleventh Century', *Annales de l'Institut Kondakov* 9 (Prague, 1937), 39–70; *The Life of King Edward who rests at Westminster*, ed. F. Barlow, 2nd ed. (OMT, 1992), pp. 105–8, n. 265; K. Ciggaar, 'L'émigration anglaise à Byzance après 1066', *Revue des études byzantines* 32

(1974), 301–42; idem, 'Une description de Constantin-ople traduite par un pèlerin anglais', *Revue des études byzantines* 34 (1976), 211–67; C. H. Haskins, 'A Canter-bury Monk at Constantinople', *EHR* 25 (1910), 293–5; V. Ortenberg, *The English Church and the Continent in the Tenth and Eleventh Centuries* (Oxford, 1992), pp. 197–217.

MICHAEL LAPIDGE

C

CÆDMON is the illiterate cow-herd *Bede credits in the *Historia ecclesiastica* (iv.24) as the first to transform the basic narratives of Christian history into classical OE verse. He spent most of his life in the secular world, presumably working on one of the estates of the monastery of *Whitby. After his startling abilities were accepted by Abbess *Hild (d. 680), Cædmon became a brother in the monastery, where he lived out his days. Bede presents Cædmon's gift of poetry as a miracle: unable to participate in secular singing, Cædmon is visited in a dream by a man who orders him to sing something. The song that results, Cædmon's *Hymn*, is a nine-line praise poem in honour of God the Creator. Cædmon's documented illiteracy makes him a central figure in analyses of *oral traditional composition in Old English even though Bede records not the *Hymn* itself, but rather a Latin paraphrase of it. However, in two of the earliest manuscripts of the *Historia ecclesiastica*, St Petersburg, Saltykov-Schedrin Public Library, Q. v. I. 18 (the 'Leningrad Bede'), and Cambridge, University Library, Kk. 5. 16 (the 'Moore Bede'), one early state of the OE poem is found, in the first instance as a kind of gloss, in the second as an addendum at the end of the manuscript. Bede's account indicates that Cædmon rendered much of biblical history into verse, and nineteenth-century scholars attributed to Cædmon *Genesis, *Exodus and *Daniel, poems in the *Junius Manuscript, then known as the Cædmon Manuscript. For stylistic and other reasons, such an attribution cannot be maintained and the *Hymn* is the only poem to which scholars now attach Cædmon's name.

D. K. Fry, 'Cædmon as a Formulaic Poet', in *Oral Literature: Seven Essays*, ed. J. J. Duggan (Edinburgh and New York, 1975), pp. 41–61 [= *Forum for Modern Language Studies* 10.3 (1974), 227–47]; A. J. Frantzen, *Desire for Origins* (New Brunswick, NJ, 1990); K. O'B. O'Keeffe, *Visible Song*, CSASE 4 (Cambridge, 1990), 23–46.

KATHERINE O'BRIEN O'KEEFFE

CÆDMON MANUSCRIPT: *see* Junius Manuscript

CÆDWALLA, king of *Wessex (685–8), was overlord of the greater part of England south of the Thames following his military conquest of *Kent, *Sussex and the *Jutes of Wight in 685–6. Kent rebelled in 687 and Cædwalla's brother Mul, who had been installed as king, was burnt to death. Cædwalla had not been baptised at the time of his accession, but, after coming under the influence of the exiled Bishop *Wilfrid I, he made generous gifts to the church. Cædwalla abdicated in 688, in order to travel to Rome to be baptised, and died there on 20 April 689.

Bede, *HE* v.7; Kirby, *Kings*, pp. 51–3, 116–22; Yorke, *Wessex*, pp. 58–9, 65–7, 73–4, 80–4.

B. A. E. YORKE

CANALS may have been more common in late Anglo-Saxon England than is usually thought. In about 1060, at the request of the men of *Oxford, *Abingdon Abbey cut a navigation channel to bypass a difficult stretch of the Thames. At *Glastonbury a man-made channel some 7 m wide, linking the abbey to the river Brue, has been dated to the mid-tenth century on radiocarbon evidence. It is possible that some riverine terms in *place-names and *charter-bounds (notably *lade*) denote such bypass channels or canals, which would have been wider than mill-leats (cf. *transport and communications).

Chronicon Monasterii de Abingdon, ed. J. Stevenson, RS (London, 1858), i.480–1, ii.282; C. and N. Hollinrake, 'The Abbey Enclosure Ditch and a Late-Saxon Canal: Rescue Excavations at Glastonbury, 1984–88', *Somerset Archaeology & Natural History* 136 (1992), 78–83; Blair, *AS Oxon*, p. 121.

JOHN BLAIR

CANON LAW is the law of the Church (in distinction to civil law), and refers in essence to the 'canons' or 'rules' promulgated by ecclesiastical councils. The earliest such council was that of Nicaea in 325, the canons of which (in Greek) form the first stage of most canon law collections, but the Nicene canons were supplemented by those of earlier and subsequent councils, notably Ancyra (314), Neocaesarea (early fourth century), Antioch (330), Gangra (c.341), Laodicea (fourth century), Sardica (343), Chalcedon (451), Constantinople (381 and 553) and Carthage (419). The fundamental basis of canon law in the Latin West is the Latin translation of the above-mentioned Greek canons made by Dionysius Exiguus (d. c.556), to which he added various decretals (that is, papal letters); however, at any time or place, the basic Dionysian collection or *Dionysiana* (as it is called) could be supplemented by the decrees of local ecclesiastical councils, so that there is considerable diversity in surviving canon law collections. It is a reasonable assumption that books of canon law will have been available in England from the period of the earliest Christianity, but in fact the earliest reference to such a book is found in *Bede's description (*HE* iv.5) of Archbishop *Theodore's convocation of the Council of Hertford in 672 or 673, at which the archbishop 'produced a book of canons' and from it promulgated certain rules. These rules, as recorded by Bede, agree in tenor but not in verbal detail with the Dionysian collection. Theodore also apparently taught canon law at Canterbury, for the early chapters of the Leiden Glossary are drawn from the canons of various early councils in a form which often agrees in verbal detail with the *Dionysiana*. But Theodore evidently had access to other sources of canon law: the second book of his *Iudicia* contains excerpts from the canons of various early councils, and in this case verbal details suggest that he was drawing on a sixth-century Italian collection known as the *Sanblasiana*. A number of Theodore's formulations were taken over by the Irish compilers of the *Collectio canonum Hibernensis* (c.725), and this compilation in turn is preserved in various Anglo-Saxon manuscripts of the later period. One of Theodore's legislative innovations was the stipulation of annual church councils to be held at *Clofesho, and the legislation enacted at these councils will have become part of English canon law. In later Anglo-Saxon England canon law underwent the influence of Carolingian reform in this domain: the council of Aachen in 802 stipulated the use of a collection entitled the *Hadriana* (a revised updating of the *Dionysiana*) in conjunction with another called the *Hispana* (a collection of Spanish conciliar canons). The impact of Carolingian legislation on canon law in later Anglo-Saxon England has scarcely been studied; a crucial figure in this domain is Archbishop *Wulfstan, whose eclectic personal collection of canons is preserved in several manuscripts in his own handwriting.

C. H. Turner, *Ecclesiae Occidentalis Monumenta Iuris Antiquissima*, 2 vols. in 7 parts (Oxford, 1899–1939); F. Maassen, *Geschichte der Quellen und der Literatur des canonischen Rechts im Abendlande bis zum Ausgange des Mittelalters* (Graz, 1870): J. A. Brundage, *Medieval Canon Law*, rev. ed. (London, 1995); P. W. Finsterwalder, *Die Canones Theodori Cantuariensis und ihre Überlieferungsformen* (Weimar, 1929); B. Bischoff and M. Lapidge, *Biblical Commentaries from the Canterbury School of Theodore and Hadrian*, CSASE 10 (Cambridge, 1994), 147–55; M. Brett, 'Theodore and the Latin Canon Law', in *Archbishop Theodore*, ed. M. Lapidge, CSASE 11 (Cambridge, 1995), 120–40; Lapidge, *ALL* i.160–2; C. Cubitt, *Anglo-Saxon Church Councils c.650–c.850* (London, 1995); H. Vollrath, *Die Synoden Englands bis 1066* (Paderborn, 1985); *Archbishop Wulfstan's Canon Law Collection*, ed. J. E. Cross and A. Hamer (Woodbridge, 1998).

MICHAEL LAPIDGE

CANONS: *see* Cathedral Clergy

CANONS OF EDGAR: *see* Wulfstan the Homilist

CANTERBURY. Principal city of the kingdom of *Kent and seat of the southern archbishop. In pre-Roman times there was an Iron Age settlement on the site, which was later to develop into the important Roman-British city known as *Durovernum Cantiacorum*, the capital of the territory of the tribe of the *Cantii*. The fate of *Durovernum* during the English invasions of the fifth century is controversial. It seems most likely that the city was wholly or partly abandoned for a time; archaeological investigation has revealed thick layers of dark earth between Roman and Anglo-Saxon levels, which would seem to indicate that the Roman buildings had been abandoned and been allowed to decay. On the other hand, there is increasing evidence for the early presence of Anglo-Saxon settlers in Canterbury. Dating the earliest Anglo-Saxon structures and finds is very difficult indeed, but some scholars would argue that they may go back as far as the late fourth century. If this is correct, then these remains could possibly be those of Germanic mercenaries engaged by the Romano-British inhabitants to defend the city (cf. *foederati).

The archaeological evidence indicates some level of occupation of the city during the fifth and sixth centuries. By the end of the sixth century Canterbury had become the *metropolis* or principal city of the kingdom of the people of Kent, a status reflected in its Anglo-Saxon name, *Cantwaraburh*: the *burh* ('stronghold', later 'town') of the *Cantware* (the Kentish people). A few Christian churches and shrines in and around the city may have continued to be used as centres of worship, perhaps by the descendants of the Romano-British inhabitants. Queen Bertha, the Christian wife of the pagan Kentish king *Æthelberht, was accustomed to visit one of these churches, perhaps surviving as the present St Martin's just outside the city walls to the east, to pray with her chaplain Bishop Liudhard. It has been speculated that there was an early Anglo-Saxon royal residence in the area of Fordwich, north-east of the city, which would have been convenient for St Martin's. When *Augustine and his fellow-missionaries arrived in Kent in 597, King Æthelberht allowed them to live in Canterbury, which became the centre of the Roman missionary effort. They reconstructed a building in the city believed to have been an ancient Roman church, which was to become the cathedral of Christ Church. Pope *Gregory the Great had intended that the new English church should have two archbishops with seats at *London and *York, but it seems rapidly to have been decided that Canterbury was a more appropriate site for the southern seat. No doubt this change of plan was due in part to the wishes of King Æthelberht and in part to Augustine's pragmatism, for the Kentish king was at that time the most powerful ruler in southern England and his close support was entirely necessary to the success of the mission. The idea of the London archbishopric was essentially abandoned once the Canterbury seat was established, apart from an abortive revival at the end of the eighth century when the Mercian king *Coenwulf tried to persuade the pope to agree to a transfer from Canterbury to London (then a Mercian city).

With the close support and encouragement of King Æthelberht, Augustine founded a monastery to the east of the city (fig. 13) which was to serve as a burial-place for the kings of Kent and the archbishops of Canterbury: this was the celebrated St Augustine's monastery, which remained an important partner of the cathedral church and community throughout the Anglo-Saxon period. The presence of these two wealthy ecclesiastical houses probably encouraged the development of Canterbury as a genuine urban centre. Canterbury was an important early *mint, where coins were struck for the archbishops in the eighth and ninth centuries, as well as for various kings. The walls of the Roman city remained and some of the great public buildings were probably still standing, even if in a ruinous state; there is good reason to think that the theatre in the city centre was an important landmark of the Anglo-Saxon city, perhaps because it was used as a tribal meeting-place or as a market. The heaviest occupation seems to have been in the eastern part of the city, especially in the area around the cathedral; the low-lying western parts were probably prone to flooding and would seem to have been used for agriculture. Most houses would have been of wood and therefore vulnerable to fire: much of the city was burned down in the time of Archbishop *Mellitus (619–24), and there are records of other disastrous fires in 756 and 1067. Another danger was assault and massive destruction in time of war. It seems very likely that Canterbury suffered badly during the Kentish revolt against Mercian rule in 796–8, which was put down with great severity: the cathedral archives up to 798 have vanished, probably destroyed at around this time. The wealthy city was also a regular target of *Viking armies. It was sacked in 850 or 851, and probably again in 893, and repeatedly threatened during the second surge of Viking activity in the late tenth and early eleventh centuries. In 1011 Canterbury was devastated and the cathedral burned by the Viking leader Thorkell the Tall. Archbishop *Ælfheah and other eminent ecclesiastics were captured and held to ransom; the archbishop was murdered in 1012.

Despite these setbacks, Canterbury was a prosperous economic centre in the last part of the Anglo-Saxon period. In the reign of *Æthelstan the city's mint employed seven moneyers, only one fewer than the largest mint at London. A specialised cattle-market existed by 923, and trading in the city was administered by a port-reeve, who represented the king's interests. Documents from the late Anglo-Saxon period give some hint of the existence of gilds and fraternities of city-dwellers. According to *Domesday Book there were 451 burgesses in Canterbury in 1066; an Anglo-Norman cleric, writing in c.1100, estimates that the total population in 1011 was about 8000. Brooks, *Canterbury*; T. Tatton-Brown, 'The Towns of Kent', in Haslam, *Towns*, pp. 1–36; idem, 'The City and Diocese of Canterbury in St Dunstan's Time', *Dunstan* pp. 75–87; D. A. Brooks, 'The Case for Continuity in Fifth-Century Canterbury Re-examined', *Oxford Journal of Archaeology* 7 (1988), 99–114; K. Blockley et al., *Excavations in the Marlowe Car Park and Surrounding Areas*, Archaeology of Canterbury 5 (Canterbury, 1995); S. Kelly, 'The Anglo-Saxon Abbey', *English Heritage Book of St Augustine's Abbey Canterbury* (London, 1997), pp. 33–49; K. Blockly et al., *Canterbury Cathedral Nave: Archaeology, History and Architecture*, Archaeology of Canterbury 1 (Canterbury, 1997).

S. E. KELLY

CARLISLE (Cumb.), a Romano-British town, was probably a base for post-Roman Christian activity. By the 680s it was the most important place in *Northumbria's province west of the Pennines, frequently visited by St *Cuthbert and containing a monastery ruled by King Ecgfrith's sister-in-law. The anonymous *Life* of Cuthbert describes his vision of Ecgfrith's death while Waga, 'reeve of the city', was showing his party the Roman walls and fountain. The churches of St Mary (now the cathedral), St Alban and St Cuthbert represent the monastic nucleus: Anglian-period buildings, coins and other finds, including fragments of two inscribed crosses, have been found nearby. The discovery of an Anglo-Scandinavian cemetery under the cathedral points to religious continuity during the ninth to eleventh centuries.

Anon., *Vita S. Cuthberti*, iv.8–9; Bede, *Vita S. Cuthberti*, cc. 27–8; M. R. McCarthy, 'Thomas Chadwick and Post-Roman Carlisle', in *The Early Church in Western Britain and Ireland*, ed. S. M. Pearce (Oxford, 1982), pp. 241–56; idem, 'The Origins and Development of the Twelfth-Century Cathedral Church at Carlisle', in *The Archaeology of Cathedrals*, ed. T. Tatton-Brown and J. Munby (Oxford, 1996), pp. 31–45.

JOHN BLAIR

CARPET-PAGES occur in some Insular *gospel-books of seventh- to ninth-century date. They carry complex ornamental designs, which invite comparison with eastern carpets, hence their name. They are largely abstract in design but frequently incorporate crosses, either overtly or ambiguously. They articulate the text by introducing each gospel and often face the decorated openings of their texts (incipit pages). Their use in Christian art may be of ultimately Coptic or Syrian origin, perhaps stemming from the decorative emphasis of the beginnings and ends of texts in Late Antique book and roll production, and from early frontispiece crosses. Mosaic pavements and *bookbindings are other possible influences. The earliest surviving Insular example is in the Milan Orosius, probably made at the Irish foundation of Bobbio (N. Italy) in the early seventh century, and is the frontispiece to a chronicle rather than a gospel. Its design features rosettes or marigolds, themselves Christian symbols. The first great Insular gospelbook, the Book of *Durrow (probably of the second half of the seventh century), contains six carpet pages located at the front and back of the book and protectively enclosing each gospel. Several of these have crosses embedded within their abstract ornament, which forms a synthesis of Germanic, Celtic and Mediterranean forms. Here the carpet-pages already form part of the characteristic Insular programme of gospelbook decoration, along with depictions or symbols of the evangelists and the decorated incipit. This programme was subsequently developed in works such as the *Lindisfarne Gospels (see pl. 5) and the Book of Kells. The decorative character of carpet-pages should not obscure their possible symbolic function as embodiments of the Word (Christ) in non-figural fashion. Other interpretations, including relationships to plans of the holy places, have also been advanced.

G. Henderson, *From Durrow to Kells. The Insular Gospelbooks 650–800* (London, 1987); C. Nordenfalk, 'An Illustrated Diatessaron', *Art Bulletin* 50 (1968), 119–40; M. Werner, 'The Cross-Carpet Page in the Book of Durrow: The Cult of the True Cross, Adomnán, and Iona', *Art Bulletin* 72 (1990), 174–223.

MICHELLE P. BROWN

CASTLES: *see* Forts and Fortification

CATHEDRALS: *see* Architecture, Ecclesiastical

CATHEDRAL CLERGY. The idea that a bishop's church should be served by *clergy (rather than, for example, monks) was deep-rooted in Christian tradition before *Gregory I launched his mission to *Canterbury in 597. *Augustine brought several clerics with him, although his senior companions were monks. He set up separate churches, presumably to be served by the two groups, one his see-church, termed *ecclesia* by *Bede, dedicated to the Saviour and lying within the walls of Canterbury, and the other a monastery (*monasterium* according to Bede), dedicated to SS Peter and Paul and lying outside the walls (later known as St Augustine's). Gregory, himself a monk, hoped that Augustine's clergy should share revenues in common. In spite of its monastic leadership, the Canterbury mission seems to have followed a policy of setting up clerical communities to support bishops, so for example we find *Nothhelm (Bede's correspondent) as a priest of *London, and *Paulinus of *York being assisted by a deacon called *James. Moreover Bede in his *Historia ecclesiastica* is always careful to describe churches where bishops had their thrones as *ecclesiae*, retaining the term *monasterium* for a community headed by an abbot. Knowledge of the *liturgy was especially valued in clerics, as we can see from Bede's accounts of the deacon James and of the education offered at Canterbury under *Theodore in the late seventh century. Canterbury exported trained chanters (precentors) to other churches, for example Maban to *Hexham in 709.

Nonetheless, although it is probable that all the cathedral churches south of the Humber and also

Pl. 5 A carpet-page from the Lindisfarne Gospels.

York were served by clerks from their foundation, clerical communities in Anglo-Saxon England failed to make the same impact as their equivalents in Francia. There are several possible explanations. Firstly, churches not headed by bishops often had much greater cultural influence than cathedral churches (with the notable exception of Canterbury, and, during the eighth and ninth centuries, York). Even more significantly, perhaps, bishops were relatively infrequently chosen from the communities they were appointed to preside over, and even among those who were designated by the outgoing bishop, and who had usually served the latter as deputy, the period of original training had often been at a different, and very often a non-episcopal, church. Monasteries such as *Breedon-on-the-Hill in Mercia, St Augustine's in Kent, and above all the Northumbrian *Whitby and *Melrose trained future bishops. In Northumbria it was (York apart) normal for see-churches to be based in monasteries. *Ripon and Hexham, founded in the 670s as monasteries, soon afterwards became sees; *Lindisfarne was founded as a monastery and a see, with both a bishop and an abbot, with the latter exercising control over the community. It is likely, however, that at Lindisfarne bishops always had a few clergy particularly associated with them; the occupants of Ripon and Hexham are harder to define – Bede terms the members of the Hexham community *fratres*. *Wilfrid had a following of clergy, who moved around with him. In his letter to Ecgberht, bishop of York, Bede advocated that the practice of turning monasteries into sees (as at Ripon and Hexham) should be followed to found new sees, provided that the monks should choose the bishops and assist them in taking care of the diocese.

Contrary to Bede's hopes, no new sees were founded between his death (735) and the early tenth century, and – although evidence for the late eighth and ninth centuries is poor – it appears that episcopal churches and their clergy began to gain in influence. Numerous small private monasteries were taken over by *Worcester cathedral and by Christ Church Canterbury; the community of Lindisfarne likewise seems to have made conscious acquisition of land and churches to act as staging posts for episcopal journeys southwards to York before the late ninth century. At the same time, clerical communities start to be referred to in charters separately from their bishops, and though the terms used (*congregatio, familia, hired* and *hine*) are not very specific, we can learn more about the composition of these groups from witness lists

from the end of the eighth century onwards at Worcester and Canterbury. Both communities were composed of clerics; *c.*800, both had high proportions of priests (about half the community or more), though the ratio shifted in the ninth century, with the number of priests falling and the number of *clerici* (presumably clerks in minor orders) increasing. At about the turn of the eighth and ninth centuries, also, the idea that some land ought to be specifically set aside for the needs of the clergy as opposed to the bishop (signified by terms like for the use – *ad opus, to bryce* – of the community, or for the refectory – *refectorium, biode*) began to gain ground in charters. Canterbury seems to have been closely associated with the contemporary developments in Francia to encourage cathedral clergy to live according to a rule which culminated in the *Rule of Aachen* of 816. Already in 805 the heads of Canterbury's community were described as *praepositi* (the term favoured in the *Rule of Aachen*), and Canterbury also used the term *mensa* to describe land set aside for its clergy. Even so, the existence of the text of any canonical rule cannot be shown in England before the tenth century, and then, to begin with, only in Benedictine houses. Even the term 'canon' to describe a member of a cathedral community does not occur in England, if we exclude the report of the papal legates of 786, before 966 (*Edgar's privilege for New Minster) and is used first by the Benedictine reformer *Æthelwold.

The relative lack of institutional structure left cathedral communities in England at a disadvantage when the Benedictine reformers, chiefly Æthelwold, bishop of Winchester 963–84, started to alter the ecclesiastical map under Edgar. Æthelwold, hostile to the clergy of the Old Minster, his cathedral in *Winchester, had them driven out by a royal *thegn and replaced them with monks. Throughout his writings Æthelwold is consistently hostile to clerics, referring to them as unclean. It was chiefly their tendency to marry which offended him. Æthelwold was greatly influenced by Bede, whose ideas about monastic cathedrals he himself adopted. *Regularis Concordia*, drafted by him, made proposals for how bishops should treat monastic communities in cathedrals. However, although his contemporary, *Oswald of Worcester, started to build a monastery (St Mary's) in the cathedral precinct at Worcester, probably in 966, Oswald did not force the existing clergy (of St Peter's) to change their way of life and Worcester cathedral had a hybrid community until at least the early eleventh century. *Dunstan, though keenly interested in Benedictine monasticism, made no attempt to introduce it into Christ Church, where the first genuine evidence for monks comes from the 1020s. Sherborne became monastic under Bishop *Wulfsige in or just after 998. No other cathedrals became monastic before the Norman Conquest, but Canterbury, Winchester and Worcester dominated the English ecclesiastical scene through their wealth, their educational attainments and their *scriptoria*, and are far better documented than all the rest.

At a few of the others, we can point to a growing interest in a more highly regulated way of life for canons from the mid-eleventh century. The enlarged *Rule of Chrodegang* (i.e. the *Rule of Chrodegang* with a large admixture of the *Rule of Aachen*) was introduced at *Exeter under the Lotharingian-trained *Leofric from 1050. Archbishop *Ealdred set up communal accommodation for canons at York. However, Exeter apart, interest in a common life was weak. At St Paul's and also at *Hereford there was already a trend before the Norman Conquest to create separate landholdings for some of the canons.

Bede, *HE*, passim; C. Cubitt, 'Wilfrid's "Usurping Bishops": Episcopal Elections in Anglo-Saxon England, *c.*600–*c.*800', *NH* 25 (1989), 18–38; Alcuin, *The Bishops, Kings and Saints of York*, ed. P. Godman (OMT, 1982); Brooks, *Canterbury*; *Oswald of Worcester*; I. Atkins, 'The Church of Worcester from the Eighth to the Twelfth Century', *AJ* 17 (1937), 371–91, and 20 (1940), 1–38; *Cuthbert*; M. Lapidge and M. Winterbottom, ed., *Wulfstan of Winchester, Life of St Æthelwold* (OMT, 1991); *Councils & Synods*; J. Barrow, 'Cathedrals, Provosts and Prebends: a Comparison of Twelfth-Century German and English Practice', *JEH* 37 (1986), 536–64; idem, 'English Cathedral Communities and Reform in the late Tenth and the Eleventh Centuries', in D. Rollason, M. Harvey and M. Prestwich, ed., *Anglo-Norman Durham* (Woodbridge, 1994), pp. 25–39.

JULIA BARROW

CELTIC INFLUENCES were as varied as the Celtic regions that fringed the Anglo-Saxon world (see *Celts; *Celtic languages), but the focus here will be on Irish cultural and literary influences (the most significant and best documented). According to *Bede, the Irish played a key role in the conversion of the Anglo-Saxons. The monasteries of *Iona (founded by St *Columba) and *Lindisfarne (under Bishops *Aidan, Finán and Colmán) became centres of Irish *missionary activity and cultural influence in *Northumbria. Irish missionaries were active as well in East Anglia, where St *Fursa experienced his vision, and in the kingdoms of *Middle Anglia and *Mercia, whose first bishop was *Diuma. Certain differences of observance between the Irish and Roman missions (see *Easter controversy) were formally resolved in favour of the Roman party at the Synod of *Whitby in 664, after which Colmán departed to found a monastery in Ireland (later called 'Mayo of the Saxons') for his English followers; but Irish cultural influences remained deeply ingrained (see Hughes). Both King *Oswald and his brother King *Oswiu (who presided at Whitby) spent periods of exile in Iona and could speak Irish. *Adomnán, ninth abbot of Iona, presented his work *De locis sanctis* to Oswiu's son and successor, the Irish-educated *Aldfrith. During the seventh century the Anglo-Saxons adopted Irish forms of script and assimilated many Irish devotional and learned traditions (see *Confession and penance; *prayer, private; *visions). The origin of the Hiberno-Saxon style of illumination exemplified in the *gospelbooks of *Durrow, Kells, and *Lindisfarne (see also *carpet-pages) is still debated, but we know from *Ædiluulf's poem *De abbatibus* that a famed Irish calligrapher named Ultán was active at a dependency of Lindisfarne in the early eighth century. As Bede relates, many Anglo-Saxons went to Ireland to seek instruction and ascetic discipline, a trend deplored by *Aldhelm, who, though probably also a student of an Irish master, had come to regard as superior the instruction of the school of *Canterbury under *Theodore and *Hadrian. Although the Synod of Chelsea (816) legislated against Irish clerics whose ordination was of questionable validity, Irish scholars continued to find welcome at Anglo-Saxon courts throughout the Anglo-Saxon period. King *Alfred maintained contacts with Irish, Welsh and Breton churches, and received three Irish pilgrims who landed in Cornwall in a rudderless boat, an event recorded by the *Anglo-Saxon Chronicle* in the entry for 891, which also records the death of a renowned Irish scholar named *Swifne* (Suibne mac Maele Umhai of Clonmacnois). The court of King *Æthelstan was likewise visited by travelling Irish clerics, and Irish (as well as Breton) books were among Æthelstan's collection. St *Dunstan is reported to have studied the books of Irish pilgrims at *Glastonbury Abbey, and owned a Welsh manuscript which contained some Hiberno-Latin material. 'Up to 1066', as Denis Bethell has remarked, 'we can still say that English and Irish monks shared a common cultural world in which the Irish could still be teachers'.

Evidence for knowledge of Hiberno-Latin exegetical and homiletic literature in Anglo-Saxon England has been collected by Wright (1990), who has also surveyed Irish literary influences in Old English religious literature (1993), with special attention to anonymous homilies that reflect apocryphal cosmology and eschatology disseminated through Irish sources (see *Apocrypha). Other Old English prose texts influenced by Hiberno-Latin texts and traditions include the Old English *Martyrology, the introductions to Psalms I–L in the Paris Psalter, and *Adrian and Ritheus and *Solomon and Saturn. Irish influences on Old English secular literature are surveyed (rather sceptically) by Reichl. Scholars have sought – with more industry than success – traces of Irish myth and secular literature in *Beowulf, and it has been argued that the poet's sympathetic portrayal of noble pagans owes something to the concept of 'natural goodness' as developed in Irish law and literature. Affinities have also been noted between the Old English *'elegies' and Celtic poetry, both Welsh and Irish, and the *Seafarer has been interpreted in the light of the Irish ideal of spiritual *pilgrimage. Some corrupt Irish words and phrases occur in the *charms.

Welsh and Breton ecclesiastical influences become more prominent in the late ninth and early tenth centuries, beginning with *Asser's role as advisor and biographer of King Alfred. A recension of the Cambro-Latin *Historia Brittonum was made during *Edmund's reign. England received Breton exiles and imported many books and relics from Brittany, particularly during the reign of Æthelstan. The Life of one Breton saint (*Machutus) was translated into Old English.

D. Bethell, 'English Monks and Irish Reform in the Eleventh and Twelfth Centuries', in *Historical Studies VIII*, ed. T. D. Williams (Dublin, 1971), pp. 111–35; P. L. Henry, *The Early English and Celtic Lyric* (London, 1966); K. Hughes, 'Some Aspects of Irish Influence on Early English Private Prayer', *Studia Celtica* 5 (1970), 48–61; idem, 'Evidence for Contacts between the Churches of the Irish and English from the Synod of Whitby to the Viking Age', in *England before the Conquest: Studies in Primary Sources presented to Dorothy Whitelock*, ed. P. Clemoes and K. Hughes (Cambridge, 1971), pp. 49–67; K. Reichl, 'Zur Frage des irischen Einflusses auf die altenglische weltliche Dichtung', in *Die Iren und Europa im früheren Mittelalter*, ed. H. Löwe, 2 vols. (Stuttgart, 1982), i.138–68; C. D. Wright, 'Hiberno-Latin and Irish-Influenced Biblical Commentaries, Florilegia, and Homily Collections', in *Sources of Anglo-Saxon Literary Culture: A Trial Version*, ed. F. Biggs *et al.* (Binghamton, NY, 1990), pp. 87–123; idem, *The Irish Tradition in Old English Literature*, CSASE 6 (Cambridge, 1993).

CHARLES D. WRIGHT

CELTIC LANGUAGES form a branch of the Indo-European family of languages and can be divided on geographical and chronological, rather than primarily linguistic, considerations into two main groups: Continental and Insular Celtic. Continental Celtic is known mainly from stone inscriptions, metal plaques, coin legends, as well as from place- and personal names; the earliest texts date from the third century BC. The evidence, though fragmentary, is such to allow us to speak of several subgroups: Gaulish, the language of the Celtic inhabitants of Gaul; Lepontic, used to describe the body of Celtic evidence from Northern Italy; and Hispano-Celtic once spoken in the Iberian peninsula. In addition, ancient authors provide us with evidence for a Celtic language, Galatian, in Asia Minor. When exactly these languages ceased to be spoken is uncertain; some of the evidence can be dated to the third and fourth centuries AD. The precise relationship of the languages to one another, as well as to Insular Celtic, is also a matter for debate. Gaulish and Lepontic are more closely related to each other than either is to Hispano-Celtic and it has been suggested that they form a Gallo-Brittonic group together with the Brittonic branch of the Insular Celtic languages.

Insular Celtic is comprised of Brittonic and Goidelic branches, also known as P- and Q-Celtic respectively since Indo-European */kʷ/ became /p/ in Brittonic and remained as /kʷ/ (which later became /k/) in Goidelic. The Goidelic languages are Irish and its sister languages, Scottish Gaelic and Manx, which are derived from the language of Irish settlers in Scotland and the Isle of Man; Brittonic consists of Welsh, Cornish and Breton, the language of British emigrants introduced into Brittany in the fifth and sixth centuries AD. Another closely related Brittonic language, Cumbric, was spoken in the area of southern Scotland south of the Firth of Clyde, as well as in northern England perhaps until the eleventh century AD.

The earliest Goidelic evidence is in the form of Ogam inscriptions written in Archaic Irish and dating from the fourth to the seventh centuries AD. Additionally, there is a large and varied body of Irish material written in the Latin alphabet dating from the sixth century onwards. Extant material in Scottish Gaelic and Manx is later, beginning in the twelfth and seventeenth centuries respectively. British, the ancestor language of Welsh, Cornish, Breton and Cumbric, is known from place-name evidence, as well as from personal and tribal names attested in Latin inscriptions and Anglo-Saxon sources. Some

Welsh material has survived from the seventh century AD, while the earliest Cornish and Breton sources are of ninth- and tenth-century date.

Distinctive phonological features of the Celtic languages include loss of Indo-European */p/ (where /p/ occurs in the individual branches it is the outcome of secondary phonological developments) and the change of Indo-European */e:/ to /i:/. On a morphological level, the occurrence of conjugated prepositions in Insular Celtic is noteworthy, so called because the preposition forms a paradigmatic unit with a following pronoun: *dom* 'to me' (preposition *do*), *frit* 'against you' (preposition *fri*). Similarly characteristic for the Insular Celtic languages is a system of morphophonemic variation of consonants in initial position, though the realisation of these mutations varies in the individual languages, e.g. Old Irish *cath* 'battle', *a chath* 'his battle'; Middle Welsh *cat* 'battle', *y gat* 'his battle'. The verbal system is characterised by double inflection with a different set of forms used when the verb is preceded by a particle; thus Old Irish *berid* '(s)he bears', *ní beir* '(s)he does not bear'. The verb-initial sentence pattern of Insular Celtic may also be noted; in Continental Celtic, the subject more commonly stands at the head of the sentence.

Contact between the Celtic-speaking peoples and their neighbours is evidenced by the occurrence both of loanwords in the Celtic languages and of Celtic loanwords in other languages. The former are derived mainly from Latin, though Old English loanwords also occur: OE *heafoc* 'hawk' was borrowed into Middle Welsh as *hebawc* and into Old Irish as *seboc*. Borrowings in the other direction include OE *brocc* 'badger' from Welsh *broch*, and OE *drý* 'magician' from Irish *druí*. The number of Celtic, and in particular British, loanwords in Old English, however, is quite small, considering the close political and cultural relationships between Anglo-Saxon England and its Celtic neighbours.

The Celtic Languages, ed. M. J. Ball and G. E. Jones (London, 1993); D. S. Evans, *A Grammar of Middle Welsh* (Dublin, 1976); K. H. Jackson, *Language and History in Early Britain* (Edinburgh, 1953); *The Celtic Languages*, ed. D. Macaulay (Cambridge, 1992); *Stair na Gaeilge in òmòs do Pádraig Ó Fiannachta*, ed. K. McCone et al. (Maynooth, 1994); P. Russell, *An Introduction to the Celtic Languages* (London and New York, 1995); R. Thurneysen, *A Grammar of Old Irish*, 2nd ed. (Dublin, 1946).

MÁIRE NÍ MHAONAIGH

CELTS is the name given to various groups of peoples in western and central Europe and Asia Minor, who appear in archaeological and documentary sources from the sixth century BC onwards. Linguistically, they are identified as speakers of one of the *Celtic languages; their earliest identifying trait, however, is a particular art style. In Anglo-Saxon times, they occupied Ireland, northern, western and south-western Britain, as well as Brittany, to which a number of Celtic Britons from the south-west migrated between the fourth and the sixth centuries AD. At an earlier period, before the onslaught first of Romans and later of Germanic tribes, the Celts occupied large tracts of land from Spain to Ireland, from Scotland to Hungary and as far as Anatolia. There they came to the attention of a number of classical writers who commented on both the geographical location and characteristic features of their neighbours, Κέλτοι, *Celtae* or *Galli* (so-called because their principal settlement area was Gaul). At the end of the sixth century BC, the geographer Hecataeus of Miletus, for example, claimed that *Massalia* (Marseilles) was occupied by Celts, and it is from approximately the same period that they are identifiable in the archaeological record. A large number of graves and residential monuments belonging to a Celtic aristocratic class survive from the late Hallstatt period c.650–400 BC (named after the type-site, Hallstatt in Austria). Equally significant are the material finds from La Tène (in Switzerland) ranging in date from the fifth to the first centuries BC which show a developing culture, and provide evidence in particular for evolving art styles.

Already before the end of this period, however, the Celts were in decline. Defeats by the Romans are recorded from the third century BC; two centuries later Gaul was taken by Julius Caesar. Their power diminished, but the Celts maintained their language for a period as indicated by the survival of Continental Celtic inscriptions from the third and fourth centuries AD. Moreover, aspects of their culture were incorporated into the emerging Gallo-Roman way of life. The pattern is similar in Britain where, despite hostile encounters between Romans and Celts, a certain accommodation was reached and cross-cultural exchange was such to enable us to speak of a Romano-Celtic society.

It was this society which attacking Angles, Saxons, Franks and Jutes encountered in the fourth and fifth centuries AD, first as raiders, later as settlers. While Roman authority collapsed, Celtic Britons sought to resist but eventually became confined to the northern, western and south-western regions of Britain. Some, as already mentioned, escaped to Brittany. The Celts in

Ireland remained secure and indeed established a number of settlements in Argyll in Scotland, Dyfed in Wales, and *Cornwall in the same period. Accounts of hostile encounters between these various groups survive from the Anglo-Saxon period: the Welsh poem, Y *Gododdin 'The Gododdin', purports to describe a sixth-century battle fought by the Gododdin of south-east Scotland against the English of *Deira and *Bernicia. Similarly, a tenth-century Welsh poem of prophecy, *Armes Prydein Vawr 'The Great Prophecy of Britain', calls on the Irish, and the Hiberno-Norse, to form an alliance with the men of Scotland, Wales, Cornwall and Brittany to expel the Saxons. Other sources, however, provide evidence for contacts of a different kind: it has been suggested that hanging bowls found in Anglo-Saxon contexts are Celtic in origin and certain techniques used by the Celts in filigree work were derived from Anglo-Saxon England. Irish *missionaries played a large role in the *conversion of *Northumbria, and one of the Northumbrian kings, *Aldfrith, son of *Oswiu, is given an Irish name, Fland Fína, in Irish annalistic *compilations.

Moreover, relations between the different Celtic groups are equally diverse. Medieval *hagiography preserves memories of visits by Welsh and Irish clerics to each other's monasteries, and Old Irish sagas provide many references to Irish kings and nobles finding refuge with kings of Alba (northern Britain). The ninth-century text, *Historia Brittonum, on the other hand, claims that one of the Gododdin princes, Cunedda, along with his eight sons, had earlier succeeded in driving the Irish from all British lands. We would do well to remember, therefore, that the term Celts implies neither unity nor uniformity, and an understanding of the various peoples identified as such can only come from an examination of their many and diverse cultures.

H. Birkhan, Kelten (Vienna, 1996); B. Cunliffe, The Celtic World (London, 1979); M. J. Green, ed., The Celtic World (London and New York, 1995); P. Mac Cana, Celtic Mythology (London, 1983); B. Raftery, ed., L'art celtique (Paris, 1990); K. H. Schmidt, ed., Geschichte und Kultur der Kelten (Heidelberg, 1986); P. Sims-Williams, 'The Visionary Celt: the Construction of an Ethnic Preconception', CMCS 11 (Summer, 1986), 71–96; The Celts / I Celti [exhibition catalogue] (Milan, 1991).

MÁIRE NÍ MHAONAIGH

CEMETERIES, FURNISHED, are burial grounds where some or all of the graves contain *grave goods. Burial with grave goods was practised on the Continent before the Germanic migration to England, and continued as a tradition amongst the pagan Anglo-Saxons in England, both in the cremation and the inhumation ritual. Furnished cemeteries occur wherever the Anglo-Saxons settled, and are often the best or only evidence for the earliest presence of Anglo-Saxons and the penetration of Anglo-Saxon culture in England. The richest furnished cemeteries with the highest concentration of gold, *jewellery and exotic imports are found in the south-east of England. Cemeteries towards the periphery of Anglo-Saxon influence, in the west and north of England, tended to be more poorly furnished, perhaps representing the lower standard of living of these communities, or perhaps reflecting the greater influence of the British population. Thousands of furnished cemeteries have been identified in England, ranging in size from under fifty burials in the smaller inhumation cemeteries to hundreds of burials in the larger cremation cemeteries. Although only a handful of furnished cemeteries have been excavated in their entirety, they provide the single greatest source of information about fifth- to seventh-century Anglo-Saxon *settlement, society and economy.

The graves within a furnished cemetery demonstrate great diversity in their grave goods, from a single clay pot or iron knife to a complex set of goods. This diversity is thought to indicate the social structure of the mortuary population, but there may be other explanations involving religious beliefs or family rituals. Furnished inhumation cemeteries may also be characterised by variations in grave structure. Graves may have been marked by barrows, cairns, ditches and one or more timber posts. Occasionally, animals may have been buried in separate graves within the furnished cemetery. Orientation within the furnished inhumation cemetery tended to be variable, and burials were loosely grouped rather than set in rows. Cremation cemeteries were considerably larger than inhumation cemeteries, but are characterised by the same loose groupings, sometimes with several cremation urns buried together in the same pit. Furnished cemeteries appear to have been located away from the area of settlement. Sometimes the earliest burials may be focused around a prehistoric barrow or a prominent geographical feature, but more commonly the earliest burial, usually the wealthiest, acted as the focus of the developing cemetery. No clear evidence of buildings has been found associated with furnished cemeteries, although timber structures defined by post-holes have been found marking cremations at Alton (Hants.).

Towards the end of the period in which furnished cemeteries were used, there was a decline in the variety of grave goods. In the seventh century, deposition of weapons became more restricted, and furnished cemeteries became more organised. Burials orientated west-east in rows predominated, and cremation disappeared as a ritual. Up to three-quarters of burials in these 'Final Phase' cemeteries may be unfurnished, and this fading-out of furnished burial may represent a transitional phase from pagan to Christian society.

The tradition of furnished burial declined with the spread of Christianity in the seventh century and early eighth, and can to some extent be ascribed to it. There are, however, notable furnished burials with Christian symbols, for example those from Roundway Down (Wilts.) and Desborough (Northants.) which include gold and garnet necklaces with crosses. These are likely to be the graves of very early Christians before the introduction of churchyard burial. The most spectacular known example of a furnished Christian burial is that of St *Cuthbert. Whilst individual furnished burial may have continued into the Christian period, furnished burials as a whole ceased when cemeteries were associated with churches. No furnished cemeteries are known to have continued into use as church graveyards, but occasionally the earliest burials within a church cemetery were furnished, as at St Paul's in the Bail, *Lincoln. By the eighth century unfurnished Christian cemeteries associated with churches came into use, and the old furnished cemeteries were finally abandoned.

The significance of furnished cemeteries to the burying population remains unclear. The majority of grave furniture is associated with apparel, and no special symbolism need be given to these items beyond indicating sex and perhaps social status. The presence of food and drink in some furnished burials may indicate a belief that the dead would need sustenance in an afterlife, or they may be part of a ritual funeral feast held by the mourners at the time of burial.

Anglo Saxon Cemeteries 1979, ed. P. Rahtz, T. M. Dickinson and L. Watts, BAR Brit. ser. 82 (Oxford, 1980); A. L. S. Meaney, *A Gazetteer of Early Anglo-Saxon Burial Sites* (London, 1964); *Anglo-Saxon Cemeteries: a Reappraisal*, ed. E. Southworth (London, 1990); *Making of England*; E.-J. Pader, *Symbolism, Social Relations and the Interpretation of Mortuary Remains*, BAR Brit. ser. 130 (Oxford, 1982)

SALLY CRAWFORD

CEMETERIES, UNFURNISHED, are those in which most or all of the graves do not have any *grave goods. Unfurnished graves are often found in cemeteries in which grave goods are frequent (cf. *cemeteries, furnished); they are attributed to people of lower status, though other ideological explanations should be allowed for. The characteristic unfurnished cemetery is, however, one in which the graves are usually set in rows, with a west-east orientation, heads to west; they do not include any cremations. Such cemeteries have their more general antecedents in Late Roman north-west Europe, but are numerous in Anglo-Saxon England from the later seventh century onwards. They are, in the seventh–eighth centuries, contemporary with furnished burial of the 'Final Phase' or 'Conversion Period'. Cemeteries of this class are frequently found in and around churches. While their characteristics became conventionally associated with churchyard burial, this is not necessarily due to the influence of Christianity; some are on sites with no known Christian nucleus or finds.

Burial in churches began, for certain sectors of society, in the earlier seventh century, and became common in churchyards from the eighth century and later. In up to two-thirds of archaeologically-dated seventh- to eleventh-century churches, the earliest data are of the burials themselves. There may be thus many cases where the cemetery preceded the building of a church; they are, nevertheless, on new sites. There is no certain instance of an unfurnished cemetery being a continuation of a furnished one of earlier date.

There is no evidence from written sources that the church discouraged grave goods. It has been suggested that they were no longer necessary in a self-proclaimed egalitarian ideology and a life after death; and less effective in the communication of ideological commitment to the church. This is in contrast to the signals transmitted by rich furnished graves or barrow burials. Another explanation has been that both general taxation (in the developing power of state and kingship) and church taxation ('gravescot') were creaming off surplus formerly used for grave goods. In the context of the church, this was directed towards ideological investment in church building, vestments, manuscript preparation, and liturgical metalwork.

The archaeological evidence for unfurnished cemeteries has accrued principally from the excavation of churchyards and monastic precincts in the last few decades, in town and country, such as *Winchester, *Repton, *Barton-on-Humber and

*Raunds. Formerly, the absence of grave goods discouraged their exploration; but the recognition of their intrinsic interest as settlement indicators; and the increase in holistic approaches to church archaeology led to an explosion of data. An associated factor is the increased interest in human remains, leading to a better understanding of community *diet, health, life-expectation, demography, and the history of *diseases.

In these cemeteries, there are many variations within the norms characterising them. Diversity is found in spatial organisation, memorials in stone or wood, grave depth, body container or wrapping, special treatment (grave structure, 'charcoal burial', or 'pillow' stones) and body position (normally supine and extended, but with arm, head or leg variation). All these are potentially meaningful in terms of mortuary behaviour and ideology related to belief, affiliation, kinship, gender, age, status, 'custom', and cultural/ethnic affinity.

The general distribution of unfurnished cemeteries is broadly similar to that of those furnished, in the conversion period. There were also, however, numerous examples further west (such as Cannington) where largely unfurnished field cemeteries of late Roman and later centuries gave way to churchyard burial as this became universal in the later eighth century onward.

A. Boddington, *Raunds Furnells: the Anglo-Saxon Church and Churchyard* (London, 1996); D. Bullough, 'Burial, Community and Belief in the early Medieval West', in *Ideal and Reality in Frankish and Anglo-Saxon Society: Studies presented to J. M. Wallace-Hadrill*, ed. P. Wormald, D. Bullough and R. Collins (Oxford, 1983), pp. 177–201; H. Geake, *The Use of Grave-goods in Conversion-period England c.600–c.850 AD*, BAR Brit. ser. 261 (Oxford, 1997); R. K. Morris, *The Church in British Archaeology* (London, 1983); P. A. Rahtz, 'Grave Orientation', *Archaeological Journal* 135 (1978), 1–14; P. A. Rahtz, T. M. Dickinson and L. Watts, ed., *Anglo-Saxon Cemeteries 1979* (Oxford, 1980).

PHILIP RAHTZ

CENSERS, in the form of cast bronze bowl-shaped containers swung on chains to disperse the scent of burning incense, are illustrated in manuscripts and were certainly used in Anglo-Saxon England, but only two certain examples survive: a sixth- to seventh-century import from *Byzantium found near the precinct of *Glastonbury Abbey, and a ninth-century example from the site of the Anglo-Saxon church at North Elmham (Norfolk), which is known to have been in existence between 803 and 840. A small group of late tenth-century tower-shaped cast openwork bronze attachments have also traditionally been identified as censer-covers, though this interpretation presents some practical problems, not least the absence of the square bowls which they would require. The recent discoveries at Thetford of two diminutive versions of the type, much too small to have served as covers, add to doubts about this identification.
D. M. Wilson, *Anglo-Saxon Ornamental Metalwork 700–1100 in the British Museum, Catalogue of Antiquities of the Later Saxon Period*, I (London, 1964), pp. 53–4, 122–4, 151–2, 157–8; *Golden Age of AS Art*, pp. 19–90; *The Making of England*, pp. 94, 238–9.

LESLIE WEBSTER

CENWALD: *see* Koenwald

CEOLFRITH, abbot of *Monkwearmouth-Jarrow (688–716). Born c.642 to a noble family, he abandoned secular life in his youth. He spent time at monasteries in both the north and the south before moving to Wearmouth at the request of *Benedict Biscop, with whom he later journeyed to *Rome. Appointed the first abbot of Jarrow (dedicated 685), he took charge also of Wearmouth on Benedict's death in 689 and presided over the twin foundation during its most thriving period. He died at Langres, Burgundy, en route to Rome to present gifts, including the Codex *Amiatinus, to St Peter's.
Sharpe, *Handlist*, 183; *VBOH*, ed. Plummer, i.388–404 [*Vita S. Ceolfridi*]; *EHD* i.697–708; P. Hunter Blair, *The World of Bede*, rev. ed. (Cambridge, 1990), chs. 15–18; I. Wood, *The Most Holy Abbot Ceolfrid*, Jarrow Lecture (1995).

RICHARD MARSDEN

CEOLNOTH, archbishop of Canterbury (833–70). Following the death of Archbishop *Wulfred, on 24 March 832, the succession at *Canterbury appears to have been disputed between two candidates, Feologild and Suithred. The dispute might in some way reflect the complexities of the prevailing political situation, with King *Ecgberht and his son King *Æthelwulf quite recently established in *Kent, and with Wiglaf more recently restored as king of the Mercians; yet whatever the immediate outcome of the dispute, we find in fact that a certain Ceolnoth was 'elected bishop and consecrated' in 833, and 'received the pallium' in 834 (*ASC*). It is not known of Ceolnoth whence he came, or where his sympathies would lie; but he would have found that Wulfred's was a difficult act to follow. It may not have been entirely clear in the early 830s how the archbishop stood in relation to the king of the Mercians, or how Ecgberht and Æthelwulf would handle their own interests in the south-east. Moreover, the *Vikings (who had ravaged Sheppey in 835) were now on the loose, and Kentish churches would need some guarantee of effective protection. In 836 Ceolnoth convened a church council at Croft, in Leicestershire, which was attended by King Wiglaf (S 190); and in 838 he came to a formal agreement with Ecgberht and Æthelwulf, at *Kingston-upon-Thames (S 1438), whereby the archbishop undertook that he and his successors would remain ever loyal to the kings and their heirs, and the kings for their part promised to respect the liberties of the church. Ceolnoth held a church council *æt Astran* (unidentified, but probably a place in Wessex) in 839 (S 1438), and another at London in 845 (S 1194); and since kings were seemingly not present on either occasion, it may be that the churchmen were being left more to their own devices. The episcopal professions surviving from Ceolnoth's period of office at Canterbury demonstrate that he maintained the authority of his church throughout the Southumbrian province; yet the quality of this evidence stands in contrast to the lack of evidence for the holding of church councils from the mid 840s onwards. It is conceivable that councils were held on a regular basis, and have simply left no trace of their activities because they were not attended by kings; but it is perhaps more likely that councils were not held, reflecting the general disruption caused by the escalation of Viking raids, or (more particularly) the archbishop's disinclination to convene councils at a time when priorities had changed. Ceolnoth's pontificate is otherwise associated with the spectacular decline of Latinity in southern England, which reached its nadir under his successor in the 870s (represented by S 344 and S 287). It would be tempting in this connection to invoke the impact of the Viking sack of Canterbury and *London in 851 (*ASC*). There is, however, a considerable amount of information, in *charters, on the lesser clergy of Kent throughout the ninth century, and if Ceolnoth lacked competent scribes in the 850s and 860s it was certainly not for lack of sufficient manpower (e.g. S 1269 (863 × 867), S 338 (867), and S 1200 (867 × 870)). The question arises, on the other hand, whether the community at Christ Church was organised in strict accordance with the Rule of Chrodegang, or whether it remained in some more general sense monastic. Archbishop Ceolnoth died on 4 February 870. He was succeeded by a certain Æthelred, who held office as archbishop from 870 to 888, and who was himself succeeded by *Plegmund (890–923).

Brooks, *Canterbury*, pp. 143–9, 160–4 [community], 167–74 [scribes], 198–206 [Kentish minsters]; M. Lapidge, 'Latin Learning in Ninth-Century England', *ALL* i.409–54, esp. 435–8, 446–54; S. Keynes, 'The Control of Kent in the Ninth Century', *EME* 2 (1993), 111–31, at 123–4, 127–8; idem, *The Councils of Clofesho*, Brixworth Lecture 1993 (Leicester, 1994), pp. 50–1; C. R. E. Cubitt, *Anglo-Saxon Church Councils c.650–c.850* (Leicester, 1995), pp. 236–8; B. Langefeld, '*Regula canonicorum* or *Regula monasterialis uitae*? The Rule of Chrodegang and Archbishop Wulfred's Reforms at Canterbury', *ASE* 25 (1996), 21–36, at 33.

SIMON KEYNES

CERDIC (d. 534?) was the founder-king from whom all rulers of the *Gewisse and *Wessex claimed descent. His arrival in the Solent and victories over the British are described in the *Anglo-Saxon Chronicle* (s.a. 495–534), but there are good reasons to doubt the accuracy of both the chronology and the mythic events. Not the least interesting fact about Cerdic is that his name appears to be a Germanisation of the British name *Caraticos. If he was a historical personage he may have been the leader of a mixed British/ Saxon group in the upper Thames where the *Gewisse* are first reliably recorded.

D. N. Dumville, 'The West Saxon Genealogical Regnal List and the Chronology of early Wessex', *Peritia* 4 (1985), 21–66; R. Coates, 'On some Controversy Surrounding *Gewissae/Gewissei*, *Cerdic* and Ceawlin', *Nomina* 13 (1989/90), 1–11.

B. A. E. YORKE

CERNE, BOOK OF (Cambridge, University Library, MS L1.1.10), is a private devotional compilation and a member of the 'Tiberius' group of Southumbrian manuscripts. Art historical and palaeographical analogies, especially with *charters, suggest that it was made in the W. Midlands (*Mercia) around 820–40. It contains an Old English Exhortation to Prayer; Passion and Resurrection narratives from the Gospels, with evangelist miniatures, decorated incipits, and an *acrostic poem (fol. 21) naming 'Aedeluald episcopus'; seventy-four prayers and hymns (some with Old English *gloss) forming a quasi-litanic invocation; a Breviate Psalter (ascribed to Bishop Aedeluald); a Harrowing of Hell text related to liturgical drama. These ninety-eight folios are sandwiched between fourteenth-century to sixteenth-century accretions relating to Cerne Abbas, Dorset – a post-Dissolution antiquarian arrangement. The volume was probably never at Cerne, annotations suggesting a medieval *Worcester provenance and with early influence upon *Winchester materials. By 1697 it belonged to John

Moore, bishop of *Norwich and *Ely. Aedeluald has been variously identified as *Æthilwald, bishop of *Lindisfarne (721–40) and as bishop of *Lichfield (818–30). Arguments presenting Cerne as substantially a copy of an earlier nucleus of texts associated with the earlier Aedeluald entail tampering with the acrostic to achieve Northumbrian spelling, whilst unconditional association with Aedeluald of Lichfield entails accepting (near-) compositional corruptions in latinity. Cerne draws heavily upon earlier Roman, Celtic and eastern material, but seems to be a conscious thematic compilation (along with related prayerbooks: BL., Royal 2.A.XX and Harley 2965), focusing primarily upon participation within the Communion of Saints. At least a secondary textual association with Aedeluald of Lichfield or his circle remains likely. The unusual evangelist miniatures likewise conflate culturally varied visual sources, to form multivalent images which explore (with the aid of their inscriptions and links to biblical and exegetical sources) the nature of Christ, the gospels and the aspirations of the Just. Cerne represents the culmination of the Insular experience, on the eve of the *Viking incursions.
A. B. Kuypers, *The Prayer Book of Aedeluald the Bishop* (Cambridge, 1902); M. P. Brown, *The Book of Cerne. Prayer, Patronage and Power in Ninth-Century England* (London and Toronto, 1996).

MICHELLE P. BROWN

CHAD, ST (= Ceadda, d. 672), abbot of *Lastingham (N. Yorks.), and first bishop of *Mercia and *Lindsey at *Lichfield, was a pupil of St *Aidan at *Lindisfarne, and gained part of his monastic training in Ireland. His brother Cedd was made bishop of the East Saxons, and had also established a monastery at Lastingham, which Chad took charge of when Cedd died of the plague in 664. This same year King *Oswiu of *Northumbria had chosen *Wilfrid to be bishop of *York, but Wilfrid, having gone to France to be consecrated bishop delayed his return to England. In Wilfrid's absence, Oswiu chose Chad to be bishop instead, sending him to be consecrated by the archbishop of Canterbury, *Deusdedit. By the time Chad reached *Kent, Deusdedit had died, so he was eventually consecrated by Wine, bishop of the West Saxons. In 669 *Theodore, archbishop of Canterbury, deposed Chad and restored Wilfrid to York. Chad retired to Lastingham, but was soon summoned to become the first bishop of Mercia and Lindsey. Chad is said to have followed Aidan's style in insisting upon travelling around his large diocese on foot, until, as *Bede tells us, Arch-

bishop Theodore man-handled him on to a horse. Chad died of the plague on 2 March 672, and was buried close to the church of St Mary in Lichfield. His remains were later translated into the newly-built church of St Peter (on the site of the present cathedral).
Bede, *HE* iii.28, iv.3.

R. C. LOVE

CHANCERY, ROYAL. A term applied to the royal writing-office of the tenth and eleventh centuries, staffed by priests who served in the royal household. The arrangements which existed in Anglo-Saxon England for the production of *charters and other written documents have long been the subject of intense scrutiny, not least because it is a matter which determines our use of the documents for historical purposes and which affects our estimation of the development of royal government in Anglo-Saxon England. The debate can be reduced to a choice between two basic positions, each of which is capable of some refinement. On the one hand, it might be supposed that charters were always drawn up by 'ecclesiastical' as opposed to 'royal' scribes, operating on behalf of the beneficiaries in the *scriptoria of 'local' religious houses, or in the entourage of a bishop or abbot on the move. On the other hand, it might be supposed that (sooner or later) kings took a more direct interest in the production of the charters which ran in their names, and, in particular, that in the tenth and eleventh centuries charters were normally though by no means invariably drawn up by a central (and thus putatively 'royal') agency staffed by priests attached to the king's household. It would be unhelpful, however, to polarise the issues at stake, and the solution is to admit the possibility of development, variation, and change. In the late seventh, eighth, and ninth centuries, charters were generally drawn up by ecclesiastical scribes, operating in the scriptoria of episcopal sees and other religious houses, and acting either on behalf of the king as grantor or on behalf of the beneficiary; indeed, subtle distinctions can be recognised between the diplomatic practices which prevailed in one centre of production (for example *Worcester) as opposed to another (for example Christ Church, *Canterbury). There is reason to believe, however, that different practices may have developed in the kingdom of the West Saxons, and that already during the ninth century charters of the West Saxon kings, for estates in *Wessex, were drawn up by a central or 'royal' agency acting in the king's name on behalf of a variety of lay and ecclesiastical beneficiaries; the agency in question was probably the succession of priests serving in the royal household.

The position is complicated in the first decade of the tenth century by the close links which existed during the reign of King *Edward the Elder between the royal court and the Old and the New Minsters at *Winchester; but production of charters by royal priests seems to have remained the norm. Not one charter survives for the period from c.910 until Edward's death in 924, suggesting that the production of new charters may have been kept under restraint or even suspended for the duration of the campaign against the Danish settlers in southern England. A single agency was responsible for the production of the remarkable series of charters issued in the name of King *Æthelstan between 928 and 935, and there can be little doubt that this agency can be personified as a priest attached to the royal household; his charters set him apart as a person of singular distinction, determined to project an image of royal power commensurate with the emergence of a new political order in 927 (the 'kingdom of the English'). The production of charters by a royal agency appears to have remained the norm in the central decades of the tenth century; and just as some of the important developments in tenth-century script may be seen on this basis to have originated in the royal writing-office, so too is it possible to explain changing patterns of diplomatic style in terms of changes in personnel at the king's court.

It should be emphasised, however, that the arrangements which existed in the tenth century for the production of charters were not inflexible, and that there was always scope for the adoption of a different procedure in a particular case. For example, a distinctive series of charters known to modern scholarship as the 'alliterative' type was apparently produced in the 940s and 950s by an agency which operated in the normal way at meetings of the king's council, and which seems to have been associated in some way with *Koenwald, bishop of Worcester (c.928–58). Another distinctive series of charters, known as the 'Dunstan B' type, appears to have been produced by an agency working perhaps at *Glastonbury abbey in the early 950s, and on occasion by special request thereafter. The most strikingly anomalous charter is also the most famous: the so-called 'Foundation Charter' of the New Minster, Winchester (S 745), produced (in book form) under the auspices of Bishop *Æthelwold at the Old Minster in 966, written throughout in gold letters and with a prefatory image of King *Edgar presenting the charter to Christ (see pl. 21).

The draftsmen of charters became more adventurous in the 990s, producing documents of considerable interest and literary sophistication; and although 'centralised' production appears to have remained the norm for the duration of *Æthelred's reign, it would appear in certain cases that the draftsmen worked in close collaboration with representatives of the beneficiaries. A particularly important charter for *Abingdon Abbey, issued in 993 (S 876), is a case in point. Practices in the eleventh century are best characterised as flexible. Certain bishops, and some other high ecclesiastics, were authorised to draw up charters on the king's behalf, for themselves as beneficiaries or for other parties; there is some evidence of 'local' production, particularly in the south-west; and, at court, the employment of 'foreign' priests in the households of *Cnut, *Harthacnut, and *Edward the Confessor finds due reflection in the adoption of 'continental' practices and terminology. The Lotharingian priest Regenbald was described in the 1060s as the king's chancellor; and it is in the same spirit that the royal writing-office of the tenth and eleventh centuries might reasonably be described as a royal chancery.

P. Chaplais, 'The Origin and Authenticity of the Royal Anglo-Saxon Diploma', and other papers by the same author, repr. in *Prisca Munimenta*, ed. F. Ranger (London, 1973); S. Keynes, *The Diplomas of King Æthelred 'the Unready' 978–1016* (Cambridge, 1980), esp. pp. 14–83; Brooks, *Canterbury*, esp. pp. 327–30; P. Chaplais, 'The Royal Anglo-Saxon "Chancery" of the Tenth Century Revisited', *Studies in Medieval History presented to R. H. C. Davis*, ed. H. Mayr-Harting and R. I. Moore (London, 1985), pp. 41–51; S. Keynes, 'Royal Government and the Written Word in Late Anglo-Saxon England', *The Uses of Literacy in Early Mediaeval Europe*, ed. R. McKitterick (Cambridge, 1990), pp. 226–57; idem, 'The Dunstan B Charters', *ASE* 23 (1994), 165–93; idem, 'The West Saxon Charters of King Æthelwulf and his Sons', *EHR* 109 (1994), 1109–49; D. N. Dumville, 'English Square Minuscule Script: the Mid-Century Phases', *ASE* 23 (1994), 133–64; S. Keynes, 'Regenbald the Chancellor [sic]', *ANS* 10 (1988), 185–222; idem, 'Giso, Bishop of Wells (1061–88)', *ANS* 19 (1997), 203–71; *Charters of Abingdon Abbey*, ed. S. E. Kelly, Anglo Saxon Charters 7–8 (Oxford, 2000). SIMON KEYNES

CHANT. Evidence concerning the nature and state of ecclesiastical chant in Anglo-Saxon England before the end of the tenth century is scarce. That no chant book copied before this period survives, despite the fact that such books are more than likely to have existed, represents an especial impoverishment. Nevertheless, a series of remarks in *Bede's *Historia ecclesiastica* suggests that, since the arrival of *Augustine and his disciples in *Kent in 597, numerous attempts had been made to teach and to spread the singing of Roman chant. At *Clofeshoh* in 747, a council decreed that 'baptism was to be performed and the mass celebrated, according to the forms received in writing from the Roman church'.

Questions concerning the level at which such an imposition of practice might be articulated can be examined in the light of *Alcuin's florilegium *De laude Dei*. 'A liturgical enthusiast, acknowledged expert and innovator' (Bullough), Alcuin included in this collection a list of around 100 liturgical texts for singing ('De antiphonario'). The assorted provenances of these – including Roman, Gallican and Hispanic material – demonstrates the degree to which in the late eighth century liturgical practice based on Roman models remained open to widespread influence and variation. While bishops were evidently concerned to promote good and proper singing of chant according to Roman procedures, the detail of what was actually sung did not follow a rigid pattern.

The revival of monastic life led by *Dunstan, *Æthelwold and *Oswald in the last half of the tenth century produced a different, more uniform, result. By this time, largely as a result of Carolingian impulses, liturgical practice throughout western Europe had become more standardised. The continental model was certainly familiar to the monastic reformers. Having consulted monks from *Fleury and Ghent, *Æthelwold himself drew up the *Regularis concordia*, a text containing extensive liturgical instructions, intended to bind together monastic houses of monks and nuns alike.

As a body of 'Roman' liturgical practice (highly shaped by practice north of the Alps, and thus 'Romano-Frankish') became more widely adopted, so local creativity found other means of expression. In the tropes and sequences composed as elaboration of existing chant–repertories in the composition of which *Winchester Cathedral took a leading role, in offices composed in honour of local saints (of which the office for St *Cuthbert copied already in the early eleventh century in Cambridge, Corpus Christi College 183 is an outstanding example), and in polyphonic settings of chant, Anglo-Saxon musicians displayed a wealth of creative talent and learning.

It was probably only at this time that conditions in England were favourable to the development of musical notation as an indigenous practice and recognised means of communicating and recording the chant repertory. The number of extant books containing notated chants copied between the late tenth and the end of the eleventh century is dominated by those of highest grade, pontificals. Books primarily intended for use in connection with chanting include Le Havre, BM 330 (Missal of the New Minster, Winchester), Durham Cathedral, Cosin V.V.6 (Gradual of Christ Church, Canterbury), Cambridge, Corpus Christi College 391 (the 'Wulstan Collectar', from Worcester, containing chants for the offices), London, BL, 2961 (the 'Leofric Collectar', an equivalent book from Exeter), London, BL, Harley 1117 (from Christ Church, Canterbury, containing offices for Cuthbert, Benedict and *Guthlac) and the three celebrated Tropers: Cambridge, Corpus Christi College 473, Oxford, Bodleian Library, Bodley 775 and London, BL, Cotton Caligula A.xiv.

Regularis Concordia, ed. T. Symons (London, 1953); A. Planchart, *The Repertory of Tropes at Winchester*, 2 vols. (Princeton, NJ, 1977); S. K. Rankin, 'The Liturgical Background of the Old English Advent Lyrics: A Reappraisal', in Clemoes FS, pp. 317–40; D. A. Bullough, 'Alcuin and the Kingdom of Heaven: Liturgy, Theology, and the Carolingian Age', in his *Carolingian Renewal: Sources and Heritage* (Manchester, 1991), pp. 161–240; L. M. Sole, 'Some Anglo-Saxon Cuthbert Liturgica: the Manuscript Evidence', *RB* 108 (1998), 104–44.

SUSAN RANKIN

CHARMS. Two scholars, Grendon and Storms, have published collections of Anglo-Saxon charms, but neither provided a succinct definition. If the equations of charm with *amulet, or with personal attractiveness, are set aside, a charm is a formula by which an end is attempted by *magic means. All charms published by the two editors have (to our way of thinking) good ends (for example, exorcism or against snake bite), but sometimes they oppose black magic or devilish tricks. The Old English word for a charm is *galdor*, related to the verb *galan*, 'to sing'; and at the heart of most (but not all) charms is an incantation or the equivalent. Perhaps the oldest of the Anglo-Saxon charms are the dozen (none, however, recorded before the mid-tenth century) which contain passages in Old English verse, usually somewhat irregular and obscure, so that a previous period of oral transmission may be indicated: they resemble some much older (for example, Babylonian) charms, and illustrate the range of charm purposes. Five of them are for medical conditions (one against *dweorh*, 'fever', one for a woman unable to raise a child, one for the 'water-elf disease', one for a wen, and one for *færstice*, 'a sudden stitch' – perhaps including lumbago), three (two nearly identical) were for lost or stolen cattle, one for the improvement of agricultural land, one, the 'Nine Herbs' charm, is against poison, one is to settle a swarm of bees, and one to assure a safe journey. In place of the vernacular incantation there is sometimes a passage of gibberish, or of Latin, appealing for help to Christ or the saints. Sometimes the 'words of power' are to be written as a kind of amulet, or are replaced by a diagram. Around the incantation are various instructions to the patient, magician or exorcist; these can include the gathering of herbs (sometimes with rituals such as silence, and at a specified time), and or their preparation as part of an ointment or potion, which may be applied or consumed with yet more ritual. Other materials, such as communion wafers, are sometimes specified.

F. Grendon, 'The Anglo-Saxon Charms', *Journal of American Folklore* 22 (1909), 105–237; K. L. Jolly, *Popular Religion in Late Saxon England: Elf Charms in Context* (Chapel Hill, NC, and London, 1996); G. Storms, *Anglo-Saxon Magic* (The Hague, 1948).

AUDREY MEANEY

CHARTER BOUNDS (also called 'perambulations') are descriptions of the boundaries of land-units, generally found in 'boundary clauses' within charters. The perambulation typically starts towards one corner of the estate (commonly the south-eastern or south-western angle) and proceeds clockwise from feature to feature around the perimeter to end back where it began. Some bounds survive in 'original' grants, where the script, formulae and witnesses are consistent with the date given in the text. Most, however, occur only in cartulary copies. In such cases, care is needed over dating: even grants considered 'authentic' on diplomatic grounds may have an interpolated boundary clause (e.g. S 99, an apparently eighth-century charter with what are clearly late Old English bounds). A number are found divorced from any charter, both in cartularies and (rarely) as separate slips of parchment. Although some later medieval cartularies are notable for texts distorted through repeated copying or perambulations comprehensively updated into Middle English, most texts reflect a conservatism on the part of their copyists, and the bounds as a whole form a relatively coherent body of material.

Our earliest 'original' charter (of Hlothhere, king of Kent, 679: S 8) notes, but does not supply, the estate's 'very well-known boundaries indicated by me and my officials'; the next (697: S 19) gives rudimentary bounds. These early boundaries are brief Latin statements of location, based ultimately on Roman models. Their evolution into the detailed vernacular descriptions characteristic of the tenth century is hard to trace, due to the uneven nature of the surviving evidence. Of the thirty-five boundaries in manuscripts generally accepted as dating before AD 900, twenty-six relate to land in Kent, and only one to 'Wessex'. With one exception, none of these thirty-five boundaries cites more than five boundary marks; typically, they name the features on the four cardinal points, with a tendency to start in the east and run clockwise. The emphatic exception is the one West Saxon charter (S 298, dated 847) with its detailed perambulation in English, mentioning some forty-five landscape features. That this text appears to depend on a written source drawn up by a Cornishman makes it all the more tantalising that there is no further 'original' evidence for Wessex until 931. To fill the gap we must turn to cumulative and circumstantial evidence from charters in later copies. Such sources indicate that the cardinal points format also prevailed in early Wessex. From the 770s, detailed Latin bounds occur sporadically, in perambulation format but with underlying reference to the compass points. Outside the conservative south-east, bounds in Latin peter out after the early years of the ninth century.

Unfortunately, however, few vernacular perambulations can be unequivocally dated earlier than the 930s. Indeed, roughly four-fifths of the extant vernacular bounds come from documents bearing tenth- and eleventh-century dates, three-quarters of which fall within the years 930–1000; many of those undated or in ostensibly earlier charters will also belong to this period. Equally distorted is their geographical distribution, the overwhelming majority of bounds relating to land south and west of *Watling Street, with over half coming from just the five (pre-1974) counties of Worcestershire, Wiltshire, Hampshire, Berkshire, and *Kent.

Evidence is as sparse for the mechanisms whereby surveys were maintained and updated as it is for procedures for compiling and recording them. In a late-ninth-century dispute one party leads the other around 'all the boundaries', reading the land-marks from *þam aldan bocum* 'the old documents' (S 1441). Similarly, in the early eleventh century the bishop of *Hereford rides round his estate together with other contending parties, the exact course of the boundary being verified by those who 'had marked the bounds for him' when he acquired the land (S 1460). And S 1603 mentions a perambulation by horseback and by boat.

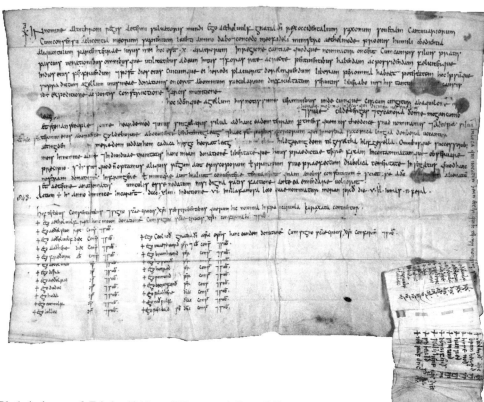

Pl. 6 A charter of Æthelwulf, king of Wessex and Kent (843).

Pl. 7 A writ of Edward the Confessor for the monastery of Saint-Denis (1053 × 1057).

The tenth-century boundary of East Woolstone, Berkshire, must suffice to illustrate the wealth of detail (topographical, archaeological, agrarian etc) contained in these surveys: 'First to the old dyke, along the lynchet to the fox holes, thence to ring pit, from the pit to watchman's barrow, thence into the narrow valley, along the valley to Ock springs, along the watercourse to the mill, then it goes up to the heathen burials, thence along the green way to stone pool, thence to the bramble bushes, thence to the northern part of the meadow . . . to Tættuca's stone, from the stone (back) to the old dyke where it began'.

There are over a thousand surviving 'Anglo-Saxon boundary clauses', although this figure includes some duplication. For example, essentially the same perambulation for Alresford, Hampshire, occurs both as a detached text and in an apparently authentic charter of *Eadwig (956), with closely related versions in spurious charters of Ecgberht (undated) and *Ine (701). Changes are illuminating: a 'ford' may become a 'bridge' in a later version, a mill might appear, adjacent lands change hands, or ploughed fields replace topographical land-marks.

Boundaries are conservative, and Anglo-Saxon estates are quite likely to survive as units into the nineteenth century or later, often as parishes or groups of parishes. Similarly, many Anglo-Saxon boundary-marks survive in place-names, recorded perhaps as minor names on the modern map or field names in the nineteenth-century Tithe Awards – e.g. *mære hrycg* 'boundary ridge' in Marriage Farm, and *blacan beorg* 'black barrow' in Blackberry Field. From these and other clues, the line of the survey can often be traced quite precisely in the modern landscape. To walk these bounds is to be struck in equal measure by those two old favourites, 'continuity and change'.

P. H. Sawyer, *Anglo-Saxon Charters: an Annotated List and Bibliography* (London, 1968); M. Gelling, *Signposts to the Past*, 2nd ed. (Chichester, 1988), pp. 191–214; J. Spittal and J. Field, *A Reader's Guide to the Place-names of the United Kingdom* (Stanford, 1990); J. Jenkyns, 'Computing in Name-Studies: the Charter Bounds', *Nomina* 12 (1988–9), 131–52; D. Hooke, *Anglo-Saxon Landscapes of the West Midlands: the Charter Evidence*, BAR Brit. ser. 95 (Oxford, 1981); idem, *The Landscape of Anglo-Saxon England* (Leicester, 1998).

JOY JENKYNS

CHARTERS AND WRITS. A charter (or diploma) is typically a short and self-contained text written in Latin on a single sheet of parchment, recording a grant of land or privileges by the king to a particular person or to a religious house, drawn up in accordance with prevailing (but changing) conventions and invested with all the force and formality of a legal instrument. The greater part of a 'standard' (tenth-century) charter is relentlessly formulaic, comprising invocation, proem, superscription, dispositive section (incorporating immunity clause, statement of powers, and reservation clause), sanction, boundary-clause (see *charter bounds), dating-clause, and witness-list, with an endorsement (normally on an outer panel created by folding the single sheet) summarising the substance of the grant. The corpus of extant charters comprises over 1000 texts, ranging in date from the last quarter of the seventh century to the eve of the Norman Conquest, with a concentration in the central decades of the tenth century (940s–960s). The majority of the charters survive because they were the title-deeds for estates which came into the possession of the religious house in whose archives they were formerly preserved; about 200 of them exist in their original form (on a single sheet, written in a hand judged to be contemporary with the given date), and the rest as copies (entered, for example, in a medieval cartulary). The study of charters is complicated by the fact that not all texts are what they purport to be; and part of their attraction lies in the need to learn how to establish the authenticity of a given text, and in understanding the variety of contexts (before and after the Conquest) in which charters were altered, improved, and forged.

Charters were introduced to England in the seventh century for recording grants of land and privileges to the Church, and were cast in a form appropriate to that elevated purpose; but while they came, during the eighth and ninth centuries, to be used increasingly for ordinary grants in favour of laymen, and while their form remained essentially the same, there was scope for considerable variety and development of substance and expression. In the simplest case, a charter created – and thereafter served as the title-deed for – an estate of bookland (see *land tenure), to be held on the terms specified in the text, including freedom from various worldly burdens and with the power to dispose of the land to any other party. Yet many more complex kinds of transaction might be concealed behind the deceptively standard formulation. A charter of *Æthelwulf, king of the West Saxons, issued in 846, records how he granted a large estate in Devon to himself (S 298: *EHD* i, no. 88), perhaps because he was consolidating his own interests in the south-west, or because he wished to enable himself to divide the land up among other parties. And although most charters represent the transaction as a royal grant, apparently for services rendered, it is always possible that a beneficiary had purchased the land from the king, or that he was exchanging it with the king for land elsewhere, or that he was converting land which he already held as folkland (see *land tenure) into land which henceforth he and his heirs would hold as bookland, or that the king was confirming the beneficiary's title to an estate which had come into the beneficiary's possession in some other way. Whatever the historical significance of the particular text, their value as evidence is transformed when charters are studied collectively. We can trace the development of a king's power (in the minds of those who drafted his charters, and also on the ground); we can observe a king's dealings with the great and the good of his realm, and his handling of religious, economic and military interests; and the attached witness-lists afford a vital guide to the changing composition of the king's household, and to attendance at meetings of the king's *council. Charters also bear directly on matters of wider cultural significance, ranging from the development of script (in the case of 'originals') to changing standards of Latinity and the variable quality of Latin learning from one centre of production to another. For an account of the arrangements for the production of charters, see *chancery.

Writs are typically much shorter documents, written in the vernacular, cast in the form of an address by the king (or other issuing party) to the persons assembled at a shire court (or a hundred court), and bearing an impression of a *seal as evidence of the authority behind them. Documents of this kind would appear to have originated in the late ninth century, and were used for a variety of different purposes (including administrative instructions, and notifications of appointment to high office, or entitlement to privileges); but the surviving examples date from the eleventh century, and the majority of them concern changes in the ownership of land or grants of privileges over land. It would appear that the king's writs were written and sealed in an office which formed part of the king's household, and were then taken by a royal agent to the shire court, where they would be read out to the assembled company; it would remain for an interested party to take the writ into its own keeping, for preservation thereafter as evidence of what it contained. Writs happen to survive in quantity from the period during which charters appear to be on the decline, but it does not follow (as might be

supposed) that the outmoded charter was superseded by the more adaptable writ. The two types of record complemented each other, and each needed the other to serve purposes which it could not serve itself: the charter was addressed in Latin to posterity, defining the estate and establishing its privileged status, whereas the writ was addressed in the vernacular to contemporaries, making it known that an estate had changed hands.

P. H. Sawyer, *Anglo-Saxon Charters: an Annotated List and Bibliography* (London, 1968); N. Brooks, 'Anglo-Saxon Charters: the Work of the Last Twenty Years', *ASE* 3 (1974), 211–31; S. E. Kelly, 'Anglo-Saxon Lay Society and the Written Word', *The Uses of Literacy in Early Mediaeval Europe* ed. R. McKitterick (Cambridge, 1990), pp. 36–62. Charters: F. M. Stenton, *The Latin Charters of the Anglo-Saxon Period* (Oxford, 1955); *EHD* i.369–84 and nos. 54–135; *Charters of St Augustine's Abbey Canterbury*, ed. S. E. Kelly, AS Charters 4 (Oxford, 1996), and other fascicules in the same series; M. Lapidge, 'Latin Learning in Ninth-Century England', *ALL* i.409–54. Writs: F. E. Harmer, *Anglo-Saxon Writs* (Manchester, 1952); T. A. M. Bishop and P. Chaplais, *Facsimiles of English Royal Writs to AD 1100* (Oxford, 1957); S. Keynes, 'Regenbald the Chancellor [*sic*]', *ANS* 10 (1988), 185–222, at 214–18.

SIMON KEYNES

CHEDDAR is a royal site and minster in North Somerset. It is referred to in *Alfred's will, but not necessarily as a palace. The estate and buildings may have been rather the residence of a branch of the royal family, or of a religious community, a 'minster'. Meetings of the king with his *witan* are recorded in three surviving charters of 941, 956 and 968 in the reigns of *Edmund, *Eadwig, and *Edgar. *Dunstan was at court here in the early 940s. He is associated with the famous story of King Edmund's narrow escape from death while hunting above Cheddar Gorge, which was followed by Dunstan's appointment as abbot of *Glastonbury.

The area south of Cheddar (the Somerset Levels) has always been rich in mineral, agricultural and grazing resources, and the Forest of Mendip also afforded splendid opportunities for hunting. There are extensive Roman finds here, including a large villa in the area around the nearby parish church. It seems likely that there is some relationship between the Roman villa estate and that of Anglo-Saxon Cheddar, which is linked in later written sources with Wedmore (where Alfred concluded a peace treaty with *Guthrum in 878), and with Axbridge. The latter was the defensible nucleus of the area, with a *mint, and figured in the *Burghal Hidage.

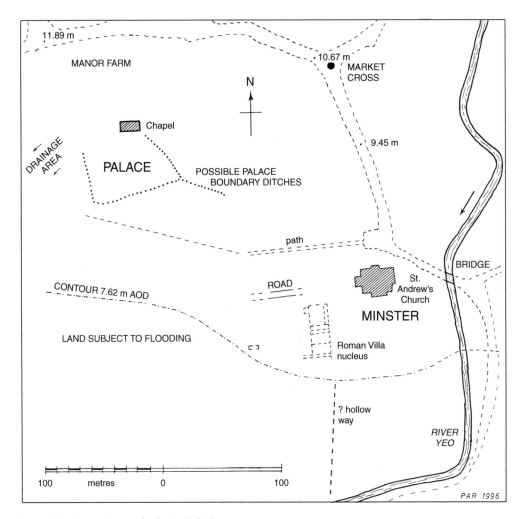

11.89 m

MANOR FARM

N

10.67 m MARKET CROSS

DRAINAGE AREA

Chapel

PALACE

POSSIBLE PALACE BOUNDARY DITCHES

9.45 m

path

BRIDGE

CONTOUR 7.62 m AOD

ROAD

St. Andrew's Church

MINSTER

LAND SUBJECT TO FLOODING

Roman Villa nucleus

? hollow way

RIVER YEO

100   metres   0   100

PAR 1996

Fig. 2 Cheddar: palace and minster (plan).

Extensive excavations in the 1960s defined a series of buildings and other features in six phases, the first three of which are pre-Conquest. The first phase is dated to the ninth/tenth century; it comprises a two-storey hall set in an enclosure with other smaller buildings, protected from periodic flooding by a storm-water ditch. There was much domestic rubbish from this phase including thousands of food bones, high-status metal objects and coins.

The second phase is attributed to King *Æthelstan, built in the 930s and the setting for the royal visit of 941. The new layout comprised further storm-water protection and an elaborate eastern enclosure façade of fence and ditch; a central gateway in this was flanked by a massive free-standing pole, which may have carried emblems

or carvings symbolic of the House of Wessex. There was a new hall, gable-end to the enclosure entrance, minor domestic buildings, and a stone-built private royal chapel. Finds were few, but included coins of Æthelstan and Edmund, and debris of fine metal-working in bronze, silver and gold.

This layout was retained in the third phase, of the late tenth or early eleventh centuries, with rebuilding of hall and chapel; finds include coins of King *Æthelred and King *Cnut.

The written sources refer also to 'Cheddar minster'. This is believed to have been in the area of the Roman villa and present parish church of St Andrew. It would have provided the facilities for major religious gatherings of the royal court, and may have been the principal

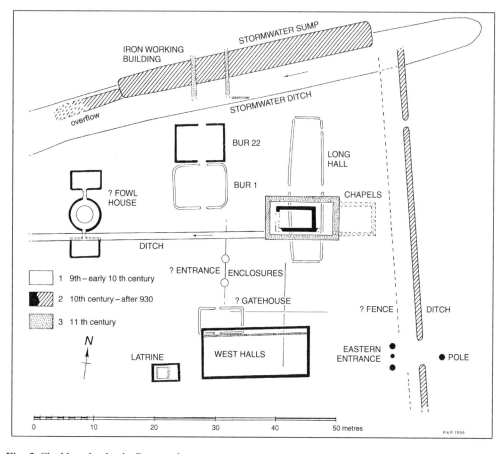

Fig. 3 Cheddar: the Anglo-Saxon palaces.

nucleus of the area, the palace being relatively subsidiary.

P. A. Rahtz, *The Saxon and Medieval Palaces at Cheddar* (Oxford, 1969); S. M. Hirst and P. A. Rahtz, 'Cheddar Vicarage 1970', *Somerset Archaeology and Natural History* 117 (1973), 65–96; J. Blair, 'Palaces or Minsters? Northampton and Cheddar Reconsidered', *ASE* 25 (1996), 97–121.

PHILIP RAHTZ

CHERTSEY (Surrey) was one of two monasteries founded by *Eorcenwald, bishop of London, in the 660s (see also *Barking). It was originally endowed by King Ecgberht of *Kent; after *Wulfhere of Mercia's incursions south of the Thames, a large estate was given in 672 × 674 by his sub-king Frithuwold, whose charter defines its bounds as the Thames, 'the boundary which is called the ancient ditch, that is *Fullingadic*', and 'the boundary of the next province which is called *Sunninges*' – the oldest extant boundary clause

(see *charter bounds). Chertsey was sacked by *Vikings in about 870, but a religious community still existed there a decade or so later; it was recolonised by monks in 964, and remained an important Benedictine abbey thereafter. The saints enshrined there were Beocca and Edor, martyrs to the Vikings, and the benefactor Frithuwold.

J. Blair, 'Frithuwold's Kingdom and the Origins of Surrey' and 'The Chertsey Resting-Place List and the Enshrinement of Frithuwold', in Bassett, *Origins*, pp. 97–107, 231–6.

JOHN BLAIR

CHESTER, termed a *civitas* by *Bede, was a Roman legionary fortress until the early fifth century and probably continued in British occupation for some time thereafter. The location of a British synod *c.*600, and of the Northumbrian king Æthelfrith's victory over the British in 616, it probably came under Anglo-Saxon control in the seventh century: a late tradition records that the minster of St John's, located by the Roman amphitheatre outside the city walls, was founded by the Mercian king Æthelred (675–704).

In 893, when it was raided by the *Vikings, Chester was allegedly deserted. However, there is evidence of ninth-century occupation south of the legionary fortress but within the medieval enceinte, and from c.890 the city was probably the site of a *mint. In 907 it was refortified by the rulers of *Mercia, *Æthelflæd and *Æthelred, apparently in response to a Hiberno–Norse raid upon Wirral; the defences then established were by the mid-eleventh century, under arrangements probably made much earlier, maintained by the men of the shire. The new *burh* was the focus of unrest after the deposition of Æthelflæd's heir, and in 924 *Edward the Elder planted a garrison there.

After the refortification and probably under Æthelflæd, the remains of the Mercian princess *Werburg were transferred from Hanbury to Chester and established in a new or refounded minster. By *Æthelstan's reign there was a major mint, the exceptional productivity of which may reflect its role as a centre for the collection of bullion and tribute and the importance of its trade – probably in salt, metalwork, cloth and slaves – with Dublin.

Although increasingly on the fringes of royal authority, Chester was the scene of *Edgar's celebrated encounter with several (probably eight) Scots, Welsh and Scandinavian rulers in 973, when he was allegedly rowed on the Dee in token of submission. In 1000 it served as the naval base for an English attack on Cumberland and Man, and thereafter it became an important centre for the Mercian earls and for *Harold Godwinsson when he attacked the Welsh king Gruffudd ap Llywelyn in the early 1060s. In 1066 Chester was a prosperous regional centre, with c.3,000 inhabitants, two minsters, and its own hundredal court, presided over by twelve doomsmen. It was in the hands of three lords – the king, earl, and bishop, of whom the earl, represented by his own reeve, was especially influential.

A. T. Thacker, 'Chester and Gloucester: Early Ecclesiastical Organisation in Two Mercian Burhs', *Northern History* 18 (1982), 199–211; idem, 'Early Medieval Chester', *VCH Cheshire*, v.17–29; D. J. P. Mason, *Excavations at Chester: 26–42 Lower Bridge St, Dark Age and Saxon Periods*, Chester Archaeological Excavation and Survey Reports 3 (Chester, 1985); S. Ward *et al.*, *Excavations at Chester: Saxon Occupation Within the Roman Fortress*, Chester Archaeological Excavation and Survey Reports [7] (Chester, 1994).

ALAN THACKER

CHILDREN. What little is known about Anglo-Saxon children must be pulled together from a variety of sources. Information about care of children, mortality rates and the size of the family can be inferred from excavated skeletal remains. Where burials are furnished, some information can be gleaned about age thresholds and status of children. Written sources such as *law-codes, the *Lives* of saints and *medical texts give further information about childrearing and the child's place in later Anglo-Saxon society.

On the whole, children seem to have been well cared for. Children's skeletons reveal little indication of *disease, trauma or *malnutrition, although a slightly higher incidence of cribra orbitalia (pepperpot lesions in the bone of the eye socket) in juveniles in some cemetery populations might reflect dietary deficiency. However, a few striking burials of adults who survived childhood with severe congenital defects, such as the burial of an adult male missing an arm from Kingsworthy (Hants.) are an indication of the care lavished on children, and the special feeding-bottle found with an infant from Castle Dyke, Beverley, is evidence of particular and focused care of a child. This feeding-bottle is a rarity, and normally infants appear to have been breast-fed: there is little later documentary evidence for the practice of wet-nursing babies. The rapid abrasion of children's teeth from the age of about two identified in some Anglo–Saxon *cemeteries has been attributed to a sudden process of weaning at this age.

Infants are an under-represented group in earlier Anglo-Saxon cemeteries, and several reasons for this have been suggested. It may be that infant burials, being smaller and shallower than adult graves, are lost from the inhumation record. Infant bones would be destroyed more easily than adult bones in both cremations and inhumations. Another possibility is that infants were given differential burial treatment, and were not buried in the pagan cemeteries at all. In later cemeteries, associated with churches, the proportion of infants is higher. Here, it seems that infant burials may clump together, often under the eaves-drip of the church as at *Whithorn (Galloway) and *Raunds (Northants).

On the whole, children were buried with fewer and less valuable grave goods than adults. Exceptionally, a young girl may be found with great wealth: a large string of beads, gilt brooches and containers. Any explanation for these rich girls must remain hypothetical, although one reasonable possibility may be that they represent girls of important families who were buried with the equivalent of their bridewealth. Whilst women are distinguished by their *jewellery and men by their weapons, there are no artefacts in furnished burials which are only associated with children. There are no certain examples of toys buried with children, but the *Lives* of the saints offer glimpses of boys playing rowdy physical games. St *Cuthbert, as a child, is described playing games and turning cartwheels with other children.

Fosterage seems to have played a key part in the upbringing of many Anglo-Saxon children. The high mortality rates in the Anglo-Saxon period may help to explain why this practice was so important: not because Anglo-Saxon parents did not care for their children, but because caring parents knew that death might overtake them before their children were old enough to survive on their own. In a society where status and safety were assured by the size and power of one's kin group, fosterage allowed vulnerable children to extend the group of people who owed them an obligation of protection. The bond between foster-parents and child seems to have been close. St Cuthbert, for example, showed a particular fondness for his foster-mother, who played a more important role in his *Life* than his own parents. In the Christian period, the practice of sending children to be brought up in monasteries was encouraged by the church. This may have been a mechanism to weaken the Germanic system of fosterage, but the monastery also provided an education and a safe environment for orphaned boys and girls. Children could be placed in monasteries from as young as two to three years of age. *Law-codes throughout the Christian Anglo-Saxon period emphasised the vulnerability of an orphaned child and made provision for the community to care for such children.

An analysis of furnished inhumation and cremation cemeteries does indicate that particular grave goods were age-related, and the inclusion of these in the grave indicates customary ages of transition from childhood to adulthood. In the furnished inhumation cemeteries, girls start to be buried with adult women's items such as chatelaines from the age of about twelve. Some boys are buried with small spears from about six, but do not receive shields until about twelve. Swords are only exceptionally buried with children or adolescents, but the written sources suggest that a spear and shield alone were sufficient to form the weapon-set of a warrior, and that adolescents could and did take part in battles. The archaeological information is supported by the law-codes, where orphans may take control of their property, and

children become legally culpable for their actions, at ten to twelve. One law of *Æthelstan attempted to raise the level of culpability to fifteen, and clearly expressed the difficulty of dealing with adolescents who were expected to be taking their place in adult society before they reached emotional maturity.

The education of boys and girls depended on their status and situation. A literary education was an important aspect of a monastic upbringing: *Ælfric's *Colloquy* is a surviving textbook for children, offering lively exercises in Latin conversation, and amongst the first efforts of *Augustine's mission was the setting up of *schools. Both boys and girls were given a literary education. *Literacy in secular society seems to have been less important: St *Guthlac's education consisted of listening to the recitation of poetry in his father's hall and learning the art of military warfare, and he remained illiterate until he entered the church.

Notwithstanding the high mortality rates and relatively poor communities, documentary sources offer irrefutable evidence that Anglo-Saxon parents cared about their offspring and gave them protected time to develop as children. The poem *The *Fates of Man* from the *Exeter Book evokes a picture of loving parents doting over their child, and illustrations of close relationships between parents and children occur in manuscripts such as the *Harley Psalter, where mothers are shown cuddling their infants and holding the hands of their older children.

S. E. E. Crawford, 'When do Anglo-Saxon Children Count?', *Journal of Theoretical Archaeology* 2 (1991), 17–24; idem, 'Age Differentiation and Related Social Status: a Study of Earlier Anglo-Saxon Childhood', unpublished D. Phil. thesis (University of Oxford, 1991); idem, 'Children, Death and the Afterlife', *ASSAH* 6 (1993), 83–92; M. Kuefler, ' "A wryed existence": Attitudes towards Children in Anglo-Saxon England', *Journal of Social History* 24 (1991), 823–30.

SALLY CRAWFORD

CHI-RHO. Latin scribes borrowed from their Greek counterparts the practice of using symbols for the holy names of the Christian faith. Christ was represented by χρ plus the final letter appropriate for the syntax. In Insular *gospelbooks, such as the Book of *Durrow and the *Lindisfarne and Lichfield Gospels, particular emphasis was given to the symbol for the name of Christ at Matt. I.18 (*Christi autem generatio sic erat*: 'Moreover the birth of Christ was thus'), reflecting the special status of this text as both the beginning of the first gospel narrative and the account of the Incarnation. The trend of enlarging and decorating this 'Incarnation initial' or 'Chi-rho' reached its apogee in the Book of Kells, where it occupies an entire page (34r). The last example to be elaborately decorated occurs in Boulogne, Bibliothèque municipale, 10, of the early tenth century; in late Anglo-Saxon gospelbooks a discreet plain gold initial sufficed.

L. Traube, *Nomina Sacra, Versuch einer Geschichte der christlichen Kürzung* (Munich, 1907); S. Lewis, 'Sacred Calligraphy: the Chi Rho page in the Book of Kells', *Traditio* 36 (1980), 139–59.

RICHARD GAMESON

CHIROGRAPH is the name given to a *charter generally copied in duplicate or triplicate onto a single sheet of membrane, divided into its separate portions after the word 'CYROGRAPHVM' (or equivalent) had been written across the line of the cut(s). *Wills, leases and other contractual agreements were frequently recorded in this manner. Over sixty charters dating from the pre-Conquest period show evidence of having been produced as chirographs. Approximately half survive as portions. The others can be identified only by the employment or retention of a clause noting the existence of duplicates.

K. A. Lowe, 'Lay Literacy in Anglo-Saxon England and the Development of the Chirograph', in *Anglo-Saxon Manuscripts and their Heritage*, ed. P. Pulsiano and E. Treharne (Aldershot, 1998), pp. 161–204.

K. A. LOWE

CHRIST I, II: see Advent Lyrics; Cynewulf

CHRIST III, a complete poem on Judgement Day (798 lines), is impressive for its powerful working of the themes of retribution and redemption. The image of the 'red' cross of Christ dominates the opening sections, its light shining on Judgement Day throughout the world in place of the sun's light. With the apocalyptic darkening of the sun, the fall of the moon and scattering of the stars, fire will come to consume this world's evil, but those who are stained with sin and blind to thought will not recognise Christ. The central division, with its focus on the need for inward recognition of wrong-doing, confession and atonement, presents both the rewards of the blessed and the damnation of the wicked, urgently warning of the brief time body and soul are joined together on earth. Later, Christ, who comes to greet the blessed, explains creation, incarnation and the agony of Calvary: there is no bypassing of Christ's sufferings in this poem, which should be read by all who admire The *Dream of the Rood*.

Overall, this well-structured poem is marked by a masterly unity of images. Even in the final picture of heaven, traditional paradisiacal motifs evoke hell vividly.

ASPR iii.27–49; A. S. Cook, *The Christ of Cynewulf* (Boston, 1900); G. Shepherd, 'Scriptural Poetry', in *Continuations and Beginnings*, ed. E. G. Stanley (London, 1966), pp. 1–36; F. M. Biggs, 'The Sources of *Christ III*: A Revision of Cook's Notes', *Old English Newsletter*, Subsidia 12 (1986); J. Roberts, 'Some Reflections on the Metre of *Christ III*', in *From Anglo-Saxon to Early Middle English. Studies presented to E. G. Stanley*, ed. M. Godden, D. Gray and T. Hoad (Oxford, 1994), pp. 33–59.

J. ROBERTS

CHRIST AND SATAN. The last item in the *Junius manuscript consists of 729 lines of verse, called *Christ and Satan*, and although doubt has been expressed about whether it constitutes one poem or many because of the lack of a coherent narrative thread, the fact that its subjects include the lament of the fallen angels, the Harrowing of Hell, the Resurrection, the Ascension, and the Day of Judgement, in that order, suggests a controlling mind at work.

ASPR i.135–58; *Christ and Satan*, ed. M. D. Clubb, Yale Studies in English 70 (New Haven, CT, 1925); C. R. Sleeth, *Studies in 'Christ and Satan'* (Toronto, 1982).

DONALD SCRAGG

CHURCHES: *see* Architecture, Ecclesiastical

CHURL (*CEORL*): *see* Peasants; Social Class

CIRENCESTER (Glos.), formerly the Roman-British town of *Corinium*, was one of the three 'chesters' which, according to the *Anglo-Saxon Chronicle* for '577', the *Gewisse captured from the British at the battle of *Dyrham*. That it became a major ecclesiastical centre is proved by its huge ninth-century basilican church (found by excavation), but nothing else is known of this establishment, and by 1086 it had dwindled to a humble two-hide minster in the hands of the royal clerk Regenbald. Probably the monastic lands were annexed by the West Saxon crown: royal assemblies are recorded at Cirencester from 935 onwards, including an Easter 'Great Council' in 1020. By 1086 it had started to re-develop as a small *town.

Archaeology and History of Cirencester, ed. A. D. McWhirr (Oxford, 1976); A. K. B. Evans, 'Cirencester's Early Church', *Transactions of the Bristol and Gloucestershire Archaeological Society* 107 (1989), 107–22; R. Gem, 'Architecture of the Anglo-Saxon Church, 735 to 870', *JBAA* 146 (1993), 29–66, at 41–4.

JOHN BLAIR

CLASSICAL LEARNING. The influence of classical learning on the Anglo-Saxons is difficult to assess, given the tendency of some Christian authors from the period to disguise or deny their debt to an evidently pagan past, coupled with the fact that so many of the patristic and Carolingian authorities upon which later writers drew so freely were themselves steeped in the classical tradition. So, for example, *Bede, composing his treatise on Latin *metre (*De arte metrica*), carefully purges his highly derivative text of illustrative examples from classical poets, substituting instead more acceptable snatches of Christian Latin verse; in the same way his textbook on rhetoric (*De schematibus et tropis*), takes its examples not from the classical authors cited in his own sources, but from the *Bible. But despite his best efforts to erase all traces of classical learning, it is abundantly clear from (for example) Bede's own verse that he was himself well acquainted with the poetry of Vergil, whom he echoes often, and who was clearly a staple of the Anglo-Saxon curriculum. Other Anglo-Saxons were less coy about their debt to classical culture: it is certain that *Aldhelm, for example, knew a range of classical poets, notably Vergil and Lucan (whose verses he quotes alongside those of Ennius, Terence, Seneca, Lucretius, Persius and Juvenal, which he more probably knew only at second hand); it is possible that he had some familiarity with some of the poems of Horace, Ovid, and Statius. Likewise *Alcuin, in his versified catalogue of the books owned by his mentor *Ælberht of *York, includes Vergil, Statius and Lucan among the Latin poets, together with (more surprisingly) Aristotle (presumably via Boethius), Pompeius Trogus (via Justinus), Pliny, and Cicero (notably his *De inuentione* and *De oratore*) among prose authors. The possibility that some of the works of Cicero were known in Anglo-Saxon England is particularly intriguing, since the influence of classical rhetoric on Anglo-Saxon literature is often asserted, but has proved difficult to demonstrate beyond doubt. Clearly, however, the classical world exerted a considerable fascination for Anglo-Saxons throughout the period, and knowledge of the works of a large number of classical and Late Latin authors seems likely in certain fields, especially *medicine (where, for example, there is evidence of the influence of Cassius Felix, Dioscorides, and Marcellus of Bordeaux), *astronomy (where some familiarity with Hyginus seems likely), and, above all, *grammar (where the works of authors such as Charisius, Consentius, Donatus, and Priscian were evidently keenly studied). Classical myth, history, and legend were apparently viewed with the same suspicion as literature, but the additions to his translation of *Orosius by a contemporary of King *Alfred, the Old English translation of a supposed letter to Aristotle by *Alexander the Great, the evidence of several *glossaries, and the oblique (and generally second-hand) references to classical learning made by *Byrhtferth in his *Enchiridion* all testify to the enduring appeal of classical authors and texts in Anglo-Saxon England.

F. Biggs, T. D. Hill, and P. Szarmach, *Sources of Anglo-Saxon Literary Culture: a Trial Version* (Binghamton, NY, 1991); G. Knappe, *Traditionen der klassischen Rhetorik im angelsächsischen England* (Heidelberg, 1996); W. M. Lindsay, *Studies in Early Mediaeval Latin Glossaries*, ed. M. Lapidge (Aldershot, 1996); J. D. A. Ogilvy, *Books Known to the English, 597–1066* (Cambridge, MA, 1967); idem, *Books Known to the English, 597–1066; Addenda and Corrigenda*, Old English Newsletter Subsidia 11 (Binghamton, NY, 1985); J. Bately, 'Those Books that are Most Necessary for All Men to Know: the Classics and late Ninth-Century England, a Reappraisal', in *The Classics in the Middle Ages*, ed. A. S. Bernardo and S. Levin (Binghamton, NY, 1990), pp. 45–78; A. Orchard, *The Poetic Art of Aldhelm*, CSASE 8 (Cambridge, 1994), 127–52; N. Wright, 'Bede and Vergil', *Romanobarbarica* 6 (1981–2), 361–79.

ANDY ORCHARD

CLERGY, a term derived from Latin *clericus* ('cleric') meaning essentially the religious as distinct from the laity. The clergy was hierarchical, consisting of various orders, described as major and minor. The major orders consisted of bishops, priests and deacons. The minor orders were four and consisted of: doorkeepers (*ostiarii*), the equivalent of modern vergers; lectors or readers (*lectores*), who were responsible for reading from the Old Testament Prophets and New Testament Epistles; exorcists (*exorcistae*), who pronounced the prayers and formulas used in expelling evil spirits; and acolytes (*acolyti*) who helped in service at the altar and in the administration of the eucharist. Admission to the major orders was by ordination (from the fourth century onwards, it was a tenet of *canon law, as promulgated by the Council of Neocaesarea, that ordination to the priesthood should not take place before the age of thirty) performed by a bishop (see *pontifical ceremonies). In Roman rite, minor orders could be conferred by commission and by the symbolic bestowal of the so-called Instruments of office (keys for the doorkeeper; a book for the lector; a booklet containing exorcisms for the exorcist; and a candle-stick (*ceroferarium*) and ewer (*urceolus*) for the acolyte); the Gallican rite, which is that represented in

Anglo-Saxon pontificals (see *liturgical books), included brief services of ordination to these minor orders. Monks were not originally regarded as clergy, but as it soon became normal for monks to be ordained to religious orders, they were inevitably considered to pertain to the clergy. With the growth of reformed Benedictine *monasticism in the tenth century, a distinction emerged between monks and secular (that is, non-monastic) clergy. Inasmuch as they were not (Benedictine) monks, secular clerics were free to marry and to own property; in many cathedral chapters, however, the secular clergy adhered to the Rule of Chrodegang and led a disciplined life parallel in many ways to that of Benedictine monks (see *cathedral canons). The secular clergy also included parish priests (see *parochial organisation).

Isidore, *Etymologiae* vii.12; *DACL* i.348–56 [acolyte], iii.1902–5 [clerk], iv.738–46 [deacon], v.964–78 [exorcist], viii.2241–69 [lector], xiv.1525–33 [doorkeeper]; M. Andrieu, 'Les Ordres mineurs dans l'ancien rite romain', *Revue des sciences religieuses* 5 (1925), 232–74; J. G. Davies, 'Deacons, Deaconesses and the Minor Orders in the Patristic Period', *JEH* 14 (1963), 1–15.

MICHAEL LAPIDGE

CLOFESHO. A place designated in 672 as the location of church *councils to be held regularly thereafter (Council of Hertford, ch. 7, in *HE* iv.5). The name means 'hillspur bisected by a cleft'. It has not been identified, but must have lain somewhere within the Mercian sphere of influence in Southumbria since the recorded meetings held there were attended by bishops of the southern ecclesiastical province and by the Mercian kings. The first reliably attested council of *Clofesho* was that convened by Archbishop Cuthbert in 747 (see *Æthelbald). Church councils are otherwise known to have met at *Clofesho* in ?792, 793 × 796, 794, 798, 803, and ?804 (during the archiepiscopate of Æthelheard), and in 824 and 825 (towards the end of the archiepiscopate of *Wulfred).

S. Keynes, *The Councils of Clofesho*, Brixworth Lecture 1993, Univ. of Leicester Vaughan Paper 38 (Leicester, 1994); C. Cubitt, *Anglo-Saxon Church Councils c.650–c.850* (London, 1995), pp. 27–39, 304–6.

C. R. E. CUBITT

CLOTHING includes garments of cloth and other materials, together with their fasteners and dress accessories. Women's dress in particular was subject to change. Archaeological evidence demonstrates that in the pagan period a traditional Germanic costume was worn in Anglian and Saxon areas. It consisted of a tubular gown, fastened at the shoulders by a pair of brooches, with a festoon of beads between, sometimes worn over an undergarment with narrow sleeves fastened by metal clasps, and sometimes with a cloak. Kentish fashion, including a centrally-fastened gown and, for the wealthy few, gold-brocaded fillets, reflected Frankish influence.

Knives, keys and other possessions were carried at the belt, which was of leather or braided textile. Braids, which were also used as cuffs and neckline borders, were sometimes woven with dyed threads in geometric patterns. The rest of the clothing was probably undyed, but not necessarily dull, since cloth-makers could exploit the variety of natural wool colours and, as surviving *textile fragments demonstrate, could produce cloths with attractive self-coloured patterns as well as simpler twill and tabby weaves.

By the seventh century the tubular gown and paired brooches disappeared, perhaps under the influence of Christian culture. Wealthy women might have a single, jewelled brooch (often of cruciform design) at neck or shoulder, which probably fastened a cloak in an adaptation of (male) Byzantine fashion. Byzantine-style necklaces of gold beads and jewelled pendants appeared. One example, from Desborough (Northants.), suspends

Fig. 4 The clothing of early Anglo-Saxon women (reconstruction).

a cross. Other women wore pairs of tiny annular broches, or suites of pins which perhaps secured head-veils.

Eighth-century art shows women in open-necked veils or hoods and front-opening cloaks over long robes. Later they are depicted in wimples which hide the neck, and robes with wide sleeves (more exaggerated in the eleventh century) over tight-sleeved undergarments. Cloaks are poncho-shaped. *Jewellery is not depicted although metalwork survives from the period, including brooches, rings and strap-ends. Textual evidence suggests head-bands were common though they are depicted only occasionally, over or under the headdress. Loose, uncovered hair is rare and associated with dissoluteness.

Men probably wore a knee-length tunic over close-fitting trousers throughout the Anglo-Saxon era since this is the Germanic costume shown in Roman art and the dress of secular men in later Anglo-Saxon art: archaeological evidence for the early period is, however, limited, being confined mainly to buckles apart from a few rich burials with unusual features (*Sutton Hoo, *Taplow). The costume depicted often includes a cloak, fastened by a circular brooch, and strips of cloth wound round the lower legs. Men are mostly bare-headed, though some manuscripts show 'Phrygian' caps. By the end of the tenth century the ruling classes sometimes wore long garments for ceremonial occasions.

Animal skin was undoubtedly exploited. Textual evidence suggests fur jerkins and fur-lined robes but they are never illustrated. Leather shoes were worn by the wealthy at least from the seventh century and are common finds from urban archaeology, though persons engaged in agricultural labour seem to have worked barefoot.

Monks and nuns did not wear distinctive habits, though they were expected to dress plainly. Priests wore short, secular dress when not celebrating mass. Ecclesiastical vestments, which derived from Roman tradition, were totally different. Bishops' vestments, purchased abroad, or made of imported silk, were sometimes lavishly embroidered with gold.

Garment-names are documented in *glossaries, but garments (mail-coats and helmets excepted) are rarely mentioned in literature. Conversely, clothing is prominent in art; the Anglo-Saxons show no interest in the nude body. However, evidence must be used with caution: depiction of dress is selective and stylised, and most art is dependent on older, foreign models. Christ, saints and angels are pictured in a 'classical' costume of Byzantine origin which probably bore no resemblance to contemporary dress, though there are also useful depictions of men in secular, medieval clothes. There is no such distinction in illustrations of women. Whether representing personifications, saints or seculars they wear similar costume, which may or may not be an accurate reflection of Anglo-Saxon fashions.

G. R. Owen-Crocker, *Dress in Anglo-Saxon England* (Manchester, 1986); idem, 'The Search for Anglo-Saxon Skin Garments and the Documentary Evidence', in *Leather and Fur. Aspects of Early Medieval Trade and Technology*, ed. E. A. Cameron (London, 1998), pp. 27–43; *The Old English Illustrated Hexateuch*, ed. C. R. Dodwell and P. Clemoes, EEMF 18 (Copenhagen, 1974); D. M. Wilson, *The Bayeux Tapestry* (London, 1985).

GALE R. OWEN-CROCKER

CNUT, king of England (1016–35), king of Denmark (*c*.1018–35), and overlord of certain parts of Norway and Sweden. Cnut had been present with the Danish fleet during the invasion and conquest of England by his father, *Swein Forkbeard, in 1013–14; and it was probably during these years that he formed a relationship with Ælfgifu of Northampton, daughter of Ealdorman Ælfhelm. Cnut returned to Denmark after his father's death, and invaded England on his own account in 1015. His arrival exacerbated latent political tensions, prompting *Eadric Streona to defect to the Danish side. After an extended campaign against *Æthelred and *Edmund Ironside, Cnut won a resounding victory at *Assandun* (Essex), on 18 October 1016, and was established thereafter as king of 'Mercia' (in effect, north of the Thames). It so happened, however, that Edmund died, on 30 November 1016, leaving Cnut well placed to gain recognition as king of all England.

Cnut's concern in 1017 was to secure his ground against threats from without and within. He divided the kingdom into four regions (*Wessex, *East Anglia, *Mercia, and *Northumbria), retaining control of Wessex for himself; he took action against certain prominent Englishmen who might be expected to challenge his position; he disposed in one way or another of Æthelred's surviving descendants by his first marriage; and by marrying *Emma, Æthelred's second wife (pl. 14), he gave her the position which would keep her on his side, and which would thereby undermine the prospects of her exiled sons *Edward and Alfred. Cnut's concern in 1018 was to prepare the ground for the cultivation of peace, justice, and the Anglo-Danish way. The tribute (*gafol*) was paid, and the army paid off, though the king retained a small but elite force of his own *housecarls; new appointments were made, and secular government was re-organised; 'and the Danes and the English reached an agreement at Oxford, according to Edgar's law' (*ASC*, MS. D). It is well established that Archbishop *Wulfstan was the principal architect of the political settlement, which found expression in a preliminary agreement drawn up at Oxford in 1018 (*EHD* i, no. 47) and which was symbolised by the consecration of a minster at *Assandun* in 1020 (*ASC*). The settlement found further expression in the production of a major code of laws (*EHD* i, no. 49), emanating from a meeting held at Winchester during the Christmas season in 1020–1 or 1021–2, and also, it seems, in the formal translation of the relics of Archbishop *Ælfheah from London to Canterbury in June 1023.

It would be difficult to construct a chronological or narrative account of Cnut's reign as king of England. The notional centre of political power seems to have moved back from *London to *Winchester; and although the conquest may have been attended by some new settlement of 'Danes' in eastern England, it seems that the housecarls gravitated more particularly towards Dorset and the west Midlands. The administrative arrangements within the kingdom underwent further development, and by 1030 secular power was balanced between Earl *Godwine, established in Wessex, and Earl *Leofric, dominant north of the Thames, with consequences which reverberated long after Cnut's death. And all the while the Danish king and his Norman queen played out their brilliantly contrived double act, earning good will where it mattered through the patronage of the church and through the public display of their royal grandeur. Yet although Cnut was first and foremost a king of the English, any account of his reign would have to be punctuated by the record of his activities as one who came to preside over a veritable 'North Sea empire'. He returned to Denmark in 1019–20, following the death of his elder brother Harold (*c.*1018); and while still abroad he despatched a remarkable letter to the English people (*EHD* i, no. 48, chs. 1–13), of which a copy was entered at the back of the 'York Gospels' and furnished with Wulfstanian additions (chs. 14–20). Cnut went to Denmark again in 1022–3, apparently to sort out a local difficulty; and it was on his return to England that he elevated Godwine to a position of primacy among his earls. In 1026–7 Cnut disposed of a Scandinavian challenge to his rule in battle at the Holy River

(1026), went on (apparently via Saint-Omer in *Flanders) to attend the imperial coronation of Conrad II at Rome (March 1027), and returned via Denmark; it was in the course of this expedition that he advertised his achievements by means of another remarkable letter to the English people (*EHD* i, no. 53). Cnut took a naval force from England to Norway in 1028, in order to make good his claim to that land, returning to England in 1029. He also mounted an expedition to Scotland, probably in 1031. Cnut was, in fact, the first ruler since *Æthelwulf of Wessex who is known to have ventured overseas during his reign; and although *Æthelstan stood high among his contemporaries, Cnut did much to revive the prestige of a battered monarchy. The marriage between his daughter Gunnhild and Henry, son of the emperor Conrad II, was arranged in 1035 and took place in 1036; and conditions were created which attracted a number of Lotharingian clerics to the royal court.

Cnut died at Shaftesbury, in Dorset, on 12 November 1035, and was buried in the Old Minster at Winchester. His death precipitated a disputed succession between *Harthacnut and *Harold Harefoot, and provided an opportunity for Queen Emma to play a more prominent part in the politics of her age. The famous story of Cnut's attempt to impose his will on the incoming tide was told in the first instance by *Henry of Huntingdon, in the first half of the twelfth century, to illustrate the king's humility when confronted with evidence of his own impunity (*Hist. Angl.* vi.17); ironically, it is now told as a way of poking fun at those so arrogant that they aspire to do what is wholly beyond their power.

M. K. Lawson, *Cnut: the Danes in England in the Early Eleventh Century* (London, 1993); *The Reign of Cnut: King of England, Denmark and Norway*, ed. A. R. Rumble (London, 1994).

SIMON KEYNES

CODICOLOGY. Medieval books were made from sheets of parchment, which were cut to size, folded, and gathered into groups to form quires. The sheets were marked with prickings to guide the rulings, which in their turn guided the script. When the sheets had been written, rubricated, and (if appropriate) decorated, the quires were finally bound together to form a codex. Each stage of this process was subject to variations according to the time and place of manufacture, and the nature and grade of the volume itself. The early medieval book was a very flexible commodity, a point underlined by the striking physical differences between individual copies of the same text: the pages of the largest eleventh-century English psalter (BN, lat. 8824), for instance, are twenty times bigger than those of the smallest one (Oxford, Bodleian Library, Laud. lat. 81). Our information about these procedures comes from a small number of medieval treatises, from scattered depictions, and from close inspection of the manuscripts themselves.

To make good parchment, the animal had to be well bled immediately after slaughter, thus preventing its veins from marking the skin. The flayed skin was soaked in a lime bath to loosen the hairs and fatty tissue, prior to being scraped smooth. It was then allowed to dry while held under tension on a frame: the simultaneous drying and stretching produced parchment as opposed to leather. The quality of the end-product varied according to the type, age and health of the animal, and the care with which the skin was treated. Correspondingly, the quality of the membrane provides a clear indication of the importance of a project and the standards of the *scriptorium responsible. The finest material was used in *liturgical service books, with particularly stout membrane sometimes being reserved for illuminated pages. Although holes (the result of damage to the skin either whilst still on the animal or during processing) are ubiquitous in early medieval manuscripts, they are much rarer in liturgical books than *library volumes; while grainy or yellow pages and irregular edges (the result of the sheet being cut from the very edge of the skin) generally appear in reading books and not liturgical ones. Particularly poor parchment, such as that in the Herbal, London, BL Harley 585, and the Homiliary, Oxford, Bodleian Library, Junius 85–6, is rare outside vernacular manuscripts.

Even with fairly well-prepared membrane, there remains a contrast in tone and texture between the hair side (H) and the flesh side (F) of the sheet. To minimise the discrepancy on a given opening, medieval scribes generally arranged the sheets so that hair side faced hair and flesh, flesh ('Gregory's Rule'). In most Anglo-Saxon manuscripts, however, the skins all face the same way (HF, HF). Thus, except at the centre of the quire and where two quires abut, hair side faces flesh. In this, Anglo-Saxon scribes followed their Irish counterparts; and it is worth stressing that this remains the case in early English manuscripts produced in centres under strong Mediterranean influence, which otherwise imitated the appearance of Mediterranean books. The membrane in the sixth-century Italian 'St Augustine's Gospels'

(Cambridge, Corpus Christi College 286) is consistently arranged FH, HF; in the eighth-century copy of Acts in Oxford, Bodleian Library, Selden Supra 30, by contrast, it is generally HF, HF; while in the coeval psalter, BL, Cotton Vespasian A. i, and the Codex Aureus (Stockholm, Kungl. Bibl. A. 135) it is fairly random. The point should, however, be made that English parchment was often of a higher quality than its Italian or Frankish counterpart, and the discrepancy in tone and texture from H to F was appreciably less. Indeed when the transition from 'Insular' to 'Continental' preparation begins in the tenth century, it often appears first in books (or indeed individual quires) of poorer membrane with greater tone contrast. Such is the case, for instance, in the OE Bede, in Oxford, Bodleian Library, Tanner 10. By the early eleventh century, most English scriptoria arranged the sheets HF, FH.

The quires themselves were generally quaternions, that is they were composed of 4 sheets, giving 8 folios, 16 pages. (Early Irish scribes, by contrast, often preferred to use five sheets.) Self-contained units of text, such as calendars or canon tables, were often given a quire of their own, which could consequently be of a different size. Individual quire structures might also be changed in response to errors in transcription: major omissions or mistakes might be rectified by the removal or insertion of half-sheets (singletons). Other half-sheets were generally confined to the interior of the quire (i.e. sheets 2 and 3, fols. 2–3 and 6–7), the innermost and outermost bifolia (fols. 1 + 8, and 4 + 5) being regarded as more vulnerable – though blank leaves at the end of a quire might also be removed ('cancelled'). Altogether exceptional is the structure of the Codex Aureus, most of whose quires are sevens, consisting of three bifolia with a central singleton.

An awl or a knife was used to prick the sheets (both were sometimes employed, as in the Lichfield Gospels); and generally one set of prickings served to mark a whole quire. The placing of the prickings varied with time. In antique manuscripts pricking was done down the centre of the page: this is the case in the Italian Gospels of St Augustine, and the practice was imitated in the eighth-century Codex Aureus. In some older Anglo-Saxon manuscripts, such as CCCC 69 (Gregory, *Homiliae*) and the Hereford Gospels, the prickings were located on the outer edge of the text block, and this is still the case is Lambeth Palace 218 (Alcuin, *Epistolae*) a century later; by the tenth century, however, pricking was almost invariably done in the margins. In Insular manuscripts, pricking was generally done with the sheets folded, not open. Consequently there are two sets of prickings on each page, one in the inner, the other in the outer margin. Even when there are no prickings in the inner margin, the nature of the punctures and the disposition of direct and indirect ruling makes it clear that the sheets were folded when pricked and ruled. This is the case, for instance, in the *Vespasian Psalter and the gospelbook, BL, Royal 1. B. VII (which were presumably, then, ruled with the aid of a set-square). In many continental scriptoria, by contrast, the sheets were pricked open, thus having only one set of prickings per page. The latter procedure became the norm in England by the eleventh century after a complicated period of transition.

Throughout the Anglo-Saxon period, the lines were ruled in hard (or 'dry') point. After *c*.1000 lead was occasionally used in special circumstances, for instance if a passage had to be reruled, or if major illumination was planned for the verso (Eadui Basan's section of the Psalter, BL, Harley 603, is a case in point). In general, lead or crayon only began to supersede hard point in the generation after the Norman Conquest, above all at Christ Church, *Canterbury. The new practice does not, however, represent 'Normanisation' for Norman scriptoria were themselves only just beginning to make the change.

Generally one horizontal line was ruled for each line of text; however, in de luxe manuscripts, such as the early gospelbooks and in late tenth-century manuscripts written in a particularly tall Square minuscule (e.g. Oxford, Bodleian Library, Bodley 718), double lines were ruled to guide the head and the foot of the letters, ensuring maximum regularity of script. Double vertical lines were generally supplied if the margins were to contain initials. If the manuscript was to have a more elaborate layout (including, for instance, interspersed illustrations or a marginal apparatus), the ruling pattern was necessarily more complicated. In Cambridge, University Library, Kk. 3. 21, a glossed copy of Boethius's *De consolatione Philosophiae*, there is an extra horizontal line for an interlinear gloss between each of the rulings for the main text, while columns of narrower rulings for marginal glosses flank the main text block. Using hard point, the ruling done on one sheet could be transmitted to those beneath it, speeding the process. The impression became fainter through the quire, and re-ruling occurred when necessary. With the exception of de luxe volumes which were carefully ruled, sometimes on both sides of each sheet, such procedures were common until the late tenth century. In the eleventh century, ruling was done on the hair sides of most sheets, which were then arranged according to Gregory's Rule.

Prior to the tenth century codicological practices varied greatly – there are almost as many procedures as there are manuscripts. If, on the one hand, this is the consequence of the poor survival rate of the material, it is also, on the other, a true reflection both of the extent to which the techniques used by the Anglo-Saxons' neighbours themselves differed, and of the intelligent flexibility with which they were adopted. The steps by which this variety had, by the eleventh century, been reduced to one fairly standard procedure are as yet imperfectly understood. In theory, codicological practices help us to chart England's relations with Irish and continental scriptoria; and it is true that 'Insular preparation' is one symptom of Anglo-Saxon or Irish personnel in continental scriptoria, while 'continental' features gradually become more prominent in English books during the tenth century. However these traditions are clearly more diverse and complicated than previous discussions have allowed, and such generalisations undoubtedly need to be refined by further research.

R. Read, *Ancient Skins, Parchments and Leathers* (London, 1972); J. Vezin, 'La réalisation matérielle des manuscrits latins pendant le haut Moyen Âge', *Codicologica* 2 (Leiden, 1978), 15–51; B. Shailor, *The Medieval Book* (New Haven, CT, 1988); E. A. Lowe, *Codices Latini Antiquiores* II, 2nd ed. (Oxford, 1972); Ker, *Catalogue*.

RICHARD GAMESON

COENWULF, king of the Mercians (796–821), and one of the last, though by no means the least, of the succession of Mercian 'overlords' (cf. *Penda, *Wulfhere, *Æthelbald, and *Offa). Following the death of King Offa on 29 July 796, and the death of his son Ecgfrith in mid-December of the same year, Coenwulf, son of Cuthberht, became king of the Mercians. The structures of power were always vulnerable when power itself changed hands; and just as a certain Eadberht Præn seems immediately to have established himself as king of *Kent, so too did a certain Eadwald begin to strike coins as king of the East Angles. Coenwulf, with Archbishop Æthelheard, raised the possibility with Pope Leo III that primacy among the Southumbrian bishoprics might be transferred from *Canterbury to *London; but the pope would have none of it (*EHD* i, no. 205), at which point (it seems) Coenwulf invaded Kent, seized Eadberht Præn, 'and brought him in fetters into Mercia' (*ASC*, s.a. 798). Coenwulf promptly installed his brother Cuthred as king of Kent, placing other members of his family, such as Eanberht (S 159), in useful positions; it was perhaps under these circumstances that he was able to implement the abolition of the archbishopric of *Lichfield in 803 (*EHD* i, nos. 209–10). Cuthred died in 807, whereupon Coenwulf assumed direct control of Kent. His interests soon began to clash and collide with those of *Wulfred, archbishop of Canterbury (805–32). Decisions made in Coenwulf's presence at the Council of Chelsea, in 816, constituted a direct challenge to the king's powers, especially with regard to *Minster-in-Thanet and *Reculver, but the dispute was still unresolved at the time of Coenwulf's death (S 1436). On his northern border Coenwulf had suffered the indignity in 801 of being invaded by Eardwulf, king of the Northumbrians; but peace was soon re-established between them. Within his own kingdom, Coenwulf took what may have been a special interest in the church which Offa had founded at *Winchcombe (Glos.), suggesting that he may have been of Hwiccian as opposed to Mercian origin; the foundation charter is not authentic in its received form (S 167), but privileges obtained by Coenwulf from Pope Leo III and Pope Paschal I (BCS 337, 363) may have a genuine basis. It would also appear that King Coenwulf granted control of *Glastonbury abbey to a certain Cynehelm in the late 790s, obtaining another papal privilege from Pope Leo III (*William of Malmesbury, *De Ant. Glast.*, cc. 49–51). If so, Coenwulf's intervention would reflect the extension of 'Mercian' interests across the Somerset Avon into a part of the kingdom of *Wessex. A book said to contain 'certain Charters of Coenwulf King of the Mercians', known to have existed in the early eighteenth century but now lost, conceivably pertained to the king's patronage of a religious house in *Lindsey; while the fact that Coenwulf sooner or later resumed 'Mercian' control of the kingdom of *East Anglia is demonstrated by numismatic evidence. A leaden *seal of King Coenwulf came to light in Italy in the mid nineteenth century, and is now in the British Museum.

Coenwulf died in 821, apparently at Basingwerk (Flintshire) and so perhaps in the course of an intervention in north Wales; he was buried at Winchcombe. According to legend, his son Cynehelm (St *Kenelm) was chosen as king, but was then murdered on the orders of his jealous sister, Cwoenthryth. A series of attestations in the name of Cynehelm, styled *princeps* or *dux*, occurs in Mercian charters between *c.*800 and 811; and on this basis it has been suggested that the *ætheling Cynehelm predeceased his father and that the legend is fictitious. It seems more likely, however, that the *ealdorman was a different person of the same name (conceivably the person put in control of Glastonbury); and there is no necessary objection, therefore, to the presumption that the ætheling Cynehelm survived his father, and then fell victim to internal dynastic rivalry. In the event, Coenwulf was succeeded by his brother Ceolwulf. Coenwulf's daughter Cwoenthryth was abbess of Minster-in-Thanet, in Kent, and was also in dispute with Archbishop Wulfred; interestingly, it emerges that ancient charters pertaining to her properties were kept at Winchcombe (S 1434, 1436). In the late ninth century, the Mercian Ealdorman Æthelwulf (d. 901) perused the 'hereditary charters' of King Coenwulf which pertained to the inheritance belonging to Winchcombe (S 1442), as if he might have had a special interest in them; in which case the same could be said of his sister Ealhswith, wife of King *Alfred the Great.

The supremacy of the Mercian kings disintegrated in the 820s, during the reigns of Ceolwulf I (821–3), Beornwulf (823–5), Ludeca (825–7), and Wiglaf (827–40). In the view of someone present at a council convened at *Clofesho* in 825, 'after the death of Coenwulf, king of the Mercians, many quarrels and innumerable disputes had arisen between important men of all kinds – kings, bishops, and ministers of God's churches – concerning a multitude of secular affairs' (S 1435). In 825 Beornwulf was defeated by *Ecgberht, king of the West Saxons, at the battle of *Ellendun* (Wroughton, Wilts.), and thereby lost control of the south-eastern provinces; in a separate though not unrelated process, the Mercians lost control of the kingdom of East Anglia in 826–7. There are also various signs during the 820s of dissension within Mercia itself. Finally, in 829 Ecgberht 'conquered the kingdom of the Mercians, and everything south of the Humber; and he was the eighth king who was *Bretwalda' (*ASC*).

Archaeologia 32 (1847), 449–50 [leaden seal]; Stenton, *ASE*, pp. 225–30; W. Levison, *England and the Continent in the Eighth Century* (Oxford, 1946), pp. 249–59 [Winchcombe]; P. Wormald, 'The Ninth Century', *The Anglo-Saxons*, ed. J. Campbell (Oxford, 1982), pp. 132–59; Brooks, *Canterbury*, pp. 120–5; S. Bassett, 'A Probable Mercian Royal Mausoleum at Winchcombe, Gloucestershire', *AntJ* 65 (1985), 82–100; P. Sims-Williams, *Religion and Literature in Western England 600–800*, CSASE 3 (Cambridge, 1990), 165–8 [Winchcombe]; Yorke, *Kingdoms*, pp. 117–24; Kirby, *Kings*, pp. 185–9; S. Keynes, 'The Control of Kent in the Ninth

Century', *EME* 2 (1993), 111–31, at 113–18; *Three Eleventh-Century Anglo-Latin Saints' Lives*, ed. R. C. Love (OMT, 1996), pp. lxxxix–cxxxix and 49–89 [St Kenelm of Winchcombe].

SIMON KEYNES

COINAGE. Coins were produced in significant quantity in England during the middle and late Anglo-Saxon periods, and their discovery in *hoards and as stray finds makes them one of the most plentiful classes of artifact surviving today. Because they can be closely dated and generally bear inscriptions indicating where and by whom they were issued, they are often a valuable source of evidence for economic, administrative and political history.

Soon after the flight of the Roman garrisons in the early fifth century, Britain lapsed into an essentially non-monetary economy. Continental gold coins, initially imported as ornaments, began to circulate as money towards the end of the sixth century. At about this time the first Anglo-Saxon coins were struck, although more sustained production was not achieved until the 630s. These small gold coins – probably the shillings (OE *scillingas*) of the Anglo-Saxon *law codes, though also known to numismatists as 'thrymsas' – were modelled on the contemporary Merovingian coinage. A few bear the name of Eadbald, king of Kent (616–40), some the name of a *moneyer (Witmen or Pada), and others the name of a *mint (*Canterbury or *London); but many merely reproduce the inscriptions of their continental or Roman prototypes.

The gold shilling was superseded *c.*675 by the silver penny (OE *pening*), which was to remain the principal denomination until the mid-fourteenth century. The earliest of these pennies were struck from cast flans producing thick dumpy coins similar to their Merovingian counterparts. These are commonly, though erroneously, known as 'sceattas' to distinguish them from the broader, thinner pennies made from sheet-silver that replaced them in southern England from *c.*760. The early pennies are rich in their iconography, displaying a wide variety of pictorial and geometric designs, some of which can be paralleled in contemporary metalwork and sculpture. Few of them bear inscriptions, and where they do these are mostly the names of moneyers. Only on the Northumbrian and latterly the East Anglian coinages do the names of kings ever appear, although that does not necessarily mean that the production of the anonymous coins was not also regulated by royal authority

The new Carolingian-style penny, introduced by *Offa probably at London in *c.*760, marked a departure not only in its thinner fabric, but more especially because henceforth coins would normally carry the names of both the ruler and the moneyer responsible for issuing them. The coinage was now overtly regal, yet the moneyers enjoyed a degree of independence and the supply of silver to the mints probably depended more on the individuals and merchants who brought old or foreign money or bullion to them than on state-owned metal. During the course of the ninth century there is evidence of increasing governmental control, as the designs used by different moneyers became more standardised, and a monetary alliance was formed between *Mercia and *Wessex in the 860s so that coinage of a common design might circulate over a wider area. This was maintained in English Mercia and Wessex throughout *Alfred's reign, but in the early tenth century regional groupings developed which may reflect local self-interest. Although *Æthelstan after the conquest of *York in 927 was styled REX TO(*tius*) BRIT(*anniæ*) on his coins, a single uniform coinage for all the kingdom was not achieved until the end of *Edgar's reign.

Edgar's great coinage reform, which may have coincided with his (second) *coronation in 973, was more radical than just the standardisation of designs. It heralded a new monetary system that would last for 150 years and be the most sophisticated in Europe. It had all the features of a strong well-controlled currency comparable to that of the Franks under Charlemagne or Louis the Pious: reliable quality, the fineness and weight having been restored to those set by Alfred; good accountability with the coins now naming both mint and moneyer; and a uniform design at all the 50 or so mints (rising to more than 70 under *Æthelred II) so that there were no barriers to coin circulation within England. However, the late Anglo-Saxon coinage went further than being an excellent medium of exchange, for it was a fiscal tool in itself. The designs used at all mints were changed every few years – initially every six years or so, but after 1036 every three years or less – and only coins of the current type could be used, at least for certain transactions. This meant that before making a payment, people had to change their old coin into coin of the current type, paying probably quite a substantial fee to the moneyer; 15 per cent has been suggested. This was, in effect, a form of wealth tax. Between *c.*973 and the abandonment of this system of periodic recoinages probably in 1125 there were some fifty successive

Pl. 8 Coinage.

issues. Not all the available money was reminted on each occasion, for the hoards show that in their savings people often retained older coins, while in the smaller 'currency' hoards the coins are generally of the latest one or two types.

The silver penny was of relatively high value – in the early tenth century a sheep was worth five pence and a pig ten (VI Æthelstan 6.2) – so in order to provide smaller change pennies were cut in two or four producing halfpennies and farthings. The weight standard for the penny had been changed on a number of occasions. The earliest Anglo-Saxon coins in principle used the Merovingian standard of c.1.30 g, but Offa increased it to c.1.40 g in the early 790s. Alfred, who was also innovative in his management of the coinage, increased the standard to c.1.60 g in c.880. In each case, however, as a result of economic cycles, the weights of the coins declined from these theoretical standards. After Edgar's reform, each substantive coin issue was struck to a series of declining standards only to be restored at the beginning of the next type. This manipulation of the weight standard appears to

have been a deliberate mechanism to encourage people to bring coin and bullion into the mint throughout the life of the issue. This would have been achieved by offering a better exchange rate, i.e. more coins to the pound of silver, towards the end of a coin type. It seems that the more detail in which we study the coinage, the more we appreciate the complexity and originality of late Anglo-Saxon government and administration.

J. J. North, *English Hammered Coinage 1. Early Anglo-Saxon to Henry III c.*600–1272, 3rd ed. (London, 1994); P. Grierson and M. Blackburn, *Medieval European Coinage 1. The Early Middle Ages (5th–10th Centuries)* (Cambridge, 1986), chs. 8 and 10; C. E. Blunt, B. H. I. H. Stewart, and C. S. S. Lyon, *Coinage in Tenth-Century England* (Oxford, 1989); K. Jonsson, *The New Era: The Reformation of the Late Anglo-Saxon Coinage* (Stockholm, 1987); I. Stewart, 'Coinage and Recoinage after Edgar's Reform', in *Studies in Late Anglo-Saxon Coinage*, ed. K. Jonsson (Stockholm, 1990), pp. 455–85; M. A. S. Blackburn, 'Æthelred's Coinage and the Payment of Tribute', *The Battle of Maldon AD 991*, ed. D. Scragg (Oxford, 1991), pp. 156–69.

M. A. S. BLACKBURN

Coinage
1. Gold shilling ('thrymsa'), c. 670, with the name of the moneyer, Pada, in runes set in a Roman standard on the reverse.
2. Aldfrith of Northumbria (685–704). Aldfrith's silver pennies ('sceattas') are quite exceptional in carrying the name of the ruler (+ALDFRIDUS), as no other contemporary Anglo-Saxon or Merovingian issues did.
3. Silver penny ('sceat'), Series J, York mint?, c. 725. Most coins of the first half of the eighth century bear no inscriptions, but their iconography is rich.
4. Offa of Mercia (757–96). This East Anglian coin of the moneyer Wilred was struck early in Offa's reign and is evidence that Offa had already subdued the East Angles by the 760s.
5. Wulfred, archbishop of Canterbury (805–32). Unlike those of his predecessors, Wulfred's coins make no reference to the authority of the king.
6. Ecgberht of Wessex (as king of Mercia, 829). These rare London coins of Ecgberht with the title REX M(*erciorum*) give welcome corroboration to the statement in the *Anglo–Saxon Chronicle* that in 829 Ecgberht conquered the kingdom of Mercia.
7. Æthelwulf of Wessex (839–58). Open Cross type, Rochester, moneyer Ethelere. Under Æthelwulf regulation of the West Saxon coinage was tightened, bringing uniformity in the designs used by all moneyers.
8. Ceolwulf II of Mercia (874–9). Most of Ceolwulf's twelve surviving coins were struck in London, demonstrating that Vikings did not control the city in the later 870s.
9. Guthrum (880–90). Soon after Guthrum and his army settled in East Anglia and the East Midlands he started striking a coinage similar to Alfred's but using the name Æthelstan, by which he had been baptised in 878.
10. Edward the Elder of Wessex and Mercia (899–924). This is one of a number of pictorial coin types struck in the West Midlands while under the control of Edward's sister Æthelflæd, but only Edward's name appears on the coinage.
11. Edgar (959–75), Reform type, Lewes, moneyer Goldstan. Edgar initiated c. 973 a system of periodic recoinages, which for its time was the most sophisticated in Europe.
12. Edward the Confessor (1042–66). Sovereign-Eagles type, Hastings, moneyer Brid. The image of the king enthroned was derived from a sixth-century Byzantine coin.

Note: All coins illustrated are in the Fitzwilliam Museum, Cambridge. Enlarged × 1.25.

Pl. 9 Images of kingship from Anglo-Saxon coins.

Images of Kingship

1. Eadbald of Kent (616–40). Eadbald (AUDVARLD REGES) was the first Anglo-Saxon king to be portrayed on a coin. The style is Frankish, and there is notable Christian symbolism in the form of a cross before the face (here off the flan) and one on the reverse.
2. Offa of Mercia (757–96). Coins provide the only contemporary images of Offa. Some represent him as a Roman emperor, while others such as this appear to be novel and may indeed reflect a contemporary hair style.
3. Cenwulf of Mercia (796–821). The diademed and draped bust are derived from Roman imperial coins, although the immediate prototype is a contemporary Carolingian coin of Louis the Pious.
4. Alfred of Wessex (871–99). Here the image of Alfred is taken directly from a gold solidus of Honorius or a near contemporary. The title accorded him on this coin struck at London *c.* 875 is REX s[*axonum et*] M[*erciorum*], 'king of the Saxons and Mercians'.
5. Æthelstan (924–39). This is the first time that an Anglo-Saxon ruler is shown on the coinage wearing a crown, and it is remarkably similar to the depiction of Æthelstan in a contemporary manuscript of Bede's *Lives of St Cuthbert* (CCCC 183).
6. Æthelred II (978–1016). A sceptre is added as symbol of authority in this, Æthelred's *Second Hand* type.
7. Cnut (1016–35). In his second type Cnut is shown wearing a helmet of contemporary form.
8. Harold II (1066). Harold is depicted with a bearded face, Germanic arched crown and sceptre, yet the form of the bust and muscular, undraped neck is taken from bronze coins of the emperor Claudius.
9. William I (1066–87). The image on this, William's first type, emphasises succession and continuity with his Anglo-Saxon predecessors, rather than the introduction of a new regime.

Note: All coins illustrated are in the Fitzwilliam Museum, Cambridge. Enlarged × 1.75.

COLDINGHAM (Berwick) preserves the name of *Colodesburg*, the main Bernician royal monastery. It was a double house, with both English and Irish inmates, and was ruled by Æbbe (d. 683), sister of King *Oswald and a major figure in Northumbrian politics. St *Cuthbert spent a nocturnal vigil in the sea while staying at this house, and St *Æthelthryth lived there for a year before moving to *Ely. For *Bede the fire which destroyed it in *c.*686 was a judgement on 'the wickedness of those who dwelt there and especially on those who were supposed to be its leaders'. His account of the complex, its 'public and private buildings' towering grandly up, its 'cells built for praying and reading' now used for luxury and vice, its nuns 'weaving elaborate garments with which to adorn themselves as if they were brides', is one of the best descriptions of an Anglo-Saxon *monastic site. The site can be identified with St Abb's Head, a coastal promontory still enclosed by the well-preserved monastic *vallum* (fig. 11).

Anon., *Vita S. Cuthberti* ii.3; Bede, *HE* iv.25; J. Blair, 'Anglo-Saxon Minsters: a Topographical Review', in Blair and Sharpe, *Past. Care*, pp. 226–66, at 227–8, 233, 259–61.

JOHN BLAIR

COLEMAN: *see* Wulfstan II

COLLECTAR: *see* Liturgical Books

COLLOQUIES (Latin *colloquia*, 'conversations') are a form of school-room exercise designed to teach young oblates how to converse in Latin (which they were required to do by various ecclesiastical legislation dating from the Carolingian period: though how widely and strictly this legislation was applied in pre-Conquest England is a nice question). A further benefit of the ability to speak Latin was the facilitation of travel to continental monasteries and monastic guesthouses; accordingly, scholastic colloquies often served the same function as modern travellers' phrase-books. The form of the colloquy was inherited from late antiquity. Because the Roman empire was bilingual in Greek and Latin, bilingual phrase-books containing conversational exercises, reading-texts and vocabularies were produced, apparently from the second century AD onwards (a characteristic form is preserved as part of the so-called 'Hermeneumata pseudo-Dositheana'). Typically the exercise is couched in the form of a dialogue between a young boy and his slave, and concerns the events of the day, beginning with getting up in the morning (hence sentences of the sort, 'Bring me my shoes', 'bring me some water so I can wash my face', etc.). At some point, somewhere in the British Isles, the utility of such colloquies for teaching Latin conversation was realised, whereupon they were adapted for monastic use by jettisoning the Greek component, and tailoring the conversation to a monastic milieu. This early type of adaptation is seen in a colloquy entitled *De raris fabulis* (of unknown origin: Wales or Ireland, between the seventh and ninth centuries?), and is parodied in the Hiberno-Latin *Hisperica famina* (mid-seventh century). By the later tenth century, and in the wake of the Benedictine reform movement (which may have enacted stricter regulations regarding the use of Latin at times when conversation was permitted in monasteries), Anglo-Saxon pedagogues such as *Ælfric, and his pupil *Ælfric Bata adapted the inherited form of the colloquy in imaginative ways with the intention of making Latin conversation an enjoyable exercise: so that in Ælfric's *Colloquium* the boys take on the roles of various craftsmen and tradesmen, whereas Ælfric Bata inserts in his colloquies the sort of scatological vocabulary which has occupied schoolboys from time immemorial.

W. H. Stevenson, *Early Scholastic Colloquies* (Oxford, 1929); *Latin Colloquies from pre-Conquest Britain*, ed. S. Gwara (Toronto, 1996); *Ælfric's Colloquy*, ed. G. N. Garmonsway, 2nd ed. (London, 1947); A. C. Dionisotti, 'From Ausonius' Schooldays? A Schoolbook and its Relatives', *Journal of Roman Studies* 72 (1982), 83–125; G. N. Garmonsway, 'The Development of the Colloquy', in *The Anglo-Saxons*, ed. P. Clemoes (London, 1959), pp. 248–61; P. Riché, 'La vie quotidienne dans les écoles monastiques d'après les colloques scolaires', in *Sous la Règle de Saint Benoît* (Paris, 1982), pp. 417–26; D. Porter, 'The Latin Syllabus in Anglo-Saxon Monastic Schools', *Neophilologus* 78 (1994), 1–20; S. Gwara and D. W. Porter, *Anglo-Saxon Conversations. The Colloquies of Ælfric Bata* (Woodbridge, 1997).

MICHAEL LAPIDGE

COLOPHONS (from a Greek word meaning 'ending', 'finishing touch') are personal comments made by scribes at the end of their scribal stints, hence often at the end of a manuscript, occasionally in metrical form, in which they often reveal their name and place of activity, or comment on the difficulty of the task; such comments are exceptionally valuable evidence in the attempt to date and localise manuscripts. A few Anglo-Saxon manuscripts contain colophons: Oxford, Bodleian Library, Laud Misc. 263 ('Willibaldus diaconus'); Vatican City, Biblioteca Apostolica Vaticana, Barberini lat. 570, the *'Barberini Gospels' ('Ora pro uuigbaldo'); the Book of *Durrow; London, BL, Cotton Nero D. iv, the *'Lindisfarne Gospels', where a tenth-century colophon has been added on 259r by *Aldred; London, BL, Add. 49598, the *'Benedictional of St Æthelwold', where the text is preceded by a metrical preface in which the scribe names himself as *Godeman; Hannover, Kestner-Museum, W. M. XXIa. 36 ('Eaduuius cognomento Basan').

A. W. Pollard, *An Essay on Colophons* (Chicago, 1905); [Benedictines of Bouveret], *Colophons de manuscrits occidentaux des origines au XVI siècle*, 6 vols, Spicilegii Friburgensis Subsidia (Fribourg, 1965–82); *CLA* Supp. **1400 [Willibald]; D. N. Dumville, *English Caroline Script and Monastic History: Studies in Benedictinism, AD 950–1030* (Woodbridge, 1993), pp. 120–4 [Eadwig].

MICHAEL LAPIDGE

COLOUR was a vital element in Anglo-Saxon art, crafts, literature and environment, with aesthetic, social, religious, technological, commercial and linguistic implications. All these aspects of colour required a vocabulary to express and discuss them. As with most languages, Old English had a group of frequently and widely used colour words which were capable of abstract use, and also, a larger, more specialised vocabulary. It should never be assumed that Old English colour words are easily translatable, since they may indicate more, or less, than one hue, or be restricted in terms of darkness, vividness or context.

The red area includes the common term *read* which means 'red', but which can also indicate parts of brown, orange, pink, and purple. *Brun* gives the modern 'brown', but it specialises in dark brown, while red-brown is more usually described as *read*, and pale brown as *fealu*. *Brun* can also denote dark red and purple, and, even stranger for modern readers, it appears to mean 'shiny' in the context of metal. More specialised words include *basu*, which usually indicates a rich and striking red, such as scarlet or crimson. When combined with *brun*, as in *brunbasu*, the colour is darkened to purple or violet. Two specialised words, both borrowed from Latin, can indicate the textile, dye or colour of luxury garments: *purpuren* and *pællen*.

The green area includes *grene*, with a meaning remarkably similar to that of modern green, and the much rarer and highly specialised *walden*, indicating greenish or hazel eyes.

The yellow area is dominated by *geolu* and *fealu*, which appear to be complementary, since *fealu* covers the less striking pale and dull yellows, but it also denotes pale and/or dull brown, and grey.

Gylden is often to be taken literally, when it means 'made of gold' or 'gilded', but it can also have a colour sense indicating yellow or yellowish orange, often shining, and always impressive. *Gecroged*, meaning literally 'saffroned', is rare, and denotes a range of yellow to orange in the context of dye, cloth or clothing.

The blue area has *hæwen*, which is very close to being a basic term but was probably not universally used as such. It can also mean 'grey', and it can be darkened by the addition of a prefix, giving *blæhæwen* 'dark blue'. Specialised terms restricted to dye, cloth and clothing include *blæwen* 'dark blue', and *wæden*, meaning literally 'woad-dyed'. *Glæsen* usually means 'made of glass' but, since early glass was often blue-green, there is sometimes a colour sense involved in its usage.

Among the non-hues, darkness has a basic term, *blæc*, meaning 'black', 'dark' (hue unspecified), or any dark hue, for example, dark blue. Several other words can mean 'dark', such as *deorc* and *mirce*. *Hwit* means 'white' but also 'shining' and 'pale'. Several other words also indicate the last two concepts, such as *blac* and *sciene*. *Græg* can mean 'grey' but it can also denote a greyish hue, such as 'dull green'. *Hasu* indicates grey and grey-brown, but is extant only in poetry. Two other grey words, commonly used of human hair, are *har*, which can also mean 'white', and *wylfen*, meaning literally 'wolf-coloured'.

W. E. Mead, 'Color in Old English Poetry', *PMLA* 14 (1899), 169–206; L. D. Lerner, 'Colour Words in Anglo-Saxon', *MLN* 46 (1951), 246–9; G. König, 'Die Bezeichnungen für Farbe, Glanz und Helligkeit im Altenglischen' (unpubl. dissertation, Johannes Gutenberg University of Mainz, 1957); N. F. Barley, 'Old English Colour Classification: Where do Matters Stand?', *ASE* 3 (1974), 15–28; C. P. Biggam, 'Sociolinguistic Aspects of Old English Colour Lexemes', *ASE* 24 (1995), 51–65; idem, *Blue in Old English* (Amsterdam, 1997); idem, *Grey in Old English* (London, forthcoming).

C. P. BIGGAM

COLUMBA (d. 597), saint and founder of *Iona, belonged to the lineage of Cenél Conaill, the ruling dynasty of Donegal. He was born around 521 but his life is not known until in 561 he is said to have prayed for the success in battle of his kinsmen. Soon afterwards he was the subject of censure at a synod convened by his family's political opponents in Meath. In 563 he left Ireland for Scottish Dalriada, where the king, Conall, gave him the island of Iona. Here his monastery flourished and he became a major holy man for Dalriada, though retaining his links with northern Ireland. He is said to have consecrated Conall's successor, Áedán mac Gabráin, as king and to have played a part in negotiating the relationship between Áedan and the saint's cousin Áed mac Ainmirech, king of Cenél Conaill, Northern Uí Néill overlord, and king of Ireland, at a royal meeting held near Coleraine at Druim Cett. Áed's presence here suggests that the date 575 given by the Irish annals is too early by more than ten years. His Life, written around 697 by *Adomnán, provides a vivid account of monastic life in Iona but offers little biographical detail. Some stories of the saint's visits to the Pictish king Bridei combined with Bede's account, derived from Pictish sources, suggest that he was active as a missionary and founder of churches among the Picts in eastern Scotland. His foundations in Ireland at Derry and elsewhere are better remembered, though many of the churches associated with Columba's name may belong to a later period. In Irish he is usually known as Columb Cille. He died at Iona on 9 June 597.

Sharpe, *Handlist*, 200; Bede, *HE* iii.4; *Adomnán's Life of Columba*, ed. and trans. A. O. and M. O. Anderson, rev. M. O. Anderson, 2nd ed. (OMT, 1991); *Adomnán of Iona: Life of St Columba*, trans. R. Sharpe (Harmondsworth, 1995); T. O. Clancy and G. Markus, *Iona. The Earliest Poetry of a Celtic Monastery* (Edinburgh, 1995); *Studies on the Cult of St Columba*, ed. C. Bourke (Dublin, 1997).

RICHARD SHARPE

COMITATUS. Since the nineteenth century the immediate followers of a king or lord have regularly been referred to as his *comitatus* (the term is taken from Tacitus, *Germania*, c. 13). He provided them with food, and they lived – and slept – in his hall. For exceptional service he gave them rich gifts of rings, weapons, armour and horses, and during times of feasting they vowed absolute loyalty. The most famous literary exponent of the relationship is in the entry for 755 in the *Anglo-Saxon Chronicle* (Cynewulf and Cyneheard). Even after the social organisation of Anglo-Saxon England had changed, in the tenth century, the concept survived as an image in *heroic literature, notably in the *Battle of Maldon*, and, by transference to God/Christ as Lord, into Christian literature. Much play is made in the *elegies of the sad lot of the man exiled from the *comitatus*.

D. H. Green, *The Carolingian Lord* (Cambridge, 1965), pp. 64–79; K. O'Brien O'Keeffe, 'Heroic Values and Christan Ethics', *CamComp*, pp. 107–25.

DONALD SCRAGG

COMPUTUS (cf. OE *gerim*, *gerimcræfi*) is the term applied both to the medieval science of com-

putation and to texts dealing with that science. Computus was concerned mainly with the calendar, and especially with the problem of the movable feasts – those holidays, like Easter, whose dates were determined by the phases of the moon and so fell on no fixed date in the Julian calendar. The various methods used in late ancient and medieval times to determine the Julian dates of the new and full moons were based on cycles, the theory being that if a particular number of lunar periods could be shown to correspond exactly to a particular number of years, one could predict the moon's phases in perpetuity. Two paschal cycles were known in early England: the 84-year cycle used by the Irish and the 19-year cycle developed in Alexandria and used at Rome. At the Synod of *Whitby (664), it was decided that the English church would conform to Roman usage (see *Easter controversy).

The two major classes of text associated with computus are textbooks and miscellanies. Preeminent among the textbooks are *Bede's short *De temporibus* (703) and his more expansive *De temporum ratione* (725), which combines instruction in the use of the calendar with natural lore and chronology. Apart from *Ælfric's *De temporibus anni*, which provides a brief overview of the subject, the only other computus textbook from Anglo-Saxon England is *Byrhtferth's OE and Latin *Enchiridion* (1011), which draws liberally on Bede's work. Both Bede and Byrhtferth based their textbooks on computistical miscellanies (called *computi*), of which there were a great variety. The *computi* known to Bede were of Irish origin and were often quite large, normally containing a perpetual calendar, an Easter table, tables for finding the moon's age and the weekday, arithmetic tables, instructions for calculating and documents relating to the history of the calendar. *Computi* of this type continued to be copied throughout the Anglo-Saxon period, but the beginning of the tenth century saw the production of smaller, more practical *computi*, suitable for inclusion in such *liturgical books as missals, homiliaries, and psalters. These omitted most of the historical and theoretical material, which had been relevant in the earlier Easter controversy. Most were in Latin, but some contained passages of OE. A practical and highly condensed computus compiled at *Winchester around the year 978 had great influence, being known to Byrhtferth as well as to computists in *Worcester, *Canterbury, and elsewhere. Beginning in the late tenth century, the computus of *Abbo of Fleury, notable for its mathematical sophistication and the clarity of its tables, had considerable influence, particularly on Byrhtferth, who around 988 compiled a large computus (the one on which he later based his *Enchiridion*). Byrhtferth's computus is predominantly Abbonian, but also contains material from the earlier Winchester and Irish *computi*; its eclecticism is typical of *computi* produced in Anglo-Saxon England.

C. W. Jones, *Bedae Opera de Temporibus* (Cambridge, MA, 1943); idem, *Bedae Pseudepigrapha* (Ithaca, NY, 1939); H. Henel, *Studien zum altenglischen Computus* (Leipzig; 1934); B. Günzel, *Ælfwine's Prayerbook*, HBS 108 (London, 1993), 16–30; *The Leofric Missal*, ed. F. E. Warren (Oxford, 1883), pp. 21–58 [*De Computo ecclesiastico*, a 'Winchester' computus]; *Byrhtferth's Enchiridion*, ed. P. S. Baker and M. Lapidge, EETS ss 15 (Oxford, 1995).

PETER S. BAKER

CONFESSION AND PENANCE. Confession of sins in Anglo-Saxon England took three forms: public acknowledgment of sins before the bishop, usually reserved for the most serious sins; private acknowledgment of sins to the priest, the form believed to have been the most common; and devotional exercise in which the sinner confessed in prayer, sometimes using a set list of sins that could not have corresponded closely to any one person's conduct. In the later Middle Ages, private confession to the priest became the norm, but the Anglo-Saxon evidence is too vague to permit any one of these modes to be seen as dominant.

Private confession in the Anglo-Saxon period was followed by the performance of various penitential acts assigned by the priest according to the catalogue of penances contained in the penitential. Continental Latin penitentials contemporary with Anglo-Saxon handbooks of penance accompany the penitential's list of sins with an *ordo confessionis* to guide the priest's interrogation of the penitent in confession. The vernacular Old English texts do not include a formal *ordo confessionis*, but some of them include detailed advice to aid the priest in such matters as ensuring the penitent's candor and sincerity. Confession and penance were most likely to be undertaken during the major holy seasons of the church year – Advent, Lent, and Pentecost.

Acts of penance were performed in one of three contexts, depending on the seriousness of the sin being atoned for. Public acts of penance, which in the early church could be undertaken only once, were required for such sins as fratricide or the murder of a cleric, which might carry the penance of exile. Private penance could be repeated and involved a range of penitential acts, the most fre-

quent being fasts lasting for periods ranging from a few days to several years. Crimes involving personal injury entailed restitution before absolution could be given, a requirement that indicates close cooperation between ecclesiastical and secular authorities. The interaction of penance and secular law is apparent as early as the laws of *Alfred and continues in the laws which *Wulfstan the Homilist wrote for *Cnut.

Sources such as parish registers of penitents are, unfortunately, unknown for the Anglo-Saxon period, so there is no consensus about such basic matters as the frequency with which confession was heard or about the uniformity or supervision of penances assigned. References to confession by homilists (e.g. Wulfstan or *Ælfric) indicate varying expectations in the practice of confession and penance for both clergy and laity.

The traditional nineteenth-century model of regular confession to the priest cannot be traced to Anglo-Saxon sources. The question of the frequency of confession, which was not an annual requirement before 1215, is related to a widespread characterisation of penitential practice as a form of social control exercised by the *clergy over the laity. Although penance was a form in which the clergy sought to direct the public and private lives of lay men and women, such direction also had educational and devotional functions which are as yet inadequately appreciated. Penance and confession also raise questions of *literacy; they required the use of written texts in a society whose literature and legal system were primarily oral, and this aspect of their cultural significance remains largely unexplored.

J.-C. Guy *et al.*, *Pratiques de la confession des pères du désert à Vatican II: Quinze études d'histoire* (Paris, 1983); R. Spindler, *Das altenglische Bussbuch (sog. Confessionale Pseudo-Egberti). Ein Beitrag zu den Kirchlichen Gesetzen der Angelsachsen* (Leipzig, 1934); R. Fowler, 'A Late Old English Handbook for the Use of a Confessor', *Anglia* 83 (1965), 1–34.

ALLEN J. FRANTZEN

CONFRATERNITY BOOK: *see* Liturgical Commemoration

CONVERSION. Any general narrative of the conversion, or more accurately Christianisation, of the English peoples is essentially that of *Bede's *Historia ecclesiastica*. The first of the pagan English kingdoms to be converted to Christianity, *Kent, was christianised initially by a group of monks, led by *Augustine, and sent by Pope *Gregory the Great, who had heard that the people of Kent were looking to be evangelised. The monks arrived in 597 and had achieved considerable success before the end of the year. Although it is not known when *Æthelberht, the king of Kent, was baptised, his conversion to Christianity prompted the conversions of the kings of *Essex and *East Anglia. On the other hand, when Æthelberht died in 616 he was succeeded by his son, Eadbald, who was still a pagan: Kent lapsed into paganism and the kingdoms of Essex and East Anglia apostasised, with King *Rædwald of East Anglia apparently adopting a syncretist religion. Eadbald, however, soon abjured paganism, and when the king of *Northumbria, *Edwin, asked to marry Eadbald's sister, Æthelburh, the king of Kent insisted on her right to remain Christian and to have with her christian priests, of whom the leader was *Paulinus. The marriage of Edwin and Æthelburh was to be one of a number of factors which in turn prompted the conversion of the Northumbrian king. As in the case of Kent, however, the king's death led to a period of apostasy, which ended with the accession in 635 of *Oswald, a prince of the rival Bernician dynasty, who had already been converted among the Irish settlers of western Scotland. As a result Oswald invited Irish missionaries from *Iona, of whom the most important was *Aidan, to work in Northumbria, notably from their base at *Lindisfarne. Oswald was also able to promote Christianity elsewhere, notably in *Wessex, where he stood as godfather to King Cynegils, who had been converted by an Italian priest named *Birinus, sent by Pope Honorius. Meanwhile the apostasy of East Anglia had been reversed under King Sigeberht, who had the support of the Frankish missionary Felix and the Irishman *Fursa, and shortly afterwards Christianity was reestablished among the East Saxons, through the help of Oswald's successor, *Oswiu, and the Northumbrian priest Cedd. Oswiu also helped spread Christianity among the Middle Angles, arranging the baptism of their ruler, Peada. The christianisation of other Mercian groups followed, although Bede fails to provide much detail. The last of the English kingdoms to be christianised was *Sussex, where Bishop *Wilfrid of Northumbria preached in the 680s, during one of his periods of exile.

Bede's narrative portrays the christianisation of the English largely in terms of the actions of saints and saintly kings. His leading saints can be categorised either as Roman, that is they were sent by a pope or had connections with *Canterbury, or as Irish, which usually means that they had come from Iona or one of its dependencies, usually *Lindisfarne. The differences between the groups

were considerable: most obviously they followed divergent liturgical practices. Yet other factors may have been more important: the Irish may have been better placed to explain a religion whose *liturgy and scriptures were in an alien language (i.e. Latin), since it had been as foreign to them as it was to the English, and they had therefore already had to face the difficulties which this presented; the Romans may have been less attuned to such problems. Equally the Irish may have had more sense of the social norms of a tribal society than did Augustine and his companions. Yet for all these differences both groups had much in common: above all they were monastic. Further, although it is often pointed out that the Irish missions always succeeded whereas the Roman missions all experienced one setback, it should be noted that the Irish in Northumbria and Essex were evangelising in areas where the Romans had previously worked. Most areas of England were converted after one relapse into paganism. The Irish may have been successful because they usually provided the second wave of missionaries.

Apart from the significance of saints in Bede's account the role of kings should also be noted. Although he does not say so directly, Bede describes a process of christianisation which was largely determined by power-politics. Overlords often saw to the conversion of inferior or client kings. The power of Æthelberht, Oswald and Oswiu was reflected in their ability to influence the religion of others.

It is also necessary to note what is left out or underemphasised by Bede. In his concern to stress the importance of *Rome and of the Irish, Bede downplays the role of Frankish clergy: one Frankish bishop, Liudhard, had accompanied Bertha when she married Æthelberht; other Frankish clerics accompanied Augustine in 597, and yet others continued to play a role in the christianisation of the English, notably in East Anglia, where Felix was active, and Wessex, where *Agilbert was bishop. Rather harder to evaluate is the possible role of British clergy. Bede claims that they did nothing for the English, and there is evidence from the Synod of the Grove of Victory that the British church was opposed to association with the English. Nevertheless it is probable that British clergy did play some missionary role in the westernmost areas of English settlement, in the West Midlands and in Northumbria, where the church of Rheged may have had some influence.

The history of christianisation in Anglo-Saxon England did not conclude with the christianisation of *Sussex. The level of christianisation achieved by the missions was variable, and in many respects Bede's account of the pastoral activities of *Cuthbert shows the need for continuing evangelisation. Equally, English missionaries turned from England itself to the Continent from the late seventh century onwards. Within England the arrival of the *Vikings in the ninth century brought a new pagan population to the British Isles. For their conversion we have no source equivalent to Bede's *Historia ecclesiastica*, but it is clear that christianisation continued to be a political issue in the Viking period. One of the conditions of the treaty which followed *Alfred's defeat of *Guthrum at Edington in 878 was the baptism of the Viking leader at Aller, with Alfred standing as his godfather.

J. Campbell, 'The First Century of Christianity in England' (1971) and 'Observations on the Conversion of England' (1973), repr. in his *Essays*, pp. 49–67, 69–84; P. Wormald, 'Bede, *Beowulf*, and the Conversion of the Anglo-Saxon Aristocracy', *Bede and Anglo-Saxon England*, ed. R. T. Farrell, BAR Brit. ser. 46 (1978), 32–95; A. Angenendt, 'The Conversion of the Anglo-Saxons Considered against the Background of the Early Medieval Mission', *Settimane* 32 (1986), 747–92; I. Wood, 'The Mission of Augustine of Canterbury to the English', *Speculum* 69 (1994), 1–17.

IAN WOOD

COPPERGATE: *see* York

CORNWALL was presumably an independent kingdom, with its own king, *c.*700, when *Aldhelm addressed a letter to King Geruntius of 'Domnonia' (which must effectively have meant Cornwall, as it cannot realistically still have included Devon); the same king also donated land to *Sherborne Abbey in Dorset. Conflicts between Cornish and English are recorded during the eighth and early ninth centuries, the last recorded battle being that of King *Ecgberht against a combined Cornish and *Viking force at Hingston Down (just within Cornwall) in 838. Thereafter the whole region must nominally have been under English rule (King *Alfred held land in more than one part), although a king of Cornwall is recorded in the Welsh Annals later in the ninth century. Grants of land by English rulers occur in the eastern part of the county during that century, and a Cornish bishop professed obedience to the archbishop of *Canterbury; but not until the mid-tenth century are grants attested in the western half of the county. During the tenth century, too, Cornishmen appear bearing two names, one English and one Cornish; and the manumissions recorded in the Bodmin Gospels also show some

cultural assimilation at that period. For about a century, from the reign of King *Æthelstan to *c.*1020, Cornwall had its own episcopal see, at St Germans; but it was then merged with the see of Crediton in Devon. At the time of *Domesday Book Cornwall's *settlement pattern can be seen to be distinctively non-English, and the county must have been predominantly Cornish-speaking, except perhaps in the *towns; administratively, however, it had by then been thoroughly incorporated into the English system.

H. P. R. Finberg, 'Sherborne, Glastonbury, and the Expansion of Wessex' (1953), repr. in his *Lucerna: Studies of Some Problems in the Early History of England* (London, 1964), pp. 95–115; M. Forster, 'Die Freilassungsurkunden des Bodmin-Evangeliars', in *A Grammatical Miscellany Offered to Otto Jespersen*, ed. N. Bogholm *et al.* (London and Copenhagen, 1930), pp. 77–99; D. Hooke, *Pre-Conquest Charter-Bounds of Devon and Cornwall* (Woodbridge, 1994); W. G. Hoskins, *The Westward Expansion of Wessex* (Leicester, 1960); L. Olson, *Early Monasteries in Cornwall* (Woodbridge, 1989); W. M. M. Picken, 'Bishop Wulfsige Comoere: an Unrecognised Tenth-Century Gloss in the Bodmin Gospels', *Cornish Studies* 14 (1986), 34–8; M. F. Wakelin, *Language and History in Cornwall* (Leicester, 1975), ch. 3.

O. J. PADEL

CORONATION. A term denoting the ritual used for the inauguration of a king, which served to differentiate the king from all Christians and (from a clerical viewpoint) to define his responsibilities. Kings were anointed in Visigothic Spain, probably from 631; and the practice began in Francia with Pippin, the first Carolingian, in 751. The English evidence is less clear cut. A practice of royal anointing is first recorded in *Mercia and *Northumbria towards the end of the eighth century. In 787 Ecgfrith, son of *Offa of Mercia, was 'hallowed (*gehalgod*) to king' (*ASC*), representing a pre-mortem association of son by father, as opposed to an accession following the death of a king; and in 796, after the death of Æthelred of Northumbria, Eardwulf 'took the kingdom and was afterwards consecrated (*gebletsod*) and enthroned in York' (*ASC*, MSS. DE). A charter of Ceolwulf I of Mercia, dated 822 and extant in its original form (S 186), grants land to the archbishop of *Canterbury in return for 'my consecration (*consecratio*) which . . . I have received from him the same day'. The practice first breaks surface in *Wessex in the second half of the ninth century. In 853 *Alfred was sent to *Rome, and Pope Leo IV 'hallowed him to king and stood sponsor to him at confirmation' (*ASC*). It is most unlikely that Alfred was anointed king at this time; and more likely that a chronicler, writing *c.*890, represented Alfred's confirmation at the pope's hands as a sign that he was destined to become king. The liturgical affinity between confirmation and royal anointing certainly facilitated such an elision. Whatever the case, it is clear that royal anointing was already considered important, even though it is otherwise absent from the *Chronicle* prior to the tenth century.

The evidence of the surviving coronation *ordines* modifies and clarifies this picture in important respects. Nelson has shown that the so-called 'First English *ordo*', preserved in its earliest form in a part of the Leofric Missal (Oxford, Bodleian Library, Bodley 579), represents an English or more specifically West Saxon tradition of royal anointing in the early ninth century, and that it served as the basis for the *ordo* composed by Hincmar of Rheims for Judith, daughter of Charles the Bald, when she married *Æthelwulf, king of the West Saxons, in 856. The 'Second English *ordo*' derives some of its forms from the much simpler 'First *ordo*', but is mainly based on late-ninth-century Carolingian *ordines*. An early version of this *ordo* was exported to Francia probably when Louis (IV) d'Outremer was recalled from exile at *Æthelstan's court in 936 to become king of the West Franks. In the anointing prayer, the king is raised to the throne 'of the Saxons, Mercians, and Northumbrians'; and other uncorrected phrases in the same prayer suggest that in a still earlier version of the *ordo* the king had been anointed as ruler of *two* peoples. Given that both Alfred in his later years and *Edward the Elder asserted that they ruled over the Angles and Saxons, or the Anglo-Saxons (meaning the West Saxons and Mercians), it is possible that the 'Second *ordo*' was first used for the coronation of Edward in 900 (cf. *Anglo-Saxons). It is more likely, however, that Æthelstan was the first king to succeed jointly to Wessex and Mercia, and that the new *ordo* was first used when he was anointed at *Kingston-upon-Thames in 925. Within two years the Northumbrians had submitted to him; and thenceforth stress was laid in the king's *charters on his hegemony over the peoples of Britain, often in imperial language. This would accord with the hypothetical original of the 'Second *ordo*', proclaiming the king's rule over two peoples, and its subsequent amendment to 'Saxons, Mercians, and Northumbrians'. The suggestion that the 'Second *ordo*' was first used for Æthelstan is strengthened by a regnal list, written during the reign of *Edward the Martyr (and appended to *ASC*, MS.

B). This list gives reign-lengths rounded to the nearest year up to and including the reign of Edward the Elder; but from Æthelstan onwards the compiler measured reign-lengths to the nearest week or even day, beginning from a date which was evidently or apparently that of a king's coronation (as opposed to his accession), suggesting that coronation had assumed a new significance in the 920s. It has been argued that King *Edgar was consecrated not long after his accession, in 959, and so that his supposedly delayed coronation at Pentecost in 973, amidst the evocative Roman remains in *Bath, was a second coronation. The precise significance of the ceremony in 973 remains a puzzle; but it was probably an 'imperial' coronation, representing a further development of the theme of hegemonial overlordship expressed in the 'Second *ordo*'. Copies of the 'Second *ordo*' are found in most of the pontificals written in England in the late tenth and early eleventh centuries.

There is reason to believe that the Danish conqueror *Cnut and his sons *Harold Harefoot and *Harthacnut were not anointed, but crowned and enthroned in secular ceremonies. If so, English tradition was reasserted in the person of *Edward the Confessor. He became king in 1042, but it was not until 1043 that he 'was hallowed to king at Winchester on Easter Day with great ceremony' (*ASC*, MSS. CE). The version of the 'Second *ordo*' probably used on this occasion also provided the format for the coronations of *Harold II and *William the Conqueror in 1066, each of whom was anxious to proclaim that he was Edward's legitimate successor. In another respect, however, Harold's and William's coronations were innovatory. Edward the Elder, Æthelstan, *Æthelred the Unready, Edward the Confessor, and possibly Eardwulf of Northumbria, can all be shown to have been anointed some considerable time *after* they had become kings. In 1066 Harold was anointed on the day after Edward's death, and William did not take the title of king until after his coronation on Christmas Day. It is arguable, therefore, that although the liturgical form of the service remained the same, in one crucial respect its meaning changed: coronation acquired a newly *constitutive* function. This new meaning persisted, even when the *ordo* changed.

P. L. Ward, 'The Coronation Ceremony in Medieval England', *Speculum* 14 (1939), 160–78; idem, 'An Early Version of the Anglo-Saxon Coronation Ceremony', *EHR* 57 (1942), 345–61; C. E. Hohler, 'Some Service Books of the Later Saxon Church', *Tenth-Century Studies*, ed. D. Parsons (Chichester, 1975), pp. 60–83; J.

L. Nelson, *Politics and Ritual in Early Medieval Europe* (London, 1986); G. S. Garnett, 'The Third Recension of the English Coronation *Ordo*: the Manuscripts', *Haskins Society Journal* (forthcoming).

GEORGE GARNETT

COTTON, SIR ROBERT (1571–1631), one of the five founding members of the Elizabethan Society of Antiquaries, assembled the single most important private library of medieval manuscripts in post-dissolution England. By the time of his death his library must have contained the equivalent of at least 800 manuscript volumes. Cotton often disbound manuscripts and reorganised sections in new combinations: perhaps more than half his manuscripts are his own composites and do not represent the original state of the codices. In 1731 a major fire destroyed or damaged over 200 of the manuscripts; some 'burnt to a crust' as J. Planta described them in his catalogue of 1802. Thomas Smith's pre-conflagration catalogue of 1696 is, therefore, a particularly important witness to the collection.

C. G. C. Tite, 'The Early Catalogues of the Cottonian Library', *British Library Journal* 6 (1980), 144–57; J. P. Carley and C. G. C. Tite, 'Sir Robert Cotton as Collector of Manuscripts and the Question of Dismemberment: British Libary MSS Royal 13 D.I and Cotton Otho D. VIII', *The Library*, 6th ser. 14 (1992), 94–9; K. Sharpe, *Sir Robert Cotton 1586–1631: History and Politics in Early Modern England* (Oxford, 1979); Thomas Smith, *Catalogue of the Manuscripts in the Cottonian Library 1696 (Catalogus librorum manuscriptorum bibliothecae Cottonianae)*, ed. C. G. C. Tite (Cambridge, 1984); C. G. C. Tite, *The Manuscript Library of Sir Robert Cotton* (London, 1994); *Sir Robert Cotton as Collector: Essays on an Early Stuart Courtier and his Legacy*, ed. C. Wright (London, 1997).

JAMES P. CARLEY

COUNCIL, KING'S, was known in Old English as the *witan*, which meant literally 'wise men'; a meeting of the council was a *witenagemot*. Those who might expect to advise the king included members of the royal house, the two archbishops, the bishops, prominent abbots, the *ealdormen and other leading laymen with administrative or military roles, such as the king's *thegns. The consultation of women was rarer, but the *queen or queen-mother and, even more infrequently, abbesses might be included on occasion. In the tenth and eleventh centuries large assemblies of these categories of persons were held regularly, as can be seen from the witness-lists of diplomas approved at the meetings, but the council should not be thought of as a representative body. Rank and position defined membership of the *witan*, and

it was far removed from the embryonic parliament, with elected representatives from the shires, conjured up by seventeenth-century radicals who liked to think they were advocating a return to a more democratic era. The concept of the *witan* as an extended folk-moot, or assembly of freemen, lingered into the nineteenth century, but has now been abandoned.

It is probable that from the earliest days Anglo-Saxon leaders would have been obliged to consult their chief men, but we can only study such meetings after the advent of Christianity. *Bede provides an early example of King *Edwin of Northumbria consulting his closest advisers, including a pagan priest, about the adoption of Christianity – though much of his description must be an imaginative reconstruction. An early principle seems to have been that the *witan* had to approve and elect a new king. The corollary of this was that they might also deselect a king who was deemed unsatisfactory. In 757 the *witan* of the West Saxons deposed King Sigebert 'because of his unjust acts' (*ASC*), and similar decisions are recorded from eighth-century *Northumbria. Consultation therefore had the imperative of self-preservation behind it.

New *laws were promulgated after consultation with leading men of the kingdom. *Ine of Wessex stated in his lawcode that he had consulted his father, his bishops and other churchmen, his ealdormen and his senior councillors (*ieldstan witum*). King *Alfred felt it necessary to have his *will approved by the West Saxon *witan*, and the text shows that earlier disputes about his father's inheritance had been resolved at meetings of the council. Fuller records for the tenth and eleventh centuries, by which time the work of the *witan* had probably become more formalised, enable us to trace a greater range of activities. In addition to the promulgation of law and authorisation of grants of land, business might include judicial judgements, the settlement of disputes, the election of archbishops and bishops, and decisions of major matters of both church and state. In the reign of King *Æthelred the Unready, for instance, king and council together decided on payment of tributes to the *Viking armies, and after the battle of *Assandun* in 1016, the *witan* advised *Edmund Ironside to come to terms with *Cnut. The bringing together of so many leading men could make meetings of the *witan* the occasion for intrigue and internal disputes; it was at a meeting of the council in 1015 at Oxford that *Eadric Streona enticed the thegns Sigeferth and Morcar into his chamber and had them killed.

Meetings might also serve other diplomatic functions. King *Æthelstan was attended at some of his councils by his Welsh underkings, who are included among the witnesses to land grants issued on these occasions, and the embassy of Hugh, duke of the Franks, was received at a meeting of the council at *Abingdon in 926.

Council meetings tended to be held at the rural residences of the kings rather than in urban or ecclesiastical centres. In the tenth and eleventh centuries the majority of sites chosen were in *Wessex, with only occasional forays into *Mercia. Residences in the country were no doubt preferred to more restricted sites in *towns or monasteries because considerable space was needed to accommodate meetings of what must often have amounted to several hundred people, if the retinues of those attending are taken into account. Most of these must have been housed in temporary accommodation such as tents. The only royal palace site of the later period to have been excavated, *Cheddar, where the *witan* may have met in 956, had a limited range of permanent buildings. Among the most significant of these was the great hall where the formal council meetings would have taken place. The *Anglo-Saxon Chronicle* entry for 977 (MSS. DE) records the collapse of the upper storey of a hall at Calne (Wilts.) in which the councillors were meeting, resulting in the death or severe injury of a number of them, although Archbishop *Dunstan was unhurt because he had the good fortune to be standing on a floor-beam. An innovation in the reign of *Edward the Confessor, based on continental practices, was the introduction of councils accompanied by religious ceremonies and formal crown-wearings at the major ecclesiastical festivals of Christmas, Easter and Whitsuntide. In the reign of his successor William the Conqueror these great meetings tended to be held respectively at *Gloucester or *Westminster, *Winchester, and Westminster or *Windsor. It was at his great Christmas court at Gloucester in 1085 that William ordered *Domesday Book to be compiled.

F. Liebermann, *The National Assembly in the Anglo-Saxon Period* (Halle, 1913); T. J. Oleson, *The Witenagemot in the Reign of Edward the Confessor* (Toronto, 1955); P. Rahtz, *The Saxon and Medieval Palaces at Cheddar*, BAR Brit. ser. 65 (Oxford, 1979); S. Keynes, *The Diplomas of King Æthelred 'the Unready' 978–1016* (Cambridge, 1980), pp. 126–34; H. R. Loyn, *The Governance of Anglo-Saxon England 500–1087* (London, 1984), pp. 96–106; M. Biddle, 'Seasonal Festivals and Residence: Winchester, Westminster and Gloucester in the Tenth to Twelfth Centuries', *ANS* 8 (1985), 51–72.

B. A. E. YORKE

COUNCILS, CHURCH. The first known meeting of the Anglo-Saxon church under the presidency of its archbishop took place at Hertford in 672 or 673 under *Theodore (*HE* iv.5). Canon 7 of the decrees published at this council ruled that church councils should meet once a year, but it is unclear whether this ruling was put into operation. From 735 and probably before, the Northumbrian church appears to have held separate meetings of its own province but these are sparsely recorded. The numerous controversies concerning Bishop *Wilfrid were debated before councils of both the Northumbrian church and of the whole Anglo-Saxon church.

Southumbrian councils under the archbishop of *Canterbury and attended by all the suffragans of the province seem to have met regularly until *c*.850, being held at a number of locations (possibly all within the diocese of *London), commonly at *Clofesho* (unidentified), *Acleah* (also unidentified) and Chelsea. These adjudicated matters of church discipline, resolved property disputes, and promulgated reforming canons. The canons issued by the 747 Council of *Clofesho* under Archbishop Cuthbert represent a thoroughgoing reform of the church, dealing with episcopal responsibilities, monastic discipline, the role of priests, pastoral care and liturgical matters; their promulgation was possibly prompted by a letter of admonition from St *Boniface. The councils also considered relations between the laity and the church, and these form the central concerns of the 816 Council of Chelsea under Archbishop *Wulfred which fostered episcopal unity and attacked royal lordship of monasteries. The attendance of the kings and their followers, usually those of *Mercia, is frequently recorded at Southumbrian councils during the eighth and early ninth centuries, and royal, secular business may also have taken place at church councils, although probably in separate sessions. The great councils which met during the second half of the eighth century and the early ninth century are a feature of the Mercian supremacy, and chiefly documented in a number of land *charters; they have been interpreted as indicating Mercian overlordship over the Southumbrian church, but the evidence is unclear and suggestive of archiepiscopal rather than royal authority at these meetings. In fact relations between the archbishops of Canterbury, other representatives of the Southumbrian church, and Mercian kings were often stormy, and church councils functioned as the forum where disputes between these parties were aired and could be used to counter royal domination.

Church councils also played a role in papal relations. For example, the Council of Hatfield was convened in 679 to affirm the orthodoxy of the Anglo-Saxon church as part of the preparations for the sixth ecumenical council. In 786 councils were held in the presence of two papal legates then visiting England, at which twenty canons were published (which may be identical to the lost *lawcode of King *Offa).

After 850, separate meetings for the church cease to be recorded; the pattern of meetings between Mercian kings and Southumbrian bishops was terminated by the West Saxon eclipse of the Mercians in Southumbria and ultimately by the *Viking raids during the second half of the ninth century. From the tenth century, church business appears to have been discussed at meetings of the king and his councillors. This new practice can be seen, for example, in a meeting held at London 941 × 946, under King *Edmund and Archbishops *Oda of Canterbury and *Wulfstan of York, from which ordinances were issued in the king's name concerning ecclesiastical discipline and spiritual matters for both the laity and ecclesiastics. The great council at *Winchester attended by bishops, abbots and abbesses, at which the *Regularis Concordia was imposed upon all English monasteries was convened by King *Edgar and held under his authority.

Smaller diocesan assemblies of bishops and the clergy for disciplinary and other purposes may have taken place throughout the period, but are poorly recorded.

H&S, Councils; Councils & Synods; C. Cubitt, Anglo-Saxon Church Councils c.650–c.850 (London, 1995); H. Vollrath, Die Synoden Englands bis 1066 (Paderborn, 1985); idem, 'König Edgar und die Klosterreform in England: die "Ostersynode" der "Vita S. Oswaldi auctore anonymo"', Annuarium Historiae Conciliorum 10 (1978), 67–81.

C. R. E. CUBITT

COUNTY HIDAGE. A document of uncertain origin, date, and purpose, listing thirteen shires (Wiltshire, Bedfordshire, Cambridgeshire, Huntingdonshire, Northamptonshire, Gloucestershire, Worcestershire, Herefordshire, Warwickshire, Oxfordshire, Shropshire, Cheshire, and Staffordshire), and indicating the total number of hides of land pertaining to each shire; cf. *Tribal Hidage and *Burghal Hidage. The figures are close enough to the reality of *Domesday Book to suggest that they were derived from an administrative record of some kind, yet in certain cases different enough from the late eleventh-century

assessments to encourage the supposition that the document might have originated before the Norman Conquest. In particular, the figures given for Cambridgeshire, Northamptonshire, Shropshire and Cheshire are significantly larger than the corresponding figures calculated from Domesday Book, suggesting that by 1066 certain adjustments had been made as requirements had changed. The document obviously reflects the extension of the shire system into the midlands, which may have taken place during the course of the tenth century, perhaps during the reign of *Edward the Elder or *Æthelstan, but which is not clearly attested until the closing years of the reign of *Æthelred the Unready. It should be noted, moreover, that the figure for Gloucestershire seems to be inclusive of 'Winchcombeshire', a shire said to have been abolished by *Eadric Streona, *ealdorman of the Mercians (1007–17). If the document is to be given the benefit of the doubt, its origins might be sought in the context of changing administrative arrangements during the period 1016–66.

F. W. Maitland, Domesday Book and Beyond (Cambridge, 1897), pp. 455–60; C. S. Taylor, 'The Origin of the Mercian Shires', Gloucestershire Studies, ed. H. P. R. Finberg (Leicester, 1957), pp. 17–45; D. P. Kirby, The Making of Early England (London, 1967), pp. 176–7; C. Hart, The Hidation of Northamptonshire (Leicester, 1970), pp. 15–16, 45–6; P. H. Sawyer, From Roman Britain to Norman England (London, 1978), pp. 228–9; S. Keynes, The Diplomas of King Æthelred the Unready 978–1016 (Cambridge, 1980), pp. 197–8; Hill, Atlas, pp. 96–7 [County Hidage], 99 [Winchcombeshire]; J. Whybra, A Lost English County: Winchcombeshire in the Tenth and Eleventh Centuries (Woodbridge, 1990), pp. 1–15 [cf. Taylor, cited above], 105–6.

SIMON KEYNES

COURTS were arenas of dispute settlement in Anglo-Saxon society. Disputes can be settled in any sort of meeting agreed by both parties; though any serious disagreement will normally need to be ironed out publicly, before witnesses. In Kentish and West Saxon legislation of the late seventh century it was already envisaged that one way in which this could be done was in formally convened bodies. These can be called law-courts, so long as it is appreciated that they worked in very different ways from their modern equivalents. The nature of law-courts in fact changed greatly as the Anglo-Saxon period proceeded. A Kentish code of the 680s speaks of bringing a charge at 'an assembly or meeting'. The word for an assembly is found in the code of *Æthelberht and is cognate with its Frankish equivalent, while the second term, þing, is common Germanic for legal/

political gatherings. The same text goes on to order that 'right' be done as 'the judges of the men of Kent prescribe'; and further envisages settlement of any outstanding grievance before an 'arbitrator'. Authority thus seems to reside with the same sort of (plural) local experts in law and custom as are well attested in continental laws. Throughout the Anglo-Saxon period, and indeed until the judicial reforms of the Angevins, judging remains an essentially plural function, the business of the court as a whole. But already in the laws of *Ine we find a 'scirman or other judge' who may fail to give satisfaction, and an *ealdorman who stands to lose his scir for failing to act against theft. Ine's prologue expressed a hope that his officials as well as subjects would respect his decrees. We may therefore conclude that royal government had made its presence felt in courts, at least to the extent that its agents were presiding and responsible for enforcing judgements.

At the same time, there is no suggestion at this stage, nor at any time till the mid-tenth century, that there were courts for what would become the English *shires. Courts are either local or held before the king himself. The first hint of a change is in *Alfred's laws, which have penalties for fighting at a 'meeting' before either an ealdorman (the 120 shilling fine reserved for disobedience to the king) or his 'deputy' (the 30 shillings later allocated to lower courts). Alfred's immediate successors made several laws about court process that would soon apply to lower courts. But the classic medieval division between the courts of the shire itself and of its subdivision, the *hundred, comes only in the laws of *Edgar (later restated and amplified by *Cnut). It was at about this time that a fairly detailed ordinance was issued for the hundred's operations; and from about then that we find shire-courts at work in recorded lawsuits. In making sense of these developments, the best guess is that, with at least half an eye on the similar Frankish arrangements, the old local court was reorganised and renamed as the hundred, while a court was created for the pre-existent *military* unit of the shire, as required by the kingdom's enlargement; Ine's scir would then have been a lesser district. Responsibility for running a shire court was assigned to the local bishop and *ealdorman*. But lawsuit evidence shows that officials corresponding to (and before long identified as) 'shire-reeves' (i.e. sheriffs; cf. *reeve) were in action by the 990s. The repeated warnings directed by Anglo-Saxon laws against corrupt officials suggest that presiding figures could affect a case's outcome, even if actual judging was not their affair.

But in one respect the locally powerful lacked the opportunity to dictate results that they by then had on the continent. There are few signs that they were entitled to hold courts by virtue of their landlordship. On the contrary, the abidingly 'public' character of Old English justice is a key reason why kings were so well-placed to introduce the changes of the twelfth century.

Liebermann, *Gesetze* i.192–5 [Hundred Ordinance], 200–3 [III Edgar 2–5:3], 318–23 [II Cnut 15:1–19:2], ii.482–3 ['Grafschaftsgericht'], 516–22 ['*hundred*'], 701–3 ['Urteilfinder']; H. M. Chadwick, *Studies on Anglo-Saxon Institutions* (Cambridge, 1905), pp. 202–92; A. Harding, *The Law-Courts of Medieval England* (London, 1965); H. R. Loyn, 'The Hundred in England in the Tenth and Eleventh Centuries', *British Government and Administration. Studies presented to S. B. Chrimes*, ed. H. Hearder and H. R. Loyn (Cardiff, 1974), pp. 1–14; P. Wormald, 'A Handlist of Anglo-Saxon Lawsuits', *ASE* 17 (1988), 247–81, at 279–80; A. Kennedy, 'Law and Litigation in the *Libellus Æthelwoldi episcopi*', *ASE* 24 (1995), 131–83; P. Wormald, 'Lordship and Justice in the early English Kingdom: Oswaldslow Revisited', *Property and Power in the Early Middle Ages*, ed. W. Davies and P. Fouracre (Cambridge, 1995), pp. 114–36; idem, 'Giving God and King their Due: Conflict and its Regulation in the Early English State', *Settimane* 44 (1997), 549–83.

PATRICK WORMALD

CREEDS are concise, authorised formulations of Christian doctrine; they are normally tripartite in form, and were used characteristically as part of the service of baptism. The transmission of various forms of creeds in the western church is exceptionally complex. The earliest form, which probably dates from the third century and was probably originally in Greek, is the so-called 'Old Roman Creed' (referred to as R by students of creeds). The creed known as the 'Apostles' Creed' is a later (western) development of R: it is first mentioned by Ambrose *c.*390 and first attested in the early eighth century. The likelihood is that it originated in southwest Francia; in any event, it was endorsed by Charlemagne and became the standard text in the Latin West (it is referred to as T = 'textus receptus'), being adopted eventually in *Rome itself, which during the intervening centuries had continued to use the 'Old Roman Creed'. The so-called 'Nicene Creed' (N) is a Greek formulation which was promulgated at the Council of Nicaea in the attempt to achieve doctrinal orthodoxy in the face of Arianism; it too underwent modifications (to result in the Constantinopolitan creed, or C), and does not appear in Latin dress in Rome before the eleventh century. A different type of creed, the so-called

'Athanasian Creed' or 'Quicumque uult' was composed probably in Gaul in the fifth century (it has nothing to do with Athanasius, and is first quoted in a sermon of Caesarius of Arles); it is found in prayerbooks and formed part of the Divine Office. In terms of Anglo-Saxon England, at least for the later period (from which most surviving liturgical manuscripts survive), the usual form of creed is the 'Apostles' Creed' in the recension known as T; but Anglo-Saxon prayerbooks often include the 'Athanasian Creed' as well. It is exceptionally interesting that one of the earliest manuscripts to preserve the Greek form of the 'Old Roman Creed' (R) is the *'Æthelstan Psalter' (London, BL, Cotton Galba A.xviii), where it has been copied along with some other Greek prayers into additional quires at the end of the manuscript (s. $x^2/^4$); there is reason to associate the presence of this prayer in England with Archbishop *Theodore, and its presence in the manuscript with *Israel the Grammarian.

A. R. Burn, *Facsimiles of the Creeds from Early Manuscripts, with Palaeographical Notes by the late Dr Ludwig Traube*, HBS 36 (London, 1909); J. N. D. Kelly, *Early Christian Creeds*, 3rd ed. (London, 1972).

MICHAEL LAPIDGE

CREMATIONS: *see* Cemeteries, Furnished; Cemeteries, Unfurnished

CRICKLADE (Wilts.) is a large, regular planned *town with well-preserved defences, probably laid out in *Alfred's reign but enclosing, on an eminence overlooking the Thames, the old minster of St Samson. The town had a possibly timber-revetted bank (re-fronted in stone *c.*1000), an external double ditch system, and an intra-mural steet. It is assessed at 1,400 or 1,500 hides in the *Burghal Hidage, and was a *mint from the reign of *Æthelred II. Excavation has shown that large areas within the walls were never developed: a good illustration that ambitious urbanisation schemes were not always fully realised.

H. R. Loyn, 'The Origin and Early Development of the Anglo-Saxon Borough with Special Reference to Cricklade', *Wilts. Archaeological Magazine* 58 (1961–3), 7–15; Haslam, *Towns*, pp. 106–10; J. Haslam, 'The Metrology of Anglo-Saxon Cricklade', *MArch* 30 (1986), 99–103; Hill and Rumble, *Defence of Wessex*, pp. 199–201.

JOHN BLAIR

CRIMES are legal wrongs which, as offences against society as a whole, are punished by society as a whole. Although they are not mutually exclusive, crimes are contrasted with torts (civil wrongs), whose consequences lie in compensation to an injured individual or group. Among the Anglo-Saxons, law addressed to the maintenance of order must have developed for the most part from the specification and apportionment of tortious liabilities. In consequence, legal texts throughout the period use the language of tort to describe wrongs against established authority or public institutions, and some late writings continue to indicate that wrongs against individuals or groups, which were treated as crimes in later medieval law, might still be amendable in the eleventh century and beyond.

But criminal sanctions were never unknown to Anglo-Saxon law and the paradigmatic description of the consequences of particular offences as compensation (OE *bot*) and punishment (OE *wite*) as early as the *laws of *Ine must speak for the sense of a general distinction between the criminal and tortious aspects of a legal wrong. In his own code two hundred years later King *Alfred rationalised widespread monetary sanctions in England in a manner which shows that he clearly understood this distinction. There are indications that Alfred and his son *Edward the Elder introduced or developed concepts concerning criminal law which were later refined and elaborated by the kings of England into a considered, although particularistic and not entirely coherent, programme of criminal justice, whose inclusiveness was at times signalled by a general pardon or a proclaimed limit to legal memory. The laws attributed to kings from *Æthelstan through to *Cnut reflect the general commitment to justice and public order enshrined in the *coronation promise, but they seem as well to represent a series of practical measures intended to suppress wrongdoing and bring the whole nation within the control of the criminal law. These measures were directed principally at theft in its various manifestations, and offences associated with homicide, but other crimes such as counterfeiting and debasement of the *coinage were also addressed. *Oaths of loyalty created a very broad conception of treason, whose sanction in forfeiture was a compelling and profitable deterrent, but these oaths seem intended also to isolate wrongdoers from protection and support. The isolation of the criminal was reinforced by a strengthened conception of outlawry, which may owe something more than the mere name to Scandinavian influence, and within which older summary procedures were subsumed. Control over potential criminals was enhanced by making lords and sureties increasingly responsible for their men and associates, and by closely regulating com-

Pl. 10 'An Anglo-Saxon king dispenses justice' (from London, BL, Cotton Claudius B.iv, 59r).

merce. To these developments were added sometimes quite remarkably harsh punishments: the foreign monk *Lantfred attributed to King *Edgar measures to suppress theft which he described as the introduction of *lex talionis* into England. One result was a reduction in the practical range of amendable wrongs. King Cnut pronounced that some serious offences were *botleas* ('unamendable') but his short list was not exhaustive, and it did not include wrongs whose criminal sanctions must have rendered their tortious component nominal.

*Charters and legal memoranda show how potent an instrument the criminal law could be, although the evidence is insufficient in volume and kind accurately to show how capable or otherwise one administration or another was in providing protection under the law for its citizens. King Æthelstan conceded in his laws that some criminals were too powerful to be brought to justice, while in the one code King *Edmund both complained of widespread violence and thanked his supporters for the current freedom from theft. Public order must have come close to disintegration during the last, difficult years of King *Æthelred the Unready. But there can be no doubt that, whatever in the end they made of it, the Norman and Angevin kings inherited a legal system in which criminal justice had become an important part.

F. Pollock and F. W. Maitland, *The History of English Law before the Time of Edward I*, 2 vols. (Cambridge, 1895; 2nd ed., with new introduction and select bibliography by S. F. C. Milsom, Cambridge, 1968), ii.448–511; P. Wormald, 'A Handlist of Anglo-Saxon Lawsuits', *ASE* 17 (1988), 247–81; S. Keynes, 'Crime and Punishment in the Reign of King Æthelred the Unready', in Sawyer FS, pp. 67–81; P. Wormald, 'Maitland and Anglo-Saxon Law: Beyond Domesday Book', *PBA* 89 (1996), 1–20.

ALAN KENNEDY

CROSSES, STONE, free-standing and elaborately decorated on all four faces, were one of the distinctive features of Christianity in pre-Norman England. Most now only survive as fragments but at sites like *Bewcastle and *Gosforth it is still possible to see near-complete monuments in their original positions and to appreciate the original impact of carvings which once stood up to 5 m high.

The origins of the Insular tradition of erecting decorated crosses carved from stone are still not fully understood, though it is now clear that the earliest developments took place in *Northumbria. The date of the first examples in England is also disputed. Current orthodoxy, however, sees such monuments as secondary to the development of architectural sculpture, which is associated with the church-building activities of men like *Benedict Biscop and *Wilfrid. The early years of the eighth century now seem the most likely context for the emergence of this form of monument, though some undecorated examples (like those known from *Whitby) may be slightly earlier in date.

If the dating of the onset of the Northumbrian tradition is unclear, then the general chronology of the subsequent series of crosses is equally uncertain. In the north and, to a lesser extent, in the Midlands it is possible to isolate carvings which must belong to the *Viking period on the basis of their use of Scandinavian-based motifs and styles. Yet even here the persistence of conservative tastes, particularly in the Cuthbert Community lands north of the Tees, causes difficulties. Within the pre-Viking period comparisons with manuscripts, metalwork and ivories (themselves not always well dated) have allowed a certain consensus on the general lines of ornamental evolution. What seems to be emerging is that the custom of carving crosses was established early in Northumbria and continued right through the pre-Norman period. In the Mercian area the tradition began slightly later, but still within the eighth century. Here also there is a continuation into the Viking period but there is a strong tendency, particularly in the eastern Midlands, for sculptors to favour slabs and small cruciform headstones in the later period. In the south of the country crosses were never as popular a form of monument as they were in the midlands and north. There are very few of any pre-Norman date in the south-east though the *Reculver cross, from *Kent, shows that work of exceptionally high quality did exist here by the ninth century. In *Winchester and to the west more has survived; again there is little pre-ninth century work but crosses from *Gloucester and East Stour in Dorset show the tradition continuing into the tenth century. By this date, however, the more advanced sculptors of *Wessex were expressing their art on slabs and in architectural decoration, notably in a series of large-scale roods.

Initially, like all sculpture, stone crosses were the products of monastic workshops, the work of masons who were also responsible for architectural decoration. Cross production seems to have remained largely, though not exclusively, in the hands of such monastic ateliers until the ninth century. The Viking invasions then accelerated a change which may already have been in train: a change to more secular patronage and production. The great popularity of crosses in tenth- and eleventh-century Northumbria is the result of the enthusiastic adoption by the new Anglo-Scandinavian aristocracy of this once monastic art. It is this change in patronage and workshops which accounts for the fact that pre-Viking crosses are relatively rare when compared with work of the tenth and eleventh centuries.

Crosses vary in both size and shape and such variation can be related to date. There is, for example, a general tendency towards smaller crosses in the later period and for monuments of that period to have shafts which are more slab-like in section. Though the dominant form of shaft is

rectangular in section, the ninth century saw several ambitious attempts to produce cylindrical forms: *Reculver in Kent, *Winchester, *Worcester, Masham in Yorkshire and Beckermet St Bridget in Cumbria show that this was a widespread fashion at that date. The type continued to be productive into the tenth century, notably in north-western Mercia but its most elegant manifestation at that date is at Gosforth in Cumbria.

The forms of cross-head also vary according to period and region. One type in particular should be noticed: the ring head in which the arms of the cross are joined by some form of circle or ring. It was only in the Viking period that this type was used in English sculpture; it seems to represent a tenth-century innovation drawing on a type of cross-head popular in the Celtic west.

The function of crosses varied through time and from area to area. Documentary evidence points to their use in marking sacred spots and boundaries. In the eighth-century *Hodoeporicon* of *Willibald they are described as marking places of prayer. Inscriptions indicate that some were memorial in function, though it is only late in the pre-Norman period that they are likely to have been used as *grave-markers. The pre-Viking distribution of crosses in Northumbria, which strongly coincides with that of known monastic sites, indicates that many would have acted as objects of contemplation, teaching and penitence within the monastic vallum. Crosses, in summary, served no single function, a fact that is emphasised by noting that some have never been exposed to the elements which have battered others.

CASSS; R. N. Bailey, *Viking-Age Sculpture in Northern England* (London, 1980); R. J. Cramp, 'Schools of Mercian Sculpture', in Dornier, *MS*, pp. 191–233; idem, 'Anglo-Saxon Sculpture of the Reform Period', in *Tenth-Century Studies*, ed. D. Parsons (Chichester, 1975), pp. 184–99; *Studies in Medieval Sculpture*, ed. F. H. Thompson (London, 1983); D. M. Wilson, *Anglo-Saxon Art* (London, 1984); R. N. Bailey, *England's Earliest Sculptors*, Publications of the Dictionary of Old English 5 (Toronto, 1996).

RICHARD N BAILEY

CROWLAND: *see* Æthelbald; Guthlac

CROWN: *see* Coronation

CRYPTS are vaulted chambers, usually below the main level of a church, serving in the Anglo-Saxon period for burials and, especially, the cult of saints. Such structures ultimately derive from the extramural cemeteries of late Roman antiquity, where altars within *memoriae* were built over the burial-chambers of those revered as saints. By the early fifth century the typical arrangement for the veneration of a saint in the Roman cemeteries comprised a tomb- or relic-chamber (*martyrium* or *confessio*), usually beneath the high altar of the basilicas that had superseded the initial *memoriae*, though sometimes located beside the basilicas and accessed from them.

The earliest Anglo-Saxon crypts resembled the burial-chambers (*hypogea*) from which they derived. St *Wilfrid's crypts at *Ripon and *Hexham (670–7) were no doubt inspired by his earlier visit to *Rome. Their central chambers, under the altar, contained *relics in the manner of a Roman *confessio*; the complex approach corridors replicated the disorientating effect of the Roman catacombs.

Excavation has revealed evidence for a number of burial-chambers of Roman type. At *Glastonbury, a rectangular burial-chamber, perhaps the grave of a king, stood immediately east of the contemporary church. There is limited evidence for a similar free-standing mausoleum crypt at *Winchcombe, possibly built for the royal child-martyr St Cynehelm or *Kenelm (early ninth century). Such burial-chambers have also been excavated beneath the church at Sidbury and within the extramural Roman cemetery at *Wells.

The surviving crypt at *Repton (pl. 15), possibly originally constructed as the royal mausoleum of *Æthelbald of Mercia (d. 757), resembled the *hypogeum* built by Mellebaude at Poitiers at slightly earlier date. It was remodelled in the mid-ninth century: first by a vault supported on spiral pillars, and subsequently with the transformation of its central entrance passage into a western *loculus*, flanked by new entrance stairs descending from the church. These changes may have been introduced at the time of the burial of King Wiglaf (d. 840), but would be equally appropriate as an architectural setting for the tomb of St Wigstan, buried 'in the mausoleum of his grandfather' in 849.

The crypt at *Wing was similarly remodelled, probably in the mid-tenth century: work which has been associated with Queen Ælfgifu, the divorced wife of King *Eadwig, on the basis of a reference in her will (966–75) to an estate there.

The more elaborate 'ring-crypt', though important in the development of continental Romanesque architecture, was more sparingly used in Anglo-Saxon England. It was first employed at St Peter's, Rome, in *Gregory the Great's remodelling, and at San Pancrazio, rebuilt by Pope Honorius I (625–38). The type was taken up again in the early ninth century, both in Rome and in the Carolingian empire. The key to its success was the way in which the curved passages within the face of the apse wall provided access to the body of the saint, located in an axial chamber under the altar.

Evidence for Anglo-Saxon ring-crypts is fragmentary. Excavation has suggested that the crypt at *Cirencester may have been of this form. At *Brixworth, a curved passage *outside* the apse of the Anglo-Saxon church seems best related to similar arrangements in churches in ninth-century *Germany.

Known only from Eadmer's description, the eastern crypt of *Canterbury cathedral appears to have conformed most closely to Carolingian exemplars: it was 'made in the likeness of the *confessio* of St Peter, at Rome'. The date is disputed: the crypt might have been built as late as the early eleventh century, as a worthy setting for the relics of Archbishop *Dunstan.

Taylor and Taylor, *AS Arch*, esp. pp. 1014–17; M. Biddle, 'Archaeology, Architecture, and the Cult of Saints in Anglo-Saxon England', in Butler and Morris, *AS Church*, pp. 1–31; J. Crook, 'The Architectural Setting of the Cult of Saints in the Early Medieval West and its Development in the English Romanesque', unpubl. D.Phil. thesis (Oxford, 1995).

JOHN CROOK

CURRICULUM: *see* Schools

CUSTOMARY: *see* Liturgical Books

CUTHBERT, ST (d. 687), bishop of *Lindisfarne, was born *c.635 in Northumbria, probably of noble parents. In 651, inspired by a *vision, he decided to become a monk and entered *Melrose, placing himself under the spiritual direction of its prior *Boisil. In the late 650s, he and his abbot *Eata briefly transferred to the monastery of *Ripon, newly founded by the Northumbrian king *Oswiu's son Alhfrith, but they were soon displaced by Alhfrith's protégé *Wilfrid and returned to Melrose. When Boisil succumbed to the plague, perhaps in 664, Cuthbert succeeded him as prior and for several years followed Boisil's example in paying pastoral visits and preaching to the surrounding districts. His reputation was such that he was summoned by King Oswiu's sister, Abbess Æbbe, to her monastery of *Coldingham to preach to its inmates.

Cuthbert had accepted King Oswiu's decision in favour of the Roman method of calculating *Easter at the synod of *Whitby in 664. Some time afterwards, probably in the 670s, he moved to Lindisfarne, at the invitation of Eata, by then its abbot and possibly also bishop. There, during a brief priorate, he reformed the rule, an activity which engendered considerable bitterness, but soon was attracted to the eremitical life, withdrawing first to St Cuthbert's Isle next to Lindisfarne and later to the much more remote island of Farne. His fame as a holy ascetic spread, and in 684 he was consulted by Oswiu's daughter *Ælfflæd about the future of her brother King Ecgfrith and about the succession.

In 685, at the instance of Ecgfrith, the reluctant Cuthbert was induced to accept episcopal orders. Initially offered the see of *Hexham, he prevailed upon Eata to exchange sees so that he could remain at Lindisfarne. As bishop Cuthbert seems to have preserved his ascetic way of life, retaining the friendship of fellow hermits such as Hereberht of *Carlisle, while pursuing an active pastoral role, preaching and ministering to the people of his large diocese and acquiring a reputation as a wonderworking seer and healer. He also maintained his links with the Northumbrian royal family, dedicating one of Ælfflæd's churches and visiting Ecgfrith's queen in Carlisle while she awaited the outcome of the king's fatal campaign against the Picts. The intimacy of his royal connexions is especially apparent in his foreknowledge of Ecgfrith's nemesis at *Nechtansmere*.

Early in 687, sensing death approaching, Cuthbert withdrew once again to Farne, where he died on 20 March. Apparently well aware of his status as a holy man, he advised the community to bury him on Farne to avoid being troubled by the influx of fugitives seeking sanctuary at his shrine. The brethren, however, insisted upon burying him in a place of honour on the south side of the altar of the abbatial church of St Peter. Eleven years later, in a ceremony intended to establish Cuthbert's sanctity as authoritatively as possible, the community caused his remains to be elevated and placed in a wooden tomb chest above the original burial place. The body was found to be incorrupt, a particularly noteworthy authentication of the saint's chastity and holiness. Such claims and observances, many of which derive ultimately from Gaulish practice, mark the Lindisfarne monks as among the most advanced English shrine guardians of their day.

Cuthbert, remarkably, was the subject of three early Lives. The earliest (*BHL* 2019), commissioned by Bishop Eadfrith of Lindisfarne and written by a monk of the community between 698 and 705, presents the saint in terms of early hagiographical prototypes such as the hermit Anthony and above all the fourth-century Gaulish bishop Martin, also portrayed as both ascetic and pastor. Shortly afterwards *Bede composed a metrical Life (*BHL* 2020), primarily as a meditation on the anonymous Life for a restricted elite audience but also to update the corpus of miracle stories. About 720 he also compiled a new prose Life (*BHL* 2021), a work intended to harness the Cuthbertine cult to his programme of spiritual reform by presenting the saint as ideal monk, spiritual teacher, and bishop. Bede's work is the product of a period when the cult was being vigorously promoted, probably in response to tensions within the Northumbrian political and ecclesiastical establishment focused on the controversial career of Bishop Wilfrid.

Despite the proliferation of material, Cuthbert's own personality is difficult to assess. Almost certainly he combined a love of ascetic solitude with genuine pastoral concern and, like other early solitaries, evinced an affinity with the natural world and in particular a friendship for animals. Besides his undoubted asceticism, however, must be set a certain magnificence: the friend of abbesses and queens, as bishop he travelled on horseback accompanied by a retinue and possessed a pectoral cross of considerable splendour.

Cuthbert's cult retained its early importance, and indeed became the greatest in the North. After Lindisfarne was exposed to *Viking attack, the incorrupt body was moved with other treasures of the community, resting apparently at Norham-upon-Tweed from the second quarter of the ninth century, and from 883 at Chester-le-Street, where it was honoured by the West Saxon royal house. In 995 it was finally laid to rest at Durham.

The saint's remains were found to be still incorrupt when they were transferred to the new Norman cathedral in 1104. Reverently buried at the Reformation, they were dug up in 1827; the corporeal relics, which by then had disintegrated, were reinterred, but many other items, including the original reliquary-coffin, early vestments, silks, and the saint's comb and pectoral cross were retained for display at the cathedral.

In Anglo-Saxon times the primary feast, the deposition (20 March), was celebrated from the late seventh century. A translation feast on 4 September occurs from the ninth century.

Two Lives of St Cuthbert, ed. B. Colgrave (Cambridge, 1940); *The Relics of St Cuthbert*, ed. G. F. Battiscombe (Oxford, 1956); Bede, *HE* iv.25–30; *St Cuthbert, His Cult and His Community to AD 1200*, ed. G. Bonner, D. W. Rollason, and C. Stancliffe (Woodbridge, 1989); D. P. Kirby, 'The Genesis of a Cult: Cuthbert of Farne and

Ecclesiastical Politics in Northumbria in the Late Seventh and Early Eighth Centuries', *JEH* 46 (1995), 383–97.

ALAN THACKER

CUTHBURG (d. 718), sometime queen of *Ald-frith, king of *Northumbria (685–705), and, after she had separated from her husband, foundress of the abbey of *Wimborne (Dorset). No contemporary *vita* of Cuthburg survives, but she is mentioned in sources of the late seventh and early eighth century, such as the dedication of *Aldhelm's prose *De virginitate*, from which it seems clear that Cuthburg was at that time a member of the community of *Barking under Abbess *Hildelith (it is also likely that Cuthburg was related in some way to Aldhelm); and in a dream *vision preserved among the correspondence of *Boniface, the anonymous visionary, writing after 757, reports that he saw Cuthburg in a pit in hell. She is not mentioned by *Bede, but her death is recorded in the *Anglo-Saxon Chronicle* s.a. 718. A late (and unreliable) *vita* is preserved in two fourteenth-century manuscripts (*BHL* 2033), and was apparently composed sometime after the Norman Conquest.

Aldhelm, prose *De virginitate* (MGH, AA xv.229); MGH, ES i.248 (no. 115); J. M. J. Fletcher, 'The Marriage of St Cuthburga, who was afterwards Foundress of the Monastery at Wimborne', *Dorset Natural History and Antiquarian Field Club* 34 (1913), 167–85; P. Coulstock, *The Collegiate Church of Wimborne Minster* (Woodbridge, 1993).

MICHAEL LAPIDGE

CUTHMAN, ST: *see* Steyning

CYNETHRYTH, wife of *Offa, king of the Mercians (757–96), and evidently a power beside, not merely behind, the Mercian throne. *Alcuin urged their son Ecgfrith to learn *auctoritas* from his father and *pietas* from his mother; he also asked Hundrud, a nun at Offa's court, to greet the queen in his name, and in another letter he asked Offa to do the same, describing her as *dispensatrix domus regiae* ('controller of the royal household'). Most importantly, Offa and Cynethryth were named jointly in a privilege of Pope Hadrian I as having an interest in various religious houses, suggesting that she was very much a part of the regime which he personified. From 770 onwards, she was often included among the witnesses in charters issued by King Offa; and she is said to have encouraged her husband to grant privileges to *Chertsey abbey (S 127, allegedly issued at a synod of *Aclea* in 787). A *coinage bearing a royal portrait and a moneyer's name (Eoba) on the obverse, and 'Cynethryth regina M[erciorum]' on the reverse, is the only Anglo-Saxon coinage issued in the name of a *queen, and is thus indicative of her high standing; it may reflect an awareness of classical Roman practice, or it may reflect an awareness of the contemporary coinage of the Empress Irene, a formidable woman who from 780 presided over the eastern empire with her young son, the Emperor Constantine VI, and who, after disposing of her son, ruled in her own right from 797 to 802. Cynethryth's daughters included Æthelburh (an abbess), Eadburh (who married Beorhtric, king of the West Saxons), Ælfflæd (who married Æthelred, king of the Northumbrians), and Æthelswith. She is found after Offa's death in charge of the monastery at Cookham, in Berkshire, and also (it seems) in charge of the church at Bedford where Offa was buried (S 1258: *EHD* i, no. 79); indeed, it was only by surrendering to *Canterbury some extensive lands in *Kent, which Offa had bequeathed to his heirs with reversion to Bedford, that she was able in 798 to recover Cookham's charters from Archbishop Æthelheard, and also to gain possession of a minster at *Pectanege* (unidentified) which her son Ecgfrith had given to Canterbury. A story to the effect that Cynethryth was implicated in the murder of *Æthelberht, king of the East Angles, in 794, is told in the *Passio S. Ethelberti*, and was known to *John of Worcester (s.a. 793); it developed further thereafter, notably in the writings of Roger of Wendover and Matthew Paris, monks of St Albans, who knew her as 'the wicked Quendrida'.

Brooks, *Canterbury*, p. 184; P. Grierson and M. Blackburn, *Medieval European Coinage* I (Cambridge, 1986), pp. 279–80.

SIMON KEYNES

CYNEWULF. Four OE poems contain the name Cynewulf in *runes, with or without -*e*-, doubtless the conceit of an ingenious poet used to Latin *acrostics and Old English *riddles: *The Fates of the Apostles* and *Elene* in the *Vercelli Book and *Christ II* and *Juliana* in the *Exeter Book. The seven or eight runes are easily grasped by readers when seen on the page, and listeners may not have found taxing the task of adding together groups of runic letter names listed in *Juliana*. In the other three poems the rune names serve both as letters and as words, but the words required contextually for some of the rune names differ from traditional equivalents and may therefore always have seemed forced. Certain other poems have been ascribed to Cynewulf, though without proof. The phrase

'Cynewulfian poetry' continues to be widely used, principally of religious poems that clearly look to Latin writings for themes and techniques. The four signed poems, even allowing for loss both from *Christ II* and *Juliana*, make up a modest corpus that is smaller than **Beowulf*.

Cynewulf's longer poems are divided into well shaped fitts, in length similar to those found in **Guthlac B* and The **Phoenix*, suggesting a shared transmissional background, but these latter poems are far more inventive in the handling of source materials. Cynewulf generally seems to follow his chosen originals closely, adding to them the passages of reflection in which he names himself and seeks, explicitly in *Fates of the Apostles* and *Juliana*, to be remembered in the prayers of his readers. The narrative figure of these elegiac closing passages may well be conventional. The *Elene* version, for example, introduces a poet who considers the cross in relation first to an individual life, to a writer now old but granted the gift of poetry, moving on into more generalised moralisation on the cleansing properties of the fire of judgement. Where Cynewulf tacks on his closing ruminations, the **Dream of the Rood* poet integrates them into his whole poem.

Nineteenth-century histories of literature present highly imaginative biographies of Cynewulf, diligently seeking to identify him, for example, with an eighth-century bishop of **Lindisfarne*, a **Clofesho* signatory of *c.*803 or an abbot of Peterborough, later bishop of **Winchester*, who died *c.*1006. There is no secure evidence to date these four poems, although it is likely that they are not early. Traditional in vocabulary, they are generally held to be Mercian rather than West Saxon in **dialect*.

The Fates of the Apostles follows *Andreas* in the Vercelli Book, and has therefore sometimes been regarded as its final division. It is however a separate, well structured poem, relating to *Andreas* positionally and thematically. No single source has been identified. Conceived as a memorial poem, it celebrates the acts and martyrdom of the apostles, recording their fame and power in terms used elsewhere of secular heroes but here entirely suited to retainers of glory. The first person narrator of the opening reappears in the closing lines, asking to be remembered in prayer and advising careful listening to discover the poet's name.

Elene relates the finding of the cross legend, based on the *Inventio* (May 3). The bare bones of the story, tales of the emperor Constantine, of his mother Helena and of the first Christian bishop of Jerusalem, are simple enough. Constantine, on the day after he sees the cross in a vision of the cross, defeats barbarian hordes. He sends Helena to look for the cross. At Jerusalem Helena interrogates senior figures among the Jews, eventually taking captive a man of great wisdom, Judas, suspected of withholding information. Judas proves a master of equivocation and denial, and he is cast into a pit until more chastened in attitude. Once released, he accompanies Helena to Calvary, where miracles reveal the burial place of the cross, identify it from among the three crosses buried there, and bring about the conversion of Judas to Christianity. In memory of the finding of the cross, Constantine directs that a church should be built on Calvary. Judas is consecrated bishop, with the name Cyriacus. Nails from the cross are worked into a jewelled bridle for Constantine's horse. Overall, *Elene* is a triumphal poem, and Helena, the emperor's envoy, is the powerful leader of a great army. Cynewulf follows his source so carefully that his fitt endings sometimes coincide with the legend's chapter divisions. Yet, he does not hold back from loading such scenes as Constantine's battle and Helena's sea journey with traditional diction. His handling of Judas's dialogue is particularly effective. Cynewulf's epilogue, which draws on some of the themes of the preceding legend, opens with a rhymed passage.

Although the three Christ poems at the beginning of the Exeter Book hold together thematically and antiphonal echoes in this poem make it seem particularly suited as the centre of a triptych, manuscript capitals clearly mark out *Christ II* both from the preceding **Advent* hymns (*Christ I*) and from the Judgement Day poem (**Christ III*) that follows it. The poems were long read as a sequence, but more recently it has been suggested that Cynewulf wrote *Christ II* as a bridge between its neighbours. The poem's 427 lines extant are usually numbered 440–866. Two folios are lost, at line 490 and at line 556, the latter accounting for an awkward jump in narrative for which the poem has been unjustly criticised. Much of the poem is loosely based on an Ascension Day sermon of **Gregory the Great*. Arguably the finest of Cynewulf's four poems, the closing sequence merits comparison with The **Seafarer*.

Juliana is sometimes regarded either as the first or the last of Cynewulf's four signed poems, equally on the grounds that it is plainer in diction and that the Cynewulf runes are merely listed. Juliana (feast day: February 16), imprisoned for her refusal to marry an unbeliever, withstands lengthy temptation by the devil, successfully defending the citadel of her soul. Before martyrdom, she instructs onlookers to secure a strong foundation (*stapol*) for themselves.

ASPR ii.51–4, 66–102; iii.15–27, 113–33; *Juliana*, ed. R. Woolf (London, 1955); *Cynewulf's 'Elene'*, ed. P. O. E. Gradon (London, 1958); J. E. Cross, 'Cynewulf's Traditions about the Apostles in *The Fates of the Apostles*,' *ASE* 8 (1979), 163–75; D. G. Calder, *Cynewulf* (Boston, 1981); E. R. Anderson, *Cynewulf: Style, Structure, and Theme in his Poetry* (Rutherford, NJ, 1983); A. H. Olsen, *Speech, Song, and Poetic Craft: The Artistry of the Cynewulf Canon* (New York, 1984); *Cynewulf: Basic Readings*, ed. R. Bjork (New York, 1996).

JANE ROBERTS

D

DANEGELD: *see* Heregeld

DANELAW. An area of England distinguished in legal terms from areas subject to Mercian and West Saxon law, which roughly comprises York-shire, *East Anglia and the central and eastern Midlands. Although none is precisely cotermi-nous, this area has other features which distinguish it from 'English' areas: shires were divided into *wapentakes, not *hundreds; geld assessed in carucates, not hides; a duodecimal counting system; and place-names of Danish origin.

The Danelaw originated in the ninth-century settlements of the Great Danish Army, recorded by the *Anglo-Saxon Chronicle* under the years 875 (*Northumbria), 876 (*Mercia) and 879 (East Anglia). The scale of the Scandinavian presence has been much debated. Interpretation of the *place-name evidence has suggested a substantial migration of Scandinavian farmers behind the screen of Danish armies into areas where Scandi-navian names are common – primarily in a band stretching from Yorkshire through Lincolnshire to Leicestershire – but there is little further evidence that such occurred (see *place-names, Scandinavian). Pagan *Viking burials barely appear and archaeological evidence is undiag-nostic. Nor do Scandinavian place-names occur frequently across all the Danelaw. Nor is there evidence of depopulation in Denmark.

Irrespective of the number of immigrants, the Danelaw began with a seizure of power in eastern England by Danish rulers and landholders during the late ninth century. Its subsequent history encouraged respect for Danish legal practices but in other respects regional diversity reasserted itself.

The Danelaw receives its earliest implicit recog-nition in an undated treaty between *Alfred and *Guthrum (d. 890). Each recognised the territorial rights of the other and gave equal legal value, or *wergild, to both Dane and Englishman. Part of its purpose was to provide protection for Eng-lishmen of free status who fell under the authority of Guthrum and 'the army', whose own customary law was already affecting land-rights.

A crucial factor in its development was the so-called 'reconquest', undertaken by *Edward the Elder (899–924) and *Æthelflæd, 'Lady of the Mercians (d. 918). Although some Viking leaders and their followers departed – as did Jarl Thur-cytel of Bedford, for example – most were reckoned to have acknowledged Edward's position as king in return for recognition of their lands and customs. This process is confirmed by reference to 'peace-writings' in Edward's second law-code. By 920, therefore, a substantial part of England was ruled beneath the crown by an Anglo-Danish gentry whose inheritance and landholding customs were protected by English kings. This situation was further complicated by the incorporation of *Northumbria into the English state in the mid-tenth century, when the customs of the men of *York seem to have been accommodated by the English crown and given protection in return for their acquiescence. York was to remain committed to Scandinavian law even as late as 1065, when the Northumbrian revolt successfully demanded of *Edward the Confessor (1042–66) the renewal of the laws of *Cnut (1016–35). The law-code III Æthelred concerning the *Five Boroughs and issued at Wantage *c.*997 is the most significant survivor of Danelaw.

Danelaw communities were among the most influential in the country throughout the tenth and eleventh centuries. They enjoyed a greater pace of urbanisation and market activity than many areas and a true coin economy developed. Allied to this was the high density of population. Areas such as the Fens provided widespread opportunity for colonisation. This may be one reason why classes of free farmers such as sokemen are so numerous in the Danelaw. Another factor was the marginalisation of the church as a landholder and instrument of royal power in the region, where the pre-Viking church had lost the bulk of its wealth and influence. The monastic revival of the tenth century found the southern Danelaw an important source of patronage.

The Danelaw was not, however, a political entity within the late Anglo-Saxon state, but divided into several sub-units. From the mid-tenth century onwards, there were normally *ealdormen or earls of Yorkshire (or Northumbria), East Anglia (which generally included the south-east Midlands) and Mercia, which on occasion stretched to the North Sea. The disparity of distribution of such characteristics as carucates and wapentakes arguably derive from the different histories of these separate parts. Carucates, for example, were the standard basis for Domesday geld liability in *Lindsey, the Five Boroughs and East Anglia, but not elsewhere, while wapentakes occur only in the first two of these regions. The Danelaw was not a uniform entity but one which, even while sharing a common respect for Danish law, was in other ways a bundle of disconnected regional communities, each of which had its own roots in the pre-Danish past as well as a common Danish inheritance.

Yet the ruling elite set over different parts of the Danelaw was frequently interconnected: ealdormen of Yorkshire and archbishops of York were often drawn from the Mercian Danelaw, Peterborough provided bishops to Durham under Edward the Confessor, and Earls Siward and Tostig of Northumbria both held substantial estates and jurisdiction in and around Northamptonshire. The Danelaw's boundaries had some political significance throughout the period. *Watling Street was named in the treaty between Alfred and Guthrum and again as the boundary dividing those who recognized *Swein in 1013 from those who still acknowledged Æthelred's kingship. It may have been the boundary of Danish customary law before the shiring of the Midlands displaced it in favour of shire boundaries.

Hill, *Atlas*, p. 98; *Alfred the Great*, pp. 171–2; P. Stafford, *The East Midlands in the Early Middle Ages* (Leicester, 1985); idem, 'The Danes and the Danelaw', *History Today* 36 (1986), 17–23; H. R. Loyn, *Anglo-Saxon England and the Norman Conquest*, 2nd ed. (Harlow, 1991); Hart, *Danelaw*.

N. J. HIGHAM

DANIEL, the third poem in the *Junius Manuscript, focuses on the struggle between the Three Children and Nabuchodonossor, king of Babylon; on Nabuchodonossor's conversion chiefly through the agency of *Daniel*; and on Baltassar's Feast, which ends with the conquest of Babylon by Darius the Mede. *Daniel* may be seen as two poems, *Daniel A* and *Daniel B*. *Daniel A* corresponds to the first five chapters of the Vulgate Daniel, including the Song of the Three Children; the last six chapters (VII–XII), containing the prophecies which, according to Jerome's commentary, made the book of Daniel important, are ignored, so in a very real sense the Old English poet has turned his back on the exegetical tradition. While following the general order of events in the Vulgate, the poem displays some differences of emphasis, indicating that it interprets its biblical source.

Immediately after the Three Children are seen to be surviving in the fiery furnace there is an interpolation, called *Daniel B*, lines 279–408 of the whole poem. *Daniel B* seems to be a version of the OE poem *Azarias*, found in the *Exeter Book. It comprises principally the Song of Azariah (283–332) and the Song of the Three Children (362–408), with a brief introduction (279–82) and a narrative 'bridge' passage between the two Songs (333–61). Most of it is direct speech. In the Song of Azariah the speaker prays for deliverance, though in *Daniel A* that deliverance has already been supplied. In the Song of the Three Children they thank God for their deliverance by Him. The main arguments for *Daniel B* as an interpolation are: the dislocation of the narrative *vis a vis* the biblical source; differences in vocabulary, especially the words used for God; and differences in metrical usage.

In *Daniel A* the main theme seems to be salvation for those who keep God's law, while those who fail to do so must take the consequences. The Three Children are plunged into a fiery furnace and emerge unscathed, saved by God because of their faith. For neglecting His law God allowed the Israelites to be conquered by Nabuchodonossor and taken off into captivity in Babylon. Like that of the Israelites, Nabuchodonossor's wickedness is also described in terms of contempt for God's law, and he too is exiled – until he sees the light and believes. Similarly, in the incomplete final episode Baltassar's sacrilege in misusing the sacred vessels from the temple in Jerusalem for a feast offends against God's law.

In *Daniel B* the emphasis is different. Azariah appeals to God to save the Three because of the covenant which the Lord gave to Abraham, Isaac and Jacob. The Song of the Three Children praises God as helper of men. In emphasizing the help of God *Daniel B* was presumably thought to complement *Daniel A* by treating a different aspect of the theme of salvation.

ASPR i.111–32; *Daniel*, ed. R. T. Farrell (London, 1974); P. G. Remley, *Old English Scriptural Verse*, CSASE 16 (Cambridge, 1996), 231–434.

P. J. LUCAS

DATING OF VERNACULAR TEXTS. It is important to distinguish between the dating of manuscripts containing Old English, about which we can be reasonably precise, and the dating of the texts they contain. Most Old English poetry is recorded in manuscripts written late in the tenth century or early in the eleventh, but scholars disagree on the date of composition of individual poems. *Beowulf, for example, is still, after two hundred years of scholarly argument, dated anywhere between the eighth century and the eleventh, and even the earlier dating may be pushed back further by those who assume oral composition. The view, held generally until the 1970s, that poems from the heroic tradition such as Beowulf and *Widsith, and those that draw on that tradition such as *Genesis and *Exodus, are 'early' (i.e. eighth-century), and *Judith and the Old Saxon interpolation in Genesis are 'late' (i.e. end of the ninth century or tenth), with *Cynewulf's poems and the *elegies lying somewhere between, is now frequently challenged. The principal difficulty is that there are no sure linguistic or metrical tests for dating Old English poems. Most poems exhibit a mixture of the linguistic forms associated with different *dialects and periods, but a similar mixture can be found in a variety of tenth-century prose texts, and appears to reflect a looser degree of tolerance of mixed forms than is found in later manuscripts. Even the traditional linguistic/metrical indicators such as the syncopation of medial e, the contraction of inflections after stressed vowels and the alliteration of g are now seen as unreliable. The *Battle of Maldon, undeniably a late poem, has very occasional lines which do not conform with the patterns of classical verse, but the tenth-century poems of the *Anglo-Saxon Chronicle have none. There appears to be no clearly marked tendency towards the looser metrical style of Middle English before the Norman Conquest.

For prose we have some better indicators, in that the works of King *Alfred and his circle can be placed at the end of the ninth century, a firm chronology has been established for the voluminous writings of *Ælfric, and the English writings of other named individuals such as Bishop *Æthelwold, *Wulfstan the homilist and *Byrhtferth of Ramsey can be dated with some precision. But there remains a large body of anonymous prose surviving only in eleventh-century copies which may have had an extended transmissional history. Many anonymous *homilies, for example, could have been composed decades earlier than the manuscripts in which they survive.

C. L. Wrenn, A Study of Old English Literature (London, 1967); A. Crandell Amos, Linguistic Means of Determining the Dates of Old English Literary Texts, Medieval

Academy Books 90 (Cambridge, MA, 1980); C. Chase, The Dating of Beowulf (Toronto, 1981); J. M. Bately, 'Old English Prose before and during the Reign of King Alfred', ASE 17 (1988), 93–138; R. M. Liuzza, 'On the Dating of Beowulf', Beowulf: Basic Readings, ed. P. S. Baker (New York and London, 1995), pp. 281–302; R. D. Fulk, A History of Old English Meter (Philadelphia, PA, 1992).

DONALD SCRAGG

DEERHURST (Glos.) was an important *Hwiccian minster, first mentioned c.804 in the will of Æthelric son of Æthelmund, who desired to be buried there. Archbishop *Ælfheah (d. 1012) spent part of his early career there. By the 1050s the minster was closely associated with Earl Odda, whose chapel there was consecrated (according to its surviving inscription) by Bishop *Ealdred of Worcester in 1056, and who died there four months later.

Two Anglo-Saxon churches remain near each other, on the eastern edge of the floodplain of the river Severn, near Tewkesbury. Odda's Chapel is a typical two-cell small eleventh-century church, unique in being precisely dated. St Mary's, the minster, is much more complex: it retains many Anglo-Saxon features, including windows, doorways and sculpture, much of it still in situ. Thanks to recent intensive investigations of St Mary's, both above and below the ground, an earlier view of it as a single-phase late Saxon building must be replaced by a complex sequence that begins several centuries before this (see fig. 5).

The sequence at St Mary's can now be shown to start with a substantial Roman background; this includes mortuary evidence from beneath the church itself and possible structural elements in both timber and stone at both the east and west ends of the present church. These may belong to the Roman period proper, or to the immediately-following centuries.

The first definite church was a stone-based 'basic rectangle' (the area of the present nave), including a possible wooden eastern apse and adjuncts to the north and west. From this core, initially of both stone and timber, the church can be followed through four further major periods of pre-Conquest alterations. Timber components were gradually replaced by stone; the number and form of adjuncts on all sides of the basic rectangle increased in number; a semi-circular eastern apse was replaced by an elaborately-decorated polygonal one; doorways, windows and other openings, floor levels, heightenings and sculpture can be detailed, as can the evolution of the western 'porch/tower'. This reconstruction demonstrates

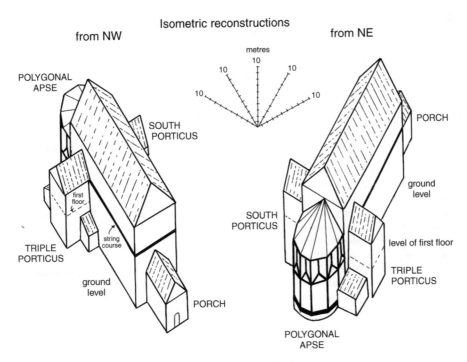

Isometric reconstructions

from NW

POLYGONAL
APSE

SOUTH
PORTICUS

metres
10

10   10

10   10

first
floor

string
course

TRIPLE
PORTICUS

ground
level

PORCH

from NE

PORCH

ground
level

SOUTH
PORTICUS

level of first floor

TRIPLE
PORTICUS

POLYGONAL
APSE

Fig. 5 Deerhurst St Mary in the ninth century (reconstruction).

activity at many different points in the church: on the ground, at first-floor level, and, higher, in the lofty spaces of the porch/tower.

The sequence is dated by radiocarbon determinations at both its beginning and end, and by art-historical criteria. These suggest a culmination in the late ninth–tenth centuries of a church both elaborate and sophisticated, whose details have been interpreted as a spiritual and liturgical expression of the tenth-century reform movement.

Outside the church, elements of the monastic complex have been identified, including part of the circuit of a possible *vallum monasterii*, sectioned at one point. Beyond again, the estates of the monastery, around Deerhurst itself and in more distant areas, have been located on the ground.

It was the post-Conquest history of the church and its estates, with relative stagnation under absentee owners, that resulted in the survival of so much of the Anglo-Saxon fabric.

P. Rahtz, *Excavations of St Mary's Church, Deerhurst 1971–73* (London, 1976); P. Rahtz and L. Watts with the late H. M. Taylor and L. Butler, *St Mary's Church, Deerhurst, Gloucestershire. Fieldwork, Excavations and Structural Analysis, 1971–84* (Woodbridge, 1997); P. Wormald, *How do we Know so Much about Anglo-Saxon Deerhurst?*, The Deerhurst Lecture for 1991 (Deerhurst, 1993).

LORNA WATTS

DEIRA. An English kingdom bounded by the Humber to the south and the Tees to the north. The name is of British derivation which suggests an English take-over of British tribal territory. Archaeological evidence shows settlement to have been underway by the middle of the fifth century. The first recorded king is Ælle (560–90), founder of the Deiran dynasty and father of King *Edwin. Deira unsuccessfully fought its northern rival *Bernicia for supremacy in the late sixth and seventh century. Oswine (*c.*642–51) was the last Deiran to rule the kingdom independently, after which it was governed by members of the Bernician dynasty. See also *Northumbria.

M. Miller, 'The Dates of Deira', *ASE* 8 (1979), 35–61.

PHILIP HOLDSWORTH

DEMESNE, ROYAL: *see* Manors and Manorial Lordship

DEMOGRAPHY: *see* Settlement Patterns

DEOR is a short Old English poem offering limited consolation on the strength of past examples of troubles overcome. It is often grouped with other *heroic poetry because the six examples allude to figures known in Germanic heroic legend, although the third example, which names

139

Mæðhild and Geat, cannot be confidently identified. In the sixth example the pseudo-autobiographical poet, Deor, juxtaposes himself with Heorrenda, a famous legendary minstrel, who has ousted him as the court *scop*; in a wry pun he explains that he, Deor, had formerly been dear (*dyre*) to his lord. Uniquely in the Old English poetic corpus, there is a refrain: *þæs ofereode*; *þisses swa mæg*, 'That passed away; so can this', which occurs after every example. 'That' can be interpreted throughout as referring to the misfortune just cited and 'this' to the reader's or auditor's own unspecified trouble; less optimistically, the final 'that' may be taken to refer to Deor's former happiness and 'this' to his present misfortune, from which release can be hoped for but not guaranteed. In offering consolation through apparently real examples and repeated assertion, the poem has a form reminiscent of a *charm, but its emotional restraint and hardwon wisdom are characteristic of much Old English poetry. *Deor* survives in the *Exeter Book. Its prior history is unknown.

ASPR iii. 178–9; *Deor*, ed. K. Malone (London, 1933; rev. ed., Exeter, 1977); *Old English Minor Heroic Poems*, ed. J. Hill (Durham, 1983; rev. ed. 1994).

JOYCE HILL

DESCENT INTO HELL is one of a group of shorter religious poems in the *Exeter Book. Although older critics found it confusing in structure, in that it begins with the visit of the two Marys to Christ's sepulchre, moves rapidly into the harrowing of hell and ends abruptly, when seen within the context of the Easter liturgy it makes perfect sense. Thematically it is related to other poems such as *Christ and Satan, *Christ III* and the conclusion of the *Dream of the Rood*, as well as the prose translation of the Gospel of Nicodemus (see *apocrypha, biblical).

ASPR iii. 219–23; P. W. Conner, 'The Liturgy and the Old English "Descent into Hell"', *JEGP* 79 (1980), 179–91; *The Exeter Anthology of Old English Poetry*, ed. B. Muir, 2 vols. (Exeter, 1994).

DONALD SCRAGG

DEUSDEDIT, a native of *Wessex and archbishop of *Canterbury (655–64), is worth recording because he was the first native Anglo-Saxon to be appointed to archiepiscopal office (his predecessors all having been Roman members of the Gregorian mission), the implication being that – as in the case of *Ithamar, the first native Anglo-Saxon bishop – it required more than a generation for the *schools established by the Gregorian mission to train a native sufficiently schooled in

*liturgy, *canon law and ecclesiastical doctrine to be appointed to high office. Nothing is otherwise known of him.

Bede, *HE* ii.20, iii.28–9.

MICHAEL LAPIDGE

DIALECTS. In speaking of dialects of Old English, scholars generally have in mind varieties of language each current in a particular region. There is virtually no evidence for other kinds of dialect variation (e.g. class dialects). The assumption is usually made that the written language of the surviving texts reflects the spoken language of the regions in question, although it is unknown to what extent it does so. The dialects have been distinguished from one another primarily on the basis of differences between their sound-systems, and certain of the surviving texts are considered to reflect these sound-systems particularly well. It is usual to reckon with four dialects: Northumbrian (in the northern part of the country), Mercian (in the Midlands), Kentish (in the South East), and the West Saxon dialect (in the South and South West), with Northumbrian and Mercian together forming the larger Anglian dialect group. West Saxon came to serve as a standard written language in the later Anglo-Saxon period. Opinions have differed as to the dialectal status of the language in which most of the extant Old English verse is recorded.

The surviving materials give at best a very incomplete picture, even of phonology. Northumbrian is represented by a handful of texts (brief verse compositions and *runic inscriptions, and records of personal names) of the mid-eighth to early ninth century, and by extensive interlinear *glosses (including that to the *Lindisfarne Gospels) of the later tenth century. Mercian is represented mainly by English words in some eighth- and ninth-century glossaries, by the mid-ninth-century interlinear gloss to the *Vespasian Psalter, by part of the interlinear glossing of the Rushworth Gospels (tenth century), and by a few minor texts. The principal evidence for Kentish consists of some ninth-century *charters, together with a small group of late-tenth-century texts found in a single manuscript (two relatively short poems and a substantial number of interlinear glosses to Proverbs). There are few texts representing West Saxon before *c*.900, but through the prose works surviving from about that time, and through a large body of prose from the later tenth century onwards, the dialect is the one for which the largest body of evidence is available.

The texts mentioned very often fail to give

evidence of some important linguistic features. They may be relied upon at best as reflecting the language of the immediate vicinity of their place of origin (known with some certainty in only a few cases), and there is therefore no textual evidence for the language used in large tracts of the four supposed dialect areas. Where earlier and later texts representative of a particular 'dialect' exist (widely separated in time in the case of, e.g., Northumbrian), the language of the later texts cannot be assumed to be the straightforward development of that in the earlier ones.

The evidence of the texts can be supplemented by the study of place-names and of Middle English and later dialects. Dialect boundaries are liable to move over time, however, and post-Anglo-Saxon evidence must be used with due caution.

A considerable amount of work has been done, starting near the beginning of this century but more extensively since about 1960, on regional differences in vocabulary in Old English. The results of this work have to a large extent been the uncovering of differences between 'Anglian' and 'West Saxon' vocabulary.

Various explanations have been offered as to the origins of dialectal distinctions in Old English. Some scholars believe that these distinctions reflect differences in the language spoken by various groups of settlers at the time of the Anglo-Saxon *settlements, others that the dialects took shape after the settlement period, as a result of political and other factors (including, according to some opinions, post-settlement contacts with the continent).

A. Campbell, *Old English Grammar* (Oxford, 1959), pp. 4–11; D. DeCamp 'The Genesis of the Old English Dialects: a New Hypothesis', *Language* 34 (1958), 232–44 (repr. in *Approaches to English Historical Linguistics*, ed. R. Lass (New York, 1969), pp. 355–68); R. M. Hogg, *A Grammar of Old English*, I (Oxford, 1992), pp. 2–9; M. L. Samuels, 'Kent and the Low Countries: Some Linguistic Evidence', in *Edinburgh Studies in English and Scots*, ed. A. J. Aitken, *et al.* (London, 1971), pp. 3–19; H. Schabram, *Superbia: Studien zum Altenglischen Wortschatz* (Munich, 1965); K. Sisam, 'Dialect Origins of the Earlier Old English Verse', *Studies in the History of Old English Literature* (Oxford, 1953), pp. 119–39; F. Wenisch, *Spezifisch anglisches Wortgut in den nordhumbrischen Interlinearglossierungen des Lukasevangeliums*, Anglistische Forschungen 132 (Heidelberg, 1979); W. Hofstetter, *Winchester und der spätaltenglische Sprachgebrauch* (Munich, 1987).

T. HOAD

DICTIONARIES, MODERN. Modern dictionaries of Old English still in use include the pioneering work by J. *Bosworth of 1838, later enlarged and completed by T. N. Toller as *An Anglo-Saxon Dictionary* (1898 and 1921); more compact are those of H. *Sweet (1896) and Clark Hall and Meritt (1894; rev. 1960). All are superseded by the computer-assisted coverage of the Toronto *Dictionary of Old English* (from 1986), and its related concordances. For the history of Old English words surviving in later periods, the *Oxford English Dictionary* is invaluable, while Ekwall (1960) is a standard work for place-names. J. Bosworth and T. N. Toller, *An Anglo-Saxon Dictionary* (Oxford, 1898) with T. N. Toller, *Supplement* (Oxford, 1921), and A. Campbell, *Enlarged Addenda and Corrigenda* (Oxford, 1972); J. R. Clark Hall, *A Concise Anglo-Saxon Dictionary*, 4th ed. with a supplement by H. Meritt (Cambridge, 1960; repr. Toronto, 1984); E. Ekwall, *The Concise Oxford Dictionary of English Place-Names*, 4th ed. (Oxford, 1960); S. A. Barney, *Word-Hoard: An Introduction to Old English Vocabulary* (New Haven, CT, and London, 1977); A. diP. Healey and R. L. Venezky, *A Microfiche Concordance to Old English* (Toronto, 1980); R. L. Venezky and A. diP. Healey, *A Microfiche Concordance to Old English: The High Frequency Words* (Toronto, 1985); A. diP. Healey, *et al.*, *Dictionary of Old English* (Toronto, 1986-).

MARK ATHERTON

DIET: *see* Food and Drink

DIPLOMA: *see* Charters and Writs

DISEASES. Evidence for diseases in the Anglo-Saxon period is derived from various sources. Palaeopathology (the scientific study of diseases in the corporeal remains of earlier peoples) provides direct evidence of trauma and chronic diseases which are mainfest in skeletal change. Acute diseases with recovery or fatal result do not generally induce skeletal change. Palaeopathology reflects, therefore, only a small part of the spectrum of disease in antiquity. Although preserved soft tissues, mainly as bog burials, are known from Britain, no such remains have been recovered from the Anglo-Saxon period. Artistic portrayal of disease is usually representative of physically deforming disease, and, because of artistic licence and possible interpretative error, cannot be unequivocally diagnostic. Documentary evidence of disease is found in medical and surgical texts, in legal documents relating to specific diseases, and in contemporary records of epidemic disease. Rarely in archaic documents are adequate and pathognomonic descriptions of disease given. Diagnoses from contemporary documents are, with few exceptions, tentative.

The diseases endemic and constant in Anglo-Saxon England differed little from those of both earlier and later periods. The problems of degenerative arthritis, non-specific infection (infections in which the cause is unknown), dental caries, and injury were really no different for the Anglo-Saxon peasant or nobleman than they were for the Romano-British or medieval inhabitants. Malignant diseases (cancers and related diseases) were, as for the period before and for several centuries later, rare indeed, and the reasons for this are obscure. Of endemic diseases in the period, leprosy and tuberculosis are singled out because of their increasing prevalence, and their legal and social significance. Both diseases, on current evidence, first appeared in Britain in the later years of the Roman period. The diseases subsequently spread geographically, and increased in prevalence. Tuberculosis, manifest as scrofula (tuberculous involvement and enlargement of lymph nodes in the neck) attracted royal interest and by the reign of *Edward the Confessor was of such significance as to inspire the practice of Touching for the Kings Evil. This ritual, of considerable emotional, an perhaps financial, benefit to the recipient, but of no therapeutic value whatsoever, became an increasing practice in post-Conquest England and was not abandoned until well after the Middle Ages. Because of inadequate sources of evidence, the true prevalence of tuberculosis in Anglo-Saxon England is not known. Basing theory on modern epidemiology, it is likely that the disease became rampant with the advent of urbanisation in the later Anglo-Saxon period. The increased population density and population aggregation in centres at this time favoured the respiratory transmission of the disease. Tuberculosis must surely have been responsible for much misery, suffering, and death in Anglo-Saxon England.

Leprosy too was a disease relatively new to the English scene at this time. From its first presence, on current evidence, at Poundbury, Dorset, the infection spread. By the Norman Conquest there can have been few villages which were not aware of the maimed and, to the uncouth medieval mind, abhorrent figure with advanced lepromatous leprosy. But, notwithstanding the illfounded opprobrium which was to develop, the Anglo-Saxon sufferer was treated no differently in death from his more fortunate kinsmen. It is likely therefore that he was an accepted, or at least tolerated, member of society. Lazar house development and a policy of segregation were features of post-Conquest society. And even on this later phenomenon, there was a bivalence of attitude towards the suf-

ferer. At one and the same time there was a movement of sympathetic beneficence and a movement of harsh rejection. Although these attitudes were, in some measure, determined by illfounded theology and unsound concepts of infection, it is strange that Anglo-Saxon England, perhaps no less Christian, demonstrated a tolerance and acceptance, in life and in death, of the maimed leprosy sufferer. This, together with palaeopathological findings of other chronic mutilating, and physically incapacitating, diseases, suggests that Anglo-Saxon society was compassionate. Support of a member, prevented from arduous work by physical disability, must surely have imposed a considerable strain upon a small Anglo-Saxon group.

These diseases, although of increasing prevalence and significance in Anglo-Saxon England, were present in Britain at an earlier period. There is, however, one disease, common today, which, on palaeopathological evidence, first appeared as a human disease during the late Anglo-Saxon period. Rheumatoid arthritis, a disease of largely unknown cause, appears to have been non-existent prior to the period. Palaeopathology affords the earliest evidence of this disease, artistic portrayal and literary record appearing several centuries later. The reason for the appearance of the disease at this time remains an enigma. Whether social, environmental, or genetic factors operated in its development is unknown.

Superimposed on the undercurrent of commonplace and endemic diseases are the epidemics. Epidemic disease is frequently devastating, personally and collectively fearsome, geographically widespread, and of short duration. Epidemic diseases are infective, caused by virus or bacterium, and are acute. Because of their acute nature, bone change rarely occurs, and the diseases have not been identified in palaeopathology of skeletal remains. Thus, the evidence for epidemic disease in the Anglo-Saxon period is documentary. The literary concern is, however, with implied social catastrophe; diagnostic precision is rarely possible with epidemic disease at this period. Contemporary documents refer to pestilence and to plague. It is noted that the history of epidemics in England before the Black Death is really concerned with sickness associated with famine. Although many of the epidemics in the Anglo-Saxon period did follow recorded periods of famine, there were outbreaks not associated with such periods. Doubtless, famine so reduced the general health status of peoples that they were more susceptible to virulent and fulminating infectious diseases. However, several outbreaks of pestilence are recorded in the *Anglo-Saxon Chronicle* and in *Bede in the second half of the seventh century which were not preceded by famine. An outbreak in 664 has carried the name *pestis ictericia*. This suggests that jaundice was a prominent feature in the disease, a feature indicating that the disease was not the plague of later years. In the absence of further contemporary description, it is impossible to differentiate several infectious diseases, amongst which are malaria, yellow fever, and Weil's disease. These are diseases requiring insect vectors for transmission which have been eradicated from Britain but which, because of different environmental conditions, were present in earlier periods. Such was the case with malaria and, perhaps, other infections now confined to tropical and subtropical zones.

C. Creighton, *A History of Epidemics in Britain* (London, 1965); K. Manchester, *The Archaeology of Disease* (Bradford, 1983); D. J. Ortner and W. G. J. Putschar, *Identification of Pathological Conditions in Human Skeletal Remains* (Washington, DC, 1985); P. Richards, *The Medieval Leper and his Northern Heirs* (Cambridge, 1977); R. T. Steinbock, *Paleopathological Diagnosis and Interpretation* (Springfield, OH, 1976); J. R. Maddicott, 'Plague in Seventh-Century England', *P&P* 156 (1997), 7–54.

K. MANCHESTER

DIUMA was an Irish priest sent from *Northumbria, with three English colleagues, to preach to the *Middle Angles in about 653. *Bede says that after the Northumbrian defeat of *Mercia in 655/656 he was ordained bishop of both the Middle Angles and the Mercians; 'in a short time he brought many people to the Lord, then died among the Middle Angles in the region called *Infeppingum*'. The central monastery of this unidentified region was possibly Charlbury (Oxon.), where the relics of one 'Dioma' were venerated in the tenth century.

Bede, *HE* iii.21; Blair, *AS Oxon*, pp. 59–60.

JOHN BLAIR

DOMESDAY BOOK is the result of the Domesday survey, ordered by William the Conqueror at his Christmas court at Gloucester in 1085 and completed by 1 August in the following year, when the returns were presented to the king at Salisbury. Apart from Domesday Book itself, some of the extensive documentation produced for and by the survey survives, including the *Inquisitio Eliensis*, a private compilation made from the Domesday returns for the abbot of *Ely, the *Inquisitio Comitatus Cantabrigiensis*, seemingly the commissioners' own report on Cambridgeshire,

and two circuit returns, *Exon Domesday*, which covers the south-west, and *Little Domesday*, the East Anglian return, which was never enrolled by the Domesday scribe, but rubricated and kept with the text of Domesday proper.

The famous description of the survey in the *Anglo-Saxon Chronicle* (s.a. 1085) shows that it consisted of two related enquiries. The first concerned the king's own lands and rights, and included an inquiry into the operation of the geld. The second comprised 'a record of how much land his archbishops had, and his bishops and his abbots and his earls, and . . . what or how much everybody had who was occupying land in England'. For the purposes of the survey, the shires were grouped into seven circuits, each with its group of commissioners, who held little or no land in the area. The royal officials in each shire, who were responsible for the king's estates and perquisites, were probably instructed to prepare reports for the commissioners. The commissioners themselves then held sessions of the shire courts, at which these officials gave testimony; and information was also gathered from the local juries assembled from the shire and from its constituent *hundreds and vills. Sometimes the local landholders also gave evidence before the shire-court; but the business of the second enquiry was largely achieved by requiring each landholder to submit a written account (*brevis*) of his estates (manors) in the shire. When using Domesday, it is important to remember that it records units of estate-management (manors) and units of taxation (vills) and is emphatically not a list of actual settlements (villages).

Once both enquiries were completed, the commissioners had to compile the returns for their circuits. The information on the king's rights and dues would be arranged geographically, by *shire, hundred and vill, the units through which geld was assessed and collected; but the descriptions of the landholders' estates would be ordered tenurially, as each described the estates (manors) which made up his total holding, his honour. The commissioners had to reconcile these differing arrangements and different expedients were adopted by the various groups. The south-western return (Exon Domesday) shows a subordination of the territorially-arranged returns, derived from the geld-accounts, to a seigneurially-based structure, which cuts across even the shire boundaries. Thus the lands of Robert, count of Mortain, in *Devonshire are immediately followed by his lands in *Cornwall and then in Somerset, and the single manor of William de Moion in Wiltshire is immediately followed by his lands in Dorset. In the east midlands, however, the commissioners took exactly the opposite line. The *Inquisitio Comitatus Cantabrigiensis* orders its material by hundred and by vill; the details of the estates derived from the seigneurial *breves* are subordinated to a 'geld-list' structure, hundred by hundred. The *Danelaw circuit (VI) may have followed the same principle, for the so-called 'Yorkshire summary', included in Domesday itself, is in effect a 'conversion-table' which can be used to transfer estates from a territorial to a tenurial format.

Domesday itself combines the two arrangements; indeed this is one of its most striking characteristics. Each shire is described in turn, and within the shire, the lands are arranged by the honours of the landowners: the king, the ecclesiastical holders and finally the lay lords. But within each holder's honour, his estates (manors) are arranged in order of the hundred and vill in which they lie. (It is striking that the honour, the private lordship, though acknowledged, is nevertheless subordinated to the public institutions of the shire and hundred.)

The returns were sent to the royal writing-office at *Winchester to be edited and abbreviated into a single text. It is essentially the work of a single scribe, the 'main scribe', though there is also a correcting hand, which makes small but significant additions to the text. Who oversaw the process we do not know, though a case can be made for William of Saint-Calais, bishop of Durham, in which case the 'main scribe' was perhaps a Durham clerk. He was no mere copyist. He was presented with a mass of material; not only the circuit-returns, but also much supplementary matter, which was coming in as he wrote, and he had to make numerous additions and corrections as he went along. Thus the Domesday text is full of interlinings, marginal additions and even specially-inserted folios and fragments of folios carrying material displaced or but lately received. The scribe sometimes writes notes of missing details to himself; sometimes they have been found and inserted, but often not. He had also to deal with disputes recorded, but rarely resolved, over the ownership of land, which largely explains the so-called 'double entries', estates and parts of estates claimed by rival landowners and entered under the names of both.

The scribe also had to impose some uniformity on the material before him; for the different groups of commissioners had interpreted their instructions in different ways. The range of material is vast, and varies from circuit to circuit

and shire to shire. In some areas, for instance, there is a detailed account of the manorial structures, while elsewhere parcels of land are largely undifferentiated from each other; again, some circuits record pasture along with meadow and *woodland, while others do not. When comparing region with region, it is important to distinguish real variations from by-products of the idiosyncracies of the circuit commissioners. Domesday is not an internally consistent text, which makes it notoriously difficult to interpret; but one is filled with admiration for the unknown compiler, and the skill which he brought to his difficult (but illuminating) task.

D. Bates, *A Bibliography of Domesday Book* (Woodbridge, 1986); *Domesday Book: a Reassessment*, ed. P. H. Sawyer (London, 1985); *Domesday Studies*, ed. J. C. Holt (Woodbridge, 1987); *Domesday Book Studies*, ed. R. W. H. Erskine and A. Williams (London, 1987); D. Roffe, 'Domesday Book and Northern Society', *EHR* 105 (1990), 310–36; D. Roffe, 'The Making of Domesday Book Re-considered', *HSJ* 6 (1994), 153–66.

ANN WILLIAMS

DORCHESTER (Dorset), a Romano-British town, could just possibly have continued as a central place into the Anglo-Saxon period. Sceattas have been found there, and *Æthelweard identifies it as the 'king's *tun*' to which a *reeve tried to force the first *Viking raiders in 789. It occurs as a royal vill in *charters of the 830s onwards, as a *mint in the tenth and eleventh centuries and as a borough in *Domesday Book.

L. Keen, 'The Towns of Dorset', in Haslam, *Towns*, pp. 203–47.

JOHN BLAIR

DORCHESTER-ON-THAMES (Oxon.) was a fortified settlement controlling the upper Thames valley in the late Iron Age and Romano-British periods. Evidently it continued as a post-Roman territorial centre, for one of the town's *cemeteries remained in use well into the sixth century. It has also produced some of the earliest fifth-century Germanic burials found in England (even though one of them is no longer identified as the grave of a mercenary in the late Roman army), and it offers unusually persuasive evidence for interaction between a British successor state and the first English settlers. In the 630s the newly-converted King Cynegils of the *Gewisse gave Dorchester (called by *Bede a *civitas*) to the missionary *Birinus as his episcopal seat; two excavated groups of large timber buildings may have housed the associated religious community. *Penda's invasion of the region led to the abandonment of the Gewissian see, though Dorchester reappears briefly as a Mercian see in the 670s, and it is likely that religious life never wholly ceased there. From the late ninth century Dorchester was again the seat of a bishop, but it failed (probably because of the proximity of *Oxford and *Wallingford) to develop as a *town, and in 1072 the bishopric was transferred to the more urban *Lincoln.

Bede, *HE* iii.7, iv.23; J. Cook and T. Rowley, ed., *Dorchester through the Ages* (Oxford, 1985); Blair, *AS Oxon*.

JOHN BLAIR

DRAGONS represent the most common type of monstrous animal in Anglo-Saxon art and literature. The Anglo-Saxon dragon (OE *draca, wyrm*; Latin *draco, serpens*) is typically serpentine in shape and associated with evil; literary descriptions disagree on more specific details, but are generally indebted to Germanic legend and biblical, classical and patristic traditions. Conventional motifs include fire-spitting (described in the famous dragon-episode in *Beowulf* 2200–3182), the ability to fly (described in *Beowulf*, The *Battle of Finnsburh* 3b and the *Anglo-Saxon Chronicle*, 793 DE), poisonous breath and monstrous proportions. Dragons are frequently located in cave-like structures, although it is not always clear whether natural caves or burial mounds (prehistoric or Anglo-Saxon) are intended. The notion that dragons guard hidden treasures is attested in *Beowulf*, the *gnomic *Maxims II* 26b–27a and more widely in Scandinavian and classical material, and provides the primary motivation for the dragon-fights of Sigemund and Beowulf (*Beowulf* 884b–97 and 2200–3182) and numerous other heroes in related traditions, notably in Old Norse sagas. To what extent the dragon-imagery of Germanic legend existed outside Anglo-Saxon literary sources as oral *folklore is difficult to determine, since surviving evidence (in the form of *place-names, for example) is scarce. The Christian dragon-imagery of Anglo-Saxon England appears in homiletic, apocryphal and especially hagiographical texts such as *Aldhelm's *De virginitate*, which describes the dragon-fights of saints Hilarion, Silvester and Victoria; other dragon-fighting saints known to the Anglo-Saxons include Michael, Margaret, and *Machutus. The association of St George with a dragon, by contrast, is a post-Conquest development. Anglo-Saxon dragon-imagery is notable primarily for the dragon-fight described in lines 2200–3182 of *Beowulf*, the longest and most complex account of its kind, whose symbolic content remains disputed, and whose idiosyncra-

cies are perhaps best explained as the result of an ingenious combination of secular and Christian traditions. The great ornamental potential of the dragon in Anglo-Saxon art (due in part to its serpentine shape and suitability for zoomorphic interlace) is exemplified in the decorative patterns particularly of the early period (such as the dragon-imagery of the *Sutton Hoo treasure, clearly indebted to Scandinavian models); particularly noteworthy are also the frequent depictions of St Michael and the dragon in eleventh- and twelfth-century stone carvings.

R. Jente, *Die mythologischen Ausdrucke im altenglischen Wortschatz*, Anglistische Forschungen 56 (Heidelberg, 1921); F. Wild, 'Drachen im *Beowulf* und andere Drachen', *Sitzungsberichte der österreichischen Akademie der Wissenschaften, phil.-hist. Klasse* 238 (1962), 3–62; K. Sisam, 'Beowulf's Fight with the Dragon', *Review of English Studies* ns 9 (1958), 129–40; M. E. Goldsmith, *The Mode and Meaning of 'Beowulf'* (London, 1970), pp. 124–45; M. E. Ruggerini, 'L'eroe germanico contro avversari mostruosi: tra testo e iconografia', in *La funzione dell'eroe germanico: storicità, metafora, paradigma*, ed. T. Paroli (Rome, 1995), pp. 201–57; J. Hoops, ed., *Reallexikon der germanischen Altertumskunde*, 2nd ed. (Berlin, 1973–), vi. 131–7; J. Simpson, *British Dragons* (London, 1980); C. Hicks, *Animals in Early Medieval Art* (Edinburgh, 1993).

CHRISTINE RAUER

DREAM OF THE ROOD. The Old English poem *The Dream of the Rood* has been preserved in two different versions, one in the *Vercelli Book, the other in extracts from the central part of the poem, or an earlier version of it, carved on the eighth-century *Ruthwell Cross (pl. 16).

The theme of the Vercelli poem is the triumph of the cross on which Christ died and the rewards gained by devotion to it. It unites images from *heroic poetry, the *liturgy and contemplative prayer but its main focus is eschatological. The first three lines of the poem define it as a dream *vision. This vision, which need not be anything more than a poetic device, takes place at midnight, the hour of Christ's birth, resurrection and return as judge: a time, therefore, when it was important to watch and pray. It is also a time of silence, and therefore conducive to prayer. In the first main section of the poem, the dreamer contemplates a shifting series of images: a tree towering up into the sky, a *beacen* or sign, sometimes bloodstained, sometimes covered in gold and jewels or decorated with hangings. The ambiguity of this description, recalling the technique of the Old English *riddles, allows the poet to introduce a number of images which he develops later in the poem. The image of the tree recalls the many liturgical references to the tree of the cross, which became the tree of life planted in the river of life in the heavenly Jerusalem. The jewels recall the jewelled crosses of the early Christian period, while the hangings are almost certainly a reference to what is called a trophy-cross, that is, a cross draped with a purple cloak in imitation of Roman military trophies.

In this first part of the poem the poet is outside the vision; in the second section of the poem he moves into the vision, to describe Christ's death as seen and experienced by the cross. Although, strictly speaking, this second part of the vision is spoken by the cross, the poet's use of phrases like 'I saw' conveys the impression that dreamer and cross are the same and that it is the dreamer who has moved back into biblical time and who watches the crucifixion. Similarly, the third and fourth sections of the poem (comprising an address by the cross to the dreamer, asking him to tell his vision to others, and the reflections of the dreamer about the part devotion to the cross plays in his life) appear to merge, allowing the poet to assume the authority of the cross. At the end, the poet, who presents himself as the typical friendless exile of Old English *elegiac poetry, takes the cross as his new lord and looks forward to the time when he can join his friends at the banquet in heaven.
ASPR ii.61–5; B. C. Raw, 'The Dream of the Rood and its Connections with Early Christian Art', MÆ 39 (1970), 239–56; The Dream of the Rood, ed. M. J. Swanton, 2nd ed. (Exeter, 1987); B. C. Raw, 'Biblical Literature: the New Testament', in CamComp, pp. 227–42.
BARBARA C. RAW

DRYHTHELM: see Visions

DUNSÆTE, a regional (that is 'settler') name, recorded only in a short statement of legal practices in force there. The text is said to have been agreed between 'English councillors' and 'Welshmen', and mainly concerns cattle-theft and homicide as affecting two communities divided by a river that was probably the Wye. That being so, the *Dunsæte* are most plausibly located in Archenfield, south-west of *Hereford. The text's legal procedures and language favour a date about the time of *Æthelstan's heavy-handed negotiations with the Welsh c.930; but it was perhaps interpolated when it was affixed to *Æthelred II's 994 treaty with Olaf, the context of its preservation in its one vernacular copy, and in the Latin *Quadripartitus*. It is an important example of the way that law could be written locally and without evident official sponsorship.
Liebermann, Gesetze i.374–9, ii/2.355–6, iii.214–19; F.

Noble, Offa's Dyke Reviewed, ed. M. Gelling (Oxford, 1983), pp. 14–18; M. Gelling, The West Midlands in the Early Middle Ages (Leicester, 1992), pp. 112–19.
PATRICK WORMALD

DUNSTAN, sometime bishop of *Worcester and *London, and archbishop of *Canterbury (959–88), was the figure-head of the tenth-century Benedictine reform movement. The early part of his life is moderately well documented in the Vita S. Dunstani by the English cleric who gives his name only as B.; but for the period of his archbishopric, much less is known of his activity. According to B., he was born in *Wessex, of parents named Heorstan and Cynethryth, in the days of King *Æthelstan (924–39); but since he is known (from other sources) to have been consecrated a priest by Bishop *Ælfheah of Winchester before Æthelstan's death in 939, and since he will have needed to have reached the canonical age of 30 for consecration to have taken place, most scholars assume that B.'s information is mistaken on this point, and hence that Dunstan was born c.910 or slightly earlier. In any event, Dunstan's family was apparently a wealthy one which owned estates near *Glastonbury (his brother Wulfric had substantial lands in Wiltshire and Surrey, and on his death c.951 bequeathed his estates to Glastonbury); and it was at Glastonbury that Dunstan received his early education. He subsequently came to the attention of King Æthelstan, and was present at his court during the 930s; after the king's death in 939, Dunstan withdrew from the royal court (his withdrawal apparently provoked by the malice of other courtiers who had the ear of King *Edmund) and, in company with *Æthelwold, later bishop of *Winchester, spent a substantial period of study during the 940s and 950s at Glastonbury, over which he was appointed abbot 940 × 946. Their study during this period, particularly of the Regula S. Benedicti and the writings of *Aldhelm, was to have important consequences for tenth-century English learning. During the reign of Edmund's successor, *Eadred, Dunstan regained a position of influence at the royal court, and figures prominently among the witnesses of Eadred's *charters. But this position of influence was once again terminated by the accession of King *Eadwig, as a result of whose personal animosity – prompted, according to B., by Dunstan's intransigent attitude to Eadwig's relationship with the noblewoman Ælfgifu (whom the king later married) – Dunstan was forced in 956 to go into exile at the monastery of St Peter's, Ghent (in *Flanders). The abbot of St Peter's at the time was one Womar, who subsequently spent some time at the Old Minster, Winchester (perhaps at Dunstan's invitation), and it is possible that Womar was one of the informants from Ghent who offered advice on the practices stipulated by the *Regularis Concordia*; in any case, during his stay at Ghent Dunstan will have been able to observe the practices of reformed Benedictine monasticism. During the two years of Dunstan's exile, political circumstances changed in southern England, so that England north of the Thames was in the control of Eadwig's younger brother *Edgar. Edgar recalled Dunstan from exile (perhaps through the intercession of Æthelwold, who was the young Edgar's tutor), and soon afterwards Dunstan was appointed to the see of London (he also acquired and held in plurality the see of Worcester on the death of Bishop *Koenwald in 958). But when Eadwig died on 1 October 959, the kingdom was reunited under Edgar, and at this point Dunstan was made archbishop of Canterbury (though his appointment involved the deposition of a previous appointee, one Byrhthelm), a position which he held until his death on 19 May 988. The period of his archbishopric is not well documented, but it is clear that he was an active member of the king's council, and (according to post-Conquest sources) that he endowed a number of monasteries, probably including *Malmesbury and *Westminster.

Dunstan was also a scholar of some standing. A number of manuscripts survive which bear his annotations (including one, the so-called 'St Dunstan's Classbook', now Oxford, Bodleian Library, Auct. F. 4. 32, which contains a famous drawing of Dunstan kneeling before Christ, accompanied by a distich composed by him), and several of his poems, including an accomplished and difficult *acrostic poem, have been preserved. After his death he was quickly and widely venerated as a saint (an ecclesiastical ordinance of King *Cnut, issued 1020 × 1022, stipulated that Dunstan be commemorated throughout England), and hymns and liturgical prayers were composed for his cult. Two Lives of St Dunstan (those by B. and by Adelard of Ghent) were written within a generation of his death, and, during the twelfth century, Lives were written by *William of Malmesbury and by Osbern and Eadmer of Canterbury.

Sharpe, *Handlist*, 246; *Memorials of St Dunstan*, ed. W. Stubbs, RS (London, 1874); *St Dunstan: his Life, Times and Cult*, ed. N. Ramsay, M. Sparks and T. Tatton-Brown (Woodbridge, 1992); M. Lapidge, *ALL* ii.146–9, 150–6; *St Dunstan's Classbook from Glastonbury*, ed. R. W. Hunt (Amsterdam, 1961); H. Gneuss, 'Dunstan und Hrabanus Maurus: zur Hs. Bodleian Auctarium F.4.32', *Anglia* 96 (1978), 136–48.

MICHAEL LAPIDGE

DURROW, BOOK OF (Dublin, Trinity College Library, 57), a Latin *gospelbook of Fischer's 'English' textual family. It is one of the great monuments of Insular art and, like the Book of Kells (to which its preliminary texts are related), remains highly contentious. Datings range from the mid-seventh to ninth centuries, with a consensus favouring the late seventh–early eighth century. Suggested origins include Ireland, *Northumbria and Scotland (possibly *Iona, whence it may have reached Ireland as part of the evacuation of St *Columba's relics in the early ninth century). It has become a focus for nationalistic debate during the twentieth century. By 877–916 the volume was at the Columban foundation of Durrow, Co. Offaly, when King Flann Mac Mael Sechnaill enshrined it in a *cumdach* as a relic of St Columba (*c.*521–97). An altered scribal *colophon (247v) may reflect a Columban exemplar. After the dissolution it appears to have remained with hereditary keepers, its use including cures for cattle, until presented by Henry Jones, bishop of Meath (1661–82), to Trinity College.

Its script is a half-uncial which, although elegant and stable is not as regular as that of the 'reformed' *Lindisfarne Gospels variety. Its programme of decoration comprises canon tables, *carpet-pages, a cross and evangelist symbols page, individual evangelist symbol pages and decorated incipits. It exhibits stylistic influences from eastern Mediterranean and Coptic art, Pictish carvings and Celtic and Germanic metalwork (especially that of *Sutton Hoo). English influences led Masai, in 1947, to question assumptions of Irish origins for Hiberno-Saxon illumination in favour of Northumbrian. Studies of the Lindisfarne *scriptorium have perpetuated this view and presented Durrow as stylistically earlier than the Lindisfarne Gospels and associates, whilst recent attempts to avoid English influence in favour of Frankish input via Ireland have swung the nationalistic pendulum too far in the opposite direction. Recent excavations at Dunadd in the Irish kindom of Dalriada in Scotland support a more balanced view of pooled cultural influences and might reinforce a possible Ionan origin. Affinities with early Echternach manuscripts, such as the Willibrord Calendar (Paris, BN lat., 10837) and with Turin, Bibl. Nat. Univ., O.IV.20 (an over-painted and burnt volume), have been used to suggest an early eighth-century dating, but this continues to be debated.

A. A. Luce, *et al.*, *Evangeliorum Quattuor Codex Durmachensis*, 2 vols. (Olten and Lausanne, 1960); G. Henderson, *From Durrow to Kells. The Insular Gospelbooks 650–800* (London, 1987); B. Meehan, *The Book of Durrow* (Dublin, 1996).

MICHELLE P. BROWN

DYNASTIES, ROYAL, were defined by their descent from a common founder king, as is recorded in the surviving *genealogies. The most detailed surviving foundation myths are those of the royal houses of *Kent and *Wessex which both describe how a pair of founders with alliterating names, *Hengest and Horsa, and *Cerdic and Cynric respectively, came to England with a small number of ships and, after battling with the British for a few years, made themselves kings. Such accounts have similarities with the foundation stories of continental Germanic kingdoms. The founders were also believed to be of divine descent. All the royal houses for which genealogies survive traced their descent from Woden, with the exception of the royal house of *Essex which claimed to be descended from Seaxnet, a god also worshipped by the continental Old Saxons.

All male descendants of the founders were apparently *æthelings eligible for the kingship, and no formal system for designating an 'heir to the throne' seems to have existed in early Anglo-Saxon England, with the result that there could be considerable competition on the death of a king for the vacant position. Few royal lines were as successful as Kent and *East Anglia in confining the succession to just one branch of the royal house for more than two or three generations. Wessex in the mid-seventh and eighth centuries, *Northumbria in the eighth century and *Mercia in the ninth suffered major periods of instability as rival branches of the royal houses fought each other for control. Women of the royal houses do not seem to have been eligible for the throne themselves, but could pass the royal blood to their offspring. *Marriage with *women of a defeated dynasty could be one way a king could strengthen his claim to a conquered kingdom. *Bede tells us that *Oswald of Northumbria was acceptable to both the Bernician and Deiran kingdoms, because his father was king of *Bernicia and his mother a Deiran princess. He also provides many other examples of the importance of marriages between the different royal dynasties of early Anglo–Saxon England in forming alliances between kingdoms and spreading common cultural norms, including furthering the adoption of Christianity.

Early Anglo-Saxon kings sometimes attempted to designate a close relative as heir by associating them with their rule as a joint or sub-king. *Offa of Mercia went further by having his son Ecgfrith anointed as king. Offa, following the Carolingian house's use of Old Testament precedents, probably hoped to found a new God-given dynasty, but his line was ended when Ecgfrith died soon after his father. In Wessex *Ecgberht and his descendants were successful in the ninth century in establishing their line as the only one from which kings of Wessex (and later England) might be chosen. From this time we find the term *ætheling* restricted to the sons of kings, and the descendants of those who did not become kings were excluded from further consideration. They might, however, like descendants of *Alfred's brother Æthelred, become *ealdormen and thus play a major role in supporting the dynasty.

Primogeniture was not introduced and fraternal succession remained a common pattern in the tenth century. There were still opportunities for disputes over the succession, which were most likely to occur when kings left sons by different mothers, as happened on the deaths of *Edward the Elder and *Edgar. Kings now tended to take their wives from the nobility, and these women and their relatives could play a key role in the factions which formed around the different candidates. The kings of England generally took care not to enlarge the dynasty by marrying their female relatives to members of the nobility, though *Æthelred the Unready was an exception. The daughters of Edward the Elder married into European dynasties and, as earlier, these marriages outside the kingdom helped forge new bonds and open up the country to new influences. The intrusion of members of the Danish royal house on to the English throne, after the military conquests of *Swein Forkbeard and his son *Cnut, weakened the Anglo-Saxon dynasty, especially after the deaths of several Anglo-Saxon *æthelings*. In 1066 *Harold Godwineson, brother-in-law of *Edward the Confessor, the last ruler of the old West Saxon royal line, was poised to establish a new dynasty.

K. Sisam, 'Anglo-Saxon Royal Genealogies', *PBA* 39 (1953), 287–346; D. N. Dumville, 'The Anglian Collection of Royal Genealogies and Regnal Lists', *ASE* 5 (1976), 23–50; A. Williams, 'Some Notes and Considerations on Problems Connected with the English Royal Succession', *ANS* 1 (1978), 144–67; D. N. Dumville, 'The Ætheling: a Study in Anglo-Saxon Constitutional History', *ASE* 8 (1979), 1–33; Yorke *Kingdoms*.

B. A. E. YORKE

E

EADBURG, abbess of Thanet in Kent, was the recipient of no fewer than three of the surviving letters of *Boniface, by whom she was evidently held in high esteem; a further letter (with accompanying gifts), from *Lull, Boniface's successor as archbishop of Mainz, testifies to her lasting influence. The correspondence began even before Boniface left for the Continent: in an early letter of 716 × 719, Boniface, using his original name of Wynfrith, writes to Eadburg giving a lengthy account of a *vision of heaven and hell by a monk at Wenlock. Later letters demonstrate Eadburg's role as a provider of both books and learning: Boniface writes from Germany around 735 to thank her for a gift of books, and again at about the same time to request that she send a copy of the Pauline Epistles written in gold, apparently to impress potential converts, while *Leofgyth, writing soon after 732 to ask for Boniface's guidance, appends an example of her own versification in Latin *metre, a skill that she says was taught her by Eadburg. The last surviving letter from Boniface to Eadburg has been dated to the period 742 × 746, but shares the same easy tone (and much of the diction) of his earlier missives, offering ample testimony to the warmth and depth of a friendship that evidently lasted at least three decades.

S. Bonifatii et Lullii Epistolae, ed. M. Tangl, MGH ES 1 (Berlin, 1916); E. Emerton, trans., The Letters of Saint Boniface (New York, 1940); E. Kylie, trans., The English Correspondence of Saint Boniface (London, 1911); C. Fell, 'Some Implications of the Boniface Correspondence', in New Readings on Women in Old English Literature, ed. H. Damico and A. H. Olsen (Bloomington, IN, 1990), pp. 29–43; P. Sims-Williams, Religion and Literature in Western England, 600–800, CSASE 3 (Cambridge, 1990), 243–72.

ANDY ORCHARD

EADGIFU, queen (b. before 902/4, d. c.966/7), was the daughter of Ealdorman Sigehelm, a Kentish noble. She married King *Edward the Elder, c.919, and was mother of Kings *Edmund and *Eadred. Her chequered career followed the fluctuations of family politics. In Edward's reign and especially in that of her stepson *Æthelstan, she appeared to have little or no prominence at court. The accession of her sons made her queen-mother and the first important *queen of the tenth century, thanks to her landed power, especially in Kent, but particularly to the protracted succession question which forefronted family politics. The crisis of this came on Eadred's death (955), in a struggle for the throne between her grandsons. The eldest, *Eadwig, deprived her of all her lands after taking the throne, though she was restored by the younger, *Edgar, after his accession to *Wessex in 959. Yet her days as queen were over. She was rarely at court after 959, and probably lived in religious retirement. Eadgifu's historical reputation has been enhanced by the supportive role she is given in the Lives of *Dunstan and *Æthelwold. This partial hagiographical view masks her wide interest in churches and in land acquisition, particularly in eastern England, and her active involvement in the extension of West Saxon power. She held large estates, perhaps even acting as a quasi-regent in *Kent. Her last public appearance was appropriately at the gathering to celebrate the birth of Edgar's second son by his third wife in 966, where her presence added to the demonstration of family unity at such a potentially divisive moment. The place and date of her death are uncertain.

C. Hart, 'Two Queens of England', Ampleforth Journal 82 (1977), 10–15, 54; M. A. Meyer, 'Women and the Tenth Century English Monastic Reform', RB 87 (1977), 34–61; P. A. Stafford, 'The King's Wife in Wessex', P & P 91 (1981), 3–27; M. A. Meyer, 'The Queen's "Demesne" in Later Anglo-Saxon England', The Culture of Christendom, ed. M. A. Meyer (London, 1993), pp. 75–113; P. Stafford, Queen Emma and Queen Edith: Queenship and Women's Power in Eleventh-Century England (Oxford, 1997).

PAULINE STAFFORD

EADGYTH [EDITH], queen (b. 1020×30, d. 19 December 1075) was the daughter of Earl *Godwine of Wessex and his Danish wife, Gytha. A learned woman, educated at the royal nunnery at Wilton, she married *Edward the Confessor on 23 January 1045. The union was later seen as chaste, though this is a retrospective view, encouraged by Eadgyth herself, inspired by its childlessness. The marriage marks the king's alliance with and reliance on her father, and Eadgyth's career follows that of her family. In 1051 their fall from favour saw an attempt at her divorce; their restoration in 1052 brought her back; and in the last decade of the reign her high profile matches the importance of her brothers, *Harold and Tostig, in court and kingdom. Eadgyth was, however, an English *queen as much as Godwine's daughter. Her patronage and her major landholding and activity in the north-east midlands and Welsh borders were part of the political structure of a unified England; it was that unification which made the queen, by 1066, the fourth richest person in England. It was as English queen that she survived the Norman Conquest of 1066, protected by William the Conqueror, anxious to stress his legitimacy. Her own arguments for survival, and her view of the recent English past, are enshrined in the *Life of King Edward*, which she commissioned. Edith may have retired to Wilton. She died in *Winchester, and was buried in *Westminster Abbey alongside Edward.

The Life of King Edward Who Rests at Westminster, ed. F. Barlow, 2nd ed. (OMT, 1992); F. Barlow, *Edward the Confessor* (London, 1970); K. E. Cutler, 'Edith, Queen of England, 1045–66', *MS* 35 (1983), 222–31; P. Stafford, *Queen Emma and Queen Edith: Queenship and Women's Power in Eleventh-Century England* (Oxford, 1997).

PAULINE STAFFORD

EADGYTH [EDITH], ST (961–84), daughter of King *Edgar by his concubine Wulfthryth, was brought up within the monastery of Wilton, where her mother had been a novice. Wulfthryth became abbess of Wilton, and, having made her profession, Eadgyth remained at the convent all her life; this was, according to her biographer, despite repeated attempts to bring her out into the world, to make her *queen, and to make her abbess of three other houses, *Winchester, *Barking and Amesbury. Most of what we know about Eadgyth's life derives from the Latin Life by *Goscelin, written *c.*1080 (*BHL* 2388), which emphasises her humility and service to others, while also highlighting Wilton's powerful connections. After her death, miracles, also recorded by Goscelin, occurred at Eadgyth's shrine, which ensured the growth and spread of her cult and established her as Wilton's principal saint (feast: 16 September; translation: 3 November).

A. Wilmart, 'La légende de Ste Édithe en prose et vers par le moine Goscelin', *AB* 56 (1938), 5–101, 265–307.

R. C. LOVE

EADRED, son of *Edward the Elder and *Eadgifu, was king of the English (946–55) in succession to his brother *Edmund. It was in Eadred's reign that *Northumbria finally became a permanent part of England, nearly three decades after the submission to *Æthelstan in 927.

The chronology of Eadred's dealings with Northumbria is not perfectly clear, but can be reconstructed from the *Anglo-Saxon Chronicle* and the alliterative *charters, which specifically call Eadred ruler of the Northumbrians in 946, 949–50, and 955. Eadred received oaths of fealty from the northerners in 947 at Tanshelf, but within the year they accepted *Eric Bloodaxe as king. Eadred retaliated in 948, leading an army up to *Ripon, where the minster was burnt down; after an attack on his retreating army drove Eadred to threaten to devastate the north, the Northumbrians abandoned Eric and returned to the English fold for a couple of years. In late 950 or 951, the Northumbrians revolted again, in favour of Olaf Sihtricsson; in 952 they threw Olaf out and brought back Eric. In 954, the Northumbrians expelled Eric for the last time and received Eadred as their king.

Eadred contributed to the groundwork of the monastic revival by granting to *Æthelwold the monastery of *Abingdon. The earliest *Life of St Dunstan* reports that Eadred suffered from an unidentified illness, which eventually killed him. He probably delegated authority to *Dunstan and others in his last years: fewer than a third of the charters of 953–5 are witnessed by the king. Eadred, who is not known to have married or to have had issue, died on 23 November 955, and was buried at the Old Minster, *Winchester. His *will, which implies that he planned to be buried elsewhere, was apparently overturned in the turmoil of the accession of his nephew *Eadwig.

C. Hart, 'The Alliterative Charters', *The Danelaw* (London, 1992), pp. 431–45; S. Keynes, 'The "Dunstan B" Charters', *ASE* 23 (1994), 165–93; P. Sawyer, 'The Last Scandinavian Kings of York', *NH* 31 (1995), 39–44.

SEAN MILLER

EADRIC STREONA ('the acquisitor'). Eadric was appointed ealdorman of the Mercians in 1007, and sooner or later married Edith, daughter of King *Æthelred the Unready. Some time between 1009 and 1012 he gained the primacy among the king's *ealdormen, and went on to play a notoriously disreputable part in the political turmoil which led to *Cnut's conquest of England. The circumstances of his defection to the Danes were perhaps more complex than we could ever hope to know, but may not have been unrelated to political tensions generated in the wake of the death of the ætheling *Æthelstan in June 1014, combined with the opportunities presented by the arrival of the Danish force in 1015. Eadric's services as ealdorman of *Mercia were initially retained by Cnut, to whom he had done good service. Nonetheless, he was killed on the king's orders at London in 1017, 'so that retainers (*milites*) may learn from this example to be faithful, not faithless, to their kings' (*Encomium Emmae* ii.15); his body was thrown over the city wall and left unburied (*'Hemming's Cartulary', ed. Hearne, p. 281; *John of Worcester, s.a. 1017). Eadric's bad reputation is already pronounced in the account of Æthelred's reign written perhaps by a Londoner, *c.*1017, and incorporated in the *Anglo-Saxon Chronicle*; and the *Encomium Emmae* shows that the chronicler was not alone in his judgement. It is worth noting, however, that the tradition which began to develop thereafter has a particular local flavour. Eadric would appear to have had roots in Shropshire, and his association was latterly with the *Magonsætan* (the people of Herefordshire and Shropshire); yet the impression of him which prevails to this day is essentially that formed at *Worcester, where he was remembered as an appropriator of estates and revenues properly belonging to the church, and as the one under whose auspices Winchcombshire (and also, it seems, a part of Herefordshire) was subsumed into Gloucestershire. Eadric Streona is a convincing villain, though of course a case could and has been made for his rehabilitation.

Hemingi Chartularium Ecclesiæ Wigorniensis, ed. T. Hearne, 2 vols. (Oxford, 1723), pp. 280–1; *Chronicle of John of Worcester* II, ed. R. R. Darlington and P. McGurk (OMT, 1995), pp. 456–504, *passim*; *Henry of Huntingdon*, ed. D. Greenway (OMT, 1996), pp. 344–62, *passim*; *Walter Map: De Nugis Curialium/Courtiers' Trifles*, ed. M. R. James, rev. C. N. L. Brooke and R. A. B. Mynors (OMT, 1983), pp. 428–9; P. Stafford, 'The Reign of Æthelred II: a Study in the Limitations on Royal Policy and Action', *Ethelred the Unready*, ed. D. Hill (Oxford, 1978), pp. 15–46, at 36–7; S. Keynes, *The Diplomas of King Æthelred 'the Unready' 978–1016* (Cambridge, 1980), pp. 211–14; idem, 'A Tale of Two Kings: Alfred the Great and Æthelred the Unready', *TRHS* 5th ser. 36 (1986), 195–217, at 213–17; A. Williams, 'The Spoliation of Worcester', *ANS* 19 (1997), 383–408, at 385.

SIMON KEYNES

EADWIG, son of King *Edmund, was king of the English (955–9) in succession to his uncle *Eadred. The chronicler *Æthelweard notes that Eadwig was called 'All-fair' by the common people for his great beauty. Eadwig started his reign by asserting his independence from the important counsellors of his uncle's and father's reigns. He apparently had a confrontation with Abbot *Dunstan at his *coronation feast, and soon afterwards drove him into exile. He also confiscated the estates of his grandmother *Eadgifu, who had witnessed many of the charters of her sons Edmund and Eadred, but no genuine charters of Eadwig. Eadwig did not remove the chief *ealdorman, *Æthelstan Half-King, but did appoint new ealdormen to parts of *Mercia which Æthelstan had previously administered himself. An unprecedented sixty-odd *charters survive from 956, presumably the results of Eadwig's attempt to create a base of retainers loyal to him. Among the new people promoted were several royal kinsmen, including Ælfheah, ealdorman of Mercia, Ælfhere, seneschal and later ealdorman of central *Wessex, and Byrhthelm, bishop of *Winchester. These three, along with Eadwig's queen Ælfgifu, probably the sister of Æthelweard the Chronicler, may all have been descended from Æthelred I. The promotion together of such a kin-group might well have alarmed already established powerful families, like those of Æthelstan Half-King and Dunstan. Eadwig's marriage to Ælfgifu might have alarmed *Edgar still more, much as *Æthelwulf's marriage to Judith had probably worried *Æthelbald a century earlier: a child of the union of two royal parents might be considered more throne-worthy than Edgar himself.

It may have been the concerted action of Eadwig's enemies that caused the division of the kingdom in the second half of 957. The exact cause of the events will probably never be clear, but the division itself was peaceful: ealdormen and bishops to the north of the Thames went to Edgar's court, and those to the south of the Thames stayed with Eadwig's court. It would appear that Eadwig retained overall authority: in his charters he remained *rex Anglorum*, 'king of the English', while Edgar was styled 'king of the Mercians'. It also seems that coins both sides of the Thames were in Eadwig's name until his death. On the other hand, Edgar was able to recall Dunstan from exile, and in 958 Archbishop *Oda divorced Eadwig from Ælfgifu on grounds of consanguinity. As their relationship was surely known from the beginning, this was a political rather than a religious move. Eadwig and Ælfgifu had no children; and when Eadwig died, on 1 October 959, Edgar became king over a once-more united realm.

Stenton, *ASE*, pp. 364–7, 448–9; B. Yorke, 'Æthelwold and the Politics of the Tenth Century', in *Æthelwold*, pp. 65–88; C. E. Blunt, B. H. I. H. Stewart and C. S. S. Lyon, *Coinage in Tenth-Century England: from Edward the Elder to Edgar's Reform* (Oxford, 1989), pp. 146–56; S. Keynes, 'England 900–1016', *The New Cambridge Medieval History* III, ed. T. Reuter (Cambridge, 1999), pp. 456–84.

SEAN MILLER

EALDORMAN. The term began as the vernacular equivalent of a range of Latin titles, such as *princeps*, *dux*, *comes*, *praefectus*. Like them it was originally applied to high-ranking men, including some of royal birth or quasi-regal status, the basis of whose power and authority was independent of the king. Like them it was a term which evolved in meaning, and before the end of the ninth century must always be interpreted carefully and in context. Its history is to a large extent the faltering story of the establishment of wider kingships or overlordships within England, of the fate of lesser kings and rulers and the opportunities for advancement within that process, and of the constant interaction of noble status and royal power and service. Thus Ealdred, king of the *Hwicce, was described in a charter of *Offa as *subregulus . . . et dux* ('underking and ealdorman'). During the second half of the ninth century the title of Oswulf in Kent, *dei gratia dux atque princeps provinciae Orientalis Cantiae* ('by the grace of God *dux* and *princeps* of the province of East Kent') was still almost royal, and his province recalls the ancient divisions of *Kent. Yet in *Wessex in the reign of *Alfred, 'ealdorman' described the leaders of individual *shires. When it was used of *Æthelred, Lord of the Mercians, especially in West Saxon sources, 'ealdorman' put a perspective on his status in which subordination to Alfred was being stressed, but not overstressed. By this date the notions of royal service, and of power exercised in the name of the king, were coming to be uppermost, but the high status of those it could describe is still evident and 'ealdorman and *thegn' were as much synonyms for the nobility as for servants of the king.

During the tenth century the term acquired greater precision as a description of a local ruler acting in the king's name and on the king's behalf, a reflection of the significance of this period in the final unification of England. By now the ealdorman was the local representative of the West Saxon overlords who had become kings of the English. An ealdorman as the local ruler might lead fighting men, as Byrhtnoth did against the Danes at Maldon in 991; sit as president of the shire and other courts, as Æthelwine did at Cambridge in

the late 970s or at Wansford with the great men of *Northampton and *East Anglia; levy taxation, as in the case of *Eadric, who was responsible for the collection of *heregeld on the lands of the church of *Worcester at the beginning of the eleventh century; and take his share of the profits of justice, as in the ubiquitous Earl's third penny in *Domesday Book. There was no fixed number nor geographical pattern of ealdormanries. In general the tenth century saw large ealdormanries, sometimes as large as the old kingdoms whose lineaments they preserved, as when ealdormen ruled the whole of *Mercia, East Anglia, *York, or *Northumbria. Wessex no longer had an ealdorman in each shire, but often two responsible for Wessex East and West of Selwood. There are some trends in the tenth century which can almost be described as royal policies. In the early to middle decades of the century West Saxon nobles were often appointed to ealdormanries north of the Thames. *Edgar and *Æthelred appointed north midlands nobles to York in an attempt to bind the area more firmly into a southern English kingdom, and displayed a tendency to replace large ealdormanries and their provincial rulers with shire *reeves in the last decades of the tenth century.

But the history of tenth-century ealdormen and ealdormanries is a political more than an administrative story. Ealdormen and ealdormanries were simultaneously royal creations linking centre and provinces, and the potential vehicles for memories of older political units and identities; the possession of powerful noble families, and the plum of royal patronage; and the king's most important subjects, and semi-independent rulers. Kings establishing new reigns and in quest of loyalty, like *Eadwig in 956 or *Edward the Martyr in 975, made appointments and even carved out new ealdormanries or revived older ones. Ealdormen from south of the Tees, and especially of the Humber, were frequent attenders at the royal court; after the king and royal family they were the most prominent and invariable lay witnesses of royal *charters. Their attendance is an index of the centripetal forces in a wealthy and aggressive kingdom, binding even the greatest nobles to the king; in the 930s and 940s *Æthelstan Half-King and his brothers between them ruled much of England south of the Humber in apparent loyalty. But these decades are poorly chronicled and loyalty could be questionable. Ealdormen could divide during succession disputes, as in 956–8, and those divisions expressed, amongst other things, revivals of separatist feeling. Southern appointees north of the Humber could be suspect, whether locally or to their royal masters; two successive ealdormen of York were exiled or murdered.

The earls of the eleventh century must be seen against this tenth-century background. During the reign of *Cnut, the vernacular term *eorl* begins to replace ealdorman. Like ealdorman originally, the wider meanings of this term are 'noble', and its adoption at this date probably relates to its common meanings for English and Danes. The change does not indicate a change in the nature and power of the men described. The taking of the throne by Earl *Harold in 1066 underlines the power of an earldom/ealdormanry, but it is not a simple symptom of an eleventh-century shift in the balance between king and ealdorman. Foreign rule and royal absence under Cnut, and the protracted succession problems of the mid eleventh century, produced a peculiar situation. One result of that was the dominance of Earl *Godwine and his sons rivalling that of Æthelstan Half-King and his brothers before. Æthelstan acted as a regent for *Eadred; *Harold took the throne. That accession might have ushered in a difficult reign in which political relations might have shifted fundamentally; *Hastings ensured that we shall never know. Ealdormen, however, lived on, in name if not in substance, in the aldermen of medieval urban government.

H. Loyn, *The Governance of Anglo-Saxon England, 500–1087* (London, 1984); idem, 'The Term Ealdorman in the Translations Prepared at the Time of King Alfred', *EHR* 68 (1953), 513–25; A. Thacker, 'Some Terms for Noblemen in Anglo-Saxon England', *ASSAH* 2 (1981), 201–36; C. Hart, 'Athelstan "Half King" and his Family', *ASE* 2 (1973), 115–44; Stafford, *Unification*; S. Keynes, 'Cnut's Earls', *The Reign of Cnut: King of England, Denmark and Norway*, ed. A. Rumble (London, 1994), pp. 43–88.

PAULINE STAFFORD

EALDRED, archbishop of York (1061–9), was a monk of *Winchester who became abbot of Tavistock (*c*.1027–*c*.1043) and then bishop of *Worcester in 1046. While bishop of Worcester he served as a diplomat of King *Edward the Confessor, making two trips to *Rome (1050, 1061) on the king's behalf, and an important embassy to the Emperor Henry III in Cologne in 1054 (to negotiate the return of prince Edward 'the Exile'); an interesting result of this embassy is that Ealdred was able to observe the liturgical customs of Cologne under Archbishop Herimann, and through this contact was able to bring a copy of the influential Romano-German Pontifical back to England (he may also have brought back from Cologne the exemplar of the 'Cambridge Songs',

a famous collection of medieval Latin lyrics). In 1058, as part of a diplomatic mission to Hungary, Ealdred continued on *pilgrimage to Jerusalem and the Holy Land. As archbishop of *York Ealdred was responsible for endowing churches in his archdiocese (including extensive building works at Beverley) as well as York Minster itself; and it was through Ealdred's patronage that *Folcard of Saint-Bertin was able to write the Lives of various saints of York, including John of Beverley. Ealdred assumed a leading role among the English in the immediate aftermath of *Hastings, and it was he who crowned William the Conqueror (25 Dec. 1066) a few years before his death on 11 Sept. 1069.

J. M. Cooper, *The Last Four Anglo-Saxon Archbishops of York* (York, 1970), pp. 23–9; F. Barlow, *The English Church 1000–66*, 2nd ed. (London, 1979), pp. 86–90; M. Lapidge, 'Ealdred of York and MS. Cotton Vitellius E.XII', *Yorkshire Archaeological Journal* 55 (1983), 11–25 (repr. in *ALL* ii. 453–67); V. King, 'Ealdred, Archbishop of York: the Worcester Years', *ANS* 18 (1996), 123–37; P. Wormald, *How do we know so much about Anglo-Saxon Deerhurst?* (Deerhurst, 1993).

MICHAEL LAPIDGE

EANFLÆD (d. *c*.704), sometime abbess of *Whitby, was the daughter of *Edwin, king of *Deira (616–33) and Æthelburg Tata, daughter of *Æthelberht, king of Kent (560–616). Eanflæd was baptized by Bishop *Paulinus (626). She was subsequently married to *Oswiu, king of *Bernicia (642–70); the marriage effected the union of the two Northumbrian kingdoms under Oswiu. After Oswiu's death, Eanflæd retired to Whitby (where Oswiu was buried), which she ruled jointly with her daughter *Ælfflæd following the death of Abbess *Hild in 680. During her abbacy the relics of her father, King Edwin, were translated to Whitby and became the focus of a royal cult.

Bede, *HE* ii.9, iii. 15, 24–5, 29, iv. 19; *The Earliest Life of Gregory the Great*, ed. B. Colgrave (Lawrence, KA, 1968), c. 18; P. Hunter Blair, 'Whitby as a Centre of Learning in the Seventh Century', Clemoes FS, pp. 3–32.

MICHAEL LAPIDGE

EARCONWALD (d. 693), bishop of *London (675–93), scion of a wealthy and possibly royal family, and founder of the monasteries of *Chertsey (Surrey) and *Barking (Essex). The care of Barking was entrusted to Earconwald's sister Æthelburg, who seems to have shared the rule with *Hildelith, whereas Earconwald maintained control of Chertsey. He was an influential bishop, as witness the preface to the *laws of

King *Ine, and was responsible for effecting the reconciliation of Bishop *Wilfrid and Archbishop *Theodore; he seems to have had an important influence on the formulation of the earliest surviving *charters of Southumbria. According to *Bede, Earconwald had so great a reputation for holiness that splinters cut from his horse-litter were able to accomplish miracles after his death. His relics were preserved at St Paul's in London, and an anonymous account of his life and miracles was composed in the early twelfth century.

Bede, *HE* iv.6; *EHD* i. 399 (no. 32), 479–80 (no. 54); Stephen of Ripon, *Vita S. Wilfridi*, c. 43; E. G. Whatley, *The Saint of London: the Life and Mircales of St Erkenwald* (Binghamton, NY, 1989); P. Wormald, *Bede and the Conversion of England: the Charter Evidence*, Jarrow Lecture (1994).

MICHAEL LAPIDGE

EARL: *see* Ealdorman; Social Class

EARLS BARTON (Northants.) was the centre of a large late Anglo-Saxon estate; the defensive earthwork beside the church probably marks the site of an important thegnly residence. The turriform nave of *c*.1000, covered with pilasters and ornamental stripwork, is the most lavishly decorated of all surviving Anglo-Saxon buildings. It exemplifies what was probably a widespread church form of the time, and it is possible that it served defensive as well as religious functions for the adjoining enclosed homestead (cf. *Barton-upon-Humber and St Michael's, *Oxford).

Fernie, *Architecture*, pp. 143–5; M. Audouy, B. Dix and D. Parsons, 'The Tower of All Saints' Church, Earls Barton', *Archaeological Journal* 152 (1995), 73–94.

JOHN BLAIR

EARTHWORKS, DEFENSIVE: *see* Forts and Fortifications

EAST ANGLIA, KINGDOM OF: a long-lived kingdom comprising Norfolk and Suffolk. Archaeological evidence suggests that this was among the earliest regions of Anglo-Saxon settlement, before *c*.450. *Bede referred to the East Angles as deriving from Anglian settlers, and finds from the numerous cremation *cemeteries support this view. The late Roman archaeology is peculiarly rich and the pagan English period is similarly well-evidenced.

The kingdom succeeded a Roman *civitas* based on the pre-Roman tribe of the Iceni, centred on Caister St Edmunds (*Venta Icenorum*), but the boundaries of neither are known, although the *civitas* was probably largely confined to Norfolk.

Pl. 11 Earls Barton tower.

The unique shire names, 'North-folk' and 'South-folk', imply that the kingdom had an early duality, but this need not pre-date the creation of two dioceses in 680. East Anglia was bounded by the North Sea, the East Saxons (primarily Essex), minor peoples such as the East and West Willa eventually incorporated into the Middle Angles from the 640s onwards, and the Fens.

Bede's reference to Rendlesham as royal, and the strong evidence for high status burials at *Sutton Hoo and Snape, imply that the dynasty was closely associated with southern Suffolk, but the history of the kingdom is poorly documented. *Rædwald – the earliest East Anglian king whose career is reconstructible – was 'the son of Tytil, whose father was Wuffa, after whom the kings of the East Angles are called Wuffings'. Wuffa could be an invention designed to explain a family name which means 'followers (or "descendants") of the wolf' – and the long reign of Aldwulf (literally 'old wolf') in the early eighth century may have encouraged this. Equally, it could be a real name, since animal-names were common (cf. *Hengest). Later commentators considered that the dynasty originated in the second half of the sixth century. The *Historia Brittonum named Wuffa's father 'the first to rule over the people of the East Angles'.

Rædwald achieved a notable military victory and recognition as an 'overking' with influence outside his own people but he died in the mid-620s. His successors were targeted by *Edwin of the Deirans, who used *conversion as a means to impose himself on Eorpwald c.627, whom the East Angles killed in reaction. His brother, Sigeberht, secured the throne c.631, returning from exile in Gaul, and introduced Christianity through the Burgundian bishop Felix, to whom he gave Dommoc (perhaps Dunwich) as his see. The distinctiveness of this conversion reflected concern to limit the power of the Northumbrian 'overking'. East Anglia was, however, hard hit by Mercian invasions led by *Penda (633–55), and rarely again enjoyed real independence. Bede recorded King Æthelhere's participation in the Mercian army which was destroyed at the Winwæd in 655, but the continuing struggle between *Northumbria and *Mercia benefited the East Angles, whose king Aldwulf was named as one of four guarantors of the synod of Hatfield (679). Mercian supremacy from 685 onwards increased pressure on East Anglia, but the dynasty survived and was even able to issue its own *coinage during the eighth century, despite encirclement by Mercian absorption of *London, *Essex and *Kent.

Mercian dynastic crises in the 820s allowed the East Angles to throw off their 'overkingship' and kill the Mercian king Beornwulf, but they accepted the supremacy of *Ecgberht of *Wessex (802–39) and were constrained by the alliance of Mercia and Wessex from the late 830s. The Chronicle account of *Viking raids is dominated by matters of interest to West Saxons, and East Anglia is barely referred to. However, an incursion in 841 and frequent reference to Vikings in Kent and London imply that East Anglia suffered from Scandinavian attacks. This is borne out by the arrival of the 'Great Danish Army' in 865, which occupied winter quarters there and secured horses. The Danes returned in 869 to winter at Thetford but were attacked by King *Edmund, who was, however, defeated and killed and they 'conquered all that land and did for all the monasteries to which they came'. Edmund may initially have been succeeded by an English tributary king but the Danes returned to settle in 879 and this became the kingdom of *Guthrum (d. 890), whose attempts to conquer Wessex were resisted by *Alfred (871–99), and who was eventually baptized as part of their reconciliation. Guthrum minted his own coinage from c.880. His followers continued to raid English territory in alliance with other Danish forces after his death – raiding *Chester, for example, in 893 – but found English resistance increasingly obdurate.

Despite this settlement, there are relatively few Danish *place-names in East Anglia but there was large-scale disruption of the ecclesiastical organisation, with both sees (at *Elmham and perhaps Dunwich) abandoned and no monasteries known to have continued. Pre-Viking architecture is comparatively scarce and no *charters survive which were issued by East Anglian kings, but something of the social and legal structure can be reconstructed from the treaty between Alfred and Guthrum. It has been suggested that the poem *Beowulf derives from this region in the late pre-Viking era.

East Anglia's history as a separate kingdom ended in the campaigns of *Edward the Elder (899–924), in 917, but its structure survived as a great ealdormanry or earldom and a diocese based on refounded Elmham. Its principal spiritual focus and richest monastery was *Bury St Edmunds, where the cult of its last English king flourished.

Hill, Atlas; Stafford, Unification; Yorke, Kingdoms; Kirby, Kings; Dumville, 'The Treaty of Alfred and Guthrum', in his Wessex, pp. 1–23; The Age of Sutton Hoo, ed. M. Carver (Woodbridge, 1992); T. Williamson, The Origins of Norfolk (Manchester, 1993); M. D. Newton, The Origins of Beowulf and the Pre-Viking Kingdom of East Anglia (Woodbridge, 1993).

N. J. HIGHAM

EASTER CONTROVERSY. According to the reports of Bede (HE iii.21) and Stephen of Ripon (Vita S. Wilfridi, c. 10), an assembly was convened at *Whitby in 664, in the presence of King *Oswiu and Abbess *Hild, to hear arguments about how best to determine future dates for the celebration of Easter. At least four different Easter tables and types of *computus were represented at this Synod of Whitby by the spokesmen: Colmán, an Irish monk of *Iona who had come to *Lindisfarne as bishop of *Northumbria; *Agilbert, a noble

Frank who was then a bishop in *Wessex, probably at *Dorchester, and later became bishop of Paris; and *Wilfrid of Northumbria who had been ordained priest by Agilbert. The context from which each one spoke cannot be ignored. Easter tables used extensively by bishops of Gaul during the fifth to eighth century and introduced to Ireland in the sixth had derived from Victorius of Aquitaine (455), famous for his book of arithmetic called *Calculus*. Victorian Easter tables were adapted from Alexandrian but set lunar limits of XVI–XXII. Their 19-year cycles could be repeated for up to 532 years before enough minutes of difference between lunar and solar cycles had accumulated for a full day to be dropped, so that the system recommenced in coordination with the stars. Agilbert came from this tradition, but during 635–40 he may have learned alternatives, including that of Dionysius Exiguus (525), at Rath Melsigi in southern Ireland. That monastery was a meeting place for Irishmen from both Ireland and Scotland as well as Britons, Saxons, Angles, and Franks and was the base for *Willibrord's mission to the *Frisians. Rath Melsigi had a *library from which many computistical tracts later reached Bede at *Monkwearmouth-Jarrow. King Oswiu invited Agilbert to speak first at the Synod, but he deferred to his protégé Wilfrid who could speak Oswiu's language and thus be understood.

Wilfrid described the Alexandrian 19-year lunar cycle which was basic for Easter tables of the Victorian and Dionysian systems, as well as that of Milan, but not any of the systems known from the diocese of *Rome. Full moon was observed on vernal equinox, and the next Sunday which fell within limits of luna XIV and XXI was chosen for the Easter celebration. From the fourth century onwards, Alexandrians had assumed that vernal equinox occurred on XII Kal. Aprilis [21 March]. They had also used a table of five 19-year lunar cycles which after 95 years would be adjusted and repeated in order to keep the table in coordination with the stars in the zodiac.

Colmán then explained the Easter tables on the basis of a treatise *De ratione paschali*, also designated *Canon paschalis*, which was used at Lindisfarne until this Synod; it was also used on the island of *Iona and in parts of Ireland and Scotland at least until 716 and in Wales until the ninth century. Its dates of Easter Sundays were determined by observing the full moon nearest the vernal equinox and by choosing the Sunday of that day or thereafter which fell within the limits of luna XIV and XX. Colmán's text also assumed that the equinox fell on XII Kal. Aprilis [21

March] of the solar calendar, and his Easter tables were based upon a 19-year cycle which continued for 84 years before they would be adjusted and repeated.

The differences between Colmán's and Wilfrid's explanations were essentially: (1) lunar limits of XIV–XX versus XIV–XXI, which meant that sometimes the Sunday chosen by Wilfrid would be later, thereby affecting other periods and liturgical celebrations during five months from the beginning of Lent to the end of Pentecost. Thus, it could be anticipated that during Holy Week of 665 this would cause problems in the household of Oswiu whose wife *Eanflæd with her chaplain and other servants were from *Kent and followed the practice of *Canterbury; (2) repetition of Easter tables after 84 years versus 95 years also meant that timing within the 19-year cycles would vary on many occasions; (3) a further complication was the *saltus lunae* which was placed differently in the two 19-year cycles, causing subsequent variations in data of the tables from which Easter Sunday would be calculated.

A element common to the two types of Easter tables was that they both counted the series of thirty lunar days from the appearance of the moon's first crescent: luna I. But at what hour did one begin a lunar day: dawn, noon, sundown, or the first appearance of the moon? Different choices were made in Alexandria and Rome, which resulted in different calendar days for the same luna I or luna XIV (vernal equinox). In his Latin adaptation of the Alexandrian computus (525), Dionysius had simplified the application of his tables by setting lunar limits of XV–XXI, rather than XIV–XXI, thus avoiding luna XIV altogether. But neither Colmán nor Wilfrid recognized that quartodeciman problem which would have further complicated each computus. (Later, Bede accepted Dionysius' lunar limits, as did most Anglo-Saxon schoolmasters.)

Wilfrid cleverly led Colmán to explain the authority of his Easter tables in terms of its attribution to Anatolius, whom he affirmed was a disciple of John, the apostle. Wilfrid however claimed that his own tables were used in Rome 'where the apostles St Peter and St Paul lived, taught, suffered, and were buried, . . . everywhere in Italy and Gaul . . ., at one and the same time in Africa, Asia, Egypt, Greece, and throughout the whole world . . .' Neither assertion was true, Wilfrid's least of all. Given a conundrum of conflicting apostolic claims, Colmán had to admit to Oswiu that Peter holds the keys to the kingdom of heaven. To this, the king responded abruptly that therefore the Roman bishop must surely know the correct Easter.

That his own conclusion lacked any logic seems to have been acknowledged by Oswiu with a smile, according to Stephen of Ripon. Bede accepted the conclusion and did not report the comedy, despite doubts which he too harboured about how the Romans did actually choose the date for Easter Sunday during his own lifetime. He adopted the Dionysian tables and adapted them for his own computus explained in *De temporibus* (703) and in more detail in *De temporum ratione* (716–25). His report of the Synod of Whitby supports adoption of Alexandrian terms as if they were Roman. In fact neither Alexandrian nor Roman terms, but rather the Bedan terms for Easter reckoning were gradually accepted throughout the British Isles and in the schools and dioceses of the Carolingian empire during the ninth century. During the tenth century there is finally evidence that Bedan tables were being used in the diocese and the province of Rome.

P. Hunter Blair, 'Whitby as a Centre of Learning in the Seventh Century', in FS Clemoes, pp. 3–32; D. P. Kirby, 'Northumbria in the Time of Wilfrid', in *St Wilfrid at Hexham*, ed. D. P. Kirby (Newcastle, 1974), pp. 1–33; D. Ó Cróinín, 'The Irish Provenance of Bede's Computus', *Peritia* 2 (1983), 229–47; W. M. Stevens, *Bede's Scientific Achievement*, Jarrow Lecture 1985, repr. in his *Cycles of Time and Scientific Learning in Medieval Europe* (Aldershot, 1995), no. II; idem, 'Sidereal Time in Anglo-Saxon England', in *Voyage to the Other World: the Legacy of Sutton Hoo*, ed. C. B. Kendall and P. S. Wells (Minneapolis, MN, 1992), pp. 125–52, repr. in *Cycles of Time*, no. V; D. McCarthy, 'The Lunar and Paschal Tables of *De ratione paschali* attributed to Anatolius of Laodicea', *Archive for the History of Exact Sciences* 49 (1996), 285–320.

WESLEY M. STEVENS

EATA (d. 686?), sometime bishop of *Hexham (678–81, 685–6) and *Lindisfarne (681–5), was a pupil of Bishop *Aidan at Lindisfarne who became a monk and later abbot of *Melrose. Among his monks at Melrose during the 650s was the young *Cuthbert. Eata and Cuthbert were involved briefly in the monastic foundation at *Ripon (which had been endowed by King Alhfrith), but after the Synod of *Whitby (664), and following the departure of Bishop Colmán, Eata became abbot of Lindisfarne, with Cuthbert as his prior. When Bishop *Wilfrid's vast Northumbrian diocese was broken up by Archbishop *Theodore in 678, Eata became bishop of its northern part (*Bernicia), with his see at Hexham; then in 681 this see too was subdivided, and Eata returned to

Lindisfarne as bishop. Then in 685, when the bishop of Hexham (one Tunberht) was deposed by Archbishop Theodore, Eata returned once again to Hexham, with his disciple Cuthbert assuming the bishopric of Lindisfarne. Eata died of dysentery, probably in 686, and was buried at Hexham. According to Bede, Eata was an extremely venerable and gentle man (*uir reuerentissimus et mansuetissimus*).

Bede, *HE* iii.26, iv. 12, 25–6, v.2, 9, 24; Bede, prose *Vita S. Cuthberti*, cc. 7, 8, 16, 25 (ed. B. Colgrave, *Two Lives of St Cuthbert* (Cambridge, 1940), pp. 174–6, 180–2, 206, 240).

MICHAEL LAPIDGE

ECGBERHT, bishop (732–5) and archbishop of *York (735–66), was the brother of King Eadberht of *Northumbria (737–58); their joint control of Northumbrian church and state was seen by later writers such as *Alcuin as a time of unparalleled peace and stability. Ecgberht was regarded as a man of considerable learning: *Bede visited him in York shortly before his death and addressed to him his *Epistola ad Ecgberhtum episcopum* on the problems facing the Northumbrian church; Ecgberht is also known as the author of a *Dialogus ecclesiasticae institutionis*, a treatise on ecclesiastical discipline and the observance of the Quatember fasts (other works which pass under Ecgberht's name, such as the *Excarpsum de canonibus catholicorum patrum* or 'Penitential of Ecgberht', and the so-called 'Pontifical of Ecgberht' in Paris, BN, lat. 10575, are certainly spurious). Ecgberht travelled at least once to Rome (to receive the *pallium), and was the recipient of letters from Pope Paul I as well as from *Boniface, in one of which the missionary bishop seeks from Ecgberht copies of various exegetical works of Bede. It is a reasonable inference that the later glory of the York school under *Ælberht and Alcuin owed much to the scholarship of Ecgberht.

Sharpe, *Handlist*, 251; MGH, PLAC i. 197–8 (lines 1247–86); *Alcuin: the Bishops, Kings, and Saints of York*, ed. P. Godman (OMT, 1982), pp. 98–100; MGH ES i. 156–8 (no. 75), 206–8 (no. 91); H & S, *Councils* iii.394–6, 403–13 [*Dialogus*].

MICHAEL LAPIDGE

ECGBERHT, king of *Wessex (802–39), was the grandfather of King *Alfred and the man who established Wessex as the dominant power in southern England. Ecgberht claimed descent from King *Ine's brother Ingeld, and his father Ealhmund may have been briefly king in *Kent in 784. Ecgberht attempted to take the throne of Wessex in 786, but was defeated and spent a period in exile at the court of the Frankish king Charlemagne. He succeeded in becoming king of Wessex in 802. Ecgberht's greatest period of success came after his defeat of the Mercians at the battle of *Ellendun* (Wroughton, Wilts.), which resulted in Kent, *Sussex, Surrey and *Essex passing from Mercian to West Saxon overlordship. These southeastern provinces were entrusted to his son *Æthelwulf to rule. In 829 Ecgberht conquered *Mercia, which led to him being hailed by the West Saxon Chronicler as the eighth *Bretwalda, and went on to receive the submission of *Northumbria. But such success was shortlived as Mercia recovered its independence the following year. Ecgberht also extended West Saxon power to the west at the expense of the Cornish (see *Cornwall), and defeated them in 838 when they joined forces with one of the *Viking fleets which began to trouble Wessex in the closing years of the king's reign.

Stenton, *ASE*, pp. 231–5; Kirby, *Kings*, pp. 189–95; S. Keynes, 'The Control of Kent in the Ninth Century', *EME* 2 (1993), 111–31.

B. A. E. YORKE

ECGWINE (d. 717), bishop of *Worcester (692–717) and founder of the monastery of Evesham. Virtually nothing is known of Ecgwine from records contemporary with his lifetime, and even the dates of his bishopric are uncertain (they derive from the twelfth-century *Chronica chronicarum* of *John of Worcester). The earliest Life of Ecgwine, which was written *c.*1020 by *Byrhtferth of *Ramsey, is a hagiographical confection of legends and spurious claims to Evesham's endowment; it throws some light on the cult of Ecgwine in the late tenth and early eleventh centuries, but contains no reliable information about the saint himself. Later hagiographers, such as Dominic of Evesham, depended wholly on Byrhtferth's Life.

Vita quorundam Anglo-Saxonum, ed. J. A. Giles (London, 1854), pp. 349–96 [Byrhtferth, *Vita S. Ecgwini*]; M. Lapidge, 'Byrhtferth and the *Vita S. Ecgwini*', *MS* 41 (1979), 331–53 (repr. *ALL* ii.293–315); idem, 'Dominic of Evesham, *Vita S. Ecgwini episcopi et confessoris*', *AB* 96 (1978), 65–104; idem, 'The Medieval Hagiography of St Ecgwine', *Vale of Evesham Historical Society Research Papers* 6 (1977), 77–93; idem, *Byrhtferth of Ramsey: the Lives of Oswald and Ecgwine* (OMT, forthcoming)

MICHAEL LAPIDGE

ECHTERNACH GOSPELS (Paris, BN, lat. 9389), a Latin *gospelbook of Fischer's 'pre-Carolingian' textual family. In the facsimile commentary volume of the *Lindisfarne Gospels,

its artist/scribe was identified with that of the Durham Gospels and termed the 'Durham-Echternach Calligrapher'. He was seen as an older contemporary member of the Lindisfarne *scriptorium and it was suggested that this volume was sent from Lindisfarne in 698 as a foundation gift to St *Willibrord's monastery at Echternach in the mission-fields. Its evangelist symbols and incipits display masterly penwork but are less fully painted than related works, whilst its script is a 'set' formal cursive rather than half-uncial, leading to the suggestion that it was produced in a hurry. These assumptions have been challenged by Ó Cróinín and others, pointing to the Irish background to the mission and suggesting manufacture at the unidentified Irish centre, *Rath Melsigi*. Netzer's work on the Echternach scriptorium has reinforced a Northumbrian origin for this volume, and discussed the interaction of English, Irish and continental elements in the scriptorium's development.

CLA v. 578; Alexander, *Insular MSS*, no. 11; T. D. Kendrick, *et al.*, *Evangeliorum Quattuor Codex Lindisfarnensis*, 2 vols. (Olten and Lausanne, 1956–60); D. Ó Cróinín, 'Rath Melsigi, Willibrord, and the earliest Echternach Manuscripts', *Peritia* 3 (1984), 17–49; N. Netzer, *Cultural Interplay in the Eighth Century, the Trier Gospels and the Making of a Scriptorium at Echternach* (Cambridge, 1994).

MICHELLE P. BROWN

EDDIUS STEPHANUS: *see* Stephen of Ripon

EDGAR, son of King *Edmund and fostered by *Æthelstan Half-King, was king of the Mercians and Northumbrians (957–9), and king of the English (959–75). According to *John of Worcester, Edgar was called *pacificus*, which should probably be rendered 'the peacemaker' rather than 'the peaceable'. The fact that *Thanet was ravaged on the king's orders in 969, and the violent reaction after his death, suggest that the peace of Edgar's reign was the result of strict control backed up by military force rather than serenity of character. The show of violence probably also helped to keep Edgar's reign free of foreign invasion: no *Viking activity is recorded in England between 954, when *Eric Bloodaxe finally left York, and 980, when the second wave of Viking attacks began.

One of the most notable events in Edgar's reign was his consecration in 973, marked in the *Anglo-Saxon Chronicle* by a poem and described at some length in *Byrhtferth's *Vita S. Oswaldi*. It took place not at *Kingston but at *Bath, a former Roman settlement, which would evoke shades of

'Britannia' and the kingship of Britain (cf. King *Æthelstan). In another carefully staged show of royal power, six or eight 'British' kings acknowledged Edgar's overlordship by rowing him along the river Dee at *Chester, while Edgar held the rudder. Another important event in 973 was a thorough reform of the *coinage, involving the establishment of new mints and a system of periodic recoinages.

The event at Bath in 973 was almost certainly Edgar's second consecration, repeating on a grander scale an earlier consecration in 960 or 961. It has been argued that Edgar's consecration was delayed until his thirtieth year in 973, by analogy with the canonical age for ordination as bishop. But in 959 it cannot have been certain that Edgar would reach his thirtieth year (his father Edmund died at 25, his brother Eadwig probably younger), and it is unlikely that Edgar or his allies would deliberately avoid a means of strengthening his authority. As *Ælfric said, the people may choose a king, but once he has been consecrated he has dominion over his people, and they cannot shake off his yoke.

That Edgar's yoke was to favour the monastic reformers, and fall heavily on the secular clergy, is shown by the *Anglo-Saxon Chronicle* for 964, which states that Edgar drove secular priests from *Winchester, *Chertsey, and Milton Abbas, and had them replaced with monks. This action, a major step in the monastic reform, was planned by *Æthelwold, but would have required Edgar's active support. The account of King Edgar's establishment of the monasteries, probably written by Æthelwold, and also the proem of the *Regularis Concordia*, show clearly the mutual esteem that existed between Edgar and his monastics.

Edgar was twice or perhaps three times married. He was involved with Wulfthryth, who was probably not his wife and later become a nun and abbess of Wilton; their daughter was St *Edith. His first wife was Æthelflæd Eneda, and either Wulfthryth or Æthelflæd bore *Edward the Martyr. By late 964 Edgar had married his second wife, *Ælfthryth, who was mother of Edmund (who died in 971) and *Æthelred the Unready. Like *Edward the Elder, Edgar thus had sons by different mothers, and it was probably clear that this was a succession crisis waiting to happen. Efforts seem to have been made to avert it. The gold-lettered refoundation charter of the New Minster, Winchester, issued in 966, gives Ælfthryth's son Edmund primacy over his half-brother Edward (Edward is a *clito* or *ætheling, but Edmund is the *legitimus clito*), and on this basis it seems likely that Edmund's position would have been inherited by Æthelred. Edgar died on 8 July 975, and was buried at *Glastonbury; the succession was then disputed between Edward and Æthelred, and in the event it was Edward who succeeded as king.

The *Anglo-Saxon Chronicle* for 959 contains a generally favourable summing-up of Edgar's reign, but notes one flaw, that he brought heathen manners and harmful foreigners into England. Similar charges were brought against *Edward the Confessor; in Edgar's case they may relate to his lawcode IV Edgar, which admits the legal separateness of the Danelaw.

Stenton, *ASE*, pp. 364–72; R. H. M. Dolley and D. M. Metcalf, 'The Reform of the English Coinage under Edgar', *Anglo-Saxon Coins*, ed. R. H. M. Dolley (London, 1961), pp. 136–68; N. Lund, 'King Edgar and the Danelaw', *Medieval Scandinavia* 9 (1976), 181–95; J. L. Nelson, 'Inauguration Rituals' and 'The Second English *Ordo*', in her *Politics and Ritual in Early Medieval Europe* (London, 1986), pp. 283–307 and 361–74; Dumville, *Wessex*, pp. 141–2, 144–5.

SEAN MILLER

EDITH: *see* Eadgyth

EDMUND, son of *Edward the Elder and *Eadgifu, was king of the English (939–46) in succession to his half-brother *Æthelstan. He was the first king to succeed to all of England, including *Northumbria; by the end of his first year, however, he had lost not only Northumbria but *Mercia north of *Watling Street. He reconquered Mercia in 942, and Northumbria in 944, but his reign shows clearly that although Æthelstan had conquered Northumbria, it was still not really part of a united England, nor would it be until the end of *Eadred's reign.

Edmund had fought beside Æthelstan at *Brunanburh in 937. Olaf Guthfrithson, the Norse king who had fought against them, took back *York before the end of 939, apparently without opposition, and raided into the midlands in 940. Olaf was besieged in *Leicester in 940, together with Wulfstan, archbishop of York. In 940, Wulfstan of York and the archbishop of *Canterbury arranged a peace whereby the border between Olaf and Edmund was set at Watling Street. Olaf Guthfrithson died on a raid into northern Northumbria in 941, and his successor Olaf Sihtricson was unable to hold the new territories. Edmund won back the territory of the *Five Boroughs in 942, in the same year crushing the Welsh revolt of Idwal of Gwynedd. The recovery of the east midlands was celebrated by a short poem in the

Anglo-Saxon Chronicle. In 944, Edmund continued north and drove from York both Olaf Sihtricson and his rival Rægnald Guthfrithson. Olaf retired to Dublin, but he came back to rule York briefly around 951–2. In 945, Edmund ravaged Strathclyde, and gave it to Malcolm, king of the Scots. The gesture was short-lived, as the deposed king of Strathclyde was soon back in power, but it shows Edmund recognizing that Northumbria was the northern limit of Anglo-Saxon England. In 946, Edmund sent a mission to Francia to negotiate for the restoration of Louis, who had been fostered at Æthelstan's court, but was killed before anything could come of it; his successor Eadred had his hands full with yet another Northumbrian revolt and is not known to have pursued the matter.

Edmund was also responsible for appointing *Dunstan as abbot of Glastonbury. Edmund was not as single-mindedly behind the monastic reform movement as his son *Edgar would prove to be, but Dunstan's introduction of the Benedictine Rule at *Glastonbury was an important step towards the reforms later in the century.

Edmund was twice married. His first wife, Ælfgifu (d. 944), was a benefactress of *Shaftesbury, where a cult of St Ælfgifu developed; she was the mother of Eadwig and Edgar. Edmund's second wife was Æthelflæd of Damerham. Edmund died on 26 May 946: he was stabbed by a man called Leofa, while trying to rescue one of his officials in a brawl at Pucklechurch, and was buried at Glastonbury. Neither of his sons was old enough to succeed on Edmund's death, and the kingship passed to his brother Eadred.

Stenton, *ASE*, pp. 356–60, 446–8, 552; A. P. Smyth, *Scandinavian York and Dublin*, 2 vols. (Dublin, 1975–9), ii. 89–125; Dumville, *Wessex*, pp. 173–84.

SEAN MILLER

EDMUND IRONSIDE, king of England (1016), 'called Ironside because of his valour' (*ASC*, MS. D, s.a. 1057). Edmund was the third son of King *Æthelred the Unready, by his first wife Ælfgifu. He appears for the first time as a witness to a charter which emanated from a meeting at *Winchester in 993, with his brothers *Æthelstan, Ecgberht and Eadred; but he cannot have been much more than five years old at the time, and was probably being brought up by his paternal grandmother *Ælfthryth, perhaps based at *Æthelingadene* (Dean), in west Sussex. Following the death of *Swein Forkbeard in February 1014, Æthelred was faced with the need to re-establish his own position and credibility as king; and the

death of the ætheling *Æthelstan, in June of the same year, would have put pressure on Edmund, as the eldest of the king's surviving sons, to assume his own part in public affairs. Edmund's actions in 1015 appear to reflect his determination to take a stand against *Eadric Streona, and against Eadric's domination of the ailing king. Sigeferth and Morcar, styled 'chief *thegns of the Seven Boroughs' and known to have been prominent among the king's advisers, were killed on Eadric's orders at *Oxford; whereupon Edmund took Aldgyth, Sigeferth's widow, from captivity at *Malmesbury, married her, and proceeded to take possession 'of all Sigeferth's estates and Morcar's, and the people all submitted to him' (*ASC*, MSS. CDE, s.a. 1015; JW, s.a. 1015). It was at this moment that *Cnut invaded England; and if Edmund's intervention had undermined Eadric's position, it may also have precipitated Eadric's decision to defect to the Danes. The details of Edmund's activities thereafter, first in association with King Æthelred and then as king following Æthelred's death on 23 April 1016, are best followed in the *Anglo-Saxon Chronicle*. He made the fatal mistake of receiving Eadric back onto the English side, leading to the defeat of the English at the battle of *Assandun* on 18 October 1016. Edmund came to terms with Cnut at Olney, near *Deerhurst (Glos.); but he died soon afterwards, on 30 November 1016, and was buried at *Glastonbury. His widow and children were forced overseas: Edward 'the Exile' returned from Hungary to England in 1057, and promptly died, leaving a son, Edgar, to complicate matters in 1066, and a daughter, Margaret, who married Malcolm III, king of Scotland (1058–93), generating a large family who could trace their descent from the ancient line of the West Saxon kings.

P. Stafford, 'The Reign of Æthelred II, a Study in the Limitations on Royal Policy and Action', *Ethelred the Unready*, ed. D. Hill (Oxford, 1978), pp. 15–46, at 35–7; S. Keynes, *The Diplomas of King Æthelred 'the Unready' 978–1016* (Cambridge, 1980), p. 187; idem, 'The Crowland Psalter and the Sons of King Edmund Ironside', *Bodleian Library Record* 11.6 (1985), 359–70; N. Hooper, 'Edgar the Ætheling: Anglo-Saxon Prince, Rebel and Crusader', *ASE* 14 (1985), 197–214; S. Keynes, 'A Tale of Two Kings: Alfred the Great and Æthelred the Unready', *TRHS* 5th ser. 36 (1986), 195–217, at 214–16.

SIMON KEYNES

EDMUND, ST, KING OF EAST ANGLIA. The *Anglo-Saxon Chronicle* (MS. A) notes the death of King Edmund of East Anglia at the hands of a *Viking army under 870 (= 869). Of his reign nothing remains but a number of coins. After his death, however, he was venerated as a saint. The conversion of the Danish inhabitants of what had become the *Danelaw saw the striking of coins in the name of St Edmund from about 890 to about 910. Possibly a process among the Anglo-Danish East Anglians towards a reconciliation of existing 'tribal' feelings with acquired Christian attitudes played a part in traditions concerning Edmund. The monastery dedicated to his cult at *Bury St Edmunds, whence his remains had been translated in the early decades of the tenth century, was another cradle of hagiographical development.

The first written treatment of Edmund's death was by the learned *Abbo of Fleury, who had taught in England at *Ramsey from 985 to 987. Although written more than a century after the event, there are sound grounds for assuming some historical accuracy. The apparent contradiction between Edmund's death in battle in the *Chronicle* and his martyrdom in Abbo's *Passio S. Eadmundi* can be explained by the telescoping of events: the king probably was executed after his capture. The *Passio* reflects the development of both popular and monastic traditions concerning Edmund. A major addition by Abbo himself consisted of a description of Edmund as an ideal Christian king. This trait is so pronounced that it has led to the assumption that Abbo may have written his final version only after his return to Francia. The accession of the Capetians there mattered intimately to his monastery, *Fleury, which had always enjoyed the protection of the Carolingian kings.

Abbo's text was translated and adapted by *Ælfric in his *Lives of Saints*. Differences between the latter's English version and the original may be explained by a difference in purpose: Ælfric wanted to write a succinct sermon, whereas Abbo had written an elaborate hagiographical text. Neither Ælfric nor any of the many later treatments of St Edmund add anything to our knowledge of the historical Edmund. The monastery of Bury was to remain the major centre of his cult. Edmund was in later centuries venerated in Scandinavia, Ireland and on the Continent as well as in England, but the development of the legend seems to have taken place entirely in England.

Abbo of Fleury, *Passio S. Eadmundi*, in *Three Lives of English Saints*, ed. M. Winterbottom (Toronto, 1972), pp. 65–87; Ælfric, *St Edmund, King and Martyr*, in Ælfric, *Lives of Three English Saints*, ed. G. I. Needham (Exeter, 1976), pp. 43–59; *Corolla sancti Eadmundi*, ed. F. Hervey (London, 1907); M. Mostert, *King Edmund of East Anglia (†869): Chapters in Historical Criticism* (Ann Arbor, MI, 1986); R. Frank, 'Viking Atrocity and Skaldic Verse: the Rite of the Blood Eagle', *EHR* 99 (1984), 332–43; J. Grant, 'A New Passio Beati Edmundi regis et martyris', *MS* 40 (1978), 81–95; A Gransden, 'Abbo of Fleury's *Passio S. Eadmundi*', *RB* 105 (1995), 20–78.

MARCO MOSTERT

EDUCATION: *see* Schools

EDWARD THE CONFESSOR (d. 5 January 1066) was the elder son of *Æthelred II by *Emma of Normandy. Æthelred had six sons by a former wife, and Edward's path to the kingship was made more precarious by the Danish conquest of England in 1016. His mother married King *Cnut, probably in 1017, but Edward fled to *Normandy with his brother and sister. On Cnut's death in 1035, the succession was disputed between *Harthacnut, Cnut's son by Emma, and Harold I, his son by Ælfgifu of Northampton. Emma supported Harthacnut, rather than her sons by Æthelred. Edward made an abortive raid on Southampton, and his brother Alfred was murdered on an expedition to England in 1036. In 1037, Harold I established himself as king, and Emma fled to Bruges. She returned, with Harthacnut, on Harold's death in 1040. Harthacnut rapidly lost favour with the English magnates, and in 1041 Edward arrived in England and was recognized as his half-brother's heir. When Harthacnut died suddenly in 1042, he was accepted as king.

Edward's success was bolstered by *Godwine of Wessex, whose elder sons became earls; in 1045 Edward married the earl's daughter *Edith. But Godwine had been implicated in the murder of Edward's brother Alfred, and the king's favour was probably expedient only. He had brought with him many friends from Normandy, notably Robert of Jumièges, who became bishop of *London. In 1050, Edward prevented the election of the earl's kinsman to the archbishopric of *Canterbury, in favour of Robert of Jumièges, and subsequently allowed his followers to build castles in Herefordshire (the command of Godwine's son Swein) and in Essex (in that of *Harold Godwineson). In 1051, Edward's one-time brother-in-law, Eustace of Boulogne, arrived, apparently to take command of a projected castle at Dover, in Earl Godwine's own sphere. The men of Dover objected, and in the ensuing fighting killed nineteen of Eustace's men. When Godwine refused to punish them, the king engineered his exile. It was about this time that Edward offered the English succession to his kinsman, William of Normandy.

Godwine, however, was too well-entrenched,

and in 1052 forced the king to reinstate him, and to exile his main enemies, including Robert of Jumièges. For the latter part of his reign, Edward seems to have concentrated on his favourite pastime, hunting, and on the endowment of *Westminster Abbey. Harold, who succeeded Godwine in 1053, was probably in charge of the administration. In 1054, Bishop *Ealdred of Worcester, a supporter of Harold, went to Germany in search of Edward ætheling, the king's nephew, who arrived in England in 1057; though he died almost immediately, he left a son, Edgar, to be raised at court. Harold's successful campaigns against the Welsh between 1055 and 1063, and his settlement of the Northumbrian rebellion in 1065 increased his popularity; and it seems that, although he had sworn to uphold the claims of Duke William, Edward nevertheless nominated him on his deathbed as his successor. Edward's widow, Edith, commissioned a *vita*, but his posthumous reputation and eventual canonization are largely due to the monks of his foundation at Westminster.

Vita Edwardi regis, ed. F. Barlow, 2nd ed. (OMT, 1992); F. Barlow, *Edward the Confessor* (London, 1970); R. Fleming, 'Domesday Estates of the King and the Godwines: a Study in Late Saxon Politics', *Speculum* 58 (1983), 987–1007; S. Keynes, 'The Æthelings in Normandy', *ANS* 13 (1991), 173–205; R. Fleming, *Kings and Lords in Conquest England* (Cambridge, 1991); P. A. Clarke, *The English Nobility under Edward the Confessor* (Oxford, 1994).

ANN WILLIAMS

EDWARD THE ELDER was king of the Anglo-Saxons (899–924), in succession to his father, King *Alfred the Great. He is first called 'the Elder' at the end of the tenth century, probably to distinguish him from King *Edward the Martyr. In his reign, under his leadership and that of his Mercian brother-in-law *Æthelred and sister *Æthelflæd, all of the 'Scandinavian' lands south of the Humber were brought back under English control.

Edward was already active against the Danes towards the end of Alfred's reign. The chronicler *Æthelweard notes that Edward led troops in 893, and one of Alfred's *charters from 898 calls Edward a king, perhaps sub-king of *Kent. On Alfred's death in 899, Edward's cousin Æthelwold rebelled: he fled north, where he was accepted as king by the Northumbrian Danes. Later he harried *Mercia and *Wessex with the East Anglian Danes, before dying at the battle of Holme late in 902. Little is known of English/Danish relations over the next several years, but in 910 a joint Mercian/West Saxon army annihilated the Northumbrian Danes so completely that they ceased

to venture south of the Humber, leaving Edward and his allies free to concentrate on the Danes in the *Five Boroughs and *East Anglia. The wars and fortress-building of the next eight years can be followed in the *Anglo-Saxon Chronicle*: by 918, all of the people of Mercia, both English and Danes, had submitted to Edward.

The submission of the English Mercians after Æthelflæd's death in 918 was not a foregone conclusion. Charters and coins demonstrate that Æthelred and Æthelflæd were acting as governors of Mercia under the overall control of Edward from the beginning of Edward's reign, but the Mercian Register makes clear that the Mercians expected Ælfwynn, Æthelflaed's daughter, to succeed as governor. Edward instead assumed direct control, and had Ælfwynn taken into Wessex.

In 920 Edward went north and received the submission of the Northumbrians, Scots and Strathclyde Britons; he probably did not exercise real authority north of the Humber, as Sihtric ruled *York and issued his own coins in the 920s. Very little is known of the last four years of Edward's reign. He died on 17 July 924, at Farndon, soon after putting down a Mercian-Welsh revolt at *Chester. This revolt is only recorded by *William of Malmesbury, but it is a plausible result of Mercian resentment over the treatment of Ælfwynn. Edward was buried at the New Minster, *Winchester, a monastery he had founded in 901, probably to emphasize the wider horizons of the new kingdom of the Anglo-Saxons that his father had founded. Another important religious event of Edward's reign was the division of the West Saxon bishoprics in 909, by which the new sees of Ramsbury, *Wells, and Crediton were carved out of the ancient sees of Winchester and *Sherborne.

Edward was married three times and had perhaps fourteen children. He was first married in the 890s, and his wife Ecgwynn was the mother of King *Æthelstan. By 901 Edward was married to Ælfflæd, who was the mother of Ælfweard (king for under a month after Edward's death in 924) and Eadwine (drowned in 933). By 920, Edward was married a third time, to *Eadgifu, who was the mother of Kings *Edmund and *Eadred.

F. T. Wainwright, 'The Submission to Edward the Elder', *History* ns 27 (1952), 114–30; Stenton, *ASE*, pp. 319–39; J. Nelson, 'Reconstructing a Royal Family: Reflections on Alfred, from Asser, chapter 2', in Sawyer FS, pp. 47–66; S. Keynes, 'The West Saxon Charters of King Æthelwulf and his Sons', *EHR* 109 (1994), 1109–49, at 1141–7; idem, *The Liber Vitae of the New*

Minster and Hyde Abbey, Winchester, EEMF 26 (Copenhagen, 1996), 16–19; S. Miller, *The Charters of the New Minster at Winchester* (Oxford, 2000).

SEAN MILLER

EDWARD THE MARTYR, king of the English (975–8), was the son of *Edgar and either Wulfthryth or Æthelflæd. On Edgar's death, the succession was disputed between Edward and his younger half-brother, *Æthelred, Edgar's son by *Ælfthryth. Edward became king, but was murdered on 18 March 978. Within twenty-five years he was an established saint and martyr.

It is surprising to find that the two pillars of monastic reform backed different candidates in the succession crisis, with *Æthelwold on Æthelred's side and *Dunstan on Edward's. The nobles were also divided, with Ealdorman Æthelwine of East Anglia and Byrhtnoth of Essex for Edward, and Ælfthryth, Edgar's widow, and Ælfhere of Mercia for Æthelred. Given that in 975 Æthelred was probably nine, and Edward only a few years older, they were surely figureheads rather than active participants. The real reasons for preferring one or the other may have lain in family alliances rather than in the relative thronewortiness of the candidates.

Edward was crowned in 975, but the unrest and resistance continued, alongside what is sometimes called the 'anti-monastic reaction'. To judge from the *Anglo-Saxon Chronicle, Ealdorman Ælfhere of Mercia and many others launched unprovoked attacks on monasteries. It emerges from other sources that some of the lands given to monasteries in Edgar's reign were seized by force, under circumstances which make it appear that the 'reaction' was more a recovery of territory than a revulsion against monastic ideals. Further, even people seen as pro-monastic, such as Æthelwine 'the friend of God', were often merely protecting their own interests: Æthelwine was a founder of *Ramsey, so naturally *Byrhtferth of Ramsey's *Vita S. Oswaldi* speaks highly of him, but the monks of *Ely remember him for stealing several of their estates.

The *Anglo-Saxon Chronicle* notes that Edward's murder took place at Corfe, on 18 March 978, in the evening, and that he was buried at *Wareham without royal honours. It notes further that in the following year Ealdorman Ælfhere recovered the body and bore it with great honour to *Shaftesbury. Byrhtferth's *Vita S. Oswaldi* adds that Edward had gone to visit his half-brother, who was staying with his mother, and certain zealous *thegns of Æthelred killed him. The late eleventh-century *Passio S. Eadwardi* adds that it was Ælfthryth who plotted the killing, so that her son could be king. Ælfthryth's complicity in Edward's death cannot be demonstrated, and without earlier evidence it is simplest to assume that Æthelred's zealous thegns acted on their own initiative, perhaps expecting more advancement under Æthelred. In 1001 Edward's body was translated within the abbey at Shaftesbury. A charter that same year (S 899) calls him a saint, the celebration of his feast-day is enforced in legislation drafted by Archbishop Wulfstan, and he appears in pre-Conquest calendars, litanies, and prayers.

D. J. V. Fisher, 'The Anti-Monastic Reaction in the Reign of Edward the Martyr', *Cambridge Historical Journal* 10 (1950–2), 254–70; C. Fell, *Edward King and Martyr* (Leeds, 1971); S. Keynes, *The Diplomas of King Æthelred 'the Unready' 978–1016* (Cambridge, 1980), pp. 163–74; S. Ridyard, *The Royal Saints of Anglo-Saxon England: a Study of West Saxon and East Anglian Cults* (Cambridge, 1988), pp. 44–50, 154–75.

SEAN MILLER

EDWIN, KING OF NORTHUMBRIA (d. 633), belonged to the Deiran dynasty. After the death of his father, King Ælle (*c.*560–90), and the subsequent annexation of *Deira by King Æthelfrith of *Bernicia (*c.*592–616), Edwin went into exile. *Bede records how he 'wandered secretly as a fugitive through many places and kingdoms' (*HE* ii. 12), and it was in this period that he married Cwenburh, daughter of the Mercian king Cearl, by whom he had two children, Osfrith and Eadfrith. He was given refuge by *Rædwald, king of the East Angles, who in 616 raised an army which defeated a Northumbrian force in battle near the river Idle during which Æthelfrith was killed. Edwin subsequently took control of Bernicia as well as Deira and drove the sons of Æthelfrith (including *Oswald and *Oswiu) into exile. Soon after his accession he enlarged the territory of Deira through conquest of the British kingdom of *Elmet. Edwin exercised authority far beyond the borders of Northumbria and his overlordship may, at various times, have been acknowledged by all the English kingdoms except for *Kent. He was one of three Northumbrian kings on Bede's list of those who held *imperium* south of the Humber, the others being Oswald and Oswiu (*HE* ii. 5; and see *bretwalda). He also controlled the British islands of Anglesey and Man, strategic places on the Irish Sea maritime routes, which implies that Edwin had a substantial fleet at his command.

It was during Edwin's reign that the Christian mission established in Kent reached *Northumbria. Sometime before July 625 he married

Æthelburh, Christian daughter of *Æthelberht of Kent, who was accompanied to Northumbria by the missionary *Paulinus. To overcome objections to the union by the church in Kent, Edwin agreed his wife should be allowed to practise her faith without hindrance and to consider accepting Christianity himself. On several occasions he drew back from *conversion despite assurances he had given to Paulinus. Bede's description of the meeting between Edwin and his councillors at which it was agreed to accept Christianity, though in large measure a literary device, illustrates the political sensitivity of the decision. To ensure that the new religion would not be a cause of disunity in his kingdom, Edwin required his chief men to be baptized with him. This took place at *York in 627 with Paulinus standing as sponsor for the king. Contact with the Christian world brought Edwin the prestige of letters and gifts from the pope in *Rome, and marriage to Æthelburh gave Northumbria contact via Kent with the Frankish world. Edwin administered his kingdom and maintained the royal household by making a circuit of his estates. He consumed food renders and met his subjects at the *villae regis* by the Derwent in Deira, *Ad Gefrin* (*Yeavering) in Bernicia, and *Campodonum* in Elmet. Bede provides a glimpse of the ceremony attached to a royal circuit when he describes how Edwin was preceded by a standard bearer, 'as he rode among his cities, estates, and kingdoms with his *thegns. Further, when he walked anywhere along the roads, there used to be carried before him the type of standard which the Romans call a *tufa* and the English call a *thuf*' (*HE* ii.16).

Edwin's far-reaching authority brought him into conflict with other rulers. In 626 he survived an attempt on his life when Cwichelm, a West Saxon king, sent an assassin disguised as an emissary. In 633 Cadwallon of Gwynedd invaded Northumbria with the help of the Mercian king, *Penda, and Edwin was killed in a battle at Hatfield Chase. Northumbrian overlordship of Anglesey (part of the kingdom of Gwynedd) may have been the cause of the conflict, for Bede describes Cadwallon's action as a rebellion. Edwin's death brought an end to Northumbrian unity: the kingdom of Deira went to his cousin, Osric, and Bernicia to Eanfrith, a son of Æthelfrith. Both kings were soon killed by Cadwallon who occupied and ravaged the Northumbrian kingdoms for a year. In the late seventh century Edwin's cult was established at *Whitby by his daughter *Eanflæd, but it failed to achieve the wide popularity enjoyed by the cult of King Oswald.

Bede, *HE* ii.9–18, 20, iii.1; *The Earliest Life of Gregory the Great*, ed. B. Colgrave (Lawrence, KA, 1968), cc. 15–19; Stenton, *ASE*, pp. 78–81, 113–16; Kirby, *Kings*, pp. 77–88.

PHILIP HOLDSWORTH

ELEGIES is a term conventionally applied to certain Old English poems, especially the following nine from the *Exeter Book: the *Wanderer*, the *Seafarer*, the *Rhyming Poem*, *Deor*, *Wulf and Eadwacer*, the *Wife's Lament*, *Resignation* (or the second half of it, 'Resignation B'), the *Husband's Message*, and the *Ruin*. Passages from longer works are sometimes included, notably *Beowulf* 2247–66 and 2444–62a (the laments of the Last Survivor and the Bereaved Father, respectively) and *Guthlac* 1348–79, the lament of *Guthlac's disciple. The *Husband's Message* and the *Ruin* are sometimes excluded from the elegies group because of the optimism of the former and the impersonal nature of the latter, which lacks the usual narrating character. The elegies have thematic and formal affinities with *wisdom literature and with *riddles.

Though doubts persist about the appropriateness of 'elegies' as a designation, the principal features of the group are clear. The genre in Old English is characterized by typical themes: exile, loss of loved ones, physical hardship, desolate landscapes and seascapes, contemplation of ruins, meditation on the inevitability of decay and the transience of all earthly things. These themes, and the *formulae associated with them, cluster in the Exeter Book elegies, but are also to be found lending an 'elegiac' colouring to many passages in Old English poetry. Greenfield defined the elegy as 'a relatively short reflective or dramatic poem embodying a contrasting pattern of loss and consolation', Klinck as 'a discourse arising from a powerful sense of absence, of separation from what is desired'. The object of desire may be an individual, as in the three love poems (*Wulf*, *Wife*, *Husband*), or, more usually, a collectivity, the warrior *comitatus*. Longing that springs from unsatisfied desire is the product of separation, and pervades all the elegies – including the *Ruin*, with its nostalgia for a vanished warrior-band, and the *Husband's Message*, with its expectation of a reunion. The scenery of elegy includes 'the sea with cliffs, hail, snow, rain, and storms', a setting which forms the narrator's present, and, in the past or far away, 'the meadhall of heroic poetry with its lords, warriors, hawks, horses, and precious cups'.

The central characters of nearly all the Exeter

Book elegies are exiles of one kind or another. The classification by Greenfield of the formulas of exile identifies some of the typical language of elegy, with its solitary (*anhaga*) or exile (*wrǽcca*), who treads the paths of exile (*wrǽclastas*), deprived (*bidǽled, bidroren*) of kinsmen and of joy. Another recurrent topos is the abandoned hall, with its contrast between present desolation and former mirth – a theme that finds poignant expression in the *Beowulf* elegies. These motifs arise from the warring, tribal culture of continental Germania, but readily lend themselves to Christian appropriation: the lord becomes Christ, the warrior-band the host of the blessed, and exile exclusion from heaven or from God's grace.

In addition to its themes and vocabulary, Old English elegy has some recurrent structural features: monologue, the form of most of the elegies; personal introduction and generalising conclusion, either gnomic or homiletic; balance of contrasting halves – in the longer, didactic poems; and formal repetition creating a leitmotiv or even a refrain. The openings of the *Seafarer* and the *Wife's Lament*, which speak of narrating (*wrecan*) a story (*giedd*) about oneself, are clearly formulaic. Similar personal introductions appear, shifted from the opening, in *Wanderer* 8, *Deor* 35, and *Resignation* 96b–97a. The gnomic ending is used in *Deor*, *Wulf*, *Wife*, and *Resignation*; the more extended homiletic conclusion in *Wanderer*, *Seafarer*, and *Rhyming Poem*. The keyword *ar* ('grace') is repeated at the beginning and end of the *Wanderer*; words for 'longing' throughout *Wife*; *Wulf* reiterates lines 2–3 in 7–8, intensifying the speaker's feeling of separation from and anxiety for her lover; *Husband* the pledge of fidelity between the betrothed in lines 16 and 53; and *Deor* repeats its consolatory refrain six times.

There is no single obvious source for this Old English genre. Its oral Germanic ancestors are lost. Perhaps the closest foreign analogues are to be found in the early Welsh Llywarch Hen cycle, especially three laments: that of the Sick Man of Abercuawg, and those for the devastated halls of Cynddylan and Urien Rheged. The influence of Boethius' *Consolation of Philosophy* lies behind *Deor*, probably the *Wanderer*, and possibly other elegies too. Though no specific models exist, parallels appear in various Latin, Celtic, and Norse texts.

B. J. Timmer, 'The Elegiac Mood in Old English Poetry', *ES* 24 (1942), 33–44; S. B. Greenfield, 'The Formulaic Expression of the Theme of "Exile" in Anglo-Saxon Poetry', *Speculum* 30 (1955), 200–6, repr. in his *Hero and Exile*, pp. 125–31; H. Pilch, 'The Elegiac

Genre in Old English and Early Welsh Poetry', *ZCP* 29 (1964), 209–24; S. B. Greenfield, 'The Old English Elegies', *Continuations and Beginnings: Studies in Old English Literature*, ed. E. G. Stanley (London, 1966), pp. 142–75, repr. in *Hero and Exile*, pp. 93–123; M. Green, ed., *The Old English Elegies: New Essays in Criticism and Research* (Rutherford, Madison, and Teaneck, 1983); J. Harris, 'Hadubrand's Lament: On the Origin and Age of Elegy in Germanic', *Heldensage und Heldendichtung im Germanischen*, ed. H. Beck (Berlin and New York, 1988), pp. 81–114; S. B. Greenfield, *Hero and Exile* (London and Ronceverte, WV, 1989); A. L. Klinck, *The Old English Elegies: A Critical Edition and Genre Study* (Montreal and Kingston, 1992); M. J. Mora, 'The Invention of the Old English Elegy', *ES* 76 (1995), 129–39.

ANNE L. KLINCK

ELMET. A British kingdom located in West Yorkshire between the Vale of York and the Pennine watershed. *Bede (HE* iv. 23) and the *Historia Brittonum* (c. 63) record its survival into the seventh century when it was conquered by King *Edwin of *Deira *c.*616. The *Elmedsaete* are the most northerly group recorded in the *Tribal Hidage, which suggests that the kingdom was an administrative sub-division of Deira (or possibly *Mercia) at the time the document was compiled. The name is preserved in the modern settlements of Sherburn-in-Elmet and Barwick-in-Elmet, both east of Leeds.

M. Faull, 'Place-Names and the Kingdom of Elmet', *Nomina* 4 (1980), 21–3.

PHILIP HOLDSWORTH

ELMHAM, NORTH (Norfolk), can almost certainly be identified with the 'Elmham' which became an episcopal seat in the 670s or 680s with the division of the see of *Dommoc*. Episcopal succession ended with the *Viking invasions but resumed, after a long gap, in the 950s; the cathedral was moved to *Norwich in 1071. Excavations beside the old cathedral site have found an eighth- and ninth-century planned settlement of small two-roomed buildings, with parallel ditches defining roads (fig. 19). After a hiatus in the Viking age the settlement, still planned around the early road layout, developed and intensified through the tenth and eleventh centuries; the cathedral cemetery seems to have remained in continuous use. The ruined church on the site, previously identified as the late Anglo-Saxon cathedral itself, has been convincingly reinterpreted as an episcopal chapel built after 1071.

S. E. Rigold, 'The Anglian Cathedral of North Elmham, Norfolk', *MArch* 6–7 (1962–3), 67–108; P. Wade-Martins, *Excavations in North Elmham Park, 1967–72*, East Anglian Archaeology 9 (Gressenhall, 1980); S.

Heywood, 'The Ruined Church at North Elmham', *JBAA* 135 (1982), 1–10; J. Campbell, 'The East Anglian Sees before the Conquest', *Norwich Cathedral: Church, City and Diocese 1096–1996*, ed. I. Atherton *et al.* (London, 1996), pp. 3–21.

JOHN BLAIR

ELSTOB, ELIZABETH (1683–1756), was introduced to Anglo-Saxon studies at Oxford by her brother William and his friend George *Hickes. When she and William moved to London in 1702, she set up a women's circle to study Old English. She published two significant works, an item from *Ælfric's first series of Catholic Homilies, *An English-Saxon Homily on the Birth-Day of St Gregory*, in 1709, and *Rudiments of Grammar for the English-Saxon Tongue* in 1715. But in that year her brother died, and her plans for a much more ambitious edition of the Catholic Homilies foundered.

Anglo-Saxon Scholarship: The First Three Centuries, ed. C. T. Berkhout and M. McC. Gatch (Boston, 1982); K. Sutherland, 'Editing for a New Century: Elizabeth Elstob's Anglo-Saxon Manifesto and Ælfric's St Gregory Homily', *The Editing of Old English*, ed. D. G. Scragg and P. E. Szarmach (Cambridge, 1994), pp. 213–37.

DONALD SCRAGG

ELVES: *see* Folklore

ELY ABBEY, Cambridgeshire. *Bede, writing in 731, described Ely as 'a district of about 600 hides in the kingdom of the East Angles, like an island in that it is surrounded by marshes or by water, taking its name from the abundance of eels which are caught in the same marshes' (*HE* iv.19). The place is associated most closely with *Æthelthryth (better known as St Etheldreda or St Audrey), daughter of Anna, king of the East Angles (d. 654), both as a person (in the mid seventh century) and as a cult (from the late seventh century onwards). In about 660, following the death of her first husband Tondberht, a *princeps* of the southern Gyrwe, Æthelthryth married Ecgfrith, son of *Oswiu, king of the Northumbrians (655–70); she was determined, however, to remain a virgin, and not long after Ecgfrith's accession in 670 she withdrew to the double house at *Coldingham (in northern *Northumbria), where she stayed for a year; but in about 672 she returned to *East Anglia, founded a religious house at Ely, and held office there for seven years as its first abbess (*HE* iv.19). Æthelthryth died on 23 June (her feast-day) in 679 (*ASC*), and was succeeded as abbess by her sister *Seaxburh. In 694, when Æthelthryth's

grave was opened, her body was found to be incorrupt; so it was wrapped in new robes, placed in a marble sarcophagus (brought to Ely from Cambridge), and (according to Bede) held in great veneration 'to this day' (*HE* iv.19).

Little is known of Ely's history in the later eighth, ninth, and first half of the tenth centuries. Monastic life at Ely is presumed to have been destroyed when the Vikings conquered the kingdom of East Anglia in 869–70, and in the 940s the shrine of St Æthelthryth was tended by a community of clerks; one of them, called *Ælfhelm, wrote an account of her miracles, incorporated in the *Liber Eliensis*, i.43–9. The isle of Ely was in royal ownership in 957, when land there was given by King *Eadwig to *Oda, archbishop of *Canterbury (see S 646); but it came back into royal ownership shortly thereafter, probably in the 960s. The abbey was re-founded by Bishop *Æthelwold, *c.*970, with the help and approval of King *Edgar, and placed under Abbot Byrhtnoth (Wulfstan of Winchester, *Vita S. Æthelwoldi*, c. 23). Ely would naturally have appealed to the monastic reformers because of its close association with St Æthelthryth, and through her with the golden age of the late seventh century; but others may have hoped that a prosperous abbey would serve as a binding force – in social, political, and economic terms – for the people who lived in this prosperous part of eastern England. With its impeccable credentials, and its powerful and wealthy backers, Ely's success was all but guaranteed. It is clear that the process of endowment generated some tension and resentment locally, yet the quality of the documentary record makes it possible in Ely's case, more so than in any other, to observe how the abbey presently came into its own as a focal point for the region. Above all, the *Libellus Æthelwoldi episcopi*, written in the early twelfth century to provide an account of the good works of Bishop Æthelwold, but based on vernacular records which had originated in the late tenth century, reveals much about the circumstances in which the abbey accumulated its land in the early 970s, and how it was obliged to defend its interests at law in the wake of the troubles precipitated by the death of King *Edgar in 975.

The compiler of the *Liber Eliensis*, working later in the twelfth century, made effective use of the *Libellus*, but also used a quantity of vernacular wills and charters, filling out his narrative with local traditions. Further material is to hand in the form of farming accounts, records of benefactors, and a small stock of royal diplomas; also of interest are the statutes of the *thegns' guild at Cambridge, entered in a gospelbook at Ely (*EHD* i, no. 136). The abbey was patronized by King *Cnut and Queen *Emma, and prospered as much under the Anglo-Danish establishment as it had done under King Edgar. When Alfred the ætheling, son of King *Æthelred the Unready, was blinded on the orders of King *Harold Harefoot, in 1036, he was entrusted to the monks of Ely, who cared for him until he died of his wounds on 5 February 1037. Latterly Ely became a centre of English resistance to the Norman regime, associated with the name and more especially the legend of Hereward the Wake. It makes a good story, though much depends on whether we show a preference for the Ely as opposed to the Peterborough tradition. The post-Conquest community at Ely was not slow to appreciate the advantages which might accrue from the cultivation of its pre-Conquest past; but while one should like to think that this was done for the noblest of reasons, one suspects that what truly counted was the registration of its landed interests, and the safe-keeping of its quite considerable store of treasures.

Bede, *HE* iv.19–20; E. Miller, *The Abbey and Bishopric of Ely* (Cambridge, 1951); *Liber Eliensis*, ed. E. O. Blake, Camden 3rd ser. 92 (London, 1962); P. Courtney, 'The Early Saxon Fenland: a Reconsideration', *ASSAH* 2 (1981), 91–9; P. A. Thompson, 'St Æthelthryth: the Making of History from Hagiography', *Studies in English Language and Literature*, ed. M. J. Toswell and E. M. Tyler (London, 1996), pp. 475–92; P. A. Thompson and E. Stevens, 'Gregory of Ely's Verse Life and Miracles of St Æthelthryth', *AB* 106 (1988), 333–90; A. Kennedy, 'Law and Litigation in the *Libellus Æthelwoldi Episcopi*', *ASE* 24 (1995), 131–83; S. Keynes and A. Kennedy, *Anglo-Saxon Ely: Records of Ely Abbey and its Benefactors in the Tenth and Eleventh Centuries* (forthcoming).

SIMON KEYNES

Fig. 6 Anglo-Saxon embroidery (drawn from the Cuthbert stole and maniple).

EMBROIDERY. The Anglo-Saxons were famed for their embroidery, the art of embellishing textiles by means of decorative stitching or other decoration applied to a previously woven fabric. However, only three substantial embroideries usually claimed to be Anglo-Saxon have survived. The largest and best known is the *Bayeux Tapestry, a 70 m. wool-embroidered linen frieze, probably designed in *Canterbury. A recent book, challenging this prevailing consensus, has asserted that a clear distinction can be made between Anglo-Saxon embroidery and that of northern Europe and particularly Scandinavia, and that therefore it is Norman work.

The *Durham embroideries of the early tenth century from the tomb of St *Cuthbert, an embroidered stole and maniple, and a possible girdle or other garment, are all closely related in material (gold thread amd silk embroidery on silk) and technique, and are stylistically southern English work of the early tenth century. The first two have embroidered inscriptions which confirm they were commissioned in southern England between 909 and 916.

The third, from Maaseik in Belgium, has been

167

compared to Anglo-Saxon work of the late eighth/ early ninth century such as the Brunswick Casket and the Book of *Cerne: it comprises several pieces of mainly gold thread and silk embroideries on linen (including appliqués which include painted decoration, and some linen with metal appliqués), put together at some later date as a relic of two Anglo-Saxon saints. The main pieces possibly originally decorated an altar frontal. However, for these also a recent survey has suggested a Rhine-Meuse origin under the influence of Anglo-Saxon art.

There is, however, no more than a handful of major western European embroideries of the period before 1100, from Merovingian and *Viking period graves, and church treasuries, and some of these may be Anglo-Saxon, or Anglo-Saxon influenced, for example pieces from Mammen (Denmark), Oseberg (Norway) and S. Ambrogio, Milan.

Embroideries are both portable and fragile (see *textiles): their study is very different from that of manuscripts, *metalwork or *sculpture, for which many more examples have survived. The few fine works are often considered in isolation from the fragments of archaeological textiles, some of which have fragments of decorative stitching. There are important fragments from *Sutton Hoo; Dover; Durham, on the border of a possibly seventh- or eighth-century dalmatic; Kempston (Bedfordshire); Mitchell's Hill, Icklingham (Suffolk), and *York: less is known about similar fragments from outside the British Isles and Scandinavia.

The available European corpus suggests that some decorative sewing was an attempt to reproduce expensive imported patterned weaves without a special loom; while other stitches, originally functional, developed a decorative element to disguise constructional features or to outline and emphasise edges and openings. The attempt to distinguish Anglo-Saxon from other north European embroideries pre-1100 on the grounds of technique cannot be upheld on the basis of present knowledge.

F. Stenton, *The Bayeux Tapestry: A Comprehensive Survey*, 2nd ed. (London 1965); M. Budny and D. Tweddle, 'The Maaseik Embroideries', *ASE* 13 (1984), 65–96; idem, 'The Early Medieval Textiles at Maaseik, Belgium', *AJ* 65 (1985), 353–89; D. M. Wilson, *The Bayeux Tapestry* (London, 1985); L. von Wilckens, *Die textile Künste von der Spätantike bis zum 1500* (Munich, 1991); W. Grape, *The Bayeux Tapestry, Monument to a Norman Triumph* (Munich and New York, 1994).

ELIZABETH COATSWORTH

EMMA OF NORMANDY, queen (b. 980×990, d. 7 March 1052), was the daughter of Richard I count of Rouen, and his Danish-descended wife, Gunnor. She married *Æthelred II in 1002, and his Danish successor, the conqueror, *Cnut, in 1017; by Æthelred she bore three children, including *Edward the Confessor, by Cnut two, including King *Harthacnut. Her marriage to Æthelred was the first foreign marriage of an English king since the mid ninth century, and was arranged in the context of *Viking attack. Her Norman/Danish origins did not prevent her playing some role at court during Æthelred's reign, but they may have inhibited any great significance for her at that time. The peak of her power belongs to Cnut's reign, when her public profile in patronage and *charter witness-lists is higher than that of any earlier English queen. Emma was important to an insecure conqueror, often absent from England, whilst symbolizing continuity with the old regime to the English. Her career represents a high-point of English *queenship, yet was shaped and dominated by the complexity of family politics. She was not the first wife of either husband. The marriage to Cnut in 1017 saved her from the obscurity which the accession of a stepson would have meant, but in 1035, on Cnut's death, the claims of *Harold Harefoot again threatened her with this fate. She struggled personally to avoid it. Supported by Earl *Godwine and the *housecarls, she held the royal treasure in her dower borough of *Winchester in 1036. Attempts to bring her son Harthacnut back from Denmark, where he was ruling, failed, but appeals to her sons by Æthelred, in exile in Normandy, resulted in their return. The younger, Alfred, was captured, blinded and died, a tragedy which became a cause célèbre of mid eleventh-century politics and hung over Emma's and Godwine's heads. Emma was exiled to *Flanders as Harold's hold on England tightened; his death in 1040 allowed her return with Harthacnut, and for the next two years she appears alongside him, as prominent as *Eadgifu had been a century before. Perhaps at her behest, Edward was brought back from *Normandy and associated in rule. It was now that Emma commissioned the so-called *Encomium Emmae reginae*, an almost unique apologia for the career of an early queen. Her power as queen-mother was short-lived. In 1042 her older son, Edward, succeeded, and proceeded in 1043 to deprive his mother of her lands and treasure, to reduce her to dowager status. Emma's attempt to resist the obscurity of widowhood was ended. She was not permanently disgraced, but her last years were lived probably at Winchester, where she was buried alongside her Danish husband Cnut in the Old Minster.

Encomium Emmae Reginae, ed. A. Campbell, Camden Soc. 3rd ser. 72 (London, 1949); M. W. Campbell, 'Queen Emma and Ælfgifu of Northampton: Canute the Great's Women', *Medieval Scandinavia* 4 (1971), 66–79; S. Keynes, 'The Æthelings in Normandy', *ANS* 13 (1991), 173–205; P. Stafford, *Queen Emma and Queen Edith: Queenship and Women's Power in Eleventh-Century England* (Oxford, 1997).

PAULINE STAFFORD

ENAMEL is coloured ground glass melted and fused into a metal setting to form a durable inlay. Opaque red champlevé enamel, i.e. in cast or engraved fields, is found in Anglo-Saxon *metalwork from the fifth century onwards; the earliest example is on a sword pommel, but it was relatively uncommon. The technique may have been brought in from Scandinavia or learnt from the British. Largely confined to eastern England, enamel was used in small amounts in the sixth century, mainly on dress fasteners. In the ninth century, red enamel appeared occasionally on strap ends and dress hooks, while polychrome enamelled brooches were imported from the Rhineland. Fine cloisonné enamels (with cell walls made of gold strip, back-plates and a variety of glass colours) were manufactured by the late ninth century to decorate finger rings and elaborate mounts, including the *Alfred Jewel; this technical development may reflect influence from *Germany and Lotharingia. The glasses are predominantly opaque white, blue, green, yellow and red with some translucent green. A related series of Anglo-Saxon gilt bronze disc-brooches with polychrome cloisonné enamels in a central roundel has been found in England and Denmark. These show a variety of floral and other patterns and date to the tenth and eleventh centuries.

V. I. Evison, 'An Enamelled Disc from Great Saxham', *Proc. of the Suffolk Inst. of Archaeol. and Hist.* 34 (1977), 1–13; D. A. Hinton, *A Catalogue of the Anglo-Saxon Metalwork 700–1100 in the Department of Antiquities, Ashmolean Museum* (Oxford, 1974), nos. 22, 23, 27, 28; C. Scull, 'Further Evidence from East Anglia for Enamelling', *ASSAH* 4 (1985), 117–24; D. Buckton, 'Late 10th- and 11th-century *cloisonné* Enamel Brooches', *MArch* 30 (1986), 8–18; idem, 'Late Anglo-Saxon or early Anglo-Norman *cloisonné* Enamel Brooches', *MArch* 33 (1989), 153–5; G. Haseloff, *Email im frühen Mittelalter. Frühchristliche Kunst von der Spätantike bis zu den Karolingern* (Marburg, 1990); J. M. Cook, 'Bronze-bound Buckets', in V. I. Evison, *An*

Anglo-Saxon Cemetery at Great Chesterford, Essex, CBA Research Report 91 (York, 1994), 22–4.

S. M. YOUNGS

ENCOMIUM EMMAE REGINAE. A work ostensibly in praise of Queen *Emma (d. 7 March 1052), commissioned by her and written by a monk of Saint-Bertin (Saint-Omer, *Flanders) in 1041–2, during the reign of King *Harthacnut. It would appear that the *Encomium* was intended not so much for the gratification of the queen's ego, as for the edification of those in positions of power and influence at the Anglo-Danish royal court. The Encomiast passes over the first phase of Emma's political career (as the wife of King *Æthelred), and focusses instead on the story of the Scandinavian conquest of England in 1013–16, paying particular attention to the role of Thorkell the Tall and creating a positive image of the regime personified by *Swein Forkbeard and by his son *Cnut. Yet the work was written at a time when there was much disquiet in England about the circumstances which had led to the capture and blinding of the *ætheling Alfred in 1036 (and to his death at *Ely in 1037), and also at a time when Harthacnut's rule was proving decidedly unpopular. Special importance attaches, therefore, to the Encomiast's treatment of political developments in the period from Cnut's death in 1035 to the accession of Harthacnut in 1040. His particular concern seems to have been to put the blame squarely on *Harold Harefoot for enticing Alfred back to England, and thereby to expose Harold's complicity in Alfred's capture, blinding, and death. More generally, he was perhaps concerned implicitly to remind his audience of Emma's pivotal role in the establishment of the Anglo-Danish regime; and by clearing her from any suspicion of blame for Alfred's death he may have sought to strengthen her position as the one who presided in England over the regime now personified by Harthacnut (with *Edward to follow). There is no reason to believe that the contemporary audience was fooled or persuaded by the artful dissimulation. The work survives in one mid-eleventh-century manuscript (BL, Add. 33241), notable for its inclusion of a prefatory image depicting the enthroned queen receiving the book from the Encomiast, with her sons Harthacnut and Edward the Confessor lurking in the background.

Encomium Emmae Reginae, ed. A. Campbell, Camden Soc. 3rd ser. 72 (London, 1949); *Golden Age of AS Art*, no. 148; P. Stafford, *Queen Emma and Queen Edith: Queenship and Women's Power in Eleventh-Century*

England (Oxford, 1997), esp. pp. 28–40; S. Keynes, 'Queen Emma and the *Encomium Emmae Reginae*', *Encomium Emmae Reginae*, ed. A. Campbell, Camden Classic Reprints 4 (Cambridge, 1998), pp. [xiii]–[lxxxvii].

SIMON KEYNES

ENGLISH PEOPLE, a formulation corresponding to *gens Anglorum*, a term coined by Pope *Gregory the Great to describe the Germanic inhabitants of south-eastern Britain, and given a wider currency by *Bede in his *Historia ecclesiastica*. Despite their different ethnic origins and separate political organisation, the Anglo-Saxon peoples of the former Roman Britain were seen by outsiders to have a single identity, which was generally before the eighth century defined as a Saxon one. The Celtic peoples of Britain consistently called their Germanic neighbours Saxons throughout the pre-Conquest period (and beyond), and the term Saxon was similarly used by most of the non-Insular authors who described affairs in Britain in the fifth and sixth centuries, such as the Gallic Chronicler of 452 and Constantius, author of the *Life of St Germanus*. The only author before the time of Pope Gregory to use any other term was the Byzantine historian Procopius, who in describing the island of *Brittia* spoke of the three populous nations inhabiting the place, the *Brittones*, the *Frisiones* and the *Angiloi* (*History of the Wars*, VIII.xx.4–8). Pope Gregory adopted the same term, *Anguli* (or *Angli*), to describe the Germanic inhabitants of Britain; his use of the label is known most famously from the story that he was persuaded to send missionaries to the English after encountering slave-boys in the Roman market ('not Angles but angels'). In a letter to Eulogius, bishop of Alexandria, describing the success of *Augustine's mission, Gregory accounted for the name differently saying that the *gens Anglorum* was found at the world's corner: *in mundo angulo posita* (Gregory, *Epistolae*, viii.29). All of Gregory's letters about the Roman mission to *Kent referred to the people as the Angles, including those written after he had received some direct information about affairs in Britain and so might have known that this was not the most appropriate term, certainly not for the Kentish people whom *Æthelberht ruled. Gregory's adoption of the *Angli/Anguli* label was only given a wider currency through Bede's use of the term.

For Bede, the Anglo-Saxon peoples, although separated by the diversity of their political arrangements, were united by their shared Christian faith into one *gens Anglorum* in the sight of God. It was Bede who gave the idea of Englishness its particular power; Bede demonstrated that the Church not only created but named this new communal identity and made the *gens Anglorum* a people with a covenant, like Israel. For Bede, the semblance of unity was created by the existence of one language distinguishing the Germanic settlers of Anglo-Saxon England from their British, Irish and Pictish neighbours (*HE* i.1). One of Bede's intentions in writing his *Historia* was to demonstrate that, despite their separate ethnic and political origins, the Anglo-Saxons had been brought together into one *gens* by the unifying power of the Christian faith, transmitted to them by *Rome. Part of what Bede had aimed to illustrate was the process by which a 'national' church was created; although his was an argument about spiritual authority not about political power, there was a potential political dimension to his historical vision, demonstrable from his list of seven kings who held *imperium*, or wide-ranging power (*HE* ii.5). Bede was not arguing here that there was one quasi-imperial office, ranking above the kingship of an individual kingdom, which passed from one king to another from the fifth to the seventh century, though a West Saxon chronicler in the late ninth century used this passage from Bede when hailing *Ecgberht of Wessex in 829 as the eighth king who was *Bretwalda. Instead Bede was hinting that, just as one faith and one language can unify disparate groups, so, bearing in mind the demonstrable unity provided by the centralising authority of the church, could a single political authority potentially bind distinct political groups into a common cause.

The notion that the *gens Anglorum* had one collective identity had an enduring currency in certain circles in England at least from the time of Bede, an identity that transcended the significant separation occasioned by the existence of multiple political organisations and ethnic groups among the Anglo-Saxons; it was also clearly recognisable to outsiders. Bede's vision received further promotion when *Alfred adopted the vernacular label of the *Angelcynn* to denote a people with a shared, Christian, past, united under West Saxon rule, fostering an awareness that English self-consciousness lay in their acknowledgement of a common Christianity centred on Canterbury. According to the *Anglo-Saxon Chronicle*, in 886 Alfred occupied *London 'and all the *Angelcynn*, those who were not under subjection to the Danes, submitted to him'. The word *Angelcynn* directly translates the Latin *gens Anglorum*, and although it is recorded in a Mercian charter of the 850s (S 207), it becomes common only at the end of the ninth century, when it appears in various vernacular texts associated with the Alfredian court or with the king's programme of educational reform, among them the Old English Bede. At the same time changing his royal style to describe himself as king of the Anglo-Saxons, or of the Angles and Saxons, Alfred promoted a label for his newly united people to signify that all his Germanic subjects belonged to one 'Englishkind' (cf. kingdom of the *Anglo-Saxons). The notion of one English people continued to have a currency in the tenth and eleventh centuries as West Saxon kings expanded their realm into the *Danelaw, frequently describing themselves as kings of the English together with other royal styles. Outsiders continued to see the Anglo-Saxons as one people, using Saxon and English as synonymous, except when distinguishing English from continental Saxons. *Cnut termed his subjects collectively the *gens Anglorum*, his realm *Engla lond*. The *gens Anglorum* still appeared one people not just to Cnut but to William the Conqueror, the referent of the word changing after each conquest to encompass first the Danish and then the Norman as well as the Germanic inhabitants of Britain.

P. Wormald, 'Bede, the *Bretwaldas* and the Origins of the *gens Anglorum*', in *Ideal and Reality in Frankish and Anglo-Saxon Society*, ed. P. Wormald *et al.* (Oxford, 1983), pp. 99–129; M. Richter, 'Bede's *Angli*: Angles or English?', *Peritia* 3 (1984), 99–114; S. Reynolds, 'What do we mean by Anglo-Saxon and the Anglo-Saxons?', *Journal of British Studies* 24 (1985), 395–414; S. Foot, 'The Making of *Angelcynn*: English Identity Before the Norman Conquest', *TRHS* 6th ser. 6 (1996), 25–49.

SARAH FOOT

ENIGMATA. As a genre, Anglo-Latin *enigmata* ('mysteries') are often equated with the Old English *riddles of the *Exeter Book, and frequently depict the same topics; indeed, two of the vernacular riddles are directly translated from Anglo-Latin *enigmata*. But, unlike their anonymous vernacular counterparts, the primary purpose of which seems in many cases to have been simple amusement, it is clear from their context that the majority of extant *enigmata*, composed in Latin verse by a handful of named authors, had a mainly educational role. So, for example, while the vernacular riddles customarily end with a challenge to say what the object depicted is called, the Latin *enigmata* very seldom do so. The earliest Anglo-Latin *enigmata* are those of *Aldhelm, who composed a hundred poems varying in length from four to eighty-three lines in imitation of the Late Latin poet Symposius

(whose name means something like 'party boy'), whose own collection of one-hundred poems of three lines each was supposedly produced extemporaneously by the poet in his cups for the amusement of fellow party-goers. The tone of Aldhelm's *enigmata* is quite different from that of his model, whose chosen topics well match their supposed setting. Aldhelm, by contrast, composes a series of closely observed *enigmata* on, for example, the natural world, daily life, church furniture, and the classroom. A bookish quality is evident in many of the other topics addressed, which would certainly have been outside the daily experience of Anglo-Saxon England, and Aldhelm claims to have composed his *enigmata* early on in his literary career, as scholarly illustrations of the principles of Latin versification. As such, Aldhelm's *enigmata* seem to have enjoyed a circulation as classroom texts, and were highly influential. *Boniface included copious echoes of Aldhelm's verse in his own *enigmata*, a series of ten poems on the Vices and ten on the Virtues produced for the moral instruction of an unnamed female correspondent, and similar verbal and thematic reminiscences link the associated collections of forty *enigmata* by *Tatwine and sixty by the otherwise unknown Eusebius sometimes identified with *Hwætberht, abbot of *Monkwearmouth-Jarrow. The combined total of one hundred *enigmata* by Tatwine and Eusebius, whose work is transmitted together in two surviving manuscripts, is identical to that of Aldhelm (and Symposius), but their chosen topics are highly idiosyncratic. Tatwine, who had himself composed a *grammar, includes a number of classroom subjects, alongside familiar everyday objects, church furniture, and an interesting selection of abstract topics: his first three *enigmata* are on 'philosophy', 'hope, faith, and charity', and 'historical, spiritual, moral, and allegorical sense'. By contrast, the first six *enigmata* of Eusebius appear to be arranged in a careful sequence ('God'; 'angel'; 'fallen angel'; 'man'; 'heaven'; 'earth') which rapidly deteriorates into a random collection of familiar classroom topics and suchlike, culminating in the final twenty *enigmata* in a bizarre gathering of outlandish creatures culled largely from the writings of Isidore of Seville. It is with such *enigmata* that we return in spirit to the exuberance of Symposius, and, in part, to that of the vernacular Old English riddles.

Variae Collectiones Aenigmatum Merovingicae Aetatis, ed. F. Glorie, CCSL 133–133A (Turnhout, 1968); M. L. Cameron, 'Aldhelm as Naturalist: a Re-examination of Some of His Enigmata', *Peritia* 4 (1985), 117–33; M. Lapidge, 'Introduction to the *Enigmata*', in *Aldhelm: the*

Poetic Works, ed. M. Lapidge and J. Rosier (Cambridge, 1985), pp. 61–9; C. Milovanović-Barham, 'Aldhelm's *Enigmata* and Byzantine Riddles', *ASE* 22 (1993), 51–64; F. H. Whitman, 'Aenigmata Tatwini', *Neuphilologische Mitteilungen* 88 (1987), 8–17.

ANDY ORCHARD

ENTERTAINMENT took a variety of forms in Anglo-Saxon England. Sport appears to have been very popular: horse-racing is mentioned in *Beowulf* (853–6) and in Bede's *Historia ecclesiastica* (v.6), and dog-racing (as enjoyed by the pre-Conquest monks of *Canterbury) by *William of Malmesbury. Swimming, ice-skating, hunting and falconry were also practised. In particular falconry and *hawking seem to have been favoured as a royal pastime: *Asser reports, for instance, that *Alfred employed falconers and hawkers, and *Æthelstan exacted birds of prey as tribute from Welsh rulers.

Less athletic pursuits included dice-games and chess, the latter arriving in England in the eleventh century. *Tæfl* (known in later centuries as 'tables') was a strategic board game played with counters; one side attacked a single 'king' piece while the other defended it. Playing-pieces for the game are found in Anglo-Saxon graves dating as far back as the fifth century, although those of the early centuries lack the 'king' figure.

Many of these amusements may have been enjoyed by children as well as adults, but some pastimes can be more precisely assigned to the young. Bede's *Life of Cuthbert* recounts an episode of children practising acrobatics, the youthful St *Cuthbert among them, and the *Colloquy* of *Ælfric Bata describes hoop-rolling. Excavations at *Winchester have also turned up leather balls and a whipping top.

Although the magnificence of Anglo-Saxon personal ornaments suggests that both men and women valued jewels and adornments, it is the *women who are credited with – and rebuked for – such love of fashion in the literature. Men, by contrast, seem to have developed boasting of heroic prowess into both competition and amusement. In literature such as *Beowulf* this boasting takes place at feasts, which also served as the setting for the telling of heroic stories.

Such stories were not always confined to secular feasts. *Alcuin's famous letter to 'Speratus', in 797, castigated the clergy for telling such stories at dinner: 'What has Ingeld', wrote Alcuin, 'to do with Christ?' Wherever it took place, the precise manner of such story-telling is uncertain: many tales were recounted in verse, accompanied by a harp, but the extent to which stories were also told in prose, or without accompaniment, is unclear.

*Music was also popular, and dancing is mentioned in various problematic contexts: one source describes women dancing in some sort of ceremony in a churchyard, another men dancing as part of their training as warriors. Finally, sources agree that the Anglo-Saxons habitually drank substantial quantities of beer, which may have sufficed to make everything that much more entertaining.

H. J. R. Murray, *A History of Board Games other than Chess* (Oxford, 1952; repr. New York, 1978); R. S. Oggins, 'Falconry in Anglo-Saxon England', *Mediaevalia* 7 (1984 for 1981), 174–20; N. Orme, *Early British Swimming, 55–1719* (Exeter, 1983); S. M. Youngs, 'The Gaming-Pieces', in R. Bruce-Mitford, *The Sutton Hoo Ship-Burial*, 3, i. and ii, ed. A. C. Evans (London, 1983), pp. 853–74.

MARTHA BAYLESS

EOSTERWINE (d. 686), sometime abbot of *Monkwearmouth. His life is known principally from the anonymous *Vita S. Ceolfrithi* and from *Bede's *Historia abbatum* (he is not mentioned in the *HE*). From these sources we learn that Eosterwine was a nobleman who had fought in the armies of King Ecgfrith, but who at the age of 24 decided to become a monk of Monkwearmouth, shortly after its foundation by *Benedict Biscop in 673 or 674 (from which it can be calculated that Eosterwine was born *c*.650). He was ordained priest in 679, and appointed abbot in 682 to rule the monastery in Benedict's absence(s). In spite of his noble origins, he was apparently a man of great humility who involved himself enthusiastically in the menial activities of the monastery. He died of the plague in 686.

Bede, *Historia abbatum*, cc. 7–8 (Plummer, *VBOH* i.370–3); Anon., *Vita S. Ceolfridi*, cc. 12–13 (Plummer, *VBOH* i.392).

MICHAEL LAPIDGE

EPISCOPAL LISTS. Lists of bishops of the various sees in the provinces of *Canterbury and *York. It would appear that the lists were compiled in the first instance as a single collection, based in part on whatever imperfect records were available at the place of compilation, and in part on whatever could be learnt from 'local' enquiry. The collection as a whole should thus be understood as the product of an exercise in 'historical' reconstruction, representing a particular conception of the political and ecclesiastical orders. It probably originated in the late eighth or early ninth century, symbolising an awareness of the sense of collective identity fostered and promoted at the church councils which met regularly during this period (see church *councils, and *Clofesho). Episcopal lists bear comparison in certain respects with royal *genealogies and regnal lists; for they can be tendentious, and are by no means necessarily authoritative or complete.

The collection exists in several manuscripts, ranging in date from the early ninth to the early twelfth century; and it is arguable that the manuscripts represent successive stages in the development of the collection as an ecclesiastical record. In its original form (represented by the lists in BL, Cotton Vespasian B.vi, fols. 108–9, written in the first quarter of the ninth century), the collection comprised episcopal lists for the sees of *Canterbury, *Rochester, the East Saxons (*London), the South Saxons (*Selsey), and the West Saxons (initially at *Dorchester, then at *Winchester and *Sherborne), followed by lists for the sees of the East Angles (*Elmham and Dunwich), the 'provinces' of the Mercians (at *Lichfield, then at *Leicester and Lichfield), the men of *Lindsey, the Hwicce (*Worcester), and the 'Uestor E [. . .]' (*Hereford), and ending with the Northumbrians (initially at *York or *Lindisfarne, then at York and *Hexham), Lindisfarne, and Casa Candida (*Whithorn). It would appear that the collection was revised during the reign of King *Æthelstan, probably c.930. The lists for Canterbury and for the West Saxon sees were brought up to date, in order to accommodate the division of the see of Winchester into two (Winchester and Ramsbury) and of the see of Sherborne into three (Sherborne, *Wells, and Crediton). Moreover, significant adjustments were made to the order in which the lists are given: the two East Anglian sees were relegated to a lower position; Worcester was promoted ahead of the two 'Mercian' sees; Hereford was promoted ahead of Lindsey; and the Northumbrian sees were left unchanged. This revised form of the collection is represented by the lists in Cambridge, Corpus Christi College 183, fols. 61–4, forming part of a manuscript commissioned by King Æthelstan in the early 930s and presented by him to the see of St *Cuthbert at Chester-le-Street. The collection was revised as it were for a second time during the archiepiscopate of *Dunstan (959–88), probably in the mid-980s. The compiler of this version retained the modified order of the lists, and attempted to bring rather more of them up to date, on the basis of whatever (generally imperfect) information was available at the place of compilation (presumably at Canterbury). Most interestingly, he introduced certain refinements in

the process, for example by naming *Wilfrid as the first bishop of the South Saxons, and by 'suppressing' several tenth-century bishops (including Ælfsige and Brihthelm between *Oda and *Dunstan in the list for Canterbury, Dunstan himself in the list for London, Brihthelm in the list for Selsey, and Bishop *Æthelwold's immediate predecessor Brihthelm in the list for Winchester); he seems at the same time to have misunderstood the nature of the division of the West Saxon sees in the early tenth century. This revised form of the collection is best represented by the lists in BL, Cotton Tiberius B. v, fols. 21–2 (written in the second quarter of the eleventh century), and by the lists in the Textus Roffensis, 110v–116r (written in the early twelfth century). It also lies behind an 'edited' version of the collection, which probably originated at Winchester in the 990s, in which the range of sees was restricted to Canterbury, Rochester, London, Selsey, Winchester, Sherborne, Ramsbury, and Crediton, omitting Wells, with some alterations to the lists themselves (e.g. the insertion of additional names for London and Selsey, to cover the early tenth century). The 'Winchester' collection is found in Cambridge, Corpus Christi College 173 (the Parker Chronicle and Laws), fol. 55; it was copied thence in BL, Cotton Otho B. xi (damaged in the Cotton fire, but known from seventeenth- and early-eighteenth-century descriptions), with additions; and it recurs in BL Stowe 944 (the 'Liber Vitae' of the New Minster, Winchester, written in 1031), 14v–17r, with the necessary addition of an independent list for the see of *Wells. The version of the whole collection added c.1100, probably at *Bath, in Cambridge, Corpus Christi College, 140, fol. 115, is basically a development of the revised form of the collection seen in Tiberius B. v and the Textus Roffensis; but the material has been drastically rearranged, an independent list for Wells has been added, and Brihthelm has been inserted in the list for Winchester. It is the case, in general, that within this pattern of development each surviving manuscript containing a collection of episcopal lists has errors, alterations, and additions peculiar to itself.

The collections of episcopal lists are naturally of the greatest value for reconstructing the details of episcopal succession during the Anglo-Saxon period, taking their place in this process beside the evidence of *charters, episcopal professions, chronicles, and the various products of *liturgical commemoration. *John of Worcester and *William of Malmesbury were among the first historians to use versions of the collection for their own purposes. Certain sees, notably those of St Cuthbert (at Chester-le-Street and Durham) and of *Cornwall, are not represented; and bishops who operated at a level lower than that of the main diocesan structure, and who are sometimes found attesting charters, are not covered.

R. I. Page, 'Anglo-Saxon Episcopal Lists, Parts I and II', and 'Anglo-Saxon Episcopal Lists, Part III', *Nottingham Medieval Studies* 9 (1965), 71–95, and 10 (1966), 2–24; S. Keynes, 'Episcopal Succession in Anglo-Saxon England', *Handbook of British Chronology*, 3rd ed., ed. E. B. Fryde *et al.* (London, 1986), pp. 209–24; *The Liber Vitae of the New Minster and Hyde Abbey, Winchester*, ed. S. Keynes, EEMF 26 (Copenhagen, 1996), 84–6.

SIMON KEYNES

ERIC BLOODAXE (Eiríkr Blóðøx), son of Harald Fairhair, was the last of the Scandinavian kings of *York. Driven out of Norway, Eric became king of York in 947. King *Eadred, to whom the northerners had already sworn allegiance, invaded in 948 and resumed control. Eric returned in 952, and Eadred retaliated by imprisoning Archbishop Wulfstan of York. Two types of silver penny for Eric survive, perhaps corresponding with his two reigns. In 954 the Northumbrians finally concluded that their interests lay with the southern English, not the Scandinavians: Eric was driven out and killed. The poem *Höfuðlausn* ('Head-Ransom'), in praise of Eric, was composed by the Icelander Egill Skallagrímsson when he met the king at York, as an alternative to decapitation. Another poem, *Eiríksmál*, describes Eric's entry into Valhalla. Eric's byname 'Bloodaxe' is recorded in Norse sagas, e.g. *Heimskringla* and *Egils Saga*.

A. P. Smyth, *Scandinavian York and Dublin*, 2 vols. (Dublin, 1975–9), ii. 155–90; P. Sawyer, 'The Last Scandinavian Kings of York', *NH* 31 (1995), 39–44.

SEAN MILLER

ESCOMB church (co. Durham) is the best preserved of the seventh- and eighth-century Northumbrian churches. It now consists of a very tall, narrow nave with a chancel or east *porticus*; further *porticus* to the west and north, now demolished but known from excavations, were added shortly afterwards. The fabric, including the entire chancel arch, consists of massive Roman masonry carefully re-used. Excavations have identified a curvilinear enclosure surrounding the church.

Taylor and Taylor, *AS Arch* i. 234–8; Fernie, *Architecture*, pp. 53–6; M. Pocock and H. Wheeler, 'Excavations at Escomb Church, County Durham, 1968', *JBAA* 3rd ser. 34 (1971), 11–29; B. H. Gill, 'Excavations at St John, Escomb, County Durham', *Universities of Durham and Newcastle-upon-Tyne Archaeological Reports* 3 (1979), 15–16.

JOHN BLAIR

ESSEX, kingdom of, was one of the middle-sized kingdoms of early Anglo-Saxon England which was rated in the *Tribal Hidage at 7000 hides. The county of Essex formed the core of the kingdom, but in the seventh century the East Saxon kings also controlled the province of the *Middle Saxons which included *London, described by *Bede as the East Saxon *metropolis*. The East Saxon bishopric was founded there, at St Paul's within the Roman walled town, during the reign of Sæbert in 604. The East Saxon kings also had interests south of the Thames in the seventh century. Ambitions to control Surrey brought them into conflict with the West Saxons which resulted in the deaths of Sæbert's three sons, who had succeeded him, in battle, and in a series of disputes between the two kingdoms in the later seventh century which were resolved at a meeting at Brentford in 704/5. Swæfheard, son of King Sæbbi (d. 693/4), ruled as king of part of *Kent from 687/8 until his expulsion by King Wihtred, sometime between 692 and 694.

The East Saxon royal house claimed descent from Seaxnet, the tribal god of the Old Saxons, and its kings were remarkably consistent in bearing names that alliterated with the letter 'S'. Sledd, the father of Sæbert, appears to have been the founder of the *dynasty, as he was the common ancestor from whom all other rulers claimed descent in the three surviving East Saxon *genealogies. No East Saxon regnal lists survive, and these would have been difficult to compile, as joint kingship appears to have been the norm. There are instances of brothers ruling together and fathers with sons, but also of quite distant cousins. No one branch of the house seems to have been able to dominate the kingship for more than two reigns in succession. Some of the joint kings may have been subkings, like Swæfheard in Kent, ruling areas subject to East Saxon overlordship.

The East Saxons themselves were often subject to the overlordship of other more powerful rulers who tried to use *conversion to Christianity as one of their means of control. Sæbert was converted at the court of his uncle, *Æthelbert of Kent, who was regarded as the main founder of St Paul's. The first bishop of *London, the Italian *Mellitus, was ejected by Sæbert's sons as part of their rejection of Kentish political authority. King Sigebert 'Sanctus' was converted at the court of the powerful Northumbrian king *Oswiu in *c.*653, which led to the Irish-trained Cedd becoming the second bishop of the East Saxons. Sigebert was murdered by two kinsmen who apparently objected to him forgiving his enemies in accordance with Christian doctrine. His successor Swithhelm was baptised at the East Anglian court. There was one further period of temporary rejection of Christianity when Sigehere and his section of the people apostatised at the time of the great plague of 663/4. *Wulfhere of Mercia saw this as a challenge to his overlordship and the Mercian bishop Jaruman was sent to oversee reconversion.

The Mercians became increasingly interested in control of *London, an important trading centre in the seventh century, as recent excavations in the Strand and Covent Garden have shown. During the reign of *Æthelbald of Mercia (716–57), London and the Middle Saxons were detached from East Saxon control and became Mercian dependencies, though the East Saxon rulers remained autonomous in Essex and issued their own coinage. Although a succession of kings can be traced, East Saxon affairs become increasingly obscure at the end of the eighth and beginning of the ninth century. In 825 when Mercian supremacy gave way to West Saxon, *Ecgberht of Wessex expelled the ruler of the East Saxons (probably Sigered) and the province became a West Saxon dependency, administered as part of a West Saxon subkingdom, and subsequently an ealdormanry, based on Kent. However, an East Saxon king, Sigeric II, was recognised in Mercia after this date though nothing can be said about the basis of his power.

B. A. E. Yorke, 'The Kingdom of the East Saxons', *ASE* 14 (1985), 1–36; K. Bailey, 'East Saxon Kings – Some Further Observations', *Essex Journal* 23 (1988), 34–40; D. N. Dumville, 'Essex, Middle Anglia and the Expansion of Mercia in the South-East Midlands', in Bassett, *Origins*, pp. 123–40; C. Hart, 'The Ealdordom of Essex' in his *The Danelaw* (London, 1992), pp. 115–40.

B. A. E. YORKE

ESTATE MANAGEMENT. Early estate management consisted of the collection and enforcement of rights and obligations rather than a direct intervention in the rural economy. The supply systems of kings and major nobility were based on their travelling to places at which supplies were assembled for their consumption (see *feorm*). Royal circuits covered kingdoms: elements of the same arrangements on a lesser scale appear in the type of major aristocratic landholding known as the 'multiple', 'federated' or 'complex' estate. Its essential features were a centre or centres, outlying settlements from which rents in kind were due, and rights over natural resources such as *woodland and pasture.

Over time landowners developed at the centre of their estates an intensively managed portion to provide them with a reliable supply of essential foods and materials (see *manors and manorial lordship). This was the 'inland' ('inner estate'). Multiple estates had several inlands, which we encounter as berewicks, often with specialised supply or husbandry functions such as the supply of honey or timber. Within their inlands monastic – perhaps also major lay – estates developed bartons, central 'home farms'. It is probable that this direct management considerably increased productivity. We know from their reading that some educated religious were interested in the classical theory and practice of estate management. A handful of texts from late Anglo-Saxon England shows an interest in efficient management on two large ecclesiastical estates: we know virtually nothing about how lesser landlords ran theirs. (Anglo-Saxon England apparently lacked the elaborate estate surveys of Carolingian France known as *polyptyques*: at least, none has survived.) *Rectitudines singularum personarum*, possibly of the tenth century, a custumal of the year 900 relating to Hurstbourne Priors (Hants.) and a survey with custumal for Tidenham (Gloucs.) of the late tenth to eleventh century show estate centres with a specialised workforce given food allowances and plots of land. Slaves worked as ploughmen, stockmen, dairy workers, probably also textile workers and smiths. Dependent peasants worked holdings which may have been interspersed with the lord's own arable; their rent mainly consisted of agricultural work, especially ploughing, and renders of essential supplies. We should not rule out the possibility of wage labourers and seasonal workers paid by the day or the job.

The OE term *gerefa* (*reeve) may have covered a considerable range of officials. The great estate would have needed both steward and treasurer: some such official must have drawn up the *Ely 'farming memoranda' which record the deployment of stock and personnel on the newly founded Thorney and Ely abbeys. A large estate entailed a deal of litigation and major landlords could be represented in the public courts by their reeves. A group of higher status 'riding-men' supervised droves and carried money and messages. Local reeves and bailiffs, sometimes rewarded with grants of land, ran the inlands of smaller bookland estates.

Of the two options open to the major landowner, to lease out land or to exploit it directly, leasing seems to have been the rule rather than the exception. Leases of the lands of the major ecclesiastical landlords, the bishops of *Worcester's being an exceptional survival rather than an exception, show leaseholds ranged from large properties to single hides. The figures for 'what it is worth and how much more could be got for it' which William required to be given for each place entered in *Domesday Book are likely to have been, or to be directly related to, its leasable value. Land was leased stocked with the ploughteams, workers and livestock needed for the home farm, and the appropriate number of each was known for each property. It is this information, whether recorded in writing or simply a matter of local knowledge, which enabled the compilers of Little Domesday, which covers *East Anglia, and Exon Domesday, which covers the West Country, to record the manorial livestock at each vill.

Most Anglo-Saxon leases were for two or more lives, and there was a tension between landlords, who wanted to retain control over their property, and lessees who wanted to establish a permanent hold on it for their family. Some gifts to the church took the form of emphyteutic leases by which the donor gave land to the church and received it back on lease, intending to secure the permanent transfer of the property at the end of the lease. Others were in effect mortgages, the lessor receiving a large sum of cash down for a lease and a set sum or renders in kind each year. Leasing was a routine way of holding land at all levels of society, not seen as inferior to outright ownership. By the early twelfth century leases for lives were treated in some judicial repects as a kind of freehold.

R. J. Faith, *The English Peasantry and the Growth of Lordship* (London, 1997); S. P. J. Harvey, 'Domesday England', in *The Agrarian History of England and Wales* II. *1042–c.1350*, ed. H. E. Hallam (Cambridge, 1988), pp. 45–136; V. King, 'St Oswald's Tenants', in *Oswald of Worcester*, pp. 100–16; R. V. Lennard, *Rural England 1086–1135: a Study of Social and Agrarian Conditions* (Oxford, 1959), pp. 105–212; P. D. A. Harvey, 'Rectitudines Singularum Personarum and Gerefa', *EHR* 108 (1993), 1–22.

ROSAMOND FAITH

EXCOMMUNICATION is the harshest penalty the church can impose upon sinners, resulting in the sinners' ostracism from the church and inability to participate in Communion. Evidence for *crimes punishable by excommunication during the Anglo-Saxon period comes from the *laws and *homilies. Such crimes include incest, and the killing of a priest. In addition, a number of contemporary Latin excommunication texts are extant and a unique Old English formula survives in a twelfth-century copy. There is, however, little documentation to indicate how often the penalty was used or how effective a punishment it might have been.

E. M. Treharne, 'A Unique Formula for Excommunication from Cambridge, Corpus Christi College 303', *ASE* 24 (1995), 185–211.

ELAINE M. TREHARNE

EXEGESIS, the interpretation of the Bible, was the higher education in Anglo-Saxon England from the late seventh century onward. It presupposed at least elementary training in reading (see *schools) and *grammar and its *scientia interpretandi*; it subsumed intermediate ecclesiastical disciplines like *liturgy and *computus. Yet for most students it seems to have consisted mainly not of direct explication, but of reading and excerpting the standard Latin commentators (Augustine, Ambrose, Augustine, *Gregory the Great, Isidore). By the mid eighth century it was widely thought that these *auctores catholici* included England's own *Bede (d. 735).

Bede is the one Anglo-Latin author who has left a substantial corpus of biblical commentary; he was not, however, the first Insular author who attempted systematic biblical exegesis. In the sixth and seventh centuries, the Irish produced a substantial corpus of biblical commentary, some of which may be presumed to have reached *Northumbria through the agency of Irish scholars such as *Aidan and *Adomnán. (The evidence for the influence of Irish exegesis on Northumbrian biblical studies is, however, tenuous, and depends on the identification of Hiberno–Latin texts which were certainly known to Anglo-Saxon authors; one such text, which was quoted by Bede in his *De natura rerum*, is the pseudo-Isidorian *Liber de ordine creaturarum*, and others no doubt await detection.) The apogee of biblical scholarship in Anglo-Saxon England was attained at the *Canterbury school of Archbishop *Theodore and Abbot *Hadrian in the late seventh century. Both of these scholars had been trained in Mediterranean schools; in the case of Theodore, it is demonstrable that he had studied in the schools of Antioch (and hence had absorbed the methods and techniques of Antiochene – that is, literal and philological – exegesis) and Edessa, where Syrian commentators, like their Antiochene masters, expounded the Bible in a literal manner. The corpus of biblical commentaries which has survived from the school of Canterbury shows that Theodore and Hadrian expounded the sacred text by means of constant repair to the text of the Septuagint and Greek New Testament (the comparison of variant versions of the sacred text was a characteristic technique of Antiochene exegesis), as well as to scientific disciplines such as grammar, rhetoric, *medicine, philosophy, metrology and chronology. The number of Greek patristic authorities laid under contribution in the Canterbury commentaries is astounding for a western text, and includes such authors as John Chrysostom, Basil of Caesarea, Epiphanius, Clement of Alexandria, Cosmas Indicopleustes, and others who were not studied again in the West before the Renaissance. The encyclopedic reading of Theodore and Hadrian gave a distinctive stamp to the exegesis produced at their Canterbury school; but, given the unusual circumstances of their advent in England, was unfortunately inimitable.

It fell to Bede to produce a corpus of biblical exegesis, particularly on those books of the Bible which were seldom commented on, for the guidance of his students. The success of Bede's exegesis was no doubt largely due to the industry and intelligence with which he selected and adapted patristic materials. In an autobiographical summary, Bede relates that he spent twenty-nine years making 'brief extracts from the works of the venerable Fathers on the Holy Scriptures', and adding 'notes of my own to clarify their sense and meaning'. This is the most important statement of his exegetical method, and it does not reflect a programme of passive copying. In some cases Bede's version of a patristic passage is clearer and more pointed than the original, and he used nothing without first understanding it. Hence his more than twenty commentaries are in no sense a mere patchwork of quoted authorities. If he preferred the thoughts and even the words of the Fathers, his own pastoral care and Latin scholarship impart purpose and shape to every work. In a few places he respectfully criticized his sources, even Jerome. More than half his biblical writings treat the Old Testament through typological and moral exegesis; the most scholarly and original of his expository works, the *Retractatio in Actus Apostolorum*, keeps to the letter, which he read in both Latin and Greek. In addition to the commentaries, he wrote fifty homilies on the Gospels, a book on biblical topography, and a grammatical treatise, *De schematibus et tropis*, which was intended as a manual for exegetes. This last book provided the definitive early medieval formulation of the patristic theory of the multiple sense of Scripture: literal, typological, moral, mystical. Bede himself practised only the first three, and never used the fourfold schema in a programmatic way.

After Bede, *Alcuin of York produced a corpus of exegetical works, all of them during his years on the Continent. The tenth century monastic reform movement prompted some biblical homilies in Old English (notably those of *Ælfric), but no biblical exegete of any standing who wrote in Latin.

B. Bischoff, 'Wendepunke in der Geschichte der lateinischen Exegese im Frühmittelalter', in his *Mittelalterliche Studien*, 3 vols. (Stuttgart, 1966–81), i.205–73; B. Bischoff and M. Lapidge, *Biblical Commentaries from the Canterbury School of Theodore and Hadrian*, CSASE 10 (Cambridge, 1994); M. T. A. Carroll, *The Venerable Bede: his Spiritual Teaching* (Washington, DC, 1946); R. Ray, 'What do we know about Bede's Commentaries', *Recherches de théologie ancienne et médiévale* 49 (1982), 5–20.

ROGER RAY

EXETER (Devon), the former Roman city of *Isca Dumnoniorum*, contained a minster by the end of the seventh century when St *Boniface was educated there. Evidently this survived two centuries later, for King *Alfred gave 'Exeter with all the *parochia* pertaining to it in Saxon territory and in *Cornwall' to *Asser. Exeter was occupied by the Danish army in 877, and occurs in the *Burghal Hidage with an assessment of 734 hides; the borough, with a new street-plan but re-using the Roman walls, had developed by 1086 into a substantial town with several churches. The minster was re-founded as a Benedictine monastery in 968, but was burnt in the early eleventh century. It continued as an impoverished community until 1050, when *Leofric established his new cathedral there, founded a chapter of strict-living *cathedral canons, and endowed it richly with ornaments and books including the *Exeter Book. The cathedral complex probably contained churches of St Peter and St Mary; excavation has revealed the tenth- or eleventh-century western church (St Mary), overlying a mid-Saxon and possibly sub-Roman cemetery.

C. G. Henderson and P. T. Bidwell, 'The Saxon Minster at Exeter', in S. M. Pearce, ed., *The Early Church in West Britain and Ireland* (Oxford, 1982), pp. 145–76; J. Allan, C. Henderson and R. Higham, 'Saxon Exeter', in Haslam, *Towns*, pp. 385–414; P. W. Conner, *Anglo-Saxon Exeter: a Tenth-Century Cultural History* (Woodbridge, 1993); F. Barlow *et al.*, *Leofric of Exeter* (Exeter, 1972); R. Gameson, 'The Origin of the Exeter Book of Old English Poetry', *ASE* 25 (1996), 135–85; J.R. Maddicott, 'Trade, Industry and the Wealth of King Alfred', *P&P* 123 (1989), 3–51.

JOHN BLAIR

EXETER BOOK. The Exeter Book is the name

given to an anthology of religious and secular vernacular poetry, Exeter, Cathedral Library, 3501,
fols. 8–130, a large handsome manuscript, without
any illustrations, from the middle of the second
half of the tenth century (*c*.975), written
throughout by a single hand which has been identified in two other books in Latin: London,
Lambeth Palace Library, 149, fols. 1–139, and
Oxford, Bodleian Library, Bodley 319. It is very
unlikely that these books were produced in *Exeter
itself, although the precise place of origin has yet
to be identified. The best that can be said is that
the Exeter Book originated somewhere in the south
of England.

The book is defective at the beginning, and
lacks a quire or quires after the present Quire 6
and single leaves at various points throughout the
codex. Because of the loss of leaves, there has been
some critical debate about the internal consistency
of a number of the poems, e.g. *Resignation*, the
Physiologus and some of the *riddles. The
linguistic uniformity of the collection (in contrast
to that of the other poetic codices) suggests that
someone (perhaps the anthologist or perhaps a
later copyist) imposed his own forms on the
material he collected. Since there is evidence that
the latest scribe was mechanical, it is likely that he
was producing a fair copy of an anthology already
in existence, rather than creating an original collection. A recently expressed view that the book
consists of three 'booklets', now disordered, has
not found favour.

It is clear that someone has ordered the items
in the collection, at least in part, for the pieces are
far from random. The first eight that survive
are longer poems, the rest shorter. The first three,
Advent Lyrics, *Cynewulf's Ascension* and *Christ
III*, which are by different authors, appear to have
been put together deliberately since they form a
sequence related to the birth, death and second
coming of Christ, and these are followed by two
poems on St *Guthlac, again of different authorship. Other religious poems follow, *Azarias* (which
parallels part of *Daniel* in the *Junius
Manuscript), the *Phoenix*, and a second signed
poem by Cynewulf, *Juliana*. Amongst the shorter
poems are the somewhat amorphous group known
as the *elegies, which the anthologist seems not
to have distinguished from other moralising and
homiletic verse in the second half of the book,
including poems such as the *Gifts of Men*, *Vainglory*, the *Fortunes of Men*, the *Order of the World*,
Resignation and the *Descent into Hell*. The
anthology also contains secular verse in the form
of the 'minstrel' poems *Widsith* and *Deor*, the
varied collection of *gnomic poetry known as
Maxims, and two large collections of *riddles.

The book is most probably to be identified with
an item in an inventory of books given to Exeter
cathedral by Bishop *Leofric some time before his
death in 1072. Two copies of the inventory survive,
both roughly contemporary with the bequest, one
of them now on the quire which opens the Exeter
Book itself where they were added only after 1566
when the manuscript to which they properly
belonged, a gospelbook (now Cambridge, University Library, Ii.4.6), was given by the Exeter Dean
and Chapter to Archbishop *Parker. The item
involved reads: 'i. mycel englisc boc be gehwilcum
þingum on leoðwisan geworht' ('one large book in
English concerning various subjects composed
in the form of verse'). We have no idea where
Leofric might have obtained the book, or why he
should have felt it appropriate to include it in his
list of donations to the regular canons at his newly
created see of Exeter. Many of Leofric's gifts can
still be identified with reasonable certainty, but the
Exeter Book is the only one which has remained
at Exeter. Recognition of its importance to Old
English studies came late. Although Laurence
*Nowell wrote an interlinear gloss to a few lines
in the sixteenth century, and *Wanley included
it in his Catalogue, modern study of the codex
and publication of its contents did not begin until
the early nineteenth century.

The Exeter Book of Old English Poetry, ed. R. W. Chambers, M. Förster and R. Flower (London, 1933); K.
Sisam, 'The Exeter Book', in his *Studies in the History
of Old English Literature* (Oxford, 1953), pp. 97–108; P.
W. Conner, *Anglo-Saxon Exeter: a Tenth-Century Cultural History* (Woodbridge, 1993); *The Exeter Anthology
of Old English Poetry*, ed. B. J. Muir, 2 vols. (Exeter,
1994); R. Gameson, 'The Origin of the Exeter Book of
Old English Poetry', *ASE* 25 (1996), 135–85.

DONALD SCRAGG

EXHORTATION TO CHRISTIAN LIVING,
an 82-line poem found in Corpus Christi College,
Cambridge, 201, is a call to the poverty, abstinence,
and prayer that were the hallmark of medieval
monastic discipline. Stylistically the poem stands
midway between the distinctive voice of Old
English *wisdom literature and that of the prose
*homilies, one of which, Vercelli homily XXI,
actually incorporates part of it. In its opening
line the poet proclaims his intention of giving
instruction to his audience, in the manner of the
conventional wise elder found in *wisdom literature, but he does so 'as one should instruct a
beloved friend', a phrase that echoes the homilist's
most common term of address, 'most beloved

men'. The poet's summing up, from line 55b, contains elements common to the Old English *elegies, emphasising the transitory and unpredictable nature of life on earth (lines 56–64) and the importance of taking thought for one's soul at dawn (lines 69–74a), a traditional time for mournful reflection in the elegies, but here given a more hopeful complexion as a moment of opportunity during which one can open the way to the eternal kingdom. Recently it has been suggested that *Exhortation* and the piece which precedes it in the manuscript, *A Summons to Prayer*, are actually part of a single poem.
ASPR vi.67–9; L. Whitbread, 'Notes on the Old English *Exhortation to Christian Living*', *Studia Neophilologica* 23 (1951), 96–102; idem, 'Notes on Two Minor Old English Poems', *Studia Neophilologica* 29 (1957), 123–9; F. C. Robinson, ' "The Rewards of Piety": Two Old English Poems in their Manuscript Context', *Hermeneutics and Medieval Culture*, ed. P. J. Gallacher and H. Damico (Albany, NY, 1989), pp. 193–200; *The Vercelli Homilies and Related Texts*, ed. D. G. Scragg, EETS 300 (Oxford, 1992).

ROBERT DINAPOLI

EXODUS, the second poem in the *Junius Manuscript and the most selective of the Old Testament biblical poems in Old English, concentrates on the departure of the Israelites from Egypt, the trek to the Red Sea, the crossing of the Red Sea by the Israelites, and the drowning of the pursuing Egyptian host. Although its main narrative thread corresponds to Exodus XIII.20 to XIV.31, a mere one and a half chapters from the biblical book, the poem also shows a familiarity with the Bible as a whole, especially Genesis, Numbers, Psalms and Wisdom. Moreover, in its treatment of biblical narrative it goes beyond what is in the text of the Bible, and reflects a knowledge of biblical *exegesis, calling for interpretation according to the Spirit as well as the Letter (523–6). Through the word *lifweg* 'life-way' (104) the exodus is equated with the journey of Christians ('without a homeland' 534) through life. On this journey, which is seen as a sea-voyage (106), Christians travel aboard the Ship of the Church with its mast and sailyard which was the Cross (80–3). The pillar of cloud and fire is equated with the Holy Spirit (96, 104a). That the Crossing of the Red Sea is to be identified with Baptism is clearly implied in lines 310–46, just as the Drowning of the Egyptians, so it is implied, is to be taken as foreshadowing the Day of Judgement for the wicked (447–515). Pharaoh is cast as the devil, Moses as a type of Christ. These exegetical ideas are referred to from time to time in the poem

and are momentarily brought to the fore, but they never become dominant overall.

Exodus also reflects the *liturgy, specifically that for Holy Saturday. Lines 113b–15a correspond closely to the wording of a statement in the *Exultet* of the Paschal Vigil, and the treatment of the fire-pillar, especially the reference to it as 'heaven-candle' (115), probably reflects the use of the Latin word *columna* with dual meaning (fire-pillar/Paschal Candle) in the Holy Saturday service.

Not only is *Exodus* rich in allusion, it is also rich in poetic quality. There is a remarkable variety of style, showing good control of tempo and of temporal and visual focus. Many passages show an allusive condensation of meaning, none more so than that describing the pillar of cloud and fire (71–97), and the poem displays a rare ability to fuse distinct concepts poetically, such as animate and inanimate, concrete and abstract. In its use of metaphor the poem is outstanding, and it has the highest proportion of different compounds per line of any of the longer OE poems.
ASPR i.91–107; *Exodus*, ed. P. J. Lucas (London, 1977); *The Old English Exodus. Text, Translation and Commentary by J. R. R. Tolkien*, ed. J. Turville-Petre (Oxford, 1981); P. G. Remley, *Old English Biblical Verse*, CSASE 16 (Cambridge, 1996), 168–230.

P. J. LUCAS

EXORCISM, the casting out of demons by the saying of a specific holy command, is relatively well-documented in the Anglo-Saxon period. The formulas for exorcism survive in a number of different forms in both Old English and Latin, and are contained in manuscripts which include other liturgical materials; the various Old English exorcism texts are found in a missal (Cambridge, Corpus Christi College 422), a *collectar (Durham, Cathedral Library, A.iv.19), and in two *pontificals (Cambridge, Corpus Christi College 146 and BL, Cotton Vitellius A.vii), all of which are datable to the eleventh century. Exorcism appears to have been used during the church service when incense, oil, and salt were cleansed of all evil spirits, for example. Exorcism was also used to free those possessed from evil spirits of these demons, and to cleanse the Holy Sacrament, or the water, or fire, or iron traditionally used in the *ordeals of God (the *Iudicium Dei*) before the ordeal actually took place. In addition to the formulas for exorcism, the practice of casting out of demons from possessed victims is exemplified in the Old English translations of the gospels, and a number of homilies and saints' lives.

Liebermann, *Gesetze*, i.401–29; Ker, *Catalogue*; *The Canterbury Benedictional (British Museum, Harl. MS. 2892)*, ed. R. M. Woolley, HBS 57 (London, 1917).

ELAINE M. TREHARNE

EXPECTATION OF LIFE: *see* Diseases

EYNSHAM (Oxon.) lies amid a concentration of early Anglo-Saxon settlement sites on the river-gravels of the upper Thames. In the *Anglo-Saxon Chronicle* for '571' it is named as one of four *tunas* captured by the *Gewisse* from the British, and although this is essentially unhistorical, it suggests that Eynsham was remembered in the ninth century as an ancient place of importance. In the 820s it occurs as the centre of a 300-hide estate, almost certainly monastic since a land-owning church at Eynsham is mentioned in a charter of 864. In 1005 the minster was re-founded by Ealdorman Æthelmær as a Benedictine abbey, with *Ælfric as its first abbot; an abbot and community still existed in the 1050s, but by the time of *Domesday Book the minster seems to have been secularised. Excavations on the site have revealed a complex sequence: a Bronze Age enclosed settlement; early Anglo-Saxon sunken-floored buildings; eighth-century timber buildings, presumably from the early minster; and the stone claustral ranges of Æthelmær's abbey. The small medieval town of Eynsham grew up at the abbey's gate.

Blair, *AS Oxon.*; A Hardy, A. Dodd and G. Keevill, *Excavations at Eynsham Abbey, 1990–2* (Oxford, forthcoming).

JOHN BLAIR

F

FARMING: *see* Agriculture; Animal Husbandry; Field-Systems; Peasants

FATES OF THE APOSTLES: *see* Cynewulf

FELIX (fl. 713 × 749), author of the *Vita S. Guthlaci* (*BHL* 3723), an account of the hermit *Guthlac of Crowland, a work which was commissioned by Ælfwald, king of the *East Angles (713–49). Nothing is known of Felix's life: though his name could be a calque on an English name with the theme *Ead-*, or could be a name taken in baptism, it is not certain that Felix was English (in c. 10 he gives the etymology of Guthlac's name hesitantly as what 'those who are familiar with that people [= the English]' say, implying that he was not himself English (cf. the bishop of East Anglia named Felix who, as Bede reports [*HE* ii.15], was of Burgundian origin). Whatever his origins, however, he was thoroughly familiar with the writings of *Aldhelm, and fashioned an elegant and flamboyant life of the hermit saint from his familiarity with the Latin translation of Athanasius's Life of St Antony, as well as with the Life of St *Fursa. The fact that he also quotes from Bede's prose *Vita S. Cuthberti* implies that his Life of Guthlac was composed after *c.*720. Given his literary accomplishment, it is a pity that nothing is known of the centre in which he wrote or the school in which he was trained.

Sharpe, *Handlist*, 296; *Felix's Life of St Guthlac*, ed. B. Colgrave (Cambridge, 1956); Bolton, *ALL* pp. 223–7; B. Kurtz, 'From St Antony to St Guthlac', *University of California Publications in Modern Philology* 12 (1926), 103–46; M. Schütt, 'Vom hl. Antonius zum hl. Guthlac', *Antike und Abendland* 5 (1956), 75–91.

MICHAEL LAPIDGE

FEORM ('renders in kind'). The provisioning of Anglo-Saxon kings is the system of which we have most evidence, but it is likely that in early Anglo-Saxon England dominant figures of all kinds were supported by levies of food and other goods from the inhabitants of the land over which they had control. The king's supplies were delivered to royal vills, which he and his entourage visited on circuit. The assignment of an area to the support of a particular royal vill was at the root of the formation of the *hundred, a unit notionally of a hundred *hides. *Ine's laws show that the kings of *Wessex had, at least in theory, regularised this system to the extent of laying down what was to be delivered at the royal vill from every ten hides: '10 vats of honey, 300 loaves, 12 ambers of Welsh ale, 30 ambers of clear ale, 2 full grown cows or 10 wethers, 10 geese, 20 hens, 10 cheeses, a full amber of butter, 5 salmon, 20 pounds in weight of fodder and 100 eels'. This seems to represent the full range of an upper-class diet (although pork and game are missing and there must have been many local variations). Grazing was probably also made available for the royal party's mounts. At ground level, so to speak, we learn from a *charter also of Ine's reign that a further stage in the process was to allot the hidage of a broad area, and thus a set share of the obligation, among individual places – farms or hamlets. This was an important step in the process by which *feorm*, essentialy a form of tribute, evolved into rent. Grants of *bookland took the process further. Such grants conveyed with the land the right to receive the food renders which had formerly gone to the king. Honey, malt, lambs, fish, firewood and pigs figure in our scanty records of rents paid by peasants, and many leases oblige the lessee to pay in food as well as cash. Minsters were probably the most dependent of all landlords on food renders, which became organized on the basis of a monthly cycle of deliveries due from the various properties on the estate. Standardisation had proceeded further by the eleventh century, when, explicitly on the king's lands and possibly, although unrecorded, on major lay estates as well, *feorm* was expressed in terms of 'the farm of one night', *firma unius noctis*, a fixed unit commutable for cash. The administration of the royal estates was in the hands of the sheriff who was answerable for their proceeds among the returns from the *shire. In spite of widespread commutation, kings and major religious houses still received large amounts of supplies in kind well after the Conquest.

As well as being able to call on the countryside for supplies, the powerful landowner developed on his or her estates inlands, land directly exploited

for production for his or her household (see also
*estate management). The many place-names
formed from 'bishop's-*tun*' 'king's-*tun*', 'ealdorman's-*tun*', 'priests'-*tun*' denote these, as do
charter references to 'the king's barns' and so on.
Royal farms of this sort may be the category of
land recorded in the Northamptonshire Geld Rolls
as *kynges ahne ferme land*, 'the king's own food-
rent land', exempt from geld, and the 'land of the
king's farm' in occasional references in *Domesday Book.

D. Banham, 'The Knowledge and Use of Food Plants in
Anglo-Saxon England', unpublished Ph.D. dissertation
(Cambridge, 1990); T. M. Charles-Edwards, 'Early
Medieval Kingships in the British Isles', in Bassett,
Origins, pp. 28–39; P. Stafford, 'The "Farm of One
Night" and the Organisation of King Edward's Estates
in Domesday', *Economic History Review* 33 (1980),
491–502; Stenton, *ASE*, pp. 218–19, 287–9, 297–8.

ROSAMOND FAITH

FEUDS were conditions of hostility between individuals or groups within the one community
caused by wrongs done by one side to the other.
The consequences of this hostility could be acts
of private revenge or settlement through the
payment of compensation for the wrongs committed. Throughout the Anglo-Saxon period
individuals relied on social structures like the ties
of lordship and kinship for protection and material
welfare, and private justice played an important
role in the resolution of disputes. Reciprocal commitments and loyalties, and the demands of
honour, put pressure on individuals and groups
to seek vengeance for wrongs done to associates
or kinsmen. But the consequences of uncontrolled
feuding could be disastrous in terms of bloodshed
and material destruction. They must always have
constituted a powerful stimulus to peaceful settlement and the policies of the early Anglo-Saxon
kings and ecclesiastical authorities were directed
at strengthening already existing means to prevent
violence and destruction. Feuds arose typically,
but not exclusively, as a consequence of homicide,
and already in the seventh-century *laws much
attention was addressed to how much should be
paid as *wergild to the kinsmen of a dead man,
or as compensation (OE *manbot*) to his lord, when
and how it should be paid, and who should share
in it. Limitations were imposed on the circumstances in which feuds might be prosecuted and
on those who might properly be involved. Neither
revenge nor compensation could be sought for
the execution of convicted criminals and thieves
caught in the act: a passage in *Beowulf* offers
poignant testimony to this prohibition (2444–59).

Kings also involved themselves directly in the
feuding process as surrogates and, at the margins,
they imposed penalties for violence, and for disturbances in public and protected places.

Later kings attempted further to restrict the
opportunities for private revenge. King *Alfred
issued detailed prescriptions for the conduct of
feuds which at face value left them so closely
circumscribed that it is only in the last resort
that an individual seems permitted his personal
revenge. The most coherent statement of royal
policy towards feuds arising out of homicide
appears as provisions in a code of King *Edmund,
some of which are elaborated in a private tract
known as *Wergeld*. These provisions invoke the full
range of royal sanctions in order to restrict the
participants in the feud and to compel them to
compound their hostilities. Such prescriptions are
consonant with the increasingly interventionist
policies of the later administrations towards the
suppression of *crime. Nothing in the Anglo-
Saxon laws, however, goes as far as the occasional
Carolingian attempt to proscribe the very existence
of organized hostilities, and it is clear that they
continued to have social importance, as indeed
the code of King Edmund acknowledged. The
members of the London peace guild towards the
middle of the tenth century, and those of the Cambridge *thegns' guild fifty years or so later, would
doubtless have regarded themselves as law-abiding
citizens: the provisions of both bind their
members to support one another in feuds. As the
blood price for a man and hence a definition of
his status, the wergild remained an indicative sum
for legal purposes, and King *Edgar prescribed
that it was the most any man should have to pay
for an amendable offence.

The *laws are witnesses both to the prevalence
of feuding and to the efforts of successive kings
to suppress its violent consequences. How far they
were successful in replacing private violence with
public settlement is unknowable. The anecdotal
evidence of feuding is uneven and often contaminated by political and racial animosities, as too
are the terms of the treaty between Danes and
Englishmen issued (probably) in 994, which seem
to countenance revenge killings in certain circumstances. The feud which began when the thegn
Thurbrand killed Earl Uhtred early in the eleventh
century, and which continued over three generations, was a quarrel between highly placed
magnates in the north where English government
was weak. On the other hand, long and deeply
held values clearly died hard: the articles of the
Cambridge thegns' guild contemplated revenge for

a slain member if compensation was not paid, and as late as the episcopate of Bishop *Wulfstan II five brothers refused to accept compensation for another who was killed by accident.

Liebermann, *Gesetze*, i. 186–91 [II *Edmund*], 392–5 [*Wergeldzahlung*], ii, *s. v. Blutrache*; D. Whitelock, *The Beginnings of English Society* (Harmondsworth, 1952, repr. with revisions, 1965), pp. 29–47; P. R. Hyams, 'Feud in Medieval England', *HSJ* 3 (1991), 1–21.

ALAN KENNEDY

FIELD SYSTEMS (the layout of *agricultural holdings and the organisation of cropping within them) displayed considerable regional and local variations by the time of the Norman Conquest. A large proportion of vills in a broad wedge of territory running across Midland England from Dorset to Yorkshire already possessed open fields on the familiar text-book pattern, associated with a *settlement pattern of nucleated villages. In such vills, the arable land was divided into strips or *lands*, grouped into bundles or *furlongs*. These in turn were grouped into two, three or four large fields, one of which lay fallow each year, and open to the grazing of the village livestock. The existence of such a continuous, extensive fallowing sector was only possible because the strips of each farmstead were distributed relatively evenly across the territory of the vill. In the post-Conquest period, at least, a manorial *court or village assembly administered this highly communal system, which included control over wastes and meadows. Not all vills which later in the Middle Ages possessed field systems of this type had gained them by 1066. Nevertheless, across large areas of the Midlands could be found the kind of landscape implied in a *charter of Charlton (Berks.) of 956 (S 634): 'The said country is not surrounded by fixed limits, but the acres (*iugera*) lie next to acres'. It is noteworthy that hedges are but rarely mentioned in the boundary clauses of late Saxon charters from areas later characterized by the Midland system, implying that extensive, continuous cropping sectors already existed in many vills (see *charter bounds).

Open field systems of this familiar 'regular' or 'Midland' type were never ubiquitous, even in lowland England. In much of *East Anglia, in the south-east of England, and in the west, the early medieval settlement pattern was more dispersed than in the Midlands, and the arable land lay in varying proportions of hedged closes and 'irregular' open fields: that is, systems of fields which were subdivided into strips but in which the holdings of each farmstead were clustered in

restricted areas, rather than being dispersed evenly across the territory of the vill. The precise nature of field systems in these areas in the pre-Conquest period remains obscure, but there is little doubt that they never developed 'regular' open field systems of Midland type to any significant extent. Some historians believe that the landscapes of these regions deviated from those of the Midlands because they were cleared and settled at a relatively late date. It is clear, however, that in many such areas the principal field boundaries evolved directly from Romano-British or prehistoric systems of land division. In parts of Essex and East Anglia, especially, Roman *roads slice through the 'medieval' fieldscape in a way analogous to a modern bypass.

It was once thought that classic open field systems of 'Midland' type were introduced by the Saxon settlers in the fifth century, but this is no longer generally accepted. Almost by definition, the Midland system was associated with villages, implying as it does a system of *agriculture based on a high degree of cooperation. It would, moreover, be difficult to institute an extensive, continuous fallowing sector within a landscape of scattered farms. Yet archaeological field surveys suggest that nucleated villages only evolved in the Midlands in the middle or later Saxon period, from a more dispersed pattern of settlement inherited from the Romano-British past. The isolated farms and hamlets of most non-Midland counties probably represent the survival and extension of this earlier pattern.

In some areas, most notably in parts of Northamptonshire and Yorkshire, the appearance of nucleated villages seems to have been accompanied by a drastic replanning of the landscape, involving the laying out of open fields with blocks of very large furlongs, sometimes as much as a mile in length. In most areas, such 'long furlongs' were eventually subdivided and realigned to produce the more familiar hotch-potch of furlongs which appear on the earliest maps. In some places, however, and most notably in parts of Holderness in Yorkshire, the original layout often survived largely intact until enclosure in the eighteenth or nineteenth century. But the development of regular open fields did not always involve large-scale planning and the concomitant erasure of earlier landscape features. Open field furlongs sometimes seem to have developed organically within an existing framework of boundaries, thus in some cases preserving elements of Romano-British or prehistoric landscapes. The semi-regular grid of furlongs at Tadlow in Cambridgeshire is one recently suggested example of this phenomenon.

There was clearly more than one way in which open field systems of Midland type could become established in the landscape: but why did they develop at all? One school of thought sees them as evolving from more irregular systems of subdivided fields, of the kind which developed in many non-Midland areas. Sub-divided fields themselves resulted in part from partible inheritance, in part perhaps from the expansion of cultivation, as areas of waste were divided in strips between the families who had formerly utilized them as grazing. The remodelling of irregular subdivided fields into the 'Midland System' came about, according to one popular view, as population growth in the later Saxon period led both to a landscape increasingly dominated by subdivided fields, and to a contraction of reserves of pasture and waste. In many cases, the shortage of grazing presented by the latter development may have been accentuated by tenurial changes, as the fragmentation of extensive early estates led to the severance of links between settlements and their traditional grazing lands. Shortage of grazing led to an increased need to graze the fallows in the aftermath of the harvest, but this would have been difficult in a landscape of intermingled strips unless continuous areas of arable were cropped and planted at the same time. The solution was the creation of a continuous fallowing sector, something which would have involved a radical reorganisation of landholding and, in many cases, settlement. While the theory that the Midland system developed as a response to a shortage of grazing has much to recommend it, it does leave certain questions unanswered. In particular, it fails to explain the curious distribution of the system, in that many of the areas with the highest density of recorded population and plough teams in the *Domesday Survey never adopted it. Many of these areas developed extensive areas of subdivided fields, but these remained of 'irregular' type; that is, the spatial distribution of property was not reorganized so as to allow for the imposition of a single continuous fallowing sector. In the centuries before and after the Norman Conquest, such areas found a variety of ways of coping with the shortage of grazing. In north-east Norfolk, for example, by the end of the twelfth century a sophisticated system of agriculture had been developed which involved the planting of fodder crops and the stall-feeding of animals: a response to the grazing shortage which, arguably, the adoption of the rigidly communal Midland system precluded. More usually, as in parts of Essex and Hertfordshire, a discontinuous fallowing sector was imposed across the irregularly distributed strips within a vill, the settlement pattern within which often remained highly dispersed. Population growth and a shortage of grazing did not automatically lead to the adoption of the Midland system.

Partly because of this, some historians have argued that the wide and even distribution of holdings which was the most prominent feature of this system may also have been encouraged by other factors. The farmers of later Saxon England were members of a complex society, and were affected not only by demographic change, but also by changes in social organisation. In particular, the burdens imposed on them by church, state, and local lords were increasing in the later Saxon period. Whether imposed through the manor, the parish, or the vill, exactions were rated on the area of land, rather than on its productivity. There would therefore have been an increasing tendency to ensure that the customary holdings of each farmer within the communities upon whom assessments were imposed were of equal quality, and perhaps equal accessibility. Some historians have therefore suggested that only the demands of strong and undivided local lordship could have provided the necessary stimulus for the adoption of the Midland system: others have gone further, suggesting that the reorganisation of holdings which the system demanded could only have been imposed from above, by local lords. Yet the Midland system was not invariably associated with strong lordship. The system was common in many areas, such as Cambridgeshire, which were by the time of Domesday characterized by a high density of free tenants, and by vills divided between several *manors.

It is possible that the adoption of the Midland system was encouraged by different combinations of factors in different areas. In some places, demographic and agricultural considerations may have been paramount; in others, and especially where manor and vill tended to be coterminous, fiscal and tenurial pressures may have been more important. What is clear is that, while our understanding of early English field systems has increased markedly in the last twenty years, there are still a great many features of their origin and distribution which we do not fully understand.

Studies of Field Systems in the British Isles, ed. A. R. H. Baker and R. A. Butlin (Cambridge, 1973); R. Dodgshon, *The Origin of the British Field System: an Interpretation* (London, 1980); D. Hall, *Medieval Fields* (Aylesbury, 1981); O. Rackham, *The History of the*

Fig. 7 An Anglo-Saxon fishweir at Colwick, Notts. (reconstruction).

Countryside (London, 1986); *The Origins of Open Field Agriculture*, ed. T. Rowley (London, 1980).

T. WILLIAMSON

FINNSBURH FRAGMENT: see Battle of Finnsburh

FISHING provided a valuable contribution to the early medieval diet, encouraged by the church's requirements for abstinence from meat through Lent and other fast-days. Marine, estuarine and freshwater sources were all exploited from the sixth century onwards, with both the level of consumption and the range of species apparently increasing in the late Anglo-Saxon period. The existence of specialist fishing communities is indicated by place-names such as Fiskerton in Northamptonshire, while *Domesday Book records considerable numbers of fishermen along the east coast, as well as smaller numbers in the midlands.

Marine and estuarine fish were caught in a variety of ways. *Bede credits Bishop *Wilfrid with teaching the South Saxons to fish in the sea using eel-nets. *Ælfric's *Colloquy* describes coastal fishing from boats using nets, baited hooks and creels, and lists sturgeon, herring, plaice, flounders, salmon, sprats, crab and lobster among the catch. Fish-hooks, stone net-sinkers and line-sinkers have been recovered from a number of sites.

A wide range of species is represented in archaeological deposits, though fish bones are small and fragile and wet-sieving is needed to ensure representative recovery. Colder climatic conditions in the eighth and ninth centuries may have extended the southerly range of species like cod and herring. Cod bones occur particularly on sites on or near the North Sea coast. The introduction of some form of drift-net by the *Vikings may explain the significant increase in herring bones reported from late Saxon *Ipswich. Domesday Book underlines the importance of herring fisheries along the east coast, with Dunwich alone rendering 68,000 herrings a year.

There was a thriving commercial market in sea fish. Fishwick at the head of the Ribble estuary was named from this trade. *Egil's Saga* records the import of dried cod from Norway into England in the ninth century, while in 982 *Æthelred II levied import duties from foreign merchants at a rate of 1d for a large shipload of fish and 6s for a ship carrying salt whale. Large cod, bones of which have been found in *Lincoln, *Durham and *Northampton, probably came from more northerly

185

waters and were imported dried. A compacted layer of scales and bones from discarded herrings or sprats on the floor of a Roman building in *York suggests that it was reused in late Anglian and Viking times for processing fish. Sea fish were relatively cheap and were being traded deep into the midlands long before the Norman Conquest.

Along the coast a variety of stake-nets and fore-shore weirs were used to trap fish on the outgoing tide. From 956 to shortly before the Norman Conquest, *Bath Abbey held an estate at the confluence of the Severn and Wye which included four *haecweras*, probably hurdle and brushwood sea-hedges, and a hundred *cytweras*, probably wooden frameworks set up in the intertidal zone with basketwork fish-traps. These fisheries were still a valuable resource at the time of the Domesday survey.

The flooding of former Roman farmland in the fens of East Anglia created a waterlogged landscape which yielded huge quantities of eels. Bede tells us that this is how *Ely acquired its name. Abbeys with fenland estates such as Ely, Thorney and *Ramsey, received tens of thousands of eels a year in rents. Eels were also obtained all over the country from traps set in mill-streams.

River fishing was sometimes carried out from boats using nets or lines. Aneirin's late sixth-century epic Welsh poem *Y *Gododdin* mentions fishing from a coracle. A late Anglo-Saxon hoard from Nazeing (Essex) contained an iron trident fish-spear, probably intended for salmon since its tines were set too wide apart for eel. *Charter references to inland river fisheries occur from the late seventh century onwards. Sometimes they imply no more than a general right to take fish, but often they indicate some form of fixed weir containing traps. Remains of such a weir, dated by radiocarbon to the eighth or ninth century, have been found at Colwick (Notts.), where two rows of holly and hawthorn posts were driven into the river bed in a V-shape, supporting wattle hurdles of hazel, willow and ash which funnelled fish towards a basketwork trap (see fig. 7). Fish-weirs have also been recognized archaeologically near Castle Donington on the Trent and in Lincoln on the Witham.

Ælfric states that eels, pike, burbot, trout, lampreys and other small fish were caught in rivers. Middens frequently contain eel bones, but other freshwater fish rarely occur in great quantity. At Coppergate in York the disappearance of barbel and grayling bones after the late ninth century may reflect the increasing pollution of the river.

A fishpond near Cumnor (north Berks.) is men-

tioned in two charters nominally of the tenth century. Excavation at Wharram Percy (Yorks.) revealed late Saxon woodwork and basketwork, probably the remains of fish-traps, set into the mill-dam funnel. However, artificial fishponds generally seem to be rare before the end of the eleventh century.

M. Aston, ed., *Medieval Fish, Fisheries and Fishponds in England*, BAR Brit. Ser. 182 (Oxford, 1988); O. G. S. Crawford, 'A Saxon Fish-Pond near Oxford', *Antiquity* 4 (1930), 480–3; C. R. Salisbury, 'Primitive British Fishweirs', *Waterfront Archaeology*, ed. G. L. Good, R. H. Jones and M. W. Ponsford (London, 1991), pp. 76–87.

C. J. BOND

FIVE BOROUGHS, a term applied to *Leicester, Nottingham, Derby, *Stamford and *Lincoln, with attendant territories, during the tenth and eleventh centuries. All were Danish strongholds conquered by *Edward the Elder (899–924) and his sister *Æthelflæd (d. 918). The earliest reference to them as a group occurs in the entry for 942 in the *Anglo-Saxon Chronicle*, as the Danish part of *Mercia reconquered from King Olaf by King *Edmund (939–46), bounded by Dore, Whitwell, the Humber and the North Sea; so they would appear to have encompassed much of what the *Tribal Hidage had termed 'original Mercia', plus *Lindsey and Hatfield. The term recurs in King *Æthelred's Wantage Code (III Æthelred, of *c*.997), and in the *Chronicle* regarding the submission to *Swein Forkbeard in 1013, but is then distinguished from Lindsey. Lincoln may, therefore, have been excluded in this instance, but a close association is upheld by the annal for 1015, which refers uniquely to 'the Seven Boroughs'. Stenton suggested Torksey and York as the additional two, but both could have been Mercian towns. In any event, the region exercised considerable political influence in the late Anglo-Saxon period. *Edmund Ironside (1016), *Cnut (1016–35) and Earl *Leofric (d. 1057) all sought the support of its leaders. *Domesday Book suggests that it was well-developed and comparatively rich.

P. Stafford, *The East Midlands in the Early Middle Ages* (Leicester, 1985).

N. J. HIGHAM

FLANDERS, corresponding approximately to modern Belgium and north-east France, was, because of its geographical proximity to England, the territory through which all travel and commerce to and from the Continent passed (principally via the port of Quentavic); the influence of Flanders on all aspects of Anglo-Saxon life was therefore very considerable. Commercial contact is poorly documented, but it is reasonable to assume that England imported cloth from Flanders (and perhaps exported wool). Cultural influence was mediated principally through the monasteries of Saint-Bertin in the town of Saint-Omer, and St Peter's and St Bavo's in Ghent, but also through Saint-Vaast in Arras, Saint-Amand, and Corbie; it is attested from the reign of King *Alfred onwards (though it is interesting to note that the Englishman Frithugils, a student of *Alcuin, was abbot of Saint-Bertin, 820–34). Alfred's youngest daughter Ælfthryth was married to Baldwin II, count of Flanders (879–918), sometime between 893 and 899, and a few years earlier *Grimbald of Saint-Bertin had been invited to England by Alfred; Grimbald had a significant effect on the revival of learning which Alfred initiated, both through his teaching and through books which he brought with him. In 944, a group of monks from Saint-Bertin, fleeing the monastic reforms of Gerhard of Brogne, were settled in St Peter's, *Bath, by King *Edmund; a decade or so later *Dunstan was exiled by King *Eadwig and spent two years (956–7) at St Peter's, Ghent, where he became familiar with these same monastic reforms. The abbot of St Peter's, Ghent, at the time was Womar (d. 981), who later visited Winchester and is commemorated in the *Liber vitae* of the New Minster. After Dunstan's return to England, and his appointment to the archbishopric of Canterbury (959), he remained in contact with colleagues in Flanders, such as Abbot Wido of St Peter's in Ghent, Count Arnulf II of Flanders, and Fulrad, abbot of Saint-Vaast. English *liturgical books of the second half of the tenth century (including the famous *'Benedictional of St Æthelwold') contain frequent commemorations of Flemish saints. Although in the eleventh century political relations between England and Flanders became strained at various times, particularly when after the death of King *Cnut (1035) the exiled Queen *Emma took refuge with Count Baldwin V, literary contacts intensified: Adelard, a monk of St Peter's in Ghent, composed a set of liturgical lections on the life of Dunstan (1006 × 1011); the anonymous author of the *Encomium Emmae* (1041–2) was apparently a monk of Saint-Bertin; and *Goscelin and *Folcard, who made a huge contribution to the *hagiography of English saints, were both monks of Saint-Bertin. After the Conquest, the abbot of St Peter's in Bath, one Sæwold, returned with his community to Arras, and left his library of books

brought from Bath to the abbey of Saint-Vaast. Judith (d. 1095), the wife of Earl Tostig (who was killed at Stamford Bridge in 1066), took refuge in Flanders for some years after his death, before moving on to southern Germany; she is known as the patron of a number of lavish *gospelbooks, some of which were written by Anglo-Saxon scribes.

P. Grierson, 'The Relations between England and Flanders before the Norman Conquest', *TRHS* 4th ser. 23 (1941), 71–112; V. Ortenberg, *The English Church and the Continent in the Tenth and Eleventh Centuries* (Oxford, 1992), pp. 21–40; D. Nicholas, *Medieval Flanders* (London, 1992); P. McGurk and J. Rosenthal, 'The Anglo-Saxon Gospelbooks of Judith, Countess of Flanders: their Text, Make-up and Function', *ASE* 24 (1995), 251–308.

MICHAEL LAPIDGE

FLEET: *see* Navy

FLEURY. The monastery of Fleury (Saint-Benoît-sur-Loire) owed its great prestige to the possession of the relics of St Benedict, whose bones had been brought there from the devastated monastery of Monte Cassino in the eighth century. It was the benevolence of this saint which brought pilgrims from far and near to Fleury, inspired them through the miracles he performed to part with some of their earthly goods, and imparted a spirit of humane asceticism to the community. It was in the tenth century, after the reform of the monastery by Odo of Cluny, that the intellectual achievements of the abbey began to have more than local importance. Fleury became active in the cause of monastic reform: French monasteries were reformed, were given teachers and books. The community also attracted clerics from beyond the borders of Francia, from *Germany, Spain and England.

Relations with England began when *Oda, the future archbishop of *Canterbury, became a monk there. Then, just before 959, *Oswald, Oda's nephew, embraced the monastic life in Fleury. Back in England, he was actively engaged in the founding of *Ramsey, becoming its first nominal abbot. Its first prior, *Germanus, also stayed at Fleury for a considerable time. Fleury monks meanwhile visited England: it has been demonstrated through a comparison with the Fleury *Consuetudines* that the Cluniac elements in the *Regularis Concordia* were introduced by them.

In 985 a delegation from Ramsey arrived at Fleury to ask for a teacher. It was *Abbo of Fleury himself, one of the most celebrated scholars of the age, who accepted the job; as a consequence, relations flourished. This may be ascertained from surviving Fleury manuscripts. Several magnificent liturgical manuscripts of English origin, such as the benedictional in Paris, BN lat. 987, given by Ramsey to Abbo's successor Gauzlinus (abbot 1004–30), and the so-called Winchcombe Sacramentary (Orléans, BM 127 (105)), ended up in the library. There were also several English scribes working at Fleury itself. An anonymous English pilgrim versed in *'Winchester School' illumination, the 'Master of Ramsey', left a memory of his stay in Fleury in a drawing of Christ in a mandorla enthroned between St Gregory and St Benedict, in Orléans, BM 175 (152).

Meanwhile, English clerics borrowed books from Fleury (*Dunstan had to be reminded to return a volume). But the main impact of Fleury culture came through Abbo's teaching. The number of manuscripts of his own scientific works are evidence for the thesis that Abbo was the most important transmitter of Carolingian science to England.

DACL v.1709–60; *DHGE* xvii. 441–76; L. Gougaud, 'Les relations de l'abbaye de Fleury-sur-Loire avec la Bretagne et les Iles Britanniques (Xe et XIe siècles)', *Mémoires de la Société d'histoire et d'archéologie de Bretagne* 4 (1923), 3–30; G. Chenesseau, *L'abbaye de Fleury* (Paris, 1931); A. Vidier, *L'historiographie à Saint-Benoît-sur-Loire et les miracles de saint Benoît* (Paris, 1965); R.-H. Bautier, 'Le monastère et les églises de Fleury-sur-Loire sous les abbatiats d'Abbon, de Gauzlin et d'Arnaud', *Mémoires de la Société Nationale des Antiquaires de France*, 9th ser. 4 (1968), 71–154; M. Mostert, *The Library of Fleury: a Provisional List of Manuscripts* (Hilversum, 1989).

MARCO MOSTERT

FLORENCE, monk of *Worcester (d. 1118). Florence is known to posterity from the entry for 1118 in the (Anglo-Norman) Chronicle of *John of Worcester: '7 July. Florence [Florentius] of Worcester died, through whose acute understanding and through the industry of whose assiduous labour this Chronicle of Chronicles prevails over all others.' On the basis of this entry, the chronicle in question was long known and cited as the 'Chronicle of Florence of Worcester'. It is clear, however, that the person responsible for the production of the chronicle in its received form was John of Worcester himself (who was seen at work on a post-Conquest section of the chronicle, probably in the 1120s, by Orderic Vitalis); and since there is no obvious trace of a distinction between the methods or styles of two different chroniclers, it is presumed that John must have worked over the whole, obscuring the

nature and the extent of Florence's own contribution. It is as well to emphasize, therefore, that John felt himself to be sufficiently in Florence's debt to warrant the generous acknowledgement in the entry for 1118; and that it may have been Florence, rather than John, who was responsible for gathering much of the material incorporated in the earlier part of the chronicle, bearing on the ninth, tenth and eleventh centuries. It is well known that *Wulfstan II, bishop of Worcester (1062–95), had instructed the monk *Hemming to set to work on the muniments of the church; and there is reason to believe that Wulfstan instructed another monk to begin work on matters of wider historical import. According to Orderic, the monk in question was John; but since John was still active in the 1140s, it may be that the task had been undertaken in the first instance by Florence, and that Florence's role was subsequently taken over by John. This is, of course, no more than a wishful thought. It makes some difference, however, whether the information on the eleventh century was gathered by a chronicler working in the reign of William I, or in the reign of Henry I, even though one still has little choice but to cite the chronicler as 'John'. Hemming, Florence and John are included in the list of the members of the community of St Mary's, Worcester, drawn up during the episcopate of Bishop Samson (1096–1112), and entered in the 'Liber Vitae' of *Durham; and Florence is listed first among the recently departed monks named in the *titulus* for the church of Worcester entered in the mortuary roll of Vitalis, abbot of Savigny (d. 1122).

Sharpe, *Handlist*, 299; *The Vita Wulfstani of William of Malmesbury*, ed. R. R. Darlington, Camden 3rd ser. 40 (London, 1928), pp. xv–xviii; *The Ecclesiastical History of Orderic Vitalis* II, ed. M. Chibnall (Oxford, 1968), pp. 186–8; *The Chronicle of John of Worcester*, II: *The Annals from 450 to 1066*, ed. R. R. Darlington and P. McGurk, trans. J. Bray and P. McGurk (OMT, 1995), pp. xvii–xviii, lxxx–lxxxi.

SIMON KEYNES

FOEDERATI, one of the terms (with *laeti/gentiles*) for barbarian peoples in the later Roman empire serving as soldiers. Literary sources are patchy and suggest variation, but a scheme may be suggested for the western provinces. *Foederati* were barbarian tribes granted *receptio* (admission) under a *foedus* (treaty). In the fourth century warriors served in the imperial army, by the fifth in royal armies (e.g. the Visigoths). Alamanni were sent to Britain possibly as *foederati* in 372/3 (Ammianus Marcellinus XXIX.iv.3). *Laeti* (also styled *gentiles*) seem to have been defeated barbarians settled on the land in the western provinces and supplying recruits to the army. They are listed in Gaul and Italy in the *Notitia Dignitatum* (*Occ.* XLII); a leaf of the manuscript is missing so they could also have been stationed in Britain.

Burials from northern Gaul containing Germanic items along with elaborate 'chip-carved' belt-suites are interpreted as graves of *foederati* or *laeti*. Such burials are not known from Britain, but the belt equipment is and was interpreted as 'Germanic'. It is now appreciated that it is from official belts issued by the late Roman state to its military and administrative servants, irrespective of ethnic origin. Thus proposed 'Germans' in late Roman Britain as a channel of continuity to the Anglo-Saxon period are unconvincing.

W. Böhme, *Germanische Grabfunde des 4. bis 5. Jahrhunderts zwischen untere Elbe und Loire* (Munich, 1974); P. Southern and K. Dixon, *The Late Roman Army* (London, 1996).

SIMON ESMONDE CLEARY

FOLCARD OF SAINT-BERTIN

FOLCARD OF SAINT-BERTIN, hagiographer and monk of Saint-Bertin, Saint-Omer, is thought to have come to England in the 1050s. We know little for certain about his activities before 1069 when he was appointed acting abbot of Thorney (Cambs.). While still at Saint-Bertin he was commissioned to rewrite the *vita* of the patron saint, Bertin. From Folcard's time in England we know of several other hagiographical works: his *vitae* of John of Beverley (*BHL* 4339), dedicated to *Ealdred, archbishop of York (to whom Folcard seems to have owed a debt of thanks for unspecified kindnesses), of *Botwulf (*BHL* 1428), dedicated to Walkelin, bishop of *Winchester, of *Tancred, Torhtred and Tova, whose relics were at Thorney, and an account of the translation of the Thorney saints. At Christmas 1085 Folcard was deposed from Thorney for unknown reasons and nothing is known of his life or whereabouts thereafter.

Sharpe, *Handlist*, 300; F. Barlow (ed. and trans.), *The Life of King Edward who rests at Westminster* (London, 1962; 2nd ed., OMT, 1992), pp. lii–lix.

R. C. LOVE

FOLKLAND: *see* Land Tenure

FOLKLORE is the traditional, unofficial culture of communities. It involves items (proverbs, *riddles, tales, customs, designs or the like), a particular group, and the process of passing items (usually orally) from one person to another within it, particularly down the generations. Only a little of general Anglo-Saxon folklore can ever have been recorded, and moreover, when folklore does occur in literature it is often difficult to disentangle from scholarly traditions: for example, much of the 'natural history' found in the OE riddles comes either from observation, or from late *classical learning, but the idea that barnacle geese were born as shell-fish apparently belongs to popular culture, as it is not otherwise recorded before Giraldus Cambrensis. Tales of the 'Heroic Age', based as they are in history (however distorted), may not be folklore, strictly speaking, but *Beowulf* has several elements which belong to folk literature: Grendel, the *dragon, Beowulf's fifty-year reign, and even the succession of conflicts. Weland the smith, creator of the best armour, had become part of literary folklore: his story is only told fully in later Norse sources, but scenes from it are depicted on the eighth-century Northumbrian box known as the *Franks Casket, and it is mentioned in the poem *Deor*.

Folklore encompasses popular religion, and is therefore often in conflict with official formal Christianity. Eighth-century *penitentials and other ecclesiastical sources contain several references to disapproved practices: to bringing in diviners and lot-casters to rid one's house of evil, to having oneself tattooed, and to wearing *amulets. In eleventh-century sources others are added: for example, calendar superstitions concerning lucky and unlucky days, performing love *magic, and bringing offerings to or keeping vigils at stones, trees or springs, usually with the aim of restoring health. *Ælfric condemned cursing cattle to make them thrive, noisy and drunken wakes, and divinations 'either by birds or by sneezing or by horses or by dogs', in undertaking new enterprises, or in brewing, or at childbirth.

Popular religion also seems to have included animistic ideas: that the countryside was populated by spirits such as dwarves and elves, which occur in some place-names, and also in some compounds in poetry, such as *elfsciene*, 'radiant as an elf'. In *medical literature and *charms, however, the elf brings disease, sometimes by 'shooting' it into a victim (perhaps with the Stone Age points known as elfshot in modern folklore). Illnesses such as *elfadl*, *elfsidenne* and *elfsogoða* (not always identifiable) were named from the disease-bringing agent. Here, evidently, Germanic spirits had been conflated with the Christian devil and become wholly evil, though perhaps originally amoral. On the other side, *hagiography contains many elements from folklore, such as the recognition of sanctity by animals, and its power to protect against fire.

A. L. Meaney, 'Anglo-Saxon Idolators and Ecclesiasts from Theodore to Alcuin: a Source Study', *AASAH* 5 (1992), 103–25; K. L. Jolly, *Popular Religion in Late Anglo-Saxon England: Elf Charms in Context* (Chapel Hill, NC, and London, 1996).

AUDREY MEANEY

FOOD AND DRINK in Anglo-Saxon England had much in common with the diet of other pre-industrial societies. Animal foods had the highest status, but plants, especially cereals, were far more significant nutritionally.

The main cereal in the early period was barley, but wheat was used increasingly, and rye and oats were also eaten. Cereals were consumed as bread, beer and 'pottage' (OE *briw*: cereals or pulses boiled with vegetables or other flavourings). Bread consumption probably went up during the period (presumably at the expense of *briw*), since the increase in wheat is mostly accounted for by types suitable for baking (see also *agriculture).

The Anglo-Saxon loaf was small and round, and normally made of wheat in the later period. Barley bread may have been more common earlier, and was considered suitable for saints and penance. Bread was baked on the hearth-stones in most households, although large establishments like monasteries had ovens. King *Alfred's 'cakes' would have been small, round, hearth-baked loaves. Flour was ground by hand in rotary querns, or later in water-*mills, and therefore stone ground and normally wholemeal. 'White' bread (darker than many modern 'brown' flours) existed, however, produced by sieving the coarser particles out of the flour (and constituted the attraction of Christianity for otherwise pagan kings of *Essex). Fancy breads seem to have been unknown.

Beer was made of barley, or sometimes wheat for special purposes, flavoured with hops or possibly other herbs. It constituted a significant dietary element, being drunk in far larger quantities than wine or mead (see below), or indeed water, which was generally unsafe.

Pulses (beans, peas and possibly vetches) were eaten as *briw* (see above), and were the most important component in the diet after cereals. Other vegetables were used mainly as flavourings, although monks ate boiled and raw 'herbs'. The leek was the Anglo-Saxon vegetable *par excellence*: a vegetable garden was a *lectun*, and onions and garlic were classed as types of leek. Other 'pot-herbs' included cabbage (probably like modern kales), turnips and beets, or their leaves. Carrots and/or parsnips (consistently confused until coloured carrots replaced white ones in the early modern period) were also known. Wild plants such as *Chenopodium* species (OE *melde*) were eaten, and possibly cultivated. Most familiar culinary herbs, however, were essentially medicinal plants at this period. Imported spices (pepper and probably ginger and coriander) used in both medicine and food, cannot have been widely available.

Native fruits (apples, pears, plums, cherries, blackberries, raspberries and strawberries) were eaten, and improved varieties probably grown. Nuts, mainly the native hazel, were also eaten. There are references to exotic fruits such as peaches and mulberries, but the only one certainly grown was the grape. Evidence for viticulture predates that for imports, but wine must have been imported for the mass before the climate improved enough to grow grapes. Wine also became increasingly popular for secular use with Anglo-Saxons who could afford it. With its religious and classical associations, wine occurs a good deal more in Anglo-Saxon literature than in the diet.

The other luxury drink was mead. Although honey was used to sweeten medicines, and presumably food, mead was its main use. Its importance to the ruling classes is shown by its regular occurrence in food rents (see *feorm) alongside such staples as corn. Honey may also have been used to sweeten beer and wine, and the mysterious *beor*. This last was a sweet drink made, or at least flavoured, with fruit. It may have included cider, but the evidence does not suggest that this was a common drink.

Milk may have been drunk fresh to some extent, but most of it was made into butter and cheese. Most cheeses, small by modern standards, would be eaten fairly young. Fresh cheese, along with curds and whey, buttermilk, and so on, were also consumed. Cows and sheep, and possibly goats as well, were milked. Eggs came mainly from hens, but also ducks and geese, and occasionally wild birds. For most Anglo-Saxons, dairy goods, including eggs, would have been their most concentrated source of protein.

All the species mentioned above were slaughtered for meat (although the bones of sheep and goat are difficult to distinguish in archaeology), but pigs were probably eaten in greater numbers. All domestic animals were smaller and lighter than modern breeds (see also *animal husbandry). Despite the prestige of muscle meat from quadrupeds (except horses, the eating of which was frowned on by the church), most Anglo-Saxons would rarely have eaten it. Only for the upper classes would 'red' meat form a regular part of the diet, and they would also eat wild animals such as deer, presumably including the products of aristocratic *hunting. For the rest of the population, the pig was the only mammal consumed regularly, usually in preserved form such as bacon or possibly sausage.

Domestic fowl were eaten, as were, to a lesser extent, wild birds (see *hawking). Less exalted Anglo-Saxons could catch birds for their own consumption, as well as their lords'. Fish, including oysters and eels, came into their own on fast days (see *fishing). The huge numbers of eels in food-rents suggest that they must have been preserved. Evidence for preservation, however, is thin. There is no firm evidence either for fish ponds before the Conquest, so presumably both freshwater and sea fish were caught in the wild.

Salt, important as a preservative and essential nutritional component, was traded from the earliest times. For the ordinary Anglo-Saxon, it must have formed a substantial item of expenditure, even if other foods were produced at home.

D. Banham, 'The Knowledge and Uses of Food Plants in Anglo-Saxon England' (unpubl. Ph.D. dissertation, Univ. of Cambridge, 1990); A. Hagen, *A Handbook of Anglo-Saxon Food: Processing and Consumption* (Pinner, 1992); idem, *A Second Handbook of Anglo-Saxon Food & Drink: Production & Distribution* (Hockwold cum Wilton, 1995).

DEBBY BANHAM

FOODRENT: *see Feorm*

FORESTS: *see* Woodland

FORMULAE: *see* Oral-Formulaic Theory

FORTS AND FORTIFICATIONS are puzzlingly absent from both the written and the archaeological record of the early Anglo-Saxons, in sharp contrast to Ireland, Scotland and the British south-west where defended citadels were prominent in aristocratic life and warfare during the fifth to seventh centuries. Strong-points mentioned in the earlier annals of the *Anglo-Saxon Chronicle* are normally prehistoric or Roman, and it is symptomatic that *burh*, the OE equivalent of Celtic *caer* or *dun*, seems in pre-Viking sources to denote Iron Age hillforts or *monastic sites, rarely *royal sites. It is a Welsh potentate whom Bede (*HE* iii.1) locates *in oppido municipio*. The 'great enclosure' at *Yeavering (in any case in a British-influenced region) probably functioned as a cattle-compound, and the royal buildings lay outside it.

Possibly the itinerant lifestyle which food-circuits imposed on warrior aristocracies was not easily compatible with fixed residential strongholds.

The duty of building or maintaining fortresses is first explicitly reserved in a Mercian royal privilege of 749, and becomes gradually more frequent (as one of the 'three common burdens'; see *trinoda necessitas*) thereafter. One probable reason for this is the growth, under *Æthelbald and *Offa, of a royal government capable of increasingly ambitious public works. *Offa's Dyke is merely the most spectacular product of an established tradition of linear earthworks, but late eighth-and early ninth-century *Mercia also provides the first archaeological evidence for major newly-constructed settlement defences, most clearly at *Hereford but also probably at *Tamworth and *Winchcombe. There is some anachronism in calling such places *'towns' (in origin they were hierarchically important sites rather than large concentrations of people; cf *monastic sites), but as stable centres of activity with public-maintained defences they mark an important new development.

Mercia seems to have been ahead of other regions: the 'common burdens' are first recorded in Kent in 792, and in Wessex not until 846. How far this reflects actual building activity is uncertain, but there is no archaeological evidence for new forts or fortified towns in Wessex before the reign of *Æthelwulf (839–58). The *Burghal Hidage of *Alfred's or *Edward the Elder's reign lists thirty-one heterogeneous places – some full-scale towns, some prehistoric and *Roman sites, some mere promontories and islands – which were built or rebuilt, maintained and manned, from hidage-based obligations. Despite the chronological problems, it cannot be doubted that there was a sharp increase in fortress-building in late ninth-century *Wessex, partly but by no means wholly prompted by the *Viking threat. A characteristic form of rampart, comprising a timber-laced and timber-revetted bank with an external ditch, has now been excavated at several sites.

The campaigns against the Vikings under Edward the Elder, *Æthelflæd and their successors extended the West Saxon techniques of fortress-building to other regions, notably north-west Mercia and the East Midlands. At the same time, defences became more substantial, as at Hereford and *Oxford where the original timber revetments were re-fronted in stone. At Portchester and *Winchester rebuilt gates in the Roman walls can plausibly be dated to the late

Anglo-Saxon period, and at Oxford St Michael's church tower was integrated into the north gate.

Minor royal strongholds in the late Anglo-Saxon countryside are possibly indicated by places called Bourton and Burton (i.e. *burh-tūn*), which often seem to be near minsters or royal vills, and by place-names containing the title *burhweard*, 'fort-guardian'. But there is an ambiguity: already in the laws of King *Ine (*c.*700) a king's or noble's residence is called a *burh*, and by the eleventh century the word was widely used for an enclosed manorial site (for instance the numerous 'Kingsburys' in small towns) rather than a fortress in the strict sense. The *Anglo-Saxon Chronicle* for 757 describes an enclosed royal residence with defensible gates at the unidentified *Meretun*, but it is uncertain how far this can be regarded as a contemporary source. A text of *c.*1000 which lists a *burhgeat* ('fortress-gate' or 'manor-house-gate'?) among the attributes of a prosperous *ceorl* aspiring to thegnhood has been much debated in the context of the origins of English castles. The distinction between enclosure and defence is not clear-cut, but it is now clear from excavations, notably at *Goltho (Lincs.) and Sulgrave (Northants.), that at least a few late Anglo-Saxon manor-houses were stoutly defended with banks, ditches and perhaps palisades.

N. Brooks, 'The Development of Military Obligations in Eighth- and Ninth-Century England', *England Before the Conquest*, ed. P. Clemoes and K. Hughes (Cambridge, 1971), pp. 69–84; Hill and Rumble, *Defence of Wessex*; M. Gelling, 'The Place-Name Burton and Variants', *Weapons and Warfare in Anglo-Saxon England*, ed. S. C. Hawkes (Oxford, 1989), pp. 145–53; B. K. Davison, 'Excavations at Sulgrave', *Archaeological Journal* 134 (1977), 105–14; A. Williams, 'A Bell-House and a Burh-Geat: Lordly Residences in England before the Norman Conquest', *Medieval Knighthood*: IV, ed. C. Harper-Bill and R. Harvey (Woodbridge, 1992), pp. 221–40.

JOHN BLAIR

FORTUNES OF MEN is a 98-line poem found on 87r–88r of the *Exeter Book (titled *The Fates of Mortals* in Muir's edition). An example of *gnomic poetry, it comprises two catalogues, the first listing a variety of ways in which human beings can meet their deaths, with an emphasis on God's command of fate, the second enumerating the many different skills and talents which God has granted to different individuals, in the manner of the poem known as the *Gifts of Men*. Much recent scholarly analysis has focused on the first catalogue, where many of the fates listed have been seen to reflect a partially submerged memory of Germanic initiatory rites, possibly the *residuum* of an earlier

pre-Christian poem appropriated into the Christian ambience of the introduction, second catalogue, and conclusion.

ASPR iii.154–6; R. H. Dammers, 'Unity and Artistry in *The Fortunes of Men*', *American Benedictine Review* 27 (1976), 461–9; K. Swenson, 'Death Appropriated in *The Fates of Men*', *SP* 88 (1991), 123–35; *The Exeter Anthology of Old English Poetry*, ed. B. J. Muir, 2 vols. (Exeter, 1994).

ROBERT DINAPOLI

FOWLING: *see* Hawking and Wildfowling

FRANKPLEDGE, 'free-pledge' (in twelfth-century Old English *fri[ð]borg/h*): a system of neighbourhood surety and policing designed to rein in and if necessary discipline society's more unruly elements. The system can only be seen clearly in practical operation in the later Middle Ages, by which time it was a method of dragooning (usually unfree) peasants. The evidence, however, suggests that it was originally aimed at free subjects, those called 'law-worthy' in Old English texts. The clearest semi-official account of its working is in the great thirteenth-century legal treatise under the name of Bracton. *Sheriffs were to hold their 'tourn' twice a year in each *hundred for the purpose of taking the 'View of Frankpledge'. This entailed ensuring that all free males who had reached the age of twelve were to take an *oath of fealty to the king and his heirs, as well as swearing 'not to be a robber nor consent to a robber'. If a felon fled from the consequences of his crime, the rest of his 'frankpledge or *tithing' (group of ten) was to be fined for its failure to control the malefactor. According to early-twelfth-century evidence, frankpledges/tithings were also responsible for launching the hue and cry after any such wrongdoer. It has justly been said that 'no more highly centralized and thoroughgoing scheme of suretyship to secure order was ever devised on European soil'.

Because the system is first clearly evident after 1100 – and, it must be said, also because of the way that the course of English history was then read – it was thought by W. A. Morris, author of this quotation, that the 'governmental action of a deliberate and rigorous nature' that must have been at work could only be Norman. Yet the post-Conquest sources themselves clearly cite the *laws of *Cnut. These do, at least implicitly, make a similar requirement: all free men who wish to have full legal rights must be 'brought, if over twelve, into a hundred or tithing': a 'surety that will hold him . . . to every legal duty'; and 'every man over twelve is to give an oath that he will not be a thief or accessory to a theft'. It is hard to deny that something very like Bracton's Frankpledge is involved here. The usual counter-argument, that these are successive but separate clauses, hence the policing tithing and the neighbourhood surety were as yet distinct and united only after 1066, has to confront the simple fact that they are *not* separate clauses in the only copy of Cnut's code that is divided into clauses at all. The harder one looks at legislation before Cnut, the more possible it seems that it too is talking about what became Frankpledge. The policing duties of groups of ten under headmen are laid out in detail in *Æthelstan's ordinance on *London's 'peace-guild'. Surety is prescribed on lines very like post-Conquest arrangements in *Edgar's 'third' (Andover) code. Sureties in *Æthelred's Woodstock code operate like the *jury of the laws he issued slightly later at Wantage. And King *Alfred's first law instructs that all are to keep their *'oath and pledge'*; before going on to issue orders on the defaulter's fate that are at least reminiscent of what would later happen to those without surety. It is therefore reasonable to suppose that the seeds of Frankpledge were planted as soon as the oath was grafted on to the subject's obligations. There were no doubt a series of refinements of detail throughout the tenth century before the medieval system became fully recognizable. There was variation between the *West Saxon core where a tithing was a tenth of a geographical (non-numerical) hundred, and *Mercia/*East Anglia, where, since the hundred was numerical, they were more likely to consist of ten *'hides'/men. But neither that nor any other consideration is sufficient grounds to deny the system's Old English origins. It was a key factor in early England's coherence – and conquerability.

Liebermann, *Gesetze* i. 46–9 [Alfred 1–1:8], 174–81 [VI Æthelstan 2–8:9], 202–5 [III Edgar 6–7:3], 322–5 [II Cnut 20–1], 488 [Art. William 8–8:1], 554 [*Leges Henrici* 8–8:7], ii. 743–8 ['Zehnerschaft']; W. A. Morris, *The Frankpledge System* (Harvard, 1910), pp. 1–41; W. L. Warren, *The Governance of Norman and Angevin England 1086–1272* (London, 1987), pp. 39–44.

PATRICK WORMALD

FRANKS. The Franks, rulers of Gaul and Western *Germany in the early medieval period, originated in the area of the Lower Rhine, but in the course of the fourth and fifth centuries moved westwards and southwards to extend their settlements to northern Gaul. Under Clovis (481–511) they conquered the remaining parts of Gaul and

consolidated their hold over the peoples to the east of the Rhine. The Franks were a confederate people and as a result of their conquests became an increasingly hetereogenous group, the term 'Frank' coming to have a cultural and political rather than ethnic significance. *Stephen of Ripon and *Bede reflect this rather open concept of 'Frankishness' by using the terms 'Frank' and 'Gaul' interchangeably to designate the inhabitants of the lands across the Channel. These lands were, likewise, sometimes referred to as 'Francia', and sometimes as 'Gaul'.

Archaeological evidence (largely of *jewellery deposited in graves) reveals that in *Kent in the first half of the sixth century there were people who were culturally 'Frankish'. Such people seem to have been of the highest social status and were often *women. Here the archaeology provides a context for what is the best known example of Frankish contact with Kent, namely, the marriage of the Merovingian Frankish princess, Bertha, to the king of Kent, *Æthelberht, which took place *c.*560. In context, therefore, this marriage took place as one of a series of high-level contacts between the two peoples, and it has been suggested that these contacts show that Kent, and possibly also areas further to the west, were actually under some sort of Frankish overlordship for much of the sixth century. That Bertha was a relatively low status Frankish princess is in this argument said to indicate that Æthelberht was treated by the Merovingian rulers as a client king not worthy of a more royal bride. If this were the case, then Æthelberht's decision to support Christian missionaries who came from *Rome rather than from Paris could indicate a successful Kentish attempt to break free of Frankish tutelage. By the same token, Anglo-Saxon England's peculiar reverence for the authority of the Roman church might well have been an insurance policy against absorbtion into a Frankish polity which increasingly drew strength from its control over the church.

From the evidence of Stephen's *Life* of *Wilfrid and Bede's *HE* it is clear that in the mid-seventh century, after the collapse of the Roman mission, Frankish churchmen played an important role in sustaining Christianity in southern England. Bishops *Agilbert (fl. 650–80) and his nephew *Leuthere (fl. 670–6) carried on the work of *Birinus in organizing a church amongst the West Saxons. The names of these two, which are the Frankish forms of Æthelberht and Hlothhere, also recall the earlier links between the Kentish kings and the Merovingian rulers. At the same time,

Erchinoald, the most important non-royal leader ('mayor of the palace') in Neustrian Francia, also had links with the Kentish dynasty. The bishop of London, *Earconwald (675–93), bore the same name as the 'mayor', suggesting continuing Anglo-Frankish family links into the 670s. In *East Anglia, the many Frankish artefacts deposited in the famous *Sutton Hoo ship burial reveal another set of Frankish contacts. It has indeed been observed that whoever was buried at Sutton Hoo had been provided with what is basically a Merovingian treasure. On the other side of the Channel, Erchinoald provided the Merovingian ruler Clovis II (d. 657) with an Anglo-Saxon bride, Balthild, who became *queen regent from 657 to c.664. Agilbert, who left England and became bishop of Paris when Balthild was driven out, took part in the ordination of Wilfrid as bishop in that year, and in 676, Wilfrid, probably with Agilbert's help, arranged for the return to Francia of a king, Dagobert II, who had been living in exile in Ireland. In the later seventh century it was also the custom, says Bede, for noble or royal Anglo-Saxon women to join Frankish convents, and these convents were institutions founded and run by the very families whose members we see appearing in England in the mid-seventh century. We also find that the earliest English *charters seem to be derived from Frankish rather than Roman models. One conclusion to be drawn from this evidence is that in the later seventh century Frankish influence upon religious life in southern England was strong, or even that southern England was being pulled into a Frankish religious orbit. What reversed the trend was the advent of Archbishop *Theodore, whose influence as a steadfast Romanist was extraordinary, and the rise of a Mercian power which distanced itself from the Frankish connection as one way of breaking Kentish influence in the south. At same time, at the beginning of the eighth century, the power of the old Neustrian Frankish families once involved in England, and the power of their patrons, the Merovingian family itself, went into rapid decline. Thereafter, cross-Channel traffic would be in one direction only, as English missionaries, scholars, and some exiles, sought patronage and protection in Francia. These people did not establish family links with their hosts as the Franks had done earlier in England. The letters of the most famous of the missionaries, *Boniface, make it clear in fact that many of the Frankish leaders actually resented the English presence, and poetry from the court of Charlemagne (768–814) reveals a certain cultural disdain for the English, despite (or possibly because of)

the fact that the leading court scholar, *Alcuin, was English.

Though English influence on the Continent in the eighth century was made famous by the celebrated activities of missionaries and scholars, we know very little about other kinds of contacts between the Anglo-Saxons and the Franks in this period. Letters from Charlemagne to King *Offa at the end of the century show that Eadberht Præn, a member of the Kentish royal line, had sought sanctuary from Offa at the Frankish court. The letters also reveal that *trade between England and Francia was regarded as an important matter, with cloaks being mentioned as one item exported from England to Francia, which might suggest a very early date for the importance of woollens in the English economy. *Coinage demonstrates that the monetary system of south-eastern England was closely tied to that of Francia, and the rapid growth of coastal trading emporia in this period similarly reflects the importance of trade with the near Continent.

P. Fouracre and R. Gerberding, *Late Merovingian France. History and Hagiography 640–720* (Manchester, 1996); E. James, *The Franks* (Oxford, 1988); W. Levison, *England and the Continent in the Eighth Century* (Oxford, 1946); A. Lohaus, *Die Merowinger und England* (Munich, 1974); P. Drewett, D. Rudling and M. Gardiner, *The South-East to AD 1000* (London, 1988); P. Wormald, *Bede and the Conversion of England: the Charter Evidence*, Jarrow Lecture (1984); I. Wood, *The Merovingian North Sea*, Occasional Papers on Medieval Topics 1 (Alingsås 1983); idem, *The Merovingian Kingdoms 450–751* (London, 1994).

PAUL FOURACRE

FRANKS CASKET. The eighth-century Anglo-Saxon whalebone box known as the Franks Casket is a unique survival which reflects central issues concerning the transmission of learning and culture following the *conversion. First recognized in the possession of a family in Auzon, France, in the early nineteenth century, it was presumably once church property, secularised during the revolutionary years. Its earlier history is unknown, but it seems likely that it was originally a prestige gift made by an Anglo-Saxon churchman or noble to a local church.

Rectangular in plan, it consists of a base constructed from four side panels which are dowelled and slotted into corner posts, and a composite flat lid which, though extensively damaged and repaired, probably represents the original form. Traces of metal hinges, a handle and a lock show that it was designed to hold precious contents. Each wall panel, and the central panel on the lid, is decorated with lively relief carving depicting events carefully selected to represent a variety of traditions. On the front, the Adoration of the Magi is paired with the Revenge of the Germanic artificer, Weland the Smith; the back has the Destruction of the Temple at Jerusalem by the Roman general (later Emperor) Titus, in AD 70; the left-hand end symbolises both the origins of Rome and the Christian church in its depiction of Romulus and Remus nurtured by the she-wolf; while the right-hand end bears an unidentified composite scene drawn from Germanic mythology. The surviving decorated lid panel was originally flanked by two other, presumably decorated, panels which may have had inscriptions or additional scenes; it also appears to depict a scene from Germanic legend, probably a lost exploit of the archer hero Egil (thus labelled) involving the defence of a fortified place.

The other panels are accompanied by extended descriptive texts, sometimes augmented by one-word labels of the kind seen on the lid. These display a deliberate linguistic and alphabetic virtuosity; though they are mostly written in *Old English and in *runes, they shift into Latin and the Roman alphabet, then back into runes while still writing Latin; on the undeciphered right-hand panel, the runes are encoded; elsewhere, the texts may be carved upside down or in retrograde, while on the front panel, this erudite playfulness is encapsulated in a text which is actually a *riddle about the whale from which the casket was made.

Nothing else like this survives. Stylistically and linguistically it is likely to have been made somewhere in Northumbria in the first half of the eighth century. Very clearly, it was modelled on a late antique ivory box, of the narrative type represented by the Brescia reliquary. Such things were certainly reaching England along with ecclesiastical books and other equipment which we know leading churchmen of the day were bringing back from *Rome. Its exuberantly learned nature and contrapuntal iconographic programme suggest production in a monastic centre; yet the mythological, even pagan, Germanic content might imply a secular purpose. Indeed a royal context would not be improbable; in the Insular tradition of complex visual and textual interaction, the casket's themes might very possibly be read as a series of texts on the nature of divine and secular kingship. Whatever its purpose, however, the casket is a remarkable work of synthesis and exploration which aptly characterizes the intellectual temper of scholarship in this period.

A. S. Napier, 'The Franks Casket', in *An English Miscellany Presented to Dr Furnivall* (Oxford, 1900), pp. 362–81; R. I. Page, *An Introduction to Old English Runes* (London, 1973), pp. 66–8, 174–82, 188–9; L. E. Webster, 'Stylistic Aspects of the Franks Casket', in *The Vikings*, ed. R. T. Farrell (Chichester, 1982), pp. 20–32; I. N. Wood, 'Ripon, Francia and the Franks Casket in the Early Middle Ages', *NH* 26 (1990), 1–19; *The Making of England*, pp. 101–3; L. Webster, 'The Iconographic Programme of the Franks Casket', in *Northumbria's Golden Age*, ed. J. Hawkes and S. Mills (Stroud, 1999) pp. 227–46.

LESLIE WEBSTER

FRISIANS. Of the Germanic languages spoken today Frisian is closest to English. The Germanic invaders of Britain must have numbered Frisians among them, as the road from the homelands of the Angles and Saxons to the island of Britain led through the coastal areas of the modern Netherlands and northern *Germany. It was this geographical area, stretching from the Sincfal in the south to the Weser in the north, that went by the name Frisia in the early Middle Ages. Neither ethnically nor politically did it form a unity: the *Franks living in the south of the area might be called 'Frisians' by contemporaries (Bede, *HE* v.10). Although there is not sufficient archaeological and linguistic evidence to suppose a common Dark Age culture involving all peoples bordering the North Sea, the Anglo-Saxons were definitely aware of their continental background. They considered the Franco-Frisians, speaking dialects which were still very close to OE., as their relatives (Bede, *HE* v.9).

The gradual incorporation of the Frisian lands into the Frankish polity ensured the success of Anglo-Saxon efforts at converting their heathen cousins. There had been a church in Utrecht before 612, but only its foundations remained when the first Insular *missionaries arrived at the mouths of the Rhine. *Wilfrid, bishop of *York, spent the winter of 678–9 as the guest of King Aldgisl and preached the gospel. However, Aldgisl's successor King Radbod reverted to the ancient gods. *Willibrord and *Boniface and their companions, with the support of the Frankish church and Frankish arms, achieved more lasting results. Nevertheless, Boniface was killed at Dokkum in 754, and when Charlemagne fought against the pagan Saxons, many Frisians attached themselves to their leader Widukind.

From the seventh century onwards there is unequivocal evidence for commerce between Frisia and England. Before 650 a *mint was established at Dorestad, a merchants' settlement which, until its decay in the second half of ninth century through the twin causes of *Viking raids and

195

changes in the course of the Rhine, was the most important trade centre in north-western Europe. The Frisians brought the Dorestad coinage into England, and in 678 the first documented Frisian merchant appeared in London (Bede, *HE* iv.22). They were also seen in *Hamwic* (*Southampton) and York, where Frisian colonies appeared in the eighth century, and, together with their Anglo-Saxon competitors, in Saint-Denis. Together they were the most important distributors of silver *coinage, which had been replacing gold, the value of which had risen so dramatically as to make it unsuitable for commercial exchange. The produce of the Rhineland was carried by the Frisian farmer-navigators to England; metals, slaves and cloth were exported. In England 'Frisian' was used as a synonym of 'long distance trader' (cf. the 'Frisian sailor passage' in the *Exeter Book *Maxims*) long after the Scandinavians together with their Anglo-Danish and Anglo-Saxon relatives had taken over the lead in commercial matters.

H. H. van Regteren Altena and H. A. Heidinga, 'The North Sea Region in the Early Medieval Period (400–950)', in *Ex Horreo*, ed. B. L. van Beek, R. W. Brandt and W. Groenman-van Waateringe (Amsterdam, 1977), pp. 47–67; *Excerpta Romana*, ed. A. W. Byvanck, 3 vols., Rijks Geschiedkundige Publicatiën 73, 81 and 89 (The Hague, 1931–47) [covering virtually all mentions of Frisians up to *c.*1500]; 'Friesen', in *Reallexikon der Germanischen Altertumskunde*, 2nd ed., 101–2 (Berlin and New York, 1996), 2–70; *Frisia before 1100 AD*, Berichten van de Rijksdienst voor het Oudheidkundig Bodemonderzoek 15–16 (1965–6); S. Lebecq, *Marchands et navigateurs frisons du haut moyen age*, 2 vols. (Lille, 1983) [which includes a full bibliography and a 'Corpus des sources écrites' from the sixth century onwards]; L. Whitbread, 'The Frisian Sailor Passage in the Old English Gnomic Verses', *RES* 22 (1946), 215–19.

MARCO MOSTERT

FRITHEGOD of Canterbury (fl. 950), a scholar of Frankish origin (his original name was presumably Fredegaud, of which Frithegod is an anglicization found in English sources), was a member of the household of Archbishop *Oda, and served as tutor for Oda's nephew, the future Archbishop *Oswald. Frithegod produced as a commission for Oda a metrical version, entitled the *Breviloquium Vitae Wilfridi*, of *Stephen of Ripon's earlier prose Life of St *Wilfrid; the occasion for the commission was the acquisition by Canterbury of the relics of St Wilfrid during King *Eadred's invasion of Northumbria and sack of Ripon in 948. This *Breviloquium* consists of

some 1,400 hexameters, and is unquestionably the most difficult Anglo-Latin product of the pre-Conquest period, in that its diction comprises archaic Latin words, words borrowed from Greek, and many words coined by the poet on the basis of Greek elements. Two other poems by Frithegod survive: a hymn for Maundy Thursday (inc. 'Dum pietas multimoda') focused on the person of Mary Magdalene, and a rhythmical poem on the twelve precious stones of Revelation (inc. 'Ciues celestis patrie'); a further poem on St Audoenus (Ouen), whose relics were acquired for Canterbury by Archbishop Oda, was seen in the sixteenth century by John *Bale, but has not survived (or been identified as yet). Various evidence suggests that, after the death of his patron Oda in 958, Frithegod returned to Francia, to the canonry of Brioude in the Auvergne.

Sharpe, *Handlist*, 301; *Frithegodi monachi Breuiloquium Vitae Beati Wilfredi et Wulfstani Cantoris Narratio Metrica de Sancto Swithuno*, ed. A. Campbell (Zurich, 1950); *Analecta Hymnica Medii Aevi*, ed. C. Blume and G. M. Dreves, 55 vols. (Leipzig, 1886–1922), xvi. 33–5 ['Dum pietas multimoda']; P. Kitson, 'Lapidary Traditions in Anglo-Saxon England: Part II, Bede's *Explanatio Apocalypsis* and Related Works', *ASE* 12 (1983), 73–123, at 109–23; D. C. C. Young, 'Author's Variants and Interpretations in Frithegod', *Archivum Latinitatis Medii Aevi* 25 (1955), 71–98; M. Lapidge, 'A Frankish Scholar in Tenth-century England: Frithegod of Canterbury / Fredegaud of Brioude', *ASE* 17 (1988), 45–65 (repr. in *ALL* ii. 157–81, with addenda at p. 481).

MICHAEL LAPIDGE

FRITHUSWITH (FRIDESWIDE), ST: *see* Oxford

FULLER BROOCH. A ninth-century disc-brooch bearing an iconographic scheme of remarkable ingenuity. It is a silver disc, 11.4 cms in diameter, whose engraved surface has been given added definition by the application of niello (black silver sulphide), and by fretwork near the edge. Two later holes have been drilled at the top, possibly to allow suspension when the fastening-pin on the reverse was removed. Two concentric circles frame sixteen roundels, containing in each quadrant one example of what appear to be four categories: a head and shoulders of a human, a quadruped, a floral motif and a bird entwined with foliate infill. In the middle, four lozenges and a central field enclose five figures, each of whom is performing a different gesture (see fig. 8).

The brooch was first brought to scholarly attention in 1910, but its unknown provenance and excellent condition led to its dismissal as a fake in the 1920s. The discovery of the comparable Strickland brooch in 1949 prompted chemical tests of the niello, which established its great antiquity. The brooch's burnished surface suggests that it has the unusual distinction of not having gone to ground, even before the seventeenth century, when a sharkskin case was made to protect it.

Disc-brooches with five bosses and a quadripartite design are a uniquely Anglo-Saxon form. First produced in *Kent in the seventh century, they became the standard means of fastening one's cloak at the shoulder in Anglo-Saxon England. The Fuller brooch combines these two distinctively Anglo-Saxon features with the 'Trewhiddle Style' of ninth-century *metalwork, which is characterized by the interplay of animal and foliate motifs, inlaid with niello. The human figures are paralleled in such early ninth-century Mercian manuscripts as the Book of *Cerne. The double-nicked lobes on the central figure's plant stems, however, are a feature of later West Saxon metalwork, such as the *Abingdon sword and the rings associated with *Æthelwulf, king of Wessex, and his daughter Æthelswith, which suggests a date rather closer to 900.

The Fuller Brooch is unique among disc-brooches in that it was designed to convey a specific iconographic message, the main feature of which is conventionally believed to be the Five Senses. Any doubts one might have about the clarity of this scheme should be ascribed to the

Fig. 8 The Fuller Brooch.

conciseness necessary to fit five complex ideas into a small area. The brooch-designer has therefore largely omitted any objects of sensation. Clockwise from the top left, Taste has his hand in his mouth, Smell has his hands behind his back yet still senses the foliate infill which points towards his nose, Touch is placing his hands palm to palm, and Hearing is running in response to a call which his right hand at his ear has amplified. Sight, given extra importance by his central position, the small cross on his vestments and the plant stems in his hands, stares out with exaggerated circular eyes.

This primacy of Sight and the different aspects of Creation in the outer roundels seem to be two additional and apparently connected features of the iconographic message. Biblical commentaries available in England show that the Five Senses must have been known from the seventh century onwards, but these do not convey what explained the primacy of Sight in medieval Christian thought: that, in addition to the corporeal eyes, there were the 'mind's eyes' (*oculi mentis*), through which the soul could perceive heavenly things. Certain *Alfredian texts reveal that these 'mind's eyes' (*modes eagan*) were of particular interest at Alfred's court. In his version of Augustine's *Soliloquia*, where Augustine argues that the Five Senses are not to be trusted, Alfred explains that this means 'neither eyes, nor ears, nor smell, nor taste, nor touch'. In long additions Alfred then describes how 'just as the visible sun illuminates the eyes of our body, so wisdom illuminates the eyes of our mind, that is, our understanding'. In another addition, he argues that whereas 'apples, grass and plants . . . and likewise all beasts and birds . . . and even the bodies of men' wither and die, men's souls are ever-living. The outer roundels may thus be drawing this distinction between man's bodily existence, which he shares with the rest of Creation, and the spiritual faculty of his immortal soul, the 'mind's eyes' of the central field.

Sophisticated Christian iconography is also a feature of the *Alfred Jewel and the Abingdon sword, both of which may have Alfredian connections. Together with these pieces, the Fuller brooch aptly reflects the inventiveness and deeply religious nature of the studies undertaken at Alfred's court and recalls *Asser's description (c. 91) of the 'treasures incomparably fashioned in gold and silver' at Alfred's instigation.

R. L. S. Bruce-Mitford, 'Late Saxon Disc-Brooches', *Aspects of Anglo-Saxon Archaeology* (London, 1974), pp. 303–45; *Golden Age of AS Art*, no. 11; *Making of England*, no. 257; C. Nordenfalk, 'The Five Senses in

Late Medieval and Renaissance Art', *Journal of the Warburg and Courtauld Institutes* 48 (1985), 1–22, at 1 n. 2.

DAVID PRATT

FURSA (d. 649), an Irish monk who left Ireland to go on *pilgrimage for the love of God. When he arrived in England *c.*630 he was given permission by King Sigeberht of *East Anglia to establish a hermitage at a former Roman camp called *Cnobheresburg* (now Burgh Castle, Suffolk). According to *Bede (who was drawing on an anonymous *Vita S. Fursei*), Fursa was devoted to the study of sacred books and monastic discipline; Bede also records a number of *visions which were seen by Fursa. Fursa subsequently went to Francia, where, with the patronage of King Clovis, he built a monastery at Lagny, where he died in 649. After his death, his remains were translated to Péronne, which subsequently became a focal point for Irish pilgrims, and is accordingly referred to in Latin sources as *Peronna Scottorum* (it was from Péronne that the Irish scholar Cellán wrote to *Aldhelm requesting copies of his writings). Fursa is commemorated on 16 January in Insular calendars.

MGH, SS rerum Merovingicarum iv. 423–49 [*Vita S. Fursei*]; Bede, *HE* iii. 19; J. Hennig, 'The Irish Background to St Fursey', *Irish Ecclesiastical Record* 77 (1952), 18–28; P. Ó Riain, 'Les vies de saint Fursy: les sources irlandaises', *Revue du Nord* 69 (1986), 405–13.

MICHAEL LAPIDGE

FYRD: *see* Army

G

GAMES: *see* Entertainment

GANDERSHEIM CASKET. This elegant house-shaped small casket is one of the finest pieces of Middle Saxon carving to have survived. It dates to the late eighth century, and was at Gandersheim Abbey in Germany during the Middle Ages, passing in 1815 into the ducal collection at Braunschweig where it remains to this day.

Constructed of carved whalebone panels set in a bronze framework, the casket's walls and lid are exquisitely decorated with an intricate chequerboard of interlacing creatures, vine-scroll and spiral ornament. The style is close to some Anglo-Saxon *stone sculpture of the late eighth and early ninth centuries, such as the Hedda Stone in Peterborough Cathedral, and the Rothbury cross-shaft. Insular animal ornament also occurs on some of the metal fittings. On the underside of the basal frame is an apparently Old English runic inscription which has not been satisfactorily read; the base itself seems to be a replacement of an earlier frame, and the possibility exists that the runes were copied from a somewhat earlier original.

The casket's house-shaped construction and small scale relate it to the Insular series of small metal-fitted wooden reliquaries, while the vine-scroll decoration also suggests a religious context. It may have served as a shrine, or perhaps as a container for the host. How it came to be at Gandersheim is unknown, though the survival of a significant number of Anglo-Saxon artefacts in continental treasuries indicates that it was not uncommon for such precious things to be presented to churches abroad. One possible contender as donor is King *Æthelstan, a noted collector and giver of relics, who had a close relationship with the Saxon court, and was himself commemorated at Gandersheim.

A. Fink, 'Zum Gandersheimer Runenkästchen', in *Karolingische und Ottonische Kunst, Werden, Wesen, Wicklung*, ed. F. Geke, G. von Opel and H. Schnitzler (Wiesbaden, 1957), pp. 277–81; D. M. Wilson, *Anglo-Saxon Art* (London, 1984), pp. 64–7; *Making of England*, pp. 177–9.
LESLIE WEBSTER

GELD: *see Heregeld*

GENEALOGIES, ROYAL. Royal genealogies describe kinship relationships between two or more members of a dynasty. Though often grouped together with *regnal lists (both in medieval manuscripts and by modern scholars), they constitute a separate medium with characteristic features and problems of their own, and should be treated separately. For Anglo-Saxon England, the earliest direct evidence of genealogies comes from the early eighth century, though it has been argued they derive from pagan Germanic practice (see below). *Bede knew a version of the Kentish royal genealogy (*HE* i.15, ii.5) and perhaps also that of *East Anglia (ii.15). The important 'Anglian' collection of genealogies was originally composed in *Northumbria, probably during the reign of Alhred (765×774), though more recent collateral lines occur in the extant copies. It contains pedigrees of the kingdoms of *Deira, *Bernicia (four lines), *Mercia (four lines), *Lindsey, *Kent, East Anglia and *Wessex, all traced to Woden, as well as some regnal, papal and *episcopal lists. Versions of some of these pedigrees also occur in the *Historia Brittonum*, the *Anglo-Saxon Chronicle* and the Chronicle of *Æthelweard. In addition, there is an account of the royal genealogy of *Essex, *c*.800, which survives in BL, Add. 23211 (copied after 871). Inevitably, the West Saxon genealogy proved to be the most durable, and over time it was regularly updated and also extended further into the past, eventually to Adam. In addition to the versions in the *Chronicle* (esp. *s.a.* 855), it occurs in the so-called 'West-Saxon Genealogical Regnal List' and in *Asser's *Vita Ælfredi* (c. 1). Later versions include an elaborate genealogy of *Edgar and his sons, composed 966×970/1; and some Anglo-Norman chronicles also contain Anglo-Saxon royal genealogies.

Most of these extant genealogies are what can be termed retrograde linear patrilines. They are linear or unilateral in form in that they give one name per generation, though the occurrence of collateral lines for Bernicia, Mercia and Essex adds a degree of segmentation; they are retrograde or 'ascending' in perspective in that they begin with the chronologically most recent name and trace the line of descent back in time (only the material in

Historia Brittonum reverses this, using the Biblical *genuit* formula). Furthermore, female ancestors are not included, though Asser does discuss briefly *Alfred's maternal ancestry (c. 2). The language of the genealogies can be either Old English (the 'Anglian' collection or the *Chronicle*) or Latin (Bede, Asser, or Æthelweard) depending on the narrative context.

Recent comparative study of royal genealogies has demonstrated that, while superficially being descriptions of kinship relationships, they can in fact be very sophisticated means of expressing political claims. As such they are prone to a high degree of ideological manipulation and falsification, which can undermine the historical reliability of the genealogical statements made therein. The 'Anglian' collection is an example of such manipulation. Each of the heptarchic dynasties is traced back to its respective eponymous founder and thence to the common ancestor Woden. It seems likely that a symmetrical and artificial scheme underlies the surviving texts, whereby fourteen generations separated the subject of each patriline and Woden. Although originally a pagan god, it has been argued that Woden functioned here as a means of defining 'Anglian' origin (or at least a belief in that origin) and thus stands in contrast to Seaxnet, the equivalent figure in the East Saxon genealogy, who defined a 'Saxon' origin. Consequently, it seems that the non-Anglian dynasties of Kent and Wessex have been artificially incorporated into the 'Anglian' scheme of the collection, by grafting them onto the lines of Deira and Bernicia respectively (causing chronological difficulties for the Kentish line). It might be argued that the purpose of this manipulation was to express in genealogical terms the predominant position of the 'Anglian' kingdoms in the eighth century, and possibly also to reflect a number of inter-dynastic marriage-alliances in the seventh. The fact that the East Saxon line was not incorporated into the scheme – even though Essex was also under the 'Anglian' overlordship (of Mercia) – may undermine this interpretation. However, the occurrence of certain conspicuously non-alliterative personal names, such as Offa (possibly inserted retrospectively in the East Saxon genealogy due to its Mercian associations) may be a reflex of similar genealogical thinking.

While the surviving Anglo-Saxon royal genealogies were clearly the products of a literate and Christian society, it has been argued that in fact they were derived from earlier, pre-literate and pagan Germanic practices. This line of argument

hinges on the occurrence of so many Germanic gods in the genealogies – notably, Woden, *Saxnot* (i.e. Seaxnet), and Geat – who, whatever their function in the eighth-century and later extant genealogies, are undeniably pagan in origin. Comparable Germanic material, quotations from classical authors, and reference to anthropological study of contemporary 'oral' societies, can all be employed to support the theory that pre-Christian Anglo-Saxon kings traced their descent from pagan gods and that this divine genealogical origin served to set these kings apart from the rest of the population. Indeed, the development of the West Saxon patriline through various distinct stages (Woden – Frealaf – Geat – Sceaf 'son of Noah' – Adam) could be seen as a progressive search for such divine ancestry, even in a Christian context, following the demotion of Woden. It should be noted here, however, that the practice of grafting royal pedigrees onto Biblical genealogy, best represented in the Table of Nations (Gen. X), was not uncommon in the Middle Ages, and no doubt in part reflects the understandable desire to find one's place in the overall genealogical scheme of things. In short, it is likely that the Anglo-Saxon genealogies tell us more about political aspirations and inter-dynastic relations at the end of the eighth century, and (possibly) the nature of pagan kingship, than they do about developments in the fifth and sixth centuries, and any attempt to use them for 'historical' purposes must be undertaken with extreme caution.

D. N. Dumville, 'Kingship, Genealogies and Regnal Lists', in *Early Medieval Kingship*, ed. P. H. Sawyer and I. N. Wood (Leeds, 1977), pp. 72–104; K. Sisam, 'Anglo-Saxon Royal Genealogies', *PBA* 39 (1953), 287–348; D. N. Dumville, 'The Anglian Collection of Royal Genealogies and Regnal Lists', *ASE* 5 (1976), 23–50; B. Yorke, 'The Kingdom of the East Saxons', *ASE* 14 (1985), 1–36; H. Moisl, 'Anglo-Saxon Royal Genealogies and Germanic Oral Tradition', *JMH* 7 (1981), 215–48; C. R. Davis, 'Cultural Assimilation in the Anglo-Saxon Royal Genealogies', *ASE* 21 (1992), 23–36

DAVID E. THORNTON

GENESIS, the first and longest of the poems in the *Junius Manuscript, deals with the events of the first biblical book from the creation to the offering of Isaac. It is in fact two poems, known for convenience as *Genesis A* and *Genesis B*. *Genesis A* is based on Gen. I–XXII. On the whole it stays close to the biblical version, keeping the same narrative content event by event. But in place of the paraphrase of Gen. III.1–7, the deception of Eve by the serpent, there is an interpolation, known as *Genesis B*, comprising lines 235–851 of the whole poem.

That *Genesis B* is a translation adapted from an Old Saxon poem was first established by Eduard Sievers in 1875 and subsequently confirmed by the discovery of fragments from an Old Saxon *Genesis* in the Vatican Library. Apart from the repetition of the fall of the angels and the obvious differences in subject-matter, Sievers's argument focused on differences in vocabulary, especially the words used for God. There are also some metrical features that reflect the OS original, such as longer initial dips than usual, the predominance in the *b*-verse of verses with a rising rhythm, and unusually frequent use of anacrusis (initial extra-metrical syllables) and unstressed infinitives.

In the treatment of episodes *Genesis A* often tends to emphasize Germanic elements. For instance, like a Germanic warlord, God exacts vengeance on men's malicious deeds (1380). In the Cain and Abel episode the *kinship of the brothers is emphasized, so that, in killing his brother, Cain is offending against one of the strongest bonds of Germanic society. When Cain is banished he is sent into exile, another common motif in Old English poetry. In the episode of Lot and Sodom and Gomorrah, the Sodomites are guilty of over-bearing behaviour (2581), like Hygelac when he took on the Frisians (*Beowulf* 1206). But the poem's principal message is inevitably religious. A theme that emerges from practically every episode is that of Salvation by the Help of God. The differences between those who are saved and those who are destroyed emerges particularly clearly in the episode of Lot and Sodom and Gomorrah. Like God, Lot is firm in his adherence to the covenant between them, as were also Abel, Noah and Abraham, whereas the Sodomites, like the fallen angels and the race of Cain before them, are covenant-breakers. The terms of the covenant are that God will protect the people if they obey Him and keep His commands. God propels his followers (2813–14), but only if they fear and respect him as Abraham does in offering Isaac (2861–7). Those who fail to follow God's directives are punished: the rebel angels are sent to hell, the Sodomites are engulfed in flames, and Lot's wife is turned into a pillar of salt. God controls everything: his moral righteousness is backed by physical power.

Genesis B treats the fall of the angels and the fall of man in a dramatic and ironic way. While this subject-matter is biblical, most of what is in *Genesis B* is not in the Bible. The events are interpreted in terms of the Germanic *comitatus*.

In heaven God is lord and the angels are His *thegns owing God loyalty in return for His favour. Satan is the senior angel. But, dissatisfied with this position, he objects to serving God, and rebels. For his pains he is thrown into hell, and there, ironically, sets up his own *comitatus* with himself as lord. Chained in hell he then makes a long appeal to the fallen angels, his thegns, for one of them to volunteer to go to earth to deceive Adam and Eve. On earth, where Adam and Eve are the Lord's thegns in paradise, this devilish emissary approaches Adam, but is rebuffed on the grounds that he cannot show Adam any sign of the benefits of eating the forbidden fruit. The devilish emissary promptly invents a heavenly vision for Eve, who falls, followed by Adam. Adam and Eve are expelled from paradise, and the devilish emissary returns exultant to hell. This version of events differs from that in Christian tradition in some notable ways. First, there is an infernal council at which the devils plot the fall of Man and one of them is chosen to go and bring it about. Secondly, the devilish emissary approaches Adam first (rather than Eve) and is rebuffed. Thirdly, Eve is the victim of a deception, acting throughout in good faith. It is possible that Milton was familiar with the contents of this poem through its first editor, Francis *Junius.

E. Sievers, *Der Heliand und die angelsächsische Genesis* (Halle, 1875); B. F. Huppé, *Doctrine and Poetry* (New York, 1959); J. M. Evans, *Paradise Lost and the Genesis Tradition* (Oxford, 1968); ASPR i.3–87; *Genesis A*, ed. A. N. Doane (Madison, WI, 1978); *Heliand und Genesis*, ed. O. Behaghel, rev. B. Taeger (Tübingen, 1984); *The Saxon Genesis*, ed. A. N. Doane (Madison, WI, 1991); P. G. Remley, *Old English Biblical Verse*, CSASE 16 (Cambridge, 1996), 94–167.

4   P. J. LUCAS

GENS ANGLORUM: *see* English People

GERMANIC LANGUAGES, a group of closely related languages originally found in north-western Europe. They derive from a single common ancestor, known as Proto-Germanic or Primitive Germanic, spoken up to about the fourth century AD and originating in southern Scandinavia and Germany roughly north of the Elbe. This language is known directly from names cited by Greek and Roman writers, and from a small number of inscriptions cut in *runes, dating from about the second century AD onward. Proto-Germanic was an Indo-European language, and shared a remote common ancestor with most of the other languages of Europe, most importantly Greek, Latin, the Celtic languages and the Baltic and

Slavonic languages, and also some Asiatic languages, most importantly Hittite and Sanskrit. It was an unusually pure Indo-European language, in that it contained very little vocabulary of external origin, though it had a few prehistoric loans from Celtic (e.g. *rich*), and some Latin loans of the Roman period (e.g. *tower, street, cheap*). It differed from other Indo-European languages by a major consonant-shift (*'Grimm's Law') and some vowel-changes. It reorganized verbs into older 'strong' such as *sing, sang, sung*, and newer 'weak' such as *love, loved*. It established a dynamic word-initial root accent: that is, the first syllable of each word carried the meaning and was spoken loudest. Consequentially following syllables were spoken more quietly and were often lost, and so the language simplified and lost many of its inflectional endings. These had shown word-function, which then had to be indicated by other means, often by 'function words' such as prepositions and auxiliary verbs, and by word-order. This process has continued in most of the subsequent languages. Proto-Germanic had several early dialects which developed into separate languages after the tribal migrations at the time of the collapse of the Roman Empire. These are, firstly, East Germanic, significantly attested only by Gothic; secondly, West Germanic, first attested by Old High German, Old Saxon, Old Frisian and *Old English; thirdly, North Germanic, attested in *Old Norse. These dialect groupings are ambiguous in that Old Norse and Old High German share different features with Gothic, while the 'North Sea' group of Old Saxon, Old Frisian and particularly Old English share other features with Old Norse. Other than in runic inscriptions, Gothic is attested in manuscripts of the sixth century AD, mostly containing parts of a translation of the Bible attributed to the late fourth century; Old English is first attested in manuscripts from the end of the seventh century onwards, Old High German and Old Saxon during the eighth century onwards, and Old Frisian and Old Norse from the twelfth century onwards. Other early Germanic dialects existed, e.g. Vandal and Lombardic, but are merely known from names and phrases cited in Latin texts, in place-names and from loan-words. Modern Germanic languages include English, Frisian, Dutch, German, Danish, Swedish, Norwegian, Faroese and Icelandic.

The early Germanic languages shared a common poetic *metre and poetic diction, and also a common body of legendary narratives transmitted in poetry, and these seem to be inherited from the Proto-Germanic period, although they are mostly recorded in Old English and Old Norse. A common body of pre-Christian mythological and religious material seems also to have been transmitted, probably in poetry, though this was largely suppressed after conversion to Christianity, and is only substantially recorded in Old Norse; it is known elsewhere only in passing references, and from names.

R. E. Keller, *The German Language* (London, 1978); H. F. Nielsen, *The Germanic Languages: Origins and Early Dialectal Interrelations* (Tuscaloosa and London, 1989).

PAUL BIBIRE

GERMANUS, sometime abbot of *Winchcombe, *Ramsey, and Cholsey (d. *c*.1013). According to *Byrhtferth, whose *Vita S. Oswaldi* contains substantial discussion of Germanus, he originated in *Winchester (though it is perhaps odd that he does not have an English name, and there is some suspicion that he may have been of British origin). He subsequently accompanied Archbishop Oscytel of *York, and Oscytel's nephew, the future archbishop *Oswald, on a trip to *Rome in 956 or 957; on the return from Rome, Germanus remained at *Fleury in order to study monastic discipline. When Oswald, then bishop of *Worcester, established a small community of monks at Westbury (963 or 964), he recalled Germanus from Fleury to be their prior. When the monastery of *Ramsey was established in 966 by Oswald, working in collaboration with Ealdorman Æthelwine of *East Anglia, the same community of monks was transferred to Ramsey; but for irrecoverable reasons, perhaps friction between Germanus and the community, Germanus was recalled from Ramsey and made abbot of the refounded monastery at Winchcombe. In the period following the death of King *Edgar in 975, monasteries in Mercia were taken into the control of Ealdorman Ælfhere, and Germanus and the Winchcombe monks were driven into exile at Ramsey. Abbot Germanus and the Winchcombe community remained at Ramsey for a considerable period of time, with (no doubt) further friction between the communities, until after the death of Ealdorman Æthelwine (992), when Germanus was transferred to Cholsey. He died as abbot of Cholsey in *c*.1013. No writings of Germanus survive; but various surviving late-tenth-century manuscripts which show links with Fleury, Winchcombe and Ramsey may arguably be seen as a reflex of Germanus's long sojourn at Ramsey, including the 'Sacramentary of Winchcombe' (Orleans, BM, 127 (105)), the 'Harley Psalter' (London, BL, Harley 2904) and the 'Cambridge Psalter' (Cambridge, UL, Ff. 1.23).

M. Lapidge, 'Abbot Germanus, Winchcombe, Ramsey and the Cambridge Psalter', in Gneuss FS, pp. 99–129; D. N. Dumville, *English Caroline Script and Monastic History: Studies in Benedictinism, A.D. 950–1030* (Woodbridge, 1993), pp. 79–85; *The Winchcombe Sacramentary*, ed. A. Davril, HBS 109 (London, 1995).

MICHAEL LAPIDGE

GERMANY in the early Middle Ages may be said to occupy a rather different territory from that occupied by the modern polity; it is convenient to regard early medieval Germany as consisting in Saxony, Thuringia, Franconia, Bavaria and Lotharingia – approximately the extent of the Ottonian-Salian empire established in 962, and having as its principal cities Aachen, Bamberg, Cologne, Eichstätt, Liège, Mainz, Trier and Würzburg, and as its principal monasteries Corvey, Einsiedeln, Fulda, and Werden. Although, broadly speaking, there was less contact between Anglo-Saxon England and Germany than between England and *Flanders, *Francia and Italy, through all of which English travellers passed on the way to *Rome, there was nevertheless frequent and influential intercourse, dating from the period in the first half of the eighth century when Thuringia and Franconia were converted to Christianity by the efforts of English *missionaries, led by *Boniface, and a number of monasteries (especially Fritzlar and Fulda) and episcopal sees (notably Mainz, Würzburg, and Eichstätt) were established. In the wake of the Bonifatian mission, many Anglo-Saxons took up the religious life in Germany, among them *Lull (who succeeded Boniface as archbishop of Mainz after the martyrdom of the latter in 754), *Willibald the hagiographer of Boniface, and *Hygeburg and her brothers *Willibald and Wynnebald. Later in the eighth century, the abbot of Werden was *Liudger, who had received part of his schooling with *Alcuin at York. A century later, in the late ninth century, the priest *John, called the 'Old Saxon', was invited to England by King *Alfred to help in the process of educational reconstruction. It is a reasonable inference that John himself was educated in one of the monasteries in Saxony, perhaps Werden or Korvey. In the early tenth century, King *Æthelstan was able to marry his half-sister Eadgyth, the daughter of *Edward the Elder, to the future emperor Otto I in 929 or 930; the link between the kingdoms was consolidated in 929 when *Koenwald, bishop of Worcester, visited 'all the monasteries throughout Germany' on Æthelstan's behalf, and dispensed his largesse to them, as a result of which he was commemor-

ated in various German confraternity-books. The link established by this marriage was still in force half a century later, when *Æthelweard, an *ealdorman of royal descent, could dedicate his *Chronicon* (*c.*975) to his kinsman Matilda, a nun at Essen and the grand-daugher of Otto and Eadgyth. At approximately the same time, according to *Goscelin of Saint-Bertin (*Vita S. Eadgithae*) a German priest from Trier, one Benno, served as chaplain to St *Eadgyth (Edith) at Wilton and designed the wall-paintings in the new church there; and an Englishman named Gregory served as abbot of Einsiedeln (964–96). In the early eleventh century, a German named Wythman was abbot of Ramsey for a short period (1016–20), and in the reign of *Edward the Confessor a number of Germans from Lotharingia assumed high ecclesiastical office in England as a result of royal patronage, such as *Adelard of Utrecht, Herman, bishop of Sherborne (1058–78) and *Giso, bishop of Wells (1061–88), and it was during the Confessor's reign that *Ealdred, then bishop of Worcester, spent part of a year at Cologne in 1054 on a diplomatic embassy to Emperor Henry III, and was hosted by Herimann, archbishop of Cologne. It is to be expected that contacts of this sort will have provided the context for the exchange of books and ideas (in the case of Ealdred, it is a reasonable assumption that a copy of the *Romano-German Pontifical* came to England through his agency, and the German exemplar of the 'Cambridge Songs' may have done so as well).

S. Keynes, 'King Athelstan's Books', in Clemoes FS, pp. 143–201, at 198–201 [Koenwald]; K. Leyser, 'The Ottonians and Wessex', in his *Communications and Power in Medieval Europe*, ed. T. Reuter (London, 1994), pp. 73–104; V. Ortenberg, *The English Church and the Continent in the Tenth and Eleventh Centuries* (Oxford, 1992), pp. 41–94; T. Reuter, *Germany in the Early Middle Ages 800–1056* (London, 1991).

MICHAEL LAPIDGE

GESITH: *see* Social Class

GEWISSE was the name of a Saxon people based in the upper Thames whose rulers subsequently founded the kingdom of *Wessex. A bishopric was founded for them in 635 at *Dorchester-on-Thames by King Cynegils, but only some thirty years later his successors had lost control of the region to *Mercia and had transferred their interests further south and west. *Cædwalla was the last of the dynasty to be described by *Bede as a ruler of the *Gewisse*. The name of Gewis, their eponymous founder, was incorporated into the prehistoric part of the West Saxon *genealogy.

H. E. Walker, 'Bede and the Gewissae: the Political Evolution of the Heptarchy and its Nomenclature', *Cambridge Historical Journal* 12 (1956), 174–86; Yorke, *Wessex*, pp. 32–64, 171–3; R. Coates, 'On Some Controversy Surrounding *Gewissae/Gewissei*, *Cerdic* and *Ceawlin*', *Nomina* 13 (1989–90), 1–11; H. Kleinschmidt, 'The Gewissae and Bede: on the Innovativeness of Bede's Concept of the *Gens*', in *The Community, the Family and the Saint*, ed. J. Hill and M. Swan (Turnhout, 1998), pp. 77–102.

B. A. E. YORKE

GIFTS OF MEN, a 113-line poem from the *Exeter Book (78r–80r), titled *God's Gifts to Humankind* in Muir's edition, is a catalogue poem in the tradition of Old English *wisdom literature, enumerating the many skills and talents that God has granted to individuals. In his introduction, the poet observes that God has left no one so lacking in abilities that he should despair, nor anyone so extraordinarily gifted that he should grow proud. The gospel parable of the talents may have had some part in the poet's inspiration, but, if it did, the parallel between the two texts remains so tenuous throughout that it can assist interpretation in only the most general fashion.

The main body of the poem opens with a contrast between the wealthy and those who, though poor, are compensated by the possession of sundry valuable skills. These the poet lists in a catalogue which has resisted critics' efforts to discern a conclusively significant pattern in its apparently random sequence of gifts: physical strength, beauty, poetic skill, eloquence, skill in hunting, the ability to charm a wealthy man, martial ability, wisdom in counsel, architectural ability, musicianship, skill in penetrating mysteries, skill at archery, a good singing voice, swiftness of foot, and nautical ability, to name only the first fifteen items. The gifts listed range across practically the entire breadth of human endeavour: from the physical to the mental, from the secular to the spiritual, from the private to the political, from the practical to the purely aesthetic. Similar lists occur in the *Fortunes of Men* and in lines 659–86 of *Cynewulf's *Christ*.

ASPR iii. 137–40; D. D. Short, 'The Old English *Gifts of Men* and the Pedagogic Theory of the *Pastoral Care*', *ES* 57 (1976), 497–501; G. R. Russom, 'A Germanic Concept of Nobility in *The Gifts of Men* and *Beowulf*', *Speculum* 53 (1978), 1–15; *The Exeter Anthology of Old English Poetry*, ed. B. J. Muir, 2 vols. (Exeter, 1994).

ROBERT DINAPOLI

GILDAS is known principally as the author of a long invective, addressed to five Romano-British princes and entitled *De excidio Britanniae*, on the ills that have befallen Britain (including recent invasion by Anglo-Saxons) as a result of its godlessness. Nothing is known of Gildas save what can be gleaned from the *De excidio* itself; from this it is clear that he was widely read and had received a sound training in Latin grammar and rhetoric (the work is cast as a forensic oration in elegant but difficult Latin, which reveals that Gildas had received excellent training at the hands of a rhetor); and this training implies in turn that his schooling – if it took place in Roman Britain – must have taken place while the Roman system of education and government was still functioning, hence, presumably, some time in the fifth century. (The *Annales Cambriae*, a compilation of tenth-century date, record his obit under 570, but this date has been questioned by some historians.) Although Gildas's principal aim was rhetorical rather than historical, he nevertheless provides certain details about Romano-British religious life (esp. the native saints Alban, Julius and Aaron) and about the encroachment of Anglo-Saxons into Britain (including the account of a great British victory, under the generalship of Ambrosius Aurelianus, over the invaders at an unidentified site named *Mons Badonicus*). Gildas's narrative was mined by *Bede for his account of the Anglo-Saxon conquest (*HE* book i), and by *Alcuin (*Ep.* xvii; cf. cxxix) for some vigorous invective against sin (Alcuin's quotation of Gildas in *Ep.* xvii was used in turn by Archbishop *Wulfstan in one of his sermons, no. xx). Gildas was also the author of a work on penitential practice which enjoyed some circulation in Ireland.

Sharpe, *Handlist*, 384; MGH, AA xiii.25–85; *Gildae de Excidio Britanniae*, ed. H. Williams, Cymmrodorion Record Ser. 3–4 (London, 1899–1901); *Gildas: The Ruin of Britain*, ed. M. Winterbottom (Chichester, 1978); *Gildas: New Approaches*, ed. M. Lapidge and D. Dumville (Woodbridge, 1984); F. Kerlouégan, *Le De excidio Britanniae de Gildas. Les destinées de la culture latine dans l'île de Bretagne au VIe siècle* (Paris, 1987); N. Wright, 'Gildas's Reading: a Survey', *Sacris Erudiri* 32 (1991), 121–62; N. J. Higham, *The English Conquest: Gildas and Britain in the Fifth Century* (Manchester, 1994).

MICHAEL LAPIDGE

GISO, bishop of *Wells (1061–88), was one of several churchmen who came from Lotharingia to England in the central decades of the eleventh century. He served as a priest in the royal household, and then, like others of his kind, moved on to higher office in the English church. He succeeded

Duduc as bishop of Wells in 1061, journeyed to *Rome for consecration, and returned to his see with a privilege granted to him by Pope Nicholas II (the earliest papal privilege for a recipient in England which survives in its original form, in the archives of Wells cathedral). Thenceforth Giso laboured most effectively to protect and to advance the interests of his church, dealing initially with *Edward the Confessor, then with *Harold, and latterly with William the Conqueror. A work known as the 'Autobiography of Bishop Giso', embedded in a twelfth-century 'History of the Church of Somerset', is probably a fabrication, and the so-called 'Sacramentary of Bishop Giso' (BL, Cotton Vitellius A. xviii) may have no genuine connection with him; but we learn much about him from the various *charters generated by his activities, and we may even gaze upon what are believed to be his bones.

Sharpe, *Handlist*, 385; F. Barlow, *The English Church 1000–1066*, 2nd ed. (London, 1979); S. Keynes, 'Giso, Bishop of Wells (1061–88)', *ANS* 19 (1997), 203–71.

SIMON KEYNES

GLASS. Glass artefacts produced during the Anglo-Saxon period include vessels, window panes, beads and inlays. Glass lamps and linen smoothers were used, although their remains are difficult to recognize in archaeological contexts. Vessels were used for storage as well as for drinking and tableware. Main types included bowls, claw beakers, pouch bottles, squat jars, cone beakers, bell beakers, bag beakers, funnel beakers and drinking horns. These names have been arbitrarily assigned by English glass historians including Thorpe and Harden. Tall bottles and stemmed beakers appear in fifth-century graves, but these types belong to the late Roman tradition and soon fell into disuse.

Evidence of manufacture is scant, causing difficulties in determining which items were produced locally. Distribution suggests that bag beakers, some claw beakers, squat jars, pouch bottles, bowls and funnel beakers were made in English glass houses, although most of these shapes were also produced in Frankish workshops. Regional variations can be detected in the decoration of vessels, the eighth-century remains from *Hamwic* (*Southampton) differing from those of *Ipswich and *York. The number of forms gradually diminished during the Anglo-Saxon period.

Fifth- and sixth-century vessels were more muted in colour, although cobalt blue glass began to appear in the second half of the sixth century. By the seventh century glassware had adopted brighter hues including light green-blue and blue-green, some vessels featuring opaque red streaking. Towards the end of the millennium, glass rich in potash began to be produced, indicating a change in production techniques and raw materials.

Most Anglo-Saxon drinking vessels are unstable, having rounded or conical bases. Claw beakers had small feet formed by pushing the bases inwards and pinching the sides to form hollow rings. This was for decorative effect, however, since they were too narrow to support the vessels. Although examples of Roman claw beakers are known from sites such as *Mucking, this form of decoration was most commonly used between the fifth and seventh centuries. The claws were formed by inflating hot blobs of glass applied to the vessel while attached to the blowpipe, and hooking them downwards. Later beakers, such as those found at *Taplow are taller with flatter claws.

Palm cups were the most common type of drinking vessel in use during the seventh century. Some had optic-blown decoration, produced by blowing the gather into a (usually ribbed) mould. It would then be removed from the mould and further inflated, softening the pattern. Designs usually included Christian *iconography in the form of crosses and/or bosses arranged to form a quincunx. The profile of palm cups became more elongated during the second half of the seventh century and early eighth, and examples are often refered to as 'tall' palm cups. This type evolved into the funnel beaker, the main form of drinking vessel used in Northern Europe between the eighth and tenth centuries.

Glass decorated with twisted multicoloured glass cables (often referred to as reticella) began to appear towards the end of the seventh century. Initially these were applied to bowls, but later were used to decorate squat jars and funnel beakers. Fragments from bowls similar to that found at Valsgärde in Sweden have been found at sites in Eastern England including Ipswich and York, and it is possible that they were produced locally. Glass decorated with applied gold leaf has been found at Ipswich. Similar pieces from vessels with geometric designs depicting crosses are known from continental sites including Dorestad and Borg.

From the seventh century glass was used to augment semi-precious stones as inlay in decorative *metalwork. The Kingston Brooch features cells of blue glass, and slices of millefiori (decorative cane composed of filaments of different coloured glass) were used in the shoulder clasps from *Sutton Hoo. Fragments from *Whitby suggest that the remains of glass vessels were occasionally used as decorative inlay. A necklace from a grave at Sarre shows that vessel shards were also used as beads.

The remains of glass furnaces have been excavated at *Glastonbury Abbey and evidence for glass working exists at other monastic sites such as *Barking Abbey. A reference to the glazing of ecclesiastical buildings at *Monkwearmouth-Jarrow has been confirmed by excavation. None of these sites has revealed archaeological evidence for the manufacture of the glass itself from primary raw materials. Window-glass fragments are often vividly coloured and may have been combined in representational or abstract designs. It is likely that monasteries became the main consumers and producers of glass during the Middle and later Saxon period.

V. I. Evison, 'Anglo-Saxon Finds from Rainham, Essex, with a Study of Glass Drinking-Horns', *Archaeologia* 96 (1955), 159–95; idem, 'Glass Cone Beakers of the "Kempston" Type', *Journal of Glass Studies* 17 (1972), 74–87; idem, 'Anglo-Saxon Glass Claw-Beakers', *Archaeologia* 107 (1982), 43–76; D. B. Harden, 'Glass Vessels in Britain, A. D. 400–100', *Dark Age Britain*, ed. D. B. Harden (London, 1956), pp. 132–67; idem, 'Domestic Window Glass: Roman, Saxon and Medieval', *Studies in Building History*, ed. E. M. Jope (London, 1961), pp. 39–63; J. R. Hunter, 'The Glass', in *Excavations at Melbourne Street, Southampton, 1971–6*, CBA Research Reports 33 (London, 1980), 59–72; U. Näsman, 'Vendel Period Glass from Eketorp-II, Öland, Sweden', *Acta Archaeologica* 55 (1986), 55–116; F. Rademacher, 'Fränkische Gläser aus dem Rheinlande', *Bonner Jahrbücher* 147 (1942), 285–344; W. A. Thorpe, *English Glass* (London, 1935); J. Ypey, 'Een zeldzaam laat-Merovingisch Glas in het Rijengrafveld te Bergeijk Noord-Brabant', *Berichten van de rijkdienst voor het oudheidkundig Bodemonderzoek* 8 (1958), 82–91.

MATTHEW STIFF

GLASTONBURY ABBEY is the principal component of a complex of monastic sites in central Somerset. The area in which they lie consists of a peninsula protruding into the Somerset Levels. At times of high sea levels relative to the land, the peninsula would have been surrounded by water on three sides, and accessible to the western seaways.

The highest part of the peninsula is a very prominent steep-sided hill, Glastonbury Tor, rising to a height of over 150 m above O. D. On the summit of this, excavations in the 1960s defined an approach way cut or worn into the rock. This led to a complex of post-holes and timber-slots of wooden buildings. There were also pits, and two south-north (head to south) orientated young adult burials in rock-cut graves. Evidence of fine *metal-working comprised two bowl hearths cut in the rock, and part of a crucible with cupreous residues. Finds include a bronze escutcheon in the form of a 'Celtic' helmeted head; this had been attached to iron, probably the handle of a bucket. There were also a few stone and metal objects, and hundreds of animal bones – these are of cattle, sheep, and pig, and represent high quality joints of meat. The settlement is dated to the later fifth or sixth century by sherds of imported Mediterranean amphorae. The site is highly defensible and remote, and is alternatively interpreted as an eyrie-like stronghold of a dark age chieftain, or an early Christian eremitical monastic site; the latter is currently the favoured interpretation.

Traditions and, indeed, the earliest reliable historical references centre, however, not on the Tor, but on the Abbey, where there remain massive ruins of the great medieval abbey of St Mary. This is built over a much larger area than that available on the Tor, and on lower ground nearer to the flanks of the peninsula. In extensive excavations over the first half of the twentieth century, there were no finds which could be firmly dated before the eighth century, though the excavator claimed that some structural remains, mausolea and graves were of pre-Anglo-Saxon date. A massive bank and ditch has been located in several places, which is believed to be the monastic *vallum*. It is again claimed to be pre-Anglo-Saxon, but the only dating evidence is that it is later than the Roman period, but earlier than the time of *Alfred; it is likely to be part of the early Anglo-Saxon monastic layout, perhaps as early as the time of *Ine, who is recorded as having 'built the minster at Glastonbury' in the late seventh or early eighth century (*ASC*). Later traditions recount the former existence of an early church of wattle (the *vetusta ecclesia*), which, it is recorded, was later encased in lead, and survived until the great fire of 1184.

Further to the east, at the west end of the nave of the medieval abbey, the foundations of an Anglo-Saxon church were excavated in the 1920s. This consisted of a nave and two *porticus* with later additions; at one phase there was an *opus signinum* floor. This church has been claimed as that of *Ine, built eastwards of the *vetusta ecclesia*. There is, however, no evidence from the excavation that it was as early as this.

In the ninth century, there was *glass-making in the abbey; debris from this was found piled against the degraded bank of the *vallum*. In the tenth century, there was a major reorganisation, and the definition of a claustral lay-out by Abbot

*Dunstan. The abbey was thus a major Anglo-Saxon monastic site by the tenth century; its importance is reflected in its being the burial place of Anglo-Saxon kings – *Edmund, *Edgar and *Edmund Ironside.

The monastery controlled extensive estates – the 'Twelve Hides' – and there were satellite chapels and monastic sites. Two of these have been excavated. On the Tor, rock-cut monastic cells were discovered, and post-holes of a possible timber church. The bones are mostly of birds (principally fowl and geese) and fish; the latter include both salt- and fresh-water species. Other finds include *pottery and part of a wheel-headed cross of late Saxon date.

The other satellite site, on lower ground at Beckery, has been totally excavated. The plan of a pre-Conquest two-celled stone-based chapel was recovered from its stone foundations. There were traces of other buildings and a *cemetery of forty-six graves. Of these, two were juvenile, one was female, and the rest male. One of the latter appears to have been a founder's grave; it was inside the western cell of the chapel and was within a setting of post-holes; these may have been of a shrine or grave-structure. Radio-carbon determination for this skeleton suggests a date in the seventh–ninth centuries. The locations of other satellite monasteries are known, but have not been excavated.

J. Carley, *Glastonbury Abbey and the Holy House of the Moors Adventurous* (Woodbridge, 1988); P. Rahtz, *Glastonbury* (London, 1993); L. Abrams, *Anglo-Saxon Glastonbury: Church and Endowment* (Woodbridge, 1996).

PHILIP RAHTZ

GLOSSARIES. There are three types of glossaries which were in circulation in Anglo-Saxon England: those formed by one or more sections of *glossae collectae*; class glossaries; and alphabetical glossaries. In all types of glossary a Latin lemma is followed by one or more *interpretamenta* in Latin or Old English. With the exception of a few subject glossaries, where all the entries have a vernacular interpretation, English compilations are characterized by the unpredictable distribution of Latin and Old English interpretations. In pre-Conquest England all-Latin glossaries were produced anew and continental compilations were copied and augmented. An intricate nexus of relationships connects Anglo-Saxon glossaries with the Continent, but each glossary has its own story and identity.

Classical, Late Antique and Medieval Latin works (including Anglo-Latin ones) were provided with *glosses which could be excerpted and gathered as *glossae collectae*. The entries were copied in the same order as they occurred in the source. The oldest compilation of *glossae collectae* of English origin probably dates from the time of Archbishop *Theodore and *Hadrian and stems from their *school at *Canterbury. The original compilation is lost, but a large family of derivative glossaries – including the glossary in Leiden, Bibliotheek der Rijksuniversiteit, Voss. Lat. Q. 69, 7r–47r (written at St Gallen *c*.800) – survives. The Leiden Glossary is made up of forty-eight chapters of *glossae collectae*, including canons and papal decretals (i), the *Benedictine Rule* (ii) and books of the Old and New Testament (vii–xxv). Further batches of biblical glosses, which were apparently omitted by the compiler of the Leiden Glossary, are found in related continental glossaries.

Independent of the Leiden family is a number of *glossae collectae* occurring in Anglo-Saxon manuscripts. In London, BL, Cotton Cleopatra A. iii, 87r–117r, there is a glossary made up of glosses drawn from the gospels, followed by entries which go back the prose and verse *De virginitate* by *Aldhelm. Also drawn from the prose *De virginitate* are the glosses copied on the borders of 11r–19r of Oxford, Bodleian Library, Auct. F. 2. 14 (S. C. 2657). In Cambridge, Corpus Christi College 183, 70r–71r, there is a short glossary with entries taken from the verse *Life of St Cuthbert* by *Bede. Glosses from Bede's *Historia ecclesiastica* were copied on 5r, 34v, 60v and 124v in London, BL, Cotton Tiberius C. ii. Other glossaries are made up by small batches of different origin: in Oxford, Bodleian Library, Add. C.144 (28188), 153v, glosses from Priscian and Donatus alternate with entries whose origin is still unidentified, and those in Bodley 163, 250r, have been traced to various sources. The process through which glossaries came into being can still be studied in surviving manuscripts of *glossae collectae*. A working model is represented by the all-Latin entries in London, BL, Cotton Domitian i (37v–38v), which go back to bk iii of the *Bella Parisiacae urbis* by Abbo of Saint-Germain-des-Prés, a work which was widely studied in English *schools in the tenth and eleventh centuries because of its unusual vocabulary. A later glossary in London, BL, Royal 7. D. II also contains entries drawn from Abbo's work. In both instances the Abbo glosses were copied from the text of the poem in Cambridge, UL, Gg. 5. 35.

At least one chapter of the Leiden Glossary (xlvii) does not go back to *glossae collectae*, but has been drawn from the topical lists of the *Hermeneu-*

mata pseudo-Dositheana. This name designates a bilingual schoolbook which was in use since Late Antiquity. Initially written for Greeks who wanted to learn Latin, the *Hermeneumata* were no longer used to teach *grammar and became a sourcebook for vocabulary in the Middle Ages. They contained a subject glossary, made up of different chapters (e.g. 'de caelo') and alphabetical word-lists of verbs, nouns and adjectives (*capitula nominum* and *capitula verborum*). The *Hermeneumata* enjoyed wide circulation in the British Isles, where they were introduced very early, although the only surviving manuscript (Brussels, BR 1828–30, fols. 36–109) is late and incomplete; what survives is one alphabetic glossary and a few sections of the class glossary (*Nomina volucrum*, *De membris hominum* and *Nomina piscium*) closely related to the corresponding sections in the Second Cleopatra Glossary. The lists of birds and fishes are also connected to those in London, BL, Harley 107, although the order of the items is different.

The entries of class glossaries belong to different subject fields: names of members of the family and society, names of animals, birds, fishes, plant names, common objects, parts of the house, furniture or seafaring implements. From the time of the tenth-century Benedictine reform movement, class glossaries were widely used in schools. One example is *Ælfric's *Glossary*. A large number of glosses in the Antwerp and London glossary (Antwerp, Plantin Moretus Museum ms. 47 + London, BL, Add. 32246) overlap with Ælfric's *Glossary*, whatever the relationship between the two compilations. Akin to the class glossaries are the short lists e.g. of animal names, provided with glosses in Old English, which are found in various manuscripts. All-Latin class glossaries, as well as Greek-Latin ones, were supplied with Old English renderings and reshaped to meet new needs. Plant names were listed in large compilations such as the Durham and the Laud Herbal glossaries.

Alphabetical glossaries drew their entries from the above-mentioned compilations (reshuffling the entries under each letter of the alphabet and combining batches from different sources). It is often possible to identify the origin of a gloss (if, for example, the lemma occurs in an inflected form), but in general sources of alphabetical glossaries are difficult to determine. Anglo-Saxon glossaries are also indebted to continental compilations such as the *Abstrusa*. The entries are arranged alphabetically in A-order (i.e. by the first letter of the lemmata) or in AB-order (according to the first two letters). An example of A-order is the Épinal-

Erfurt Glossary (preserved in two manuscripts, Épinal, BM 72 and Erfurt, Amplon. Fol. 42, both copied from a lost archetype datable to the last quarter of the seventh century); examples of AB-order are the Second Corpus Glossary (CCCC 144, 4r–64v) and the Harley Glossary (London, BL, Harley 3376). Of these, the Second Corpus Glossary is very substantial, and is drawn from Épinal-Erfurt as well as the source of the Leiden Glossary; it later served in turn as a source of the First Cleopatra Glossary, which in turn is related to the glossary in London, BL, Cotton Otho E. i and to the Harley Glossary, which was once a vast compilation but now is preserved only in part (letters A–F).

In CCCC 144 there is another glossary (1r–3v) made up of 342 entries, listed in A-order. Most of the entries are proper names occurring in the Bible which are given an interpretation in the works of Jerome, Eucherius (*Instructiones*) and Isidore (*Etymologiae*). This is the largest collection of its kind in Anglo-Saxon England. In the Middle Ages there were also in circulation trilingual glossaries whose lemmata were Hebrew words, followed by their equivalents both in Greek and Latin. There is no certain evidence for the existence of trilingual glossaries in England, but both the First Corpus Glossary and the Harley Glossary contain trilingual entries. In the First Corpus Glossary there are also 'Greek' glosses, that is loanwords from Greek or transcriptions of Greek words. These items (52 in all) are drawn from a collection of glosses on grammar and metrics, occurring in several continental manuscripts. The entire glossary – bearing the title 'Grammaticae artis nomina graece et latine notata' – is found in London, BL, Harley 3826, where it occurs within a longish compilation of all-Latin glosses.

T. Wright, *Anglo-Saxon and Old English Vocabularies*, rev. R. P. Wülcker (London, 1884); G. Goetz, *Corpus Glossariorum Latinorum*, 7 vols. (Leipzig, 1888–1923); J. Zupitza, *Ælfrics Grammatik und Glossar* (Berlin, 1880); J. H. Hessels, *An Eighth-Century Latin – Anglo-Saxon Glossary preserved in the Library of Cambridge, Corpus Christi College (Ms no. 144)* (Cambridge, 1890); idem, *A Late Eighth-Century Latin – Anglo-Saxon Glossary preserved in the Library of the Leiden University* (Cambridge, 1906); W. M. Lindsay, *The Corpus Glossary* (Cambridge, 1921); idem, *Studies on Mediaeval Latin Glossaries*, ed. M. Lapidge (Aldershot, 1996); M. Lapidge, 'The School of Theodore and Hadrian', *ASE* 15 (1986), 45–72; J. D. Pheifer, 'Early Anglo-Saxon Glossaries and the School of Canterbury', *ASE* 16 (1987), 17–44; B. Bischoff *et al.*, *The Epinal, Erfurt, Werden and Corpus Glossaries*, EEMF 22 (Copenhagen, 1988); B. Bischoff and M. Lapidge, *Biblical Commen-*

taries from the Canterbury School of Theodore and Hadrian, CSASE 10 (Cambridge, 1994); J. D. Pheifer, Old English Glosses in the Epinal-Erfurt Glossary (Oxford, 1974); R. T. Oliphant, The Harley Latin-Old English Glossary edited from British Museum Harley 3376 (The Hague, 1966); J. R. Stracke, The Laud Herbal Glossary (Amsterdam, 1972); P. Lendinara, 'Il glossario del ms. Oxford, Bodleian Library, Bodley 163', Romanobarbarica 10 (1988–9), 485–518; idem, 'The Abbo Glossary in London, BL, Cotton Domitian i'; ASE 19 (1990), 133–49; idem, 'L'attività glossatoria del periodo anglos-assone', in Les manuscrits des lexiques et glossaires de l'antiquité tardive à la fin du moyen âge, ed. J. Hamesse (Louvain, 1996), pp. 615–55; H. Gneuss, 'A Grammarian's Greek-Latin Glossary in Anglo-Saxon England', in From Anglo-Saxon to Early Middle English, ed. M. Godden et al. (Oxford, 1994), pp. 60–86.

PATRIZIA LENDINARA

GLOSSES. The interactions between the two languages spoken and written in Anglo-Saxon England can be observed nowhere better than in the interlinear and marginal glosses to Latin texts, and such additions, in Old English or Latin, of translations, synonyms or explanations (usually consisting of no more than a single word) open a window on the texts which were most carefully studied in Anglo-Saxon England and on the ways these texts were interpreted and understood. The density of glossing ranges from a few interpretamenta scattered throughout the text to full interlinear versions where each Latin lemma has a corresponding English gloss. Occasionally, in the layout of the text, extra space has been provided for glossing, but usually glosses are entered in much smaller (and often later) script than the main text. Glosses may be entered in ink or with a stylus; such 'scratched' or 'dry-point' glosses are often visible under special lighting conditions only, and their original purpose is difficult to define. Many of these scratched glosses have not yet been published; presumably many more still await detection. Old English glosses often aim to clarify the morphological and semantic structure of the lemma by close imitation (loan renditions), for example: inscriptio: inwriting or conlaudare: efenherian. As a result, it is often difficult to estimate to what extent such neologisms were coined for permanent incorporation into the Old English lexicon. Not infrequently, Old English glosses appear in abbreviated form; such 'merographs' either aim to convey semantic information only (e.g. dælni [= dælnimung or dælnimendnes] for participatio), or they seek to define no more than word-class and case of the lemma (e.g. cere [= ?werlicere] for uirili). This last type of merograph

bears some resemblance to 'syntactical glosses', that is diacritical marks or letters aiming to clarifiy the structure of a Latin sentence by linking the various constituent parts of the subject, object etc. Ample supply of Latin synonyms will have been a special desideratum for students of Anglo-Latin texts, characterized by a difficult 'hermeneutic' vocabulary (protoplastus glossed primogenitus and prius plasmatus, or circumgyrat glossed complectitur and circuit are examples from glosses to *Aldhelm's prose De uirginitate). Latin synonyms, and explanatory glosses (principally in Latin but also in Old English) are often drawn from works such as Isidore's Etymologiae or Latin-Latin *glossaries or from patristic *exegesis (cf. congregatio and gesamnung for synagoga or heahtorras 'high mountains' for Alpes). With such explanatory interpretamenta, the boundary between glosses (usually single words) and scholia (brief exegetical remarks) is difficult to draw. Glosses were entered in biblical and religious texts (psalter, gospels, prayers etc.) and in the works of a variety of curriculum authors (such as Prudentius, Sedulius, Prosper or Aldhelm). There is proof that glossing (in Latin and Old English) was undertaken from the late seventh century onwards. Such early interlinear and marginal glosses and scholia (from the *Canterbury *school of *Theodore (d. 690) and *Hadrian (d. 709)) have survived almost exclusively in the form of glossaries compiled from them (such as the Leiden Family of glossaries). The only substantial corpus to have survived in interlinear form from the pre-Viking age is the psalter gloss (s. ix[1]) in London, BL, Cotton Vespasian A. i (the *Vespasian Psalter). Otherwise, glossed manuscripts have been preserved from the mid-tenth century onwards and much of the glossing activity is apparently a reflex of the intellectual revival brought about by the Benedictine reform. Continuous interlinear versions (in English) are restricted almost exclusively to biblical and religious texts, such as the psalter (ten manuscripts), the gospels (two manuscripts), the Regula S. Benedicti (one manuscript) or the *Regularis concordia (one manuscript). Most important among the gloss corpora not amounting to complete interlinear versions are the glosses to Aldhelm's prose De uirginitate. Almost all surviving manuscripts of this text are encrusted with often thousands of Latin and Old English glosses, often intricately related. Outstanding among these manuscripts is Brussels, Bibliothèque Royale 1650 (glosses entered s. xi[1], perhaps at *Abingdon), where many of the (almost 5400) lemmata bear several Latin and/or Old English glosses, thereby pointing to continuous accretions to the corpus over the generations and revealing how effectively Latin and English could be combined to facilitate the understanding of a difficult text. Thus far glosses have primarily been studied for their textual relationships, though Old English glosses are also studied for their dialect features and word-formation. Some of the questions still awaiting attention are: on which sources did the glossators draw for their *interpretamenta*, and what was their intellectual background? Did they aim to respond to the stylistic level of the text they glossed and what readership did they have in mind for their glosses?

A. Cameron, 'A List of Old English Texts', in *A Plan for the Dictionary of Old English*, ed. R. Frank and A. Cameron (Toronto, 1973), pp. 25–306, at 224–47 [a bibliography of glossed manuscripts and their editions]; L. Goossens, ed., *The Old English Glosses of MS. Brussels, Royal Library, 1650 (Aldhelm's De Laudibus Virginitatis)* (Brussels, 1974); F. C. Robinson, 'Syntactical Glosses in Latin Manuscripts of Anglo-Saxon Provenance', *Speculum* 48 (1973), 443–75; M. Korhammer, 'Mittelalterliche Konstruktionshilfen und altenglische Wortstellung', *Scriptorium* 34 (1980), 18–58; M. Lapidge, 'The Study of Latin Texts in Late Anglo-Saxon England. 1. The Evidence of Latin Glosses', in *Latin and the Vernacular Languages in Early Medieval Britain*, ed. N. Brooks (Leicester, 1982), pp. 99–140; R. I. Page, 'The Study of Latin Texts in Late Anglo-Saxon England. 2. The Evidence of English Glosses', ibid., pp. 141–65; G. R. Wieland, *The Latin Glosses on Arator and Prudentius in Cambridge University Library, MS Gg. 5. 35* (Toronto, 1983); R. Derolez, ed., *Anglo-Saxon Glossography* (Brussels, 1992); H. Gneuss, '*Anglicae linguae interpretatio*: Language Contact, Lexical Borrowing and Glossing in Anglo-Saxon England', *PBA* 82 (1993), 107–48, at 144–8.

MECHTHILD GRETSCH

GLOUCESTER, formerly the Roman town of *Glevum*, was one of the three 'chesters' which, according to the *Anglo-Saxon Chronicle* for '577', the *Gewisse* captured from the British at the battle of Dyrham. There is some evidence that sub-Roman church sites and ecclesiastical organization were assimilated by the seventh-century English, especially at the church of St Mary-de-Lode where excavation suggests ritual continuity. In about 679 a minster ('old St Peter's') was founded in a corner of the Roman fortress by the sub-king Osric. This continued as an important church, and was reformed as a Benedictine abbey before 1022.

In the aftermath of the *Viking invasions Gloucester acquired a new importance as the headquarters of *Æthelred and *Æthelflæd, rulers of English *Mercia. In about 890 they founded a second minster ('new St Peter's', later known as St Oswald's), outside the Roman walls. Their church was of proto-cruciform plan with a west-facing apse; it was richly decorated and furnished, and lavish sculpture survives. In 909 the relics of St *Oswald were brought from Bardney to Gloucester, where a square mortuary building with a *crypt at the east end of 'new St Peter's' may have been built to house them. Meanwhile Æthelflæd was re-establishing a *town within the Roman walls on the West Saxon burghal model: the grid of streets may well date from her time, and in 914 the Gloucester men helped to repel a Viking attack. Gloucester was a *mint under *Alfred and *Æthelstan, and then regularly from *Edgar onwards; by the eleventh century it had become a substantial town and the head of a shire.

C. Heighway, 'Saxon Gloucester', in Haslam, *Towns*, pp. 359–83; idem, *Anglo-Saxon Gloucestershire* (Gloucester, 1987); S. Bassett, 'Church and Diocese in the West Midlands', in Blair and Sharpe, *Past. Care*, pp. 26–9; M. Hare, *The Two Anglo-Saxon Minsters of Gloucester* (The Deerhurst Lecture, 1992); C. Heighway and R. Bryant, 'A Reconstruction of the Tenth-Century Church of St Oswald, Gloucester', in Butler and Morris, *AS Church*, pp. 188–95.

JOHN BLAIR

GNOMIC POETRY is a term used to distinguish a special class of Old English *wisdom literature, with which it shares an impulse to investigate the most fundamental aspects of human thought and experience and to present them in a striking and memorable form. What distinguishes gnomic poetry is its form, which tends toward sequences of short, tightly-structured proverbial utterances, not unlike those found in examples of near-eastern wisdom literature such as the Old Testament book of Proverbs. Clearly a popular form with roots reaching back into pre-Christian Germanic antiquity, the genre poses interesting questions about the relationship between Christian and pagan elements in Old English poetry generally, and much modern study of the gnomic poems has centred on attempts to distinguish their pre-Christian substrata. The best known gnomic poems in Old English are *Maxims I and II. *Precepts has occasional gnomic passages, and certain of the Old English *riddles, tightly structured and deploying first-person speakers who challenge their audience to deeper thought, have been seen by some critics to have distant affinities with gnomic poetry.

Individual Old English gnomes (the term used to denote a single gnomic utterance) tend to use fairly simple constructions, most employing one of two Old English verb forms: *sceal* ('ought to' or 'must') or *bið* ('is' or 'will be'). *Sceal*-gnomes tend to express what is customary, obligatory, or otherwise expected: *forst sceal freosan* ('it is the nature of frost to freeze', *Maxims* I, line 71a), *cyning sceal rice healdan* ('a king is obliged to preserve his kingdom', *Maxims* II, line 1a); *bið*-gnomes, on the other hand, tend to articulate universals and unchanging truths: *wyrd bið swiðost, winter bið cealdost* ('fate is the strongest, winter is coldest', *Maxims* II, line 5).

The subject matter of Old English gnomic utterances ranges from observations on natural processes (*Fugel uppe sceal / lacan on lyfte*, 'it is the nature of a bird to sport above in the air', *Maxims* II, lines 38b–39a), to matter of legend (*þyrs sceal on fenne gewunian*, 'A giant tends to dwell in the fen', *Maxims* II, line 42b), to social prescriptions (*Wel mon sceal wine healdan on wega gehwylcum*, 'A man ought to be true to his friend on every path', *Maxims* I, line 144), to the sometimes mysteriously philosophical (*Deop deada wæg dyrne bið lengest*, 'The deep path of the dead shall long remain hidden', *Maxims* I, line 78), to the overtly religious (*God sceal mon ærest hergan*, 'A man must first praise God', *Maxims* I, line 4b).

R. MacGregor Dawson, 'The Structure of the Old English Gnomic Poems', *JEGP* 61 (1962), 14–22; P. B. Taylor, 'Heroic Ritual in the Old English Maxims', *NM* 70 (1969), 387–407; *The Exeter Anthology of Old English Poetry*, ed. B. J. Muir, 2 vols. (Exeter, 1994).

ROBERT DINAPOLI

GODEMAN, monk of Winchester and sometime abbot of Thorney (the precise dates of his abbacy are uncertain, but he is known to have succeeded Bishop *Æthelwold in the office, probably before Æthelwold's death in 984, and is found witnessing charters from 990 onwards, his last attestation apparently occurring in 1013). It is probable that Godeman abbot of Thorney is identical with the 'Godemannus' who is known as the scribe of the *'Benedictional of St Æthelwold', and who prefaced that lavish manuscript with a fittingly flamboyant poem of thirty-eight hexameters displaying all the features, especially Greek-based vocabulary, which characterizes the so-called 'hermeneutic' style, of which Æthelwold himself was a proponent.

Sharpe, *Handlist*, 387; M. Lapidge, 'The Hermeneutic Style in Tenth-Century Anglo-Latin Literature', *ASE* 4 (1975), 67–111, esp. 86, 105–6 (repr. *ALL* ii.105–49, at 124, 143–4); *Wulfstan of Winchester: Life of St Æthelwold*, ed. M. Lapidge and M. Winterbottom (OMT, 1991),

pp. 40–2; *The Liber Vitae of the New Minster and Hyde Abbey Winchester*, ed. S. Keynes, EEMF 26 (1996), 88.

MICHAEL LAPIDGE

GODIVA [= Godgifu], wife of Earl *Leofric of Mercia. Leofric died in 1057, but Godiva survived until some time between 1066 and 1086 (the date of *Domesday Book). Leofric and Godiva were generous patrons of the church, founding and endowing the monastery of Coventry, as well as making gifts to the monasteries at Leominster, Much Wenlock, Chester (both St John's and St Werburg's), *Worcester and Evesham, and to the secular minster of St Mary's, Stow. Both Leofric and Godiva were buried at Coventry. She lives on in legend as Lady Godiva of Coventry fame.

F. E. Harmer, *Anglo-Saxon Writs* (Manchester, 1952), pp. 216, 226, 561; John of Worcester, *Chronica*, ed. Darlington and McGurk, ii.582 (s.a. 1057).

R. C. LOVE

GODODDIN. A Welsh poem (1480 lines, of which about 200 are duplications) commemorating heroes who died fighting the English in an otherwise unrecorded battle at *Catraeth* (Catterick in Yorkshire). The poem is attributed to Aneirin, who flourished in the mid-sixth century, according to the *Historia Brittonum*; it survives in two versions, both incomplete, in the thirteenth-century Book of Aneirin. Heroic in tone, it is not narrative but a series of elegies, commemorating either individual named heroes (otherwise unknown) or collectively 'the men who went to Catraeth'. The heroes mostly belonged to the British tribe of Gododdin, in south-eastern Scotland, centred on Edinburgh. It is unknown how much of the poem dates from the sixth century, though the language indicates that parts go back at least to the tenth. The enemy are described as heathens, of *Deira (*Deor*), *Bernicia (*Brenneych*, not certainly in the oldest stratum of the text) or England (*Lloegr*). Although the uncertainties surrounding the text make it almost unusable as a historical source, it is generally accepted that the poem may incorporate a genuine sixth-century nucleus, informing us credibly of an unsuccessful defence by the Scottish Britons against the English, and of the ethos and attitudes behind it.

K. H. Jackson, *The Gododdin. The Earliest Scottish Poem* (Edinburgh, 1969); *Aneirin: Y Gododdin. Britain's Oldest Heroic Poem*, ed. and trans. A. O. H. Jarman (Llandysul, 1984); L. Alcock, *Economy, Society and Warfare among the Britons and Saxons* (Cardiff, 1987), esp. ch. 16 ['Warfare and Poetry among the Northern Britons'];

Early Welsh Poetry. Studies in the Book of Aneirin, ed. B. F. Roberts (Aberystwyth, 1988).

O. J. PADEL

GODWINE, earl of Wessex (d. 15 April 1053), son of the Sussex *thegn Wulfnoth *cild*, was made earl, probably of the south-east, by *Cnut in 1018. After visiting Denmark with the king, probably in 1022–3, he became earl of *Wessex. He married Gytha, whose brother Ulf had married Cnut's sister Estrith; another, Eilaf, was earl in Gloucestershire. After Cnut's death in 1035, there was a disputed succession. Earl *Leofric, with the Mercians, Northumbrians, and the royal fleet at London, backed *Harold, Cnut's son by Ælfgifu of Northampton; *Harthacnut, his son by *Emma, was supported by his mother, the royal *housecarls at *Winchester, and Godwine (*ASC* E, 1035). A compromise recognized Harold as regent for his brother, but in 1036, Alfred, Emma's son by *Æthelred II, landed in *Kent. Godwine intercepted him and delivered him to Harold I, who had him killed. Godwine's defection to Harold was fatal to Harthacnut's cause, and only when Harold died, in 1040, did Harthacnut become king; in 1042, he himself was suceeded by Alfred's full-brother, *Edward the Confessor.

Godwine's power continued to grow throughout these crises. His sons, Swein and Harold, became earls in 1043 and 1044 respectively, and in 1045, King Edward married Godwine's daughter *Edith. Godwine's power would have been even greater had the monks of Christ Church, *Canterbury, succeeded in electing his kinsman Ælric as archbishop in 1050; but the king appointed his own nominee, Robert of Jumièges. Edward's favour to Godwine had probably been a matter of expediency rather than choice, and throughout the 1040s he had built up a following of men who had accompanied him from *Normandy.

In 1051 the tensions between king and earl erupted. Edward's Norman followers had built a castle in Herefordshire, within Swein's earldom (*ASC* E, 1051), and another at Clavering, Essex, in the earldom of Harold (*ASC* E, 1052). It seems that a third was projected at Dover, for the king's former brother-in-law, Count Eustace of Boulogne. Dover lay in Godwine's own territory; the completion of its castle would compromise the 'shires' of all three Godwinist earls. Eustace attempted to occupy Dover in 1051, but on his arrival a fight broke out in which nineteen of his followers and more than twenty townsmen were killed. Eustace complained to the king, who ordered Godwine 'to carry war into Kent toward Dover'. The earl refused, and when the king called a council at Gloucester, 'the foreigners went beforehand to the king and accused the earls'.

Godwine and his sons gathered their men at Beverstone (Gloucs.), and the king summoned the levies of Earls Leofric and Siward to Gloucester. Edward's counsellors urged caution, saying that 'it would be a great piece of folly if they joined battle, for in the two hosts was most of what was noblest in England, and they considered that they would be opening a way for our enemies to enter the country' (*ASC* D, 1051). A council was called to meet at London on 25 September. When Godwine was refused safe-conduct to attend, he fled to Bruges. Edward gave the family's earldoms to his own supporters, and repudiated Edith. The *Anglo-Saxon Chronicle* comments that 'it would have seemed remarkable to everyone in England if anybody had told them that it could happen, because [Godwine] had been exalted so high, even to the point of ruling the king and all England' (*ASC* D, 1051).

In Bruges Godwine allied with Count Baldwin V of *Flanders, while in Ireland Harold received aid from Diarmid, king of Leinster, and in 1052 the family returned. The south-east rose for Godwine, and at a council at *London, he was allowed to clear himself of all charges. The king restored him and his sons to land and office, and received Edith as his queen; Godwine's chief enemies, including Robert of Jumièges, were banished. Within a year, however, Godwine was dead. On Easter Monday, 1053 (April 12) he was dining with the king at *Winchester, when 'he suddenly sank towards the foot-stool, bereft of speech and of all his strength' (*ASC* C, 1053). He died the following Thursday and was buried in the Old Minster.

Godwine's reputation suffered after 1066, when he and his sons became easy targets for criticism. He was accused of despoiling the church (*ASC* C, 1052), although he was remembered as a benefactor at the Old Minster, Winchester, and *Abingdon Abbey. He may have been patron of St-Mary-in-Castro, Dover. Walter Map, who admired his intelligence and courage, provides a fitting epitaph: 'I do not say he was a good man, but a mighty, and an unscrupulous one'.

The Life of King Edward (Vita Ædwardi regis), ed. F. Barlow, 2nd ed. (OMT, 1992); *Walter Map's De Nugis Curialium*, ed. M. R. James, R. A. B. Mynors and C. N. L. Brooke (OMT, 1983); F. Barlow, *Edward the Confessor* (London, 1970); R. Fleming, 'Domesday Estates of the King and the Godwines: a Study in Late Saxon Politics', *Speculum* 58 (1983), 987–1007; T. Tatton-Brown, 'The

Churches of Canterbury Diocese in the Eleventh Century', *Minsters and Parish Churches*, ed. J. Blair (Oxford, 1988), pp. 105–18, at 110; D. G. J. Raraty, 'Earl Godwine of Wessex: the Origins of his Power and his Political Loyalties', *History* 74 (1989), 3–19; S. Keynes, 'Cnut's Earls', *The Reign of Cnut*, ed. A. Rumble (London, 1994), pp. 43–88.

ANN WILLIAMS

GOLTHO (Lincs.) provides the clearest case so far identified of a defended late Anglo-Saxon *thegn's residence transformed into a Norman castle. Middle Saxon houses were replaced, probably in the early tenth century, by a hall, bower, kitchen and weaving-shed within a banked and ditched enclosure. About a century later, but still before the Conquest, the complex was rebuilt within a much larger defended circuit. In the twelfth century a typical earthwork castle, comprising a motte and a massively-defended (though tiny) bailey, was superimposed. Goltho illustrates tenurial continuity, but also the contrast between the residential priorities of its late Anglo-Saxon lords and the defensive priorities of its Norman ones.

G. Beresford, *Goltho: the Development of an Early Medieval Manor, c.850–1150* (London, 1987); P. Everson, 'What's in a Name?', *Lincolnshire History and Archaeology* 23 (1988), 93–9.

JOHN BLAIR

GOSCELIN OF SAINT-BERTIN, the foremost hagiographer of eleventh-century England, was originally a monk of Saint-Bertin (at Saint-Omer in *Flanders), who came to England to join the household of Herman, bishop of Ramsbury and *Sherborne, in about 1058. He seems initially to have been attached to Sherborne Abbey, but also to have served as chaplain and tutor to the nuns at Wilton, while at the same time travelling with Herman as he went about his episcopal duties, perhaps as a personal secretary. At Herman's instigation the first of Goscelin's many Lives of the Anglo-Saxon saints were composed. Not long after his patron's death in 1078, on account of some disagreement, possibly with Herman's Norman successor, Osmund, Goscelin was obliged to leave Wiltshire, and embarked upon the itinerant existence of an exile. We cannot be certain where he went and when, but, to judge from the *hagiography he produced during this period, presumably to earn his keep, he seems to have passed through *Barking, *Ramsey, *Ely, perhaps Peterborough, and possibly *Winchester. In about 1089, certainly by 1090, Goscelin found a final haven at St Augustine's Abbey, *Canterbury,

where his hagiographical skills were soon put to use in commemorating the grand scheme of relic-translations which took place there in association with rebuilding works. He may have held the post of precentor there, since he seems also to have composed texts for use in the liturgy, with music to go with them. Goscelin was still alive in 1107, when his friend Reginald sent him a copy of his newly-composed life of St Malchus, but we do not otherwise have any precise record of when he died.

The canon of Goscelin's works has yet to be established with absolute certainty; his known works are *vitae* of Amelberga (apparently written before he came to England); *Eadgyth of Wilton; *Wulfsige of Sherborne; *Kenelm, Wulfhild, Hildelith, and Æthelburh of Barking; Ivo; Werburg; *Sexburg and Eormenhild of Ely; *Mildburg of Much Wenlock; *Mildrith, *Augustine and his successors at Canterbury; and Abbot *Hadrian of Canterbury. Goscelin's only non-hagiographical work is his *Liber confortatorius*, a profoundly moving and partly autobiographical letter, chiefly concerning the eremitical life, which he sent to one Eve, who as a young girl had been his pupil at Wilton, before leaving to become an enclosed anchoress in France. Other hagiography sometimes attributed in the past to Goscelin, but probably not in fact his work, includes Lives of *Æthelthryth and Withburg of Ely; of *Æthelred and Æthelberht, martyrs; of *Edward, king and martyr; and of *Edward the Confessor.

Sharpe, *Handlist*, 395; F. Barlow, ed. and trans., *The Life of King Edward who rests at Westminster*, 2nd ed. (OMT, 1992), appendix C [includes a list of works and printed editions]; R. C. Love, ed. and trans., *Three Eleventh-Century Anglo-Latin Saints' Lives* (OMT, 1996), pp. xl–xliv; T. J. Hamilton, 'Goscelin of Canterbury; a Critical Study of his Life, Works and Accomplishments' (unpublished Ph.D. thesis, Univ. of Virginia, 1973); A. Wilmart, 'La légende de sainte Édithe en prose et vers par le moine Goscelin', *AB* 56 (1938), 5–101, 265–307; C. H. Talbot, 'The *Liber Confortatorius* of Goscelin of Saint-Bertin', *Analecta Monastica* 37 (1955), 1–117; M. L. Colker, 'Texts of Jocelyn of Cantebury which relate to the History of Barking Abbey', *Studia Monastica* 7 (1965), 383–460; R. Sharpe, 'St Augustine and St Mildreth: Hagiography and Liturgy in Context', *JTS* n.s. 41 (1990), 502–16.

R. C. LOVE

GOSFORTH CROSS. A tenth-century carving of startling iconographic originality, depicting episodes from Scandinavian mythology at a date several centuries before they were recorded in extant literary sources. Its artist seems to have worked exclusively in Gosforth, Cumbria, where

Pl. 12 The Gosforth Cross.

he was responsible for six of the monuments now preserved at the church. Among these is the 'fishing stone' showing the popular story of Thor's encounter with the World Serpent. Both on this stone and on the large cross the same scheme is discernible: the exploitation of Scandinavian mythology in a Christian context and for Christian purposes.

The slender cross stands complete, 4.42m high, in its original socket on the south side of the church; an eighteenth-century record suggests that there was at least one other cross of similar type in the churchyard. The shape of the shaft, which combines cylindrical and squared sections, is an elegant variation on a form which was developed in the pre-Viking period in England, but the tenth-century date of the carving is clear from such details as the ringed form of the head, the Borre-style ring chain motif and the Scandinavian links of the figural ornament.

The lower, cylindrical, part of the shaft is decorated with a Cumbrian form of multiple ring-chain. Above are four full-length panels of figural and zoomorphic ornament. At the bottom of the east face is the crucified Christ flanked by Longinus, the spear-bearer, and a female figure. This is the only Christian scene on the cross; the rest of the ornament, with varying degrees of ingenuity and plausibility, can be identified with episodes from the Scandinavian story of Ragnarǫk, the tale of the overthrow and destruction of the gods of Norse mythology by the monstrous forces of evil led by Loki. Three such episodes are clearly recognisable: Viðarr's vengeful rending of the wolf's jaw is depicted at the top of the east face; the watchman god Heimdallr with his Gjallar horn is on the west side, set above the bound and tortured Loki who is attended by his faithful wife Sigyn.

The decoration on the cross is patterned to bring out a series of parallels and contrasts. On the smaller scale these operate between individual scenes and figures, such as link the two pigtailed females on the west and east panels. More important, however, is the way in which the iconographic organisation draws attention to the end of three different worlds and uses the one as commentary on the others. Two of these worlds are immediately apparent: the rule of the Norse gods which culminated in Ragnarǫk and the end of the Old Covenant which came with Christ's crucifixion. The third climactic event is present in allusive form – that of Doomsday. Christ's second appearance on earth was always closely linked in Christian thought and liturgy with His crucifixion; contemplation of his death led naturally, as can be seen in The *Dream of the Rood*, to the hope of His final coming. Against this theological background it is not irrelevant that much of the accompanying symbolism of Doomsday is present in the Ragnarǫk narrative. The Gosforth cross is thus making a Christian point in a radical manner by drawing on the traditional mythology of Cumbria's Scandinavian settlers.

CASSS ii.33, 100–4; R. N. Bailey, *Viking-Age Sculpture in Northern England* (London, 1980), pp. 125–32; R. N. Bailey and J. T. Lang, 'The Date of the Gosforth Sculptures', *Antiquity* 49 (1975), 290–3; K. Berg, 'The Gosforth Cross', *Journal of the Warburg and Courtauld Institutes* 21 (1958), 27–43.

RICHARD N. BAILEY

GOSPELBOOKS are the most numerous class of surviving Latin luxury manuscripts. Their association with relics (Stonyhurst Gospel of St John), their gift as a memorial to the dead

(Rheims, BM, 9), their preservation in treasuries (Judith Gospels: New York, Pierpont Morgan Library, 708 and 709), and their great value have ensured their survival in relatively large numbers. Sufficiently sought after to be exchanged for a best horse (Lichfield Gospels) or for much gold (Stockholm, Royal Library, *Codex Aureus*), their leaves gave enduring homes to records of guilds or estate boundaries, to a charter or a *Liber vitae*. Lists of appropriate liturgical readings (known as capitularies) were appended to many. While the most sumptuous show few signs of use, liturgical or otherwise, some were clearly extensively used (London, BL, Add. 40,000, 'Thorney Gospels').

There are only two surviving imported gospelbooks from the earlier period, the sixth-century Italian uncial books (Cambridge, Corpus Christi College 286, and Oxford, Bodleian Library, Auct. D.II.14) which have been traditionally associated with St *Augustine, but a fair number of imports survive from the tenth and eleventh centuries. Of these all, with the exception of the so-called Coronation Gospels (London, BL, Cotton Tiberius A. ii), originated in Celtic lands (e.g. the Irish 'MacRegol Gospels', Oxford, Bodleian Library, Auct. D.II.19, or the Breton 'Harkness Gospels', New York Public Library, 115).

The earliest surviving native product is the fragment at Durham (Cathedral Library, A.II.10 + C.II.13 + C.III.20). Written by an Irish scribe in Northumbria, its large decorated initial and line of larger letters at the opening of Mark is the precursor of the elaborate initial pages found in examples like the Book of *Durrow, the *Lindisfarne Gospels and the Book of Kells and which came to distinguish Insular Gospels from their contemporaries. The initial page's emphasis on the opening of the Gospel text was heightened by another novelty, a decorated *carpet-page, accompanied sometimes by an evangelist and symbol page. If only a few books are so elaborately decorated, their larger dominant initials, their lines of larger angular capitals, and their ornamental repertoire were adopted in less ambitious codices (e.g. Hereford, Cathedral Library, P.I.2). This repertoire included interlace, zoomorphic, curvilinear, straight line and red dot patterns, and was adopted in a book like the already-mentioned Stockholm *Codex Aureus*, where it merged with a different tradition of uncial script, purple leaves and evangelist portraits which looked back to late antique models. It was probably made at *Canterbury, but the *scriptorium of *Monkwearmouth-Jarrow produced three single-volume Bibles (the one complete survivor being the Codex *Amiatinus)

and the exquisite Stonyhurst St John in a very pure uncial tradition. If the innovations in bookmaking seen in the Lindisfarne Gospels had some continuing influence, the uncial masterpieces of *Bede's monastery do not seem to have had imitators.

The ninth century has left us no certain gospels as the splendid Canterbury gospelbook, London, BL Royal 1.E.VI, must be excluded as a Bible fragment, and there is a gap of over a century between the last eighth-century book and the Boulogne Gospels of the first half of the tenth century (Boulogne, BM, 10). At least nineteen gospelbooks exist from the period *c.*990–1066, and many of these are closely interconnected through scribes, capitularies and text. In nearly all of them Carolingian influence is obvious, whether in the *script of Anglo-Caroline, the restrained page lay-out, or the use of rustic and mixed capitals for rubrics and explicits. Four of the later ones are associated with Judith of *Flanders, and the interconnections of some of the others (e.g. London, BL, Royal 1.D.IX, Loan 11, and Cambridge, Trinity College B.10.4) might also suggest that they were made for a patron like *Cnut. However close some of the books were to each other textually and scribally, there was sufficient variety in accessory texts to indicate the presence of different exemplars. After 1066 pre-Conquest exemplars were copied as can be seen in different ways in Paris, BN, lat. 14782, Cambridge, St John's College 73, and London, BL, Add. 17789.

In the earlier period at least two textual families can be identified in native products, the Lindisfarne Gospels text which is that found in the gospels of the Codex Amiatinus, and a text of the 'Celtic' family as in the Lichfield Gospels; but other strands are identifiable. In the later period, the text seems not unexpectedly to have been exposed to Carolingian influence, but there is much textual variety as can be seen in the different order of the Gospel prefaces, the mixed families of chapter lists, and the varying number of canon tables.

Most of the books have architectural canon tables which enclosed the Eusebian concordance lists. In the earlier books Insular ornament invaded the flattened columns and arcades, but the later tables often have a wide variety of illustrations.

P. McGurk, *Latin Gospel Books from AD 400 to AD 800*, Publications de Scriptorium 5 (Antwerp-Brussels, 1961); Alexander, *Insular MSS*; Temple, *AS MSS*; H. H. Glunz, *History of the Vulgate in England, from Alcuin to Roger Bacon* (Cambridge, 1933); N. Barker, ed., *The York Gospels* (London, 1987); T. A. Heslop, 'The Production of *de luxe* Manuscripts and the Patronage of King Cnut and Emma', *ASE* 19 (1990), 151–96; P. McGurk and J. Rosenthal, 'The Anglo-Saxon Gospelbooks of Judith, Countess of Flanders: their Text, Make-up and Function', *ASE* 24 (1995), 251–308.

P. MCGURK

GOSPEL TRANSLATION. Bede is said to have spent his last hours translating part of the Gospel of John, but the earliest written evidence of any gospel translation is the tenth-century gloss added to the *Lindifarne Gospels (London, BL, Cotton Nero D. iv), which later served in part as the source for a gloss added to the Rushworth (MacRegol) Gospels (Oxford, Bodleian Library, Auct. D. 2. 19). Though the reading of the gospel was a regular part of the mass, gospel translation and exegesis were apparently not common in vernacular preaching before *Ælfric, who provided translations of gospel passages at the beginning of many of his *Catholic Homilies*. However, these are unrelated to the continuous prose translation of the four gospels, the so-called *West-Saxon Gospels*, which survives in six eleventh-century copies, four complete manuscripts (Cambridge, Corpus Christi College 140; Cambridge, University Library, Ii. 2. 11; London, BL, Cotton Otho C. i vol. I; Oxford, Bodleian Library, Bodley 441) and two fragments (New Haven, Beinecke Library 578, endleaf; Oxford, Bodleian Library, English Bib. C. 2), and two twelfth-century copies (London, BL, Royal 1. A. XIV; Oxford, Bodleian Library, Hatton 38). The translation is not much earlier than the surviving witnesses; the nature of the Latin original (insofar as it can be reconstructed from the translation) suggests a date sometime after the middle of the tenth century. The translation is literal but idiomatic, though not always entirely accurate; explanatory additions or omissions of more than a word or two are rare. Its origins are unknown, though linguistic evidence points to the south-east. Likewise the purpose and audience of the translation are uncertain. Surviving copies are from both monastic establishments (Cotton Otho C. i from *Malmesbury, Corpus 140 from *Bath) and cathedrals (CUL Ii. 2. 11 from *Exeter); copies for lay patrons may have existed, but none has survived. The translation probably served as a homiletic aid, or as a supplement to the Latin text for younger monks and less learned clergy. CUL Ii. 2. 11, a modest revision of the text to which has been added the apocryphal *Gospel of Nicodemus*, contains a series of Latin headings and English directions before most paragraphs, indicating the liturgical occasion on which the passage was to be read. These raise the possibility that the translation was used during mass, but this remains conjectural. In the twelfth-century copies, both from Canterbury, the text has been revised and the language has been altered to twelfth-century norms. The Hatton copy (*c.*1200) is among the latest OE works to be copied; it suggests that the text attracted continuing interest well into the early Middle English period.

The Holy Gospels in Anglo-Saxon, Northumbrian and Old Mercian Versions, Synoptically Arranged, ed. W. W. Skeat, 4 vols. (Cambridge, 1871–87); M. K. Morrell, *A Manual of Old English Biblical Materials* (Knoxville, TN, 1965); *The Old English Version of the Gospels*, ed. R. M. Liuzza, EETS 304 (Oxford, 1994); U. Lenker, *Die westsächsische Evangelienversion und die Perikopenordnungen im angelsächsischen England* (Munich, 1997).

R. M. LIUZZA

GRADUAL: *see* Liturgical Books

GRAMMAR, LATIN (STUDY OF). The *conversion introduced a new linguistic problem to seventh-century England: the need to learn the language of the Roman church. The Anglo-Saxons, like the Irish before them, faced the challenge of having to learn a foreign language without regular contact with native speakers. Such textbooks as they had were intended for Latin speakers in the fourth- and fifth-century Roman Empire. Their aim was to introduce the reader to the principles of grammatical analysis while taking a knowledge of the forms – noun declensions and verb conjugations – for granted. Thus, the standard beginners' grammar, the *Ars minor* by Donatus (Rome, *c.*350), discusses properties of the verb like mood, tense, person and voice at length, but conjugates only one verb. At the other extreme, the *Institutiones grammaticae*, by Priscian (Constantinople, *c.*500), took a thousand pages to set out all the minutiae of Latin grammar. The discussion of the noun alone occupied six books, some three hundred printed pages. Works of this kind were of little use to Anglo-Saxons needing to be taught Latin from scratch. During the seventh century a first attempt was made to remedy the obvious deficiencies of Late Latin grammars like those of Donatus. Collections of paradigms, each one accompanied by a list of anything up to a hundred words that inflected similarly, were compiled (*Declinationes nominum*, *Coniugationes verborum*). Toward the end of the century the first descriptive grammars of Latin designed for non-native speakers appeared. Their best-known Anglo-Saxon representatives are the grammars of *Tatwine (*c.*700) and *Boniface (before 716).

These two works take Donatus's longer grammar, the *Ars maior*, as their basis, expanding it with material from other *classical authors and with paradigms and lists from one of the *Declinationes nominum* texts. Other, anonymous, authors made the *Ars minor* their starting-point, arriving at a new genre – the foreign-language textbook – which remained standard until the beginning of the ninth century. Such textbooks, although the ancestors of those in use today, differ from their modern descendants in that they were structured like reference grammars, dealing with each part of speech in turn. They contain no exercises or practice material (apart from lists of examples); the beginner would practise what he had learnt in reading the psalter or the moral precepts of the *Disticha Catonis* or some other elementary work.

Although elementary foreign-language teaching was the most urgent task confronting Anglo-Saxon teachers in the first century after the conversion, a few Anglo-Saxons, at least, advanced to a higher stage of study. The flowering of Anglo-Latin literature in the decades around 700 shows that some writers had mastered the use of the hexameter (but of no other *metre) as well as the essentials of Latin grammar. *Aldhelm and *Bede, both capable hexameter poets, wrote treatises on the hexameter.

After this burst of grammatical and literary activity around 700 little more is heard of Anglo-Saxon grammarians until *Alcuin (d. 804). Among his numerous works are three on grammar. The *Dialogus Franconis et Saxonis de octo partibus orationis* ('Dialogue of the Frank and the Saxon on the eight parts of speech'), apparently written during his sojourn on the Continent in Charlemagne's entourage, extends the traditional question-and-answer framework often used in elementary grammars (including Donatus's *Ars minor*) into a lively dialogue between two teenagers, a Frank and a Saxon. Quite apart from its vivacious presentation, Alcuin's dialogue breaks with Insular tradition in being based almost exclusively on classical sources, lacking the paradigms and lists characteristic of the earlier generation of grammars. Anomalous too is its heavy dependence upon another of the famous grammars of late Antiquity, Priscian's *Institutiones grammaticae*. This unwieldy work was little used in England during the seventh and eighth centuries, except by Aldhelm, and seems to have been no more popular on the Continent. Its rise is associated with Alcuin: he compiled a series of excerpts from it and used it in his dialogue; and, suggestively, the first wave of Carolingian manuscripts of

it and of a minor work of Priscian's, the *Partitiones*, emanates from the monastery of Tours, where Alcuin was abbot from 796 to 804.

Although Alcuin's dialogue was read fairly widely in the ninth and tenth centuries, the popularisation of the *Institutiones grammaticae* and the *Partitiones* was in the long term of far greater significance. At the elementary level, a new kind of grammar inspired by the *Partitiones*, the parsing grammar, replaced Insular elementary grammars. These new grammars were structured differently from their predecessors in that they took one particular example, such as *dominus*, 'lord', as their starting point, and in a series of questions and answers focussing on that word conveyed basic grammatical information. At a more advanced level, teachers and students alike were absorbed in the task of digesting the overwhelming mass of facts offered in the *Institutiones*. Commentaries, abbreviated versions, collections of excerpts and paraphrases of the *Institutiones* proliferated. To what extent ninth-century Anglo-Saxon teachers were engaged in this laborious task is uncertain, given the paucity of English grammatical manuscripts of that period.

Only from the middle of the tenth century, in the wake of the Benedictine Reform movement, do grammatical texts appear in English manuscripts in any quantity. Almost without exception, they are elementary works: Bede's and Alcuin's tracts on orthography, Priscian's brief *Institutio de nomine*, a fourteen-page summary of the inflecting parts of speech, Donatus's grammars, a couple of parsing grammars. The continental impetus behind the revival of the study of grammar is signalled not only by the presence of the parsing grammar, but also by the appearance of other grammars popular on the Continent: a commentary by Remigius and grammars by Eutyches, Phocas, Servius and Sergius, and, toward the end of the century, the first signs of interest in Priscian's *Institutiones grammaticae*. Left to themselves, Anglo-Saxon teachers would no doubt have pursued their subject along lines similar to their French contemporaries, composing parsing grammars and gradually, as they grew in confidence, turning their attention to the *Institutiones grammaticae*.

At the end of the tenth century a radical departure from traditional approaches intervened. Between 992 and 1002 *Ælfric, then at the monastery of Cerne Abbas, Dorset, composed three textbooks designed to help students master Latin: a grammar, a Latin-English *glossary arranged by subjects, and a Latin *colloquy designed to teach

217

everyday vocabulary. The grammar, called by Ælfric *Excerptiones de arte grammatica anglice* ('Excerpts from a grammar textbook rendered into English'), is virtually unique among grammars written before the fourteenth century in being written in the native language of the students rather than in the target language. Far from considering this an important pedagogical breakthrough, Ælfric himself is apologetic, saying defensively that his grammar was intended for 'ignorant little boys', not for learned greybeards. As he reminds the reader, it was not so long since Latin learning had been in danger of disappearing. Implicit throughout his introduction is the pragmatic assumption that even if Latin studies were again to decline, nevertheless readers literate in the vernacular would always be able to teach themselves Latin by studying his grammar.

Ælfric's starting-point was an abbreviated version of Priscian's *Institutiones grammaticae*, called *Excerptiones de Prisciano*. He condensed it still further (adding occasional details – such as examples from the Bible – from other sources) and translated the skeleton text which remained into Old English. The resulting work is an adequate introduction to the main phenomena of Latin grammar. Ælfric deals with the traditional subjects: the utterance in general, the speech-sound, the syllable and diphthongs, the eight parts of speech (noun, pronoun, verb, adverb, participle, conjunction, preposition, interjection), and some miscellaneous topics like numerals and weights and measures. Syntax is not discussed: it was not until the thirteenth century that it came to form a regular part of grammatical instruction. Ælfric's contemporaries learnt Latin syntax by studying texts, as we can see from the syntactical *glosses in tenth- and eleventh-century manuscripts. The emphasis in Ælfric's grammar falls on the inflection of Latin nouns, pronouns and verbs and on vocabulary-building. He gives a relatively generous selection of paradigms and extensive lists of similarly-inflected words, each item with its Old English translation.

Together with Bede's works on metrics, figures of speech and orthography, Ælfric's grammar provided a complete introductory course in Latin. It achieved almost instant popularity: remarkably few copies of other grammars at the same level are to be found in English manuscripts of the eleventh century. Some thirteen pre-Conquest manuscripts of Ælfric's grammar survive, and several more date from the post-Conquest period, two of them glossed in Norman French – an interesting reminder of the grammar's continued usefulness.

But Norman teachers brought their own favourite textbooks with them, and English grammarians found themselves once more expected to conform to the Continental model. Not until the middle of the fourteenth century did they venture to use the vernacular again in writing about Latin.

MGH, AA xv. 59–204 [Aldhelm]; CCSL cxxiii A [Bede], cxxxiii [Tatwine], cxxxiii B [Boniface]; PL ci. 849–902 [Alcuin]; *Ælfrics Grammatik und Glossar*, ed. J. Zupitza (1880; repr. with preface by H. Gneuss, Berlin, 1966); V. Law, *The Insular Latin Grammarians* (Woodbridge, 1982); idem, 'The Study of Latin Grammar in Eighth-Century Southumbria', *ASE* 12 (1983), 43–71; idem, *History of Linguistic Thought in the Early Middle Ages* (Amsterdam, 1993); idem, *Grammar and Grammarians in the Early Middle Ages* (London, 1997).

VIVIEN LAW

GRAVE GOODS, artifacts deposited in furnished graves with the deceased, belong to the earlier period of Anglo-Saxon burial and are generally associated with paganism, although their use did continue into the Christian period, most spectacularly with the burial of St *Cuthbert.

Grave furniture includes several categories of items. Dress fittings are the most common; artefacts such as brooches, buckles, knives, purses and even weapons are all part of funerary apparel. Grave goods may also include other objects deliberately placed in or around the grave, such as animals, pots and containers. Analysis suggests that some of the containers may have contained food or drink. Many burials appear to have been laid directly in the ground, but a coffin, where present, should also be considered a grave-good, part of the equipment of the deceased deliberately consigned to the grave. Boats, beds, small wooden chambers and biers were all used as resting-places for the dead.

The number and quality of goods within a furnished *cemetery varied greatly from burial to burial, and may have expressed social status. The clearest message conveyed by the grave-goods in the inhumation ritual was the sex of the deceased. Weapons, including spears, shields and swords, were associated with male burials, while *jewellery such as strings of beads, brooches, and wristclasps and other dress fittings such as work-boxes, bunches of keys and items designed to dangle from a waist-belt (girdle hangers and chatelaines) accompanied female ones. Some items, such as pots, knives and belts (indicated in the archaeological record by buckles) were buried with both sexes, and these are the most common grave-goods recovered from furnished inhumations. Women tended to be buried with a greater number of grave goods than men, including more gold, silver, garnet and other precious materials, perhaps because their costume was designed to show off more jewellery than the male counterpart. *Children were generally buried with fewer grave goods than adults. Sometimes they were given smaller versions of an adult artefact – small iron brooches at Sewerby (Yorks.), for example, and scaled-down spears for boys – but children were more normally buried with adult artefacts, emphasising the ritual and symbolic, rather than the personal, aspect of furnished burial. In the cremation ritual, portions of animal carcass were often included in the interment. A correlation between gender, age and the species of animal cremated with the individual has been identified. The patterns on cremation urns have also been shown to reflect the gender, age and perhaps social status of the deceased. Grave goods within the cremation ritual show much less variety than those recovered from inhumations.

Sometimes grave furniture shows signs of having been old or broken at the time of the burial, and may include heirlooms or personal possessions of the deceased, but damaged or broken items may also have fulfilled a role as token artefacts, again emphasising the symbolic significance of grave goods. Many of the dress items in the graves may have had more than a functional role. Workboxes and their contents, fossils, crystal balls and necklaces made up of amber, pierced Roman *coins and animal teeth may have been *amulets. Similarly, the decoration on deposited artefacts may have been symbolic. Grave goods do not provide a simple reflection of the everyday equipment of the Anglo-Saxons. Cremation urns are more highly decorated than the plain domestic settlement equivalents, and comparisons of artefacts found in cemetery contexts against those found in associated settlements indicate that only selected items were used in graves. Tools, in particular, are a regular find in settlement archaeology but rare as grave-goods.

In the fifth and sixth centuries, grave goods demonstrated regional patterning, especially apparent in female graves. 'Saxon', 'Anglian' and 'Kentish' cultural groupings are clearly demonstrated in the type, number and dress positions of brooches, presumably reflecting distinct regional or tribal formal dress.

In the seventh and early eighth centuries, the 'Final Phase' of furnished burial, the percentage of burials with grave goods within the mortuary population declined to less than 25% in some cemeteries. At the same time, the repertoire of grave goods changed and became more constrained. Regional variations were replaced by a new cultural assemblage common across Anglo-Saxon England. Brooches and long strings of beads for women were largely replaced by pins and smaller necklaces with gold pendants and monochrome beads. Weapon burial became infrequent: male burials were characterized by small buckles, knives, the occasional shoe-tags and seaxes (long knives with angled backs). Nonetheless, it is in the seventh century that the very wealthiest assemblages of grave goods in *'princely burials' such as *Sutton Hoo, *Taplow and Cuddesdon occur. These were rich, isolated burials, usually under mounds, and included cremations at a time when cremation burial was almost unknown in the furnished cemeteries. These burials displayed dramatic excesses of wealth, not just in terms of dress fittings in the form of lavishly decorated gold and garnet buckles, sword fittings and expensive *textiles, but also in additional kit such as cauldrons, drinking equipment, gaming pieces, musical instruments and exotic imports. The dedication of such wealth to the oblivion of the grave underlines the fact that one of the functions of grave goods in these princely burials in particular, but in furnished burials in general, was to offer the opportunity for the burying community to display conspicuous consumption of wealth. The homogeneity of the seventh century grave goods throughout England, and the increasing concentration of grave wealth in fewer burials, point to emergent kingdoms within Anglo-Saxon England and increasingly polarized power and wealth in the hands of an Anglo-Saxon aristocracy.

Artifacts from furnished burials provide some of our most important material evidence for early Anglo-Saxon costume, art styles, ethnicity, belief systems, social structure, technology, *trade and wealth. It must be remembered, however, that only part of the grave assemblage may be archaeologically recoverable. Artefacts made of organic materials, such as drinking horns, bags, fine clothing and furs, can only rarely be detected. Rich though the corpus of Anglo-Saxon grave goods may be, it still represents only a part of the wealth that the earlier Anglo-Saxon population consigned to the earth.

J. D. Richards, *The Significance of Form and Function of Anglo-Saxon Cremation Urns*, BAR Brit. ser. 166 (Oxford, 1987); E.-J. Pader, *Symbolism, Social Relations and the Interpretation of Mortuary Remains*, BAR Brit. ser. 130 (Oxford, 1982); *Making of England*; J. W. Huggett, 'Imported Grave Goods and the Early Anglo-

Saxon Economy', *MArch* 32 (1988), 63–96; E. T. Leeds, *Early Anglo-Saxon Art and Archaeology* (Oxford, 1936); *The Age of Sutton Hoo: the Seventh Century in North West Europe*, ed. M. O. H. Carver (Woodbridge, 1992).

SALLY CRAWFORD

GRAVE-MARKERS. Postholes found during excavations at sites like Sewerby (Yorks.) suggest that some graves were marked by wooden posts in *cemeteries of the pagan period. After the *conversion a variety of stone markers was employed, alongside equivalent forms in wood. The evidence from the late Saxon cemetery at *Raunds (Northants.) suggests, however, that graves identified in this way were always in the minority, and even these exceptional examples were often only marked by roughly hewn slabs.

Among the more ambitious forms of grave-marker are two types which seem to be restricted to seventh- and eighth-century *Northumbria. The first, found at *York, is a tapering shaft, flat-topped and about 1 m high; these carry a restrained decoration on one face (an incised cross and an inscription) and seem to have been used with burials inside the church building. The second early form is a small, carefully dressed, stone slab which is usually no larger than *c.*15 cm by 20 cm. These carvings, often called 'name stones', carry incised cruciform decoration accompanied by an *inscription. They have been found at monastic sites in eastern *Bernicia, and both Irish and Merovingian origins have been claimed for the type. Nineteenth-century accounts suggest that some were placed within the grave itself.

The dominant form of grave-marker throughout the Anglo-Saxon period, however, was a large slab, usually decorated in relief with some type of cruciform ornament. It is often difficult to know whether such slabs were set upright or in recumbent position, though the latter seems to have been the more usual. Both forms existed by *c.*700 in Northumbria and spread into other areas in the course of the eighth century. The large collection from St Mark's in *Lincoln shows the continued popularity of the type into the tenth and eleventh centuries. In this late period the evidence from sites as widely scattered as *Winchester, Peterborough and York shows that recumbent slabs were often accompanied by small head and foot stones.

There is no doubt that other forms of *sculpture were probably also used as grave-markers though we are hindered in identifying them as such by the fact that carvings are rarely found in association with graves. It is however likely that, by the late Saxon period, many *crosses were used to mark graves and this is also the most plausible function for the *hogbacks of the Anglo-Scandinavian north. The ninth-century round-headed stone from Whitchurch (Hants.), with its high relief figure, or the Viking-age zoomorphic pillar from Mirfield (Yorks.) are, however, salutary reminders that we are still far from recognising the full range of regional and period varieties of sculptures which served this function.

R. N. Bailey, *England's Earliest Sculptors*, Publications of the Dictionary of Old English 5 (Toronto, 1996), 36–8, 40–1; R. J. Cramp, in CASSS i. 5–8; B. J. Gilmour and D. A. Stocker, *St Mark's Church and Cemetery*, The Archaeology of Lincoln 13.1 (London, 1986), 55–82; J. T. Lang, in CASSS iii. 18–19, 28; D. Tweddle, in CASSS iv. 22–3.

RICHARD N. BAILEY

GREENSTED (ESSEX): *see* Timber Building

GREGORY THE GREAT was born *c.*540, into one of the leading senatorial families of the city of *Rome. By 573 he had become city prefect, the leading secular official in the city, although he resigned the office in 574 to set up a monastery dedicated to St Andrew on a family estate on the Caelian Hill. In 579, however, he was sent as papal legate (*apocrisiarios*) to Constantinople. A few years later he returned to Rome to become deacon under Pope Pelagius II, whom he succeeded as pope in 590. He died in 604.

Much of his pontificate was taken up with organisational matters, notably with the defence of Rome against the Lombards, with organising the papal patrimony and, in times of crisis, with provisioning the city of Rome. He had also to deal with problems of ecclesiastical jurisdiction throughout the Byzantine Empire, to which Rome itself belonged, especially in the Balkans, where Slav expansion was the cause of considerable dislocation. In addition Gregory's position involved him, at a distance, with Byzantine politics. His enthusiastic support for the usurper Phocas, after the fall of the Emperor Maurice in 602, is often seen as misguided.

In Western Europe he had little influence in Visigothic Spain, despite personal friendship with Leander, bishop of Seville. He had some impact on the Frankish church, defending the papal estates and attacking simoniac practices. What success he achieved there, however, was largely a spin-off from the mission led by *Augustine which he sent to *Kent in 596 (arriving 597) and which he reinforced in 601.

According to the anonymous *Life of Gregory*, written at *Whitby *c.*700, Gregory wished to evangelize the English before he became pope. As it stands this story is apocryphal. On the other hand Gregory did instruct Candidus, his agent in the Frankish kingdom, to buy Anglian boys, to baptize them, and commit them to monasteries for education, as early as 595. This may indicate that Gregory was interested in the possibility of evangelising the English before 596. He does not, however, appear to have used the Angles purchased by Candidus in the mission of 596, which seems to have been prompted by information which the pope received from England.

Gregory hoped to recreate a church in England similar to what might have existed in *Britannia* at the end of the Roman Empire, but with archdioceses in *London and *York. Circumstances in England prevented realisation of this plan. Gregory also seems to have seen the evangelisation of the English in a millennarian context, being determined to spread the Word of God before the Second Coming. More immediately significant was his ability to respond flexibly in his letters written in response to Augustine's concerns – and in this he was to set a precedent for later papal responses, notably that of Pope Nicholas I to Khan Boris of the Bulgars.

The chief evidence for the mission to England comes from Gregory's *Register*, or letter-collection, which was compiled from the papal archives some considerable time after Gregory's death. The majority of Gregory's other writings are biblical commentaries, many of them originally delivered as sermons. In some ways even more important than these works were Gregory's *Regula pastoralis*, a handbook for bishops in particular and more generally for all in authority, and the pope's work of hagiography, the *Dialogues*, in which he set down accounts of near contemporary saints of Italy, most notably St Benedict, who is the sole subject of the second book of the work. This interest in Benedict and a concomitant interest in monasticism has led some to see Gregory, anachronistically, as a supporter of Benedictine monasticism: the Benedictine Rule only gradually became the touchstone of the monastic life, and there are only few indications that Gregory himself knew the work.

Despite his later reputation Gregory was not particularly well regarded in Rome in the century immediately following his death. His interest in mission, which seems any way to have been limited to what had once been part of the Roman Empire, was not followed up until the eighth century, notably by two popes who also took the name of Gregory. Gregory I was, however, thought of by the English as their apostle. This line was taken initially by the first author of a *Life of Gregory*, the anonymous of Whitby, and was pursued by *Bede. Gregory's reputation in England remained high, and his *Dialogues* as well as the *Regula pastoralis* were among those works translated into English at *Alfred's court (see *Alfredian texts).

F. Homes Dudden, *Gregory the Great. His Place in History and Thought*, 2 vols. (London, 1905); C. Dagens, *Saint Grégoire le Grand. Culture et expérience chrétiennes* (Paris, 1977); P. Meyvaert, *Benedict, Gregory and Others* (London, 1977); R. Godding, *Bibliografia di Gregorio Magno, 1890–1989* (Rome, 1990); *Grégoire le Grand*, ed. J. Fontaine *et al.* (Paris, 1986); *Gregorio Magno e il suo tempo*, 2 vols. (Rome, 1991); H. Chadwick, 'Gregory the Great and the Mission to the Anglo-Saxons', ibid. i. 199–212; R. A. Markus, *Gregory the Great and his World* (Cambridge, 1997); A Thacker, 'Memorialising Gregory the Great: the Origin and Transmission of a Papal Cult in the Seventh and Eighth Centuries', *EME* 7 (1998), 59–84.

IAN WOOD

GRIMBALD OF SAINT-BERTIN (d. 901) was one of the scholars who was invited to England by King *Alfred to help in the reestablishment of English *schools and learning. Something of the circumstances of this invitation are known from a letter addressed to Alfred by Fulco, archbishop of Rheims (883–900), in response to a request from the king for a scholarly advisor. From this and other evidence it can be deduced that Grimbald had been a monk of Saint-Bertin when Fulco was abbot there (878–83), having entered the community 834 × 844, and had been marked out by Fulco for episcopal office in Francia. Grimbald seems to have arrived in England in 887, and although no writings of his survive, his influence is traceable in manuscripts he may have brought to England (including a copy of Prudentius, now Cambridge, Corpus Christi College 223, and a lavish psalter which, to judge from its litany, was originally written for use in the archdiocese of Rheims, now Cambridge, Corpus Christi College 272), as well as in certain liturgical prayers in the 'Durham Collectar' (Durham, Cathedral Library, A.IV.19). Later tradition records that, on the death of Archbishop Æthelred in 888, Grimbald was offered the archbishopric of Canterbury, but declined it. On his arrival in England, Grimbald had been given a *monasteriolum* in *Winchester by King Alfred, and it is likely that the New Minster, Winchester, was planned with Grimbald in mind; but Grimbald's death on 8 July 901, before the completion of the New Minster, put paid to any such plans. After his death Grimbald was comme-morated particularly by the community of the New Minster; a now-lost Life of Grimbald, apparently compiled in the later tenth century, seems to lie behind the liturgical lections for St Grimbald in the fourteenth-century 'Breviary of Hyde Abbey'.

P. Grierson, 'Grimbald of St Bertin's', *EHR* 55 (1940), 529–61; J. Bately, 'Grimbald of St Bertin's', *Medium Ævum* 35 (1966), 1–10; *Councils & Synods* i.6–13 (nos. 4–6); *Alfred the Great*, pp. 26–8, 182–6, 331–3; *The Durham Collectar*, ed. A. Corrêa, HBS 107 (London, 1992), 121–2; *The Liber Vitae of the New Minster and Hyde Abbey, Winchester*, ed. S. Keynes, EEMF 26 (1996), 16–18.

MICHAEL LAPIDGE

GRIMM'S LAW is so-called after the philologist and folklorist Jakob Grimm (1785–1863) who first gave currency to a coherent account of this *sound-change. Grimm showed that there was a predictable set of consonantal differences between the *Germanic languages and the others of the Indo-European family, dating from the period of divergence of Proto-Germanic from other Indo-European dialects. The effects of Grimm's Law in Old English can be seen through comparing groups of cognates, that is, words in different languages with a presumed common ancestor, e.g. Old English *fæder*; *fisc* correspond to Latin *pater*, *piscis* (cf. Italian *padre*, *pesce*). Some apparent exceptions to Grimm's Law are accounted for by *Verner's Law.

C. L. Barber, *The English Language* (Cambridge, 1993).

JEREMY J. SMITH

GUTHLAC, ST (*c.*674–714), a celebrated anchorite who lived in the fens near Crowland. Nothing beyond their names, Penwalh (or maybe Penwald) and Tette, is known of his parents. He was descended from Icel, who appears five generations above *Penda in the Mercian *genealogies, and stories were handed down two generations later about his people, the Guthlacingas. A sister named *Pega lived as a hermit at Peakirk (Northants.). As a young man, Guthlac spent nine years fighting on the western borders of *Mercia, then a troubled area, and he may have lived for a time in exile among the Britons, whose language he understood. By the age of twenty-four, despite his success as a leader (men travelled from far away to serve under him), he no longer found the heroic ideal sufficient. He decided therefore to enter religion and was received by Abbess Ælfthryth into the double house at *Repton

where, for two years, he learned the psalms and church services. Then, together with a companion named Beccel, he sought out the lonely hermitage where he was to live the rest of his life, arriving there on St Bartholomew's day. The central events of the *Vita S. Guthlaci* deal with his temptation to despair, from which he was saved by the appearance and teaching of Bartholomew; and his deliverance from the gates of hell through Bartholomew's intervention. Many were attracted to Crowland for healing and teaching, among them the future King *Æthelbald of Mercia.

The main source for the life of Guthlac is the *Vita S. Guthlaci* by *Felix. *Bede does not mention Guthlac in the *Historia*, but the *Anglo-Saxon Chronicle* records his death. The great abbey at Crowland is unlikely to have been founded earlier than 971.

There are a number of Old English witnesses to the life of Guthlac. A translation of Felix's *Vita* survives in a late manuscript, London, BL, Cotton Vespasian D.xxi. This shows signs of having been modernized from what must have been a fairly literal translation of Felix's life of the saint. On the evidence both of its vocabulary and morphology the Guthlac prose translation can be categorized as Anglian and dates probably from *Alfred's age or not much later. Enough by way of obsolescent vocabulary and Latinate syntax remains in the Vespasian Life for its affiliations with the Old English Bede and *Werferth's *Dialogues* to be generally accepted. Some of the miracles have been refurbished very efficiently, for example the stories of thieving ravens, which are told with simplicity and humour. A short extract from the translation, in a much earlier version, survives as the final item in the *Vercelli Book, so-called Vercelli homily 23.

There are also two Guthlac poems, by separate authors, which follow one another in the *Exeter Book, the first a meditative poem focused on the saint's struggles, in his island hermitage, against the onslaughts of demons (A), the second a narrative of his pain-wracked death (B). *Guthlac B* draws heavily on Felix, particularly on c. 50. *Guthlac A* has often been thought to present an independent account of the temptations to vainglory and despair that form the nucleus of Felix's life. Unfortunately neither poem is complete because of loss of leaves in the manuscript.

At the beginning of *Guthlac A* an angel greets a blessed soul, making three observations, that the soul will now travel on pleasant ways, that it will see glory's bright light, that it will arrive at a home where there is no sorrow; and the question is posed: how is one to behave in this world in order to merit a place in heaven? The poet is drawing on the archetypal utterances of soul and body traditions familiar in homily, and he ends with these same themes, assuring all who love truth that God will make life's ways pleasant for them and that they will have no sorrow after death. Guthlac is presented in the body of the poem as an exemplary soldier of Christ who, unmoved by threats of death, withstands the attempts made by demons to oust him from his chosen hermitage.

In *Guthlac B* the saint is a teacher beloved of his disciple and a brother who sends dying messages to his sister, rather than the solitary soldier of Christ at the heart of *Guthlac A*. *Guthlac B* is an assured and showy piece of writing, often termed Cynewulfian. Here are the most elaborate tricks of Anglo-Saxon poetic diction: successive and crossed alliteration, compounds piled high, heavy assonance and sporadic decorative rhyme, lengthy simile. This writer manages in English as fine a death-bed scene as the Evagrian Anthony and Bedan *Cuthbert which lie behind Felix's account. Particularly effective is the personification of Death, a strong and cruel warrior who draws ever nearer to Guthlac with stealthy paces and savage clutches (a similar figure appears in The *Phoenix* (482ff.) and in the *Metres of Boethius* (27.6ff.)). The description of Beccel's journey to Pega and his words of sorrow spoken to her are much admired.

ASPR iii.49–88; *Felix's Life of St Guthlac*, ed. B. Colgrave (Cambridge, 1956); P. Gonser, *Das angelsächsischen Prosa-Leben des hl. Guthlac*, Anglistische Forschungen 27 (Heidelberg, 1909); J. Roberts, ed., *The Guthlac Poems of the Exeter Book* (Oxford, 1979); J. Roberts, 'An Inventory of early Guthlac Materials', *MS* 32 (1970), 193–233; idem, 'The Old English Prose Translation of Felix's *Vita Sancti Guthlaci*', *Studies in Earlier Old English Prose*, ed. P. E. Szarmach (Albany, NY, 1986), pp. 363–79; *The Vercelli Homilies and Related Texts*, ed. D. G. Scragg, EETS 300 (London, 1992).

JANE ROBERTS

GUTHRUM (d. 890) was the leader of a *Viking force which joined the Great Army in England in 871. He came close to overcoming King *Alfred of *Wessex in 878 when he forced him into hiding after a surprise attack. Later in the same year Guthrum was decisively defeated at the battle of Edington and agreed to be baptised with Alfred as his godfather. Guthrum retreated to rule the Viking settlers in *East Anglia and issued *coins there in his baptismal name of Æthelstan. The text of a treaty survives which Guthrum made with Alfred between 878 and his death in 890.

R. H. C. Davis, 'Alfred and Guthrum's Frontier', *EHR* 97 (1982), 803–10; Dumville, *Wessex*, pp. 1–23; C. Hart, 'The Eastern Danelaw', in his *The Danelaw* (London, 1992), pp. 25–114.

B. A. E. YORKE

H

HABITATION NAMES are *place-names which from their creation denoted inhabited sites such as homesteads, villages, fortified towns and even shelters of various kinds. Particular attention has been given to the study of these names because they indicate without ambiguity the former presence of Anglo-Saxons settled at readily identifiable locations. Attempts have been made to establish a relative chronology of habitation name types in order to chart the progress of Anglo-Saxon *settlement. However, there are problems attendant on this approach. The belief in the value of a relative chronology for habitation names depends to some extent on a model of the history of English settlement that was developed largely by nineteenth-century historians. This saw early medieval settlement as the progressive extension of a cultivated landscape with Anglo-Saxon and Scandinavian pioneers founding new villages, clearing new sites, bringing virgin *woodland, moorland and fen under the plough. No doubt this was indeed a process which in part obtained. However, archaeology and historical geography increasingly demonstrate that the countryside in which the Anglo-Saxons settled was far less unexploited than was once believed. Some estates and land boundaries reach back through Roman Britain to the Iron Age. Place-name creation, it must be emphasized, was not place creation. Not all habitation names compounded of an Anglo-Saxon personal name and a habitative generic such as are Godmersham (*Godmæreshām* 'Godmær's village') and Barnston (*Beornestūn* 'Beorn's farmstead') record founding fathers establishing new settlements on virgin soils. Surviving Anglo-Saxon habitation names no doubt reflect in very many instances various changes in land organization, ownership and tenure which took place between the migrations and the Norman Conquest.

It is unusual except in the broadest of terms to know the date of a name's creation and place-name generics must have undergone semantic changes in the same way as any other lexis in Old English. For example, *worð* and its derivatives *worðig*, *worðign* have a primary sense 'enclosure'. About seventy-five per cent of habitation names in *-worð*

have OE *personal names as their specifics which suggests that these enclosures were personal possessions and perhaps were small compounds in which single dwellings stood. No examples of habitative names in *-worð*, *-worðig(n)* appear in Anglo-Saxon records before *c.*730, but by 781 when *Tamworth, the royal *caput* of the kings of *Mercia is first recorded, a *worð(ig)(n)* clearly signified something more than a humble enclosure. A number of variables seem to have been at work in the use of generics in habitation names: for example, a range of related structures could synchronically occasion the use of the same generic so that a *burh* might refer both to a major stronghold and to a fortified manor; semantic change could dictate which generic was applied to a particular type of site at a particular date so that, for example, an estate earlier styled a *hām* with all its paraphernalia of contained homesteads and farm buildings (*hām-stede* and *hām-tūn*) could later be styled a *tūn*; a place-name's meaning could atrophy so that the site of a serf's cot could become that of a *thegn's *burh* but still retain the name of the manor's humble antecedent; increasingly successful exploitation of land for whatever reason could turn a minor habitation site such as a *worð* into a village. No doubt all the elements used as generics in habitation names throughout the Anglo-Saxon period were present in the *dialects of Primitive Old English at the time of the migrations to this island but as usage appears to have differed according to date and fashion, it is worth attempting to form a relative chronology for them, however unsubtle such a sequence may be.

An analysis of habitative names in English records to *c.*730 shows the overwhelming presence of place-names in *-hām* ('a village, an estate') by this date. Their distribution is predominantly in the east and south-east of England and they bear a significant relationship to the routes of Roman *roads, to the sites of Romano–British settlements and to pagan Anglo-Saxon *cemeteries. Names in *-hām* rapidly dwindle westwards towards the Midlands. Since so few *charters survive for the areas in which habitation names in *-hām* occur, their major presence in records to *c.*730 is doubly significant. The habitative name in *-hām* must be seen as one of great importance in the pagan period. Some of these names seem to have been given to estates which may have been expropriated as going concerns from the Romano-British inhabitants. For example, places denoted by the compound wīc-hām (giving modern names in Wickham) appear to be estates based on the territories of small Romano-British townships, styled in Latin vicus, a word borrowed early by the Anglo-Saxons, seemingly in its classical sense.

Place-names in -ceaster ('an old fortification') such as *Rochester and *Winchester also form a high percentage of habitation names in the earliest records. Of the fourteen individual sites mentioned up to c.730, nine were ecclesiastical centres. This reflects the practice of the establishment of seats of Christianity in Romano-British *towns and related fortified sites. Thirteen of the examples recorded are found in religious prose writings: but their presence there offers a salutary warning of the way in which the survival of particular kinds of documents may give evidence a bias.

The final habitation name generic which figures importantly to c.730 is burh. This has a long history in Anglo-Saxon England and it has already been noted in the senses 'fortress' and 'manor (house)'. It is reasonable to suppose that 'fortress' gave way to 'fortified manor house' to 'manor house' as less hostile environments developed and more peaceful times ensued.

Habitation names in -tūn 'a farmstead, a village, an estate' such as Clifton and Milton are the commonest of all in our modern landscape. However, such names are extremely sparse in the records to c.730. This suggests that before that date they represented only unimportant homesteads which were unlikely to figure in charters, and that only later did tūn begin to signify villages or estates, probably replacing the use of hām for such features.

A. H. Smith, *English Place-Name Elements*, English Place-Name Society 25–6 (Cambridge, 1956); B. Cox, 'The Place-Names of the earliest English Records', *Journal of the English Place-Name Society* 3 (1976), 12–66; idem, 'Aspects of Place-Name Evidence for early Medieval Settlement in England', *Viator* 11 (1980), 35–50; M. Gelling, *Signposts to the Past* (London, 1978).

B. COX

HADRIAN (d. 709 or 710), sometime abbot of the monastery of SS Peter and Paul (later St Augustine's) in *Canterbury and, in concert with his friend and colleague Archbishop *Theodore, one of the most influential figures in the early English church. Hadrian's later career, especially after his arrival in England, is known from *Bede's *HE*; his earlier life must be inferred from a collection of biblical commentaries which emanated from the *school which he and Theodore established at Canterbury. From these sources it seems probable that Hadrian was born c.635 in the Greek-speaking part of North Africa, probably in Libya Cyrenaica, and that he fled to Naples while still a youth (c.645) as a refugee from the Arab conquest of North Africa. Naples at the time was an outpost of the Byzantine empire, a bilingual (Greek-Latin) community which housed large numbers of monasteries, some of them preserving distinguished intellectual traditions. In due course Hadrian became abbot of one of these, situated on an island in the Bay of Naples called Nisida. In 663 the Byzantine emperor, Constans II (641–68) spent part of a year in Naples while he was trying to recover for the empire lands in southern Italy which had fallen into the control of the Lombards; in view of the fact that Hadrian subsequently served twice as an ambassador for Constans II on embassies to various northern European courts, it is a reasonable assumption that he first came to know the emperor during the latter's sojourn in Naples (perhaps by serving as an interpreter for the Greek-speaking emperor). In any event, while he was domiciled in Naples, Constans II visited the pope (Vitalian) in Rome, and this visit may have been the occasion on which Hadrian got to know Vitalian well enough to be able to act as his confidant and adviser in the matter of the vacancy in the archbishopric of Canterbury, as Bede reports. Vitalian's intention was to appoint Hadrian himself to the vacant archbishopric; Hadrian declined, but suggested the name of Theodore, who was then living in a community of Greek monks in Rome; Vitalian agreed to appoint Theodore on the condition that Hadrian accompany him to England. Theodore set out for Rome in 668 and arrived a year later; Hadrian travelled separately and arrived a year or so after Theodore, probably in 670. He immediately took over from *Benedict Biscop the charge of the abbey of SS Peter and Paul in Canterbury, and held this post until his death. With Theodore he established a school in Canterbury which represented one of the high points in Greek and Latin scholarship in early medieval Europe. Although no writings of Hadrian survive, his views on the interpretation of various biblical passages are reported at various points in the corpus of biblical commentaries surviving from the Canterbury school, and the presence in English liturgical books of commemorations for Neapolitan and Capuan saints can reasonably traced to (lost) liturgical books, including at least a gospelbook and a sacramentary, brought to England by Hadrian.

Sharpe, *Handlist*, 426; Bede, *HE* iv. 1–2; M. Lapidge, 'The School of Theodore and Hadrian', *ASE* 15 (1986), 45–72 (repr. in *ALL* i.141–68); B. Bischoff and M. Lapidge, *Biblical Commentaries from the Canterbury School of Theodore and Hadrian*, CSASE 10 (Cambridge, 1994), 82–132.

MICHAEL LAPIDGE

HÆDDI, bishop of Wessex (676–705). Very little is known of Hæddi's episcopate, save that it was he who persuaded the West Saxon king *Cædwalla to resign his crown and go on pilgrimage to *Rome, and who translated the remains of St *Birinus from *Dorchester-on-Thames to *Winchester. *Bede reports that his excellence as bishop depended more on his innate virtue than on book-learning; Hæddi nevertheless appears in the literary record as the recipient of an *octosyllabic poem by Archbishop *Theodore; another octosyllabic poem commemorating Hæddi was composed posthumously. After his death, the large West Saxon see was divided (with Daniel becoming bishop of Winchester, and *Aldhelm bishop of the western region, having his see at *Sherborne).

Sharpe, *Handlist*, 418; Bede, *HE* iii.7, iv. 12, v. 18; M. Lapidge, *ALL* i.376–7; A. Orchard, *The Poetic Art of Aldhelm*, CSASE 7 (Cambridge, 1994), 30–3.

MICHAEL LAPIDGE

HAGIOGRAPHY, the literary expression of the cult of the saints, survives in reasonable quantities, both in Latin and in the vernacular, from Anglo-Saxon England. The earliest surviving Latin hagiography is the anonymous Life of St *Cuthbert (*BHL* 2019), completed shortly after Cuthbert's translation in 698 by someone who had known him well. Next comes the anonymous Life of *Gregory the Great (*BHL* 3637), composed in about 710 at *Whitby, a rather eccentric piece written with very little information about the saint to go on. Between about 710 and 720, *Stephen of Ripon wrote a Life of St *Wilfrid (*BHL* 8889), a partisan account of the troublesome bishop's life. Contemporary with these is an anonymous Life of *Ceolfrith, abbot of *Monkwearmouth-Jarrow (*BHL* 1726), by a member of that community. At about this time, *Bede turned the anonymous Life of Cuthbert into a poem of 979 hexameters, which he later matched (in about 720) with a prose version. He also completed a prose version of Paulinus of Nola's Life of St Felix (*BHL* 2873), and a revision (*BHL* 408) of an earlier *Passio* of

St Anastasius, translated from the original Greek possibly by Archbishop *Theodore. In about 740, one *Felix, otherwise unknown, wrote a Life of St *Guthlac of Crowland (*BHL* 3723). At *York, a student of *Alcuin (who himself produced hagiography on the Continent), made a verse account of the Miracles of St Nynia (*BHL* 6240b). Another anonymous author from the same milieu produced (between 754 and 766) the *Metrical Calendar of York, a poem (82 hexameters) on the saints of *Northumbria. After this, on account of the *Viking depredations in England, there was little scholarly activity for the much of the ninth century, and no hagiography was produced (or at least, none has survived) from the period between 800 and 950.

In the tenth century, largely through the agency of continental scholars, hagiography again began to be produced. The first to survive is a poem (1,400 hexameters), by a continental scholar, Fredegaud (*Frithegod) of Brioude, commissioned by *Oda, archbishop of *Canterbury (941–58), to commemorate the acquisition from Ripon, in 948, of the relics of St Wilfrid. Fredegaud's *Breuiloquium vitae Wilfridi* (*BHL* 8891–2), written in terrifyingly obscure Latin, is based mainly on Stephen of Ripon's earlier account. At *Winchester in 971, under the supervision of Bishop *Æthelwold (d. 984), the translation of St *Swithun, an otherwise obscure bishop of Winchester, took place; Æthelwold commissioned a foreign scholar working in Winchester, *Lantfred, to compose a prose account of Swithun's translation and miracles (*BHL* 7944–6) to mark the occasion, and this was completed in about 975. Also probably connected with Æthelwold was the hexametrical *Passio* of St Eustace/Placidas (*BHL* 2767), whose relics were claimed by *Abingdon Abbey. Another versification datable to this time and connected with Winchester is of the Life of St *Judoc (*BHL* 4512), whose relics New Minster, Winchester, had acquired from France. Continuing the tradition of versification, *Wulfstan the Cantor, a disciple of Æthelwold, composed his *Narratio metrica de S. Swithuno* (*BHL* 7947), a 3,300-line hexametrical version of Lantfred's text, completed by 996. Wulfstan's other major work was a Life of his master Æthelwold (*BHL* 2647), completed in 996. *Ælfric (d. *c.*1010), monk of Cerne, and abbot of *Eynsham, another of Æthelwold's disciples, produced, in the year 1006, an abbreviated version of Wulfstan's Life (*BHL* 2646), as well as an epitome of Lantfred's text on Swithun (*BHL* 7949). Following a stay at *Ramsey abbey, during the years 985–7, *Abbo, an eminent scholar from France, wrote his *Passio* of St *Edmund (*BHL* 2392), the king of East Anglia murdered by the Danes in 869. Possibly inspired by the teaching of Abbo, *Byrhtferth (*c.*970–*c.*1020) produced some hagiography at Ramsey. His *Passio* of the martyred brothers *Æthelred and Æthelberht (*BHL* 2643), whose relics were brought to Ramsey shortly before 992, survives only as incorporated into his *Historia regum*. He also produced two substantial texts which do survive, his Life of St *Oswald, archbishop of York (d. 992), based on personal reminiscence (*BHL* 6374), and produced between 997 and 1002; and his Life of St *Ecgwine (*BHL* 2432), an obscure bishop of Worcester (d. 717) who founded Evesham Abbey. The latter, produced between 1016 and 1020, demonstrates in particular the hagiographer at his most inventive, since Byrhtferth had extremely little information about Ecgwine with which to construct what is nevertheless a lengthy text. At about the same time an Anglo-Saxon cleric in exile at Liège, who signed himself only as B. (perhaps Byrhthelm), sent a Life of St *Dunstan, archbishop of Canterbury (*BHL* 2342), to Archbishop Ælfric (995–1005). This text draws mainly on the author's personal recollection of the saint. Another Life of Dunstan (*BHL* 2343) was produced at roughly the same time, by Adelard of St Peter's, Ghent, where Dunstan had spent some time in exile; although produced outside England, Adelard's text seems to have been more popular than B.'s, perhaps because more readable.

After these texts, there is little evidence of hagiography in England until after the Norman Conquest. Just a few anonymous texts may date from the middle years of the century. The community at Eynesbury, now St Neots (Hunts.), acquired the relics of the Cornish saint *Neot by devious means, and the acquisition, together with accompanying miracles, is recorded in the anonymous *Vita prima S. Neoti* (*BHL* 6054–5). At *Glastonbury, an anonymous author produced a *Passio* of St *Indract (*BHL* 4271), an Irish pilgrim (properly Indrechtach) murdered at Glastonbury in the ninth century, whose relics were venerated there. A *Passio* of *Æthelbert, king of the East Angles (d. 794), survives in a single manuscript (*BHL* 2627), and is thought to have been written at *Hereford, which housed Æthelbert's relics, at some point in the eleventh century, possibly on the basis of pre-Conquest material. Around the middle of the century an anonymous cleric of Buckinghamshire produced the Life (*BHL* 7382)

of the three-day-old St *Rumwold, whose relics rested at Buckingham.

Immediately after the Conquest a remarkable flood of hagiography, principally relating to earlier Anglo-Saxon saints, was produced in England, mainly the work of *Goscelin and *Folcard, but two Englishmen, Osbern of Canterbury, and his younger contemporary Eadmer, also made notable contributions. The vast output of this period makes the pre-Conquest Latin hagiography of England seem meagre by comparison; this and the fact that much of the later hagiography was written by foreigners, has invited the conjecture that on the whole the Anglo-Saxons were relatively reticent about commemorating their saints in writing.

On the vernacular side, much of the surviving material consists of translations of earlier Latin texts, for example *Cynewulf's *Juliana* (based on a Latin version similar to *BHL* 4522–3), the poem *Guthlac B* from the *Exeter book (based on Felix's Life, c. 50), and a prose Life of Guthlac in the *Vercelli Book (Vercelli Homily XXIII, also based on Felix's text); Homily XVIII of the Blickling Homilies (and of the Vercelli Book) a version of the Life of St Martin by Sulpicius Severus; and Blickling Homily XV, based on the *Passio* of Peter and Paul; a handful of others, Lives of John the Baptist, Michael, Andrew, Mary also survive. By contrast *Guthlac A*, a late-ninth- or early-tenth-century Mercian composition, appears to be independent of Felix's Life, drawing upon the same informants and current stories about the saint. Also surviving from the ninth century is the Old English *Martyrology, a collection of notices on saints throughout the liturgical calendar drawn from a variety of sources. From the later period (950–1150), there are some thirty anonymous Old English saints' Lives, and Ælfric of Eynsham (see above) produced over sixty hagiographical texts mainly based on Latin saints' Lives; some of these occur in his collection of homilies intended for preaching on major feast days, the Catholic Homilies (completed by 994), and the rest in his Lives of Saints (written between 995 and 1002), for devotional reading. His Lives include both international saints, such as Benedict, Clement, Gregory the Great, Lawrence, Martin, and various early martyrs, but also indigenous ones: Cuthbert, Edmund, *Oswald, Swithun, *Æthelthryth. In the years following Ælfric's time individual anonymous texts continued to be composed, mainly intended for private reading. These include Lives of *Augustine of Canterbury, *Machutus, and the international saints Eustace, Mary of Egypt, the Seven Sleepers, Christopher. Later in the eleventh century more were composed: James the Great, Margaret, *Mildred, Pantaleon, Paulinus, Sexburg; and datable to the late eleventh century or early twelfth, are Lives of Giles, Neot, Margaret, and Nicholas. In the late eleventh century Coleman (d. 1113) composed an Old English Life of *Wulfstan of Worcester, which has not survived except in the Latin translation made by *William of Malmesbury in the 1120s.

M. Lapidge, 'The Saintly Life in Anglo-Saxon England', *CamComp*, pp. 243–63; M. Lapidge and R. C. Love, 'England and Wales (600–1550)', in *Hagiographies*, ed. G. Philippart (Turnhout, 1994–), iii.1–120; J. E. Cross, 'English Vernacular Saints' Lives before 1000 AD', *Hagiographies*, ii.413–27; E. G. Whatley, 'Late Old English Hagiography, *c*.950–1150', *Hagiographies*, ii.429–99; *Holy Men and Holy Women: Old English Prose Saints' Lives and their Contexts*, ed. P. E. Szarmach (Albany, NY, 1996); R.C. Love, *Three Eleventh-Century Anglo-Latin Saints' Lives* (OMT, 1996).

R. C. LOVE

HALLS: *see Comitatus*; Royal Sites

HAMWIC: *see* Southampton

HANGING-BOWLS are thin metal vessels mostly of lathe-turned bronze, sometimes of silver, with a recessed base. Three or four hooks on decorative mounts spaced around the rim held rings for suspension, an echo of Roman practice. Some bowls have elaborate external strip-work. Most bowls have been recovered from furnished early Anglo-Saxon burials, as at *Sutton Hoo, where they were included as valued items. These are dated by association to the sixth and seventh centuries and a later Irish series has been recovered from *Viking burials and markets, mainly in Norway. The hook mounts and other applied fittings are often decorated with Celtic mouldings and motifs, such as peltas, triskeles and spirals, and many are *enamelled and inlaid with *millefiori glass; some bear Christian symbols. Tin was often used to give a silvery finish to the mounts. Workshop evidence, repairs and changes of style show that the early bowls were not made directly for Anglo-Saxon patrons but were probably of contemporary British manufacture, obtained perhaps as tribute or by marriage and exchange. Their original use is not known, although hand-washing at table has been suggested and in furnished graves they were occasionally filled with food. Individual mounts were prized and reused as pendants. In the eighth century a few mounts and bowls are known from Christian England, including finds from *Whitby Abbey and the elaborate Witham

bowl. The Irish Viking series is dated to the ninth century or later.

D. M. Wilson, 'The Bowls and Miscellaneous Silver', *St. Ninian's Isle and its Treasure*, ed. A. Small, C. Thomas and D. M. Wilson, 2 vols. (Oxford, 1973), i. 108–12; S. M. Youngs, ed., '*The Work of Angels': Masterpieces of Celtic Metalwork, 6th–9th Centuries AD* (London, 1989), pp. 22, 47–52; J. Brenan, *Hanging Bowls and their Contexts*, BAR Brit. ser. 220 (Oxford, 1991); G. Haseloff, *Email in frühen Mittelalter. Frühchristliche Kunst von der Spätantike bis zu den Karolingern* (Marburg, 1990); R. L. S. Bruce-Mitford, 'Late Celtic Hanging-Bowls in Lincolnshire and South Humberside', in *Pre-Viking Lindsey*, ed. A. Vince (Lincoln, 1992), pp. 45–70.

S. M. YOUNGS

HARLEY PSALTER (London, BL, Harley 603), was made at Christ Church, *Canterbury, from *c*.1010–*c*.1130, and was left unfinished. Closely modelled on the *Utrecht Psalter, the Harley Psalter also has literal illustrations of the text heading each psalm, and the text is laid out in three columns. However, the Harley Psalter differs from the Utrecht Psalter in important respects; it is a Roman psalter, written in Caroline minuscule, and illustrated in colour. The Harley Psalter is the most extended essay in tinted line drawing by Anglo-Saxon artists. It is an extremely complicated manuscript made by eight main artists and three scribes, including Eadui Basan who wrote other *de luxe* manuscripts at Christ Church.

T. H. Ohlgren, *Anglo-Saxon Textual Illustration* (Kalamazoo, MI, 1992); W. Noel, *The Harley Psalter* (Cambridge, 1995).

WILLIAM NOEL

HAROLD II (d. 14 October 1066) was the second son of *Godwine of Wessex and his Danish wife Gytha. His parents were probably married *c*.1023, and since Harold was made earl of *East Anglia in 1044, he was born not much later than 1026. In 1051, Godwine fell out with King *Edward and Harold supported his father. When Godwine was exiled, he fled to Diarmid, king of Leinster, and raised a fleet to harry western *Wessex in 1052. At a council held in *London, Edward was forced to reinstate both Godwine and Harold.

On Godwine's death in 1053 Harold succeeded to Wessex. In 1055, the incompetence of Edward's nephew, Earl Ralph of *Hereford, made him responsible for the defence of western England against the Welsh, and thenceforth he was also earl of Hereford. By 1063, his successful campaigns had brought North Wales under English influence. Harold's immense wealth made him the second man in England after the king, and much of the administration was probably in his hands by the 1060s. Thus when, in 1065, the Northumbrians rebelled against their earl, Tostig, Harold's brother, and chose instead Morcar, brother of Edwin of *Mercia, Harold persuaded the king to ratify the choice.

Edward died on 5 January 1066, having (allegedly) made Harold his heir, and he was crowned in *Westminster Abbey on 6 January, most probably by *Ealdred, archbishop of *York. It seems, however, that Harold, on a visit to *Normandy, had sworn to uphold the king's earlier promise of the succession to William of Normandy, and his assumption of the kingship was seen by William's supporters as an act of perjury.

First, however, Harold had to face a Norwegian invasion. The aggrieved Tostig had found an ally in Harald Hardrada, whose fleet arrived in the Humber in September 1066, scattering the force brought against them by Earls Edwin and Morcar at the battle of Fulford. Harold's famous forced march to York resulted in the great English victory at Stamford Bridge, but he was unable to repeat the feat, falling to the victorious Duke William on 14 October. He was probably buried at Waltham Holy Cross, where he was regarded as the second founder, since he had rebuilt its church and increased the number of priests to thirteen, including the German scholar, Master *Adelard.

Harold was a skilful diplomat and politician and all sources, hostile or favourable, praise his good looks, intelligence and wit. His reputation suffered after 1066, and even the sympathetic author of the *Vita Edwardi regis* laments that he was 'too free with his oaths'. His memory is best preserved at his own church of Waltham Holy Cross, and at the cathedral priory of *Worcester, with which his family had long associations; Godwine had been the friend of Bishop Lyfing (1038–46), and Harold was particularly associated with Bishop Ealdred, promoted to York in 1060, and Ealdred's successor, St *Wulfstan. He was married twice, firstly to Edith 'Swanneck' and later to Ealdgyth, sister of Earl Edwin, and left numerous children. Few can be traced, but Harold's daughter Gytha is said to have married Vladimir Monomakh, prince of Kiev.
Vita Edwardi regis, ed. F. Barlow, 2nd ed. (OMT, 1992); H. Loyn, *Harold Son of Godwin* (Hastings and Bexhill, 1966); F. Barlow, *Edward the Confessor* (London, 1970); A. Williams, 'Land and Power in the Eleventh Century: the Estates of Harold Godwineson', *ANS* 3 (1981), 171–87, 230–4; R. Fleming, 'Domesday Estates of the King and the Godwines: a Study in late Saxon Politics', *Speculum* 58 (1983), 987–1007; idem, *Kings and Lords in Conquest England* (Cambridge, 1991); *The Waltham Chronicle*, ed. L. Watkiss and M. Chibnall (OMT, 1994); I. W. Walker, *Harold: The Last Anglo-Saxon King* (Stroud, 1997).

ANN WILLIAMS

HAROLD HAREFOOT, king of England (1037–40). Born c.1015; presumed by his supporters to be the son of *Cnut, by Ælfgifu of Northampton, but alleged by his opponents to be of less exalted parentage. Following the death of King Cnut, on 12 November 1035, the division of political loyalties in England found expression in a disputed succession: Earl *Leofric and the majority of the *thegns north of the Thames gave their allegiance to Harold Harefoot, while Earl *Godwine and all the chief men in *Wessex declared their support for *Harthacnut, Cnut's son by *Emma of *Normandy. The outcome was a period of shared rule (1035–7), and it was under these circumstances that Æthelnoth, archbishop of Canterbury, seems to have refused to consecrate Harold as king (*Encomium Emmae* iii. 1). In 1036 Ælfgifu of *Northampton campaigned strenuously on Harold's behalf. Sooner or later it became apparent that Harthacnut would not be able to leave Denmark; whereupon Queen Emma turned instead to her exiled sons *Edward and Alfred, an action which appears to have prompted Earl Godwine to switch his support to Harold and which led at the same time to Edward's aborted invasion and to Alfred's capture and death. In 1037 Harold was duly 'chosen as king everywhere' (*ASC*, MSS. CD), and Emma was driven in exile to *Flanders. Harold fell seriously ill at Oxford (S 1467), died there on 17 March 1040, and was buried at Westminster. Following their return to England, Emma and Harthacnut were able to vent their contempt for Harold: Emma commissioned the *Encomium Emmae*, while Harthacnut had Harold's body dug up and thrown into a bog (*ASC*). Harold's son Ælfwine, by a certain Ælfgifu, was reputedly the founder of the monastery of Sainte-Foi, Conques (Aquitaine).
Encomium Emmae Reginae, ed. A. Campbell, Camden 3rd ser. 72 (London, 1949), 38–50; *The Chronicle of John of Worcester*, II: *The Annals from 450 to 1066*, ed. R. R. Darlington and P. McGurk (OMT, 1995), pp. 520–8; W. H. Stevenson, 'An Alleged Son of King Harold Harefoot', *EHR* 28 (1913), 112–17; Stenton, *ASE*, pp. 419–22; F. Barlow, *Edward the Confessor* (London, 1970), pp. 42–8.

SIMON KEYNES

HARPS: *see* Musical Instruments

HARTHACNUT, king of England (1040–2). Son

of King *Cnut by *Emma of Normandy. He was brought up in Denmark, apparently with the expectation that he would succeed his father as king of Denmark and of England; but following Cnut's death, in November 1035, he had first to secure his position in Denmark against Magnus of Norway and had then to wait until the death of *Harold Harefoot in March 1040 before he was able to assert his position in England. Harthacnut's reign was characterized by resentment of heavy taxation (leading to the death of two of his *house-carls at *Worcester on 4 May 1041), galloping inflation, and further political intrigue. In the judgement of one contemporary chronicler, Har-thacnut 'did nothing worthy of a king as long as he ruled' (*ASC*, MSS. CD, s.a. 1040). According to *John of Worcester, Earl *Godwine was obliged to clear himself of a charge of complicity in the death of the *ætheling Alfred, and did so by presenting the king with a splendid ship, fully equipped and manned with 80 picked soldiers, and by insisting that he was only following Harold's orders; the same chronicler also provides a detailed account of the punitive ravaging of Worcestershire in November 1041. It was in the climate of growing hostility to Harthacnut's regime that the ætheling *Edward (the Confessor) was invited to return from *Normandy to England, and that Emma commissioned the *Encomium Emmae*. Har-thacnut died at Lambeth on 8 June 1042, while attending the wedding of Gytha, daughter of Osgod Clapa, to Tofi the Proud, and was buried beside his father in the Old Minster at *Win-chester.

Encomium Emmae Reginae, ed. A. Campbell, Camden 3rd ser. 72 (London, 1949), 38–50; *The Chronicle of John of Worcester* II: *The Annals from 450 to 1066*, ed. R. R. Darlington and P. McGurk (Oxford, 1995), pp. 520–34; Stenton, *ASE*, pp. 419–23; F. Barlow, *Edward the Con-fessor* (London, 1970), pp. 42–50.

SIMON KEYNES

HARTLEPOOL (Northumb.) was a double mon-astery founded in the 640s on a coastal promontory by Heiu, who was consecrated by St *Aidan as the first Northumbrian nun. She was succeeded by *Hild, who in *Bede's words 'set about estab-lishing there a rule of life in all respects like that which she had been taught by many learned men'. Excavations have found important remains of the seventh- and eighth-century monastic settlement: two phases of small rectangular buildings, clus-tered against a boundary ditch which contained mould and crucible fragments from the making of elaborate religious metalwork. Nothing more is known of the nunnery beyond the normal legend of *Viking destruction, though the location of the later parish church on the end of the peninsula, next to the excavated monastic remains, points to some religious continuity.

Bede, *HE* iv.23; R. Cramp, 'Monastic Sites', in Wilson, *Archaeology*, pp. 201–52, at 220–3; R. Daniels, 'The Anglo-Saxon Monastery at Church Close, Hartlepool, Cleveland', *Archaeological Journal* 145 (1988), 158–210.

JOHN BLAIR

HASTINGS, BATTLE OF. The Battle of Hastings was fought at Battle, Sussex, on Saturday 14 October 1066. There William the Conqueror, duke of *Normandy (1035–87), defeated King *Harold Godwineson who was killed in action together with his brothers Gyrth and Leofwine as well as the majority of the English male nobility. At stake was William's claim to the English throne based on, according to the Norman chronicles, a promise by King *Edward the Confessor (1042–66) dating as far back as 1051 and renewed *c.*1064 during a visit of the then Earl Harold to William in Normandy. Harold, however, claimed his accession and *coronation as king were legit-imate on the basis of the king's promise of the throne to him prior to his death. William's use of force to settle the dispute was backed by Pope Alexander II and many soldiers recruited from the Continent. In terms of military achievement the naval expedition, invasion, battle and subsequent campaigns in England had no parallel since Roman times. In terms of political and moral debate the Normans defended their action, claiming the right of a Christian ruler (William) to punish a tyrannical ruler who had perjured himself (Harold), while others in Europe accused the Normans (and the pope) of unjustifiable bloodshed and murder.

R. A. Brown, 'The Battle of Hastings', *ANS* 3 (1981), 1–21; *The Carmen de Hastingae Proelio of Guy of Amiens*, ed. C. Morton and H. Muntz (OMT, 1972); E. M. C. van Houts, 'The Norman Conquest through European Eyes', *EHR* 110 (1995), 832–53.

ELISABETH VAN HOUTS

HAWKING AND WILDFOWLING provided both an aristocratic recreation and a means of supplementing the winter diet. In the eighth century falcons were sent from *Germany to the kings of *Mercia and *Kent. *Asser records that King *Alfred trained his own falconers, and the Welsh sent hawks as tribute to *Æthelstan. A twelfth-century treatise on the care of hawks referred back to practices described in King *Harold's books, and the *Bayeux Tapestry shows

Harold and his nobles riding out with hawks at their wrists. William the Conqueror retained in his service several falconers who had previously served *Edward the Confessor. The *Domesday survey recorded hawks' eyries as a resource, particularly in Cheshire, and renders of hawks from various counties: Worcestershire had to provide a Norwegian hawk, probably the expensive but highly esteemed gerfalcon. The native peregrine falcon could be trained to take large prey like heron. Goshawks, which once bred in Britain though many were imported from Scandinavia, could be used against partridges, woodcock and sometimes hares. The female sparrowhawk was mainly used to take pigeons and smaller birds.

The cost of paying professional falconers and looking after the hawks was a heavy burden and often outweighed the value of the food they caught. Hawks eat voraciously, and some hawkers preferred to release them in the spring and train new ones in the autumn rather than feed them throughout the summer. Some landholders owed services of feeding the king's hawks, and in 855 the minster community of Blockley paid King Burgred of Mercia to release them from this obligation. Other methods of catching wild birds with nets, snares, birdlime, whistlelures and traps are described in *Ælfric's Colloquy.

Archaeological evidence for hawking and wildfowling is limited. Bird bones are small and fragile, and easily overlooked on excavations unless sieving is routinely carried out. Bones of peregrine falcon, goshawk and sparrowhawk have been recorded from several Anglo-Saxon sites. While there is no certain way of distinguishing captive birds from wild specimens, it is likely that these birds were used in hunting, since if they had been netted or trapped accidentally with other wildfowl they would probably have been discarded where they were captured. Bones of a wide range of wild birds, including swan, heron, bittern, various seabirds, wild geese and ducks, grey and golden plover, partridge, woodcock, curlew, rock dove, wood pigeon and many smaller birds have been reported from rural, aristocratic and urban sites throughout the Anglo-Saxon period. Cranes were bred in early medieval England, and are witnessed both in written sources and in the archaeological record, but are now only a rare passage migrant, whereas pheasant were introduced from the Continent shortly before the Norman Conquest. Direct evidence of butchery and consumption is rare, though knife marks have been found on bones of edible wild birds from mid-Saxon *Southampton.

Generally domestic geese, ducks and fowl made a far greater contribution to the diet.

A. Hagen, *A Second Handbook of Anglo-Saxon Food and Drink: Production and Distribution* (Hockwold-cum-Wilton, Norfolk, 1995), pp. 141–6.

C. J. BOND

HELMETS: *see* Arms and Armour

HEMMING, monk of *Worcester in the second half of the eleventh century. Hemming the 'sub-prior' was cited by Coleman as his authority for a story concerning *Wulfstan II, bishop of Worcester (1062–95); see *William of Malmesbury, *Vita S. Wulfstani*, i.1. He is associated more particularly with the important collection of Worcester charters and other records loosely known as 'Hemming's Cartulary'. It has long been recognized that the manuscript in question, now BL, Cotton Tiberius A. xiii, in fact comprises two cartularies of the church of Worcester, put together at different ends of the eleventh century and arguably under very different circumstances. The earlier of the two cartularies (Tiberius A. xiii, fols. 1–109 + 111–18, ptd *Hemingi Chartularium*, ed. Hearne, pp. 1–247) was compiled by at least five scribes, working presumably under the direction of *Wulfstan, bishop of Worcester (1002–16) and archbishop of York (1002–23), and comprises a series of mainly royal *charters, arranged topographically, followed by a series of episcopal leases dated between 957 and 996. The later of the two cartularies (Tiberius A. xiii, fols. 119–200), compiled by at least three scribes, is the part which might properly be called 'Hemming's Cartulary'. The original arrangement of the later cartulary has been disturbed, and it is only with difficulty that one can begin to appreciate its complexities as an account of Worcester's rights and privileges, put together in the mid-1090s. In a 'Prefatio istius libelli' (ed. Hearne, pp. 391–2), which appears to refer to the work as a whole, it is said that the book was written at Bishop Wulfstan's behest. In the 'Enucleatio libelli' (ed. Hearne, pp. 282–6, trans. Jones, pp. 160–3), Hemming names himself as the compiler, and represents his work as in some way the product of the interest which Wulfstan had taken in the re-organisation of the Worcester archives. The cartulary itself comprises a variety of material, and is best approached as an exercise in the assertion of monastic rights against external powers, whether secular or ecclesiastical. Pride of place belongs to the 'Codicellus possessionum huius ecclesie' (ed. Hearne, pp. 248–81), which reviews the circumstances in which many of the church's lands had been lost, whether as a consequence of the Danish wars during the reign of *Æthelred the Unready, or as a consequence of the activities of unjust *reeves and royal tax-gatherers, or in the aftermath of the Norman Conquest. Among other documents we find material relating to Oswaldslow, an abstract of the Domesday survey of the estates of Worcester, copies of royal charters relating to lands outside Oswaldslow, copies of charters relating to lands said to belong to the monks, and a series of 'detached' boundary clauses for estates within Oswaldslow. The cartulary ends with an account of the activities of Bishop *Ealdred and Bishop Wulfstan, mainly in connection with their acquisition of land for the church (ed. Hearne, pp. 395–425). Hemming deserves better than merely to be regarded as the compiler of a monastic cartulary. A more detailed understanding of his work would emerge from his identification as one or other of the main scribes in the second part of Tiberius A. xiii, perhaps 'Hand 1' (cf. Ker, pp. 41–2, 56). Yet he was, in effect, the historian of his own house; and his cartulary might be studied as an aspect of the response, at Worcester, to the upheavals of the Norman Conquest, and compared in this respect with responses at other major religious houses, such as *Glastonbury, *Ely, and Christ Church, *Canterbury. Hemming is prominent in the list of the members of the community of St Mary's, Worcester, drawn up during the episcopate of Bishop Samson (1096–1112), and entered in the 'Liber Vitae' of *Durham; among his colleagues were *Florence and *John of Worcester. It is not known when he died.

Sharpe, *Handlist*, 424; *Hemingi Chartularium Ecclesiæ Wigorniensis*, ed. T. Hearne, 2 vols. (Oxford, 1723); J. H. F. Peile, *William of Malmesbury's Life of S Wulstan, Bishop of Worcester* (Oxford, 1934), p. 9; N. R. Ker, 'Hemming's Cartulary: a Description of the Two Worcester Cartularies in Cotton Tiberius A. XIII' (1948), repr. in his *Books, Collectors and Libraries*, ed. A. G. Watson (London, 1985), pp. 31–59; A. E. E. Jones, *Anglo-Saxon Worcester* (Worcester, 1958); E. Mason, *St Wulfstan of Worcester c.1008–95* (Oxford, 1990); A. Williams, 'The Spoliation of Worcester', *ANS* 19 (1997), 383–408.

SIMON KEYNES

HENGEST AND HORSA. These two brothers are by far the most celebrated of the Germanic war-leaders who are supposed to have carved out kingdoms for themselves in Britain after the withdrawal of the Romans. Traditionally they were the leaders of the first wave of Anglo-Saxon invaders

in the fifth century. According to later legend, they were first invited to Britain by a 'tyrant' named Vortigern, but subsequently revolted, called in reinforcements and conquered his lands. They are particularly associated with the creation of the kingdom of *Kent, and Hengest (through his son Æsc or Oisc) was remembered as the founder of the Kentish royal dynasty.

N. Brooks, 'The Creation and Early Structure of the Kingdom of Kent', in Bassett, *Origins*, pp. 55–74.

S. E. KELLY

HENRY OF HUNTINGDON, author of a Latin chronicle entitled *Historia Anglorum* ('History of the English People'), was born *c.*1088 and died *c.*1157. His father was Nicholas, a Norman clerk and member of the Glanville family, who was appointed archdeacon of Huntingdon before 1092, and whom Henry succeeded on his death in 1110. Henry was active in the post of archdeacon, which carried a canonry of *Lincoln cathedral, until the mid 1150s, and lived with his wife and son in Little Stukeley, near Huntingdon. His mother was an English woman, from whom he seems to have learned English. He could remember old men speaking about the massacre of the Danes on St Brice's Day 1002, and his knowledge of the language is attested also by his use of Old English texts, and especially by his treatment in Latin of the alliteration and rhythms of the poem on the battle of *Brunanburh.

The *Historia Anglorum* has as its theme 'the history of this kingdom and the origins of our people', and covers the 1200 years between the invasions of Julius Caesar (55–54 BC) and the coronation of Henry II in 1154. About half the narrative relates to the Anglo-Saxon period: here Henry's account is largely dependent on *Bede's *Historia ecclesiastica* and the *Anglo-Saxon Chronicle, sources he acknowledges in his Preface. He used two identifiable versions of the *Chronicle*: one was closely allied to that at Peterborough ('E'), and another was similar to that at *Abingdon ('C'). He also witnesses one or more versions now lost, in some entries in the *Historia* which are shared with *John of Worcester, and in others also echoed by *William of Malmesbury. In addition to these two main sources, Henry quotes from Bede's *Chronica maiora*, the *Historia Brittonum* (Vatican recension), an unidentified set of Norman annals, and a lost Old English poem on battles. Oral tradition seems to lie behind other passages that cannot be traced to written sources, particularly stories from the first half of the eleventh century, including *Cnut and the waves, stories about Earl Siward, and the death of Earl *Godwine.

In his interpretation of Anglo-Saxon history, Henry develops an idea found in *Gildas and Bede, that the English invasions were God's punishments on a faithless people. Confronted by sparse annals and confused events in the early period of the *settlement, Henry imposes a framework in which, after early disorder and war, the invaders settle in the seven kingdoms of the *Heptarchy. Thereafter, a central theme of the *Historia* is the unification of the English monarchy under the kings of *Wessex. Henry quite naturally adds *Alfred and *Edgar to the number of *bretwaldas* found in Bede and the *Chronicle*. The Norman Conquest came about according to God's long-conceived plan 'to exterminate the English people for their compelling crimes . . . slaughter and treachery . . . drunkenness and neglect of the Lord's house'. The *Historia Anglorum* became a popular work: aspects of its interpretation, such as the notion of the Heptarchy, have survived into the latter part of the twentieth century.

Sharpe, *Handlist*, 461; *Henry, Archdeacon of Huntingdon: Historia Anglorum, The History of the English People*, ed. and trans. D. Greenway (OMT, 1996).

DIANA E. GREENWAY

HEPTARCHY. *Bede, following Pope *Gregory the Great, referred to the Germanic inhabitants of Britain (*Garmani*) as the *Angli*, but was not oblivious to their separate origins on the Continent. In his famous passage locating the progeny of the three component groups of settlers in terms of the political orders which prevailed in his own day, he derived the people of *Kent, the Isle of Wight and the mainland opposite from the Jutes; the East Saxons, South Saxons and West Saxons from the Saxons; and the East Angles, Middle Angles, Mercians, Northumbrians and other Anglian peoples from the Angles (*HE* i.15); he was also aware of deeper complications (cf. *HE* v.9). The notion that political organisation in early Anglo-Saxon England could be formulated as a 'Heptarchy', comprising the seven kingdoms of Kent, *Sussex, *Wessex, *Essex, *East Anglia, *Mercia, and *Northumbria, seems to have arisen in the early twelfth century (*Henry of Huntingdon, *Hist. Angl.* i. 4), as a helpful simplification of Bede's scheme. It was given expression in graphic form in a map accompanying Lambarde's *Archaionomia* (London, 1568), and, often in conjunction with the notion of the *Bretwalda, has exercised a powerful influence on the conceptions of early Anglo-Saxon history which still prevail.

It represents a most interesting idea in the search for organising principles; but of course it involves a gross distortion of what we may judge to have been the truth. In particular, it obscures the complexities which lie behind the political development of each kingdom, and conceals the deep-rooted differences between the kingdoms which helped to determine their respective fortunes.

D. P. Kirby, *The Making of Early England* (London, 1967), pp. 54–71; J. Campbell, 'Some Twelfth-Century Views of the Anglo-Saxon Past', *Essays*, pp. 209–28; D. Dumville, 'Essex, Middle Anglia and the Expansion of Mercia in the South-East Midlands' (1989), repr. in his *Britons and Anglo-Saxons in the Early Middle Ages* (Aldershot, 1993), pp. [IX] 1–30, at 6–7; Kirby, *Earliest English Kings*, pp. 1–9; S. Keynes, 'Rædwald the Bretwalda', *Voyage to the Other World: the Legacy of Sutton Hoo*, ed. C. B. Kendall and P. S. Wells (Minneapolis, MN, 1992), pp. 103–23; W. Goffart, 'The First Venture into "Medieval Geography": Lambarde's Map of the Saxon Heptarchy (1568)', Bately FS, pp. 53–60.

SIMON KEYNES

HERBALS. From classical antiquity until the late Middle Ages, 'herbal' (Latin *herbarius*) meant a *pharmacopoeia* whose main ingredients were of vegetal origin. Herbals acquired a distinctive literary form in the early centuries AD, when illustrations were added to the descriptions of plants and their medical uses. Toward the second half of the tenth century, a translation from Latin into OE was made of a group of medical documents which together can be considered to form the common *pharmacopoeia* of the early Middle Ages before the expansion of the great medical schools of Salerno and Montpellier. Originally separate Latin treatises at a very early date became part of the textual tradition of one of them, the *Herbarius pseudo-Apulei*, and the OE translation combined them in two major works. The first, the 'enlarged herbal', contained vegetable-based remedies and the second, the so-called *Medicina de quadrupedibus*, featured treatments derived from wild and domestic animals. The enlarged herbal comprises 185 chapters and an index with herb names in both Latin and OE. Its first chapter, on betony, is a partial translation of the *De herba vettonica liber* falsely attributed to Antonius Musa; chs. 2–131 contain the *Pseudo-Apulei herbarius*; and the remaining 53 chapters describe herbs taken either from the *Liber medicinae ex herbis feminis*, wrongly attributed to Pedanius Dioscorides, or the *Curae herbarum*, compiled mainly from Dioscorides's *De materia medica* and Pliny's *Naturalis historia*. The fourteen chapters of *Medicina de*

233

quadrupedibus translate the anonymous *De taxone liber* on the medicinal virtues of the badger, another tract on the qualities of the mulberry tree, and the abridged version (on four-legged mammals only, hence F. Junius's title was accepted by O. Cockayne) of the *Liber medicinae ex animalibus* attributed to one Sextus Placitus Papiriensis.

The reasonably accurate translation has been preserved in four manuscripts: London, BL, Harley 585 (H); Cotton Vitellius C.iii (V), whose vivid and apparently naturalistic illustrations are actually faithful reproductions of models in the original Latin texts; Oxford, Bodleian Library, Hatton 76 (B), which was prepared for illustration but never completed; and London, BL, Harley 6258B (O). H, V and B, copied in the late tenth century (H) or early eleventh (V, B), belong to the same textual tradition. O (s. xii) contains a later version with the herbs ordered alphabetically.

The Old English Herbarium and Medicina de Quadrupedibus, ed. H. J. De Vriend, EETS os 286 (London, 1984); L. E. Voigts, 'Anglo-Saxon Plant Remedies and the Anglo-Saxons', *Isis* 70 (1979), 250–68; W. Hofstetter, 'Zur lateinischen Quelle des altenglischen Pseudo-Dioskurides', *Anglia* 101 (1983), 315–60; H. Sauer, 'Towards a Linguistic Description and Classification of the Old English Plant Names', in Gneuss FS, pp. 381–408; M. A. D'Aronco, 'L'erbario anglosassone, un'ipotesi sulla data della traduzione', *Romanobarbarica* 13 (1994–5), 325–65; *The Old English Illustrated Pharmacopoeia: British Library Cotton Vitellius C. III*, ed. M. A. D' Aronco and M. L. Cameron, EEMF 27 (Copenhagen, 1998).

MARIA A. D'ARONCO

HERE. The word *here* was used to denote an *army, a large band of marauders or an armed troop of men. The late seventh-century *laws of the West Saxon king *Ine (§ 13) define *here* as a troop of marauders consisting of more than thirty-five men. The terms *here* and *sciphere* ('ship-*here*') are used in the *Anglo-Saxon Chronicle* mostly to denote *Viking armies, whereas English armies are usually referred to as *fyrd*s. The typical Scandinavian *here* of the ninth century was a composite force, comprising the crews of a number of small fleets, each under the command of its own sea-captain. These 'armies' usually numbered no more than a few hundred. Even the 'great heathen army' (*micel hæðen here*) that the *Anglo-Saxon Chronicle* reports as having landed in East Anglia in 866 was a fluid and shifting combination of fleets that conquered the kingdoms of *Northumbria, *East Anglia and (eastern) *Mercia with only a few thousand men. The *hergas* (*heres*?) that raided England in the late tenth century and which, under the command of the Danish kings

*Swein Forkbeard (d. 1014) and his son *Cnut (king of England, 1016–35), were larger and better organized, still should be thought of as composite fleets or war bands rather than 'national armies'. The *Anglo-Saxon Chronicle* also used the term *here* to describe the groups of Scandinavians who settled in the *Danelaw in the early tenth century under *jarls* in districts organized around towns such as *Northampton, *Leicester, *Lincoln, Derby, *Stamford, Bedford, Huntingdon and Cambridge. *Here* also appears as the first element in a number of compound words, such as *heregeld* and *heriot* (*heregeatu*).

Liebermann, *Gesetze* ii.499–500; A. diP. Healey and R. Venezky, *A Microfiche Concordance to Old English* (Toronto, 1980), s.v. *here*; A. Smyth, *Scandinavian Kings in the British Isles, 850–880* (Oxford, 1977); N. Lund, 'The Armies of Swein Forkbeard and Cnut: *leding* or *lið*', *ASE* 15 (1986), 105–18.

RICHARD ABELS

HEREFORD, at a major crossing of the Wye, was the episcopal seat of the *Magonsæte* by 801, and perhaps from the creation of the diocese in 676 when, according to later legend, the sub-king Milfrith built the cathedral. The cult of King *Æthelberht of East Anglia, 'martyred' by *Offa in 794, was established in the cathedral. Another (and perhaps the earliest) religious focus lay 300 m. eastwards, where burials from the seventh century onwards have been found. It is unknown when the cult of St *Guthlac was established on this site, but there are references from the 970s to the dual communities of St Æthelberht's (i.e. the cathedral) and St Guthlac's (fig. 19).

Hereford means 'army-ford', and it was always a frontier settlement; the Welsh Annals record a battle there between Welsh and English in 760. Perhaps developed by Mercian kings for its strategic importance, it has revealed some of the earliest town planning known on any inland site: eighth-century *timber buildings aligned on a street, overlying slightly earlier grain-drying ovens. In the mid-ninth century the rectilinear core, including the cathedral, was enclosed by a bank and ditch. This small early *town was enlarged eastwards (encapsulating St Guthlac's) and re-fortified, probably by *Æthelflæd, and in 914 the Hereford men helped to repel a *Viking attack. There was a *mint under *Æthelstan, and regularly from 973. By the eleventh century Hereford was the centre of a shire, and a growing town; Earl Ralph built a castle there *c.*1052. The Welsh burnt Hereford in 1055, but *Domesday Book shows a well-developed commercial town.

P. Sims-Williams, *Religion and Literature in Western England, 600–800*, CSASE 3 (Cambridge, 1990); M. D. Lobel, 'Hereford', *Historic Towns Atlas: I* (London and Oxford, 1969); R. Shoesmith, *Hereford City Excavations, I–II*, CBA Research Reports 36 (1980) and 46 (1982); M. Gelling, *The West Midlands in the Early Middle Ages* (London and Leicester, 1992), pp. 159–64.

JOHN BLAIR

HEREGELD ('army-tax'). A form of annual taxation instituted in 1012, during the reign of *Æthelred the Unready, in order to pay Scandinavian mercenaries (notably Thorkell the Tall), and used thereafter to finance the military force which maintained the Anglo-Danish regime in power. The *heregeld* was formally abolished by *Edward the Confessor, in 1051, though it may well have been revived following the restoration of Earl *Godwine and his family in 1052. The *heregeld* was the model for one of the forms of taxation levied by the Anglo-Norman kings, and came to be known as the 'Danegeld'. A careful distinction has to be maintained, however, between the *heregeld*, or Danegeld, and the massive payments of *gafol* ('tribute') which had been made to marauding *Viking armies during Æthelred's reign, rising from £10,000 in 991 to £48,000 in 1012, and (under more complex circumstances) to £72,000 + £10,500 in 1016–18. The *heregeld* was a form of taxation on owners of land, levied at a specified but variable number of pence per hide of land (e.g. 12d per hide), and collected by local officials at fixed times each year. The quantities of gold and silver needed for the payments of *gafol*, on the other hand, were raised (whenever the need arose) by whatever means were at the disposal of those obliged or inclined to make them, including the sale of land and privileges, taxation, and the use of available reserves of treasure and coin. The confusion between *heregeld* and *gafol* is compounded by modern usage, in which the term 'Danegeld' is transferred from the former to the latter, and in which considerations properly applicable to one are transferred improperly to the other.

S. Keynes, *The Diplomas of King Æthelred 'the Unready' 978–1016* (Cambridge, 1980), pp. 221, 225; J. A. Green, 'The Last Century of Danegeld', *EHR* 96 (1981), 241–58; M. K. Lawson, 'The Collection of Danegeld and Heregeld in the Reigns of Æthelred II and Cnut', *EHR* 99 (1984), 721–38; J. Gillingham, ' "The Most Precious Jewel in the English Crown": Levels of Danegeld and Heregeld in the Early Eleventh Century', *EHR* 104 (1989), 373–84; further contributions to this debate in *EHR* 104 (1989), 385–406, and in *EHR* 105 (1990), 939–50, 951–61; S. Keynes, 'The Historical Context of the Battle of Maldon', *The Battle of Maldon AD 991*, ed. D. Scragg (Oxford, 1991), pp. 81–113, at 99–102.

SIMON KEYNES

HERIOT (*heregeatu*), literally 'war-gear', was a death-due that originated in the return of the weapons with which a lord had outfitted his man. The payment of a heriot was a symbolic expression of the mutual obligations between a lord and his man. That heriots continued to be rendered in weapons and horses by the higher nobility of *Wessex and *Mercia, rather than commuted into cash payments, right up to the Conquest, indicates the persistence of the military ethos among the Anglo-Saxon aristocracy.

The growth of royal power in the tenth century helped regularize the payment of heriots, though regional differences persisted. Both are seen in the normative table of heriot payments included in the *laws of *Cnut (*c*.1020–3). *II Cnut*, c. 71 stipulates the heriot payments owed by individuals belonging to different status groups in the three main 'legal' regions comprising the kingdom of England. An earl's heriot, according to Cnut's laws, consisted of eight horses, four saddled and four unsaddled, four mail coats and four helmets, eight spears and eight shields, four swords and fifty mancuses of gold – sufficient armament to outfit a troop of four fully armed warriors with four mounted attendants. King's *thegns in *Wessex and *Mercia gave four horses, two saddled and two unsaddled, two swords, four spears and four shields, a helmet and coat of mail, and fifty mancuses of gold. Lesser thegns in Wessex paid with a horse, its trappings, and their personal weapons. Lesser thegns in Mercia and *East Anglia and king's thegns in the *Danelaw paid in cash. Helmets and byrnies are rarely found in the heriots preserved in tenth-century *wills. Eleventh-century wills, on the other hand, mention them as a matter of course. It has been suggested that the heriot table in Cnut's laws reflects an attempt by King *Æthelred the Unready (d. 1016) and his advisers to improve the military gear borne by English soldiers in their war with the *Vikings.

By the end of the Anglo-Saxon period heriots had become associated with tenurial succession. A lord's reception of a heriot payment obliged him, in general, to support the deceased's testamentary bequests. The acceptance of a heriot by the king was a necessary prelude to the descent of *bookland. To the Norman commissioners who compiled *Domesday Book, heriots looked very much like 'reliefs', payments proffered by an heir to a lord for succession to a fief, and the term most often used to translate heriot in the Inquest is *relevium*. The heriot survived into the twelfth and thirteenth centuries as a *peasant inheritance due. Shedding its former military associations, the heriot was converted into the payment of livestock to a manorial lord by the heir to a peasant tenancy. The transformation of the heriot reflects the persistence of Anglo-Saxon customs into the Middle Ages as well as the degradation of the English landed elite after *Hastings.

Liebermann, *Gesetze*, ii.500–2; D. Whitelock, ed., *Anglo-Saxon Wills* (Cambridge, 1930), p. 100; N. P. Brooks, 'Arms, Status and Warfare in Late-Saxon England', in *Ethelred the Unready: Papers from the Millenary Conference*, ed. D. Hill, BAR Brit. ser. 59 (Oxford, 1978), 81–103; R. Abels, *Lordship and Military Obligation in Anglo-Saxon England* (Berkeley, CA, 1988), pp. 137–8, 149, 265–6.

RICHARD ABELS

HEROIC POETRY is the generic term for a tradition of narrative poetry in many ancient, medieval and modern cultures, which celebrates the mighty deeds of heroes, whose socially determined code of honour is tested in circumstances commonly involving physical risk. The tone is usually restrained, and exaggeration and the marvellous are kept within bounds. The extant heroic poems from Anglo-Saxon England are late-tenth or early-eleventh-century copies. Their prior history is unknown, but they draw upon legends that had developed, originally in oral tradition, around kings, heroes, and tribal conflicts of the period of the Germanic migrations and the fall of the Western Roman Empire. The earliest datable figure in *Widsith's comprehensive catalogues is Ostrogotha, who flourished *c*.218–50; the most prominent is the Ostrogothic leader Eormanric, who died in 375; the latest is Ælfwine (Alboin), king of the Lombards, who was assassinated in 572. Other notable historical figures in the heroic tradition are Guthhere, king of the Burgundians (d. 436/7), Attila, leader of the Huns (d. 453), and Theodoric the Ostrogoth (d. 526). Legends associated with these names were elaborated throughout the Germanic world, from Austria to Iceland. Apart from the Old High German *Hildebrandslied*, preserved in a manuscript of *c*.810, the Old English poems are the earliest surviving in any Germanic language, but there is a particularly rich vernacular legacy in thirteenth-century manuscripts from Scandinavia and Germany, including the *Poetic Edda*, the prose *Vǫlsunga saga*, and the *Nibelungenlied*. Although there are variations across time and place, the legends are clearly part of a tradition whose historical origins can be glimpsed through late classical and early medieval Latin historians and chroniclers, such as Ammianus Marcellinus, Jordanes, and Paul the Deacon. As the legends developed, the original circumstances were often simplified almost beyond recognition, minor tribes and heroes were forgotten and their deeds were reassigned to more significant figures whose stature was thereby further increased, chronology was reorganized so that men and tribes from different centuries came to co-exist in an undefined past, and the historical realities of tribal movements and large-scale conflict were replaced by a concentration on the individual hero and his *comitatus*, with the poems' events thus being motivated by individuals responding to personal pressures and the demands of their own heroic moral code.

The Anglo-Saxons also drew upon Scandinavian legend-cycles, but the fifth- and sixth-century historical events from which they evolved were unknown to the historians of the imperial and post-imperial world, except for Hygelac's raid on the Frisians (*c*.520), which was recorded by Gregory of Tours because it involved the Franks. The extant Scandinavian witnesses to this general body of legends are from the early thirteenth-century and later, notably the Latin history of Denmark by Saxo Grammaticus, Snorri Sturluson's *Ynglinga saga* (using *Ynglingatal*, from perhaps the early tenth century), and *Hrólfs saga kraka*.

The Old English heroic poems which exploit Germanic legend-cycles are *Beowulf*, the *Battle of *Finnsburh*, *Deor*, *Waldere*, and *Widsith*, but it is clear from their chance survival and the confident nature of their extra-textual allusions that they were part of a larger corpus. *The Battle of *Maldon* and the *Battle of Brunanburh*, which celebrate tenth-century events, exploit the values of the heroic tradition, whilst the *elegies give powerful expression to the negative aspect: the loss of past glories and the misery of exile from the kin-groups and lord-groups which were the focus of heroic life, providing the rich material context, confirming the warrior's heroic identity, and paradoxically being the source of the recurrent dilemma of conflicting loyalty which, along with the accepted risk of death, invests the poems with their characteristically tragic dynamism.

H. M. Chadwick, *The Heroic Age* (Cambridge, 1912); C. M. Bowra, *Heroic Poetry* (London, 1952); D. G. Calder, R. E. Bjork, P. K. Ford and D. F. Melia, trans., *Sources and Analogues of Old English Poetry. II: The Major Germanic and Celtic Texts in Translation* (Cambridge, 1983);

R. Frank, 'Germanic Legend in Old English Literature', in *CamComp*, pp. 88–106; L. Musset, *The Germanic Invasions: The Making of Europe AD 400–600*, transl. E. and C. James (London, 1975).

JOYCE HILL

HEWALD, the name borne by two Northumbrian missionaries who were murdered in Saxony *c*.695. Bede, who provides the sole surviving account of their mission, notes that they were distinguished by being called 'the Black Hewald' and 'the White Hewald' because of the colour of their hair (see *by-names). They had spent some time in Ireland before joining the mission of *Willibrord in *Frisia. Their method of preaching, including the use of a portable altar, so incensed the Old Saxons that they murdered the two men and threw their bodies into the Rhine. A miraculous pillar of light subsequently revealed where the bodies had washed up, and they were duly translated to the church in Cologne. They are commemorated in some Anglo-Saxon liturgical calendars on 3 October.

Bede, *HE* v.10.

MICHAEL LAPIDGE

HEXHAM (Northumb.) was a monastery founded by Bishop *Wilfrid in 671–3 on a promontary overlooking the river Tyne. Though there were several churches on the site it is only within the present priory church that substantial remains of seventh-century architecture can now be seen. Nineteenth-century records and more recent excavations combine to suggest that Wilfrid's main church, dedicated to St Andrew, stood within the area of the existing nave and *Stephen of Ripon's description shows that this was a building with several stories, linked by passages and staircases; *Bede records that Wilfrid's successor *Acca (709–732/3) subsequently modified this structure by adding *porticus* within the building. Most of this ambitious church was destroyed by later medieval works but surviving fragments of its architectural sculpture suggest that it was decorated in a distinctively non-Insular, Mediterranean, style. Under the present chancel, axially aligned with Wilfrid's large church, are the foundations of a small apsed structure of pre-Norman date which may have functioned as a mausoleum.

The main architectural interest of Hexham for the Anglo-Saxonist, however, lies in the surviving *crypt belonging to the principal monastic church. This, on Stephen's evidence, is Wilfrid's work. It is constructed with re-used stone from the nearby Roman site at Corbridge, and its plan, like many of its constructional details and measurement units, echoes the earlier crypt built by Wilfrid at *Ripon. Both, for example, have a vaulted and plastered main chamber with an ante-chamber to the west, and both have a flanking northern passage. But, whilst Ripon has only two entrances, Hexham has three – an enhancement which was no doubt designed to improve circulation arrangements for pilgrims. Hexham's two eastern passages tunnelled under the main walls of the church and were presumably entered from *porticus* lying outside the chancel; using these entrances it would thus have been possible for pilgrims to venerate relics in the main crypt chamber without entering the main body of the church. The plans of these two Wilfridian crypts have no close parallels in western Europe, though it has been argued that Wilfrid took his inspiration from models as various as the catacombs of *Rome and literary descriptions of Christ's tomb in Jerusalem. Whatever their source, both powerfully exploit the contrast between disorienting, sharply-turning, dark passages and candle-lit chambers to produce an appropriate architectural setting for the drama of Divine Revelation.

The history of the monastery after Acca is not well documented. The last record of the bishopric at Hexham is in *c*.821 and there is no reliable documentary evidence about the site thereafter until the eleventh century, when the lands were being administered by provosts associated with *Durham and the church was in the hands of hereditary priests. Sculptural evidence, however, shows continued use of the *cemetery between the ninth and eleventh centuries, whilst the deposition of the Hexham *hoard of *c*.8000 *coins in the middle years of the ninth century gives some indication of the wealth of the post-Wilfridian community.

R. N. Bailey, 'St Wilfrid, Ripon and Hexham', *American Early Medieval Studies* 1 (1990), 3–25; E. Cambridge and A. Williams, 'Hexham Abbey: a Review of Recent Work and its Implications', *Archaeologia Aeliana* 5th ser. 23 (1995), 51–138; R. J. Cramp, in CASSS i.174–93; *St Wilfrid at Hexham*, ed. D. P. Kirby (Newcastle, 1974); Taylor and Taylor, *AS Arch* i. 297–312, iii. 1014–17.

RICHARD N. BAILEY

HICKES, George (1642–1715), philologist and Anglo-Saxonist. Destined for a distinguished career in the Church of England, Hickes became Dean of *Worcester in 1683, and there began to develop the interest in ancient northern languages which is represented in the first instance by his *Institutiones grammaticae Anglo-Saxonicae* (Oxford,

1689). He was deprived of his ecclesiastical office following his refusal to take the oath of allegiance to William and Mary in 1689, and throughout the 1690s was obliged to tread carefully as a nonjuror. It was during this period that he began work on the major collaborative project which bore fruit some ten years later in the form of his 'Two Books of Ancient Northern Literature' (*Antiquæ Literaturæ Septentrionalis Libri Duo* (Oxford, 1703–5)), generally but perhaps mistakenly known as Hickes's *Thesaurus* (after the title proper to the first volume only). The first volume of this remarkable work comprised Hickes's composite 'Grammatico-Critical and Archaeological Treasury of Ancient Northern Languages' (*Linguarum Vett. Septentrionalium Thesaurus Grammatico-Criticus & Archæologicus*), which in addition to a set of grammatical treatises contained an important tract on charters by Hickes himself (the *Dissertatio Epistolaris*), as well as a tract on coinage by Andrew Fountaine. The second volume comprised Humfrey *Wanley's 'Historico-Critical Catalogue of Ancient Northern Books preserved in the Libraries of England' (*Librorum Vett. Septentrionalium, qui in Angliæ Biblioth. extant, Catalogus Historico-Criticus*), covering manuscripts in London, Oxford, Cambridge, and elsewhere, and containing detailed accounts of their contents. An abridged version of Hickes's *Thesaurus*, prepared by William Wooton, was published in 1708, and was later translated into English by Maurice Shelton, *Wooton's Short View of G. Hickes's Grammatico-Critical and Archaeological Treasure of the Ancient Northern-Languages* (London, 1735). Hickes died on 15 December 1715, and is buried in the churchyard of St Margaret's, Westminster. J. A. W. Bennett, 'Hickes's *Thesaurus*: a Study of Oxford Book-Production', *Essays and Studies* n.s. 1 (1948), 28–45; *A Chorus of Grammars: the Correspondence of George Hickes and his Collaborators on the 'Thesaurus linguarum septentrionalium'*, ed. R. L. Harris, Publications of the Dictionary of Old English 4 (Toronto, 1992).

SIMON KEYNES

HIDE. In a society without maps or any means of measuring large areas of land the hide provided the basis for rough estimates: the *Tribal Hidage tells us that 'the land of the Mercians . . . is 30,000 hides', and *Bede expressed kingdoms and small estates alike in hides. In early Anglo-Saxon England the hide was used as the basis for assessing the amount of *feorm* due from an area – *Ine's *laws refer to what was due from ten hides – and it was a short step from this overall assessment to assigning the obligations to smaller groups of hides and eventually to the single hide. The land which owed these obligations was hidated, reckoned in hides, while land which was exempt, such as many monastic inlands, was commonly, although not invariably, unhidated. As the unit on which public obligations were assessed, the hide was essential to the workings of the Anglo-Saxon state: as well as food rents, manning and maintaining the walls of *burhs*, and the payment of geld were assessed on the hide. There is a connection between hides, liability to public service, and free status. Possession of a given number of hides conferred superior status (see *social class) and traces of a five-hide unit from which military service was due can be seen, foreshadowing the knight's fee, in *Domesday Book and in Fyfield ('five-hides') place-names. The term hide seems never to have taken on the connotations of tenancy which became attached to *mansus*, although many hides did in fact become tenancies, their tenants known in some places as *hidarii* or 'hydars', their rents sometimes reflecting the obligations which had once been assessed on the hide.

OE *hiwisc* means 'family', 'household' and like the continental *mansus*, the hide was thought to be equivalent to the land farmed by, and supporting, a peasant family. Bede thought that describing land as 'of x families' was 'the English way of reckoning'. Anglo-Saxon *charters use the terms 'land of x hides' interchangeably with 'land of x families', 'land of x *cassati*', 'land of x *mansae*' (this term appears to have had a feminine form in England, a masculine one in France), 'land of x *tributarii*'. If a typical hide supported a single family in Bede's time, by the eleventh century in many places it supported four (each with a quarter of a hide or yardland), eight, or more. Elsewhere, single hides survived as isolated family farms, notably in the west country where some have the element *huish*, from the OE form *hiwisc* as, or in, their names. Hide Farms elsewhere are their equivalent. In areas of common field husbandry, holdings which consisted of scattered strips were nevertheless sometimes reckoned in hides. The size of the hide differed according to the value and resources of the land involved. Over time, it was assigned a set acreage, which could vary from place to place, but was commonly 120 acres, and there is some evidence of 'small hides' of sixty acres or fewer. That the hidages of some places remained the same from their first appearance in the charters to the figures for manors recorded in Domesday Book and sometimes for centuries afterwards shows how artificial the hide had become as a unit of area. However, it continued to be used as a nominal unit on the basis of which villagers continued to arrange communal rights and obligations: thus the villagers of Cassington, Oxfordshire, were allotted their hay-meadows by the hide into the nineteenth century.

F. W. Maitland, *Domesday Book and Beyond* (London, 1897), pp. 416–62; T. M. Charles-Edwards, 'Kinship, Status and the Origins of the Hide', *P&P* 56 (1972), 3–33; R. J. Faith, *The English Peasantry and the Growth of Lordship* (London, 1997), pp. 109–52.

ROSAMOND FAITH

HILD or HILDA (d. 680), abbess of *Whitby, and one of the principal proponents of monastic life in early *Northumbria. She was born (*c.*614) to parents named Hereric and Breguswith, who were connected with both the East Anglian and Northumbrian royal houses, and was baptized in the company of King *Edwin (her father Hereric's uncle) by Bishop *Paulinus in 627. Although she seems to have spent the early part of her life as a laywoman (little is known of her life in the period following the death of Edwin in 633), she subsequently developed enthusiasm for the monastic life, and planned to become a nun at Chelles (near Paris) which had been founded by an English-woman and where her sister Hereswith was then domiciled. However, she was persuaded to remain in England by Bishop *Aidan, and was given a small plot for a monastery on the river Wear (precise location unknown); she subsequently became abbess of *Hartlepool (between 647 and 651), where she remained until in 657 she was given land to establish a monastery at Whitby. During the twenty-three years that Hild was abbess of Whitby, the monastery was a focal point for the religious life: it was there that the famous synod on the dating of *Easter was held in 664 and the cowherd *Cædmon created the first recorded religious verse in Old English. According to Bede, Whitby under Hild's guidance was a nursery of bishops: five bishops (*Bosa, Ætla, Oftfor, John of Beverley, and *Wilfrid II) who had been trained at Whitby were consecrated to English sees. It was also at Whitby in Hild's time that the anonymous *Vita S. Gregorii*, the earliest life of Pope *Gregory the Great, was composed. Hild died aged 66 on 17 November 680; her feast was commemorated in numerous Anglo-Saxon liturgical calendars, and a number of churches were dedicated to her; in the tenth century her relics were translated to *Glastonbury, before the refoundation of Whitby in the eleventh century.

Bede, *HE* iv. 23; C. E. Fell, 'Hild, Abbess of Streonaes-halch', in *Hagiography and Medieval Literature*, ed. H. Bekker-Nielsen *et al.* (Odense, 1981), pp. 76–99; J. E. Cross, 'A Lost Life of Hilda of Whitby: the Evidence of the *Old English Martyrology*', *Acta* 6 (1979), 21–43; P. Hunter Blair, 'Whitby as a Centre of Learning in the Seventh Century', Clemoes FS, pp. 3–32.

MICHAEL LAPIDGE

HILDELITH (fl. 700), abbess of *Barking (*Essex), a double monastery which was founded during the decade 665 × 675 by *Earconwald, later bishop of *London (675–93) and whose first abbess was Earconwald's sister, Æthelburg (d. 675). After Æthelburg's death, Hildelith became abbess; according to Bede, who was drawing on a lost *libellus* of Hildelith's life, she presided over the monastery for many years, but the date of her death is unknown. Bede reports that Hildelith was energetic in the observance of monastic discipline, and it was to Hildelith and her community of religious women that *Aldhelm dedicated his massive prose *De virginitate*; at another time, Boni-face described in a letter (*Ep.* x, datable to 716) to Abbess *Eadburg the events of a *vision seen by a monk of Much Wenlock which had been described to him by Abbess Hildelith. This implies that Hildelith was in close communication with the principal scholars of her time.

Bede, *HE* iv. 6–11; MGH, AA xv. 228–9, ES i.7–15 (no. 10).

MICHAEL LAPIDGE

HISTORIA BRITTONUM, a synchronizing history extending from Creation to the 680s, composed anonymously at an unidentified centre in north Wales in the fourth year of the reign of Merfyn Frych, king of Gwynedd (826–44), hence in 829 or 830. The text in its original form does not survive, but is known through a large number of later redactions (one of which is ascribed to one 'Nennius', hence the *Historia Brittonum* itself is often ascribed, mistakenly, to Nennius). Its contents include accounts of the Six Ages of the World, of the origins of Britain and Ireland, of Britain under the Romans, of the lives of St Ger-manus of Auxerre and St Patrick, and of the campaigns of King *Arthur; its interest for Anglo-Saxon history is that it includes extracts from a Kentish Chronicle (concerned *inter alia* with Vortigern and Hengest) and royal *genealogies of *Bernicia, *Kent, *East Anglia, *Mercia, and *Deira. To judge from these contents, the anony-mous author was probably a native of the Anglo-Welsh border who was almost certainly a speaker of Old English; he was also a man of some learning

(he is able to quote from Vergil), and may have been familiar with *Bede's *Historia ecclesiastica*.
Sharpe, *Handlist*, 1072; MGH, AA xiii.111–222; E. Faral, *La légende arthurienne*, 3 vols. (Paris, 1929), iii. 5–44; *The Historia Brittonum 3. The 'Vatican' Recension*, ed. D. Dumville (Cambridge, 1985); *Nennius*, ed. J. Morris (London and Chichester, 1980); D. N. Dumville, *Histories and Pseudo-Histories of the Insular Middle Ages* (Aldershot, 1990), esp. nos. II–VII; idem, '*Historia Brittonum*: an Insular History from the Carolingian Age', in *Historiographie im frühen Mittelalter*, ed. A. Scharer and G. Scheibelreiter (Vienna and Munich, 1994), pp. 406–34.

MICHAEL LAPIDGE

HOARDS. Some three hundred coin hoards of the Anglo-Saxon period have been found in the British Isles, varying in size from small groups of just a few coins to massive treasures such as that from Cuerdale in Lancashire, deposited *c.*905, with some 7,000 coins and four times their weight in silver bullion. Such hoards generally represent money that has been stored by individuals and not recovered by them. There can be many reasons for non-recovery, and only very occasionally can a hoard be associated with a specific historical event, as in the case of the Chester (1914) hoard which was probably lost when Cheshire was ravaged by the *Vikings in 980. More significant can be the overall pattern of hoarding, so that the concentration of hoards from the 860s and 870s undoubtedly reflects the activities of the Viking Great Army in England, and the quite exceptional six hoards from *Sussex deposited in 1066 vividly show the disruption caused by the Norman invasion. Interestingly, the Danish conquest of England in 1013–16 left no discernible sign in the hoards, raising questions about the nature of that campaign. Some 60,000 late Anglo-Saxon coins have been found in hoards from Scandinavia, Poland and Russia, many times more than found in the British Isles. For long these were thought to have been the result of tributes and Danegeld payments to the Vikings, but they are now regarded as primarily the fruits of trade either direct with Scandinavia or via northern Germany.
M. Blackburn and H. Pagan, 'A Revised Check-list of Coin Hoards from the British Isles, *c.*500–1100', in *Anglo-Saxon Monetary History*, ed. M. A. S. Blackburn (Leicester, 1986), pp. 291–313; N. P. Brooks and J. A. Graham-Campbell, 'Reflections on the Viking-Age Silver Hoard from Croydon, Surrey', in *Anglo-Saxon Monetary History*, ed. Blackburn, pp. 91–110; M. Blackburn and K. Jonsson, 'The Anglo-Saxon and Anglo-Norman Element of the North European Coin Finds', in *Viking-Age Coinage in the Northern Lands*, ed. M. A. S. Blackburn and D. M. Metcalf, BAR Internat. ser.

Pl. 13 A hogback at Ingleby Arncliffe (Yorks.).

122(i) (Oxford, 1981), 147–255; K. Jonsson, 'The Routes for the Importation of German and English Coins to the Northern Lands in the Viking Age', in *Fernhandel und Geldwirtschaft*, ed. B. Kluge (Sigmaringen, 1993), pp. 205–32.

M. A. S. BLACKBURN

HOGBACKS are a Viking-period innovation in the sculptural repertoire of northern England. They are solid stone monuments, usually 1 to 1.5 m long, which take the form of a building. Their roof ridge has a distinct curve, a feature which accounts for the name of these sculptures, whilst the side walls have the curving, bombé, lines of what is sometimes misleadingly called a 'boat-shaped' house. Many hogbacks are equipped with end-beasts which are placed on the gables. These vary in form from simple zoomorphic heads, gazing inwards along the line of the ridge, to the type seen at Brompton (Yorks.) where the whole of the gable end of the monument is dominated by the powerful shoulders of muzzled animals which clasp the sides of the structure with their paws. The ornament and the distribution of hogbacks suggests that the type is a tenth-century development within the *Viking settlement areas of north Yorkshire and Cumbria. Outside this region there are only isolated English examples, whilst in Scotland the relatively few hogbacks have a coastal distribution and are demonstrably reflexes of Northumbrian forms. Wales and Ireland have yielded only single occurrences and there are none on the Isle of Man.

In part the shape and decoration of these carvings can be related to contemporary architecture. Thus the bombé plan of the side-walls is well known from buildings excavated at such Viking-age sites as Fyrkat and Trelleborg in Denmark whilst the existence of curved ridge lines in this period is well attested by evidence like that of the small model house from Klinta in Sweden. Links to Scandinavian building practices do not however provide a total explanation for the origin and development of this form of monument. More important is its relationship to various types of shrine which were known in Anglo-Saxon England, as in the rest of early Christian Europe. A persistent feature of these shrines, which were worked in various media and at differing sizes, was that they were given the shape of a building. *Bede's account (*HE* iv. 3) of St *Chad's shrine which was 'in the shape of a little house' provides a well known seventh-century example of the type. Among this cluster of shrine material were solid stone structures like the eighth-century Hedda's tomb at Peterborough which probably stood over the relics of a saint. This is a highly decorated piece, with distinct walls and roof, and has a length of 1.05 m; it is thus of about the same size as many hogbacks. The hogback is best seen therefore as an adaptation of the kind of monument represented by Hedda's tomb, but with a modification in shape to reflect contemporary Viking-age architectural forms.

The origins of the end-beast motif have been much discussed. It may have been suggested by contemporary architectural decoration. Alternatively it also could have been dependent on the ornament of shrines, for both on the Continent and in Ireland there are portable *shrines with zoomorphic ornament attached to the ridge. Whatever its ultimate source, the hogback end-beast motif seems to have carried a now irrecoverable significance, for it is noticeable that, however degenerate the rendering, muzzled jaws are very persistent.

The decoration of these stones firmly fixes them within the Viking period. This is the implication of the Jellinge ornament on hogbacks from Aspatria, *Gosforth and Plumbland in Cumbria, Pickhill in Yorkshire or the stone from Derby. It is further confirmed by the use of Borre-style ring-chain ornament at Crosscanonby in Cumbria, the ring-knots on hogbacks from Brompton in Yorkshire and the depiction of the Vǫlundr narrative on the stone from Bedale in the same county.

Several of the hogbacks carry explicit Christian decoration: there are crucifixion scenes at Gosforth and *York, an *orans* at Crosscanonby, raised crosses on the gables at Dewsbury in Yorkshire and Lowther in Cumbria. A Christian significance may also have been present in the scrollwork which decorates a large group of hogbacks at sites like *Repton in Derbyshire, York, or Appleby in Cumbria. There is therefore little basis for the oft-repeated assertion that these are pagan monuments. There are, however, among the *c.*115 hogbacks surviving in England, some four or five whose decoration, if not pagan, then certainly draws on secular narrative. The Vǫlundr stone from Bedale has already been cited and to it can be added stones from Gosforth and Lowther in Cumbria which depict armed encounters whose closest parallels are to be found on the pagan stones of Gotland. Their occurrence on hogbacks does not, however, necessarily indicate pagandom; rather it reflects the secular patronage of sculpture in the Viking-period north and the traditional interests of a new warrior aristocracy.

Hogbacks vary in form. Some have large end-beasts like the group of eleven which survive at Brompton in north Yorkshire. Others have a simple zoomorphic head, whilst many have no beasts whatsoever. There are also clearly regional preferences. In Cumbria, for example, there is a marked emphasis on tall narrow hogbacks which may all derive from the work of the Gosforth master on the so-called 'Saint's Tomb' – many of the hogbacks at Govan on the Clyde, which are linked to the Cumbrian group, show the same slender proportions. Across on the east coast, by contrast, hogbacks tend to be relatively small and flat.

Hogbacks are thus a peculiar manifestation of that fusion of cultures which took place in the Anglo-Scandinavian north of England in the tenth century. The stone shrine, a traditional Insular form of monument, was given a new function in an adapted form in the villages of Viking-age Yorkshire and Cumbria.

R. N. Bailey, *Viking-Age Sculpture in Northern England* (London, 1980), pp. 85–100; J. Lang, 'The Hogback; a Viking Colonial Monument', *ASSAH* 3 (1984) 85–176; idem, 'Hogback Monuments in Scotland', *Proceedings of the Society of Antiquaries of Scotland* 105 (1976) 206–35; H. Schmidt, 'The Trelleborg House Reconsidered', *M Arch* 17 (1973), 52–77.

RICHARD N. BAILEY

HOMILIARY: *see* Homilies; Liturgical Books

HOMILIES and homiletic material are the most numerous of all vernacular items to survive from the period. Almost half are by *Ælfric, about 130, there is a much smaller number, more than twenty, by *Wulfstan, and the rest, another 120 or so, are anonymous. Amongst the latter, it is rare to find examples of more than one that can with certainty be attributed to a single person. It is difficult to be more precise about numbers because of the propensity of the named authors to rework their own material, and of anonymous preachers in the eleventh century to create compilations from earlier works in a cut-and-paste method, sometimes building new homilies almost entirely from existing materials. The term homily is used in Old English studies to cover both an exposition of the pericope read during the mass (a true homily) and a more general exhortation (in precise terms a sermon). Most of Ælfric's homilies are the former, whilst Wulfstan's and most of the surviving anonymous pieces are sermons. Another fine line divides the homily from the saint's life, especially when the latter is appropriate for liturgical use.

The earliest manuscript containing homilies is the *Vercelli Book, written in the middle of the second half of the tenth century. Another early collection of anonymous pieces is in the Blickling manuscript (now Princeton, Princeton University Library, Scheide Library 71), dating from the end of that century. But the homilies they contain, as well as many recorded only in later manuscripts, may well have been composed earlier (see *dating vernacular texts). The latest 'Anglo-Saxon' collections of homilies, Anglo-Saxon because they contain copies of homilies composed during the previous century or earlier, are Cambridge, University Library, Ii.1.33 and Oxford, Bodleian Library, Bodley 343, both of which were written in the second half of the twelfth century in a language which is still recognisably Old English. These may be compared with the late twelfth-century Trinity and Lambeth Homilies (Cambridge, Trinity College B.14.52 and London, Lambeth Palace Library, 487), both of which contain items which draw on Old English material although they are written in a language usually judged to be Middle English. The recopying of homilies into the late twelfth century, and that century's re-use of earlier homiletic material, both verbatim and in terms of themes and ideas, shows the survival of the pre-Conquest tradition into the later Middle Ages.

Vernacular homilies contain little 'original' material in the sense that most can be shown to draw on surviving sources, usually in Latin. Ælfric and Wulfstan are careful to use only the most orthodox material, relying heavily on patristic and Carolingian writings. Although some anonymous authors used those sources too, others drew upon *biblical apocrypha or on Hiberno-Latin literature. The most popular subject for sermons (and also many liturgical homilies) is the end of the world, writers waxing most eloquent on the horrors of hell that will afflict the unrighteous.

The study of the sources of Old English homilies began more than a century ago, but the fact that the sources of most surviving homilies is now known in detail does not mean that the homilies themselves contain little of interest. Study of their sources can tell us much about the books available to the Anglo-Saxons, the choice of subject matter helps us to understand Anglo-Saxon culture, their language illuminates their authors' ability to translate Latin and to express complex ideas in their native tongue, and the multiplicity of copies of many items (and their relationship) gives us an insight into scribal attitudes to copying and to the origin and dissemination of manuscripts. It is perhaps symbolic that the first Old English text to be printed at the instigation of Matthew *Parker in 1566 was an Ælfric homily for Easter in *A Testimonie of Antiquitie*.

P. A. M. Clemoes, 'The Chronology of Ælfric's Works', *The Anglo-Saxons: Studies . . . presented to Bruce Dickins*, ed. P. Clemoes (London, 1959), pp. 212–47; M. McC. Gatch, *Preaching and Theology in Anglo-Saxon England* (Toronto and Buffalo, 1977); *The Old English Homily and its Background*, ed. P. E. Szarmach and B. F. Huppé (Albany, NY, 1978); D. G. Scragg, 'The Corpus of Vernacular Homilies and Prose Saints' Lives before Ælfric', *ASE* 8 (1979), 223–77; C. D. Wright, *The Irish Tradition in Old English Literature*, CSASE 6 (Cambridge, 1993).

DONALD SCRAGG

HONORIUS (d. 653), fifth archbishop of Canterbury, was one of the second wave of Roman missionaries sent to Kent by Pope *Gregory, arriving in 601. He succeeded *Justus as archbishop sometime between 627 and 631, and was consecrated at *Lincoln by Bishop *Paulinus. According to *Bede (*HE* v.19), Honorius was 'thoroughly well instructed in ecclesiastical affairs'; Bede also preserves (ii.18) the text of the letter sent by Pope Honorius I (625–38) to Archbishop Honorius to accompany the *pallium. During his long archiepiscopate, the *conversion of England proceeded apace: *East Anglia was converted by the Burgundian bishop Felix, who was given a see at Dunwich by Honorius, and the *Middle Angles under King Peada accepted Christianity. Honorius was able to consecrate the first native Anglo-Saxon bishop, *Ithamar of Rochester, in 644. He died on 30 September 653, and was succeeded by the first native Anglo-Saxon archbishop, *Deusdedit.

Bede, *HE* ii.15, 18, iii. 14, 20, v. 19.

MICHAEL LAPIDGE

HOSTAGES were sureties of peace in Anglo-Saxon England, given by conquered peoples or exchanged between hostile neighbours. Two *law-codes mention them, the *Dunsæte Ordinance*, by which the *Wentsæte* were to give hostages to the

West Saxons, and the *Treaty of Alfred and Guthrum*, by which people wishing to trade across the English/Viking border were to give hostages as proof of their peaceful intentions. Most of the recorded examples occur in the ninth to eleventh centuries in truces between English and *Viking forces, but other examples involve different factions of the English (Byrhtnoth had a Northumbrian hostage at the *Battle of Maldon, and in 1051 hostages were exchanged to facilitate a peaceful meeting between King *Edward and the family of *Godwine), or the English taking British hostages (seen in the eighth-century feud of Cynewulf and Cyneheard, and the eleventh-century Welsh conquests of *Harold Godwinesson). In practice, the exchange of hostages often did not prevent further hostilities. The fact that their prince Ecgfrith was a hostage of the Mercians did not prevent the Northumbrians from killing the Mercian king *Penda in 655. The Vikings in the 870s twice gave hostages and swore oaths to leave *Wessex, though in 876 they did not leave at all and in 877 they left only to return the following year. It was a measure of *Alfred's victory at Edington in 878, after which the Vikings swore a third time to leave and this time kept their promise, that the Vikings gave hostages without demanding any in return. *Asser notes that this had never happened before, which suggests that earlier references to Alfred receiving Viking hostages also involved the surrender of English hostages. The fate of hostages when truces were broken could be gruesome: when in 1014 the English reneged on their submission to the Danish king *Swein and drove out his son *Cnut, Cnut retaliated by having his English hostages set ashore with their hands, ears, and noses cut off.

K. Cutler, 'The Godwinist Hostages: the Case for 1051', *Annuale Mediaevale* 12 (1972), 70–7; Keynes and Lapidge, *Alfred the Great*, p. 249 n. 108.

SEAN MILLER

HOUSECARLS appear in the last fifty years of Anglo-Saxon England. Osbern of *Canterbury, speaking of the translation of *Ælfheah in 1023, notes that *Cnut's household troops were called housecarls in Danish. While it was once thought that these housecarls followed elaborate codes of conduct like those set out in late-twelfth-century Danish sources, there is no clear evidence of this, and it is more plausible that in eleventh-century England 'housecarl' is simply a Danish variant term for a king's *thegn. Records of Bovi and Urk, two eleventh-century housecarls who are nonetheless called thegns for most of their careers,

tend to confirm this view, and there are several others variously called housecarl or thegn in *Domesday Book. The vast majority of individual housecarls have Norse names, which probably reflects their origin as Cnut's followers or a belief that the term, borrowed from Old Norse, is more appropriate to people of Norse descent. As such, it is tempting to see the block of about thirty Norse names in the Thorney Abbey *Liber Vitae* as the housecarls of Cnut or of one of his earls. However, this racial distinction may not always apply to 'housecarls' used as a collective term: the men who died in Siward's campaign against Macbeth in 1054 are called housecarls in *ASC* 1054D but both Danes and English in the parallel passage in *ASC* 1054C.

D. Whitelock, 'Scandinavian Personal Names in the Liber Vitae of Thorney Abbey', *Saga Book of the Viking Society* 12 (1940), 127–53; N. Hooper, 'The Housecarls in England in the Eleventh Century', *ANS* 7 (1985), 161–76; idem, 'Military Developments in the Reign of Cnut', in *The Reign of Cnut*, ed. by A. Rumble (London, 1994), pp. 89–100.

SEAN MILLER

HUNDREDS were local administrative units of later Anglo-Saxon England, both a measure of land and the area served by a hundred-court (cf. *courts). They appeared in the tenth century, but some such local arrangements must have existed much earlier. The name corresponds neatly with the sizes of hundreds in the Midlands, which were often assessed at about a hundred hides. No such clear relationship exists in the south; this might suggest that an ancient West Saxon measure was applied much more rigidly over the rest of the country in the first half of the tenth century. The mid-tenth-century *Hundred Ordinance* sets out some of the duties of the hundred-court: the court is to meet every four weeks, thieves are to be pursued by all the chief men of the hundred, people who oppose the decisions of the hundred are to be fined (and outlawed if they persist), and days are to be appointed for the trying of cases and those who fail to appear on those days are to be fined. Some similar provisions occur in the codes of *Edward the Elder and *Æthelstan, though the term 'hundred' is first recorded in *Edmund's laws. Since the shire-courts met only twice a year, the monthly hundred-courts must have been the main contact most people had with royal government. Later *law-codes confirmed this importance: *Cnut ruled that no one should appeal to the king unless he had failed to get justice from his hundred-court.

O. Anderson, *The English Hundred-Names* (Lund, 1934);

H. R. Loyn, 'The Hundred in England in the Tenth and Early Eleventh Centuries', in *British Government and Administration: Studies presented to S. B. Chrimes*, ed. H. Hearder and H. R. Loyn (Cardiff, 1974), pp. 1–15.

SEAN MILLER

HUNTING, according to *Gildas, was vital for subsistence in the period after the collapse of the Roman administration. His lament is supported by evidence from the Latimer villa (Bucks.), where the decline of farming in the early fifth century seems to be compensated for by increased consumption of venison. As *agriculture revived, hunting ceased to be essential for food supply, becoming instead a form of recreational training designed to develop strength, stamina and weapon-handling skills which were also useful in warfare. *Asser regarded hunting as a fitting pursuit for a nobleman, and praised King *Alfred's skill in the chase. King *Edmund narrowly escaped death while hunting in Somerset, when the hart which he was chasing plunged over the precipice of Cheddar Gorge, followed by his hounds, the king saving himself on the very brink of the cliff by repenting his decision to exile *Dunstan from the royal court. It was said of King *Harold Harefoot that he regularly hunted with his dogs while others were in church, and even *Edward the Confessor was reputed to have hunted every morning.

Professional huntsmen were important figures, and were often rewarded with grants of land: for example, in 957 King *Eadwig gave his huntsman Wulfric several small estates in Wiltshire. Landholders obliged to feed the king's huntsmen, horses and hounds on request sometimes successfully sought relief from this burden: in 843–4 King Beorhtwulf of *Mercia granted to his *ealdorman Æthelwulf an estate at Pangbourne (Berks.), freed from the duty of entertaining 'men who bear hawks and falcons, or who lead dogs and horses'. Several hunters who had served King Edward are named as holders of lands in the *Domesday survey.

At first anyone was free to hunt, except on Sundays, and could claim a share of the meat even if he killed on someone else's land. Some limitations were probably imposed as common land became apportioned to particular estates. *Cnut permitted every man to hunt in woods and fields on his own property, but forbade hunting where this was reserved for the king alone. The early place-name Waltham (*weald-ham*), which occurs in several wooded districts, may indicate a royal property reserved for hunting. However,

restrictions before the Norman Conquest were far less punitive than the new game laws imposed by William of Normandy, so deplored in the Peterborough version of the *Anglo-Saxon Chronicle.

Hunting and trapping were carried out in various ways. *Ælfric's *Colloquy* includes an interview with a hunter, who describes how he caught harts, boars, roe deer and sometimes hares, using hounds, nets and spears. Hunting on horseback with hounds was probably the preserve of nobles, because of the costs. Good hunting dogs were highly valued: King Alfred sent two hunting dogs to the archbishop of Rheims as a gift, while *Æthelstan exacted a tribute of hunting dogs from the Welsh. The duty of supplying beaters to drive deer for the king was a common obligation of land tenure. In 964 Bishop *Oswald of Worcester required his lessees to erect a hedge for his hunt and to lend their own hunting-spears on request. Spears were used particularly for wild boar, while bows were used for deer. Early Welsh laws mention pit traps, while smaller game were caught by snares.

Red deer were the principal quarry of the chase. Roe deer were scarcer, more localized, and less valued because of their small size. Generally venison appears to have made only a minor contribution to the diet, and deer bones rarely comprise more than 5 per cent of the total animal bone recovered from Anglo-Saxon contexts. Even at the royal palace at *Cheddar, a location abounding in game and known to have been used as a hunting base, deer was poorly represented in the bone record. However, animal bones are prolific in Danish *York, and almost a quarter of the bones examined from two sites in Pavement were of red deer. Part of the late Saxon ditch of *Southampton also produced an unusually large quantity of red deer bones, all from food remains. Unusually, at mid-Saxon Ramsbury (Wilts.), where wild animals were also well represented, young roe deer were more common than red deer.

Around thirty deer parks are mentioned in Domesday Book, but it is unclear whether any of these were of pre-Conquest origin. Evidence of place-names and charter boundary landmarks does reveal some landscape features associated with deer management. The name of Dyrham (Gloucs.) implies some sort of deer enclosure, while Hindlip (Worcs.) indicates a deer-leap. The term *haga* commonly occurs in *woodland districts, and seems to mean either a hedge or fence set up along the edge of a woodland, or an area of woodland enclosed by such a hedge. They may be identical with the *haiae* of the Domesday Survey, which are recorded mainly in the Welsh border counties. Occasionally they are specifically said to be for roe deer.

Wild boar were still sufficiently widespread to generate a number of Old Engish *place-names incorporating the word *eofer*, for example Everley (Yorks.) and Everdon (Northants.). However, their numbers were declining, and by the Norman Conquest they survived only in the most remote and densely-wooded areas. Wild boar bones have been identified at Thetford, but they are often difficult to distinguish from bones of domestic pig. Hares were also hunted for food, while foxes and badgers were hunted for their pelts. Wolves and beavers had not yet been hunted to extinction in Britain, but fallow deer and rabbits were not introduced until after the Norman Conquest.
A. Grant, 'The Significance of Deer Remains at Occupation Sites of the Iron Age to the Anglo-Saxon Period', in *The Environment of Man: the Iron Age to the Anglo-Saxon Period*, ed. M. Jones and G. Dimbleby (Oxford, 1981), pp. 91–108; A. Hagen, *A Second Handbook of Anglo-Saxon Food and Drink: Production and Distribution* (Hockwold-cum-Wilton, Norfolk, 1995), pp. 132–41; J. Clutton-Brock, 'The Animal Resources', in Wilson, *Archaeology*, pp. 373–92; J. Bourdillon, 'Countryside and Town: the Animal Resources of Saxon Southampton', *Anglo-Saxon Settlements*, ed. D. Hooke (Oxford, 1988), pp. 177–95.

C. J. BOND

HUSBAND'S MESSAGE is a poem of approximately 53 lines in the *Exeter Book. It has occasionally been linked with the *Wife's Lament* on the basis that the same story may lie behind both. Because of its elegiac motifs, the *Husband's Message* is often included among the *elegies, although its mood is optimistic. The narrator conveys to the wife or betrothed of his lord a message to join him in his new-found prosperity over the sea, the troubles which sent him into exile now being over. Two passages in the text suffer from burn damage. The first of these obscures part of the beginning, where the speaker gives a brief account of his (or its) history. The word *treocyn* ('kind of wood or tree') appears in line 2; the author of the message is referred to as 'the one who engraved this piece of wood' in line 13; and a cryptogram in *runes confirming the lovers' pledge of fidelity is given in lines 49–50. These indications suggest that the speaker either actually is or is carrying a rune-stave – a stick with a runic message. The *Husband's Message* may thus share with the *riddles the device of prosopopoeia, whereby an object speaks. Because *Riddle 60*, 'Reed-Pen', the poem immediately preceding in

the manuscript, also focusses on an object made from a tree or plant for the purpose of private communication, it has been argued, by Pope and others, that *Riddle 60* is the beginning of the *Husband's Message*.
ASPR iii.225–7; R. F. Leslie, *Three Old English Elegies* (Manchester, 1961; repr. with corrections 1966); J. C. Pope, 'Palaeography and Poetry: Some Solved and Unsolved Problems of the Exeter Book', *Medieval Scribes, Manuscripts and Libraries: Essays presented to N. R. Ker*, ed. M. B. Parkes and A. J. Watson (London, 1978), pp. 42–63; P. Orton, 'The Speaker in *The Husband's Message*', *LSE* 12 (1981), 43–56.

ANNE L. KLINCK

HWÆTBERHT was the successor of *Ceolfrith (d. 716) as abbot of *Monkwearmouth-Jarrow. According to Bede, Hwætberht had been brought up as a child-oblate in the monastery, and was remarkable for the energy which he devoted not only to observance of monastic discipline but also to reading, writing, chanting and teaching. He visited *Rome on one occasion (possibly in the company of Ceolfrith) during the papacy of Sergius I (687–701), and spent some considerable time there, learning and copying out things which he deemed useful. When Ceolfrith decided to resign the abbacy and go to Rome, Hwætberht was chosen abbot in his place (*Bede preserves the text of the letter of commendation addressed by Hwætberht to the pope on Ceolfrith's behalf; a reply by Pope Gregory II to Hwætberht is preserved in the anonymous *Vita S. Ceolfridi*), and was subsequently consecrated by Bishop *Acca. As abbot, Hwætberht was able to implement the monastic discipline which he had studied in his youth; he also translated the remains of Abbots *Eosterwine and Sigfrith. That he was a scholar of some standing is indicated by the fact that Bede dedicated to him various of his works, including the treatise *De temporum ratione*, as well as the commentaries on Acts and Revelation. In the preface to bk iv of his commentary on Samuel, Bede refers to Hwætberht, 'to whom he gave the name "Eusebius" because of his love and concern for holiness'; a collection of sixty Latin *enigmata* which were composed as a complement to the forty *enigmata* of *Tatwine, are transmitted under the name of Eusebius, and it is possible that Eusebius the enigmatist is identical with Hwætberht. Some years after Bede's death, perhaps *c.*747, *Boniface wrote to Hwætberht requesting copies of works of Bede. The date of Hwætberht's death is unknown.
Sharpe, *Handlist*, 534; *Vita S. Ceolfridi*, cc. 28–30, 39 (Plummer, *VBOH* i.398–403); Bede, *Historia abbatum*,

cc. 18–20 (ibid. i.382–5); MGH, ES i. 158–9 (no. 76); CCSL cxxxiii.209–71; Bolton, *ALL*, pp. 219–23.

MICHAEL LAPIDGE

HWICCE. The kingdom of the Hwicce was situated in the West Midlands. Its episcopal see, *Worcester, may have been a British ecclesiastical centre in the sub-Roman period, and it is possible that the Anglo-Saxon kingdom was based upon a British predecessor. The province was assessed at 7000 hides in the *Tribal Hidage. Its royal house is known primarily from *charters, and is first recorded in the last quarter of the seventh century. Five generations can be traced, though no *regnal lists or *genealogies survive. There are several instances of joint rule by brothers. The family is notable for founding a number of religious houses, including *Gloucester, *Bath, Fladbury and Withington, many of which were governed by its female members. The Mercians seem to have been significant overlords of the province following *Penda's victory at the battle of *Cirencester in 628. In the time of *Offa the Hwiccian kings are referred to as *subreguli*, but by the end of his reign the Hwiccian province had become a Mercian ealdormanry and no more is heard of its royal house. In the tenth century the greater part of Hwiccian territory was divided between the shires of Gloucestershire and Worcestershire, but parts were incorporated into Warwickshire and the shortlived Winchcombeshire.

H. P. R. Finberg, *The Early Charters of the West Midlands*, 2nd ed. (Leicester, 1972); D. Hooke, *The Anglo-Saxon Landscape: the Kingdom of the Hwicce* (Manchester, 1985); S. Bassett, 'Churches in Worcester before and after the Conversion of the Saxons', *AntJ* 69 (1989), 225–56; P. Sims-Williams, *Religion and Literature in Western England, 600–800*, CSASE 3 (Cambridge, 1990).

B. A. E. YORKE

HYGEBURG (fl. 780) was an Englishwoman who went to *Germany in the wake of the mission of St *Boniface and became a nun at the double monastery of Heidenheim in Thuringia. The first abbot of Heidenheim had been *Wynnebald (d. 761), and it was perhaps in 777 when his brother *Willibald (d. *c.*787), then bishop of Eichstätt, translated Wynnebald's remains, that Hygeburg had the opportunity of recording from dictation Willibald's recollections of his remarkable travels in the Near East during the years 723–9. She incorporated this record, which she named the *Hodoeporicon* ('Travellers Book'), into her Life of Willibald, the *Vita S. Willibaldi* (*BHL* 8931), written 767 × 778. She subsequently composed

(782 × 785) a Life of Wynnebald, the *Vita S. Wynnebaldi* (*BHL* 8996). The style of Hygeburg's Latin is much indebted to *Aldhelm, especially for its use of unusual vocabulary (some of it derived dubiously from Greek), and is often impenetrable. Nevertheless her Lives of the two brothers are a remarkable witness to the level of Latin training which could be attained by an educated woman in the late eighth century.

Sharpe, *Handlist*, 536; MGH, SS xv.86–117; B. Bischoff, 'Wer is die Nonne von Heidenheim', *Studien und Mitteilungen zur Geschichte des Benediktiner-Ordens* 49 (1931), 387–8; E. Gottschaller, *Hugeburc von Heidenheim* (Munich, 1973); W. Berschin, *Biographie und Epochenstil im lateinischen Mittelalter*, 3 vols. (Munich, 1986–), iii. 18–26.

MICHAEL LAPIDGE

HYMNAL: *see* Hymns; Liturgical Books

HYMNS were sung daily as part of the Divine Office (but not the Mass), and may be defined as stanzaic poems in either quantitative or rhythmical Latin verse; because they consist usually of eight, sixteen or thirty-two stanzas, it is probable that they were sung antiphonally. The early Anglo-Saxon church inherited from late antiquity a small corpus of some sixteen hymns, known as the 'Old Hymnal' (made up largely, but not entirely, of hymns by Ambrose); this cycle of hymns had apparently been specified for use in Benedictine monasteries, and is known through various sources, including the Rules of Caesarius and Aurelianus of Arles, some early manuscripts from Canterbury (one lost, one preserved as BL, Cotton Vespasian A.i), and Bede's treatise *De arte metrica*. The likelihood is that the 'Old Hymnal' was brought to England by the monks of the Gregorian mission. The limited scope of the 'Old Hymnal' meant that the hymns needed to be repeated in the Office day in, day out (only four of the hymns were specified for feasts of the Sanctorale); and it is not surprising that eventually further hymns were composed in order to provide greater variety and to cater in particular for the numerous feast days of the Sanctorale. *Bede composed a small corpus of eleven hymns (all cast in highly compressed but extremely elegant Latin diction) which were evidently intended to supplement the 'Old Hymnal' on feasts of the Sanctorale. Continental scholars in the early ninth century seem to have felt misgivings similar to Bede's concerning the restricted scope of the 'Old Hymnal', and it was at this time that the 'New Hymnal', consisting of some hundred hymns, came into being. The compilers of the 'New Hymnal' drew on the 'Old Hymnal', as well as on Late Latin poets such as Prudentius, Caelius Sedulius and Venantius Fortunatus; they also included one hymn of Bede in their compilation. The 'New Hymnal' was apparently introduced into England by the tenth-century Benedictine reformers; the earliest Anglo-Saxon manuscript to contain it is a manuscript associated with *Dunstan (London, BL, Add. 37517), and the *Regularis concordia assumes use of the 'New Hymnal' in its stipulations. At this time too a small number of hymns were composed to commemorate Anglo-Saxon saints, including SS *Æthelwold, *Augustine and *Oswald of Worcester. And because of the compressed nature of the diction of Latin hymns, they appear to have been studied carefully in Anglo-Saxon schools by way of a treatise known as the *Expositio hymnorum*.

H. Gneuss, *Hymnar und Hymnen im englischen Mittelalter* (Tübingen, 1968); idem, 'Latin Hymns in Medieval England: Future Research', in *Chaucer and Middle English Studies in Honour of Rossell Hope Robbins*, ed. B. Rowland (London, 1974), pp. 407–24, repr. in his *Books and Libraries in Early England* (Aldershot, 1996), no. XI; M. Lapidge, *Bede the Poet*, Jarrow Lecture 1993 (Jarrow, 1994), repr. in *ALL* i.313–38; *The Canterbury Hymnal*, ed. G. R. Wieland (Toronto, 1982) [= BL, Add. 37517]; I. B. Milfull, *The Hymns of the Anglo-Saxon Church*, CSASE 17 (Cambridge, 1996).

MICHAEL LAPIDGE

I

ICONOGRAPHY (USE OF SYMBOLISM).
Symbolism in Anglo-Saxon art includes three
separate kinds of symbolic representation: symbols
which can stand alone, such as those for the evangelists; symbolic motifs in larger compositions;
and figures or scenes which are linked to one
another typologically or which are presented in a
non-historical way.

Symbols of the four evangelists (images of a
man or angel, a lion, a bull or calf, and an eagle)
feature regularly in Anglo-Saxon *gospelbooks,
either alone, or accompanying representations of
the evangelists in human form. These symbols
derive from the description of God's throne in
the Apocalypse (IV.6–8) and recall Jerome's gospel
preface, *Plures fuisse*, and works by Ambrose,
*Gregory and *Bede, in which each gospel is
associated with some characteristic of the related
symbol. Other commonly found symbols are those
for the three persons of the Trinity: the *dextera
Dei*, the Lamb and the Dove. The Trinity, being
without form, cannot be depicted directly, but only
through metaphors, symbols and analogies: the
dextera Dei, for example, involves a visualization
of the many references in the Old Testament to
God's right hand; it does not imply that God has a
human form. The Lamb is a metaphor for Christ,
recalling the passover lamb of Exodus XII.3 and
John the Baptist's words about Christ, 'Look,
there is the lamb of God that takes away the sin
of the world' (John I.29). The Dove recalls the
dove which appeared at Christ's baptism (Matt.
III.16); it is an example of the use of a created
being as a vehicle for the manifestation of the
divine. The Dove and the Lamb appear in symbolic images of the Trinity (BL, Cotton Tiberius
C. vi; Paris, BN, lat. 6401) and the *dextera* in
scenes such as the crucifixion, placed above the
head of Christ to symbolize God's approval of
Christ's sacrifice. The Lamb sometimes embodies
a eucharistic reference (e.g. on an Anglo-Saxon
portable altar in the Musée de Cluny, Paris) but
is also used as an identifying motif (or emblem)
in representations of John the Baptist such as those
on the *Ruthwell and *Bewcastle Crosses.

This emblematic use of symbols is common:
evangelists are portrayed holding books, St Peter

is identified by the keys he holds, saints who were
martyred hold palm branches, while Mary is
shown holding the Christ Child in scenes unrelated to the nativity story to indicate her role as
mother of the Saviour. Angels placed above the
canon tables in gospelbooks hold orbs and sceptres
as a sign of Christ's royal status, or blow trumpets
and hold scales in reference to the coming judgement. Other motifs are used to vary the meaning
of a scene such as the crucifixion, where Christ is
depicted wearing a diadem, and symbols of the
sun and moon are placed above the arms of
the cross to remind the viewer of the darkness
which covered the earth at Christ's death and the
belief that the world mourned the death of its
creator.

These motifs form part of a wider symbolic
approach to religious themes. Pictures of David
defeating Goliath are linked to gospel scenes to
become prophetic symbols of Christ's defeat of
the devil (BL, Cotton Tiberius C. vi). A small
cross is placed in the centre of one of the trees in
the Garden of Eden (Oxford, Bodleian Library,
Junius 11) to recall the link between the tree of
life in the garden and the cross, Christ's tree of life.
Mary holds a book in pictures of the annunciation
to remind the viewer of Isaiah's prophecy of the
Messiah's birth (Benedictional of *Æthelwold:
London, BL, Add. 49598). Representations of
Christ above the beasts do not simply recall the
words of Ps. XC.13: they symbolize Christ's more
general triumph over evil and, sometimes, His
resurrection – a subject more generally represented, obliquely, by the scene of the women at
the empty tomb. Representations of the baptism
show the Dove carrying a double ampulla of oil,
to symbolize Christ's anointing as both king and
priest, and the river Jordan standing up in a hill,
a reference to the words of Ps. CXIII.3–5
(Benedictional of Æthelwold, BL, Add. 49598).
Pictures of the crucifixion do not attempt to
recreate the scene described in the gospels, but
show Mary as an orant, interceding for the human
race, and John writing in a book as guarantor of
the truth of what is portrayed. Standing figures
are classified as helpers (as in Stephen's vision of
Christ, Acts VII.56) whereas seated figures are

symbols of judgement. Finally, the location of statues and paintings in churches was used to recall the symbolic relationship between the altar and Christ's tomb and between the eastern end of the church and heaven.

A. Grabar, *Christian Iconography: a Study of its Origins* (London, 1969); B. C. Raw, *Anglo-Saxon Crucifixion Iconography and the Art of the Monastic Revival*, CSASE 1 (Cambridge, 1990); idem, *Trinity and Incarnation in Anglo-Saxon Art and Thought*, CSASE 21 (Cambridge, 1997); K. Weitzmann, ed., *Age of Spirituality: a Symposium* (New York, 1980).

BARBARA C. RAW

ILLUMINATION is the practice of enhancing books with decoration, a custom which the Anglo-Saxon church adopted from its Irish and continental neighbours. Mediterranean exemplars supplied models for the earliest figural art, while Irish scribes provided the concept of enlarging and embellishing initial letters to provide graphic punctuation. Illumination not only beautified a book, it also added to its value symbolically by the ornament and imagery, and materially by dint of the extra labour and pigments required.

The surviving evidence presents *gospelbooks and psalters as the major recipients of illumination in the pre-Viking Age church, and they remained the principal focus for decoration in the late Anglo-Saxon period. Yet other liturgical books such as pontificals, benedictionals and sacramentaries were also decorated, as were certain other texts, notably the *Marvels of the East*, Prudentius' *Psychomachia*, and the calendar. There is evidence to suggest that an illustrated copy of Caelius Sedulius's *Carmen paschale* was produced in early Anglo-Saxon England, based directly on a late Antique model; however Carolingian manuscripts supplied the immediate exemplars for the surviving cyclical illustrations which all date from the tenth and eleventh centuries. In addition, in outstanding scriptoria, such as St Augustine's and Christ Church, *Canterbury, a high percentage of library texts received decorated initials.

Although all religious centres required books, not all of them needed or produced illuminated copies. Our knowledge of early *scriptoria is shadowy in the extreme, but it is clear that illumination was practised at *Lindisfarne and *Monkwearmouth-Jarrow from the seventh century, and at Canterbury and *Minster-in-Thanet from the eighth century. In the late Anglo-Saxon period decorated books can be associated with *Winchester, Canterbury, Crowland, Peterborough, Thorney, *Ramsey, *Glastonbury and *Exeter. The case of *Worcester, an important ecclesiastical centre which seems not to have produced major decorated books, suggests that not all houses practised illumination, preferring to acquire major illuminated books from other centres that specialized in it. The distribution of manuscripts produced at Winchester and Canterbury implies that these places played an important role in supplying other centres, and, perhaps, individuals, with handsome volumes.

The earliest surviving certainly Anglo-Saxon illuminated manuscripts were produced in *Northumbria *c.*700 (though the Book of *Durrow is probably earlier, it remains a matter of debate whether it was made in Ireland, *Iona, or England). They are mature rather than experimental volumes, presupposing earlier work both in England and Ireland, little of which has survived; and they show that within a century of the coming of Christianity, the Anglo-Saxons were able to produce decorated books equal to anything in contemporary Europe. The *Lindisfarne Gospels and the Codex *Amiatinus, though broadly contemporary products of two Northumbrian houses, vary greatly in the style of their artwork, reflecting the different cultural traditions of Lindisfarne and Monkwearmouth-Jarrow respectively. Both depended upon Mediterranean exemplars for their figural subject matter, but whereas the image of Ezra in the Codex Amiatinus faithfully reproduces a semi-three-dimensional late Antique image, in the evangelist portraits of the Lindisfarne Gospels, Insular love of pattern vies with illusionism. Furthermore, whereas the Codex Amiatinus reproduces the pure text aesthetic of antiquity, Lindisfarne apotheosises text into symbol by elaborating the major initials with a wealth of Insular decoration. This tension between figural imagery and abstract Insular ornament is central to the art of the gospelbooks, such as the Lichfield, *Barberini, and St Petersburg Gospels, which are the major surviving monuments of Anglo-Saxon illumination from the eighth century. The conflation of word and art reached its logical conclusion in the historiated initial, where the letter is decorated with imagery of relevance to the textual content. As the two earliest examples of the genre, dating from the first half of the eighth century (the *Vespasian Psalter: BL, Cotton Vespasian A. i, and the St Petersburg Bede: Public Library, Q. v. I. 18) both appear in Anglo-Saxon books, it would seem to have been an English invention.

The earliest Southumbrian books date from the eighth century, and their aesthetic reveals a stronger debt to Mediterranean models which, reflecting the ecclesiastical history of the south, were presumably more numerous. The image of David in the Vespasian Psalter and, above all, the evangelist portraits in the Codex Aureus (Stockholm, Kungl. Bibliotek, A. 135) are well modelled, semi-three-dimensional figures. Insular ornament is present in both books – attesting to the availability of Northumbrian manuscripts – but its role is more circumscribed. Though the initials in the Vespasian Psalter, for instance, are rich in Insular ornament, they are strictly defined and do not spread far into the text itself. On the other hand, these are distinctly Anglo-Saxon books: although the creators of the Codex Aureus revived the antique practice of writing in coloured and metallic ink on purple parchment, the surfeit of pattern makes the general effect far from classical.

Book illumination continued during the first half of the ninth century, with, seemingly, a stronger tradition in the south than the north: the masterpiece of this period is the Royal Bible from Canterbury (BL, Royal 1. E. VI), which originally had illustrative pages as well as evangelist portraits and canon tables, and whose conception hints at incipient Carolingian influence. But in the second half of the century, book production as a whole declined dramatically. Though revived under the aegis of *Alfred the Great, the products of the 890s were rudimentary, their decoration confined to simple initials: those in the contemporary copy of the king's translation of Gregory's *Regula pastoralis* (Oxford, Bodleian Library, Hatton 20), a royal commission, are qualitatively very poor. The book decoration of the early tenth century was similarly limited to initials constructed from birds and beast, albeit of increasing robustness. Towards the middle of the tenth century, with growing continental contacts and the beginnings of the monastic revival, figural subjects reappear. The images in the Hrabanus Maurus, Cambridge, Trinity College, B. 16. 3, are painterly and sophisticated, and, like the frontispiece to St Dunstan's 'Classbook' (Oxford, Bodleian Library, Auct. F. 4. 32) reflect direct contacts with Carolingian art – the first probably depending upon a Fulda model, the second echoing the 'Ada' group manuscripts of the court school of Charlemagne.

In the second half of the tenth century, allied to the rise of the monastic reform movement, Winchester and Canterbury rose to prominence as centres of book decoration, the former specialising in rich miniatures within lavish foliate frames with much use of gold, best exemplified by *Æthel-wold's Benedictional; the latter in vivacious coloured line drawings under the influence of the *Utrecht Psalter. The importance of this Rheimsian manuscript for the art of Christ Church is underlined by the fact that *c.*1000 the community embarked upon making a new, more colourful version of it, the *Harley Psalter, in accordance with contemporary tastes (BL, Harley 603). By the early eleventh century the Winchester and Canterbury traditions had intermingled, and similar work flourished at other scriptoria in the south – best represented by a series of opulent gospelbooks – continuing until after the Conquest. Alongside this continuity with later tenth-century work, the eleventh century saw several more innovative artistic projects, most notably the production of an elaborately illustrated vernacular Hexateuch (BL, Cotton Claudius B. iv). There was also, seemingly, a slight change in the pattern of patronage, with wealthy lay folk being increasingly documented as the patrons and owners of decorated books. Although Anglo-Saxon traditions of illumination survived the Norman Conquest, the different conception of a monastic library which the Normans fostered, redirecting scriptorium effort to the copying of patristic texts (which had rarely received much decoration in previous centuries) led to a re-orientation of artwork: few full page miniatures were produced, but there was a steady rise in the use of decorated initials.

Two general points apply to early and late Anglo-Saxon illumination alike: the love of decoration – to the extent that ornamental effect was often preferred to clarity of figural subject matter – and secondly the high respect which it commanded on the Continent, as the many pastiches and variants first of 'Insular', and then of the *'Winchester School', attest.

Alexander, *Insular MSS*; C. Nordenfalk, *Celtic and Anglo-Saxon Painting* (London, 1977); T. D. Kendrick et al., *Codex Lindisfarnensis*, 2 vols. (Olten and Lausanne, 1956–60); T. J. Brown et al., *The Durham Gospels*, EEMF 20 (Copenhagen, 1980); G. Henderson, *From Durrow to Kells* (London, 1987); D. H. Wright, *The Vespasian Psalter*, EEMF 14 (Copenhagen, 1967); Temple, *AS MSS*; F. Wormald, *English Drawings of the Tenth and Eleventh Centuries* (London, 1952); T. Ohlgren, *Anglo-Saxon Textual Illustration* (Kalamazoo, MI, 1993); R. G. Gameson, *The Role of Art in the Late Anglo-Saxon Church* (Oxford, 1995); C. R. Dodwell and P. Clemoes, *The Old English Illustrated Hexateuch*, EEMF 18 (Copenhagen, 1974); F. Wormald, *Collected Writings I* (London, 1984).

RICHARD GAMESON

INDRACT, ST, an Irish pilgrim who was murdered in the vicinity of *Glastonbury (probably at some point in the ninth century) and was subsequently venerated there as a martyr. The name 'Indract' represents the Irish form *Indrechtach*, and the saint is probably identical with an abbot of *Iona bearing that name who is recorded in the Annals of Ulster s.a. 848 [849] as having transported the relics of St *Columba to Ireland (from Iona, presumably); the same abbot is said s.a. 853 [854] to have been martyred 'among the Saxons', apparently while on a *pilgrimage to *Rome. The account of his martyrdom is recorded in an eleventh-century Anglo-Latin *passio* composed at Glastonbury; *William of Malmesbury also composed a Life of Indract, but this has been lost.

G. H. Doble, 'Saint Indract and Saint Dominic', *Somerset Record Society Publications* 57 (1942), 1–24; M. Lapidge, 'The Cult of St Indract at Glastonbury', in *Ireland in Early Mediæval Europe: Studies in Memory of Kathleen Hughes*, ed. D. Whitelock *et al.* (Cambridge, 1982), pp. 179–212 [with text of the *passio* at pp. 199–204], repr. in *ALL* ii.419–52.

MICHAEL LAPIDGE

INE, king of Wessex (688–726), played a major role in consolidating the conquests of his predecessors in the south and west of England; he laid the foundations which enabled Wessex to withstand Mercian pressure in the eighth century and to establish itself as a major power in the ninth. Ine had no overlordship in *Kent, but was able to exact compensation for the death of *Cædwalla's brother Mul. He continued West Saxon control of *Sussex where the king Nothhelm was his kinsman, and was also ruler of Surrey where his interests brought him into conflict with the kings of *Essex. Battles are also recorded with King Geraint of *Dumnonia* (710) and King Ceolred of *Mercia (715) as the West Saxons sought to maintain and extend their western and northern borders. Friendlier contacts are recorded with *Northumbria, whose king *Aldfrith (685–705) married Ine's sister *Cuthburg.

However, it is not so much for the scale of his military victories, but for his statecraft that Ine deserves to be remembered. He issued the earliest known written West Saxon *laws and these have come down to us through their inclusion as an appendix to the lawcode of King *Alfred. They are described as being produced with the advice of Ine's father Cenred, who seems to have been associated with his rule, and with that of the bishops and leading laymen of the kingdom. The laws show Ine striving to extend the *jurisdiction of royal justice, and include provision for his newly conquered British subjects in the south-west. They also enforce Christian practices (such as infant baptism and the payment of tithes) on the West Saxon people. The church was aided further (after some initial resistance from the king) by the division in 705 of the large West Saxon diocese into two sees based on *Winchester and *Sherborne, with *Aldhelm appointed as first bishop of the latter. There was royal patronage for major religious houses, especially those in the diocese of Sherborne which had earlier Celtic origins, such as *Glastonbury and *Malmesbury. A major new house was founded at *Wimborne where Ine's sister Cuthburg was the first abbess.

Ine's laws also contain the earliest reference to West Saxon *ealdormen and their *shires, and *charter evidence also suggests that the office was introduced during his reign. It may therefore be Ine who was responsible for the division of Wessex into the shires of Hampshire, Wiltshire, Dorset, Somerset and Devon, though their boundaries would have been influenced by earlier administrative subdivisions and were subject to further modifications in the following centuries. The introduction of ealdormanries coincided with the disappearance of subkings who were such a feature of West Saxon politics in the seventh century. Ine did not, however, bring an end to competition for the throne between rival branches of the West Saxon *dynasty. Possibly Ine's wife Æthelburg was involved in one such challenge, as the *Anglo-Saxon Chronicle* records her demolition in 722 of Taunton 'which Ine had built' at a time when Ine was under threat from the *ætheling Ealdberht. Archaeological and numismatic evidence suggests that it was during Ine's reign that the international trading-base (*wic*) at *Hamwic* (*Southampton) was established, and that the first West Saxon *coinage was minted. A common clause in the laws of Ine and his Kentish contemporary Wihtred concerning the way foreign travellers should move around the country may illustrate the interest King Ine had in controlling mercantile activities through the extension of royal 'protection'. Laws, coins, ealdormanries and the *wic* are all testimony to Wessex under Ine being brought into line with the most advanced of the other Anglo-Saxon kingdoms.

In 726, like his predecessor Cædwalla, Ine resigned his throne to travel to *Rome, where he died. His brother Ingeld was the ancestor of King *Alfred, but Ine's immediate successor was Æthelheard, whose relationship to Ine is not known, though some later sources believed him to be his brother-in-law.

Stenton, *ASE*, pp. 71–3; H. Edwards, *The Charters of the Early West Saxon Kingdom*, BAR Brit. ser. 198 (Oxford, 1988); Kirby, *Kings*, pp. 124–31; D. M. Metcalf, *Thrymsas and Sceattas in the Ashmolean Museum Oxford* (Oxford, 1993-94), i. 152–7; iii. 321–40; P. Wormald, ' "Inter cetera bona . . . genti suae": Law-Making and Peace-Keeping in the Earliest English Kingdoms', *Settimane* 42 (1995), 963–93; B. A. E. Yorke, *Wessex in the Early Middle Ages* (Leicester, 1995), pp. 58–66, 79–84, 90–1, 259–62, 299–309.

B. A. E. YORKE

***-INGAS, -INGA* NAMES**. Place-names such as Hastings and Reading belong to an early period of Anglo-Saxon settlement in England. They were formed by the addition of the Old English suffix *-ingas* to a personal name. The function of this suffix was to denote a group or association of people who depended on a common leader and lived together in a particular location or territory. These names, then, were originally folk-names rather than *place-names. Hence, Hastings is a modern form of *Hæstingas* 'the people of Hæst' and Reading a modern spelling of *Rēadingas* 'the people of Rēad' (or possibly Rēada). It is unusual for the final syllable of *-ingas* to survive as it does in the case of Hastings. Much more usual is a reduction of *-ingas* to *-ing* as in Reading.

Until the 1960s, *-ingas* place-names were thought to be the oldest identifiable stratum of Anglo-Saxon village names. They were considered to belong to the period of Germanic migration from the Continent when folk groups with their war lords were carving out territories for themselves in a hostile landscape. There were three principal reasons for this view. First, the distribution of such place-names is predominantly in the east and south-east of England, the area of earliest Anglo-Saxon penetration and *settlement where the largest number of early pagan Anglo-Saxon *cemeteries has been found. Secondly, the folk-name formation in *-ingas* is one shared by other Germanic languages where its first use is also very old. Thirdly, the personal names compounded in the folk-names are predominantly of an archaic type, some of which can only be paralleled in Continental Germanic. However, when place-names in *-ingas* are plotted against known pagan Anglo-Saxon cemetery sites, they show an overwhelming lack of congruity. Apart from the occasional coincidence of pagan cemetery with *-ingas* name, such original folk-names are divorced in their distribution from the areas of the earliest Anglo-Saxon settlements signalled by such cem-

eteries. It is now believed that place-names in *-ingas* represent a colonizing phase of Anglo-Saxon settlement. They may indicate an epoch of territorial expansion where settlers were moving away from the areas of the earliest immigrant occupation marked by pagan cemeteries. It would seem that because so few *-ingas* names coincide geographically with pagan Anglo-Saxon cemeteries, this colonizing phase developed at about the beginning of the Christian era in England, after which changing burial practices demanded a move to churchyard interment without *grave goods, a move to 'undiscoverable' cemeteries. A sixth-century date is suggested for the beginning of the *-ingas* phase in place-names.

J. M. Dodgson, 'The Significance of the Distribution of English Place-Names in *-ingas*, *-inga* in southeast England', *MArch* 10 (1966), 1–29, repr. in *Place-Name Evidence for the Anglo-Saxon Invasion and Scandinavian Settlements*, ed. K. Cameron, English Place-Name Society (Nottingham, 1975); J. Kuurman, 'An Examination of the *-ingas*, *-inga* Place-Names in the East Midlands', *Journal of the English Place-Name Society* 7 (1974), 11–44.

B. COX

INSCRIPTIONS, NON-RUNIC, remain or are recorded in a wide variety of ecclesiastical and secular contexts: on buildings, on memorial stones, on stone *crosses and on portable objects. Most of the texts are short and are in Latin or Old English, if they consist of more than names. (The commonest non-runic inscriptions, those on *coins, are conventionally excluded from epigraphic studies and left to numismatists.) Coins apart, most inscriptions cannot be very precisely dated, although examples survive from throughout the Anglo-Saxon period from the later seventh century onwards.

Most of the inscriptions are in capitals derived from Roman 'square capitals' but frequently including non-classical forms. Initially (around the seventh century) the models came from Italy and Gaul. The Carolingian revival of square capitals in manuscripts and for inscriptions had some impact in the last century or so before the Conquest. There were sometimes very close links between the lettering of manuscripts and that of inscriptions, as can be seen in the 'Insular' decorative capitals used in several inscriptions of about the eighth century from the north of England. These capitals are very similar to the display script of manuscripts such as the *Lindisfarne Gospels. All the non-runic inscriptions are in the Roman alphabet with the exception of occasional uses of

Greek alpha and omega and an ogam-like cryptic script on the Hackness cross (eighth century).

The earliest extant and datable inscription on stone is that recording the dedication of the church of St Paul at *Jarrow in 685. Most of the surviving inscriptions on stone are north of the Humber but this may well be explained by a combination of greater destruction and less suitable stone further south. Nevertheless, the early Northumbrian church is comparatively well represented, with inscriptions found for example at several documented ecclesiastical sites (Hackness, *Hartlepool, *Hexham, Jarrow, *Lindisfarne, *Monkwearmouth, *Whitby and *York). The more important monastic houses seem to have developed distinctive house-styles for their inscribed stones and perhaps maintained their own designers and stone-cutters. The inscriptions of the twin monasteries of Monkwearmouth and Jarrow are closely related and seem deliberately to have imitated lettering and formulae with Roman connotations. Of particular interest at Jarrow are the dedication inscription and an inscription in honour of the Cross in words intended to recall a Constantinian inscription. At Lindisfarne the small *grave-markers carry names in decorative capitals very like those of the Lindisfarne Gospels. Those at Hartlepool are not dissimilar, whilst the typical inscribed memorial at Whitby was a small inscribed cross.

Several Anglo-Saxon stone crosses, nearly all of the eighth and ninth centuries, are inscribed. Most have memorial texts which name the commemoratee and may name the patron and sometimes include a request for prayers. Occasionally inscriptions identify or complement figure sculpture. The Latin texts that surround and gloss the sculpture on the *Ruthwell Cross are quite exceptional in their length and sophistication. Nearly all Anglo-Saxon carved figures appear without inscriptions.

There are several striking architectural inscriptions from the century before the Conquest. Most are from minor churches, the major churches having largely disappeared. Of those that record details of church dedications some, such as *Deerhurst, also commemorate a secular patron. This period sees a fashion for inscribed *sundials, some like Kirkdale doubling as building or dedication inscriptions. The obscure inscription around the crossing arch at Breamore is unusually monumental in scale and effect.

The surviving inscriptions are not fully representative. None of the longer architectural inscriptions or epitaphs in Latin verse that were composed and recorded by *Bede and others is now extant. These often imitated examples in Roman and other continental churches known through manuscript collections of *tituli. Longer inscriptions may sometimes have been painted onto plaster rather than carved. (Two small fragments of plaster with painted lettering have been excavated at Heysham.) The present condition of the inscriptions on stone may also be misleading in that originally most were probably picked out in paint.

A wide range of portable objects attracted inscriptions. Ecclesiastical examples include portable altars in Durham and Paris, the processional cross in Brussels with verses reminiscent of the *Dream of the Rood, reliquaries, a *censer and the *embroidered stole and maniple from *Winchester (now at *Durham). The texts are various but may relate to imagery or, as on the *'Alfred Jewel' (perhaps a book-pointer) from Athelney, record patronage. The inscriptions on the secular objects such as rings, brooches, knives and leather sheaths were mainly concerned with identifying owners, patrons or makers, often in short vernacular or Latin formulae in which the object 'speaks' (' . . . me worhte', ' . . . me ah' etc.). (Similar texts recording maker or patron appear on some ecclesiastical objects.) Unaccompanied personal names probably had similar meanings, although the ninth-century rings with the names of King *Æthelwulf and Queen Æthelswith (from Laverstock and Sherburn) perhaps marked them as royal gifts. The invocation of the Trinity on the eighth-century York helmet, however, was clearly intended to protect the wearer. There is a small group of inscribed *seal matrices belonging to ecclesiastical and secular individuals.

Anglo-Saxon inscriptions raise some interesting questions about the uses of *literacy. In the pre-Viking period the inscriptions are primarily monastic in origin; later the laity are much more frequently represented. The increasing use of the vernacular in later centuries probably indicates growing secular involvement, both in patronage and in the audience, which may have extended, through literate intermediaries, beyond those who could themselves read. The Roman *alphabet was the normal choice for texts in Latin and by the tenth century had taken over from *runes for Old English.

E. Okasha, 'The Non-Runic Scripts of Anglo-Saxon Inscriptions', *Transactions of the Cambridge Bibliographical Society* 4 (1968), 321–38; idem, *Hand-List of Anglo-Saxon non-runic Inscriptions* (Cambridge, 1971); idem 'A Supplement to Hand-List of Anglo-Saxon Non-Runic Inscriptions', *ASE* 11 (1983), 83–118; idem, 'A

Second Supplement to Hand-List of Anglo-Saxon Non-Runic Inscriptions', *ASE* 21 (1992), 37–85; idem, 'The Commissioners, Makers and Owners of Anglo-Saxon Inscriptions'; *ASSAH* 7 (1994), 71–7; J. Higgitt, 'The Dedication Inscription at Jarrow and its Context', *AJ* 59 (1979), 343–74; idem, 'Words and Crosses: the Inscribed Stone Cross in Early Medieval Britain and Ireland', in *Early Medieval Sculpture in Britain and Ireland*, ed. J. Higgitt, BAR Brit. ser. 152 (Oxford, 1986); idem, 'The Stone-Cutter and the Scriptorium', in *Epigraphik 1988: Fachtagung für mittelalterliche und neuzeitliche Epigraphik, Graz 10–14. Mai 1988*, ed. W. Koch (Wien, 1990), pp. 149–62; CASSS 1; L. Wallach, 'The Urbana Anglo-Saxon Sylloge of Latin Inscriptions', *Poetry and Poetics from Ancient Greece to the Renaissance: Studies in Honor of James Hutton*, ed. G. M. Kirkwood (Ithaca, NY, and London, 1975), pp. 134–51; M. Lapidge, 'Some Remnants of Bede's Lost Liber Epigrammatum' *EHR* 90 (1975), 798–820; *Literaturbericht zur mittelalterlichen und neuzeitlichen Epigraphik (1976–84)*, ed. W. Koch, MGH, Hilfsmittel 11 (Munich, 1987); *Literaturbericht zur mittelalterlichen und neuzeitlichen Epigraphik (1985–91)*, ed. W. Koch, MGH, Hilfsmittel 14 (Munich, 1994).

JOHN HIGGITT

INSCRIPTIONS, RUNIC: *see* Runes

INVASIONS: *see Adventus Saxonum*

IONA, founded as a monastery off the west coast of Scotland by *Columba in 563, had already provided a home for two English Christians, Pilu and Genereus, before Columba's death in 597. Having in this way anticipated the first dated English *conversions, the island monastery continued in the seventh century to provide a refuge for Northumbrian exiles. After 617 the fugitive sons of King *Æthelfrith, Eanfrith, *Oswald, and *Oswiu, stayed some time in Iona and were baptized there. When Oswald reclaimed the kingdom, his victory in 634 was achieved with the help of St Columba, and he turned to Iona for a bishop to convert his people. *Aidan was consecrated and sent out to preach to the English, establishing his see at *Lindisfarne. For thirty years Iona's influence was strong, particularly during the reigns of Oswald and Oswiu, who spoke Irish themselves and trusted the Irish clergy. Those who came from Iona were for the most part monks; and Bede says that they came 'to those English provinces over which Oswald was king' (*HE* iii.3). They established monasteries on lands given by the rulers, they trained English children, and they taught monastic ways. How far the influence of Iona spread among the territories over which Oswald held lordship is unclear. There were Irish monks active in England from other parts of Ireland, and

it was through one of these, Rónán, that the *Easter controversy flared up in *Northumbria in the 650s. While the monks of Iona had taken a pluralist view up to this point, accepting that the king followed their customs but his Kentish queen the Roman practice, in 664 they did not accept King Oswiu's decision taken at *Whitby and most returned to Iona. From there some moved on to Ireland, establishing themselves at Inishboffin.

Twenty years later, in the spring of 685, Oswiu's Irish-born eldest son Aldfrith was staying in Iona when his brother King Ecgfrith was killed in eastern Scotland. Ecgfrith's body was brought to Iona and Aldfrith was hailed as his successor. During the next two years Abbot *Adomnán of Iona twice visited England, on the first occasion as an ambassador for the Southern Uí Néill king to recover captives. He may have been chosen for this role because of his friendship with the scholarly Aldfrith. On his next visit he began to take a close interest in the Roman calculation of Easter, and it is possible that he and Aldfrith hoped to heal the rift on that subject and to bring Iona back into active participation in the Northumbrian church. Nothing came of this in England, though Adomnán is said by Bede to have played the major part in bringing most of the northern Irish churches to the orthodox practice. After his death it was an English monk, Ecgberht, called by God to give instruction to the monasteries of St Columba, who brought Iona into conformity with Roman practice – an act which for Bede represented a repayment by the English church for its debt to Iona.

The Columban monastery in Iona continued to flourish in the eighth century, though it later declined in importance. One aspect of Bede's account of this community has had a particular influence on the study of Irish church history: 'This island always has an abbot for its ruler who is a priest, to whose authority the whole kingdom, including even bishops, have to be subject. This unusual arrangement follows the example of their first teacher, who was not a bishop but a priest and monk' (*HE* iii.4). The unusual custom of Iona, not followed even at Lindisfarne, was treated as the key to understanding the stress on monastic terminology in the records of the Irish church, and led to the development of a theory in which the role of bishops in the Irish church was underestimated.

Adomnán of Iona: Life of St Columba, trans. R. Sharpe (Harmondsworth, 1995); Bede, *HE* iii.3–4, v.22; [Royal Commission on Ancient and Historical Monuments] *Argyll IV. Iona* (Edinburgh, 1982); M. Herbert, *Iona,*

Kells and Derry. The History and Hagiography of the Monastic Family of Columba (Oxford, 1988); T. O. Clanchy and G. Markus, *Iona. The Earliest Poetry of a Celtic Monastery* (Edinburgh, 1995); A. Ritchie, *Iona* (London, 1997).

RICHARD SHARPE

IPSWICH. Archaeological excavation in Ipswich since 1974 has confirmed that the town was founded in the early seventh century to serve as the major commodity production centre and international trading port of the kingdom of *East Anglia. The earliest settlement, of the late sixth or early seventh century, is associated with handmade local *pottery, and imported wares paralleled in the Merovingian *cemeteries of *Flanders and Holland. It was a *de novo* settlement on unoccupied heathland at the head of the Orwell Estuary, just nine miles south-west of the East Anglian royal cemetery at *Sutton Hoo. Seventh- to early eighth-century occupation appears to be restricted to twenty hectares on the north bank of the river with a major inhumation cemetery of this date to the immediate north, and evidence of a field system to the east. From the mid-eighth century the settlement grew to cover about fifty hectares both north and south of the river. Commodity production included spinning, weaving, *bone/antler working, bronze and iron working and *leather working. These craft industries were overshadowed by the mass production of Ipswich ware pottery located in the north-east sector of the settlement. The scale of production is evidenced by the distribution of the product. Ipswich ware is found on all settlements of Middle Saxon date throughout the kingdom of East Anglia and beyond as far as *Kent and Yorkshire. Outside the kingdom it appears to be restricted to privileged settlements, with ecclesiastical or aristocratic connections, which may indicate a prestige value in areas where handmade pottery only was being made, or the trade network for other products.

The evidence of trade consists mainly of imported pottery which forms up to fifteen per cent of the ceramic assemblage. The majority originates from the Rhineland, but there are also wares from northern France, Flanders and Holland. Some of the pottery may indicate traders in residence rather than traded goods. The traded pottery was probably an accoutrement to a trade in Rhenish wine of which few other traces remain. Excavations have revealed part of a wooden barrel, reused to line a well, with staves made from a tree of Rhenish origin felled shortly after 873. Two large-scale excavations have revealed contrasting townscape patterns between the centre of the settlement and its eastern margin. The St Stephen's Lane excavation, in the centre, revealed buildings close together and built against the street edge, in characteristically urban fashion. At Foundation Street, on the eastern fringe, the buildings were sparser and set back from the street in a more rural pattern. This apparent difference was reflected in activities at each site. At Stephen's Lane there was abundant evidence of craft production, including a potter's kiln, bronze and ironworking, bone/antler working and weaving. In contrast, there was little craft activity at Foundation Street and the environmental evidence indicates an agrarian element.

The *town grew very little in the later Anglo-Saxon period. It was surrounded with defences, for the first time, in the early tenth century, probably by the Danes. The late Saxon economy continued to be based on commodity production and trade, but the latter is almost exclusively regional. International trade revives in the early eleventh century. Buildings at this period are normally set back from the street frontage and mostly two storied with the lower storey a cellar or half cellar.

R. Hodges, *Dark Age Economics: The Origins of Towns and Trade AD 600–1000* (London, 1982); K. Wade, 'Anglo-Saxon and Medieval Ipswich', *An Historical Atlas of Suffolk*, ed. D. Dymond and E. Martin (Ipswich, 1988), pp. 122–3; idem, 'Ipswich', in *The Rebirth of Towns in the West, AD 700–1050*, ed. R. Hodges and B. Hobley (London, 1988), pp. 93–100; idem, 'The Urbanisation of East Anglia: the Ipswich Perspective', in *Flatlands and Wetlands: Current Themes in East Anglian Archaeology*, ed. J. Gardiner (Gressenhall, 1993), pp. 144–51.

KEITH WADE

ISRAEL THE GRAMMARIAN, a scholar of Breton origin who spent some time at the court of King Æthelstan (924–39), probably as a refugee from political turmoil in Brittany; he subsequently returned to the Continent where he served (from *c.*940 onwards) as tutor to Bruno, later archbishop of Cologne (953–65), and ended his life as a monk in the monastery of St Maximin in Trier. Israel was an accomplished grammarian and poet, and one of the few scholars of this time to have first-hand knowledge of Greek. His presence in England is recorded in a brief text known as the *Alea euangelii* ('Gospel Dice'), and is reflected in various texts which passed through his hands (such as the Greek prayers copied in the last folios of the *Æthelstan Psalter) or which were composed by him (such as, probably, the immensely

255

difficult poems *Rubisca* and *Adelphus adelphe*) and transmitted in English manuscripts (such as the poem *De arte metrica*, which was dedicated to Archbishop Robert of Trier).

MGH, PLAC v. 501–2; C. Jeudy, 'Israël le grammairien et la tradition manuscrite du commentaire de Remi d'Auxerre à l'*Ars minor* de Donat', *SM* 3rd ser. 18 (1977), 751–71; E. Jeauneau, 'Pour le dossier d'Israel Scot', *Archives d'histoire doctrinale et littéraire du moyen âge* 52 (1985), 7–71; M. Lapidge, 'Israel the Grammarian in Anglo-Saxon England', in *From Athens to Chartres: Neoplatonism and Medieval Thought*, ed. H. J. Westra (Leiden, 1992), pp. 97–114, repr. in *ALL* ii. 87–104.

MICHAEL LAPIDGE

ITHAMAR, bishop of *Rochester (d. *c.*664), deserves to be recorded because he was the first native Englishman after the Augustinian mission who was sufficiently well trained (presumably in Anglo-Saxon *schools) to be appointed to a bishopric. Bede tells us that he was a native of *Kent and was comparable to his (Roman) predecessors in virtue and learning; the date of his accession is unknown.

Bede, *HE* iii.14, 20.

MICHAEL LAPIDGE

IVORY: *see* Bone Working; Bone and Ivory Carving

IWIG, St, trained as monk under *Cuthbert in seventh-century *Northumbria, was inspired to follow the Irish tradition of exile for Christ's sake, and therefore got into the first boat he found, which took him to Brittany, where he settled to the eremitical life, until his death. This story occurs in *Goscelin's Life of St *Eadgyth of Wilton, which includes the account of how a group of Breton clergy arrived at Wilton Abbey seeking hospitality. They had with them Iwig's relics, which they deposited, for the duration of their visit, on St Eadgyth's altar in the abbey church. When they decided to leave, the reliquary was found to be immovable, resisting all the Bretons' best efforts, so the abbess, Wulfthryth, gave them 2,000 *solidi* as a consolation, and they returned to Brittany. This story may have been the hagiographer's circumlocution for the purchase (or possibly theft) of Iwig's relics. His feast was celebrated on 8 October at Wilton, and also at *Winchester and *Worcester.

A. Wilmart, 'La légende de Ste Édithe en prose et vers par le moine Goscelin', *AB* 56 (1938), 5–101, 265–307, at 273–4.

R. C. LOVE

J

JÆNBERHT, abbot of St Augustine's abbey, *Canterbury (762–5), archbishop of Canterbury (765–92), and an adversary in *Kent of *Offa, king of the Mercians (757–96). When Offa is first seen developing interests in west Kent, in 764 (S 105), he acted at Canterbury with the consent of the east Kentish establishment, represented by King Heahberht and Archbishop Bregowine (760–4). Bregowine was succeeded as archbishop by Jænberht, who was consecrated on 2 February 765, apparently at a church council attended by King Offa (S 107), and who received his *pallium in 766 (*ASC*). Offa seems soon to have extended his authority over east Kent; but in 776 the men of Kent, perhaps with encouragement from Jænberht, fought against the Mercians at Otford (in west Kent), and broke free from Mercian control. By 785 Offa had managed to recover his position in the south-east, and began to tighten his grip. It was probably at about this time that Offa conceived his plan to have his son Ecgfrith consecrated king, transforming the ideological basis of Mercian kingship and helping at the same time to secure the succession. It is conceivable that Jænberht refused to be party to this scheme, and that when Offa sought a more compliant archbishop it was Jænberht who attempted to undermine Offa's relations with Pope Hadrian I by spreading a (false) rumour that Offa had been plotting with Charlemagne to depose the pope; if so, the plan came to nought. In 786 two papal legates were despatched to England in order to prepare the ground: on their arrival, they advised Jænberht 'of those things which were necessary', and then went about their proper business (*EHD* i, no. 191). In 787, 'there was a contentious synod at Chelsea, and Archbishop Jænberht lost a certain part of his province, and Hygeberht [bishop of *Lichfield] was chosen by King Offa, and Ecgfrith was consecrated king' (ASC). We learn from a letter from King *Coenwulf to Pope Leo III, written in 798, that Offa had moved for the creation of the archbishopric of Lichfield 'on account of the enmity he had formed against the venerable Jænberht and the people of Kent' (*EHD* i, no. 204). Hygeberht assumed responsibility, as archbishop, for a province which presumably included the 'Mercian' sees of Lichfield, *Leicester, *Lindsey, *Worcester, and *Hereford, and which may also have included the East Anglian sees of Dunwich and *Elmham; he is called 'bishop' in a *charter issued at a council of Chelsea in 788 (S 128), which may reflect a 'Canterbury' view of his position, or which may indicate that he had not then received his pallium (cf. S 129), but he then took his place, after Jænberht, in the episcopal hierarchy. Jænberht issued *coins in his own name ('Ienberht pontifex'), perhaps in the years immediately following the battle of Otford; and coins bearing the name and title of Jænberht on one side, and the name and title of Offa on the other side, were struck at Canterbury in the later 780s. Jænberht is known to have convened *councils of the Southumbrian church at Brentford and Chelsea (Middlesex), and at *Aclea* (? in Kent); and he tried unsuccessfully on such occasions to recover control of the monastery at Cookham, Berks., initially from Cynewulf, king of the West Saxons (757–86), and latterly from King Offa (S 1258: *EHD* i, no. 79). It is striking, however, that Jænberht seems not to have used *Clofesho as a meeting-place, perhaps because it was too closely identified with Mercian political interests. Jænberht died on 12 August 792, and was buried not in Christ Church but by his own choice in St Augustine's abbey. He was succeeded as archbishop by Æthelheard, formerly abbot of Louth (in *Lindsey), and evidently a 'Mercian' appointee; significantly, one of Æthelheard's first actions seems to have been to secure a grant of privileges for the Kentish churches from King Offa, in a council convened at *Clofesho* in 792 (S 134).

Brooks, *Canterbury*, pp. 81, 111–20; P. Grierson and M. Blackburn, *Medieval European Coinage* I (Cambridge, 1986), pp. 278–9; S. Keynes, *The Councils of Clofesho*, Brixworth Lecture 1993 (Leicester, 1994), pp. 6–8; C. Cubitt, *Anglo-Saxon Church Councils c.650–c.850* (London, 1995), pp. 215–16, 217–18; *Charters of St Augustine's Abbey Canterbury and Minster-in-Thanet*, ed. S. E. Kelly, AS Charters 4 (Oxford, 1995), pp. xv, 208; R. Fleming, 'Christ Church Canterbury's Anglo-Norman Cartulary', *Anglo-Norman Political Culture and the*

Twelfth-Century Renaissance, ed. C. W. Hollister (Woodbridge, 1997), pp. 83–155, at 100–1 and 115.

SIMON KEYNES

JAMES THE DEACON (*Iacobus diaconus*) was the deacon and assistant of *Paulinus during the latter's mission to *Northumbria; when after the death of King *Edwin (633) Paulinus retired to *Kent, James bravely remained at York to continue the mission. Like Paulinus, he was presumably of Italian origin. According to Bede, he was a man of great energy and sanctity; and Bede records in particular that he was skilled in ecclesiastical *chant 'after the manner of *Rome' (though with adaptations which had been introduced in Kent), and that, during the Synod of *Whitby when the *Easter controversy was being settled, he adhered to the Roman method of calculation. He lived until Bede's own days in a village near Catterick, and died at a venerable old age.

Bede, *HE* ii.16, 20, iii.25.

MICHAEL LAPIDGE

JARROW *see* Monkwearmouth (or Wearmouth) and Jarrow

JEWELLERY, decorative ornaments of dress made from a range of materials, most notably *metals, played an important role in Anglo-Saxon society. Whether they served as practical fasteners (e.g. brooches, belt-fittings) or costume access-ories (e.g. bracelets, girdle-collections), all might be vehicles for the expression of personal and social identity. This is especially evident in the Migration Period (fifth – sixth centuries), when clothed burial was a prominent and widespread rite. Then jewellery-use was constrained primarily by gender: men rarely had ornamental adjuncts beyond those for belts, whereas women had access to a wide range, depending further on their political or territorial affiliation, family wealth and age.

In the initial phase of Anglo-Saxon activity (early to mid-fifth century), the jewellery reper-toire included Late Roman forms (e.g. belt fittings, bracelets), but was marked by the import and copying of brooch-forms from northern *Germany: supporting arm, equal-arm, cruci-form, and applied and cast saucer brooches are found mostly from the Thames valley to the North Sea/Wash, and reflect the wearing of a *peplos*-style overdress fastened at the shoulders by a pair of brooches, sometimes with a third display brooch. To the south, quoit brooches, the finest in zoomor-phic-decorated ('Quoit Brooch Style') silver, were more often worn singly; like belt-fittings in the same style, they continued to be placed in graves in southern England for a long time, complicating arguments about their dating and cultural context – Germanic or British. The origins of broad-band annular and penannular brooches are equally debated. Nonetheless, by the later fifth century, through selective development of these types and further continental imports, the classic 'English Migration Period' regional costumes had come into being.

North of the Thames valley ('Anglian' region), cruciform, small-long, narrow-band annular, pen-annular and swastika brooches were particularly favoured, though pairs were not necessarily matched and the addition of a third brooch, or even more, was popular. Grander ensembles often involved items derived from southern Scandinavia, such as great square-headed brooches (with their characteristic animal-ornament, 'Salin's Style I'), clasps for fastening the cuffs of an underdress, and gold or silver bracteates or shield-shaped pendants enhancing a standard festoon of glass and/or amber beads between the shoulder-brooches. Bucket-shaped pendants and key-shaped girdle-hangers are also typically 'Anglian', while silver bracelets and finger-rings are characteristic, if not exclusively so.

South of and along the Thames valley ('Saxon' region), paired round brooches, especially relief-decorated saucer or simple disc brooches, were preferred, supplemented by button, broad-band annular, penannular and small-long or small square-headed brooches, with great square-headed brooches occasionally as a third piece. Necklaces and girdle-collections feature commonly, but lack types exclusive to the region, though festoons of beads at the hip, three-piece toilet sets hung on the chest, and a slightly greater tendency to adorn young *children lavishly are distinctive features.

In *Kent, Quoit-Brooch-Style jewellery and cruciform brooches gave way to new fashions. Silver square-headed brooches, later produced in pairs, button brooches and gold bracteates with Style I decoration, as well as the application of Style I to belt-fittings, reflected Scandinavian links. Imported radiate-headed, bird- and rosette brooches, amuletic crystal balls and sieve-spoons hung from the waist, and the application of garnet-inlays to jewellery showed Merovingian connec-tions. In the second quarter of the sixth century pairs of silver garnet-inlaid disc brooches were produced; later they replaced the square-headed series, came to be worn singly at the throat, perhaps on an open-fronted gown, and sported

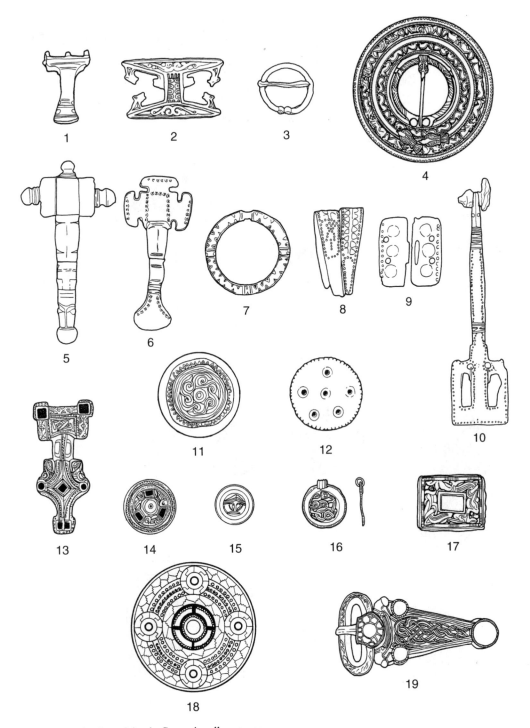

Fig. 9 A selection of Anglo–Saxon jewellery types.

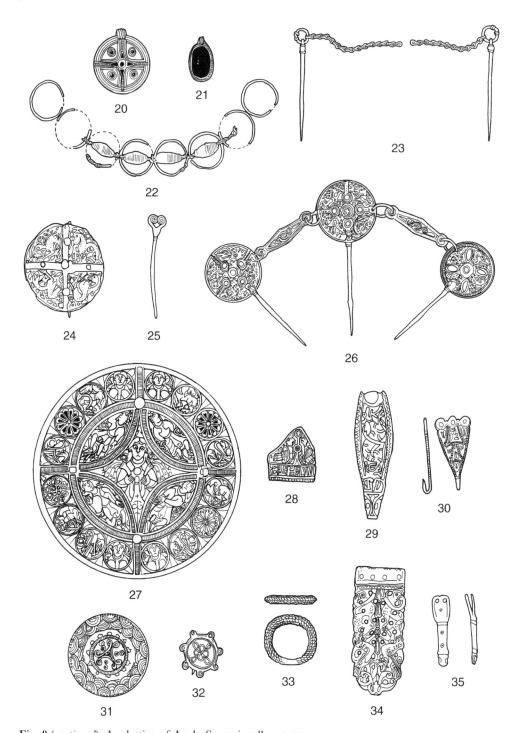

Fig. 9 (*continued*). A selection of Anglo-Saxon jewellery types.

the latest Scandinavian zoomorphic art, 'Salin's Style II'. From the late sixth to mid-seventh century gold was increasingly available, especially in Kent, and Style II was a favourite embellishment for luxuries, e.g. on plated and composite disc brooches with filigree and cloisonné ornament, bracteate-pendants, and triangular-plated belt-buckles, these last marking the return of some grandeur to male costume (with *Sutton Hoo the pinnacle). Other innovations at this date were amethyst beads and metal fittings for shoes and leggings.

These changes presaged a fundamental change nationwide. Jewellery-burial became rarer in the seventh century, and those women who retained it abandoned 'tribal' dress for Late Antique/ Byzantine-inspired costumes, the most complete ornamented with delicate necklaces of plain glass and metal beads, wire rings and sheet-metal and/or inlaid pendants, a belt with châtelaine, and small, often linked, pins,

perhaps for a veil; brooches became rare. These developments are best documented in the second half of the seventh century. They may be less a consequence of *conversion to Christianity (though crosses do make their first appearance) and more an aspect of the institutionalising of status, especially of a landed aristocracy, and the reassertion of an ideal of *Rome as the fount of power.

For the eighth century onwards, information is restricted mainly to finds from *settlements (rural, ecclesiastic and urban) and *hoards, supplemented by pictorial representations in manuscripts or on sculpture. Gold became scarce again, and castwork was preferred to sheet-metal working. Pins (with globular, faceted, spiraliform, or flat heads) became the dominant type; the showiest, with zoomorphic or vegetative decoration, might be worn in linked sets, smaller ones, with hipped shafts, for veils still. Investment in jewellery returns in the ninth century, associated with the

---

Fig. 9 A selection of Anglo-Saxon jewellery types (see pp. 259–60). Left-hand page illustrates the fifth to early seventh century: the top row (1–4) shows items from the earlier fifth century; the three central rows show items from the classic English Migration period by region – Anglian (5–10), Saxon (11–12) and Kentish 13–17); the bottom row (18–19) shows Kentish material of the late sixth-/early seventh century. The right-hand page illustrates in four rows material from the seventh (20–3), eighth (24–6), ninth (27–30) and tenth to eleventh centuries (31–5) respectively. All items are at 1/2.

Detailed Source-Data:
1. Supporting-arm brooch, Mucking II, 989 (Evison 1981, fig. 4a). 2. Equal-armed brooch, Mucking I, 90 (Jones and Jones 1975, pl. 28b). 3. Penannular brooch, Mucking II, 979 (Evison 1981, fig. 6d). 4. Silver quoit brooch, Sarre (Hawkes 1961, pl. 14). 5. Cruciform brooch, Spong Hill 46 (Hills, Penn and Rickett 1984, fig. 101). 6. Small-long brooch, Great Chesterford 73 (Evison 1994, fig. 36). 7. Narrow annular brooch, Spong Hill 29 (Hills, Penn and Rickett 1984, fig. 85). 8. Silver bracelet, Holywell Row 11 (Lethbridge 1931, fig. 2, 3). 9. Sleeve clasp, Spong Hill 37 (Hills, Penn and Rickett 1984, fig. 90). 10. Girdle hanger, Sewerby 49 (Hirst 1985, fig. 52, 10). 11. Cast saucer brooch, Berinsfield 54 (Boyle, Dodd, Miles and Mudd 1995, fig. 64). 12. Disc brooch, Beckford B, 6 (Evison and Hill 1996, fig. 18). 13. Silver square-headed brooch, Finglesham E2 (Chadwick 1958, fig. 11b). 14. Garnet-inlaid disc brooch, Buckland Dover 14 (Evison 1987, fig. 10). 15. Button brooch, Buckland Dover 48 (Evison 1987, fig. 27). 16. Gold bracteate, Finglesham D3 (Chadwick 1958, fig. 9e). 17. Garnet-inlaid belt plate, Royal Museum, Canterbury. 18. Composite brooch, Sarre (Avent 1975, map 6, cf. pl. 66). 19. Triangular-plated belt-buckle, Sarre 68 (Speake 1980, pl. 6f). 20. Gold pendant, Sibertswold 172 (Faussett 18, pl. 4, 13). 21. Gold cabochon-garnet pendant, Sibertswold 172 (Faussett 18, pl. 4, 16). 22. Silver wire rings and wound-wire beads, Chamberlain's Barn II, Bd 9 (Hyslop 1962). 23. Silver linked pins, Winnall II, 8 (Meaney and Hawkes 1970, fig. 9). 24. Disc brooch, Ixworth (Wilson 1964, pl. 19, 25). 25. Spiral-headed pin, Brandon (Webster and Backhouse 1991, 85 no. 66g). 26. Silver disc-headed linked pins, River Witham, Fiskerton (Wilson 1964, pl. 18). 27. Silver disc brooch known as the 'Fuller brooch' (Wilson 1964, pl. 44, 153). 28. Gold finger ring, Laverstock (Wilson 1964, pl. 19, 31). 29. Strap-end with Trewhiddle Style, Whitby (Webster and Backhouse 1991, 142 no. 107b). 30. Silver hooked tag, Winchester (Biddle et al. 1990, fig. 148, 1408). 31. Pewter disc brooch, London (Wilson 1964, pl. 26, 51). 32. Cloisonné enamelled brooch, Saunderton (Buckton 1986, fig. 1). 33. Bold twisted-wire finger ring, Winchester (Biddle et al. 1990, fig. 175, 2000). 34. Strap-end, Winchester (Biddle et al. 1990, fig. 124). 35. Strap-end, Winchester (Biddle et al. 1990, fig. 126,1070).

---

widespread use of the zoomorphic 'Trewhiddle Style' and, towards the end of the century, with overt expressions of Christian ideology and royal power, most notably in series of fine silver disc brooches and precious-metal, and, sometimes inscribed, finger rings. But the ninth-century corpus is dominated by belt-fittings, notably strap-ends (but *not* buckles) and hooked tags, a type recorded from the late seventh to eleventh centuries, but whose function (for laces on leggings, purses, etc.) is obscure. The Late Saxon corpus (tenth-eleventh centuries) is again limited. Men and women continued to wear single disc brooches and finger rings, but types are simpler. Brooches are often in base metal (including lead/pewter), with nummular (coin-like) and, in eastern counties, enamelled forms being distinctive developments; rings, relief-cast or of twisted wire, might be of gold. Strap-ends were still numerous, but apart from some fine relief-cast pieces, plainer types, perhaps with an animal-head tip, were dominant; pins appear less distinctive and perhaps were less popular. Debate continues about whether these fluctuations in later Saxon jewellery were caused by mere vagaries of survival or fashion, by changing access to precious metals, contexts of production (especially urban), patterns of gift-giving (ecclesiastic and secular), or rather, as in the earlier period, by fluctuating social need to communicate identity, status and relationship.

G. Baldwin Brown, *The Arts in Early England*, III–IV: *Saxon Art and Industry in the Pagan Period* (London, 1915); K. Brush, 'Adorning the Dead: the Social Significance of Early Anglo-Saxon Funerary Dress in England (Fifth to Sixth Centuries AD)', unpublished PhD dissertation (Univ. of Cambridge, 1993); T. Dickinson, 'Fibel und Fibeltracht. II.L: Völkerwanderungszeit in England', in *Reallexikon der germanischen Altertumskunde* VIII.5–6, ed. H. Beck, H. Jankuhn, H. Steuer and R. Wenskus (Berlin, 1994), 582–5; J. Hines, *The Scandinavian Character of Anglian England in the Pre-Viking Period*, BAR Brit. ser. 124 (Oxford, 1984); D. Hinton, 'Late Anglo-Saxon Metalwork: an Assessment', *ASE* 4 (1975), 171–80; G. Owen-Crocker, *Dress in Anglo-Saxon England* (Manchester, 1986); *Making of England*.

TANIA M. DICKINSON

JEWS. There does not appear to be any evidence for the presence of Jews in England before the Norman Conquest, though of course it is likely that English travellers and pilgrims would have met Jews on the Continent, and that Jewish merchants may on occasion have found their way across the Channel. In effect, therefore, consciousness of the Jewish people and their customs was disseminated among the English by the Old Testa-

ment and by Christian teaching: examples abound from the *school of *Theodore and *Hadrian, in the late seventh century, to the works of *Ælfric and *Wulfstan, in the eleventh. The English were thus imbued with all the conventional Christian prejudice against a people supposed to have betrayed and rejected Christ. It is a prejudice which sometimes manifests itself, for example, in the sanctions of tenth-century royal diplomas which stipulate that the infractor will perish 'with the impious and unfaithful Jews, blaspheming Christ with sacrilegious mouth on the altar of the cross'; and it may be that Jews were excluded from England by royal authority. It is generally supposed that the first Jewish community in the country was that established by William the Conqueror at *London.

C. Roth, *A History of the Jews in England*, 3rd ed. (Oxford, 1964), pp. 2, 271; R. Mellinkoff, 'The Round, Cap-Shaped Hats Depicted on Jews in BM Cotton Claudius B. iv', *ASE* 2 (1973), 155–65, at 159–60; C. N. L. Brooke with G. Keir, *London 800–1216: the Shaping of a City* (London, 1975), pp. 222–7; Bischoff and Lapidge, *Biblical Commentaries*, p. 246 n. 14; R. DiNapoli, *An Index of Theme and Image to the Homilies of the Anglo-Saxon Church* (Hockwold cum Wilton, 1995), pp. 55–7; J. Campbell, 'The Late Anglo-Saxon State: a Maximum View', *PBA* 87 (1995), 39–65, at 61–2.

SIMON KEYNES

JOHN, monk of Worcester (d. *c.*1140). Compiler of the *Worcester *Chronicon ex chronicis*, formerly attributed to *Florence of Worcester. The underlying framework for the narrative was provided by the Universal Chronicle of Marianus the Scot, who died at Mainz in 1082/3. This was given an English dimension by inserting extensive extracts from *Bede, *Asser, a Latin translation of the *Anglo-Saxon Chronicle*, the lives of saints, notably *Oswald of Worcester and *Dunstan, and from Eadmer's *Historia novorum*. However, the chief value of the Worcester *Chronicon* for the pre-Conquest period lies in its use of some earlier sources which otherwise appear to be lost. The nature of the *Anglo-Saxon Chronicle* used by the Worcester chronicler is not easily determined. Although it must often have been closest to the 'D' text, there are a number of passages which are only found in others. While John might have created his own eclectic text, there are close parallels between his *annals and those now known only from the 'E' chronicle, at least as far as 1106, which makes it more likely that he was using a version which no longer survives. How much of the relatively abundant material in the *Chronicon*, notably for the reigns of *Æthelred the Unready and *Cnut, for which there is no earlier authority, came from this source, and how much from local knowledge, saga or elsewhere, has not been established. Some further passages between the mid-tenth century and the end of the eleventh are also found in *William of Malmesbury's *Gesta regum*, apparently from another shared but lost source.

In all the manuscripts the *Chronicon* is preceded by a set of chronological tables modelled on those of Marianus, but enlarged to include the succession to the English kingdoms and bishoprics from their foundation, with occasional historical notes. Most, but not all, of this information is also found in the *Chronicon* itself. Both tables and text were extensively revised by John, whose manuscript (Oxford, Corpus Christi College 157) survives as the ancestor of all surviving copies. He made numerous additions to the text, drawn from William of Malmesbury's *Gesta regum*, *Symeon of *Durham's history of his church, and elsewhere, and re-wrote the conclusion from 1128 to 1131, replacing it with a narrative to 1140 at least (the manuscripts are incomplete). He also made an abbreviation of the whole to 1123, which includes some new information, notably extracts from a chronicle close to the 'F' text of the *Anglo-Saxon Chronicle*.

Where the Worcester *Chronicon* can be compared with its known sources, it proves to be a trustworthy if unimaginative compilation. Particularly for the tenth and eleventh centuries it preserves a significant amount of credible information known from no other source, which needs to be treated seriously. John's work also appealed to many later compilers of like tastes, and was widely excerpted.

Sharpe, *Handlist*, 984; *The Chronicle of John of Worcester, II: The Annals from 450 to 1066*, ed. R. R. Darlington and P. McGurk, trans. J. Bray and P. McGurk (OMT, 1995); M. Brett, 'John of Worcester and his Contemporaries', *The Writing of History in the Middle Ages: Essays presented to R. W. Southern*, ed. R. H. C. Davis and J. M. Wallace-Hadrill (Oxford, 1981), pp. 101–26; P. McGurk, 'The *Chronicon ex Chronicis* of "Florence" of Worcester and its Use of Sources for English History before 1066', *ANS* 5 (1982), 185–96; C. Hart, 'The Early Section of the *Worcester Chronicle*', *JMH* 9 (1983), 251–315.

MARTIN BRETT

JOHN THE OLD SAXON (fl. 890), a monk, priest and scholar who, according to *Asser (cc. 78, 94–7), was invited to England by King *Alfred to help in that king's programme of educational renewal. Asser reports that John was a man 'of most acute intelligence, immensely learned in all fields of literary endeavour, and extremely

ingenious in other forms of expression'. His origin in Saxony is unknown (possibly he was a monk at one of the Saxon monasteries, such as Werden or Korvey). While in England John (and others) helped Alfred prepare his English translation of *Gregory's *Regula pastoralis*, and Alfred subsequently appointed him abbot of Athelney. While at Athelney he survived an assassination attempt by two French priests in the newly-established community. Little is known of his subsequent career (he last witnesses a charter of King *Edward the Elder in 904). In the domain of Latin scholarship John has been recognized as the author of a brief *acrostic poem dedicated to King *Æthelstan while he was still a child, and it is possible that he was also the author of two acrostic poems dedicated to King Alfred. The poem to Æthelstan is embellished with the recherché vocabulary (often called 'hermeneutic') which characterizes much later tenth-century Anglo-Latin verse. It is tempting to associate the presence in England of the Old Saxon poem *Genesis (and its partial translation as *Genesis B*) with John the Old Saxon; but as yet no firm proof has been adduced in support of this association.

Sharpe, *Handlist*, 825; Keynes and Lapidge, *Alfred the Great*, pp. 26–7, 103–5, 260 n. 169; M. Lapidge, 'Some Latin Poems as Evidence for the Reign of Athelstan', *ASE* 9 (1981), 61–98, at 72–83, repr. in *ALL* ii.49–86, at 60–71.

MICHAEL LAPIDGE

JUDITH is a poem based on the Old Testament *Liber Judith* which describes how the eponymous heroine saves her people from the Assyrian army by decapitating the general Holofernes while he lies in a drunken stupor. The only extant copy of the poem is in the *Beowulf* Manuscript. The opening section of the poem has been lost and although there has been much speculation about the original length of the work, it is virtually impossible to draw any firm conclusions on this matter from the evidence of the manuscript.

The poem is not a direct translation of its biblical source and it is clear that the treatment of the story has been influenced by patristic interpretations of the *Liber Judith* and by the conventions of Latin *hagiography. Judith is portrayed as a handmaiden of the Lord who, made strong by her faith, fights and destroys the heathen. It has been suggested that the poem can also be read as a call to the English to take up the fight against the heathen armies who threatened them.

ASPR iv. 99–109; *Judith*, ed. B. J. Timmer (London, 1952, rev. repr. Exeter, 1978); *Judith*, ed. M. Griffith (Exeter, 1997); D. Chamberlain, '*Judith*: a Fragmentary and Political Poem', in *Anglo-Saxon Poetry: Essays in Appreciation*, ed. L. E. Nicholson and D. W. Frese (Notre Dame, IN, 1975), pp. 135–59; I. Pringle, '*Judith*: the Homily and the Poem', *Traditio* 31 (1975), 83–97; A. W. Astell, 'Holofernes's Head: *Tacen* and Teaching in the Old English *Judith*', *ASE* 18 (1979), 117–33; P. J. Lucas, '*Judith* and the Woman Hero', *Yearbook of English Studies* 22 (1992), 17–27.

SUSAN ROSSER

JUDOC, ST (d. *c.*668), a Breton prince who abandoned his wealthy origins, was ordained a priest and, after making a *pilgrimage to *Rome, spent the rest of his life as a hermit in Ponthieu, at a place which later took his name (Saint-Josse-sur-Mer). The hermitage was subsequently used as a guest-house for English travellers (*Alcuin was at one time abbot of the house), and it was possibly through contacts of this sort that the cult of St Judoc was established in England. In any event, the *relics of St Judoc were acquired in about 901 by the New Minster, *Winchester, supposedly having been brought there by refugees from Saint-Josse; they were enshrined in the new church just then under construction by *Edward the Elder. Judoc's feast was prominent among those observed at Winchester, and at some point in the late tenth century, someone at Winchester composed an unprinted metrical life of St Judoc (*BHL* 4512), now preserved in London, BL, Royal 8.B.XIV, fols. 137–44, based on an earlier prose life of continental origin (*BHL* 4504). At approximately this time the community of Saint-Josse made a counter-claim (expressed in a *vita* of the saint by one Florentinus) to possess Judoc's body intact; possibly this claim was made in response to Winchester's claims. Feast: 13 December; translation, 9 January.

J. Trier, *Der heilige Jodocus*, Germanistische Abhandlungen 56 (Breslau, 1924); *The Ecclesiastical History of Orderic Vitalis*, ed. M. Chibnall, 6 vols. (OMT, 1969–80), ii. 156–66, 366–7; J. Howe, 'The Date of the "Vita Judoci" by Abbot Florentius', *AB* 101 (1983), 25–31; M. Lapidge, 'Tenth-Century Anglo-Latin Verse Hagiography', *Mittellateinisches Jahrbuch* 24–5 (1989–90), 249–60; H. Le Bourdellès, 'Vie de St Josse avec commentaire historique et spirituel', *SM* 3rd ser. 34 (1993), 861–958.

R. C. LOVE

JULIANA: see Cynewulf

JUNIUS, Franciscus (1591–1677), pioneer Anglo-Saxonist and 'father' of Germanic philology, styled F. F. [= Francisci Filius] to distinguish him from his eponymous father, a professor of theology at Leiden University. After a humanist classical edu-

cation in the Netherlands, in 1621 Junius became librarian to the Earl of Arundel, a renowned collector, and became an authority on the historical criticism of art. Later, already fascinated by the similarities between Dutch and English, he took up his interest in Germanic languages by looking for historical links as an explanation of modern differences. Making frequent long visits to London and Oxford from his base in the Netherlands, he worked from original sources transcribing texts, recording comments, and compiling word-lists with references to examples in the texts. In 1655 he published the *Cædmon* containing the biblical poems in the *Junius Manuscript (*Genesis, *Exodus, *Daniel, *Christ and Satan*), the first major edition of Old English poetry, for which he used specially made Anglo-Saxon types. His etymological method is demonstrated in his 1665 publication of the Gothic and Anglo-Saxon Gospels with a Gothic glossary. Junius left his books, manuscripts and 'printing utensils' to Oxford University.

K. Aldrich, P. Fehl and M. R. Fehl, *Franciscus Junius: The Literature of Classical Art*, 2 vols. (Berkeley, CA, 1991); R. H. Bremmer, Jr, ed., *Franciscus Junius and his Circle* (Amsterdam, 1997); Franciscus Junius, F. F., *Quatuor D. N. Jesu Christi Evangeliorum Versiones perantiquae duae, Gothica scil.* [by Junius] *et Anglo-Saxonica* [by Thomas Marshall] (Dordrecht, 1665); P. J. Lucas, *Franciscus Junius Cædmonis Monachi Paraphrasis Poetica Genesios ac praecipuarm Sacrae paginae Historiarum* (Amsterdam, 1997) [facsimile of 1655 edition]; F. Madan, H. H. E. Craster and N. Denholm-Young, *Summary Catalogue of Western Manuscripts in the Bodleian Library at Oxford* (Oxford, 1937), ii/2. 962–90.

P. J. LUCAS

JUNIUS MANUSCRIPT. The Junius manuscript, now Oxford, Bodleian Library, Junius 11, is a unique and enigmatic member of the small group of books preserving substantial amounts of Old English verse. The long sequence of biblical poetry in Junius 11 comprises verse now identified by the titles *Genesis (or *Genesis A* and *B*), *Exodus, *Daniel and *Christ and Satan. The book's collective contents strikingly resemble the body of work ascribed by *Bede to the oral poet *Cædmon, who is said to have sung about 'the Creation of the world, the origin of the human race and the whole history of Genesis, and the departure of Israel from Egypt', among other topics of the Old and New Testaments. However, the stylistic variation evinced by different parts of the biblical sequence, along with certain literary-historical considerations (such as the Old Saxon basis of *Genesis B*), mark them decisively as products of multiple authorship. The attribution of the collection as a whole to Cædmon has long since been abandoned by literary scholars, but the designation 'Cædmon manuscript' is still employed occasionally by historians of art.

Alone among surviving collections of Old English verse, Junius 11 was designed from the start as a generously illustrated picture-book. A series of spaces, accommodating (or intended to accommodate) scriptural illustrations, spans the whole length of the Old Testament sequence. Spaces adjoining the text of approximately the first five-eighths of *Genesis* display the work of two main artists, who are jointly responsible for almost fifty completed line-drawings in brown ink, the second artist employing a limited amount of coloured ink to embellish his contributions. For reasons unknown, the illustrations were never executed for which the blank spaces in the remainder of the Old Testament sequence were set aside. The completed illustrations include remarkable depictions of God enthroned above the primordial chaos; of Adam and Eve, who stand undraped and bashful after their Fall; and of a snaky-locked Satan chained in hell.

The palaeography and *codicology of Junius 11 pose many problems, notably regarding the unity of the volume. A single scribe has copied out the verse of *Genesis, Exodus* and *Daniel*, which occupy 212 of the book's 232 extant leaves. The distribution of the Roman numerals which precede certain sections of the sequence suggests that all of the Old Testament verse in Junius 11 had already been joined together in the scribe's exemplar. Leaves containing the last part of *Daniel* appear to have been lost during the Anglo-Saxon period. In their place we find an atypical gathering of leaves on which the verse of *Christ and Satan* has been entered by several hands, none of which may be identified securely as that of the main scribe of Junius 11. The independent character of these *Christ and Satan* leaves is further indicated by the width of their written area, which is notably greater than that observed elsewhere in Junius 11, and by the intrusion of a pronounced horizontal crease running across the middle part of every page. The crease plausibly attests to the former use of these leaves as part of a folded, portable booklet. Yet another scribal hand has copied (or, more precisely, recopied) the final lines of *Christ and Satan*, followed by the words *finit liber .ii. amen* ('The second book is finished. Amen'), on the final, uncreased leaf of Junius 11, which is physically conjoint with the last surviving *Daniel* leaf. It is thus apparent that the parchment formerly serving as the outer wrapper of the booklet preserving *Christ and Satan* (and containing the final lines of its verse) was discarded before the creased leaves were inserted into the remains of the final *Daniel* gathering. Accordingly, the manuscript in its present state must be viewed as forming a composite codex in two books (*libri*). Nevertheless, it is worth stressing that Junius 11 was conceived as such during the Anglo-Saxon period, having been intended by the architects of the volume itself – though not, perhaps, by the main scribes of either the Old Testament sequence or *Christ and Satan* – as a collection of biblical verse treating themes of both the Old Testament and the New.

The existence of Junius 11 was first brought to the attention of the public by Francis *Junius, who received the manuscript around 1651 as a gift from the archbishop of Armagh, James Ussher (1581–1656), known as a prolific book-buyer and patron of libraries. Junius issued the first edition of the volume's biblical verse, now known accordingly as the Junius poems, in 1655. The place of origin and the provenance of the manuscript are uncertain, centres at *Canterbury (notably Christ Church), *Winchester and *Malmesbury having occasioned the greatest amount of speculation in these regards. A series of illustrations depicting the virtues and vices (as allegorized in Prudentius's *Psychomachia*), preserved in the so-called Corpus Prudentius (Cambridge, Corpus Christi College 23, fols. 1–40), is almost certainly to be identified as the work of the second artist of Junius 11, an artist whose training in techniques of *illumination appears to have taken in styles originating at Christ Church, Canterbury. To judge by an inscription in Latin verse near the beginning of the Corpus Prudentius, the donation of that book to Malmesbury Abbey before *c.*1050 is probable. There is no evidence, however, to indicate any similar donation of Junius 11 to Malmesbury, and the production of either of the manuscripts (or both) in the *scriptorium at Malmesbury, though possible, remains doubtful. An entry in a medieval booklist treating the holdings of Christ Church, Canterbury, prepared by Prior Eastry (1283–1331), mentions a *Genesis Anglice depicta* ('an illustrated Genesis in English'), which has been seen as a reference to the whole sequence of verse in Junius 11. The phrase *Genesis Anglic[e]*, however, elsewhere refers to an illustrated copy of the so-called Old English Hexateuch associated with *Ælfric, once housed at St Augustine's, Canterbury (the present London, BL, Cotton Claudius B. iv). The use of cord to secure the gatherings of leaves in

Junius 11 to the oak boards of their binding recalls a practice observed in Anglo-Saxon *bookbindings dated before *c.*1050. The present configuration of the volume's vellum-covered boards, however, has sometimes been dated to the post-Conquest period. In any case, the binding shows signs of formerly having been chained in place, suggesting that the extraordinary value of the codex was perceived in the Middle Ages. Wholly obscure is the identity of one Ælfwine, whose likeness is depicted (without monastic tonsure or dress) in a portrait-medallion on the second page of Junius 11 and who possibly commissioned the production of its text and illustrations.

The 'Cædmon Manuscript' of Anglo-Saxon Biblical Poetry, facs. ed., introd. I. Gollancz (London, 1927); G. Henderson, 'The Programme of Illustrations in Bodleian MS Junius XI', *Studies in Memory of David Talbot Rice,* ed. G. Robertson and G. Henderson (Edinburgh, 1975), pp. 113–45 with pls. 59–71; P. J. Lucas, 'MS Junius 11 and Malmesbury', *Scriptorium* 34 (1980), 197–220, and 35 (1981), 3–22; R. Thomson, 'Identifiable Books from the Pre-Conquest Library of Malmesbury Abbey', *ASE* 10 (1982), 1–19; B. C. Raw, 'The Construction of Oxford, Bodleian Library, Junius 11', *ASE* 13 (1984), 187–207; *Anglo-Saxon Textual Illustration,* ed. T. H. Ohlgren (Kalamazoo, MI, 1992); P. G. Remley, *Old English Biblical Verse,* CSASE 16 (Cambridge, 1996); M. Budny, *Insular, Anglo-Saxon, and Early Anglo-Norman Art at Corpus Christi College, Cambridge* (Kalamazoo, MI, 1997).

PAUL G. REMLEY

JURISDICTION, the range of the judicial or administrative capacity of a court. The *laws of *Kent and *Wessex show that local *courts had a place in the administration of justice in the early English kingdoms but little more than this is known about them. Local justice becomes more approachable in the tenth century, and the laws of King *Cnut in the early eleventh show that a hierarchical system of courts, in which both secular and ecclesiastical authorities had integral functions, had been in place for some decades. Litigants were expected to seek justice in the *hundred court before approaching the king, and in some circumstances they had to do the same before taking claims to the *shire court. But it is doubtful whether this system involved in practice rigid jurisdictional rules. Kings reserved to their own courts serious crimes with a political colour to them, but they often adjudicated other suits at first instance when they chose to do so. On the other hand they also sent disputes to the shire courts for resolution. It was important to publicize judgements, and proceedings were sometimes rehearsed in several forums. At lower levels jurisdiction based on local relevance must have been complicated by those borough courts which shared meeting places and suitors with shire courts, groups of hundreds which regularly met as a single court, and groups of shires which sometimes did. Sometimes local suits followed the hierarchical course laid down in the laws, but often enough they did not, and it is nowhere recorded that a claimant failed on the principle that he had begun his action in the wrong court. It was a principle that a litigant should make his claim or defence known as early and as publicly as possible; it would seem to follow that any convenient gathering ought be competent at least to hear the beginning of a suit.

How much of this system of 'public' courts came into private hands is difficult to assess. Shire courts remained public forums but courts at the hundred level may have become private franchises during Anglo-Saxon times. Kings had alienated some of the profits of justice perhaps as early as the seventh century, and the kings of England in the later tenth and eleventh centuries made very substantial grants of this kind, especially to the great religious houses. It is reasonable to suppose that those who took the penalties controlled the courts which imposed them, but it is in fact quite uncertain to what extent and how often these congeries of entitlements amounted to courtholding rights, especially the right to exclude royal officials from the deliberations of the court. The later laws assume that public courts are the norm, and it requires some ingenuity to find in them even oblique references to private jurisdiction. Some genuine Anglo-Saxon *writs of the eleventh century go some way towards making explicit grants of exclusive courtholding rights, but most such purported grants are Norman concoctions, and scarcely any is entirely above suspicion. Forgeries were not produced to no purpose and it may well be that the great immunities claimed by Norman landlords had as much to do with what they wanted as what they in fact acquired from their Anglo-Saxon predecessors.

At all events it is clear that neither manorial nor franchisal justice was as important in England as in the lands from which the new masters came. Circumstantial records of endowment and litigation concerning the monastery of *Ely in the late tenth century illuminate a regional world in which public courts flourished at some odds with the claims of the supposed 'foundation' *charter. Although *ealdormen and bishops exercised their considerable inherent authority to do sometimes very rough justice, there are no clear indications in these records that private courts had to this time made substantial encroachments upon public justice.

F. W. Maitland, *Domesday Book and Beyond* (Cambridge 1897, reissued with forward by J. C. Holt, 1987), pp. 80–107, 258–92; J. Goebel, *Felony and Misdemeanor. A Study in the History of English Criminal Procedure* (New York, 1937), pp. 336–440; H. Cam, 'The "Private" Hundred in England before the Norman Conquest', *Studies Presented to Sir Hilary Jenkinson*, ed. J. C. Davies (Oxford, 1957), pp. 50–60, repr. in H. Cam, *Law-Finders and Law-Makers in Medieval England* (London, 1962), pp. 59–70; A. Kennedy, 'Law and Litigation in the *Libellus Æthelwoldi Episcopi*', *ASE* 24 (1995), 131–83; P. Wormald, 'Lordship and Justice in the Early English Kingdom: Oswaldslow Revisited', in *Property and Power in the Early Middle Ages*, ed. W. Davies and P. Fouracre (Cambridge, 1995), pp. 114–36.

ALAN KENNEDY

JURY. Traditionally the talisman of English liberties and once traced back to Old English times, the panel of fellow-citizens commissioned to decide one's guilt or liability is so difficult to find in Anglo-Saxon laws or legal practice that historians since the German Heinrich Brunner and his English friend F. W. Maitland have tended to write it off altogether. The jury as such, that is a panel of twelve local men under oath to denounce persistent malefactors to the king's justices, is not well attested before Henry II's Assize of Clarendon (1166). It does not appear in the relatively copious if largely unofficial legal writing of the earlier twelfth century. There is no clear evidence of its activity in accounts of lawsuits from either side of the Conquest. Yet if it is to be ruled out as an institution of Anglo-Saxon *law, we are left with the problem of how there comes to be a single reference to something very like it in the 'third' code of *Æthelred II, issued at Wantage probably in 997: 'Let there be a meeting in each *wapentake; and let the twelve senior *thegns go out and swear on the relics . . . that they will not accuse any innocent man nor accuse any guilty one. And let them then take the suspect men against whom the *reeve proceeds . . .'. These thegns are undeniably fulfilling a role very like that of Henry II's juries of 'presentment' (i.e. indictment). The first clue to the resolution of this conundrum is to appreciate that the provisions of the Wantage code are at this point very close to, and to an extent the equivalent of, those issued by Æthelred at Woodstock shortly before. Here, it is the business of a man's sureties to bring him to justice if he be charged; and those so suspect as to lack surety

may be summarily despatched by the king's reeve. Surety in later Anglo-Saxon law was a function of the *frankpledge to which one belonged, as was everyday policing. It was thus a frankpledge that normally discharged the job assigned at Wantage to twelve senior thegns. The Wantage code was directed especially at the *Danelaw, for which previous legislation by *Edgar had established standing bodies of 'witnesses' (under oath), twelve for each *hundred (equivalent to wapentake). Hence, the twelve thegns are an aspect of the particular way that English justice worked in one-time Danish territory. A second and even more important point, however, is that from at the latest *Alfred's time, Englishmen were under an *oath, probably then, as certainly later, taken at the age of twelve, which bound them not to conceal robbery by their neighbours. This oath was quite possibly linked from the outset – as once again it certainly was at a later date – to enrolment in a frankpledge or surety-police group. The Carolingian system to which Brunner and Maitland traced the jury in fact involved no more (or less) in matters of *crime than a duty arising from a general oath of loyalty and good citizenship, like the one taken in tenth-century England. It thus becomes possible to suggest that the reason why Anglo-Saxon juries are heard of only in special circumstances is that the task they performed for Henry II was carried out by the citizenry at large, organized as it was in groups entrusted with that job. It was the English, not Henry, who borrowed from the Carolingians. As for Henry's jury itself: the likeliest people to have been recruited to its ranks were the heads of frankpledges; it was a new tactic, not, a revolutionary strategy, in a campaign against obdurate crime that began at least 250 years before.

Liebermann, *Gesetze* i. 228–9 [III Æthelred 3:1–2], ii. 466 ['Geschworene']; F. Pollock and F. W. Maitland, *The History of English Law*, 2 vols., reissued with introduction by S. F. C. Milson (Cambridge, 1968) i. 138–44; R. V. Turner, 'The Origins of the Medieval English Jury: Frankish, English or Scandinavian?', *Journal of British Studies* 7 (1968), 1–10; R. C. van Caenegem, 'Public Prosecution of Crime in Twelfth-century England', *Church and Government in the Middle Ages. Essays presented to C. R. Cheney on his 70th Birthday* (Cambridge, 1976), pp. 41–76.

PATRICK WORMALD

JUSTUS, ST (d. 627), was sent to England in 601 by Pope *Gregory the Great to reinforce the missionary work of St *Augustine of *Canterbury. He became the founding bishop of *Rochester in 604, and was subsequently elevated to the archiepiscopal see in 624. Like the other early archbishops of Canterbury, he was buried in St Augustine's Abbey, where there was an attempt to honour his memory in the 1090s. His body was translated to a new shrine behind the high altar, while *Goscelin of Saint-Bertin composed a short Life (*BHL* 4601) and Reginald of Canterbury a brief poem.

Sharpe, *Handlist*, 997; Bede, *HE* i.29, ii.3–17; *Acta SS*, Nov. iv. 535–6; F. Liebermann, 'Raginald von Canterbury', *Neues Archiv der Gesellschaft für ältere deutsche Geschichtskunde* 13 (1887–8), 519–56, at 550.

PAUL ANTONY HAYWARD

JUTES are one of the three 'very powerful Germanic tribes' whom *Bede believed had colonized Britain in the fifth century. It is usually assumed that they came from Jutland in Denmark. Bede identified as Jutish areas of settlement *Kent, under the leadership of *Hengest and Horsa, the Isle of Wight, and the southern part of Hampshire. The *Anglo-Saxon Chronicle* claims that the founders of the latter two provinces were, respectively, Stuf and Wihtgar and Port and his two sons.

N. Brooks, 'The Creation and Structure of the Kingdom of Kent', in Bassett, *Origins*, pp. 55–74; B. A. E. Yorke, 'The Jutes of Hampshire and Wight and the Origins of Wessex', ibid., pp. 84–96.

B. A. E. YORKE

K

KALENDAR: *see* Liturgical Books; Metrical Calendar, Latin; Metrical Calendar, OE

KEMBLE, J. M. (1807–57), Anglo-Saxonist. John Mitchell Kemble, elder brother of the renowned actress Fanny Kemble, was an undergraduate at Trinity College, Cambridge, and a prominent member of the free-thinking society known as 'The Apostles'. A trip to Germany in 1829–30 converted him from philosophy to philology, and, after a brief venture as a revolutionary in Spain (1830–1), he settled down in Cambridge where he embarked upon his edition of *Beowulf* (published in 1833) and lectured to dwindling audiences on the history of the English language (1834). Always a controversial figure, Kemble left Cambridge in 1835, and made his way as editor of a literary and political journal in London. He continued his work as an Anglo-Saxonist, publishing a six-volume edition of Anglo-Saxon charters (*Codex Diplomaticus Ævi Saxonici* (1839–48)), an edition of the legend of St Andrew in the *Vercelli Book (1843), an edition of *Solomon and Saturn (1848), and a two-volume historical work on *The Saxons in England* (1849); but he was unable all the while to gain the kind of advancement he sought. Kemble moved to Hanover in 1849, and undertook pioneering work on early Germanic archaeology, published posthumously as *Horae Ferales* (1863). He returned to London in 1855, and died on a visit to Ireland in March 1857; he is buried in St Jerome's Cemetery, Dublin. Kemble's books and working papers, kept together by his family for many years, are now widely dispersed.
B. Dickins, 'John Mitchell Kemble and Old English Scholarship' (1939), repr. in *British Academy Papers on Anglo-Saxon England*, ed. E. G. Stanley (Oxford, 1990), pp. 57–90; R. A. Wiley, ed., *John Mitchell Kemble and Jakob Grimm: a Correspondence 1832–52* (Leiden, 1971); P. Allen, *The Cambridge Apostles: the Early Years* (Cambridge, 1978); R. A. Wiley, 'Anglo-Saxon Kemble: the Life and Works of John Mitchell Kemble 1807–57, Philologist, Historian, Archaeologist', *ASSAH* 1 (1979), 165–273; S. Keynes, *Anglo-Saxon Manuscripts in the Library of Trinity College, Cambridge*, OEN Subsidia 18 (Binghamton, NY, 1992), 54–61; idem, 'Black Jack Kemble: Apostle, Revolutionary, and Anglo-Saxonist' (forthcoming).

SIMON KEYNES

KENELM, ST, the son and heir of *Coenwulf of *Mercia (d. 821), was supposedly, on succeeding to the throne at the age of seven, brutally murdered in Clent Forest (Worcs.) by his tutor Æscberht, at the behest of his sister Cwoenthryth. Although at first the body lay hidden, its whereabouts were miraculously revealed to the pope as he celebrated mass in *Rome. Once exhumed, Kenelm's remains were triumphantly carried to the royal palace and monastery at *Winchcombe (Glos.), where they were laid in a *shrine which immediately became the focus for miracles. This story, first recorded in the mid-eleventh-century, in a Latin Life of Kenelm (*BHL* 4641n–4641t) probably composed for Winchcombe by *Goscelin, contains some anachronisms, and it is difficult to be sure about the precise identity of Kenelm, and about the origins of the cult, which, judging from liturgical evidence, was already in existence by the later tenth century (feast: 17 July).
R. C. Love, ed. and trans., *Three Eleventh-Century Anglo-Latin Saints' Lives* (OMT, 1996), pp. lxxxix–cxxxix, 50–89.

R. C. LOVE

KENNING: *see* Poetic Technique, OE

KENT, KINGDOM OF. The Anglo-Saxon kingdom of Kent seems to have covered approximately the same area as the modern county, although it may at times have included parts of eastern Surrey. In Roman times Kent was the territory of the tribe known as the *Cantiaci*, whose capital lay at *Canterbury. Archaeological evidence from Canterbury suggests that Germanic settlers may already have been present in Kent in the later fourth century, perhaps employed as mercenaries or federates. The foundation-legend of the Kentish kingdom relates to the celebrated brothers *Hengest and Horsa, reputedly the ancestors of the Kentish royal dynasty, the *Oiscingas* (through Hengest's son Oisc). According to the developed versions of the story, the two brothers were invited to Britain by King Vortigern to defend his people, and were given the south-eastern corner of the island (i.e. Kent) in return for their services or as

269

a bride-price for Hengest's daughter. While the legendary details are easy to dismiss, there may be some grounds for the view that the Anglo-Saxon take-over of Kent was the result of a negotiated treaty rather than of a brutal invasion. Institutional continuity is difficult to prove, but it may be significant that the newcomers became known as the *Cantware*; it is rare in Anglo-Saxon England for a Romano-British tribal name to be preserved in that way. In later times Kentish customs in some respects differed from the Anglo-Saxon norm, for instance in the measurement of land and in inheritance patterns, and it may be that these differences go back to pre-English practices.

The English settlers in Kent were traditionally *Jutes, but they probably included members of other tribal groups. *Grave-goods from Kentish *cemeteries have strong cultural links with similar items from across the Channel, which may reflect an influx of *Franks or perhaps simply regular contact. Kent lay on the trading-route between *London and the Continent, and exploitation of this good fortune (in the form of taxes and tolls) may account for the wealth of the Kentish kingdom, already evident in the sixth-century cemeteries. Contact with the Frankish rulers led to marriage links: *Æthelberht (d. 616) married Bertha, the daughter of a former king of Paris, while his son Eadbald (d. 640) married another Frankish aristocrat. Æthelberht was an extremely powerful ruler, one of those whom *Bede mentions as holding *imperium* or rule over all the English kingdoms south of the Humber (*HE* ii. 5). In 597 he welcomed *Augustine and his fellow-missionaries, and established them in Canterbury, which is described as his *metropolis* or principal city; soon after this he was baptised, and encouraged the conversion of his people. Canterbury became Augustine's episcopal seat, but a second see was established at *Rochester in 604 (*HE* ii. 3), even though during the early stages of the conversion it was usual for only one bishop to be appointed for each Anglo-Saxon kingdom.

Kent remained a strong independent kingdom until a brief civil war in 685 and the death in the following year of the usurper Eadric. Intruders backed by other kingdoms briefly installed themselves, but by 694 the ancient Kentish line had been restored in the person of Wihtred (d. 725). Wihtred ruled a strong and united kingdom, but after his death Kent was divided between his three sons. One of these disappeared almost immediately, while the remaining two seem to have established themselves respectively in east and west Kent. The senior partner was Æthelberht II

(d. 762), who was based in the wealthier eastern half of the kingdom (including Canterbury); his brother Eadberht II (d. 748) took the western portion, which was inherited by his son Eardwulf. Both these men probably recognised the overlordship of the Mercian king *Æthelbald (see *HE* v. 23). After the death of Æthelberht II, political stability in Kent seems to have disintegrated. Over the next few years there was a rapid turnover of kings, some of them probably foreign nominees, and by 764 it would seem that Kent had fallen under the firm control of *Offa, king of *Mercia. There is some sign that the Kentish people resented this level of domination. In 776 there was a battle at Otford between the Mercians and the men of Kent. No contemporary source reports the outcome, but it may be significant that there is no evidence of Kentish submission to Offa for another nine years; local rulers granted away land without acknowledging Offa's permission for the transaction. This situation had come to an end by 785, in which year Offa issued the first in a series of *charters disposing of land in Kent without reference to a Kentish king: it would seem that he had ejected or killed the local rulers. Kentish rebellion was not dead, and after Offa's death in 796 there was a full-scale revolt led by a certain Eadberht Præn, a former priest who may have been a representative of the ancient Kentish dynasty. This revolt was put down with chilling severity by the Mercian king *Coenwulf in 798; Eadberht was horribly mutilated and imprisoned. Perhaps as a conciliatory measure, Coenwulf gave Kent its own king in the shape of his brother Cuthred, who ruled as his subordinate; but after Cuthred died in 807 Coenwulf ruled the province directly. Like Offa, he seems rarely if ever to have set foot in the province, preferring to administer it through decrees issued at *councils held elsewhere. Kent remained a Mercian possession until the Mercian domination collapsed in the 820s; it then fell to *Ecgberht of Wessex, whose father may have ruled briefly in Kent in the period after the battle of Otford.

N. Brooks, 'The Creation and Early Structure of the Kingdom of Kent', in Bassett, *Origins*, pp. 55–74; Brooks, *Canterbury*; A. Everitt, *Continuity and Colonization: the Evolution of Kentish Settlement* (Leicester, 1986); *The Charters of St Augustine's Abbey, Canterbury, and Minster-in-Thanet*, ed. S. E. Kelly, Anglo-Saxon Charters 5 (Oxford, 1995); T. Tatton-Brown, 'The Towns of Kent', in Haslam, *Towns*, pp. 1–36; S. Keynes, 'The Control of Kent in the Ninth Century', *EME* 2 (1993), 111–31.

S. E. KELLY

KENTISH DIALECT: *see* Dialects

KINGS AND KINGSHIP were the dominant political organisation in England during the Anglo-Saxon period. The foundation myths which survive for some of the Anglo-Saxon kingdoms depict their founders as military leaders who won their kingdoms by defeating British rulers in battle in the late fifth and sixth centuries. Whatever the truth of these accounts, warleadership can be seen to be a major activity of kings in the seventh and eighth centuries, and a major source of revenue through the collection of tribute. Early Anglo-Saxon kings strengthened their positions by drawing upon traditional attributes of Germanic kingship, which included custodianship of the law and a belief in descent from the gods. In the surviving *genealogies, Anglo-Saxon kings traced descent from Woden, except the East Saxons who claimed descent from the Saxon god Seaxnet. Anglo-Saxon kings may also have inherited facets of their power from British rulers who came to pre-eminence following Britain's separation from the Roman empire in the early fifth century. The kingdom of *Kent, for instance, preserves both the name and territory of a Roman *civitas*.

In the seventh century we can identify at least twelve provinces whose rulers are regularly described as kings (*reges*). It is a moot point whether smaller territories, which tend to appear in sources of the seventh and eighth centuries as subdistricts (*regiones*) of the larger kingdoms, had once had their own 'tribal' kings, but, if they had, little confirmation of such a status appears in the written records. Competition and intermarriage led to the amalgamation of kingdoms so that at the beginning of the ninth century only four Anglo-Saxon kingdoms remained: *East Anglia, *Mercia, *Northumbria and *Wessex. Former kingdoms might retain some territorial identity as *shires, or similar subdivisions of the larger kingdoms, managed by *ealdormen on behalf of the rulers. Kings regularly travelled within their kingdoms, being supported as they did so by the foodrents or *feorm* which they could claim from the substantial estates of the royal demesne. Although kings came under increasing pressure to grant land to their followers, an important principle was established, developed particularly by the Mercian kings *Æthelbald and *Offa, that kings retained certain inalienable rights over land, including the right to exact military services (cf. *trinoda necessitas*).

The development of kingship was also aided by the advent of Christianity which was adopted by all the Anglo-Saxon royal houses in the course of the seventh century. Christianity was attractive to kings because of the respect they could command as Christ's representatives on earth. It carried the prestige of the late Roman empire, and brought *literacy and *classical learning to the Anglo-Saxons, as well as new concepts such as Roman land *law. Christianity's efficacy as a religion would have seemed guaranteed through its adoption by the most powerful kingdoms in Europe, including that of the Anglo-Saxons' nearest continental neighbours, the *Franks. Advances in the Christian concepts of kingship under the Carolingian rulers were copied in Anglo-Saxon England, as can be seen in the introduction of the *coronation ritual and in the lawcodes of *Alfred of Wessex and his successors.

Attacks by pagan *Vikings in the ninth century encouraged kings like Alfred to present themselves as patrons of the church and the protectors of Christianity among the Anglo-Saxon peoples. After the 'great army' had deposed the royal houses of East Anglia, Northumbria and Mercia, the West Saxon royal house under *Edward the Elder and his sons were able to win the submission of the other Anglo-Saxon provinces and so become kings of England. Military achievements were underpinned by ceremonial. *Edgar had a second coronation at Bath in 973 as part of his successful bid to be recognised as the most powerful of the rulers of the British Isles. Edgar's reign saw a further strengthening of the bonds of church and state when the king supported major monastic reforms instigated by Bishop *Æthelwold and Archbishop *Dunstan. However, stress on the priestly nature of the office of king was not sufficient to prevent the murder of Edgar's son King *Edward the Martyr, though it may have helped make him a saint.

The united kingdom of England was very effectively controlled through royal officers and a network of local administration based on the *hundreds and *wapentakes. The strength, if not the oppression, of royal government is demonstrated by the regularity with which *coinage was renewed at the *mints, and by King *Æthelred the Unready's ability to collect large sums in tribute to pay the Vikings and to institute the *heregeld*. Although the scale was greater, the forms of government available to the later Saxon kings had evolved out of earlier systems. Restrictions on royal power continued to exist. The king's *council may have become more elaborate, but it remained vital for kings to rule with the consent and advice of their leading men. In spite of the wealth and grandeur surrounding later Anglo-Saxon kingship (or perhaps because of its allure), the country was vulnerable to foreign attack. Military strength never ceased to be the basis of royal power in the early middle ages. With the conquests of *Swein Forkbeard, *Cnut and William of Normandy we appear to come full circle, with successful, invading warleaders able to establish new dynasties in England.

J. M. Wallace-Hadrill, *Early Germanic Kingship in England and on the Continent* (Oxford, 1971); J. Campbell, E. John and P. Wormald, *The Anglo-Saxons* (Oxford, 1982); Loyn, *Governance*; S. Reynolds, *Kingdoms and Communities in Western Europe, 900–1300* (Oxford, 1984); Campbell, *Essays*; Bassett *Origins*; Kirby, *Kings*; Stafford, *Unification*; Yorke, *Kingdoms*; S. Keynes, 'England, 700–900', in *The New Cambridge Medieval History*, II *c.*700–*c.*900, ed. R. McKitterick (Cambridge, 1995), pp. 18–42; J. Nelson, 'Kingship and Royal Government', ibid. pp. 383–430.

B. A. E. YORKE

KINGSTON-UPON-THAMES, Surrey. A royal estate situated on the south bank of the river Thames, at about its highest tidal point. It was in a meeting convened at Kingston in 838 that *Ecgberht, king of the West Saxons, and his son King *Æthelwulf, reached an agreement with *Ceolnoth, archbishop of *Canterbury, symbolising the culmination of the process whereby the south-eastern provinces (*Kent, *Surrey, *Sussex, *Essex) were brought into the realm of the West Saxon kings (S 1438). In the tenth century (if not before) Kingston became the favoured site for royal ceremonial, perhaps reflecting the importance of the Thames, and *London, in the emergence of the 'kingdom of the *Anglo-Saxons' and the 'kingdom of the English'. *Æthelstan was consecrated at Kingston on 4 September 925; King *Eadred was consecrated there in August 946; and King *Æthelred the Unready was consecrated there on 4 May 979. There is some evidence that *Edward the Elder (900), *Edmund (939), *Eadwig (956), *Edgar (*c.*960) and *Edward the Martyr (975) were also consecrated at Kingston. According to John Stow, writing in the late sixteenth century, King Æthelstan's coronation 'was celebrated in the market place [at Kingston] upon a stage erected on hie, that the king might be seene the better of the multitude'. It was later presumed that the kings were crowned in the ancient chapel of St Mary, which adjoined the south side of the parish church and which collapsed in 1730. A large stone recovered from the ruins of the chapel has been regarded since the eighteenth century as a 'coronation stone'; it was set up initially beside the town hall, and used as mounting block, but in 1850 it was accorded a more dignified station in the market place, where it remains. A number of late-fifteenth-century paintings of kings crowned at Kingston, seen by John Aubrey in the chapel of St Mary, were removed to Baston House, in Kent, and are now preserved in the rooms of the Society of Antiquaries (London).

W. E. St L. Finny, 'The Saxon Church at Kingston-upon-Thames', *Journal of the Archaeological Association* n.s. 32 (1926), 253–64; J. Blair, *Early Medieval Surrey: Landholding, Church and Settlement before 1300* (Stroud, 1991), pp. 99–101; Brooks, *Canterbury*, pp. 197–203, 323–5 (for S 1438); S. Keynes, *The Diplomas of King Æthelred 'the Unready' 978–1016* (Cambridge, 1980), pp. 270–1; idem, 'The West Saxon Charters of King Æthelwulf and his Sons', *EHR* 109 (1994), 1109–49, at 1112–14.

SIMON KEYNES

KINSHIP played a central part in the structural framework of Anglo-Saxon society. The maintenance of law and order depended to a large extent on the collective responsibility of individual kindreds for the safety and good conduct of their members; and the rights and obligations of kinship groups feature prominently in the *laws. It was the duty of the kindred to seek justice for a member who was killed or injured, either by prosecuting a *feud or by exacting the appropriate financial compensation: cf. *wergild. Conversely, they were required to ensure that an accused member appeared to answer the charge. If convicted, a member could expect food and support from the kindred while in prison as well as assistance in meeting the prescribed penalty; but no aid could be given to an outlaw. A woman's interests continued to be safeguarded after *marriage by her own kindred, and the paternal kin were responsible for administering the property of orphaned minors. Certain types of heritable land were inalienable from the kin group: cf. *land tenure.

Unlike the extended kin groups of early Scandinavian and Celtic societies, the focal unit in Anglo-Saxon England was the nuclear family. This is reflected both in the imprecision of Old English terminology for more distant degrees of kinship, and in legislation pertaining to inheritance and to compensation. According to II Cnut 70, the property of a man who died intestate belonged exclusively to his *widow, *children, and close relatives; and similarly the first instalment of *wergild was payable to close relatives of the deceased (*Wer* 5). Spiritual kinship, through sponsorship at baptism, was also formally recognised, with godfathers and godsons being entitled to the same amount of compensation as a dead man's lord in seventh-century Wessex (Ine 76), and *marriage being forbidden between spiritual relatives by the reign of *Æthelred the Unready (VI Æthelred 12, I Cnut 7).

The plight of the kinless man is movingly depicted in Old English poetry; and the importance of kinship within the legal system made it necessary to provide safeguards for people without an effective kin group, including foreigners, foundlings, ecclesiastics, and emancipated slaves. In such cases, the role of the kindred was commonly transferred either to the king or to a group of associates. According to the laws of *Ine, the wergild of an illegitimate child disowned by its father was to be divided between its lord and the king (ch. 27), and that of a kinless foreigner between his *gesith* (variously interpreted as protector or associates) and the king (ch. 23). *Alfred's law-code directs that if a kinless man was killed, his associates were to receive half the wergild and the king the other half (ch. 28). The king was also to act as kinsman and protector towards an ecclesiastic or a foreigner who was robbed or killed (Edward and Guthrum 12, VIII Æthelred 33, II Cnut 40), and received the share of wergild for a nun's child that would normally have been payable to the maternal kin (Alfred 8). The wergild of an emancipated slave belonged to the former owner (Wihtred 8).

The extent of the kin-group's obligation to contribute to the payment of compensation incurred by one of its members is uncertain. Æthelberht 23 states that the relatives of an absconding homicide were responsible for half the amount; but it is unclear whether this applied only in the event of the slayer's flight. Alfred's law-code may indicate that a homicide was personally responsible for only part of the compensation, since ch. 27 directs that if a man without paternal kin committed murder, his maternal relatives were to pay one third of the wergild and his associates another third, while if there were no maternal kin, the associates were to pay half. Again, however, an allusion to the slayer's flight makes it possible that their liability was conditional only. Later legislation refers to the kindred's responsibility to provide surety for payment (II Edmund 7), and it has been suggested that this may have replaced the obligation to contribute. As late as the eleventh century, however, the relatives of a priest accused of homicide were obliged either to assist in clearing him of the charge or to share with him in the feud

or compensation payment (VIII Æthelred 23, I Cnut 5,2b).

The potential for conflict between the dual obligations of kinship and of lordship is already reflected in the account of Cynewulf and Cyneheard in the *Anglo-Saxon Chronicle* entry for 757. Secular law supported the lord's authority – for instance, Alfred 42 forbids a man to fight against his lord in defence of a kinsman – and kinship ties tended to become progressively weaker during the later Anglo-Saxon period. Nonetheless, certain kindreds remained so strong that it was necessary for III Æthelstan 6 to direct that where a kindred was powerful enough to protect one of its members from the law, the wrongdoer should be moved to another part of the kingdom. There were also situations where a kin group could choose to renounce its rights. According to II Edward 6, the kindred could disclaim responsibility for a convicted thief, thereby forfeiting their subsequent right to his wergild; and II Edmund 1 also allows the kindred to disown a murderer, granting them exemption from the feud provided they give him no support. A freeman had the right not to associate himself with a relative who was a slave, and a slave had a similar right not to associate himself with a free relative (Ine 74,2).

L. Lancaster, 'Kinship in Anglo-Saxon Society, Parts I and II', *British Journal of Sociology* 9 (1958), 230–50, 359–77; D. A. Bullough, 'Early Medieval Social Groupings: the Terminology of Kinship', *P&P* 45 (1968), 3–18; T. M. Charles-Edwards, 'Kinship, Status and the Origins of the Hide', *P&P* 56 (1972), 3–33; H. R. Loyn, 'Kinship in Anglo-Saxon England', *ASE* 3 (1974), 197–209; C. Fell, 'Family and Kinship', in her *Women in Anglo-Saxon England* (London, 1984), pp. 74–88; S. D. White, 'Kinship and Lordship in Early Medieval England: the Story of Sigeberht, Cynewulf, and Cyneheard', *Viator* 20 (1989), 1–18.

CAROLE HOUGH

KOENWALD (Cenwald), bishop of *Worcester (928/9–58). Koenwald was probably of Mercian origin, and would appear to have served as a priest in the household of King *Æthelstan; in which capacity he may have been responsible for drafting the inscription which recorded how Æthelstan, 'king of the Anglo-Saxons', presented the 'Mac-Durnan Gospels' (London, Lambeth Palace Library, 1370) to the see of *Canterbury. (The *inscription anticipates the distinctive formulation of a group of *charters associated with Koenwald, on which see further below.) Koenwald was appointed bishop of Worcester some time between 16 April 928 (the date of the latest charter attested by his predecessor, Wilferth) and October 929 (when, as a bishop, his presence was recorded in *Germany). Hrotsvitha of Gandersheim relates in the *Gesta Ottonis* (written in the 960s) how Henry the Fowler set about finding a suitable bride for his son Otto (the future emperor Otto I), and how Æthelstan responded by giving him a choice between two of his half-sisters, Edith and *Adiva*; in the event, Otto married Edith, towards the end of 929 or early in 930. It is known that in 929 Koenwald was entrusted by King Æthelstan with the leadership of an expedition to Germany: he arrived at the abbey of St Gallen on 15 October 929, and it was in connection with this expedition that the names of King Æthelstan and others were entered in the confraternity books of St Gallen and Reichenau (cf. *liturgical commemoration). The possibility arises, therefore, that it was Koenwald who accompanied the king's half-sisters to the German court, and that the bishop went on in the course of the same expedition to advertise the king's distinction by distributing quantities of silver entrusted to him for the purpose, to visit religious houses throughout the kingdom of Germany (his stated purpose at St Gallen), to establish personal contacts, and perhaps to collect relics and books. In this way Koenwald would have acquired some knowledge of the monastic reform movement gathering pace on the Continent, and it might well have been through him that this knowledge passed to others at King Æthelstan's court, including *Dunstan and *Æthelwold. Little is known of Koenwald's activities as bishop of Worcester in the 930s and 940s, though there is reason to believe that he took monastic vows, that he was a prominent figure at court, and, in particular, that he was entrusted on occasion with the production of royal charters. The charters in question, ranging in date from 940 to 956, were drawn up in a self-consciously 'literary' style (replete with alliterative and rhythmical phrases), and display a combination of distinctive features which set them apart from what may be identified as the diplomatic mainstream. For example, the text is cast in the third person; the king is conceived as one who ruled the 'Anglo-Saxons', with (or without) the Northumbrians, pagans, and Britons; and certain unusual categories of witnesses – notably Welsh sub-kings, northern earls, assistant bishops, and abbots – are admitted into the witness-lists, in apparent imitation of a practice employed by the draftsman of charters issued in the name of King Æthelstan between 928 and 935. The circumstances in which the so-called 'alliterative' charters were produced are not yet fully understood; but there can be little doubt that they are the work of a single agency, operating for various beneficiaries (though generally in respect of estates lying north of the Thames) on the occasion of meetings of the king and his councillors held in different parts of the kingdom. The identification of the agency responsible for the production of these charters depends on a number of seemingly insignificant details which in combination point towards Bishop Koenwald, or a member of the bishop's entourage. In terms of their diplomatic, the charters have Mercian antecedents, and in other respects a Mercian complexion. Koenwald is the only witness who occurs in all the charters with unabbreviated witness-lists; and although the type was revived on at least one later occasion (in 1013), the main series ends with a charter dated 956, before Koenwald's death in 958. Koenwald is explicitly described in the witness-lists of four charters as *monachus* (S 544, 566, 569, 633), suggesting respect for the condition which set him apart from other bishops; in S 544, his name was displayed in larger script. An inscription added in the mid tenth century on the last page of the famous copy of the OE *Pastoral Care* which King Alfred had sent to *Werferth, bishop of Worcester, incorporates an innocuous phrase tellingly reminiscent of the charters; the inscription ends 'Koenwald monachus. Ælfric clericus hoc conposuit' (Oxford, Bodleian Library, Hatton 20, 98v), as if it had been entered by Ælfric on Koenwald's authority. Finally, a lease issued by Bishop Koenwald in 957, which happens to be the first of the important series of Worcester leases stretching forwards into the 990s and beyond, also displays unmistakable elements of the 'alliterative' style (S 1290). The clerk Ælfric was presumably a member of the bishop's community at Worcester; interestingly, the witnesses to Koenwald's lease include an Ælfric, who recurs as a deacon and a priest in leases issued by Bishop *Oswald in 962–3. Koenwald attested one of the charters issued by King *Edgar in 958, but was succeeded in that year, or in 959, by Dunstan. The obit of a 'Bishop Koenwald' who had been a monk of Glastonbury was recorded in a Glastonbury calendar on 28 June (William of Malmesbury, *De antiquitate Glastonie*, c. 67), suggesting that Koenwald may have been attached in some way to the community over which Dunstan had presided from *c.*940 to 956. He was remembered at Worcester as 'a man of great humility and a professed monk' (*Chronicle of John of Worcester*, s.a. 957).

Stenton, *ASE*, p. 444; C. R. Hart, *The Early Charters of Northern England and the North Midlands* (Leicester,

1975), pp. 310–11; S. Keynes, 'King Athelstan's Books', Clemoes FS, pp. 143–201, at 153–9 [alliterative charters], 198–201 [visit to Germany]; *Facsimiles of Anglo-Saxon Charters*, ed. S. Keynes (Oxford, 1991), p. 12 [no. 43]; Hart, *Danelaw*, pp. 431–53.

SIMON KEYNES

L

LABOUR SERVICE. Most rulers and land-owners in early medieval northern Europe could demand labour in some form from the inhabitants of the land they ruled or owned: the extreme form of labour rent extracted from the servile tenants of the post-Conquest manor has come to stand for what was once a much wider category. We may divide labour rent, as contemporaries probably did, according to the circumstances under which it was performed, rather than the task itself. It was these circumstances which determined whether the performance of labour rent was compatible with the personal freedom of those who performed it (see *social class).

Most rural societies embody a generally-accepted obligation of neighbours to help each other at times of the greatest and most urgent need for labour: harvest and haymaking. Dominant figures were able to channel these obligations to service central places. The customs owed by the people of the early land unit known as the *scir* included labour of this sort, as did the service owed at royal vills. Typical customs were a limited number of days' ploughing, harvesting and hay-making. As the recipient of dues which had once gone to the king, the owner of even a small book-land estate could probably expect inputs of this kind from the local peasantry. Many customs were connected with the visits of powerful figures on circuit from centre to centre. Locally-provided services were essential to the running of these itinerant courts: the collection of **feorm*, attendance on the powerful and the administration of their property, carrying messages, supplying animals for transport, guarding prisoners. Services connected with *hunting figure largely: building hunting lodges, driving game, feeding and training dogs, keeping up deer-hedges. The repair of buildings and the surrounding fence or palisade, for which expensive timber was needed, also figure. These more responsible tasks, and especially those for which riding-horses were required, were due from an upper echelon in rural society, below the rank of the nobility, a class called in some texts *geneats*, in others *thegns or drengs. In some areas they were referred to as 'riding-men'.

The purely agricultural services endured to appear on the post-Conquest estate as boon-works, a set number of days' seasonal work due from all the tenants at ploughing, haymaking and harvest, often with strict conditions about what the tenant was entitled to in food and drink and the number of hours he or she must work. None of the services just described was seen as dishonourable.

As well as these episodic and limited services, regular labour rent was essential to the exploitation of the inland (see *estate management). Insofar as it is recorded in the scanty documentation this took the form of 'week-work', later limited to a set number of days a week but possibly once unlimited, in return for a plot of land. An important *law of *Ine reveals that a landlord who had supplied his tenant with a house as well as a 'yard of land' (this is generally taken to mean an arable holding) could demand labour from him as well as cash rent.

Landlords deployed week-work on the major agricultural tasks: ploughing, harrowing, weeding, harvesting, ditching. Ploughing was sometimes measured in a fixed amount of land to be ploughed with the tenant's own team. The *gebur* is likely to have been this kind of *peasant, heavily dependent on a landlord for the land which was his livelihood. Smaller plots were leased to inland worker-tenants such as the people recorded in *Domesday Book as 'bordars' and cottagers who probably worked as general agricultural labourers, although those who had a share in a plough-team would be expected to contribute to ploughing the lord's arable.

The terms on which these dependant tenants rented land, sometimes even the tenancies themselves, were very much the same as those of post-Conquest customary tenants with a yardland or fraction of one. With the development of the common law categories of villein and villeinage these tenants, their land, and the terms on which they held it, came to be seen as legally unfree: hence the week-work they typically owed became *par excellence* a mark of serfdom.

R. J. Faith, *The English Peasantry and the Growth of Lordship* (London, 1997); H. P. R. Finberg, 'Anglo-Saxon England to 1042', in *The Agrarian History of England and Wales* I. AD 43–1042, ed. H. P. R. Finberg (Cambridge, 1972), pp. 385–525; R. V. Lennard, *Rural*

England 1086–1135: a Study of Social and Agrarian Conditions (Oxford, 1959), pp. 364–92.

ROSAMOND FAITH

LAMBETH PSALTER: *see* Psalter Glosses

LANDSCAPE: *see* Aerial Reconnaissance; Agriculture; Field Systems; Settlement Patterns; Woodland

LAND TENURE. The best-known tenure in pre-Conquest England is probably *bookland, sometimes contrasted with folkland. Bookland, like the royal *charter or *landboc* which established it, was introduced by and for the church in the seventh century. Religious houses needed stable endowments, and the charter granted tenure in perpetuity, with freedom of alienation. The latter stipulation may seem contradictory, since the land was intended to remain in the grantee's possession. The explanation may lie in a common distinction between property which was inherited from an ancestor, and that which was acquired in the lifetime of the testator. Disposition of the latter was more or less free, whereas the descent of the former was limited by the customary rights of kinsmen, though precisely what they were is never specified. Bookland may be regarded as a type of acquisition, whereas folkland, references to which are rare and difficult to interpret, may be land governed by the customary laws of inheritance. The charter, which creates a perpetual right of free bequest, enables the grantor to donate to the church land on which his kin had no claim.

When bookland was itself bequeathed, testators might set limits on its freedom of alienation. King *Alfred's *will requires some who have received his booklands not to dispose of them outside his kindred and then only in the male line, though other estates can be given 'on the female side as well as the male side'. Alfred's *laws allow similar arrangements to his subjects: a man who has inherited bookland may not dispose of it outside his kindred, if there is a document or witness to show that those who acquired it had prohibited this. By the eleventh century, any distinction between bookland and inherited land had probably largely vanished, and any inherited land was likely to be regarded as bookland, whatever its original status. This could create problems in the case of temporary grants (see discussion of loanland, below).

Bookland was also freed from worldly dues, so that the religious communities for which it was first intended could concentrate on their spiritual duties. It is unlikely, however, that all secular service was ever remitted, especially after kings began to issue charters for lay nobles. From the eighth century in *Mercia and the ninth in *Wessex, military service and the more serious judicial fines were always reserved from exemption, and by the eleventh century, bookland could be forfeited to the king if the military service was not performed (see *Trinoda necessitas*).

All the lesser dues which were exempted could be diverted by the beneficiary for his own benefit. These rights are summarized as 'sake and soke', but jurisdiction was only one of the mediatized dues; sake and soke covered other renders, in cash and kind, which *Domesday Book describes as *consuetudines*, customary dues. Those who dwelt on the land covered by the book continued to hold their property, but the services which they had once performed for the king, at a royal vill, were now due to the hall of the beneficiary and their lands were appurtenant to the vill where that hall lay. The tributary holdings are often called sokeland, to distinguish them from the property of the landlord (OE *landhlaford*, *landrica*). The holders could still (as Domesday says) 'give or sell' their lands, though the service due could not be withdrawn. Nor did the *landrica* automatically hold the personal commendation of the holders of sokeland; they were free (to quote Domesday again) 'to commend themselves (*se vertere*) to whatever lord they would' (there are numerous variants of this formula but the import is the same). It is in this sense that men could have two lords: a personal lord (*hlaford*), to whom they were commended, and a landlord who was entitled to the service from their lands.

Unlike sokeland, loanland (*lænland*) belonged to the lord (*hlaford*) who bestowed it, in return for service, upon his man; *lænland* reverted to the donor if the service was not performed. The usual term for such grants was three lives (recipient, widow and one heir), but single-life terms are also known. *Lænland* could be difficult to recover at the end of the term if the heirs proved obstructive; there are cases of priests and monks being bribed to hand over the landbooks relating to such estates, so that the tenants could claim outright ownership. It sometimes happened too that the *lænland* of a miscreant was confiscated along with his own land, even though it should have reverted to the original grantor. Similar to *lænland* is thegnland, again land granted by a lord in return for service; the distinction seems to be that grants of thegnland involved smaller amounts of land, and perhaps more specific services. Virtually all known *læns* are granted by ecclesiastics, but this is a function of the way in which the evidence has survived, and it is unlikely that lay lords did not make similar grants to their men.

A. G. Kennedy, 'Disputes about *Bocland*: the Forum for their Adjudication', *ASE* 14 (1985), 175–95; S. Reynolds, 'Bookland, Folkland and Fiefs', *ANS* 14 (1992), 211–27; D. Roffe, 'From Thegnage to Barony: Sake and Soke, Title and Tenants in Chief', *ANS* 12 (1990), 157–76; P. Wormald, *Bede and the Conversion of England: the Charter Evidence*, Jarrow Lecture 1984 (Jarrow, 1985); idem, 'Charters, Laws and the Settlement of Disputes in Anglo-Saxon England', *The Settlement of Disputes in Early Medieval Europe*, ed. W. Davies and P. Fouracre (Cambridge, 1986), pp. 149–68.

ANN WILLIAMS

LANTFRED (fl. 975), sometime monk of the Old Minster, Winchester, and author of the earliest account of the miracles which took place following the translation of the relics of Bishop *Swithun into the Old Minster on 15 July 971 (the *Translatio et miracula S. Swithuni: BHL* 7944–6). Very little is known of Lantfred's life, save that he was of continental Frankish origin (Ælfric describes him as *se oferscæwisca*, and various Latinized French words occur in his *Translatio*), and that after a sojourn in England he went to *Fleury, from where he wrote to Archbishop *Dunstan (in a letter datable 974 × 984) requesting the return of a book which he had left in England on his departure. In his preface to the *Regularis concordia, *Æthelwold states his gratitude to monks of Ghent and Fleury for advice concerning monastic custom, and this statement is best explained on the assumption that Lantfred was one such monk from Fleury who had been invited to Winchester by Æthelwold. His *Translatio* is a highly polished piece of Latin prose, abounding in learned-sounding Greek words (though errors in declension make it unlikely that Lantfred had first-hand knowledge of Greek) and is cast in a kind of rhyming prose which has no correlate in earlier Anglo-Latin prose. It provides a valuable account of the medieval process of establishing a saint's cult, and is a primary witness to various aspects of Anglo-Saxon life, including *pilgrimage, *slavery, *law and capital punishment, and the operation of the *ordeal.

Sharpe, *Handlist*, 1001; *ActaSS*, Iulii ii.331–7 + *AB* 4 (1885), 365–410; M. Lapidge, *The Cult of St Swithun*, Winchester Studies iv.2 (Oxford, forthcoming); J. P. Carley, 'Two Pre-Conquest Manuscripts from Glaston-bury Abbey', *ASE* 16 (1987), 197–212; K. O'Brien O'Keeffe, 'Body and Law in late Anglo-Saxon England', *ASE* 27 (1998), 209–32.

MICHAEL LAPIDGE

LAPIDARIES are treatises concerning the appearance, nature and medical properties of precious stones. In antiquity various scholars had treated the subject (including Pliny the Elder, Solinus and Isidore); in the Christian period, various church fathers devoted attention to the jewels described in Exodus and in Revelation, notably Epiphanius (who wrote in Greek an account of the 'Twelve Precious Stones' on Aaron's breastplate in Exodus XXVIII). Epiphanius's treatise was used at the *Canterbury *school by *Theodore and *Hadrian in their commentary on Exodus, and their explanations concerning the precious stones of the Heavenly Jerusalem in Revelation are preserved in the Leiden Glossary (see *glossaries). At approximately the same time an anonymous author, perhaps an Anglo-Saxon, compiled a Latin treatise on precious stones which has been preserved as part of the so-called *Collectanea pseudo-Bedae*; *Bede drew on this anonymous treatise in his *Explanatio Apocalypsis*. In the later Anglo-Saxon period, *Frithegod drew in turn on Bede's treatise for his poem 'Ciues celestis patrie' (an account of the precious stones in Revelation), and an anonymous scholar compiled the earliest surviving lapidary in any vernacular language (this 'Old English Lapidary' is preserved in London, BL, Cotton Tiberius A.iii).

B. Bischoff and M. Lapidge, *Biblical Commentaries from the Canterbury School of Theodore and Hadrian*, CSASE 10 (Cambridge, 1994), 213–14; *Collectanea pseudo-Bedae*, ed. M. Bayless and M. Lapidge, Scriptores Latini Hiberniae 14 (Dublin, 1998); P. Kitson, 'Lapidary Traditions in Anglo-Saxon England, part I, the Background; the Old English Lapidary', *ASE* 7 (1978), 9–60; idem, 'Lapidary Traditions in Anglo-Saxon England, part II, Bede's *Explanatio Apocalypsis* and Related Works', *ASE* 12 (1983), 73–123.

MICHAEL LAPIDGE

LASTINGHAM (Yorks.) was a monastery founded in the 650s by Bishop Cedd on land given him by King Æthelwald of *Deira. *Bede says that Cedd chose a site 'among bleak and remote hills' and describes the fasts and abstinence with which he purified it; the church stands on a rocky outcrop at the interface between Spaunton Moor and the Vale of Pickering. Both Cedd and his brother *Chad (d. 672) were buried at Lastingham. The surviving sculpture, which includes high-quality eighth-century pieces, parts of two tenth-century crosses and a *hogback, illustrates Lastingham's prestige in the pre-Viking period and its survival as an important religious site thereafter.

Bede, *HE* iii.23, 28, iv.3; CASSS iii: = J. Lang, *York and Eastern Yorkshire* (Oxford, 1991), 167–74.

JOHN BLAIR

LAURENTIUS (d. 619), second archbishop of *Canterbury, was one of the original Roman missionaries who came to England with *Augustine in 597. According to Bede, it was Laurentius who in late 600 travelled to *Rome to meet Pope *Gregory and to announce the success of the mission; he also delivered to the pope a number of questions from Augustine concerning ecclesiastical discipline, and, on his return to England, brought the booklet of Gregory's replies known as the *Libellus responsionum*. Because Augustine was anxious about the stability of the English church and the succession to Canterbury in particular, he consecrated Laurentius as his successor while still living (against *canon law), and Laurentius duly succeeded Augustine on the latter's death (between 604 and 609). As archbishop he attempted to exert some measure of pastoral control over the native Britons, and was the first to direct his attention to the Irish, whom he knew to be celebrating Easter according to outdated procedures (Bede preserves the text of a letter addressed by Laurentius, *Mellitus and *Justus to the bishops and abbots of Ireland). When after *Æthelberht's death (616) the kingdom of Kent reverted to paganism under his son Eadbald, Laurentius stood firm (while Mellitus and Justus retreated to Gaul), and by means of a miraculous *vision was able to convert Eadbald to Christianity. It was Laurentius who consecrated the church of SS Peter and Paul (later St Augustine's) outside Canterbury, where archbishops of Canterbury and kings of Kent were to be buried; he himself died on 2 February 619 and was buried there with his predecessor.

Bede, *HE* i.27, 33; ii.4, 6.

MICHAEL LAPIDGE

LAWS, defined as written statements of observed and enforceable social norms, are among the most distinctive and important memorials of Old English history. Unlike some other Anglo-Saxon records, they have been more fortunate in their editors than their commentators. In particular, a crucial point missed by most discussions is the degree to which law and legislation changed between the first codes in the seventh century and the long series of texts from *Alfred to *Cnut.

The law-code of *Æthelberht of *Kent is the earliest extended piece of writing in English. It is said by *Bede to have followed 'the examples of

the Romans'. Whatever he meant by this phrase, the code did follow the general lines of the legislation of Merovingian Europe, though it is unlike continental European texts in being couched entirely in the vernacular. It is 'Germanic' law, in so far as it is predicated on the mechanisms of *feud. Redress of injury to person or property is left to victims and/or their associates, typically kin. The king's part was to protect those with no kin; to penalize abuse of feuding convention, like avenging a thief legitimately slain because caught in the act; and generally to underwrite social peace, thus taking fines from thieves convicted by process rather than caught red-handed. An important feature of seventh-century law, however, was growing royal involvement. Æthelberht's code makes strikingly few claims to payment for offences against the social order that he embodied. His successor *Wihtred was notably more active, as well as doing more to accommodate the church in society. *Ine, the first law-maker in *Wessex, was more aggressive still. Though preserved as a single statement, his laws in fact look like a *series* of successive pronouncements, each responding to problems confronting him and his subjects. The penalties to purse and body that he exacted were also a lot more prominent than in Kent.

Law-making then recedes from view for two centuries. Alfred could refer to laws made in the time of *Offa of *Mercia, as if he had issued a code; but he may have meant the extant 'capitulary' promulgated by papal legates in 786 at the Northumbrian and Mercian courts. A more important point is that a number of later-eighth- and ninth-century *charters which grant the perquisites of punishment to the beneficiary show that kings remained active in repressing disorder, even without legislating. The series of laws resumed with Alfred, who stressed how little he was innovating, and whose laws are highly traditional in subject-matter and language. Nevertheless, his code made some radical departures. He acknowledged the inspiration not only of Ine, whose code was appended to his own, but also of Æthelberht as well as Offa. More important, he prefaced his whole 'law-book' with a translation of Mosaic law: the logic of the evident parallels between Israelite and English custom was that the English could *and should* themselves be a Holy People, answerable for their shortcomings to God. From his time to Cnut's, all but three short-lived kings issued at least two codes; and though the influence of Carolingian models is detectable, this was, most significantly, at a time when there was no longer much European law-making west of *Byzantium. Two other points deserve note. Some tenth-century laws had a perceptibly less formal style, one whose use of a royal first person and of greeting formulae recalls the *writ. Secondly, there is a considerable body of apparently unofficial legal statements, ranging from the local ordinance of the *Dunsæte* to a tract on Judges and texts gathered by Archbishop *Wulfstan on social ranks (which incorporate the only records of Northumbrian and Mercian law).

The law made by kings from Alfred to Cnut differs in critical ways from that of the seventh century. Codes have a well-developed notion of *crime as an injury not just to the victim but to society at large. Death penalties are ubiquitous – till replaced by hardly less grisly mutilations. *Wergild and *bot* ('compensation') are payable no longer to aggrieved parties only but to the king and his officials, and not only for offences threatening the crown directly but also (for example) for precipitate second marriage: this was the one period in English legal history other than the Commonwealth when adultery was a secular crime. Feud is contained; kins need no longer be answerable for a member's misdeeds. At the heart of this harsh approach was an *oath, taken by all freemen aged twelve, to abstain from and denounce any major crime: theft thus amounted to disloyalty. Whereas *courts in the early period were local moots or the royal court itself, there was now a hierarchy of courts, with those of the shire or borough interposed between local moots that were renamed *hundreds and the king's court proper. Their presiding officials were in effect royal appointees. *Bookland, title vested in a *charter of which possessors had free disposition, showed signs in the ninth century of becoming the vehicle of conventional land transactions between subjects. After laws made by Alfred and *Edward the Elder (among the very few on this topic in the whole Anglo-Saxon series), it was more clearly a privilege that only kings could bestow, guarantee – or remove.

There is no extant legislation that can be safely dated after 1023, and little after 1066 other than a few legislative writs. Legal texts before Henry II were overwhelmingly of the unofficial variety and very largely, it seems, written by Frenchmen. Because they had no more to help them grasp the system than the texts we have ourselves, their picture of it often misleads. In particular, the author of the *Leges Henrici Primi* (who translated most codes in the Latin *Quadripartitus*) reproduced all texts as if they had equal validity; and

so concealed from Maitland and later commentators the extent to which tenth-century law represented vigorous change. The 'archaic' image of pre-Conquest law is in fact quite misconceived. Its aggressive conception of royal justice laid the essential foundations of Angevin 'Common Law'.

Liebermann, *Gesetze*; translations of most texts and introduction in *EHD* i; F. Pollock and F. W. Maitland, *A History of English Law*, ed. S. F. C. Milsom, 2 vols. (Cambridge, 1968), ch. 2; J. Goebel, *Felony and Misdemeanour*, 2nd ed. E. Peters (Philadelphia, PA, 1976), chs. 1, 6; H. Cam, *Law-Finders and Law-Makers in Medieval England* (London, 1962), chs. 1, 3; P. Wormald, 'Charters, Law and the Settlement of Disputes in Anglo-Saxon England', in *The Settlement of Disputes in Early Medieval Europe*, ed. W. Davies and P. Fouracre (Cambridge, 1986), pp. 149–68; idem, '*Inter Cetera Bona . . . Genti Suae*: Law-Making and Peace-Keeping in the earliest English Kingdoms', *Settimane* 42 (1995), 963–96; idem, 'Maitland and Anglo-Saxon Law', *History of English Law: Centenary Essays on 'Pollock and Maitland'*, ed. J. Hudson (Oxford, 1996), ch. 1.

PATRICK WORMALD

LEATHER-WORK in Anglo-Saxon England followed a Late Roman tradition involving thin skin products over a wooden foundation, probably using glues, with decoration raised in relief and emphasized by colour. Evidence for the use of leather by the Anglo-Saxons before *c.*700 is scarce. *Cemetery evidence suggests that it was used for horse harnesses, knife sheaths and sword scabbards, shields (for covering the wooden board), and for some belts and thongs. Traces of decoration by relief moulding, tooling and by the application of gold occasionally survive upon such finds. Other examples of seventh-century English leatherwork are to be seen on the bindings of the *Stonyhurst Gospel of St John in the British Library and Codex Bonifatianus in the Landesbibliothek, Fulda. The bindings of these two manuscripts were dyed red, and it is also recorded that purple dye was occasionally used on seventh-century parchments (Stephen, *Vita S. Wilfridi*, c.17). Types of leather identified from the settlement period are of sheep or goat, calf and occasionally deer. Methods of tannage included vegetable tanning and alum tawing. There is no evidence to suggest the existence of an organized leather industry at this early date.

A more robust form of leatherwork, introduced in the seventh century, used thicker leather that was more easily decorated by tooling and incision. Leather finds surviving from the eighth to the late eleventh century include the binding of Codex Bonifatianus 1 (*c.*700), sheaths of knives and seaxes, sword scabbards and shoes. Leather of this date is characteristically 1.5 mm or more in thickness and was frequently unsupported by wood. By the tenth century calf predominates over sheep or goat, a shift of emphasis which is attributed to changes in trade patterns as well as perhaps to increased guild control. Evidence of leather production first appears in association with urban development, but is scarce. Remains of a tannery, possible of *Viking date, were found at High Ousegate, *York. From the eighth to the eleventh centuries the strongest influences in style and technique seem to have come from Southern Scandinavia, and it is probably from this northern source that English medieval leatherworking tradition developed.

T. J. Brown, ed. *The Stonyhurst Gospel of St John* (Oxford, 1969); E. A. Cameron, 'Pre-Conquest Leather on English Bookbindings, Arms and Armour, AD 400–1100', in *Leather and Fur. Aspects of Early Medieval Trade and Technology*, ed. E. Cameron (London, 1998), pp. 45–56; A. MacGregor, 'Hides, Horns and Bones: Animals and Interdependent Industries in the early Urban Context', ibid. pp. 11–26; H. M. Nixon and M. M. Foot, *The History of Decorated Bookbindings in England* (Oxford, 1992); D. M. Wilson, 'An Anglo-Saxon Bookbinding at Fulda (Codex Bonifatianus 1)', *AJ* 41 (1961), 199–217.

ESTHER CAMERON

LEBUIN: *see* Leofwine

LECTIONARY: see Gospelbooks; Liturgical Books

LEICESTER, the Roman town of *Ratae*, was the ecclesiastical centre of the *Middle Angles. From the division of the Mercian province into dioceses in about 690 the bishop of *Lichfield kept a secondary seat at Leicester, which became an independent bishopric in 737. The site of the cathedral remains uncertain: a strong candidate on physical evidence is the church of St Nicholas, which is built into the *palaestra* of the Roman bath complex and retains late Anglo-Saxon fabric (fig. 15), but St Mary-de-Castro had the later parochial status normally associated with minsters. After *Viking disruption in the 870s the see was abandoned. In the late ninth century Leicester was established as a Danish borough (see *Five Boroughs), which submitted to *Æthelflæd in 918. In the eleventh century it was the centre of a *shire, probably based on an older territory; it had a *mint under *Æthelstan, and then regularly from the 970s. In *Domesday Book it appears as a substantial *town, with perhaps around 2,000 inhabitants and six churches.

T. H. McK. Clough *et al.*, *Anglo-Saxon and Viking Leicestershire* (Leicester, 1975); R. Bailey, *The Early Christian Church in Leicester and its Region*, University of Leicester Vaughan Paper 25 (1980); D. Parsons, 'Before the Parish: the Church in Anglo-Saxon Leicestershire', *Anglo-Saxon Landscapes in the East Midlands*, ed. J. Bourne (Leicester, 1996), pp. 11–35; A. Chinnery, 'Leicester at Domesday', *The Norman Conquest of Leicestershire and Rutland*, ed. C. Phythian-Adams (Leicester, 1986), pp. 43–7.

JOHN BLAIR

LELAND, JOHN (1503?–1552), reorganized Henry VIII's libraries at Greenwich Palace, Hampton Court and Westminster Palace as repositories for manuscripts retrieved from the dissolved monastic houses. Although there is no evidence that he ever was 'King's Antiquary' as such, he did have some sort of authorisation, a 'diploma' as he called it, from the king in this endeavour. Interested primarily in British authors, his earliest collecting activities related to Henry VIII's first divorce and the supremacy, but he later concerned himself with wider bibliographical questions. For well over a decade he travelled the length and breadth of England and Wales, taking notes of the contents of libraries and, especially in the 1540s, describing topographical and other features. Many of the extracts in his *Collectanea* are transcriptions from medieval manuscripts, some subsequently destroyed or lost. According to *Bale, Leland was himself a pioneer in the study of Old English: certainly he took notes from *Ælfric's *Glossary*, presumably recognizing the importance of this sort of word list for language acquisition. Criticized by Bale for his promiscuous antiquarianism, that is his refusal to dismiss medieval authors on theological grounds, he intended to publish a comprehensive dictionary of British writers, 'de illustribus viris'. Although this work was nearing completion when he became insane in 1547, it did not appear in print until 1709.

Sharpe, *Handlist*, 778; *Joannis Lelandi Antiquarii De rebus Britannicis Collectanea*, ed. T. Hearne, 3rd ed., 6 vols. (London, 1774); *Commentarii de scriptoribus Britannicis, auctore Joanne Lelando Londinate*, ed. A. Hall, 2 vols. (Oxford, 1709); *The Itinerary of John Leland in or about the Years 1535–43*, ed. L. Toulmin Smith, 5 vols. (London, 1906–10); C. Brett, 'John Leland and the Anglo-Norman Historian', *ANS* 11 (1988), 59–76; idem, 'John Leland, Wales, and Early British History', *Welsh History Review* 15 (1990), 169–82; R. E. Buckalew, 'Leland's Transcript of Ælfric's *Glossary*', *ASE* 7 (1978), 149–64; J. P. Carley, 'John Leland and the Contents of the English Pre-Dissolution Libraries: Lincolnshire', *TCBS* 9 (1989), 330–57; idem, 'John Leland and the

Foundations of the Royal Library: the Westminster Inventory of 1542', *Bulletin of the Society for Renaissance Studies* 7 (1989), 13–22.

JAMES P. CARLEY

LEOFGYTH, also known as Leobgytha or Leoba, was one of the most important and influential of the women who followed *Boniface on his mission to *Germany. Educated in the convent of *Wimborne in Dorset, Leofgyth wrote soon after 732 to Boniface, to whom she was evidently related through her mother, requesting his prayers for her parents, and asking for his guidance and protection. Her letter closes with a further request that Boniface correct the 'rustic style' of her Latin, followed by some halting verses in Latin *metre heavily indebted to *Aldhelm, from whose metrical treatises (which are also echoed) Leofgyth had clearly derived her verse technique. Two further letters survive to her from Boniface, and another from his successor as archbishop, *Lull, and together testify to the twin success of her requests: under Boniface's guidance Leofgyth went on to become abbess of Tauberbischofsheim and the subject of a Life by Rudolf of Fulda, written in 836, while elsewhere Lull closely echoes the diction of her original letter to Boniface in his own writings.

Sharpe, *Handlist*, 1016; *S. Bonifatii et Lullii Epistolae*, ed. M. Tangl, MGH, ES 1 (Berlin, 1916); E. Emerton, trans., *The Letters of Saint Boniface* (New York, 1940); E. Kylie, trans., *The English Correspondence of Saint Boniface* (London, 1911); C. Fell, 'Some Implications of the Boniface Correspondence', in *New Readings on Women in Old English Literature*, ed. H. Damico and A. H. Olsen (Bloomington, IN, 1990), pp. 29–43; C. H. Talbot, *The Anglo-Saxon Missionaries in Germany* (London, 1954), pp. 203–26; C. Wybourne, 'Leoba: a Study in Humanity and Holiness', in *Medieval Women Monastics*, ed. M. Schmitt and L. Kulxer (Collegeville, MN, 1996) pp. 81–96.

ANDY ORCHARD

LEOFRIC, earl of Mercia (d. 31 August or 30 September 1057), son of Ealdorman Leofwine of the *Hwicce, rose to power under *Cnut, but was overshadowed by *Godwine of Wessex. His family were perhaps related by marriage to that of Ælfgifu of Northampton, Cnut's first wife, and on Cnut's death in 1035, Leofric supported *Harold I, Ælfgifu's son, against *Harthacnut, Cnut's son by *Emma. In the crisis of 1051, Leofric supported King *Edward against Earl Godwine, but helped broker the eventual agreement between them. He was a noted benefactor of the church, founding Stow St Mary (Lincs.) and Coventry Abbey, but the church of *Worcester remembered

his family as spoliators. His son Ælfgar succeeded to his earldom, and his wife Godgifu (*Godiva) became the subject of a celebrated legend.

J. Hunt, 'Piety, Prestige or Politics? The House of Leofric and the Foundation and Patronage of Coventry Priory', *Coventry's First Cathedral*, ed. G. Demidowicz (Stamford, 1994), pp. 97–117; S. Keynes, 'Cnut's Earls', *The Reign of Cnut*, ed. A. Rumble (London, 1994), pp. 43–88, at 74–5, 77–8.

ANN WILLIAMS

LEOFRIC (d. 1072), bishop of Devon and *Cornwall [later, *Exeter], was probably born in either Devon or Cornwall before 1016 (he is described by *John of Worcester as *Brytonicus*, although his name is unambiguously English: perhaps he was born to an English family living in a British-speaking area). His early training took place in Lotharingia, presumably in a reformed house of secular canons; he met the future king *Edward the Confessor at Bruges in 1039, and accompanied him to England two years later, where he served as a scribe (*cancellarius*) at the royal court. To judge from the *library which he bequeathed on his death, he was a scholar of very considerable range and learning. He was promoted to the bishopric of Devon and Cornwall in 1046, with their sees in Crediton and St Germans respectively (and which he held in plurality); he subsequently transferred the two sees to one at Exeter in 1050, where he established a community of regular *cathedral canons ('regular' insofar as they followed the *Regula canonicorum* of Chrodegang of Metz; Leofric's own copy of this text, in Latin and Old English, survives as CCCC 191). Leofric was able to acquire various estates for his new see, and to furnish his church at Exeter properly, though he undertook no new building works. On his death in 1072 he bequeathed his substantial collection of some fifty-five books to his cathedral chapter; a number (perhaps as many as seventeen) of these books survive and have been identified by his *ex-libris* inscriptions, including the famous *Exeter Book of Old English poetry.

F. Barlow, *The English Church 1000–66*, 2nd ed. (London, 1979), pp. 83–4; F. Barlow, K. M. Dexter *et al.*, *Leofric of Exeter* (Exeter, 1972); M. Lapidge, 'Surviving Booklists from Anglo-Saxon England', in Clemoes FS, pp. 33–89, esp. 64–9.

MICHAEL LAPIDGE

LEOFWINE or LEBUIN, an Anglo-Saxon missionary who joined the Bonifatian mission during its final phases in *Germany and *Frisia, probably shortly after the death of *Boniface in 754. Upon arrival, Leofwine was sent by Boniface's pupil Gregory (who was acting, but had not been consecrated, bishop) of Utrecht, to the borderland of Franks and Saxons on the river Yssel, and established his centre of activity in Deventer. According to later *hagiography, he had considerable success in converting the heathen Saxons. The date of his death is unknown, though it may have occurred *c.*775, since it was approximately at that time that *Liudger went to Deventer to continue the conversion of the Saxons, implying that Leofwine was by then dead; he is commemorated (under the continental form of his name, Lebuin) on 12 November in some calendars from the Low Countries. What is known of his life derives from an anonymous mid-ninth-century prose *vita* (*BHL* 4810b), which is based on the *Vita S. Gregorii abbatis* of Liudger as well as Altfrid's *Vita S. Liudgeri*; this work contains a dramatic account of Leofwine's preaching to the heathen Saxons at their Thing at Marklo.

MGH, SS xxx.789–95 [*Vita I. S. Lebuini*; trans. C. H. Talbot, *The Anglo-Saxon Missionaries on the Continent* (London, 1954), pp. 229–34]; A. Hofmeister, 'Über die älteste Vita Lebuini und die Stammesverfassung der Sachsen', in *Geschichtliche Studien Albert Hauck zum 70. Geburtstage dargebracht* (Leipzig, 1916), pp. 85–107; W. Levison, *England and the Continent in the Eighth Century* (Oxford, 1946), pp. 108–10; H. Löwe, 'Entstehungszeit und Quellenwert der Vita Lebuins', *Deutsches Archiv* 21 (1965), 345–70; W. Berschin, *Biographie und Epochenstil in lateinischen Mittelalter*, 3 vols. (Stuttgart, 1986–), iii.57–60.

MICHAEL LAPIDGE

LETTER COLLECTIONS. The vast majority of extant medieval letters are transmitted in association with larger or smaller groups of other letters, in letter collections. Some awareness of the genesis of such compilations is therefore essential to interpreting their significance. Because they usually lacked legal value, early medieval letters only survive as loose originals in the most exceptional cases: two famous examples from Anglo-Saxon England are the Fonthill letter (addressed to *Edward the Elder) and a letter of Bishop Wealdhere of London, datable to 704/5. Almost all other medieval letters, however, owe their survival to recopying, at some stage, into parchment codices, or, in the case of the *papacy until the ninth century, papyrus registers. Recopying entails the loss of information about the physical format of the letter and may imply that some criteria of selectivity were applied. In many cases, copyists omitted salutations and reduced proper names to *N.* (for *nomen*), which has led to the assumption that letters were most often copied or preserved

as formularies, that is, to assist others in letter-writing. The sparse information about the reception of letter collections that can be derived from marginal annotations and references in other sources does not always bear out this assumption. The vicissitudes of preservation and selection may also account for the fact that extant letters indicate that correspondence in Anglo-Saxon England was almost always conducted in Latin. Yet the OE poem known as the *Husband's Message* could be regarded as evidence for the possible existence of vernacular messages in Anglo-Saxon England. Such lay and vernacular letters as might have existed were most unlikely to be preserved or recopied.

Letter collections can be broadly characterized as derived from either 'sender transmission' (*Absenderüberlieferung*) or 'receiver transmission' (*Empfängerüberlieferung*), that is, copied from the sender's drafts, or else from the recipient's texts. The distinction between the two processes is not absolute and they may overlap. After the sixth century there are virtually no examples of authorially selected and produced letter collections until the eleventh century (*Alcuin's possible role in supervising the diffusion of groups of his own letters is a salient exception). During this time, awareness of a letter collection as a literary whole is eclipsed, although two fictional letter-collections (of Alexander and Dindimus and of Seneca and St Paul) were recopied by Alcuin and presented to Charlemagne. Most non-fictional early medieval collections were apparently copied from the sender's drafts by someone other than the sender, sometimes generations later. This type of 'sender transmission' might be characterized as 'archival transmission' and here too, selectivity and judgement will have guided the choice of material and sometimes dictated adjustments in content, although these motives may not be apparent. Finally, in rare cases, letters of special interest are transmitted in non-epistolary contexts (for example, *Bede's inclusion of letters of *Gregory the Great in the *Historia ecclesiastica*).

Important letter collections for the Anglo-Saxons included the letters of Jerome, Ambrose, and Augustine, the Pauline Epistles, and, not least, the letters of Gregory the Great. Patristic letters at first circulated in disparate small groupings; larger collections begin to be assembled in Carolingian centres. Bede and *Boniface revealed their awareness of the inadequacy of available Gregorian collections when each sent a messenger to search the papal archives for letters of Gregory not available in England.

Whatever the apparent pattern of compilation and preservation, it is clear that most letter collections would have included only a small fraction of a sender's epistolary output, while extant collections, in turn, can be demonstrated to comprise only a small proportion of the letters that once existed. For a number of reasons, the transmission of English letters (apart from those of Alcuin and Boniface) is scanty and haphazard. A mere handful of letters from the prolific *Aldhelm survive and the letters home of many missionaries to the Continent were not transmitted to posterity. Bede's letter to *Egcberht and Cuthbert's letter on the death of Bede demonstrate that some letters on topics of special interest might find their best chances of transmission outside the context of letter collections. Letters of dedication may or may not be preserved in letter collections separately from the work to which they were originally attached, and can remind us that many works which we think of as independent were originally in some sense epistolary; all of Aldhelm's writings fall into this category. Testimony from *William of Malmesbury and John *Leland can occasionally establish the existence of letters and collections no longer extant.

P. Chaplais, 'The Letter from Bishop Wealdhere of London to Archbishop Brihtwold of Canterbury: the Earliest Original "Letter Close" Extant in the West', in *Medieval Scribes, Manuscripts and Libraries: Essays presented to N. R. Ker*, ed. M. B. Parkes and A. G. Watson (London, 1978), pp. 3–23; G. Constable, *Letters and Letter Collections*, Typologie des sources du moyen âge occidental 17 (Turnhout, 1970); H. Hoffmann, 'Zur mittelalterlichen Brieftechnik', in *Spiegel der Geschichte: Festgabe für Max Braubach*, ed. K. Repgen and S. Skalweit (Münster, 1964), pp. 141–70; C. Lanham, *Salutatio Formulas in Latin Letters to 1200: Syntax, Style and Theory*, Münchener Beiträge zur Mediävistik und Renaissance-Forschung 22 (Munich, 1975); J. J. Murphy, '*Ars dictaminis*: The Art of Letter Writing', in his *Rhetoric in the Middle Ages: A History of Rhetorical Theory from Saint Augustine to the Renaissance* (Berkeley, CA, 1974); R. H. Robbins and G. Sauer, 'B. Briefwesen und Briefliteratur in den Volkssprachen Mittell-, West- und Südeuropas: IV. Englische Sprache und Literatur', in *Lexikon des Mittelalters* ii. 670–1; F. J. Schmale, 'Brief, Briefliteratur, Briefsammlungen I. Allgemein', ibid. p. 648; 'IV [i] Lateinisches Mittelalter', ibid. pp. 652–6; 'IV [ii] Briefsammlungen', ibid. pp. 656–9; I. Wood, 'Letters and Letter-Collections from Antiquity to the Early Middle Ages: The Prose Works of Avitus of Vienne', in *The Culture of Christendom: Essays in Medieval History in Commemoration of Denis L. T. Bethell*, ed. M. A. Meyer (London, 1993), pp. 29–43.

MARY GARRISON

LEUTHERE (fl. 670–6), was a *Frank who was the nephew of *Agilbert (fl *c.*650–*c.*680), one-time bishop of the West Saxons and later bishop of Paris. Leuthere originated from the Soissons area in Francia, and since his name is a form of Clothar, a name borne by three Frankish kings, it is likely that he was related to the Merovingian royal family. His name is also basically the same as that of the contemporary king of *Kent, Hlothere, which suggests that Leuthere had family links with the Kentish royal house. His uncle, Agilbert, likewise had the Frankish form of a Kentish royal name, *Æthelberht. According to Bede (*HE* iii.7), in 670 Cenwalh, king of the West Saxons, wished to recall Agilbert to become once more a bishop in his kingdom; but Agilbert declined the offer because he was now bishop of Paris. In his stead he sent his nephew Leuthere, who was already a priest. Leuthere was consecrated bishop by *Theodore of Canterbury in 670, and he held the see of *Winchester from 670 to 676. As bishop he attended the *council of Hertford in 672. In 675 he appeared in a charter granting land at *Malmesbury for the foundation of a monastery there (S 1245). The beneficiary of this grant was *Aldhelm, later bishop of *Sherborne, whom Leuthere may have ordained priest. Leuthere's successor *Hæddi witnessed the Malmesbury charter as abbot, but later in the same year Haeddi appears in another charter as bishop, alongside Leuthere (S 51). This may suggest that at least briefly Leuthere ruled Winchester jointly with his successor. In both *charters the style of Leuthere's witness reveals use of a so-called Frankish 'humility formula', an observation which supports recent arguments that it was Frankish, rather than Italian, models which formed the basis of early charter writing in England. Leuthere, therefore, might well have been a key figure in the introduction of the Latin charter into England.

W. Levison, *England and the Continent in the Eighth Century* (Oxford, 1946), pp. 226–8; A. Lohaus, *Die Merowinger und England* (Munich, 1974); P. Sims-Williams, 'Continental Influence at Bath Monastery in the Seventh Century', *ASE* 4 (1975), 1–10; P. Wormald, *Bede and the Conversion of England: the Charter Evidence*, Jarrow Lecture (1984).

P. FOURACRE

LIBER MONSTRORUM ('book of monsters'), as its name suggests, offers a description of around 120 examples of the monstrous in myth and nature, divided into three books which treat in turn human-shaped monsters, marvellous beasts, and serpentine wonders. For reasons of style, content, and transmission, the anonymous *Liber* *monstrorum* is considered an Anglo–Latin work, probably composed during the last half of the seventh century or the first half of the eighth, and closely asssociated with the figure of *Aldhelm, although it seems unlikely that he was himself the author. In drawing on a wide range of both Christian and pagan sources, the latter of which are consistently disparaged or undermined, the evidently learned author of the *Liber monstrorum* implicitly warns his audience of the seductive dangers of *classical learning, and the whole work explores the tensions between past and present, Christian and pagan, and truth and lies. There are a number of intriguing connections between the *Liber monstrorum* and *Beowulf, not least the appearance in both of the figure of Hygelac, king of the Geats, and the *Liber monstrorum* has a number of other connections with two of the other exts in the *Beowulf-manuscript, deriving much of its material from Latin versions of the *Marvels of the East and *Alexander's Letter to Aristotle.

Liber Monstrorum, ed. F. Porsia (Bari, 1976); A. Orchard, *Pride and Prodigies: Studies in the Monsters of the 'Beowulf'-Manuscript* (Cambridge, 1995), pp. 86–115, 254–320; idem, 'The Sources and Meaning of the *Liber monstrorum*', in *I monstra nell' Inferno dantesco: tradizione e simbologie* (Spoleto, 1997), pp. 73–105.

ANDY ORCHARD

LIBRARIES. During the Anglo–Saxon period, and particularly before the *Viking invasions of the ninth century, England was in the vanguard of European scholarship, and it is clear that this scholarship was underpinned by extensive library resources. Unfortunately, there is very little direct evidence for the nature of Anglo–Saxon libraries: the full library catalogue (with or without shelf-marks for retrieving volumes) is an invention of post-Conquest times, and the few surviving book-lists (thirteen in number) from the pre-Conquest period are, in comparison with surviving lists from continental monasteries, of limited value in assessing what library books were owned in England. The evidence of the booklists must therefore be supplemented by other sorts of evidence: in particular, the books which Anglo–Saxon authors can be demonstrated to have studied (by means of quotations and verbal reminiscences) and the manuscripts written or owned in Anglo–Saxon England which happen to have survived until the present day (some 1,200 such manuscripts have thus far been identified). Of these two categories of evidence, the former can often depend on subjective judgement as to what does, or does not,

constitute a verbal reminiscence, while the value of the latter is much reduced by the fact that many Anglo-Saxon books and libraries were destroyed and dispersed during the ninth century, so that more English books exported to the Continent by the Anglo–Saxon *missionaries before *c.*835 have survived in continental libraries than in England. Nevertheless, although the evidence is uneven and disparate, it is clear that there were very substantial libraries at various times in the pre-Conquest period.

Depending on the owner, there were various kinds of libraries in Anglo-Saxon England (all ecclesiastical institutions will have possessed *liturgical books, but these scarcely constitute libraries, and will in any case have been housed separately from books intended for teaching and private study). In Benedictine monasteries, books were owned corporately by the institution, insofar as no monk was permitted to own so much as a pen of his own, let alone a book (*Regula S. Benedicti*, c. 33). In the case of secular (that is, non-monastic) *clergy, such as *cathedral canons, such a stipulation did not obtain; in the case of such clergy, there was often evidence of private ownership of books (for example, the library which was amassed and owned by *Ælberht of York, which he bequeathed to *Alcuin, or the library owned by Bishop *Leofric, which on his death passed to the cathedral chapter of *Exeter). It is also probable that Anglo-Saxon laymen owned books, although here the evidence is less full than might be desired: King *Æthelstan is known to have owned books, to judge from the various volumes which he donated to various churches, and his grandfather *Alfred also presumably had a modest personal library at his disposal (including the *enchiridion* or 'handbook' which is described by *Asser). In the early twelfth century, Adelard of Bath composed a work on falconry in which he states his indebtedness to 'books of King *Harold' and a book of *Edward the Confessor; but there is no way of knowing what these books might have been. A final class of evidence may be mentioned. Narrative sources very often contain references to books and libraries: thus *Bede in his *Historia abbatum* refers to the large number of books which were brought back to England by *Benedict Biscop in the course of his six trips to Rome, and *Boniface in letters to English correspondents frequently requests specific books.

The history of Anglo-Saxon libraries has yet to be written, but from the various categories of evidence mentioned above, it is clear that some individuals and institutions owned very substantial libraries. The biblical commentaries which were compiled at the school of *Canterbury from the teaching of Archbishop *Theodore and Abbot *Hadrian make reference to (and quote from) a vast range of patristic literature, most of it in Greek; given that some of the quotation from Greek sources is extensive and verbatim, there is some presumption that some of the texts were being quoted from books then existing at Canterbury, even though all trace of these books has perished. *Aldhelm, who was at one time the student of both Theodore and Hadrian, also quotes from a vast range of literature, *classical and patristic, but in Latin (in fact Aldhelm quotes from various classical works, such as the *Orpheus* of Lucan, which have not come down to us, but were still available to Aldhelm in the late seventh century); Aldhelm's most recent editor, Rudolf Ehwald, has identified quotations in his writings from some sixty separate authors (not including the substantial number of individual *passiones* and saints' *vitae* on which he drew for his prose *De virginitate*, and bearing in mind that some authors would be represented by more than one volume): in sum, it is reasonable to think in terms of a (personal?) library in excess, probably, of two hundred volumes (of which a fragment of only one volume, a copy of Junilius, appears to have survived). The library at *Monkwearmouth-Jarrow which was assembled by Benedict Biscop and *Ceolfrith, and which was drawn on by Bede, was of a similar size, to judge from the number of authors quoted in Bede's writings (and identified by M. L. W. Laistner); again, only a single volume (a copy of the *Carmina* of Paulinus of Nola) has been conjecturally identified. It is certain that other Northumbrian monasteries – notably *Lindisfarne, *Ripon and *Hexham – will have had libraries to support the studies of scholars such as *Wilfrid and *Acca, but of these we know nothing. The library assembled by Ælberht at *York is known in broad outline from a poem on the saints of York by Alcuin, who lists some forty authors who were represented in Ælberht's library; Ælberht bequeathed this library to Alcuin, who later in life requested that it be shipped to him in Francia, with the result that not a single volume has been convincingly identified. In contrast with these very substantial pre-ninth-century Anglo-Saxon libraries, the number of books which were available at King Alfred's court seems extremely modest; and it was only through the efforts of patrons of learning such as Alfred that the process of restocking English libraries began in earnest from the late ninth century onwards. Substantial numbers of manuscripts survive from the later tenth century onwards, and many of these can be assigned (on palaeographical grounds) to individual centres, so that it is possible to form some notion of institutional libraries, especially at centres such as the two Canterbury houses (Christ Church and St Augustine's) and the two principal *Winchester houses (the Old and New Minsters), from the witness of surviving manuscripts. Evidence drawn from palaeography can be supplemented in turn from the quotations and sources used by individual authors, notably *Æthelwold, *Ælfric, *Wulfstan Cantor and *Byrhtferth, all of whom were scholars of impressively wide learning. It will be possible to form a more complete notion of what books were available in Anglo-Saxon England when the work of the collaborative project known as 'Fontes Anglo-Saxonici' (which has as its goal the identification of all works quoted or paraphrased by Anglo-Saxon authors writing in Latin or English) is complete; but even then it will be necessary to correlate the evidence of surviving manuscripts if even a partial picture of the contents of Anglo-Saxon libraries is to be achieved.

M. Lapidge, 'Surviving Booklists from Anglo-Saxon England', in Clemoes FS, pp. 33–89; S. Keynes, 'King Athelstan's Books', ibid. pp. 143–201; H. Gneuss, 'Anglo-Saxon Libraries from the Conversion to the Benedictine Reform', Settimane 32 (1986), 643–88, repr. in his *Books and Libraries in Early England* (Aldershot, 1996), no. II; idem, 'King Alfred and the History of Anglo-Saxon Libraries', in his *Books and Libraries in Early England*, no. III; D. N. Dumville, 'The Importation of Mediterranean Manuscripts into Theodore's England', in *Archbishop Theodore*, ed. M. Lapidge, CSASE 11 (Cambridge, 1995), 96–119; Bischoff and Lapidge, *Biblical Commentaries*, pp. 190–242; *Aldhelmi Opera*, ed. R. Ehwald, MGH, AA 15 (Berlin, 1919), 544–6 [Aldhelm]; M. L. W. Laistner, 'The Library of the Venerable Bede', in *Bede, his Life, Times, and Writings*, ed. A. H. Thompson (Oxford, 1935), pp. 237–66; W. Levison, *England and the Continent in the Eighth Century* (Oxford, 1946), pp. 139–48; M. Lapidge, 'Latin Learning in Ninth-Century England', in his *ALL* ii.409–54.

MICHAEL LAPIDGE

LICHFIELD (Staffs.) succeeded the nearby Romano-British town of *Letocetum* (now Wall). There is archaeological evidence for Christianity in the late Roman town, and a reference in the *Marwnad Cynddylan* to a Welsh raid on *Caer Lwytgoed* in the 630s, which gave no protection to the bishop and the 'book-holding monks' there, implies a British Christian community surviving under *Penda's pagan rule. It is unclear why the religious centre moved soon afterwards from Wall to Lichfield, which King *Wulfhere gave to Bishop *Wilfrid in the 660s as 'a place made ready (*paratum*) as an episcopal see for himself or for any other'.

*Chad established his seat at Lichfield in 669, and also had a nearby retreat-house for private prayer, perhaps the present St Michael's church. Bede recounts miracles attending Chad's death, and describes the 'wooden tomb made in the shape of a little house' over his grave. This account shows that the cathedral complex had twin churches dedicated to St Peter and St Mary, one evidently on the present cathedral site where a *porticus* containing mid-Saxon burials has recently been excavated. In 787 King *Offa had Lichfield raised to the status of an archiepiscopal see, but the reform was bitterly opposed by *Canterbury and was reversed in 803. Lichfield nonetheless remained a cathedral, which seems, during the tenth and eleventh centuries, to have attracted limited proto-urban growth which had some impact on the later *town plan.

Stephen of Ripon, *Vita S. Wilfridi*, c. 15; Bede, *HE* iv.3; N. Brooks, 'The Formation of the Mercian Kingdom', in Bassett, *Origins*, pp. 159–70, at 168–9; J. Gould, 'Lichfield – Ecclesiastical Origins', *In Search of Cult*, ed. M. Carver (Woodbridge, 1993), pp. 101–4; W. Rodwell, 'Lichfield: Lichfield Cathedral', *MArch* 39 (1995), 241–2; M. O. H. Carver, 'Archaeology of Early Lichfield', *Transactions of the South Staffordshire Archaeological and Historical Society* 22 (1980–1), 1–12; S. R. Bassett, 'Medieval Lichfield: a Topographical Review', ibid. 22 (1980–1), 93–121; T. Slater, 'Topography and Planning of Medieval Lichfield', ibid. 26 (1986), 11–35.

JOHN BLAIR

LINCOLN, the Roman town of *Colonia Lindensium*, was the centre of the post-Roman province of *Lindsey. *Bede says that in the 620s *Paulinus converted Blæcca, 'ruler of the city' (*praefectus civitatis*), and built 'a stone church of remarkable workmanship'. Lindsey had bishops from 678, though their seat is not certainly located; in 803 one of them called himself bishop of the unidentified *Syddensis civitas*. It is arguable that the episcopal seat was in fact at Lincoln, perhaps in the Roman suburb of Wigford; in the early ninth century there were dual episcopal and monastic communities.

Excavations on the site of St Paul's church revealed a building with an eastern apse, set squarely within the Roman forum courtyard. A grave containing a seventh-century bronze *hanging-bowl had been dug either inside this building or in a small rectangular structure on its site. The date of this early church remains controversial: was it the cathedral of a fifth-century sub-Roman bishop, or was it Paulinus's church (as the close similarity of its plan to the seventh-century Kentish churches might suggest)? At all events St Paul's is evidence for Christian continuity at the heart of the Roman town from at least the early seventh century.

Urban planning and re-growth began, as normally in the East Midlands, with Lincoln's adoption as a Danish borough from the 870s. It probably fell to the English in 918–20; in the tenth and eleventh centuries it emerged as the head of an enormous *shire. From the 960s the *town grew rapidly, with an exceptionally high *mint output, and under *Cnut it became a major international port trading with the Scandinavian world and north-eastern Europe. Excavations, notably at Flaxengate, show the intensification of industry and urban-style living during these years, and in *Domesday Book Lincoln appears as by far the biggest East Midland town.

Bede, *HE* ii.16; M. J. Jones, 'St Paul in the Bail, Lincoln: Britain in Europe?', '*Churches Built in Ancient Times': Recent Studies in Early Christian Archaeology*, ed. K. Painter, Society of Antiquaries of London, Occasional Paper 16 (London, 1994), 325–47; *Pre-Viking Lindsey*, ed. A. Vince (Lincoln, 1993); S. R. Bassett, 'Lincoln and the Anglo-Saxon See of Lindsey', *ASE* 18 (1989), 1–32; P. Stafford, *The East Midlands in the Early Middle Ages* (Leicester, 1985); M. J. Jones, 'Archaeology in Lincoln', *Medieval Art and Architecture at Lincoln Cathedral* (London, 1986), pp. 1–8; *The Archaeology of Lincoln* series (Lincoln Archaeological Trust, in progress).

JOHN BLAIR

LINDISFARNE (Northumb.), also known as 'Holy Island', is an island off the Northumbrian coast, cut off by high tides twice daily but otherwise accessible along a causeway. It adjoins the Bernician royal fortress of Bamburgh, and the rocky outcrop where Lindisfarne Castle now stands is a natural strong-point: the *Historia Brittonum* states that a late sixth-century Bernician king fortified it against a British siege.

In 635 King *Oswald gave the island to the Irish monk *Aidan, who established there his episcopal seat and a monastic dependency of *Iona. *Bede gives a detailed account of its constitution, whereby the bishop and his priests followed monastic observance together with the abbot and monks. For thirty years Lindisfarne was the undisputed mother church of *Northumbria, and the centre of the Irish monastic mission to the English.

The year 664 brought troubles: the triumph of the Roman *Easter at the Synod of *Whitby split the Lindisfarne community, and the island was temporarily eclipsed by *York as the Northumbrian bishop's seat.

For some decades, which included the episcopate of *Cuthbert (685–7), the community was embroiled in factional court politics, jockeying with its formidable rival *Wilfrid for status and influence. Cuthbert's death in 687 was followed by a phase of extraordinary cultural activity. In 698 his incorrupt body was opulently enshrined; his rapidly growing cult stimulated the production both of the incomparable *Lindisfarne Gospels and of the anonymous *Prose Life of St Cuthbert*, followed shortly afterwards by Bede's *Verse Life*. In about 720, at the community's request and perhaps in reaction to the developing cult of Wilfrid, Bede completed his enlarged and re-written version of the *Prose Life*. Here he celebrated the union at Lindisfarne of what he considered best in the Irish and Roman traditions: austerity and pastoral zeal on the one hand, liturgical orthodoxy on the other.

We know relatively little about the physical appearance of the monastery, which occupied the present village site on the south-west edge of the island. It is possible that the village street-plan reflects a boundary (*vallum*) enclosing a rectilinear monastic precinct. Bede tells us that Bishop Finan (651–61) built a timber church dedicated to St Peter, in which Cuthbert was buried and which Bishop Eadberht (688–98) encased in lead, and calls this the 'greater church' (*basilica maior*). The existing Romanesque priory church of St Peter and parish church of St Mary are axially aligned (fig. 13), and it seems highly likely that they perpetuate pre-Viking twin churches (see *monastic sites). There is a small group of early inscribed *grave-markers and cross-shaft fragments. The recent excavation of a small mid ninth-century *peasant *settlement at Green Sheil, on the north coast of the island, gives some glimpse of the economic base of the late pre-Viking monastery.

In 793 the monastery was sacked in a shockingly unexpected attack by *Vikings. St Cuthbert's community continued on the island for several decades, but as Viking raids intensified the bishop and monks moved inland to safer sites, taking his body with them. Apparently some kind of religious life continued at Lindisfarne: there is a substantial collection of ninth- to eleventh-century monumental *sculpture, and when *Durham monks re-colonized the site from the 1090s they seem to have taken over the ancient pair of churches.

Two Lives of St Cuthbert, ed. B. Colgrave (Cambridge, 1940); D. O'Sullivan and R. Young, *Lindisfarne: Holy Island* (English Heritage, 1995); *Cuthbert*; R. Cramp, CASSS 1: *Co. Durham & Northumberland* (Oxford, 1984), 194–208 and pls. 188–203; J. Blair, 'The Early Churches at Lindisfarne', *Archaeologia Aeliana*, 5th ser. 19 (1991), 47–53.

JOHN BLAIR

LINDISFARNE GOSPELS (BL, Cotton Nero D.iv) is a Latin *gospelbook of the 'Northumbrian' textual family, thought to have been made at *Lindisfarne, perhaps in connection with the translation of the relics of St *Cuthbert in 698. An interlinear Old English *gloss was added by *Aldred, who was provost of the community of St Cuthbert at Chester-le-Street, in 970. Aldred's *colophon associates his work in completing the gospelbook by translating it with an original production team consisting of the artist/scribe, Eadfrith, bishop of Lindisfarne (698–721); the binder, Ædiluald, prior of *Melrose; the maker of the *metalwork fittings or shrine (*cumdach*), Bilfrith the anchorite. Their actual participation, or patronage, cannot otherwise be proven, but it is remarkable that such an elaborate work was largely made by one artist/scribe, when lower-grade Lindisfarne products (such as the Vatican Paulinus) involved teams of scribes. This is a cult item, the *opus Dei* of an important and gifted individual, and would have demanded considerable spiritual, physical and material resources, including the finest vellum and lapis lazuli from the Near East. The volume assimilates varied cultural influences: its 'Italo-Northumbrian' text exhibits Neapolitan liturgical features; its elegant, 'reformed' Insular half-uncial *script reflects the influence of Roman uncials; its evangelist portraits are indebted to Italo-Byzantine painting, interpreted in stylized form; its *carpet-pages (pl. 5) betray possible Coptic influence; its canon tables, decorated incipit pages and initials apply the status-laden repertoires of Celtic and Germanic ornament to the new medium of the book.

The book was associated in the facsimile commentary (1960) with the Durham and Echternach Gospels, which have been suggested as the work of an older contemporary in the Lindisfarne scriptorium. The Gospels seem to have accompanied the community from Lindisfarne to Chester-le-Street and *Durham, and passed to Robert Bowyer in the early seventeenth century, thence via Sir Robert *Cotton (1571–1631) to the British Museum in 1753.

CLA ii. 187; Alexander, *Insular MSS*, no. 9; T. D. Kendrick *et al.*, *Evangeliorum Quattuor Codex Lindisfarnensis*,

2 vols. (Olten and Lausanne, 1956–60); J. M. Backhouse, *The Lindisfarne Gospels* (Oxford 1981).

MICHELLE P. BROWN

LINDSEY, kingdom of. The district of eastern England between the river Witham and the Humber, in the northern part of modern Lincolnshire. Lindsey would appear to have enjoyed an identity as a separate kingdom in the sixth and seventh centuries, and may have retained this identity into the early eighth century; but it is a kingdom without a history, whose rulers succumbed sooner rather than later to more powerful neighbours, whose bishops established themselves in a place (*Syddensis ciuitas*) which cannot be securely identified, and whose people have to be recovered from what little trace they have left in the archaeological record. *Bede, writing in 731, had much to say of the bishops and monasteries of Lindsey (*HE* Pref., ii.16, iii.11, iii.27, iv.3, iv.12), but nothing to report of its kings. The *Lindesfarona*, with Hatfield, were assessed in the *Tribal Hidage at 7000 hides, which would put them on a par with other 'minor' kingdoms like the *Hwicce and the *East Saxons; and a genealogy for the kings of Lindsey, ending with a certain Aldfrith, son of Eatta, was included in the 'Anglian Collection' of royal genealogies. It was argued by Stenton that King Aldfrith attested King Offa's confirmation of a South Saxon charter (S 1183), *c.*790, representing the one and only appearance of a king of Lindsey in the historical record; sadly, the reference is to 'Ealfrid rex', which in context is more likely to be a scribal error for Offa's son Ecgfrith (cf. S 1184). Excavations at Flixborough, South Humberside, have done much to compensate for the inability of historians to be more constructive.

F. M. Stenton, 'Lindsey and its Kings' (1927), repr. in *Preparatory to Anglo-Saxon England*, ed. D. M. Stenton (Oxford, 1970), pp. 127–35; Stenton, *ASE*, pp. 48–50; S. Bassett, 'Lincoln and the Anglo-Saxon See of Lindsey', *ASE* 18 (1989), 1–32; B. Eagles, 'Lindsey', in Bassett, *Origins*, pp. 202–12, 280–4; S. Foot, 'The Kingdom of Lindsey', *Pre-Viking Lindsey*, ed. A. Vince, Lincoln Archaeol. Stud. 1 (Lincoln, 1993), 128–40; B. Yorke, 'Lindsey: the Lost Kingdom Found?', *Pre-Viking Lindsey*, ed. Vince, pp. 141–50.

SIMON KEYNES

LITANY OF THE SAINTS: *see* Prayer, Private

LITERACY. The question of literacy in Anglo-Saxon England is a complicated one. Because literacy is a social phenomenon, rather than a transcendent category of perception, the dimen-sions of medieval literacy are markedly different from our own. The medieval application of the Latin pair *litteratus-illitteratus* provides some help in defining literacy, but it is limited because of the social dimensions of the phenomenon. Grundmann has shown how the term *litteratus* was delimited to members of the clergy who could read and write in Latin. Its contrasting term, *illitteratus*, which denoted both a layman and one who could not read in that language, can offer no information on the cases where clergy could read but not write, or could read only the vernacular, or cases of lay people who could read either language. A second, contrasting pair, 'literate-oral', deriving from the modern understanding of literacy, provides limited insight into Anglo-Saxon literacy. The dichotomy in this pair sets off the ability to read and write against ignorance of these skills, but it ignores the fact that in the early Middle Ages reading and writing were separable skills, and that people who were non-readers could function in textual culture through the mediation of others. The circumscribed denotations of these pairs of terms suggest that a historically nuanced definition of literacy and its conditions in Anglo-Saxon England must take into account the language(s) of literacy, the clerical or lay status of a possible reader, and the specific features of early medieval literate practice.

Latin was the language of worship (for Mass, the sacraments, and the Divine Office), of ecclesiastical administration, and of the monastic *school. Primarily a textual language, it was as well the medieval language of power. The learning process for literacy in Latin, however, had a considerable admixture of oral processes: the boy was expected to memorize the psalms and *hymns (without necessarily understanding what he would speak). Only afterwards would he learn the *grammar and proceed to read increasingly advanced texts. Throughout his life he would hear texts as well as read them. The processes of literacy in Latin were inflected throughout with memory techniques from earlier centuries of oral learning. Works written in Latin were expected to be heard as well as read (e.g. the Preface to *Bede's *Historia ecclesiastica*). While the evidence for Latin literacy in England is primarily for the male clergy, there are clear indications that a number of women had achieved high degrees of literacy. The community of Abbess *Eadburg was asked to provide for *Boniface a copy of the epistles of Peter; *Aldhelm composed the *De virginitate* for the nuns of *Barking Abbey, Essex; *Hygeburg, an English nun at Heidenheim in *Germany, wrote the *Vita*

SS. Willibaldi et Wynnebaldi. There is restricted evidence as well for lay literacy. Bede indicates that King *Aldfrith of Northumbria (d. 705) was a learned man who had studied with *Adomnán; and King *Alfred (d. 899) translated *Gregory's *Regula pastoralis*, Boethius's *De consolatione Philosophiae*, Augustine's *Soliloquia*, and the first fifty psalms. While it is clear that Alfred could read, it is not as clear that he could write. The evidence of *Asser's biography (c. 88) suggests that it was Asser himself who copied passages into Alfred's *Enchiridion*.

Whatever the earliest identification of literacy in England with learning in Latin, Alfred, perhaps after 887, launched his project to translate those books 'most needful for men to know' into English. In his Preface to the translation of the *Regula pastoralis*, Alfred comments on the sad state of learning in England following upon the *Viking depredations. In the now famous lines, Alfred notes that 'there were very few on this side of the Humber who knew how to understand the divine service in English or further who could translate a letter from Latin into English; and I expect that there are not many beyond the Humber'. Finding this account somewhat exaggerated, Parkes has distinguished between two forms of literacy, professional (the ability to read and write to monastic standards) and practical (the ability to use writing to conduct business).

Alfred's Preface has further implications for the social conditions of literacy, since it outlines an ambitious programme of education for young free men, who have the opportunity (or 'wealth', OE *speda*) to study and who are required for no other tasks. They would be educated to read English. Further study in Latin would be for those intended for the *clergy. While it is unclear that Alfred's programme was ever formally adopted, manuscript evidence from the tenth and eleventh centuries indicates that English developed as an important language for study and thought in writing.

D. A. Bullough, 'The Educational Tradition in England from Alfred to Aelfric: Teaching *Utriusque Linguae*', *Settimane* 19 (1972), 453–94; M. T. Clanchy, *From Memory to Written Record: England 1066–1307*, 2nd ed. (Oxford, 1994); D. H. Green, *Medieval Listening and Reading: The Primary Reception of German Literature 800–1300* (Cambridge, 1994); H. Grundmann, 'Litteratus-Illitteratus', *Archiv für Kulturgeschichte* 40 (1958), 1–65; S. Kelly, 'Anglo-Saxon Lay Society and the Written Word', in *The Uses of Literacy in Early Mediaeval Europe*, ed. R. McKitterick (Cambridge, 1990), pp. 36–62; M. B. Parkes, 'The Literacy of the Laity', in *The Mediaeval World*, ed. D. Daiches and A. Thorlby (London, 1973), pp. 555–77, at 555–6.

KATHERINE O'BRIEN O'KEEFFE

LITURGICAL BOOKS, codices that contain the texts (and sometimes directions, commonly called rubrics) out of which the various services of the Christian liturgy are performed, are distinguished either by type of service or by intended user. Certain kinds of books are used for the Mass, the central sacrament at which bread and wine are offered and communion received; others for the Divine (or Daily) Office, services which combine elements of praise, prayer, and sometimes readings during seven or eight occasions in every twenty-four hours; still others for services performed only occasionally when there is need for them. The latter can range from simple pastoral offices like baptism and burial to services of great complexity like the consecration of churches or even the *coronation of monarchs. Alternatively, some books needed for only certain parts of a given service are specific as to user. Examples are a *gospelbook, or evangeliary, used by the deacon at Mass, or a benedictional, out of which a bishop pronounced solemn blessings at the time of communion.

The principal kind of liturgical book used at Mass in Anglo-Saxon England is the sacramentary, which contains the formulas, mostly prayers, used by the celebrant (the bishop or priest who presides). The variable *chants comprise a second main group of Mass texts; there are sometimes also tropes, verbal and musical elaborations of these chants or of the fixed chants like *Kyrie* and *Gloria in excelsis*. The primary book containing texts and, especially, music for these chants is the gradual, but there is also the troper, for the more specialized trope repertory. Finally, the biblical readings are either specified from a readings-list (mass lectionary) or contained entire as epistle-books or gospelbooks (evangeliary). When all these sets of elements – celebrant's formulas, chant texts, and readings – are combined into a single codex it is called a *missale plenum*, or missal for short.

The numbers of each of these kinds of books that survive vary widely. A relatively large number of gospelbooks are extant, but no epistle-books; of chant books, three or four (depending on how far the Anglo-Saxon period is extended; here the approximate terminus is *c.*1100); of massbooks proper (sacramentaries or missals) there are five complete, two very substantial, and several others in a more or less fragmentary state. Outstanding among the massbooks is the Leofric Missal (Oxford, Bodleian Library, Bodley 579), at its core a Gregorian sacramentary written in Lotharingia around AD 900 to which various English layers, including both calendar and mass forms, have been added; the latest of these additions date from the time of Bishop *Leofric (Exeter 1050–72). Next in age comes the Winchcombe Sacramentary (Orléans, Bibl. mun. 127), written almost certainly by an English scribe at the end of the tenth century, perhaps at the Gloucestershire abbey of *Winchcombe; but the book has been in France since the early eleventh century. The Missal (properly, sacramentary) of Robert of Jumièges (Rouen, Bibl. Mun. 274/Y.6) is also of monastic origin, *Ely and Peterborough being the likeliest places of writing; it was given to Jumièges by its eponymous owner when he was bishop of London, 1044–51. The only plenary missal to survive at all extensively is one from the New Minster, *Winchester (Le Havre, Bibl. mun. 330) from, probably, the 1070s. The plenary missal form has nothing intrinsically to do with the Norman Conquest; it is evident in some fragments (four gatherings) from a mid-eleventh century book from the Old Minster at *Winchester (now Worcester Cathedral, F. 173).

Celebrated among the very few chant books are two copies of what is generally termed the Winchester Troper (Cambridge, Corpus Christi College 473 and Oxford, Bodleian Library, Bodley 775); another troper (London, BL, Cotton Caligula A.xiv) has notable illustrations. Only one true gradual, and that of the late eleventh century (Durham, UL, Cosin V.v.6), is extant.

Books containing texts for the Daily Office include at a minimum the psalter, the collectar, and a chant book often called the antiphonary; these would suffice for the services of Lauds, Prime, Terce, Sext, Nones, Vespers, and Compline. For the readings at the 'night' Office – Nocturns, later and more normatively called Matins – some elements of Bible, homiliary (containing patristic sermons for certain occasions) and legendary or passional (providing saints' legends for their specific days) would also be required. Many psalters survive, although few of them are unarguably liturgical. The collectar contains variable prayers and brief biblical passages. The earliest surviving example (Durham, Cathedral Library, A.IV.19) dates to c.900 in its original core. The mid-eleventh-century Leofric Collectar (London, BL, Harley 2961) has much more extensive material than its nickname would suggest; it is thus moving towards being a breviary or portiforium, the omnibus book for Daily Office

texts. The late-eleventh-century Wulstan Portiforium (Cambridge, Corpus Christi College 391) moves a long way in this direction. No antiphonaries survive as such.

The bishop's distinctive book, the pontifical (and its offshoot, the benedictional) tends to be physically august, as befits its owner. As with the other books considered here, the pontificals that survive anything like entire date only from about 970. One can with some confidence be assigned to *Dunstan (Paris, BN, lat. 943), and the splendidly-illustrated *Benedictional of St Æthelwold (London, BL Add. 49598) was almost certainly used by that prelate. Roughly twenty such bishops' books are extant, entire or in substantial fragments. Three of the latest (including Cambridge, Corpus Christi College 163) are copies or versions of the Romano-German Pontifical developed in imperial circles in the mid-tenth century. The frequent inclusion of coronation rites in pontificals makes them compelling objects of study. At the other extreme of dignity would come the manual, the collection of pastoral rites used on needed occasions by a simple priest; but no manual survives, as a discrete book, from Anglo-Saxon England.

The Liturgical Books of Anglo-Saxon, England, ed. R. W. Pfaff, OEN Subsidia 23 (Kalamazoo, MI, 1995); D. N. Dumville, 'On the Dating of Some Anglo-Saxon Liturgical Manuscripts', TCBS 10 (1991–5), 40–58; H. Gneuss, 'Liturgical Books in Anglo-Saxon England', Clemoes FS, pp. 91–141; K. D. Hartzell, 'An Unknown English Benedictine Gradual of the Eleventh Century', ASE 4 (1975), 131–75; F. E. Warren, The Leofric Missal (Oxford, 1883); H. A. Wilson, The Missal of Robert of Jumièges, HBS 11 (London, 1896); A. Davril, The Winchcombe Sacramentary, HBS 109 (London, 1992); A. Corrêa, The Durham Collectar, HBS 107 (London, 1992); D. H. Turner, The Claudius Pontificals, HBS 97 (London, 1971); H. A. Wilson, The Benedictional of Archbishop Robert, HBS 24 (London, 1903).

RICHARD W. PFAFF

LITURGICAL COMMEMORATION. The practice whereby any person of high or good standing might ask to be remembered in the prayers of a particular religious community, or whereby members of one religious community would enter into a reciprocal agreement of a similar kind with another community, or whereby churchmen were encouraged by their leaders formally to commemorate other churchmen as and when they died. The practice found expression in various forms, and led to the development of complex webs linking the secular and ecclesiastical worlds. Some religious communities would have

Pl. 14 King Cnut and Queen Ælfgifu from the New Minster *Liber vitae*

maintained a 'Liber Vitae', or its equivalent, in which they kept a record of persons who entered into confraternity with them; the names which accumulated in this way were commemorated in daily services by their inclusion in the book, and by figurative extension were written in the 'Book of Life' which would be opened at the Last Judgement (Revelation XX.12). Communities also kept records of the obits of their friends and benefactors, as well as of their own members, and entered them in the margins of their martyrologies, or in the calendars of their service books, or in dedicated necrologies; of course, such records throw much light on a community's place in a wider context, and were subject to manipulation and adjustment in many ways. Among the various products of the practices of liturgical commemoration in Anglo-Saxon England are: the 'Liber Vitae' of the community of St *Cuthbert at *Lindisfarne (*c.*840), continued in the tenth century at Chester-le-

Street, and in the eleventh century at *Durham (BL, Cotton Domitian A. viii); the 'Liber Vitae' of the New Minster, later Hyde abbey, *Winchester, put together from earlier records in 1031 and also with layer upon layer of later additions (BL, Stowe 944: see pl. 14); the obits entered in a copy of the Martyrology of Usuard, from *Abingdon abbey (Cambridge, Corpus Christi College 57); and the obits entered in the calendar in the Prayerbook of *Ælfwine, dean (later abbot) of the New Minster, Winchester (BL, Cotton Titus D. xxvi + xxvii). Records of the same kind lie behind the pre-Conquest material incorporated in later (post-Conquest) manifestations of the same liturgical practices, for example at Christ Church, *Canterbury, and at *Ely abbey. Special interest attaches to the circumstances in which the name of a layman or ecclesiastic from Anglo-Saxon England might come to be entered in the 'Liber Vitae' of a religious house on the Continent. In some instances the practice might reflect an actual visit to the house in question; in other instances, it might reflect an agreement made from a distance, or an entry made by a visiting party on behalf of an absent party. Examples include certain ninth-century entries in the 'Liber Vitae' of Brescia (north Italy), and the tenth-century entries relating to King *Æthelstan, and others, in the *libri vitae* of St Gallen, Reichenau, and Pfäfers (Switzerland).

J. Gerchow, *Die Gedenküberlieferung der Angelsachsen, mit einem Katalog der* libri vitae *und Necrologien* (Berlin, 1988); R. Fleming, 'Christchurch's Sisters and Brothers: an Edition and Discussion of Canterbury Obituary Lists', *The Culture of Christendom*, ed. M. A. Meyer (London, 1993), pp. 115–53; S. Keynes, 'King Athelstan's Books', Clemoes FS, pp. 143–201, at 198–201; *The Liber Vitae of the New Minster and Hyde Abbey, Winchester*, ed. S. Keynes, EEMF 26 (Copenhagen, 1996), 49–65; S. Keynes, 'Anglo-Saxon Entries in the "Liber Vitae" of Brescia', Bately FS, pp. 99–119.

SIMON KEYNES

LITURGY, here defined as the performance of public services of Christian worship, was practised in some degree in Anglo-Saxon England from the time *Augustine of *Canterbury and his companions arrived in 597. At that point it would have been basically what is now called Early (or Old) Roman liturgy, itself in a state of flux and evolution. Subsequent development of liturgy in England reflects not only that evolution but also the very considerable reworking and adaptation of Roman liturgy to Frankish conditions, above all in the Carolingian and post-Carolingian periods. (It is possible that there was also some Celtic influence, but this is hard to pin down, save for a Breton strain in the last century or so of Anglo-Saxon England.)

In the time of *Bede (d. 735) a full liturgical regime was being followed in at least a few great establishments – most obviously, *Benedict Biscop's two houses, the monastery and cathedral at Canterbury, *York, and *Lindisfarne – but even for those churches no service book survives anything like entire. Evidence from fragments of books, from archaeology, and from literary texts witnesses to the evolution of a liturgical year which includes English saints like *Oswald, *Cuthbert, and *Æthelthryth, as well as retaining many Roman martyrs and other saints from the remote Mediterranean past. The vitality of English liturgy c.800 may be inferred from *Alcuin's writings, but for the ninth century there is very little direct evidence; the Old English *Martyrology provides ancillary, and tantalizing, hints.

When fuller evidence begins to be available, in roughly the last third of the tenth century, certain characteristics are plain. The mass-liturgy is fundamentally of the Gregorian type, mediated through the supplemented form developed by Carolingian liturgists. Against a central framewok of fixed formulas runs a contrapuntal pattern of variable prayers, chants, and readings. The Divine Office is celebrated according to either a monastic form, deriving ultimately from the Rule of Benedict and characterized by twelve lessons on great feasts, or a secular form in which the maximum number of lessons is nine. Much less evidence survives for the secular form than for the monastic; the Benedictine reform is both context and impetus for the production of much of what is extant in the way of *liturgical books. In either form the Daily Office is a highly complex mixture of sung and spoken elements, with at its heart the recitation of the psalter, usually within a single week. Liturgies for pastoral occasions such as baptism, visitation of the sick, burial, and (to some degree) marriage are discernible, partly as a kind of appendix to massbooks and partly through the emerging genre of the pontifical. Here the English strand appears to be quite original, as shown by several pontificals, fragmentary or whole, which until the mid-eleventh century seem to be quite independent of the predominant continental type, from c.950 the so-called Romano-German Pontifical.

By the mid-eleventh century the Anglo-Saxon liturgical year, in its core identical to that of other Western European areas which followed the Roman liturgy, tends to feature many English saints. Although there is much regional variation, several such saints are widely celebrated, like *Edmund of East Anglia, *Edward the Martyr, and *Mildred. There are also a few distinctively English observances like the Conception of John the Baptist and the Oblation of the Virgin.

Inferences drawn from the few major liturgical books that survive whole, like the *Benedictional of Æthelwold or the Missal of Robert of Jumièges, might lead to the supposition that the liturgical life of England was as rich and complex c.1000 as it was in, say, 1400. This is almost certainly a false impression. The sophisticated and elaborate liturgy practised at *Æthelwold's *Winchester or *Dunstan's Canterbury or (to take a secular example) *Leofric's *Exeter cannot safely be extrapolated beyond a couple of dozen major establishments. Surprisingly little is known about liturgical performance even in minster churches, and very little indeed about that in the emerging parish churches.

E. Bishop, *The Bosworth Psalter* (London, 1908); C. R. E. Cubitt, *Anglo-Saxon Church Councils c.650–c.850* (London, 1995); D. N. Dumville, *Liturgy and the Ecclesiastical History of Anglo-Saxon England* (Woodbridge, 1992); H. Gneuss, *Hymnar und Hymnen, im englischen Mittelalter*, Buchreihe der Anglia 12 (Tübingen, 1968); *Regularis concordia*, ed. T. Symons (London, 1953); *English Kalendars before AD 1100*, ed. F. Wormald, HBS 72 (London, 1934).

RICHARD W. PFAFF

LIUDGER (d. 809) was a native of *Frisia who was active in the Anglo-Saxon mission on the Continent. The precise date of his birth is unknown; but given that he was ordained priest in 777, he was presumably born no later than 747. He received his early training under Gregory (who was a Frankish pupil of *Boniface) at Gregory's school in Utrecht, which is known to have attracted Anglo-Saxon pupils. Through contact with these Anglo-Saxons, presumably, Liudger took the decision to go to *York, where he spent some time studying with *Alcuin (hence before 781, when Alcuin left England to join Charlemagne's court). Liudger subsequently returned to Frisia, where he restored the church at Deventer which had been established by *Leofwine (Lebuin), and built a church at Dokkum, the scene of Boniface's martyrdom. In the mid-780s, in the face of Saxon invasions of Frisia, Liudger travelled to *Rome; from there he went to Monte Cassino, where he spent two years studying Benedictine monasticism. When he returned to Frisia (786), he established the monastery of Werden, which became an important centre for the diffusion of

Anglo-Saxon learning and a repository of Anglo-Saxon books. His sole literary creation is the *Vita S. Gregorii abbatis* (*BHL* 3680), a Life of his master Gregory of Utrecht, which was completed *c*.790. He was appointed first bishop of Münster in 804, a post which he held until his death in 809. He was commemorated as a saint in the Low Countries, and one of his relatives, the Frisian Altfrid, who became the third bishop of Münster (839–49), composed a *Vita S. Liudgeri* (*BHL* 4937) sometime during the years of his bishopric.

MGH, SS xv.66–79 [Liudger, *Vita S. Gregorii abbatis*]; MGH, SS ii.404–19 [Altfrid, *Vita S. Liudgeri*]; A. Schröer, 'Chronologische Untersuchungen zum Leben Liudgers', in *Liudger und sein Erbe*, ed. H. Börsting and A. Schröer, Westfalia Sacra 1 (Münster, 1948), 85–138; idem, 'Das geistliche Bild Liudgers', in *Das erste Jahrtausend*, 2 vols. (Düsseldorf, 1962), i.194–215; R. Drögereit, *Werden und der Heliand* (Essen, 1950), esp. pp. 66–82; H. Löwe, 'Liudger als Zeitkritiker', in his *Von Cassiodor zu Dante. Ausgewählte Aufsätze* (Berlin, 1973), pp. 111–22; W. Berschin, *Biographie und Epochenstil im lateinischen Mittelalter*, 3 vols. (Stuttgart, 1986–), iii.41–50; R. Schieffer, 'Liudger', *Verfasserlexikon* v.852–4.

MICHAEL LAPIDGE

LOAN-TRANSLATIONS, or calques, are terms in which each element corresponds to an element of a term in another language. A Modern English example is *loan-word*, based on the German *Lehnwort*, where *loan* translates *Lehn*, and *word* translates *wort*. Most Old English loan-translations are based on terms from Latin, although there are a few from Old Norse. Latin terms which are calqued in Old English include *misericordia* 'mercifulness', rendered by the Old English *mildheortnes*; *circumcidere* 'circumcize', for which the Old English equivalent is *ymbsniþan* 'to cut round', and *illuminatio* 'illumination', translated as *inlihtnes*. Latin *trinity* is found as *prines* 'threeness' in Old English, and *Spiritus Sanctus* as *Halig Gast* 'holy spirit'. Where Modern English has the borrowed the term *unicorn* from Latin, Old English has *an-hyrne* 'one-horned'. It is less easy to identify loan translations from Old Norse with any certainty. Possible examples include *botleas* 'that cannot be compensated for', *hamsocn* 'attacking an enemy in his home', *lahceap* 'payment for reentry into lost legal rights', and *landceap* 'tax paid when land was bought'. It is sometimes possible to make a distinction between loan-translations and loan-renditions. The elements of a loan-rendition do not all correspond to elements in the foreign model. For instance, Latin *superbire* 'be proud', is paralleled by Old English *oferhygdian* from

oferhygd 'proud', in that *super-* is translated by *ofer-*, but *-bire* and *-hygdian* do not correspond. Another example is Latin *domus*, in the sense 'family, race', rendered by Old English *gehusscipe* 'house-ship', rather than *hus* 'house'.

H. Gneuss, *Lehnbildungen und Lehnbedeutungen im Altenglischen* (Berlin, 1955).

JULIE COLEMAN

LOAN-WORDS are words borrowed from another language. Most OE loan-words came from Latin or Old Norse, though a scattering of terms were also borrowed from Greek, Celtic, French, Frisian and Old Saxon. Loan-words represent a much smaller proportion of Old than of Modern English vocabulary. Where new concepts needed expression, the tendency in OE was to create self-explanatory compounds from within native resources, sometimes in the form of *loan-translations, or to use an existing term in a slightly altered sense. It should also be noted that many loan-words are recorded only once, so there is little evidence of their entry into the language in any meaningful sense.

A few Latin terms, largely plant names and terms belonging to the fields of agriculture, the military, government, and commerce, were adopted before the Anglo-Saxons left the Continent. Contact with the spoken language of the Romano-Britons led to the introduction of a smaller number of more general terms, usually nouns, such as *pærl* 'pearl', *oele* 'oil', and *copp* 'cup'. One result of the Anglo-Saxons' conversion to Christianity was an influx of Latin terminology from the mid-seventh century onwards. Borrowings during this period were largely religious, but by the end of the tenth century they were joined by learned terms, some of them ostentatiously obscure. Where Latin terms occur in OE texts, however, particularly in translations from Latin, they are often explained or presented alongside a synonymous OE word.

Scandinavian loan-words began to enter English after the end of the eighth century. Many of them belong to the fields of government and the military, but terms as basic as *tacan* 'to touch, take', *husband* 'householder, husband', and *feolaga* 'fellow', are also borrowed during this period. Much of the evidence for Old Norse influence on English dates from after the Conquest, with many terms restricted to the dialects and place-names of the *Danelaw. Greek terms in OE are largely adopted via Latin, though *engel* 'messenger, angel', *deofol* 'adversary, devil', *cirice* 'church', and *preost* 'priest' were borrowed directly into the continental Germanic dialects. Like these, the later borrowings through Latin are also largely ecclesiastical in nature: *(a)postol* 'apostle', *abbod* 'abbot', *paradis* 'paradise'. A few more general terms, such as *meregreot* 'pearl', *butere* 'butter', and *coper* 'copper', are also found.

If *place-names are excluded, *Celtic influence on OE is surprisingly small. It can be divided into three periods, of which the first two correspond roughly to those used to discuss Latin loans. The continental period can be represented by *dun* 'hill, down', borrowed into all Germanic dialects before the Anglo-Saxons left the Continent. The second period saw loans such as *brocc* 'badger' and *binn* 'manger, bin' adopted within Britain after the Anglo-Saxons arrived in the fifth century. The third period dates from the tenth-century, when renewed borrowing took place under the influence of Irish missionaries and reformers. Most of the loans from this period are no longer in use.

Loans from other sources are rarer still. French influence on English begins slightly before the Conquest, largely through Norman influence at the royal court (see *Anglo-Norman). Most Old Saxon loans are found only in *Genesis B*, a translation of an Old Saxon original, but the verb *(ge)macian* 'to make, do' is more widely used. From Frisian comes the compound *iegland* 'island'. A. C. Baugh and T. Cable, *A History of the English Language*, 4th ed. (London, 1993), ch. 4; A. Campbell, *Old English Grammar* (Oxford, 1959), ch. X; D. Kastovsky, 'Semantics and Vocabulary' in CHELang, i. 290–408; R. Lass, *Old English* (Cambridge, 1994), ch. 8; M. S. Serjeantson, *A History of Foreign Words in English* (London, 1935), pp. 11–103; B. M. H. Strang, *A History of English* (London, 1970) §§175–7, 187, 188, 202; H. Gneuss, '*Anglicae linguae interpretatio*: Language Contact, Lexical Borrowing and Glossing in Anglo-Saxon England', *PBA* 82 (1993), 107–48, repr. in his *Language and History in Early England* (Aldershot, 1996), no. V [with addenda].

JULIE COLEMAN

LONDON was the most important city of Roman Britain, and excavation outside its walls shows that its *cemeteries continued to be used after *c.400*. However, little trace survives of the late Roman *town itself other than the walls. Evidence for post-Roman political control comes from a few written, Christian sources. Although the story of the visit of St Germanus makes no mention of London, for this visit to take place implies that the Thames was still in British hands. In the sixth century, by contrast, *Gildas lamented that it was not possible for pilgrims to visit *St Alban's shrine since by then the British in the Chilterns were

completely encircled by heathens. At present, however, no type fossil which would allow us to identify fifth-to-sixth-century British occupation sites or burials on the ground is known.

Early Anglo-Saxon cemeteries and occupation sites are common in the Thames valley. Some had their origins in the fifth century and there is no reason to doubt that by *c.500* there were Germanic communities occupying most of the lighter soils of the valley. The first post-Roman polity in the London area known to history is the kingdom of the East Saxons. By the end of the sixth century there seems to have been a single authority ruling the area north of the Thames from the east coast through to the Chilterns. London lay in Middlesex, a western province of this kingdom. The first bishop of the East Saxons (*Mellitus) had his cathedral in London.

The first archaeological evidence for activity to the east of the walled city is of late sixth- or early seventh-century date, and there is numismatic evidence, in the form of a small issue of gold thrymsas, to suggest that London was a place of some importance by *c.640*. By *c.680* both archaeological and documentary sources agree that there was a major port at London. Stray finds and excavations show that an extensive settlement existed behind the Strand, probably that known from documents as *Lundenwic*. *Lundenwic* was originally undefended, although its boundary would probably have been marked by a ditch. If its inhabitants needed protection they would have had to seek it within the walls of the Roman town. Patches of metalling have been found on several excavations in *Lundenwic*, but only in those at the Royal Opera House in Covent Garden can these be dignified with the name 'street', where a major north-south street lined with timber buildings and with metalled lanes gave access from the street to presumed industrial and horticultural land behind.

A few excavations at the periphery of *Lundenwic* have produced evidence which suggests that they were located in a ring of farms and quarries surrounding the main settlement. Observations in Whitehall between Downing Street (a mid Saxon farm site) and Charing Cross (within the emporium) have failed to produce evidence of mid Saxon settlement, so there was probably open land between the focus at Thorney (*Westminster) and *Lundenwic*.

Evidence for overseas contacts comes in the form of imported *pottery, *glass and other items. All were presumably incidental to the main traffic passing through the port, which according to *Bede included *slaves. A high proportion of the pottery used in *Lundenwic* is *Ipswich ware, made in the contemporary East Anglian port and testifying to a thriving coastal *trade.

There is little evidence for the large-scale production of goods in *Lundenwic*. Loom-weights occur in large numbers, but are also a ubiquitous feature of rural early-to-mid Anglo-Saxon *settlements. Pottery was not made in the London area and evidence for *metalworking, though present, is not notable. As in other English emporia, the scale of the documented manufacturing capability of the settlement is uncertain and the known crafts could easily have been involved solely in supplying the needs of the indigenous population.

From *c*.820 London suffered a number of attacks, mainly at the hands of the *Vikings, culminating in an overwintering in the Thames valley by a Viking band in the late 870s. Ninth-century artefacts are absent from within the walls of Roman London but occur in *Lundenwic*, although the Strand excavations typically fail to produce artefacts dated later than *c*.850. It is likely that the inhabitants of London were severely affected by this social unrest but still clung onto the Strand settlement.

That London was refounded by *Alfred in 886 is well-known from the entry under that year in the *Anglo-Saxon Chronicle*. What 'refoundation' actually meant is now much clearer as a result of a combination of documentary and archaeological research. These show that there was a wholesale abandonment of *Lundenwic*; on the other hand, settlement and trade was encouraged within the walls of the Roman city, which had been sparsely occupied before *c*.880, except for the cathedral precinct, and a putative royal palace possibly occupying the site of the Cripplegate fort. The first activity was concentrated in the western half of the walled city, in the shadow of the cathedral, and seems in the beginning to have consisted of two north-south streets running back from the river at Queenhithe. A decade later, plots of land between these streets were defined in relation to east-west streets and one minor north-south lane. Dating of timbers from excavations at Queenhithe confirm that post-Roman activity began in the late 880s.

The subsequent growth of the late Saxon *town is shown in outline by the distribution and frequency of stray *coin finds, which suggest that London grew slowly before *c*.950 but then took off spectacularly. This sequence is confirmed by excavations to the north of the London Bridge, in the eastern part of the walled city, where a second nucleus seems to have been established by *c*.900.

Little is known of any refurbishment of the Roman defences. The ditches were redug but the walls seem to have survived.

The distribution of late Saxon pottery shows that *c*.1000 the town was concentrated around the west and east market streets, Cheapside and Eastcheap, with another probable focus around the site of the Roman basilica. Expansion from these nucleii took place before the Norman Conquest onto the waterfront, in front of the City wall. At a later date, perhaps even after the Conquest, the land between the initial nucleii and the landward walls was occupied. Excavations in the Aldgate, Bishopsgate and Aldersgate suburbs shows that ribbon development had taken place alongside approach roads to the city by *c*.1050.

Traded goods found in Late Saxon deposits in the City of London include pottery from the Rhineland, Belgium and northern France; Rhenish lava, Scandinavian honestones and silks from *Byzantium and China. Evidence for crafts and industries in Late Saxon London is sparse. The most frequently-found waste consists of fragments of crucibles from the working for both copper alloys and precious metals.

V. Horsman, C. Milne and G. Milne, *Aspects of Saxo-Norman London I*, London and Middlesex Archaeological Society Special Paper 11 (London, 1988); A. Vince, *Saxon London: an Archaeological Investigation* (Seaby, 1990); A. Vince, ed., *Aspects of Saxo-Norman London II*, London and Middlesex Archaeological Society Special Paper 12 (London, 1991).

ALAN VINCE

LORDSHIP: *see* Manors and Manorial Lordship

LULL (*c*.710–86), a native of Wessex who received his early training at the monastery of *Malmesbury in the time of Abbot Eaba (fl. *c*.730). It is probable that the name Lull (from the Latin form *Lullus*) derives from the *by-name *Lytel* ('Little') by which he was known at Malmesbury. As a young man he went to *Germany to join the mission of *Boniface, with whom he was closely associated during the latter's lifetime, and whom he succeeded as archbishop of Mainz following Boniface's martyrdom in 754. The exact date of his arrival in Germany cannot be determined, but the earliest of his letters preserved among the corpus of Bonifatian correspondence date from the early 740s, and by 751 he was sufficiently well established to be entrusted by Boniface with a mission to Pope Zacharias in Rome. He was a deacon by 740, a priest by 751, and Boniface's chorepiscopus by 752. Among his various accomplishments was the foundation of the monastery of Hersfeld. He assumed the archbishopric of Mainz when Boniface departed for *Frisia in 754, but, probably as a result of his enduring struggle with Sturmi, the abbot of Fulda, concerning episcopal jurisdiction over that monastery, he did not receive the *pallium until 780. Unusually, Lull's profession of faith to the pope made in that year has been preserved. Like Boniface, Lull was a scholar of some attainment (it has been thought that the annotating hand which accompanies that of Boniface in various manuscripts preserved at Fulda is that of Lull); and his letters to correspondents in England contain insistent requests for books, especially the works of *Aldhelm and *Bede. Among the corpus of Bonifatian correspondence are preserved some sixteen letters addressed by Lull to various recipients, as well as some twenty-three letters to Lull. Lull's own letters show him to be a prose-writer of some competence (much indebted to the model of Aldhelm) as well as a competent poet in hexameters and *octosyllables. He was buried at Hersfeld where he was commemorated on 16 October; a *vita* of Lull was composed in the eleventh century by Lambert of Hersfeld (*BHL* 5065), but this contains little reliable detail concerning his life.

Sharpe, *Handlist*, 1025; *ActaSS*, Oct. vii. 1083–9 [Lambert, *Vita S. Lullii*]; MGH, SS xv. 135–48 [Lambert, *Vita S. Lullii*]; M. Tangl, ed., *Epistolae S. Bonifatii et Lullii*, MGH, ES 1 (Berlin, 1916); W. Levison, *England and the Continent in the Eighth Century* (Oxford, 1946), pp. 233–40 [Lull's profession of faith]; H. Hahn, *Bonifaz und Lul* (Leipzig, 1883).

MICHAEL LAPIDGE

LYMINGE (Kent) was a royal double monastery founded for Æthelburh (d. 647), daughter of King *Æthelberht of *Kent and widow of King *Edwin of *Northumbria. It may also have been a royal centre: a charter of 689 grants an iron-mine belonging to the 'court' of Lyminge. Priest-abbots occur in 689 and 732, and many endowments are recorded during the eighth century. In the reigns of *Offa and *Coenwulf it was one of the minsters disputed between the archbishops and the Mercian kings. Sacked by *Vikings, it passed into the hands of the West Saxon dynasty and eventually of Christ Church, *Canterbury; *Dunstan may have partly rebuilt it. Excavated footings suggest a complex group of buildings centred on the apsidal seventh-century church.

D. W. Rollason, *The Mildrith Legend* (Leicester, 1982); Brooks, *Canterbury*, pp. 183–7, 202–6; H. M. Taylor, 'Lyminge Churches', *Archaeological Journal* 126 (1969), 257–60; S. E. Kelly, *Charters of St Augustine's, Canterbury*, Anglo-Saxon Charters 4 (Oxford, 1995).

JOHN BLAIR

M

MACHUTUS, ST [= St Malo], a sixth- or seventh-century bishop, perhaps of Welsh birth, founder of the church of Saint-Servan (Aleth), whose centre is the present-day Saint-Malo, and is thus known as the apostle of Brittany. Two recensions of a Life of Machutus by one Bili survive from the ninth century (*BHL* 5116a, b), depicting the saint as a vigorous and challenging preacher who travelled on horseback, but these texts shed little light on his true origins and ministry. *Relics of Machutus were claimed at several places in England, including *Winchester, and his feast was quite widely celebrated (feast 15 November; translation 11 July). An OE Life of Machutus, based on the long recension of Bili's Life, was composed probably at Winchester in the time of Bishop *Æthelwold.

F. Plaine, 'Vie inédite de Saint Malo, évêque d'Aleth (510–621?), par Saint Bili, évêque de Vannes et martyr', *Bulletin et mémoires de la Société archéologique du département d'Ille-et-Vilaine* 16 (1884), 137–256; A. de la Borderie, *Deux vies inédites de S. Malo* (Rennes, 1884); G. Le Duc, *Vie de Saint Malo, évêque d'Alet: Version écrite par le diacre Bili* (Rennes, 1979); D. Yerkes, *The Old English Life of Machutus* (Toronto, 1984); E. G. Whatley, 'Lost in Transmission: Omission of Episodes in some Old English Prose Saints' Legends', *ASE* 26 (1997), 187–208, at 198–207.

R. C. LOVE

MAGIC. Scholars unfortunately disagree on the definition of magic. In 1948 Storms repeated the *Oxford English Dictionary*: 'the pretended art of influencing the course of events . . . by processes supposed to owe their efficacy to their power of compelling the intervention of spiritual beings, or of bringing into operation some occult controlling principle of nature'; and went on to quote Frazer's two 'Laws': of Similarity – 'that like produces like, or that an effect resembles its cause'; and of Contagion – 'that things which have been in contact . . . continue to act on each other . . . once the physical contact has been severed'. The traditional distinction between science and magic is that the former is rational and the latter irrational, and between magic and religion (including prayer) is that the former is manipulative, the latter supplicative and/or worshipful. If so, pagan priests may (as often elsewhere) have practised magic; for example, *Stephen of Ripon described a high priest attempting by means of spells to bind *Wilfrid's hands. In practice, too, it is often difficult to make a distinction between supplication to and attempted manipulation of the supernatural; for example, in the so-called *Æcerbot*, a ritual recorded in the eleventh century to improve agricultural land, to be performed at the beginning of ploughing, which combines traditional with Christian elements. Flint argued that the church 'rescued' from paganism some kinds of relatively harmless magic for its own ends; Jolly, however, claimed that to speak of Christian magic is anachronistic, since to a Christian Anglo-Saxon magic was evil and associated with the devil. However, there does not seem to have been one comprehensive Old English word which expressed our idea of 'magic', but many, for different aspects. Perhaps religion and magic should be regarded as at either end of a spectrum: at one end an official, public ritual worshipping a deity at a recognized sanctuary, and at the other end a secret, individual action like that mentioned in a tenth-century charter, where a woman was drowned, and her son (who escaped) declared an outlaw, because they had driven iron pins into [presumably an effigy of] a man. Many rituals fall in between; for example, a community ceremony to bring rain, or an individual's invocation, in church, of a saint to help in healing, might have been condemned by strict churchmen, but accepted as Christian by rural priests and people.

Among the primary sources for Anglo-Saxon magic are the *laws against idolatry and the condemnations of ecclesiastics in *penitentials and sermons. Penalties were prescribed, for example, for those, often women, who performed divinations or love magic. In the Anglo-Saxon *medical literature magic elements (such as wearing *amulets and using certain apparently irrational rituals) are employed, especially for 'conditions intractable to rational treatments' (see also *charms). However, churchmen condemned as idolatrous women who put their daughters on the roof or in an oven to cure fever, or who 'pulled their children through the earth' at crossroads for their health's sake.

A. L. Meaney, 'Ælfric and Idolatry', *The Journal of Religious History* 13 (1984), 119–35; A. Davies, 'Witches in Anglo-Saxon England', *Superstition and Popular Medicine in Anglo-Saxon England*, ed. D. G. Scragg (Manchester, 1989), pp. 57–71; V. I. J. Flint, *The Rise of Magic in Early Medieval Europe* (Oxford, 1991); K. L. Jolly, *Popular Religion in Late Anglo-Saxon England: Elf Charms in Context* (Chapel Hill, NC, and London, 1996); A. L. Meaney. 'Anglo-Saxon Idolators and Ecclesiasts from Theodore to Alcuin: a Source Study', *ASSAH* 5 (1992), 103–25.

AUDREY MEANEY

MAGONSÆTAN: *See* Hereford, Mercia

MALMESBURY (Wilts.) was notable in the Anglo-Saxon period for its monastery, founded within the ramparts of an Iron Age hillfort overlooking the river Avon, around which a small town developed. *Bede records the earliest form of the *place-name as *Maildubi Urbs* and this is believed to indicate, as later Malmesbury tradition asserted, that its first religious house had been founded by an Irish monk Maildubh. When the area was conquered by the West Saxons in the late seventh century, control of the foundation passed to the leading West Saxon churchman and scholar *Aldhelm, who may himself have been educated by Maildubh. Under Aldhelm Malmesbury became famed as a centre of learning where, among others, the Anglo-Saxon missionary *Lull was trained. Aldhelm became the most significant saint of the foundation and attracted continuing royal patronage. King *Æthelwulf of Wessex presented a silver shrine decorated with miracles of the saint, while King *Æthelstan chose Malmesbury as his place of burial. The Iron Age defences made Malmesbury an obvious choice for one of King *Alfred's burhs, and it is listed in the *Burghal Hidage with an assessment of 1200 hides. Urban development was encouraged by the establishment of a *mint in the tenth century, and Malmesbury was described in *Domesday Book as a borough.

M. Lapidge and M. Herren, *Aldhelm: the Prose Works* (Cambridge, 1979); J. Haslam, 'The Towns of Wiltshire', in Haslam, *Towns*, pp. 111–17; Yorke, *Wessex*, passim.

B. A. E. YORKE

MALNUTRITION is a condition in humans which signifies a nutritional status significantly different from some standard, or a loss of balance between consumption and expenditure of energy. There are three categories of malnutrition: marasmus (a decline to 60% of expected weight for age), kwashiorkor (deficient protein), and wasting (a body height less than 90% of ideal for age). Famine may be an intermittent or continuous state where a population is deprived of its normal sources of food, for example a harvest failure, or does not receive enough food because of overpopulation; famine can lead to malnutrition. Biocultural factors cause malnutrition, such as household income, *social class and often *disease, especially infection. Malnutrition is more often seen in agriculturists and lower socioeconomic groups today in developing countries, and some individuals may become malnourished because of their age and sex, through neglect.

In the Anglo-Saxon period direct evidence for malnutrition and famine may be found both in human remains and documentary sources. Although in human remains many signs of malnutrition are only revealed in the soft tissues, in the skeleton and teeth markers of nutritional stress may be present, reflecting undernutrition. Dental enamel defects, and radiographically opaque horizontal (Harris) lines in the ends of arm and leg bones, reflect stress most likely caused by malnutrition during growth. Decreased stature for age, reduced thickness of cortical (outer) layer of bones, osteoporosis (reduced bone quantity), cribra orbitalia/porotic hyperostosis (iron deficiency anaemia), scurvy (vitamin C deficiency) and rickets (vitamin D deficiency) also reflect an individual's lack of access to an adequate diet. The presence of disease in the skeleton may also represent a response to malnutrition and/or famine since a malnourished body is more susceptible to health problems. In studies of skeletons from Anglo-Saxon *cemeteries the evidence for malnutrition is mainly on the basis of dental enamel defects and cribra orbitalia. For example, at *Raunds, a third of the adult and nearly two thirds of the non-adult population had cribra orbitalia, whilst at Caister-on-Sea a quarter of the adults and a third of the non-adults suffered. Dental defects were seen in 13.1% of the total teeth at Addingham and in over half of the dentitions at Eccles, and in around half of the non-adults at Raunds. Harris Lines have been noted in a third of the non-adults at Raunds, occurring mainly at age 2–4 years, whilst the average number of lines per person in one study appeared to fall from the early to late Saxon period, possibly indicating a reduction in stress; scurvy, rickets, reduced cortical thickness and osteoporosis have rarely been reported. In the majority of instances, stature has been noted as normal for the period in most population studies, which suggests that nutrition was adequate in this respect. The Anglo-Saxon period, from published evidence, suggests a mixed economy involving cultivation of crops and *animal husbandry but their relative contributions varied in different geographical regions; an interpretation of the results of studies of stress in cemetery populations in relation to questions of malnutrition and famine is difficult.

S. A. Quandt, 'Nutrition in Medical Anthropology', in *Medical Anthropology. Contemporary Theory and Method*, ed. C. F. Sargent and T. M. Johnson (London, 1996), pp. 272–89; D. L. Martin, A. H. Goodman and G. J. Armelagos, 'Skeletal Pathologies as Indicators of Quantity and Quality of Diet', in *Analysis of Prehistoric Diets*, ed. R. I. Gilbert and J. H. Mielke (London, 1985), pp. 227–79; J. Rackham, ed., *Environment and Economy in Anglo-Saxon England*, CBA Research Report 89 (York, 1994).

CHARLOTTE A. ROBERTS

MANORS AND MANORIAL LORDSHIP.

The term *manor* (Latin *manerium*, French *manoir*) came into England with the Normans and many of the difficulties surrounding its use stem from the fact that a word used in France to denote a type of building – a seigneurial residence – came to be used in England to denote a type of social structure. What became known as the 'manorial system' (on the Continent more commonly the 'bi-partite system') essentially comprised two elements, the 'demesne' (*la réserve*), land devoted to production for the lord of the manor (a term taken here to include institutional as well as private landowners), and land held by tenants in return for a variety of services in cash, kind, and labour.

The extent to which the manorial system had developed in England before the Conquest is a matter of debate. It is important not to read back into the period developments which happened after it, and *Domesday Book is not as unambiguous a witness to the existence of manorialism in eleventh-century England as is sometimes assumed. Nevertheless, these key elements – demesne and tenant land – were undoubtedly present, some in embryo, some well developed.

The context for the development of the manor before the conquest is the growth in the amount of private property. Bookland, land given by *charter (OE *boc*) by kings, by lay people in the guise of gifts by kings, or by leading ecclesiatics, was heritable, transferable and, unlike traditionally inherited land, owned outright by an individual (see *land tenure). Originally introduced for the secure transfer of property to the church, bookland granted to individuals became the agent of effective family strategies (including church

endowment) and the favouring of particular heirs, retainers or blood lines. Private ownership also encouraged the owners of bookland to establish seigneurial centres on the inlands of their estates, the portion devoted to cultivation of food for their table (this area was sometimes called 'bordland' or 'table-land': see *estate management). A late Anglo-Saxon text shows that the most important status indicators at these were an enclosed and well-defined central space or *burh*, with its 'burh-gate' or entrance, and a kitchen building: many included a private church or chapel and a burial ground and land to support a resident priest. Some of these centres can be recognized in place-names composed of an individual's name in the genitive and *-tun*, such as Woolstone, 'Wulfric's *tun*', named from the *thegn who acquired it in the late tenth century, or similar names in *-burh* (see *forts and fortifications).

Also part of the inland were plots of land assigned to *slaves and estate workers, and the larger holdings of very dependent tenants who held their land in return for rents which included a large component of labour (see *labour service). The smaller category of these holdings was held by the people that the Domesday clerks categorized as *bordarii*, bordars, who approximated to servile smallholders known in Normandy and other parts of northern France as *bordiers* or tenants in *bordage*. The larger tenant holdings were thought of in the seventh-century *laws of *Ine to be typically a yardland (arable land measured by the ploughman's rod, which may or may not have approximated to the thirty acres of the later medieval yardland). They were held under varying degrees of dependence: one of Ine's laws shows that such a holding could be taken on for a mixture of rent and labour, and the lease could be given up at the end of the year, but if the lord had provided a house for his tenant and wished to charge labour alone, he could enforce a permanent tenancy. Three late Anglo-Saxon texts show that at least on the great ecclesiastical estates, week work – labour of unlimited amounts in some cases – could be demanded from these dependent tenants, in one document (from Hurstbourne Priors, Hants.) referred to as *ceorls*, in another (from Tidenham, Gloucs.) as *geburs*. The tenants of the inland were tied to their holdings, and were effectively unfree (see *estate management). It was probably only from the twelfth century that lordship of a manor, however small, would convey the right to hold a court for its tenants, a 'hall-moot'.

The extent to which the entire peasantry of a particular locality was involved in such arrangements before the Conquest varied widely. In the case of the small bookland estate, it is likely that most of the local peasantry rented their land from the lord and worked on his inland. The centres of large estates, where high rates of production were required to support the landowner, were similarly likely to have relied on an intensively exploited peasantry – monastic inlands and the centres and berewicks of lay multiple estates are examples. But, particularly in areas of Scandinavian settlement and in regions of scattered settlement, many *peasants may have had only a tangential involvement with the lord's economy, typically obliged to work and lend their equipment for a limited number of days at the peak times of the agricultural year.

It is these wide differences which made the Domesday clerks' job so difficult and Domesday such a problematic guide to the extent of dependent social relations within the manor. The compilers were required to collect information about the major landholders, their properties, physical assets and the people of various categories of the rural population at each vill. The information was returned in each county vill by vill but was reorganized under the holdings of the major landholders and those who held land from them. The term manor is not used for all entries. When it is used, it denotes the smallest unit of lordship. (As it is lordship that is being recorded, not physical geography, there might be more than one manor in a single vill, and a manor might comprise more than one vill.) The purpose of assigning all land, where possible, to a manor may be more to do with the collection of geld than with the recording of landlord-tenant relationships. A typical entry records demesne land, with its associated plough-teams and slaves on the one hand, and on the other the *villani*, *bordarii*, cottagers, freemen and sokemen, and their land and plough-teams. What Domesday never records is the relationship between the landowner and these people.

T. H. Aston, 'The Origins of the Manor in England', *TRHS* 5th ser. 8 (1958), 59–83; R. J. Faith, *The English Peasantry and the Growth of Lordship* (London, 1997); F. W. Maitland, *Domesday Book and Beyond* (Cambridge, 1897), pp. 140–75; J. J. Palmer, 'The Domesday Manor', in *Domesday Studies*, ed. J. C. Holt (Woodbridge, 1987), pp. 139–53; P. Vinogradoff, *The Growth of the Manor*, 2nd ed. (Oxford, 1911), pp. 304–470.

ROSAMOND FAITH

MANUAL (RITUAL): *see* Liturgical Books

MANUMISSION is a legal act whereby a person is freed from a state of servitude. It also denotes the record of such an act (hereinafter called a manumission-document). The exiled Bishop *Wilfrid's freeing in 681 × 686 of 250 slaves on his *Selsey estate in *Sussex (*Bede, *HE* iv.13) is the earliest known English manumission. Wihtred's Kentish code of 695, the first incorporation of manumission into English *law, required a person to be freed in church, a Roman form known as *manumissio in sacrosanctis ecclesiis*. As in Lombard Italy, the liberated *slave was declared to be *folcfry* (publicly free) but the manumittor retained certain rights in the freedman. Manumission at the crossroads, another legal form otherwise known only from Lombard sources, is recorded from Devon and Cambridgeshire. Both forms may have been borrowed early from Italy, possibly when *Theodore came to England in 669 to reorganize the church.

*Æthelberht's laws (597×616) mention three classes of *læt*, the highest having a *wergild twenty shillings less than a freeman. The word is almost certainly related to the Latin *lætus* (a bondman given land to till) and to the *litus*, *latus* and *lazzus* of continental Germanic laws. These classes may represent freedmen moving towards the full integration into the free community attainable only in the fourth generation.

The Scandinavians practised a similar system of inter-generational status change. The higher type of freedman, the *leysíngr*, attained full freedom, embracing the rights of marriage, disposal of property and inheritance, after three generations. The word (in the form *lising*) appears in an agreement of 880×890 between *Alfred and *Guthrum; its use as a personal name and in *place-names such as Lazenby suggests this practice existed in the *Danelaw and the use of the term 'half-free' in a Danelaw *will implies that the lower category of freedman, who gained freedom after nine generations, was also known in England.

Some 120 manumission-documents from *Bath, Bodmin, *Exeter and *Durham survive, mostly entered in *gospelbooks. The earliest dates from 924×925 and is untypical only in that the manumittor was a king, *Æthelstan of *Wessex. Entry in a gospelbook, which does not seem to have been a continental practice, may have been of Celtic origin: the earliest manumission-document from Britain, dating from before 840, appears in the Welsh Lichfield Gospels. Its record here gave sacred authority to and permanent, written public recognition of the act while also acknowledging the manumittor's charity. Erasures in two of the gospelbooks suggest that the act could be revoked.

The practice survived the Conquest: some Old English entries in the *Exeter Book date from the 1130s.

As to the nature of the ceremony, one record from the 1090s mentions the prior sale of a person at the church door, followed by a ceremony at the altar, where the purchaser subsequently manumitted the slave. Witnesses included both clerics and laymen. The sacredness of the altar could be transferred to a saint's tomb or even to religious relics outside a church. This last occurred when one Ordgar 'was very sick'; a ceremony at the altar followed, presumably to validate what must have been a testamentary manumission. Most records claim the act was performed for the good of the manumittor's soul; although motives must often have been mixed, the example of Ordgar and the growing numbers of testamentary manumissions to be found in late Anglo-Saxon wills show that this pious motive should not be disbelieved.

Ties binding freemen to the land gradually grew tighter in England. A late-tenth-century *Ely document claimed possession over persons called *geburas* ('boors'), two with great-grandparents who had lived on its Hatfield estate. Two mid-tenth-century Wiltshire records reveal that *geburas* were having to pay to become *færfrige* ('free to go'). Apart from granting this right these Wiltshire records are like other manumission-documents: the ambiguous diplomatic form reveals the shift from *slavery to serfdom taking place in late Anglo-Saxon society, a change completed in the first half of the twelfth century whereby the right to move from an estate became a mark of a free person.

Diplomatarium Anglicum Ævi Saxonici, ed. and trans. B. Thorpe (London, 1865), pp. 623–48; D. A. E. Pelteret, *Slavery in Early Mediaeval England from the Reign of Alfred until the Twelfth Century* (Woodbridge, 1995), esp. ch. 5; idem, 'Two Old English Lists of Serfs', *MS* 48 (1986), 470–513.

DAVID A. E. PELTERET

MANUSCRIPTS *see* Script; and see also entries for individual named manuscripts.

MARKETS AND FAIRS must have had a major, though largely unrecorded, place in Anglo-Saxon social and economic life. It is likely that sites of regular popular assembly, whether for religion, *law or *entertainment, were also used for regular local *trade. Concentrations of eighth-century *coins, hooked tags and dress-fittings found (mainly by metal-detecting) in the open country, often on border zones or within prehistoric earth-works, seem to identify a range of fair and market sites in use when coinage first became widespread; major regional fairs were held in some Iron Age hillforts down to modern times. *Monastic sites in particular may have attracted regular long-term markets, perpetuated in the market-places adjoining many ex-minsters in late medieval small *towns, and in the churchyard markets which sometimes continued as late as the thirteenth century.

The growth of fortified towns during *c.*870–920 gave kings the incentive to restrict major transactions to boroughs and ports, where they could be supervised by royal officials. It is doubtful if these measures were ever practicable, given the likely volume of low-level exchange at rural fairs and markets. The list of some sixty English markets in *Domesday Book (1086) must be grossly incomplete. Later evidence suggests the possibility of a regular system of *hundredal markets, and there are abundant references to informal but ancient assemblies (*congregationes*). Many of the ostensibly new markets and fairs in twelfth- and thirteenth-century planned towns may in fact have been long-standing gatherings, newly brought under royal and seigneurial control.

P. H. Sawyer, 'Fairs and Markets in Early Medieval England', *Danish Medieval History: New Currents*, ed. N. Skyum-Nielsen and N. Lund (Copenhagen, 1981), pp. 153–68; R. Morris, 'Baptismal Places', Sawyer FS, pp. 15–24; R. H. Britnell, 'English Markets and Royal Administration before 1200', *Economic History Review* 2nd ser. 31 (1978), 183–96; idem, *The Commercialisation of English Society 1000–1500* (Cambridge, 1993); C. Dyer, 'The Hidden Trade of the Middle Ages: Evidence from the West Midlands of England', *Journal of Historical Geography* 16 (1992), 141–57.

JOHN BLAIR

MARRIAGE AND DIVORCE. Marriage in Anglo-Saxon society took the form of a contract between the bridegroom and the bride's kindred. Two marriage agreements survive from the early eleventh century, and further evidence is contained in a late text 'On the Betrothal of a Woman' and in the seventh-century *laws of *Æthelberht (chs. 77–81). The prospective bridegroom was required to pledge a substantial sum in return for the acceptance of his suit. This is sometimes interpreted in terms of the sale of the bride; but it is clear that at least during the later period the woman was a consenting party and herself the recipient of the 'bride-price', the role of the kindred being to safeguard her interests. As part of the marriage settlement, she also received a 'morning-gift' from the bridegroom the morning after the consummation of the marriage. This became her personal property, reverting to her own kindred if she died childless. Æthelberht (77,1) provides for the annulment of the contract in the event of fraud, but it is uncertain whether this refers to unchastity on the part of the bride or to the groom's failure to meet his financial commitments.

By the eleventh century, marriage was forbidden between fourth cousins, as also between spiritual relatives (VI Æthelred 12, I Cnut 7). Earlier provisions were less strict; and so too penalties for adultery became harsher towards the end of the Anglo-Saxon period. II Cnut 53 orders the mutilation of a guilty woman, whereas under Æthelberht 31, her partner was to pay the appropriate *wergild and meet the expense of another wife for the wronged husband. Divorce for reasons other than adultery is not mentioned in the secular laws but was recognized by the church: the text known as 'Theodore's Penitential' (2, 12) allows a woman to repudiate her husband on the grounds of impotence, and sanctions remarriage if a spouse had been taken into captivity or penally enslaved (cf. *penitentials), while the Law of the Northumbrian Priests 65 states that a couple could also separate in order to preserve chastity (cf. St *Æthelthryth).

Husband and wife were separately accountable under the law, with independent property rights. A woman was implicated in a crime committed by her husband only if she was a willing accessory (Wihtred 12, Ine 7, Ine 57, VI Æthelstan 1, II Cnut 76); and her share of the household goods is defined as one third in Ine 57 and VI Æthelstan 1. A wife's interests continued to be protected by her own kindred, and her wergild was unaffected by her marriage.

R. Hill, 'Marriage in Seventh-Century England', in Saints Scholars and Heroes: Studies in Medieval Culture in Honour of Charles W. Jones, ed. M. H. King and W. M. Stevens, 2 vols. (Collegeville, MN, 1975) i. 67–75; C. Fell, 'Sex and Marriage', in her Women in Anglo-Saxon England (London, 1984), pp. 56–73; A. Fischer, Engagement, Wedding and Marriage in Old English (Heidelberg, 1986); T. J. Rivers, 'Adultery in Early Anglo-Saxon Society: Æthelberht 31 in Comparison with Continental Germanic Law', ASE 20 (1991), 19–25; C. Hough, 'The Early Kentish "Divorce Laws": a Reconsideration of Æthelberht, chs. 79 and 80', ASE 23 (1994), 19–34.

CAROLE HOUGH

MARTYROLOGIES: see Liturgical Books; Martyrology, OE

MARTYROLOGY, OE. The 'Old English Martyrology' is the earliest 'historical' or narrative martyrology preserved in the vernacular. The term 'historical martyrology' describes a work which contains brief notices of the Life or passio of a saint, rather than the telegraphic entries, giving merely date and place of martyrdom, which are found in the late fifth-century Martyrologium Hieronymianum (the text which lies at the base of the western cult of saints). The earliest 'historical' martyrology is that of *Bede, and it is possible that Bede's Martyrologium served as a model, though not demonstrably a source, for the OE Martyrology. The OE Martyrology, in the form in which it has been preserved, contains narrative notices (sometimes consisting of a brief paragraph, sometimes extending over several pages) of some 200 saints or groups of saints. It is not, however, preserved complete; the five extant manuscripts are all fragmentary to a greater or lesser extent (most of February and much of December are lacking from all these witnesses). The *dialect of the text is Mercian, and the earliest of the manuscript witnesses (BL, Add. 23211) dates from the late ninth century, which is the terminus ante quem for the work's composition. Unfortunately nothing is known of the identity, date (ninth-century?) or locale of the author, who was in any event a scholar of considerable learning, inasmuch as entries in the OE Martyrology are drawn from a wide range of sources, including Bede, HE, Historia abbatum and prose Vita S. Cuthberti; *Aldhelm, prose and verse De uirginitate; *Stephen of Ripon, Vita S. Wilfridi; *Felix, Vita S. Guthlaci; *Adomnán, De locis sanctis; a number of works of *Gregory the Great; the treatise De ortu et obitu patrum of Isidore; the Liber pontificalis; and the Verba seniorum. It is clear that the author of the OE Martyrology was able to draw on the resources of a substantial *library, and it is unfortunate that the location of the library is as yet unknown.

Das altenglische Martyrologium, ed. G. Kotzor, Bayerische Akademie der Wissenschaften, phil.-hist. Klasse, Abhandlungen 88 (Munich, 1981); An Old English Martyrology, ed. G. Herzfeld, EETS os 116 (London, 1900); J. E. Cross, 'The Influence of Irish Texts and Traditions on the OE Martyrology', Proceedings of the Royal Irish Academy 81C (1981), 173–92; idem, 'Saints' Lives in OE: Latin Manuscripts and Vernacular Accounts: the OE Martyrology', Peritia 1 (1982), 38–62; idem, 'The Latinity of the Ninth-Century OE Martyrologist', in Studies in Earlier Old English Prose, ed. P. E. Szarmach (Albany, NY, 1985), pp. 275–99; idem, 'On the Library of the Old English Martyrologist', in Clemoes FS, pp. 227–49; G. Kotzor, 'The Latin Tradition of Martyrologies and the OE Martyrology', in Studies in Earlier

303

Old English Prose, ed. P. Szarmach (Albany, NY, 1986), pp. 301–33.

MICHAEL LAPIDGE

MARVELS OF THE EAST is an eclectic collection offering brief descriptions of purported wonders from eastern parts, ranging from rams as big as oxen to dog-headed men. The most sumptuous version of the text, including parallel descriptions of some thirty-seven marvels in both Latin and Old English, together with a splendid set of illustrations, is found in London, BL, Cotton Tiberius B.v. A later English manuscript, Oxford, Bodleian Library, Bodley 614, contains a derivative but expanded version in Latin alone of forty-nine illustrated marvels, whilst the briefest version of the text, comprising only thirty-two marvels with illustrations, and this time only in Old English, is found in the **Beowulf*-manuscript. All the Anglo-Saxon versions derive ultimately from a continental group of Latin texts, almost all of which share a basic epistolary framework entirely lacking in the Anglo-Saxon versions, and in which a variously-named traveller reports back to his emperor. The general scheme is thus somewhat similar to that of *The Letter of *Alexander to Aristotle*, which immediately follows *The Marvels of the East* in the *Beowulf*-manuscript, and Latin versions of both these texts provided major sources for the equally exotic and eclectic collection of around 120 monstrosities known as the **Liber monstrorum*.

An Eleventh-Century Anglo-Saxon Illustrated Miscellany (British Library Cotton Tiberius B. V Part I), ed. P. McGurk, D. N. Dumville, and M. R. Godden, EEMF 21 (Copenhagen, 1983); A. Orchard, *Pride and Prodigies: Studies in the Monsters of the Beowulf-Manuscript* (Cambridge, 1995), pp. 173–203.

ANDY ORCHARD

MAXIMS: *see* Gnomic Poetry

MEDICAL LITERATURE AND MEDICINE were well developed in Anglo-Saxon England. Medical texts were written in both Old English and Latin; the Old English texts are the only surviving medical works from this period in Europe in a language other than Greek or Latin, and thus have a unique place in medieval medical literature. Some five hundred leaves of connected medical texts in Old English survive, which, considering the loss of manuscripts, indicates a very large vernacular medical literature during the period. Of these the most extensive and important are the two treatises in London, BL, Royal 12.D. XVII of the mid-tenth century, but apparently a copy of an exemplar compiled some fifty years earlier. It contains the two books of *Bald's Leechbook* and *Leechbook III*. *Bald's Leechbook* gives an enlightening picture of the medical attainments of at least one Anglo-Saxon physician, showing him to have been on a par with the more famous medical writers of the school of Salerno of the ninth and tenth centuries. It is a compilation made up from the best of Latin and Greek works of the Roman and Byzantine world available in Latin, drawing from Oribasius, Alexander of Tralles, and Cassius Felix (by way of the *Petrocellus* and *Passionarius*) and thus ultimately derived from Galen. It drew on the less sophisticated work of Marcellus and from the *Medicina Plinii* and the *Physica Plinii*, and on traditional English medicine. Given that it and *Leechbook III* are the oldest medical works from northern Europe, we cannot estimate their debt to Northern European cultures.

The *Lacnunga*, found in London, BL, Harley 585 (very late tenth century) is a haphazard collection of medical and related materials, and gives no indication that its compiler had any knowledge of medicine. Although its medical value is small, it is important for showing the non-rational side of Anglo-Saxon medicine, especially as it concerns the use of *charms. To the *Lacnunga* we owe the best of these, such as the 'Nine Herbs Charm' which contains the only reference to a pagan god (Woden) in the whole of the Anglo-Saxon medical repertoire. It is the *Lacnunga* which has given Anglo-Saxon medicine a name for magical dealings, whereas the amount of non-rational material in the *Leechbooks* is relatively small, no greater than that in the Latin and Greek literature. A single leaf (the Omont Fragment) attests to other collections, now lost.

Also in Old English are two treatises translated from Latin. The translation of the *Herbarium of Pseudo-Apuleius* and the *Medicina de quadrupedibus* survive together in four manuscripts. One of these, London, BL, Cotton Vitellius C.iii (see *herbals), is carefully indexed and has marginal notations which indicate that it was frequently consulted. The *Herbarium* owes much to Dioscorides and in its Old English form is supplemented by extracts from other collections, the *Ex herbis femininis* and the *Curae herbarum*, and a few quite short treatises on single plants and animals. The *Peri didaxeon* is a very late translation (incomplete) of the *Petrocellus* with material taken from other unidentified sources. There are also short articles found as entries on fly-leaves and margins of non-medical manuscripts; many of these are charms.

It is not easy to identify as of English origin works in Latin in manuscripts from English scriptoria. But two manuscripts containing extensive recipe collections in Latin seem to have been compiled in their respective monasteries: the *Cambridge Antidotary* from St Augustine's, *Canterbury (Cambridge, University Library, Gg. 5. 35), and a collection from *Ramsey Abbey in Oxford, St John's 17. Other Latin collections, which cannot claim to be of English origin, but were found in English libraries, are important for the use made of them by English physicians. Among these are the *Aurelius* and *Esculapius* (derived from Caelius Aurelianus), the three treatises addressed to Glauco (derived ultimately from Galen) and the *Passionarius* and *Petrocellus*. The last two are especially important because their contents drew heavily on much Latin and Greek medicine not otherwise available to Anglo-Saxons. One must conclude that Anglo-Saxon physicians had an extensive medical tradition to draw on, from native and Mediterranean sources, so that some at least of them were acquainted directly or indirectly with most of the medical ideas from the time of Galen to their own time.

The little that is known about physicians and their patients can be learned only by inference from non-medical sources. In the *Historia ecclesiastica* Bede tells how the physician Cynefrith was called in to treat St *Æthelthryth of *Ely in 679, and how John of Beverley turned over to a physician a patient he was treating by miraculous means. This suggests that these physicians may have been laymen. We also find Cyneheard, bishop of *Winchester (about 754), complaining that the medical books in his monastery prescribed foreign ingredients which were unknown to him and difficult to obtain. This suggests physicians attached to a monastery and so probably clerics. From such accounts we may conclude that both clerics and laymen practised medicine.

In spite of Cyneheard's complaint, it is clear that by the time of the *Leechbooks* a very large pharmacopoeia was available to the Anglo-Saxon physician, most of it of plant origin, some of it from as far away as India, China and the Moluccas, from where pepper, cinnamon, cumin, ginger and other exotic ingredients reached England through the intermediary of Arabic traders. Some things were useful, more were useless or positively harmful. But some remedies contained such things as garlic, onion, oxgall and copper salts, all useful to combat bacterial infections, others contained iron salts, useful to replace loss of iron from the body during attacks of malaria. Others, such as lichen, are still used to combat tuberculosis.

*Surgery was attempted; there are details of the lancing of a liver abscess. There are descriptions of amputations for gangrenous limbs, the cutting to be done in the sound flesh proximal to the gangrene. Surgical treatment for closure of hare-lip prescribed a silk suture, as does one for closure of an abdominal wound. Gynaecological advice was sensible and in accord with that of today.

A close examination of extant texts indicates that *magical practices were mostly invoked for ailments which did not yield to rational treatment. With no knowledge of the existence of bacteria and viruses, the Anglo-Saxon physician could not know that dirty lancets and not the phase of the moon or time of the day or year were the cause of infections following blood-letting. With no knowledge of immune reactions he could not know how best to treat asthma, eczema, and other such allergic reactions. That he used magical measures is only an indication that he knew of no rational way to handle such problems. If we can trust the evidence of the surviving medical literature it appears that Anglo-Saxon medicine was no worse than any other of its day, and that at its best it was probably better than most.

M. L. Cameron, *Anglo-Saxon Medicine*, CSASE 7 (Cambridge, 1993); idem, 'Bald's *Leechbook*: its Sources and their Use in its Compilation', *ASE* 12 (1984), 153–82; idem, 'Bald's *Leechbook* and Cultural Interactions in Anglo-Saxon England', *ASE* 19 (1990), 5–12; *Leechdoms, Wortcunning and Starcraft of Early England*, ed. O. Cockayne, 3 vols., RS (London, 1864–6); J. H. G. Grattan and C. Singer, *Anglo-Saxon Medicine and Magic Illustrated Specially from the Semi-Pagan Text 'Lacnunga'* (Oxford, 1952); J. F. Payne, *English Medicine in the Anglo-Saxon Times* (Oxford, 1904); B. Schaumann and A. Cameron, 'A Newly-Found Leaf of Old English from Louvain', *Anglia* 95 (1977), 289–312; G. Storms, *Anglo-Saxon Magic* (The Hague, 1948); C. H. Talbot, *Medicine in Medieval England* (London, 1967); S. Rubin, *Medieval English Medicine* (London, 1974); L. E. Voigts, 'Anglo-Saxon Plant Remedies and the Anglo-Saxons', *Isis* 70 (1979), 250–68; H. J. De Vriend, *The Old English Herbarium and Medicina de Quadrupedibus*, EETS os 286 (Oxford, 1984).

LAURENCE CAMERON

MELLITUS was the third archbishop of *Canterbury (619–24); he was a Roman monk sent to England by Pope *Gregory in 601, as one of the reinforcements (which included *Justus and *Paulinus) for the original mission under the direction of *Augustine. *Bede (*HE* i.30) preserves the text of a letter sent by Gregory to

Mellitus soon after his arrival in England, offering guidance on various matters pertaining to pagan worship (the instructions in this letter supersede some of the advice given by Gregory to Augustine in the *Libellus responsionum*). In 604 Mellitus was consecrated (first) bishop of the East Saxons (Justus meanwhile was consecrated bishop of *Rochester), with the see of his bishopric at *London; and after the East Saxons had been satisfactorily converted, King *Æthelberht built for Mellitus a church dedicated to St Paul in *London. As bishop of London Mellitus travelled to *Rome to confer with Pope Boniface IV (608–15) about the requirements of the English church; while there he took part in a synod (not otherwise recorded) of Italian bishops concerning monastic discipline, in order that he might bring back to England the ratified *acta* of the synod. In the period of apostasy following the death of King Æthelberht in 616, Mellitus was expelled from London; he and Justus withdrew to Gaul, leaving *Laurentius in charge of the English church. By means of a miraculous *vision, Laurentius was able to persuade Æthelberht's successor (Eadbald) of the virtues of Christianity, and Mellitus and Justus were recalled from Gaul; although the people of London refused to receive Mellitus, the death of Laurentius (2 February 619) enabled Mellitus to be promoted to the archbishopric of Canterbury. Bede relates that, although Mellitus was troubled by gout, he was sound of mind; on one occasion, he was able by his prayers to avert the danger of fire from the church of the Four Crowned Martyrs in Canterbury. He died on 24 April 624.

Bede, *HE* i.29–30. ii.3–4, 7; Brooks, *Canterbury*, pp. 11–13.

MICHAEL LAPIDGE

MELROSE (Berwick) preserves the name of *Mailros*, an early Anglo-Irish monastery closely linked to *Lindisfarne. *Cuthbert entered it in 651, attracted by the reputation of *Boisil who was prior there under Abbot *Eata. In the 650s *Ripon was first (and briefly) founded as a dependency of Melrose, observing its rule. In 664 Cuthbert became prior at Melrose and stayed there for some years, using it as a base for energetic pastoral activities, described by *Bede, before leaving for Lindisfarne. The site (Old Melrose) is on a promontory in a loop of the Tweed, still cut off by a substantial *vallum*.

Bede, *Vita S. Cuthberti*, cc. 6–15; *HE* iii.26, iv.27, v.12; C. Stancliffe, 'Cuthbert and the Polarity between Pastor and Solitary', in *Cuthbert*, pp. 21–44; C. Thomas, *The*

Early Christian Archaeology of North Britain (Glasgow, 1971), pp. 35–6.

JOHN BLAIR

MENOLOGIUM: *see* Metrical Calendar, OE

MERCIA, kingdom of. The 'Mercians' were by definition a border people (OE *mierce*, 'boundary'), though it is not clear what border those who named them had in mind. The natural presumption is that the Mercians were so called because they inhabited the land bordering with the British of north Wales. It has been suggested, however, that the border in question was the line of the Humber estuary, between the Northumbrians and the Southumbrians, or that the Mercians were seen as the people who lived to the north and west of the concentration of Anglian peoples in the midlands, with little thought of what lay beyond. In *Bede's day (*c.*730), the kingdom of the Mercians comprised land assessed at 5000 hides (i.e. sufficient for the support of 5000 households) lying to the south of the river Trent, and land assessed at 7000 hides lying to the north (*HE* iii.24); the river Idle, which flows into the Trent north of Gainsborough, was considered by him to lie in the (eastern) extremities of the Mercian kingdom (*HE* ii.12). It was probably during the course of the eighth century that the term 'Mercia' came under unfolding political circumstances to be applied more loosely to a much larger area, comprising the greater part of midland England: east of the border with Wales, south of the Humber estuary, north of the rivers Avon and Thames (extending as far downriver as *London), but west of the two 'eastern' kingdoms of *East Anglia and *Essex. In this sense, the term represents not so much a consolidated and homogeneous political entity as an amorphous supremacy established over various other peoples: the *Wreocensætan* (around the Wrekin), the *Westerna* or *Magonsætan* (west of the river Severn, in Herefordshire and Shropshire), the *Pecsætan* (in the Peak district), the *Hwicce (east of the Severn estuary, around *Gloucester, *Winchcombe and *Worcester), the men of *Lindsey, the *Middle Angles (comprising about twenty other peoples each with their own separate identity), and the *Middle Saxons. The Mercian heartland ('that part first called Mercia') was assessed at 30,000 hides in the *Tribal Hidage, representing an advance on Bede's figures which would appear to reflect the more intensive exploitation of the same area by the late eighth century. The profusion of other peoples who made up 'Mercia' in its larger sense were assessed in the same document at a further 55,000 hides (or thereabouts), making roughly 85,000 hides for 'Mercia' as a whole. Beside this total should be set the figures for East Anglia (30,000), Essex (7000), *Kent (15,000), *Sussex (7000), and *Wessex (100,000). The principal royal centre of the Mercian kingdom was at *Tamworth, on the river Tame (a tributary of the Trent), in 'southern' Mercia; the see of the Mercians was established at *Lichfield (*HE* iv.3), and was accorded archiepiscopal status in the period 787–803. The other 'Mercian' sees – at *Leicester (serving the Middle Angles), in *Lindsey, at Worcester (serving the Hwicce), and at *Hereford (serving the *Magonsætan*) – pertained to different elements of the greater Mercian realm. London, which had formerly pertained to Essex (*HE* ii.3), fell under the sway of the Mercian kings in the eighth century; and although it retained its 'Mercian' identity, it was by the mid-ninth century in an interestingly ambivalent position.

The earliest known king of the Mercians was a certain Cearl, whose daughter Cwenburh married *Edwin, later the king of the Northumbrians, some time before 616 (*HE* ii.14). Thereafter we encounter, among others, the succession of powerful rulers who gave changing shape to what has come to be known as the 'Mercian Supremacy': *Penda (*c.*632–55) and *Wulfhere (658–74), representing a first phase of supremacy south of the Humber, when circumstances obliged the kings to focus their attention on developments across the border in Northumbria; *Æthelbald (716–57) and *Offa (757–96), representing a second phase, when the kings were able to give rein to their predatory instincts in the south, and when correspondingly grandiose notions of their station gained some currency; and *Coenwulf (796–821), Ceolwulf I (821–3) and Beornwulf (823–5), representing a third phase, when the supremacy began to fall apart at the seams. The dominance of these kings was central to the political history of the English peoples for a period of almost two hundred years; but while they did much to shape the course of English history, it is questionable whether they made a significant or lasting contribution to the process which in retrospect is recognized as the 'making' of England. It is true, of course, that we lack substantive material from many places of interest in 'Mercia' (e.g. Lichfield, Winchcombe, Hereford, *Repton, Leicester, Crowland, Louth, *Brixworth, *Medeshamstede*, *Breedon-on-the-Hill, *Northampton, Cookham, Bedford, St Albans); that we have nothing for Offa to set beside Einhard's *Life* of *Charlemagne* or

*Asser's *Life* of *Alfred the Great; and that a tantalising allusion to what would appear to be a *law-code of King Offa serves only to remind us of what we have lost. It is also true that the Mercian kings are known largely if not entirely from (supposedly) biassed sources (notably the West Saxon *annals in the *Anglo-Saxon Chronicle*), or from their 'victims' (whether the Northumbrians, the Welsh, or churches and other landholders in Kent and elsewhere), or from parties simply not interested in them for their own sake (for example Bede, *Boniface, and *Alcuin). It is arguable, therefore, that if only the Mercians could have had their own say, we would understand them better and properly appreciate their intentions. Yet to suppose that but for the loss of all this material Mercia would stand on comparable terms with Wessex and Kent is perhaps to expect uniformity among the kingdoms where we would do better to respect diversity. The Mercian overlords of the eighth century were the product of an old and increasingly outmoded political order. Little seems to have changed in their world from the confederacies of a former age, and the closer one looks the clearer it becomes that their kingdom differed in certain respects from the polities established in Wessex and Kent. There was a strong monarchy, in preference to multiple kingship, yet the forms and institutions of royal government seem not to have developed in ways conducive to the emergence of a monarchy which enjoyed dynastic security. Kings appear to have emerged from the body of *ealdormen, and can often be spotted attesting the *charters of their predecessors; ealdormen were themselves the leaders of the constituent peoples of the confederacy, as opposed to men appointed by the king to exercise power in a specific district on his behalf; and there was less sense than in Wessex of the coalescence of a nobility defined by their service to the king. We hear in the mid ninth century of Humberht, 'ealdorman of the Tomsætan' (S 197), presumably those dwelling in the vicinity of the river Tame; and while King Alfred's (West Saxon) mother was the daughter of Oslac, King Æthelwulf's butler, his (Mercian) wife was the daughter of Æthelred, 'ealdorman of the Gaini' (Asser, cc. 2, 29). It is also arguable that the Mercian overlords exercised power in ways which were not likely to endear them to the peoples who fell under their sway.

Latterly the Mercians seem to have contained themselves in the west Midlands: our attention shifts to the development of an alliance between the Mercians and the West Saxons in opposition to their common enemies, and to the emergence of a political order with a much stronger basis. The last independent ruler of the Mercians was Burgred (852–74), who was driven out of his country by the *Vikings. It is possible, however, that the distinction in fact belongs to Ceolwulf II (874–9), supposedly a Viking puppet but perhaps misrepresented as such by a West Saxon chronicler c.890, sensitive to other political interests. In the late ninth century 'English' Mercia was subsumed into a new polity, conceived at the court of King Alfred the Great. *Æthelred, styled 'Lord of the Mercians', and his wife *Æthelflæd, styled 'Lady of the Mercians', were empowered to issue charters in their own right, but in other respects appear to have been subordinate to the 'king of the *Anglo-Saxons'. It seems that Mercia's time had passed, though it is apparent that Mercian sensitivities in fact had some way to run in the formation of the kingdom of the English. Sooner or later a system of *shires was imposed on English and Danish Mercia, though the ancient tribal names persisted into the second half of the tenth century and beyond: we encounter the *Magonsætan* in 958 (S 677), the *Pecsætan* and the *Wreocensætan* in 963 (S 712a, 723), and the *Magonsætan* again in 1016 (*ASC*) and 1041 (John of Worcester).

Stenton, *ASE*, pp. 38–42, 201 [map], and 336–8 [shires]; D. P. Kirby, *The Making of Early England* (London, 1967), pp. 61–5; C. Hart, 'The Kingdom of the Mercians', in Dornier, *MS*, pp. 43–61; P. H. Sawyer, *From Roman Britain to Norman England* (London, 1978), pp. 38–40; N. Brooks, 'The Formation of the Mercian Kingdom', in Bassett, *Origins*, pp. 159–70; D. Dumville, 'Essex, Middle Anglia and the Expansion of Mercia in the South-East Midlands' (1989), repr. in his *Britons and Anglo-Saxons in the Early Middle Ages* (Aldershot, 1993), pp. [IX] 1–30; Yorke, *Kingdoms*, pp. 99–127; Kirby, *Kings*, pp. 113–17, 129–36, 163–89; M. Gelling, *The West Midlands in the Early Middle Ages* (Leicester, 1992), pp. 79–85; N. J. Higham, *An English Empire: Bede and the Early Anglo-Saxon Kings* (Manchester, 1995), pp. 143–51.

SIMON KEYNES

MERCIAN DIALECT: *see* Dialects

MEREWENNA, ST, was appointed abbess of Romsey by King *Edgar (959–75) when it was reformed in about 967. A cult must have arisen before 1031, since her tomb is noted in an Old English 'List of Saints' *Resting Places' which was copied into London, BL, Stowe 944, in that year. Later manuscripts of the List add the name of her disciple and successor, Æthelflæd, with whom she was later venerated. A later life (*BHL*

2471) is preserved in London, BL, Lansdowne 436 (s. xiv).

Acta SS, Oct. xii. 922–3; John of Worcester, *Chronicon*, ed. R. R. Darlington and P. McGurk (OMT, 1995), ii. 416–18; F. Liebermann, *Die Heiligen Englands* (Hanover, 1889), pp. 15, 19.

PAUL ANTONY HAYWARD

METALWORKING was practised in a variety of metals with differing levels of skill by the Anglo-Saxons. By examining surviving examples of *jewellery and weapons a great deal can be learnt about their method of manufacture and the skill employed.

The mechanical process of forging metal – shaping an object by blows whilst the metal is hot – was common to both the iron-smith and the jeweller. There are numerous examples amongst Anglo-Saxon metalwork of composite objects which employ both ferrous and non-ferrous metals in their construction and decoration. From this common foundation specialist skills developed which proceeded to distinguish the iron-smith from the jeweller.

Elaborate techniques were developed for producing iron weapons and tools with hardened edges. Piling – repeatedly heating, folding and hammering iron – created a laminated structure of wrought iron and thin bands of low carbon steel. Due to the relatively high phosphorus content of much early iron, difficulties were encountered in diffusing carbon into the iron. As a result, sword blades were produced as composite structures, made up with both high phosphorus and low carbon iron rods, welded together and twisted into decorative patterns.

Both piling and pattern-welding were attempts by early smiths to obtain a hard metal. However, there is some doubt about the effectiveness of these techniques. Their survival well into the late Anglo-Saxon period was due to the value placed upon the patterning and not the resilience of the blades. By the eighth century smiths had a growing understanding of the effects which heat treatment had on the physical properties of iron. Quenching hot iron in a liquid produced hardness whilst tempering – reheating the metal – removed any attendant brittleness. High carbon iron is found inserted between the soft iron cheeks of swords and knives, suggesting the deliberate production of steel from the tenth century onwards.

Amongst non-ferrous metalworkers some smiths possessed the ability to cast metals in complex moulds. Ingot casting was a necessary precursor to the forging of rod and wire used in the production of pins and dress fasteners. But the casting of brooches required the making of piece moulds from clay and the use of models made in a variety of materials. Identical brooches could be cast repeatedly with the use of a permanent model – an existing brooch, for example – embedded in clay to form a mould of two halves and extracted prior to casting. Serial production of this kind is rare amongst pagan Anglo-Saxon jewellery, although it is increasingly recognisable amongst later jewellery produced in the area of the *Danelaw.

The early Anglo-Saxon period is typified by individual brooches of varying degrees of similarity – but rarely identical – cast in enclosed moulds. Using models made from wax, hand-decorated and invested with a clay coating, a hollow mould could be formed by melting-out or removing the wax prior to casting. The manner in which the models were made, and the degree of hand-carving prior to investment, varied greatly. The use of a pattern at an intermediary stage was important. Bearing the basic elements of shape and decoration, either in relief or as deep impressions, wax models could be made from a pattern, and further decorated by hand before investing with the clay of a mould. Like iron-working techniques, there is a strong impression of a chronological development in casting technology during the Anglo-Saxon period. From the third quarter of the sixth century multiple brooch production becomes more prevalent and casting technology is adapted accordingly. In the late Anglo-Saxon period complex castings are reserved for objects of high value, such as liturgical items – serial casting is used to mass produce smaller items of personal ornament in a range of base metals. But for lavish pieces of jewellery sheet metalworking in silver and gold is preferred, especially outside the area of the *Danelaw.

Beyond the objects, it is possible to identify the metalworking sites themselves using debris recovered from archaeological excavations. Smelting and smithing waste-slags are to be found on a variety of sites. When associated with metalworking structures – hearths and furnaces – identification is most secure. Otherwise, deposition can be the product of numerous agencies unrelated to metalworking activity.

A discernible division between smelting and smithing arises at an early stage in the Anglo-Saxon period. Smelting, especially iron-smelting (for which the most evidence exists), frequently occurs in a rural context by virtue of its dependence upon natural materials such as ore, wood and clay. But smithing, both ferrous and non-ferrous, occurs on a greater range of sites in town and country. But mixed slag assemblages from smelting and smithing occur throughout the period, in urban as well as rural contexts. Large quantities of debris rarely accumulate as the product of continuous activity but are frequently broken by periods of abandonment, whilst the focus of metal-working moves from one location to another within the same site.

All these things hint at an industry operating in various ways and at different levels of production. At its most basic, metalworking can be a purely domestic activity, geared to supplying the immediate needs of a single household or small community. The technology employed is of a low level and there are few signs of specialization amongst the mixed collection of residues, which may include smithing, smelting, ferrous and non-ferrous slags. At the other end of the spectrum there are the purpose-built workshops of smiths who display a high level of craft specialisation: standardized forms of objects and fabrication methods.

Unfortunately, these modes of metalworking appear to represent only a small number of sites. A far greater quantity falls between the two. Some signs of specialization are present: the residues are the product of one process and of one metal; the level of technology has advanced beyond that associated with domestic metal-working; purpose-built structures are recognisable. However, the quantity of residues is still comparatively small and although metalworking may take place over a long period of time, it is not continuous nor fixed to any one location like a workshop. To complicate matters further this group of sites may in fact comprise two modes of activity: semi-specialist and itinerant production. The two are difficult to distinguish archaeologically, yet one represents the activities of a craftsman working part-time, the other full-time.

There is no reason to believe that these various modes of production form a continuous chain of development which commences with domestic metalworking in the early Anglo-Saxon period and stretches through part-time craftworking, itinerant smiths and finally workshop production. It appears more likely that each mode of production represents a response to a particular set of circumstances – level of demand, availability of resources, settlement status. Thus, some early Anglo-Saxon jewellery could be produced in workshops at the same time as most ironwork was made by semi-specialists who practised the craft on a part-time basis to supplement their basic agricultural economy. Even in the late Anglo–Saxon period domestic metalworking can be observed. However, itinerant smiths appear to be a phenomenon associated with the development of *towns and as such can be no earlier than the middle Anglo–Saxon period.

D. M. Wilson, *Anglo–Saxon Ornamental Metalwork 700–1100 in the British Museum* (London, 1964); D. A. Hinton, *Anglo–Saxon Ornamental Metalwork 700–1100 in the Department of Antiquities, Ashmolean Museum* (Oxford, 1974); idem, 'Late Anglo–Saxon Metal-Work: an Assessment', *ASE* 4 (1975), 171–80; Wilson, *Archaeology*, pp. 261–9; J. Haslam, 'A Middle Saxon Smelting Site in Ramsbury, Wiltshire', *MArch* 24 (1980), 1–68; C. F. Tebutt, 'A Middle Saxon Iron Smelting Site at Millbrook, Ashdown Forest, Sussex', *Sussex Archaeological Collections* 120 (1982), 19–36; D. A. Hinton and R. White, 'A Smith's Hoard from Tattershall Thorpe, Lincolnshire', *ASE* 22 (1993), 147–66.

KEVIN BROWN

METRE, LATIN. The technical difficulties of the composition of Latin metrical verse for non-native speakers unused to the idiosyncrasies of Latin prosody evidently exerted considerable fascination on some of the most learned of Anglo–Saxons: *Aldhelm, *Boniface, and *Bede all wrote treatises on Latin metre, and (unlike Old English poetry, where few named authors are known), the poems of more than thirty identifiable Anglo–Latin poets have survived. Old English *metre is quite different, being based on the relative stress of syllables rather than their length, and although some Anglo–Latin authors did compose rhythmical verse in Latin, notably in *octosyllables, the amount of Latin metrical verse surviving from Anglo–Saxon England is very considerable. The great majority of this verse is composed in hexameters, the metre employed by most of the classical and Christian-Latin poets whose works were studied throughout the period, such as Vergil, Prudentius, and Caelius Sedulius. As the name suggests, each hexameter verse consists of six metrical feet, each of which (except the last) must be either a dactyl (a long syllable followed by two short syllables) or a spondee (two long syllables); the final foot must be either a spondee or a trochee (a long syllable followed by a short syllable). Occasionally, Anglo–Latin poets combined hexameters alternately with verses of five metrical feet (pentameters), to form so-called elegiac couplets: as an added conceit such couplets sometimes begin and end with the same words, producing so-called epanaleptic verses, of which examples survive by authors as diverse as Bede

and *Wulfstan of Winchester, and the latter went further, experimenting with still more obscure metres, including sapphics, as *Alcuin had done before him. The general technique for the composition of Anglo–Latin hexameter verse can be seen in the poems of Aldhelm, who consistently limits the metrical possibilities in his verses (three-quarters of which conclude with the same four metrical feet – spondee, spondee, dactyl, spondee (or trochee) – leaving only the first two feet variable), and effectively divides his lines into three segments generally built from a combination of remembered and repeated phrases, very much after the fashion prescribed by the so-called *oral-formulaic theory. Such a technique is abundantly clear in some extant verse addressed to Boniface by *Leobgyth, who echoes precisely in the preceding prose a number of phrases from Aldhelm's own metrical treatises, rather like an undergraduate copying sentences from a textbook. Indeed, it is striking just how much later Anglo–Latin metrical verse is confected from a combination of formulaic phrasing, often Aldhelm's own, and how such a strategy sometimes leads to the inadvertent juxtaposition of syllables which in classical Latin verse would be slurred or 'elided'; failure to elide is therefore often a sign of formulaic composition.

P. Godman, ed., *Alcuin: the Bishops, Kings, and Saints of York* (OMT, 1982), pp. civ–cx; A. Orchard, *The Poetic Art of Aldhelm*, CSASE 8 (Cambridge, 1994), 73–125; D. Norberg, *Introduction à l'étude de la versification latine médiévale*, Acta Universitatis Stockholmiensis. Studia Latina Stockholmiensia 5 (Stockholm, 1958); N. Wright, 'Appendix: Aldhelm's Prose Writings on Metrics', in *Aldhelm: the Poetic Works*, trans. M. Lapidge and J. Rosier (Cambridge, 1985), pp. 61–9.

ANDY ORCHARD

METRE, OE, the measured arrangement of words in a half-line of verse, is a field sustained by modern hypotheses because the Anglo-Saxons left no descriptive metrical treatise of any kind. The half-line must have a minimum of four syllables, but it displays a number of intricately regulated variations depending on syllable length, count, and stress. In the late nineteenth century Eduard Sievers classified the patterns under five categories, given the unpoetic names A, B, C, D, and E in descending order of frequency. If / represents a full stress on a syllable and x an unstressed syllable, they are:

Type A	/ x / x
Type B	x / x /
Type C	x // x
Type D	// x x
Type E	/ x x /

On these basic patterns many variations can be built, as the following *riddle from the *Exeter Book illustrates:

	Wer sæt æt wīne	mid his wīfum twām	
A	/xx/x	xx/x/	B
	ond his twēgen suno	ond his twā dohtor,	
B	xx/x/	xx//x	C
	swāse gesweostor,	ond hyra suno twēgen,	
A	/xx/x	xxx//x	C
	frēolico frumbearn;	fæder wæs þæs inne	
A	/xx/\	/x/\x	D
	þāra æþelinga	æghwæðres mid,	
light	xx/xx	/\x/	E
	ēam ond nefa.	Ealra wæron fife	
A?E?		/xx/x	A
	eorla ond idesa	insittendra.	
A	/xx/x	/\xx	D

'A man sat feasting with his two wives, his two sons and two daughters, dear sisters, and their two noble first-born sons; the father of each prince was inside there too, uncle and nephew. In all five lords and ladies were sitting there.'

The *alliteration of each line links one or two stressed syllables in the on-verse with the first stressed syllable in the off-verse. The first three lines give examples of Types A, B, and C, each with a syllable (or two) added to the first unstressed position. Secondary stress (indicated by \) usually arises from compound elements (*frumbearn* 4, *æghwæðres* 5, *insittendra* 7). In the second and third lines *suno* is scanned as if it were a single syllable, a feature called 'resolution', which can apply to two syllables of which the first is short; other examples in this passage are *fæder* 4, *æþel-* 5, and *ides-* 7. A common variant called a 'light verse' is illustrated in *þāra æþelinga* 5, which has one stressed syllable instead of the more usual two. One ambiguous half-line remains, *ēam ond nefa* 6, which can be scanned either as Type A (/ x / x) if *nefa* does not undergo resolution, or as Type E (/ x x /) if *nefa* undergoes resolution and if the historically contracted *ēam* is expanded to scan as two syllables. Despite such occasional ambiguities, the basic principles of versification are clear, so that the affiliations of Sievers's five types are less enigmatic than that of Lot and his four offspring.

A. J. Bliss, *An Introduction to Old English Metre*, OEN Subsidia 20 (Binghamton, NY, 1993); idem, *The Metre of Beowulf* (Oxford, 1967); T. Cable, *The English Alliterative Tradition* (Philadelphia, PA, 1991); R. D. Fulk, *A History of Old English Meter* (Philadelphia, PA, 1992); J. C. Pope, *The Rhythm of Beowulf* (New Haven, 1966); G. Russom, *Old English Meter and Linguistic Theory* (Cambridge, 1987).

DANIEL DONOGHUE

METRICAL CALENDAR, LATIN. A metrical calendar is a poem in hexameters, designed probably as a mnemonic aid, each line of which contains the name of a saint and the date on which s/he is commemorated, in Roman date-reckoning (e.g. 'Hinc idus Martis quartas Gregorius aurat': 'St Gregory here adorns the fourth ides of March'). The earliest surviving metrical calendar was composed at *York in the later eighth century (hence it is known as the 'Metrical Calendar of York'); in its original form it consists of 82 hexameters, and commemorates a number of Northumbrian saints, especially those of York itself. This 'Metrical Calendar of York' enjoyed wide circulation, both in England and Ireland as well as on the Continent, where it underwent successive phases of redaction aimed at eliminating little-known English saints and replacing them with saints commemorated in the locality where the redaction took place. In the very early tenth century it served as the inspiration for a more elaborate undertaking known as the 'Metrical Calendar of Hampson' (named after its first editor); this elaboration consists of 365 lines, commemorating a saint on each day of the calendar year. The 'Metrical Calendar of Hampson' contains commemorations of King *Alfred and Queen Ealhswith (d. 902); on the other hand, one of the manuscripts in which it is preserved is the *Æthelstan Psalter, which implies that the poem was composed in the first decade of the tenth century. In expanding the poem from 82 to 365 lines, the anonymous poet included commemorations of a large number of northern Frankish saints from the Pas de Calais, and also numerous Irish saints (which seem to have been drawn from a *félire* similar to the *Félire Óengusso* or 'Martyrology of Oengus'). In the late tenth century a poet at *Ramsey, who was familiar with both the 'Metrical Calendar of York' and the 'Metrical Calendar of Hampson', composed a new metrical calendar (known as the 'Metrical Calendar of Ramsey'), consisting of 128 lines and commemorating various Anglo-Saxon saints whose cults had developed during the tenth century. Although it is preserved uniquely in a manuscript of the early twelfth century (Oxford, St John's College, 17), the fact that several of its lines are quoted by *Byrhtferth of Ramsey in his *Vita S. Oswaldi* (composed 997 × 1002) shows that it was known at Ramsey at that time; its commemoration of Ramsey's founder, Archbishop *Oswald, suggests that it was composed there as well.

A. Wilmart, 'Un témoin anglo-saxon du calendrier métrique d'York', *RB* 46 (1934), 41–69; P. McGurk,

'The Metrical Calendar of Hampson', *AB* 104 (1986), 79–125; M. Lapidge, 'The Metrical Calendar of Ramsey', *RB* 94 (1984), 326–69, repr. in *ALL* ii.343–86, 489.

MICHAEL LAPIDGE

METRICAL CALENDAR, OE. Corresponding to the Latin *metrical calendars is a poem of 231 lines which is prefixed to the C-version of the *Anglo-Saxon Chronicle* (BL, Cotton Tiberius B.i). It commemorates some twenty-eight liturgical feasts and saints (most of whom were culted by the universal church; the only English saint who is commemorated is *Augustine of Canterbury); the feasts are set out serially without any indication of date-reckoning (unlike a Latin metrical calendar), and are arrived at by counting forward from the last feast or from the beginning of the month. Since the nineteenth century the poem has been mistakenly known as the 'Menologium' (a *menologion* is a Greek liturgical book containing Lives of saints arranged in calendar order). It is worth noting the existence of a brief OE prose text which is preserved in two computistical manuscripts (BL, Harley 3271; CCCC 422) which is also mistakenly described as a 'menologium'; this prose text simply lists some thirty-five feasts serially, without any specification.

ASPR vi.49–55 (trans. K. Malone in *Studies in Language, Literature and Culture of the Middle Ages and Later*, ed. E. B. Atwood and A. A. Hill (Austin, TX, 1969), pp. 193–9); M. Lapidge, 'The Saintly Life in Anglo-Saxon England', *CamComp* pp. 243–63, at 249–50; H. Henel, 'Ein altenglisches Prosa-Menologium', in his *Studien zum altenglischen Computus* (Leipzig, 1934), pp. 71–91.

PETER S. BAKER

MIDDLE ANGLES. A collective term for the multiplicity of different peoples who inhabited the region of midland England between the Mercians (notionally the 'west' Angles) and the East Angles, though not with any implication that they constituted a coherent social entity which found political expression in the form of a separate 'Middle Anglian' kingdom. The peoples of this region would appear to have fallen under Mercian overlordship in the first half of the seventh century, perhaps in the course of extended conflict between the Mercians and the East Angles, and not unnaturally were regarded or treated by their overlords as one people. *Penda set up his son Peada as their *princeps* or ruler, and when Peada sought to marry Alhflæd, daughter of King *Oswiu, his request was granted only on condition that he accept Christianity 'with the people over

whom he was set' (*HE* iii.21); after Oswiu's victory over Penda at the battle of *Winwæd*, in 655, Peada was given the kingdom of the 'southern Mercians' (in addition to what he had already), but he was then murdered in the spring of 656 'by the treachery of his wife' (*HE* iii.24). At this point, the Middle Angles may have reverted to their separate identities under their separate rulers; but soon afterwards they fell under the overlordship of *Wulfhere, king of the Mercians. Episcopal care for the Middle Angles was provided initially by the line of bishops 'of the Mercians, Lindsey, and Middle Angles', culminating with Seaxwulf, founder of *Medeshamstede* [Peterborough] (*HE* iii.24, iv.3, iv.6, iv.12, iv.23). After Seaxwulf's death, *c.*690, this sprawling diocese was reorganized, and a separate see for the Middle Angles was presently established at *Leicester. By *c.*730 it was natural enough for *Bede to write of the Middle Angles as one people (e.g. *HE* i.15). A rather different and more revealing impression of the Middle Anglian peoples may, however, be gained from the *Tribal Hidage. It is arguable that this document dates from the latter part of the eighth century, or even the early ninth century; if so, it would suggest that the Middle Anglian peoples managed to retain their separate identities under Mercian overlordship. Little is known of their political organisation, though one might suppose that their leaders are to be found among the *ealdormen who attest 'Mercian' *charters of the eighth and ninth centuries. It should otherwise be emphasized that the region supported some important religious houses, including *Medeshamstede*, Crowland, and *Ely; the structure still standing at *Brixworth begs a place in the same context. It is all the more unfortunate that so little survives of the records of the churches of the Middle Anglian region for the early period, and that the rest is lost, presumed destroyed as a direct or indirect consequence of the Danish conquest and settlement of the eastern midlands in the 870s. D. Dumville, 'Essex, Middle Anglia and the Expansion of Mercia in the South-East Midlands' (1989), repr. in his *Britons and Anglo-Saxons in the Early Middle Ages* (Aldershot, 1993), pp. [IX] 1–30; Yorke, *Kingdoms*, p. 107; Kirby, *Kings*, p. 93; S. Keynes, *The Councils of Clofesho*, Univ. of Leicester Vaughan Paper 38 (Leicester, 1994), 30–48; idem, 'England, 700–900', *The New Cambridge Medieval History* II: *c.700–c.900*, ed. R. McKitterick (Cambridge, 1995), pp. 18–42, at 21–5 [Tribal Hidage].

SIMON KEYNES

MIDDLE SAXONS, province of, is first recorded in a *charter of 704 as a dependency of the East

Saxon kings, who had controlled the territory since the beginning of the seventh century. There is no evidence that the Middle Saxons ever had their own royal house. The East Saxons lost control of *London and the Middle Saxons to *Mercia during the reign of *Æthelbald. The Middle Saxon province included parts of southern and eastern Hertfordshire as well as Middlesex, but the former were probably detached in the aftermath of *Edward the Elder's conquest of the area in 912.

B. A. E. Yorke, 'The Kingdom of the East Saxons', *ASE* 14 (1985), 1–36; K. Bailey, 'The Middle Saxons', in Bassett, *Origins*, pp. 108–22.

B. A. E. YORKE

MILDBURG, ST (d. 715), great-granddaughter of King *Æthelberht of *Kent, daughter of Mere-walh, king of the *Magonsætan* and sister to St *Mildrith, was abbess of the abbey of Much Wenlock (Shropshire), founded by her father in about 670. Knowledge of Mildburg derives mainly from an unpublished eleventh-century Life by *Goscelin. Supposedly her remains, accompanied by a collection of ancient documents, lay hidden for years in the disused abbey church, and were rediscovered during rebuilding works, when Much Wenlock was refounded as a Cluniac priory in 1079. Goscelin probably derived the core of his information about Mildburg's origins from a late-tenth-century Old English account of the Kentish royal family, and he claimed also to have incorporated within his text the original record of endowments with which Merewalh founded Much Wenlock; these documents, known as 'Mildburg's Testament', are regarded by some as authentic seventh-century charters. Feast: February 23.

A. J. M. Edwards, 'An Early Twelfth-Century Account of the Translation of St Milburga of Much Wenlock', *Transactions of the Shropshire Archaeological Society* 57 (1961–4), 134–51; H. P. R. Finberg, *The Early Charters of the West Midlands*, 2nd ed. (Leicester, 1961), pp. 197–224.

R. C. LOVE

MILDRITH, ST (= Mildred; d. *c.*700), daughter of Merewalh, king of the *Magonsætan* and Eor-menburh (Domne Eafe), and great-granddaughter of King *Æthelberht of *Kent, was abbess of *Minster-in-Thanet from 694. Educated at Chelles (near Paris), Mildrith became a nun at Minster-in-Thanet, a monastery founded by her mother, and was subsequently buried there. In 1035 her relics were translated to St Augustine's Abbey, *Canterbury. The neighbouring hospital of St Gregory, founded in the eleventh century by

Lanfranc, also rather controversially laid claim to Mildrith's remains, a claim refuted in a strongly-worded polemic by *Goscelin, who also composed a Life of Mildrith, and an account of her translation and miracles (*BHL* 5960–2). Feast: July 13; translation: May 18.

D. W. Rollason, *The Mildrith Legend. A Study in Early Medieval Hagiography in England* (Leicester, 1982); idem, 'Goscelin of Canterbury's Account of the Translation and Miracles of St Mildrith: an Edition with Notes', *MS* 48 (1986), 139–210; M. L. Colker, 'A Hagiographic Polemic', *MS* 39 (1977), 60–108.

R. C. LOVE

MILLEFIORI glass is a made from coloured rods of glass fused together, stretched and cut across to give patterned slices which can themselves be fused into complex sheets. In parallel with its use on *hanging bowls, fine imported millefiori from the Near East was first set in late sixth- and seventh-century cloisonné *jewellery of quality, principally in the *Sutton Hoo ship burial, and with occasional use on gold pendants. It remained rare and was even imitated in the foils of the Kingston Down brooch. Millefiori glass beads, possibly imported, were used in necklaces of the same period in combination with many other types of bead. A millefiori rod and complex slices excavated at the monastery of *Monkwearmouth-Jarrow suggest later local manufacture, as does the simple blue and white chequer recorded on the missing Witham hanging bowl, but there is no evidence for the use of millefiori in Anglo-Saxon England after the eighth century.

S. Chadwick Hawkes and L. A. Groves, 'Finds from a Seventh-Century Anglo-Saxon Cemetery at Milton Regis', *Archaeologia Cantiana* 78 (1963), 22–38; R. J. Cramp, 'Decorated Window-Glass and Millefiori from Monkwearmouth', *AJ* 50 (1970), 327–35; M. Bimson, 'Aspects of the Technology of Glass and Copper Alloys. A. Coloured Glass and Millefiori in the Sutton Hoo Grave Deposit', in *The Sutton Hoo Ship-Burial*, ed. R. L. S. Bruce-Mitford, 3 vols. (London, 1975–83), iii.924–44; V. I. Evison, *Dover: The Buckland Anglo-Saxon Cemetery*, Historic Buildings and Monuments Commission for England, Archaeological Report 3 (London, 1987), 64–5 and pl. IV; J. Carroll, 'Millefiori in the Development of Early Irish Enamelling', in '*From the Isles of the North': Early Medieval Art in Ireland and Britain*, ed. C. Bourke (Belfast, 1995), pp. 49–57.

S. M. YOUNGS

MILLS were used in Anglo-Saxon England for the grinding of corn, and possibly for other purposes. Written sources, relating principally to associated rights and values, attest the presence of mills from the seventh century onwards. There

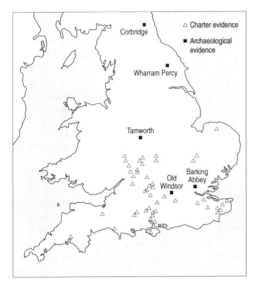

Map 1 Anglo-Saxon mills.

are references to water mills, leats, millponds and boundaries. One reference seems to refer to an over-shot or breast-shot wheel, another to a tidal mill. The terminology used can be seen as part of a widespread north-west European context. Hand-mills (rotary querns) are common finds on settlement sites. They were made both of local stone and also imported Rhenish lava. There were doubtless also animal-powered mills, though none is attested from either written sources or archaeology (Map 1).

Watermills seem to have provided the principal means of grinding grain in household, high-status and urban contexts. By the time of *Domesday Book, no fewer than 5624 watermills were recorded, varying in 'value' from three pence to four pounds. The watermill had been used extensively as a power source in Roman Britain, and was a well-known and sophisticated machine throughout the classical world. All these seem to have been of vertical-wheeled type (as described by Vitruvius). There were probably numerous mills of this type in Anglo-Saxon England. One very elaborate example is reported from Old *Windsor. Here was a seventh-century vertical-wheeled mill, powered by three massive leats in parallel, diverted from the river Thames.

Above the silted-up remains of this was a later horizontal-wheeled mill. It seems likely that most of the Anglo-Saxon watermills were of this latter type (often referred to as 'Greek' or 'Norse' mills). These machines, normally without gears, are known as early as the seventh century in Ireland,

and have been in continuous use in Europe ever since; working examples can still be found in Turkey, Crete, France and northern Spain.

An example of this type of mill, in a well-preserved condition, was excavated in *Tamworth in 1971 (fig. 10). It is dated by dendrochronology to 955 ±9. A leat was diverted from the river Anker, which filled a millpond. From this a chute directed water onto a wooden-paddled horizontal wheel, which caused it to rotate clockwise. The wheel was pivoted on a steel bearing; this was set in a plank which could be raised or lowered by remote control from the mill-house above, by means of a vertical rod attached to one end. This allowed the raising and lowering of the plank, the steel gearing, and wheel. Through the main vertical shaft extending upwards from the wheel-assembly into the mill-house, this rod could adjust the space between the millstones to allow for different kinds of grinding, or to take up wear on the stones. In the mill-house, grain from a hopper was fed into the central hole of the turning upper millstone. It was then forced outwards between the upper and lower stones, the flour being collected from a trough in the mill-house. In this type of mill, one revolution of the wheel equated with one revolution of the stone, at a speed of about sixty revolutions a minute. The stones themselves were both of local origin and of Mayen lava, imported from the Rhineland. Grain ground included oats and barley. The mill may have been associated with the royal palaces of the kings and *queens of *Mercia in the nearby *burh.

Other examples of this type have recently (1995–6) been reported from Corbridge and from *Barking Abbey (both eighth century); many others must await discovery. The horizontal-wheel type of watermill died out in England in the Middle Ages, being largely superseded by vertical-wheeled mills and by the windmill, the latter unknown in Anglo-Saxon England.

M. T. Hodgen, 'Domesday Watermills', *Antiquity* 13 (1939), 261–79; P. A. Rahtz, 'Medieval Milling', in *Medieval Industry*, ed. D. W. Crossley (London, 1981), pp. 1–5; P. A. Rahtz and D. Bullough, 'The Parts of an Anglo-Saxon Mill', *ASE* 6 (1977), 15–37; P. A. Rahtz and R. Meeson, *An Anglo-Saxon Watermill at Tamworth* (London, 1992); O. Wikander, 'Archaeological Evidence for early Watermills', in *History of Technology*, ed. N. Smith (London, 1985), pp. 151–80.

PHILIP RAHTZ

MILRED (d. 774), bishop of *Worcester, one of the most powerful churchmen during the reign of King *Offa of Mercia, and a scholar of some standing. Nothing is known of Milred's birth or

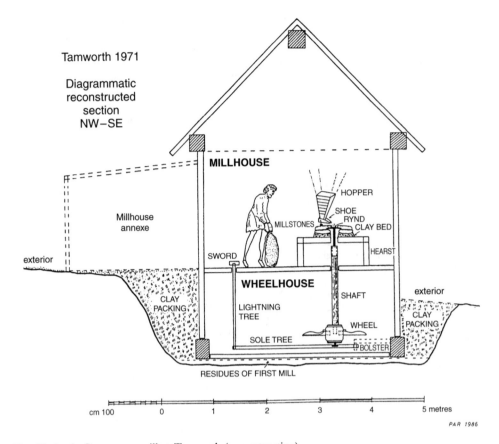

Tamworth 1971

Diagrammatic
reconstructed
section
NW–SE

MILLHOUSE

Millhouse
annexe

exterior

MILLSTONES

HOPPER

SHOE
RYND
CLAY BED

HEARST

SWORD

WHEELHOUSE

CLAY
PACKING

LIGHTNING
TREE

SOLE TREE

SHAFT

WHEEL

BOLSTER

exterior

CLAY
PACKING

RESIDUES OF FIRST MILL

cm 100   0   1   2   3   4   5 metres

PAR 1986

Fig. 10 Anglo-Saxon watermill at Tamworth (reconstruction).

background, but he was appointed to the see of Worcester between 743 and 745, and attended the important *council of *Clofesho in 747. In either 753 or early 754 he visited both *Boniface and *Lull in Germany, and a letter addressed by Milred to Lull concerning the recent martyrdom of Boniface survives among the corpus of Bonifatian correspondence. Interestingly, this letter contains unmistakable reminiscences of both Vergil and Horace, as well as a request for the return of a copy of the *acrostic poems of Porphyrius, which indicates that Milred had acquired a respectable education. One of his scholarly achievements was the compilation of a *sylloge of metrical inscriptions or *tituli; this sylloge includes a number of Anglo-Latin epigrams and epitaphs of Anglo-Saxon ecclesiastics not otherwise attested. It was prefaced by an epigram composed by Milred himself. Milred's sylloge has unfortunately not survived intact; but a single leaf written perhaps at Malmesbury in the mid-tenth century and now in Urbana, Illinois, preserves some of the

tituli, and in the sixteenth century John *Leland transcribed some further poems from parts of the Urbana manuscript which have since been lost.

Sharpe, Handlist, 1064; MGH, ES i.243–5 (no. 112); H. Hahn, Bonifaz und Lul (Leipzig, 1883), pp. 256–9; M. Lapidge, 'Some Remnants of Bede's Lost Liber epigrammatum', EHR 90 (1975), 798–820, repr. in ALL i.357–79 [with addenda at pp. 510–12]; D. J. Sheerin, 'John Leland and Milred of Worcester', Manuscripta 21 (1977), 172–80; P. Sims-Williams, 'Milred of Worcester's Collection of Latin Epigrams and its Continental Counterparts', ASE 10 (1982), 21–38; idem, Religion and Literature in Western England, 600–800, CSASE 3 (Cambridge, 1990), 328–59.

MICHAEL LAPIDGE

MINING and QUARRYING for metalliferous ores and stone was begun as early as the sixth century and increased in intensity throughout the whole Anglo-Saxon period until, by the eleventh century, both had developed into recognisable industries. Britain's mineral resources were well known to classical authors and heavily exploited by the Roman army and civilian entrepreneurs. But by the time the Anglo-Saxons arrived very little of this extractive industry survived.

Ironworkings appear in the earliest archaeological record of the Anglo-Saxons. Evidence for mining has to be inferred from the identification of smelting sites; the majority lie within 2.5 km of a known ore source. The most productive ores were limonites – hydrated iron oxides – a form of ore which was easy to smelt in the primitive bloomery furnaces employed by Anglo-Saxon smiths. Lower grade ores, commonly iron pyrites and other forms of concretionary nodules, were also used often in conjunction with the more productive types.

Extensive deposits of the richer iron ores existed in a number of places. In both the Sussex Weald and Northamptonshire Heights major industries operated from the earliest stages of the Roman occupation and other ironworkings grew up subsequently in the Forest of Dean, South Humberside, north-east Norfolk and the South-West. It is in these same areas that the clearest evidence of Anglo-Saxon smelting and mining occurs. But there is little to suggest continuity. The pattern of exploitation is closely linked to the history of the Anglo-Saxon *settlements.

It would, however, be wrong to assume that these were the only areas in which ironworking took place. A number of early sites fall outside those areas possessing the limonitic ores. But such workings were incapable of supporting a high level of production and as time progressed the traditional ironworking areas asserted their superiority. Such a pattern of events follows the model of increasing specialization observed in *metalworking and reflects the change from domestic to semi-specialist and workshop production.

An early decline in the working of some ore deposits is one reason for the complete lack of any evidence for the extraction of non-ferrous ores at the beginning of the Anglo-Saxon period. By the mid-fourth century little, if any, gold, copper, lead or tin was mined in Roman Britain and the province was a nett importer of metals. Indeed, by the end of the Roman period much metalworking depended upon the recycling of metal in the form of scrap objects and *coinage. It is not surprising, therefore, to find that early Anglo-Saxon *jewellery was produced from a similar stock of metal. Late Roman copper-alloy jewellery and coinage, silver plate and gold coins from *Byzantium and Merovingian Gaul were all consigned to the crucible.

The manner in which the ores were mined may have been one reason for the failure of the non-ferrous metals extraction industry. The Romans had to sink shafts and use galleries to mine gold, copper and some lead ores. Even the working of alluvial deposits, such as tin, could necessitate the removal of a considerable depth of overburden. This was both labour intensive and costly, demanding the provision of shoring, lighting and drainage. In contrast, Anglo-Saxon iron mines were little more than a series of pits dug through the topsoil to the iron-bearing strata beneath. Fortunately, examples dated to the late Anglo-Saxon period have been recorded in north-east Norfolk, showing that pitting took place where the ore outcropped at the head of stream courses.

When the extraction of non-ferrous ores was revived, at the beginning of the ninth century, it is quite likely that the mines were no more than pits and channel addits. None of the workings have been identified and we must rely upon documentary references. Lead mines are mentioned in charters relating to the Derbyshire Peak District, dated c.835 and c.883. By the time of *Domesday Book there are references to twenty-eight mines or works in the area. Lead ore has been recovered from metalworking contexts at *Coppergate.

The mining of copper, tin, silver and gold goes unnoticed in the documentary sources and very little archaeological material remains to suggest their extraction at any time during the Anglo-Saxon period. Like pagan jewellery, non-ferrous metalwork in the middle and later periods was dependent upon the recycling of broken and damaged objects. From time-to-time new metal from external sources was introduced into this enclosed system. Copper-alloy objects from the eastern Mediterranean, gold coinage from Carolingian France, and silver produced from metal mined in France and Germany and imported as coinage supplemented the basic stock of metal.

There is no firm evidence of stone quarrying in the early Anglo-Saxon period, but by the eleventh century the range of freestones to be found in quoins, dressings, architectural and free-standing *sculpture marks the development of an extensive industry. Similarly, the repeated use of a particular stone over wide areas suggests a high degree of organization. Barnack Stone – a type of oolitic limestone – became the predominant building stone of eastern England. Quarr stone – shell-brash limestone – has a marked distribution along the south coast, from the Isle of Wight eastwards, whilst Bath Stone is best represented in the West Country and South Cotswolds. Its northerly spread is impeded by the southerly extent of Taynton Freestone from Oxfordshire.

A great deal more is known about these late Anglo-Saxon quarries than the contemporary mines. Domesday Book contains seven references, four in Sussex and one each in Surrey, Nottinghamshire and Oxfordshire. Only the products of the Taynton (Oxon.) quarry are sufficiently distinctive to be recognisable today. The other named quarries produced stone from the Upper Greensand and Keuper Beds: sandstones which provided the decorative elements for late Saxon churches.

Only the medieval quarries at Barnack survive today, incorporating some part of the late Saxon workings. The striking feature is the small size of the workings. Each quarry comprises a number of pits dug down from the surface to the bedded freestone. The stone blocks would have been removed with the aid of iron-wedges, heavy mallets and crowbars. Tool marks on existing stonework suggest coarse dressing with an axe, whilst finer work was carried out using hammers, punches and chisels of various sizes. Both land and water were used to transport the bulky stone to the building site. Barnack Stone was shipped along the Fenland waterways and river Nene; Quarr stone by sea, along the coast to Hampshire and Sussex. Written sources suggest that stone was taken to *Lindisfarne in the late eleventh century by ox-pulled wagons and carts.

The earliest phase of stone building – beginning in the seventh century – is marked by the re-use of Roman stonework, particularly amongst the churches of northern England (cf. *Roman remains). In the south, Roman brick and tile supplement the use of rubble-stone hand-picked from the surface or quarried by means of pits and linear ditches – *fossae* and *gedelf*. It is assumed that the quarrying of bedded freestone did not continue beyond the end of Roman rule. Yet fresh supplies of dolomite were provided from the Roker and Hartlepool districts of the North-East for the preparation of architectural and free-standing sculpture at the late seventh- and eighth-century monastic foundations of *Monkwearmouth and *Hartlepool. *Benedict Biscop's Gaulish masons may have been responsible for the opening of these quarries.

Wilson, *Archaeology*, pp. 260–1, 266–7; D. Parsons, 'Stone', in *English Medieval Industries*, ed. J. Blair and N. Ramsay (London, 1991), pp. 1–27.

KEVIN BROWN

MINSTER-IN-SHEPPEY (*Kent) was a nunnery founded for Seaxburh, daughter of King Anna of *East Anglia and widow of King Eorconberht of Kent, after her husband's death in 664. It continued as a royal family monastery, Seaxburh being succeeded in turn by her daughter and grand-daughter. *Asser, describing the *Vikings' wintering on Sheppey in 851, notes that 'an excellent monastery is established on the island'. The minster stood on a commanding site, overlooking the Thames estuary. The core of the existing parish church is an impressive Anglo-Saxon building with windows turned in Roman brick, perhaps dating from the original foundation, and there are hints of a further church to the east. Excavations north of the nave recovered high-quality eighth-century pottery and other artifacts. D. W. Rollason, *The Mildrith Legend: a Study in Early Medieval Hagiography in England* (Leicester, 1982); Taylor and Taylor, *AS Arch*, i. 429–30.

JOHN BLAIR

MINSTER-IN-THANET (Kent) was one of the richest and most important royal *nunneries of early England. It was reputedly founded in the 660s by King Ecgberht for Æbba ('Domneva'), daughter of the Kentish sub-king Eormenred and widow of Merewalh of the *Magonsæte*, who was succeeded as abbess by her daughter *Mildrith. Between 675 and 780 Minster received numerous land-grants in *Kent, as well as toll-remissions on *ships which show that the nuns were actively involved in trade between *London and the Frankish ports. From *Offa's reign the nunnery became increasingly a pawn in power-struggles between the archbishop and the kings of *Mercia and *Wessex. Late hagiographic sources describe the sacking of Minster by the Danes and the flight of the nuns to *Lyminge, with which it had already been closely linked. There is evidence, however, that a reduced religious community continued to exist through the tenth century; the dual sites of Minster Court and the parish church may perpetuate twin foci within a large monastic precinct. S. Kelly, *Charters of St Augustine's Abbey, Canterbury, and Minster-in-Thanet*, Anglo-Saxon Charters 4 (Oxford, 1995); idem, 'Trading Privileges from Eighth-Century England', *EME* 1 (1992), 3–28; D. W. Rollason, *The Mildrith Legend: a Study in Early Medieval Hagiography in England* (Leicester, 1982).

JOHN BLAIR

MINSTERS: *see* Monastic Sites; Monasticism; Parochial Organization

MINTS AND MINTING. The location of mints in England before the later ninth century primarily reflects access to the principal source of bullion, namely continental trade. From the inception of the Anglo-Saxon *coinage in the early seventh century the most important mints were situated in the south-east, in *Kent and *London. The mid-seventh century saw the opening of a Northumbrian mint, presumably at *York, while in the early eighth century minting spread into *East Anglia, *Wessex (*Southampton) and probably southern and eastern *Mercia. For most of the ninth century the principal mints remained London, *Canterbury, *Rochester (from c.810), and *Ipswich (?), with another in Wessex producing occasional coinages, and York issuing debased coins for local circulation in *Northumbria.

Towards the end of the ninth century the geographical pattern of minting changed due in part to increased governmental intervention by *Alfred (871–99) and his successors, who developed a network of new mints covering most of Wessex and Mercia, but in part also to the *Vikings who established major mints in the *Danelaw. Their abundant coinages in fine silver were produced in both Northumbria and the southern Danelaw, and the relatively high output of these regions was sustained even after their reconquest during the tenth century.

Few coins struck before the reign of *Æthelstan (924–39) carry the name of a mint. London (Lundonia) is found on a series of gold shillings of the 630s and on some early silver pennies (the so-called 'sceattas') of the 720s and 730s. Thereafter it occurs only on a special issue marking the capture of the city by *Ecgberht of Wessex in 829 and on Alfred's famous London Monogram issue of c.880. *Canterbury (Dorovernia or Dorobernia) is named on a single coin of the early seventh century and thereafter not again until the ninth century when it occurs, usually in the form of a monogram, on coins of Ceolwulf I of Mercia (821–3) and of Archbishops *Wulfred (805–32) and *Ceolnoth (833–70). *Rochester (Dorobrebia) is also named on Ceolwulf's coinage, but later issues have the ambiguous form DORO or DOROB which could stand for either city, and in *Æthelwulf's coinage it probably served for both; on Ecgberht's and Alfred's coins it is thought to refer only to Canterbury.

At the end of the ninth and beginning of the tenth century other mint-names occur: on Alfred's last coinage, *Exeter (Exa), *Gloucester (Gleawa), *Oxford (Ohsnaforda) and *Winchester (Win); on *Edward the Elder's, *Bath (Bað); and in the Viking coinages, York (Ebraice or Eborace), *Lincoln (Lincolla), and *Leicester (Licira).

Thirty-five mints are named on Æthelstan's coinage and after *Edgar's reform of c.973, when the mint-name was always given, some 60–70 mints were normally in operation. Descriptive terms occasionally qualified the mint-name in the tenth century: civitas for Bath, Canterbury, Chichester, Exeter, London, Winchester, and York, and urbs for Lewes, Oxford, *Southampton, and an unidentified 'Darent'.

The Grateley code (II Æthelstan, ch. 14) shows that in the tenth century every borough in the south was entitled to at least one *moneyer, and hence to operate a mint, though not all exercised that right. Later, north of the Thames where mints were less plentiful, there seems to have been a mint in every shire. The term 'mint' may, however, be misleading – Stenton preferred 'minting-place' – for it seems that moneyers normally operated, not from a single building, but from their own private workshops, which may have been gathered in a particular area of the *town as in the case of eleventh-century Winchester.

I. Stewart, 'The English and Norman Mints, c.600–1158', in A New History of the Royal Mint, ed. C. E. Challis (Cambridge, 1995), pp. 1–82; M. Blackburn, 'Mints, Burhs, and the Grately Code, cap. 14.2', in The Defence of Wessex. The Burghal Hidage and Anglo-Saxon Fortifications, ed. D. Hill and A. R. Rumble (Manchester, 1996), pp. 160–75; M. Biddle and D. J. Keene, 'Winchester in the Eleventh and Twelfth Centuries', in Winchester in the Early Middle Ages, ed. M. Biddle, Winchester Studies 1 (Oxford, 1976), 241–448, at 396–422 [iii. The mint].

M. A. S. BLACKBURN

MISSIONARIES. The christianisation of England and the *conversion of its kings was carried out largely at the hands of continental and Irish missionaries, beginning with *Augustine of Canterbury's arrival in 597, and continuing with *Aidan's establishment at *Lindisfarne in 635. *Canterbury and Lindisfarne continued to act as missionary centres within England, with *Paulinus travelling to *Northumbria from *Kent, and Aidan's disciples, the brothers Cedd, Cynebill, Cælin and *Chad, working in much of midland and eastern England. In addition Frankish missionaries worked in eastern England, most notably the Burgundian Felix, and the Italian *Birinus worked in *Wessex.

Having been christianized, the Anglo-Saxons in their turn provided a substantial number of missionaries for the evangelization of the Germanic regions east of the Rhine. The earliest Englishman known to have acted as a missionary on the Continent was the Northumbrian bishop,

*Wilfrid, who spent time working in *Frisia while en route to *Rome in *c.*679. The notion of missionary work on the Continent was then taken up by another Northumbrian, the monk Ecgberht, who was living in Ireland at the monastery of *Rathmelsigi*, and who wished to evangelize peoples whom he regarded as continental cousins of the English. Although prevented from working on the Continent himself he sent a number of pupils, including Wihtberht, *Willibrord and Swithbert, and he inspired a separate mission to the continental Saxons which was undertaken by the two *Hewalds. Of Ecgberht's pupils Willibrord (d. 739) was by far the most successful, working in Frisia, becoming archbishop of the Frisians, with his base in Utrecht in 695, and founding the monastery of Echternach. From the start Willibrord sought backing from the *papacy, travelling to Rome in *c.*690 and 695, and he collaborated with the leading aristocratic family of the Frankish kingdom, the Pippinids. Although Willibrord, who was himself a Northumbrian, maintained close connections with northern England, his most famous helper was the West Saxon, *Boniface, who made an initial attempt to work in Frisia in 716, which came to nothing because of the political situation, but then worked with Willibrord in the region between 718 and 721. Thereafter he worked largely in the already christianized regions of Hesse, Thuringia and Bavaria, where he reorganized the church. Like Willibrord, Boniface made great use of Pippinid and papal support, travelling to Rome in 718, 722 and 738–9. In 738, following Charles Martel's defeat of the continental Saxons, it seemed as if Boniface would be able to work among that people, whom, like Ecgberht, he saw as being related to the Anglo-Saxons, and to this end he appealed to a number of English contacts for help. In the event the opportunity to work among the Saxons passed, and it was not until 754, the year of his death, that Boniface was able to return to work among pagans, once again in Frisia, where he was martyred. Through his connections in Wessex and Kent, Boniface was able to draw a number of Englishmen and women to work on the Continent, most notably *Wynnebald, abbot of Heidenheim, *Willibald, bishop of Eichstätt, and *Leobgyth, abbess of Tauberbischofsheim. Nor did the arrival of English missionaries on the Continent come to an end with Boniface's martyrdom. Among the latest missionaries were two other Northumbrians: *Leofwine (Lebuin), who worked largely in Frisia, and *Willehad, who was bishop of Bremen 787–9. Interestingly, these men did not initially work

under the aegis of Charlemagne: indeed Willehad was sent to the Continent by the Northumbrian king Alchred (765–74) and by the bishops of Northumbria. Like a number of missionaries he was also a friend of *Alcuin, who, although not a missionary himself, contributed much to Carolingian missionary theory in his letters and in his *Life of Willibrord*.

The English missionaries on the Continent are remarkably well represented both in *Bede's *Historia ecclesiastica*, which portrays the work of Wilfrid, Ecgberht and Willibrord as a logical extension of the christianization of England, and in a large number of saints' Lives, as well as in the letters of Boniface and his disciple *Lull. By contrast there is no comparable documentation for Frankish and Irish missionaries who are known from fragmentary evidence to have been active east of the Rhine before the arrival of the English. It is, therefore, important to be aware that outside Frisia and Saxony the English missionaries were acting in regions which were already Christian, even if the standards of Christianity in those areas were not high. Boniface's great achievement was, therefore, organisational rather than missionary, and much of the continental impact of his Anglo-Saxon disciples lay in their promotion of *monasticism, and more especially the Rule of St Benedict.

I. Wood, 'The Mission of Augustine of Canterbury to the English', *Speculum* 69 (1994), 1–17; P. Hunter Blair, 'The Letters of Pope Boniface V and the Mission of Paulinus to Northumbria', in *England Before the Conquest. Studies in Primary Sources presented to Dorothy Whitelock*, ed. P. Clemoes and K. Hughes (Cambridge, 1971), pp. 5–13; S. J. Crawford, *Anglo-Saxon Influence on Western Christendom, 600–800* (Oxford, 1933), pp. 32–71; W. Levison, *England and the Continent in the Eighth Century* (Oxford, 1946), pp. 45–69 [Willibrord], 70–93 [Boniface]; C. H. Talbot, *The Anglo-Saxon Missionaries in Germany* (London, 1954); J. M. Wallace-Hadrill, 'A Background to St Boniface's Mission', in his *Early Medieval History* (Oxford, 1975), pp. 138–54; D. Parsons, 'Sites and Monuments of the Anglo-Saxon Mission in Central Germany', *Archaeological Journal* 140 (1983), 280–321; R. McKitterick, 'Anglo-Saxon Missionaries in Germany: Reflections on the Manuscript Evidence', *TCBS* 9 (1986–90), 291–329; idem, *Anglo Saxon Missionaries in Germany: Personal Connections and Local Influences*, University of Leicester Vaughan Paper 36 (Leicester, 1991); H. Mayr-Harting, *The Coming of Christianity to Anglo-Saxon England*, 3rd ed. (London, 1991).

IAN WOOD

MONASTERIALIA INDICIA ('Monastic Signs') are a text preserved on 97r–101v of

319

London, BL, Cotton Tiberius A.iii (under the ungrammatical rubric 'Monasteriales indicia'), a manuscript written at Christ Church, Canterbury in the first half of the eleventh century which has been described as the 'manifesto of the monastic reform'. The text itself consists of 127 manual signs for use, as the *incipit* explains, 'if one wishes to observe diligently God's service', that is to say, to keep silence, as enjoined by the *Benedictine Rule (c. 42), in church, at meals, and at night. The signs include those for *liturgical books and furniture, *food and drink and eating utensils, and *clothing and personal possessions (including writing equipment), as well as persons both within the community and outside. The text cannot be localized to a particular establishment, although it assumes a male readership. It may have been intended as a template for each house to adapt to its own circumstances (including, where applicable, female gender). The signs depend on those used at Cluny, and there is no evidence for signing in pre-reform English monasteries, so presumably the practice was intended to facilitate the reformed way of life. The *indicia* give us a unique insight (albeit probably idealized) into Anglo-Saxon monastic life, including, for example, signs for use 'if you need salt meat for any reason' (evidently an excuse was needed in reformed houses), for the schoolmaster (made of up signs for 'to look (after)' and 'small'), and for both celibate priests and 'a priest who is not a monk'.

Ker, *Catalogue*, no. 186; D. Banham, *Monasteriales Indicia: the Anglo-Saxon Monastic Sign Language* (Pinner, 1991; rev. ed. Hockwold cum Wilton, 1996).

DEBBY BANHAM

MONASTICISM is a distinctive feature of Christendom, and is, in simplest form, the expression of an urge to seek God through prayer and abstinence. This expression takes two principal forms: cenobitic (the word derived from Greek *koinos* and *bios*: 'life in common') and eremitic (from Greek *eremos*, 'desert'). Both these forms are attested in Anglo-Saxon England: the former by communities of monks living under the rule of an abbot according to a common discipline (as, say, at St Augustine's, *Canterbury) or of nuns living according to a common rule (see *nunneries); the latter by hermits or anchorites – the word deriving from the Greek verb *anachoreo*, 'to retreat' – living the eremitic life (e.g. *Guthlac at Crowland). (A combination of the two forms, known as a *laura*, in which monks lived separately as anchorites who were nevertheless under the rule of a single abbot, is not attested in Anglo-Saxon

England.) The earliest Christian monasticism is attested in the ascetics of fourth-century Egypt (characteristically by St Antony) and Palestine (characteristically by St Hilarion); but their practices became known in the West, both through the reports of travellers who had known and studied with oriental monks, such as Cassian, who recorded the conversations and practices of these monks in his *Conlationes*, and through the Lives of exemplary saints such as Athanasius's Life of Antony (in the Latin translation of Evagrius) and Jerome's Life of Hilarion. The result is that various monastic communities were established in the West by the early fifth century, notably at Lérins, and from there the practice spread throughout Europe. The major monastic foundations in Ireland, for example, date from the mid-sixth century. And as monasticism became established, Rules were promulgated to direct the lives of monks, notably those of St Benedict (d. *c.*550), St Honoratus of Lerins, Caesarius and Aurelian of Arles, Columbanus of Bangor and Bobbio, and many more, including the *Regula magistri* (which is thought by some to be source on which the *Regula S. Benedicti* is based).

The first Christians who arrived in Anglo-Saxon England with *Augustine were monks of Pope *Gregory's monastery of St Andrew, and they no doubt brought their own practices with them to England, even though these practices cannot now be determined. During the course of the seventh century, the various Irish monks who came to England as *missionaries (notably *Aidan of *Iona; but he is only one among many) will have brought their monastic practices with them; and various Northumbrian monasteries such as *Lindisfarne and *Melrose may be assumed to have followed Irish practice, at least in their earliest phases. Anglo-Saxon travellers who went to *Rome during the seventh century will have had the opportunity of observing Roman monastic custom at first hand, notably *Wilfrid, *Benedict Biscop, *Ceolfrith, and *Aldhelm; in particular, Benedict Biscop was tonsured and spent two years at Lérins, and will have returned to England thoroughly familiar with Lerinian custom. The point is that, during the first century or so of English Christianity, there was considerable variety in the models of monastic discipline (*Bede reports in his *Historia abbatum* c. 11 that Benedict Biscop based the custom of *Monkwearmouth-Jarrow on those of seventeen monasteries which he had visited during the course of his travels) and considerable flexibility in the structure of monastic communities: for example, the so-called 'double monastery', a community housing both monks and nuns, is a feature of English religious life at this time, practised successfully with strict separation of the sexes at *Barking and *Whitby (and, according to Bede, less successfully at *Coldingham, where the community lapsed into intimate familiarity and was divinely chastized by a fire which destroyed the monastic buildings). In many cases such monasteries will have served primarily as retirement homes for pious gentlefolk. Furthermore, many private monasteries were established on the lands of noblemen, no doubt in many cases for the laudable purpose of having a private chaplain at hand; but because monasteries were also exempt from royal taxation, there were undoubtedly many which were established solely for the purposes of tax evasion, and in a letter to *Ecgberht of York, Bede warns his colleague of the perils of such abuse. In any event, the strict discipline of Benedictine monasticism is a much later phenomenon. The earliest certain evidence for study of the *Regula S. Benedicti* in England is found in the Leiden Glossary which derives from the late seventh-century *school of Archbishop *Theodore and Abbot *Hadrian at Canterbury (and recall that Theodore was a Greek monk, familiar through his oriental training with the Rule of St Basil rather than with western rules such as that of Benedict), and the earliest Anglo-Saxon manuscript of the *Regula S. Benedicti* (Oxford, Bodleian Library, Hatton 48) dates from the first half of the eighth century; but there is no evidence that any monastery followed strict Benedictine custom before the mid-tenth century.

During the following centuries, monastic life – such as it was – was disrupted by *Vikings, beginning with the sack of Lindisfarne in 793, and the depredations which continued during the ninth century may be assumed to have brought it almost completely to extinction. In the preface to his translation of Gregory's *Regula pastoralis*, King *Alfred noted that, on his accession in 871, the religious orders (among which he evidently included monks) who had formerly excelled in learning, teaching and religious services, had so declined in numbers that there was not a single one south of the Thames who could understand divine services or translate a sentence from Latin into English. Alfred made his own contribution towards remedying this situation by providing revenue for the foundation of a monastery at Athelney and a nunnery at *Shaftesbury, but it was not until the mid-tenth century that a vigorous attempt at monastic reform was undertaken. Religious leaders at this time were well aware of the monastic reform movements taking place on the Continent in Lotharingia and *Flanders (under the inspiration of Gerhard of Brogne) and at *Fleury (under the inspiration of Odo of Cluny and of Cluniac monasticism in general). The first stirrings of English reform took place at *Glastonbury, where *Dunstan had become abbot sometime between 940 and 946, and where during the 940s and early 950s he was joined by his colleague *Æthelwold, the future bishop of *Winchester. Among the texts which were studied at Glastonbury were the *Regula S. Benedicti* and commentaries on it (including that by Smaragdus of Saint-Mihiel). Accordingly, when Dunstan became archbishop of Canterbury in 959, there was a splendid opportunity to implement the reforming principles which had been incubated at Glastonbury: Æthelwold was appointed bishop of Winchester in 963, and *Oswald, who had studied and been tonsured at Fleury, was appointed bishop of *Worcester in 961. In February 964 Æthelwold, with the support of King *Edgar (and his troops), expelled the secular *clergy from the Old Minster – thus depriving them of their wealthy benefices – and replaced them with his monks from *Abingdon, who were by now strict Benedictines, and who will therefore have owned the Winchester benefices communally (according to c. 33 of the *Regula S. Benedicti*, no Benedictine monk was permitted to own so much as a stylus: all property was owned by the community). Æthelwold translated the *Benedictine Rule into Old English, and it was he who composed the *Regularis concordia* – the customary which, insofar as it was intended to supplement the Benedictine Rule, prescribed and defined the reformed Benedictine discipline – on the basis of advice given by monks from Ghent and Fleury as well as on Carolingian conciliar legislation (decrees of councils of 816 and 817, as well as on the 'Memoriale qualiter' of Benedict of Aniane). From this period, substantial numbers of monasteries were founded or refounded, and monks from these reformed houses were very frequently appointed to bishoprics, so that monastic cathedrals become a characteristically English feature of ecclesiastical life in the late tenth and earlier eleventh centuries. Although in the years immediately following the death of King Edgar in 975 there was a reaction in *Mercia against monastic ownership of estates led by Ealdorman Ælfhere, with the result that certain refounded Benedictine communities were forced to leave Mercia (for example *Winchcombe, which removed itself entire to *Ramsey), on the whole the influence of Benedictine monks remained in the ascendant until the Norman Conquest.

It is difficult, because of insufficient evidence, to form a clear picture of what life in an early Anglo-Saxon monastery entailed, and even for the period of the Benedictine reform much must be deduced from analogy with continental institutions (even the *Regularis concordia* is frustratingly vague on details of everyday life in a Benedictine monastery). Much of the monks' day was taken up with the Divine Office, consisting of psalmody, prayers, *hymns and, on saints' days, readings from the Life of the saint in question. The day began *c*.2.00 a.m. with the three Nocturns (or Matins) which made up the Night Office, followed just before dawn by Lauds, then the so-called Little Hours of Prime, Terce, Sext, None, Vespers and Compline; following Terce was the Morrow Mass, which in turn was followed by Chapter, where the monks assembled to receive instructions from the abbot, and to hear the reading of the day's martyrology (see *liturgy). The community consisted of oblates (children who had been offered to the monastery at the age of seven), novices (young men who were under probation for approximately a year before becoming monks), and professed monks (that is, those who had made the threefold vow of poverty, chastity and obedience). The officers of the monastery consisted of the abbot and the provost (*praepositus*) who was in effect second-in-command, and then one or more deans (*decani*, the name originally meaning someone responsible for ten people); the word *prior* also occurs in the *Regularis concordia*, and apparently refers to someone in charge who may be either the abbot or the provost. In addition there were various specialized officers: the precentor (*cantor*) who was responsible for the *music and also (usually) the *library; the sacristan (*aedituus*) who was responsible for the shrines of the church's saints; the master of the *school (*custos*), who was responsible for the oblates; and a disciplinary officer called a *circator* who, as the name implies, circulated about the monastery looking for infractions of discipline. In short, although Anglo-Saxon monasteries were in theory retreats from the world, because of their great landed wealth they were often in a position to play a significant role in worldly affairs.

DACL xi.1774–1947; G. Constable, *Medieval Monasticism: a Select Bibliography* (Toronto, 1976); D. Knowles, *The Monastic Order in England*, 2nd ed. (Cambridge, 1963); T. Symons, *Regularis Concordia* (London, 1953); *Heads of Religious Houses, England and Wales 940–1216*, ed. D. Knowles, C. N. L. Brooke and V. London

(Cambridge, 1972); *Tenth-Century Studies*, ed. D. Parsons (Chichester, 1975); A. Gransden, 'Traditionalism and Continuity during the Last Century of Anglo-Saxon Monasticism', *JEH* 40 (1989), 159–207, repr. in her *Legends, Traditions and History in Medieval England* (London, 1992), pp. 31–79; M. Lapidge and M. Winterbottom, ed., *Wulfstan of Winchester: the Life of St Æthelwold* (OMT, 1991), pp. li–lx; D. J. V. Fisher, 'The Anti-Monastic Reaction in the Reign of Edward the Martyr', *Cambridge Historical Journal* 10 (1950–2), 247–70; F. Barlow, *The English Church 1000–1066*, 2nd ed. (London, 1979), esp. pp. 311–38; *Æthelwold*; C. Cubitt, 'The Tenth-Century Benedictine Reform', *EME* 6 (1997), 77–94.

MICHAEL LAPIDGE

MONASTIC SITES were established in England in their hundreds during the seventh to ninth centuries. A minority were transformed from the tenth century onwards after being re-founded as regular monasteries; most of the rest are now marked by substantial parish churches. Given the complex and diverse nature of the communities which they housed, it is unsurprising that pre-Viking sites reveal no clear-cut distinction between monastic and clerical, or between 'Roman' and 'Celtic'. Instead they show a broad continuum of practice in the planning of ecclesiastical sites across Britain, Ireland, Gaul, and the regions of northern Europe which were converted by Anglo-Saxons and Irish.

Religious communities tended to be prominently sited, on hills, coastal headlands or bluffs overlooking rivers; along the Thames, for instance, a line of important minsters can be traced from source to estuary. Such locations do not, on the whole, suggest seclusion, but rather a proximity to the main communication arteries, and a centrality amid the dispersed *settlement patterns of mid-Saxon England. Monastic sites, unlike *royal sites, were generally enclosed by a bank and ditch (the *vallum monasterii* of texts) defining a substantial circular or curvilinear zone. For this purpose Iron Age forts were sometimes reused; more commonly, *Roman towns and forts provided ready-made enclosures and formal settings, and were frequently given by seventh-century kings to bishops and monastic founders (for instance *Dorchester-on-Thames and *Reculver).

Churches dominated the buildings of the precinct. In England the tradition of twinned or multiple churches (general throughout early Christendom on sites of any importance) often took the form of two or more churches aligned on a west–east axis (fig. 13). Sometimes the Anglo-Saxon churches survive or are known from exca-

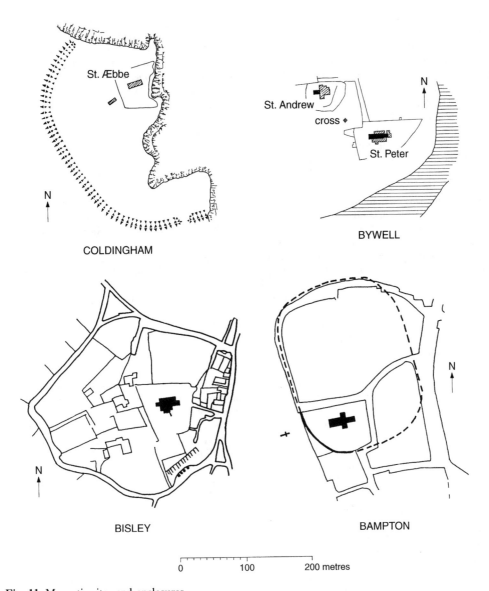

Fig. 11 Monastic sites and enclosures.

vation, as at *Canterbury St Augustine's, *Glastonbury, *Monkwearmouth–Jarrow, *Lind-isfarne and *Wells; more often, late medieval rebuildings perpetuate the early layout (as for instance at *Winchcombe). Functions are poorly recorded, but it is evident that multiple church sites reflect specialized uses (for instance by distinct groups of people, or to honour different saints), as well as processional liturgies which sometimes embraced dependent holy sites well outside the precincts.

Other buildings are known only from descrip-tions and from excavation. The main domestic ranges at Jarrow were finely built of masonry, and *Northampton minster (if the monastic interpre-tation is accepted) had a huge stone hall in the early ninth century. Generally, though, the dom-estic quarters of pre-Viking minsters were of timber, and comprised one or more large communal buildings, associated with dense clus-ters of small rectangular 'halls' (excavated at *Brandon, *Hartlepool, *Whithorn and *Whitby) which probably functioned as private accom-modation and workshops. Excavations on eighth-

323

century sites in northern and eastern England have found distinctive assemblages of rich objects, including elaborate pins and other dress fittings, writing styli and imported *pottery and *glass. Written sources give an impression of complexity and of high density: Bede describes the impressive sight of *Coldingham with its 'communal and private buildings' (*HE* iv.25), and mentions the building-over of a *cemetery at *Barking because of space problems (iv.10). Nonetheless, only a proportion of the large zone which a typical *vallum* enclosed can have been filled with buildings: there were probably also kitchen gardens, space for stock, and perhaps even arable 'infields'.

After *c*.850, to judge from the excavations, monastic settlements contracted and prestige goods disappeared, even though most of the sites retained locally important churches and (presumably) basic accommodation for the groups of priests which they now housed (see *parochial organization). The impact of tenth- and eleventh-century planning on the minority of sites which were reformed as strict monasteries is surprisingly obscure, even though a good deal is known about the liturgical enlargement of churches. Fragments of early cloisters have been found at Canterbury St Augustine's, *Glastonbury, *Eynsham and *Winchester, and there is written evidence that in the early to mid eleventh century the canons of the strictest minsters, including the reformed cathedral chapters at *Wells, *Exeter and *Hereford, were required to have common refectories and dormitories (see *cathedral clergy). Except at *Westminster, where the works still in progress in 1066 had always envisaged a true cloister, the buildings of English abbeys must have looked very inadequate to Norman eyes.

In England as in Ireland, it is as *towns that early monastic sites are most evident in the modern landscape: as religious functions declined during the ninth to twelfth centuries, commercial and industrial ones developed. Thus the street-plans of many small towns retain traces of the curvilinear precincts out of which they developed. R. J. Cramp, 'Monastic Sites', in Wilson, *Archaeology*, pp. 201–52; J. Blair, 'Minster Churches in the Landscape', *Anglo-Saxon Settlements*, ed. D. Hooke (Oxford, 1988), pp. 35–58; idem, 'Anglo-Saxon Minsters: a Topographical Review', in Blair and Sharpe, *Past. Care*, pp. 226–66; R. Morris, *Churches in the Landscape* (London, 1989).

JOHN BLAIR

MONEYERS were the individuals responsible for organizing the production of coins. They had their origins in the Roman office of the *monetarius*. They are one of the best recorded group of people in Anglo-Saxon England since most coins bear the name of the moneyer who issued them. There could be between one and fifteen or more moneyers operating in a *mint town depending on its size and importance, and the total number of moneyers recorded from the Anglo-Saxon period runs to several thousand.

Moneyers were of men of relatively high status. They can be found among the witnesses to *charters; in *Winchester in the mid-eleventh century most or all were of burgess rank; in *Lincoln some also seem to have held the office of lawman; and two *York moneyers are described on their coins as *thegns. The moneyers were the wealthiest occupational group in Winchester in 1148, comparable with royal officials; and in the trade regulations for London (IV Æthelred, ch. 9.1), moneyers are made responsible for the *coinage produced by their employees. One should probably think of moneyers as financiers rather than as people who were physically striking the coins, although some may also have played a role in that.

It is possible to follow the careers of particular moneyers over periods of up to thirty or forty years, and sometimes moving between mints or holding positions at several simultaneously. In the late eighth and early ninth centuries, when control of *Kent and *East Anglia changed several times between *Mercian or *West Saxon and local rulers, operation of the mints of *Canterbury, *Rochester and *Ipswich (?) was not appreciably disrupted, and the same moneyers would strike coins for successive rival dynasties, suggesting that the moneyers were not political appointees but people prominent in the local commercial community.

The moneyers' names as they appear on the coins are a rich source of material for the study of personal names since they can be closely dated and localized. The majority of them are Old English, though the forms in which they occur sometimes reflect the influence of local *dialects. In the *Danelaw many of the names are of Scandinavian origin, a higher proportion at York and Lincoln than in East Anglia and the east Midlands, where Scandinavian influence was less intense. A number of Frankish names also occur in the Danelaw, as a result, it would seem, of the earliest Scandinavian settlers in the late ninth century bringing a number of Carolingian moneyers over to establish mints for them.

I. Stewart, 'Ministri and monetarii', *Revue numismatique*, 6th ser. 30 (1988), 166–75; V. Smart, 'Scandinavians,

Celts, and Germans in Anglo-Saxon England: the Evidence of Moneyers' Names', in *Anglo-Saxon Monetary History*, ed. M. A. S. Blackburn (Leicester, 1986), pp. 171–84.

M. A. S. BLACKBURN

MONKWEARMOUTH (OR WEARMOUTH) AND JARROW

(Tyne and Wear) were monastic houses founded in *c*.673 and *c*.681 respectively. As a twin institution, they contributed significantly to European culture and learning, not least through the works of their most famous inmate, *Bede. It is through his work that so much is known of their early history, and the aspiration of their founder – the Northumbrian noble *Benedict Biscop – which resulted in a foundation very different from the colonies of monasteries founded earlier by the Irish mission.

Benedict Biscop, who had become a monk at Lérins, had travelled extensively in Gaul and Italy, for twenty years, before he returned to his native kingdom and received a major land grant from the king to build a monastery, at the mouth of the Wear, 'in the Roman manner' which, as Bede recorded, he had always admired. To that end he went to Gaul for capable masons, and between 674/5 a stone church was built. As it neared completion, he sent to the Continent for glaziers to glaze the windows of the church and *porticus* and to instruct the English in the craft of *glass-blowing. To the extensive *library he had already accumulated, Benedict sought to add liturgical vessels, vestments, and icons to enrich his church, and when the church was dedicated to St Peter in 675/6, he made his fifth visit to *Rome taking with him *Ceolfrith, who later was his successor as sole abbot of the monastery. When the travellers returned they brought with them not only more books, relics, and pictures, but also John, abbot of St Martin's monastery and archicantor of St Peter's in *Rome, in order to ensure that ceremonial singing and reading aloud conformed to Roman practice.

So great was the success of the foundation that King Ecgfrith gave a second endowment for a monastery on a tributary of the Tyne about seven miles north, at Jarrow. This was colonized, and presumably built, by twenty-two of the Monkwearmouth community under Abbot Ceolfrith. In the third year from the foundation of the monastery the building of the church began, and in the second year afterwards it was dedicated to St Paul. The dedication stone, providing a date of 23 April 685, survives in the church today.

At St Peter's, the larger of the twinned houses, the only Anglo-Saxon structure surviving above ground today is the west wall of the church and the lower two stories of the west tower, which was originally an entrance porch. From nineteenth-century excavations it can be deduced that the nave was *c*.19.8 m long and 5.64 m wide, with a funerary adjunct to the east. Recent excavations to the south of the churches have demonstrated that the site was carefully laid out with a central covered way or *porticus*, over 35.5 m long, leading from the churches through a range of buildings towards the river. This covered way seemed to divide off the monastic from an earlier lay *cemetery to the west, and it may be compared with similar long corridors in Roman and Gaulish sites. It should be emphasized that neither here nor at Jarrow has the complete area of the *monastic site been determined, but the excavated area demonstrates that the final plan of the liturgical heart of Monkwearmouth, with its formal layout and two ranges enclosed within surrounding walls, presented a very continental appearance. This impression was accentuated by the painted and striped walls, painted balusters at openings, red concrete floors, and the coloured window glass.

The present chancel of St Paul's church at Jarrow, which was originally an independent building, is the only Anglo-Saxon structure of that monastery surviving above ground. The 'basilica' described in the dedication stone was rebuilt in the eighteenth and again in the nineteenth centuries, but excavations in the interior of the modern nave have revealed the foundations of the Anglo-Saxon nave, of the same dimensions as Wearmouth, and with a square-ended chancel, separated from the funerary chapel to the east.

The general topography of Jarrow (fig. 13) resembled that of Monkwearmouth, but the buildings were laid out in detached parallel rows rather than organized around an enclosed space as at Monkwearmouth. Between the churches and a range of buildings 15.24 m to the south was a cemetery. The buildings were divided by a very narrow passage, and it is assumed that they were two-storied. The western building has been identified as a refectory, with an added kitchen to the south and sleeping-quarters above, and the eastern building as a general-purpose hall with a private oratory and cell at the east and again sleeping quarters above. About 15.24 m south of this range were other buildings on the waterfront, one of which has been interpreted as a guest-house, later a workshop, with other flimsy workshops attached, in which *metal- and glass-working took place. The major stone buildings were enriched with coloured plaster, *sculpture and coloured window-glass, and finds from the site demonstrated wide-ranging external contacts.

The twin monastery flourished in the eighth century, and when Abbot Ceolfrith left on his last journey to Rome in 716 the joint community numbered about six hundred brethren. At the height of its achievement, Monkwearmouth/Jarrow was highly influential in Britain, Ireland, and beyond. Naiton, king of the Picts, asked for its masons to build him a church of stone, and sought advice on church doctrine; its library and its scholars, particularly Bede, were widely admired.

Excavation has revealed a context for these achievements which is probably unlike most other Anglo-Saxon monasteries. In its allegiance to Roman traditions, Monkwearmouth/Jarrow pre-figured the greater Carolingian monasteries, and it was unfortunate that the wars and disturbances of the *Viking Age in *Northumbria put an end to further development. There is no evidence for occupation on these sites after the mid-ninth century, and the buildings were abandoned and ruinous at the time of the refoundation of the sites by southern monks in the late eleventh century.

P. H. Blair, *The World of Bede* (London, 1970); R. Cramp, 'Excavations at the Saxon Monastic Sites of Wearmouth and Jarrow Co. Durham: an Interim Report', *MArch* 13 (1969), 21–36; idem, 'Decorated Window-Glass and Millefiori from Monkwearmouth', *AJ* 50 (1970), 327–35; idem, 'Window Glass from the Monastic Site of Jarrow', *Journal of Glass Studies* 17 (1975), 88–96; idem, 'Monastic Sites', in Wilson, *Archaeology*, pp. 201–52; idem, 'Jarrow Church', *Archaeological Journal* 133 (1976), 220–8; idem, 'Monkwearmouth', ibid. pp. 230–7; idem, 'Monkwearmouth and Jarrow in their European Context', in '*Churches Built in Ancient Times*', *Recent Studies in Early Christian Archaeology*, ed. K. Painter, (London, 1994), pp. 279–94; *Bede and his World: The Jarrow Lectures, 1958–93*, ed. M. Lapidge, 2 vols. (Aldershot, 1994); Taylor and Taylor, *AS Arch* i.338–49, 423–46; iii.740–1, 749, 752–3.

ROSEMARY CRAMP

MUCKING, an Anglo-Saxon settlement on the north bank of the Thames estuary in Essex, occupies a unique place in the history of early medieval archaeology. Excavated almost continuously between 1965 and 1978 under the direction of Margaret and Tom Jones in advance of gravel-quarrying, Mucking was until recently by far the most extensive excavation undertaken in Britain. At the end of the excavation, some eighteen hectares of ancient landscape had been revealed. This was the first time that most (though perhaps not

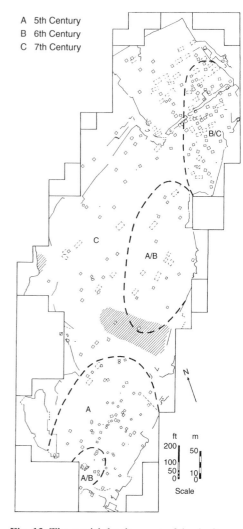

A 5th Century
B 6th Century
C 7th Century

Fig. 12 The spatial development of Anglo-Saxon Mucking.

all) of an Anglo-Saxon *settlement was uncovered, together with its associated *cemeteries. In all, the remains of some 203 sunken huts (small buildings with dug-out floors) and at least fifty-three rectangular 'halls' built of earth-fast timber posts were identified, spread out along nearly a kilo-metre of gravel terrace.

A wide range of artifacts derive from the settlement, including *pottery imported from Francia, late Roman military-style belt fittings, three silver *coins (*sceattas*) of *c.*680–5, a wide range of iron tools, spinning and weaving equipment, cast lead rings and a mould for casting a brooch. A number of hearths and pits were associated with the buildings, as well as workshop debris primarily derived from *textile production, iron and lead working. What has survived archaeologically, however, reflects only a fraction of the economic activities in which the community at Mucking was engaged.

Full analysis of the cemeteries has yet to be completed, but it is clear that both Cemetery I (with some sixty inhumations) and Cemetery II (with over 700 burials, one-third inhumations and the rest cremations) were, like the settlement, established in the first half of the fifth century. While most burials were relatively ordinary, both cemeteries contained rich 'founder' graves and a number of well-equipped burials, perhaps representing the heads of households, containing high-status *grave goods such as swords and *glass vessels.

In the early years of the excavation it was believed that Mucking originated as a settlement of Germanic mercenaries guarding the Thames estuary against invasion. This hypothesis remains plausible, although the archaeological evidence is insufficient to prove it. The Anglo-Saxon settlement was sited on a parcel of former Romano-British farmland with several Romano-British cemeteries and structures. Apart from this continuity of land use, however, direct evidence for socio-economic continuity at a deeper level, or for Romano-Saxon overlap or integration is lacking. The Roman ditches had largely silted up by the time the Anglo-Saxon settlement was established and the Anglo-Saxon cemeteries were founded on new sites, entirely separate from the Romano-British cemeteries.

The association of two cemeteries with a single settlement remains puzzling. The buildings lay in two main concentrations, but analysis of the pottery and finds revealed that these represented neither two contemporary settlements nor a single, sprawling village, but instead different phases of the same settlement as it gradually shifted northwards in the course of some three hundred years, from the first half of the fifth century to at least the beginning of the eighth. Mucking in this way resembled many Migration Period settlements in north-west Europe which shifted periodically while continuing to utilize ancestral burial grounds. Although the settlement varied somewhat in size and layout over time, groups of buildings lay together without well-defined properties or boundaries. Despite the rich burials, no exceptionally large or central buildings were identified, nor was clear planning apparent in the layout of the settlement. A tentative assessment of population size suggests an average of around one hundred occupants, with at least ten 'halls' and fourteen sunken huts standing at any one time.

M. U. Jones and W. T. Jones, 'The Crop-Mark Sites at Mucking, Essex' in *Recent Archaeological Excavations in Europe*, ed. R. Bruce-Mitford (London, 1975), pp. 133–87; H. Hamerow, *Excavations at Mucking Vol. 2: The Anglo-Saxon Settlement* (London, 1993); S. Hirst and D. Clarke, *Excavations at Mucking Vol. 3: The Anglo-Saxon Cemeteries* (London, forthcoming).

HELENA HAMEROW

MUSIC. References in both OE and Latin texts to the lives, lifestyles and artistic milieux of Anglo-Saxon musicians seem to indicate intensive creative activity spread across both sacred and secular traditions. The division between the religious and the popular is to some extent an arbitrary one for, as *Bede's account of *Cædmon illustrates, the evolution of Christian musical expression must from the outset have benefited greatly from the vigour and diversity of indigenous popular music. Certainly archaeological finds of simple yet musically expressive instruments recovered from Middle and Late Saxon towns, notably in the east of England, confirm that at least instrumental music (but almost certainly song as well) figured strongly in everyday work and *entertainment: in the house, street and market-place; in the countryside and at sea. From similarities in instrument forms an element of continuity from earlier Roman and native popular traditions seems increasingly likely.

What is still unclear is the precise relationship between these informal, unselfconscious modes of expression and those traditions which are most prominently documented in the literature: in particular any musical components there may have been in the original performance of surviving vernacular poetry. Latin verse, of which good examples occur in the collection known as the *Cambridge Songs* (Cambridge, UL, Gg.5.35) and elsewhere, is sometimes annotated, its melodic lines inscribed using various neumatic notations which adopt northern French models. As yet the earliest examples in the English language are still of distinctly post-Conquest date; yet the texts of the poems themselves include sufficient association of *scop* (poet) with *hearpe* (stringed instrument) to leave us in little doubt as to the existence of musical accompaniment. Indeed, the excavated remains of such instruments show them to be well adapted to, and acoustically compatible with, this role.

The *hearpe* is documented most often in the context of the aristocratic mead-hall, whether in the hands of the *scop* or played by the head of the household. In **Beowulf* the Danish king Hrothgar, seated in his hall Heorot, himself entertains his assembled retainers with tales of the remotest past whilst now and then playing a pleasant melody on the *hearpe*. At other times they are regaled instead by his *scop*'s heroic lays. The exact identity of this figure the *scop* remains something of a mystery, in spite of the descriptions provided by the poems **Widsith* and **Deor*: whether the term implied designation of a specific status, for example, is not at all clear. However, archaeological discoveries in pagan inhumation *cemeteries in *East Anglia, most recently at Snape in Suffolk, reveal the existence there of no fewer than four (and therefore, originally, probably many more) lyre-players between the sixth century and the early seventh. This cluster, together with its proximity to the royal ship-burial at *Sutton Hoo – which also contained such an instrument – is strongly suggestive of a local concentration of some importance, perhaps under royal patronage, and if so may have implications for our appreciation of the early context of such musical-poetic expression. Curiously, no such marked concentration has been observed elsewhere where such things might be expected, for example in *Northumbria or in *Wessex – or indeed on the Continent, despite careful survey and comparable soil-conditions.

Sources of information concerning church music (see *chant) and musicians are, on the whole, entirely separate from those which evoke other musical situations. One notable exception is the mention in *William of Malmesbury's *Vita S. Dunstani* of Dunstan's proficiency as a stringed-instrument (*cithara*) player. Within the limits of vocal performance imposed by the church, musical traditions flourished in the later tenth and eleventh centuries. The practice of elaborating existing (monophonic) chant with a second vocal line, creating a polyphonic texture, is documented at *Winchester, in the form of over 160 notations for added voices. Written down *c.*1000 (in CCCC 473), this notated repertory of organa predates by over 150 years any other European collection of liturgical polyphony. In writing down what was elsewhere practised orally, the monks of Winchester were showing not so much their precocity as the high regard in which they held these new (and by them, well understood) musical techniques.

A. Holschneider, *Die Organa von Winchester* (Hildesheim, 1968); S. Rankin, 'Winchester Polyphony: the Early Theory and Practice of Organum', in *Music*

in the *Medieval English Liturgy*, ed. S. Rankin and D. Hiley (Oxford, 1993), pp. 58–99.

GRAEME LAWSON AND SUSAN RANKIN

MUSICAL INSTRUMENTS. Some remarkable discoveries made during recent archaeological excavations lend both fine detail and new depth to our knowledge of Anglo-Saxon *music. Literary and historical records have long indicated the existence and diversity of music and musical instruments in Anglo-Saxon England and, together with illustrations in manuscripts and other art, hint at the contexts and ways in which they were performed. Such sources have contributed to the construction of elaborate theoretical models which form the basis of our developing understanding of music's evolution during the early Middle Ages. Yet they give us only the vaguest idea of location and distribution and, most tantalisingly, of what things really *sounded* like. By contrast, archaeology provides us with some very specific evidence indeed: nothing less than the preserved remains of the instruments which were actually used. These too display a remarkable diversity, from small, tinkling metal bells and shrill pipes made from bird-bones, to large stringed instruments of elaborate and sophisticated design. Application of ergonometry, surface-wear analysis, replication and acoustimetry permits reconstruction of both their original acoustical flavour and their technical capabilities. This constantly expanding resource brings with it two further important advantages: find-contexts offer firm dates and precise geographical, even cultural parameters for the evidence each instrument preserves; and the finds themselves are a source apparently uncompromised by later, deliberate human intervention.

Anglo-Saxon wind instruments are known from documentary sources to have included horns, trumpets and – in due course – even large, keyboard-operated devices such as the *Winchester organ. But the archaeological record is without question dominated by small, apparently homemade, flutes and pipes. This is fortunate because their forms preserve valuable evidence of performance practices and especially of ancient tuning specifications and procedures. Flutes and pipes of wood must have been popular, if the handful of surviving finds is anything to go by, for this material survives rarely and only in very special soil-conditions. In spite of this difficulty two especially important finds have emerged from excavations of later levels at *York: during the 1950s at St Peter's, Hungate, substantial portions were found of a small reed-pipe of fruit-wood with neatly carved decoration, rather like a bag-pipe chanter although missing its reed and its horn 'bell'. More recently an almost complete set of Pan-pipes, carved and drilled from a single block of box-wood, was discovered at Coppergate. Both of these instruments represent a high degree of craftsmanship, perhaps even the use of simple machine-tools, and are clearly the products not of idle whittling but of workshops – perhaps of the same kind as produced the earlier (and remarkably similar) box-wood Pan-pipes of the Roman period. An organized trade in such items cannot be ruled out. By contrast the vast bulk of surviving Anglo-Saxon wind-instruments are plain, hand-made items utilizing the natural hollow bones of sheep and large birds and shaped with the aid of a simple knife-point and blade. Most beautiful are those made from the wing-bones (*ulnae*) of geese, swans and even exotic species such as cranes. At Thetford in Norfolk three such pipes ranging from Late Saxon to post-Conquest date appear to be associated with a cellared building at a street-corner, suggesting a site of recreational activity – perhaps a tavern.

Most recently, among more fragmentary examples, research suggests that there may be pieces of bone instruments of an altogether different type, reed-pipes, which typically use instead the lower leg-bones (metapodials) of deer. Bone equivalents of the York apple-wood horn-pipe, and perhaps identifiable with the OE *swegelhorn*, have been found. In place of the bird-bone instrument's high-pitched, fluting tone, the deer-bone pipe's inserted reed, made probably from local thatching reeds (*Phragmytes communis*), produces the full-bodied skirl of later folk-clarinets, shawms and bagpipes. In one such find, from Middle Saxon *Ipswich, the effect is enhanced by the addition of a second pipe, the pair tied together and played simultaneously. For such doubling there are, besides continental parallels, once again closely similar Roman precursors.

In sharp contrast with such bucolic pastimes many OE texts allude to stringed instruments of more formal, primarily household, indeed courtly character, both under the generic title *hearpe* and by means of such kennings as *gomen-wudu* (joy-wood) and *gleo-beam* (glee-beam). Archaeological discoveries confirm both the identity and the high status of such equipment. Tiny bridges of wood, bone and amber from instruments closely similar to the lyres shown in eighth-century manuscript illustrations occur amongst the occupation debris of early medieval towns such as York and Birka, and the type may have survived in use well into post-Conquest times. However it is in the instruments preserved in Anglo-Saxon *cemeteries of the fifth to seventh centuries that they are best represented, notably amongst the *grave goods accompanying two royal barrows, at *Sutton Hoo (Suffolk) and *Taplow (Bucks.). Such finds are remarkably consistent through space and time in several important technical details, particularly their rigorous adherence to six strings and to bridges of unusually small size – which profoundly affect their musical character. They are also elegantly designed and manufactured to very high specifications, each employing a range of different timbers (maple, oak, willow and fruit-woods; compare *Exeter Book riddle no. 53) in such a way as to show a keen appreciation of their different structural properties. Such instruments are usually assumed to have been strung with sheep-gut, although the form of a tuning-peg from a grave in Suffolk suggests that it could have been intended to receive horse-hair, a material popular later in the Middle Ages especially in North European traditions. First indications of the lyre's decline to eventual extinction in Britain appear in the iconography of King David as psalmist. In early manuscript art and sculpture, including the ninth-century stone pillar at Masham (N. Yorks.), David is shown playing a lyre, illustrating *cithara*. After around 900 this gives way to the recently imported triangular harp, and even bowed instruments. However, for these new arrivals, all well attested amongst later medieval finds, there is as yet no archaeological corroboration in the Anglo-Saxon period.

R. L. S. Bruce-Mitford, 'The Lyre', in *The Sutton Hoo Ship Burial* III (London, 1983), pp. 611–731; G. Lawson, 'The Lyre Remains from Grave 97', in *Morning Thorpe Anglo-Saxon Cemetery, Norfolk I*, ed. B. Green, A. Rogerson and S. White, East Anglian Archaeology Series 36 (Gressenhall, 1987), 166–71; idem, 'Bone Flutes', in *Excavations in Thetford by B. K. Davison between 1964 and 1970*, ed. C. Dallas, East Anglian Archaeology Series 62 (Gressenhall, 1993), 159–60.

GRAEME LAWSON

N

NAVY. Naval forces constituted a critical arm of the Anglo-Saxon military establishment in the tenth and eleventh centuries. There was, in fact, little distinction made between a land (*fyrd*) and a sea force (*scipfyrd*) in the late Anglo-Saxon period. Both were recruited on the basis of the 'common burdens' incumbent upon landed estates (**Trinoda necessitas*), while the leaders and personnel of the two forces, professional sailors aside, were probably identical. Naval battles *per se* were discouraged by the type of ships used, Viking-style longships and cogs, better suited for troop transport, blockades of estuaries and rivers, and coastal raiding. The **Anglo-Saxon Chronicle*'s entry for 896, our one extended account of a 'naval engagement', describes an attempted blockade followed by hand-to-hand fighting on the shore between the crews of nine English ships and six Danish ships.

Despite the continental origin of the Angles, Saxons and Jutes who established kingdoms in fifth- and sixth-century Britain, there is little evidence of wide-spread naval activity in the centuries immediately following the **Adventus Saxonum*. King **Edwin's (d. 633) conquest of Anglesey and Man and Ecgfrith's devastating raid upon Ireland in 684 suggest that the rulers of seventh-century **Northumbria possessed considerable naval resources. A century later, however, **Viking fleets were able to sack without challenge the island monastery of **Lindisfarne (793) and religious houses along the coasts of **Kent. It was not until 851 that an English fleet is recorded as engaging the Vikings at sea. In that year, according to the *Anglo-Saxon Chronicle*, King Æthelstan of Kent, son of King **Æthelwulf of Wessex, and Ealdorman Ealhhere 'fought in ships and slew a great army at Sandwich in Kent, and captured nine ships and put the others to flight'. King Æthelwulf's youngest son King **Alfred (d. 899) fought small-scale naval engagements against the Danes in 875 and 882. In 885 Alfred dispatched a naval force from Kent to raid **East Anglia. After seizing sixteen Danish ships at the mouth of the river Stour, the English fleet was intercepted on its return and routed by a much larger Viking naval force. Most famously, Alfred was responsible for reforming the design of royal warships. In 896, in response to Viking raids along the southern coast of **Wessex, Alfred ordered a fleet to be built. The ships were to be constructed 'neither on the Frisian nor the Danish pattern, but as it seemed to King Alfred himself that they could be most useful' (*ASC*, s.a. 896). Alfred, apparently, employed professional sailors, among them a number of Frisians, to man these vessels. Despite the chronicler's boast that Alfred's new model ships not only were almost twice as long as the Viking ships they opposed but were also swifter, steadier, and rode higher, the new fleet met with only mixed success in its only recorded engagement, a skirmish in an estuary against a Danish raiding party consisting of six ships. Nevertheless, Alfred's interest in naval matters led to the popular, though mistaken, idea that he was the founder of the Royal Navy. It was for 'Alfred: A Masque' (1740) that James Thompson wrote 'Rule Britannia'.

Alfred's successors in the tenth century expanded English sea-power. In 910 King **Edward the Elder (d. 924) raised a fleet of 100 ships against the Vikings, and the number of warships at his disposal undoubtedly increased with the submission of the Vikings of the eastern **Danelaw. His son and successor King Æthelstan (d. 939) supported Louis d'Outremer's claims to Lotharingia with naval forces, and in 934 dispatched a joint naval and military expedition against Scotland, during which the English fleet ravaged the Scottish coast to Caithness. **John of Worcester's report that King **Edgar (d. 975) possessed a fleet of 3,600 ships deployed in three squadrons of 1,200 is clearly an exaggeration. Nonetheless, there can be little doubt that English naval power lay behind the chronicler's boast that there was no 'fleet so proud nor host so strong that it got itself prey in England' during Edgar's reign. Edgar's hegemony over a maritime empire was symbolized by the manner in which eight British sub-kings demonstrated their submission to the English king at Chester in 973: they rowed him on the Dee, as Edgar himself piloted the vessel. It was perhaps during Edgar's reign that 'ship sokes' were established to provide the king with the warships that he needed.

In the last two decades of the tenth and the first sixteen years of the eleventh century, English naval resources proved inadequate to defend the kingdom against renewed Viking activity, despite considerable efforts on the part of King *Æthelred 'the Unready' (d. 1016) and his councillors. English fleets were raised in 992 and 999, but met with no success. Raiding expeditions were sent against the Isle of Man and the Norman Cotentin around the year 1000 in an attempt to deprive the Vikings of naval bases. To increase his naval forces, Æthelred in 1008 ordered that one warship and a crew be raised from every 300 (or 310) hides throughout the kingdom. The great armada assembled at Sandwich in 1009 accomplished nothing. Soon after, the king and his advisors turned for protection to the very Danes who had been ravaging their kingdom. In 1012 the Danish mercenary leader Thorkell the Tall, who had been raiding in England since 1009, took service with Æthelred along with the crews of forty-five ships. *Cnut retained a standing fleet of forty ships after his victory in 1016, and levied a tax, the *heregeld, to pay the professional warriors, lithsmen, who manned these vessels. The size of this stipendiary fleet fluctuated greatly over the reigns of Cnut and his sons, falling to sixteen ships in the last year of Cnut's reign and rising to sixty ships under *Harthacnut in 1040. Between 1049 and 1050 *Edward the Confessor (d. 1066) disbanded the fleet, then consisting of fourteen ships, and abolished the heregeld. Thereafter he and his successor *Harold (d. 1066) relied upon ship levies supplemented by the naval services of what were to be known as the Cinque Ports (Hastings, Romney, Hythe, Dover and Sandwich). During Edward's and Harold's reigns, English naval forces were used mainly for coastal defence in squadrons stationed off Sandwich and the Isle of Wight, though Edward did support the German emperor Henry III with a naval blockade of the ports of *Flanders. King Harold spent much of his brief reign preparing for invasions. Fearing an attack from Duke William of *Normandy, Harold assembled 'a naval and land force larger than any king had assembled before in this country' (*ASC* s.a. 1066 CD) at Sandwich in the early summer of 1066 and maintained it on the Isle of Wight throughout the summer and autumn. Scouting ships kept tabs on William's fleet, reputedly unable to sail because of adverse winds. The 'E' version of the *Anglo-Saxon Chronicle* alludes to a naval skirmish fought in the Channel, but details are lacking. Finally on 8 September provisions ran out and the fleet disbanded. This, coupled with the invasion of Harold Hardrada in the North, permitted William the Conqueror, duke of Normandy, to land his fleet unopposed at Pevensey on 28 September.

N. Hooper, 'Some Observations on the Navy in Late Anglo-Saxon England', in *Studies in Medieval History Presented to R. A. Brown*, ed. C. Harper-Bill, C. J. Holdsworth and J. L. Nelson (Woodbridge, 1989), pp. 203–13; M. Strickland, 'Military Technology and Conquest: The Anomaly of Anglo-Saxon England', *ANS* 19 (1997), 353–82, esp. 373–80; C. W. Hollister, *Anglo-Saxon Military Institutions on the Eve of the Norman Conquest* (Oxford, 1962), pp. 103–26; J. Haywood, *Dark Age Naval Power: A Reassessment of Frankish and Anglo-Saxon Seafaring Activity* (London and New York, 1991).

R. ABELS

NENNIUS: *see Historia Brittonum*

NEOT, ST (d. *c.*877), supposedly of royal descent (either East Anglian or West Saxon), joined the community of *Glastonbury in his youth, but went to become a hermit near Bodmin Moor, and founded there a small monastery; the place came to be called Neotstoke. Supposedly King *Alfred went to visit Neot to seek his advice; the other anecdote recorded about Neot was that he was so short that he was obliged to stand on a stool to say the Mass. He was buried in the church at Neotstoke. Over a hundred years later, the community at Eynesbury, founded in the 970s, now known as St Neots (Hunts.), acquired the relics of the Cornish saint by devious means, possibly pure theft. The acquisition, together with accompanying miracles, is recorded in the anonymous eleventh-century *Vita prima S. Neoti* (*BHL* 6054–5). The relics were inspected in the late eleventh century, and certified to be authentic by Anselm, archbishop of Canterbury. One arm remained at St Neot's in Cornwall. Feast: 31 July.

D. N. Dumville and M. Lapidge, ed., *The Annals of St Neots with Vita Prima Sancti Neoti* (Woodbridge, 1985).

R. C. LOVE

NOBILITY: *see* Social Status

NORMANDY, province of France. As a principality Normandy was founded between 905 and 918, probably in 911, when King Charles the Simple (879–922) granted Rouen and its surroundings to the 'Norsemen of the Seine, Rollo and his companions, for the defence of the realm', that is to say, to defend it against attacks from other groups of *Vikings. Rollo's dynasty ruled

Normandy, which took its name from its new settlers, in direct line till 1204 when King Philip Augustus annexed the duchy to the royal French domaine and abolished the office of duke. Within three generations of its foundation Normandy more or less covered the area it covers today: from Eu on the north coast to Mont Saint-Michel in the south, and from the Atlantic coast in the west to the rivers Epte and Avre on the eastern border with the Ile-de-France. This area also coincides with the ecclesiastical province of Rouen, which itself constituted the western tip of the Romano-Carolingian province of Neustria.

Rollo (d. *c.*928), his son William Longsword (*c.*928–43) and his grandson Richard I (943–96) ruled Normandy as a county, while Richard II (996–1026) styled himself as duke. It was during the latter's reign that the first dynastic history of a French principality was written, by Dudo of Saint-Quentin, claiming that Normandy had been given to Rollo as an allodial possession and not as a fief of the French crown. Until the demise of the duchy in the early thirteenth century the relationship between the Norman dukes and the kings of France was tense and fraught with difficulties, centring on conflicting interpretations of their feudal ties, especially when after 1066 the Norman duke as king of England was of equal rank as the French king but as a duke was the king's subject.

Normandy's fame, however, derived from its relations with its western neighbour, the kingdom of the English. Both countries had strong economic, cultural and political ties. In 991 a treaty between Richard I and King *Æthelred of England was concluded with the aim, presumably, to end Norman support for the Scandinavian raiders of the English harbours. Ten years later the political friendship was sealed when Æthelred married the duke's daughter *Emma. Ultimately, in 1066, it was this particular bond of kinship which formed the basis for the claim to the English throne by Duke William the Conqueror (1035–87). As Emma's great-nephew he considered himself the closest relative of Emma's son King *Edward the Confessor, who died without offspring. There were other reasons as well. After her husband's death Emma remarried, produced a male heir for her second spouse, King *Cnut (1016–35), and denounced the children of her first marriage, Edward, Alfred and Godgifu, who were left on the Continent under the care of her brother Duke Richard II. When in 1042 Edward finally recovered the English throne he remained grateful to his Norman cousins, and according to the Norman chroniclers, promised his throne to Duke William in the event of his childless death. Such a promise might well have been made *c.*1051, by which time Duke William's son, Robert Curthose (duke 1087–1106, d. 1134) by his Flemish wife Matilda, had been born, representing the best hope for the continuation of both families' line. However, in 1066 Edward's brother-in-law *Harold Godwineson became king and was immediately challenged by Duke William, who accused him of perjury of the faith sworn to him on a visit to Normandy a few years earlier. The result was the Norman invasion of England, Harold's death on the battlefield, and the subsequent subjection of the English to Norman rule.

Whereas contacts between Normandy and England had been steady before 1066, after that year they obviously increased. Scholarly debate continues as to the effects of the Conquest on both countries. For England possible consensus could be reached by arguing that short term political upheaval did not seriously disrupt the development of Anglo-Saxon customs and practices in the long term. As far as English influence in Normandy is concerned there is no doubt that the financial boost to the treasury of the dukes (deriving from English taxation) helped to finance the many wars fought on the Continent and in particular with Normandy's neighbours in Maine, Brittany, the French royal domaine and *Flanders. Such warfare continued even during the reign of Henry II (1154–89), who added to his father's inheritance of Anjou his wife's inheritance of Aquitaine. The accumulation of continental possessions by the king-dukes ultimately dwarfed Normandy's role and led to its acquisition by the French king in 1204.

C. H. Haskins, *Norman Institutions* (New York, 1918); R. H. C. Davis, *The Normans and their Myth* (London, 1976); D. Bates, *Normandy before 1066* (London, 1982); E. Searle, *Predatory Kinship and the Creation of Norman Power 840–1066* (Berkeley, CA, 1988); *The Gesta Normannorum Ducum of William of Jumièges, Orderic Vitalis and Robert of Torigni*, ed. E. M. C. van Houts, 2 vols. (OMT, 1992–5); D. Bates, 'The Rise and Fall of Normandy *c.*911–1204', *England and Normandy in the Middle Ages*, ed. D. Bates and A. Curry (London, 1994), pp. 19–34; idem, 'Normandy and England after 1066', *EHR* 104 (1989), 853–61; S. Keynes, 'The Æthelings in Normandy', *ANS* 13 (1991), 173–206.

ELISABETH VAN HOUTS

NORTHAMPTON is first mentioned in 913, when a *Viking army was based there, but excavations reveal it as a centre of major importance under the Mercian kings. Its nucleus, a promontory in a bend of the river Nene, contains a scatter of seventh- to ninth-century *settlement remains around the paired churches of St Peter and St Gregory. Between these churches was a large eighth-century timber hall, replaced in the ninth century by a massive stone hall of a form and scale unparalleled in England (fig. 13). This hall, like nearby *Brixworth, reflects Carolingian influence and patronage at the highest level, but its function is controversial. Originally published as a royal palace, it is perhaps better seen as the central building of a great monastic site. St Peter's is recorded as an old minster in the eleventh century, when a saint named Rægner was enshrined there, and the growth of the town around a monastic core during the post-Viking period would follow the normal pattern (see *monastic sites and *towns). A scatter of tenth- and eleventh-century sunken-floored buildings over and around the site of the halls illustrate unusually clearly this earliest stage of urbanisation.

J. H. Williams, M. Shaw and V. Denham, *Middle Saxon Palaces at Northampton* (Northampton, 1988); J. H. Williams, 'From "Palace" to "Town": Northampton and Urban Origins', *ASE* 13 (1984), 113–36; J. Blair, 'Palaces or Minsters? Northampton and Cheddar Reconsidered', *ASE* 25 (1996), 97–121.

JOHN BLAIR

NORTHERN ANNALS. Bede's *Historia ecclesiastica*, especially v.24, which summarises the period from 60 BC to 731 in annalistic form, seems to have inaugurated a process of keeping *annals of Northumbrian history, for it is clear that such annals were preserved from 732 until perhaps 806. These annals have not survived in their original form, but their content can be partially surmised from their preservation to a greater or lesser extent, first in the Moore manuscript of *Bede's Historia ecclesiastica* (which has annals for 731–4), and then in the following later works: the Continuations to Bede's *Historia ecclesiastica* found in twelfth-century and later manuscripts and comprising annals from 732 to 766; the northern recension of the *Anglo-Saxon Chronicle; *Symeon of Durham's *Libellus de exordio atque procursu istius hoc est Dunhelmensis ecclesie* (also known as the 'History of the Church of Durham'); the *Historia regum* ('History of the Kings') which was associated in the twelfth century with the same writer and may well have been compiled by him; the *Chronicle of Melrose*; and the work of Roger of Hoveden in the late twelfth century. This last writer incorporated wholesale into his own history a work called the *Historia Saxonum uel Anglorum post Bede obitum* ('History of the Saxons and Angles after the Death of Bede') which seems to have been compiled in Durham largely on the basis of an early version of the *Historia regum*, perhaps in the 1120s.

Comparison between the sources listed above makes it possible to reconstruct with some confidence part at least of the content of the annals from 732 to 806, known here as the Northern Annals. That they are based on authentic information is shown partly by the details which they contain (for example, the names of otherwise unknown Northumbrian princes and aristocrats), which are unlikely to be the work of a later compiler, partly by the accuracy of their recording of astronomical information which can be shown by modern computation to be correct and can only have been known by a contemporary. A good example is the account given under the year 756 of how a 'bright star', now known to be the planet Jupiter, passed behind the eclipsed moon. The exact place of composition of these annals has been debated, but the level of detail relating to *York and the indications in their Latin style that their composition may have been influenced by *Alcuin point to their having been written at York. Some scholars refer to them as the 'York Annals'. It is possible to discern several phases in their composition: a phase in the early to mid-eighth century on which the Continuations to Bede's *Historia ecclesiastica* drew; a phase in the mid-eighth-century, material from which entered the northern recension of the *Anglo-Saxon Chronicle; and a late eighth-century phase, characterised by continental information, perhaps connected with Alcuin, which was ultimately absorbed into the *Historia regum* and the *Historia Saxonum uel Anglorum post Bede obitum*. It is possible that the tradition of keeping annals was continued in *Northumbria after 806, but if so all that has been preserved are some annals of dubious accuracy in Roger of Wendover's *Flores historiarum* ('Flowers of History'), and a set of annals from 888 to 957 relating principally to the *Viking kingdom of York, preserved in the *Historia regum*.

Chronica Rogeri de Houedene, ed. W. Stubbs, 4 vols., RS (London, 1868–71), i, pp. xxviii–xxix; *Two of the Saxon Chronicles Parallel with Supplementary Extracts from the Others*, ed. C. Plummer, 2 vols. (Oxford, 1892–9), ii, pp. lxviii–lxx; P. Hunter Blair, 'Some Observations on the *Historia Regum* Attributed to Symeon of Durham', in *Celt and Saxon: Studies in the Early British Border*, ed. N. K. Chadwick (Cambridge, 1963), pp. 63–118, at 98–9; A. Gransden, *Historical Writing in England c.550 to c.1307* (London, 1974), pp. 31–2; J. E. Story, 'Charlemagne and Northumbria: The Influence of Francia on

Northumbrian Politics in the Later Eighth and Early Ninth Centuries' (unpubl. Ph.D. dissertation, Univ. of Durham, 1995); D. N. Dumville, 'Textual Archaeology and Northumbrian History Subsequent to Bede', in *Coinage in Ninth-Century Northumbria: The Tenth Oxford Symposium on Coinage and Monetary History*, ed. D. M. Metcalf, BAR Brit. ser. 180 (Oxford, 1987), 43–55, repr. D. N. Dumville, *Britons and Anglo-Saxons in the Early Middle Ages* (Aldershot, 1993), no. X.

DAVID ROLLASON

NORTHUMBRIA, an Anglo-Saxon kingdom formed by the amalgamation of *Bernicia and *Deira and enlarged through the conquest of British kingdoms to the west and north. The term Northumbria was popularised by *Bede in the *Historia ecclesiastica* to promote a view of the Bernicians and Deirans as a single people (*Nordanhymbrorum gens*), and the debate continues as to whether or not it was coined by him. If Bede's account of the Council of Hertford is faithful to his source, the term was current in 673, for *Wilfrid is described in the proceedings as *Nordanhymbrorum gentis episcopus*. However, in Bede's report of the Council of Hatfield held in 679 King Ecgfrith (670–85) is called *rex Humbronensium*, and in *Stephen's *Vita S. Wilfridi*, completed shortly before the *Historia ecclesiastica*, a variety of terms is used, most frequently *Ultrahumbrensis*. Unification of the English kingdoms of Bernicia and Deira was first forged in the seventh century during the reign of King Æthelfrith of Bernicia (*c.*592–616). His successor in both kingdoms was *Edwin of Deira (616–33), but for a time after his death, and after that of *Oswald (634–42), Bernicia and Deira were ruled separately. The last independent king of Deira was Oswine until his murder in 651 by *Oswiu of Bernicia (642–70). Thereafter Deira was governed by Bernician kings of Northumbria until the *Viking seizure of *York in the ninth century.

Northumbria reached its greatest territorial extent and the height of its political and military powers during the seventh century. Once conquered, the British kingdoms of the Pennines and further west (among them Elmet, Craven and Dent) remained part of Northumbria; however, overlordship of the Picts, Scots, Strathclyde Britons, and other Anglo-Saxon kingdoms was personal and each king had to establish his own authority beyond the borders of Northumbria. Edwin's power reached the isles of Anglesey and Man, but unlike Oswald he had no influence in *Kent; Ecgfrith was able to establish a Northumbrian bishopric for a brief period at Abercorn on the Forth; and Edwin, Oswald, Oswiu and Ecgfrith

had each to establish their own control of *Lindsey. A persistent challenge to Northumbrian overlordship came from *Mercia whose kings killed in battle seven members of the Bernician and Deiran dynasties between 616 and 679. But the end of Northumbrian supremacy came not in the familiar battleground of its southern border but at Dunnichen Moss near Forfar in Angus, where King Ecgfrith was killed and his army routed by Picts in 685 at the battle of *Nechtansmere*. The result was the end of Northumbrian hegemony in the north and political involvement south of the Humber. The kingdom ruled by Ecgfrith's successor, King *Aldfrith (686–705), was smaller than that of his seventh-century predecessors. It was still, however, of considerable extent, for *Whithorn in Galloway was a Northumbrian see in 731.

The political history of Northumbria during the eighth century is dominated by the feuding of rival families, not all of royal descent, who claimed kingship. Of fourteen kings who reigned between 705 and 806, four were murdered, six were deposed, tonsured or exiled, and two chose to abdicate and enter religious life. Only King Eadberht (737–58) attempted to restore Northumbria's power and influence. His campaign against the Picts in 740 came to a premature end when *Æthelbald of Mercia invaded Northumbria, but he detached the plain of Kyle from the kingdom of Strathclyde in 750 and in 756 successfully attacked Dumbarton (this time in alliance with the Picts) although the British reversed the victory only nine days later. Sources for the history of Northumbria in the ninth century are few. The *Royal Frankish Annals* record that after King Eardwulf was deposed in ?806 he was restored through the intervention of Charlemagne, but there is no confirmation of this from English sources. The *Anglo-Saxon Chronicle* claims that in 829 the Northumbrians submitted to the West Saxon king, *Ecgberht, at Dore in Derbyshire on the southern border of Northumbria. This statement suggests the meeting may have amounted to no more than a show of strength by Ecgberht, but in Roger of Wendover's *Flores historiarum*, written in the thirteenth century and drawing on earlier (lost) *northern annals, Ecgberht is said to have pillaged and laid waste Northumbria and to have made King Eanred (?810–40/1) pay tribute. *Viking raids began with the sack of *Lindisfarne in 793, and attacks on other monastic houses followed. King Rædwulf and many of his followers were killed in battle against Vikings in 844, and in 867, after defeating King Osberht, the 'Great Heathen

Army' took York and brought to an end the Anglo-Saxon kingdom of Northumbria. The province of Deira remained under Scandinavian control as the Viking kingdom of York until 954 when King *Eadred expelled the Viking king *Eric Bloodaxe, while Bernicia continued to be ruled by native kings until 927 when it submitted to the West Saxon king, *Æthelstan. The name of Northumbria was preserved as the territory governed by *ealdormen under kings of a unified England.

J. M. Wallace-Hadrill, *Bede's 'Ecclesiastical History of the English People': a Historical Commentary* (OMT, 1988), pp. 226–8: T. Charles-Edwards, 'Bede, the Irish and the Britons', *Celtica* 15 (1983), 42–52, at 49; P. H. Blair, *Anglo-Saxon Northumbria* (London, 1984); Kirby, *Kings*, pp. 77–112; Yorke, *Kingdoms*, pp. 86–95; N. J. Higham, *The Kingdom of Northumbria AD 350–1000* (Stroud, 1993).

PHILIP HOLDSWORTH

NORWICH began during the eighth century as a trading settlement with scattered nuclei, one of them the original 'north *wic*', on the river Wensum. An Anglo-Scandinavian borough probably developed from the 880s, and by *c.*900 the area north of the river was defended by a ditch. Soon afterwards the community expanded southwards, to the zone which was to be the core of the later town. This south-bank settlement grew spectacularly during the late tenth and early eleventh centuries, and cellared buildings have been excavated; there was a *mint from *Æthelstan's reign. By 1086 Norwich was one of the biggest English *towns, with a population probably well over 5,000. The multiplication of tiny urban churches – some fifty by 1086 – reflects, as in other eastern towns, intensified activity during these years. Norwich was also a major port, with wide trading contacts both inland and overseas.

J. Campbell, 'Norwich', *Historic Towns Atlas: II*, ed. M. D. Lobel (London, 1975); A. Carter, 'The Anglo-Saxon Origins of Norwich', *ASE* 7 (1978), 175–204; Hart, *Danelaw*, pp. 54–7; B. Ayers, *The English Heritage Book of Norwich* (London, 1994).

JOHN BLAIR

NOTHHELM, archbishop of *Canterbury (735–9). Nothhelm is renowned chiefly as the 'godly priest of the church of *London' through whom information about the Gregorian mission in Kent was transmitted by *Albinus, abbot of the monastery of St Peter and St Paul, Canterbury, to *Bede, 'either in writing or by word of mouth' (Bede, *HE*, Preface); in which case he must have played a part in expounding to Bede the inwardness of Canterbury's vision of Pope *Gregory's

conception of the *gens Anglorum*. Bede remarks that Nothhelm afterwards 'went to Rome and got permission from the present Pope Gregory [Gregory II (715–31)] to search through the archives of the holy Roman church and there found some letters of St Gregory and of other popes'; and on Albinus's advice Nothhelm 'brought them to us on his return' (*HE*, Preface). The process may be reflected in the construction of Bede's account of the Gregorian mission, in which a distinction is maintained between the Canterbury traditions (*HE* ii.25–6, 33) and the documentary record (*HE* ii.23–4, 28–32). Nothhelm had occasion on his own part to ask Bede to comment upon various points of difficulty which he had encountered in the Book of Kings. Bede put together his responses to what struck him as the thirty more weighty questions (*In Regum librum XXX Quaestiones*), and made a separate collection of notes on the less important matters (perhaps the treatise entitled *Nomina locorum*), remarking in his covering letter that there were many more obscure matters in the Book of Kings about which Nothhelm had not asked. Bede's treatise *De VIII Quaestionibus*, transmitted in association with *XXX Quaestiones*, may also have been produced for Nothhelm's benefit. Nothhelm thus emerges as a prominent member of the ecclesiastical establishment in London, with good connections in *Kent and *Northumbria; and it was perhaps through the influence of *Æthelbald, king of the Mercians, that he gained his appointment as archbishop of Canterbury, in succession to *Tatwine (731–4). He was consecrated archbishop in 735. In a letter written to Nothhelm in 736 (*EHD* i, no. 171), Boniface asked the archbishop to send him a copy of Gregory's *Libellus responsionum*, and also asked to be told 'in what year from the incarnation of Christ the first preachers, sent by St Gregory, came to the nation of the English'; from which we may infer that Boniface had not yet seen Bede's *Historia ecclesiastica*. A document preserved at *Worcester shows Nothhelm acting with his episcopal colleagues in a church *council (S 1429: *EHD* i, no. 68). He died in 739.

Brooks, *Canterbury*, pp. 80, 99; M. L. W. Laistner and H. H. King, *A Hand-List of Bede Manuscripts* (Ithaca, NY, 1943), pp. 155–7 [*De VIII Quaestionibus*]; *Bedae Venerabilis Opera*, II: *Opera Exegetica* 2, ed. D. Hurst, CCSL cxix. 273–87 [*Nomina locorum*] and 293–322 [Bede, *In Regum librum XXX Quaestiones*], at 293 [Bede's letter to Nothhelm]; J. McClure, 'Bede's Old Testament Kings', *Ideal and Reality in Frankish and Anglo-Saxon*

Society, ed. P. Wormald (Oxford, 1983), pp. 76–98, at 80–1, 85, 86, 92–3.

SIMON KEYNES

NOWELL, LAURENCE (*c.*1510/20–*c.*1571), was a major figure in the revival of Anglo-Saxon studies in the second half of the sixteenth century. Until recently he was mistakenly identified as the Dean of Lichfield, who was actually his cousin. Although he has long been recognized as 'the father' of Old English studies, none of his own work appeared in print during his lifetime, nor indeed till the mid-twentieth century. He compiled an Old English dictionary, the *Vocabularium Saxonicum*, entered a glossary in the margins of a copy of Richard Huloet's *Abecedarium Anglico-Latinum*, and fabricated a portion of Old English text of the Anglo-Saxon *laws in Lambarde's *Archaionomia* (1568). Both the *Exeter Book and the *Beowulf* manuscript passed through his hands. London, BL, Add. 43703 contains his transcript of *The *Battle of Brunanburh*. He also made a transcript of a lost manuscript of Ælfric's *Grammar* and *Glossary* and of the now largely destroyed BL, Cotton Otho B.xi.

C. T. Berkhout, 'The Pedigree of Laurence Nowell the Antiquary', *ELN* 23 (1985), 15–26; R. E. Buckalew, 'Nowell, Lambarde, and Leland: the Significance of Laurence Nowell's Transcript of Ælfric's *Grammar* and *Glossary*', in *Anglo-Saxon Scholarship: the First Three Centuries*, ed. C. T. Berkhout and M. McC. Gatch (Boston, 1982), pp. 19–50; R. Flower, 'Laurence Nowell and the Discovery of England in Tudor Times', *PBA* 21 (1935), 47–73; R. J. S. Grant, 'Laurence Nowell's Transcript of BM Cotton Otho B.xi', *ASE* 3 (1974), 111–24; idem, *Laurence Nowell, William Lambarde and the Laws of the Anglo-Saxons* (Amsterdam, 1996); A. Lutz, 'Das Studium der Angelsächsischen Chronik im 16. Jahrhundert: Nowell und Joscelyn', *Anglia* 100 (1982), 301–56; *Laurence Nowell's 'Vocabularium Saxonicum'*, ed. A. H. Marckwardt (Ann Arbor, MI, 1952); J. L. Rosier, 'A New Old English Glossary: Nowell upon Huloet', *Studia Neophilologica* 49 (1977), 89–94; K. Sisam, 'The Authenticity of Certain Texts in Lambard's *Archaionomia* 1568', *Studies in the History of Old English Literature* (Oxford, 1953), pp. 232–58; R. M. Warnicke, 'Note on a Court of Requests Case of 1571', *ELN* 11 (1974), 250–6.

JAMES P. CARLEY

NUNNERIES were congregations of religious women, described simply as *monasteria* with or without such qualification as *sanctimonialium*; there is no gender-specific noun for female monastic houses in either Latin or Old English (cf. *monasticism; *monastic sites). Female enthusiasm for conventual forms of religious life is apparent in England from at least the middle years of the seventh century, the first female religious houses being founded in *Kent from the 630s with the active support and participation of members of the Kentish royal house. Before that time, according to *Bede, aspiring English nuns had to travel to Francia (*HE* iii.8).

When the first English nunneries were established they quickly attracted members, and the generosity of lay, especially royal, patrons. The later seventh century was the most active period for new foundations; at various times before the end of the ninth century as many as sixty female congregations may have been created throughout Anglo-Saxon England, although several were perhaps relatively short-lived institutions, housing religious women for only one or two generations. The majority of the first Anglo-Saxon nunneries were royal foundations, governed by royal abbesses; indeed many of these houses (such as *Whitby, *Repton, and *Minster-in-Thanet) served important memorial functions in maintaining the cults of the families of their first members, and played a significant political role.

In the absence of surviving monastic customaries or rules from pre-Viking Age England, little is known about the internal organisation of early Anglo-Saxon nunneries other than that a substantial proportion (although possibly not all) housed men and women, living together with varying degrees of internal segregation under the overall authority of an abbess. Among the most celebrated of these early double houses are *Barking, *Coldingham, *Ely, Repton, Minster-in-Thanet, Wenlock, *Wimborne and Whitby, all of which were royal foundations. The Anglo-Saxon double house has parallels only in contemporary Francia. The institution differs both from Eastern and later medieval mixed congregations (such as the Gilbertines) governed by men; these were not groups of women seeking to live under the shelter of male communities, nor were the men brought into the nunnery for economic or liturgical purposes. The origin of the Anglo-Saxon double house (and probably also of its demise beyond the ninth century) should be attributed to the particular status of women within early Germanic society, a status denied them once the ecclesiastical doctrine that women should be under the spiritual direction of men predominated. The last certainly identifiable double house is the minster of Abbess Æthelthryth, still functioning in 796 (Alcuin, *Ep.* cvi); there are examples of male and female religious apparently living together in the late ninth century (at *Cheddar, Wenlock and

*Winchcombe) and of communities which had housed women being later governed by men (for example Berkeley or the three houses of Stonegrave, Coxwold and *Donæmuthe*), but these were not true double houses.

Nunneries ostensibly played a part in the so-called golden age of the tenth-century English church. The rhetoric surrounding the revolution in monastic organisation in mid-tenth-century England clearly included female alongside male congregations of religious; according to the *Regularis Concordia* agreed at the Council of *Winchester in the 970s, nunneries were to be reordered according to the precepts of the *Benedictine Rule, and placed under the protection of the queen. Prominent among these nunneries were the royally-founded and patronised houses at *Shaftesbury, Wilton and the Nunnaminster at Winchester, and another half-dozen or so houses almost all of which lay in *Wessex (the exceptions are *Barking in *Essex, and Chatteris in Cambridgeshire). Yet these nunneries are less well attested in the contemporary sources than many male houses lacking royal associations, and an account of the reform survives only for the Nunnaminster at Winchester (*Wulfstan of Winchester, *Vita S. Æthelwoldi*, c. 22). Beyond this group approximately forty further places in southern and midland England are known to have housed religious women in the tenth or eleventh centuries, but histories for these establishments can frequently be constructed only with recourse to later medieval evidence, and sometimes only from antiquarian accounts.

The clear diminution in the quality and quantity of the sources relating to nuns before and after the First *Viking Age requires explanation. It is possible that the nunnery (the enclosed congregation of professed religious women only) was in fact a relatively rare occurrence throughout the Anglo-Saxon period. Before the mid-ninth century at least half of the known houses for women were double. When that institution ceased to be acceptable among the English, the opportunities for women to express a monastic vocation were more restricted. Outside the royal nunneries of tenth- and eleventh-century Wessex, devout women chose other forms of religious life, living as *widows under vows on their own estates, or under the protection of male monastic or cathedral communities. It is probably for this reason that so many later Anglo-Saxon women's religious houses appear to have been ephemeral, with no permanent landed endowment, sustaining a congregation for only one or two generations. Royal patronage was essential to the success of female religion throughout the pre-Conquest period; in the seventh and eighth centuries royal interest was predominantly in the double house; during and after the monastic revolution of the tenth century it lay exclusively in the female nunnery, and was directed to the geographically restricted group of houses closely associated with the West Saxon royal house and the maintenance of its cult.

M. A. Meyer, 'Patronage of West Saxon Royal Nunneries in late Anglo-Saxon England', *RB* 91 (1981), 332–58; D. B. Schneider, 'Anglo-Saxon Women in the Religious Life: a Study of the Status and Position of Women in an Early Mediaeval Society' (unpublished PhD thesis, Univ. of Cambridge, 1985); B. Yorke, ' "Sisters under the skin?" Anglo-Saxon Nuns and Nunneries in Southern England', in *Medieval Women in Southern England*, Reading Medieval Studies 15 (1989), 95–117

SARAH FOOT

O

OATHS, sworn statements of what the oath-taker is or believes, will do or not do, have been central to the social cohesion of many pre-modern societies. They were undeniably important for the Anglo-Saxons, but in ways and for purposes that changed as the period advanced. In the early period, there is no good evidence that oaths were sworn either to lords generally or to kings specifically: the warrior's loyalty to his lord arose from the latter's generosity, not from any ceremonial pledge. (It should, nevertheless, be noted that *Æthelberht legislates about men whom he calls his *leode*, and the cognate Frankish *leudes* certainly took an oath.) Oaths in the early sources are usually found in the context of 'oath-helping', oaths sworn by an appropriate number of people to the good character of a party in dispute, and hence the probable justice of his case: an elaborate and far from wholly clear mechanism in the *laws of *Ine reckons oath-helping in numbers of *hides. Traditional medieval legal history distinguishes sharply between this sort of support and the actual evidence of witnesses as to particular facts at stake. All the same, reflection suggests that there may not have been a lot of difference in practice between backing a litigant's general record and his specific claim; nor, in some cases on record, is it at all obvious whether oath-helping or witnessing is what was involved. We can say only that the process of 'compurgation' was going out of use by the later twelfth century, whereas witnessing is of course integral to modern law – or almost any other legal system.

In the first clause of the laws of King *Alfred, we meet something that is to all appearances new: 'we teach, as is most necessary, that each man keep his oath and pledge'. As it stands, this need not mean anything special. But a charter of Alfred's son and successor, *Edward the Elder, mentions an oath of loyalty taken to Alfred, and speaks in his laws of an 'oath and pledge that the whole people has given', in a context suggesting its relevance to harbouring criminals in general; and his grandson *Æthelstan explained, in launching his brutal campaign against thieves, that 'oaths, pledges and sureties are all disregarded and broken'. In providing the formula for swearing loyalty, *Edmund at once went on to stigmatize thieves. By the next century, *Cnut was quite explicit, first that an oath was to be taken by all aged twelve or over; and secondly that it was an oath to avoid theft. It is noteworthy in this context that Æthelstan at first ordered the summary execution of thieves caught in the act *if aged twelve*. Three things in fact suggest that an oath of loyalty was introduced by Alfred and from the first covered a much wider range of *crime than disloyalty. First, this was the exact pattern of the oath that the Carolingians enforced: the model was therefore no less available to him than to his successors. Second, from Alfred's time *but not before*, there are regular references in *charters to property forfeit for crime and often for theft. Forfeiture for theft suggests that this too was now seen as the sort of disloyalty for which loss of property was the logical penalty. Third, theft and treason actually are equated by laws of both *Edgar and Cnut. All this has major implications for the history of English law. For one thing, it was always axiomatic that loyalty to the king overrode that owed to any more immediate lord. This seems to be the point of the oath levied by William the Conqueror in 1086 at Salisbury. Since this looks so like the Carolingian oath, of which there is yet no trace in tenth- or eleventh-century *Normandy, it is more likely to be an Anglo-Saxon legacy than a Norman import. Another point is that English law was from at least Henry II's time marked by the nasty principle of felony: any serious crime was punished as if it were treasonable. There seems no reason why 'mere' crime should be regarded as treason unless loyalty were already stretched to cover it; which is what the pre-Conquest oath appears to do. The significance of the Anglo-Saxon loyalty oath is thus that, from the genesis of the English kingdom as an organized state, the government was in the front rank of the battle to control social deviance and disorder (cf. *frankpledge).

Liebermann, *Gesetze* i.46–9 (Alfred 1–1:8), 142–5 (II Edward 5–5:2) 150–1 (II Æthelstan 1–1:5), 166–7 (V Æthelstan Pr. – Pr.:3), 190 (III Edmund 1), 324–5 (II Cnut 21), ii.374–5 ('Eid'), 377–81 ('Eideshelfer', 'Eideshufen'); W. Kienast, *Untertaneneid und Treuvor-*

behalt (Weimar, 1952), pp. 172–89; J. Campbell, 'Observations on English Government from the Tenth to the Twelfth Century', *TRHS* 5th ser. 25 (1975), 39–54, at 46–7.

PATRICK WORMALD

OBLATURE: *see* Monasticism

OCTOSYLLABLES, LATIN. Two distinct kinds of Latin octosyllables, an eight-syllable rhythmical verse-form, are known from Anglo-Saxon England, apparently stemming from two quite separate traditions. The first, closely associated with *Theodore of Canterbury, requires an absolutely regular rhythm of alternately long and short syllables, with pairs of verses linked by end-rhyme, and can be traced back to an accentual form of Greek anacreontics that was certainly used in seventh-century *Byzantium; only four poems employing this rhythm survive (of which one, a greeting to Bishop *Hæddi of *Winchester, was certainly composed by Theodore, and the other three, all hymns or prayers to Christ, were plausibly composed by Theodore himself, or at least under his supervision). The second kind of Latin octosyllables are equally closely associated with *Aldhelm, who had been a student of Theodore at *Canterbury, but these have a much less insistent rhythm. In this case, the only regular rhythm within each octosyllabic verse is supplied by a single stress on the antepenultimate syllable; once again, pairs of verses are linked by end-rhyme; it has been argued that this model derives from earlier octosyllabic forms in Latin *metre, such as the so-called iambic dimeter, which proved popular in *hymns and was used in both metrical and rhythmical forms by, for example, Ambrose and Caelius Sedulius. But the best model for this 'Aldhelmian' form of the Anglo-Latin octosyllable is found in certain seventh-century Hiberno-Latin hymns, notably the so-called 'Altus prosator', which Aldhelm seems to have known, perhaps while a student at *Malmesbury. Aldhelm's main octosyllabic composition is a poem of 200 verses describing a trip back from *Cornwall to Devon, in the course of which he experienced a mighty storm. Aldhelm went much further than earlier poets in his use of aural effects such as *alliteration and assonance in octosyllabic verse, particularly in the highly effective storm-sequence, but it was left to his student, *Æthilwald, radically to change the octosyllabic verse form by increasing dramatically the amount of alliteration, much of it clearly modelled on the idiosyncratic alliterative patterning of vernacular Old English verse. Significantly, it was Æthilwald's model, rather than that of Aldhelm, which was largely followed on the Continent in a number of octosyllabic poems contained in correspondence associated with the mission to *Germany by *Boniface and his followers, including *Lull and the English nun *Beorhtgyth, who produced some affecting and effective verse. Outside the Bonifatian correspondence, evidence for later Anglo-Latin octosyllbles is notably sparse: a few verses by *Lantfred and *Frithegod survive, along with a handful of hymns, including one on St *Cuthbert.

M. Lapidge, 'Theodore and Anglo-Latin Octosyllabic Verse', in his *ALL* i.225–45; idem, 'The *Carmen* rhythmicum', in *Aldhelm: the Poetic Works*, trans. M. Lapidge and J. Rosier (Cambridge, 1985), pp. 169–79; M. Herren, 'The Stress Systems in Insular Latin Octosyllabic Verse', *CMCS* 15 (1988), 63–84; A. Orchard, *The Poetic Art of Aldhelm*, CSASE 8 (Cambridge, 1994), 19–72.

ANDY ORCHARD

ODA, archbishop of Canterbury (941–58), was of Anglo-Danish extraction (his father is alleged to have come to England with Ívarr and Hubba in the 870s) but was raised in the household of an English *thegn named Æthelhelm, probably in the *Danelaw. On one occasion he and Æthelhelm, who is otherwise unknown, travelled to *Rome together. Oda was appointed *c.*927 to the see of Ramsbury by King *Æthelstan, and is known to have travelled to the Continent on royal business (that of negotiating with Duke Hugh the safe return to France of Æthelstan's nephew, Louis d'Outremer, as king of the Franks) in 936; it was possibly on this trip that he was tonsured at *Fleury. He continued to enjoy the royal favour of Æthelstan's successor, *Edmund, and was appointed archbishop of *Canterbury in 941. He negotiated a truce with Archbishop *Wulfstan I concerning the *Five Boroughs, and together with Wulfstan was the motivating force behind King Edmund's first *law-code, which contained various stipulations pertaining to ecclesiastical discipline. A similar concern is seen in his *Constitutiones* (issued between 942 and 946, and based largely on the Legatine *Council of 786) as well as in a letter addressed to his suffragan bishops which is preserved by *William of Malmesbury. It was probably at Oda's instigation that the see of *Elmham was re-established in the *Danelaw. Oda was also active on behalf of his own church at Canterbury: he rebuilt the cathedral church (by raising the height of the nave some 20 feet), and acquired the relics of St *Wilfrid and St Ouen (Audoenus). He then commissioned *Frithegod, a continental clerk in the archiepiscopal household, to composed poems to commemorate these acquisitions. Frithegod's poem on Wilfrid, the *Breviloquium vitae Wilfridi*, survives as one of the most difficult Anglo-Latin works of the period; his Life of St Ouen is unfortunately lost. The *Breviloquium* is prefaced by a flamboyant prose account, ostensibly composed by Oda, of the acquisition of Wilfrid's relics from *Ripon, but the likelihood is that Frithegod was its author. Oda also acquired substantial estates for Canterbury, and was reportedly known to contemporaries as 'Oda the Good' (*Oda se goda*). The principal source for his life is pt i of *Byrhtferth's *Vita S. Oswaldi*; the post-Conquest Life by Eadmer, which draws on Byrhtferth, contains many additional statements (such as the report that Oda fought alongside Æthelstan at the battle of *Brunanburh* in 937) which are interesting but unverifiable. He died on 2 June 958.

Sharpe, *Handlist*, 1132; *Historians of the Church of York*, ed. J. Raine, 3 vols., RS (London, 1879–94), i.401–10 [Byrhtferth of Ramsey, *Vita S. Oswaldi*, pt i]; *Anglia Sacra*, ed. H. Wharton, 2 vols. (London, 1691), ii.78–87 [Eadmer, *Vita S. Odonis*; repr. PL cxxxiii.933–44]; J. Armitage Robinson, *St Oswald and the Church at Worcester*, British Academy Supplemental Papers 5 (London, 1919), 38–51; C. R. Hart, *The Early Charters of Northern England and the North Midlands* (Leicester, 1975), pp. 347–50; Brooks, *Canterbury*, pp. 222–37; *Councils & Synods* i. 65–7 [Oda's letter to his suffragans], i.67–74 [Oda's *Constitutiones*].

MICHAEL LAPIDGE

OFFA, king of the Mercians (757–96). When *Æthelbald, king of the Mercians, was killed by his bodyguard in 757, he was succeeded by Beornred; in the same year, Offa 'put Beornred to flight and attempted to conquer the Mercian kingdom with sword and bloodshed' (*HE Continuatio*, s.a. 757). Under circumstances of this kind, it seems unlikely that Offa could have inherited much from his predecessors, and more likely that he would have drawn upon his own resources and his own network of personal loyalties in rebuilding Mercian power. He would soon have been able to re-establish Mercian control of the *Hwicce and the *Magonsætan*, in the west Midlands, and one imagines that the men of *Lindsey, and the conglomeration of peoples known as the *Middle Angles (separately itemised in the *Tribal Hidage), would have had little choice but to submit to Offa in much the same way. Offa also lost little time in asserting his commercial interests in *London, inaugurating a new *coinage there and bringing the *Middle Saxons under his sway; doubtless his influence spread thence into Surrey. Elsewhere it may not have been so simple, and perhaps more a matter of degree, as Offa came to terms with rulers of peoples who may have been more determined to maintain their independence. It seems that he was able to take control of *Kent in the 760s, and that he moved westwards from Kent into *Sussex in 771. In 776, 'the Mercians and the people of Kent fought at Otford' (*ASC*), which probably signifies that the people of Kent rose up against Mercian oppression; certainly, there are indications that the rulers of Kent, and Sussex, enjoyed freedom from Mercian domination for a short while thereafter. Offa had recovered his position in the south-east by 785, and proceeded to tighten his grip; but he had incurred the enmity of Archbishop *Jænberht (765–92), and may have found it difficult to have all things his own way. Offa's reach also extended in one form or another into *East Anglia and *Essex; and, like *Æthelbald before him, he had interests in Somerset, and along the Thames valley. So, in addition to patronising monasteries established in different parts of his extended realm (e.g. *Medeshamstede* and Crowland), and founding others (e.g. *Winchcombe, *St Albans, and Bedford), he also took control of religious houses in sensitive locations (e.g. *Bath, Cookham, and perhaps *Glastonbury); and, crucially, he prevailed upon Pope Hadrian I (772–95) to grant special privileges in respect of at least some of these minsters to himself and to his wife *Cynethryth, no doubt as a means of consolidating his control. There is, however, no evidence to substantiate the notion that the kingdom of *Wessex, as a whole, was at any time subjected to Offa, or that the kingdom of *Northumbria ever fell under his sway. Offa died on 29 July 796, and was buried in the church which he had founded at Bedford; perhaps significantly, the bishops of Lindsey and London 'left the country' (*ASC*). He was succeeded by his son Ecgfrith; but Ecgfrith died in December 796, and it was *Coenwulf who took up the Mercian cause.

Offa must have struck his contemporaries as a ruler of awesome power. Many would have become familiar with his name or image on his coinage, and some would have been grateful to him for promoting good business practices. The bishops and abbots who gathered at *councils convened under the auspices of the archbishops of *Canterbury would have seen much evidence of imperious behaviour; and both Charlemagne and Pope Hadrian were party to the machinations which led to the despatch of papal *missionaries to England in 786, to the creation of a new archbishopric of

*Lichfield at the 'contentious synod' of Chelsea in 787, and so, indirectly, to the consecration of Ecgfrith in the same year. The Welsh, who had experienced Mercian oppression in 778 and 784, were doubtless greatly impressed by the effort and expenditure which went into the construction of *Offa's Dyke. For his part, *Alcuin, the expatriate Northumbrian scholar observing affairs in his homeland from his vantage point at Charlemagne's court, warmly approved of Offa's determination to reinvent Mercian kingship in the Carolingian mould, which culminated with the consecration of Ecgfrith, though he was forced after the death of Offa and Ecgfrith, in 796, to acknowledge the bitter truth that Ecgfrith's position had been secured by the ruthless suppression of political opponents. Yet Offa was no match for Charlemagne, and no model for *Alfred the Great. He may have lacked a contemporary biographer, and it may be that we are dependent on reports emanating from his 'victims', whether at *Worcester, or at Canterbury, or in Wales; but even to suggest the comparison is to set him up as something which would misrepresent the kind of ruler that he was, and the kind of ruler that he claimed to be. Offa was driven by a lust for power, not by a vision of English unity; and what he left was a reputation, not a legacy. Alfred made a point in his *law-code of remembering Offa's legislation for his people; the chronicler *Æthelweard described him as 'an extraordinary man' (uir mirabilis); and *Æthelstan, son of King *Æthelred the Unready, bequeathed to his brother *Edmund Ironside 'the sword which belonged to King Offa'.

The act which proved in time to contribute most to the formation of King Offa's historical identity was his foundation of St Albans Abbey (Herts.), probably in the early 790s. Offa may have had it in mind to promote a cult which would take precedence over the cult of St *Augustine (cf. Bede, HE i.7), at an abbey very well placed on the road leading from Mercia into London. Alas, little is known of the abbey's fortunes in the first two hundred years of its history, though it is known to have prospered under royal patronage during the reign of King *Æthelred the Unready. The abbey's pretensions in the thirteenth century are not in doubt, and it was at the hands of two monks of St Albans that Offa achieved his apotheosis. The story was first told in connected detail by Roger of Wendover, in his Flores historiarum, and it only remained for Roger's successor, Matthew Paris, to establish the legend. We can read all about it in the first part of Matthew's Chronica majora, or in the more parochial Gesta abbatum,

or in the remarkable Vitae duorum Offarum (first Offa of Angeln, then Offa of Mercia). Matthew also devised a splendid sequence of illustrations depicting events in the life of King Offa for inclusion in his miscellany of material on the cult of St Alban (Dublin, Trinity College, 177).

Offa was remade in the twentieth century as a unifying principle of early English history, not so much on the basis of the legend generated at St Albans as on the basis of the analysis of his charters. The notion that Offa claimed to be 'king of the English', or 'king of the whole country of the English', has been shown to depend, however, on charters forged in the tenth century. In his own day he was 'king of the Mercians', and proud enough to be so.

Stenton, ASE, pp. 206–24; R. Vaughan, Matthew Paris (Cambridge, 1958), esp. pp. 189–94; P. Wormald, 'The Age of Offa and Alcuin', The Anglo-Saxons, ed. Campbell, pp. 101–28; Making of England, pp. 193–253; S. Keynes, 'Changing Faces: Offa, King of Mercia', History Today 40.11 (1990), 14–19; Yorke, Kingdoms, pp. 112–17; Kirby, Kings, pp. 163–84; S. Keynes, 'England, 700–900', The New Cambridge Medieval History, II: c.700–c.900, ed. R. McKitterick (Cambridge, 1995), pp. 18–42; D. Chick, 'Towards a Chronology for Offa's Coinage: an Interim Study', Yorkshire Numismatist 3 (1997), 47–64; Charters of Selsey, ed. S. E. Kelly, AS Charters 6 (Oxford, 1998).

SIMON KEYNES

OFFA'S DYKE was built by *Mercia against Powys; it was sixty-four miles (103 km) long and ran between Rushock Hill on the north side of the Herefordshire Plain to Llanfynydd, near Mold in Clwyd. A formidable barrier, it consists of an earthen bank thirty feet (10 m) wide with a ditch six feet (2 m) deep and twelve feet wide (4 m) on the Welsh side. No evidence has been found for a palisade or walkway on the bank. Sixty-eight excavations on Offa's Dyke have provided no artefacts or timber by which to date it but there is no reason to doubt the long standing and traditional belief that it is the 'great dyke' which *Asser tells us was built by King *Offa (757–96). The earthwork was carefully engineered to create the most effective barrier and to keep the best view into Wales, suggesting that its primary function was military and that the Mercians had a free choice of where to site it: it cannot have been an agreed frontier as all the advantage is to the Mercians. It is unlikely that it would have been continually garrisoned; this would not have been normal Anglo-Saxon practice and no associated *forts have been found. A warning that Mercia was being entered, it would have made it difficult for the

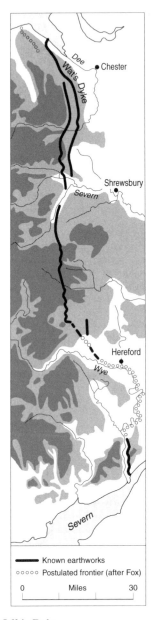

Map 2 Offa's Dyke.

Welsh to drive stolen livestock back into their own territory and it would have provided time to raise a local group to prevent too much damage. Asser's statement that the dyke ran ' . . . from sea to sea . . .' has encouraged people to seek further lengths but extensive archaeological research since 1971 has shown that only the continuous sixty-four mile length is to be considered a part of the original design. Original gateways through the

Dyke were postulated by Fox and by Noble, but excavations designed to test this hypothesis have shown that the earthwork was a continuous barrier acting as a deterrent to incursions by the Welsh. Whilst the work of Fox needs serious revision in the light of new evidence, it remains a valuable record of the monument in 1931, as many lengths have subsequently been damaged or destroyed.

C. Fox, *Offa's Dyke: a Field Survey of the Western Frontier Works of Mercia in the Seventh and Eighth Centuries* AD (London, 1955); F. Noble, 'Offa's Dyke Reviewed. A Critical Re-assessment of Published Work and Accepted Opinions, with Detailed Reconsideration of the Course of the Dyke through the Diocese of Hereford' (unpubl. M. Phil. dissertation, Open Univ., 1978); idem, *Offa's Dyke Reviewed*, BAR Brit. ser. 114 (Oxford, 1983) [part of thesis only]; D. H. Hill, 'Pattern and Purpose: Offa's Dyke', *AJ* (forthcoming).

MARGARET WORTHINGTON

OFFICE: *see* Liturgy

OHTHERE was a Norwegian chieftain who in the reign of King *Alfred (871–99) visited the court in *Wessex and gave accounts of three voyages in Scandinavia and of his way of living. His information was included, together with Wulfstan's account of his voyage into the Baltic, in the Old English *Orosius*. One of Ohthere's voyages took him round the North Cape and along today's Lapmark, vast areas inhabited only by nomadic *Finnas*, and round Kola peninsula, home of the *Terfinnas*, into the White Sea. Here he reached the permanently settled areas of the Biarmians but did not venture into them for lack of a peace agreement. His main reason for undertaking this journey, apart from exploring the land, was to hunt walruses; a party of six men had been able to kill sixty walruses in two days, he claimed. The *ivory from their teeth was highly valued, and Ohthere brought some to the king (see also *bone-working). The scholars at Alfred's court were particularly keen to learn whether, when Ohthere changed direction, the land was turning, or the sea was penetrating the land. This would help them establish whether Ohthere had been travelling along the utmost edge of the world, or was merely entering another inland sea like the Baltic, said to penetrate the land. Another part of the account describes the journey from Ohthere's home to the port of *Sciringesheal* in southern Norway. Ohthere told his hosts that he lived furthest to the north of all Northmen and archaeology suggests that his home may have been on the island of Bjarkøy; the traditional boundary between the areas of *búmenn*, permanent settlers, and those of the nomadic Samians is the Malangen Fjord some forty miles northeast of Bjarkøy. *Sciringesheal* has been identified as Kaupang near Larvik, an important market in *Viking age Norway. This journey could, under adverse conditions, take as long as a month. Reference is made to the location of Ireland and Britain, though hardly for any purpose of practical navigation.

From *Sciringesheal* Ohthere continued his journey to Hedeby in the south of Jutland, which was reached in five days. He reports that for the three days he had Denmark to port and the open sea to starboard. Then for two days he had Jutland and *Sillende* (South Jutland) and many islands to starboard; his interviewer comments that the Angles lived in those parts before they came to 'this land', i.e. England. And on the port side he had those islands which belong to Denmark. This distinction between Jutland and *Sillende* and many islands on one side, and 'Denmark' and the islands belonging to it on the other, is matched in the introductory description of Europe beyond Danube and the Rhine by a distinction between South Danes in *Sillende* and Jutland, and North Danes in Denmark.

An account of a voyage by a certain Wulfstan, by his name apparently an Englishman, follows that of Ohthere's voyages in the OE *Orosius*. Wulfstan's journey begins at Hedeby where Ohthere's ends. He travelled across the Baltic to modern Poland, and the report tells of the economy of the region and in particular the funerary arrangements of the wealthy.

The Old English Orosius, ed. J. Bately, EETS s.s. 6 (London, 1980); *Ohthere and Wulfstan. Two Voyagers at the Court of King Alfred*, ed. N. Lund and C. E. Fell (York, 1984); M. Korhammer, 'Viking Seafaring and the Meaning of Ohthere's *ambyrne wind*', in *Problems of Old English Lexicography*, ed. A. Bammesberger (Regensburg, 1985), pp. 151–73.

NIELS LUND

OLD ENGLISH, the language of the Anglo-Saxons, sometimes called Anglo-Saxon, though that term is now outmoded. Old English is a *Germanic language. Traditionally it is derived from the West Germanic branch, closely akin to the languages of North *Germany and the Low Countries. None of these tongues evidence the High German consonant shift which characterises modern German. More recently scholars have preferred to see Old English as part of a language continuum, distinguished by certain phonological features, called North Sea Germanic (also known

as Inguaeonic), spreading from Schleswig-Holstein across *Frisia to the coasts of the Netherlands. Old English has a few specific affinities with early Frisian which have led some scholars to suggest an 'Anglo-Frisian phase' of the language.

From the early Anglo-Saxon period few language records survive and they are short inscriptions often hard to interpret. Written documents begin in the late seventh century, and thereafter there is a continuous series of manuscripts down to the period after 1100 when Old English developed into Middle English. They record a number of local *dialects.

Compared with modern English, Old English is a quite highly inflected language: the relationship between words in a sentence is indicated not so much by word order or an extended use of prepositions, as by the different inflexional endings added to nouns, adjectives, articles, pronouns and verbs. In this respect the structure of Old English is closer to that of modern German than to modern English.

There are three genders of noun, called for convenience masculine, feminine and neuter though these do not necessarily coincide with natural gender in any noun: for instance, *wif*, 'woman', and *cild*, 'child', are both neuter, while *stan*, 'stone', is masculine and *boc*, 'book', is feminine. Nouns are declined in singular and plural, in four grammatical cases in each: nominative (subject), accusative (object), genitive (possessive) and dative (indirect object or prepositional). These cases and numbers have different endings in different noun classes: so, for instance, the word *stan* has the following singular forms: nom.acc. *stan*, gen. *stanes*, dat. *stane*; plural forms: nom.acc. *stanas*, gen. *stana*, dat. *stanum*. *Sunu*, 'son', has singular forms: nom.acc. *sunu*, gen.dat. *suna*: plural forms: nom.acc.gen. *suna*, dat. *sunum*. Old English has some half a dozen major noun classes, and there are also several minor ones, including those nouns that form their plurals by mutating the vowel of the stem: as *fot*, pl. *fet* (= foot, feet), and *mon*, pl. *men* (= man, men) – these two mutation plurals survive in English – and *boc*, pl. *bec* (= book, books), which does not. Articles and demonstratives decline according to number, case (the four listed for nouns together with an occasional additional one known as the instrumental) and gender. Adjectives decline according to number, case and gender, and there are two forms of each, the weak (used after a definite article or a demonstrative or personal pronoun) and the strong (used when the adjective stands without such an article). First and second person pronouns have four cases and, as well as singular and plural forms, also the dual: *ic*, 'I', *we*, 'we', *wit*, 'the two of us': *þu*, 'thou, you (sg.)', *ge*, 'you (pl.)', *git*, 'you two'. The third person pronoun has only singular and plural forms, but is declined for gender as well as case.

As modern English, Old English has only two simple tenses, present and past. Other tenses are formed with auxiliaries, the verbs 'be', 'have', 'will', etc. However, as well as the indicative of these tenses, Old English also has the subjunctive, which is practically defunct in the present-day language. Verbs, again as in modern English, are either strong or weak. The strong, representing a type that derives from the Indo-European verbal form, are those that form past tenses and past participles by a change in the stem vowel: *singan, ic sang, we sungon, sungen* (= sing, sang, sung, but note that in Old English the past singular may have a different vowel from the past plural). The weak verb, a characteristic feature of Germanic languages, forms its past tense and past participle by adding a dental suffix: *fylgan, ic fylgde, we fylgdon, gefylgod* (= follow, followed, followed). There are also a few important anomalous verbs: *beon/wesan*, 'be', *don*, 'do', *gan*, 'go', *willan*, 'will'; and a distinctive group of common verbs called preterite-present, which show strong past tense forms with present meaning, and weak past tense forms with past meaning; this includes *witan*, 'know', *cunnan*, 'know how to, be able to', *sculan*, 'shall', *magan*, 'can'. The verb must be conjugated in first, second and third person singular and in the common plural, for tense and mood.

In its surface structure, then, Old English is quite a complex language, but even this complexity represents a simplification of the earlier language forms it developed from. Old English is an early stage of the movement from a synthetic language (relying on inflexional endings for indicating the relationship between words) to the analytical language that modern English is (using word order and prepositions to show relationship). It is in the change from Old to Middle English that the language loses a good deal of its inflexional precision, with the levelling out of endings and the consequent need to establish other methods of relating words together. Northern and eastern dialects move in this direction earlier than those of the south and west.

Our knowledge of Old English is inevitably minimal. We have only the formal registers recorded in documents, and know little about the informal or spoken registers. In some ways the language of Anglo-Saxon poetry differs from that of prose, and there may be other differences of usage

of this sort that have not survived. Pronunciation we have to deduce, partly from written forms, partly from the more recent forms of words, partly from closely related words in contemporary languages; but obviously pronunciation would vary with region, and perhaps with class or education. The language seems to have had a strong stress rhythm, with stress falling on the first syllable of nouns and the root syllable of verbs, inflexional endings being lightly stressed. We can know nothing about the intonation or 'tune' of the language. Finally, there are many subjects not dealt with in surviving literature, and the vocabulary for dealing with them has been lost forever.

B. Mitchell and F. C. Robinson, *A Guide to Old English*, 5th ed. (Oxford, 1992); A. Campbell, *Old English Grammar* (Oxford, 1959); H. Gneuss, 'The Old English Language', *CamComp*, pp. 23–54; CHELang I, ed. R. Hogg (Cambridge, 1992).

R. I. PAGE

OLD NORSE is the *Germanic language spoken by most of the inhabitants of Scandinavia in the early and High Middle Ages, and so the language of the *Vikings. It developed from North Germanic by several major changes of phonology and morphology occurring around the seventh century AD. This development is shown in inscriptions cut in *runes, which first appear in perhaps the second century AD and continue into the late medieval period. In and after about the tenth century Norse divides into distinct dialects, initially into West and East Norse. West Norse then subdivides into Old Icelandic, Old Faroese, Norn (the varieties of Norse spoken in the British Isles), and the dialects of Old Norwegian. East Norse subdivides into the dialects of Old Danish and Old Swedish, and Old Gutnish (the dialect of Gotland). These probably all remained mutually intelligible until the late medieval period, when they must be considered separate languages. Old Icelandic is the earliest dialect of Old Norse to be substantially attested in writing in the roman alphabet, from the twelfth century onward, and it uniquely developed a large original literature in the high medieval period; Norse forms are usually cited from it. This literature gives an important but frequently untrustworthy account of the Viking period, several centuries earlier. It also preserves much poetry, some of which may be much older, and which records Germanic myths and legends, as well as possibly historical accounts of the Viking period.

Old Norse was related to *Old English, but mutual intelligibility is unlikely in the Viking period beyond very simple sentences and limited wording. Bilingual populations probably existed in the east and north of England (the *Danelaw) after aristocratic Viking conquest and Norse peasant settlement. Norse words appear occasionally in English poetry during the tenth century, and are used in legal contexts in the eleventh century. These are high-status words which imply the use of Norse in bilingual courts of kings and noblemen. Modern English *earl* derives its sense from Norse *jarl* 'nobleman next in rank beneath a king', but its form comes from Old English *eorl*, a poetic word meaning 'man'; the modern use is first attested in texts of around the beginning of the eleventh century. Norse words do not appear in the general language in large numbers, however, until the twelfth and thirteenth centuries, together with apparently Norse-derived syntax and idiom; their distribution is then largely but not entirely restricted to dialects of eastern and northern English, and must be derived from a partly Norse-speaking population. Norse also appears in many place-names of the Danelaw; some of these may show features specific to East or West Norse, though most instances are uncertain.

A. Noreen, *Altnordische Grammatik* I, *Altisländische und altnorwegische Grammatik*, 4th ed. (Halle, 1923); II, *Altschwedische Grammatik mit Einschluss des Altgutnischen* (Halle, 1904); E. Haugen, *The Scandinavian Languages* (London, 1976).

PAUL BIBIRE

ORAL-FORMULAIC THEORY is based on the notion that the high level of verbal and thematic repetition in orally-derived texts may imply a compositional technique enabling illiterate poets to extemporise compositions of extraordinary length. By analogy with contemporary Serbian poets it was suggested that Homeric verse might derive from oral composition by an illiterate poet recasting and combining more or less traditional formulas, and when F. P. Magoun first applied the theory to Old English he concluded that *Beowulf* too was an oral-formulaic work. The logical fallacy of assuming that if oral compositions are formulaic, formulaic compositions must be oral was exposed by Larry D. Benson, who demonstrated that much Latin-derived (and therefore literate) verse in Old English is also highly formulaic; so too is the Latin poetry of *Aldhelm, whose method of recycling remembered phrases from previous poets and combining them with repeated phrases of his own provides an exact parallel for the 'oral-formulaic' techniques found in Homer. If poetic tradition in Anglo-Saxon England was ultimately orally derived, literate Anglo-Saxons were still able to exploit those traditional techniques. Likewise *Wulfstan in his *preaching offers a number of points of comparison, while it is becoming clear that there is an oral-traditional element not only in the composition of some Anglo-Saxon texts, but also in their transmission.

F. P. Magoun, 'The Oral Formulaic Character of Anglo-Saxon Narrative Poetry', *Speculum* 28 (1953), 446–67; L. D. Benson, 'The Literary Character of Anglo-Saxon Formulaic Poetry', *PMLA* 81 (1966), 334–41; J. M. Foley, ed., *Oral-Formulaic Theory and Research: an Introduction and Annotated Bibliography* (New York, 1985); A. H. Olsen, 'Oral-Formulaic Research in Old English Studies: I', *Oral Tradition* 1 (1986), 548–606; idem, 'Oral-Formulaic Research in Old English Studies: II', *Oral Tradition* 3 (1988), 138–90; A. Orchard, 'Oral Tradition', in *Approaches to Reading Old English Texts*, ed. K. O'Brien O'Keeffe (Cambridge, 1997), pp. 101–23.

ANDY ORCHARD

ORDEAL. The forms of service for the ordeal in Anglo-Saxon England are preserved in the pontificals of that period, that is the *liturgical books which developed from the tenth century onwards and came to contain the services reserved for the bishop. The purpose of the ordeal was simply to determine whether someone accused of a crime was guilty or innocent. Four types of ordeal seem to have been in use in Anglo-Saxon England. First, there was the ordeal by fire, in which the accused had to carry a piece of red-hot iron of a defined weight over a specified distance. The resultant burns on the accused's hand were then bandaged; if after three days, they were found to have healed cleanly the accused was innocent; if they had festered, they were guilty. In a second form of ordeal, the accused had to retrieve a stone suspended in boiling water. The resulting scalds were treated in the same way as the burns in the ordeal by fire. Thirdly, the ordeal of cold water involved binding the accused and lowering them into a large tank of cold water. If they sank to a specified depth, they were innocent; if they did not, they were guilty. The fourth type of ordeal, which was probably restricted to the clergy, involved swallowing a consecrated portion of dry barley bread and goat's cheese. If the accused succeeded in swallowing it, they were innocent; if they choked on it they were guilty. A fifth type of ordeal, that by battle, does not seem to have been known in England until after the Norman Conquest.

Although found already in the *laws of King *Ine, ordeals are unlikely to have been pagan in origin. In any case, by the late Anglo-Saxon period they were thoroughly Christianised, involving for example fasting, *relics, communion for the accused, processions and blessings. Their significance can be variously interpreted: as an instance of the early medieval belief in the working of the miraculous in society which could be harnessed for purposes of judgement; as a mechanism within society by which judgements were reached by human deliberation but were attributed to supernatural intervention so that no one need take personal responsibility (in this interpretation, it is necessary to postulate that the results of the ordeals were not clear-cut and needed to be interpreted in the light of the consensus reached, for example, amongst those supporting the accused and those supporting the accusers); and as a mechanism by which kings sought to establish judgements in cases where more prosaic mechanisms could not function.

D. Rollason, *Two Anglo-Saxon Rituals: The Dedication of a Church and the Judicial Ordeal*, Vaughan Papers in Adult Education 33 (Leicester, 1988); R. Bartlett, *Trial by Fire and Water: The Medieval Judicial Ordeal* (Oxford, 1986); C. Morris, 'Judicium Dei: the Social and Political Significance of the Ordeal in the Eleventh Century', *Studies in Church History* 12 (1975), 95–111; S. L. Keefer, 'Ut in omnibus honorificetur Deus: the Corsnæd Ordeal in Anglo-Saxon England', in *The Community, the Family and the Saint*, ed. J. Hill and M. Swan (Turnhout, 1998), pp. 237–64.

DAVID ROLLASON

ORDER OF THE WORLD, a poem of 102 lines from the *Exeter Book. A prime example of Old English *wisdom literature, it opens with the poet challenging his audience to question him about the wonders of creation, likening the song he will sing to similar songs composed by poets in the distant past, who have been identified variously by modern critics as either the poets and prophets of the Old Testament or earlier practitioners of Germanic verse. Its opening verses display certain affinities with Ps. XVIII in the Vulgate Bible, while the heart of the poem, a forty-line visionary representation of the sun voyaging from its rising to its setting, has been fruitfully compared with the song of creation sung by Hrothgar's *scop* in lines 90b–98 of *Beowulf.

ASPR iii. 163–6; N. Isaacs, *Structural Principles in Old English Poetry* (Knoxville, TN, 1968); B. F. Huppé, *The Web of Words* (Albany, NY, 1970); *The Exeter Anthology of Old English Poetry*, ed. B. J. Muir, 2 vols. (Exeter, 1994).

ROBERT DINAPOLI

ORMSIDE BOWL. This eighth-century Anglo-Saxon bowl, one of the treasures of the Yorkshire Museum, was found in Ormside churchyard, Cumbria, where it had probably been buried in a *Viking grave. It consists of a gilt-bronze inner shell and a silver-gilt outer bowl decorated with repoussé bush-vine motifs, in which birds and curious beasts clamber and feed. Bosses and *glass insets also embellish it. In its form and size, it is related to some of the silver bowls from the St Ninian's Isle hoard, and in decorative detail to the lost river Witham *hanging-bowl. However, the exuberant inhabited vine-scroll decoration, with its Christian message, relates it stylistically to the decoration of the *Barberini Gospels, to the *Breedon-on-the-Hill sculptural friezes, and most of all to the great Northumbrian altar cross from Bischofshofen in Austria. These ecclesiastical parallels, and the explicit cruciform design of the inner and outer base-plates, suggest that its original function was liturgical.

G. Baldwin Brown, *The Arts in Early England*: IV. *The Christian Arts of Northumbria* (London, 1921), pp. 318–28; E. Bakka, 'Some English Decorated Metal Objects found in Norwegian Viking Graves', *Årbok for Universitetet i Bergen: Humanistik Serie* 1 (1963), 8–11, 22–3; *Making of England*, pp. 172–3.

LESLIE WEBSTER

ORNAMENT: *see* Anglo-Saxon Art, Chronology

OROSIUS, OE TRANSLATION OF. The OE *Orosius* is a translation of Orosius' world history, the *Historiae aduersum paganos*, produced during the reign of King *Alfred (871–99), and generally linked with Alfred's programme of education. Although *William of Malmesbury stated that Alfred translated this text, recent studies of the the vocabulary, syntax, and style suggest he was not its author. The translator's syntactical sophistication, use of alliteration, and attention to the rhythm and balance of his sentences have made a place for the OE *Orosius* in discussions of early English prose writing. The text is usually dated from internal evidence – such as *Ohthere's report to Alfred, the section describing the geography of Europe, and similarities in phrasing with the *Anglo-Saxon Chronicle – to no earlier than 889 and no later than 899. Four manuscripts, two of which are fragments, are extant; the earliest, the Lauderdale or Tollemache manuscript, connected by palaeography to *Winchester, is often used as a source for early *West Saxon *dialect forms.

The translator generally retains the broad outlines of Orosius's history, but he treats his source text freely, often supplementing Orosius with references to a variety of well-known classical texts.

Though he expands some sections – his account of the rape of the Sabines and description of the geography of northern and western Europe, for example – the OE text is markedly shorter than the original. Tracing the passage of dominion from the reign of King Ninus of Assyria to the sack of Rome, the *Orosius*-translator reshapes his text for a late ninth-century audience by clarifying potentially obscure allusions, institutions, and events and excising much of Orosius's moral commentary on human moral weakness. In his expanded interpretation of Roman history, the translator lingers over the Roman rulers and suggests that the people's welfare is directly connected to their leader's character. Of particular interest to scholars have been the interpolated voyages of Ohthere and Wulfstan which provide expanded descriptions of the geography of Northern Europe, brief images of its people and culture, and a glimpse into contemporary systems of navigation.

J. M. Bately, 'King Alfred and the Old English Translation of Orosius', *Anglia* 88 (1970), 433–60; *The Old English Orosius*, ed. J. M. Bately, EETS ss 6 (London, 1980); J. M. Bately, 'Old English Prose Before and During the Reign of Alfred', *ASE* 17 (1988), 93–138; *The Tollemache Orosius (British Museum Additional MS 47967)*, ed. A. Campbell, EEMF 3 (Copenhagen, 1953); W. A. Kretzschmar, Jr., 'Adaptation and *anweald* in the Old English Orosius', *ASE* 16 (1987), 127–45.

ALICE SHEPPARD

OSGYTH (fl. *c*.660–80), abbess and saint, is known only from late legends, one derived from Aylesbury (Bucks.) and the other from Chich (Essex), which have been confused with other material. These sources make her daughter of the Mercian sub-king Frithuwold and his wife Wilburh, sister of King *Wulfhere of *Mercia, and state that she was born in her father's palace at Quarrendon (Bucks.) and brought up in a family *nunnery at Aylesbury. She was married unwillingly to King Sigehere of the East Saxons (*c*.664–88), but was saved from consummating the marriage and founded a nunnery at Chich (Essex), finally being martyred by pirates. How much, if any, of this has a historical basis is doubtful; it is even uncertain whether there were two Osgyths or one, since both Aylesbury and Chich claimed her relics.

D. Bethell, 'The Lives of St Osyth of Essex and St Osyth of Aylesbury', *AB* 88 (1970), 75–127; C. Hohler, 'St Osyth and Aylesbury', *Records of Buckinghamshire* 18 (1966–70), 61–72; K. Bailey, 'Osyth, Frithuwold and Aylesbury', *Records of Buckinghamshire* 31 (1980), 37–48.

JOHN BLAIR

OSWALD, king of *Northumbria (d. 642), was a son of Æthelfrith of *Bernicia (*c*.590–616). During the reign of King *Edwin (616–33) he was exiled among the Scots of Dal Riada where he was converted to Christianity. In 634 he defeated Cadwallon of Gwynedd in battle at Heavenfield near *Hexham and was afterwards acknowledged as king in both Bernicia and *Deira. He had a legitimate claim to kingship in Deira through his mother, Acha, a daughter of King Ælle and Edwin's sister. Oswald was a powerful overlord although the extent of his authority is difficult to determine. *Bede's claim that he was ruler of all the British, Pictish, Irish and English peoples cannot be confirmed and is probably inflated, and *Adomnán's description of him in the *Life of St Columba* as emperor of all Britain is undefined. There is no evidence that by his defeat of Cadwallon, Oswald exercised power among the British kingdoms of North Wales as did his predecessor Edwin, or that his authority was acknowledged in Pictland. The overlordship and alliances created by Oswald appear to have been made with the intention of containing the growing power of *Penda of *Mercia. He ruled *Lindsey and the kingdom of the South Saxons and demonstrated his superiority over the West Saxon king, Cynegisl, by standing as his sponsor at baptism. He also joined in, or confirmed, Cynegisl's grant of *Dorchester-on-Thames to Bishop *Birinus as the site of the first West Saxon see. Relations with the West Saxons were strengthened when he took Cynegisl's daughter as his wife. Oswald also exercised influence in *Kent, a kingdom which Bede specifically excluded from King Edwin's authority. After the death of Edwin, his widow Æthelburh returned to Kent with Edwin's daughter, son and grandson, where she was given refuge by her brother, King Eadbald. Later, fearful that Oswald and Eadbald might plot to murder Edwin's male heirs, she sent them to her kinsman in Francia, King Dagobert I.

Soon after he became king Oswald asked the monastery of *Iona for help to convert Northumbria to Christianity. He was sent Bishop *Aidan to whom he gave as his see the island of *Lindisfarne, close to the principal Bernician stronghold of Bamburgh. Bede describes Oswald as 'the most Christian king', who was personally involved in the development of the church in Northumbria; he interpreted Aidan's words to his *ealdormen and *thegns because the bishop had a poor command of English, and he donated lands and property from royal estates to establish monasteries. Oswald was killed in 642 at the battle of *Maserfeld* (Oswestry?) by Penda of Mercia and immediately afterwards miracles were reported as having occurred at the spot where he died. His cult was established at the monastery of Bardney in Lincolnshire where he became venerated as the first Anglo-Saxon royal saint, whose popularity reached continental Europe.

Bede, *HE* iii. 1–7, 9–13; P. Clemoes, *The Cult of St Oswald on the Continent*, Jarrow Lecture (1983), repr. in *Bede and His World: the Jarrow Lectures 1958–1993*, ed. M. Lapidge (Aldershot, 1994), pp. 587–610; *Oswald: Northumbrian King to European Saint*, ed. C. Stancliffe and E. Cambridge (Stamford, 1995).

PHILIP HOLDSWORTH

OSWALD, bishop of *Worcester (961–92) and archbishop of *York (971–92), was one of the principal figures in the tenth-century Benedictine reform movement and one of the most powerful bishops of his time. Oswald was born to an influential and wealthy family (to judge from his own subsequent wealth) of Anglo-Danish origin: he was the nephew of *Oda, archbishop of *Canterbury (941–58) and was related to Oscytel, archbishop of York (956–71). Although the precise date of his birth is unknown, he was at some point raised in the household of his uncle Oda at Canterbury, where his tutor was the continental scholar *Frithegod. From Frithegod, we may assume, he will have learned to write Latin in a flamboyant manner, and it is unfortunate that no composition in his name has come down to us, save perhaps for a block of attestations in an original charter (S 690) of King *Edgar dated 961, which he drafted and possibly wrote. While he was still a young man a 'monastery' (*monasterium*) was purchased for him in *Winchester, the location of which is unknown, but at some point in the early 950s he was trained and ordained as a monk at *Fleury, where he remained until shortly after the death of his uncle Oda in 958. He was appointed to the bishopric of *Worcester in 961, and with the reforming zeal for Benedictine *monasticism which he had learned at Fleury, he established a number of monasteries, including Westbury-on-Trym (963 × 964), *Ramsey (in 966, in collaboration with the *ealdorman of East Anglia, Æthelwine) and Pershore (*c.*970), and helped to refound others, including *Winchcombe, where his colleague *Germanus, who had previously been prior of Westbury and Ramsey, became first abbot. There is, however, some debate about how quickly and thoroughly the *cathedral clergy of his own church at Worcester was reformed, the debate turning on the evidence of nearly eighty leases in his name to

land in the region of Worcester. In 971 he was appointed to the archbishopric of York on the death of his relative Oscytel, and he held York in plurality with Worcester until his death. Much of what we know of Oswald's life and personality derives from the *Vita S. Oswaldi* by *Byrhtferth of Ramsey, written 997 × 1002; Byrhtferth's principal concern was to portray Oswald as an icon of Benedictine monastic ideals, but almost incidentally includes a number of personal details concerning Oswald's imposing physique and gout, and a moving account of his final visit to Ramsey in 991 on the occasion of the dedication of a new tower. Oswald died at Worcester on 28 February 992; his remains were translated a decade later, on 15 April 1002 (JW, s.a. 1002).

Sharpe, *Handlist* 1150; *Historians of the Church of York*, ed. J. Raine, 3 vols., RS (London, 1879–94), i.399–475 [Byrhtferth of Ramsey, *Vita S. Oswaldi*]; J. Armitage Robinson, *St Oswald and the Church at Worcester*, British Academy Supplemental Papers 5 (London, 1919); I. Atkins, 'The Church of Worcester from the Eighth to the Twelfth Century', *AJ* 17 (1937), 371–91; D. J. A. Fisher, 'The Anti-Monastic Reaction in the Reign of Edward the Martyr', *Cambridge Historical Journal* 10 (1950–2), 254–70; E. John, 'St Oswald and the Tenth-Century Reformation', *JEH* 9 (1958), 158–72; P. H. Sawyer, 'Charters of the Reform Movement: the Worcester Archive', in *Tenth-Century Studies*, ed. D. Parsons (Chichester, 1975), pp. 84–93; *Æthelwold*, pp. 92–3 [charter drafted by Oswald]; *Oswald of Worcester*.

MICHAEL LAPIDGE

OSWALD THE YOUNGER (fl. 1010), a poet and scholar at the abbey of *Ramsey who was the nephew of *Oswald, archbishop of York (971–92), and was evidently a major literary figure in his own day, although his writings have almost all been lost. He was an oblate at Ramsey in the time of Abbot Eadnoth (992–1006), and is remembered in the *Liber benefactorum* of Ramsey as one of four schoolboys who cracked one of the monastery's bells by pulling frivolously on the bell-ropes. He subsequently travelled to the Continent, visiting Saint-Omer and Arras in *Flanders, then Corbie, Saint-Denis in Paris and Lagny; he ended up this period of travel by studying in *Fleury, as his uncle had done before him. His accomplishments at Fleury were recorded in a poem by one Constantine, a monk of Fleury and later abbot of Micy (d. 1021); although the poem is lost, it was reportedly composed in elegiacs and was seen in manuscript by John *Leland in the sixteenth century. Oswald later returned to Ramsey to a life of quiet study, becoming a man 'renowned for his erudition and piety', according to the *Liber* *benefactorum.* The same source records that he turned down the offer of a bishopric, preferring to remain ensconced in study at Ramsey. On the occasion of a visit by King *Edward the Confessor to Ramsey, Oswald was able successfully to petition the king for a grant of estates at Wimbotsham (Norfolk) and Downham Market (the original *charter does not survive, but a later forgery based on it is preserved as S 1030). According to Leland, Oswald composed a *Liber sacrarum precationum* (partly in prose, partly in verse), and a treatise *De componendis epistolis* cast in the form of a letter. John *Bale added to this list a treatise *De edendis carminibus.* All of these works have apparently been lost. But two short poems of Oswald have been identified in Cambridge, UL, Gg.5.35; both are composed in the fiendishly difficult form known as *versus retrogradi* (that is, the hexameter metre is preserved whether the lines are read forwards or backwards).

Sharpe, *Handlist* 1149; M. Lapidge, 'The Hermeneutic Style in Tenth-Century Anglo-Latin Literature', *ASE* 4 (1975), 67–111, at 106–7, repr. in *ALL* ii.105–49, at 144–5; P. Dronke, M. Lapidge and P. Stotz, 'Die unveröffentlichten Gedichte der Cambridger Liederhandschrift (CUL Gg.5.35)', *Mittellateinisches Jahrbuch* 17 (1982), 54–95, at 66–8.

MICHAEL LAPIDGE

OSWIU, king of *Northumbria (d. 670), was a son of King Æthelfrith of *Bernicia. In the reign of King *Edwin of *Deira (616–33) he was exiled among the Scots of Dal Riada, and during this period may have married a princess of the Uí Neill dynasty by whom he had a son, *Aldfrith, king of Northumbria 685–705 (*Bede describes him as illegitimate). After the death of his brother King *Oswald (634–42), Northumbria separated into its constituent kingdoms of Bernicia (ruled by Oswiu) and Deira (ruled by Oswine, a son of King Edwin's cousin Osric). The overlordship ascribed to Oswiu by Bede (*HE* ii.5) took a long time to establish and was short-lived; his reign was punctuated by attacks by *Penda of Mercia and rebellion by his nephew and son. Oswiu (whose mother may have been Acha, a daughter of King Ælle and Edwin's sister) disputed Oswine's right to rule Deira and to strengthen his own claim married Edwin's daughter *Eanflæd in 643. In 651, after Oswine had refused to engage a large army raised by the Bernician king, Oswiu ordered the murder of his rival. The act failed to secure him Deira which passed to his nephew Oethelwald who may have had support from King Penda of Mercia. In 655, after Mercian forces had pillaged Bernicia, Oswiu

killed Penda in battle near the river *Winwæd* in South Yorkshire. Oswiu appointed his son Alhfrith as sub-king in Deira, and Penda's son Peada (who had become his son-in-law, *c.*653) as sub-king in southern Mercia. When Peada was murdered one year later, Oswiu extended direct rule to the whole kingdom until Mercian *ealdormen revolted and set up Penda's youngest son, *Wulfhere, as king in 658. Although Bede describes this as the period when Oswiu was ruler of all the southern kingdoms there is no evidence to substantiate the claim, but it was doubtless the time when his influence was greatest. In the north his authority reached the Firth of Forth, for according to an entry in the *Historia Brittonum* Oswiu took refuge at *urbs Iudeu* (possibly Stirling) sometime before the battle at *Winwæd.* However, there is no support for Bede's claim that he made tributary the Scots of Dal Riada. The decision by Oswiu's predecessor, King Oswald, to invite Gaelic missionaries to Northumbria had resulted in the introduction of usages which *Rome considered to be irregular. This led to divisions within Oswiu's kingdom, for while he observed Gaelic practices his wife, Eanflæd, and his son, Alhfrith, conformed to the teachings of Rome. Alhfrith may have attempted to exploit the issues to detach Deira from Oswiu's overkingship; if so his attempt was unsuccessful. In 664 Oswiu convened a synod at *Whitby to resolve, among other matters, the *Easter controversy, and decided in favour of Rome. He died of natural causes in 670.

Bede, *HE* iii.14, 24–9; Kirby, *Kings*, pp. 92–104.

PHILIP HOLDSWORTH

OTLEY (Yorks.) was an estate of the see of *York by the tenth and probably the late ninth century. Its importance as a religious centre is proved by its two great Anglian *crosses, one probably late eighth century and the other ninth, and by some Anglo-Danish grave-slabs (see *grave-markers). The *iconography of the crosses is strongly evangelistic, suggesting that Otley may have been a minster of pastorally-active clergy under the archbishop's control.

R. Cramp, 'The Position of the Otley Crosses in English Sculpture of the Eighth to Ninth Centuries', *Kolloquium über Spätantike und frühmittelalterliche Skulptur* 2 (Mainz, 1970), 55–63; I. Wood, 'Anglo-Saxon Otley: an Archiepiscopal Estate and its Crosses in a Northumbrian Context', *NH* 23 (1987), 20–38.

JOHN BLAIR

OXFORD occurs, in late sources, as a double monastery ruled by the royal abbess Frithuswith (trad. d. 727). Her church stands at the Thames-

Cherwell confluence, overlooking the 'oxen-ford' which carried long-distance traffic from central *Mercia to *Southampton. Excavation has revealed eighth-century activity at the head of the crossing, which probably had a causeway or *bridge. A fortified planned *town, encapsulating the minster, was laid out in the 890s (fig. 19): a coin of *Alfred was minted at Oxford, and the *Burghal Hidage lists it with an assessment of 1300 or 1500 *hides. From the late tenth century the town grew rapidly; by the Conquest it was a centre of commercial and political importance, and had already spread outside the original walls. Excavation has revealed sections of the original timber-faced bank and street-surfaces, as well as dense groups of early eleventh-century cellar-pits on the commercial frontages.

Blair, *AS Oxon*, pp. 52–4, 61–3, 87–92, 99–101, 145–70.

JOHN BLAIR

P

PAGANISM. The Germanic tribes who came to Britain shared the system of beliefs and mythology (ultimately deriving from Indo-European) which Christians called heathenism or paganism. Since they were then illiterate, contemporary Anglo-Saxon textual evidence for paganism is lacking, and we are mainly dependent upon references, often incidental, by later, Christian writers. It is unsafe to take the much later sophisticated Norse mythology as applicable to pagan England several centuries earlier, except where it confirms our deductions from the limited local evidence.

Four gods' names are found in the days of the week (replacing Roman gods): Tiw (or Tig), Woden, Thunor, and the goddess Frig (or Freo); they also occur in English *place-names, but only in the south, the south-east and the Midlands. Only Woden is mentioned in Old English texts (often as the ancestor of nearly all the royal lines, once in poetry compared to the Christian God, once in a charm acting as a magician), and is the most frequent in place-names, often combined with words for man-made objects, for example, a mound (e.g. Wenslow = *Wodnes-hlaw*), as well as with words for natural features such as clearings in *woodland (e.g. Wensley = *Wodnes-leah*). Names with Thunor (a thunder god) resemble Woden names (e.g. Thunderlow, Thunderley), but are not found in Anglian areas. Tiw's name is rarely found in place-names, most probably for a high hill spur at Tysoe in Warwickshire; it is cognate with that of Zeus, but in Tuesday was equated with Mars, a war god. Frig's name occurs only once in a reliable early form, in Friden, for a Derbyshire valley. Since these theophorous place-names sometimes occur within a few miles of each other, they may represent cultic sanctuaries. Two place-name elements (never combined with words for man-made objects, but with a similar distribution to the 'god's name' sites) appear to have been used for pagan shrines, perhaps shared between several deities. *Hearh* usually appears in modern English as Harrow, often combined with words for 'hill'; it may have indicated a tribal sanctuary, perhaps (on the evidence of etymology) centred upon stone altars or idols. In Old English texts the word *wig/ weoh* was used for 'idol'; in modern place-names it appears as Wye (e.g. in *Kent), or as Wee (as in Weedon, Northants.); some sites were on low-lying ground; most are close to Roman *roads and may have been road-side shrines.

All these sanctuaries deduced from place-names (or by Blair at square-ditched or fenced enclosures) may have been open air. However, a small sturdy building excavated at *Yeavering in Northumberland may have been a temple, since it had contained three free-standing wooden pillars and a pit filled with heads of oxen, but no domestic rubbish. Letters from popes to England during the *conversion envisaged temples as buildings, and *Bede related that a chief priest who turned against his gods (on the pragmatic grounds that the king favoured others over him), mounted a stallion and armed himself (actions forbidden to priests), and threw a spear into the temple at Goodmanham (Yorks.), which was afterwards burnt, with its enclosures. Another priest mentioned in *Stephen of Ripon's *Life of Wilfrid* acted more as a magician (see *magic).

In his *De temporum ratione* Bede devotes a chapter to the pre-Christian English calendar, which was luni-solar (like the modern Jewish calendar), and referred to various festivals which he may have heard about from oral tradition. Some kind of harvest festival may have been celebrated in *Halegmonath* (September), 'the month of sacred observances'. The year began on 25 December, which the pagans called *Modranect*, 'the night of the mothers', and since mother goddesses are known among the continental Germans and Celts, Bede's conjecture of an overnight ceremony is feasible. However, no evidence exists for an English word *sol* meaning 'cakes' which Bede says were offered to the gods in *Solmonath* (more or less equivalent to February); the goddesses from whom *Hrethmonath* (March), and *Eosturmonath* (April) were named were probably imaginary; and 'the month of sacrifices' (November), *Blotmonath* in some manuscripts, might have been *Blodmonath*, 'bloodmonth', with reference to blood puddings, eaten after the autumn slaughter of beasts.

A few archaeological artifacts are ornamented with scenes perhaps of ritual dancing. Archaeologists have looked in vain, however, for Anglo-

Saxon pagan shrines within the *cemeteries, though some sites had structures associated with individual graves. Burials were of two kinds: in inhumation graves the bodies were apparently buried in their best clothes, and men's burials were often supplied with weapons. Occasional provision of food or drink may indicate a belief in a continuing existence within the grave, but may have simply shown respect, if the social aspect of the inhumation rite was predominant. Cremation, in which the (again apparently fully-clothed) body was burned on a pyre, and (some of) the ashes usually placed in a decorated urn, may have been for the more convinced pagans, who may have believed that their spirits were carried to an afterlife in the smoke. Animals, whether sacrificed or as part of a funeral feast, are more often associated with cremations than with inhumations, but weapons are exceptional. The idea of a journey after death may also be exemplified in the rare rite of boat burial, for example at *Sutton Hoo.

There is, therefore, very little undoubted evidence for Anglo-Saxon paganism, and we remain ignorant of many of its essential features of organisation and philosophy. Many have assumed animistic beliefs: that the Anglo-Saxons thought the landscape peopled with spirits such as elves, dwarves and *dragons; in view of some place-names and *charms, this may well have been so, but their connection with the deities and with organised worship is problematic (see also *folklore).

G. R. Owen, *Rites and Religions of the Anglo-Saxons* (Newton Abbot, 1981); D. Wilson, *Anglo-Saxon Paganism* (London, 1992); J. Blair, 'Anglo-Saxon Pagan Shrines and their Prototypes', *ASSAH* 8 (1995), 1–28; A. L. Meaney, 'Pagan English Sanctuaries, Place-Names and Hundred Meeting-Places', *ASSAH* 8 (1995), 29–42; R. I. Page, 'Anglo-Saxon Paganism: The Evidence of Bede', in *Pagans and Christians*, ed. T. Hofstra, L. A. J. R. Houwen and A. A. MacDonald, Germania Latina 2 (Groningen, 1995), 99–129; R. North, *Heathen Gods in Old English Literature*, CSASE 22 (Cambridge, 1997).

AUDREY MEANEY

PALAEOGRAPHY: *see* Script

PALLIUM, a white woollen band decorated with six black crosses worn around the neck of the pope and symbolizing his authority, was bestowed by the pope on archbishops as a token of papal authority. The origin of the usage is obscure: the *Liber pontificalis* attributes the ceremony of bestowal to fourth-century popes; but in fact it is securely attested only from the sixth century,

where it is portrayed in mosaics from Ravenna, and only appears in the documentary record from the time of *Gregory the Great. By then it was apparently customary for the bishop of Arles to receive the pallium as symbolizing the extension of papal authority into Gaul; and as *Augustine passed through Arles on his way to Canterbury he will have been aware of the symbolic authority which the pallium entailed. Accordingly, Gregory bestowed the pallium on Augustine (Bede, *HE* i.29), and his successor Pope Honorius (625–38) sent pallia to Archbishops *Honorius of Canterbury (627×631–653) and *Paulinus of York (625–33)(*HE* ii.17, 18). After these precedents it became normal (if not compulsory) for English archbishops to go to Rome to receive the pallium (in itself a reflection of the intimate relationship between the English church and the *papacy); and from the later tenth century there are numerous records of English archbishops travelling to *Rome to obtain the pallium. The understanding was that English archbishops should only wear the pallium on important liturgical feasts (e.g. Christmas, Epiphany, Easter and Pentecost) or for the consecration of bishops, as is made clear in the privilege granted by Pope John XII (955–64) to Archbishop *Dunstan in 960.

DACL xiii.931–40; H. Thurston, *The Pallium* (London [1893]); J. W. Legg, 'The Blessing of the Episcopal Ornament called the Pall', in his *Essays Liturgical and Historical* (London, 1917), pp. 108–56; Plummer, *VBOH* ii. 49–52; *Councils & Synods* i.88–92 (no. 25).

MICHAEL LAPIDGE

PAPACY. 'And I say also unto thee, That thou art Peter, and upon this rock I will build my church; and the gates of hell shall not prevail against it. And I will give unto thee the keys of the kingdom of heaven: and whatsoever thou shalt bind on earth shall be bound in heaven: and whatsoever thou shalt loose on earth shall be loosed in heaven' (Matt. XVI.18–19). The bishops of *Rome were the successors of St Peter the Apostle; St *Augustine had been despatched to England by Pope *Gregory the Great; and later popes, bathing in the reflected glory of their distinguished predecessors, personified the source of inspiration and authority for those who practised their faith in the church of the English people. Kings, churchmen, envoys, and many others of lesser degree, travelled from England to Rome for a variety of different reasons. Some were moved to undertake a *pilgrimage in order to visit the shrines of the apostles, or to pass the rest of their lives in their company; some took payments of *alms to Rome, whether for themselves or on behalf of others; some went in search of *relics; and some had a particular advantage to gain from an encounter with the pope. For their part, popes found cause to encourage particular kings and other laymen to conduct their lives in the appropriate manner, to remind them of their obligations, and to insist that they respect the rights and privileges of the church; or they were moved to give advice to archbishops and bishops on matters of particular concern, or more generally to investigate the state of the English church. Popes also had the authority if not always the inclination to modify the organisation of the church, in response to changing circumstances; they granted the licence, in the form of the *pallium, which empowered an archbishop to consecrate other bishops; and they could be prevailed upon to make general grants of privileges, for example in favour of particular persons (affirming their rights in respect of a religious house), or in favour of particular religious houses (affirming freedom of abbatial election, protecting a house and its estates from any form of external interference, and extending other desirable immunities). Yet these are only the more obvious aspects of a relationship which in truth went to the core of religion and learning in Anglo-Saxon England: whatever articulates is merely symbolic of the English debt to 'Rome'.

In the period which in retrospect is identified as the age of the *conversion, relations between England and the papacy were close, verging on intense. The correspondence of Pope Gregory the Great (590–604) reveals his abiding concern for the people conceived by him as the *'English people' (gens Anglorum). Letters addressed by Pope Gregory to King *Æthelberht of Kent (and to his wife, Bertha) and by Pope Boniface V (619–25) to King *Edwin of Northumbria (and to his wife Æthelburh) illustrate how the pressure was applied. After a period of diversions and distractions, proceedings at the Synod of *Whitby in 664 were settled in Rome's favour by an affirmation of the Lord's mandate to St Peter (Stephen of Ripon, Vita S. Wilfridi, c. 10; Bede, HE iii.25). The decisive event was, however, the outcome of an accident of death. The priest Wigheard had journeyed to Rome in order to fetch his pallium, but died there, of the plague; whereupon Pope Vitalian (657–72), having despatched a holding letter to King *Oswiu of Northumbria (HE iii.29), chose *Theodore as the new archbishop of Canterbury, with far-reaching results (HE iv.1–2). It became increasingly common for the heads of religious houses to secure privileges from Rome, albeit

under different circumstances. *Benedict Biscop obtained one from Pope Agatho (678–81), for his monastery at *Monkwearmouth; *Wilfrid obtained one, also from Agatho, for *Ripon and *Hexham; *Ceolfrith obtained one from Pope Sergius I (687–701), for Monkwearmouth-Jarrow; and Abbot Hædda obtained one from Pope Constantine I (708–15), for Bermondsey and Woking (in Surrey). Other houses which liked to think that they had obtained papal privileges in the late seventh or early eighth century include St Augustine's *Canterbury, *Chertsey, Evesham, St Paul's London, *Malmesbury, and Medeshamstede (Peterborough). By the same token, the roads which led from England to Rome became increasingly busy. Oswiu died in 670, before he could fulfil his intention to end his days in Rome (HE iv.5); *Cædwalla, king of the West Saxons, set off for Rome in 688, and died there in 689 (HE v.7); Coenred, king of the Mercians, and Offa, king of the East Saxons, followed suit in 709 (HE v. 19); and *Ine, king of the West Saxons, resigned his throne in 726 and went to Rome, where he is presumed to have died (HE v.7). Indeed, it is likely that it was the popularity of *pilgrimage to Rome that led, during the course of the eighth century, to the establishment of the colony of Englishmen on the Vatican hill, protected by successive popes and known locally as the 'Schola Saxonum'. In 731 Bede, who would have witnessed Abbot Ceolfrith's departure for Rome in 716 (HA, cc. 15–23), put his own feelings into his extended account of Pope Gregory the Great (HE ii.1); and just as this passage served thereafter as a model of episcopal virtue, so too did the Historia ecclesiastica itself serve to formulate the view from Jarrow of a people's debt to Rome.

The maintenance of good relations with the papacy was no less important to the English during the period of Mercian supremacy in the eighth and early ninth centuries. It was *Boniface who pushed for reform in the mid-740s, duly implemented at the council of *Clofesho in 747 and at Gumley in 749; but one suspects that Pope Zacharias (741–52), and the spirit of Gregory the Great, lay not far behind him. In the mid-780s King *Offa found that he had need of an archbishop less obstructive than *Jænberht of Canterbury, and sought to make changes; whereupon Pope Hadrian I (772–95) despatched papal legates to England (786), leading to the elevation of *Lichfield to archiepiscopal status and to the coronation of Offa's son Ecgfrith (787). It is significant in the same connection that Offa and his wife *Cynethryth secured from Pope Hadrian special privileges in respect of a number of religious houses, all of which were dedicated to St Peter. Matters became more complex during the reign of *Coenwulf, king of the Mercians (796–821), the pontificate of Pope Leo III (796–816), and the archiepiscopate of *Wulfred (805–32). Canterbury recovered its former status in 803; certain monasteries, such as *Glastonbury, *Abingdon and *Winchcombe, gained (or claim to have gained) useful or distinctive privileges; and both king and archbishop were determined to have their own way. When Eardwulf, king of the Northumbrians, was driven from his kingdom, in 806, he went first to Charlemagne at Nijmegen and then on to Leo in Rome; he returned to Northumbria in 808, accompanied by a papal envoy, identified as a 'Saxon' deacon called Aldulf, and by two of Charlemagne's abbots (*Royal Frankish Annals*, s.a. 808, 809). Little is known of the circumstances behind these remarkable events; but letters from Pope Leo to Charlemagne, written in 808, hint at the complications. In 824 Pope Eugene II (824–7) was represented at a council of *Clofesho* by an envoy called Nothhelm (S 1433), who to judge from his name was (like Aldwulf before him) of English origin. Perhaps it was papal practice to recruit envoys to England from the 'Schola Saxonum' in Rome.

The rulers of the West Saxons in the ninth century, and their successors in the tenth and eleventh centuries, were no less eager to seek help and advantage from Rome at every opportunity. King *Ecgberht may have planned to go there in 839, only to be prevented from doing so by his death. King *Æthelwulf sent his son Alfred to Rome in 853; he travelled there himself in 855, taking Alfred with him; and he made generous provision for Rome in his will. Pope John VIII (872–82) told Burgred, king of the Mercians, that the *Viking invasions were punishment for the sins of his people (*EHD* i, no. 220); and when Burgred was deposed, in 874, he went to Rome with Queen Æthelswith (Alfred's sister) and was buried there 'in the church of St Mary in the English quarter' (*ASC*). Pope John also wrote to Æthelred, archbishop of Canterbury, urging him to stand up to King *Alfred (*EHD* i, no. 222); and it seems that he wrote at the same time to Alfred himself, urging the king to be obedient to the archbishop. In 883 Alfred sent alms to Pope Marinus I (882–4), and asked him to free the 'English School' from taxation; and he made regular payments of alms to Rome in the later 880s. Like John before him, Pope Formosus (891–6) seems to have taken a close interest in

the state of the English church; the division of the West Saxon bishoprics in 909 was perhaps the belated response. Relations between the English church and the papacy in the tenth century have, however, left less of a trace than one might expect. Archbishop Wulfhelm went to Rome in 927, for his pallium; but when Bishop Ælfsige did the same, in 958, he froze to death in the Alps (*Vita S. Dunstani*, c. 26). In 963 Pope John XII (955–64) authorised the ejection of secular clergy from the Old Minster, *Winchester, and the monks of Glastonbury claimed to have a privilege from John XIII (965–72); but in other respects the reform movement made its own way forward. In 990–1 Pope John XV (985–96) instigated a peace process between England and *Normandy, and it was also a Pope John who at about this time wrote to Ealdorman Ælfric, castigating him for injuring Glastonbury abbey (*EHD* i, no. 231). There were still many who travelled to Rome for their different reasons, though kings were not among them. The pattern was broken, however, in 1027, when King *Cnut went to Rome for the coronation of the emperor Conrad II by Pope John XIX (1024–32); and the impression of a king still learning the rules of Christian kingship emerges from his expressed wish to inform the people that he had gone to Rome because he had learnt from wise men of the powers given by the Lord to St Peter, 'and thus more especially I considered it very profitable to seek diligently his special advocacy with God' (*Letter of 1027*).

If it seems that the relationship between England and the papacy had long been allowed to fester, a change took place during the pontificate of the reforming Pope Leo IX (1049–54). There were English representatives at the synod of Rheims convened by Leo in 1049; English chroniclers began to take more consistent notice of papal succession; and there was a renewed enthusiasm among churchmen for obtaining privileges from Rome. Leo himself granted a papal privilege to Ælfwine, abbot of *Ramsey; Pope Victor II (1055–7) issued privileges for Chertsey and *Ely, and also (it seems) for St Mary's, Stow; Pope Nicholas II (1058–61) issued privileges for *Giso, bishop of Wells, and for Wulfwig, bishop of Dorchester; and Pope Alexander II (1061–73) granted another privilege to Abbot Ælfwine. It is all the more striking, of course, that this flurry of activity coincided with the archiepiscopate of Stigand, who displaced Archbishop Robert in 1052, who received the pallium from the antipope Benedict X (1058–9), and who in these and other respects provided the papacy with a pretext for its support of *William, duke of Normandy, in 1066.

In 1839 John Mitchell *Kemble planned to produce an edition of papal privileges, but the plan came to nothing. It is a subject which would respond well to further investigation.

J. N. D. Kelly, *The Oxford Dictionary of Popes* (Oxford, 1986); W. J. Moore, *The Saxon Pilgrims to Rome and the Schola Saxonum* (Fribourg, 1937); W. Levison, 'England and the Church of Rome', in his *England and the Continent in the Eighth Century* (Oxford, 1946), pp. 15–44; J. M. Wallace-Hadrill, 'Rome and the Early English Church: Some Questions of Transmission' (1960), in his *Early Medieval History* (Oxford, 1975), pp. 115–37; M. Deanesly, 'The Anglo-Saxon Church and the Papacy', *The English Church and the Papacy in the Middle Ages*, ed. C. H. Lawrence (London, 1965), pp. 31–62; F. Barlow, *The English Church 1000–1066*, 2nd ed. (London, 1979), pp. 289–308; V. Ortenberg, *The English Church and the Continent in the Tenth and Eleventh Centuries* (Oxford, 1992), pp. 127–96.

SIMON KEYNES

PARASITES are organisms which live temporarily or permanently within (endoparasites) or upon (ectoparasites) the body of another organism, known as the host. They derive nourishment from the host but do not provide any benefits; they may damage bodily functions and cause death. Parasitism can occur among all groups of infective agents such as fungi, worms, bacteria, viruses, arthropods, protozoa and helminths and it can cause disease in humans and non-humans; humans contract many parasitic diseases from animals (zoonoses). The transition to *agriculture in all parts of the world appears to have increased parasitic disease.

Helminths (worms) are the commonest endoparasite, with different types apparent: trematodes (flukes – e.g. schistosomiasis or bilharzia, spread via infected freshwater), cestodes (tapeworm – e.g. echinococcus, or dog and cat tapeworm, transmitted through fur or contaminated food and water), acancephalans (thorny headed worm) and nematodes (round worm – e.g. filiariasis, transmitted by mosquitoes). Most archaeoparasitological work is concerned with helminths and arthropod parasites and, to a lesser extent, fungal disease. Head and body lice, fleas, bedbugs, mosquitoes, mites and ticks can all be responsible for the transmission of parasitic infection. Protozoa, or unicellular animals, may also cause a variety of conditions ranging from toxoplasmosis (a common parasite of birds and mammals and contracted by humans from raw or undercooked

meat) to leishmaniasis (a skin disease transmitted to humans by sandflies).

Most parasitic diseases do not cause any specific skeletal damage and have soft tissue involvement only. However, in the later stages of some conditions, for example toxoplasmosis and leishmaniasis, the skeleton may be affected, and in the fungal diseases such as blastomycosis (contracted via the skin and respiratory tract), where the spine and ribs are primarily involved, the skeletal abnormalities may be easily detected.

Direct evidence for the parasites themselves in archaeological contexts is found in coprolites often in dry environments, the intestinal contents of bodies (e.g. bog bodies of Europe), latrine and cess deposits, and in preserved hair and combs. Preservation depends on the condition of the containing deposits. Unless parasites are found undisturbed within a human body it may be difficult to determine whether they are of human origin. Little research on archaeoparasitology has been undertaken to date worldwide, and even less on Anglo-Saxon contexts, although published work illustrates human infestation with intestinal parasites (on the basis of pit fills), and lice, in many contexts of late Saxon date from Coppergate, *York; in addition, contemporary documentary sources make reference to intestinal worms and to the treatment of the sheep liver fluke.

R. J. Donaldson, *Parasites and Western Man* (Lancaster, 1979); A. K. G. Jones, 'Human Parasitic Remains: Prospects for a Quantitative Approach', in *Environmental Archaeology in the Urban Context*, ed. A. R. Hall and H. K. Kenward (London, 1982), pp. 66–70; H. K. Kenward and A. R. Hall, *Biological Evidence from 16–22 Coppergate. The Archaeology of York. The Environment 14/7* (York, 1995); K. F. Kiple, ed., *The Cambridge World History of Human Disease* (Cambridge, 1993); K. J. Reinhard, 'Archaeoparasitology in North America', *American Journal of Physical Anthropology* 82 (1990), 145–63.

CHARLOTTE A. ROBERTS

PARIS PSALTER: *see* Psalter Glosses

PARKER, MATTHEW (1504–75), archbishop of Canterbury, bequeathed the largest part of his collection of manuscripts to Corpus Christi College, Cambridge, of which he had been Fellow and Master. Three official audit lists of this gift exist; these provide a more or less complete documentation of his library as it was *c.*1574. Not all of his manuscripts, however, went to Corpus: twenty-five were given to the Cambridge University Library and others fetched up elsewhere. In Parker's view the Anglo-Saxon church was much closer to his own reformed church on many doctrinal matters than it was to the church of Rome, and in his letters he referred to the corruption introduced into the indigenous church by the emissaries from Rome. His sizeable collection of Anglo–Saxon manuscripts thus reflected his desire to justify the doctrines of the church of England through appeal to historical precedents. Because they could not be easily read in post-Conquest times, moreover, he considered Old English manuscripts to have been less susceptible to Catholic censorship than were Latin writings. Apart from collecting primary materials (and Stephen Batman, for example, claimed to have gathered at least 6,700 books for him) he instigated and oversaw the publication of polemical texts incorporating Anglo–Saxon materials and was responsible for introducing Anglo–Saxon typeface into printing through his 1566 commission to John Day to print *A Testimonie of Antiquitie*, the first edition of Old English texts. J. Bromwich, 'The First Book Printed in Anglo-Saxon Types', *TCBS* 3 (1959–63), 265–91; J. C. T. Oates, *Cambridge University Library: a History: From the Beginnings to the Copyright Act of Queen Anne* (Cambridge, 1986), pp. 96–110; R. I. Page, *Matthew Parker and His Books* (Kalamazoo, MI, 1993); V. Sanders, 'The Household of Archbishop Parker and the Influencing of Public Opinion', *JEH* 34 (1983), 534–47; S. Strongman, 'John Parker's Manuscripts: an Edition of the Lists in Lambeth Palace MS 737', *TCBS* 7 (1977–80), 1–27.

JAMES P. CARLEY

PAROCHIAL ORGANIZATION of some kind must have existed in pre-Viking England. The lack of references to organized *paganism (as distinct from folk-magic) after the late seventh century, and the apparent impact of Christianity on furnished *cemeteries, suggests that once kings had converted, an infrastructure for establishing formal Christian observance was put in place relatively quickly. That the *laws of *Ine of *Wessex (*c.*700) could impose penalties for neglecting infant baptism suggests high expectations, whatever the reality. Widespread and serious acceptance of Christianity below the top levels may be less unlikely than some have found it: Anglo–Saxon society was hierarchical, and once the aristocracy had converted the imperative to follow one's lord must have been a powerful stimulus (cf. *conversion).

In the theory of the western Church, pastoral care was the work of bishops and of priests under their direction. Prescriptive sources, especially the canons of the 747 *Council of *Clofesho, imply that this was so in England, but how far ideal became reality is another matter. In contrast to the regions of Europe where late Roman adminis-

tration had to some extent survived, and where bishops had a major role in shaping the pastoral structures of their dioceses, there is very little sign that English bishops before the eleventh century exercised much real authority at a local level by virtue of their office alone. Well-documented bishops' careers, above all *Wilfrid's, suggest rather that they built up power through networks of monasteries, which they controlled very much as did kings and nobles.

Indeed, there are strong grounds for thinking that the hundreds of rich *monastic sites, with their complex communities of monks, nuns and priests, were the main foci for pastoral care as they were for all other aspects of ecclesiastical culture. Defining these communities is extremely difficult, and research has been hampered by anachronistic conceptions of what a 'monastery' should be like. In pre-Viking sources the Latin word *monasterium* was used much more broadly than its modern derivative: many modern scholars prefer a less loaded term, 'minster' (from the Old English *mynster*, itself simply a *loan-word from *monasterium*). The fact nonetheless remains that many minsters contained monks, and the extent of their involvement in pastoral care has occasioned much debate. In early England the seclusion of the monastic life always had its ambiguities, not least to *Bede who, though he knew that sacraments were the preserve of ordained priests, set great store by the monastic example to the laity: it is mainly monks whom he presents as models of pastoral diligence. The problem becomes less intractable when we remember that minsters of professed religious also housed priests: even when monks and nuns did not perform pastoral work, they were in a position to organize it.

The few explicit early references show that priests and clerks were envisaged as living in minsters: *Guthlac entered the *Repton community as a clerk; *Ecgberht's *Dialogue* locates *clerici* in *monasteria* and assumes that a priest or deacon needing to travel requires the consent of his *prior*; and canon 29 of the *Clofesho* council in 747 requires clerks, monks and nuns to return to the houses of their profession. Centralised groups of clergy going out to preach in the countryside are sometimes indicated: thus *Willibald's *Life* of *Boniface mentions times when 'priests or clerics went out to preach to the people, as is the custom in those parts, and came to the settlement where his father dwelt'. Whether this already took place within defined territories, the mother-parishes recorded from the tenth century, is controversial. The widespread continuity of site from pre-Viking

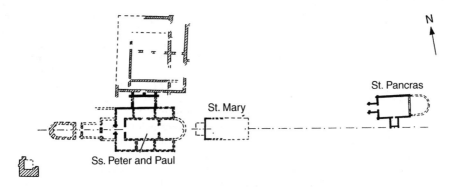

CANTERBURY, ST AUGUSTINE'S

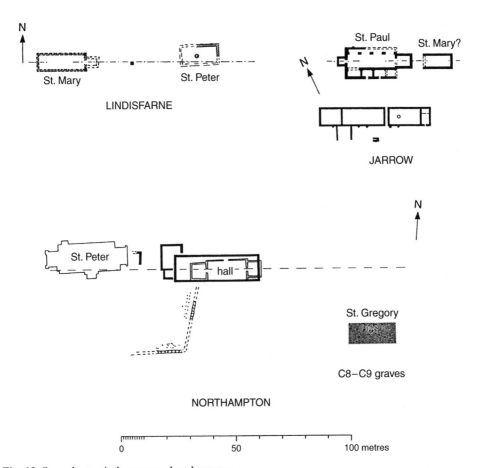

Fig. 13 Seventh- to ninth-century church groups.

minsters to eleventh- and twelfth-century mother-churches (see *monastic sites) points in that direction, and in a world where land-based food-renders (see *feorm) owing to *royal sites were already strictly assessed, an early and precise definition of 'minster parishes' need not have been difficult.

Viking-age devastation is undeniable, yet it was not the only cause of the minsters' decline, nor was it total. On the one hand, the absorption of monastic sites and estates into royal hands had started in the mid-eighth century and was to continue through the tenth; on the other, there is abundant written, topographical and sculptural evidence for Christian continuity on the old minster sites, if at a much reduced level. Monks and nuns were succeeded by groups of priests, many of them still visible in *Domesday Book, onto whom any continuing pastoral duties must have devolved. At the same time, tenth-century kings were becoming more insistent about the parochial duties of the laity. *Æthelstan's first law-code makes tithe payment compulsory, and in a crucial passage *Edgar's second code (959 × 72) enjoins that 'all tithe is to be paid to the old minster to which the obedience (hernes) belongs'; a *thegn who has on his *bookland a church with a graveyard should give it a third of his demesne tithes, but if it has no graveyard he must 'pay to his priest from the [remaining] nine parts what he chooses'. Clearly this buttresses an established system whereby 'old minsters' had vested rights to take the tithes of the laity, and by implication to control their burials.

Why legal defence of these rights should have started to seem necessary is explained by the appearance, also in the mid- to late tenth century, of the first references to *manorial churches in aristocratic *wills, and of the earliest archaeological evidence for village churches and graveyards (for instance *Raunds). The expanding class of manorial gentry were starting to build little churches next to their manor-houses, where they were encouraging their dependants to pay their tithes, to be buried, and presumably to hear mass. In a more developed and manorialised countryside, where nucleated villages and open fields were developing (see *field systems and *settlement patterns), a more localised structure of pastoral care was becoming appropriate for both lords and villagers. Seigneurial patronage was crucial, though the bias of record may have distorted our perceptions: it is quite possible that significant numbers of churches were founded communally

by groups of *peasants. But in either case the trend was to the long-term detriment of the minsters.

Domesday Book (1086) portrays an England containing thousands of local churches and local priests, but the replacement of 'minster parishes' by the local parishes of modern England still had a long way to go. Minsters remained powerful, and at least in some regions new churches could only be built with their consent: the free-for-all in private church-building may only have been gathering momentum from the 1050s. The granting of permanent glebeland (first in *East Anglia), and the widespread replacement of timber or rubble with permanent masonry structures (see *architecture, ecclesiastical), seem also to be features of the eleventh century rather than earlier. Nor can we yet speak of local parishes in a formal institutional sense: manorial churches simply served their lords' lands and tenants, and parish boundaries were not to crystallise until well into the twelfth century.

The presence of so many more locally-based priests must have brought the church's pastoral and sacramental activities closer to the ordinary laity. Yet the new type of priest was characteristically low-status and ignorant – *Ælfric's 'backwoods priest' (uplendisc preost) – and the decline of the cultured and cosmopolitan minsters, the natural ritual and social foci of the pre-Viking countryside, must have left some voids. Christianity for many can have been little more than sacramental, even if creatively fused with an older tradition of folk beliefs with which it was not in inevitable opposition.

Blair and Sharpe, Past. Care; S. Foot, 'Parochial Ministry in Early Anglo-Saxon England: the Role of Monastic Communities', Studies in Church History 26 (1989), 43–54; E. Cambridge and D. Rollason, 'The Pastoral Organization of the Anglo-Saxon Church: a Review of the "Minster Hypothesis" ', EME 4 (1995), 87–104; J. Blair, 'Ecclesiastical Organization and Pastoral Care in Anglo-Saxon England', EME 4 (1995), 193–212; Minsters and Parish Churches: the Local Church in Transition, 950–1200, ed. J. Blair (Oxford, 1988); J. Blair, 'Secular Minster Churches in Domesday Book', Domesday Book: a Reassessment, ed. P. H. Sawyer (London, 1985), pp. 104–42; idem, 'Local Churches in Domesday Book and Before', Domesday Studies, ed. J. C. Holt (Woodbridge, 1987), pp. 265–78; K. L. Jolly, Popular Religion in Late-Saxon England: Elf-Charms in Context (Chapel Hill, NC, 1996).

JOHN BLAIR

PASTORAL CARE: *see* Parochial Organization

PAUL, ST, VISION OF: *see* Apocrypha, Biblical; Visions

PAULINUS, bishop of *York (625–33), was one of the second wave of Roman monks sent to England by Pope *Gregory to reinforce the mission of St *Augustine, arriving with *Mellitus, *Justus and Rufinianus in 601. His activities during his early years in England are unknown (and were presumably spent in *Kent), but when King *Edwin of *Northumbria, then a pagan, sought to marry the Christian princess Æthelburg (daughter of King *Æthelberht of Kent), Æthelburg was permitted to travel north on the condition that she be accompanied by her Christian retinue, that she be allowed to practise her religion, and that Edwin himself consider the possibility of adopting Christianity. Paulinus was consecrated bishop by Archbishop Justus in 625, with the intention that he accompany Æthelburg to Northumbria, and help to establish Christianity in that region (it has also been suggested that he and Æthelburg went north as early as 619, six years before his consecration). He succeeded to the extent that Edwin and his daughter *Eanflæd were baptized at York in 627; this baptism was anticipated by letters addressed by Pope Boniface V (619–25) to both Edwin and Æthelburg (both recorded by Bede, *HE* ii.10–11), and the reflections which led Edwin to convert are symbolically expressed in Bede's memorable anecdote (put in the mouth of one of Edwin's nobles) of the sparrow passing through the hall on a winter's night as a metaphor of human life. Paulinus, in collaboration with his colleague *James the Deacon, was able to baptize many other Northumbrians, once spending thirty-six days with the king and queen at *Yeavering catechizing and baptizing. He was also successful in converting the kingdom of *Lindsey to Christianity, and establishing a church at *Lincoln. Unfortunately Paulinus's Northumbrian mission was terminated by the death of Edwin in battle against *Penda of *Mercia in 633: Æthelburg and Paulinus retreated to Kent (the *pallium sent by Pope Honorius arrived in England too late to be of use), where Paulinus served as bishop of *Rochester until his death on 10 October 644. According to Bede (*HE* ii.16), he was tall with a slight stoop, had black hair, a thin face and hooked nose, and was at once both venerable and terrifying in appearance; but there is no doubt that he was an effective *missionary.

Bede, *HE* i.29, ii.9–20, iii.1, 14; Stenton, *ASE*, pp. 113–16; D. P. Kirby, 'Bede and Northumbrian Chronology', *EHR* 88 (1963), 514–27; P. Hunter Blair, 'The Letters of Pope Boniface V and the Mission of Paulinus to Northumbria', in *England before the Conquest. Studies in Primary Sources presented to Dorothy Whitelock*, ed. P. Clemoes and K. Hughes (Cambridge, 1971), pp. 5–13, repr. in his *Anglo-Saxon Northumbria*, ed. Pauline Hunter Blair and M. Lapidge (London, 1984), no. XI; H. Mayr-Harting, *The Coming of Christianity to Anglo-Saxon England*, 3rd ed. (London, 1991), pp. 66–8.

MICHAEL LAPIDGE

PEASANTS. Anglo-Saxon society was based on *agriculture. By 1086 its farmers were able to produce a surplus capable of supporting an urban population of perhaps one in ten of the total and a non-productive landowning class. *Domesday Book, *charters and *wills are informative about larger landholdings, but the peasant farm is elusive. It is likely, but ultimately unproveable, that the typical early Anglo-Saxon farm was run and owned by a single family and its *slaves. *Bede remarked that the unit of land known as the *hide was considered by the native English to be 'the land of one family' (see also *hide). It is the size and nature of the family that is still in doubt. The eponymous founders or rulers of places with names in *-ingas may have been the heads of large family units or small tribes. Yet it is often individuals, not families, that seem to own the ploughland, woods and valleys that are named in the *charter bounds of the ninth to eleventh centuries. Actual arrangements may have been less individualistic. The primary labour supply on the peasant farm is the peasant family, and to secure this labour family members must have an interest in remaining on the farm. The inheritance customs of free peasants after the Conquest, which may preserve Anglo-Saxon practice, gave all sons rights in the family holding and women members a claim to support from it. On the great estates women worked in dairying and *textile production, but we know very little about the gender division of labour on the peasant farm. It is likely that the family labour supply proved insufficient at times: *Ine's *laws show that *ceorls*, many of whom must have been peasants, commonly employed *slaves and labourers. It is probable that where *settlement was dense enough neighbours were another source of labour. The boon works which became part of tenants' obligations to landlords (see *labour service) may be a relic of older communal obligations to provide mutual help at haymaking and harvest. The evolution of common *field systems was the culmination of co-operative farming.

By 1066 single farms of as much as a hide (later reckoned at *c.*120 acres) were rare and the Domesday entries for Middlesex show that the mass of holdings in that county were of a yardland (quarter of a hide) or half a yardland. Slaves' plots and the holdings of particularly dependent tenants were smaller. The farms of independent peasants may have been much larger, as would farms with their own pasture land, such as those in the west country and upland regions. As far as Domesday yields figures for the size of holdings, they seem to have been particularly large in Gloucestershire, Herefordshire and Worcestershire and particularly small in the eastern coastal counties south of the Humber. Some peasants became dependent tenants, taking on landholdings for which they owed rent in kind and in labour on the inland of the lord of a bookland estate: such were the people known as *geburas* (see *manors and manorial lordship). Independent farmers, perhaps the majority, formed the largest group in the class of people known as *ceorls*, with a *wergild of two hundred shillings, the obligation to pay tax and perform public duties such as *bridge and *fortification work, and the right to participate in the public *courts.

As revealed by archaeology, early Anglo-Saxon settlers appear typically to have established themselves in small groups of farmsteads (see *settlement patterns), but *place- and field-names indicate that the discrete farm, although as yet little investigated, was important too. The *timber buildings on sites such as *Mucking (Essex) fall into two broad types: the residential 'hall' and the 'sunken-featured building' which has been assigned a variety of functions: storage, textile production, possibly slaves' housing. Earlier views that the settlers were pioneers of land clearance are now discarded, and they seem often to have picked sites which had been intensively cultivated by the British; but the settlement period may have seen some fall-back in production and an increase in pastoralism.

Early settlements were unstable, shifting over an area as buildings decayed, were abandoned and rebuilt elsewhere. Possibly encouraged by the advent of a more benign climate from around the year 800, settlement seems to have stabilised. Population increase would explain much that happens about this time, but we have no direct evidence. In some areas the separate fields of discrete farmsteads began to be combined in common field systems. This made it necessary to resite the farm buildings in nucleated settlements – the forebears of the village. Both seigneurial and peasant initiative have been proposed as the major influence behind this development: where the lord's land was integrated with peasant field systems, both may have been at work. Villages

and common-field agriculture were not universal: there were field systems which were a mixture of enclosed and common and in many areas isolated farmsteads or small hamlets and agriculture carried out in individual enclosed fields have remained the norm until the present day. Whatever the field system, communally-used pasture and *woodland were an important supplement to the arable surrounding the settlement.

Perhaps the most useful piece of equipment on the Anglo-Saxon farm was the slave. It is only on the large estate, where they were specialist stock and dairy workers, that we know what jobs slaves did, and we do not know what the specifically 'slave-work' of the laws was, but there was no shortage of heavy manual and dirty labour on the Anglo-Saxon farm, such as ditching and spreading animal and human manure on the fields.

Improved methods of exploiting animal power, especially the heavy wheeled plough which replaced the scratch plough or ard, and the collar which replaced the throat harness, were widespread in western Europe by the ninth century. Domesday Book assumes an eight-ox team and seems to measure land in terms of the number of such teams that would be required to plough it, but heavy ploughs and large teams may have been only those which belonged to lords, or were at work on his land: actual peasant ploughs and plough-teams were probably smaller. (Thus most peasants are recorded as owning only a fraction of a team.) Well-off farmers, whose social ranking would put them among those responsible for services involving long-distance droving, carrying messages and so on, may well have owned horses, and there was a category of people – whether affluent peasant or the lowest class of landowner is a moot point – known as 'riding-men' who certainly did.

The skills of drainage and water management were evidently understood. *Mills are documented from the ninth century as appurtenances of royal and ecclesiastical estates. Those serving a peasant community are harder to detect but just over a quarter of the settlements recorded in Domesday had a mill. These were watermills: windmills were not introduced until the late twelfth century. Much peasant corn must have been milled by hand, in querns or between small flat millstones.

When the laws of the sixth and seventh century refer to *trade it appears to involve local transactions and itinerant traders rather than organised *markets. Fair dealing is ensured by witness. The exception is *London, where Kentishmen were trading in the seventh century. London (the

Strand and Aldwich areas) is an example of a *wic*. *Wics* fall into the category of *emporia*, markets which were stages in long-distance, large-scale trading systems. Another was *Hamwic* (*Southampton), a trading settlement from which cattle were exported in the eighth century, in numbers large enough to suggest the existence of specialist producers. It had a market area which had regularly laid out streets and plots and hence some overall planning. From the tenth century 'ports' – small market towns, or large market villages – appear in the laws. They were protected by the king, who profited from the tolls levied on their traders, they had market officers, and trading and minting were officially confined to them. This is not to say that informal trade between farmers, or with itinerant traders, did not continue.

When the laws refer to trade it is generally in cattle, a valuable commodity. There is not likely to have been either a purely pastoral or a purely arable peasant economy anywhere in pre-Conquest England, but the small amount of archaeological evidence shows some specialisation in stock farming, such as for sheep in East Anglia. The size, sex and age of animals in bone assemblages are a guide to consumption on higher status or urban sites: these were produced by peasant farmers whose own consumption patterns may have differed but they show cattle, sheep, and pigs bred for the market. The peasant economy was supplemented by by-occupations and while the products of some of these, like *fishing and *fowling, probably went on mainly to vary the diet, others like salt and lead working were part of a small industrial sector. Markets of all kinds are testimony to the ability of late Anglo-Saxon agriculture to produce a surplus, but we do not know what proportion of that surplus was produced on the great estates, and what by peasant farmers.

R. Faith, *The English Peasantry and the Growth of Lordship* (London, 1997), chs. 4–5; P. J. Fowler, 'Agriculture and Rural Settlement', in Wilson, *Archaeology*, pp. 23–48; *Environment and Economy in Anglo-Saxon England*, ed. J. Rackham, CBA Research Report 89 (London, 1994); C. Scull, 'Archaeology, Early Anglo-Saxon Society and the Origins of Anglo-Saxon Kingdoms', *ASSAH* 6 (1993), 1–18.

ROSAMOND FAITH

PEGA, ST (d. *c.*719), sister of St *Guthlac, lived as an anchoress at Peakirk (Northants.), only a short distance from Guthlac's hermitage at Crowland. The Life of Guthlac, our only source of information about Pega, describes how, at her brother's summons, she sailed down the river Welland to his funeral (d. 714). She then set out on a *pilgrimage to *Rome and died there. Her feast was kept on 8 January at Crowland.

B. Colgrave, ed. and trans., *Felix's Life of St Guthlac* (Cambridge, 1956).

R. C. LOVE

PENANCE: *see* Confession and Penance; Penitentials

PENDA (son of Pybba), pagan king of *Mercia (*c.*632–55), and scourge of Christian kings and kingdoms; perhaps the most powerful Southumbrian ruler of the seventh century. A West Saxon chronicler, writing in the late ninth century, believed that Penda reigned for 30 years, putting his accession in 626, and adding (somewhat improbably) that he was then 50 years old. The chronicler states further that Penda fought against Cynegils and Cwichelm at *Cirencester in 628, perhaps representing a decisive stage in the extension of Mercian control over the *Hwicce. *Bede, on the other hand, implies that Penda did not become king until the early 630s. In his view, Penda was 'a most energetic member of the royal house of the Mercians', who had supported Cadwallon, king of Gwynedd, in the defeat of King *Edwin at the battle of Hatfield in 633, and who from about that time ruled over his kingdom for 22 years, 'with varying success' (*HE* ii.20). Penda was the first of the succession of Mercian overlords who were dominant south of the Humber in the seventh, eighth and early ninth centuries; for while it is difficult in his case to do much more than draw general inferences from the particular incidents registered by Bede, there can be no doubt that his power and influence were felt widely outside his own kingdom. In 645, when Cenwealh, king of the West Saxons, repudiated his wife (Penda's sister), Penda attacked and drove him out of his kingdom (*HE* iii.7; *ASC*). Penda also had occasion to attack *East Anglia, causing the death of Sigeberht, formerly king of the East Angles, and of King Ecgric; he attacked again in 654, leading to the death of King Anna (*HE* iii.18). Yet the point of balance between the dominant political powers in the seventh century lay along the line of the Humber estuary, and Penda's attention was thus directed in particular towards the kingdom of *Northumbria. According to a ninth-century Welsh source, Penda was the first to 'separate' the kingdom of the Mercians from the kingdom of the Northerners (**Historia Brittonum*, c. 65), which may indicate that he was seen by the

Welsh as one who had asserted Mercian resistance to predatory Northumbrian overlords. On 5 August 642 Penda defeated *Oswald, king of the Northumbrians, at the battle of *Maserfelth* [Oswestry?] (*HE* iii.9); Penda's brother Eowa is said to have died in the same battle (*Historia Brittonum*, c. 65). Penda was at the head of a Mercian army which ravaged Northumbria later in the 640s, while *Aidan was still bishop of *Lindisfarne (635–51), reaching on that occasion as far north as Bamburgh itself (*HE* iii. 16); and he ravaged Northumbria again a few years later, while Finan was bishop (651–61), affording another opportunity for thaumaturgical display (*HE* iii.17). In 655 Penda went north yet again; and although *Oswiu offered to pay tribute, Penda was determined to destroy the Northumbrian people. In the event, Penda was defeated and killed at the battle of the *Winwæd* (an unidentified river in the vicinity of Leeds, conceivably the river Went), with thirty 'royal *ealdormen' (*duces regii*), including Æthelhere, king of the East Angles, and doubtless other leaders of the various peoples in the Mercian confederacy (*HE* iii.24; *Historia Brittonum*, c. 64). Penda's role in Bede's *Historia ecclesiastica* was essentially to act as an instrument of pagan aggression; yet Bede admitted that Penda did not forbid preaching of the faith in his own kingdom (*HE* iii.21), and it may be that the truth was more complex. Penda had placed his son Peada over the *Middle Angles, who soon embraced Christianity under Northumbrian influence (*HE* iii.21); in 655, after the battle of the *Winwæd*, Oswiu gave the kingdom of the southern Mercians to Peada (*HE* iii.24), but soon afterwards Peada was killed. Penda was succeeded in Mercia by his younger sons *Wulfhere (658–75) and Æthelred (675–704). Merewalh, ruler of the *Magonsætan*, is also said to have been Penda's son, perhaps by an earlier marriage.

Stenton, *ASE*, pp. 81–4; P. H. Sawyer, *From Roman Britain to Norman England* (London, 1978), pp. 31–2, 38–9; N. Brooks, 'The Formation of the Mercian Kingdom', in Bassett, *Origins*, pp. 159–70, at 164–70; M. Gelling, *The West Midlands in the Early Middle Ages* (Leicester, 1992), pp. 77–9; Yorke, *Kingdoms*, pp. 103–11; Kirby, *Kings*, pp. 81–96; N. J. Higham, *An English Empire: Bede and the Early Anglo-Saxon Kings* (Manchester, 1995).

SIMON KEYNES

PENITENTIALS or handbooks of penance are catalogues listing sins and the penances assigned to each by the priest in confession. In manuscript form, penitentials survive more often as parts of larger codices rather than as the small, self-contained handbooks presumably common in the Middle Ages, although a few handbook-sized manuscripts do exist. Penitentials appear to have originated in Ireland and reached England through the work of Irish *missionaries. By the late seventh century, the handbook was recognized in England as an important pastoral text. *Theodore of *Canterbury was the first non-Irish authority to issue a penitential; early handbooks attributed to other English ecclesiastics (e.g. to *Ecgberht and *Bede) suggest that the form was quickly assimilated into the disciplinary literature of the English church. During the ninth century, penitentials of Irish origin were the subject of prolonged controversy on the Continent, but disputes about the orthodoxy of private penance and the literature that regulated it do not appear in English records.

Penitentials in Anglo-Saxon England were written in both Latin and the vernacular (the Latin texts being more numerous) and took various forms; those with elaborate prefatory apparatus circulated alongside those which merely listed tariffs for sins. Four Anglo-Saxon vernacular texts can be distinguished, although only three are well attested: the *Confessionale Pseudo-Egberti*, the *Poenitentiale Pseudo-Egberti*, 'A Late OE Handbook for the Use of a Confessor'; and the 'Canons of Theodore'. The 'Canons of Theodore' exist in complete form in two manuscripts and as a fragment in a third manuscript. This text is a translation of parts of the two-book form of the Penitential of Theodore; it lacks introductory matter for the priest that is found in the other three texts.

Found in a small number of important eleventh-century manuscripts, the vernacular texts are anonymous. Dating from the tenth and eleventh centuries, they list penances largely identical to those found in eighth-century Latin texts. Since it is expected that penitential tariffs would have been revised as the handbooks passed from region to region and century to century, this uniformity is significant. It is possible that the conservatism of the system is primarily a feature of textual culture and that in practice penances were adjusted within limits sometimes specified in the texts. It is also possible that variations within penitential standards were not as great across time as might be assumed.

England was second only to Ireland in developing a vernacular literature of penance built around the private penitential system. In addition to the penitentials there are confessional prayers, liturgies, and other forms, including homilies, *laws, and clerical letters, which quote the penitentials or share textual sources with them. The Anglo-Saxons seem to have been the first to organize comprehensive collections which included penitentials, ceremonies for public penance, and confessional prayers, and to excerpt these sources to form collections for devotional reading and instruction (e.g. *Ælfric's collection at the end of Cambridge, UL, Gg.3.28).

R. Fowler, 'A Late OE Handbook for the Use of a Confessor', *Anglia* 83 (1965), 1–34; A. J. Frantzen, 'The Tradition of Penitentials in Anglo-Saxon England', *ASE* 11 (1983), 23–56; F. J. Mone, *Quellen und Forschungen zur Geschichte der teutschen Literatur und Sprache* (Aachen and Leipzig, 1830), pp. 514–28 [The Canons of Theodore]; J. Raith, ed., *Das altenglische Version des Halitgar'schen Bussbuches (sog. Poenitentiale Pseudo-Egberti)* (Hamburg, 1933); R. Spindler, ed., *Das altenglische Bussbuch (sog. Confessionale Pseudo-Egberti)*. (Leipzig, 1934); B. Thorpe, *Ancient Laws and Institutes of England*, 2 vols. (London, 1840), ii.228–31, 232–9 [Canons of Theodore]; C. Vogel, *Les 'Libri Paenitentiales'*, Typologie des sources du moyen âge occidental 27 (Turnhout, 1978; corr. and rev. A. J. Frantzen, 1985); T. Charles-Edwards, 'The Penitential of Theodore and the *Iudicia Theodori*', in *Archbishop Theodore*, ed. M. Lapidge, CSASE 11 (Cambridge, 1995), 141–74.

ALLEN J. FRANTZEN

PERSONAL NAMES, CELTIC, like Germanic names, may be either monothematic or dithematic. In Anglo-Saxon sources they occur in two main contexts: Anglo-Saxon royal *genealogies, towards their heads; and named immigrants from Celtic lands (primarily, though not solely, clerics, and particularly from Ireland). The royal dynasty of *Wessex traced its line back through *Cerdic (Neo-Brittonic *Ceredig*); he was supposed to have come to Britain with his son Cynric, in the late fifth or early sixth century, with five ships. The arrival from overseas is unlikely for someone with a Brittonic name; it may be an attempt to disguise a Brittonic ancestry. A later ruler of the same dynasty (late seventh century) had the Brittonic name *Cædwalla (Welsh *Cadwallon*), although intervening and subsequent rulers bore English names. These and a few other such names suggest intermarriage between early English rulers and native Britons; an attested example is Rieinmelth, a wife of *Oswiu, king of *Northumbria 654–70 (Welsh *rhiain* 'maiden' + *mellt* 'lightning'). The case of the poet *Cædmon (British *Catumandos*) shows that such names could also extend lower down the social scale, though wider evidence is lacking. In general, Brittonic personal names, never common, seem to occur in English contexts down to the seventh century, and rarely after that

date. There are also some names which have no clear derivation within either Germanic or Celtic; the best explanation is that they were based on the first syllables of Brittonic names, but took on a life of their own as Old English ones (undergoing English sound-changes, such as palatalisation of c). An example is *Ceadda* or *Cedda*, possibly based on Brittonic *Cad-* ('battle-'), as in names such as *Cadwallon* (but not found as a monothematic name in Brittonic). These names appear, not only as those of non-royal Englishmen, but also in place-names. Similarly the name *Penda does not appear to be native English, and it has been suggested that it could be an abbreviated form of an early Welsh name, or perhaps of a title such as *Pendevic* 'ruler'.

The most famous Irish cleric in England is probably the *Maeldub* who was believed to have founded *Malmesbury (*Maildufi urbs*, Bede); others include three Irishmen, named as *Dubslane*, *Machbethu* and *Maelinmum*, who came ashore in a boat on the Cornish coast in 891 according to the *Anglo-Saxon Chronicle*; and an eighth-century abbot of Evesham called *Credan* (probably Old Irish *Crítán*). However, the best-known Welsh cleric who lived in England, *Asser, had an Old Testament, not a Brittonic name; the Book of Llandaf shows further examples of this name in south Wales in the ninth to eleventh centuries, and other instances of biblical names (such as that of St David) also occur.

The Text of the Book of Llan Dâv, ed. J. G. Evans and J. Rhys (Oxford, 1893), Index; M. A. O'Brien, 'Old Irish Personal Names', *Celtica* 10 (1973), 211–36; D. N. Dumville, 'The Anglian Collection of Royal Genealogies and Regnal Lists' (1976), and 'Kingship, Genealogies and Regnal Lists' (1977), repr. in his *Histories and Pseudo-Histories of the Insular Middle Ages* (Aldershot, 1990), chs. V, XV; idem, 'The West Saxon Genealogical Regnal List and the Chronology of Early Wessex' (1985), repr. in his *Britons and Saxons in the Early Middle Ages* (Aldershot, 1993), ch. VIII; idem, [review of A. P. Smyth, *King Alfred the Great*] *CMCS* 31 (1996), 90–3; B. Ó Cuív, 'Aspects of Irish Personal Names', *Celtica* 18 (1986), 151–84; C. Clark, 'Onomastics', in CHELang i.452–89, at 462–4; J. Uhlich, *Die Morphologie der komponierten Personennamen des Altirischen* (Bonn, 1993); D. Parsons, 'British *Caratīcos, Old English *Cerdic*', *CMCS* 33 (1997), 1–8.

O. J. PADEL

PERSONAL NAMES, OLD ENGLISH. OE personal names are of two types: dithematic or compounded, and monothematic or uncompounded. Dithematic names consist of two elements in conjunction. The two elements could

363

be either OE nouns or adjectives, as *Wulf-gar* (noun + noun), *Wulf-beorht* (noun + adjective), *Beorht-helm* (adjective + noun), *Beorht-swiþ* (adjective + adjective). Sometimes the compound makes sense, as *Æþel-red* (Æthelred), 'noble counsel', *Wig-heard*, 'battle-hardy'. Sometimes it makes no obvious sense, as *Wulf-stan*, 'wolf-stone', *Ælfric*, 'elf-powerful'. Some elements are recorded only in first place, as *Æþel-*, *Os-*, others only in second, as *-lac*, *-laf*. Many of the commonest elements can be either, as *beorht*, *wulf*. There are both male and female dithematic names, the grammatical gender of the second element being significant. Many first elements are found in both male and female names, as in *Æþelbeorht* (male) and *Æþelflæd* (female). Under monothematic or uncompounded can conveniently be grouped a variety of shorter names, some of them not strictly monothematic or uncompounded: (i) the simplest type: an OE strong noun or adjective used as a name: *Beorn*, 'bear, warrior', *Wine*, 'friend', *Brun*, 'brown', *Leof*, 'dear'; (ii) the so-called weak names in *-a* (masculine) or *-e* (feminine): *Eadda*, *Monna*, *Dunne*, *Gode*, *Tate*; (iii) masculine names in *-i*, later *-e*: *Dynne*, *Ini/Ine*; (iv) original diminutive names, with various endings as *-il/-el*, *-ul/-ol*, *-la*, *-ele*, *-ic*, *-uc/-oc*, *-ca*, *-ig*: *Tatel*, *Bercul*, *Hiddila*, *Winele*, *Dunic*, *Lulluc*, *Maneca*; (iv) names in *-ing*; this ending was at one time a patronymic, with the meaning 'son of', but developed into a simple name suffix: *Maning*, *Roting*, *Leofing*.

These types of uncompounded name produce groups of related forms: so, related to *Brun* are *Bruna*, *Brune*, *Brunel*, *Brunic*, *Bruning*; to *Leof* are *Leof(f)a*, *Leofe*, *Leofeca*, *Leofig*, *Leofing*. Other uncompounded names, which are not recorded independently, may be deduced from early *place-name forms, as *Hæsta* from *Hastingas/Hæstinga-*, Hastings. Evidence suggests that uncompounded names were less common during the later Anglo-Saxon period, when native names, at any rate for people of higher rank, tended to be dithematic. Some of these dithematic names survive to the present day, as Edward, Alfred, Oswald.

Also from Anglo-Saxon times are hypocoristic or pet-names. These are shortened forms originating in familiar use. They are often hard to distinguish from uncompounded names. Bede gives the example of the East Saxon king *Saberct* whom his sons called *Saba*, and *Cuþuulf* (Cuthwulf)/*Cupa* are alternative name forms within the West Saxon *dynasty.

W. G. Searle, *Onomasticon Anglo-Saxonicum* (Cambridge, 1897); T. Forssner, *Continental-Germanic Personal Names in England in Old and Middle English Times* (Uppsala,

1916); M. Redin, *Studies on Uncompounded Personal Names in Old English* (Uppsala, 1919); O. von Feilitzen, *The Pre-Conquest Personal Names of Domesday Book* (Uppsala, 1937); idem, 'Some Old English Uncompounded Personal Names and Bynames', *Studia Neophilologica* 40 (1968), 5–16; idem, 'Personal Names', in *Winchester in the Early Middle Ages*, ed. M. Biddle, Winchester Studies 1 (Oxford, 1976), 145–91; C. Clark, 'Onomastics', CHELang i.452–89, esp. 456–71; idem, *Words, Names and History: Selected Writings of Cecily Clark*, ed. P. Jackson (Cambridge, 1995).

R. I. PAGE

PERSONAL NAMES, SCANDINAVIAN, were introduced to England by Danes and Norwegians who arrived as raiders or settlers. After the partitions of land in the ninth century, in which members of the Danish armies were granted land on which to settle, Scandinavian forenames became extremely popular in parts of northern and eastern England and their popularity increased in the reigns of *Cnut and his sons. Over 75 per cent of the names in an early eleventh-century list of sureties from *York are of Scandinavian origin and about two-thirds of the householders in York in 1065 bore Scandinavian names. After the Norman Conquest, however, names introduced by the Normans, mainly of continental Germanic or biblical origin such as *William* and *John*, quickly ousted from use both Scandinavian names and names of English origin. By the year 1250 it is very rare for forenames of Scandinavian origin to occur in England.

The Scandinavian forenames were of the same basic types as the English names current at that period. They fall into three main classes: compound names of the type *Ásketil* and *Óláf*, original by-names such as *Halfdan* 'half-Dane', *Svart* 'black' and *Óspak* 'unwise, unruly', and derivative formations such as *Gunni*, from compound names in *Gunn-*, and *Tóki*, probably from *Thorketil*.

The first Scandinavian names to arrive in England were anglicised by the English scribes who recorded them. *Halfdan*, for example, is recorded as *Healfdene* and *Ásketil* as *Oscetel*. In East Anglia, where there is no evidence for Scandinavian immigration after the original settlement in the late ninth century, the anglicised forms survived to the time of *Domesday Book. Further north, however, where the Danish settlement was denser and more long lasting, it became normal to retain the Scandinavian spelling of the names. A sound-development which took place about the year 1000 in Denmark, the contraction of *-ketil* as a second element to *-kel* or *-kil*, e.g. in *Áskil*, is reflected in names in the *Danelaw, suggesting that these name-forms must have arrived in England with the followers of Cnut in the early eleventh century.

Unlike the names introduced by the Normans, the Scandinavian personal names that are recorded in England are not just a comparatively small body of stereotype names. A very large number of different names are recorded and there is evidence for the development of many new Scandinavian names, e.g. several compound names in *-grím*, *-ketil* and *-ulf*, such as *Alfgrím, Hafgrím, Ketilgrím, Ulfgrím, Grímketil, Ulfketil, Ligulf* and *Steinulf*. There are also many original *by-names that would seem to have been coined in England, for example the names indicating a lack of something, such as *Bróklaus* 'without breeches' and *Serklaus* 'without a shirt', and names such as *Dragmál* 'slow of speech' and *Sumarlithi* 'summer traveller'. Many of these names coined in the Danelaw later found their way to Denmark, Sweden, Norway and Iceland.

G. Fellows-Jensen, *Scandinavian Personal Names in Lincolnshire and Yorkshire*, Navnestudier 7 (Copenhagen, 1968); J. Insley, *Scandinavian Personal Names in Norfolk*, Acta Academiae Regiae Gustavi Adolphi 62 (Uppsala, 1994); G. Fellows-Jensen, *The Vikings and their Victims: the Verdict of the Names* (London, 1995).

GILLIAN FELLOWS-JENSON

PETER'S PENCE: *see* Alms

PHOENIX. The OE *Phoenix* is preserved in the *Exeter Book. Its author is unknown and its date of composition (perhaps late ninth century) is uncertain. The poem, composed of 677 lines, shows an interesting conflation of texts and traditions: the first 380 lines freely follow the Latin poem *De ave phoenice*, attributed to Lactantius (fourth century), and deal with the story of oriental origin of this mythical, eternal sun bird (including a description of the bird and of its habitat); the remaining lines, devoted to the allegorical interpretation in Christian terms of the first half, combine different exegetical sources, including Ambrose's *Hexameron*.

The story of the phoenix which cyclically, once grown old, burns itself and after its death returns to life, suitably represents the Christian doctrine of the resurrection. This theme, which plays a central role in the Old English poem, is developed in various ways by the poet, who establishes analogies between the phoenix, Christ and the faithful man, underlines the natural aspect of resurrection through examples taken from the natural world, and, quoting the *Physiologus*, joins the phoenix

to the eagle, both used to represent the renewal of life.

The poem has been variously interpreted by critics: some have read it in the light of the fourfold exegetical interpretation of medieval texts, some have seen in it the representation of the chaste monastic life, others have focused their attention on the Mariological aspect. But the importance of the poem rests in the way the author selects and expands the source material, reworking a traditional subject within the refined frame of Old English poetic diction.

ASPR iii.94–113; *The Phoenix*, ed. N. F. Blake (Manchester, 1964); J. E. Cross, 'The Conception of the Old English Phoenix', in *Old English Poetry: Fifteen Essays*, ed. R. Creed (Providence, RI, 1967), pp. 129–52; D. G. Calder, 'The Vision of Paradise: a Symbolic Reading of the Old English *Phoenix*', *ASE* 1 (1972), 167–81; J. Bugge, 'The Virgin Phoenix', *MS* 38 (1976), 332–50; C. F. Heffernan, 'The Old English *Phoenix*. A Reconsideration', *NM* 83 (1982), 239–54.

DORA FARACI

PHYSIOLOGUS. The anonymous OE *Physiologus* belongs to the long tradition of the Physiologus and bestiary genre, going back to the second century AD. In such works each of the many chapters is divided into two sections, the second offering a moral, allegorical and didactic interpretation of the physical nature of the animal described in the first. The three chapters of the OE text (in the *Exeter Book) deal with the panther, the whale and a bird identified as the partridge. Its date of composition is uncertain and the question of the completeness of the poem is still open. Although it has been argued that the extant text is only a fragment, the poem shows a formal unity and a harmonic, symbolic design which reflects homiletic influence. The animals dealt with form a sort of microcosm of God's creation, representing creatures of land, sea and air and, according to Christian doctrine, they symbolize respectively Christ, the devil and man's achievement of eternal glory.

ASPR iii. 169–74; D. R. Letson, 'The Old English Physiologus and the Homiletic Tradition', *Florilegium* 1 (1979), 15–41; P. W. Conner, 'The Structure of the Exeter Book Codex', *Scriptorium* 40 (1986), 233–42; *The Old English Physiologus*, ed. A. Squires (Durham, 1988).

DORA FARACI

PICTS. *Picti* was the name given by Roman writers from the third century on to the confederation of tribes living north of the Antonine Wall. The name may be the Latin for 'painted ones', referring to the native custom of tattooing, or be

365

a latinisation of either a native collective name or the unit of land implied in their *pett*-place-names. *Bede considered Pictish to be different from Welsh, but how different it was is not clear: as evidenced by place-names in the southern part of their territory (Fife to Moray), it was a P-*Celtic language, akin to Welsh but dialectically distinguishable from it; however, some thirty inscriptions, from all parts of Pictland, and written in the Ogham alphabet borrowed from the Irish, have so far mostly eluded satisfactory decipherment. If these Ogham inscriptions are evidence of a non-Celtic element in Pictish society then they can be set alongside the similarly inconclusive evidence of another potentially non-Celtic Pictish practice, that of inheritance through the female.

In the sixth century the Picts lost what is now Argyll and its islands, to colonising Irish. These 'Scots' established a kingdom there known as Dál Riata. The lands bordering the Forth-Clyde estuaries were thereafter occupied by the Picts, the Scots, the Angles of *Northumbria and the Britons of Strathclyde. Changes of alliance between all four peoples characterise the political history of the north from the sixth century to the ninth. At the time of *Edwin of *Deira's accession one of the exiled sons of Æthelfrith of *Bernicia went to Pictland and married into the Pictish royal line. His son, Talorcan, was king of the Picts at the time that his uncle, *Oswiu, achieved his great victory over *Penda of Mercia on the banks of the river *Winwæd* in 655. To consolidate Northumbria's influence in Pictland Oswiu campaigned in Pictland with the result that the regions from the Forth to the Tay were subjugated to the Northumbrians for a generation. The Picts eventually recovered their lands by defeating Oswiu's son and successor, Ecgfrith, at the battle of Nechtansmere in 685.

The *conversion of the Picts to Christianity began in the sixth century with the establishment of good relations between the powerful Pictish king Bruide, son of Maelchon, and *Columba of *Iona. By 700 Columban monasteries were to be found throughout Pictland. Contacts with the Columban foundations in Northumbria would have been frequent. Even after the Northumbrian church broke away from Iona in 664, *Cuthbert, as prior of *Melrose, had fraternal relations with Pictish communities. For eight years of the Northumbrian occupation *Wilfrid of *York had episcopal authority over the Pictish church, thus paving the way for a 'Roman' party in Pictland. In 717 the Pictish king Nechtan, son of Derilei, after taking advice from Abbot *Ceolfrith of

*Monkwearmouth/Jarrow, expelled those Pictish Columban clergy unwilling to accept the authority of *Rome.

Nechtan was caught up in a civil war which led to the ascendancy of Pictland's most powerful king, Oengus, son of Fergus (729–61). Alternately enemy or ally, Oengus held his own against the warlike Eadberht of Northumbria. The onset of *Viking attacks affected both Dál Riata in the west and the Pictish heartlands. The military effectiveness of the Dál Riadan leader Cinaed mac Alpin (d. 858), eventually led to the permanent establishment of the Scots in the east, based in the Pictish royal centre of Forteviot in Perthshire. The mechanisms whereby the two peoples united to form a new political entity known as Alba remain unclear.

Although no native narrative or annalistic texts survive there is evidence in their king-lists that the Picts were interested in keeping track of their past and in controlling lines of legitimate descent. The culture of the Picts is best represented by their art which survives as *metalwork and *sculpture. The art displays easy acquaintance with the decorative repertoire of contemporary Insular productions. The technical development of stone sculpture can be attributed to the Northumbrian stonemasons in Pictland at the time when Nechtan was building a Pictish St Peter's. However, there are distinctive aspects of Pictish art: a pervasive system of symbolism and a naturalistic animal art which began as superb stylised individual portraits of animals and expanded into fully descriptive hunting-scenes and animal combats, sometimes involving exotic or non-naturalistic animals. Any attempt to play down the distinctiveness of the Picts has to account for these highly individual traits in their art, which lasted well into the period of the take-over by the Scots.

M. O. Anderson, *Kings and Kingship in Early Scotland*, 2nd ed. (Edinburgh, 1980); A. A. M. Duncan, 'Bede, Iona and the Picts', in *The Writing of History in the Middle Ages: Essays presented to R. W. Southern*, ed. R. H. C. Davis and J. M. Wallace-Hadrill (Oxford, 1981), pp. 1–42; Kirby, *Kings*; L. Alcock and E. A. Alcock, 'Reconnaissance Excavations on Early Historic Fortifications and other Royal Sites in Scotland', *Proceedings of the Society of Antiquaries of Scotland* 122 (1992), 215–87; J. R. Allen and J. Anderson, *The Early Christian Monuments of Scotland*, 3 pts (Edinburgh 1903; repr. with an Introduction by Isabel Henderson, 2 vols., Balgavies, 1993); *Scotland in Dark Age Britain*, ed. B. E. Crawford (St Andrews, 1996).

ISABEL HENDERSON

PILGRIMAGE. A journey made for spiritual reasons. Three kinds of pilgrimage may be distinguished: those in the Irish tradition of exile from one's homeland; those made to a holy shrine or place; and those imposed for judicial reasons. The prominent place which *Bede gives to Ecgberht (d. 729) makes him the best known English example of the exile who early in life vowed never to return to his native land (*HE* iii.4, 27; v.9, 22). The mission of *Willibrord to *Frisia was inspired by Ecgberht, and can be regarded as a development of Irish *peregrinatio*, a tradition which declined as Irish influence waned.

Ecgberht had hoped to visit *Rome, and *Wilfrid I, the pupil of the Irish monastery of *Lindisfarne, and *Benedict Biscop, were the first Northumbrians to undertake the journey to Rome. The journey to Rome was the best recorded of pilgrimages in the second category, and kings, ecclesiastics and laymen are recorded making the trip in the seventh and eighth centuries: *Cædwalla of Wessex, for example, was baptised in Rome; Offa of the East Saxons ended his life as a monk there; *Ceolfrith, accompanied by a party of about eighty, carried the 'Codex *Amiatinus' as a gift; and *Boniface's friend, Wiethburg, found spiritual happiness. The *Schola Saxonum* in Rome and Boniface's concern about the moral and physical dangers for English women of the Roman pilgrimage bear witness to its popularity. *Cnut's concern in 1027 for juster exactions from merchants and pilgrims journeying to Rome, and Archbishop Sigeric's itinerary to Rome and list of Roman stations (990) are the background to its continued popularity, as evidenced by the visits of kings like *Æthelwulf of Wessex in the ninth century and of *Cnut in the eleventh. Among pilgrims travelling further afield, *Willibald in the eighth century, and Bishop *Ealdred of Worcester in the eleventh, journeyed to Jerusalem. Local pilgrimages were less spectacular, but those of English kings in the tenth and eleventh centuries to the shrine of St *Cuthbert (usually made as part of a northern expedition), or visits to *St Albans, to *Glastonbury or to St *Swithun at *Winchester, are among known examples.

In the third category, judicial pilgrimages, journeys to Rome are imposed in some laws for non-payment of *Peter's Pence, and exile for certain crimes in other laws and penitentials. The journey of Swein, the son of Godwine, to Jerusalem may be an example of an expiatory pilgrimage.

K. Hughes, 'The Changing Theory and Practice of Irish Pilgrimage', *JEH* 11 (1960), 143–51; W. J. Moore, *The Saxon Pilgrims to Rome and the Schola Saxonum* (Fribourg, 1937); *Pellegrinaggi: Pellegrinaggi e culto dei santi in Europa fino alla Ie crociata*, Convegni del Centro di studi sulla spiritualità medievale 4 (Todi, 1963); B. Colgrave, 'Pilgrimages to Rome in the Seventh and Eighth Centuries', *Studies in Language, Literature, and Culture of the Middle Ages and Later*, ed. E. B. Atwood and A. A. Hill (Austin, TX, 1969), pp. 156–72; V. Ortenberg, 'Archbishop Sigeric's Journey to Rome', *ASE* 19 (1990), 197–246; S. Keynes, 'Anglo-Saxon Entries in the *Liber Vitae* of Brescia', Bately FS, pp. 99–119; D. J. Birch, *Pilgrimage to Rome in the Middle Ages* (Woodbridge, 1998).

P. MCGURK

PLACE-NAMES, CELTIC. The evidence of Celtic place-names in England is of particular value in two fields: the phonological development of the British language, and the *settlement of the Anglo-Saxons, since borrowed place-names have implications for the degree of survival and intercourse of the native British population with the incoming Anglo-Saxons. In most of England (with a few westerly exceptions, such as *Cornwall, Cumberland and Herefordshire), remarkably few British place-names survive. A reasonable sample of pre-English place-names is provided by the recorded Romano-British (RB) place-names (467 approximately, including river-names and tribal names). Most are of Celtic derivation (though in Latin guise); but the sample may not be representative. It may contain very few native names for minor settlements; and in latinizing the Celtic names, the Romans may have altered them, or tended to select names of types which were easier to latinize. Some RB place-names were adopted into English with little change, such as RB *Londinium* > *London*, *Eburacum*, probably 'place of Eburos (god or man)' > OE *Ēoforwīc* (showing re-interpretation) > Scandinavian *Jórvík* > *York*, and *Pennocrucio* 'chief-tumulus' > *Penkridge* (Staffs.). Rather more (about 20) were adopted with the addition of an English element, as in *Danum* > *Don-caster* (Yorks.) and *Venta* > *Win-chester*. Sometimes the RB name was shortened, as in *Branodunum* > *Bran-caster* (Norfolk) and *Mamucio* > *Man-chester*; but the shortening may be a process which occurred within English after borrowing, as in *Letocetum* > OE *Lyccid-felth* > *Lichfield* (Staffs.) and *Durnovaria* > OE *Dornwara-ceaster* > *Dorchester* (Dorset). In general, the rate of survival of attested RB place-names, poor everywhere, is no worse in eastern England than in the west, and may even be slightly better.

The reverse is true of Celtic place-names which are not recorded in the RB period. All types of these – river-names, settlement-names and others – decrease in frequency from west to east.

Although re-interpretation ('folk-etymology'), as in *Eburacum* > *Ēoforwīc*, may sometimes have rendered a Celtic name unrecognizable, it is considered unlikely that this has significantly altered the number of identifiable Celtic place-names.

English place-names of Celtic origin are of several types: names of rivers and other major natural features, such as RB *Tamēsa* > river Thames; later *Moil-vrinn* 'bare-hill' > Malvern Hills (Worcs.) and *Coid* 'wood' > Chute Forest (Wilts.); *towns with Roman origins; and other significant places, usually of some administrative significance ('major names'), typically manors recorded in *Domesday Book or earlier (e.g. Penge, Surrey > *Penn-kēd* 'wood's end'). The incidence even of these names decreases from west to east, and some areas of eastern England are almost devoid of native place-names. There are no instances in eastern England of British settlement-terms (such as *tref*, *bod* and *caer*, all found in Wales, Cornwall and Brittany). In most of England it would be hard to argue convincingly for a Celtic derivation of a place-name which was not recorded till the fifteenth century or later, or of a minor name or field-name. It has been observed that surviving Celtic place-names are not evenly distributed across England, but tend to occur in clusters. These clusters serve to emphasise the paucity elsewhere; they also, by suggesting a degree of British survival in those areas, beg the question of what happened to the British elsewhere.

Tautological hybrids, such as Chetwood, Breedon, Crookbarrow (Hill), and river Avon, require explanation. The conventional account is that in Neo-Brittonic these were common nouns in use locally (*kēd*, *brē*, *crüg*, *avon*), misunderstood as proper nouns by the English, who then added their own synonymous element (*Ced-wudu*, *Bre-dūn*, etc.). Alternatively a clue may be provided by a phrase in an early charter of 682 (S 237): 'juxta collem qui dicitur brittannica lingua *Cructan*, apud nos *Crycbeorh*' 'near the hill called in the British tongue *Cructan*, and among us *Crycbeorh*' (Creechbarrow Hill, by the river Tone, in Somerset). The English borrowed only the first of the two elements in the Celtic place-name, and added their own synonymous word; note the different spelling of the element in the two forms. Other tautologous place-names could have arisen in this way.

Overall, the paucity of Celtic place-names in England demands explanation, particularly by those who consider that the Anglo-Saxon settlement was a process of peaceful co-operation. Two explanations could be invoked: preservation with re-interpretation on a massive scale (as in *Eburacum* > *Ēoforwīc*), which most philologists would find improbable; or the role of written forms. Most Celtic place-names did not exist in written form; this could have promoted their disappearance. The corollary would be that the survival of RB place-names was partly due to their existing in written form. Against this can be set the poor rate of survival even among attested RB place-names.

E. Ekwall, *English River Names* (Oxford, 1928); M. Gelling, *Signposts to the Past* (London, 1978), chs. 2 and 4; K. Jackson, *Language and History in Early Britain* (Edinburgh, 1953); A. L. F. Rivet and C. Smith, *The Place-Names of Roman Britain* (London, 1979); P. Sims-Williams, 'Dating the Transition to Neo-Brittonic: Phonology and History, 400–600', in *Britain 400–600: Language and History*, ed. A. Bammesberger and A. Wollmann (Heidelberg, 1990), pp. 217–61.

O. J. PADEL

PLACE-NAMES, OE. By the date of the Norman Conquest, the place-name stock of England was an accumulation of the *habitation names, *topographical names and *river names of its waves of British-, OE- and Scandinavian-speaking settlers. The great majority of these names of places in England were created in the Anglo-Saxon period by English-speaking peoples. The Germanic immigrants into Britain found a landscape whose *settlements and physical features already bore names formed by its British-speaking inhabitants. Some of these Celtic names (see *place-names, Celtic) were adopted by the Anglo-Saxons and survive almost intact, especially those of rivers such as the Avon, Severn, Thames and Trent, larger hill groups such as the Malverns, the Cheviots and the Quantocks, and important fortified sites in the south-east like Dover (*Dubris*), Lympne (*Lemanis*) and Reculver (*Regulbium*). Some Celtic names were incorporated into new English place-names such as Doncaster, Gloucester and Manchester (from *Dano*, *Glevo* and *Mamucio* respectively). But in general the Anglo-Saxons used their own word-hoard to describe their new environment and burgeoning settlement.

The Anglo-Saxons created place-names which were principally of two types: those which designated habitation sites (see *habitation names) and those which described aspects of topography (see *topographical names). Many English village names originally denoted features of topography; that is to say they were nature names. Settlements which developed near such features in the landscape frequently assumed their names. Names of this kind were elliptical. For example, Stratford

(Warwicks.) originally designated a ford over the river Avon carrying a Roman *road (*strǣt*). The village which developed at the ford was named from it. When the name Stratford was used of this village, it meant 'the settlement at Stratford'. The Anglo-Saxon topographical place-name consists usually of two parts which may be termed the specific and the generic: the specific invariably precedes the generic. OE *dun* 'a hill' (normally giving *don* in modern spellings) appears frequently as a generic in topographical names and may serve as a model to illustrate the immense variety of the type. Thus specifics compounded with *dun* may emphasize natural features of the particular hills: hence Clevedon (*clif* 'a steep slope, a cliff'), Grandon (*grene* 'green'), Hambledon (*hamol* 'mutilated, cut off', i.e. 'flat-topped'), Longdon (*long* 'long'), Standon (*stan* 'stone'). They may be words for trees, vegetation or crops: thus Ashendon (*æscen* 'growing with ash trees'), the common Farndon (*fearn* 'fern'), Haddon (*hǣð* 'heather'), Whaddon (*hwǣte* 'wheat'). They may be names of animals: hence Cauldon (*cælf* 'a calf'), Oxendon (*oxa* 'an ox'), Swindon (*swin* 'a pig'); or words for artefacts, as in Maldon (*mæl* 'a cross') and Quorndon (*cweorn* 'a quern' i.e. 'the hill where quern-stones are obtained'). Personal names may form specifics too, suggesting either an individual's ownership of the hill or his association with it in some significant way. Thus we find Baldon (*Bealda*), Cheldon (*Ceadela*) Luddesdown (*Hlud*) and Ockendon (*Wocca*).

Common generics in topographical names are *burna* 'a stream' (Fishbourne, Pangbourne), *eg* 'land partly surrounded by water, a piece of dry ground in fenland' (Maxey, Forksey), *feld* 'open country' (Marefield, Sheffield), *ford* 'a ford' (Fulford, Twyford), *leah* 'a clearing in woodland' (Bentley, Lambley), *wella* 'a spring, a stream' (Caldwell, Prittlewell) and *wudu* 'a wood' (Charnwood, Harewood). Topographical features were more likely than habitation sites to occasion a variety of simplex place-names. The simplex name consists of an unqualified substantive. This may describe a major physical feature as does the common Combe (*cumb* 'a valley') and Ness (*næss* 'a promontory, a headland') or a smaller feature as does Bourne (*burna* 'a stream') and Hoole (*hol* 'a hollow'). Habitation sites may also appear as simplex place-names as with Cote (*cot* 'a cottage'), the ubiquitous Stoke (*stoc* 'a cattle farm'), Thrup (*þrop* 'a hamlet') and Wick (*wic*, often 'a dairy farm').

A third type of Anglo-Saxon settlement was once the name of a minor folk unit: see *-ingas*

names. Finally, the Scandinavian settlements in Anglo-Saxon England created a new stratum of place-names (see *place-names, Scandinavian).

A. H. Smith, *English Place-Name Elements*, English Place-Name Society 25–6 (Cambridge, 1956); K. Cameron, *English Place-Names* (London, 1961); E. Ekwall, *The Oxford Dictionary of English Place-Names*, 4th ed. (Oxford, 1960); *Place-Name Evidence for the Anglo-Saxon Invasion and Scandinavian Settlements*, ed. K. Cameron (Nottingham, 1975); M. Gelling, *Signposts to the Past* (London, 1978).

B. COX

PLACE-NAMES, SCANDINAVIAN, are found over most of northern and eastern England and spill over into southern Scotland. They confirm the written evidence that land was divided out between Scandinavian settlers in Yorkshire in 876, in the East Midlands in 877, in East Anglia in 880, and in Wirral and Durham early in the tenth century. They also indicate that there must have been settlement in the north-west. Hardly any Scandinavian place-names are to be found south and west of the boundary of Danish territory drawn in the treaty concluded between King *Alfred and the Danish leader *Guthrum in about 880.

There are also, however, areas where there are few Scandinavian names even though there is documentary evidence for Scandinavian activity. Topography alone cannot explain the absence of Scandinavian place-names, since these are quite common in some inhospitable areas, such as the remote valleys of the Cumbrian Dome and the marshy areas around the Ouse in Yorkshire and along the coasts of *Lindsey and eastern Norfolk. The explanation for the absence of Scandinavian place-names from some areas where the *Vikings are known to have been active is probably the speed with which English rule was restored there.

To begin with, the Vikings must have taken over English *settlements as going concerns. Most names of major settlements survived the take-over unchanged, although the English name of *York, *Eofor-wīc*, developed to *Jórvík*, while the borough known to the English as *Norð-worðig* was renamed Derby (*djúra-bý*). The names of some villages were partially scandinavianised by the substitution of a Scandinavian word or sound for its English equivalent, for example *karl* replaced *ceorl* in Carlton (cf. Chorlton), /k/ replaced /tʃ/ in Kirkton (cf. Churchton) and /sk/ replaced /ʃ/ in Skelton (cf. Shelton).

Other old villages received new names in *-bý*. The first element of these names was generally a Scandinavian word which revealed something

369

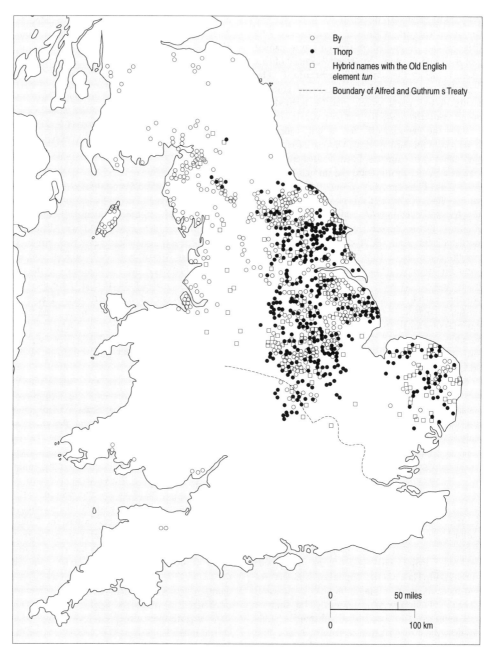

Map 3 The main Scandinavian settlement-names in southern Britain.

about the settlement, e.g. Lazenby 'the settlement of the freedmen (*leysingjar*)', Dalby 'the settlement in a valley (*dalr*)', Kirkby 'the settlement with a church (*kirkja*)'. Later the Danes in eastern England began to break up the existing estates into small independent agricultural units. This process of fragmentation is marked by place-names

consisting of a Scandinavian personal name in the genitive plus -*by*, for example Aismunderby in Yorkshire (*Ásmundar*). In Lancashire, Cheshire and Westmorland, there are no certain instances of names of this type, probably because these counties were only ever partly under Scandinavian control and that for a comparatively short period of time. Further north, in Cumberland and Dumfriesshire, there are several place-names in which personal names that were introduced into England by the Normans are combined with *by*, for example Rickerby (*Richard*). These names probably indicate settlements whose names in -*by* had been altered to incorporate the names of the new Norman tenants.

The element *thorp* was used in Scandinavia to denote a secondary dependent settlement, and place-names in -*thorp* in England have been thought to represent a later stage in the Scandinavian colonisation, since the settlements with such names are generally not only smaller and poorer than places with names in -*by* but are also found in inferior situations. There is, however, good reason to believe that the foundation of many of the settlements bearing names in -*thorp* antedates the Viking invasions and the distribution pattern of the *thorps* may in part reflect a pre-Viking distribution pattern of English names in related -*throp*. Evidence for settlements established on land first cleared for cultivation by the Scandinavian settlers must be sought from the names in -*thveit* 'clearing'.

Names such as Normanby, Danby, Irby and Gautby point to isolated enclaves of Norwegians, Danes, Irishmen or Norwegians from Ireland, and Gauts respectively. The best indicator of Danish influence is the element *by*. Settlers coming to England from the Scandinavian colonies in Gaelic-speaking areas brought with them the Gaelic loan-word *ærgi* for a shieling and the spread of this element reveals their presence not only in the north-west, e.g. in *Grimsargh*, but also, although less markedly, in Yorkshire, e.g. in *Arram*.

Viking settlement east of the Pennines was basically Danish, whereas to the west of the Pennines, men from the Danelaw settled side by side with men of Norwegian origin who had come there from the Gaelic-speaking colonies, some few of whom in turn made their way eastwards across the Pennines.

G. Fellows Jensen, *Scandinavian Settlement Names in Yorkshire*, Navnestudier 11 (Copenhagen, 1972); idem, *Scandinavian Settlement Names in the East Midlands*, Navnestudier 16 (Copenhagen, 1978); idem, *Scandinavian Settlement Names in the North-West*, Navnestudier 25 (Copenhagen, 1985); *Place-Name Evidence for the Anglo-Saxon Invasion and Scandinavian Settlements*, ed. K. Cameron (Nottingham, 1975).

GILLIAN FELLOWS JENSEN

PLEGMUND, archbishop of *Canterbury (890–923). Plegmund is said to have lived as a hermit at Plemstall ('Plegmund's stow'), in Cheshire; but he is more reliably introduced as one of the several Mercian ecclesiastics recruited by King *Alfred the Great in the early 880s to assist in the king's programme of revival and reform. In this context he was described by *Asser as 'a Mercian by birth and an estimable man richly endowed with learning' (*Vita Ælfredi*, c. 77); on which basis we may feel justified in presuming him to have been a significant figure at court. Æthelred, who had succeeded *Ceolnoth as archbishop of Canterbury in 870, died on 30 June 888. There is reason to believe that King Alfred offered the post to *Grimbald, who had recently arrived in England from Saint-Bertin, and who had been installed by the king in a small monastery at *Winchester, pending an opportunity to grant him a bishopric; but Grimbald declined the offer, and the choice fell on Plegmund, who was appointed archbishop in 890 (*ASC* MS. F) and received the *pallium from Pope Formosus (891–6). Plegmund would seem to have been instrumental in the early stages in the revival of the English church, after years of decline and neglect under adverse circumstances. We learn from Flodoard's 'History of the Church of Rheims' not only that King Alfred had been congratulated by Fulk, archbishop of Rheims, for appointing Plegmund as archbishop, but also that Plegmund had himself been complimented by Fulk for working so hard 'to cut off and extirpate the incestuous heats of lasciviousness . . . which would seem to have sprung up in that race' (*EHD* i, nos. 224–5); and Formosus was pleased enough to withdraw a threat of general excommunication (*EHD* i, no. 227). Plegmund was named by Alfred as one of those (with Asser, Grimbald, and *John) who helped in the translation of Pope *Gregory's *Regula pastoralis*. He may have played a part in the formation of the distinctive polity known to contemporaries as the kingdom 'of the *Anglo-Saxons'; and King Alfred's grant of adjacent properties at 'Æthelred's hithe' [Queenhithe], on the Thames, to him and to *Werferth, bishop of Worcester, in 898 (S 1628), reflects the advantages of convenient access from the river to the restored city of *London, now emerging into its own. It might also have been Plegmund who determined the choice of *Kingston-upon-Thames as the place for royal ceremonial, and it would have been he who officiated at the coronation of *Edward the Elder at Kingston in 900. Two documents show Plegmund operating in Kentish circles. In 905 he leased an estate in *Kent to a certain Byrhtræd, recorded in a *charter which survives in its original form (S 1288); and it was probably at about the same time that he confirmed an older private charter, also preserved in single-sheet form (S 1203). In their own modest way the charters symbolize the revival of Latin *literacy during Plegmund's pontificate; and it is interesting in both cases to find him in company with a certain Beornhelm 'priest-abbot', who flourished in the period c.865–905, and who was apparently abbot of St Augustine's, Canterbury. In 908 Plegmund dedicated 'a very high tower in the city of Winchester' (part of the New Minster, or of the Nunnaminster), and then 'conveyed *alms to *Rome for the nation and also for King Edward' (**Æthelweard*, *Chronicon* iv.4). In Rome Plegmund would have encountered the virulently anti-Formosan Pope Sergius III (904–11); yet soon after his return he effected the division of the West Saxon bishoprics, perhaps in necessarily belated response to papal stricture. Denewulf, bishop of Winchester, died in 908 and was succeeded by Frithestan; and Asser, bishop of Sherborne, died in 909 or 910. Where there had previously been two large dioceses, of Winchester and *Sherborne, five were created, with sees at Winchester (Hampshire) and Ramsbury (Wiltshire), and at *Sherborne (Dorset), *Wells (Somerset) and Crediton (Devon), providing a firm basis for the revival of the church in *Wessex. Archbishop Plegmund died on 2 August 923. The circumstances behind the division of the bishoprics were later recalled in a document produced at Crediton (*Councils & Synods* I.i, no. 35 (i)), and in a letter from Archbishop *Dunstan to King *Æthelred (ibid. no. 35 (ii); *EHD* i, no. 229); but certain elements of the story, including the supposed role of Pope Formosus, reflect a process of embroidery after the passage of time.

Brooks, *Canterbury*, pp. 152–4, 173–4, 209–14; T. Dyson, 'King Alfred and the Restoration of London', *London Journal* 15 (1990), 99–110; S. Keynes, 'King Alfred and the Mercians', *Kings, Currency, and Alliances: The History and Coinage of Southern England, AD 840–900*, ed. M. A. S. Blackburn and D. N. Dumville (Woodbridge, 1998), pp. 1–45.

SIMON KEYNES

POETIC TECHNIQUE, LATIN. Pre-Conquest Anglo-Latin poets, from *Aldhelm to *Wulfstan Cantor and beyond, imitated the poetic techniques of classical and Christian-Latin poets; but there were also various devices adopted (and often abused) by Anglo-Latin poets which helps to set Anglo-Latin poetic diction apart from that of contemporary Irish and continental poets. At the same time, there were various more subtle poetic devices employed by earlier poets which apparently eluded Anglo-Latin poets; but it is well to remember that the Anglo-Saxons were the first non-Latin-speaking peoples to attempt quantitative verse composition on any substantial scale, and that they succeeded in mastering this difficult medium in a way that, for example, Irish poets were unable to equal before the mid-ninth century at earliest. For example, in matters of prosody (that is, the correct scansion of long and short syllables) Anglo-Latin poets were remarkably accurate. Aldhelm, the earliest Anglo-Latin poet, had difficulty with enjambement (most of his hexameter lines are end-stopped, and were apparently conceived one at a time, and usually built up from preconceived formulaic expressions), and used elision only sparingly; but a generation later *Bede had no difficulty with these techniques, and it can be said that Bede's Latin verse is technically flawless. Similarly, as far as hexametrical rhythm is concerned, it may be said that Aldhelm's hexameters are rhythmically monotonous (he employs a small number of patterns repetitively; the pattern dactyl–spondee–spondee–spondee in the first four feet of the hexameter occurs in some 30 per cent of his hexameters, a monotony unthinkable, say, in Vergil); but Aldhelm's successors, especially Bede and Wulfstan, achieved pleasing variety in this respect. Other devices used by classical and Christian-Latin poets for metrical variety, such as the use of monosyllables in the sixth foot of a hexameter, or the use of pentasyllabic words to fill up the fifth and sixth feet at once, were practised confidently by Anglo-Latin poets; Wulfstan is particularly noteworthy in this respect (he was even confident enough to compose a hypermetrical line, in which an extra syllable at the end of a hexameter elides with a word beginning with a vowel at the start of the next), and it is not surprising that, of all Anglo-Latin poets, Wulfstan attempted composition in the widest variety of metres, including *octosyllables, *hymns, sapphic stanzas and epanaleptic verses. Anglo-Latin poets employed, sometimes to excess, various metrical helpmeets which were used sparingly by their predecessors, such as the use of the archaic passive infinitive ending *-ier* before a word beginning with a vowel in the cadence, or the use of nouns terminating in *-amen*, declined in the abl. sg. or nom./acc. pl., to fill out the fifth foot of the hexameter, and it is the use of such devices which imparts to Anglo-Latin verse a distinctive diction.

A. Campbell, 'Some Linguistic Features of Early Anglo-Latin Verse and its Use of Classical Models', *Transactions of the Philological Society* (1953), 1–20; idem, *Æthelwulf de abbatibus* (Oxford, 1967), pp. xxxv–xlvii; M. Lapidge,

'Aldhelm's Latin Poetry and Old English Verse', *Comparative Literature* 31 (1979), 209–31, repr. in his *ALL* i.247–69; idem, *ALL* ii.226–9; A. Orchard, 'After Aldhelm: the Teaching and Transmission of the Anglo-Latin Hexameter', *The Journal of Medieval Latin* 2 (1992), 96–133; idem, *The Poetic Art of Aldhelm*, CSASE 8 (Cambridge, 1994).

MICHAEL LAPIDGE

POETIC TECHNIQUE, OE. Vernacular poetic technique, with its roots in an oral tradition which predates the arrival of *literacy, differs from prose conventions in four principal areas: diction, syntax, metre, and figures of speech. Poetic diction employs a range of synonyms, useful in the alliterative scheme, for such traditionally fixed concepts as 'weapon', 'woman', and 'leader'. Most are common words, though some like *brim* 'flood, sea' are restricted exclusively or primarily to verse. The most distinctive elements of poetic diction are compounds, many of which are repeated as *formulae. Their constitutive elements can stand in a range of relations with each other, from the descriptive (*brim-ceald* 'cold as the sea', *brim-liðende* 'traveller on the sea') to the more figurative. For example, *brim-wudu* 'sea wood' and *brim-hengest* 'sea horse' both mean 'ship', the former by metonymic extension and the latter by a compressed metaphoric substitution known as a kenning: a ship sails across the sea just as a horse gallops on land.

Compounding illustrates how the metre encourages an economy in the selection of words, a principle which can be extended to verse *syntax. Semantically weighty nouns, adjectives, and non-finite verbs are favoured in the alliterative scheme at the expense of other elements. Where prose uses connectives between clauses, verse may prefer to juxtapose them, resulting in more parataxis. The tendency to juxtapose extends to words and phrases in what is known as variation or apposition. Apposed elements must be the same part of speech, have the same referent, and not show any grammatical relation other than syntactic parallelism. The element order in verse clauses has often been called 'free' in comparison with prose, but the variations are the result of the overlapping constraints of OE *metre and syntax. In dependent clauses, for example, the tendency to postpone the verb and the tendency to give it metrical stress necessarily influence each other.

The figure of speech commonly mislabelled as 'understatement' works by asserting the categorical exclusion of a contrary state. 'He was no coward' says little, literally, about bravery. Yet figuratively it means that the bravery was untouched by any taint of cowardice, hence extraordinarily brave. While Anglo-Saxon poets display a knowledge of figures derived from *classical learning, especially in poems from Latin sources, figurative language does not depend on learned rhetoric. Metaphoric language abounds: treachery is a cunning net, the bride is a peace-weaver, ice is bound with fetters. Some *riddles work by unpacking metaphoric resemblances. Metonymy, as in the compound *brim-wudu*, is another favourite figure.

J. J. Campbell, 'Learned Rhetoric in Old English Poetry', *Modern Philology* 63 (1966), 189–201; B. Mitchell, *Old English Syntax* (Oxford, 1985), esp. §§3952–76; F. C. Robinson, *Beowulf and the Appositive Style* (Knoxville, TN, 1985); D. Donoghue, *Style in Old English Poetry: The Test of the Auxiliary* (New Haven, CT, 1987); M. Godden, 'Literary Language', in CHELang i.490–535.

DANIEL DONOGHUE

PONTIFICAL CEREMONIES are those liturgical services which can only be performed by a bishop (rather than a priest) such as the consecration of an abbot or another bishop, the dedication of a church, the *coronation of a king or *queen, or the conduct of an *ordeal. In the early medieval period, the instructions pertaining to the performance of these ceremonies were contained in a book(let) called an *ordo*, and from the eighth century onwards various *ordines* survive which describe pontifical ceremonies at Rome itself (such as *Ordo romanus primus*). These *ordines* were subsequently augmented and transmitted to Francia, where they are preserved from the eighth and ninth century onwards; the type of book known as the pontifical (see *liturgical books) is attested from the mid-tenth century onwards, and characteristically combined the directions for liturgical rite contained in the *ordines* with the text of prayers pronounced by the bishop (a separate type of bishop's book, called the benedictional, contained the blessings pronounced by the bishop when he officiated at mass on Sundays and feast-days). The *Regularis concordia* draws *inter alia* on *Ordo romanus primus*, and the earliest Anglo-Saxon pontificals, which are attested from the mid-tenth century (or slightly earlier), include the 'Pontifical of St *Dunstan' (Paris, BN, lat. 943) and the 'Egbert Pontifical' (Paris, BN, lat. 10575). At about this time the compilation which determined the shape of pontifical ceremony in the Christian West for the next millennium, known as the 'Romano-German Pontifical', was produced at the church of St Alban in Mainz (perhaps as a result of the patronage of the Ottonian court) in the 950s. Because of its comprehensiveness and accessibility, it was soon adopted by continental churches, and a century or so later was brought to England by *Ealdred, bishop of *Worcester and archbishop of *York, as a result of a visit by Ealdred to Cologne in 1054. It quickly became the standard text for pontifical services in England, and it is likely that the coronation *ordo* used by Ealdred in the coronation of William the Conqueror was taken from the Romano-German Pontifical. Pontifical ceremonies are frequently illustrated in later medieval manuscripts, but only a few such illustrations are known from Anglo-Saxon England.

C. Vogel, *Medieval Liturgy: an Introduction to the Sources*, trans. W. G. Storey and N. K. Rasmussen (Washington, DC, 1981), pp. 135–247; M. Andrieu, *Les Ordines romani du haut moyen âge*, 5 vols. (Louvain, 1931–61); C. Vogel and R. Elze, *Le Pontificale romano-germanique du dixième siècle*, 3 vols., Studi e testi 226, 227, 269 (Rome, 1963–72); W. H. Frere, F. C. Eeles and A. Riley, *Pontifical Services*, 4 vols., Alcuin Club Collections 3, 4, 8, 12 (London, 1901–8); M. Lapidge, 'Ealdred of York and MS. Cotton Vitellius E.xii', *Yorkshire Archaeological Journal* 55 (1983), 11–25, repr. in his *ALL* ii.453–67.

MICHAEL LAPIDGE

POPULATION: *see* Settlement Patterns

POTTERY. The earliest published description of Anglo-Saxon pottery dates from the seventeenth century, but it was not until the pioneering work of J. N. L. Myres, beginning in the 1920s, that Anglo-Saxon pottery was subjected to detailed study. His series of papers on the subject culminated in two major works in which he constructed a detailed typology of early Anglo-Saxon pottery based on form and decoration. His primary objective was to attribute different pottery types to the Angles, Saxons or Jutes and to trace the movements and interaction of these tribes through the distribution of their pottery.

Early Anglo-Saxon pottery, however, is remarkably resistant to typological classification. It was hand-built and decorated using a wide range of incised designs as well as stamped and embossed motifs; profiles range from globular to straight-sided and include bowls with angled carinations, but most vessels are roughly globular jars. Countless variations exist, and the same pot may appear quite different in both form and decoration when viewed from different angles.

As a result of this variability, few motifs, fabrics or forms can be attributed with certainty to a particular ethnic group, region, or century, although some trends are apparent, such as the decline during the seventh century in the proportion and quality of decorated pottery. Although early Anglo-Saxon pottery closely followed the potting traditions of the continental homelands, there were significant differences; for example, stamped decoration and grass-tempered pottery were much more popular in England.

The essentially art-historical approach to early Anglo-Saxon pottery has given way to analyses (see Richards 1987) of the links between the form and decoration of cremation urns and the social identity (especially age, gender and status) of the individual buried in them. Many pots, especially in the sixth century, were decorated with stamped designs using clay or bone/antler dies. The repertoire of stamped motifs is broad though fairly standardised, ranging from simple circles and crosses to highly elaborate and zoomorphic designs. It seems almost certain that these were symbols, but of what? One theory is that they were totemic and related to different lineages, but this tantalising question remains unanswered. The designs found on pottery are, furthermore, not unique to ceramics; they are closely echoed on *metalwork and could also have been used on wooden and leather objects.

The pottery from early Anglo-Saxon *settlements is essentially the same as that found in pre-Christian *cemeteries, although settlements produce, not surprisingly, a higher proportion of wide-mouthed cooking pots and bowls and a smaller proportion of decorated pottery. Early Anglo-Saxon pottery was probably manufactured by part-time potters working within a domestic context, although the finest vessels reflect a high degree of skill. A few sixth-century 'workshops' did exist, as indicated by groups of closely similar vessels distributed within a limited region, the best-known example being the 'Illington-Lackford' group in *East Anglia. These pots were decorated with the same 'tool kit' of stamps using almost identical decorative schemes, and were clearly made by the same potter or by a group of potters working closely together.

The quantity and quality of hand-made pottery declined in the seventh century, when the first mass-produced, wheel-turned wares were manufactured, presumably by specialist potters. Hand-made pottery died out at different times in different regions and in some areas continued to be made into the Late Saxon period. Firing technology also changed. Prior to the seventh century, pottery was fired in pits or bonfires, covered with fuel which then smouldered at a relatively low temperature. Middle Saxon wares, however, were generally fired in more sophisticated kilns which reached higher temperatures. The result was harder, fairly coarse pottery, usually plain or with simple linear or stamped decoration, some of which was made in somewhat clumsy imitation of Frankish wares. The earliest of these wares was produced in *Ipswich, where a kiln of this period has actually been excavated. Ipswich Ware was widely traded within East Anglia from c.650–850. Whether it was prized primarily for itself or for its contents we do not know, but it seems that outside of East Anglia, it reached primarily 'special function' settlements such as monasteries, trading and estate centres. Many other Middle Saxon pottery wares were traded locally and regionally, for example Maxey Ware, which was widely exported throughout the East Midlands, or the coarse wares produced at the trading town of *Hamwic* (mid-saxon *Southampton) which were distributed within Hampshire.

By the mid-tenth century pottery had come into widespread, everyday use and its production was increasingly (though not exclusively) based in *towns; while the most precocious Late Saxon pottery industry was based at *Stamford, *Norwich, Stafford, *Thetford, Ipswich, Torksey, and *Lincoln all had pottery industries, although few production sites have been excavated on any scale. Oddly, *London does not seem to have produced its own pottery but instead imported much of its pottery from Oxfordshire. The Late Saxon period also saw the appearance of new forms such as pitchers, lamps and large storage vessels, the last presumably introduced in response to increased trade in the commodities they contained. Carolingian influence can be seen in some of these, such as some amphorae-style Thetford Ware storage jars. The productivity of these Late Saxon pottery workshops was matched by efficient distribution networks. Study of pottery fabrics shows that shelly wares made at Lincoln in the first half of the tenth century were widely traded across the east Midlands, just as Stafford wares were marketed throughout the west Midlands. This was also a period of technological innovation in both the *Danelaw and *Wessex, and a wide range of techniques was used to produce and fire pottery, ranging from hand-building to wheel-throwing, and from bonfires to updraught kilns.

P. Blinkhorn, *The Ipswich Ware Project* (London, forthcoming); T. Briscoe, 'A Classification of Anglo-Saxon Pot Stamp Motifs and Proposed Terminology', *Studien zur Sachsenforschung* 4 (1983), 57–71; Sir Thomas Browne, *Hydriotaphia, Urn-burial, or, A Discourse of the Sepulchral Urns Lately Found in Norfolk* (1658; repr. Oxford, 1972); J. Hurst, 'The Pottery', in Wilson, *Archaeology*, pp. 283–348; K. Kilmurry, *The Pottery Industry of Stamford, Lincs. c. AD 850–1250*, BAR Brit. ser. 84 (Oxford, 1980); M. McCarthy and C. Brooks, *Medieval Pottery in Britain c. AD 900–1600* (Leicester, 1988); J. N. L. Myres, *Anglo-Saxon Pottery and the Settlement of England* (Oxford, 1969); idem, *A Corpus of Anglo-Saxon Pottery*, 2 vols. (Cambridge, 1977); J. Richards, *The Significance of Form and Decoration of Anglo-Saxon Cremation Urns*, BAR Brit. ser. 166 (Oxford, 1987).

HELENA HAMEROW

PRAYER, PRIVATE. Whereas the prayers of the faithful were formally expressed through public *liturgy, it was possible for an individual Christian to pray to God in secret (cf. Matt. VI.6) and to seek forgiveness for sins. Accordingly, a layman could follow a course of private prayer and devotion, and religious were free (and indeed encouraged) to pray outside the requirements of the formal liturgy. Private prayers took various forms: antiphons and hymns; mass-sets (usually extracted from sacramentaries: see *liturgical books); petitions to individual saints for intercession; prayers for the protection of all parts of the body from the assaults of the devil (the so-called *loricae*); breviate psalters; and passages from gospels (particularly the Passion). A particularly suitable type of prayer for private devotion was the litany of saints, which included formulaic petitions to numbers of saints that could be expanded or curtailed as the occasion demanded. That laymen owned books containing prayers of this type is clear from the example of King *Alfred and his *Enchiridion* (as recorded by *Asser in his Life of Alfred, c. 88); but religious also assembled books of prayers, examples being the *Collectio psalterii* of *Bede (a breviate psalter which could be committed to memory) and *Alcuin's (unprinted) *De laude Dei*. A small number of private prayerbooks, which may have belonged to laymen or laywomen, survives from early Anglo-Saxon England, including the 'Book of *Cerne' (Cambridge, UL, Ll. 1. 10: Mercia, s. ix^{in}), the 'Book of Nunnaminster' (London, BL, Harley 2965: s. viii/ix), and several others; surprisingly, there are almost no analogous books from the Continent. A prayerbook of the earlier eleventh century, *'Ælfwine's Prayerbook', contains prayers for personal devotion alongside various *computistical, prognostic and scientific materials which reflect the personal interests of the book's owner. H. Gneuss, 'Liturgical Books in Anglo-Saxon England and their Old English Terminology', in Clemoes FS, pp. 91–141, at 137–8; CCSL cxxii.452–70 [Bede, *Col-

lectio psalterii]; R. Constantinescu, 'Alcuin et les "Libelli precum" de l'époque carolingienne', *Revue d'histoire de la spiritualité* 50 (1974), 17–56; M. Lapidge, *Anglo-Saxon Litanies of the Saints*, HBS 106 (London, 1991); A. B. Kuypers, *The Prayer Book of Aedeluald the Bishop, commonly called the Book of Cerne* (Cambridge, 1902); W. de G. Birch, *An Ancient Manuscript of the Eighth or Ninth Century* (London, 1889); B. J. Muir, *A Pre-Conquest English Prayer-Book*, HBS 103 (London, 1988); B. Günzel, *Ælfwine's Prayerbook*, HBS 108 (London, 1993).

MICHAEL LAPIDGE

PRAYERBOOK: *see* Liturgical Books; Prayer, Private

PREACHING in Anglo-Saxon England has been described as essentially conservative, and it is true to say that the great majority of preaching texts look for inspiration to the same handful of patristic and Carolingian sources. That regular preaching to lay congregations was held to be a key duty of the church is stressed again and again by Anglo-Saxon authors, particularly those associated with the period of the Benedictine reform, and both *Ælfric and *Wulfstan repeatedly underline its importance. A distinction is sometimes made between a liturgical address based on the biblical passage or 'pericope' proper to the day, and a more generally didactic or catechetical discourse on a Christian theme; some scholars label the former *homilies, the latter sermons: in practice the difference can sometimes be quite difficult to determine. As a result the assumption that the bulk of the preaching performed in Anglo-Saxon England took place in a liturgical setting, with a member of the clergy reading to the people, is difficult to demonstrate, and relies to a large extent on drawing analogies from Carolingian practice, where the evidence is much fuller. Such Carolingian evidence suggests that the exegetical preaching of homilies in the strictest sense was generally derived from the homiletic works of a handful of Fathers, notably Augustine, Jerome, *Gregory, and *Bede, and was mainly associated with the night Office on Sundays and feast days; these same Latin fathers certainly also provided much material for vernacular Anglo-Saxon preachers of both homilies and sermons. As an aid to Carolingian preaching appropriate homilies had been assembled into homiliaries by figures such as Paul the Deacon, Smaragdus of Saint-Mihiel, and Haymo of Auxerre, and the purpose of these anthologies seems to have been more to provide meditational reading or material for adaptation than simply providing lections; once again such Carolingian homiliaries were to offer ample material for later Anglo-Saxon preachers.

The style of Anglo-Saxon preaching differs greatly across authors and texts; that the twelfth canon of the *Council of *Clofesho held in 747 should apparently prohibit clerics from performing before congregations 'in the manner of secular poets' is especially interesting in the light of the fondness of later preachers, including both Ælfric and Wulfstan, to employ precisely the kind of *alliteration and rhythmical phrasing so favoured in Old English verse. As in their verse, it often seems in their preaching texts that one can almost hear the animated and authentic voice of individual authors, and it is perhaps unsurprising that aspects of *oral-formulaic theory have been applied successfully to both kinds of discourse.

T. L. Amos, 'Preaching and the Sermon in the Carolingian World', in *De Ore Domini: Preaching and Word in the Middle Ages*, ed. T. L. Amos, E. A. Green, and B. M. Kienzle, Studies on Medieval Culture 27 (Kalamazoo, MI, 1989), 41–60; M. Clayton, 'Homiliaries and Preaching in Anglo-Saxon England', *Peritia* 4 (1985), 207–42; M. McC. Gatch, *Preaching and Theology in Anglo-Saxon England: Ælfric and Wulfstan* (Toronto, 1977); J. Hill, 'Reform and Resistance: Preaching Styles in Late Anglo-Saxon England', in *De l'homélie au sermon: Histoire de la prédication médiévale*, ed. J. Hamesse and X. Hermand (Louvain, 1993), pp. 15–46.

ANDY ORCHARD

PRECEPTS: *see* Gnomic Poetry

PRINCELY BURIALS. Amongst the large number of human burials (see *cemeteries) known from the fifth to eighth century in England, a small group can be isolated by virtue of their high investment in burial rite and *grave goods. Termed 'princely' by Tania Dickinson in 1974, and analogous to Fürstengräber or Adelsgräber in continental cultures, the group is generally held to include *Sutton Hoo in East Anglia, *Taplow in Buckinghamshire, Caenby in Lincolnshire, Asthall and Cuddesdon in Oxfordshire, Broomfield in Essex and perhaps Coombe in Kent (Map 4). More examples could be included and more no doubt await discovery, but it seems safe to assume that a 'princely group' is neither illusory nor without meaning. The princely burials are dated to the early seventh century, and are recorded, or suspected, as having been covered by earth mounds 10–20 m in diameter, and originally up to 3 m high, located in prominent positions, so as to see from and be seen. Coombe had a view of the sea, Sutton Hoo of the Deben valley, Cud-

Map 4 Princely burials.

desdon, Taplow and Asthall of the Thames Valley. Caenby was sited on a locally prominent limestone ridge overlooking the Roman Ermine Street.

The burial rite varies widely. Coombe and Asthall were cremations, as were Sutton Hoo 3–7 and 18. At Sutton Hoo the cremated material was gathered in a bronze bowl and covered with a cloth. At Taplow the body was interred on the back, with the feet to the west. Sutton Hoo 1 and 2 were ship burials; in Mound 2, the body lay in a chamber beneath a ship which was positioned at ground level and then buried. In Mound 1, the body was placed in a coffin in a chamber in the centre of a ship buried in a trench and covered by a mound, and this is likely to have been true also of a neighbouring example at Snape. The majority of the persons being honoured are held to be males by virtue of their skeletal remains or grave-goods. But female princely burials are not excluded: Swallowcliffe Down, in which a woman 18–25 years old was interred on a bed with a rich assemblage might qualify as a member of an aristocratic group.

Exotic grave goods, such as bronze vessels from the eastern Mediterranean (Cuddesdon) or glass from the Rhineland (Coombe), are important indicators of wealth in a grave. At Sutton Hoo Mound 1, nearly half the objects placed in the chamber were originally from abroad. The majority of the assemblages comprise a particular set of weapons and other objects thought to celebrate the male warrior: the jewelled sword, ornamented shield and helmet, lyres, and playing pieces. Equipment

for eating, and more particularly drinking, form part of the kit: cauldrons, buckets, drinking horns, glass bowls, cups and beakers.

Unfurnished burials with evidence for violent death were found in close association with mounds at Cuddesdon and Sutton Hoo 5. These are now known to belong to execution sites (*cwealmstow*) rather than sacrifices. They are generally tenth century and later in date, but in the case of Sutton Hoo, at least, began at the time of the mound burial.

Rich mound burial was a feature of Bronze Age Britain and occasionally known in the Roman period (at Bartlow Hills, Essex). Its reappearance in Anglo-Saxon England may be attributable to Frankish influence: the burial of Childeric (in 482) represented a model for pagan kingship, while Christian kingship was offered a model by the burial of his son Clovis in a timber church he had constructed on the site of the later Sainte-Geneviève in Paris. But Scandinavia provided an equally potent influence for England and offered contemporary examples of cremation under mound and ship-burial. Mound-burial had flour-

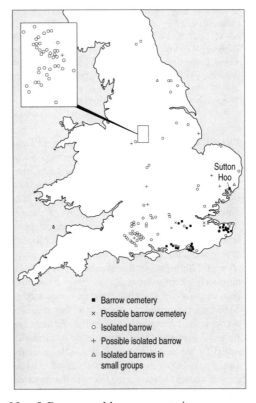

Map 5 Barrows and barrow cemeteries.

377

ished in sixth-century *Kent in the form of cemeteries of small mounds, but extended to the rest of England in the early seventh century in the form of the larger, apparently isolated mounds of the princely group (Map 5). Given the short and sudden period of their appearance, the context could well have been the attempts at *conversion to Christianity and the associated political pressure of Francia. In this case they may be seen as the demonstrative reaction of an aristocracy anxious to maintain their ideology and their allegiance to the peoples of the pagan North Sea cultural region.

VCH Essex i.220–6 [Broomfield]; VCH Buckinghamshire i.199–204 [Taplow]; A. Meaney, *A Gazeteer of Early Anglo-Saxon Burial Sites* (London, 1964); H. R. Ellis Davidson and L. Webster, 'The Anglo-Saxon Burial at Coombe (Wodenesborough), Kent', *MA* 11 (1967), 1–41; T. M. Dickinson, *Cuddesdon and Dorchester-on-Thames, Oxfordshire. Two Early 'Princely' Sites in Wessex*, BAR Brit. ser. 1 (Oxford, 1974); J. F. Shepherd, 'The Social Identity of the Individuals in Isolated Barrows and Barrow Cemeteries in Anglo-Saxon England', in *Space, Hierarchy and Society*, ed. B. Burnham and J. Kingsbury, BAR Brit. ser. 59 (Oxford, 1979), 47–80; G. Speake, *A Saxon Bed Burial on Swallowcliffe Down* (London, 1989); T. M. Dickinson and G. Speake, 'The Seventh-Century Cremation Burial in Asthall Barrow, Oxfordshire: a Reassessment', in *The Age of Sutton Hoo*, ed. M. O. H. Carver (Woodbridge, 1992), pp. 95–130; P. Everson, 'Pre-Viking Settlement in Lindsey', in *Pre-Viking Lindsey*, ed. A. Vince (Lincoln, 1993), pp. 91–100 [Caenby]; M. Müller-Wille, 'Königtum und Adel im Spiegel der Grabfunde', in *Die Franken–Wegbereiter Europas* (Mannheim, 1996), pp. 206–21.

M. O. H. CARVER

PROSE STYLE, LATIN. A great range of Latin prose styles was employed by Anglo-Saxon authors from the earliest period, and many individual authors seem to have been keen to develop their own distinctive 'voice', by adopting an idiosyncratic set of stylistic pretensions: no one would mistake (for example) the limpid and direct prose style of *Bede, with its basically biblical vocabulary and syntax, for the highly elaborate and ornate style of *Aldhelm, with a vocabulary and syntax ultimately derived from Latin verse. Much has been made of the so-called 'puerile pomposity' of Aldhelm's extraordinary prose style, but this is to overlook the twin issues of intended audience and authorial purpose: Bede's prose style is admirably suited to his didactic aim, while Aldhelm is the first Anglo-Saxon who can be observed striving for self-consciously artistic effects in Latin prose. Since it was Aldhelm's prose style, rather than Bede's, which was to prove popular in later Anglo-

Saxon England, and since it has been so misrepresented and misunderstood, it is worth considering certain aspects of his style in some detail.

The chief features of Aldhelm's prose style can all be explained by a desire to imitate and extend certain aspects of Latin verse style, and can indeed be matched in Aldhelm's own Latin poetry. So, for example, Aldhelm shows in his prose a marked tendency to favour certain suffixes such as *-fer*, *-ger*, and *-fluus* (for adjectives) or *-amen* (for nouns), as well as a penchant for archaic and obsolete words; precisely the same forms have been much favoured by Latin poets through the ages for their metrical usefulness. Characteristically, Aldhelm goes further in his taste for ornate vocabulary, adopting many grecisms and glossary terms to pep up his prose. Another favoured feature of Latin verse style is based on the so-called 'golden' line, in which (usually) two nouns are separated from their dependent adjectives by a medial verb; Aldhelm's own verse is largely patterned on just this arrangement. At the heart of this pattern is the rhetorical device of *hyperbaton* (literally 'going over'), whereby words in agreement are kept separate. In Aldhelm's prose, hyperbaton is employed routinely, often with artistic purpose: Aldhelm greatly favours both alliteration and *paronomasia* or punning sound-play, and often uses hyperbaton to point up these effects. A further otherwise baffling aspect of Aldhelm's style is best explained with recourse to verse: when (eschewing hyperbaton) Aldhelm does arrange a noun and its accompanying adjective consecutively, he scrupulously sees to it that the noun and adjective in question come from different declensions. Such a strategy is precisely echoed in Latin hexameter verse (for example that of Vergil, with whose work Aldhelm was extremely familiar), to avoid *homoeoteleuton* or end-rhyme in consecutive words. A number of these aspects of Aldhelm's Latin prose style are clearly intended for the ear rather the eye, and some localised effects, such as the opening of a letter where fifteen of the first sixteen words begin with the letter 'p', or the rhyming and rhythmical prose to be found at the end of his letter to King *Aldfrith of Northumbria, only emphasise this point. By contrast, *Boniface, who follows closely many features of Aldhelm's prose style, seems more interested in the repetition of key words and phrases (particularly in his letters), often employing paronomasia and repeated or parallel syntax to emphasise his point. Echoes of Aldhelm's prose style (and often his very words) are also evident in many *charters, where the bombastic diction and sonorous prose was evidently thought well suited, even if, in some cases, it is clear from the bungled syntax that the composer of the charter has not understood the sense of what is being copied. The same interest in the wilder aspects of Aldhelm's vocabulary, rather than the subtleties of his syntactical patterning, is also evident throughout much of the tenth and eleventh centuries, when the so-called 'hermenuetic style', with its characteristic reliance on archaisms, neologisms, and loan-words became extremely prominent. Examples of the hermeneutic style, the roots of which can also be seen in developments on the Continent, and which became current through its adoption by the most senior figures of the Benedictine reform, are found from all the most important monastic centres: *Canterbury (where the main exponent was *Frithegod), *Winchester (where *Æthelwold fostered its use), *Ramsey (where *Byrhtferth proved most prolific), and *Glastonbury (where *Dunstan left several examples). Not all the writers of the period were affected by the sonorous magniloquence of the hermeneutic style: some seem to have looked back to Bede, rather than Aldhelm, as a model, of whom perhaps the most prominent was *Ælfric, but the point to be stressed is that towards the end of the Anglo-Saxon period, as at the beginning of the literary record, Anglo-Saxon authors retained a keen sense of individual style, in Latin as well as in Old English.

M. Lapidge, 'The Hermeneutic Style in Tenth-Century Anglo-Latin Literature', in his *ALL* ii.105–49; idem, 'Schools, Learning, and Literature in Tenth-Century England', in *ALL* ii.1–48; idem, 'Byrhtferth and the *Vita S. Ecgwini*', in *ALL* ii.293–315; M. Winterbottom, 'Aldhelm's Prose Style and its Origins', *ASE* 6 (1977), 39–76.

ANDY ORCHARD

PROSE STYLE, OLD ENGLISH. The documented history of OE prose begins in the reign of King *Alfred, with the translations of Alfred himself and his intellectual circle, but the great flowering of prose, and the largest number of manuscripts containing it, dates from the Benedictine Revival of the 960s. In the last century of the Anglo-Saxon state, prose was written in a remarkable variety of styles to suit the considerable range of subjects covered, from *Ælfric's lucid, meticulously ordered style used for a clear exposition of patristic doctrine, through the anonymous highly patterned description in the *Anglo-Saxon Chronicle* of the pathos of the martyrdom of Archbishop *Ælfheah, to *Wulfstan's fulminations

against the lawlessness of the nation in his sermon of 1014 after the exile of King *Æthelred. The prose is capable of adaptation to the needs of writers explaining either the growth of the foetus in the womb or the complex calculations of the *computus. It describes vividly man-eating ants the size of dogs in the *Marvels of the East* and the hairy, misshapen devils that afflicted St *Guthlac. The reader gains the impression that the medium is so flexible and the vocabulary and syntax so full that a competent writer could express himself clearly on any subject he liked.

The composition of ordered prose is not simply a matter of putting speech into writing. Writers must convey meaning without the benefit of intonation or gesture to avoid ambiguity. Early prose writers had models in legal documents, in poetry and in Latin, as well as Latin books of rhetoric which were aimed at improving both oral and written expression. The composers of vernacular prose at the end of the ninth century used Latin models with greater or lesser success, King Alfred having the former and Bishop *Werferth the latter in his very literal translation of Gregory's *Dialogues*. The earliest entries in the *Anglo-Saxon Chronicle* are stylistically simplistic, repetitive in sentence structure and phraseology, and with little clause subordination. But by the last decade of the ninth century, subordination of clauses was sufficiently complex to show cause and effect in the events recounted, and a century later the chroniclers regularly charged their prose with their feelings and prejudices.

Some of the writings of named OE authors are attributed on the basis of style. Not all of the works said by *William of Malmesbury to be by King Alfred, for example, are now accepted as the king's because the style does not fit. Wulfstan's style is so distinctive that it helps in the attribution of his work. Although his homilies and legal writings show appreciation of the need to vary style according to purpose, as all competent stylists recognise, his very frequent use of intensive words and phrases is characteristic of all his writings, and passages containing pairs of words that alliterate or rhyme are widespread. Ælfric's style varies considerably, as one would expect of such a prolific writer, but it is noticeable that in all his work, the frequency of subordinate clauses and of successive sentences with linking adverbs such as 'therefore' or 'however' means that the reader is led carefully through his argument. During the composition of his Second Series of Catholic Homilies, Ælfric perfected a rhymical prose with a loosely metrical alliterating line which he used regularly in the Lives of Saints and later work.

If Ælfric is the master of the simple prose style, the writer who is keenest to show his ability to produce the most elaborate is *Byrhtferth of Ramsey. He has the distinction too of being the only writer to make observations on the rhetoric that he uses, naming and illustrating at one point in his *Enchiridion* a series of rhetorical figures, at another explaining how an adept rhetorician puts together words in the most elegant way. Although he is here writing about metrical composition in Latin, his comments include observations of and examples in the vernacular.

The Homilies of Wulfstan, ed. D. Bethurum (Oxford, 1957), pp. 87–98; *Homilies of Ælfric: A Supplementary Collection*, ed. J. C. Pope, 2 vols., EETS 259–60 (London, 1967–8), i.94–136; C. Clark, 'The Narrative Mode of *The Anglo-Saxon Chronicle* before the Conquest', *England Before the Conquest: Studies . . . presented to Dorothy Whitelock*, ed. P. Clemoes and K. Hughes (Cambridge, 1971), pp. 215–35; *Studies in Earlier Old English Prose*, ed. P. E. Szarmach (Albany, NY, 1986); J. M. Bately, 'Old English Prose before and during the Reign of Alfred', *ASE* 17 (1988), 93–138; idem, 'The Nature of Old English Prose', *CamComp*, pp. 71–87.

DONALD SCRAGG

PROSTITUTION. The large number of terms for prostitution in Old English imply that it was a widespread practice amongst the Anglo-Saxons. However, analysis of their contexts demonstrates that all of the terms for organized prostitution ('brothel', 'bawd', etc.) are found in *glosses, *glossaries or in retellings of stories, often saints' lives, set elsewhere. Of the few terms for 'prostitute' which do occur outside these contexts, it is impossible to define them any more specifically than as denoting 'promiscuous woman'. For the Anglo-Saxons, the prostitute and promiscuous woman were morally equivalent; for us, the payment of money sets the two apart. That there is little solid evidence for prostitution in the modern understanding of the term is indicated by the tendency for studies of the subject to begin with the later medieval period, when urbanization, the growth of capitalism, and greater individual mobility provided the necessary market, funds and anonymity.

C. E. Fell, *Women in Anglo-Saxon England* (London, 1984); C. Hough 'The Ladies of Portinscale', *The Journal of the English Place-Name Society* 29 (1997), 71–8; K. S. Kiernan '*Cwene*: The Old Profession of Exeter Riddle 95', *MP* 73 (1975), 384–9.

JULIE COLEMAN

PROVERBS: *see* Gnomic Poetry

PSALTER: *see* Liturgical Books; Psalter Glosses; Vespasian Psalter

PSALTER GLOSSES. Of the forty psalters and psalter fragments surviving from Anglo-Saxon England, eleven contain more or less complete continual interlinear glossing in Old English, one is partially glossed, two contain scattered glosses, two are binding strips from the same manuscript, and one contains a prose translation of Ps. I-L and a metrical translation of Ps. LI-C. The manuscripts range in date from the late eighth to the twelfth century. Seven of these manuscripts contain the *Romanum* version of the psalms (the text adopted by the church at *Rome and representing a revision of the Old Latin), while twelve manuscripts contain the *Gallicanum* version (so called from the ninth century because of its use in Gaul; a revision based on the Hebrew and Greek [Septuagint] versions). Two manuscripts, Cambridge, Trinity College R. 17. 1 (= E), and its copy, Paris, Bibliothèque Nationale, lat. 8846 (= O), are triple psalters, containing the *Romanum* (with Old English gloss), *Gallicanum* (with Latin gloss) and *Hebraicum* (with Anglo-Norman gloss) versions in parallel columns. Both contain extensive illustrations that ultimately derive, along with those in London, BL, Harley 603, from the *Utrecht Psalter (Utrecht, Universiteitsbibliotheek, 32).

Relations among the psalters are complex. Scholars distinguish between an A-type (London, BL, Cotton Vespasian A. i [= A]) and D-type (London, BL, Library, Royal 2.B. V [= D]) gloss tradition, the first associated with *Canterbury, the second with *Winchester, and exhibiting distinguishing traits in lexical choice that underlie the basis for the distinct traditions (although they share a common core vocabulary). The earlier notion that both gloss traditions derived from an archetype has been discarded. Other psalters complicate the picture: Junius (= B), Regius (= D), Stowe (= F), Vitellius (= G), Tiberius (= H) and Arundel (= J).

It has been argued that GJ were in direct contact (an unsubstantiated view), but other scholars suppose that H derived its glosses directly from D. While the older (red ink) glosses in New York, Pierpont Morgan Library, M.776 (= M) are independent, the later glosses (Latin and Old English) have been shown to depend directly upon D; E was heavily corrected from D or a D-type exemplar, although its original stratum of glosses often stand independent of other glossed psalters. The gloss in London, Lambeth Palace 427 (= I), the most scholarly of the psalters, containing multiple glosses and syntactical construe marks, is related to D but shows many independent additions, some of which are reflected also in F. The originality of the *Vespasian Psalter (= A) has been at issue for nearly a century, it being argued that the gloss is not a copy but an original addition that gave rise to the glosses in BC. While the glosses in B and C (Cambridge, University Library, Ff.1.23) derive from an A-type exemplar, evidence argues against direct copying from A. Scribal lapses, misspellings, and dittographic slips demonstrate that A is a copy of a lost gloss and opens the possibility that BC could have derived their glosses from another exemplar.

P. Pulsiano, *Psalters I*, Anglo-Saxon Manuscripts in Microfiche Facsimile 2 (Binghamton, NY, 1994); idem, 'Psalters', *The Liturgical Books of Anglo-Saxon England*, ed. R. W. Pfaff, *OEN* Subsidia 23 (Kalamazoo, MI, 1995), 60–85 [with bibliography to the end of 1992]; idem, 'The Originality of the Old English Gloss of the *Vespasian Psalter* and Its Relation to the Gloss of the *Junius Psalter*', *ASE* 25 (1996), 37–62.

PHILLIP PULSIANO

PUNCTUATION is a means of disambiguating visually elements of meaning in written discourse which are otherwise clearly conveyed in speech. In the nearly five centuries of writing in Anglo-Saxon England, conventions of punctuation may be distinguished according to a number of variables, including date, language used (whether Latin or Old English), and purpose (primarily, whether liturgical or not). Because *literacy itself is a historical condition, punctuation, an invention to make writing readable, shows a clear development in the range and meaning of its marks over time, as texts become increasingly dissociated from oral/aural performance. In addition to the marks of punctuation, developments in the conventions of textual layout (spacing between words, lineation, division of sections) contribute to the disambiguation of meaning in written texts.

Two overlapping interests combine to determine the development of punctuation in Anglo-Saxon England. Since Latin was the language of both written culture and public worship, for the former, punctuation was needed to assist in the grammatical construction of meaning; for the latter, punctuation was needed to divide texts for appropriate performance in the liturgy. While this need was not peculiar to the English church (St Jerome had adapted classical rhetorical textual division to scripture), *Alcuin's remarks in *Carmen* lxvii.7–10 ('Let them punctuate the meaning according to cola and commata, and place the points in correct order, lest the lector misread or fall suddenly silent before his devout brothers in the church') indicates that in the early Middle Ages concern for correct liturgical performance was the Christian analogue for the classical orator's care in construing and marking a text before reading it aloud. Alcuin's terms *cola* and *commata* call on a system of punctuation Isidore of Seville usefully outlines in *Etymologiae* I.xviii–xx. In his analysis, marks of punctuation distinguish three units of meaning in written discourse: the *comma* (pl. *commata*), smallest portion of the complete thought (*periodus*, rhetorical period, also called a *sententia*), and the *colon* (pl. *cola*), a major division of the *periodus*. The practical application of *comma* and *colon* varied, depending on whether the *sententia* to be construed was prose or verse. While Isidore refers to these marks as *positurae*, the marks he actually discusses are a development of the classical system of *distinctiones*. *Positurae* is generally the term reserved for the later system of marking liturgical texts.

The earliest markings of texts in Anglo-Saxon England used a modification of the classical system of *distinctiones*. Whereas the system Isidore outlines uses three points, a *sub-distinctio* (a low point to mark the *comma*), a *media-distinctio* (a point mid-way up the space of writing to mark the *colon*) and a *distinctio* (a point at the top right of the letter to indicate the *periodus*), this system was difficult to read in minuscule script. Latin manuscripts written in Anglo-Saxon England before the tenth century follow the Irish convention of grouping points to indicate the level of pause. By contrast, the *positurae* were more elaborate marks developed for liturgical punctuation and designed to assist performance of the liturgy by marking sense to assist intonation in reading aloud. The basic marks in this system are the *punctus elevatus* (to indicate a medial pause), *punctus versus* (to mark the completion of the sensus) and *punctus interrogativus* (to mark completion of a question). These signs of punctuation, in origin monastic, were extended from liturgical contexts to punctuate other texts, and they appear particularly clearly in corrections to manuscripts, some made, for example, by *Wulfstan and *Ælfric.

The difference between punctuation of Latin and Old English is most clearly seen in the presentation of verse. In England before the twelfth century, verse in Old English was laid out in long lines (like prose) while verse in Latin was laid out in metrical lines, each line set off by a *littera notabilior* (in effect, a capital). While Latin verse shows efforts to punctuate for sense and metre, Old English verse in the earliest manuscripts does not. By the eleventh century, however, Old English verse is more frequently pointed to distinguish lines and even half-lines. See, for example, Oxford, Bodleian Library, Junius 11 (the *Junius Manuscript), the punctuation of whose biblical poetry may have been influenced by liturgical models. While most of the half-lines are pointed in this manuscript, the virgules added to form the *punctus elevatus* and *punctus versus* are almost certainly later. Similarly, the OE *Metrical Calendar in London, BL, Cotton Tiberius B.i (s. xi[med]), whose half-lines are set off by medial points was 'corrected' by the additions of virgules to produce the *punctus versus* and *elevatus*. The religious verse in the late Oxford, Bodleian Library, Junius 121 (s. xi^3/$_4$) shows consistent metrical pointing. It is not until the Middle English period that vernacular verse is laid out in metrical lines.

T. J. Brown, 'Punctuation', *Encyclopaedia Brittanica*, 15th ed., xv.274–7; P. Clemoes, *Liturgical Influences on Punctuation in Late Old English and Early Middle English Manuscripts* (Cambridge, 1952); B. Mitchell, 'The Dangers of Disguise: Old English Texts in Modern Punctuation', *RES* ns 31 (1980), 385–413; J. Moreau-Maréchal, 'Recherches sur la ponctuation', *Scriptorium* 22 (1968), 56–66; K. O'Brien O'Keeffe, *Visible Song: Transitional Literacy in Old English Verse*, CSASE 4 (Cambridge, 1990); M. Parkes, *Pause and Effect: an Introduction to the History of Punctuation in the West* (Aldershot, 1993).

KATHERINE O'BRIEN O'KEEFFE

Q

QUEENS. Growth in the power of early medieval kings usually entailed a rise in the status of the king's wife. The influence of continental models and of the Christian church strengthened this tendency in England. The first known Anglo-Saxon queen was Bertha, whose husband *Æthelberht of *Kent was the most powerful English king of his day. Bertha was a Frankish king's daughter and a Christian. Pope *Gregory I wrote to her as *regina* (queen), urging her to 'incline your husband's mind' to support *Augustine's mission. *Bede gives the title *regina* to some eight Anglo-Saxon kings' wives, most (perhaps all) themselves daughters of kings; but he does not otherwise distinguish them from other royal consorts. Bede, and the *Beowulf*-poet, show royal marriages were negotiated to forge alliances or enhance the power of one king over another. Queens had retinues, hence political resources. Queens were not always peace-bringers, however. When King Cenwealh of Wessex repudiated *Penda's sister, Penda deprived him of his kingdom for three years. Peada of Mercia was allegedly murdered at the instigation of his Northumbrian wife. *Æthelthryth, Bede says, refused intercourse with her husband Ecgfrith of Northumbria and finally got his permission to take the veil. Perhaps she was barren. A claim to virginity won prestige in ecclesiastical quarters; but others may have thought her conduct unqueenly. *Stephen of *Ripon recounts the career of Ecgfrith's second wife Iurminburg, who, 'tortured with envy' of Bishop *Wilfrid's wealth, sought 'to defraud him of the gifts kings had given him'. She also appropriated Wilfrid's reliquary and wore it 'in her bedchamber', perhaps as a fertility charm. Childlessness increased the chances of a queen's being repudiated; but even a queen with offspring was insecure, given the volatile relationships underpinning early medieval politics. A king's death could expose his *widow to such risks that her only options were flight or retirement to a convent. *Edwin's widow Æthelburh fled from *Northumbria with her son and step-grandson to seek refuge with her brother King Eadbald of Kent. Later, fearing both Eadbald and the Northumbrian king *Oswald, she sent the boys overseas to the protection of her Frankish kin.

The persisting weak institutionalisation of Anglo-Saxon kingship and the uncertainties of royal succession precluded the dynastic continuity that in Francia sometimes allowed a queen-mother years of power as regent during a son's minority. Yet the *Anglo-Saxon Chronicle* reveals that when King Cenwealh died in 672, 'his queen (*cwen*) Seaxburg ruled for one year after him', apparently in her own right.

In the later eighth century, the unprecedented prominence of the Mercian queen *Cynethryth reflected the power and dynastic ambitions of her husband *Offa, and perhaps her own. She subscribed his *charters, sometimes with the title *dei gratia regina Merciorum*. *Coins were issued in her name, uniquely for an early medieval queen outside Italy, perhaps to mark the consecration in 787 of her son Ecgfrith as Offa's co-ruler and successor. Ninth-century Mercian queens regularly subscribed their husbands' charters. Æthelswith granted in her own right, 'with the consent of my magnates . . . part of my own lands' to a 'most faithful *thegn'. A ring possibly given by her to such a thegn survives, inscribed with her name. *Alfred's daughter *Æthelflæd, 'Lady of the Mercians', continued the activities of Mercian queens, adding success as a military strategist.

In ninth-century *Wessex, by contrast, the king's wife, says *Asser, 'was not allowed to be called queen'; Alfred attributed this to the wickedness of Queen Eadburh, daughter of Offa and wife of King Beorhtric of Wessex: 'as soon as she had won the king's friendship, and power throughout almost the entire kingdom, she began to behave like a tyrant, to denounce [men] before the king, and thus by trickery to deprive them of life or lands, or kill them with poison'. After accidentally poisoning her husband, she fled 'with countless treasures' overseas, to die in penury in Italy, 'thrown down from the queenly throne' (Asser, cc. 13–15). This story contains various kinds of truth. The Carolingian princess Judith, marrying *Æthelwulf in 856, was specially consecrated before leaving Francia to guarantee her status in Wessex. Some West Saxon kings, including Alfred, may have downplayed the status of their wives, to make repudiation easier, or, by keeping royal succession more open, to ease conflict between *æthelings. Whatever her formal status, the effective power of a king's wife depended on her natal family, her relationships with husband, children and stepchildren, and her capacity to build up support at court. Alfred's mother Osburh lacked a queen's title but had prestige through her own lineage and wielded influence through her sons' education.

From the tenth century, the formation of a single English kingdom meant that queens, chosen from the high nobility, acquired more conspicuous political leverage. Testators left bequests to the *hlæfdige* (queen-consort or queen-mother), and litigants sought her favour with gifts. She had some control over royal treasure, parts of the royal demesne were earmarked for her endowment, and she operated within and through the royal family. Especially if longlived, a queen could wield considerable power. *Eadgifu, third wife of *Edward the Elder, was influential in the reigns of her sons and grandson *Edgar. The consecration of *Ælfthryth, third wife of Edgar, in 973 indicated a certain institutionalisation of queenship. Ælfthryth gained friends and influence by patron-ising monastic reform: Bishop *Æthelwold supported the succession in 978 of her son *Æthelred. Ælfthryth oversaw her grandson's upbringing.

Two particularly influential queens arranged for their own literary commemoration. The *Encomium* written for *Emma, wife successively of Æthelred and *Cnut, stressed her role in her second marriage as uniter of English and Danes, an 'imperial spouse' (*Encomium*, ii.16). *Edith, wife of *Edward the Confessor, commissioned the *Vita Ædwardi* as an apologia for herself and her powerful Godwinson kin, as well as for Edward. It makes his sanctity explain her childlessness and depicts her maintaining the dignity of royal household, and presiding with her husband over the royal table. With the palace the centre of an earlier-medieval kingdom, such tasks set the queen at the heart of Anglo-Saxon royal government.

P. Stafford, 'The King's Wife in Wessex 800–1066', *P&P* 91 (1981), 3–27; idem, *Queens, Concubines and Dowagers: the King's Wife in the Early Middle Ages* (London, 1983); idem, *Queen Edith and Queen Emma: Queenship and Women's Power in Eleventh-Century England* (Oxford, 1997); J. L. Nelson, 'Medieval Queenship', in L. Mitchell, ed., *Women in Medieval Western European Culture* (New York, 1998).

JANET L. NELSON

R

RÆDWALD was the earliest king of the *East Angles of whom more than the name is known and probably the most influential of all. Rædwald's reign is undated but overlapped with those of *Æthelberht of *Kent (d. c.616) and *Edwin of *Northumbria (d. 633) and he probably died c.624. Knowledge of him comes primarily from four passages in Bede's *Historia ecclesiastica* and one in the anonymous *Whitby *Life of Gregory the Great*. He was reputedly the son of Tytil and grandson of Wuffa, after whom the dynasty was named.

Before Æthelberht's death, Rædwald was subject to his 'overkingship' and was baptised in Kent, perhaps as early as c.604. His name occurs after that of Æthelberht in Bede's list of 'over-kings' (*HE* ii.5) but his meaning is somewhat ambiguous: it should probably read 'Rædwald, king of the East Angles, who while Æthelberht lived, even conceded to him the military leadership of his people'. He was later reputed to have placed both Christian and pagan altars in a single temple (*HE* ii.15) and was clearly far from committed to Christianity, so gaining the enmity of Bede and his sources, who considered him apostate.

It was primarily Rædwald's part in promoting Edwin that interested Christian writers. He gave sanctuary to Edwin of the Deirans (c.616), who had fled to escape from his Bernician rival, King Æthelfrith; Rædwald defeated and killed the latter and replaced him with his own guest (*HE* ii.12). This battle, fought by the river Idle, was arguably the basis of his 'overkingship', which Bede considered extended across all the kingdoms south of the Humber, but his patronage of Edwin may well have carried his influence into Northumbria as well.

Rædwald was, therefore, a powerful king in the years around 620, whose influence was extensive. It is possible that it was his religious views that encouraged the East Saxons to expel Bishop *Mellitus from London, who departed with *Justus of Rochester to Gaul leaving *Canterbury the only diocese in England. Equally, it was perhaps his death that led to the alliance between Edwin and Eadbald, king of Kent (d. 640), and enabled Eadbald to revive his father's cult of Christianity and then encourage Edwin to accept baptism.

Rædwald's life coincided with the appearance of the Scandinavian rite of ship-burial in the vicinity of royal Rendlesham at Snape and *Sutton Hoo; and he remains one of the strongest candidates as the individual for whom the rich ship-burial excavated at Sutton Hoo in 1939 was intended.

S. Keynes, 'Rædwald the Bretwalda', in *Voyage to the Other World: the Legacy of Sutton Hoo*, ed. C. B. Kendall and P. S. Wells (Minneapolis, MN, 1992), pp. 103–23; *The Age of Sutton Hoo*, ed. M. Carver (Woodbridge, 1993); M. D. Newton, *The Origins of Beowulf and the Pre-Viking Kingdom of East Anglia* (Woodbridge, 1993); N. J. Higham, *An English Empire: Bede and the Early Anglo-Saxon Kings* (Manchester, 1995), pp. 183–217.

N. J. HIGHAM

RAMSEY (Hunts.) was a Benedictine abbey founded in 966 by Ealdorman Æthelwine for Bishop *Oswald of *Worcester, who was its first (titular and non-resident) abbot. Unusually, it seems to have been a completely new foundation; its dedication to St Benedict underlines Oswald's debt to his early training at *Fleury. Thanks largely to Oswald's own wealth and family connections the house prospered, and by the end of the tenth century was one of the richest of all English monasteries, attracting donations from a wide aristocratic circle (by the time of *Domesday Book, and again at the time of the Dissolution, it was roughly the tenth-richest monastery in England). During the 'anti-monastic reaction' following the death of King *Edgar in 975, the community of *Winchcombe and its abbot *Germanus were housed at Ramsey. Ramsey became a major centre of scholarship, with a remarkable literary output: *Abbo of Fleury lived there for two years (985–7), teaching *grammar, metrics and *computus and composing his *passio* of St *Edmund. His pupil *Byrhtferth followed his inspiration, and composed a large corpus of *hagiographical and computistical works (one of these, his *Enchiridion*, contains various passages describing his affection for Ramsey). Some years later *Oswald the Younger also acquired a reputation as scholar. Ramsey was also notable for promoting saints' cults (notably those of SS *Æthelred and Æthelberht, as well as St Ivo, an alleged Persian bishop whose relics were discovered at nearby *Slepe* (St Ives) in 1001), and was an avid collector of relics. Oswald's church, of which nothing survives, was – according to the descriptions in Byrhtferth's *Vita S. Oswaldi* and the Ramsey *Liber benefactorum* – a complex building with side *porticus*, an axial tower, and a western tower which probably contained a gallery for the organ and singers.

VCH Huntingdonshire i.377–9; J. Wise and W. M. Noble, *Ramsey Abbey: its Rise and Fall* (Huntingdon [1881]); J. A. Raftis, *The Estates of Ramsey Abbey* (Toronto, 1957), pp. 1–21; Fernie, *Architecture*, p. 114; *Oswald of Worcester*; C. R. Hart, 'The Foundation of Ramsey Abbey', *RB* 104 (1994), 295–327; *Byrhtferth's Enchiridion*, ed. P. S. Baker and M. Lapidge, EETS ss 15 (London, 1995), xv–xxv.

JOHN BLAIR

RAUNDS (Northants.) contained the best example yet excavated of a late Anglo-Saxon *thegn's church (see *parochial organization). The tiny single-cell church had a pot (previously used for wax-making) half-buried in the floor in front of the altar, serving as a *sacrarium* drain; a 'chancel' (but with a clergy-bench along its east wall) and a probable west bellcote were added *c.*1000. Meanwhile a graveyard developed, with social gradations expressed in location and in the use of coffins, linings and markers. The church was rebuilt in the late eleventh century, illustrating a process known from innumerable standing examples. Altogether more exceptional is the cessation of burial, and the abandonment of the church during the twelfth century. Excavations still in progress are also revealing a large mid to late Anglo-Saxon settlement complex.

A. Boddington, *Raunds Furnells: the Anglo-Saxon Church and Churchyard*, English Heritage Archaeological Report 7 (London, 1996).

JOHN BLAIR

RAWLINSON, RICHARD (1690–1755), antiquary and non-juror like his contemporaries Thomas Hearne and George *Hickes, was a great collector of *coins, *charters and manuscripts, many of which were acquired during travels abroad in the 1720s. The largest part of his collections, including thousands of manuscripts, was bequeathed to the Bodleian Library, Oxford. He also made provision for the founding of the chair of Anglo-Saxon at Oxford which still bears his name. Amongst the voluminous papers he was responsible for preserving were letters and transcripts

of Anglo-Saxon scholars of the previous century, including our only witness to the *Battle of Maldon*.

G. R. Tashjian, D. R. Tashjian and B. J. Enright, *Richard Rawlinson: A Tercentenary Memorial* (Kalamazoo, MI, 1990).

DONALD SCRAGG

RECULVER (Kent), a late Roman coastal fort, illustrates the widespread practice of re-using Roman walled places for major churches (see *Roman remains). In 669, according to the *Anglo-Saxon Chronicle*, King Ecgberht of *Kent gave Reculver to the mass-priest Bassa to build a minster; the earliest extant original Anglo-Saxon *charter, issued in 679 *in ciuitate Recuulf*, thus records an assembly in what had by then become an ecclesiastical 'city' (S 8). The church, in the centre of the square fort (fig. 15), was mostly demolished in 1809, but even the surviving fragments constitute the best surviving example of a seventh-century Kentish church: it has a polygonal apse and *porticus* flanking the nave, and follows Roman prototypes closely. A triple arcade between the nave and the apse formed a screen behind the high altar, in front of which stood an elaborate stone cross, of disputed date but possibly contemporary with the building.

Taylor and Taylor, *AS Arch*, ii. 503–9; Fernie, *Architecture*, pp. 35–6; R. Kozodoy, 'The Reculver Cross', *Archaeologia* 108 (1986), 67–94.

JOHN BLAIR

REEVE is a general term denoting a man with administrative responsibilities. There were royal reeves, bishops' reeves, nobles' reeves; reeves on royal estates, in *towns and *boroughs; *shire reeves, reeves over *wapentakes and probably *hundreds. There was a reeve of the *Five Boroughs, and the terms of *Domesday Book imply a reeve in every village. *Æthelstan called on his reeves to enforce his ordinances on tithe payments, and expected that any noble who had more men than he could personally supervise would have a reeve who could do so, whilst the late tract *Gerefa* deals with the reeve's duties in *estate management. As this variety indicates, few generalizations would hold good for all reeves.

Those about whom we are best informed are the royal reeves. As with the *ealdormen these were often originally men of high status, already in the late seventh and early eighth centuries in charge of great royal estates, and securing grants of land from the king. Late seventh-century Kentish kings already had a *wicgerefa* in *London, who acted as witness if any inhabitant of *Kent bought goods there. He probably had oversight of the king's residence in London. Such residences, in towns and elsewhere, were the site at which the king's judgement could be sought, the place where royal dues were collected and often the centres of later hundreds. The reeve's responsibility for royal estates is, no doubt, an important origin of his wider judicial powers and activities.

By the end of the ninth century *Asser placed the reeves alongside the bishops, ealdormen, *thegns and nobles as lynch-pins in the control of the kingdom, whose unjust judgements were one of the prompts for *Alfred's concern with education. The tenth-century *laws make clear the significance of the royal reeves. *Edward the Elder called on them to ensure a meeting every four weeks at which days for the hearing of cases could be assigned: an early stage in the formalization of the hundred *court. In Æthelstan's laws they were responsible for the taking of pledges to keep the peace, for implementing the rulings on theft and the harbouring of criminals, for nominating men who would be witnesses at pleas in their districts. This gave them great potential power; they must not take bribes. By the early eleventh century abuses of that power were highlighted. *Cnut enjoined his sheriffs and other reeves not to manipulate justice or exact money unjustly, to give just judgements, to provide for the king from his own property and to limit their demands for royal provisioning. Asser's statements suggest that some of these were old problems. The nature of Cnut's laws and letters, which form an extended commentary on good rule and abuses of it, reveal the extent of royal power by the early eleventh century, and the extent to which that of reeves had grown with it.

Cnut's letter of 1027, unfortunately preserved only in Latin translation, appears to refer to sheriffs and reeves. Much other evidence points to the importance of the *scirgerefa*, or sheriff, by *c.*1000. Tenth-century rule had emphasized the shire; and coupled with the large ealdormanries, which meant that the ealdorman could not fulfil all the needs of royal rule, this encouraged the emergence of a noble, royal official whose responsibilities lay here, especially one whose role grew out of his concern with the king's interests in his boroughs and estates. By 1066 almost every shire south of the Tees and Mersey had its own sheriff, and one of the purposes of the Domesday Survey was to check on this major local agent of royal power. It was intended that each shire in the Survey should begin with an account of local customs, the shire town and the royal lands, for all of which the

sheriff was responsible. Edward of Salisbury received renders of enormous quantities of food stuffs (see *feorm) from which he was expected to make up any deficiencies in the reeves' provisioning for the royal court. The continuity of his activities, like theirs, with those reeves of Æthelstan's estates providing royal charity from the *feorm*, is clear.

Reeves at all levels were a point of contact between royal government and the locality. Domesday's focus on royal concerns inevitably obscures the sheriff's possible role in the shire community itself. The village reeve substituting for the lord in the shire court was there as a lord's man, as a member of his community, and to some extent as an agent of royal power.

H. M. Chadwick, *Studies on Anglo-Saxon Institutions* (Cambridge, 1905); W. A. Morris, *The Medieval English Sheriff to 1300* (Manchester, 1927); H. Loyn, *The Governance of Anglo-Saxon England 500–1087* (London, 1984); J. Campbell, 'Some Agents and Agencies of the Late Anglo-Saxon State', *Domesday Studies*, ed. J. C. Holt (Woodbridge, 1987), pp. 201–18.

PAULINE STAFFORD

REGALIA. The origin and development of formal regalia in Anglo-Saxon England is imperfectly understood. We know that by the tenth century a *coronation ritual was in place, and that kings were by that time traditionally designated by certain physical signs – a crown, a sword and its sword-bearer, and by other symbols derived from Carolingian and classical tradition, such as the orb and sceptre, as shown for example in the *Bayeux Tapestry image of *Harold enthroned, bearing these attributes of kingship. No regalia of the period survive, however, and the dependence on external models of Anglo-Saxon *coin and manuscript depictions of royalty always requires circumspect interpretation.

Nevertheless, something of the stages whereby the outward and visible signs of a king were created can be seen in material from a few graves of the sixth and early seventh century – in particular the great Mound I ship burial at *Sutton Hoo. Here, like some other Germanic *dynasties, the upwardly mobile East Anglian rulers adopted certain high-status Roman objects into a local vocabulary of kingship, presumably to legitimise the claim to authority. The helmet, derived from those worn by late Roman officers, signals exceptional status through its rarity, its Germanic iconographic content and, most of all, its Roman form. In continental contexts, it is clear that helmets played a significant part in the development of the royal crown. Other items of the strictly ceremonial *arms and armour, such as the sword and its belt fittings, and of the formal dress, such as the gold buckle, certainly symbolised power and status, as, in a wider sense, did the deliberately selected nature and geographical range of treasure in the burial. But if anything can be regarded as regalia in this grave, it is undoubtedly the unique stone sceptre, which grafts Germanic images onto a native version of the Roman consul's sceptre topped by a victor's wreath. It seems likely that the origins of Anglo–Saxon regalia lie essentially in a late Roman tradition, subsequently augmented by Christian symbolism and by the powerful example of the Carolingian emperors.

P. Schramm, *Herrschaftzeichen und Staatsymbolik* I. (Stuttgart, 1944); R. L. S. Bruce-Mitford, *The Sutton Hoo Ship Burial*, II. *Arms, Armour and Regalia* (London, 1978); D. M. Wilson, *The Bayeux Tapestry* (London, 1985), pp. 182, 226; L. E. Webster, 'Death's Diplomacy: Sutton Hoo in the Light of other Male Princely Burials', in *Sutton Hoo: Fifty Years After*, ed. R. Farrell and C. Neuman de Vegvar, *American Early Medieval Studies* 2 (1992), 75–82; M. Archibald, M. Brown and L. Webster, 'Heirs of Rome: the Shaping of Britain AD 400–900', *The Transformation of the Roman World AD 400–700*, ed. L. E. Webster and M. P. Brown (London, 1997), pp. 209–11, 221–4; W. Filmer-Sankey, 'The "Roman Emperor" in the Sutton Hoo Ship Burial', *JBAA* 148 (1996), 1–9.

LESLIE WEBSTER

REGNAL LISTS. Regnal or 'king' lists are lists of the successive kings of a kingdom, often supplying their respective reign-lengths and also very occasionally additional information, such as *genealogies. Though often grouped together with genealogies (both in medieval manuscripts and by modern scholars), they constitute a separate medium with characteristic features and problems of their own, and should be treated separately. For Anglo-Saxon England, the earliest direct evidence of regnal lists comes from the early eighth century. *Bede appears to have had access to regnal lists for *Northumbria, *Essex and *Kent and (possibly) *Mercia. Furthermore, in a famous passage (*HE* iii.1), he stated that those calculating the reigns of kings agreed to 'expunge the memory' of the apostate successors of *Edwin and to assign that year (633–4) to the reign of *Oswald. Other eighth-century regnal lists include the Northumbrian and Mercian lists in the 'Anglian' collection of genealogies (765×774) and the Northumbrian list in the Moore Memoranda (737). Updated versions of these regnal lists survive from the ninth and tenth centuries. There is also a Kentish regnal list

up to Æthelberht II (d. 762) which omits reign-lengths. These early lists pale to some extent when compared with the so-called 'West Saxon Genealogical Regnal List', composed in its present form during the reign of *Alfred, which describes the succession to the kingship of *Wessex from the arrival of *Cerdic and Cynric (dated here AD 494) to the late ninth century. It provides additional information for many of the kings, including genealogical details and some full patrilines. A later continuation of this 'List' survives in three versions: one, extending to *Edward the Martyr, is appended to *ASC* MS. B; another, to *Æthelred the Unready, in the 'Textus Roffensis'; and a third version, to *Cnut, in the *Liber Vitae* of the New Minster, Winchester. This continuation is of historical interest in that in many cases it recounts the specific reign-lengths (including the number of months, weeks and days) from the coronation to death of each king. There are also two versions of a 'tabular abstract' of the West Saxon Regnal List, originating in the reign of *Edgar but now extending to Æthelred the Unready. The New Minster *Liber Vitae* also contains an interesting, but selective, list of kings' sons or *æthelings to the late tenth century.

Although regnal lists may have performed an originally chronological function, their form and content made them perfect means of expressing political claims. Like genealogies (though probably to a lesser extent), they are prone to ideological manipulation and consequently are not necessarily reliable historical accounts of the kingdoms from the fifth and sixth centuries onwards. Indeed, by their very form, regnal lists can simplify political relations and ignore changes in kingship over time, implying continuous lineal succession. The names of kings could be omitted for a variety of reasons – the Bedan example of Edwin's apostate successors being a case in point. Similarily, rulers regarded (retrospectively at least) as usurpers could be omitted, as could periods of external rule and interregnum. All these factors might cause cumulative chronological problems, though, in the case cited by Bede, the relevant year was duly assigned to the next reign. On a larger scale regnal lists were manipulated to project into the past the political circumstances which prevailed at the time of composition. For example, the Northumbrian list in the Moore Memoranda is a confused and difficult document, but seems to be implying that seventh-century Bernician control of Northumbria had also obtained in the sixth. Similarly, the West Saxon 'List' seeks to demonstrate that the ninth-century monarchy of Wessex had existed continuously since Cerdic and Cynric in the fifth century, whereas evidence for the seventh century indicates it had then constituted a confederacy of petty kingdoms under an overlord. Explicit statements of Cerdicing ancestry no doubt reinforced the legitimacy of individual kings; and in fact analysis of the accompanying patriline of *Æthelwulf shows that none of his direct ancestors since Ceawlin (grandson of Cerdic) were included in the 'List' as kings.

D. N. Dumville, 'Kingship, Genealogies and Regnal Lists', in *Early Medieval Kingship*, ed. P. H. Sawyer and I. N. Wood (Leeds, 1977), pp. 72–104; idem, 'The Anglian Collection of Royal Genealogies and Regnal Lists', *ASE* (1976), 23–50; idem, The West-Saxon Genealogical Regnal List: Manuscripts and Texts', *Anglia* 104 (1986), 1–32; idem, 'The West-Saxon Genealogical Regnal List and the Chronology of early Wessex', *Peritia* 4 (1985), 21–66; *The Liber Vitae of the New Minster and Hyde Abbey, Winchester*, ed. S. Keynes, EEMF 26 (Copenhagen, 1996).

DAVID E. THORNTON

REGULARIS CONCORDIA, the customary sanctioned by the Council of *Winchester (*c.*973), constitutes the major document of the Benedictine Reform in England. As indicated by its programmatic title – *Regularis concordia Anglicae nationis monachorum sanctimonialiumque* – it was intended to establish a uniform observance for monks and nuns throughout the country on the basis of the *Regula S. Benedicti* and to consolidate the achievements of the monastic revival. The work was traditionally attributed to *Dunstan, yet there is compelling evidence that this largely derivative compilation was drawn up by *Æthelwold. The text is preserved in two loosely related copies, both of which were most probably produced at Christ Church, *Canterbury, around the middle of the eleventh century: in BL, Cotton Tiberius A. iii, a full version of the *Regularis concordia* with a continuous Old English interlinear *gloss and a thematic frontispiece was combined with a set of closely related Benedictine items including the Rule, whereas BL, Cotton Faustina B. iii contains a defective reproduction of the Latin text in which the epilogue has been supplanted by three model obituary notes adapted to Christ Church. Written in the so-called 'hermeneutic style' as practised by Æthelwold, the prologue and the epilogue of the document codify the mutually profitable alliance between King *Edgar, Queen *Ælfthryth, and the monastic reform party and seek to protect the property of religious houses against powerful secular interests. The main body of the *Regularis concordia* consists of twelve chapters dealing with liturgical practice throughout the year and various other aspects of monastic life and claustral organization. The code shows a special indebtedness to Carolingian reform decrees as well as to contemporary reformed monasticism on the Continent, above all to *Fleury, but there are also some genuinely English traits like the daily series of intercessory prayers for the royal house. Another remarkable feature of the customary is its inclusion in the Easter office of the *Quem quaeritis*-trope that marks the beginnings of liturgical drama in England. Evidence for the appreciation and use of the *Regularis concordia* throughout the late Anglo-Saxon period is provided by an abbreviated and supplemented Latin version known as *Ælfric's 'Letter to the Monks of Eynsham', by two fragmentary Old English prose translations and a number of more or less faithful verbal echoes in other liturgical documents.

Regularis Concordia Anglicae Nationis Monachorum Sanctimonialiumque: the Monastic Agreement of the Monks and Nuns of the English Nation, ed. and trans. T. Symons (London, 1953); 'Regularis concordia Anglicae nationis', ed. T. Symons, S. Spath, M. Wegener and K. Hallinger, in *Consuetudinum saeculi X/XI/XII monumenta non-Cluniacensia*, ed. K. Hallinger, Corpus Consuetudinum Monasticarum 7.3 (Siegburg, 1984), 61–147; *Die 'Regularis Concordia' und ihre altenglische Interlinearversion. Mit Einleitung und Kommentar*, ed. L. Kornexl, Münchener Universitäts-Schriften: Texte und Untersuchungen zur Englischen Philologie 17 (Munich, 1993); *Tenth-Century Studies*, ed. D. Parsons (London, 1975); L. Kornexl, 'The *Regularis Concordia* and its Old English Gloss', *ASE* 24 (1995), 95–130; J. Hill, 'The "Regularis Concordia" and its Latin and Old English Reflexes', *RB* 101 (1991), 299–315.

LUCIA KORNEXL

RELICS AND RELIC-CULTS. Saints' relics were an important part of Christianity from at least the second century onwards, and Anglo-Saxon England was no exception. Pope *Gregory the Great sent relics to *Augustine; Pope Vitalian sent an impressive collection of Roman relics to King *Oswiu of the Northumbrians and his queen; and relics were amongst the items that *Benedict Biscop and *Wilfrid of *Ripon brought back to England from *Rome. The relics in question were probably secondary relics, that is inanimate objects or even cloths (*brandea*) which had been in contact with the corporeal remains of the saints. Soon, however, cults developed of the relics of native Anglo-Saxon saints. The relics involved were often secondary also, as in the case of the dust said to have been taken from *Chad's shrine, or the earth from the place where St

*Oswald, king of the Northumbrians, was killed. But corporeal relics were also of great importance, notably the complete and, as it was believed, undecayed bodies of saints such as *Cuthbert and *Æthelthryth, but also under certain circumstances parts of bodies, as with St Oswald who was dismembered on the battlefield and whose head, arms, and body were venerated respectively at *Lindisfarne, Bamburgh, and Bardney. The placing of the bodies of saints in elevated shrines was probably influenced by the Gaulish church, and in some cases involved equipping the shrine with rich objects, some of which from the shrine of St Cuthbert (together with the reliquary coffin) have survived at *Durham.

Relics continued to be of importance throughout the Anglo-Saxon period, and cults seem to have been fostered especially by the reformed Benedictine communities of the tenth century. These often built up substantial relic-collections, frequently by means of translating the remains of saints from lesser or decayed churches to their own, as was the case notably at *Ely, Thorney, *Ramsey, and *Glastonbury which claimed to have acquired numerous relics, including those of Patrick, David, *Aidan, *Bede, and *Boisil. Although not a reformed Benedictine monastery in the pre-Conquest period, Durham was also prominent in this process and built up a substantial collection of relics from northern England. Relic-cults had an influence on the development of architecture. *Crypts such as those at *Repton and *Brixworth may have been built or modified to permit access to relics; and the elaborate 'westwork' constructed at the Old Minster, *Winchester, was almost certainly in part intended to glorify the grave of St *Swithun. In general, pontificals of the late Anglo-Saxon period show that relics were essential for the dedication of churches and altars. Kings had substantial collections of relics, which figured as diplomatic gifts. Relics were also important in royal government; documents were kept alongside the royal relics, and relics were used in oaths, as when King *Alfred made the *Viking army swear an oath to him on relics. They were used in manumissions, *ordeals, and *penitential processions, and as objects on which *oaths were sworn. Some relic-cults, notably those of St *Edmund, king of the *East Angles, and St *Edward, king and martyr, had potential political implications; and the patronage of the relics of St Cuthbert by the *Wessex kings may have been an element in their policy towards the north. Relic-cults retained their importance in England throughout the

Middle Ages, and it is notable that post-Conquest churchmen were often active in promoting the cults of Anglo-Saxon saints, whose remains they translated into their grand new churches, thus establishing direct continuity between pre-Conquest and post-Conquest England.

D. Rollason, *Saints and Relics in Anglo-Saxon England* (Oxford, 1989); S. Ridyard, *The Royal Saints of Anglo-Saxon England* (Cambridge, 1988); I. G. Thomas, 'The Cult of Saints' Relics in Medieval England' (unpubl. Ph.D. dissertation, Univ. of London, 1974).

DAVID ROLLASON

REPTON was a Middle Saxon royal monastery, a *Viking winter fortress, and the principal Late Saxon church of Derbyshire south of the Trent. The monastery seems to have been founded *c*.675 on land granted by Friduricus *princeps* to Hædda, abbot of Bredon, and was thus ultimately within the influence of *Medeshamstede* (Peterborough). It was a double house for men and women ruled by an abbess in which, before the end of the seventh century, *Guthlac had taken his vows and Merewalh, king of the *Magonsætan*, is said to have been buried. There followed a series of royal burials: *Æthelbald in 757, Wiglaf *c*.840, and in 849 his grandson Wigstan (Wystan). A cult soon grew up at Wigstan's tomb, and he appears in the *Secgan* as 'St Wigstan who rests in the minster at Repton by the River Trent' (see *Resting-Places of the Saints). The community survived for almost

Pl. 15 The Repton crypt.

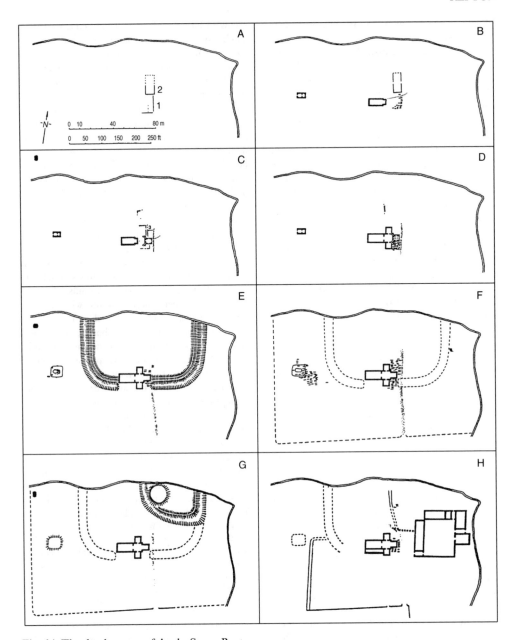

Fig. 14 The development of Anglo-Saxon Repton.

exactly two centuries until the winter of 873–4 when religious life was disrupted by the establishment of the *wintersetl* of the Danish Great Army. There is no indication that monastic life revived after the departure of the Vikings in 874, but the church was rebuilt and became the focus of a large *cemetery containing by the twelfth century perhaps as many as 16,000 burials. The size of this cemetery suggests that the church then functioned as the head minster of a *parochia* covering a large region probably equivalent to Derbyshire south of the Trent, a role probably reflected in the presence of two priests in 1086 and by the fact that in the later Middle Ages Repton had as many as seven chapelries. In 1153–9 Matilda, countess of Chester, gave the church to the Augustinian canons of Calke who migrated to Repton *c.*1172. Their priory was suppressed in 1538 and in 1557 Repton

School was established in the surviving west range of the cloister.

The east end of the parish church of St Wystan is one of the most important survivals of Anglo-Saxon architecture. The chancel, decorated externally by tall arcades of pilaster strips, and the central space of the church still stand to a great height, while beneath the chancel there is a crypt approached by diagonal passages, evidently the setting for *pilgrimage to the tomb of Wigstan. The columns supporting the vault of the crypt are crude but real *tornatile*, twisted not merely fluted, copies of those erected by Constantine before the grave of St Peter in *Rome. These structures were evidently erected in several stages but have proved very difficult to untangle, although the subject of intensive study over more than fifty years (1935–87) by Dr H. M. Taylor.

The excavations around the east end and elsewhere at Repton have however provided a clear sequence for the occupation of the sandstone bluff at the confluence of the Trent and the Repton Brook. This shows that the monastery was founded in a pre-existing estate centre comprising a number of massive timber buildings, and that these were initially adapted for monastic use, before being gradually replaced. The first church (of still unknown type) was extended east by a building which included a semi-subterranean chamber, approached from the west by diagonal passages, with a rectangular recess in each wall, and drained by a stone-lined channel. This is best interpreted as a baptistery. During the ninth century, probably in the reign of King Wiglaf of Mercia (d. *c*.840), this sunken room was converted into a mausoleum by the insertion of the pillared vault already described. It was *in mausolio Wiglavi regis avi sui* ('in the mausoleum of his grandfather Wiglaf') that Wigstan was buried in 849. A fragment of a standing cross found outside the east end of the church bears on one face the figure of a mounted ruler dressed in mail armour, wearing a diadem around his head, brandishing a sword in one hand and a small round shield in the other. This has been interpreted as a memorial to King Æthelbald, buried at Repton in 757, who is shown with Germanic weapons but in the guise of a triumphing emperor. One of the narrow faces carries a depiction of hell-mouth, and the other broad face is now thought to show the crucifixion.

This was the state of the church when in the autumn of 873 it was incorporated by the Vikings into the line of a D-shaped rampart enclosing an area of 1.46 ha. (3.65 acres) on the south bank of the Trent. The stone structure of the church

seems to have served as a strongpoint, perhaps a gatehouse. A series of burials of Scandinavian type were now made to north and south of the east end of the church, including the burial of a man who had been killed by a massive cut to the inside of his left thigh. He had a silver Thor's Hammer around his neck and his sword by his left side, and lay beside a second grave containing the body of a young man, both covered by a stone setting including fragments of a carved cross. Another burial nearby contained a gold ring of Scandinavian type and five silver pennies datable to the mid 870s. Fifty metres west of the church, outside the Viking defences, a mass burial of the disarticulated remains of at least 249 individuals was found under a mound, laid in a sunken chamber converted out of a pre-existing Anglo-Saxon building, perhaps itself a mortuary chapel. This deposit was dated by a further five silver pennies which can be ascribed on numismatic grounds alone to *c*.873–4, the precise period of the wintering the Great Army at Repton recorded in the *Anglo-Saxon Chronicle*. The mass burial, which was closed by an elaborate pagan ritual, appears to be of 'royal' status and was perhaps that of one of the leaders of the Great Army surrounded by the remains of others of the army brought together from elsewhere for burial at Repton.

After the interlude of 873–4, the Viking defences were levelled, the church rebuilt, and intensive burial took place on all sides until interrupted to the east in the twelfth century by the construction of a motte and bailey castle of the earls of Chester. When the site was given to the canons of Calke for their priory, the castle was levelled and the priory built in part above it.

H. M. Taylor, 'Repton Reconsidered', in *England Before the Conquest. Studies in Primary Sources Presented to Dorothy Whitelock*, ed P. Clemoes and K. Hughes (Cambridge, 1971), pp. 351–89; M. Biddle and B. Kjølbye-Biddle, 'The Repton Stone', *ASE* 14 (1985), 233–92; M. Biddle, 'Archaeology, Architecture, and Cult of Saints in Anglo-Saxon England', in Butler and Morris, *AS Church*, pp. 1–31, at 14–22; H. M. Taylor, 'St Wystan's Church, Repton, Derbyshire. A Reconstruction Essay', *Archaeological Journal* 144 (1987), 205–45; idem, *St Wystan's Church, Repton. A Guide and History* ([Repton], 1989); M. Biddle and B. Kjølbye-Biddle, 'Repton and the Vikings', *Antiquity* 66 (1992), 36–51; *The People of Early Repton*, ed. M. Biddle and B. Kjølbye-Biddle, Investigations at Repton 1 (Oxford, in preparation).

MARTIN BIDDLE AND BIRTHE KJØLBYE-BIDDLE

RESIGNATION. As it stands in Krapp and Dobbie's edition of the *Exeter Book, *Resignation*

(entitled *Contrition* in Muir's edition) is a poem of 118 lines, sometimes classified among the Old English *elegies, though it lacks the closing note of consolation common to that genre. Critical discussion of the poem has centered on the question of its unity, since it has been demonstrated that one folio of the Exeter Book has been lost between fos. 118 and 119, after line 69 of the poem. Some critics have noted an abrupt shift of tone at this point, from genuine penitence to more generalised lament, and have suggested *Resignation* might comprise the beginning of one poem and the end of another. The first half resembles the penitential psalms in tone and theme, while the second contemplates an exile's sea journey in a fashion that recalls the *Seafarer*.
ASPR iii.215–18; A. Bliss and A. J. Frantzen, 'The Integrity of *Resignation*', *RES* n.s. 27 (1976), 385–402; M. Nelson, 'On *Resignation*', in *Old English Elegies: New Essays in Criticism and Research* (Rutherford, NJ, and London, 1983), pp. 133–47; *The Exeter Anthology of Old English Poetry*, ed. B. J. Muir, 2 vols. (Exeter, 1994).

ROBERT DINAPOLI

RESTING-PLACES OF THE SAINTS. The *Secgan be þam Godes sanctum þe on Engla lande ærost reston* ('Concerning God's saints who formerly rested in England') is the only list of saints' resting places from Anglo-Saxon England. It consists of entries such as, 'St *Æthelberht rests at Hereford near the River Wye'. Compiled *c.*1031 but incorporating an earlier, probably ninth-century, list, it may have been a pilgrims' guide, as well as a celebration of the saints of England. Other lists probably existed in Anglo-Saxon England and are reflected in post-Conquest lists, notably one in the chronicle of Hugh Candidus.
D. Rollason, 'Lists of Saints' Resting-Places in Anglo-Saxon England', *ASE* 7 (1978), 61–93; L. Butler, 'Two Twelfth-Century Lists of Saints' Resting-Places', *AB* 105 (1987), 87–103.

DAVID ROLLASON

RHYMING POEM. The *Rhyming Poem* is the only example of sustained end-rhyme in Old English *metre. Generally, half-lines are simultaneously linked in pairs by *alliteration, and in quatrains by rhyme (predominately based on grammatical endings). The rhythmical regularity of the verse is also uncharacteristic. J. J. Conybeare, who first drew attention to the poem in 1813, suggested that the author had imitated an Old Norse scaldic form (*runhenda*). Modern scholars consider that the author was influenced by Latin hymns (particularly the 'Ambrosian'

quatrain), and was refining a technique with which *Cynewulf had experimented briefly. The *Rhyming Poem* is preserved among the *elegies found in the *Exeter Book. Its sketchily-characterized narrator is best interpreted as a king fallen from prosperity.
ASPR iii.166–9; *The Old English Riming Poem*, ed. O. D. Macrae-Gibson (Cambridge, 1983).

STEPHANIE HOLLIS

RIDDLES, OLD ENGLISH. The OE riddles are mostly short poems (usually about a dozen lines, although occasionally extending to over a hundred) which describe aspects of the Anglo-Saxon world in enigmatic ways. The riddles present a playful universe in which inanimate objects like a battering ram or a book, an iceberg or a weathercock are treated as living sentient beings with a point of view of their own, while animals like the badger or the nightingale take on human characteristics. Sometimes the riddle object describes itself in the first person; in other cases it is often characterized by the catch-all noun *wiht*, 'creature'.

The OE riddles are recorded in three sequences at the end of the *Exeter Book. One riddle is copied out twice and one is also preserved in an earlier Northumbrian version (known after the location of the manuscript as the Leiden Riddle). The text of the Exeter Book is damaged in places so that it is impossible to know the precise number of riddles once assembled there: Williamson's edition comprises ninety-one, but there may once have been a hundred, matching some of the collections of Latin *enigmata. The numbering of riddles varies in different editions and translations. The Old English riddles are presented with no title (as with all other Exeter Book poems) and no solution (although a subsequent user seems to have scratched some enigmatic clues, such as the runic first letter of an answer, beside some). As a result, there is still no consensus on the solution to a few of the riddles. Oftentimes, however, the solution is not especially difficult and the pleasure of the poem lies in contemplating the paradoxical nature of the world. The nature of the displaced description in the riddles parallels the Anglo-Saxon poetic technique of kennings.

Sometimes a consistent deceptive solution is built up in tandem with the main solution and, in about a dozen cases, that alternative is deliberately salacious. For example, a rising and swelling boneless object grabbed and covered by a prince's daughter is dough, the small miracle hanging near a man's thigh is a key, and the fecund activity of a young man thrusting with something stiff is the churning of butter. In addition to such scenes of domestic life, other riddles cluster around aspects of the heroic world, describing the various uses of a horn or the paradoxical potential of a coat of mail. A few belong to the world of learning, some translating Latin *enigmata*, such as an account of creation drawn from *Aldhelm; others describe activities of the *scriptorium, such as an account of the making of a Bible, or the surprising flight of a quill and three fingers engaged in writing. Many other riddles revel in the world of natural history, describing, for example, the manifold realms of the swan, the short-lived innocence of an ox calf, or the ceaseless motion of a fish in a river. The range of subject matter suggests both that the riddles were enjoyed by an extensive cross-section of Anglo-Saxon society and that the tastes of the compilers of the Exeter Book were more eclectic than a modern reader might expect. ASPR iii.180–210, 224–5, 229–43; *The Old English Riddles of the 'Exeter Book'*, ed. C. Williamson (Chapel Hill, NC, 1977); *A Feast of Creatures: Anglo-Saxon Riddle-Songs*, trans. C. Williamson (Philadelphia, PA, 1982); *The Exeter Book Riddles*, trans. K. Crossley-Holland (Harmondsworth, 1993).

JONATHAN WILCOX

RINGS: *see* Jewellery

RIPON (Yorks.) was a monastery founded by *Eata on land granted by King Alhfrith. Shortly afterwards, in *c.*660, the king gave the site to *Wilfrid and, with *Hexham, it then formed part of the saint's widespread 'family' of monasteries. Recent excavations, antiquarian records and topographical analysis combine to suggest that the Anglo-Saxon monastic *vallum* enclosed several scattered foci, sited on glacial banks and mounds: at Ailcy Hill for example, lying 200 m east of the Minster, there was a *cemetery in use between the seventh and ninth centuries and another, possibly associated with a church, is known at Ladykirk (100 m north-east of the Minster) from the eighth century. In addition 'Scott's Monument Yard', some 200 m north of the Minster, falls within the presumed *enceinte* and this is traditionally believed to be the site of Eata's church; ninth-century *coins are recorded from that area.

Wilfrid's main monastic church occupied the site of the present minster, set on a dominating ridge overlooking the river Skell. This location can be deduced from the crypt underlying the east end of the existing nave, which is very close in plan, constructional techniques and measurement units to the *crypt at Hexham, which *Stephen of Ripon describes as Wilfrid's work. At its centre is a vaulted chamber, lit by lamps set in niches around its walls; a large shallow niche at the east end presumably housed a major *relic. Steps and a passage give access to this chamber from the south-west whilst another passage runs from the east, alongside the main chamber, into a half-vaulted western ante-chamber. The crypt was built of re-used Roman stone, was heavily plastered internally and had an *opus signinum* floor similar to those known from contemporary *Jarrow. Excavations in 1930 revealed two substantial wall foundations, of pre-Norman date, running east/west on either side of this crypt system. These probably belong to the seventh-century church but might date from the period of Archbishop *Oswald (971–92) who is recorded as restoring the church (and even perhaps re-founding the site as a monastery) after its destruction by the West Saxons in 948. This destruction was followed by the removal of Wilfrid's relics to *Canterbury. The Cuthbert community took temporary refuge at Ripon in 995 but, in general, documentary history about the post-Wilfridian history of the site is sparse; its continued importance throughout the pre-Norman period is, however, signalled by the surviving stone *sculpture and by the density of coin *hoards belonging to the mid-eighth/mid-ninth-century period.

R. Hall, 'Observations in Ripon Cathedral Crypt', *Yorkshire Archaeological Journal* 65 (1993), 39–53; idem, 'Antiquaries and Archaeology in and around Ripon Minster', in *Yorkshire Monasticism. Archaeology, Art and Architecture from the 7th to 16th Centuries*, ed. L. R. Hoey, British Archaeological Association Conference Transactions 16 (1995), 12–30 R. A. Hall and M. Whyman, 'Settlement and Monasticism at Ripon, North Yorkshire, from the 7th to 11th Centuries AD', *MArch* 40 (1996), 62–150; Taylor and Taylor, *AS Arch*, ii.516–18, iii.1014–17.

RICHARD. N. BAILEY

RIVER NAMES for the purpose of the historian of the *settlement of England comprise those names given to all natural waterways, from major watercourses to minor streams. The names of the great rivers such as the Avon, Humber, Severn, Thames and Trent are pre-English (cf. *place-names, Celtic). A large proportion of river names appear to be the creation of British-speaking *Celts, although a few names less tractable to interpretation may be even more ancient and may have been adopted from the pre-Celtic population of the island.

British river names are chiefly uncompounded. Many, such as the Avon, Dour and Goyt, simply mean 'river, stream, water'. To the Romano-British population, the local watercourse was simply 'the river' and Anglo-Saxon immigrants in these cases seem to have adopted in ignorance British common nouns meaning 'river, stream, water' rather than proper names. Others describe the contemporary nature of the watercourse or its environment. The Cam, Camlad, Croome and Crummock are all based on British adjectives meaning 'winding'; the Aire, Hether, Taw and Tern mean 'swift, strong'; the Lugg, Luke, Nidd, Peover and Perry mean 'white, bright'. By contrast, the Devy and Dove bear the sense 'dark, black'. Humber is a common British stream name meaning 'good'. Some river names are derived from the predominant flora along their courses. The Dart, Darent and Derwent are names based on a British word meaning 'oak'; the Leam, Lymn and Lympne signify 'elm'. The Trent and Tarrant both mean 'trespasser', indicating a river liable to flooding. The names of some rivers point to river worship by the Celts: the Brent and the Dee are both 'the holy river'. In general, the proportion of river names of British origin increases towards the west of England.

Compounded river names conform to the pattern of English *place-names with specific preceding generic. As with British river names, some OE river names are derived from adjectives describing the character of the current or river bed or the colour of the water, e.g. the various Blythes are from OE *bliðe* 'gentle', hence 'the gentle one'. The final stratum of river names formed in Anglo-Saxon England was that of the Scandinavians. Their stream names are common in Yorkshire, Lancashire, Cumberland and Westmoreland and denote watercourses of small or medium size only. E. Ekwall, *English River-Names* (Oxford, 1928); M. Förster, *Der Flussname Themse und seine Sippe* (Munich, 1942).

B. COX

ROADS. The Anglo-Saxons inherited an extensive network of roads, some of Iron Age origin or older such as the Icknield Way, others metalled roads of Roman origin such as Ermine Street, the Foss Way and *Watling Street, all four being known as 'royal roads' in twelfth-century legal sources. Many Roman roads retained their importance; the origin of other Anglo-Saxon routeways is not known, however, though their existence is well attested, such as the saltways that radiated out from the brine pits of Droitwich. The ten layers of gravelled north-south streets carefully laid down at *Hamwic* (see *Southampton) shows

that by the seventh century there was a centralized authority powerful enough to organize this community. Excavations in *London and *Winchester provide later illustrations of urban roads and it is evident from the analysis of early town maps that many had a grid layout, though often independent of any underlying Roman plan. *Worcester's grid, for instance, had a high street where a market was probably located; the siting of ecclesiastical foundations dictated the location of some other streets. Several former West Saxon *burh*s such as *Wareham provide evidence of intra-mural streets following the line of the town defences. The sources are silent as to who maintained the main routeways of England, but this was done probably under royal authority since the king's protection was extended to travellers on the highways. There are quite a few roads known in the sources as *herepæpas* or *army roads: these could have gained their name because they were maintained by those doing military service and not simply because they were used for military purposes. Certainly from the reign of *Offa onwards the royal right to have *bridges maintained was reserved when property was being bestowed by *charter. Bridges were an important part of the road system, serving as a communications link and a place for collecting tolls but also providing, once the *Viking attacks started, a vital means of controlling traffic upstream, possibly inspired by Frankish fortified models. We are particularly well-informed about the bridges at *London and *Rochester. Fords and causeways were also part of the road system: one of the most famous of the former has been discovered by archaeologists at *Oxford and one of the latter played a pivotal role in the skirmish memorialized in the OE *Battle of Maldon*. The importance of Anglo-Saxon roads has been much underrated: *Harold, for instance, took only a fortnight to travel with his army from Yorkshire *via* London to *Hastings. Identification of further charter *boundaries, close examination of town plans in association with selective archaeological excavations and analysis of primary literary sources bearing local topography in mind should present us with a much clearer picture of Anglo-Saxon roads in years to come (see also *transport and communication).

N. Baker and R. Holt, 'The City of Worcester in the Tenth Century', in *Oswald of Worcester*, pp. 129–46; M. Biddle and D. Hill, 'Late Saxon Planned Towns', *AJ* 51 (1971), 70–85; M. Brisbane, 'Hamwic (Saxon Southampton): an 8th-Century Port and Production Centre', in *The Rebirth of Towns in the West AD 700–1050*, ed. R. Hodges and B. Hobley, CBA Research Report 68

(London, 1988), 101–8; N. P. Brooks, 'Rochester Bridge AD 43–1381', in *Traffic and Politics*, ed. N. Yates and J. M. Gibson (Woodbridge, 1994), pp. 1–40, 362–9; idem, 'Medieval Bridges: A Window onto Changing Concepts of State Power', *HSJ* 7 (1997), 11–29; R. H. C. Davis, 'The Ford, the River and the City', in *From Alfred the Great to Stephen* (London and Rio Grande, OH, 1991), pp. 281–91; J. M. Hassall and D. Hill, 'Pont de l'Arche: Frankish Influence on the West Saxon *Burh*?', *Archaeological Journal* 127 (1970), 188–95; B. P. Hindle, *Roads, Tracks and their Interpretation* (London, 1993); M. B. Honeybourne, 'The Pre-Norman Bridge of London', in *Studies in London History presented to Philip Edmund Jones*, ed. A. E. J. Hollaender and William Kellaway (London, 1969), pp. 17–39; D. Hooke, *The Anglo-Saxon Landscape: the Kingdom of the Hwicce* (Manchester, 1985), esp. pp. 124–6; D. A. E. Pelteret, 'The Roads of Anglo-Saxon England', *Wiltshire Archaeological and Natural History Magazine* 79 (1985), 155–63; C. Taylor, *Roads and Tracks of Britain* (London, Toronto and Melbourne, 1979); A. Vince, *Saxon London: an Archaeological Investigation* (London, 1990).

DAVID A. E. PELTERET

ROCHESTER (Kent), a Romano–British walled town, was the seat of a bishopric founded by King *Æthelberht for *Justus in 604. It lies less than thirty miles from *Canterbury, where *Augustine's see had been established seven years earlier: the two tiny dioceses are oddities suggesting that *Kent was itself a recent amalgamation of two distinct kingdoms. At all events Rochester was destined to be overshadowed by Canterbury, and developed much less than might have been predicted from its Roman past, its episcopal status and its esturine location. The apse of a seventh-century church, presumably built by Justus and possibly the western church of an axially-aligned pair, has been found under the west end of the Norman cathedral.

In 885 a *Viking army established a siege-camp outside Rochester, which was relieved by King *Alfred. There were *three moneyers in *Æthelstan's reign, and the *town developed during the tenth and eleventh centuries, when the street-plan probably crystallised. Little is known about late Anglo-Saxon Rochester, though the eleventh-century bridge-work list, which describes the obligations (assessed on manors in the lathe of Aylesford) to replace the timber superstructure of the great Roman bridge across the Medway, is a major source for the maintenance of *bridges and for public obligations in general.

T. Tatton-Brown, 'The Towns of Kent', in Haslam, *Towns*, pp. 12–16; Taylor and Taylor, *AS Arch* ii. 518–19; N. P. Brooks, 'Rochester Bridge AD 43–1381', in *Traffic*

and Politics, ed. N. Yates and J. M. Gibson (Woodbridge, 1994), pp. 1–40.

JOHN BLAIR

ROMAN REMAINS, like prehistoric standing stones and earthworks, were visible reminders to the Anglo-Saxons that others had occupied England before them. In the fifth century, all such ancient monuments were far more numerous and prominent in the landscape than they are today: testimony to manpower, organization and engineering that must have been beyond the settlers' comprehension. This impact will have decreased steadily through the Anglo-Saxon centuries, as monuments were effaced or adapted and as English society itself grew more complex.

Both archaeological evidence and common-sense suggest that the fifth-century English, with their radically different lifestyle, did not view Roman stone structures as viable dwellings; generally they kept clear of them, at least until time had sanitized them and made them safe. 'Squatter' occupation on villa sites, or within *town walls, may imply awareness that the places had economic or defensive importance, but does not represent informed use of the remains as monuments or architecture. With uncomprehending awe, *The *Ruin* describes crumbling walls (probably at *Bath) as 'old work of giants'. On the other hand the very consistent use of the term *ceaster*, a *loan-word from Latin *castrum*, in the names of towns and *forts shows awareness that a stone-walled enclosure was a distinct and special kind of place. The name Fawler (from *fāg-flōr*, 'variegated floor', a term used in *Beowulf*) refers to mosaic pavements, presumably lying open in the countryside. *Bede lists structures still visible in his day as 'cities, lighthouses, bridge and streets', and in 685 the walls and fountain of *Carlisle were displayed as wonders to *Cuthbert and his party.

In the late sixth and seventh centuries a growing habit of using villas for groups of burials, often accurately aligned on the still-standing walls, suggests a new interest in monumentality and a desire to identify with the past. This behaviour foreshadows the main *in situ* use of Roman remains in Anglo-Saxon England: as settings for seventh- and eighth-century minsters and later churches. Kings gave small towns, forts and military installations (such as *Dorchester-on-Thames and *Reculver) to bishops and monastic founders, while some of the main towns of Roman Britain, including *Canterbury, *Cirencester, *London and *York, were reborn as grand settings for cathedral and monastic communities. Probably there was little

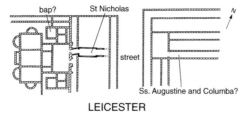

LEICESTER

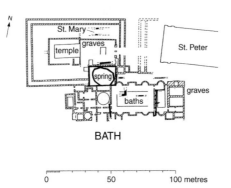

BATH

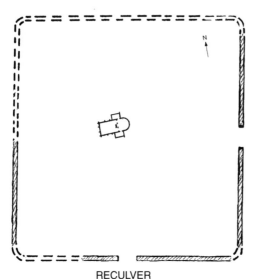

RECULVER

Fig. 15 The ecclesiastical re-use of Roman remains.

of the numerous churches built on villas mark pre-English cult sites, though even here archaeological confirmation is elusive.

The seventh-century *conversions also taught the English how to build in stone, and this needed raw materials. The early seventh-century church of St Pancras at *Canterbury is built of re-cycled Roman brick, and major Northumbrian churches such as *Hexham and *Escomb made extensive and creative use of the large ready-squared blocks freely available on Hadrian's Wall and military sites nearby. In early ninth-century *Mercia, *Brixworth church may consist largely of material carted twenty miles from the public buildings at *Leicester, and its monumental arches borrow the design as well as the materials of Roman engineering. *Bede describes how a party sent to the ruins of Cambridge to find material for St *Æthelthryth's tomb in about 695 'found near the walls of the city a coffin most beautifully made of white marble'; the carved coffin of St *Augustine at Canterbury, as described by *Goscelin, was also probably Roman. Before the eleventh century the evidence for new freestone quarrying is exiguous (see *mining and quarrying), and it may be that requirements for quoins, jambs and arches were largely met from Roman spoil.

With the rise of planned towns in late ninth-century *Wessex, new streets and plots were laid out within the still-standing walls of such former towns as Chichester, *London and *Winchester, and by the Conquest Romano-British towns across England had become sites of urban re-growth. As occupation intensified from the 980s onwards, the need to clear sites encumbered by ruins must have become more urgent; at the same time, the hundreds of small rural churches which were now for the first time being built in good masonry offered a growing market. Transactions of mutual advantage between site-clearing townsfolk and church-building lords are reflected in, for instance, the village churches around *York in which blocks with Roman tooling and cramp-holes can be recognized. The point by which easily-recovered spoil had been used up must have varied regionally, but the rise of quarrying in the eleventh century suggests a growing scarcity. As late as the 1080s, though, the vast abbey church of *St Albans could still be built entirely of Roman brick from *Verulamium*.

M. Hunter, 'Germanic and Roman Antiquity and the Sense of the Past in Anglo-Saxon England', *ASE* 3 (1974), 29–50; J. C. Higgitt, 'The Roman Background to Medieval England', *JBAA* 3rd ser. 36 (1973), 1–15; R. Morris and J. Roxan, 'Churches on Roman Buildings',

genuine continuity in all this: Italian and Gallic *missionaries were familiar with ecclesiastical re-cycling of the Roman past, and would have guided their patrons in patterns of behaviour which can leave a spurious impression of continued Christian use. In the south-west, where there was no significant pagan interlude between British and English Christianity, a case can be made that some

Temples, Churches and Religion, ed. W. Rodwell (Oxford, 1980), pp. 175–209; S. M. Pearce, 'Estates and Church Sites in Dorset and Somerset', *The Early Church in Western Britain and Ireland*, ed. S. M. Pearce (Oxford, 1982), pp. 117–38; J. Blair, 'Anglo-Saxon Minsters: a Topographical Review', in Blair and Sharpe, *Past. Care*, pp. 226–66; S. E. Rigold, '*Litus Romanum*: the Shore Forts as Mission Stations', in *The Saxon Shore*, ed. D. E. Johnston (London, 1977), pp. 70–5; R. Morris, 'Churches in York and its Hinterland: Building Patterns and Stone Sources in the Eleventh and Twelfth Centuries', in *Minsters and Parish Churches: the Local Church in Transition, 950–1200*, ed. J. Blair (Oxford, 1988), pp. 191–9; D. Parsons (ed.), *Stone* (Chichester, 1990).

JOHN BLAIR

ROME was the focal point of western Christianity and the seat of the *papacy. From the very earliest period of English Christianity, Anglo-Saxon England was in intimate contact with Rome, and this contact gave a distinctive shape to English culture and religious life (in contrast, say, with Ireland, which enjoyed only intermittent contact with Rome before the twelfth century). Christianity was brought to England by Roman monks from Pope *Gregory's monastery of St Andrew, led by *Augustine and followed a few years later by a second wave of Roman monks including *Mellitus, *Justus and *Paulinus. The Roman orientation initiated by the Augustinian mission was reinforced by the advent (in 669 and 670 respectively) of *Theodore and *Hadrian, who had been sent from Rome by Pope Vitalian. Approximately a decade later, the archcantor of St Peter's in Rome, one John, was brought to England by *Benedict Biscop, in order to teach Roman *chant and *liturgy to the English monks at *Monkwearmouth; John also served as a papal legate charged with seeking the views of the English church on the monothelete controversy and the *acta* of the Lateran Council (649), and died on the way back to Rome carrying the decisions of the English synod of Hatfield (679). A later papal legation, led by Bishops George of Ostia and Theophylact of Todi, toured England in 786 and promulgated various decrees concerning the discipline of the English church. Numerous letters from various popes to English kings and bishops survive.

Anglo-Saxons also travelled frequently to Rome, both as *pilgrims to the shrines of saints in Rome and on ecclesiastical business with the papacy. A complete list cannot be given here, but already by the seventh century a number of English ecclesiastics had travelled to Rome, including *Wilfrid (whose study at Rome proved decisive in settling the *Easter controversy at the synod of *Whitby in 664), Benedict Biscop, *Ceolfrith, *Hwætberht, *Eosterwine and *Aldhelm; and in later centuries many made the journey even if they were not on official business, such as *Oda, before he became a bishop. A principal reason for going to Rome, however, was that of obtaining papal endorsement for ecclesiastical enterprises (*Willibrord and *Boniface both travelled to Rome to secure permission and papal authority for their *missionary undertakings) or papal rulings intended to overturn the rulings of an English synod (as when Wilfrid sought papal authority to be restored to his Northumbrian see after he was expelled by King Ecgfrith). A continuing pretext for contact between England and Rome was the bestowal of the *pallium on archbishops: Pope Honorius sent a pallium to Paulinus at about the time he was forced to retire from his Northumbrian see; Wigheard was in Rome to receive the pallium when he died of the plague in 667; and from that time onwards we have frequent records of English archbishops travelling to Rome for this purpose (including Eanbald, Cynesige and *Ealdred of York, and *Plegmund, Ælfsige, *Dunstan, Sigeric, Ælfric, Æthelnoth and Robert of Canterbury). Laymen also travelled to Rome. A number of kings – of whom the first was apparently *Cædwalla in 688 – made the trip as an act of piety: Coenred of *Mercia and Offa of the East Saxons (709) and *Ine of *Wessex (726) in the eighth century, Æthelwulf (855) and Burgred (874) in the ninth; *Cnut (1027) in the eleventh. That a number of women also made the trip is apparent from references in the correspondence of Boniface (e.g. *Ep.* lxii). By the mid-eighth century the English traffic to Rome was so frequent that the pope endowed a hospice for English pilgrims known as the *schola Saxonum* (near the present church of S. Spirito in Sassia, the name of which preserves the association with 'Saxons'); and the hospice was maintained by donations sent from England, known as *Romscot* or 'Peter's Pence' (see *alms).

The *schola Saxonum* was located near St Peter's; but of course the English pilgrims also wished to visit the numerous other churches in Rome. In the early eighth century a pilgrim from *Malmesbury compiled a rudimentary guidebook (known as the 'Malmesbury Itinerary') to the location of some forty of these churches; the text survives only as it is preserved in the *Gesta regum* of *William of Malmesbury, and there are reasons for associating it with Aldhelm. Some three hundred years later Archbishop Sigeric, who travelled to Rome in 990 to receive his pallium, kept a detailed record of the churches which he visited in Rome.

The influence of Rome is palpable in many aspects of Anglo-Saxon culture. It is obvious that the earliest *liturgical books in England were brought from Rome by the Augustinian missionaries; although none of these books (with the exception of the gospelbook known as *'St Augustine's Gospels', now CCCC 286) has survived, the nature of the Roman sacramentaries (principally of the type called 'Old Gelasian') used in early England can be deduced from later evidence. Augustine probably brought with him a copy of the *Martyrologium Hieronymianum* (a redaction of which is preserved as the Martyrology of Echternach, a book compiled for the use of Willibrord), and the Roman saints commemorated in this text form the basis of all subsequent English liturgical calendars. *Relics were brought back from Rome by English travellers, and became the focus of cults in English churches. Books imported from Rome stocked many early Anglo-Saxon *libraries, and these books served as the model for Anglo-Saxon scribes, who were able to imitate Roman uncial *script to such perfection that, for example, the famous Codex *Amiatinus, which was taken by Ceolfrith to Rome as a gift to the pope, has only been recognized as an English product during the past century. The *tituli* or inscriptions which decorated Roman churches were copied into books called *syllogae* and served as models for Anglo-Latin poets such as Aldhelm and *Bede. Anglo-Saxon churches, such as those at Monkwearmouth and Jarrow, were decorated with painted panels brought back from Rome. In short, the evidence for contact between Rome and Anglo-Saxon England is vast, and deserves to form the subject of a (substantial) monograph.

DACL xiv.2514–3122; P. Llewellyn, *Rome in the Dark Ages* (London, 1971); R. Krautheimer, *Rome: Profile of a City, 312–1308* (Princeton, NJ, 1980); B. Colgrave, 'Pilgrimages to Rome in the Seventh and Eighth Centuries', in *Studies in Language, Literature and Culture of the Middle Ages and Later*, ed. E. B. Atwood and A. A. Hill (Austin, TX, 1969), pp. 156–72; M. Deanesly, 'The Anglo-Saxon Church and the Papacy', in *The English Church and the Papacy in the Middle Ages*, ed. C. H. Lawrence (London, 1965), pp. 29–62; W. J. Moore, *The Saxon Pilgrims to Rome and the Schola Saxonum* (Fribourg, 1937); WMalm, *GR* iv.352 [Malmesbury Itinerary]; V. Ortenberg, *The English Church and the Continent in the Tenth and Eleventh Centuries* (Oxford, 1992), pp. 127–96; idem, 'Archbishop Sigeric's Journey to Rome', *ASE* 19 (1990), 197–246; P. Meyvaert, 'Bede and the Church Paintings at Wearmouth-Jarrow', *ASE* 8 (1979), 63–77; D. J. Birch, *Pilgrimage to Rome in the Middle Ages* (Woodbridge, 1998).

MICHAEL LAPIDGE

ROYAL SITES comprise a series of so-called 'palaces' in town and country, defined both historically and archaeologically. The concept of a palace is that of a place visited by the king and queen and his or her family, with a suitable retinue of people and horses. Here the king or queen met his or her council (the *witan* – high-status representatives of the ecclesiastical or secular nobility, including archbishops, bishops, abbots, earls and other important people such as visiting foreigners). The palace would normally be one over which the crown had some control or direct ownership. The locations were in some cases well-known places, notably the urban ones such as *London, *Winchester, *Oxford and *Gloucester; or near prominent rural landmarks such as the gorge at *Cheddar (figs. 2–3).

The resources for such periodic visits were obtained from the surrounding estates by a food-rent (see *feorm*), later commuted for cash. There would in these places have been up to several hundred people, staying for days or weeks. Such occasions demanded considerable advance organisation by the local *reeve. The function of palace assemblies included crown-wearing (the king or

Map 6 Anglo-Saxon high status sites.

queen being seen by his or her regional subjects), discussions on home or foreign policy and defence, dispensations of royal justice, and especially the implementation and confirmation of land-grants by *charters and other rights and duties. There was also an important element of *entertainment, notably *hunting and feasting. Lists of provender survive which enumerate large quantities of ale and mead; cattle and sheep; birds, salmon and eels; cheeses and honey; hundreds of loaves and kilograms of butter; and meal and fodder for the horses.

Some royal sites are referred to in unequivocal terms such as *palatium regis* or *sedes regalis*. Certain major urban centres were favourites for the time of the great festivals of Easter and Christmas. These urban palaces must have been built on a massive scale and of more durable materials (i.e. stone) than the more numerous rural sites of timber and other organic construction. They may well have compared with the great palaces of Charlemagne such as Aachen or Paderborn.

One hundred and fifty-five locations of palaces are known and a further thirty-eight are known by name but unlocated; there is thus a total of 193 sites known from written sources. These give few details, however, of the material culture associated with these places. Literary sources do add some detail, however difficult it may be here to separate symbol or concept from fact. Pictorial evidence is little concerned with palaces before the (retrospective) depictions of elements of palaces in the *Bayeux Tapestry.

It is also possible to say something about the range of buildings and other features. Halls figure prominently, as both buildings and 'institutions'. There are also mentions of the *bur*, the domestic apartment or building. King Cynewulf was trapped and killed in a *bur* (*ASC* 757) while visiting his mistress; and this is also the name given to the women's apartments in *Beowulf*, where the men might be found who were anxious to escape the attentions of the monster Grendel. There are also records of royal chapels, agricultural buildings and other features; and accommodation on a considerable scale must be assumed for nobles, retinues, and their horses.

Details of buildings are provided only incidentally. A chamber at Calne was of two storeys; it collapsed in 977 at a meeting of the royal council. Several people were killed; others, including *Dunstan, were left hanging on beams. Such details are, of course, of interest to the archaeologist. The attributes of the hall at Heorot, in *Beowulf*, have engendered a long debate on the

relationship of the literary description to what such a hall might actually have been like in contemporary north-western Europe.

The discovery and excavation of royal sites in rural Anglo-Saxon England has been one of the major achievements of medieval archaeology in the last forty years. This has been due partly to the massive contribution of *aerial photography, which has shown up the ditches, pits, and foundation holes of many sites; and partly to the increasing ability of archaeologists to excavate and interpret the residual evidence of *timber buildings.

At two of the sites that have been extensively excavated, *Yeavering and *Cheddar, the archaeological detail could be related to written sources in ways that left no doubt of royal presence and involvement. The constructional techniques and sizes of the buildings excavated were of an appropriately impressive scale, representing the highest achievements of contemporary secular timber architecture.

Other sites, such as Sprouston, Foxley and Hatton Rock, appear to be complexes of similar status, with building plans closely parallelled at either Yeavering or Cheddar; or which have other indirect archaeological or historical evidence. It is uncertain whether any or some of these sites are 'royal', in the absence of direct evidence from written or other sources. None is included as far as is known in the list of 193 places mentioned earlier. It may be more circumspect to refer to them as of 'high status', while stressing analogies to the known royal sites.

Discussion of these royal or high status sites has been concerned with local topographic, social and economic contexts; the technology of the construction and demolition of timber buildings; space-function, regional and national typology; and units of mensuration. Especially prominent has been the development of the theory of reconstruction of such buildings from the archaeological evidence: essays in two and three dimensions.

Further research will be concerned with function, and especially with the wider question of the role these royal palaces had in the whole Anglo-Saxon economic and social world: whether this represents something new in contemporary society, or whether comparisons can usefully be drawn with either Roman 'villa-palaces' or later medieval hunting-lodges and manors. At Cheddar the continuity from Anglo-Saxon palace to medieval palace/hunting lodge is clearly displayed, and there may be continuity here too with the underlying Roman villa or its estate.

P. A. Rahtz, 'Buildings and Rural Settlement', in Wilson, *Archaeology*, pp. 49–98; J. K. S. St Joseph, 'Sprouston. Roxburghshire: an Anglo-Saxon Settlement Discovered by Air Reconnaisance', *ASE* 10 (1982), 191–9; S. James, A. Marshall and M. Millett, 'An Early Medieval Building Tradition', *Archaeological Journal* 141 (1985), 182–215; J. Blair, 'Palaces or Minsters? Northampton and Cheddar Reconsidered', *ASE* 25 (1996), 97–121.

PHILIP RAHTZ

RUIN, a poem of approximately 49 lines in the *Exeter Book, is a meditation on the remains of a Roman city. It is commonly included among the Old English *elegies, although, as an impersonal description, it lacks the usual monologue form. The *Ruin* is also related to poems in a *de excidio* or *encomium urbis* tradition, lamenting the fall of a city or praising its splendour. The text has been badly affected by burn damage, and two passages, including the ending, contain large lacunae. Like the similar meditation in the *Wanderer*, the *Ruin* describes a decaying fortress, imagining what it was like in its heyday, when many a warrior, splendidly arrayed, looked on treasure, on silver, and on fine-wrought jewels (32–5). The scene then shifts to the marvellous hot baths, and it seems to be with the amenities of the city that the poem ends. Early discussion centred on the identity of the city, *Bath being the favourite candidate. The ruined city has also been taken as a symbol of spiritual decay, like Babylon in the biblical Revelation. But the poem contains no overt moralisation to support such an interpretation, and no more critical message may be intended than *sic transit gloria mundi*.
ASPR iii. 227–9; R. F. Leslie, *Three Old English Elegies* (Manchester, 1961; repr. with corrections 1966); H. T. Keenan, 'The Ruin as Babylon', *Tennessee Studies in Literature* 11 (1966), 109–17; K. Wentersdorf, 'Observations on *The Ruin*', *MÆ* 46 (1977), 171–80; P. Zanna, '*Descriptiones urbium* and Elegy in Latin and Vernaculars in the Early Middle Ages', *Studi medievali* 3rd ser. 32 (1991), 523–96.

ANNE L. KLINCK

RUMWOLD, ST, the miraculous infant, was, according to an anonymous mid-eleventh-century Latin Life (*BHL* 7385), born in the middle of a field, to an unnamed daughter of King *Penda of *Mercia, and her unnamed husband, a king of *Northumbria. Emerging from the womb, the baby exclaimed 'I am a Christian', demanded baptism, preached a sermon on Divine Wisdom and the Trinity, and on the Christian life, prophesied his own death in three days' time, and gave instructions about the burial and two translations of his remains. It is difficult to find a context for this extraordinary tale, full of anachronisms, and Rumwold's cult can only be traced back to the tenth century from liturgical evidence. The places named in the text are King's Sutton, Brackley and Buckingham, all close together and all, quite remarkably, still preserving traces of a popular cult of Rumwold (healing wells). Church dedications, apparently to this saint, are scattered across England, and at the Dissolution, Boxley Abbey in *Kent supposedly possessed an image of the infant. Feast: 3 November.
R. C. Love, ed. and trans., *Three Eleventh-Century Anglo-Latin Saints' Lives* (OMT, 1996), pp. cxl–clxxxvii, 92–115.

R. C. LOVE

RUNE POEM gives definitions for twenty-nine *runes. Each runic letter is followed by a description which evokes the thing or person by whose name it was known. Where the order and naming of runes was fixed, the poet generally followed tradition, but the poem is not based on any of the surviving Anglo-Saxon sequences. It has been suggested that the poem was modelled on Latin *Abecedaria* which devote a stanza of description to letters of the Roman alphabet. Recent comparative study re-instates the belief that, despite discrepancies between the Old English and Scandinavian rune poems, all three poems were descended from a common Germanic archetype. All three poems, however, demonstrate Christian re-shaping of their Germanic heritage, and the suppression of pagan reference is particularly marked in the Old English poet's treatment of *Ing* and *Tir*. Faint traces conceivably remain, such as the divinatory use of runes suggested by the appearance of *hleotan* ('to cast lots') in the definition of the first symbol. The sole authority for the text is the printing in 1705 by George *Hickes of a transcription made by Humfrey *Wanley. The poem was recorded on a single leaf (lost in the Cotton fire of 1731) which had been inserted, probably in the sixteenth century, into an early eleventh-century collection of saints' lives.
The Old English Rune Poem, ed. M. Halsall, McMaster Old English Studies and Texts 2 (Toronto, 1981); M. Clunies Ross, 'The Anglo-Saxon and Norse *Rune Poems*, a Comparative Study', *ASE* 19 (1990), 23–39.

STEPHANIE HOLLIS

RUNES are characters of the runic alphabet. OE *run* and its cognates in other languages have meanings like 'council, counsel, consultation', and often carry the sense of secrecy, mystery, isolation, and sometimes of esoteric knowledge, even of secret scripts. Hence some scholars have thought that runes were in origin a magical script, to be used on *amulets and for magico–religious formulae. In contrast other runologists, particularly in modern Scandinavia, believe that runes were from the beginning a script employed for ordinary practical, mercantile and administrative purposes. There can be no final conclusion about this; in historical times runes were used both in religious/magical and in practical texts.

Various Germanic peoples used runes: some of the continental *Germani*, the Scandinavians, the Goths, the Frisians and the Anglo-Saxons. The script varies a good deal from place to place and from time to time. Where it originated is disputed. Some would say in Switzerland/northern Italy, others further east on the Danube, others again in the Danish–German borderlands. A profusion of early finds has recently strengthened the latter hypothesis. Wherever the place of origin was, it was a region where Germanic peoples had contact with Roman civilization, for several runic letter forms show similarities with their Latin equivalents.

Runes were designed for inscriptional use, primarily for cutting in wood. Hence curved lines are avoided; the earliest letter forms usually have a vertical stem (cut against the wood grain, and therefore easily distinguished from it), and one or two arms or bows (cut slanting to the grain). Little incised wood survives from Anglo-Saxon times; most English runic inscriptions are in stone, metal or bone. However, the characteristic straight-line forms remain in most cases.

The earliest rune-rows, from the Continent and Scandinavia, consist of twenty-four characters, which were divided into three groups of eight. There was a characteristic fixed letter order to the rune-row, which, from the values of its first six characters, is called the *futhark*. The Anglo-Saxon rune-masters added and adapted letters so that a total of thirty-one distinct characters (some with variant forms) occurs in English inscriptions, while there are a few pseudo–runes that are found only in early manuscript accounts of runes.

The English rune-row, with letter values given in lower-case Roman characters, is:

f u þ o r c g w h n i j ʒ p x s

t b e m l ŋ d œ a æ y ẽa ḡ k k̄

This is called the *futhorc*. The runes *o* and *a* are paralleled in *Frisia (as in the fronted value *a* for

æ), so these are sometimes called Anglo-Frisian runes. Two other added runes, *y* and *ẽa*, have so far been found only in England and they are presumably Anglo-Saxon creations. The runes *g*, *k* and *k̄*, representing distinctive variants of the voiced and voiceless back stops, are also found only in Anglo-Saxon England, but are restricted to the north-west. *Futhorcs* are drawn in a few manuscripts from the late Old English period, but the only epigraphical example is that inlaid on a decorated *scramasax* (short sword) from the river Thames at Battersea.

As well as having a sound value, each rune had a name; this usually began with the sound the rune represented but was also an OE common noun or name: the rune *d* was called *dæg* 'day', *w* was *wynn* 'joy', *i* was *is* 'ice', and *m* was *man* 'man'. Name and rune were closely linked, so that if the name underwent a change in pronunciation over the years, the rune might change its sound value in agreement. Moreover in a manuscript text a scribe might put a rune as an abbreviation of the word corresponding with its name: instead of writing *man* he could draw the rune *m*.

Runes presumably came to England with the Anglo-Saxons. The earliest known runic inscription in this country is probably that cut on a roe-deer's astragalus (ankle-bone) deposited with other bones (apparently used as playing-pieces) in a cremation urn at Caistor-by-Norwich, Norfolk. This may date from the fourth or fifth century. During the pagan period, say up to *c.*650, runes are scattered through the south-east, the Isle of Wight and the mainland nearby, *East Anglia and the east Midlands. Examples are the runes of the Chessell Down Isle of Wight scabbard mount and pail, the Dover brooch, the Gilton (Kent) runic pommel, and the rune-inscribed urns of Spong Hill (Norfolk) (actually rune-stamped) and Loveden Hill (Lincs.).

In the mid-seventh century the Anglo-Saxons began striking *coins and early types, particularly in the south-east and East Anglia, have runic legends (e.g. sceat coinages, many of the East Anglian king Beonna and the Mercian *Offa, and some styca types of *Northumbria).

During the later Anglo-Saxon period runes declined in the south-east and east Midlands though there are a few late examples. In contrast, in the north and north Midlands runes had their most flourishing use in Christian times, particularly in commemorative texts. Examples are the memorial stones from Thornhill, south Yorks (3×), Great Urswick, Cumbria (Lancs.), *Hartlepool (2×), *Monkwearmouth (2×), Chester-le-Street, and a group of name-stones and fragments from *Lindisfarne. In this area too are the great crosses of *Bewcastle and *Ruthwell and the coffin of St *Cuthbert, while from it, the dialect of its texts suggests, came the *Franks Casket though that has no known English provenance. Altogether there are, besides the coins, some seventy Anglo-Saxon runic monuments, and they supply important information on the OE language at various dates and in various places.

R. Derolez, *Runica Manuscripta*, 2 vols. (Bruges, 1954); R. W. V. Elliott, *Runes*, 2nd ed. (Manchester, 1989); R. I. Page, *An Introduction to English Runes* (London, 1973); idem, *Runes and Runic Inscriptions* (Woodbridge, 1995).

R. I. PAGE

RUSHFORTH GOSPELS: *see* Gospelbooks

RUTHWELL CROSS, the most important sculptural monument of the Northumbrian Renaissance to survive. The Cross, 6 m high, is made of two blocks of red sandstone. As these are different shades of red (hence from different quarries), it is likely that the monument was originally covered in gesso, and brightly painted like contemporary illuminated manuscripts. It is dated to the eighth century (perhaps 730–50), when the Anglo-Saxons controlled the northern shore of Solway Firth. In the sixteenth century it stood within the parish church; in 1642 it was pulled down and badly damaged by Protestant iconoclasts. It was reconstructed in the eighteenth or nineteenth century (the transom is a nineteenth-century substitution); in 1887 it was placed in an apse added to the north wall of the church.

Four carefully edited sentences from an early version of The *Dream of the Rood* are inscribed in *runes on the narrow sides of the lower stone. The poem fills the flat borders around foliage scrolls, inhabited by birds and animals. The first sentence of the poem (east side) fills the top border, then continues down the right hand border in short lines of two to four runes, without word-division: 'Almighty God stripped himself. When he willed to mount the gallows, courageous before all men, <I dared not> bow . . .'. The second sentence occupies the left hand border: 'I <lifted up> a powerful king – the lord of heaven I dared not tilt. Men insulted the pair of us together; I was drenched with blood po<ured from the man's side>'. The poem gives the monument a personality and a voice. The stress on the human courage of Christ reflects the concern of the western church to emphasise Christ's human will against

Pl. 16 The Ruthwell Cross.

Monotheletism (the theory that Christ merely participated in the divine will).

To read the two columns of runes one has to move from right to left; continuing this movement, the first half of the poem leads to the first half of the iconography (south side). The poem had dramatized the encounter between the Cross, shocked at the dilemma which requires it to bear its lord to his death, and Christ (at once God and a courageous man) who wills his death. Now the first half of the iconography shows the implications of this narrative. It begins with a crucifixion scene (on the base), and continues (reading upwards on the shaft) with four large images of encounter with Christ: the Annunciation, the healing of the man

403

born blind (John IX.1–41), the woman who was a sinner bathing the feet of Christ (Luke VII.37–8), and the Visitation. In these encounter-scenes, an image of conversion (the blind man) and of repentance (the woman who was a sinner) are flanked by two images of the growth of Christ in Mary's womb (the Annunciation below them, the Visitation above). The sequence emphasises the role of 'worthy women' (runic inscription to the Visitation scene) in Christ's incarnation and ministry.

On the second narrow side (west) the second half of the poem (top and right hand column of runes) emphasizes the union between Christ and the Cross ('Christ was on the Rood'). From afar, Christ's followers, noble and eager, come together at the Cross, which bows to present Christ's body to their hands. In the fourth sentence (left hand column) they contemplate his body, pierced with arrows and limb-weary. The iconography of the second broad side (north) completes this uniquely original narrative. On the four large scenes of the shaft, Christ's body is presented returning as a child on Mary's lap from Egypt, as the heavenly bread broken by the first monks, Paul and Anthony of Egypt, recognized by beasts and dragons, and adored as the Agnus Dei. All of these scenes are associated with the desert (the symbolic setting of the monastic life) and with the Eucharist (the Christian fulfilment of the manna of the desert in Exodus).

In the Cross's design, there is a hierarchy of languages and scripts. Pride of place is given to the panels on the broad sides, Mediterranean in style and with Latin inscriptions (usually in Roman capitals). The runic English poem on the narrow sides plays a secondary, but essential role. It reshapes the events of Good Friday into a twofold pattern: the Cross's encounter with Christ (first half) and its handing on of his body (second half). Each half of the iconography in turn explores the implications of this two-fold pattern for a clerical (monastic?) community at Ruthwell. Poem and iconography together provide a coherent synthesis of what they considered central to communal life: encounter with an heroic Christ, leading to conversion and repentance; and the sacramental recognition of Christ's body in the Eucharist.

K. E. Haney, 'The Christ and the Beasts Panel on the Ruthwell Cross', *ASE* 14 (1985), 215–31; É. Ó Carragáin, 'The Ruthwell Crucifixion Poem in its Iconographical and Liturgical Contexts', *Peritia* 6–7 (1987–8), 1–71; *The Ruthwell Cross*, ed. B. Cassidy (Princeton, NJ, 1992).

ÉAMONN Ó CARRAGÁIN

S

SACRAMENTS: *see* Liturgy

ST ALBANS (Herts.) is the site of the only Romano-British martyr-cult which can be shown to have survived into Christian England. The martyrdom of Alban in the amphitheatre outside the walls, probably in the third century, is described in an early source; *Gildas mentions the cult, and St Germanus visited Alban's shrine in 429. *Bede, writing *c.*730, notes that 'a church of wonderful workmanship' was built there, and that 'to this day . . . the working of frequent miracles continues to bring it renown'. Excavations have now shown that the abbey church, on the hill east of the Roman city, overlies a late Roman *cemetery which (it seems reasonable to assume) would have contained Alban's grave. The regrouping of cult activity around an extra-mural martyrial tomb is a common phenomenon in early Christian Europe; the unique English case becomes explicable if it is accepted that a British-ruled enclave survived in the Chilterns and eastwards until the late sixth century. In later tradition, King *Offa founded a monastery on the site in 793. The community was re-founded in the 970s as a Benedictine abbey, around which a small *town was growing by the Conquest.

Bede, *HE* i.7; E. Roberts, *The Hill of the Martyr* (Dunstable, 1993), pp. 13–29; D. Rollason, *Saints and Relics in Anglo-Saxon England* (Oxford, 1989), pp. 12–14; M. Biddle, 'Archaeology, Architecture and the Cult of Saints in Anglo-Saxon England', in Butler and Morris, *AS Church*, pp. 12–16; T. R. Slater, 'Benedictine Town Planning in Medieval England: Evidence from St Albans', in *The Church in the Medieval Town*, ed. T. R. Slater and G. Rosser (Aldershot, 1998), pp. 155–76.

JOHN BLAIR

ST AUGUSTINE'S GOSPELS (CCCC 286) is a Vulgate *gospelbook made in Italy during the sixth century. Annotations indicate that it was in England by the late seventh or early eighth century, and it has been suggested that it may have accompanied St *Augustine's mission in 597. Its uncial *script is typical of that which influenced English uncial; its registers of narrative images of the life of Christ and its evangelist miniatures (of which only Luke remains) with seated author

under an arch, the tympanum of which contains a half-length evangelist symbol, influenced English art, especially southern English works such as the Royal Bible and the Book of *Cerne. The inscription accompanying the Luke portrait derives from Sedulius' *Carmen Paschale*. The volume was at St Augustine's, *Canterbury, by the eleventh century where documents were added to it and where it was traditionally associated with St Augustine and acted as the oath-book for incoming archbishops. It passed to Corpus *via* Matthew *Parker.

CLA ii.126; F. Wormald, 'The Miniatures in the Gospels of St Augustine, Corpus Christi College, Cambridge, MS 286', in *Francis Wormald: Selected Writings* I, ed. J. J. G. Alexander *et al.* (London, 1984), pp. 13–35.

MICHELLE P. BROWN

SAINTS' LIVES: *see* Hagiography

SAKE AND SOKE: *see* Land Tenure

SALISBURY PSALTER: *see* Psalter Glosses

SANDBACH (Cheshire) has two of the most ambitious Mercian stone *sculptures to survive. Though damaged by seventeenth-century iconoclasts, the crosses still stand 4.8 m and 3.2 m high. They share *iconographic and stylistic traits which indicate that they are near-contemporary monuments; analogues for their zoomorphic ornament suggest a date of *c.*800. The larger cross carries figural scenes from Christ's life, alongside animal, interlace and vine-scroll ornament. The other shaft is less ambitious iconographically but amongst its small-scale decoration it is possible to distinguish the Transfiguration and an Adoration of the Virgin and Child. The organisation of the ornament on both crosses reflects contemporary *metalworking tastes.

J. Hawkes, 'A Question of Judgement: The Iconic Programme of Sandbach, Cheshire', in *From the Isles of the North*, ed. C. Bourke (Belfast, 1995), pp. 213–20; C. A. R. Radford, 'Pre-Conquest Sculpture at Sandbach', *The Cheshire Historian* 7 (1957), 1–6.

RICHARD N. BAILEY

SATIVOLA, ST (= ST SIDWELL), supposedly born in *Exeter, was murdered at the instruction of her stepmother, and the site of her burial outside the east gate of the city was thereafter the scene of miraculous healings. A church still stands in this place, though the healing well is now gone; there was also formerly another well, at the church of Laneast (*Cornwall), which is dedicated to Sativola and her sister Wulvella. Bishop *Leofric of Exeter is recorded as having given Sativola's relics to the cathedral in the eleventh century. The earliest surviving account of the saint is found in a fourteenth-century manuscript. The historical facts about her are thus a matter of uncertainty. According to a brief account included by *Goscelin in his eleventh-century Life of St *Eadgyth, another sister, St Juthwara, was supposed similarly to have been murdered by the same stepmother; this rather suggests that some confusion of identity has arisen, which probably cannot now be accounted for. Feast: either 31 July, 1 or 2 August. P. Grosjean, 'Legenda S. Sativolae Exoniensis', *AB* 53 (1935), 359–65.

R. C. LOVE

SCANDINAVIAN INFLUENCE ON ENGLISH ART and *iconography was already apparent in the pagan period. The Swedish links of some of the finds from *Sutton Hoo have long been recognised whilst other parts of eastern England have yielded material which reveals strong ties to Norway and Denmark. The main impact of Scandinavian art, however, dates to the period after the *Viking division of lands around *York in 876, their subsequent settlement in the *Five Boroughs area of *Mercia and the early tenth-century take-over of north-west England by Gaelic Norse groups. In the late ninth, and through the first half of the tenth century, this impact is naturally most evident in the north of the country. In the early years of the eleventh century, however, there is clear evidence of Scandinavian tastes in the south at places like *London and *Winchester; this no doubt reflects the accession of King *Cnut to the English throne in 1016 and the influence of his followers.

The dominant style in the art of the Scandinavian homeland at the time of the capture of York was the Borre style, named after a Norwegian ship burial containing objects decorated in this form of ornament. Its most recognisable elements are a cat-like mask and types of ribbon ornament based upon split bands; these bands frequently take on a ring-chain form. There are pure examples of Borre ornament surviving among *metalwork finds in England and some of these were certainly manufactured in this country. A striking illustration of this is provided by a lead alloy matrix of sub-cruciform shape from York, which was used to make moulds for casting pendants of a kind familiar from east Scandinavian hoards. Other Borre-influenced pieces, however, show modifications of the Scandinavian style in the direction of native taste. Typical of such hybrid art is a copper alloy strap end from St Mary Bishophill Senior in York which is decorated with a Borre-style ring-chain. Yet the precise form of ring-chain cannot be exactly matched in Scandinavia and it is associated with an animal-head terminal of traditional English type and occurs on a strap end of characteristic Insular form. The clay mould for a trefoil brooch found at York tells the same story of assimilated traditions: the brooch form is Scandinavian and the cat-like masks reflect the Borre style but the associated bird ornament has a long Anglo-Saxon pedigree. In another medium the same absorption and adaptation can be traced; crosses at sites like *Gosforth in Cumbria or Burnsall in Yorkshire employ the ring-chain in a variety of locally-developed forms and do so in a medium which was totally unfamiliar to the Scandinavian settlers before they came to Britain.

The Borre style flourished into the second half of the tenth century and overlaps in time with the Jellinge style, named after the Danish town of Jellinge where a small cup was found which carries the characteristic animal ornament of this style – a sleek S-shaped ribbon beast with contoured outline, spiral hips and a body which is enmeshed in the trailing extensions of its head and lip lappets. This style is a prevailing fashion throughout the first half of the tenth century though it may already have been established in the later years of the ninth. Once more York provides examples which are virtually indistinguishable from material found in Scandinavia. One of the scabbard chapes from the city, for example, is almost identical to chapes found in Iceland and Finland and belongs to a type which was particularly common around the Baltic. Some Anglo-Scandinavian artists fully understood this style. No better example of this comprehension can be found than the slick, powerful curving animals found on one of the cross-shafts from York Minster; this is clearly local work. But most York and Yorkshire carvings either fail to sympathise with the style – and here the slack and sagging forms of the ribbon animals on Ryedale sculpture can be cited – or they apply elements from Jellinge art onto animals of Insular pedigree. Such adaptations can be seen in the bird and animal chains on several York carvings. In other media the same hybrid art can be traced: a silver casket in the British Museum fuses English Trewhiddle forms with Jellinge characteristics whilst a strap end from Winchester equips its Jellinge ribbon animal with an English foliate tongue.

It is perhaps significant that the favoured Scandinavian style of the latter half of the tenth century, the Mammen style, seems to have had little impact on the Anglo-Scandinavian north. By this date the last of the Viking rulers of York, *Eric Bloodaxe, was dead and, however grudgingly, *Northumbria now owed allegiance to southern English kings. A bone plaque from the Thames in London and a cross-shaft from Workington (Cumbria) both carry ornament which employs the unruly tendril and substantial pelleted bodies of the Mammen style, but they are isolated examples of a fashion which was much more influential among the Viking colonists on the Isle of Man.

Cnut's accession to the English throne is no doubt responsible for the appearance in the south of England of material decorated in the eleventh-century Ringerike style, named after a region in Norway where it is particularly strongly represented. The symmetrically ordered plant tendrils and the pear-shaped lobes which characterise this style can be seen on a painted sarcophagus from St Paul's in London, casket mounts from Smithfield, such everyday objects as a bone pin from the river Thames and, more impressive, copper and brass inlaid stirrup irons from Seagry in Wiltshire. A rare northern example of the style can be seen on a stone slab from *Otley in Yorkshire.

The elegant, smooth and looping contours of the final Viking style, named after the Norwegian site of Urnes, belong to the Norman period of English art rather than to its Anglo-Saxon predecessor. The Pitney brooch from Somerset can stand as a representative example from England, combining a characteristic Scandinavian animal with tightly scrolled terminals which draw upon an English tradition. The Southwall tympanum in Nottinghamshire, the Jevington Christ in Majesty from Sussex and a Norman bishop's crosier from Durham provide widespread testimony to the way in which this final Viking style was absorbed into Norman work and the emerging Romanesque.

The evolving sequence of Scandinavian art is thus mirrored in England, though the enthusiasm with which it was adopted and the extent to which the successive styles were transformed varied from area to area. These zoomorphic and band styles are not, however, the only motifs which reached England in the Viking period. On perishable media like wood carvings, shield paintings and fabrics the iconography of Scandinavian mythology and heroism was carried here and reproduced in the Insular medium of stone. The Gosforth cross with its depictions of Scandinavian deities provides the best known example but elsewhere on northern carvings we find Weland and Sigurd, repeated in forms which show that there was a long established iconography to aid interpretation. To the same world must be attributed the armed warriors who appear on Yorkshire carvings; they celebrate the martial tastes of the Anglo-Scandinavian aristocracy but, typically, their bold carving is the legacy of an earlier Anglo-Saxon tradition of figure sculpture.

CASSS iii.33–42; R. N. Bailey, *Viking-Age Sculpture in Northern England* (London, 1980); S. H. Fuglesang, 'The Relationship between Scandinavian and English Art from the late Eighth to the mid-Twelfth Century', in *Sources of Anglo-Saxon Culture*, ed. P. E. Szarmach (Kalamazoo, MI, 1986), pp. 203–41; *The Vikings in England and in their Danish Homeland*, ed. E. Roesdahl (London and Copenhagen, 1981); D. M. Wilson, *Anglo-Saxon Art* (London, 1984); D. M. Wilson and O. Klindt-Jensen, *Viking Art* (London, 1980).

RICHARD N. BAILEY

SCEATTA: see Coinage

SCHOOLS were a prominent feature of ecclesiastical life in Anglo-Saxon England from the time of the Augustinian mission for, if Christianity was to flourish there, it was necessary to have native clergy sufficiently trained in Latin to be able to expand and continue the work of the original Roman *missionaries. Accordingly, one of the first priorities for Augustine and his companions must have been that of establishing a school in *Canterbury; that their efforts were successful is clear from the fact that by the 630s Sigeberht, king of *East Anglia, was able to establish a school in his kingdom with masters sent to him from *Kent (Bede, *HE* iii.18), and at approximately the same time King *Oswald (634–42) provided Irish monks with land so that they could train Anglo-Saxon children and their parents as well (*HE* iii.3). In the following decades the first native clergy were trained well enough to be able to be appointed to bishoprics (the first being *Ithamar, who was elected bishop of *Rochester some time after 644) and the archbishopric of Canterbury (*Deusdedit, who was elected in 655, being the first). As more and more monasteries were founded during the course of the seventh century (see *monasticism), many, if not all, will have received oblates (children, that is, who were given to a monastery as an act of piety), and it will have been necessary to establish schools and appoint masters to train them; although the evidence for such schools is sparse and uneven, schools are unambiguously attested for such monasteries as *Melrose, *Whitby, *Ripon, *Repton, *Monkwearmouth-Jarrow and *Malmesbury. Similarly, although the evidence is sparse once again, it may be inferred that many, if not all, English cathedrals established schools to train future clergy: such schools are attested for *Lindisfarne, *Hexham, *York and Canterbury. By the eighth century schools and a tradition of learning were sufficiently well established that England could provide schoolmasters for continental churches of the Bonifatian mission (both *Beorhtgyth and *Leobgyth are known to have acted as *magistrae* in such schools), and *Boniface himself could write in 752 that in English monasteries monks were specially designated for the task of teaching oblates (*Ep.* xciii). A few years earlier the council of *Clofesho in 747 had stipulated that oblates in monastic schools should even be 'coerced into the love of sacred learning, so that learned men will be available for the benefit of the church'. In any event, by the end of the eighth century, English schools were among the finest in Europe, and products of English schooling, such as *Aldhelm, *Bede, and *Alcuin determined the course of European learning for several centuries.

During the ninth century, as a result of repeated *Viking assaults, monastic life in England came more or less to an end, and with it the tradition of English schooling (the abysmal level of English schooling at this period, particularly between 835 and 885, is reflected in the illiteracy both of *charters and episcopal professions). King *Alfred did his best to remedy the situation by importing scholars from outside England (such as *Asser, *Grimbald, and *John the Old Saxon) and by providing substantial endowment for the establishment at his court of a school which was attended by children of the nobility as well as of lower classes. Alfred's palace school was continued by his successors *Edward the Elder and notably by *Æthelstan, whose court became a focal point for the scholarly activities of men such as *Israel the Grammarian, *Æthelwold and *Dunstan. By the time of Æthelstan's death in 939, however, the initiative in education passed back to the monasteries; both Dunstan and Æthelwold spent long periods of study at *Glastonbury during the 940s and early 950s, and Æthelwold subsequently established schools at *Abingdon during his abbacy there (*c*.954–63) and *Winchester, where he was bishop from 963 until his death in 984, and where

he himself taught young men in the monastic school attached to the Old Minster. Æthelwold numbered among his pupils two of the most learned men of the later Anglo-Saxon period, namely *Ælfric and *Wulfstan Cantor. Winchester was perhaps the outstanding school in the country at that time; but there were certainly others, notably at Glastonbury, Abingdon, *Worcester, Canterbury, and especially *Ramsey, where the great polymath *Abbo of Fleury taught for two years (985–7) and numbered among his pupils *Byrhtferth, who was less of a polymath than his master, but was nevertheless a scholar of very considerable learning. In spite of the prestige and achievements of these monastic schools, however, it is well not to overestimate their number (not all monasteries and cathedral chapters can be demonstrated to have schools), nor to overestimate the number of pupils which may have been in such a school at any one time: even the great continental schools of Rheims and Chartres did not have more than ten or twelve pupils, and a Cluniac customary (PL cxlix.742) envisages only six oblates in the school. Anglo-Saxon schools are likely to have had a similarly small number of pupils. Only from the later period is there evidence that, in addition to the small numbers of oblates and novices, secular *clergy received some training in monastic schools (Byrhtferth's *Enchiridion*, for example, is addressed to a classroom comprising both Ramsey monks and country priests).

The curriculum of Anglo-Saxon schools can be determined from various sources: narrative accounts such as Bede's *Historia ecclesiastica* (which includes, for example, a detailed description of the curriculum taught at Canterbury by *Theodore and *Hadrian: *HE* iv.2) or *Alcuin's poem on York, which contains a lengthy description of the curriculum taught there by his master *Ælberht; scholarly correspondence (Aldhelm's Letters to *Leuthere and Hadrian contain accounts of the curriculum which he studied at Canterbury, and the letters of Boniface contain many incidental references to English schooling); surviving manuscripts which show some sign of having been used in a classroom by a master, or annotated by students; and repeated quotation in Anglo-Latin authors. From these various sources it can be deduced that the young oblate was set first to memorizing the psalter, followed by the wisdom books (Wisdom, Proverbs, Ecclesiastes, Sirach and the book of Job). As progress in Latin continued, the somewhat more difficult poetic texts of the late antique curriculum (which were also studied in continental schools) would be studied, perhaps in a graded sequence of difficulty, beginning with the anonymous *Disticha Catonis* and/or the *Epigrammata* of Prosper of Aquitaine, then the *Euangelia* of Juvencus, the *Carmen paschale* of Caelius Sedulius, and the *Historia apostolica* (or *De actibus apostolorum*) of Arator. This sequence could be amplified so as to include other Christian-Latin poets: Avitus, Dracontius, Venantius Fortunatus, Prudentius (especially the *Psychomachia*); to these at a later period were added various works of Aldhelm (whose prose *De virginitate* was intensely studied in tenth-century schools) and Bede (especially the metrical *Vita S. Cuthberti*). The only *classical poets for whom there is any evidence of intensive study are Vergil, Horace and Persius (Alcuin also mentions Statius among the books in Ælberht's library). Curriculum texts such as these formed the basis for study of the *trivium*, what we would now call 'arts subjects' (*grammar, rhetoric, dialectic); and it is clear that the texts served as the basis for the master's further exposition of grammar, metrics, rhetoric and dialectic as these concerns arose in the texts under study. There is less evidence from Anglo-Saxon England for study of the scientific subjects or *quadrivium* (arithmetic, geometry, *astronomy and harmony/musical theory). Very few Anglo-Saxon manuscripts pertaining to these subjects survive (in particular, there is a paucity of manuscripts of Martianus Capella, from which the parameters of *quadrivium*-subjects could be learned); but against the absence of manuscripts of scientific texts, must be set Alcuin's statement in his poem on York (lines 1439–46) that Ælberht taught astronomy and cosmology (astronomy was also taught at Canterbury by Theodore and Hadrian). Only from the end of the tenth century, particularly from the period of Abbo's sabbatical leave at Ramsey (985–7), is there evidence that the scientific *quadrivium* was introduced, fitfully, to English schools.

Evidence of various kinds throws light on classroom procedures. In Cuthbert's *Epistola de obitu Bedae*, we have a moving account of Bede, in his last days, expounding the meaning of scriptural passages to his circle of disciples. From this description it would appear that Bede first dictated a passage of scripture to the students, and then expounded its meaning orally. A more detailed portrait of the procedures of an Anglo-Saxon school is found in the early eleventh-century *colloquies of *Ælfric Bata, from whom we learn that the students met with the master daily, and were expected to show mastery of the set text (*acceptum*) which he had dictated to them the previous day.

If they showed mastery, the master moved on to the consequential passage of text (if they failed to show such mastery, they were flogged). The passage was copied by the students from the master's dictation on to wax tablets (it can be calculated that passages of, say, 20–40 lines' length could be copied onto a diptych) or parchment scraps, and then committed to memory. At this rate it would take some 80 days to read Arator's *Historia apostolica*, and about a year to read Vergil's *Aeneid*. To judge from Ælfric Bata's colloquies, Anglo-Saxon students were very high-spirited, and these high spirits are reflected in a metrical debate between a master (a Welshman named Ioruert) and students composed at Winchester during the bishopric of Æthelwold.

DACL iv.1739–1883; P. Riché, *Éducation et culture dans l'Occident barbare, VIe–VIIIe siècles* (Paris, 1962), pp. 419–49; idem, *Les écoles et l'enseignement dans l'Occident chrétien de la fin du Ve siècle au milieu du XIe siècle* (Paris, 1979); P. F. Jones, 'The Gregorian Mission and English Education', *Speculum* 3 (1928), 335–48; M. Lapidge, 'The School of Theodore and Hadrian', *ASE* 15 (1986), 45–72, repr. in *ALL* i.141–68; idem, 'Three Latin Poems from Æthelwold's School at Winchester', *ASE* 1 (1972), 85–137, repr. in *ALL* ii.225–77; idem, 'The Study of Latin Texts in Late Anglo-Saxon England: the Evidence of Latin Glosses', in *Latin and the Vernacular Languages in Early Medieval Britain*, ed. N. Brooks, (Leicester, 1982), pp. 99–140, repr. in *ALL* i.455–98; idem, 'Latin Learning in Ninth-Century England', *ALL* i.409–54; idem, 'Surviving Booklists from Anglo-Saxon England', Clemoes FS, pp. 33–89; D. W. Porter, 'The Latin Syllabus in Anglo-Saxon Monastic Schools', *Neophilologus* 78 (1994), 463–82; S. Gwara and D. W. Porter, *Anglo-Saxon Conversations. The Colloquies of Ælfric Bata* (Woodbridge, 1997).

MICHAEL LAPIDGE

SCRIBES: *see* Colophons; Scriptorium

SCRIPT, ANGLO-SAXON. The history of handwriting in Anglo-Saxon England is bound up with the religious history of the British Isles. Christianity spread in conjunction with *literacy, and during the Anglo-Saxon period religious houses had a near-monopoly on literate education and the copying of manuscripts. The Anglo-Saxons were introduced to Latin script via two separate waves of *missionary activity. The first of these was the mission of *Augustine from *Rome to *Kent at the end of the sixth century; but the more significant for script-development was the contribution of missionaries from Ireland to *Northumbria in the first half of the seventh century. The Insular script-system which was brought to England by the Irish was distinctive and highly flexible. Derived from the scripts of the Roman empire, it had developed in Ireland after the christianisation of Ireland from Britain, and owed its idiosyncracies to the relative isolation of the British Isles from the Continent during most of the fifth and sixth centuries. It consisted of a hierarchy of scripts, of various degrees of formality, allowing scribes to adapt their handwriting to suit the status of their texts or the space available. The most formal script was Insular Half-uncial; beneath this in the hierarchy came various grades of Insular minuscule: Hybrid minuscule, Set minuscule, Cursive minuscule, and – at the bottom – Current minuscule. (There were also distinctive Insular methods of parchment-preparation, abbreviation, and decoration: see *codicology.)

Meanwhile, the Augustinian mission had brought Roman scripts to Southumbria. The most influential of these scripts was Roman Uncial (Uncial was the most formal Christian bookhand on the Continent between the fifth and eighth centuries). When practitioners of the Insular and Roman scripts met in seventh-century England, the result was that the flexible and practical Insular script-system was adopted by scribes across the country. However, Uncial was retained as the most formal script in the repertoire of English scribes, while access to the formal majuscule scripts of Rome impelled a neatening and regularisation of Insular script in England.

By the ninth century, Uncial and Half-uncial had been abandoned, leaving Hybrid minuscule at the top of the hierarchy. Partly as a result of *Viking raids, Insular literacy and calligraphy were in decline. Revival came only with the accession of *Alfred. The ecclesiastical and intellectual reforms which he promoted produced – after a few decades of experimentation – a new variety of Insular minuscule: English Square minuscule, essentially a version of Set minuscule but influenced by Hybrid minuscule, as well as Welsh, Cornish, and possibly Irish models. Its use was effectively confined to tenth-century Southumbria, and it evolved rapidly. Its use in royal diplomas means that specimens of Square minuscule may be dated with unusual precision.

Square minuscule was not the only new script of the tenth century. As a result of the continentally-inspired Benedictine reform of the mid-century, the Caroline minuscule which had developed in Francia during the ninth century – and which was almost universal in France and *Germany by the tenth – finally entered English scriptoria. By the 960s, two main styles of Anglo-Caroline seem to have developed. There may be a link between

the practice of one or other of these styles and particular reform-parties: one style, based wholly on continental models, was apparently written at monasteries connected with *Æthelwold and *Oswald, while the other, which retains Insular traits, is associable with *Dunstan.

The introduction of Caroline minuscule to English writing-houses was not immediately disastrous for Square minuscule. Although scribes at the Æthelwoldian and Oswaldian houses adopted Anglo-Caroline for high-status manuscripts, the scriptoria connected with Dunstan preferred to use Caroline for workaday texts, retaining Square minuscule for their most important material. However, Caroline minuscule – attractive and clear – gradually achieved the dominance. The use of Square minuscule was increasingly confined to vernacular material, and, by the beginning of the new millennium, Square minuscule had been abandoned as a vehicle for Latin writing in favour of Caroline.

During the first decade of the eleventh century, Square minuscule underwent a change in proportions: the result was a fresh variety of Insular minuscule, used in English vernacular manuscripts of the eleventh century. By c.1020, a new style of Anglo-Caroline minuscule had developed as well, blending features of earlier styles (its creator may have been a monk of Christ Church, Canterbury, called 'Eadwig Basan'). This style of Anglo-Caroline had gained currency all over England by the time of the Norman Conquest.

The Conquest had a dramatic impact on English scriptoria. In some houses Norman script replaced English almost immediately; in a few (notably *Bury St Edmunds and St Augustine's, Canterbury), Anglo-Caroline script remained in use until well into the twelfth century. Insular minuscule survived for even longer, though confined to vernacular use.

Golden Age of AS Art; B. Bischoff, *Latin Palaeography. Antiquity and the Middle Ages*, trans. D. Ó Cróinín and D. Ganz (Cambridge, 1990); M. P. Brown, *Anglo-Saxon Manuscripts* (London, 1991); T. J. Brown, *A Palaeographer's View* (London, 1993); T. A. M. Bishop, *English Caroline Minuscule* (Oxford, 1971); D. N. Dumville, *English Caroline Script and Monastic History. Studies in Benedictinism, A. D. 950–1030* (Woodbridge, 1993); idem, 'English Square Minuscule Script: the Background and Earliest Phases', *ASE* 16 (1987), 147–79 + plates I–VII; idem, 'English Square Minuscule Script: the Mid-Century Phases', *ASE* 23 (1994), 133–64 + plates I–VI; Ker, *Catalogue*; idem, *English Manuscripts in the Century after the Norman Conquest* (Oxford, 1960); *CLA*; E. A. Lowe, *English Uncial* (Oxford, 1960).

HELEN MCKEE

SCRIPTORIUM. During the Anglo-Saxon period, the scriptorium or 'writing office' was normally housed in cathedral churches and monasteries, although there is evidence that King *Alfred had at his disposal a writing office in which the copies, say, of his translation of Gregory's *Regula pastoralis* were produced for distribution to his various bishops, and his successors *Edward the Elder and *Æthelstan may similarly have maintained a royal scriptorium for the copying of books (rather than merely documents or *charters; see *chancery). Because scribes in a monastery or cathedral at any one time were (presumably) taught by one master scribe, their work will inevitably have a certain stylistic resemblance; and it is this resemblance which allows manuscripts now dispersed to be associated with one another and, providing one or more of these associated manuscripts can be linked to a house, to identify the scriptorium in which they originated. From the manuscripts associated in this way it is often possible to calculate how many scribes were active at the same (approximate) time, and thus to estimate the size of the scriptorium, which might vary from one or two scribes to the group of twenty-two scribes whose work appears in early eleventh-century manuscripts from Christ Church, *Canterbury, or the approximately coeval group of ten or more scribes active at St Augustine's, Canterbury. In most cases the work of the scribes will have been done in the cloisters of the monastery or church in question, rather than in a room designated for the purpose; although there may have been some panelling to protect the scribes from the worst weather, a severe winter would have brought scribal activity to a standstill (as is clear from the observation of Archbishop Cuthbert writing to *Lull in the aftermath of the severe winter of 764, to the effect that the past winter was so cold 'that the hand of the scribe was hindered from producing a great number of books': *EHD* i.832). Scribes presumably learned to write by imitating the work of the master scribe, and some pre-Conquest manuscripts (for example Rouen, BM, 1385) show the first pages to have been written by the master, and subsequent pages written by several inept imitators and later corrected by the master. The production of a scriptorium depended on the relative wealth of the monastery: the huge number of calves (*c.*1,550) which were slaughtered to produce the Codex *Amiatinus and its two companion volumes shows graphically the wealth in livestock possessed by *Monkwearmouth-Jarrow in Bede's day. The activity of a scriptorium is vividly described in a *colloquy by *Ælfric Bata, where the apprentice scribes are portrayed assembling their styluses, penknives, awls and vellum scraps for writing practice, and subsequently negotiating with a potential customer about the price for copying a manuscript missal (*Colloquia*, cc. 14, 24). Manuscripts were apparently copied one at a time from an exemplar (exemplars were frequently exchanged between scriptoria), rather than from dictation; there is no trace in Anglo-Saxon England of the mass-production of manuscripts associated with the university book-trade of the later Middle Ages. T. A. M. Bishop, 'Notes on Cambridge Manuscripts, Part IV: MSS. Connected with St Augustine's, Canterbury', *TCBS* 2 (1954–8), 323–36; idem, 'Notes on Cambridge Manuscripts, part VII: the Early Minuscule of Christ Church, Canterbury', *TCBS* 3 (1959–63), 413–23; Brooks, *Canterbury*, pp. 266–78; D. N. Dumville, *English Caroline Script and Monastic History: Studies in Benedictinism, AD 950–1030* (Woodbridge, 1993); S. Gwara and D. W. Porter, *Anglo-Saxon Conversations. The Colloquies of Ælfric Bata* (Woodbridge, 1997), pp. 112–15, 132–7.

MICHAEL LAPIDGE

SCULPTURE, STONE. The human masks on the whetstones from *Sutton Hoo and Hough on the Hill are reminders that pagan Anglo-Saxon England had its stone carvings. Yet the very rarity of such examples emphasises the fact that Anglo-Saxon sculpture is essentially a Christian art form, one of the technologies of the Mediterranean world which was transplanted to England with the new religion.

The earliest surviving sculpture dates to the later years of the seventh century and is architectural in function. Though there is some restrained cable and fret decoration on the chancel columns from *Reculver in *Kent, the most impressive work of this early period comes from *Northumbria and is associated with the churches and monastic buildings of *Wilfrid at *Hexham, and of *Benedict Biscop at *Monkwearmouth–Jarrow in the 670s and 680s. Much of this ornament, like the modelled animals or the diamond and circle decoration from Hexham, reflects the decorative tastes of Gaul and Italy. In Northumbria the continued use of sculpture for architectural purposes can be traced through to the Anglo-Scandinavian period. Further south, in *Mercia, the practice was established slightly later than in Northumbria, but sites like *Breedon and Fletton preserve fine examples of eighth-century date. It is not until the ninth century that we have evidence from Britford in Wiltshire of similar fashions in *Wessex but thereafter there are impressive survivals of sculptured wall plaques and large-scale roods, many of them dating to the Benedictine reform period of the late tenth century.

By c.700 Northumbrian sculptors were producing *crosses and *grave-markers in stone. In the course of the eighth century these forms were adopted in Mercia but there is little evidence that they had spread to Wessex or Kent before the ninth century. Indeed these southern areas never seem to have displayed the same enthusiasm for crosses as more northerly regions, even though they produced some work of very high quality like the ninth-century shafts from Reculver in Kent, Codford St Peter in Wiltshire and *Winchester itself.

Stone sculpture was used in other fields. From pre-Viking Northumbria, for example, we have a fine series of decorated stone seats or thrones whilst fragments from other furnishings, such as chancel screens and reading desks, have been identified at northern sites. Stone *shrines are also represented among the surviving sculptures; this seems to be a type which was first developed in eighth-century Mercia.

The contexts and methods of production of sculpture are not yet fully understood but work on the prolific Northumbrian material is now beginning to shed light on the problem. There is no doubt that, in its earliest phases, the production of sculpture was an ecclesiastical affair; the distribution, *iconography and *literacy of the monuments, indeed, strongly suggest that the art was largely confined to monastic houses in the seventh and eighth centuries in both Mercia and Northumbria. An increasing lay involvement may be traceable in the ninth century as *monasticism declined, but certainly by the tenth century the role of the laity as both patrons and artists was dominant, as the emergent Anglo-Scandinavian aristocracy adopted this form of art with great enthusiasm. In the south of the country the evidence for production is less clear though the Benedictine revival of the latter half of the tenth century undoubtedly strengthened the element of monastic patronage which is so markedly absent in the contemporary north.

The motifs and the monumental forms of sculpture reflect these changing patterns of patronage and production and are also inevitably influenced by the political affiliations of differing regions. Throughout the period it is possible to trace regional responses to period tastes and to see the way in which decorative organisation and ornamental motifs were constantly modified by the ebb and flow of ideas between workshops, by the impact of exotic imports, and by conservative revivals of earlier types of ornament.

The stone used for carvings is usually local. In this context, however, 'local' can mean two things: either the stone has been won from a local quarry or it lay to hand in ready-cut ashlar blocks brought to the site in the earlier, Roman, period. Re-use of Roman stones is particularly noticeable in Northumbria and is strongly evident among the carvings from *York where neither the limestone nor the millstone grit employed in so much of the pre-Norman sculpture could be quarried locally (see *Roman remains). Despite this general reliance on local sources, it is clear that from a fairly early date stone was being moved over considerable distances, particularly in the south of the country; the ninth-century carvings from Britford and Codford St Peter in Wiltshire for example seem to have been drawn from quarries which are at least 35 miles away (see *mining and quarrying).

In the early, monastic, phase of sculpture the atelier was probably within the monastery but the close links between Jarrow and the *Ruthwell and *Bewcastle crosses suggest that some sculptors may have worked further afield even at this date. In the later period there seems to have been a range of kinds of sculptor. In large towns like *Chester, *Lincoln and York there were clearly workshops supplying near-standard forms of crosses and gravemarkers to various graveyards both within the city and in the immediately surrounding area. In the country, neighbouring villages like Brompton, Kirkleavington and Sockburn in the Tees valley seem to have drawn upon the same workshop which was providing carvings over a five-mile radius. Other sculptors may have worked more independently. The Gosforth master, for example, seems to have been employed solely for a patron or patrons at *Gosforth in the tenth century. Others were no doubt itinerant.

It is clear from fragmentary survivals that many, if not most, carvings were painted and that others were also covered in gesso. In this way additional details could be added, the carved outlines modified, the intricacies clarified or (if necessary) made ambiguous. Apart from gesso all that now usually remains of this colouring are traces of red and black pigments. These may merely be sealing or primer paints; across the range of Anglo-Saxon sculptures we have records of white, blue, green, brown/yellow, pink and orange. Metal-work, *glass and coloured paste could also be added. Such attachments explain the lead settings of some carvings and the drilled holes which can still be seen on the Reculver shaft in Kent and the Breamore crucifixion in Hampshire. The original polychrome effect of these carvings was far removed from their present reticent appearance.

Like all of the arts in Anglo-Saxon England the surviving sculpture is necessarily only a fragment of what once existed. But by its very nature sculpture has survived in greater quantities than other forms. It might be broken up, re-used as rubble in later buildings, but this has often merely preserved it until it emerged again in Victorian restorations. Other arts like fabrics and wood were in perishable media, or like metalwork and precious stones were subject to looting, re-melting in the crucible or removal to museums. Sculpture, in its humble form, usually remains in its original site, the most accessible of the surviving arts.

CASSS; R. N. Bailey, *Viking-Age Sculpture in Northern England* (London, 1980); R. J. Cramp, 'Schools of Mercian Sculpture', in Dornier, *MS*, pp. 191–233; idem, 'Anglo-Saxon Sculpture of the Reform Period', in *Tenth-Century Studies*, ed. D. Parsons (Chichester, 1975), pp. 184–99; W. Rodwell and E. C. Rouse, 'The Anglo-Saxon Rood and other Features in the South Porch of St Mary's Church, Breamore, Hampshire', *AJ* 64 (1984), 298–325; R. N. Bailey, *England's Earliest Sculptors*, Publications of the Dictionary of Old English 5 (Toronto, 1996).

RICHARD N. BAILEY

SEAFARER. The 124-line *Seafarer*, in the *Exeter Book, like the *Wanderer*, is one of the Old English *elegies, and also belongs to the larger category of *wisdom literature. The speaker describes in compelling language the cold, hunger, loneliness, and danger which he has suffered at sea. Nevertheless, he longs for a voyage to a far-off land, a journey to which he is prompted by the burgeoning of life in spring. He repeatedly asserts that the man who lives comfortably on land cannot understand his feelings. His spirit ranges far and wide, and comes back to him eager and greedy, 'for the joys of the Lord are warmer to me than this dead life, loaned on land' (lines 64b–66a). Thereafter, the narrator says nothing further about seafaring, but speaks in general terms about the transience of earthly wealth and power, and the need to prepare for the life to come. The ideas in the second half are presented in a somewhat disjointed fashion, and the text at lines 111–15a is corrupt. Because of the apparent inconsistency between the speaker's attitudes in the first half, early scholars postulated a change of speaker. Another view sees two kinds of voyage: one representing the trials of this life, and the other the journey to the next. Whitelock explains the sea-

farer's painful but wished-for voyaging as *peregrinatio pro amore Dei* in the manner of Irish penitential exile. The poem is now generally accepted as a relatively unified monologue, in which the evocative descriptions of seafaring also symbolise the life of the Christian ascetic.

ASPR iii. 143–7; D. Whitelock, 'The Interpretation of *The Seafarer*', *The Early Cultures of Northwest Europe*, ed. C. Fox and B. Dickins (Cambridge, 1950), pp. 259–72, repr. in J. B. Bessinger and S. J. Kahrl, ed., *Essential Articles for the Study of OE Poetry* (Hamden, CT, 1968), pp. 442–57; I. L. Gordon, ed., *The Seafarer* (London, 1960); S. B. Greenfield, '*Sylf*, Seasons, Structure and Genre in *The Seafarer*', *ASE* 9 (1981), 199–211, repr. in his *Hero and Exile* (London and Ronceverte, WV, 1989), pp. 171–83; also in *Old English Shorter Poems: Basic Readings*, ed. K. O'Brien O'Keeffe (New York, 1994), pp. 231–49; P. Orton, 'The Form and Structure of *The Seafarer*', *Studia Neophilologica* 63 (1991), 37–55.

ANNE L. KLINCK

SEALS and sealing practice in Anglo-Saxon England are known to us from three kinds of evidence: written references, surviving sealed documents, and matrices which have been found by chance or which continued in use on post-Conquest documents. The sealed *writs of *Edward the Confessor constitute the entire category of extant sealed documents. Characteristically they are small pieces of membrane containing a short message with a relatively large two-sided seal (72 mm diameter) attached to a thin tongue cut parallel with the bottom of the sheet. Another thin strip served as a wrapping tie, and demonstrates that these were envisaged as patent documents (ones that could be opened without breaking the seal). Almost certainly this form derived from

Pl. 17 The seal of Godwine (matrix and impression).

413

close sealed letters or writs, which seem to have been in existence from at least the 860s, though this is a contentious issue. From the 860s survive both our earliest seal matrix, of Æthilwald, bishop of *Dommoc* (*East Anglia), and the earliest document to retain traces of a wrapping tie which might have borne a seal (S 1199). Some three decades later there is a significant reference in King *Alfred's 'translation' of St Augustine's Soliloquies, when he mentions a lord's writ and seal as a means of conveying 'his will'. Subsequent references to *gewrit* and *insegel* (sometimes just *insegel*), or the Latin equivalent, occur in various contexts such as the granting of a pardon (the Fonthill Letter, S 1445), a greeting to the *witan* conveyed from the king by Abbot Ælfhere of Bath (Harmer, Appendix IV no.1), diplomatic negotiations (King *Æthelred to the duke of Normandy: *EHD* i.894–5), or the introduction of a protegé (see *colloquies). While there is no proof in any of these cases that the seal was joined to a document, the alternative solution that the seal was carried separately from the message is open to serious objections.

The use of seals was quite widespread in the upper levels of late Anglo-Saxon society. Two matrices belonging to secular lords, both showing them holding swords point-upright, are extant: the earlier in bronze for one Ælfric (perhaps the infamous ealdorman Ælfric of Hampshire) and the later in walrus *ivory, datable to *Harthacnut's reign, for an otherwise unidentified *thegn called Godwine. His matrix was reused by a nun called Godgyth, whose die was engraved on the reverse. Another nun who had a seal was St *Edith of Wilton; its use in the later Middle Ages as the seal of Wilton Abbey has meant that several impressions are preserved. Like Godwine's matrix, Edith's had an elaborate handle, and this is a feature of several others: an ivory matrix belonging to Wulfric (status unknown, shown seated and again holding a sword point upwards), and later impressions of seals from the monasteries of *Sherborne, Athelney and *Glastonbury.

So far as the limited numbers give us a basis for extrapolation, it seems that the seals of individuals generally represent them as either shoulder-length or three-quarter length and in profile, whereas the seals of institutions depict a building. The former category is thus generally comparable with surviving personal seals from the Continent from the century up to 1066. The 'topographical' seals, though, seem to be peculiarly English. One or two of the latter may have quite accurate depictions of the church they belonged to. The recent exca-

vations under the nave of *Canterbury cathedral found the western apse and transeptal projections shown on the priory's seal. All the seals are circular and small (40–50 mm in diameter), and this again squares with contemporary practice in Western Europe.

There are indications that seals were used for closing boxes, and even for securing the bandages used after an *ordeal by hot iron. However, it is hard to imagine that the latter were more than occasional supplementary functions of a class of object made primarily for closing *letters, whether formal or informal. Again, in this respect, England was in tune with those neighbours who inherited Carolingian practices. Where the Anglo-Saxons differed was in refusing to use seals on *charters. Presumably, as letters were often sent long distances, they were more likely to be part of a common culture, whereas charters were generally for local consumption and therefore relatively immune from such influence.

F. E. Harmer, *Anglo-Saxon Writs* (Manchester, 1952); T. A. M. Bishop and P. Chaplais, *Facsimiles of English Royal Writs to AD 1100* (Oxford, 1957); P. Chaplais, 'The Anglo-Saxon Chancery: from the Diploma to the Writ', in *Prisca Munimenta*, ed. F. Ranger (London, 1973), pp. 43–62; T. A. Heslop, 'English Seals from the mid-Ninth Century to *c.*1100', *JBAA* 133 (1980), 1–16.

T. A. HESLOP

SEASONS FOR FASTING, an OE poetic fragment of 230 lines, was originally contained in BL, Cotton Otho B. xi; but that manuscript having been almost entirely destroyed by fire in 1731, we are dependent on a transcript made by Laurence *Nowell in 1562 (BL, Add. 43703) and brief extracts printed in *Wanley's *Catalogus* (1705) and Abraham Whelock's edition of Bede's *History* (*Historiae Ecclesiasticae Gentis Anglorum Libri V* (Cambridge, 1643), p. 96). The poem is unusual in being arranged in eight-line stanzas. It opens with an account of Moses's laws and the fasts observed by the Hebrews, and continues by listing the dates of the Ember fasts observed by the English and warning against the usage of the Bretons and the *Franks. It recommends the strict observance of Lent and cites as precedents for fasting in Lent the forty-day fasts of Moses, Elijah and Christ. It warns priests against sin, but encourages parishioners to follow the good precepts of the priest whether he is sinful or not. It breaks off while criticizing priests who indulge in oysters and wine immediately after celebrating mass. Given the poem's loose structure, it is difficult to estimate how much may be missing at the end. According to *Seasons for Fasting* and other sources, Pope *Gregory the Great appointed the days on which the English should fast, namely Wednesday, Friday and Saturday in the first week of Lent, the week after Pentecost, the week before the autumnal equinox and the week before Christmas. During the Benedictine reform, some churches, presumably under the influence of reformers from the Continent, began to hold the first fast in the first week of March and the second in the second week of June. It is this disagreement over dates that the poet refers to in stanzas 12 and 13; the reference points to a date of composition in the late tenth or the eleventh century. In style and vocabulary, *Seasons for Fasting* is connected with the poems of the Benedictine Office in Oxford, Bodleian Library, Junius 121, and particularly *The Creed*, which also is stanzaic and may be by the same author. The prose parts of the Benedictine Office are attributed to *Wulfstan, bishop of *Worcester and archbishop of *York, and although he probably did not write the verse, *Seasons for Fasting* was very likely produced in Worcester during his time.

ASPR vi.98–104; K. Sisam, 'Seasons of Fasting', in his *Studies in the History of Old English Literature* (Oxford, 1953), pp. 45–60.

PETER S. BAKER

SELSEY (Sussex), a peninsula on the south coast, was given by King Æthelwalh of the South Saxons to Bishop *Wilfrid, who founded a religious community there, and perhaps also (though the sources are ambiguous) an episcopal seat. During 705 × 709 the *Winchester diocese was divided and a see established at Selsey, with Eadberht as its first bishop. A grant to St Peter's church there was made in 772 × 787 (S 1183), and the see continued until 1075 when it was re-located at Chichester. The cathedral site can be identified with the now-isolated parish church of Church Norton.

Stephen of Ripon, *Vita S. Wilfridi*, c. 41; Bede, *HE* iv.13; J. Munby, 'Saxon Chichester and its Predecessors', in Haslam, *Towns*, pp. 317–20; S. E. Kelly, *Charters of Selsey*, Anglo-Saxon Charters 6 (London, 1998).

JOHN BLAIR

SEMANTIC CHANGE is alteration in the meaning of words. Within Old English it can be difficult to identify semantic change, especially in infrequently recorded terms, since it is hard to determine the precise connotations of a term without seeing it used in numerous contexts. If a semantic change is said to have occurred in Old English it is necessary to prove that the new sense is not found for cognate terms in other Germanic languages. The problems of *dating OE texts, as opposed to manuscripts, also complicate the issue. One area of vocabulary in which semantic change clearly took place during the Old English period is religious terminology. *God* 'God', *heofon* 'heaven', and *helle* 'hell', for example, necessarily adopted new meanings when they were applied to Christian rather than pagan concepts. Semantic change can also take the form of the development of a metaphorical meaning. In Old English this sometimes took place under the influence of Latin. Examples include *tunge* 'tongue', which was extended to mean 'language', possibly modelled on Latin *lingua*, and *wit(e)ga* 'wise man', used for 'prophet', perhaps influenced by Latin *propheta*. After the establishment of the *Danelaw, OE terms also underwent semantic development under the influence of their *Old Norse cognates. Modern English *bloom* 'flower' takes its form from either Old English *bloma* 'ingot of iron' or Old Norse *blom* 'flower', but its sense is clearly from Old Norse. In Old English, *plog* (ModE *plough*) was used for the measure of land which a yoke of oxen could plough in a day; its use with reference to an agricultural implement developed under the influence of Old Norse *plogr*. Similarly, Old English *eorl* 'man, warrior' (ModE *earl*) developed the sense 'chief, ruler of a shire' under the influence of Old Norse *jarl*.

D. Kastovsky, 'Semantics and Vocabulary', CHELang i.290–408; M. S. Serjeantson, *A History of Foreign Words in English* (London, 1935); B. Weman, *Old English Semantic Analysis and Theory* (Lund, 1933).

JULIE COLEMAN

SERMONS: *see* Homilies

SETTLEMENT, ANGLO-SAXON: the movement in the fifth and sixth centuries of Germanic peoples from North *Germany and Southern Scandinavia to the former Roman province of Britain (cf. *Adventus Saxonum*). Although it is accepted that such a migration took place, many other aspects of the process are the subject of active debate. Uncertainty arises because of the shortage of written sources, and difficulties in interpreting those which do exist. The Germanic peoples were pre-literate at this stage and later accounts from the Anglo-Saxon kingdoms describing the exploits of *Hengest and Horsa and *Cerdic and Cynric, among others, are foundation myths rather than realistic records of what actually occurred in the fifth and sixth centuries.

Any narrative of the period of Anglo-Saxon settlement has to rely heavily on information provided by *Gildas in his *De excidio Britanniae*. He describes how, after the Roman authorities had informed British leaders that they could no longer provide them with an effective defence against Irish, Pictish and Saxon raiders – an event generally dated to *c*.410 – the 'proud tyrant' (later identified as Vortigern) recruited some of the Saxon aggressors to provide a defence against the *Picts 'in the eastern part of the island'. More and more Saxon warriors came to join the initial three boatloads until they were strong enough to challenge their British paymasters and seize control of part of Britain for themselves. Such use of Germanic federate forces can be paralleled in other areas of the Roman empire in the fifth century. Further support for this aspect of Gildas's account appears to come from his use of technical terms for the treaty arrangements, from finds of Roman military metalwork from some of the earliest Germanic graves in Britain and the distribution of such finds in strategic positions close to Roman sites. *Bede subsequently identified the leaders of the Germanic forces with Hengest and Horsa, founding figures of the Kentish royal house, but, as the federate forces were deployed against the Picts from northern Scotland, the first Germanic base, as portrayed by Gildas, is likely to have been further north on the east coast.

Bede's interpretation of Gildas's account led him to date the recruitment of the Germanic federates to the joint reigns of the emperors Marcian and Valentinian (449–56) (*HE* i.15, v.23), while the Gallic Chronicle of 452 records that in 441 'Britain, abandoned by the Romans, passed into the power of the Saxons'. However, at the most, Germanic control had only been established over part of Britain by the end of the fifth century. The western half of the country was divided between British kingdoms in the sixth century, in one of which Gildas probably wrote his account. There is a marked contrast in the archaeological record between the 'Celtic' culture of western Britain and the 'Anglo-Saxon' culture of the east, especially in the sixth century. Gildas's highly coloured description of the wholesale destruction of Roman sites and murder or enslavement of the British population has not been supported by the results of excavations. Roman *towns and villas were already being abandoned or adapted to simpler forms of life in the fourth century, and their 'disappearance' is as much a feature of western as eastern Britain. Recent studies have stressed the likelihood of acculturation of the British into Germanic communities in the east of the country.

Bede identified the three main Germanic groups who settled in Britain as the Angles, Saxons and Jutes (*HE* i.15). The Angles were to be found in the north and east, and the Saxons in the south, as the names of kingdoms current in his own day suggested. Jutish settlement was located in *Kent, the Isle of Wight and southern Hampshire. Archaeological studies have broadly confirmed this pattern though geographical boundaries were not as rigidly adhered to as later nomenclature implies. Archaeological and *place-name evidence also suggests that other Germanic peoples, including *Frisians, *Franks and Norwegians, settled in Britain though not in such substantial numbers. It seems to have been in the sixth century that clear distinctions between the Anglian, Saxon and Jutish areas were marked by variations in material culture, especially noticeable in female dress (see *clothing), and in *dialect. In the seventh century a more uniform Anglo-Saxon material culture emerged. However, the scale of the Germanic migration to Britain is still debated. Some would argue that the dominance achieved by Germanic culture and language argues for the movement of large numbers of people at all levels of society, while other scholars believe the arrival of a much smaller warrior elite with their families may have been all that was required to bring about such changes.

C. Hills, 'The Archaeology of Anglo-Saxon England in the Pagan Period: a Review', *ASE* 8 (1979), 297–329; P. Sims-Williams, 'The Settlement of England in Bede and the *Chronicle*', *ASE* 12 (1983), 1–41; M. E. Jones and J. Casey, 'The Gallic Chronicle Restored: a Chronology for the Anglo-Saxon Invasions and the End of Roman Britain', *Britannia* 19 (1988), 369–98; J. N. L. Myres, *The Anglo-Saxon Settlements* (Oxford, 1986); J. Hines, 'Philology, Archaeology and the *adventus Saxonum vel Anglorum*', in *Britain 400–600: Language and History*, ed. A. Bammesberger and A. Wollmann (Heidelberg, 1990), pp. 17–36; N. J. Higham, *Rome, Britain and the Anglo-Saxons* (Manchester, 1992); idem, *The English Conquest: Gildas and Britain in the Fifth Century* (Manchester, 1994).

B. A. E. YORKE

SETTLEMENT PATTERNS. The relationship between Anglo-Saxon settlement patterns and geographical features such as soil types, Roman and medieval settlements, communication routes and territorial boundaries reveals much about changes in population size and density, agricultural practices, territorial formation, the emergence of central places and other historical developments. Yet compiling an accurate distribution map of settlements is fraught with difficulties: archaeologists can never be certain that they have identified all or even most settlements in a given region, and even once a settlement has been identified, nothing short of total excavation, a luxury very rarely afforded, will indicate its exact lifespan and thus whether it was earlier than, later than or contemporary with neighbouring settlements. These complications notwithstanding, the study of settlement patterns has a great deal to teach us about Anglo-Saxon England.

According to convention, the earliest English settlements were restricted to light soils on river terraces and other elevated locations which could be easily ploughed. Expansion onto heavier soils in valleys occurred later, with the widespread adoption of the heavy plough, these later settlements lying beneath medieval villages. While this model largely still stands, we now know that the very high proportion of early Anglo-Saxon settlements which have been identified on light soils such as river gravels is partly due to the greater effectiveness of *aerial photography on such soils and the great rate of destruction of the gravels (e.g. through quarrying) and hence of excavation there. A small but growing number of early Anglo-Saxon settlements have been recognised on the slopes and in the bottoms of river valleys, for example in Hampshire, and on clay soils, notably in Norfolk.

This bias notwithstanding, the distribution of early Anglo-Saxon sites clearly indicates that river valleys, especially confluences with tributaries, formed a major focus for settlement as they did before the establishment of Roman roads. A post-Roman retreat of settlement from waterlogged terraces and clay subsoils is apparent in many regions such as the Upper Thames Valley, north-west Essex and south-east Suffolk, while early *charters, *place-names and archaeology all indicate that heavier soils were generally not exploited until the middle and late Saxon periods. There are, of course, exceptions. In east *Kent, it appears that early Anglo-Saxon settlements occupied not only the same prime soils as Roman villas, but in some cases the same sites, though this is based on the evidence of place-names and *cemeteries, not on excavated settlements, of which there are very few. In general, however, despite growing evidence for the maintenance of Roman farmland in the early Saxon period, evidence for unbroken continuity of individual settlements from Roman Britain to Anglo-Saxon England is scarce. A dramatic decline in the number of known settlements after the end of Roman rule is, furthermore, apparent. Nevertheless, Anglo-Saxon settlement patterns were in part conditioned by Romano-British settlement. In the Midlands, East Anglia, Kent, Surrey and Sussex, a correlation exists between the distribution of Anglo-Saxon place-names ending in -ham (indicating an early settlement) and Roman settlements and roads, though how such correlations should be interpreted is far from straightforward – in Hampshire, for example, early Saxon cemeteries show no clear correlation with Roman settlements, yet the relationship of the latter and -ham place-names is unmistakable.

One key to understanding the settlement patterns of early and middle Saxon England is settlement mobility. Most settlements of this period gradually shifted over short distances to new sites. The cause of this shifting probably relates in part to agricultural practice; at a number of early medieval settlements on the Continent, it is clear that farmyards, once abandoned, were brought under cultivation. In densely settled regions such as the Thames valley, such shifting settlement creates the impression of almost continuous occupation across large swathes of landscape and nearly every remnant of gravel terrace yields traces of Anglo-Saxon occupation. At the settlement of *Mucking (Essex), for example, occupied for some three hundred years, buildings were scattered over nearly a kilometre, yet only relatively small areas were occupied at any one time. In view of the growing evidence for settlement mobility, the traditional image of the early Anglo-Saxon hamlet as the direct ancestor of the medieval village is no longer tenable.

From the later seventh century onwards, settlement patterns indicate a substantial growth in the number of communities and presumably in population, as well as an expansion into new regions such as the fenlands. The identification of settlements in this period is facilitated by new, more durable, mass-produced middle Saxon *pottery wares, although settlements in regions where such wheel-turned wares were not produced, such as the Upper Thames valley, are extremely difficult to identify. In addition to this expansion, a widespread displacement of settlement in the seventh and eighth centuries (a 'Middle Saxon Shift') has been postulated to explain why most early Anglo-Saxon settlements fail to produce finds which post-date the seventh century. This thesis posits a shift of settlements to agriculturally superior sites which then became the centres of new territories, some of which became fossilised as parishes, leaving the abandoned cemeteries and settlements at their edges. Attempts to interrelate the distribution of pagan Saxon cemeteries, late Saxon churches and parish boundaries, however, have been inconclusive and the recognition of settlement mobility largely explains why we are unlikely to find both the early and middle Saxon phases of an incompletely excavated settlement. The evidence from most counties is so far insufficient to adduce a widespread reorganization of settlement as early as the seventh and eighth centuries (with some exceptions, notably Norfolk), although the establishment of many new settlements in this period is beyond doubt.

Yet the contrast between the dispersed pattern of early Saxon settlement and the increasingly nucleated pattern apparent in much of England by 1200, still requires explanation. Excavation confirms that generally, while late Saxon settlements often lie beneath medieval villages, they do not in turn overlie early or middle Saxon settlements, suggesting that in most regions, settlement nucleation did not become widespread until the Late Saxon period. The breaking of the link between settlements and cemeteries, which generally lay in close proximity during the pagan period, must be related to a series of wider changes in middle and late Saxon England. The increased power of kings and the foundation of religious communities must have had a profound impact on the pattern of rural settlement as new landlords exercised increasing control over their estates (see *estate management). Population growth would also have acted as a catalyst for settlement nucleation, as would the increased use of the heavy plough and of open fields.

Although our perception of Anglo-Saxon settlement has undoubtedly been somewhat distorted by the small scale of most excavations and by inevitable lacunae in the archaeological record, the study of settlement patterns has greatly enhanced our understanding of the key processes of settlement mobility, expansion and nucleation.
H. Hamerow, 'Settlement Mobility and the "Middle Saxon Shift": Rural Settlements and Settlement Patterns in Anglo-Saxon England', *ASE* 20 (1991), 1–17; idem, 'Settlement on the Gravels in the Anglo-Saxon Period', in *Developing Landscapes of Lowland Britain. The Archaeology of the British Gravels*, ed. M. Fulford and E. Nicholson (London, 1992), pp. 39–46; D. Hooke, ed., *Anglo-Saxon Settlements* (Oxford, 1988).

HELENA HAMEROW

SEXBURG, ST, abbess of *Ely from 679 to about 700, was a daughter of King Anna of the East Angles, and sister to St *Æthelthryth. *Bede recounts that Sexburg was given in marriage to Earconbert, king of *Kent. When her husband died in 664, she retired to the convent at *Minster-in-Sheppey which she had founded. On the death of Æthelthryth in 679, Sexburg succeeded her sister as abbess of Ely. Little else is known of her; an eleventh-century Life by *Goscelin (*BHL* 7693) adds nothing to Bede's account. Sexburg's daughter Eormenhild followed her to Minster-in-Sheppey on the death of her husband *Wulfhere, king of *Mercia (d. 674), and she succeeded her mother as abbess of Ely. In 1106, the relics of Sexburg and the other Ely saints were translated into new shrines in the Norman cathedral at Ely. Feast: 6 July; translation, 17 October.
Bede, *HE* iii.8, iv.19–21; E. O. Blake, ed., *Liber Eliensis*, Camden 3rd ser. 92 (London, 1962).

R. C. LOVE

SHAFTESBURY (Dorset), a naturally defensible hill-spur, is listed in the *Burghal Hidage with an assessment of 700 hides. An inscription, now lost, recorded that 'in the year of the Lord's Incarnation 880 King *Alfred made this town'. Asser's statement that Alfred built a *nunnery, ruled by his daughter Æthelgifu, 'near the east gate of Shaftesbury' implies that the fort occupied the central and western parts of the spur, though it is possible that the abbey was just inside rather than just outside the gate. A case has been made for an earlier monastic presence, which, though not currently provable, is plausible enough on general grounds. Shaftesbury was a middle-ranking *mint from *Æthelstan's reign onwards, and *Domesday Book shows it as a fully-developed *town. Alfred's nunnery also prospered: it retained close royal associations, strengthened after 979 by the cult of *Edward the Martyr, and at the Conquest it was easily the richest nunnery in England.
Alfred the Great, pp. 105, 272, 340; S. Kelly, *Charters of Shaftesbury Abbey*, Anglo-Saxon Charters 5 (London, 1996); E. Murphy, 'Anglo-Saxon Abbey of Shaftesbury: Bectun's Base or Alfred's Foundation?', *Dorset Natural History & Archaeological Society Proceedings* 113 (1991), 23–32; K. J. Penn, *Historic Towns in Dorset* (Dorchester, 1980), pp. 84–90; L. Keen, 'The Towns of Dorset', in Haslam, *Towns*, pp. 203–47; Hill and Rumble, *Defence of Wessex*, pp. 216–17.

JOHN BLAIR

SHERBORNE (Dorset), originally a British monastery called *Lanprobus*, was patronised by West Saxon kings from Cenwalh (643–72) onwards. In about 705 Sherborne became the site of a new West Saxon see, with *Aldhelm its first bishop; this diocese was divided in about 909, but an episcopal seat remained at Sherborne until 1078. In 998 the religious community was re-founded as a Benedictine abbey, and large portions of the imposing cathedral church, rebuilt or extended under Bishop Ælfwold II (1045–58), still remain there. It is generally agreed that this was the cathedral site from Aldhelm onwards, but the location of the earlier Celtic monastery is controversial. The most convincing identification for *Lanprobus* is the hill, half a mile east of the town, where the Norman castle now stands and where human burials have been found.

Charters of Sherborne, ed. M. A. O'Donovan, Anglo-Saxon Charters 3 (Oxford, 1988); H. P. R. Finberg, *Lucerna* (London, 1964), pp. 95–115; B. Yorke, *Wessex in the Early Middle Ages* (London, 1995), pp. 60, 178; K. Barker, 'Sherborne in Dorset: an Early Ecclesiastical Settlement and its Estate', *ASSAH* 3 (1984), 1–33; L. Keen, 'The Towns of Dorset', in Haslam, *Towns*, pp. 203–47; J. H. P. Gibb, 'The Anglo-Saxon Cathedral at Sherborne', *Archaeological Journal* 132 (1975), 71–110; Fernie, *Architecture*, pp. 121–4.

JOHN BLAIR

SHERIFF: *see* Reeve

SHIELDS: *see* Arms and Armour

SHIPS performed a central role in Anglo-Saxon history. They were instrumental in the early raiding which prompted the Romans to fortify the Saxon Shore and in the subsequent migrations. *Trade, *fishing and communications depended on shipping. The *Vikings came by ship and the Anglo-Saxons built ships to oppose them. Ultimately the arrival of the Norman fleet brought the Anglo-Saxon kingdom to an end.

Structurally, Anglo-Saxon ships shared some common features. They were double-ended (similarly shaped at stem and stern) and clinker built. This means that runs of planking ('strakes') were fastened to a backbone of keel and stem and stern posts so that the lower edge of each strake overlapped and was fastened to the top edge of the one below. Strakes can be made up of several planks scarfed together, and later shipbuilders did this more than earlier ones. The strakes of the Nydam ship from Jutland, which dates to about 400 AD and is therefore often cited as the type of vessel in which the Anglo-Saxon migrations might have been accomplished, were continuous single planks running for more than 23 m from stem to stern. Later ships tended to be built with a greater number of strakes (Nydam had five each side while the *Sutton Hoo and Graveney ships, described below, had nine and probably eleven respectively), allowing a more complex curve to be built into the sides of the hull. Planking was usually fastened together with rivets or 'clench nails', round-headed iron nails driven in from outboard and clenched over rectangular roves on the inside. The planking was internally supported by frames or ribs, made from timbers specially selected for their natural curves. These could be fastened by lashing them to cleats on the planking or by means of wooden pegs ('treenails').

The date when northern European ships started using sail is open to debate. It seems that the example of Roman ships was not followed and the first firm evidence is provided by Gotland picture stones of the eighth century. Ships were then equipped with a single square sail. They were controlled by a side rudder mounted on the starboard ('steerboard') quarter. Anglo-Saxon ships were undecked and cargo was stowed in an open hold. In port ships were anchored or run up a beach.

The magnificent burial ship of Sutton Hoo in Suffolk was discovered in 1939. The wood from which the ship was built had completely decayed but its form was preserved as a crust and staining in the sand under the mound. Rows of clench-nails defined the edges of the strakes. Repairs show that the ship was not new at the time of the burial in about 625 AD. The ship was of great size with an overall length of 27.15 m, maximum beam of 4.6 m and maximum internal depth of 1.3 m. The ship's nine strakes each side were made up of several planks, each about 5.5 m long. Traces of timber adhered to some of the nails and analysis suggests that it was oak. The shallow keel was scarfed horizontally to the stems. Twenty-six frames were fitted into the hull, apparently fastened by treenails. If the ship originally had rowing benches or crossbeams, the construction of the burial chamber would have required their removal from the midships area and the excavators did not detect any elsewhere.

The vessel was propelled by oars; no traces of a mast step or provision for rigging were found but thirty-eight or forty oar-pivots, carved from natural forked timbers, were spiked to the gunwales. A side rudder would have been used for steering; two strengthened frames in the stern indicate where it hung.

Finds of clench nails, and other as yet not fully understood evidence, indicate that boats or ships were buried in at least two other mounds at Sutton Hoo.

Two other Anglo-Saxon ships have been found in Suffolk. That excavated at Snape in 1862–3 was buried in a mound field like that at Sutton Hoo, with which it was closely contemporary, and was similarly preserved. It was much less adequately recorded. The excavators found the rows of clench nails difficult to interpret and described the boat, which had been truncated at one end, as 'square-sterned'. It was smaller than the Sutton Hoo ship, surviving to about 14.5 m with a beam of about three metres. The boat discovered at Ashby Dell in 1830 might be Anglo-Saxon but no dating evidence was found with it and its features are puzzling and not chronologically diagnostic. The carpenter of the estate on which it was found described it but his original report has been lost and we have only a newspaper article published at a much later date. The vessel is said to have been 16.5 m long and the wood was well preserved except for the upper portions of the stem and stern. The planking was said to have been of larch, a surprising identification as larch was not indigenous in England in the Anglo-Saxon period, but one which cannot be dismissed out of hand in view of the fact that it was made by a carpenter. He said that the keel, stem and stern were of elm and that the stern post was mortised to the keel. He said that no metal was present so the method of fastening the planks together remains a mystery. Pegs or lashings were used in other parts of northern Europe. Fourteen frames were lashed to cleats which had been treenailed to the planking, and crossbeams which functioned as thwarts were fastened to the frames and the gunwale with tree-nails and cords. There were vestiges of seven oar-pivots on each side but no evidence for a mast.

Some of the graves in the seventh-century *cemetery at Caister-on-Sea in Norfolk contained planking, two to four strakes wide, cut from the sides of ships.

After these East Anglian finds of the seventh century there is a dearth of excavated material dating to the period of the expansion of trade and the Viking incursions. There is however a compensating increase in documentary references to ships.

The history of the activities of Viking ships on the English coast begins with an incident recorded in the *Anglo-Saxon Chronicle* for 789. The English were soon to become well aquainted with Viking ships. That the ninth century was a period of rapid technological innovation in shipbuilding in Scandinavia is well attested by the Oseberg and Gokstad ships. The *Anglo-Saxon Chronicle* for 896 records that King *Alfred responded with a design of his own: 'long ships' with sixty or more oars. But trade continued despite the Vikings. The *laws of Æthelred refer to Billingsgate (London) as a place where cargoes including planks and cloth, fish and wine were handled. Elsewhere ships serving religious houses were granted immunity from tolls.

The ship which was excavated at Graveney in the north Kent marshes in 1970 was a seagoing merchantman, originally about 14 m long with a beam of 3.9 m. The boat was built in the last quarter of the ninth century and laid up and abandoned on a hard made of branches in the mid tenth century. The great contrast between the Sutton Hoo and Graveney ships reflects the differences in status and function of the two vessels. The Sutton Hoo ship was long, lightly framed and contained royal possessions. The Graveney ship was beamy, very heavily built and carried unfinished millstones.

The stern post, keel and almost half of the planking survived. It is probable that there were eleven strakes each side, and these were made up of planks up to 4.5 m long. The keel had cracked badly and had been repaired. The heavy ribs were treenailed to the planking, spaced only 0.5 m apart as compared with about 1 m in the Sutton Hoo ship. Seatings in the tops of the ribs in the mid-ships area suggest that the ship had had a mast-step which had been removed.

A century after King Alfred's shipbuilding experiments the Viking fleet still had the upper hand (*ASC* 1008, 1009).

An involvement with ships was widespread through Anglo-Saxon society. Part of the duties of a *thegn was to equip a guard ship and guard the coast. Bishop Ælfwold of Crediton, who died in 1016, left a sixty-four oared ship to the king in his *will. The contemporary pictorial evidence for Anglo-Saxon ships, including *coins, graffiti and manuscript illumination, tends to be impression-istic. The *Bayeux Tapestry is exceptional in its realism and detail; the depictions of Anglo-Saxon and Norman ships and activities such as ship-building and sailing are most informative.

G. F. Bass, *A History of Seafaring Based on Underwater Archaeology* (London, 1972); R. Bruce-Mitford, ed., *The Sutton Hoo Ship Burial*, I (London, 1975); V. Fenwick, ed., *The Graveney Boat*, BAR Brit. ser. 53 (Oxford, 1978); S. McGrail, *Ancient Boats in Northwest Europe*, 2nd ed. (London, 1998).

GILLIAN R. HUTCHINSON

SHIRE. A district, in most cases conceived as a part of a larger whole, which served as a unit or organising principle of local government for military, legislative, financial, and other adminis-trative purposes. The great majority of the shires familiar in modern usage existed at the time of the *Domesday survey; but if their history is pursued beyond that point it is found that they originated at different times and under various circumstances. The main shires of *Wessex were probably created in the seventh or the eighth century as divisions of the kingdom apparently administered from particular royal estates: Dorset and Somerset took their names from the people who inhabited the districts associated with *Dorchester and Somerton respectively; and Hampshire and Wiltshire were the districts associated with 'Hamton' (*Southampton) and Wilton. In the far south-west, *Cornwall and Devonshire represent the ancient kingdom of *Dumnonia*, absorbed into the kingdom of Wessex during the eighth and ninth centuries; and in the south-east, the shires of *Kent, *Sussex, Surrey and *Essex also represent politically distinctive regions taken over by the kings of Wessex in the second quarter of the ninth century. Berkshire, lying between the river Thames and the northern boundaries of Wiltshire, Hampshire and Surrey, took its name from a natural feature (Asser, c. 1), and may have originated in the mid-ninth century (cf. *ASC*, s.a. 860), when the region was transferred from Mercian to West Saxon jurisdiction. The system of shires as the administrative sub-divisions of a larger kingdom was presently extended across the Thames into what was formerly Mercian territory, though the question arises whether this occurred in the heyday of the kingdom of the *Anglo-Saxons (in connection with the campaign against the Danes), or in *Æthelstan's reign as 'king of the English' (as part of a larger process of political consolidation), or not until the early eleventh century (e.g. by act of *Eadric Streona); cf. *Burghal Hidage and *County Hidage. Middlesex, named from the people wedged between the East Saxons and the West Saxons, may have taken shape by the end of the ninth century, providing necessary support for *London. In other cases, the new shires were named from the place which served as the administrative or defensive centre of the district in question, without any respect for the underlying 'tribal' complexion of the region, and with the appearance, therefore, of a system imposed from above: Cheshire (*Chester), Derbyshire, Shropshire (Shrewsbury), Staffordshire; Herefordshire, Worcestershire, and Warwickshire; Gloucestershire, Winchcombeshire, and Oxfordshire. The system was also extended into the east midlands, with shires named from Nottingham, *Lincoln, *Leicester, *Northampton, Huntingdon, Cambridge, Buckingham, Bedford, and Hertford. Norfolk and Suffolk retained their identity as ancient divisions of the former kingdom of the East Angles.

In ninth-century Wessex each shire would appear to have had its own *ealdorman, with two in Kent. Administrative arrangements were necessarily adjusted in the tenth century, as the kingdom of the Anglo-Saxons gave way to the kingdom of the English, as the power of the ealdormen became more entrenched, and as royal government continued to develop. In the mid-tenth century, a borough-meeting (*buruhgemot*) was convened three times a year and a shire-meeting (*scirgemot*) twice a year, in the presence of the diocesan bishop (*scire biscop*) and the ealdorman (III Edg., ch. 5.1–2). There was, however, an increasing dependence on the power of the reeve; and in the late tenth century we begin to hear of the 'shire-reeve', or sheriff, who seems to have been the king's personal representative in the shire (or in the shire town), and who in this capacity may have assumed powers which had previously belonged to the ealdorman. Moreover, it seems that by this stage the ealdormen operated on a different level, or rather on a variety of different levels: a charter issued in 997 (S 891) was attested by the ealdorman 'of the western districts [*prouinciae*]', 'of the Winchester districts', 'of the Northumbrian districts', 'of the East Saxons', and 'of the districts of the Hwicce'. Certainly, it becomes increasingly difficult to relate the office or status of the ealdorman, or earl, to administrative arrangements at shire level.

The *Libellus Æthelwoldi episcopi*, based on records compiled in the 970s, affords some impression of meetings of shire-courts of Northamptonshire (c. 10), Huntingdonshire (c. 35), and Cambridgeshire (cc. 13, 34, 45); records also survive of proceedings conducted at shire-courts of Berkshire (S 1454), Worcestershire (S 1460), and Herefordshire (S 1462). Apart from litigation over land, normal business on such occasions would have included the reading or announcement of directives emanating from the king or from meetings of the king's councillors (laws, notice of appointments, etc.), other administrative, legal and financial matters, and doubtless a great deal of gossip, intrigue, and social networking.

Stenton, *ASE*, pp. 292–3, 336–8, 502–5; C. S. Taylor, 'The Origin of the Mercian Shires', *Gloucestershire Studies*, ed. H. P. R. Finberg (Leicester, 1957), pp. 17–45; K. Cameron, *English Place-Names*, 3rd ed. (London, 1977), pp. 51–8; S. Keynes, *The Diplomas of King Æthelred 'the Unready' 978–1016* (Cambridge, 1980), pp. 197–8; Loyn, *Governance*, pp. 133–40; S. Keynes, 'Crime and Punishment in the Reign of King Æthelred the Unready', Sawyer FS, pp. 67–81, at 69–70; Blair, *AS*

Oxon, pp. 102–5; A. Kennedy, 'Law and Litigation in the *Libellus Æthelwoldi Episcopi'*, *ASE* 24 (1995), 131–83, at 134–52.

SIMON KEYNES

SHOES: *see* Leather-Work

SHRINES AND RELIQUARIES. A shrine (*scrinium*) is a primarily a casket for holy *relics, and in this sense is synonymous with 'reliquary'. However, the extension of the term means that 'shrine' has come to denote a tomb-like ensemble comprising a stone base supporting a large reliquary-coffin, usually for a whole body: the typical arrangement of the later Middle Ages.

The veneration of the physical remains of those revered as saints (first martyrs, who had died for the faith, then confessors, who had led exemplary lives) is attested from as early as the mid-second century. Initially these relics were revered at the extra-mural grave, over which an altar was placed, for Roman custom demanded that the body should remain in place, but by the fourth century fragmentary relics were circulating which were placed in small reliquaries (*scrinia*), often on altars.

From the late seventh century, the arrangements in England for the display and veneration of the remains of local saints followed patterns which had recently evolved in Merovingian Francia. Usually these saints were bishops, abbots, or abbesses, often of royal blood. Their cult was established by their successors, who thus basked in reflected

Pl. 18 The Winchester purse reliquary.

glory. Typically, the bodies were exhumed after a few years, and the relics were placed in opulent reliquaries, usually displayed behind the high altar where they might 'shine forth' within the church. Thus St *Æthelthryth, abbess of *Ely (d. 679) was exhumed after sixteen years, and her miraculously incorrupt body was placed in a re-used Roman sarcophagus. St *Cuthbert, bishop of *Lindisfarne, was buried in 687; eleven years later his intact corpse was exhumed, vested, and placed in a full-length wooden chest, rediscovered in 1827.

In a few cases, the bodies may have remained *in situ*, being marked by 'tomb-shrines': monuments constructed *over* burials. But Anglo-Saxon England does not appear to have shared in the Carolingian reversion to the 'Roman' practice whereby whole bodies were housed in ring-crypts.

The opulent monuments erected to house the elevated remains of saints are known only from contemporary descriptions. The mid-ninth century shrine of St *Aldhelm made at *Malmesbury displayed miracles of the saint in relief. Many shrines were produced under royal patronage: *Alcuin describes how King *Offa of Mercia adorned and enriched the tomb of the royal saint *Oswald at Bardney. At *Winchester, King *Edgar constructed a reliquary for the remains of St *Swithun, exhumed in 971. Weighing 300 lb., it was of silver-gilt and was decorated with scenes including Christ's Passion, Resurrection, and Ascension. It may have survived until the 1450s. According to *Goscelin, *Cnut had a shrine made for the relics of St *Eadgyth (Edith) of Wilton, which was similarly adorned with New Testament scenes illustrating Christ's triumph over death.

There is abundant literary evidence for small Anglo-Saxon reliquaries, compensating in some measure for the lack of physical survival. King *Æthelstan is remembered for his donation of an impressive collection of relics to the monastic church at *Exeter *c*.932. Just before the Conquest Abbot Mannig of Evesham created an opulent new shrine for the relics of St Odulf; it was eventually used for St *Ecgwine. Shortly before his death, William the Conqueror is said to have given to Battle Abbey 300 reliquaries of gold and silver, which had formerly been kept in the royal treasury.

J. Blair, 'A Saint for Every Minster? Local Cults in Anglo-Saxon England', in *Local Saints and Local Churches*, ed. J. Blair, A. T. Thacker and R. Sharpe (Oxford, forthcoming); J. Crook, 'The Typology of early Medieval Shrines – a Previously Unidentified "Tomb-Shrine" Panel from Winchester Cathedral', *AJ* 70 (1990), 49–64; C. Dodwell, *Anglo-Saxon Art: a New Perspective* (Manchester, 1982); M. Förster, *Zur Geschi-*

chte des Reliquienkultus in Altengland (Munich, 1943); S. Ridyard, *The Royal Saints of Anglo-Saxon England* (Cambridge, 1988); D. Rollason, *Saints and Relics in Anglo-Saxon England* (Oxford, 1989); idem, 'Lists of Saints' Resting-Places in Anglo-Saxon England', *ASE* 7 (1978), 61–93; A. Thacker, 'The Making of a Local Saint', in *Local Saints and Local Churches*, ed. J. Blair, A. T. Thacker and R. Sharpe (Oxford, forthcoming).

JOHN CROOK

SIEVERS' FIVE TYPES: *see* Metre, OE

SLAVERY existed throughout the Anglo-Saxon period, though England was never totally economically dependent on slave labour. The sixth-century writer *Gildas mentions the enslavement of native Britons after the Anglo-Saxons seized parts of Britain; in 1086 *Domesday Book records that slaves still formed 10% of the population, rising to 25% in *Cornwall, an area that came late under Anglo-Saxon control. As England was predominantly an agrarian society, slaves were largely farm labourers, the lowest in a hierarchy of rural statuses (cf. *estate management). Many male slaves worked in pairs as ploughmen, a physically taxing occupation that included the daily care of the oxen used as draught animals. Women are several times mentioned in the role of *dæge* or dairymaid. The tenth-century *will of Æthelgifu reveals, however, that slaves could perform a wide range of functions; her wealthy household included a priest, women who could sing the daily offices, and a goldsmith.

Warfare was probably the major source of slaves throughout the Anglo-Saxon era. As Gildas implies, the first slaves were probably indigenous Britons. Wales and Scotland, beyond Anglo-Saxon hegemony, offered a continuing source of potential slaves: the *Life* of St *Wulfstan of Worcester mentions many young people in eleventh-century Bristol destined for foreign slave markets who probably came from neighbouring Wales. The Anglo-Saxons also enslaved one another in the internecine wars that lasted up to the eighth century, especially women and children. Brihtwold, archbishop of *Canterbury, for instance, sought the release in *c.*712 of an enslaved Kentish girl from the abbot of *Glastonbury. (Captured warriors were probably slaughtered, as the story of Imma in Bede, *HE* iv.22[20], suggests.) The Scandinavian incursions offered further opportunities for enslavement. As ship-borne warriors, the *Vikings could transport captured persons (especially those who could not be ransomed) across the seas to slave markets such as the one at Rouen. Archbishop *Wulfstan's strictures against

the sale of persons abroad suggests that this was especially prevalent during the late-tenth-century Viking assaults on Britain.

As in the Roman world, slaves were commodities who could be bought and sold. In the early period their owners could kill them, though *Alfred's *laws subsequently placed restrictions on this. Their characteristic punishment was a lashing, whereas a free person could compound for an offence with a monetary payment. Manumission-documents record modes of freeing slaves (see *manumission) but little survives on the status of *children born to slaves of different owners: presumably this was dictated by local custom.

East Anglian wills from the late tenth century onwards show testators requesting the release of substantial numbers of slaves on their demise. Slaves could own a cow according to the late custumal called *Rectitudines singularum personarum* and late wills reveal they occupied what were *de facto* their own dwellings. Slavery depends for its survival on a sense of 'otherness': by the eleventh century England was becoming unified under a single king and possessed a relatively stable rural population. Probably already on the decline before 1066, slavery disappeared in the decades following the Norman Conquest. William the Conqueror had sought the support of a reformed church which opposed the trading in slaves. His success in suppressing revolt in England combined with Norman control of the English seas discouraged fresh enslavement, and legal distinctions based on the slave or free origin of the peasantry held little meaning for the foreigners who supplanted the Anglo-Saxon aristocracy. The Normans found labour services in return for land or the use of labourers (*famuli*) more advantageous than feeding slaves daily. Thus slavery transmuted into serfdom. The change is of more significance to us today, with our knowledge of the horrors of eighteenth- and nineteenth-century slavery, than it was to those in eleventh- and early-twelfth-century England, where the passing of the institution went unremarked.

H. P. R. Finberg, 'Anglo-Saxon England to 1042', in *The Agrarian History of England and Wales* I.ii: AD *43–1042*, ed. H. P. R. Finberg (Cambridge, 1972), pp. 383–525; J. S. Moore, 'Domesday Slavery', *ANS* 11 (1989), 191–220; D. A. E. Pelteret, *Slavery in Early Mediaeval England from the Reign of Alfred until the Twelfth Century* (Woodbridge, 1995); M. M. Postan, *The Famulus. The Estate Labourer in the XIIth and XIIIth Centuries* (London, [1954]); *The Will of Æthelgifu: a Tenth-Century Anglo-Saxon Manuscript*, ed. D. Whitelock (Oxford, 1968).

DAVID A. E. PELTERET

SOCIAL CLASS. Archaeologically, the small farming communities of the period of migration look like rather flat little societies: the burials in their *cemeteries do not show great extremes of rank. Early *agriculture in the *settlement period may have gone through a period of fall-back, if not outright recession, and there are no signs of a surplus being produced capable of supporting an elite. Pronounced social differentiation begins to appear in the sixth century and great riches in the seventh, when *princely burials denote the dominance of local potentate families. The written sources tell of kings, underkings and an aristocracy from this period. It does not seem likely that early rural society had produced from within its own ranks a landowning class supported only by locally produced surplus. More likely, a politically dominant class had won power by warfare and become able to extract surplus from the peasantry of a wide area. Elites in early Anglo-Saxon England, insofar as we can judge from the arrangements made for kings (see *feorm), were supported by tribute collected from their own people and from the people of subject territories.

It may be connected with this fact that rank was not defined only, or at first, by the ownership of land. From the earliest codes, the *laws rank people by reference to the maintenance of peace by means of systematized retribution – the exaction of compensation for death or injury. There is an important distinction between the kind of people for whom compensation is payable to their owner or employer and those for whom it is owed to their kin. The first category included throughout the period a substantial underclass of workers, *slaves and dependent tenants. Slaves, captured in war, enslaved for debt, or selling themselves in extreme poverty were not only a workforce but a traded commodity and a valued export. Freedpeople (who in *Kent included a higher status group, the *læts*) settled on smallholdings, and peasants who had taken on holdings on very restrictive terms (see *peasants) were also part of this underclass. *Wergilds, the sums due to the kin for homicide, broadly differentiated between classes of 'twelve-hundred', 'six-hundred' and 'two-hundred' shilling people. There were local variations, in *Wessex, to accommodate Britons brought within the kingdom, and in Kent there was a smaller gap between highest and lowest. The 'two-hundred' category embraced the great residuary category of the population, free but not noble, the *ceorls*. These must have included the mass of the independent peasantry owing tax and public service and participating in the public *courts.

The spread of bookland greatly stimulated the emergence of a seigneurial class which directly supported itself from the produce of privately owned land and the labour of the people living there (see *estate management). The possession of land became one of the definers of social rank and by the eleventh century five hides or more were the essential basis for social advancement.

An important factor in rank was personal service to the king, and the highest wergilds were of those close to him: in Northumbria such persons were given especially high status and described as *gesithcund* or *eorlcund*. We should probably imagine that the same applied to proximity to lesser figures too: the *clientela* was a feature of Anglo-Saxon politics at every level. Loyalty in battle could expect to be rewarded with land. So too could the performance of 'state' or 'public' functions, by grants of bookland as a reward for service by kings to such 'agents of the state' as judges, major administrators, *ealdormen and *'reeves' of varied status, and to powerful local figures to buy support (and quite possibly to raise cash). Thus the increasingly sophisticated state apparatus of late Anglo-Saxon England was run by major landowners and the economic power of its landowning class was reinforced by their participation in state power. In the aftermath of the unification of the kingdom in the tenth century a few outstanding families within the major landowners became established as earls, with control over areas as large as Kent or *East Anglia and estates in many counties: Earl *Harold Godwineson had land in almost every county south of the Trent. However, the power base of the English earls was less entrenched than that of the French counts: an earl could be brought down and deprived of office as a count could not, and not all an earl's property was in the region over which he governed.

R. J. Faith, *The English Peasantry and the Growth of Lordship* (London, 1997); H. P. R. Finberg, 'Anglo-Saxon England to 1042', in *The Agrarian History of England and Wales* I.ii AD 43–1042, ed. H. P. R. Finberg (Cambridge, 1972), pp. 385–525; W. G. Runciman, 'Accelerating Social Mobility: the Case of Anglo-Saxon England', *P & P* 104 (1984), 3–30; Stafford, *Unification*, pp. 150–61; F. M. Stenton, 'The Thriving of the Anglo-Saxon *ceorl*', in *Preparatory to Anglo-Saxon England: being the Collected Papers of Frank Merry Stenton*, ed. D. M. Stenton (Oxford, 1970), pp. 383–93.

ROSAMOND FAITH

SOKEMEN: *see* Danelaw; Land Tenure

SOLOMON AND SATURN, POETIC. The

SOUL AND BODY

name *Solomon and Saturn* is given to two separate verse texts copied (separated by a prose text of the same name) in Cambridge, Corpus Christi College 422. The two verse texts purport to be dialogues between the biblical king Solomon and a Chaldean prince, named Saturn, but neither is very convincing as such. The first text (a portion of which also appears in CCCC 41) is only superficially an exchange between the two contestants. Saturn, having searched Libya, Greece and India in vain for the truth, asks Solomon to complete his knowledge and, indeed, overcome him with the Pater Noster. Solomon obliges with a description of the power of the Pater Noster found in the individual letters making up the prayer. The poem transforms the prayer into a material being, with clothing, weapons and jewels, and describes how each letter does battle against the devil and sends him back to hell. By contrast, *Solomon and Saturn II* is framed more clearly as a contest in which the participants attempt to gain mastery in an exchange of difficult riddles. The 'rules' for such a contest are not always clear, though the riddle reply seems at least partly determined by the content of the preceding riddle. The subject of the riddles covers a range of interest from the bizarre and exotic (*vasa mortis*, *wellende wulf*) to traditional sapiential themes (good and evil, the unequal fates of twins). The list of places Saturn visits in the poem suggests extensive geographic knowledge lying behind the poem, possibly (though not certainly) derived by way of the *Cosmographia* of Aethicus Ister.

ASPR vi. 31–48; *The Dialogue of Solomon and Saturn*, ed. R. Menner (New York, 1941); K. O'Brien O'Keeffe, 'The Geographic List of *Solomon and Saturn II*', *ASE* 20 (1991), 123–41; T. D. Hill, 'Tormenting the Devil with Boiling Drops: An Apotropaic Motif in the Old English *Solomon and Saturn I* and Old Norse-Icelandic Literature', *JEGP* 92 (1993), 157–66; P. P. O'Neill, 'On the Date, Provenance, and Relationship of the "Solomon and Saturn" Dialogues', *ASE* 26 (1997), 139–68.

KATHERINE O'BRIEN O'KEEFFE

SOLOMON AND SATURN, PROSE. There are two separate prose 'dialogues' known as *Solomon and Saturn*. The lengthier of them is also the later, occurring in the twelfth-century portion of London, BL, Cotton Vitellius A. xv, 86v–93v (the Southwick Codex of the *Beowulf* manuscript). In this text, the same figures of the poetic dialogue are named as participants, but the text proper is simply a congeries of unattributed questions and answers. Its subject matter ranges from simple catechetical questions ('What is God?'), to exactingly literal points of Bible

knowledge ('Who planted the first vineyard?'), and biblical amusements ('Who was the first man to talk with a dog?') as well as folk wisdom. This prose *Solomon and Saturn* shares a number of questions with another twelfth-century text, *Adrian and Ritheus*, and both are connected to lists of Latin questions and answers known as the *Joca monachorum*, though there is no straightforward source relationship. The second, lesser known 'dialogue' is a prose fragment included without any sign of separation between **Solomon and Saturn I* and *II* in Cambridge, Corpus Christi College 422. This text contains a treatment of the Pater Noster in even more fanciful terms than in *Solomon and Saturn I*. Here, Saturn inquires about the thirty shapes the Pater Noster and the devil will assume in their struggle: the odd numbered shapes are assumed by the devil; the even numbered ones by the Pater Noster. The 'dialogue' also considers the body of the Pater Noster (primarily in terms of the size and power of its supposed body parts), and then the raiments of the Pater Noster, each composed of a different gorgeous fabric with an individual name. The dialogue breaks off with the seventh fabric and *Solomon and Saturn II* begins.

The Prose Solomon and Saturn and Adrian and Ritheus, ed. J. E. Cross and T. D. Hill (Toronto, 1982); *The Poetical Dialogues of Solomon and Saturn*, ed. R. J. Menner (New York, 1941); P. P. O'Neill, 'On the Date, Provenance and Relationship of the "Solomon and Saturn" Dialogues,' *ASE* 26 (1997), 139–68.

KATHERINE O'BRIEN O'KEEFFE

SOUL AND BODY is a verse address from a soul to its body extant in both the **Exeter Book* and the **Vercelli Book* and as such is one of the few Old English poems that survives in more than one version. Both poems urge the penitent Christian to reflect on the fate of his own soul, which after death is destined to return to its body once a week for three hundred years unless Doomsday intervenes. The damned soul castigates its body for its earthly sins and warns of Christ's severity at Judgement. Then follows a gruesome description of the body's decay. The Exeter version of the poem ends after 126 lines devoted exclusively to the damned soul's harangue, but the Vercelli version includes a corresponding address between a blessed soul and its body, ending incomplete at line 166. Several aspects of the poems' eschatology show signs of Irish influence, including the claim that at Doomsday the sinful body must endure punishments proportionate to each of its 365 joints. The language of the poems is

425

predominantly late West Saxon, and while precise dating is elusive, some features of style and phraseology are closely parallelled in other Old English texts, notably the two *Solomon and Saturn poems, the prose *Solomon and Saturn Pater Noster Dialogue and Vercelli Homily IV, which on the basis of language and content have been tentatively ascribed to an Irish-influenced Mercian literary school active in the late ninth or early tenth century, plausibly during the reign of *Æthelstan. ASPR ii. 54–9, iii. 174–8; T. D. Hill, 'Punishment According to the Joints of the Body in the OE Soul and Body', Notes and Queries 213 (1968), 409–10 and 214 (1969), 246; A. J. Frantzen, 'The Body in Soul and Body I', Chaucer Review 17 (1982), 76–88; The Old English 'Soul and Body', ed. and trans. D. Moffat (Woodbridge, 1990).

THOMAS N. HALL

SOUND CHANGE. Sound-change is a phenomenon whereby speakers adjust their *phonologies*, or sound-systems. The raw material for sound-change always exists, in the continually-created variation of natural speech, but sound-change only happens when a particular variable is selected in place of another as part of systemic regulation. Such processes of selection take place when distinct systems interact with each other through linguistic contact, typically through social upheavals such as invasion, revolution or immigration.

It may be assumed that, in Anglo-Saxon England as in present-day societies, a range of sound-systems existed as a continuum of accents. However, the evidence for this continuum is problematic. Our understanding depends on interpreting surviving contemporary *spelling-systems, and (indirectly) on comparative and internal reconstruction. The remains from the period – *place-names, *runes and, above all, vernacular manuscript texts – do not supply a thorough diachronic and diatopic record.

Nevertheless, enough material survives to enable some broad typological classifications of accent during the period. *Old English is most closely related to the variety known as Old Frisian, and both dialects have accentual features in common which distinguish them from the other West Germanic languages, like High German and Dutch; cf. Old English *dæg*, Old Frisian *dei* (with front vowels) beside present-day High German *Tag*, Dutch *dag* (with back vowels). These similarities date back, it would appear, to the period before the *adventus Saxonum. Also dating from this period, it appears, are the earliest distinctions

between the Saxon and Anglian accents, some of which may derive from the interaction between the latter and the North Germanic dialects of Scandinavia, its original geographical neighbours. Such distinctions, originally minor, led ultimately to major accentual divergences between these varieties.

Since many major sound-changes from Proto-Germanic through Old English took place before the Anglo-Saxons became literate, it is only possible to reconstruct the sequence of development by logical means. Thus, e.g., the diphthongisation called 'breaking', whereby West Saxon *eald* derived from Proto-West Germanic reconstructed *alða*, could only take place after the Anglo-Frisian sound-change called 'first fronting', whereby Proto-West Germanic *a* became *æ*. In breaking, an earlier front vowel accommodates itself to a back consonant, and it would not have occurred had the vowel been already in the back series.

Sound-changes account for many apparent morphological irregularities. Thus, e.g., the West Saxon alternation *dæg* 'day'/*dagas* 'days' is the result of two successive sound-changes: first fronting produced *dæg*/*dægas*, and a second sound-change, 'restoration of a', took place when a back vowel appeared in the following syllable, producing the attested form *dagas*.

C. L. Barber, The English Language (Cambridge, 1993); A. Campbell, Old English Grammar (Oxford, 1959); R. Hamer, Old English Sound-Changes for Beginners (Oxford, 1967); CHELang I; R. Hogg, A Grammar of Old English I: Phonology (Oxford, 1992); B. Mitchell and F. Robinson, A Guide to Old English, 5th ed. (Oxford, 1995); H. F. Nielsen, The Germanic Languages (Tuscaloosa, 1989); M. L. Samuels, Linguistic Evolution (Cambridge, 1972); J. J. Smith, An Historical Study of English (London, 1996).

JEREMY J. SMITH

SOUTHAMPTON, a thriving urban centre and port in Middle Saxon England, is known almost exclusively from archaeological investigations. A small number of texts, together with *mint marks on *coins, name the *town as *Hamwic*, *Hamtun*, or variations of these, but it has also been known (wrongly) as *Hamwih* in the archaeological literature. Located on the west bank of the river Itchen some 1.7 km downstream from where the Roman town of *Clausentum* had once stood, *Hamwic* was laid out on a site previously unoccupied in the Anglo-Saxon period. Around 700 a planned, regularly laid-out town was constructed with a grid-like pattern of streets comprising three main north-south streets and probably around fourteen east-west streets. The town covered some 45 hectares (112 acres) and was fairly densely occupied with timber-built houses and structures with wattle and daub walls. It was one of the largest centres in eighth-century England, and was one of a number of towns, like *Ipswich, which entered into extensive cross-channel *trade with Merovingian France and the Rhineland and had contact with other ports in Scandinavia and the Baltic.

A great deal of evidence for the crafts and industries practised by the town's inhabitants has been recovered from archaeological excavations. These included *metalworking (in particular iron and bronze smithing, but also lead, *glass, and gold working), *bone-working, *textile production, *pottery making, and *leather and wood working. In addition coins, notably *sceattas* which circulated widely within the town, were minted in the town.

Artifacts also provide direct evidence for long-distance trade: pottery from Belgium, the Rhineland, Normandy, and the Loire Valley, Niedermendig lava quernstones from the Eifel Mountains, mica-schist whetstones from Norway, and glass vessel fragments probably from the Rhineland. Exotic finds include a bone of a green turtle normally found south of the Canary Islands, a *spondylus* shell, and an Islamic dirham from Cordoba struck sometime between 765 and 815.

The town prospered during the eighth century, but decline set in as the *Viking raids disrupted cross-channel trade in the ninth. The *Anglo-Saxon Chronicle* records a raid on Southampton in 842 and other raids are noted during the tenth and eleventh centuries. By 900 *Hamwic* was largely depopulated. In its place, just over 1 km to the southwest on higher ground overlooking the river Test and Southampton Water, was located a new settlement, defended by bank and ditch enclosing some 6 hectares (15 acres).

This borough, listed in the *Burghal Hidage with an assessment of 150 hides, was the site of a mint from the reign of *Æthelstan. Although this numismatic evidence identifies Southampton as a centre in the early tenth century, the archaeological evidence from the town itself indicates that it was not intensively occupied, and that its defences were backfilled by the mid-tenth century. Such material as survives suggests that settlement was subsequently scattered over a wide area, beyond the confines of the later medieval walled area. It was this scattered settlement that was the subject of *Viking attacks in the late tenth century. Settlement appears to have become more intensive from the early eleventh century, and was augmented by the deliberate plantation of a group of French, and English, after 1066.

P. V. Addyman and D. Hill, 'Saxon Southampton: a Review of the Evidence, Parts I and II', *Proceedings of the Hampshire Field Club and Archaeological Society* 24–5 (1968), 61–93, and 26 (1969), 61–96; M. Brisbane, 'Hamwic (Saxon Southampton): an Eighth-Century Port and Production Centre', in *The Rebirth of Towns in the West AD 700–1050*, ed. R. Hodges and B. Hobley, CBA Research Report 68 (London, 1988); P. Holdsworth, 'Saxon Southampton: a New Review', *MArch* 20 (1976), 26–61; D. M. Metcalf and J. Timby, *Southampton Finds: the Coins and Pottery from Hamwic* (Southampton, 1988); *Excavations at Hamwic* I, ed. A. Morton, CBA Research Report 84 (London, 1992); *Excavations at Hamwic* II, ed. P. Andrews, CBA Research Report 109 (York, 1997).

MARK BRISBANE

SPELLING AND PRONUNCIATION, OE.

Spelling systems consist of sets of conventions, understood by writers and readers. Although written *Old English looks superficially very different from present-day English, this is often because of changes in the spelling system; e.g. there has been little change in pronunciation in the word *scip* 'ship' during the last thousand years, but the Anglo-Saxons used a different convention, *sc*, for the sound which we regularly represent by 'sh'. However, in present-day English, we have a variety of overlapping conventions (e.g. we use 's' for the 'sh'-sound in 'sugar') whereas in Old English such variants are rare. In this sense, Old English is more regular or 'phonetic' than current usage.

There are some qualifications to be made to this statement, however. A few symbols, notably *c* and *g*, represented different sounds in different linguistic contexts, and the pronunciation of words containing them can only be determined through their etymology (cf. present-day *get* and *gem*). Other symbols changed their representation according to their position within the word, e.g. whereas we change 'f' to 'v' in 'loaf: loaves', Anglo-Saxon scribes retained the symbol, *hlaf: hlafas*, even though the sound changed in exactly the same way. There is no real distinction between thorn and eth (see *alphabet), although some scribes exhibit a preference for one shape or the other or alter by word position. The seventeenth-century assumption (still accepted by some) that these two symbols represent the different sounds of present-day '*th*in' and '*th*en' is wrong. Scribes also regularly simplified double symbols, e.g. *man* for *mann*, especially in word-final position but occasionally elsewhere (*manes* for *mannes*), and by the late tenth century regularly alternated *i* and *y*

427

e.g. *bysig, bisig* 'busy'. Some variation of spelling is the result of different scribal conventions or training in different geographical areas, and hence is usually regarded as representative of regional *dialects.

We have no native informants for Old English, and no handbooks of pronunciation such as exist for later centuries. Consequently the study of Old English pronunciation is not an exact science. Amongst observations which can be made with some certainty, though, are that all symbols represent sounds, e.g. Old English *same* rhymes with present-day 'drama' and is not pronounced like our 'same', and there are no silent letters as in present-day 'daughter' or 'should'; combinations of consonants as in *writ* and *leoht* were pronounced as we combine the consonant sounds in 'free' and 'act'; and patterns of stress are similar to those of today, e.g. heavy stress on the first syllable of 'houses', not on its plural marker. In many printed texts, especially those in introductory grammars, Old English vowels are marked with a horizontal bar (macron) when long. These are philological aids to pronunciation unwarranted by the texts as transmitted in manuscript.

A. Campbell, *Old English Grammar* (Oxford, 1959); D. G. Scragg, *A History of English Spelling* (Manchester, 1974); R. M. Hogg, 'Phonology and Morphology', CHE Lang i.67–167.

DONALD SCRAGG

STAMFORD (Lincs.), so named from the nearby crossing of Ermine Street over the river Welland, apparently began as a nucleus on the north bank, around St Peter's church, enclosed by large ninth-century ditches. Immediately east of this was established a Danish borough, the core of the later *town. In 918, according to the *Anglo-Saxon Chronicle*, 'King Edward went with the army to Stamford, and ordered the borough on the south side of the river to be built, and all the people who belonged to the more northern borough submitted to him and sought to have him as their lord'. The evidence for this southern fortification is tenuous, though it contained a *mint and was evidently more than a temporary camp. The town on the north bank grew rapidly during the tenth and eleventh centuries, when it was both a major territorial centre and a place of outstanding commercial importance. Above all, Stamford owed its success to the *pottery industry which can be traced from the late ninth century onwards. 'Stamford Ware', a range of bowls, spouted pitchers and other vessels made in a very fine, pale-yellow-glazed fabric, is found over much of southern

England: it is perhaps the supreme Anglo-Saxon example of an attractive but mass-produced consumer product.

K. Kilmurry, *The Pottery Industry of Stamford, Lincolnshire, c. AD 850–1250* (Oxford, 1980); M. Mahany and D. Roffe, 'Stamford: the Development of an Anglo-Scandinavian Borough', *ANS* 5 (1982), 197–219; M. Mahany, A. Burchard and G. Simpson, *Excavations in Stamford, Lincolnshire, 1963–9* (London, 1982).

JOHN BLAIR

STATUS: *see* Social Class

STEPHEN OF RIPON (often referred to, mistakenly, as Eddius Stephanus) was apparently a disciple of Bishop *Wilfrid who was trained at *Ripon and who accompanied Wilfrid on his many travels to *Frisia in 678 and to *Rome in 679 and again in 704, so that, after Wilfrid's death in 709, Stephen was well placed to compose a *vita* of his master. His *Vita S. Wilfridi* (*BHL* 8889) was probably composed within a decade of Wilfrid's death (hence 710 × 720; the absolute *terminus ante quem* is 731, the date of Bede's *Historia ecclesiastica*, which draws on the Life); it was commissioned by Tatberht, abbot of Ripon, and *Acca, bishop of *Hexham (the reference to Bishop Acca in c. 22 as being *beatae memoriae* – Acca died in 740 – sits ill with the remainder of the sentence, which describes him as *adhuc vivens*, and is to be regarded as a later scribal interpolation). The earlier, but now rejected, attribution to 'Eddius Stephanus' derives from the mention in c. 14 of the precentor Aedde (Latinized as 'Eddius') who was brought by Wilfrid from *Kent to *Northumbria in the 660s and Bede's mention of the same precentor as *Aeddi cognomento Stephanus* (*HE* iv.2). Since 'Aeddi Stephanus' will have been too old to have written the work in the years following Wilfrid's death in 709, the author of the Life must have been another monk called Stephen. The Life is important not only as a record of Wilfrid's life and travails by a blatant apologist, but also as one of the earliest Anglo-Latin essays in *hagiography (it relies very heavily on the anonymous Lindisfarne Life of St *Cuthbert); it has added value for students of the early English church in that Stephen took care to reproduce various documents and letters (including one by Archbishop *Theodore) not otherwise preserved. Stephen's account of Wilfrid was used (and comprehensively revised) by Bede in *HE* v.19; in the mid-tenth century, Stephen's Life was recast into hexameters by *Frithegod at the invitation of Archbishop *Oda (941–58), the pretext being *Canterbury's acquisition from Ripon of the *relics of Wilfrid.

Sharpe, *Handlist*, 1672; MGH, Scriptores rerum Merovingicarum vi. 163–263; B. Colgrave, *Eddius Stephanus' Life of Bishop Wilfrid* (Cambridge, 1927); Bolton, *ALL*, pp. 210–14; B. W. Wells, 'Eddi's Life of Wilfrid', *EHR* 6 (1891), 535–50; D. P. Kirby, 'Bede, Eddius Stephanus and the Life of Wilfrid', *EHR* 98 (1983), 101–14; W. Goffart, *The Narrators of Barbarian History (AD 550–800)* (Princeton, NJ, 1988), pp. 281–90.

MICHAEL LAPIDGE

STEYNING (Sussex) traditionally began as a minster founded by St Cuthman, whose relics were venerated there in the tenth century. His late-attested *Life* contains reflections of early Irish *hagiography, possibly associated with the early Irish monastery at *Bosham. It was certainly an important religious site by 858, when King *Æthelwulf of Wessex was buried there. Excavations have produced unusually clear evidence for the growth of lay settlement around the monastic nucleus during the tenth and eleventh centuries, including an enclosed homestead where a gold ring bearing the name Æscwulf was found.

T. P. Hudson, 'The Origins of Steyning and Bramber, Sussex', *Southern History* 2 (1980), 11–29; M. Gardiner, 'The Excavation of a Late Anglo-Saxon Settlement at Market Field, Steyning, 1988–89', *Sussex Archaeological Collections* 131 (1993), 21–67; J. Blair, 'St Cuthman, Steyning and Bosham', *Sussex Archaeological Collections* 135 (1997), 173–92.

JOHN BLAIR

STONYHURST GOSPEL OF ST JOHN (English Province of the Society of Jesus, British Library, Loan 74) was discovered in the coffin of St *Cuthbert at Durham in 1104. It may have been placed there as a gift during the translation of his relics at *Lindisfarne in 698, perhaps commemorating a St John Gospel owned by his master, *Boisil, mentioned in the *vitae*. Marked readings suggest that it was used in the mass of the dead, presumably of Cuthbert himself. The text is of Fischer's 'Northumbrian' family. The romanising uncial *script is that of the scriptoria of *Monkwearmouth and Jarrow and the whole volume is an essay in Mediterranean techniques. The parchment is prepared in late Antique / continental fashion and the *binding, the earliest western example, employs 'Coptic' or unsupported sewing with red leather over wooden boards, moulded over a classical plant-scroll motif and tooled with interlace infilled in blue and yellow.

CLA ii.260; T. J. Brown, *The Stonyhurst Gospel of St John*, Roxburghe Club (Oxford, 1969).

MICHELLE P. BROWN

STOWE PSALTER: *see* Psalter Glosses

STRESS: *see* Metre, OE

STRONG VERB: *see* Old English

STYCA: *see* Coinage

SUNDAY LETTER. The 'Sunday Letter' purports to be an epistle direct from Christ to the clergy urging strict observance of Sunday, and dwelling on the terrible consequences for those who fail to comply. It first appears in the sixth century, and is widespread in Latin and vernacular languages throughout the Middle Ages. Six OE anonymous *homilies incorporate material from the Sunday Letter tradition, and *Wanley's *Catalogue* indicates that a seventh was lost in the Cotton fire. They draw on different Latin rescensions, two that are related (Napier pseudo-Wulfstan homilies 43 and 44) having Irish connections.

K. Jost, *Wulfstanstudien* (Bern, 1950); C. A. Lees, 'The "Sunday Letter" and the "Sunday Lists"', *ASE* 14 (1985), 129–51; idem, 'Sunday Letter', *Sources of Anglo-Saxon Literary Culture: a Trial Version*, ed. F. M. Biggs, T. D. Hill and P. E. Szarmach (Binghamton, NY, 1990), pp. 38–40.

DONALD SCRAGG

SUNDIALS in the form of vertically set, south-facing semicircular or circular dials cut in stone were used in ecclesiastical contexts from at least the eighth century. Time was marked by the shadow of a centrally fixed, probably metal, gnomon (all now lost) as it moved in relation to varying numbers of radiating lines. There is one dial on a stone cross (the probably eighth-century cross at *Bewcastle). The other known stone dials are architectural and, when still *in situ*, are set into walls of churches. That at *Escomb is probably of the eighth century, while a number, some with *inscriptions, belong to the century before the Conquest, that at Kirkdale being datable to 1055–65. The semicircle (or on circular dials the lower half of the circle) corresponding to the period of daylight is subdivided into units whose length varies with the season. The dials at Bewcastle and Bishopstone have twelve divisions corresponding to the twelve hours of daylight of Roman and ecclesiastical practice. Those like Escomb that divide the day into four and those (such as Kirkdale, Great Edstone and Orpington) that divide the day into eight may perhaps reflect a vernacular 'octaval' division of the hours of day and night. The main purpose of these ecclesiastical

Pl. 19 The Kirkdale sundial and inscription.

dials, however, was to mark liturgical time; the radii at 45°, 90° and 135° from the horizontal, which correspond to the liturgical hours of terce, sext and none, are often specially emphasized and may be the only divisions marked. A small tenth-century portable dial of gold and silver found at *Canterbury has variable settings for each month; it is held vertically towards the sun and, with the shadow of a horizontal pin, uses the altitude of the sun to indicate the time against a division of the daylight into four sections.

A. R. Green, 'Anglo-Saxon Sundials', *AJ* 8 (1928), 489–516; *Bedae Opera De Temporibus*, ed. C. W. Jones (Cambridge, MA, 1943), p. 321; E. Okasha, *Hand-list of Anglo-Saxon Non-Runic Inscriptions* (Cambridge, 1971); CASSS; A. L. Binns, 'Sun Navigation in the Viking Ages, and the Canterbury Portable Sundial', *Acta Archaeologica* 42 (1971), 23–34; *Golden Age of AS Art*, p. 94.

JOHN HIGGITT

SURGERY is the branch of medicine concerned with treating diseases or injuries by means of manual or operative procedures, especially by incision into the body. Sources of information for Anglo-Saxon surgery come mainly from documentary and skeletal evidence. Documentary evidence, when considered in isolation, suggests that surgery in this period was a relatively infrequent event. However, even though *medical literature of the period is dominated by herbal prescriptions, e.g. *Bald's *Leechbook*, there are indications of knowledge of surgical procedures within the field of medicine. Furthermore, late Anglo-Saxon illustrations of doctors in medical manuscripts sometimes show them performing minor surgical operations. Surgery, as opposed to medicine, is a practical subject not necessarily learnt by reading books. Experience was probably gained by practice handed down from generation to generation. There must be a systematic art of surgery before there is a surgical literature, and surgery books therefore come late in the development of the profession.

There are some references to the presence of surgeons in the later Anglo-Saxon period but it is likely that in the earlier years the word leech (OE *læce*) was used simultaneously to describe physicians and surgeons. Evidence suggests that leeches formed a professional group of people and that both lay and monastic physicians appeared to co-exist. However, the association of religion with surgery hindered the development of anatomical knowledge, knowledge which was an essential component of correct surgical procedure. Dissection of human bodies was prohibited in the Anglo-Saxon period because the body was considered sacred. There is no documentary evidence to show that human dissection was being practised but Latin works from the eighth century onwards do mention anatomical matters, albeit of a rudimentary and conventionalised kind.

It is commonly believed that anaesthesia prior to surgery was not widely available to people in the Anglo-Saxon period. However, there are documentary sources which mention specific plants with sleep inducing or pain relieving properties. Opium, henbane, hellebore and alcohol, drugs also used in the Roman period, are frequently cited in the *herbals. However, even though these drugs were available, the Anglo-Saxon leech had no way of measuring them so it may be that if the operation did not lead to death then the anaesthesia did. Cold water is recommended for local anaesthesia in the *Lacnunga* (see *medical literature).

Direct evidence for surgery in skeletal remains comes from trepanations, or the purposeful surgical removal of a piece of bone from the skull, and amputations, or the removal of part of the body, the latter being less prominent in the archaeological record. Evidence for trepanation in Britain is relatively scarce, the few examples coming mainly from the early and mid Anglo-Saxon periods. In the literature, trepanation is mentioned as a remedy for ailments ranging from headaches to head injuries but the main purpose in every case seems to have been to relieve pressure inside the skull.

The method used consisted of scraping the

skull surface with a sharp tool, for example a piece of flint, until the full thickness of the skull had been perforated. The scraping method was, without doubt, the safest way to perforate the skull. The amount of control which the surgeon had over the tool and the procedure would have prevented serious brain damage. The remarkable success of these trepanations can be seen in the evidence for healing of the edges of the trepanation hole. All the individuals who were trepanned survived their ordeal, some for many years hence.

Perhaps a necessary accompaniment to trepanations were post-operative dressings to the affected area. It is likely that these dressings would also have been applied to wounds. The Anglo-Saxons were knowledgeable about herbal remedies. More elaborate and perhaps more familiar methods of treating gaping wounds by stitching are described in some sources. Cautery (or burning the body tissue with a hot iron) was used extensively for treating wounds especially when the edges had overgrown. In addition, cautery was utilised for treating many diseases and there are several illustrations of the period showing the areas of the body which should be cauterized to treat specific ailments.

Surgical operations where amputation of limbs or part of a limb was recommended are evident in the medical literature, although amputation appears to have been carried out mainly for gangrene of a limb or as punishment for a crime (see *laws). An essential aspect of any amputation was the control of inevitable bleeding. Very primitive methods of haemostasis (stopping or arresting blood circulation) were practised. Kettle soot, horse dung and dried blood are all mentioned as haemostatic agents. There are also occasional indications of the recognition of pressure bandages for haemorrhage. Post-operatively, there appears to have been some attempt to dress the stump and one such dressing was of boiled sheep's marrow bound tightly around the stump.

Direct evidence of the treatment of fractured bones is infrequent. However, it is generally accepted that the Anglo-Saxons knew that fractures needed to be reduced and splinted to promote healing and prevent deformity. In one case, their recognition of the muscle contraction accompanying fractures (especially of the long bones) is evident. A hot bath was recommended to relax the muscles and enable the reduction of the fracture.

It appears that the most common surgical procedure in the period was the long established medical practice of blood letting. The belief was that excess blood in the body caused disease. It was also used as a general means to health. Specific veins were opened to cure particular illnesses. *Magic and superstition pervaded this procedure and it was deemed more beneficial to employ this treatment on certain days and in particular seasons or times of the year. The vein was opened with a lancet or knife and blood allowed to drain into a bowl. An alternative method used was cupping to draw blood, or indeed any body fluid, to the surface of the body. A cup of glass or horn was heated, its lip greased and then inverted over the skin which had already been broken. Suction developed within the cup as burning material inside it consumed the oxygen. Blood was thus drawn through the skin opening. Cutting the skin without applying a cup was called scarification and was also commonly used for many diseases.

More elaborate surgical operations are occasionally referred to in the medical literature, e.g. the opening of an abscess in the liver using a cutting iron and a primitive form of plastic surgery for a hare-lip.

The general impression of Anglo-Saxon surgery as seen in the literature and skeletal remains is that the practice appeared to be infrequent and there is a notable absence of surgical instruments in the archaeological record. Nevertheless, it is likely that there was widespread knowledge of surgical procedures, especially the minor ones such as blood letting.

D. Brothwell and V. Moller-Christensen, 'Medico-historical Aspects of a Very Early Case of Mutilation', *Danish Medical Bulletin* 10 (1963), 21–7; *Leechdoms, Wortcunning and Starcraft of Early England*, ed. T. O. Cockayne, 3 vols., RS (London, 1864–6); J. H. G. Grattan and C. Singer, *Anglo-Saxon Magic and Medicine* (London, 1952); S. Parker, C. A. Roberts and K. Manchester, 'A Review of British Trepanations with Reports on Two New Cases', *Ossa* 12 (1985–6), 141–57; S. Rubin, *Medieval English Medicine* (London, 1974).

CHARLOTTE A. ROBERTS

SUSSEX, KINGDOM OF. The modern county of Sussex approximates to the area of the ancient kingdom of the South Saxons. The legendary founder of the kingdom was Ælle, said to have landed in 477 at *Cymenesora* (probably near *Selsey), to have fought energetically with his sons against the Romano-British inhabitants of the region, and to have sacked the Roman fort at *Anderida* near Pevensey in 491 (*ASC*). Archaeology gives a rather different picture of South Saxon settlement. Germanic tribes probably first arrived in Sussex rather earlier in the fifth century. The pattern of early *cemeteries points to an initial concentration of *settlement in the area between the rivers Ouse and Cuckmere; it has been suggested that this territory may have been ceded to the South Saxons under a treaty negotiated with the Romano-British inhabitants. Whatever the truth of this, it would seem that the Germanic settlers (or at least their culture) quite rapidly came to dominate the whole of Sussex. Most people lived in the coastal plain and in the river valleys which cut north-south through the downs, and there was little permanent settlement in the forest area of the Weald, which then covered a vast area of north-eastern Sussex. In part due to the barrier of the Weald, the South Saxons tended to be isolated from the main trends of development elsewhere in Anglo-Saxon England; they were the last of the English tribes to be converted to Christianity (see *Wilfrid).

The political history of the independent South Saxon kingdom is largely obscure. King Ælle would seem to have been a considerable figure in his time, for he was remembered by *Bede as the first of a select band of English kings who held *imperium* or rule over all of the Anglo-Saxon kingdoms south of the river Humber (*HE* ii.5). No South Saxon royal *genealogy survives, so it is impossible to tell whether later rulers in Sussex claimed descent from Ælle. *Charters preserve the names of a number of South Saxon kings from the later seventh and eighth centuries, but their origins and interrelationships are for the most part irrecoverable. What does seem clear is that at times there were several kings ruling simultaneously, which probably implies some form of (perhaps temporary) territorial division. The people living in the eastern part of the kingdom, around Hastings, appear to have retained a separate group identity as the *Hæstingas*, and it seems possible that they did have their own ruler. Another division may perhaps have been along the line of the river Adur.

Political fragmentation could have left the South Saxons vulnerable to invasion. The weakest frontier was that to the west, with the powerful West Saxon kingdom. Until the second half of the seventh century there may have been a buffer zone between *Wessex and Sussex in the form of a territory inhabited by a tribe of *Jutes living in the Meon Valley in Hampshire and on the Isle of Wight. This buffer was removed in the time of the Mercian king *Wulfhere (d. 674), who conquered both Wight and the *Meonware* ('Meon people') and granted them to the South Saxon king Æthelwealh, his godson; at this period it would seem that Sussex (or at least the part of it ruled

by Æthelwealh) recognised Mercian overlordship. It may have been this barbed gift which prompted West Saxon aggression against Sussex in the 680s, leading to Æthelwealh's death and a subsequent successful conquest by the West Saxon king *Cædwalla. There followed some years of harsh West Saxon rule over the South Saxons. Nothhelm (usually known as Nunna), who ruled in Sussex in the 690s and early eighth century, was a kinsman of the West Saxon king *Ine and perhaps a West Saxon nominee. Responsibility for the fledgling South Saxon church, established by Wilfrid, was taken over by the bishops of Wessex. Some measure of renewed independence may have been initiated by the appointment of a separate bishop for the South Saxon kingdoms in around 705; his see was located in Wilfrid's monastery at Selsey. By 731 Sussex, along with the other kingdoms of the south, seems to have acknowledged the overlordship of the Mercian king *Æthelbald, and it probably remained a nominal Mercian dependency for the next forty years. In the early 770s the Mercian king *Offa initiated a full-scale invasion of the region, perhaps from *Kent where he was already supreme. He vanquished the *Hæstingas* in 771, and seems to have moved on from there to subdue the rest of Sussex up to the border with Wessex. This conquest marked the end of an independent kingdom in Sussex. A group of men who had previously ruled as kings over the South Saxons now appear in charters with the title *dux* or *ealdorman, which indicates that submission to Offa had brought a reduced status. Sussex remained under direct Mercian rule until it was conquered by the West Saxon king *Ecgberht in *c.*825, after which it was absorbed permanently into the West Saxon realm.

Charters of Selsey, ed. S. E. Kelly, Anglo-Saxon Charters 6 (Oxford, 1998); P. Brandon, *The South Saxons* (Chichester, 1978); M. Welch, *Early Anglo-Saxon Sussex*, BAR, Brit. ser. 112 (Oxford, 1983); idem, 'The Kingdom of the South Saxons: the Origins', in Bassett, *Origins*, pp. 75–96; S. E. Kelly, 'The Bishopric of Selsey', *Chichester Cathedral: an Historical Survey*, ed. M. Hobbs (Chichester, 1994), pp. 1–10.

S. E. KELLY

SUTTON HOO is a small barrow *cemetery situated on the east bank of the river Deben opposite Woodbridge in south-east Suffolk. At least fifteen mounds are currently visible, of which ten have been wholly or partially investigated. Mounds 5, 6 and 7, which form a north-south alignment, had covered cremations deposited in bronze bowls accompanied by grave goods, which, although largely rifled and dispersed, had included playing

Pl. 20 Aerial view of Sutton Hoo.

pieces and horses or large ungulates. Mounds 3, 4, and 18 were similar, except that the Mound 3 cremation was apparently placed on a wooden tray. Mound 14 had contained the inhumation of a woman, furnished with a chatelaine and a box with silver fittings. Mound 17 was the burial of a young man with a horse. The grave contained a sword, spears, shield, cauldron, bucket, haversack and the remains of an elaborate harness with a snaffle bit and gilt and silver fittings; a saddle was probably also present. The horse was buried in an adjacent pit. Three children or adolescents were buried in coffins in a row to the east of Mound 5. Mound 2 had covered the richly-furnished inhumation of a man in a chamber, on top of which had been placed a *ship about 20 m long.

Sutton Hoo's most famous burial, Mound 1, contained a ship 27 m long (fig. 17), in the centre of which was a chamber containing one of the wealthiest assemblages yet to be discovered in England. According to the latest interpretation, the dead man was laid in a large coffin, on top of which were laid a sword, an iron helmet, a purse containing Merovingian tremisses and a great buckle of solid gold. The ornament of the sword hilt, purse lid and connectors features some of the finest polychrome *jewellery known from England. These, together with playing pieces, silver bowls

and spoons, drinking vessels and a great silver dish carrying a stamp of the Byzantine emperor Anastasius, were originally laid on a yellow cloak imported from Syria, which had been thrown over the coffin. Inside the coffin was a heap of clothing and toilet articles. To the west of the coffin were three cauldrons and a tub; and to the east was a shield, an iron 'standard' and a whetstone 'sceptre'. A set of spears and angons leant against the chamber wall, on which was suspended a lyre in a beaver-skin bag. Many of these objects were imported directly or indirectly from the Continent or the Mediterranean (Map 7).

Thirty-seven other burials have been excavated at Sutton Hoo, arranged in two groups: twenty associated with Mound 5, and seventeen on the eastern periphery of the cemetery. These are all held to be victims of execution by hanging or possibly beheading. The practice began at a time contemporary with the construction of Mound 5 and continued into the Middle Ages. There was still a gibbet at Gallows Hill, Wilford, one mile away, in the seventeenth century.

The period of use of the Sutton Hoo cemetery has been determined from the ornament and character of the objects and by radiocarbon dating. The earliest burial was probably Mound 5, followed by Mounds 6, 7, 3 and 4. The two ship

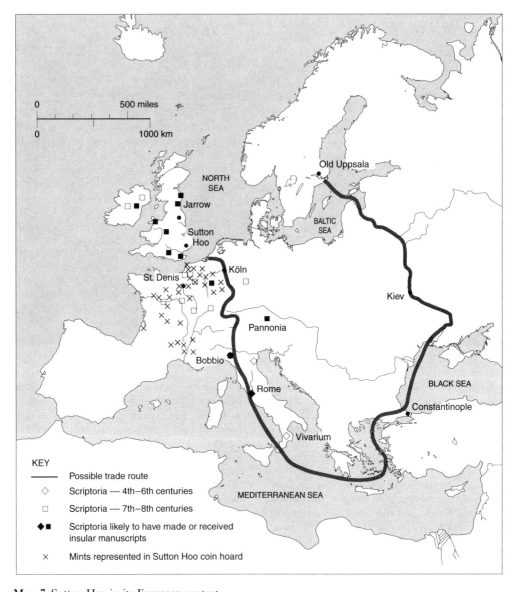

Map 7 Sutton Hoo in its European context.

burials probably came last. From the objects in them, all the mounds appear to have been erected during the seventh century.

Sutton Hoo has been claimed as the burial ground of the kings of *East Anglia, and a number of the kings named in the East Anglian *genealogy have been cited as the likely occupant of Mound 1. Bruce-Mitford argued that the richness of the Mound 1 burial, its inclusion of symbolic objects, its location and its date strongly suggested the

identification of its occupant as *Rædwald, who died between 617 and 631. He also emphasised a link with Sweden, which may have been dynastic. These attributions remain possible but unproven. As so far known, the cemetery was short-lived, belongs to the seventh century, contains only wealthy burials and executions, is remarkable for its variety of burial rite, and shows strong links with Scandinavia and France. It was a cemetery separated from the folk cemeteries, and could well

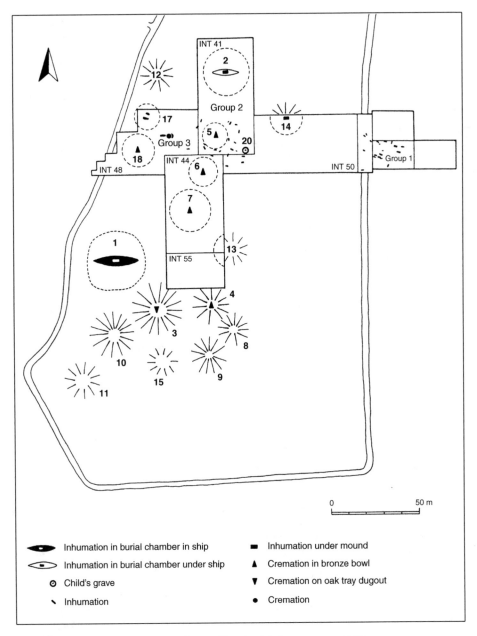

Fig. 16 The Anglo-Saxon cemetery at Sutton Hoo: burials known up to 1992.

represent the adoption of kingship of an innovative, pagan, kind. The burial rites (cremation,
ship-burial) suggest allegiance to Scandinavia and
apprehension of Frankish domination, which was
then making itself increasingly felt in south-east
England. The adoption of kingship would appear
to have had as a concomitant the adoption of
capital punishment.

After the Anglo-Saxon period, the Sutton Hoo
site reverted to sheep-walk, but remained as a
landmark and a place of execution into the Middle
Ages. In the sixteenth century, most of the mounds
were dug into with central pits, and in 1860,
several were trenched. In 1938, Basil Brown investigated Mounds 2, 3 and 4 at the instigation of
the landowner, Mrs Edith Pretty. In 1939, Basil

435

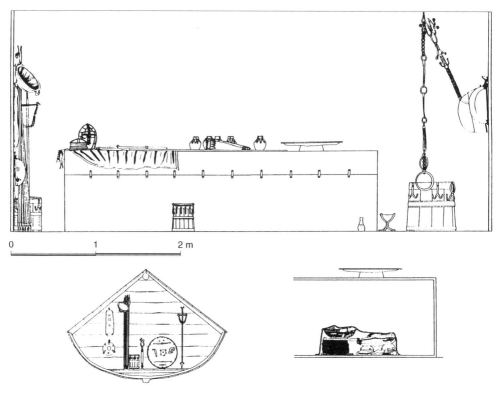

Fig. 17 Reconstruction of the burial deposit in Sutton Hoo Mound 1.

Brown trenched Mound 1, discovering the boat and the burial chamber which were excavated under the supervision of Charles Phillips. At an inquest, the coroner found the assemblage to be the property of the landowner, Mrs Pretty, who promptly donated it to the British Museum where it can now be seen. After the Second World War, the ship burial was studied by Rupert Bruce-Mitford, who returned to the site between 1966 and 1971 to complete the excavation of Mound 1 and conduct other investigations. Mound 1 was eventually published in 1975–1983, and in 1983 a fifth campaign began, intended to investigate the cemetery as a whole and put the ship-burial into context. This was carried out by the University of York for the Sutton Hoo Research Trust and involved the excavation of 1 hectare of the cemetery and a survey of the Deben Valley and the East Anglian kingdom. It was completed in 1997.
R. L. S. Bruce-Mitford, *The Sutton Hoo Ship Burial*, 3 vols. (London, 1975–83); A. C. Evans, *The Sutton Hoo Ship Burial* (London, 1986); M. O. H. Carver, 'Anglo-Saxon Objectives at Sutton Hoo, 1985', *ASE* 15 (1986), 139–52; idem, *Sutton Hoo: Burial Ground of Kings?* (London, 1998); idem, 'Sutton Hoo in Context', *Setti-mane* 32 (1986), 77–123; M. O. H. Carver and M. R. Hummler, *Sutton Hoo. The Early Medieval Cemetery and its Context* (London, forthcoming).

M. O. H. CARVER

SWEET, HENRY (1845–1912), linguist, was a major influence in the development of Anglo-Saxon studies as a modern academic discipline, producing such basic editions as the *Pastoral Care* (1871–2) and the *Oldest English Texts* (1885). Famously celebrated in Shaw's *Pygmalion*, Sweet did pioneering work in phonetics, which he regarded as the foundation of all linguistic study, including the history of the English language, where he was the first to make the distinction between 'Late' and 'Early' West Saxon *dialects. His classic *The Practical Study of Languages* (1899) outlined the principles behind his primers and readers, while his standard textbook *An Anglo-Saxon Reader* (1876) helped promote a 'canon' of texts for the study of Old English literature.
M. Atherton, 'Henry Sweet's Psychology of Language Learning', *Theorie und Rekonstruktion: Trierer Studien zur Geschichte der Linguistik*, ed. K. D. Dutz and H.-J. Niederehe (Münster, 1996), pp. 137–68; M. K. C.

MacMahon, 'Henry Sweet's Linguistic Scholarship: The German Connection', *Anglistik* 5 (1994), 91–101; C. L. Wrenn, 'Henry Sweet', *Transactions of the Philological Society* (1946), 177–201.

MARK ATHERTON

SWEIN FORKBEARD, king of Denmark (*c.*987–1014) and king of England (1013–14). Swein rebelled against his father, King Harold Bluetooth (*c.*958–87), in the 980s, and also experienced various difficulties of his own. It is not entirely clear, therefore, what his position may have been in Denmark when he participated with Olaf Tryggvason in *Viking raids on England in the early 990s. When next reported in England, in 1003, Swein was ostensibly a Christian king of the Danes, and had apparently decided to rejoin the force which had been there since 991. He was active in *Wessex and *East Anglia in 1003–4, but in 1005 a famine forced the Danes to return to their own country. Swein may or may not have given his support to either or both of the invasions of England in 1006–7 (apparently led by a certain Tostig) and 1009–12 (led by Thorkell the Tall); whatever the case, he was quick to exploit the disruption caused by the activities of Thorkell's army. He brought an army to England in the summer of 1013, and conquered the country; King *Æthelred was driven out, and joined Queen *Emma and their children Edward and Alfred in exile at the court of Richard II, duke of Normandy. Swein died on 3 February 1014. He was succeeded in Denmark by his eldest son, Harold, but the fleet at Gainsborough chose his son *Cnut as king. The English councillors sent for Æthelred, who returned to England in the spring and drove Cnut from the land. Swein's embalmed body was later removed to Denmark, and buried in the church which he had built at Roskilde.

Thietmar of Merseburg, *Chronicle*, vii.36–9, in *EHD* i, no. 27; *Encomium Emmae Reginae*, ed. A. Campbell, Camden 3rd ser. 72 (London, 1949), pp. 8–14, 18; F. J. Tschan, *Adam of Bremen: History of the Archbishops of Hamburg-Bremen* (New York, 1959), pp. 72, 75, 81–3, 90; P. Sawyer, 'Swein Forkbeard and the Historians', *Church and Chronicle in the Middle Ages*, ed. I. Wood and G. A. Loud (London, 1991), pp. 27–40; S. Keynes, 'The Historical Context of the Battle of Maldon', *The Battle of Maldon AD 991*, ed. D. Scragg (Oxford, 1991), pp. 81–113; N. Lund, 'The Danish Empire and the End of the Viking Age', *The Oxford Illustrated History of the Vikings*, ed. P. Sawyer (Oxford, 1997), pp. 156–81, at 167–71.

SIMON KEYNES

SWITHUN, bishop of *Winchester (852–63), an obscure ninth-century prelate, the details of whose life are unknown, save for the fact that he witnessed various *charters of King *Æthelwulf (it is from these charters that the dates of his episcopacy can be precisely determined); his episcopal profession to Canterbury survives, and a brief but undatable (tenth-century?) poem preserved as an eleventh-century addition to a Winchester manuscript (now BL, Royal 15.C.VII) which records that Swithun built a bridge at the East Gate of Winchester. Swithun's widespread reputation as a saint derives from the fact that his remains were translated from a conspicuous tomb outside the west door of the Old Minster into a more fitting shrine by Bishop *Æthelwold on 15 July 971, and that Winchester scholars such as *Lantfred, *Wulfstan Cantor and *Ælfric recorded at length the miracles which were accomplished at the new *shrine. As a result of this Winchester publicity, Swithun is commemorated in all later Anglo-Saxon liturgical calendars, and prayers and mass-sets for his cult were circulated widely in England. A late eleventh-century *vita* of Swithun is an impressive piece of *hagiography, but contains no verifiable historical fact.

S. Keynes, 'The West Saxon Charters of King Æthelwulf and his Sons', *EHR* 109 (1994), 1109–49, at 1129–30; H&S, *Councils*, iii. 633–4 [profession]; M. Biddle, *Winchester in the Early Middle Ages*, Winchester Studies 1 (Oxford, 1976), 271–2; M. Lapidge, *The Cult of St Swithun*, Winchester Studies 4.2 (Oxford, forthcoming).

MICHAEL LAPIDGE

SWORDS: *see* Arms and Armour

SYLLOGAE were manuscript collections of inscriptions or *tituli*, transcribed originally from inscriptions found *in situ* in churches and on tombs largely in *Rome, but later supplemented by epigrams of various kinds. The earliest *syllogae* appear to date from the mid-seventh century; the best known early *syllogae* include *Sylloge Turonensis* (from Tours, containing 42 *tituli*) and the *Sylloge Laureshamensis quarta* (from Lorsch, containing 104 *tituli*). *Syllogae* such as these had travelled to Anglo-Saxon England by the late seventh century: *Aldhelm quotes an early sixth-century *titulus* on the Roman church of S. Maria Maggiore which he presumably derived from a *sylloge* (the poem in question is found in both the Tours and Lorsch *syllogae*); a century later *Milred of Worcester compiled his own *sylloge* of epigrams, apparently drawing on one or more earlier *syllogae*, but incorporating *tituli* of a number of Anglo-Latin poets, including Aldhelm and *Bede. In the late seventh or early eighth century an Anglo-Saxon traveller to Rome – Aldhelm himself? – compiled a *sylloge* by transcribing various papal epitaphs; these epitaphs were incorporated by *William of Malmesbury into his personal redaction of the *Liber pontificalis* (now Cambridge, UL, Kk.4.6). Because of their preservation in the Cambridge manuscript, the hypothetical collection on which William drew is known as the *Sylloge Cantabrigiensis*; it is possible, but unprovable, that William took the epitaphs from the copy of Milred's *sylloge* which now survives only in a very fragmentary form.

DACL vii.850–1089; G. B. De Rossi, *Inscriptiones Christianae Vrbis Romae*, 2 vols. (Rome, 1857–88); A. Silvagni, *Inscriptiones Christianae Vrbis Romae* nuova serie (Rome, 1922); idem, 'La silloge epigrafica di Cambridge', *Rivista di archeologia cristiana* 20 (1943), 49–112; P. Sims-Williams, 'Milred of Worcester's Collection of Latin Epigrams and its Continental Counterparts', *ASE* 10 (1982), 21–38; idem, 'William of Malmesbury and *La silloge epigrafica di Cambridge*', *Archivum Historiae Pontificiae* 21 (1983), 9–33; idem, *Religion and Literature in Western England, 600–800*, CSASE 3 (Cambridge, 1990), 345–9; A. Orchard, *The Poetic Art of Aldhelm*, CSASE 8 (Cambridge, 1994), 203–12.

MICHAEL LAPIDGE

SYMEON OF DURHAM, monk of *Durham Cathedral Priory, was present at the translation of St *Cuthbert to the new cathedral in 1104, and was cantor of the cathedral in 1126. Two signed works are extant: a letter to Dean Hugh of York on the history of the archbishops of *York, and a letter to Hildebert of Lavardin on the errors of Origen. In addition, Symeon was almost certainly the principal author of the *Libellus de exordio atque procursu istius hoc est Dunhelmensis ecclesie* (also known as the 'History of the Church of Durham'), and it is very likely that he had a large part in the compilation of the *Historia regum* ('History of the Kings'), as well as of other Durham historical works, notably sets of *annals and a tract on the history of Carlisle. The recognition of Symeon's handwriting in some thirty manuscripts, mostly from Durham, has made it possible to suggest that he was born in northern France or Normandy, that he came to Durham in the early 1090s, that he was responsible for supervising the production

of manuscripts as well as for writing texts, and that he died after 1129/30, a date which strengthens the idea that he was principally concerned with the *Historia regum* which finished in 1129.

Sharpe, *Handlist*, 1625; *Symeon of Durham, On the Origins and Progress of this the Church of Durham*, ed. D. Rollason (OMT, 2000); *Symeon of Durham: Historian of Durham and the North*, ed. D. Rollason (Stamford, 1998).

DAVID ROLLASON

SYNOD: *see* Councils, Ecclesiastical

SYNTAX has been defined as the 'traffic rules' of language. Like its Germanic cognates, but unlike Modern English, *Old English has an inflexional system which includes strong and weak forms of adjectives and distinguishes only the simple present and past tenses, and employs a third element (or word) order Subject . . . Verb as well as the familiar Subject Verb and Verb Subject. Other differences between Old and Modern English exist in the use of negatives and prepositions; in sentence structure, including recapitulation and anticipation, splitting of groups joined by coordinating conjunctions, and correlation of adverbs and conjunctions; in frequent non-expression of 'definite articles' and subjects; and in the syntax of subordinate clauses.

Yet an outstanding feature of Old English syntax is its Englishness. It is clearly in transition to Modern English. The inflexional endings are less reliable than most grammars imply and there is an increasing reliance on the order Subject – Verb – Object to distinguish subject from object and on prepositions to make distinctions which the ambiguous case-forms no longer could. There is also a gradual development of the modern system of resolved moods and tenses. It is the Germanic vocabulary of Old English, rather than its syntax, which presents real difficulty to the beginner.

B. Mitchell, *Old English Syntax*, 2 vols. (Oxford, 1985); idem, *A Critical Bibliography of Old English Syntax* (Oxford, 1990) with supplements by B. Mitchell and S. Irvine, *NM* 93. 1 (1992) and 96. 1, 2, and 3 (1996); B. Mitchell and F. C. Robinson *A Guide to Old English*, 5th ed. (Oxford, 1992).

BRUCE MITCHELL

T

TALBOT, ROBERT (*c.*1505–58), antiquary and friend of John *Leland, was the earliest modern authority on Roman Britian, and an important collector of Anglo-Saxon manuscripts. Talbot was born in Northamptonshire, educated at Winchester and New College, Oxford; he was a prebendary in turn at Wells and Norwich. His Romano-British scholarship consisted in topographical analysis of the *Antonine Itineraries*; a substantial number of Anglo-Saxon manuscripts passed through his hands (he was, significantly, the first disciplined collector following the Dissolution of the monasteries), and his annotations – in a distinctive italic hand – are found in copies of the *Anglo-Saxon Chronicle* (BL, Cotton Domitian viii and Tiberius B.i), the OE *Orosius* (Tiberius B.i), *Ælfric's *Grammar* (Cambridge, UL, Hh.1.10) and the huge corpus of computistical writings now in Oxford, St John's College, 17.

Sharpe, *Handlist*, 1521; T. D. Kendrick, *British Antiquity* (London, 1950), pp. 134–6; C. E. Wright, 'The Dispersal of the Monastic Libraries and the Beginnings of Anglo-Saxon Studies', *TCBS* 1 (1949–53), 208–37, esp. 214–15, 235–7; N. R. Ker, 'Medieval Manuscripts from Norwich Cathedral Priory', *TCBS* 1 (1949–53), 1–28, at 3; idem, *Catalogue*, p. 1.

MICHAEL LAPIDGE

TAMWORTH (Staffs.) can perhaps be identified with *Tomtun*, where Æthelred of Mercia issued a *charter in 675 × 692 (S 1804). Between the 780s and the 850s it was the most important Mercian royal residence, and the most regular site for attesting charters in pre-Viking England. The *Viking invasions left Tamworth on the frontier of 'free' *Mercia. *Æthelflæd re-fortified it during her 913 campaign, and seems to have re-established it as her capital: she died there in 918, and it was to Tamworth that *Edward the Elder immediately came to secure the allegiance of the Mercians. There was a small *mint from *Æthelstan's reign, but tenth- and eleventh-century Tamworth was so thoroughly eclipsed as a territorial and commercial centre that the shire boundary bisects it. Excavations have traced the Æthelflædan defensive circuit, in places superimposed on a pre-Viking rampart; the most remarkable discovery is the well-preserved sequence of ninth- and tenth-century *mills (fig. 10).

M. Gelling, *The West Midlands in the Early Middle Ages* (London, 1992), pp. 146–53; C. Cubitt, *Anglo-Saxon Church Councils c.650–c.850* (London, 1995), pp. 312–13; P. Rahtz and R. Meeson, *An Anglo-Saxon Watermill at Tamworth* (London, 1992).

JOHN BLAIR

TANCRED, TORHTRED AND TOVA, SS, hermits at Thorney (Cambs.), were, according to a short Latin Life (not in *BHL*) written in the later eleventh century by *Folcard, murdered by the Danes in 870. Their relics were translated at Thorney by Bishop *Æthelwold, in the late tenth century. Folcard says that the only record of their lives that he could find at Thorney was a brief mention in the abbey's *priuilegia*, perhaps endowment *charters, written by Æthelwold himself. Their feast was observed on 30 September.

C. Clark, 'Notes on a Life of Three Thorney Saints Tancred, Torhtred and Tova', *Proceedings of the Cambridge Antiquarian Society* 69 (1979), 45–52.

R. C. LOVE

TAPESTRY is a technical term for a decorative weave with coloured pattern wefts which are interwoven with the warp to produce blocks of colour. This is an ancient technique, but is unknown from Anglo-Saxon England except for one example from Sutton Hoo (SH 14), although there is evidence of patterned textiles created by brocading (in which a supplementary weft is woven into the ground weave to produce a pattern), soumak (in which supplementary wefts are wrapped round the warp threads) and embroidery (where pattern thread is inserted into the woven cloth with a needle). The *Bayeux Tapestry, which takes its name from the french *tapisserie*, is technically an *embroidery.

E. Crowfoot, 'The Textiles', in R. L. S. Bruce-Mitford, *The Sutton Hoo Ship Burial*, 3 vols. (London, 1978–83), iii. 415–16, 428–35, and figs. 305, 309–11.

GALE R. OWEN-CROCKER

TAPLOW BURIAL. The seventh-century barrow at Taplow (Bucks.) was the most prestigiously furnished Anglo-Saxon burial known until the discovery of the *Sutton Hoo Mound 1 ship burial. The imposing burial-mound is sited in the churchyard of the former parish church (demolished in the 1830s). In 1883, its dominant presence prompted an investigation by local excavators who injudiciously chose to tunnel beneath the mighty yew which stood upon the mound. The subsequent collapse of the mound's superstructure, and the tree with it, resulted in irretrievable damage to the complex assemblage of grave structures and many of the grave-goods which lay within. Inadequate recording added to the confusion; as a result, the surviving material has taken many years to unscramble, and can never reveal all that it might have done.

However, despite the damage and muddle, the burial's remarkable status is apparent. It contained an adult male accompanied by many of the formal accoutrements of power current among the Germanic ascendancy in the sixth and seventh centuries. Under the earthen barrow, and below the original ground-level, a substantial wooden chamber had been constructed; within this, and unusually facing the east, the dead man was laid out on a feather mattress. Wearing a gold-embellished tunic girded by a massive gold and garnet buckle and accompanying gold-sheeted clasps and a sword, his attire alone signalled his status. This is confirmed by many other of the grave-goods; for example, the symbols of lordly hospitality and responsibility for a war-band, which are signalled in the numerous drinking horns, cups and glasses, as well as by massive cooking and storage vessels, and multiple weapons. A lyre and board-game, and a prestigious imported Byzantine bowl and stand, symbolise a courtly life-style.

The assemblage is not as rich or as eclectic as the Sutton Hoo royal burial, and is presumably of somewhat lesser status; nevertheless, its dominant situation on a high bluff overlooking the Thames, and the presence of a significant number of Kentish items in the burial, suggest that it may have been that of a local ruler who controlled a key section of the Thames valley on behalf of Kentish overlords. This scenario may tentatively be confirmed by later documentary evidence, but the bridge between written evidence and archaeology is one that should always be trodden cautiously.

Finally, the relationship of this massive burial mound to an adjacent church of likely Anglo-Saxon origin raises fundamental questions about the mechanisms of *conversion and the assertion of secular power in the conversion period.

R. A. Smith, 'Anglo-Saxon Remains', *Victoria History of Buckinghamshire* i. 199–204; A. Meaney, *A Gazetteer of Early Anglo-Saxon Burial Sites* (London, 1964), p. 59; J. Blair, 'Frithuwold's Kingdom and the Origins of Surrey', in Bassett, *Origins*, pp. 97–107; *Making of England*, pp. 55–6; L. E. Webster, 'Death's Diplomacy: Sutton Hoo in the Light of other Male Princely Burials', in *Sutton Hoo: Fifty Years After*, ed. R. Farrell and C. Neuman de Vegvar, *American Early Medieval Studies* 2 (1992), 75–82; K. East and L. E. Webster, *The Anglo-Saxon Princely Burials from Taplow, Broomfield and Caenby* (London, forthcoming).

LESLIE WEBSTER

TATWINE, archbishop of Canterbury (731–4), was a scholar of considerable standing who according to Bede (*HE* v.23) had been a priest in the monastery of *Breedon-on-the-Hill before his elevation to the archbishopric; Bede notes that he was known for his piety and wisdom, and his excellent training in the Scriptures, but no other reason is given for the surprising promotion. Tatwine is known as the author of two Latin works: a collection of forty *enigmata, which are indebted in their conception to the *Enigmata* of *Aldhelm, but attempt to articulate a sophisticated theological framework based on the theme of the human mind's attempt to understand divine mysteries (Tatwine's competence of a poet is reflected in his use of the *acrostic form which frames the collection); and a Latin *grammar, the *Ars de partibus orationis*, which is one of the earliest surviving Anglo-Latin grammars, and a good specimen of the sort of elementary grammar (using ecclesiastical vocabulary to illustrate grammatical points) which Anglo-Saxon masters had the task of composing if they were to succeed in communicating the complexities of Latin to their charges. Nothing further is known of Tatwine's life; he died on 30 July 734, and an anonymous epitaph is preserved in Bishop *Milred's *sylloge of Latin epigrams.

Sharpe, *Handlist*, 1681; CCSL cxxxiii.1–141 [*Ars de partibus orationis*], 143–208 [*Enigmata*]; M. Lapidge, 'Some Remnants of Bede's Lost *Liber epigrammatum*', *EHR* 90 (1975), 798–820, at 811–12, repr. in *ALL* i.357–79, at 370–1 [epitaph]; V. Law, 'The Study of Latin Grammar in Eighth-Century Southumbria', *ASE* 12 (1983), 43–71, at 61–2, 66–9, repr. in her *Grammar and Grammarians in the Early Middle Ages* (London, 1997), pp. 91–123, at 105–6, 109–12.

MICHAEL LAPIDGE

TAXATION. The ability of rulers to exploit the financial and other resources of their subjects was central to the operation of the powerful, sophisticated states over which many Anglo-Saxon kings arguably presided. If *Bede was correct in believing that the fifth-century South Saxon king Ælle (the first in his list of seven such rulers) had overlordship over all the territory south of the Humber, such exploitation, and on no small scale, may have existed at a very early date; perhaps it occasionally included the continuance of renders and services once due to Roman and British lords. The *laws of *Æthelberht of *Kent, third in Bede's list, refer only to the payment of judicial fines to the king, but the probable existence of other levies is indicated by the exemption from *gafol* (taxation) granted by Wihtred of Kent (d. 725) to the church, by the mention of men who pay *gafol* in the laws of Wihtred's contemporary *Ine of *Wessex, and by the known power of some seventh-century monarchs. It is difficult to believe, for example, that the achievements of *Edwin and *Oswald of *Northumbria and *Penda of *Mercia were not based on extensive administrative networks, such as are hinted at in Bede's remarks to the effect that Anglesey and the Isle of Man were assessed according to the unit known in English as the *hide (a word not used by Bede, who wrote in Latin). Ine's laws reveal that the hide could be the basis for levies of food and livestock (see *feorm*); and the document known as the *Tribal Hidage, probably from the seventh or eighth century, reveals that hidage figures had been assigned to much of England and possibly Celtic areas too.

Certainly, the creation in the late eighth century of *Offa's Dyke, one of the most astonishing feats of English government, demonstrates a remarkable facility for organising labour and resources. A land *charter issued in 749 by *Æthelbald of Mercia, a predecessor of *Offa, in exempting the church from all state demands except work on *bridges and *fortresses, implies that such demands were onerous. Others of his charters grant freedom from tolls due in *London, and prove that taxation extended to *trade. A concern to maximise such revenues by fostering the economy probably lies behind the introduction of the silver penny in Offa's time, and doubtless kings also profited from the production of *coin (virtually a royal monopoly), and used it as a medium for the payment of taxes. The *Vikings who began to raid England in the 790s found wealthy kingdoms capable of being exploited in various ways.

The tributes paid on occasion to Scandinavian raiders must themselves have necessitated heavy financial burdens on the English. A charter of *Alfred (S 354) records how the bishopric of *Winchester was unable to meet the demands

made on it, and over a century later, under *Æthelred the Unready, churches were forced to melt down precious objects and sell estates in order to fulfil their obligations. The tributes of Æthelred's time seem to have been on an unprecedented level, but no single payment equalled the £82,500 levied by his successor *Cnut in 1018, when failure to render the sum due from an estate resulted in forfeiture to whoever could meet the debt. Cnut almost certainly made the most of the taxable resources of his kingdom, both to maintain powerful military forces in England (see *heregeld) and to create his Scandinavian empire. When *Edward the Confessor abolished the *heregeld* in 1051, the *Anglo-Saxon Chronicle* reported that it had always come before other taxes, and oppressed people in many ways.

However, Viking armies were as likely to be resisted as paid off, and Alfred and his successors (who from the time of *Æthelstan ruled over a single kingdom of England) created a formidable military machine which must have made great demands on their people. Alfred's burghal system (see *Burghal Hidage) covered southern England with a network of fortresses which had to be built and garrisoned; Æthelstan demanded two mounted soldiers from every plough (in 1086 *Domesday Book was to record over 80,000 plough-teams); Æthelred the Unready levied a ship from (probably) every 300 hides, and a helmet and mailcoat from every eight. Some indication of the expense involved in such measures is furnished by evidence from eleventh-century *Normandy that a mailcoat might be worth £7: a country assessed at around 80,000 hides ought to have produced some 10,000 mailcoats for Æthelred's fleet, valued at perhaps £70,000; this is to say nothing, of course, of the cost of the *ships.

The ability to tax on such a scale is matched by other evidence of the close control exercised over their subjects by Anglo-Saxon kings. Late in his reign, *Edgar introduced the system known as *renovatio monetae*, by which millions of silver pennies were periodically recalled and reissued at a rate of exchange beneficial to the authorities (see *coinage), while hundreds of *moneyers had to pay the king for the new dies which a change of coin type necessitated. Such operations doubtless also meant the keeping of detailed records, of which documents like the Burghal Hidage and the *County Hidage are among the few survivors. Much of what we know about Anglo-Saxon taxation is gleaned from fragments of evidence, fragments which only imperfectly represent the operations set in train by elaborate and powerful systems of government.

N. P. Brooks, 'The Development of Military Obligations in Eighth- and Ninth-Century England', in *England Before the Conquest*, ed. P. Clemoes and K. Hughes (Cambridge, 1971), pp. 69–84; Campbell, *Essays*; idem, 'Some Agents and Agencies of the Late Anglo-Saxon State', in *Domesday Studies*, ed. J. C. Holt (Woodbridge, 1987), pp. 201–18; M. K. Lawson, 'The Collection of Danegeld and Heregeld in the Reigns of Æthelred II and Cnut', *EHR* 99 (1984), 721–38; F. W. Maitland, *Domesday Book and Beyond* (Cambridge, 1897).

M. K. LAWSON

TEXTILES. The study of textiles is an umbrella under which is subsumed the analysis of fibres and threads (animal, vegetable, and metallic) and their indigenous or trade sources; spinning; woven and non-woven fabrics and cords; the tools and methods used in their construction; techniques for cutting and sewing these materials into garments and other objects for use; the textile objects themselves; various forms of embellishment, including dyes, weave patterns, applied decoration (*embroidery); and the *iconography of woven and embroidered designs. Modern scientific tools, such as spectrographic analysis and the Scanning Electron Microscope, mean that there is now a considerable battery of techniques which can be deployed in their study, as well as the traditional methods of the study of visual and documentary sources. Since textiles in the broadest sense, as *clothing, animal trappings, wrappings, ties of all kinds, sails and ropes, house and grave furnishings (see *grave goods), must have touched every aspect of the daily and ceremonial lives of the Anglo-Saxons, and their production must have been one of the most ubiquitous and visible industries, the remains constitute a most important primary source for the study of the period.

Research into textiles in general, however, apart from a few special examples of embroidery, and especially the *Bayeux Tapestry, is a recent development. The presence of textiles in Anglo-Saxon graves was occasionally noticed, but even finds associated with known personalities, such as the embroideries, linen, and silks from the tomb of St *Cuthbert in Durham, opened in 1827, or the scraps of silk in the Victoria and Albert Museum said to have been removed from the tomb of *Edward the Confessor in 1685, were not much studied before the 1950s. Work on the relics of St Cuthbert in 1956 first demonstrated a methodology for the systematic analysis of the material, and subsequent work on the much less promising-looking archaeological textiles showed its potential.

As archaeological sites are the major source of new material, this information is often published as an appendix to archaeological reports, but the long time-scale for publication of major sites, and in some cases the lack of money to complete the work, means that much material sadly remains unpublished.

The potential of the material is also limited by the date range of the sites which have produced the most material, and by its fragmentary nature. Most of the remains come from graves of the 'pagan' period (from *c.*450 to the mid-seventh century), before the *conversion to Christianity ended the practice of burying grave goods with the dead, and also largely before any possible cross-reference to visual or documentary sources. The majority of textiles, mainly from inhumations, survive only as tiny fragments in the corrosion products adhering to brooches or buckles, mainly in a mineralised form or as a textile impression (*Sutton Hoo, in this as in other respects, is exceptional). It was the practice until relatively recently to clean all corrosion products off *metalwork objects, especially *jewellery: in this way much evidence from earlier excavations was lost. There are still, however, examples of uncleaned metalwork, especially iron, from eighteenth- and nineteenth-century excavations in museums. Until very recently most graves recognised as having textiles (only a small percentage of graves found) were female graves, because only women wore brooches. However, as awareness of the importance of textiles has risen, they are now looked for on all metal objects, such as girdle hangers, or knives and swords: the position may reveal the presence of a wrapping for a precious object, or, if on the body, provide evidence of garments apart from the points at which they were fastened: skirts and trousers, for example. These fragments, unpromising as they sound, provide evidence of weaves, sometimes elaborate, and the starting and finishing borders of particular types of weave; non-woven structures; stitches, including embroidery, dyes, and the characteristic structures of wool and flax fibres. Gold thread in some cases has been found still folded in its embroidered, brocaded or woven pattern, even where the animal or vegetable fibre with which it was interwoven has disappeared.

Some attempts have been made to define regional types, for example of weaves, on the basis of the distribution of the 'cemetery textiles', but some of the earlier published material does not contain all the information which specialists now look for, and all results are extremely provisional, since the publication of one new cemetery, for example Cleatham, immediately doubled the count of known textiles from the Lincolnshire area.

Since the 1960s, textiles of the later Anglo-Saxon and *Viking and the Saxo-Norman period have been recovered from urban sites, especially *London and *York: the textile history of these later periods was previously known only from the rare grand examples mainly considered under embroidery. These survivals depend on different conditions from those in graves: in York at 16–22 Coppergate, for example, survival depended on the high moisture level and low oxygen content of the soil. From this site we have complete or almost complete recognisable objects, such as an embroidered silk pouch, possibly a reliquary; a silk headdress; and a wool sock in a looped technique well known from other Viking period finds. As the study of the pouch has also shown, metalwork and other skeuomorphs of textile objects are another possible source of textile study.

C. F. Battiscombe, *The Relics of St Cuthbert* (Oxford, 1956); C. R. Dodwell, *Anglo-Saxon Art: a New Perspective* (Manchester, 1982), chs. 3, 5, 6; G. R. Owen-Crocker, *Dress in Anglo-Saxon England* (Manchester, 1986); P. Walton [Rogers], *Textiles, Cordage and Raw Fibre from 16–22 Coppergate*, The Archaeology of York 17.5 (York, 1989); L. Bender Jørgensen, *North European Textiles until c. AD 1000* (Copenhagen, 1991); E. Coatsworth, M. FitzGerald, K. Leahy, and G. Owen-Crocker, 'Anglo-Saxon Textiles from Cleatham, Humberside', *Textile History* 27 (1996), 5–41.

ELIZABETH COATSWORTH

THEGN. In the terminology of *social class in Anglo-Saxon England, a thegn (literally 'one who serves', cf. OE *thegnian*) was a person with a combination of attributes which put him into the highest rank: he was *eorlisc* as opposed to *ceorlisc*, and in later parlance he would be described as a member of the nobility or landed aristocracy. A thegn would own a substantial amount of *bookland in one or more counties, whether by inheritance or acquisition; he would also hold some *folkland, which had passed to him in accordance with customary law; and he might own some property in a *town. He would have useful social connections, and would be lord on his own estate or in his own right to many men of lesser degree, with all which that entailed. All thegns would be expected to perform military and administrative services; a number of them might hold a special position in the king's household; others would be appointed to the office of *reeve or shire-reeve (sheriff); and the most favoured or prominent among them might be promoted to the office of *ealdorman. They would be jealous of their rights, but conscious of their obligations; and although they would owe their loyalty to their lord the king, they might be inclined for whatever reason to give it to another party, and predisposed under certain conditions to protect their own interests. Collectively, the thegns were the very fabric of social and political order: they were the ones with local power and influence, who moved naturally from the locality to the centre (wherever it happened to be); it was their *oaths of loyalty which made the difference between kingship and royal power, by helping to extend the king's reach into the localities; and it was the king's ability (or otherwise) to command their support which determined his ability (or otherwise) to pursue a particular course of action. Kings gained much from their royal office, and ealdormen had much to gain from exploiting their own positions of power; but in the final analysis it was the thegns who counted.

The thegns who are so familiar from the records of the tenth and eleventh centuries formed the tail-end of a long process of social and political development. In late-seventh-century *Kent there was already a basic distinction between a *ceorl* (ordinary freeman) and an *eorlcundman* (nobleman or thegn), with a *wergild three times that of the *ceorl*, matched in *Wessex at the same time by the distinction between a *ceorl* and a man of an intermediate class, putting the West Saxon nobleman or thegn, with a wergild six times that of the *ceorl*, in an even higher class; unfortunately, the position reached at this early date in the Anglian kingdoms of *Mercia, *East Anglia, and *Northumbria is far from clear. It may be that a class of men set apart from others by their service and access to the king coalesced in Wessex at a relatively early stage, and that the emergence of this class contributed to the resilience of the West Saxon polity in the face of Mercian pressure in the eighth century and in the face of *Viking pressure in the ninth. By the time we reach the reign of *Alfred the Great, it is apparent that there was a considerable degree of organisation among the thegns at the royal court (*Asser, *Vita Ælfredi regis*, c. 100), and as we move on into the tenth and eleventh centuries the quality of available evidence affords an increasingly clear impression of the part which the king's thegns played in the affairs of the realm. *Law-codes are replete with references to thegns, showing how they functioned or what was expected of them in one context or another; *charters give us their names, and a sense of their political importance; and *wills and other private documents put flesh upon a select few of their

443

number. In certain cases it is possible to reconstruct the landed interests, religious and political affiliations, and family connections of particular thegns in some detail, and in these cases the prosopographical approach to Anglo-Saxon history comes into its own. The thegns who are most prominent in the witness-lists probably or demonstrably held office in the royal household; for while a thegn is generally described in such contexts as a *minister* (or *miles*), he might be, more specifically, a *discifer* (OE *discðegn*, 'dish-thegn', or seneschal), a *cubicularius* or *camerarius* (OE *hræglðegn*, 'rail-thegn', or *burðegn*, 'chamber-thegn'), or a *pincerna* (OE *byrele*, 'butler'). A judge who gave a false judgement would forfeit his rank as a thegn (III Edgar ch. 3), and later in the tenth century we hear how the 'the twelve leading thegns, and with them the reeve' would conduct themselves in court (III Æthelred ch. 3); and for their own part, as a general principle, 'No one is to have any jurisdiction over a king's thegn except the king himself' (III Æthelred ch. 11). Thegns were not, however, politically inert. Meetings of the *shire *court, and of the king's *council, might appear from surviving records to have been occasions for law-making, legal proceedings, and other formal business; but when thegns came together, as at a meeting at Cookham in the 990s, 'from far and wide, both West Saxons and Mercians, Danes and English' (S 939: *EHD* i, no. 121), we may suspect that the intrigue started and the gossip flowed.

While kings had trouble maintaining law and order, thegns were on a roll. The regulations of the thegns' gild of Cambridge were entered in a gospelbook at *Ely abbey (*EHD* i, no. 136). Archbishop *Wulfstan's compilation on status (*EHD* i, no. 51) reveals what one needed in order to become entitled to the rights of a thegn: fully five hides of land, a bell and a castle-gate, plus a seat and special office in the king's hall. The tract on *estate management known as 'Rectitudines Singularum Personarum' (*EHD* ii, no. 172) begins with a section on 'the law of the thegn', that he be entitled to his 'book-right' (the privileges of bookland), that he perform the requisite military services, and (in respect of many estates) provide further services for the king. We also hear from Wulfstan of the *heriot payable on the death of thegns of various kinds (II Cnut ch. 71). Most intriguing are the various indications that thegns were entrusted with official business on the part of a shire-court, or on the part of the king. Three thegns were appointed by a shire-meeting in *Cnut's reign to ascertain a mother's response to

a charge brought against her (in her absence) by her son. 'Act well like thegns, and announce my message to the meeting before all the good men, and inform them to whom I have granted my land and all my possessions, and to my own son never a thing' (S 1462: *EHD* i, no. 135). The surviving seal matrices of Godwine *minister*, of Ælfric, and of Wulfric, suggest that thegns needed *seals of their own, if not for sealing documents then at least for use as tokens of credence to guarantee their status when acting in an official capacity. The last generation of Anglo-Saxon thegns feature prominently in *Domesday Book, and many of them survived into the 1080s, albeit in somewhat reduced circumstances.

H. Loyn, 'Gesiths and Thegns in Anglo-Saxon England from the Seventh to the Tenth Century', *EHR* 70 (1955), 529–49; idem, *Anglo-Saxon England and the Norman Conquest*, 2nd ed. (London, 1991), pp. 223–7; F. M. Stenton, 'The Thriving of the Anglo-Saxon Ceorl', *Preparatory to Anglo-Saxon England*, ed. D. M. Stenton (Oxford, 1970), pp. 383–93; S. Keynes, *The Diplomas of King Æthelred 'the Unready' 978–1016* (Cambridge, 1980), pp. 138–40 [seals], 158–62 [thegns]; A. Thacker, 'Some Terms for Nobleman in Anglo-Saxon England c.650–900', *ASSAH* 2 (1981), 201–36; R. Fleming, 'Rural Élites and Urban Communities in Late-Saxon England', *P&P* 141 (1993), 3–37; P. A. Clarke, *The English Nobility Under Edward the Confessor* (Oxford, 1994); A. Williams, *The English and the Norman Conquest* (Woodbridge, 1995), pp. 71–125

SIMON KEYNES

THEODORE (602–90), archbishop of *Canterbury, was a monk of Greek origin and training, a biblical scholar and exegete of exceptional learning, and an important influence on the structure and discipline of the early English church. The principal source for Theodore's life after he was first invited to accept the archbishopric of Canterbury in 667 is *Bede's *Historia ecclesiastica*, but details of his earlier life can be gleaned from the corpus of biblical commentaries which record his teaching at the school of Canterbury. Theodore was born in Tarsus (now Gözlü Kule in south-eastern Turkey) in 602, in the Greek-speaking province of Cilicia. To judge from the scholarly orientation of his later biblical teaching, which is thoroughly Antiochene (that is, literal as distinct from the allegorical approach practised at Alexandria: see *exegesis) in character, it seems probable that Theodore studied at some point in Antioch, the nearest large city to Tarsus; among the authorities which inform the Canterbury commentaries are John Chrysostom (d. 407), who is the most frequently quoted authority, and Theodore of Mopsuestia (d. 428), two of the most important exegetes of the Antiochene school. Antioch was a city bilingual in Greek and Syriac, and it was there that Theodore came into contact with the Syriac exegetical tradition, especially the writings of Ephrem the Syrian (d. 373), which also informs the commentaries; inland from Antioch lies Edessa (now Sanlifurfa in Turkey), the centre of Syriac Christianity, and a comment in the Canterbury biblical commentaries on the size of watermelons available in Edessa (PentI 413) seems to imply first-hand experience of the city, which implies that Theodore had studied there at some point, if only briefly. Syria was twice invaded in the early seventh century: by the Persians in 613 (the Canterbury biblical commentaries contain some first-hand observations on the habits of the Persians: PentI 206, 303), and by the Arabs in 637. It is probable that the young Theodore, who may already have been a monk, left Syria as a refugee from one or other of these invaders. He is next attested in Constantinople, which in the early seventh century (especially in the reign of Heraclius, 610–41) was one of the most important centres of learning in the Mediterranean: the biblical commentaries contain an eye-witness report, attributed verbatim to Theodore (Wb1 13), of the famous Porphyry Column in Constantinople, which housed the relics of the Twelve Baskets. Constantinople housed a university and several large libraries, including those at the university and the patriarchal library of Hagia Sophia; it was also home to the great polymath Stephen of Alexandria, who lectured on philosophy and medicine, as well as to the historian Theophylact Simocatta and the poet George of Pisidia. The intellectual complexion of the Canterbury commentaries suggests that Theodore's scholarly orientation was derived from his period of study in Constantinople, particularly his interest in philosophy, rhetoric, *medicine, *computus, *astronomy, and astrology (several passages in the commentaries have close parallels in the *scholia* or lecture-notes of Stephen of Alexandria, for example, which suggest that Theodore attended Stephen's lectures).

For reasons which are now irrecoverable, Theodore left Constantinople for *Rome, where he seems to have been a monk of the community of Cilician (i.e. Greek-speaking) monks at the monastery of St Anastasius *ad aquas Salvias* (at the Tre Fontane, outside the southern gate of the city). As such, Theodore was involved with the other Greek monks of St Anastasius in drafting the *acta* of the Lateran Council of 649, the document in which

Pope Martin (649–53) repudiated the imperial doctrine of 'one will in Christ' (monotheletism), arguing instead, in the light of the theology of Maximus the Confessor (d. 662) who was also a Greek refugee in Rome at this time, that there were two wills in Christ. It is possible that one of the signatories of the Lateran *acta*, a *Theodorus monachus*, is identical with the later archbishop of Canterbury; in any event, the Canterbury biblical commentaries are indebted in many ways to the exegesis of Maximus the Confessor.

Some years later, when the archbishop-elect of Canterbury (one Wigheard) who was in Rome to collect the *pallium, died of the plague in 667, Pope Vitalian (657–72) consulted *Hadrian, the abbot of a monastery near Naples, who, after refusing the archbishopric himself, suggested the name of Theodore. Theodore was elected on condition that he be tonsured with a crown in the western manner (eastern monks shaved their heads completely), and was duly consecrated on 26 March 668; he arrived in England a year later on 27 May 669, then aged 67. He set about reforming the English church with the urgency of an old man in a hurry. He filled a number of vacancies in the bishoprics of his province, making appointments to *Rochester, Dunwich and *Winchester; and with the episcopate restored to strength, he summoned a national synod which met under his presidency at Hertford in September 672 or 673 (see *councils, ecclesiastical). Among the *acta* of this synod (as reported by Bede, *HE* iv.5) were the provisions that the number of dioceses should be increased (the intention being to break up vast dioceses such as that of Bishop *Wilfrid in Northumbria) and that national synods should be held twice-yearly at the unidentified site of *Clofesho. The first of these provisions led Theodore in 677 to depose Wilfrid and to break up the Northumbrian see into three: one in *Bernicia, one in *Deira, one in *Lindsey. Wilfrid went to Rome to appeal to the pope, and was later reinstated by Theodore as bishop of Deira with his see at *York; the reconciliation between archbishop and bishop was announced in a letter (preserved by *Stephen of Ripon in his Life of Wilfrid) which Theodore addressed to various English authorities. Theodore was deeply concerned with orthodox belief; for example, he convened the synod which met at Hatfield on 17 September 679 to endorse the *acta* of the Lateran Council of 649 (in the promulgation of which Theodore had probably participated) which with papal approval were adopted by the universal church at the Sixth Oecumenical Council of 680.

He was also concerned to establish and teach *canon law (the *acta* of the synod of Hertford were based on a *liber canonum*; the second book of the *Iudicia*, which record Theodore's answers to questions put to him by a pupil, is based on this same *liber canonum*, probably a modified copy of the collection of canons and decretals assembled by Dionysius Exiguus, a text which was also expounded at Theodore's Canterbury school) and *penitential discipline (the first book of his *Iudicia* reports Theodore's judgements on matters of penance). Theodore also exerted a decisive influence on the *liturgy: the prayer known as the litany of the saints, which is now used universally in the western church, originated in the patriarchate of Antioch and was first brought to the West, and translated into Latin, through Theodore's agency.

It was perhaps in the field of scholarship that Theodore had his most decisive impact. Bede reports (*HE* iv.2) that Theodore and Hadrian attracted crowds of students to their *school at Canterbury, where they gave instruction especially in Scripture but also in metre, astronomy and computus. Some of these students can be identified from Bede's *HE* (*Albinus, Tobias and Oftfor), and *Aldhelm is also known to have studied at Canterbury. The nature of the teaching can be gauged from the corpus of biblical commentaries which originated in their school, and are the notes taken by pupils from the *viva voce* teaching of Theodore and Hadrian. The range of learning in these commentaries is extraordinary by early medieval standards: the basis of the instruction seems to have been word for word comparison of the Latin Vulgate Bible with the Greek Septuagint and New Testament, supplemented by the opinions of various Greek Church Fathers, such as Basil of Caesarea, Clement of Alexandria, Cosmas Indicopleustes, Epiphanius of Salamis and John Chrysostom, who are quoted (and translated into Latin) at length. Other evidence of their teaching is preserved in the Leiden Glossary (see *glossaries), a manuscript copied *c*.800 at St Gallen from a collection of notes and glosses to various Latin texts (including Sulpicius Severus, Rufinus, *Gildas, Isidore, Jerome, Cassian, Orosius, *Gregory the Great and the Benedictine Rule) assembled in their Canterbury school.

In addition to these commentaries and glosses, which are the record of his oral teaching, Theodore also composed a small corpus of writings. These include: an *octosyllabic poem addressed to *Hædди, bishop of Winchester, in a metrical form indebted to Greek anacreontic verse; an unprinted Latin translation of the Greek *Passio S. Anastasii*, a Life of the Persian martyr (d. 628) who was the patron saint of the monastery *ad aquas Salvias* in Rome where Theodore had been a monk; and a work called the *Laterculus Malalianus*, based partly on the Greek *Chronographia* of John Malalas (d. 578) and partly consisting of original exegesis of the life of Christ, from conception to death. The *Laterculus* draws on some of the Greek authorities (such as Epiphanius) cited in the corpus of biblical commentaries, and shares a similar scholarly orientation. In a word, Theodore was one of the greatest scholars ever to adorn the see of Canterbury. He died on 19 September 690 and was buried in the the cathedral church at Canterbury, where he was commemorated by an epitaph (probably composed by Aldhelm) which is partially preserved by Bede, *HE* v.8.

Sharpe, *Handlist*, 1686; Bede, *HE* iv.1–2; B. Bischoff and M. Lapidge, *Biblical Commentaries from the Canterbury School of Theodore and Hadrian*, CSASE 10 (Cambridge, 1994); *Archbishop Theodore*, ed. M. Lapidge, CSASE 11 (Cambridge, 1995); J. Stevenson, *The 'Laterculus Malalianus' and the School of Archbishop Theodore*, CSASE 14 (Cambridge, 1995); Brooks, *Canterbury*, pp. 71–6, 94–9; M. Lapidge, 'The School of Theodore and Hadrian', *ASE* 15 (1986), 45–72, repr. in *ALL* i.141–68; idem, 'The Study of Greek at the School of Canterbury in the Seventh Century', *ALL* i.123–39; P. W. Finsterwalder, *Die Canones Theodori Cantuariensis und ihre Überlieferungsformen* (Weimar, 1929).

MICHAEL LAPIDGE

THEODULFI CAPITULA, an instructional work for parish priests compiled by Theodulf, bishop of Orléans (*c*.760–821), is accompanied by an OE translation in two eleventh-century manuscripts from Exeter. In the earlier of the two manuscripts (Oxford, Bodleian Library, Bodley 865), chapters of Latin and Old English alternate. The text is incompletely preserved, beginning towards the end of ch. 25. A less literal translation is found in a mid-eleventh-century manuscript (CCCC 201). In this manuscript, the Latin and the Old English are consecutive texts, separated by a homily. A Latin text with a few OE glosses is found in a mid-eleventh-century manuscript associated with *Wulfstan the Homilist (CCCC 265).

Theodulfi Capitula in England, ed. H. Sauer, Texte und Untersuchungen zur Englischen Philologie 8 (Munich, 1978).

STEPHANIE HOLLIS

THORKELIN, GRIMUR JONSSON (1752–1829), an Icelander by birth, was the first to recognise the importance of **Beowulf*. In 1787 he commissioned a copyist to make a transcript of the poem, known today as Thorkelin A, and two years later he himself made another, Thorkelin B. Despite many inaccuracies, the two are important early witnesses to the manuscript. In 1815 he published the *editio princeps* of the poem in Copenhagen, believing it to be an early Danish epic, originally composed in Danish.

The Thorkelin Transcripts of Beowulf, ed. K. Malone, EEMF 1 (Copenhagen, 1951); K. S. Kiernan, *'Beowulf' and the 'Beowulf' Manuscript* (New Brunswick, NJ, 1984); J. R. Hall, 'The First Two Editions of *Beowulf*: Thorkelin's (1815) and Kemble's (1833)', *The Editing of Old English*, ed. D. G. Scragg and P. E. Szarmach (Cambridge, 1994).

DONALD SCRAGG

THORPE, BENJAMIN (1782–1870), was an immensely productive scholar in Anglo-Saxon and Scandinavian studies and advocate, along with John Mitchell *Kemble (1807–57), of a more scientific approach to philology based on the work of Danish and German scholars. Thorpe trained in Copenhagen under Rasmus Rask (1787–1832), and came to England shortly thereafter, where he published in 1832 *Cædmon's Metrical Paraphrase*, England's 'first native volume of Old English verse'. His works, primarily editions and translations, include *Analecta Anglo-Saxonica* (1834), *Apollonius of Tyre* (1834), *Paris Psalter* (1835), *Ancients Laws and Institutes* (1840), the Old English Gospels (1842), *Codex Exoniensis* (1842), Ælfric's *Catholic Homilies* (1843–6), a translation of *Orosius* (1853), *Beowulf* (1855), *Anglo-Saxon Chronicle* (1861), and *Diplomatarium Anglicum Ævi Saxonici* (1865), along with an unpublished text of the *Vercelli Book*. He was founder of the Ælfric Society.

P. Pulsiano, 'Benjamin Thorpe', in *Medieval Scholarship. Biographical Studies on the Formation of a Discipline* II. *Literature and Philology*, ed. H. Damico (New York, 1998), pp. 75–92.

PHILLIP PULSIANO

TILES with elaborate relief-impressed geometrical designs and coloured glazes have been found on several important tenth- and eleventh-century religious sites. It seems likely that they decorated the floors, steps and perhaps wall-surfaces of liturgically important areas. They provide a valuable glimpse of the texture and colour of Anglo-Saxon church interiors, otherwise largely lost to us.

R. Gem and L. Keen, 'Late Anglo-Saxon Finds from the Site of St Edmund's Abbey', *Proceedings of the Suffolk Institute of Archaeology and History* 35 (1981),

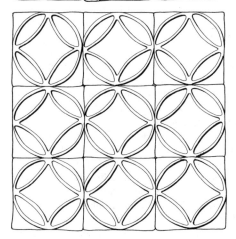

Fig. 18 Late Anglo-Saxon tiles from Winchester.

1–30; *Golden Age of AS Art*, pp. 136–7; M. Biddle and B. Kjølbye-Biddle, 'An Early Medieval Floor-Tile from St Frideswide's Minster', *Oxoniensia* 53 (1988), 259–63; L. Keen, 'Pre-Conquest Glazed Relief Tiles from All Saints, Pavement, York', *JBAA* 146 (1993), 67–86.

JOHN BLAIR

TIMBER BUILDING was ubiquitous in Anglo-Saxon England, apart from the more important churches and a limited range of monastic and defensive structures. As only Greensted church survives as a standing timber construction, the dated evidence for timber building techniques comes mostly from waterlogged deposits where timber survived as parts of wells, piles and *mills. These remarkably preserved timbers give us clues from the toolmarks and joints to the way timber was prepared and worked. The other evidence for buildings comes from stains in the ground left where timber has rotted in post-holes. These 'post-ghost' impressions give us the outline of the buildings and the positions of the principal earth-fast posts.

From surviving timbers waterlogged at the bottom of post holes we know that oak was used almost exclusively by Anglo-Saxon builders, often as small sections from large slow-grown trees of up to 1 m diameter. These axe-felled trees were converted by splitting with wooden wedges struck by wooden beetles and were cleft into both radial and tangentially split planks and posts. Posts 0.3 m square were usually made from one quarter of a large-diameter tree, rather than a smaller tree squared up. The unseasoned split timber was then hewn to shape with thin-bladed steel-edged broad axes. Some axed surfaces are so flat that the individual axe-strokes cannot be seen. Despite the clear tool-marks occurring on many waterlogged timbers, there is no evidence that saws were used in converting timber or cutting joints.

The joints themselves rarely survive. When they do, toolmarks clearly show that the wood was shaped unseasoned. Lap-joints were cut with axes; mortice-holes were first drilled out with a spoon auger, then axe-cut or chiselled out. Tenons were axe-cut and sometimes tusked (that is, pegs were driven through the protruding tenon tongues). Grooves were chiselled, and some timbers were simply pegged. Scarf-joints only survive in boats. The clearest indication of timber-working skills come from the points of wooden piles. Squared piles have long axe-tapered points with up to eight facets. Often this work had been lovingly and artistically done despite the fact that the craftsman must have assumed that the points would never

be seen again. Occasionally very crudely shaped piles occur in the same structures.

Wattle and daub were two building materials which were regularly used together, not only as infill between timbers but also for the construction of walls or small buildings on their own. Wattle walls were not always daubed but could be closely enough woven to be weatherproof; alternatively, the clay component could be used on its own as cob. The technique of wattle and daub is important as it enables simple strong structures to be put up quickly provided that there is a supply of coppice rod and poles from managed *woodland.

There were two types of buildings in the pagan Anglo-Saxon period for which some evidence of building techniques survive. Most commonly found are *Grubenhäuser*, or sunken-featured buildings, which continue a Germanic tradition of construction. These typically have a subrectangular pit underneath the building up to 1 m deep, 3 m wide and 4 m long. These irregular pits have one constant feature, a post-hole near the centre of each end indicating a ridge-beam structure. The use of the pit varies. At West Stow the pits were floored over with wooden planks and the buildings had wooden sidewalls and thatched roofs. At Colchester the trampled pit bottom was the floor of the building, and double stake-holes around the outside suggest wattle or wattle-and-daub walling. Generally neither the pits nor the post spacings are regular, and it is unlikely that these buildings were carefully framed structures.

The second type of building from the pagan Anglo-Saxon period is built of posts along the line of the walls, with no internal posts supporting the roof. The walls were probably a combination of earth-fast posts, wattle and daub, and/or cob. The post spacings are neither in straight lines nor regular enough to suggest a wallplate running along the top of the posts making a rigid frame. Sometimes post-holes may be paired across the structure, and these might have held tiebeams. The Germanic tradition of aisled buildings was not carried over to England until the tenth century. No evidence of roof structures survives and it has to be assumed that these early buildings used poles rather than jointed framing.

Cowdreys Down and a number of other sites provide post-plans from the sixth to the eighth century, and give the clearest indication for complex timber buildings up to 8.5 m wide and 22 m long. They have regular 0.5 m deep earth-fast posts set either in individual post-holes or in pick-cut trenches. The wall posts of up to 0.4 m wide by 0.08 m thick were often buttressed by external lines of posts, and the excavators were able to calculate the wall height from the angles of the buttress ghosts surviving in the ground. The technique seems to have been to use massive strength in the walls, provided by deep posts and buttressing, to oppose the outward thrust of the roof. The gable-ends of vertical planking usually suggest a ridge-beam. There was evidence of continuous wattle-and-daub walling between the timber uprights. Many buildings represent a massive investment in timber: the walls of one building alone might contain twenty cubic metres of shaped timber.

Tenth- and eleventh-century *towns contained buildings with timber-lined cellars, sometimes apparently with a full storey above. The clearest evidence for late Saxon buildings is at Coppergate in Anglo-Scandinavian *York. Tenth-century wattle structures were followed by a series of late tenth-century timber semi-basements cut up to 1.5 m into the accumulating soils. Waterlogged timber walls survive 1.8 m high. Here wide horizontal oak planks rest behind rectangular posts made from whole trees. Despite the high quality of the plank-work, no pegs, nails or joints were used to hold the heavy planks against posts, which in turn rested on, but were not jointed to, either small oak pads or foundation beams. In one building cavity walling had been created by fixing an inner skin of planks to the posts, and in another similar results were obtained with wattle screening. The only clue to the upper part of the structure was a series of lap-joints at the broken tops of the posts. In *London, re-used building timbers recently recovered from water-fronts show a form of construction in which squared upright posts passed through holes in timber 'base-plates', which gave them stability.

Evidence for roof structures is very slight. The weather was kept out by thatch, oak shingles, lapped boards, stone tiles and lead, but the structures that support these claddings have not been identified. Parts of timber roofs may survive in churches, but none have been dated by dendrochronology to the period. Ground-plans occasionally suggest ridge beams or cruck construction, but there is still little evidence for the purlins, principal rafters and windbracing which would generally be required, especially in wide roofs.

Some groups of buildings were carefully laid out, and units of measurement have been calculated from the ground plans. However, most corners were not square, the walls were rarely straight, and the posts, though regular, were not quite evenly spaced, as though the buildings had

been laid out by eye rather than with mathematical precision. The buildings were generally twice as long as they were wide.

Two jointed timber buildings survive, the heavily restored Greensted church (Essex), dated by dendrochronology to 1063 × 1108, and the waterlogged base of the *Tamworth mill, dated by dendrochronology to 846 × 864. Greensted was of stave construction, with originally continuous walls of earthfast half round staves carefully made from half trees, the inside surface hewn flat, the outside stripped of sapwood and rounded off. These massive timbers up to 0.6 m wide were grooved down each side. Separate tongues of wood joined the upright timbers together, making the wall weatherproof and allowing some movement as the timber dried. The deep chisel marks in the grooves indicate that the timber was shaped when freshly felled. The tops of the half-round timbers were cut in an external splay which probably tenoned into a wallplate, supporting tiebeams which were clasped by a second wallplate. The end walls were built as gables. This unique building confirms the Anglo-Saxons' readiness to use very large amounts of timber. The undercroft of the Tamworth mill had timber sills strong enough to withstand the force of water driving the horizontal wheel. This base was built of heavy beams 0.3 m × 0.4 m tusk-tenoned together, with a floor of planks 0.3 m wide resting on joists. When excavated the horizontal plank walls of the structure survived to 0.5 m. Finally, the recent discovery of re-used arcade posts from a substantial tenth-century building in London shows that large-aisled buildings existed, possibly with several tiers of arcading.

H. Christie, O. Olsen and H. M. Taylor, 'Greensted Church', *AJ* 59 (1979), 92–112; C. Hewett, *Early English Carpentry* (Chichester, 1980); *Wood-working Techniques before 1500*, ed. S. Macgrail (Oxford, 1982); S. James, A. Marshall and M. Millet, 'An Early Medieval Building Tradition', *Archaeological Journal* 141 (1984), 182–215; G. Milne, *Timber Building Techniques in London c.900–1400* (London, 1992); D. Goodburn, 'London's Early Medieval Timber Buildings', in *Urbanism in Medieval Europe. Papers of the Bruges Medieval Conference 1997* 1 (1997).

R. J. DARRAH

TITHING: *see* Courts; Hundreds

TITULI are Latin *inscriptions, usually metrical in form; the term originally referred to the inscription which prefaced a book (signalling author and content), but subsequently came to refer to inscriptions engraved in churches (recording the dedication) and on tombs (recording the name of the deceased). The churches and cemeteries of *Rome were filled with monuments bearing *tituli*; in the fourth century in particular Pope Damasus (366–84) composed a number of elegant epigrams which were engraved lavishly on Roman monuments by his engraver Filocalus. Anglo-Saxon pilgrims will have had many opportunities to observe (and perhaps to record) them. Collections of *tituli*, known as *syllogae, were made from the seventh century onwards, and some of these *syllogae* were early transmitted to England, where they provided models for Anglo-Latin poets who wished to compose *tituli* to commemorate in particular the dedication of churches. *Aldhelm's small corpus of so-called *Carmina ecclesiastica* are in fact *tituli* composed for churches and altars in *Malmesbury. In the reign of King *Ine someone composed (by recycling the earlier verse of Venantius Fortunatus) a *titulus* for the church at *Glastonbury. *Bede composed at least one such *titulus* to record the dedication of the church in *Lindsey by his colleague Bishop Cyneberht, and it is known (from notes made by John *Leland on a manuscript now lost) that his *Liber epigrammatum*, of which only fragments survive, contained more such *tituli*. *Milred, bishop of *Worcester (d. 774) assembled a collection or *sylloge* of inscriptions which included Bede's epigram for the church of Cyneberht, as well as other *tituli* by various English ecclesiastics, including Abbot *Ceolfrith of *Monkwearmouth-Jarrow, Cuthbert, bishop of *Hereford (736–40) and archbishop of Canterbury (740–60), and unknown abbots named Cyneheah and Cumma; Milred's *sylloge* also included epitaphs for Archbishops *Berhtwald and *Tatwine of Canterbury, Bishop *Hæddi of *Winchester, and several other otherwise unattested English ecclesiastics. *Alcuin, too, was adept at composing *tituli*, and his poetic corpus includes many poems intended to decorate Carolingian churches, as well as an epitaph for his master *Ælberht at York. The practice seems to have been discontinued in the later Anglo-Saxon period.

MGH, AA xv.11–32 [Aldhelm]; MGH, PLAC i.206–7, 304–12 [Alcuin]; M. Lapidge, 'Some Remnants of Bede's Lost *Liber epigrammatum*', *EHR* 90 (1975), 798–820, repr. in *ALL* i.357–79 [addenda at 510–12]; idem, *ALL* i.313–38, at 314–17 [Bede], and 402–3 [Glastonbury].

MICHAEL LAPIDGE

TOPOGRAPHICAL NAMES created by the Anglo-Saxons described the natural features of the landscape as they existed when the English settled and as such features developed through the processes of clearance and cultivation. Until the mid 1970s, relatively little attention had been given to this type of name, interest having been focused more on *habitation names which, it was thought, could best chart the development of English *settlement in this island. It is now clear, however, that certain kinds of topographical name were amongst the earliest created by the Anglo-Saxons. Such original nature names soon became attached to settlement sites. In records to *c.*730, a range of topographical elements appears compounded in Anglo-Saxon place-names. By far the most prevalent early generic of this sort is Old English *ēg* 'land partly surrounded by water, a piece of dry ground in a fen'. Names in *-ēg* represent nine per cent of all place-names recorded before *c.*730, names such as Bardney, Battersea, Bermondsey and Chertsey. The generics *burna* 'a stream', *ford* 'a ford' and *hamm* 'land in a river bend, dry ground in a marsh' (giving topographical names like Aldingbourne, Littlebourne, Brentford, *Stamford, Farnham and Fulham) were also important, evidently coined, as were names in *-ēg*, by farmers who were much concerned about dry sites for villages, water supply and water crossings. In north-west Berkshire such toponyms have a real coincidence of locality with pagan Anglo-Saxon *cemeteries. In addition to topographical names concerned with water and drainage, two other important generics in the earliest recorded names of this category are *dūn* 'a hill, an expanse of open hill-country' and *feld* 'open country'. These gave names like Ashdown, *Breedon and Farndon, Austerfield, Hatfield and Lichfield.

One of the commonest of all topographical generics in place-names in the modern landscape is Old English *lēah*. This had a range of meanings depending on date and location: it could signify 'a *wood, woodland', 'a woodland glade', 'a rough clearing in a wood', 'a cultivated or developed glade or woodland clearing (especially one used for pasture or arable)'. Later it came to mean 'a piece of open land, a meadow'. It has given a host of names such as Bromley (*brōm* 'broom'), Oakley (*āc* 'oak'), Oteley (*āte* 'oats'), Ryley (*ryge* 'rye'), Cowley (*cū* 'cow'), Shipley (*scēap* 'sheep'), Bradley (*brād* 'broad'), Brindley (*brende* 'burnt, cleared by burning'). It has been convincingly argued that *lēah* became the regular term for a settlement in a *woodland environment as opposed to *tūn* for one in open country. The word *lēah* appears not to belong as a name-forming generic to the earliest stratum of Anglo-Saxon toponyms. It became more important as a name-forming category after *c.*730.

B. Cox, 'The Place-Names of the Earliest English Records', *Journal of the English Place-Name Society* 8 (1976), 12–66; M. Gelling, 'Some Notes on Warwickshire Place-Names', *Transactions of the Birmingham and Warwickshire Archaeological Society* 85 (1974), 59–79; idem, 'Introduction', in *The Place-Names of Berkshire* III (Cambridge, 1976).

B. COX

TOWNS, defined as concentrations of people engaged in craft, *trade and industry, and supported by the agricultural labour of others, require forms of social organization and economic activity which were unknown to the earliest Anglo-Saxons. Continuity of *urban life* from Roman Britain is therefore impossible, though a case can be made for some continuity of *life in towns*, in the sense that the walled areas may have been used as power-centres both by British successor rulers and by the English immigrants who replaced them. *Canterbury, where over fifty early Anglo-Saxon sunken buildings have been found within the Roman walls, may never have been wholly depopulated. But in general *Roman remains seem not to have been re-occupied until the seventh century, and then usually as *monastic sites: it is above all the later urbanisation of minsters which explains why so many Roman towns are again towns today. Nonetheless, the creation of stable pre-urban foci in this period, above all ecclesiastical ones, had a major impact on the location and character of urban growth during later centuries.

In the later seventh century trading emporia began to develop along the east and south coasts of England, a response to commercial growth in north-western Europe. By *c.*700 each of the four dominant kingdoms had a major port or *wic*: *London (*Lundenwic*) for *Mercia, *Southampton (*Hamwic*) for *Wessex, *Ipswich for *East Anglia and *York (*Eoforwic*) for *Northumbria. Excavations, principally at Southampton and London, have revealed boundaries, planned streets, settlement of some density, and evidence both for imported goods and for craft production. Whether these major *wics* were under tight royal control, whether their populations were permanent or seasonal, and whether they were channels for bulk trade or merely for the exchange of prestige goods, are controversial. It does, however, seem very likely that the interest of Frankish and Frisian merchants in English bulk exports, notably wool and cloth, had a major impact on their development, and that prestige goods such as *pottery and *glass

entered England through them. That the reverberations of this trade extended far inland is suggested by the spread of the *sceatta* *coinage over lowland England between the late seventh and mid eighth centuries.

*Viking attacks were the immediate cause of the decline and (in most cases) abandonment of the *wics* in the mid-ninth century, but the re-formation of London, York and Southampton on nearby sites after only brief intervals is one illustration of an economic and political growth capable of supporting towns of a new kind, more firmly rooted in their localities. From the late eighth century onwards there is evidence for defended proto-towns in Mercia such as *Hereford, *Tamworth and *Winchcombe, their appearance perhaps coinciding with the reservation of fortress-work as a public burden in royal *charters (see *forts and fortifications, *trinoda necessitas*). By the late ninth century ambitious planned towns were being laid out in Wessex and its dependencies, some within existing Roman walls (such as *Winchester, *London and Chichester), others with new ramparts (such as *Cricklade, *Oxford and *Wareham). Archaeology demonstrates a striking consistency in the planning and engineering of the timber-laced ramparts and the rammed gravel streets. The *Burghal Hidage shows that these places, together with smaller and non-urban fortresses, were maintained by hidage-based obligations laid on the surrounding territories.

The new southern English boroughs contained *mints and *markets, bases for major rural landlords, and refuges in times of danger; many of them assumed the role of shire towns as *shires emerged during the ninth and tenth centuries. But a town is something more than a defensive or administrative centre, and could not be created by royal command alone: the urbanisation even of the major Burghal Hidage sites was a lengthy process. Canterbury, where a charter of 868 (S 1204) mentions a local bye-law that at least two feet should be left between properties as eave-drip, may have been exceptionally precocious. Many excavations suggest a low density of settlement through the period *c.*900–60, the large, open properties between the streets resembling farmsteads more than town houses. In the mid to late tenth century the Danish areas of the east and north-east saw a rapid intensification of urban activity, most impressively revealed by the excavations at *York, which spread westwards and southwards during the next hundred years. Frontages were built up and equipped with cellar-pits, small churches multiplied, specialised craft and marketing zones

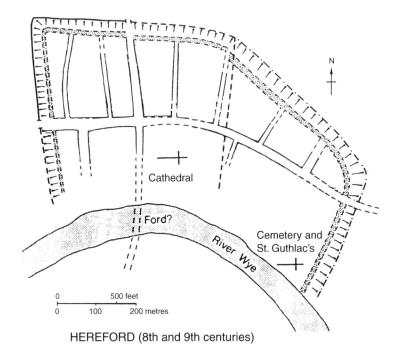

HEREFORD (8th and 9th centuries)

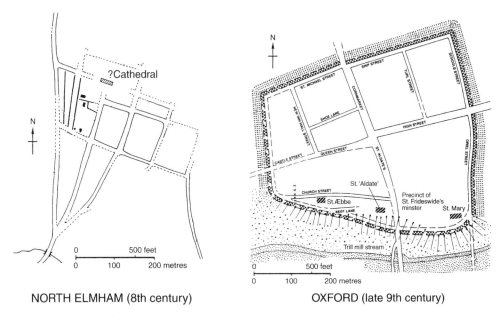

NORTH ELMHAM (8th century)

OXFORD (late 9th century)

Fig. 19 Planned towns, eighth to late ninth centuries.

developed, and populations must have risen steeply towards their Domesday levels. The importance of towns in English life grew correspondingly after *c.*980; leading citizen families (often including *moneyers) emerged, and political activity became more town-based.

During the same period a much larger number of hierarchically important centres, mainly minsters and royal vills, become archaeologically and topographically visible as nuclei for lay settlement. Excavation, where it has occurred on an adequate scale (as at *Northampton, *Steyning and *North Elmham), shows tenth- and eleventh-century homesteads and sunken-floored buildings clustered around and eventually within the pre-urban enclave. Such agglomerations, re-planned with streets and house-plots in the late eleventh to thirteenth centuries, underlie the complex topography of innumerable English small towns.

The Cambridge Urban History of Britain: I. the Middle Ages, ed. D. M. Palliser (Cambridge, forthcoming); *The Rebirth of Towns in the West*, ed. R. Hodges and B. Hobley (London, 1988); M. Biddle, 'Towns', in Wilson, *Archaeology*, pp. 99–150; R. Hodges, *The Anglo-Saxon Achievement* (London, 1989), ch. 4; P. Rahtz, 'The Archaeology of West Mercian Towns', in Dornier, *MS*, pp. 107–29; Hill and Rumble, *Defence of Wessex*; Haslam, *Towns*; G. Astill, 'Towns and Town Hierarchies in Saxon England', *Oxford Journal of Archaeology* 10 (1991), 95–117; C. Dyer, 'Recent Developments in Early Medieval Urban History and Archaeology in England', *Urban Historical Geography*, ed. D. Denecke and G. Shaw (Cambridge, 1988), pp. 69–80.

JOHN BLAIR

TRADE and exchange are mechanisms by which wealth can be transferred. Trade is usually discussed in two, by no means mutually exclusive, ways. It can be seen as an independent economic transaction by which demand is satisfied and shortages replenished, for which a charge (or profit) is made by the middleman – a 'modern' economic interpretation. Trade can also be regarded as one element of a more complicated set of interactions which could include ideas and information as well as commodities. In this, anthropologically derived, reading, the economic character of trading is subsumed within the wider spectrum of social relationships, and the nature and frequency of exchange is determined by the particular structure of society.

Most evidence for Anglo-Saxon trading comes from a high social level. The documentary references are qualitative and are mainly concerned with the royal supervision of foreign merchants, and the location and maintenance of peaceful trading. From the late seventh century, *laws are concerned with witnessing of transactions, often by a king's representative, and the exaction of tolls. By the tenth century more strenuous, and only partially successful, attempts were made to control commerce by restricting it to towns and by an efficient management of the *coinage.

The archaeological evidence is dominated by the imported products, mainly *pottery, metalwork and stone, which can be sourced and allow some quantification; thus periods of intense (eighth century) and intermittent (tenth century) long-distance trading can be crudely identified. Distribution of materials (albeit in secondary contexts) and coins can also be used to indicate exchange mechanisms.

Because of its predominantly high-status character, it is assumed that Anglo-Saxon exchange practices reflected the increasing complexity of the political structure, particularly the development of kingship and the church. A major issue is how and when exchange systems changed: an evolutionary sequence whereby one exchange mechanism replaced another, ending in a *market system, is too simplistic, and different trading methods probably existed concurrently. The small-scale nature of the power structures between *c.*500 and 700–750 could imply that exchange was an integral part of the social organization, and that it took the form of gift- or reciprocal-exchange of prestige goods which underpinned the leaders' status. Such goods were obtained from traders at periodic beach markets in exchange for, perhaps, metals, *slaves or *agricultural products such as wool – the staple English exports.

Kings in the eighth century attempted to accumulate wealth by taking control of and increasing the trade in exotic goods (which had gone on for at least 200 years): this was to be the function of the newly constructed emporia (see *towns). The distribution of material produced at these sites, such as the silver *sceatta* *coins and pottery made at *Ipswich, shows that goods were brought in from the countryside, probably in the form of tribute. A more aggressive form of kingship seems to be indicated, based not only on prestige goods, but also on the granting of land from which dues were extracted – and converted into portable coin. Coin distributions show that royal control of trade was incomplete. Coins occur on the coast away from emporia; and their occurrence at minster sites and hill forts show that exchange took place inside kingdoms, on a scale which may not have been surpassed until the later tenth and eleventh centuries.

The shift from prestige goods to the control of land as an expression of status was complete with the demise of the emporia in the ninth century. Tribute served to fuel aristocratic consumption which was then met by trading based in administrative and religious centres, and perhaps the military burhs. Exchange was clearly intended to take place within a well-regulated, royally controlled environment with a royal coinage – that is a market town; but it is unclear for whom such sites were functioning, and indeed how developed they were, in the ninth and most of the tenth centuries. Many towns (with the exception of those in the north and north midlands which were engaged in industrial production) may have predominantly catered for aristocratic needs, and it was not until the currency had fully penetrated the countryside in the later tenth century that the majority of the population perceived a need for urban markets.

P. Andrews, ed., *The Coins and Pottery from Hamwic* (Southampton, 1988); P. Grierson, 'Commerce in the Dark Ages: a Critique of the Evidence', *TRHS* 9 (1959), 123–40; P. Grierson and M. Blackburn, *Medieval European Coinage I: the Early Middle Ages (5th–10th Centuries)* (Cambridge 1986); J. Hines, 'North-Sea Trade and the Proto-Urban Sequence', *Archaeologica Polona* 32 (1994), 7–26; R. Hodges, *Dark Age Economics. The Origins of Towns and Trade AD 600–1000* (London, 1982); J. Huggett, 'Imported Grave Goods and the early Anglo-Saxon Economy', *MArch* 32 (1988), 63–96; P. H. Sawyer, 'Kings and Merchants', in *Early Medieval Kingship*, ed. P. H. Sawyer and I. N. Wood (Leeds, 1977), pp. 139–58; idem, 'The Wealth of England in the Eleventh Century', *TRHS* 9 (1965), 145–65.

GRENVILLE ASTILL

TRANSPORT AND COMMUNICATION. England's seas and rivers shaped the initial patterns of *settlement and much of the subsequent economic and political history of the Anglo-Saxon Age. The first settlers' *ships were propelled by oars, so naturally they sought the nearest landfall: *East Anglia, *Kent, and the south coast as far as the Isle of Wight, all within a hundred miles of the Continent. This coastline offered navigable rivers that penetrated well inland, notably the Thames, the rivers of the Wash and, a little later, those of the Humber estuary. By the end of the fifth century much of East Anglia, the upper Thames valley, and river valleys near the Isle of Wight were settled, even though the Romano-British inhabitants may have thrown up dykes in the Cambridge area to impede the Anglo-Saxon advance. (*Offa imitated this more successfully in his great dyke that even today is close to much of the English-Welsh border: see *Offa's Dyke.) Distance and the treacherous seas round *Cornwall meant that the Severn and the surrounding areas did not see Anglo-Saxon settlement until the sixth century – and that probably by land routes. But Gallic travellers, with superior sail technology, still sailed up the west coast in the seventh century, bringing distinctive *pottery and providing the Celtic-speaking realms with an intellectual lifeline to the Mediterranean and beyond. In the seventh century eastern and southern shorelines suitable for beaching boats became the sites for *emporia* or trading settlements: *London (*Lundenwic*), at the upper tidal reach of the Thames, Hamwic (later *Southampton) on the river Itchen, *Ipswich on the Essex coast, and *York (*Eoforwicceaster*), another riverine location. At the end of the eighth century Scandinavian raiders, utilizing the advantage of sail, initiated the depredations that doomed these unprotected *wics*. In their place near the end of the ninth century *Alfred, king of *Wessex, founded a network of defended settlements or *burhs*, supplemented at some point by a system of beacons. The *burhs* directed trade inland. Rivers nevertheless retained their importance: stone from Barnack, Taynton, Box and Quarr for building churches must have been transported at least some distance by water (see *mining and quarrying), and the accessibility to Scandinavian invaders of interior settlements such as *Repton encouraged the maintenance and development of *bridges as a means of controlling river traffic (both for defensive purposes as well as for tolls) from the time of King Offa onwards (see *canals). Ferries were also used for river crossings, as *Domesday Book attests. Water provided the passage for Duke William to bring the Anglo-Saxon era to a close in a daring late-season crossing from *Normandy to Pevensey in 1066.

Anglo-Saxon England was never a trackless waste and many people of all backgrounds travelled both locally and abroad throughout the period (cf. *pilgrimage). Shanks's pony was the main mode of transportation. The eleventh-century OE illustrated *Hexateuch* (BL, Cotton Claudius B. iv) shows men at harvest carrying sacks of corn over their shoulders; some hold the bags in position with cleft poles. The *Bayeux Tapestry depicts men dragging a four-wheeled wagon bearing a wine keg. Sleds, a primitive transportation device that survived in Britain until the nineteenth century, may have been used for heavy loads, though they are unattested in Anglo-Saxon sources. Extant bone slides show that ice-skates were used.

Kings and nobles constantly travelled round their estates, living off their lands. Throughout the period the elite (and also the Scandinavian invaders) used horses. Tents, presumably carried on sumpter horses or carts, were erected when they were benighted: several *wills contain bequests of tents and some Domesday Book entries record the obligation to provide the king with pack horses. Horses were also used for the aristocratic occupations of falconry and war, both mentioned in the Old English *Battle of Maldon. (Unlike the Normans, the Anglo-Saxons probably did not use horses as cavalry, however.) As for a horse's accoutrements, Old English had words for a bit, bridle, saddle, pommel, saddle-bag, stirrup and spur: an eleventh-century prick-spur contemporary with its illustration in the *Hexateuch* has been found in Oxfordshire.

Horses may have become more common in the late Anglo-Saxon period: one Bayeux Tapestry scene portrays a horse dragging a harrow. The words 'ass' and 'mule' have Old English antecedents: the former appears in place-names and one or the other is depicted in manuscript illuminations as a pack animal. The main beast of burden was, however, the ox. The typical Domesday plough was drawn by a team of eight oxen.

The Old English words *cræt* and *wægn* attest to the importance of wheeled transport. The *Hexateuch* depicts (67r) a two-wheeled cart drawn by two yoked pairs of oxen. Such vehicles were particularly important in the transportation of salt from Droitwich and in carrying lead from mines in Derbyshire. Mention of an elderly bishop brought on a cart to Penenden Heath for a consultation with William the Conqueror suggests that luxury vehicles may also have existed.

The transportation system was a valuable source of royal, ecclesiastical and aristocratic revenue, with renders payable on fish and tolls levied on wagon- and pack-loads (see also *roads, *Watling Street).

R. H. C. Davis, *The Medieval Warhorse: Origin, Development and Redevelopment* (London and New York, 1989); D. Hill, *An Atlas of Anglo-Saxon England* (Oxford, 1981), esp. Maps 15, 135, 145–8, 150–66, 198–200; A. C. Leighton, *Transport and Communication in Early Medieval Europe AD 500–1100* (Newton Abbot, 1972); J. le Patourel, 'The Reports of the Trial on Penenden Heath', in *Studies in Medieval History presented to Frederick Maurice Powicke*, ed. R. W. Hunt, W. A. Pantin and R. W. Southern (Oxford, 1948), pp. 15–26; G. H. Martin, 'Eleventh-Century Communications', in *Domesday Book: Studies*, ed. A. Williams and R.W.H. Erskine (London, 1987), pp. 61–4; T. H. Ohlgren, *Insular and Anglo-Saxon Illuminated Manuscripts: an Iconographic*

Catalogue, c. AD 625 to 1100 (New York and London, 1986); *The Rebirth of Towns in the West AD 700–1050*, ed. R. Hodges and B. Hobley, CBA Research Report 68 (London, 1988); C. Thomas, ' "Gallici Nautae de Galliarum Provinciis" – a Sixth/Seventh Century Trade with Gaul, Reconsidered', *MArch* 34 (1990), 1–26.

DAVID A. E. PELTERET

'TREMULOUS HAND' is the name given by modern palaeographers to an early thirteenth-century scribe at *Worcester who annotated some twenty surviving Anglo-Saxon manuscripts, providing some 50,000 *glosses – usually in Latin, occasionally in Middle English – to Old English words. He also copied a manuscript of *Ælfric's *Grammar and Glossary* (now Worcester, Cathedral Library, F.174). It is possible that his scholarly activity in Old English was in some way connected with the canonization of St *Wulfstan II of Worcester in 1203; in any case his glossing, and his apparent progress in learning Old English, constitute precious testimony to the ways in which Old English could still be understood in the early thirteenth century. Whereas it used to be believed that the trembling nature of his script was due to extreme old age, there are grounds for thinking that it may have been due to a congenital defect, and hence have no implications for his age at the time he was learning to read Old English.

C. Franzen, *The Tremulous Hand of Worcester. A Study of Old English in the Thirteenth Century* (Oxford, 1991).

MICHAEL LAPIDGE

THE TRIBAL HIDAGE is a list, with assessments in *hides, of thirty-four kingdoms and tribal territories south of the Humber. The opening entry for the 30,000 hides of 'first *Mercia' (the Mercian heartland in the Trent valley) is followed by five substantial peoples in the West Midlands, the Peak District and Lincolnshire. Entries 7 to 29, the core of the list, are a miscellany of peoples with assessments ranging between 7,000 and 300 hides, concentrated heavily in the East Midlands and often small and obscure. The last five entries cover major kingdoms: *East Anglia, *Essex, *Kent, Surrey, *Wessex. The stated total is slightly less than the actual total of 244,100 hides.

The text survives in an eleventh-century manuscript, much later than the material which it contains; it has no heading or other explanation, and was evidently transcribed for its topographical and antiquarian interest. Given the tendency to call it a 'tribute list', the many attempts to give it a precise date and context, and the elaborate models of political hegemony which have been built upon it, these facts are important. Its context

Elmedsaetna
Heath
feld
land
PECSAETNA
LINDES
FARONA
MYRCENES (Bilmiga)
LANDES
WOCEN
SAETNA
?Widerigga North gyrwa
(Wigesta)
South gyrwa
Sweordora
West Wixna / East Wixna
(Spalda)
EAST
ENGLE
Arosaetna
?WESTERNA
HEREFINNA
(West East)
HWINCA
(Willa)
Gifla
Hicca
?Faerpinga
CHILTERN
SAETNA
EAST
SAXENA
(UNECUNG-GA)
(NOXGAGA)
?HENDRICA (OHTGAGA)
CANTWARENA
WEST SEXENA
SUTH SEXENA
Wihtgara

(Possible identification)
?Probable identification
High ground tinted

0   100 miles

Map 8 The Tribal Hidage.

must be greater Mercia at some date between the mid-seventh and late ninth centuries, but we do not know what it was for, nor even whether it is all of one date. In view of the huge range in size between the peoples and hidages listed, a composite origin must be a serious possibility. The cluster of tiny *Middle Anglian peoples, such as the North and South *Gyrwe*, the *Spalda*, the *Gifla* and the *Færpingas*, seems different in kind from the rest, and records an altogether lower level of social organization. It could be that aggregate hidages for the big kingdoms, and data for a few smaller peoples which happened to be available, have been grafted onto a genuine Middle Anglian survey or tribute list by a topographically-minded scholar in the tenth or eleventh century.

If the Hidage cannot be used to chart Mercia's political fortunes, it remains crucially important evidence for an early layer in state formation. The sub-stratum of small tribal groups, here recorded mainly for Middle Anglia, illustrates a wider pattern being revealed by local studies: similar entities, often with clan names in *-ingas* and often perpetuated as hundreds or mother-parishes, underlie the territorial geography of much of England. At least some of the material in the Tribal Hidage must date from a time when these building-blocks of larger kingdoms, which exerted a powerful if now obscure influence on the emerg-

ence of English institutions, had a social and political life of their own.

W. Davies and H. Vierck, 'The Contexts of the Tribal Hidage: Social Aggregates and Settlement Patterns', *Frühmittelalterliche Studien* 8 (1974), 223–93; Bassett, *Origins*; Yorke, *Kings and Kingdoms*, pp. 9–15; M. Gelling, *The West Midlands in the Early Middle Ages* (Leicester, 1992), pp. 79–85; S. Keynes, 'England 700–900', *New Cambridge Medieval History* II, ed. R. McKitterick (Cambridge, 1995), pp. 18–42, at 21–5.

JOHN BLAIR

TRINODA NECESSITAS. The military charges of bridge-work (*brycggeweorc*), fortress-work (*burhbot*) and service upon military expeditions (*fyrdfæreld*) incumbent upon *bookland are often referred to as the *trinoda necessitas*, 'the threeway necessity'. This phrase, however, occurs only in a single charter, a forged landbook of the late seventh-century West Saxon king *Cædwalla concocted in the tenth century (S 230). Some historians, consequently, have preferred to call these obligations the 'common burdens'. From the late ninth century until the Norman Conquest the military defence of England rested on the three common burdens. All who held land by royal *charter were duty-bound to answer the king's summons to war, whether by land or by sea, along with a specified number of warriors determined by the amount of tax assessed against their landed property (see *taxation). Local landowners were also responsible for providing labourers for the maintenance and repair of borough defences and *bridges.

The common burdens apparently originated in Mercia in the mid eighth century during the reign of King *Æthelbald (d. 757) in response to the proliferation of bookland and the immunities associated with that tenure. Holders of *folkland, possibly, and of royal loanland (*lænland*), more probably, had been expected to render military services to the king, though so little definite is known about folkland that it is impossible to be certain of the matter. The introduction of a tenure, bookland, that permanently alienated land from the royal fisc threatened to deprive kings of the wherewithal needed to retain and reward military followers (as *Bede observed in the famous letter he wrote to *Ecgberht, bishop of *York). The 'common burdens' was the solution that the Mercian kings devised. King *Offa (d. 796) of *Mercia extended the common burdens to the lands of Kentish churches in 792, as a defence measure 'against pagan seamen'. By the mid-ninth century West Saxon kings were also requiring bridge- and fortress-work and host duty from lands under their control. The military reorganization of *Wessex undertaken by King *Alfred (d. 899) in the 880s and 890s made the three military obligations more burdensome, as Alfred drew upon them to establish a network of fortifications throughout his realm (see *Burghal Hidage). The obligations and the penalties for failing to fulfil them were further regularized in *laws issued by Alfred's successors. By the reign of *Æthelred II 'the Unready' (d. 1016), the 'common burdens' had been extended to the building and manning of fleets as well as to the recruitment of armies.

W. H. Stevenson, 'Trinoda Necessitas', EHR 29 (1914), 689–703; E. John, Land Tenure in Early England (Leicester, 1960), pp. 64–79; C. W. Hollister, Anglo-Saxon Military Institutions on the Eve of the Norman Conquest (Oxford, 1962); N. Brooks, 'The Development of Military Obligations in Eighth- and Ninth-Century England', in England Before the Conquest, ed. P. Clemoes and K. Hughes (Cambridge, 1971), pp. 69–84; G. Dempsey, 'Legal Terminology in Anglo-Saxon England: The Trinoda Necessitas Charter', Speculum 57 (1982), 843–49; R. Abels, Lordship and Military Obligation in Anglo-Saxon England (Berkeley, CA, 1988).

RICHARD ABELS

TROPER: see Chant; Liturgical Books; Wulfstan Cantor

TURNER, SHARON (1768–1847) was a historian whose most enduring work is the four-volume The History of the Anglo-Saxons, published from 1799 to 1805. He had become interested in Anglo-Saxon and Norse materials in his youth, and his review of the pre-Conquest language and its literature in his fourth volume which drew heavily on the manuscripts of the *Cotton collection did much to foster interest in the subject in the early nineteenth century. He has the distinction of being the first to recognise and publish part of *Beowulf.

D. G. Calder, 'Histories and Surveys of Old English Literature; a Chronological Review', ASE 10 (1982), 201–44, esp. 205–6; Anglo-Saxon Scholarship: The First Three Centuries, ed. C. T. Berkhout and M. McC. Gatch (Boston, 1982).

DONALD SCRAGG

U

UTRECHT PSALTER. The Carolingian Utrecht Psalter (Utrecht, University Library, 32), was made at Hautvillers near Rheims *c.*830. It is a Gallican Psalter, written in Rustic capitals. Each psalm is literally illustrated by a bistre line drawing. It was in England by *c.*1000, and the importance of its images for Anglo-Saxon artists in the eleventh century is hard to over-estimate: in psalters, such as the *Harley Psalter and the Paris Psalter, Anglo-Saxons used Utrecht's illustrations of specific verses; in other works artists applied Utrecht's motifs in different contexts. Moreover, the style of Utrecht Psalter and other manuscripts from Rheims had great appeal for Anglo-Saxon artists and patrons.

Utrecht Psalter, ed. with commentary by K. van der Horst and J. H. A. Engelbregt (Graz, 1982–4); K. van der Horst, W. Noel and W. Wustefeld, ed., *The Utrecht Psalter in Medieval Art* ('t-Goy, 1996).

WILLIAM NOEL

V

VAINGLORY is an 84-line poem from the *Exeter Book. An example of OE *wisdom literature, it draws the core of its matter from the teachings of the Church Fathers on the sins of pride and vainglory. The poet vividly portrays the contrasting mental and spiritual states of the proud and the humble, tracing the former's evil back to Lucifer's haughty refusal to serve God. The poem's occasionally difficult syntax has been seen by some critics as part of the poet's design for a special degree of verbal density, capable of encompassing multiple and contrasting meanings simultaneously. It also contains an unusually high percentage of unique poetic compounds.

ASPR iii. 147–9; B. F. Huppé, *The Web of Words* (Albany, NY, 1970); C. A. Regan, 'Patristic Psychology in the Old English *Vainglory*', *Traditio* 26 (1970), 324–35; *The Exeter Anthology of Old English Poetry*, ed. B. J. Muir (Exeter, 1994).

ROBERT DINAPOLI

VERCELLI BOOK (Vercelli, Biblioteca capitolare CXVII), one of the oldest of the four so-called Poetic Codices, is an anthology of religious prose and verse in Old English, dated palaeographically in the middle of the second half of the tenth century. It is written throughout by a single scribe who copied entirely mechanically and who shows no understanding of such brief quotations in Latin as appear. No satisfactory principle of arrangement has been adduced for the items, twenty-three of which are in prose (usually called *homilies, although some have little homiletic content) and six of which are verse (including *Andreas, The *Dream of the Rood and two with *Cynewulf's signature, The Fates of the Apostles and *Elene*. The verse items appear in three groups randomly amongst the prose. *Codicological evidence suggests that the scribe assembled the material piecemeal, perhaps over an extended period of time, and drew upon a number of different copy-texts. The appearance in some later manuscripts of independent copies of more than one item from different sections of the codex suggests, however, that the same range of copy-texts was available to other scribes, and it seems probable that the Vercelli scribe drew principally on the resources of a single *library. Linguistic evidence points to the scribe having been trained in the south-east, and the closest textual links of items in the book are with manuscripts associated with *Canterbury and *Rochester.

We have no knowledge of the book's earliest provenance, but eleventh-century pen-trials suggest that it remained in England long enough to be used as a copy-text, while a Latin psalter quotation in a north Italian form of the early twelfth century shows that it had reached Italy by c.1100. It was almost certainly in Vercelli, an important stopping place on the *pilgrim route to *Rome, throughout the later Middle Ages, although the inscription on the early nineteenth-century spine, *Homiliarum liber ignoti idiomatis, saeculo X*, shows that its owners had no understanding of the language in which it was written. Modern scholars became aware of the existence of the book only in the early nineteenth century, when a German jurist, Friedrich Blume, recognized and transcribed part of the text. A full description and transcription (now London, Lincoln's Inn Library, Misc. 225, fol. 43, and 312) was made in 1834 by a young German scholar, C. Maier, and this formed the basis for early editions of the poetry. Some of the prose remained unpublished until 1981.

K. Sisam, 'Marginalia in the Vercelli Book', in his *Studies in the History of Old English Literature* (Oxford, 1953), pp. 109–18; M. Halsall, 'Vercelli and the *Vercelli Book*', *PMLA* 84 (1969), 1545–50; D. G. Scragg, 'The Compilation of the Vercelli Book', *ASE* 2 (1973), 189–207; *The Vercelli Book*, ed. C. Sisam, EEMF 19 (Copenhagen, 1976); *The Vercelli Homilies and Related Texts*, ed. D. G. Scragg, EETS 300 (Oxford, 1992).

DONALD SCRAGG

VERNER'S LAW is so-called after the philologist Karl Verner (1846–96), who accounted for some apparently anomalous developments in the *sound-change known as *Grimm's Law. Verner noticed that certain voiceless fricative consonant-sounds in Proto-Germanic were realized as voiced in a voiced environment (e.g. between vowels), and when the stress was not on the immediately preceding syllable. A subsequent stress-shift meant that this environment was subsequently obscured. An OE example illustrating the process is *fæder*, with medial *d* (from earlier ð), as opposed to medial θ; cf. Proto-Indo-European **pǝtēr*.) Verner's Law has morphological implications in Old English; medial *-r-* in *curon* 'chose' (plural) is derived from earlier *z*: cf. infinitive *cēosan* 'choose'. C. L. Barber, *The English Language* (Cambridge, 1993).

JEREMY J. SMITH

VERSIFICATION: *see* Metre, Latin; Metre, OE

VESPASIAN PSALTER (BL, Cotton Vespasian A.i) is thought to have been made at St Augustine's, *Canterbury, around 720–30. Its text is the Romanum and initials mark liturgical divisions. Its script is a romanising uncial and its decoration, which includes a miniature of King David and his musicians set beneath an arcade, conflates a naturalistic, painterly figure style and exotic foliate ornament influenced by Italo-Byzantine models with Germanic and Celtic ornament. It introduces the earliest historiated (story-telling) initials, which were to be so influential in western medieval art, featuring episodes from the life of David, who is a 'type' of Christ. It is the earliest member of the 'Tiberius' group of manuscripts. In the midninth century an interlinear OE gloss was added – the earliest extant biblical translation into English. Described by Thomas of Elmham, *c.*1414–18, as kept on St Augustine's high altar, it passed from Sir William Cecil to Matthew *Parker and Sir Robert *Cotton, thence to the British Museum in 1753.

CLA ii. 193; Alexander, *Insular MSS*, no. 29; D. H. Wright, *The Vespasian Psalter*, EEMF 14 (Copenhagen, 1967).

MICHELLE P. BROWN

VIKINGS. A term of convenience applied indiscriminately by modern scholarship to the inhabitants of the Scandinavian countries (Denmark, Sweden, and Norway), before and after they achieved separate or more distinctive identities, and to the men, women and children of Scandinavian extraction who at various times left their homelands in search of a better or more exciting life overseas (whether the Baltic, the North Sea, or the Atlantic Ocean). The term is supposed by some to have originated as a name for those who came from the shores of the Oslo Fjord, known as the Viken, and by others, more generally, as a term denoting 'men of the fjords' (*vel sim.*). Among the English it was soon taken into the general vocabulary used for describing the pirates with whom they were most painfully

familiar. The pirates in question were known in the late ninth century as 'northmen', 'Danes' (or 'Danish men'), 'heathens', or 'Vikings'; and while the Alfredian chroniclers display a preference for 'Danes', reflecting the presumed origin, if not necessarily the more immediate provenance, of the forces which were causing so much disruption, it is striking that *Asser fastened on 'pagans' as the term which for his purposes best conveyed his own conception of their distinctive identity. A West Saxon chronicler describing a force which assembled in East Anglia, in 917, made a distinction between 'the army of the district' (*landhere*) and 'the Vikings whom they had enticed to their assistance' (*ASC*, MS. A), as if 'Vikings' was used in his parlance for a band of hired killers. In the terminology of later chroniclers, a 'naval force' sacked *Southampton in 980, and three ships 'of Vikings' ravaged Dorset in 982; but from the perspective of the chronicler responsible for the 'main' account of *Æthelred's reign, the invaders of this later period were again most clearly identified as 'Danes'. In the mind of an English poet, 'Vikings' remained the preferred term for those who confronted Ealdorman Byrhtnoth at the battle of Maldon in 991.

The Vikings who attacked England in the 'First Viking Age' (*c.*780–900) and in the 'Second Viking Age' (*c.*980–1066) became the victims of a hostile press; but while we may seek to explain their unfriendly behaviour, there is no good reason to excuse them for it. It would indeed be a shame to reduce such men to 'little more than groups of long-haired tourists who occasionally roughed up the natives' (Wallace-Hadrill), or to parties of merchant-adventurers who simply indulged from time to time in rather sharp trading practices. The Vikings were probably uncouth, certainly unpleasant, and decidedly unwelcome. Contemporary commentators, including *Alcuin, *Alfred and *Wulfstan, regarded them as the agents or instruments of divine punishment for the sins of the English people; and their views were shared by an English priest upon whom it was impressed, in a *vision, that only if the people atoned for their sins would they escape wholesale devastation (*Annals of Saint-Bertin*, s.a. 839). Ironically, the Vikings who attacked the kingdoms of *East Anglia, *Mercia, *Northumbria and *Wessex in the ninth century are judged by modern historians to have served as the common enemy which helped to bind the English together, while those who invaded the unified kingdom of England in the late tenth and early eleventh centuries constituted a force which broke the English apart. And while it is the case that *Cnut (1016–35), son of *Swein Forkbeard, earned his place among the most distinguished of the kings of the English, the same could not be said of his successors, *Harold Harefoot (1037–40) and *Harthacnut (1040–2).

The reputation earned by the Vikings in the British Isles, and on the Continent, should not be extended to those of their number who settled in eastern and northern England, and who played a significant part in shaping the character of the region which came to be known as the *Danelaw. Nor, of course, should it be allowed to affect our judgement of all those people who remained in Scandinavia, or who sought pastures new across the Atlantic. These men and women may have lacked (at least for the time being) some of the accoutrements or trappings of a Christian civilization, but they displayed evidence in abundance of their own resourcefulness, material culture, technological skill, powers of thought and expression, and forms of social, economic and political organisation.

The Vikings, ed. R. T. Farrell (Chichester, 1982); *Medieval Scandinavia: an Encyclopedia*, ed. P. Pulsiano (New York, 1993); *Cultural Atlas of the Viking World*, ed. J. Graham-Campbell (Abingdon, 1994); *The Oxford Illustrated History of the Vikings*, ed. P. Sawyer (Oxford, 1997); C. E. Fell, 'Modern English *Viking*', *Leeds Studies in English*, new ser. 18 (1987), pp. 111–22; L. Abrams, 'Eleventh-Century Missions and the Early Stages of Ecclesiastical Organisation in Scandinavia', *ANS* 17 (1995), 21–40.

SIMON KEYNES

VILLAGES: *see* Settlement Patterns; Towns

VIRGIN, CULT OF. Devotion to the mother of God, although not a feature of the Bible, was established as an essential feature of Christianity by the fourth century and, by the time Christianity was introduced in England, the Virgin was a universal saint of the church. Her cult seems to have reached England largely from *Rome: early dedications to Mary are in imitation of Roman dedications; the four principal feasts of Mary, the Purification, Annunciation, Assumption and Nativity, introduced gradually in the course of the seventh and eighth centuries, came from Rome; Mediterranean images provided models for English ones; and liturgical texts were imported from Italy. The cult flourished particularly in two periods: from the late seventh to the early ninth centuries and again in the Benedictine Reform period. Evidence for the early period comes especially from Anglian areas, both *Northumbria

and *Mercia: here Marian prayers were composed; *sculptures, most notably the *Breedon Virgin and the Wirksworth slab, survive; Marian texts, including *Apocrypha dealing with her nativity and death, circulated (*Bede challenged both the authenticity and the chronology of one apocryphal legend on Mary's death, but without taking a definite stance on the subject) and were composed (Bede composed the first western homily for the feast of the Purification); and the only major poem to deal in detail with the Virgin, the *Advent Lyrics* or *Christ I*, from the *Exeter Book, may also date from this period. Its view of Mary is largely that of the church fathers and the liturgy.

The second flowering of Marian devotion is associated with the Benedictine Reform movement: almost all the reformed houses were dedicated, or even rededicated, to the Virgin, monastic devotions testify to her increased importance and the cult seems to be associated with an aspiration towards a unified and uniform celibate movement under the patronage of the Virgin. Manuscript illuminations, most notably the *Benedictional of St *Æthelwold, and *ivories are innovative in their Marian images, with a new emphasis on the royalty of the Virgin. Eleventh-century prayers to Mary from *Winchester are of a devotionally very advanced nature. In the late Anglo-Saxon period, *c*.1030, as a result of eastern influence, the feasts of the Conception of Mary and her Presentation in the Temple, not celebrated anywhere else in western Europe at this date, were introduced in Winchester and spread from there to *Canterbury and *Exeter. Texts for an Office of the Virgin, among the earliest extant, are found, first as a private devotion, then as a communal one, in English manuscripts from the same period, and from the very end of the Anglo-Saxon period we have a text for a Saturday Office of Mary: these texts seem to have been composed in England, almost certainly in Winchester and Canterbury. Latin homiliaries from England contain a wide range of Marian texts, and vernacular homilies for all the major Marian feasts, both anonymous and by *Ælfric, outnumber homilies for any other saint: the most important are in the *Blickling Homilies*, the *Vercelli Book and Ælfric's two series of *Catholic Homilies*. Ælfric, following Carolingian sources, takes issue with the apocryphal narratives concerning Mary's nativity and death, but even in Winchester, the centre of the reform movement, these texts seem to have been eagerly accepted. There is some evidence to suggest that the importance of the cult waned in the second generation of the reform,

461

becoming more confined to Winchester and related houses as the forces of localism reasserted themselves throughout the country at large.

M. Clayton, *The Cult of the Virgin Mary in Anglo-Saxon England*, CSASE 2 (Cambridge, 1990); idem, 'Centralism and Uniformity versus Localism and Diversity: the Virgin and Native Saints in the Monastic Reform', *Peritia* 8 (1994), 95–106; idem, *The Apocryphal Gospels of Mary in Anglo-Saxon England*, CSASE 26 (Cambridge, forthcoming).

MARY CLAYTON

VISIONS were a genre of literature much practised in antiquity and late antiquity, but which apparently reached their apogee in eighth-century England, when the literary form was used by Anglo-Latin authors as a vehicle for contemplation on the achievements of the present life, on the terrifying threat of the Day of Judgement, and on the need for immediate and significant repentance if the Judgement is to be faced. In the surviving visions the dreamer has characteristically died in this life but, while mourners attend the corpse, has the privilege of various 'extra-body' experiences, in which he is vouchsafed a glimpse both of hell and its attendant torments, and heaven with its attendant bliss; on completion of the vision the visionary's soul returns to the body from which, revivified, he is able to describe the terrors of hell and the delights of heaven to those who will listen. There were various antique predecessors of tales of this sort: the myth of Er in Plato's *Republic* (614b–621d) who awakened on the funeral pyre in order to recount a voyage to the underworld where impure souls lived in indescribable suffering whereas pure souls experienced a vision of celestial harmony; and the latinization of this myth in Cicero's *De re publica*, where the character of the great Scipio Africanus is vouchsafed a vision of the heavenly spheres. (Plato's *Republic* could not have been read in Anglo-Saxon England; and the earliest evidence that the text of Cicero was known – in conjunction with the commentary on it by Macrobius – dates from the stay of *Abbo of Fleury at *Ramsey during the years 985–7.) More accessible was the account in Vergil's *Aeneid* Book VI of Aeneas's visit to the underworld *via* the cave of the Cumaean Sibyl to seek a prophecy on the outcome of his forthcoming voyage to Rome (once in the underworld, Aeneas is able to meet Palinurus, his recently-drowned ship's pilot, Dido, his spurned lover, and his father Anchises). Biblical dream-visions also served as antecedents for medieval visions: the dream of Nebuchadnezzar in the book of Daniel, and the account by the visionary John which forms the substance of Revelation. All these sources may have supplied descriptive details to later dream-visions: Revelation, in particular, supplied the vision of the Judge dressed in a white cloak, surrounded by (twenty-four) wise men (Rev. IV), and of the Book of Life in which the names of the dead are listed, to be judged according to their deeds in this life (Rev. XX). Many of these motifs recur in late antique visions: in the *Visio S. Pauli*, one of the most widely influential essays in the genre (and one which circulated in many recensions, some at least of Insular origin), particularly for its portrayal of the fiery rivers and pits of hell (the *Visio S. Pauli* was translated into Old English, and also provided a number of motifs used in *Beowulf* and in Blickling Homily XVI); in book IV of Pope *Gregory's *Dialogi*, which contains a number of accounts of near-death visions (including one in particular where the dreamer was obliged to pass the test of crossing a bridge over a stinking river); and in the *Visio Baronti* (composed *c.*678–9), describing the *post mortem* visions of a monk of a monastery near Bourges who, after seeing various familiar faces in Paradise, returns to his body and urges repentance on all his fellow monks.

Against the background of these various classical, biblical, late antique and continental visions, the distinctive genre of Anglo-Latin visions was forged. In his *Historia ecclesiastica* (iii. 19) *Bede excerpted from the anonymous *Vita S. Fursei* accounts of the visions experience by the Irish monk *Fursa; later in the same work (v. 12) Bede recounted in his own words the extra-body visions of a Northumbrian nobleman named Dryhthelm who, accompanied by a celestial guide, witnessed four separate stations of souls (a valley blasted by ice and heat; a pit of burning souls; a fragrant field of bright light; a place of brilliant light); of these the first and third are intermediary stations, forerunners in effect of the later medieval purgatory, between hell and heaven (the second and fourth stations respectively); after returning to life, Dryhthelm abandoned his wife and earthly wealth and entered the monastery of *Melrose where he spent the remainder of his life in penitence. In the following chapter (*HE* v. 13) Bede reports another vision, this time of a man who fell sick and was vouchsafed the vision of the accomplishments of his life as recorded in two books, a tiny one containing his virtues, and a huge one containing his sins (the man nevertheless died unrepentant). In a similar vein *Boniface reports in detail (*Ep.* x) the vision of a monk of Much Wenlock who in an extra-body vision saw fiery pits belching flames, followed by a place of wondrous beauty, so much so that when he returned to his body he regarded it ever after with loathing; in another letter (*Ep.* cxv) Boniface reports a vision of sinners immersed in a fiery river (a detail from the *Visio S. Pauli*). At the end of his poem on the saints of *York, while expressing his grief for the death of his master *Ælberht, *Alcuin includes a vision experienced by a dying oblate of a heavenly place where the alumni of the school of York were reassembled; and in his poem on the brethren of an unidentified cell dependent on *Lindisfarne, the poet *Aediluulf describes various visions (some of them in significant architectural detail), including one similar to Alcuin's, in which the brethren of the cell are seen reunited in heaven. By the early ninth century, however, the genre seems to have been exhausted, although various visions are recorded in later saints' lives, including a detailed account in *Lantfred's account of the miracles of St *Swithun, in which a crippled man is vouchsafed a vision of Swithun in a heavenly church, and subsequently cured. Among the corpus of OE verse, the *Dream of the Rood* is cast as a vision, and contains many details drawn from the Latin tradition. From the very end of the period is a vernacular prose account of visions seen by *Leofric, earl of Mercia, which contain interesting architectural information.

Bede, *HE* v. 12–14; Boniface, *Ep.* x and cxv (MGH, ES i. 7–15, 247–50); MGH, PLAC i. 205–6 [Alcuin]; A. Campbell, *Æthelwulf de abbatibus* (Oxford, 1967); P. Ciccarese, *Visioni dell'aldilà in Occidente: Fonti, modelli, testi* (Florence, 1987); P. Dinzelbacher, *Vision und Visionsliteratur im Mittelalter* (Stuttgart, 1981); J. Amat, *Songes et visions. L'au-delà dans la littérature latine tardive* (Paris, 1985); C. Carozzi, *Le voyage de l'âme dans l'au-delà d'après la littérature latine (Ve–XIIIe siècle)* (Rome, 1994); T. Silverstein, *Visio S. Pauli. The History of the Apocalypse in Latin together with nine Texts* (London, 1935); *The Old English Vision of St Paul*, ed. A. diP. Healey (Cambridge, MA, 1978); P. Sims-Williams, *Religion and Literature in Western England 600–800*, CSASE 3 (Cambridge, 1990), 243–72; C. D. Wright, *The Irish Tradition in Old English Literature*, CSASE 6 (Cambridge, 1993), 106–74; J. I. McEnerney, 'The Dream of Aedilvulf', *Mittellateinisches Jahrbuch* 23 (1988), 28–36; A.S. Napier, 'An Old English Vision of Leofric, Earl of Mercia', *Transactions of the Philological Society* (1907–10), 180–8; M. McC. Gatch, 'Piety and Liturgy in the Old English Vision of Leofric', Gneuss FS, pp. 159–79; idem, 'Miracles in Architectural Settings: Christ Church, Canterbury and St Clements, Sandwich, in the Old English *Vision of Leofric*', *ASE* 22 (1993), 227–52.

MICHAEL LAPIDGE

W

WALBURG, ST (d. 779), abbess, trained at Wimborne minster (Dorset), was sent to join *Leobgyth (Lioba), another nun from the same community, who had been appointed by the missionary *Boniface as abbess of Tauberbischofsheim in Germany. After two years, Walburg went to become abbess of the double monastery of Heidenheim, which had been established by her brother *Wynnebald (d. 761). No early Life of Walburg has survived, so little is known about her work at Heidenheim. In 870, Walburg's relics were translated to rest with those of Wynnebald at Eichstätt, and miracles were believed to have taken place at their tomb. In 893 her relics where scattered to a variety of destinations in *Germany, France and *Flanders. Feast: 25 February; local translation feasts: 1 May (known as Walpurgisnacht), 12 October and 24 September.
Acta SS., Februarii, iii.511–72; W. Levison, *England and the Continent in the Eighth Century* (Oxford, 1946), pp. 79–81.

R. C. LOVE

WALDERE was an OE poem which, to judge from the leisured narrative style of the two surviving fragments (Copenhagen, Kongelike Bibliotek, Ny Kgl. Sam. 167b (4°)), must have been at least 1000 lines long. It is the only evidence for knowledge of the story of Walter of Aquitaine in Anglo-Saxon England. Versions of the narrative, probably not identical with that circulating in England, survive as a tenth-century Latin verse-epic *Waltharius*, and in prose from thirteenth-century Scandinavia and Poland. The OE fragments, discovered in the Royal Library by Werlauff in 1860, had probably been taken to Denmark by *Thorkelin. Each is half of a single fold, not sequential, but possibly from the same gathering. They record stages in the fight between Waldere and the Burgundians Guthhere and Hagena, all of whom, along with Waldere's female companion Hildegyth, had been hostages at Attila's court. Hildegyth's exhortation of Waldere is traditionally regarded as Fragment I, with Fragment II being a taunting confrontation between the men, in which Waldere is probably the speaker throughout. The fragments illustrate heroic imprudence, the dilemma of conflicting loyalties, the role of *women in *heroic poetry, and the significance of treasure and weapons. The language is late West Saxon and the hand is datable to *c.*1000. Nothing is known of the poem's prior history.
ASPR vi.4–6; *Waldere*, ed. F. Norman (London, 1933; 2nd. ed., 1949); *Waldere*, ed. A. Zettersten (Manchester, 1979); *Old English Minor Heroic Poems*, ed. J. Hill (Durham, 1983; rev. ed. 1994).

JOYCE HILL

WALLINGFORD (Berks.), a planned and fortified town listed in the *Burghal Hidage with an assessment of 2,400 hides, may have been newly created in the Alfredian period. It is strategically sited on a major Thames crossing, and adjoins the minster of Cholsey. The ramparts and street-plan remain unusually complete, and the Norman castle in the north-east corner overlies standing late Anglo-Saxon buildings. It had a *mint from *Æthelstan's reign; by the Conquest it was the shire town of Berkshire, with at least 500 houses and a base for the king's *housecarls.
Historic Towns in Oxfordshire, ed. K. Rodwell (Oxford, 1975), pp. 155–62; Hill and Rumble, *Defence of Wessex*, pp. 19–21.

JOHN BLAIR

WALL-PAINTING is one of the least understood art forms in the Anglo-Saxon period, since so little survives. In recent decades, however, fragments have been excavated from a range of sites; one painting has been identified still *in situ* in a parish church; and the sparse but significant documentary evidence has been studied in detail. Of the excavated material, the single most important find is a painted stone discovered at *Winchester in 1966. It shows the remains of three figures and a border of pelta-pattern – a type of sub-antique ornament sometimes employed in Carolingian manuscripts. Although its figure-style is comparable to manuscript illumination of the second quarter of the tenth century, such as the miniatures added to the *Æthelstan Psalter (London, BL, Cotton Galba A. xviii), the Winchester painting was found re-used in the foundations of the New Minster, dedicated in 901, and therefore indicates that this style had already appeared

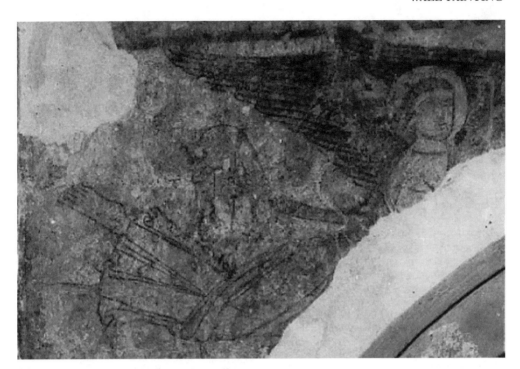

Pl. 21 Wall painting in the church of Nether Wallop

somewhat earlier in monumental painting. Anglo-Saxon painted plaster has now been recovered from some nine other sites. These include *Monkwearmouth-Jarrow (late seventh- or early eighth-century fragments, from monastic buildings); St Oswald's minster at *Gloucester; and *St Albans. Of particular interest are remains discovered at Colchester, in a timber and wattle building which may well have been a royal chapel in the early tenth century. These fragments include an eye and what appear to be draperies, and may derive from a series of life-size figures. The only Anglo-Saxon wall painting known to survive in a standing building is in the parish church of Nether Wallop, near Winchester (pl. 21). Remains of four angels and the top of a mandorla survive on the nave east wall, and though the centre of the composition was destroyed by a later enlargement of the chancel arch, the angels were presumably shown supporting a figure of Christ in Majesty. The agitated linear style of the painting derives from Carolingian illumination, and compares closely to late tenth-century Winchester manuscripts such as the New Minster Charter (BL, Cotton Vespasian A. viii, of 966). Particularly characteristic are such details as the fluttering hem-lines, and bulky flying folds over the angels' bodies, though the outline drawing at Nether

Wallop seems rather harder and firmer, indicating a slightly later date of *c.*1000.

Documentary references add to our knowledge of monumental painting in this period. *Bede describes paintings taken from *Rome to Monkwearmouth and Jarrow in the late seventh century by *Benedict Biscop, but there can be little doubt that these were panel paintings. Writing in the eleventh century, however, *Goscelin of Saint-Bertin provides an account of what was clearly a major scheme of wall painting executed at the royal nunnery of Wilton (Wiltshire) in the second half of the tenth century. One of the nuns at that time was *Edith, a daughter of King *Edgar, and Goscelin records that she added a timber chapel to the main church, and that this was decorated with paintings of Christ's Passion. The paintings are said to have been executed by one of the chaplains, Benno, a former canon of St Maximin in Trier. Presumably, they were purely Ottonian in style, and Ottonian influences may also have been introduced to England in the painted ceiling at Beverley minster executed in the time of Archbishop *Ealdred (1060–9), who also provided a *pulpitum* 'of German work'.

If evidence for Anglo-Saxon wall painting is meagre, the situation is very different for the first half century after the Norman Conquest, from which a number of major schemes survive. The most notable are those of the so-called 'Lewes Group', in various Sussex parish churches including Clayton and Hardham, and which all date from the years around 1100. Although aspects of their style and iconography appear to derive from Anglo-Saxon painting, the overall effect of these monumental, hieratic wall paintings is thoroughly Romanesque. This is not true, however, of the paintings discovered in 1996 at Houghton-on-the-Hill (Norfolk), probably of c.1090, and showing the Trinity combined with the Last Judgement. This unusual combination is reminiscent of the early eleventh-century Grimbald Gospels (BL, Add. 34890), while the quatrefoil motif on the draperies over God's knee was a standard device in pre-Conquest illumination of the eleventh century. It is clear, therefore, that, as in manuscript illumination, 1066 did not mark a clear break with Anglo-Saxon traditions of painting.

Early Medieval Wall Painting and Painted Sculpture in England, ed. S. Cather, D. Park and P. Williamson, BAR Brit. ser. 216 (Oxford, 1990); R. Gem and P. Tudor-Craig, 'A "Winchester School" Wall-painting at Nether Wallop, Hampshire', *ASE* 9 (1981), 115–36; F. Wormald, 'Anniversary Address', *AJ* 47 (1967), 159–65.

DAVID PARK

WALTHEOF, ST (d. 1076), earl of Northampton and Huntingdon, and martyr, son of Siward, earl of *Northumbria, fought against the Normans in 1066 and at the siege of *York, and subsequently received pardon from William (as well as the hand of his niece, Judith, in marriage). He was involved in 1075 in a rebellion of the earls. When this failed, Waltheof went to *Normandy to seek a second pardon, but was imprisoned for a year, and beheaded as a traitor at *Winchester in 1076. He was buried at Crowland (Lincs.) of which he had been a prominent benefactor. Quickly a local cult, venerating Waltheof as an Anglo-Saxon martyr, grew up, with a strongly nationalist flavour, and in 1093 his relics were translated at Crowland. From 1112 miracles were claimed and at this time the surviving hagiography of Waltheof was written (*Vita et Passio, BHL* 8778–9, and *Miracula, BHL* 8782). Feast: 31 August.

F. Michel, 'Vita et Passio Waldevi Comitis', *Chroniques Anglo-Normandes*, 2 vols. (Rouen, 1836), ii. 111–23, 131–42; F. S. Scott, 'Earl Waltheof of Northumbria', *Archaeologia Aeliana* 30 (1952), 149–213.

R. C. LOVE

WANDERER. The 115–line *Wanderer* in the *Exeter Book, like the *Seafarer* with which it is often linked, is one of the Old English *elegies and also belongs to the larger genre of *wisdom literature. The poem's speaker is a homeless man who has lost his lord and friends and suffers alone; after many years he achieves a stoic wisdom. The poem ends with the admonition to seek comfort in heaven, where our only real security lies. The 'autobiographical' first half, describing the narrator's experiences as an *eardstapa* ('wanderer', line 6), is balanced by a more general second half, conveying the narrator's reflections as *snottor* ('wise man', line 111). The *Wanderer* is distinguished by its vivid and emotional images, which contrast present desolation with past joy. In a dream, the lonely man lays his head and hands on his lord's knee as he receives gifts in the hall, only to awaken before a wintry sea where his only companions are birds. The wise man, in a famous rendition of the *ubi sunt* theme, contemplates a ruined fortress, and asks what has become of all life's joys. Although there is some disagreement about the poem's speech boundaries and its possible religious symbolism, the *Wanderer* is now generally accepted as a unified and thoroughly Christian poem.

ASPR iii. 134–7; R. M. Lumiansky, 'The Dramatic Structure of the Old English *Wanderer*', *Neophilologus* 34 (1950), 104–12; J. E. Cross, '*Ubi Sunt* Passages in Old English – Sources and Relationships', *Vetenskaps-Societeten i Lund Årsbok* (1956), 23–44; R. F. Leslie, *The Wanderer* (Manchester, 1966; repr. with additional bibliography Exeter, 1985); T. P. Dunning and A. J. Bliss, *The Wanderer* (London, 1969); G. Richman, 'Speaker and Speech Boundaries in *The Wanderer*', *JEGP* 81 (1982), 469–79 (repr. in *Old English Shorter Poems: Basic Readings*, ed. K. O'Brien O'Keeffe (New York, 1994), pp. 303–18).

ANNE L. KLINCK

WANLEY, HUMFREY (1672–1726), palaeographer and Anglo-Saxonist. Wanley developed a strong interest in ancient script and language as a young man, and in 1695 abandoned his job as a draper's apprentice in Coventry and moved to Oxford. He established himself at University College, and soon became an Assistant at the Bodleian Library. In 1697–9 Wanley made a series of facsimiles of the script and decoration of ancient manuscripts, in what became known as his 'Book of Specimens' (Longleat House MS. 345); and it was on the strength of this book that he acquired the reputation which gained him preferment elsewhere. He moved to London in 1700; and, though employed for the time being as secretary of the S.P.C.K., he soon began to prosper under the patronage of the statesman Robert Harley

(1661–1724), then Speaker of the House of Commons. Wanley was one of three scholars appointed to report on the condition of the Cottonian library in 1703; he was advising Harley on the purchase of manuscripts (notably the library of Sir Symonds D'Ewes) in the same year; and sooner or later he set to work on an ambitious catalogue of the Harleian manuscripts (his 'Catalogus Maior', now BL, Add. 45699–700). Wanley is chiefly renowned for his catalogue of 'ancient northern books', begun while he was based in Oxford and published in 1705 (see *Hickes); it retains its value not least for its detailed descriptions of Cottonian manuscripts lost or damaged in the fire of 1731, and is the forerunner of Neil Ker's *Catalogue of Manuscripts containing Anglo-Saxon* (1957). In 1708 Wanley took office as full-time librarian to Robert Harley, and at once began his work on what would later become the first published catalogue of the Harleian library ('Catalogus Brevior', now BL, Add. 45701–7). A portrait painted by James Hill in December 1711, now in the Library of the Society of Antiquaries, shows Wanley with his 'Book of Specimens' and various other artifacts (*Letters*, ed. Heyworth, Frontispiece). Robert Harley, created 1st Earl of Oxford in 1711, died in 1724; but responsibility for the library seems to have passed in 1714 to Robert's son Edward (1689–1741), 2nd Earl of Oxford, of Wimpole Hall, Cambridgeshire. Miscellaneous papers and notes by Wanley, including many of considerable interest to modern Anglo-Saxonists, abound among the Harleian manuscripts in the British Library (e.g. BL, Harley 7055). His 'Memorandum Book' (BL, Lansdowne 677) is ptd in *Diary*, ed. Wright and Wright, ii. 427–37; his diary (BL, Lansdowne 771), covering the period 1715–26, affords a view of his day-to-day activities as librarian; and his letters to other scholars (collected and edited by Heyworth) give full vent to his character, powers, and scholarly aspirations. Six volumes of letters to Wanley on antiquarian and other matters, full of incidental interest, are in BL, Harley 3777–82; further volumes of his notes and correspondence, formerly preserved among the Portland papers at Welbeck Abbey, are now readily accessible in the British Library (Add. 70469–92). Wanley died on 6 July 1726, and is buried in the parish church of St Marylebone, London.

R. Nares, *et al.*, *A Catalogue of the Harleian Collection of Manuscripts in the British Museum*, 4 vols. (London, 1808–12), iii [description of Wanley's correspondence in BL, Harley 3777–82, and other papers]; C. E. Wright, 'Humfrey Wanley: Saxonist and Library-Keeper', *PBA*

46 (1961), 99–129; *The Diary of Humfrey Wanley 1715–1726*, ed. C. E. Wright and R. C. Wright, 2 vols. (London, 1966); C. E. Wright, *Fontes Harleiani* (London, 1972); *Letters of Humfrey Wanley: Palaeographer, Anglo-Saxonist, Librarian 1672–1726*, ed. P. L. Heyworth (Oxford, 1989); M. McC. Gatch, 'Fragmenta Manuscripta and Varia at Missouri and Cambridge', *TCBS* 9 (1986–90), 434–75, at 439–44; S. Keynes, 'The Reconstruction of a Burnt Cottonian Manuscript: the Case of Cotton MS. Otho A. I', *Brit. Lib. Jnl* 22 (1996), 113–60, at 126–35 [Wanley's 'Book of Specimens'].

SIMON KEYNES

WANSDYKE (east) consists of 20 km of earthwork across the north Wiltshire Downs, south of the river Kennett. The northern ditch is some 5 m wide and 2 m deep. The work post-dates the Roman *road on Morgan's Hill, to the north of Devizes, and probably predates the formation of *Wessex in the late sixth or early seventh century and was possibly built by the British against the Saxons. By the eighth century it was a well documented estate boundary but no longer served a military or political purpose. A separate 20 km earthwork (west Wansdyke) of a similar scale and purpose is 25 km to the west. Here it is situated to the south of the Somerset Avon and again faces north. Two hillforts are incorporated into its length.

H. S. Green, 'Wansdyke, Excavations 1966 to 1970', *Wiltshire Archaeological and Natural History Magazine* 66 (1971) 129–46; B. Cunliffe, *Wessex to AD 1000* (Harlow, 1993).

MARGARET WORTHINGTON

WAPENTAKES were the equivalent of hundreds for the northern Danelaw: they were used instead of hundreds in *Domesday Book for the area of the *Five Boroughs. They also sometimes alternated with (rather than replaced) hundreds in Northamptonshire and in parts of Yorkshire. The term is Norse (*vápnatak*, 'a taking of weapons'), and in Scandinavia referred to a vote passed in an assembly, where consent was once shown by the brandishing of weapons (Tacitus, *Germania*, c. 11). It seems likely that the wapentake in England was substantially the same as the English hundred, though *Edgar's ruling that the Danes had some freedom to make their own *laws, and *Æthelred's Wantage code which included provisions specific to wapentakes, suggest that there may have been minor variations.

Loyn, *Governance*, pp. 142–5; Stenton, *ASE*, pp. 504–5.

SEAN MILLER

WAREHAM (Dorset), on a peninsula site, was a British Christian centre in the seventh century, to

467

judge from five inscribed stones which resemble the early inscriptions of *Dumnonia*. King Beorhtric of *Wessex was buried there in 802, and the former existence at St Mary's of a basilican church (a smaller and perhaps slightly later verson of that at *Brixworth) shows that it was a religious centre of importance in the ninth century. *Asser, describing the *Viking occupation of Wareham in 876, calls it both 'a fortified site' and 'a convent of nuns'. Wareham was one of the many religious centres which the aftermath of the Viking invasions transformed into *towns. The *Burghal Hidage lists it with an assessment of 1,600 hides; it was a *mint under *Æthelstan, and regularly from 973. *Domesday Book shows it as a developed town, one of the four main boroughs of Dorset. The late Anglo-Saxon town was laid out on a grid-plan, encapsulating the old minster of St Mary in its south-east quarter, and its street layout and defensive banks are unusually well-preserved.

Royal Commission on Historical Monuments, *An Inventory of the Historical Monuments of the County of Dorset:* II: South-East (London, 1970), pp. 303–12; R. Gem, 'Architecture of the Anglo-Saxon Church, 735 to 870', *JBAA* 146 (1993), 29–66, at 39–42; B. Yorke, *Wessex in the Early Middle Ages* (London and Leicester, 1995); Hill and Rumble *Defence of Wessex*.

JOHN BLAIR

WATLING STREET, now the name for the Roman road running from Dover past *London to Wroxeter (the A2 and A5), in Anglo-Saxon times was probably first used of the stretch near *St Albans (*Wæclingastræt* from *Wæclingatun*, 'the settlement of the followers of Wæcel or Wacol'); subsequently the form *Wætlingastræt* was the name for more extensive sections north of London. The treaty between *Alfred and Guthrum (880×890), where it formed part of the boundary between Danish and English territory, reveals its importance. An entry in the *Anglo-Saxon Chronicle* implies that it still was a *Danelaw boundary in 1013 (see also *roads).

E. Ekwall, *The Concise Oxford Dictionary of English Place-Names*, 4th ed. (Oxford, 1960); I. D. Margary, *Roman Roads in Britain*, 3rd ed. (London, 1973).

DAVID A. E. PELTERET

WAT'S DYKE was forty-nine miles (62 km) long; it shows a similar careful construction, siting and scale as *Offa's Dyke, and stretched from a tributary of the river Vyrnwy, south of Oswestry, to Basingwerk on the Dee Estuary. For most of its length it runs parallel to and a few kilometres east of Offa's Dyke. There is no archaeological or historical dating for the construction of Wat's Dyke: dates before and after Offa's Dyke have been suggested; but whether it was a model for, or a copy of, Offa's Dyke, it must have served a similar purpose.

M. Worthington, 'Wat's Dyke: an Archaeological and Historical Enigma', *Bulletin of the John Rylands University Library of Manchester* 79 (forthcoming).

MARGARET WORTHINGTON

WEAPONS: *see* Arms and Armour

WEARMOUTH: *see* Monkwearmouth

WELLS (Somerset) takes its name from a group of five natural springs. Excavation shows that they were a focus of ritual activity from at least the fifth or sixth century, when a stone-lined burial chamber was built between them. In the mid Anglo-Saxon period this was replaced by a small mortuary chapel, to the west of which stood St Andrew's minster church, the east apse of which, probably enclosing a *crypt, has also been located. In 909 *Edward the Elder created a diocese of Somerset, with its seat at the existing minster of Wells. By the mid-eleventh century the cathedral and its community were in decay; *Giso, *Edward the Confessor's reforming bishop, built a dormitory, refectory and cloister for the common life of the canons.

W. Rodwell, 'The Anglo-Saxon and Norman Churches at Wells', in *Wells Cathedral: a History*, ed. L. S. Colchester (Wells, 1982), pp. 1–23; idem, 'Above and Below Ground: Archaeology at Wells Cathedral', in *The Archaeology of Cathedrals*, ed. T. Tatton-Brown and J. Munby (Oxford, 1996), pp. 115–33.

JOHN BLAIR

WENLOCK: *see* Mildburg, St

WERBURG, ST, was the daughter of Wulfhere, king of Mercia (658–74), and his wife, Eormenhild, the daughter of Eorcenberht, king of *Kent (640–64), and St *Seaxburg. The most plausible of the several discrepant accounts of her career relate that her uncle, Æthelred, king of Mercia (675–704), put her in charge of the monasteries in his kingdom, that she was buried at Hanbury after some dissension as to which of her houses should possess her remains, and that her body was found incorrupt and elevated nine years after her death by her cousin, Ceolred, king of Mercia (709–16). *Chester, whose principal church had been dedicated to the saint since before the reign of King *Edgar (957–75), later claimed possession of the decayed remains of this corpse. Her cult was also prominent at *Ely, where her *vita* (*BHL* 8855) was probably composed in the early twelfth century.

S. J. Ridyard, *The Royal Saints of Anglo-Saxon England* (Cambridge, 1988), pp. 60, 209–10; D. W. Rollason, *The Mildrith Legend* (Leicester, 1982), pp. 26–7; A. T. Thacker, 'Chester and Gloucester: Early Ecclesiastical Organisation in Two Mercian Burhs', *NH* 18 (1982), 199–211, at 203–4.

PAUL ANTONY HAYWARD

WERFERTH, bishop of *Worcester from about 872 to 915. We know from King *Alfred's biographer, *Asser, that Werferth was a Mercian, who was involved in the literary activities promoted by the king. It is unclear precisely when Werferth first became associated with Alfred, but that the king had named him as a beneficiary in his *will suggests a close connection between the two men by the time his will was drawn up in the 880s. Though Werferth's name is nowhere mentioned in the OE translation of *Gregory's *Dialogues*, and although the preface to the text, written in Alfred's voice, records that the king requested his 'loyal friends' to undertake this work, Asser attributes it solely to Werferth. The preface claims that Alfred commissioned the work for his personal use, but the surviving manuscript evidence indicates that it had been distributed to others. Werferth's translation, which is a literal rendering of the Latin original, is not a particularly competent one and may have contributed to the marginal status his work occupied in the prose of Alfred's reign. The production of a heavily revised version of his translation by an anonymous reviser between *c*.950 and 1050 suggests dissatisfaction with Werferth's work in the later Anglo-Saxon period. In addition to Werferth's intellectual interests, his concern with public affairs is reflected in his involvement in constructing fortifications at Worcester (about 889–99), which is recorded in a grant of privileges made to him by Ealdorman *Æthelred and his wife *Æthelflæd. Werferth had also been granted land and privileges in Worcestershire by King Ceolwulf II of Mercia in 875 and in *London by King Alfred in 899.

Bischof Wærferths von Worcester Übersetzung der Dialoge Gregors des Grossen, ed. H. Hecht (Hamburg, 1907); D. Yerkes, *The Two Versions of Wærferth's Translation of Gregory's Dialogues* (Toronto, 1979); D. Whitelock, 'The Prose of Alfred's Reign', in *Continuations and Beginnings*, ed. E. G. Stanley (London, 1966), pp. 67–103; J. Bately, 'Old English Prose before and during the Reign of Alfred,' *ASE* 17 (1988), 93–138; M. Godden, 'Wærferth and King Alfred: the Fate of the Old English *Dialogues*', Bately FS, pp. 35–51.

ROHINI JAYATILAKA

WERGILD, literally 'man-payment', was the legal value set on a person's life. All classes of society excepting *slaves were protected by a wergild, the sum payable to their relatives to buy off the *feud if they were killed (see also *kinship). Under the seventh-century Kentish *laws of Hlothhere and Eadric, the wergild of a nobleman was 300 shillings, and that of an ordinary freeman 100 shillings. The corresponding sums under the West Saxon laws of *Ine were 1200 shillings and 200 shillings, with an intermediate class of 600 shillings; but the West Saxon shilling was worth much less than its Kentish counterpart (cf. *coinage). Ecclesiastics were fitted in at appropriate points on the scale according to *Law of the North People* (?early eleventh century), which defines the king's wergild as 30,000 *thrymsas* (90,000 pence), half payable to the kindred and half to the people, and equates an archbishop with an *ætheling at 15,000 *thrymsas*, a bishop with an *ealdorman at 8,000 *thrymsas*, a *hold* (nobleman) with a high-reeve at 4,000 *thrymsas*, and a mass-priest with a *thegn at 2,000 *thrymsas*: a *ceorl* is valued at 266 *thrymsas*. Mercian wergilds of the same period are defined in *Law of the Mercians* as 30,000 *sceattas* (120 pounds) for the king, 1200 shillings for a thegn, and 200 shillings for a *ceorl*.

The procedure for payment of wergild is set out in II Edmund 7, with further details in an anonymous eleventh-century text known as *Wer*. The slayer first had to provide surety for payment, with eight members of the paternal kin and four of the maternal kin acting as sureties for a wergild of 1200 shillings. The king's peace was then raised, and twenty-one days later, an initial payment (*healsfang*) of 120 shillings was divided between the children, brothers, and paternal uncle of the deceased. Twenty-one days later, compensation (*manbot*) was paid to the lord, and after a further twenty-one days, the fine for fighting (*fihtwite*). The rest of the wergild was paid in instalments, beginning with the *frumgyld* twenty-one days later.

Although originating as compensation for murder, the wergild also came to be used as the fine for various offences, and as the value of a person's *oath. Æthelberht 31 stipulates payment of wergild (whether of the offender or of the injured party is uncertain) in compensation for adultery; and under later law-codes the wergild could be forfeited for a range of crimes including theft (II Cnut 63) or accessory to theft (II Æthelstan 3.1), taking bribes (II Æthelstan 17), harbouring a fugitive (II Æthelstan 20.8) or excommunicated person (II Cnut 66), violating an ordinance (II Æthelstan 25.2), desertion from the army (V Æthelred 28), incest (II Cnut 51), sexual assault (II Cnut 52), breach of the peace (II Cnut 61), and marrying a widow within a year of her husband's death (II Cnut 73.1). The *healsfang* too was used as a fine for offences such as working on the Sabbath (Wihtred 11) or during a church festival (II Cnut 45.1), idolatry (Wihtred 12), breaking a religious fast (Wihtred 14), perjury (II Cnut 37), and unjustly disarming another person (II Cnut 60). The fine payable by a woman for sexual misconduct was in proportion to her wergild (Alfred 18), as was the compensation she received for sexual assault (Alfred 11). Similarly, the compensation for fighting indoors was assessed according to the wergild of the householder (Alfred 39). Under Ine 15 and Ine 30, a person accused of taking part in a raid or of harbouring a fugitive was to pay his own wergild or clear himself by an oath of equal value; and III Edgar 2.2 stipulates that the wergild was the maximum amount payable in compensation for any offence. The personal injury tariffs in Æthelberht 33–72 and Alfred 44–77 are commensurate with the wergild of a *ceorl*, but it is nowhere stated whether these sums too were variable in accordance with *social class.

A woman's wergild was determined by the class she was born into, and was unaffected by her *marriage. A pregnant woman was protected by her own wergild and that of her unborn child, assessed at half the value appropriate to its father's kin group (Alfred 9). No wergild was payable for a thief killed in the act (Wihtred 25, Ine 35).

H. M. Chadwick, *Studies on Anglo-Saxon Institutions* (Cambridge, 1905), pp. 76–114; G. MacCormack, 'Inheritance and Wergild in Early Germanic Law, Parts I and II', *Irish Jurist* ns 8 (1973), 143–63, and ns 9 (1974), 166–83; S. Rubin, 'The *Bot*, or Composition in Anglo-Saxon Law: a Reassessment', *Legal History* 17 (1996), 144–54.

CAROLE HOUGH

WESSEX, kingdom of, was one of the most powerful of the early Anglo-Saxon kingdoms. The term 'West Saxon' only came into regular use in the eighth century. As *Bede tells us, the West Saxon royal house were originally known as the rulers of the *Gewisse, and their base seems to have been in the upper Thames valley – notwithstanding the reputed activities of their founder King *Cerdic in the Solent. There are no written records to tell us how or when the *Gewisse* established control of other groups of Saxons in Hampshire and Wiltshire. But we can learn something of their conquest in the seventh century of the *Jutes of southern Hampshire and the Isle of Wight, under King *Cædwalla, and of the British kingdoms in the west country (though *Cornwall retained its independence into the ninth century). West Saxon kingship in the seventh century presents a rather confused picture. Multiple kingship seems to have been the norm, as represented in the annals of the *Anglo-Saxon Chronicle*, though the *regnal lists only acknowledge one ruler at any one time. The West Saxon regnal lists are the only ones from Anglo-Saxon England to include the reign of a queen, namely that of Seaxburh, who ruled 672–3, following the death of her husband King Cenwalh. The family of Cenwalh seem to have been dominant in the first three-quarters of the seventh century, but, after his death, the annals give the impression of increasing competition between rival branches of the royal house, all of whom apparently claimed descent from Cerdic.

Stability and abolition of the subkingships seems to have been achieved in the reign of *Ine (688–726), the most powerful of the West Saxon kings to date, though he built upon the military successes of his predecessor Cædwalla. It seems to have been during his reign that the form 'West Saxon' came into regular use. It is also in Ine's reign that the first references are found to the major subdivisions of Wessex, the *shires, which were controlled by officials called *ealdormen, appointed by the king. Berkshire, Hampshire, Wiltshire, Dorset, Somerset and Devon are generally considered the core West Saxon shires, and all these were under Ine's control. However, the history of the borders is very complex and the northern territory of Wessex, particularly Berkshire, was under Mercian rule during parts of the eighth century and only came permanently under West Saxon control in the ninth century. Ine also seems to have exercised overlordship over *Sussex and Surrey, but here too the West Saxons lost out to the Mercians after Ine's death.

Ine's successes did not include leaving a son who was able to succeed him, and for the rest of the eighth century there appears to have been competition once again between rival branches for the throne. *Mercia was the main enemy and, although Wessex was probably not in serious danger of being conquered by Mercia, nevertheless it does sometimes appear in a position of dependence on its more powerful neighbour. This may have been particularly the case during the reign of Beorhtric (786–802), who was married to a daughter of King *Offa. A major reversal of fortunes occurred during the reign of *Ecgberht (802–39), after which no more is heard of competing branches of the royal house. In 825, after a battle at *Ellendun* (Wroughton, Wilts.), *Kent, Sussex, Surrey and *Essex passed from Mercian to West Saxon control. To begin with they were managed as a subkingdom of the West Saxon royal house, but in 860 when Æthelberht, who had been subking, succeeded to the main throne, Wessex – that is England south of the Thames (plus Essex) – became a fully unified kingdom. Even after its rulers became kings of England in the tenth century, Wessex remained a significant unit and was the area in which the kings spent most of their time, held their most significant estates and dispensed most patronage.

The West Saxon royal dynasty was one of the last to embrace Christianity as King Cædwalla appears not to have been baptised until shortly before his death in 688. The first West Saxon king to accept Christianity was Cynegils who was baptised in 635 by Bishop *Birinus, with King *Oswald of *Northumbria as his sponsor. Birinus was given *Dorchester-on-Thames as his episcopal seat, but in the 660s the West Saxon bishopric was moved to *Winchester. Although Mercian military successes in the Thames valley may have forced the move, the West Saxon kings were becoming increasingly interested in the Solent area where *Hamwic* was founded as their *wic* site in the early eighth century. In 705 a new bishopric was established at *Sherborne with the notable West Saxon scholar *Aldhelm, abbot of *Malmesbury, as its first bishop. A major difference between the two bishoprics was that in the west the Anglo-Saxons were taking over an established British church structure. The church in Wessex was probably more affected by the attempts of its kings to reclaim church lands than by the *Vikings, but King *Alfred initiated a period of renewal in the church which was to be underpinned by the great wealth which his sucessors could command as kings of England.

H. E. Walker, 'Bede and the *Gewissae*: the Political Evolution of the Heptarchy and its Nomenclature', *Cambridge Historical Journal* 12 (1956), 174–86; D. P. Kirby, 'Problems of Early West Saxon History', *EHR* 80 (1965), 10–29; Stenton, *ASE*, pp. 62–73, 203–6, 231–5; D. N. Dumville, 'The West Saxon Genealogical Regnal List and the Chronology of Early Wessex', *Peritia* 4 (1985), 21–66; H. Edwards, *The Charters of the Early*

West Saxon Kingdom, BAR 198 (Oxford, 1988); B. A. E. Yorke, 'The Jutes of Hampshire and Wight and the Origins of Wessex', in Bassett, *Origins*, pp. 84–96; idem, *Wessex in the Early Middle Ages* (London, 1995).

B. A. E. YORKE

WESTMINSTER, on the small gravel island of Thorney beside the Thames, is identified in late tradition as a seventh-century monastic site. Other 'directional' minster names on the Thames estuary apparently describe dependencies of larger houses (e.g. Southminster in relation to Bradwell-on-Sea, or 'Northminster' at Broadstairs in relation to *Minster-in-Thanet): Westminster may originally have been a satellite of St Paul's cathedral, the two minsters being separated by the emporium of mid-Saxon *London. In *c*.959 *Dunstan re-founded Westminster as a Benedictine abbey, where King *Harold I (Harefoot) was buried in 1040. Probably in the late 1040s, *Edward the Confessor began his great scheme to rebuild the abbey. His church was the first English building in a mature Romanesque style, and one of the grandest in contemporary Europe, using an innovative system of pier alternation. The conception is clearly Norman, but two of the three known masons (Teinfrith the churchwright, Leofsige Duddlesunu and Godwine Greatsyd) had English names, and there are hints of rich surface decoration which would have reflected English taste: this was as much the last great Anglo-Saxon building as the first Anglo-Norman one. It is probable (though the evidence is later) that Edward the Confessor also established the palace of Westminster, ranged rather awkwardly along the river-front of the earlier monastic precinct.

R. Gem, 'The Origins of the Abbey', *Westminster Abbey*, ed. C. Wilson (London, 1986), pp. 6–21; J. Blair, 'The Minsters of the Thames', *The Cloister and the World*, ed. J. Blair and B. Golding (Oxford, 1996), pp. 5–28; R. D. H. Gem, 'The Romanesque Rebuilding of Westminster Abbey', *ANS* 3 (1981), 33–60; Fernie, *Architecture*, pp. 154–7.

JOHN BLAIR

WEST SAXON DIALECT. The majority of the vernacular prose texts surviving from the Anglo-Saxon period are written in a form of what is known as West Saxon dialect, generally assumed to reflect a variety of language spoken in some part of the kingdom of *Wessex. It is customary to distinguish 'Early West Saxon' and 'Late West Saxon', and insofar as these reflect spoken dialects, the latter appears not to be the direct development of the former. Early West Saxon is represented primarily in the prose translations of the Alfredian period. Particularly important are the two earliest manuscripts of the Old English translation of Pope *Gregory the Great's *Regula pastoralis*, the Lauderdale (Tollemache) manuscript of the OE translation of Orosius, and the Parker manuscript (the 'A' text) of the *Anglo-Saxon Chronicle* up to 924. These texts differ from one another in some features of their written language, and the explanation for these differences is not settled. Many scholars believe that they result at least in part from the intrusion of features from other dialects, especially Mercian. Late West Saxon is well represented at the end of the tenth century in the works of *Ælfric, but essentially the same variety of written language had come before the eleventh century to be widely used in other parts of Anglo-Saxon England and is therefore to be considered an early standard literary language.

As in the case of the other Old English dialects, West Saxon has long been primarily identified on the basis of features of the sound-system supposedly reflected in the spellings, and to some extent by features of the inflectional forms of words. More recently, however, increased attention has been given to the vocabulary of Late West Saxon. It has been forcefully argued, primarily on the basis of studies of vocabulary, that the crucial role in the establishment of a standardized literary Old English was played by the school at the Old Minster at *Winchester under *Æthelwold (bishop of Winchester 963–84), whose pupils had included Ælfric.

P. J. Cosjin, *Altwestsächsische Grammatik*, 2 vols. (The Hague, 1883–6); C. L. Wrenn, ' "Standard" Old English', *Transactions of the Philological Society 1933*, 65–88 (repr. in *Word and Symbol: Studies in English Language* (London, 1967), pp. 57–77); J. C. Pope, 'The Language of the Manuscripts', in *Homilies of Ælfric*, 2 vols., EETS 259–60 (Oxford, 1968), i.177–85; C. Sprockel, *The Language of the Parker Chronicle*, 2 vols. (The Hague, 1965–73); H. Gneuss, 'The Origin of Standard Old English and Æthelwold's School at Winchester', *ASE* 1 (1972), 63–83; J. Bately, 'The Language of the Manuscripts', in *The Old English Orosius*, EETS ss 6 (Oxford, 1980), pp. xxix–lv; J. M. Bately, 'Language', in *The Anglo-Saxon Chronicle* III: *MS A* (Cambridge, 1986), pp. cxxvii–clxiv; W. Hofstetter, *Winchester und der spätaltenglische Sprachgebrauch* (Munich, 1987); idem, 'Winchester and the Standardization of Old English Vocabulary', *ASE* 17 (1988), 139–61.

T. HOAD

WHITBY (Yorks.), called *Streanæshalch* in pre-Viking sources, was the leading royal *nunnery of *Deira and the burial-place of the royal house. It was a double community, and included lay 'brethren' (*fratres*) of relatively humble status under the abbess's control. It was founded *c.*657 as a thank-offering by King *Oswiu, whose daughter *Ælfflæd was a nun from infancy there and eventually abbess. The first abbess, *Hild (d. 680), is praised by *Bede for her energy in establishing the house, for the quality of her rule and for the famous bishops whom she educated; she encouraged the poetic skills of the cow-herd *Cædmon, and in her time the Synod of Whitby (664) was held there. In the late seventh century a member of the community wrote the *Vita S. Gregorii* (*BHL* 3637), a Life of Pope *Gregory, and probably the first significant work of English *hagiography. At this date Whitby was one of the great centres of learning and religious culture; it had daughter houses, notably Hackness, and it was large enough to give house-room between *c.*685 and 704 to part of the displaced Abercorn community with its bishop. However, its later Anglo-Saxon history is obscure. Like most minsters it presumably suffered impoverishment and disruption, though the first of the two Scandinavian names for the site (*Prestebi* on the headland as distinct from *Witebi* in the harbour) implies a group of priests.

The monastery, now represented by the post-Conquest churches of St Peter and St Mary, occupied an eroding coastal headland. *Bede interprets the original name as *sinus fari* or 'bay of the lighthouse', and it seems likely that a Roman lighthouse stood on a promontory since lost to the sea; there are no good grounds for doubting that *Streanæshalch* is Whitby, or for identifying it with Strensall near York. St Peter's was already the main church in the later seventh century, when King *Edwin's *relics were buried there; St Mary's is first mentioned *c.*1110, but is likely on general grounds to have formed part of an early twin-church group. The seventh- and eighth-century *monastic site around St Peter's, one of the most important excavated in England, comprised dense and organized groups of small structures aligned along paths. A *vallum* or other boundary feature seems to have marked a retrenchment, as the early structures extended beyond it. The finds are remarkably rich and numerous, including pins, styli and exotic imports; there is also an important collection of stone sculpture and inscriptions.

Bede, *HE*, iii.24–5, iv.23–6; P. Hunter Blair, 'Whitby as a Centre of Learning in the Seventh Century', in Clemoes FS, pp. 3–32; R. J. Cramp, 'Monastic Sites', in Wilson, *Archaeology*, pp. 223–9 (with appendices by R. J. Cramp and P. Rahtz, pp. 453–62); P. Rahtz, 'Anglo-Saxon and Later Whitby', *Yorkshire Monasticism*, ed. L. R. Hoey (London, 1995), pp. 1–11; R. Cramp, 'A

Reconsideration of the Monastic Site of Whitby', *The Age of Migrating Ideas*, ed. R. M. Spearman and J. Higgitt (Edinburgh, 1993), pp. 64–73; J. Higgitt, 'Monasteries and Inscriptions in Early Northumbria: the Evidence of Whitby', *From the Isles of the North*, ed. C. Bourke (Belfast, 1995), pp. 229–36; *The Earliest Life of Gregory the Great*, ed. B. Colgrave (Lawrence, KA, 1968).

JOHN BLAIR

WHITBY, SYNOD OF: *see* Easter Controversy

WHITHORN (Galloway) was in tradition, and perhaps in fact, the cradle of Scottish Christianity. *Bede preserves a legend that the southern *Picts were converted by a bishop Nynia, who built his church of St Martin at Whithorn (i.e. *Hwitærn*, 'white building'), so called because it was made of stone 'in a manner unusual among the Britons'. It is generally thought that Nynia was a British bishop of the early to mid fifth century. Bede's story is supported by a Latin inscription from Whithorn for one Latinus and his daughter, and still more by the recent discovery there of graves and structures spanning the fifth to seventh centuries, and associated with imported Mediterranean *pottery.

During the seventh century Dumfries and Galloway came under Northumbrian rule, and shortly before 731 Whithorn was re-constituted as a bishop's see. The excavations have found remarkable evidence for an eighth- and ninth-century Northumbrian monastery, including regularly-planned groups of timber halls, and a church and stone-built mausoleum aligned along a raised terrace. No bishops are recorded after the 830s, but Whithorn continued through the tenth and eleventh centuries as a Scandinavian settlement engaged in trade and manufacture. The stone *crosses of the 'Whithorn School' suggest that it also survived through these years as a religious centre: very probably the new see of the 1120s was based on a long-standing community of clergy.

Bede, *HE* iii.4; P. H. Hill, *Whithorn and St Ninian: the Excavation of a Monastic Town* (Stroud, 1997); I. Smith, 'The Origins and Development of Christianity in North Britain and Southern Pictland', *Church Archaeology: Research Directions for the Future*, ed. J. Blair and C. Pyrah (York, 1996), pp. 19–37; C. Thomas, *Whithorn's Christian Beginnings* (First Whithorn Lecture, 1992).

JOHN BLAIR

WIDOW. A woman predeceased by her husband was entitled to a substantial share of the joint property, as well as to the continuing possession of her 'morning-gift' (cf. *marriage). A widow who had borne a child was in a particularly favourable position, receiving half the property under early Kentish law, and the whole according to a late text 'On the Betrothal of a Woman'. She also had custody of her children, their property being administered by the paternal kin. On remarriage, a widow forfeited some or all of her inheritance from her first husband, but retained possession of her own property unless she remarried within a year of his death. As in other Germanic societies, her custody rights could also be affected by remarriage.

The special status of widows is reflected in a number of *laws. Several emphasise widows' freedom of choice (V Æthelred 21, VI Æthelred 26, II Cnut 73) and right of protection over dependants (Æthelberht 75); but legislation to the effect they were not to be forced into second marriages or *nunneries suggests that their position may sometimes have been vulnerable (II Cnut 73, 74). Assaults on widows were treated seriously, and by the eleventh century were penalised by forfeiture of the offender's *wergild (II Cnut 52).

T. J. Rivers, 'Widows' Rights in Anglo-Saxon Law', *American Journal of Legal History* 19 (1975), 208–15; C. Hough, 'The Early Kentish "Divorce Laws": a Reconsideration of Æthelberht, chs. 79 and 80', *ASE* 23 (1994), 19–34; idem, 'The Widow's *Mund* in Æthelberht 75 and 76', *JEGP* (forthcoming).

CAROLE HOUGH

WIDSITH is an OE poem in the *Exeter Book cataloguing kings, tribes and heroes, mostly from Germanic heroic legends originating in the period of migrations (fourth to sixth centuries), although some of the names listed may be fictitious. The brief references to oriental and biblical tribes are commonly regarded as interpolations. The pseudo-autobiograpical poet Widsith, 'far traveller', validates his ability to sing of legendary figures by claiming to have visited the heroes and tribes named. On one level the poem can be interpreted as a display of the poet's repertoire; on another, it celebrates the poet as a figure of extraordinary knowledge and insight. The chronological levelling, in which heroes from different dates are juxtaposed in one undefined legendary past, is characteristic of Germanic *heroic poetry. The concentration and range of the allusions have led to *Widsith* being studied mainly as a key to Germanic legend and there has been a predisposition to attribute it to the seventh century as the earliest possible date for its written form, although the linguistic evidence for this is not compelling since the non-late-West Saxon forms may be part of the poetic *dialect. If it is

473

early, there is the unresolved question of how much it might have been changed in transmission, particularly given its adaptability as a catalogue poem.

ASPR iii. 149–53; *Widsith: A Study in Old English Heroic Legend*, ed. R. W. Chambers (Cambridge, 1912); K. Malone, *Widsith*, Anglistica 13 (Copenhagen, 1962); *Old English Minor Heroic Poems*, ed. J. Hill (Durham, 1983; rev. ed. 1994).

JOYCE HILL

WIFE'S LAMENT. The 53-line *Wife's Lament* in the *Exeter Book, like *Wulf and Eadwacer*, is one of the *elegies, and also a *Frauenlied* or female-voice love-lyric. The poem has sometimes been linked with the *Husband's Message*, postulated as its sequel, but the two are very different in tone and style. Although feminine inflections at the opening point to a female narrator, some scholars have thought the speaker to be a man separated from his lord. But it is a private, not a social, relationship, that the speaker misses. Her 'lord' has banished her to a cave under an oak-tree; here, her loneliness and alienation are feelingly described. Her dwelling is mysterious, and has been variously explained: as a grave, a heathen shrine, or merely a hiding-place where she has been sent for her own protection.

ASPR iii. 210–11; R. F. Leslie, *Three Old English Elegies* (Manchester, 1961; repr. with corrections 1966); K. Wentersdorf, 'The Situation of the Narrator in the Old English *Wife's Lament*', *Speculum* 56 (1981), 492–516 (repr. with minor changes in *Old English Shorter Poems: Basic Readings*, ed. K. O'B. O'Keeffe (New York, 1994), pp. 357–92); P. A. Belanoff, 'Women's Songs, Women's Language: *Wulf and Eadwacer* and the *Wife's Lament*', *New Readings on Women in Old English Literature*, ed. H. Damico and A. H. Olsen (Bloomington, IN, 1990), pp. 193–203.

ANNE L. KLINCK

WILFRID, ST (d. 709), bishop and abbot, was born about 634, the son of a Northumbrian nobleman. Leaving home as a youth for the royal court, he found favour with Queen Eanflæd, who sent him first to be trained in the religious life at *Lindisfarne and later to the court of her kinsman, King Earconberht of *Kent. From there in the early 650s he left for *Rome with another of the queen's associates, Biscop Baducing (*Benedict Biscop), but parted from Biscop at Lyon where he remained for a while the favoured guest of the local bishop.

Wilfrid was clearly impressed by Rome, especially its liturgical ceremonial and its great store of holy *relics. He made friends there with the archdeacon Boniface, learned the current methods of calculating the date of *Easter, and conceived a devotion to the apostles Peter and Andrew, to be reflected in his ecclesiastical foundations in England. Equally formative were his experiences at Lyon where he remained for a further three years after leaving Rome, during which he received the tonsure and imbibed high notions of the status and authority of bishops.

After arriving back in England, Wilfrid was taken up by the Northumbrian king's son, Alhfrith, and intruded as abbot into the recently established monastery of *Ripon. In 663 he was ordained priest by the Frankish *Agilbert, former bishop of the West Saxons, and in 664 he acted as Agilbert's spokesman at the synod of *Whitby, where his outspoken and ultimately victorious advocacy of Roman observance caused deep offence within the Northumbrian ecclesiastical establishment. Although thus already a controversial figure, Wilfrid nevertheless succeeded to the Northumbrian see when it became vacant a second time in 664. Acting on ideas imbibed on his travels, he moved the seat of his see to *York and chose to be consecrated with splendid ceremony at the Frankish royal palace of Compiègne. Delays in his return from Gaul, however, gave his enemies their chance and when he finally arrived in *Northumbria in 666 his patron Alhfrith had been eclipsed and a new bishop, *Chad, intruded into the Northumbrian see. Wilfrid withdrew to act as bishop in *Mercia and Kent under the protection of their friendly kings.

In 669 *Theodore, the new archbishop of Canterbury, restored Wilfrid to his see. From then until 678 he was at the height of his power and influence and able to implement the ideas he had acquired in Rome and Gaul. At York he rebuilt *Paulinus's ruined cathedral, and he also invested heavily in the monasteries which he controlled both in Northumbria and Mercia, especially Ripon and his great new foundation of *Hexham, endowed by the Northumbrian queen *Æthelthryth. Into these and other churches, he introduced relics from Rome, splendid *gospel-books, vestments, *shrines, and ornaments, and elaborate liturgical observances; he claimed, indeed, to have brought the Rule of St Benedict to Northumbria, although almost certainly his own observance was, like that of his Gaulish teachers, eclectic.

Although Wilfrid, according to *Stephen, his biographer, was personally ascetic, he lived in considerable style, maintaining a large quasi-royal entourage of armed followers. The sole bishop in Northumbria, he appears to have nurtured metropolitan ambitions over the whole of northern Britain which he claimed to represent at a synod held in Rome in 679. His international contacts were demonstrated in 676, when he successfully responded to a request from the Franks of Austrasia to secure the return from Ireland of their exiled prince Dagobert.

Despite his pretensions, Wilfrid's power base was insecure. The Northumbrian king, Ecgfrith, had personal reasons for disliking his bishop, who had encouraged his first wife Æthelthryth in her decision to become a nun. Wilfrid's position was further weakened by enemies within the Northumbrian church, led by Abbess *Hild of Whitby, who had resisted Wilfrid at the synod of 664, and who seems to have sought control of the see of York. Hild had close relations with Archbishop Theodore, who had his own reasons for opposing Wilfrid, most notably his desire to subdivide the great Northumbrian diocese. In 678, therefore, at Ecgfrith's behest and with Theodore's full cooperation, Wilfrid was driven from his see; new and unsympathetic bishops were established at Ripon and Hexham, and another intruded into York itself.

Wilfrid responded by embarking upon a personal appeal to Rome, where in 679, at a synod convened to condemn the Monothelete doctrine, he demanded full restitution. The pope, Agatho, trod carefully. Although Wilfrid was to be restored to the see which he had lately held and the intruding bishops were to be expelled, he was then to chose fellow bishops who were to be *consecrated by Theodore. Wilfrid's monasteries, however, were to be exempted from diocesan control and placed directly under the Holy See.

Ecgfrith remained unmoved by the papal judgment and Wilfrid was eventually forced into exile in the still pagan kingdom of *Sussex. There in the early 680s King Æthelwalh granted him an estate at *Selsey upon which he founded a monastery and which formed a base for the *conversion, with the king's support, of the South Saxons. Wilfrid soon, however, transferred his allegiance to Cædwalla, an exiled West Saxon prince who invaded Sussex and killed Æthelwalh. In 685 when he became king of the West Saxons Cædwalla made Wilfrid his bishop and gave him a vast estate on the newly-conquered Isle of Wight. Shortly afterwards King Ecgfrith died and Archbishop Theodore determined to make peace, recommending a settlement to *Aldfrith, the new king of Northumbria, and to Abbess *Ælfflæd, Hild's successor at Whitby. Wilfrid returned to his reduced see of York and his two great monasteries,

Ripon and Hexham. He never, however, recovered the postion he enjoyed in the 670s. Although he administered temporarily Lindisfarne and Hexham, two of the new sees carved out his original diocese, by 688 both had new incumbents. Further conflict was inevitable, and in 692 after plans to turn Ripon into the seat of a bishopric Wilfrid once again left for exile in Mercia, where he remained under the protection of King Æthelred for about eleven years. During this period he fostered Anglo-Saxon *missionary activity in *Frisia, where he had preached in 679 and where from 690 his pupil *Willibrord was active.

In 703 *Berhtwald, archbishop of Canterbury, presided over a church council in Northumbria at which, with Aldfrith's consent, it was resolved that Wilfrid should be suspended from the exercise of his episcopal office and deprived of all his possessions except the monastery of Ripon. Wilfrid once more took his case in person to Rome, a move which led to the excommunication of himself and his followers. Again the pope was circumspect. Berthwald was ordered to convoke a synod together with Wilfrid, to be attended by the bishops of York and Hexham. Wilfrid thereupon returned to England, but en route suffered a seizure at Meaux, from which he probably never fully recovered and which perhaps weakened his resolve. In 705 he was reconciled with Berhtwald. With the death of Aldfrith shortly afterwards, the way lay open for at least a partial restoration. By a strange reversal Wilfrid adopted as a spiritual son the young Osred, Aldfrith's heir, and in 706 after Osred had succeeded to the kingdom a settlement was reached: the bishop of Hexham was translated to the then vacant see of York, leaving Wilfrid in full control of his former monastery.

Wilfrid survived a further four years. Some eighteen months before he died he suffered a further seizure, and thereafter disposed of his possessions in a manner more appropriate to a contemporary aristocrat than a Benedictine abbot, nominating successors at Ripon and Hexham, and dividing his portable treasure between them, other faithful followers, the poor, and (the best portion) two great basilicas in Rome. He died at Oundle, probably on Thursday 24 April 709 (or possibly 710), and was buried at Ripon, where he was immediately treated as a saint.

As the subject of one of the most vivid biographies to survive from the early medieval West, Wilfrid's career, aims, and to some extent his personality can be reconstructed in exceptional detail. Ambitious, worldly, and with a highly developed sense of his rights and privileges, Wilfrid undoubtedly cared for his own and could elicit fierce loyalty. Nevertheless, his pursuit of the welfare of the church was genuine: an ardent missionary, he founded many new communities and sought to enhance the physical environment and sacred ceremonial of many more. Such ambiguities are reflected in Bede's portrait in the *Historia ecclesiastica*, with its discreet omissions and careful neutrality. Ultimately, Wilfrid's zeal in controversy and his fatal inability to achieve a working relationship with his own people's kings and religious leaders nullified many of his most immediate plans. Above all, he was unable to preserve the Northumbrian see intact, or to place it at the head of a vast northern province. His religious connexion, which encompassed communities reaching from Northumbria to Sussex, was deeply troubled at his death and probably did not long endure. Wilfrid's main legacy lay in his missionary activities in England and Frisia and his crucial contribution to the flowering of ecclesiastical art and culture in seventh-century England.

Eddius Stephanus, Life of Bishop Wilfrid, ed. B. Colgrave (Cambridge, 1927); Bede, *HE* v. 19; Stenton, *ASE*, pp. 135–9; H. Mayr-Harting, *The Coming of Christianity to Anglo-Saxon England*, 3rd ed. (London, 1991), pp. 129–47; D. P. Kirby, *St. Wilfrid at Hexham* (Newcastle, 1974); idem, 'Bede, Eddius Stephanus and the Life of Wilfrid', *EHR* 97 (1983), 101–14; W. Goffart, *The Narrators of Barbarian History* (Princeton, NJ, 1988), ch. 4; C. Cubitt, 'Wilfrid's Usurping Bishops: Episcopal Elections in Anglo-Saxon England', *NH* 25 (1989), 18–38.

ALAN THACKER

WILFRID II, bishop of *York (?714–32), is known to have been an alumnus of *Hild's school at *Whitby (Bede, *HE* iv.23); he served as priest to another alumnus of that school, *John of Beverley, bishop of York (706–14?), until, owing to John's poor health, Wilfrid was consecrated to the bishopric of York (*c.*714). For reasons not entirely clear, Wilfrid was deposed (or resigned) in 732 and *Ecgberht, brother of the Deiran king Eadberht, was elevated in his place, and assumed for the first time (from 735) the rank of archbishop, whereupon Wilfrid went into retreat at an unspecified place. He was nevertheless remembered with great affection at York (in particular, *Alcuin in his poem on the saints of York devoted an extensive account to his benefactions, and to the fact that he adorned the church of York with many *tituli*; the day of his death was commemorated in the *metrical calendar of York). He died at *Ripon on 29 April in either 745 or 746.

Bede, *HE* iv.23; MGH, PLAC i.196–7 [Alcuin, *Carmen* i, lines 1215–46].

MICHAEL LAPIDGE

WILLEHAD, a Northumbrian friend of *Alcuin (*Ep.* vi) who in *c.*770, inspired by the martyrdom of *Boniface, went to *Frisia to continue the Anglo-Saxon *mission among the pagans in that country. Some years later (*c.*780) he was instructed by Charlemagne to direct his attention to the conversion of the Saxons, but an uprising led by Duke Widukind caused Willehad to abandon Saxony and travel to *Rome. He returned to Frisia and spent some time (783 × 785) in the monastery of Echternach (a foundation of *Willibrord) under the abbacy of another of Alcuin's English companions, Beornræd. After Duke Widukind (under compulsion from Charlemagne) accepted Christianity in 787, Willehad returned to Saxony; he was consecrated first bishop of Bremen in 787, but died in 789 soon after the consecration of his cathedral. In the ninth century (*c.*840 × *c.*860) a Life of Willehad (*BHL* 8898) was composed, apparently at Bremen (though arguments in favour of Echternach have been advanced).

MGH, SS ii.379–84; PL cxviii.1013–24; W. Levison, *England and the Continent in the Eighth Century* (Oxford, 1946), p. 110; G. Niemeyer, 'Die Herkunft der Vita Willehadi', *Deutsches Archiv* 12 (1956), 17–35; W. Berschin, *Biographie und Epochenstil im lateinischen Mittelalter*, 3 vols. (Stuttgart, 1986–), iii. 61–2.

MICHAEL LAPIDGE

WILLIAM OF MALMESBURY (d. *c.*1143), historian, hagiographer and man of letters, was the most important Anglo-Norman interpreter of the history of England from *Bede's time until his own. From childhood on he was a monk of *Malmesbury abbey, holding the office of precentor (therefore effectively librarian), but otherwise eschewing high position or public influence. Like Bede, his model as scholar and monk, William devoted his life to Christian learning, above all to the writing of history. Conscious of his mixed (English-Norman) parentage, his vision is at once pan-European and yet focussed on the special achievements of the English past, which he saw as the work of its kings and saints.

He gives a description of his earliest studies but does not say where they were undertaken. By 1119 his interest in history was sufficiently developed for him to have compiled a unique edition of the papal chronicle known as *Liber pontificalis*. Among several now-lost sources which he used was a collection of inscriptions from churches in England and elsewhere put together for *Milred, bishop of

Worcester (745–75); this in turn had drawn upon Bede's lost *Liber epigrammatum* (see *tituli*; *syllogae*). Perhaps it was this project that brought him to the attention of his monastery's patron, Queen Matilda. On a visit to the house she asked him to give an account of the alleged relationship of her own family to Malmesbury's founder St *Aldhelm. The response was William's most famous and popular work, the *Gesta regum Anglorum* in five books, completed in 1126, sporadically revised into the early 1130s. Organized chronologically (though the first book treats the Anglo-Saxon kingdoms *seriatim*), it fills in the gap which William perceived in English historiography from the death of Bede (735) until his own day. Even before it was finished William had envisaged, and begun, a companion work of similar scale, the *Gesta pontificum Anglorum*, also in five books, organized topographically, beginning with *Canterbury and terminating with the history of his own monastery.

The research for these works had William travelling throughout Britain, and perhaps to Normandy as well. The range of his sources – chronicles, documents, monuments, the memory of individuals and communities – is as impressive as the intelligent and imaginative use he made of them. Few sources available today for the history of Anglo-Saxon England were unknown to William, and in addition he had some – though not many – now lost to us.

In the course of his research, William was prevailed upon to stay for a time at *Glastonbury, where he wrote a remarkable history of the house. His account of its remote origins was too circumspect for the local monks, who later bowdlerized it and ensured its survival only in their preferred form. What William originally wrote can be partly reconstructed from the extracts which he incorporated in a later recension of the *Gesta regum*. During the same stay he wrote Lives of the local saints, notably *Dunstan. At about the same time he also wrote, for *Worcester, a Life of St *Wulfstan, adapted from a lost OE Life by the local monk Coleman.

By about 1135 William seems to have felt that this prolonged emphasis on historical writing was inappropriate for a monk. He announced, and demonstrated, his intention of turning to more serious matters in his *Commentary on Lamentations*, written soon after this year. But by 1141 he had returned to his old love with his last work, the *Historia novella*, which covers the reign of King Stephen to the end of 1142; soon after William is presumed to have died.

William's writing of the history of England has to be seen as part of his much wider interest in the development of civilization – as he conceived it – from ancient Greece and Rome to the Europe of his day; it has also to be seen in the context of William's prodigious reading and active library-building, both with special attention to the Latin classics. These interests make him one of the last major figures in a tradition of Christian scholarship dominated by Benedictine monasticism.

Sharpe, *Handlist*, 2114; *Gesta Regum Anglorum*, ed. W. Stubbs, 2 vols., RS (London, 1887–9), new ed. with trans. and commentary by R. A. B. Mynors, R. M. Thomson and M. Winterbottom, 2 vols. (OMT, 1998–9); *Gesta Pontificum Anglorum*, ed. N. E. S. A. Hamilton (RS, 1870); *Historia Novella*, ed. and trans. K. Potter (London, 1955), new ed. with trans. and commentary by E. King (OMT, 1998); *De Antiquitate Glastonie Ecclesie*, ed. and trans. J. Scott, *The Early History of Glastonbury* (Woodbridge, 1981); *Vita Dunstani*, in *Memorials*, pp. 250–324; *Vita Wulfstani*, ed. R. Darlington, Camden Soc., 3rd ser, 11 (London, 1928); R. M. Thomson, *William of Malmesbury* (Woodbridge, 1987).

RODNEY M. THOMSON

WILLIBALD (*c.*700–*c.*787), bishop of Eichstätt (741–*c.*787) and one of the most remarkable of the missionaries who followed *Boniface to Germany. He was born in Southumbria (probably in Wessex) and was a monk at Bishops Waltham (Hants.) when he conceived the plan to go on *pilgrimage. In 720 he and his brother *Wynnebald left England for *Rome, where they remained together for nearly three years (to 723). Willibald then set out on his own for the Near East, passing through Naples and Sicily (where he saw Mt Etna and visited the grave of St Agatha), then to Monemvasia in the Peloponnese and so to Ephesus in Asia Minor (where he visited the tomb of the Seven Sleepers), from whence he went *via* Cyprus to Palestine (then in the hands of the Arabs) and visited Jerusalem on four occasions; he then went to Constantinople, where he remained for two years (727–9) in the monastery of the Holy Apostles. He then returned to southern Italy, where he remained a monk at Monte Cassino for ten years (729–39), until he was sent by Pope Gregory III to join the mission of Boniface. He returned to Thuringia where he met up with his brother Wynnebald and sister *Walburg (then abbess of the double monastery of Heidenheim), and was appointed to the new bishopric of Eichstätt by Boniface in 741. The details of his eastern pilgrimage are known because late in life Willibald dictated them to a young English nun of Heidenheim named *Hygeburg, who incorporated them (as a so-called *Hodoeporicon*) into her Life of Willibald (*BHL* 8931), composed 767 × 778; the origin in Willibald's dictation is reflected in the frequent fluctuation between first- and third-person narrative. The *Hodoeporicon* is a fascinating travelogue by an extraordinary Anglo-Saxon, and it is unfortunate that little is known of his life and activities as bishop of Eichstätt.

MGH, SS xv.86–106 [Hygeburg, *Vita S. Willibaldi*]; J. Wilkinson, *Jerusalem Pilgrims before the Crusades* (Warminster, 1977), pp. 124–35, 206–8; W. Levison, *England and the Continent in the Eighth Century* (Oxford, 1946), pp. 43–4, 80–1, 102–3; C. H. Talbot, *The Anglo-Saxon Missionaries in Germany* (London, 1954), pp. 153–77; *St Willibald 787–1987*, Studien und Mitteilungen des Benediktiner-Ordens 98 (1987); W. Berschin, *Biographie und Epochenstil im lateinischen Mittelalter*, 3 vols. (Stuttgart, 1986—), iii. 18–26.

MICHAEL LAPIDGE

WILLIBALD OF MAINZ was the Anglo-Saxon author of a Life of *Boniface (*BHL* 1400) composed at Mainz *c.*760, soon after the saint's martyrdom (754), and based on authentic information, though not on personal knowledge; much of the information was presumably supplied to Willibald by Boniface's companion *Lull, to whom the Life is dedicated. (Note that this Willibald of Mainz is not to be confused with the Anglo-Saxon *Willibald who was bishop of Eichstätt.) Nothing is known of Willibald's English origins, although to judge from the pervasive influence of *Aldhelm's Latin *prose style, he received his training in a Southumbrian *school where Aldhelm's writings were studied intensively. In his preface Willibald stated that his literary models were Hegesippus, the *Historia ecclesiastica* of Eusebius (in Jerome's translation), and the *Dialogi* of *Gregory the Great. The work is probably the earliest Latin work written in Germany, and was very influential on later hagiographers of the English mission (it served as a model, for example, for *Hygeburg and *Liudger, and is preserved in some forty manuscripts and several recensions). It is probable that Willibald is identical with the 'Willibaldus diaconus' who wrote the *colophon to a copy of Gregory's *Regula pastoralis* now preserved in Oxford (Bodleian Library, Laud misc. 263; see *CLA* S.**1400).

MGH, SS ii.143–88; PL lxxxix.603–34; W. Levison, ed., *Vita Sancti Bonifatii Archiepiscopi Moguntini*, MGH SS rerum Germanicarum in usum scholarum (Hannover, 1905), pp. 1–58; idem, *England and the Continent in the Eighth Century* (Oxford, 1946), pp. 54, 76, 289; C. H. Talbot, *The Anglo-Saxon Missionaries in Germany* (London, 1954), pp. 25–62; W. Berschin, *Biographie und*

Epochenstil im lateinischen Mittelalter, 3 vols. (Stuttgart, 1986—), iii.6–13.

MICHAEL LAPIDGE

WILLIBRORD. Born in 658, an oblate at *Ripon, Willibrord joined the English community at *Rath Melsigi* (Ireland). In 690 Abbot Ecgberht sent Willibrord to convert the *Frisians. In 695 Pope Sergius consecrated him archbishop of the Frisians with Utrecht as his see. From the beginning progress of the mission depended on Frankish military support. Whenever the pagan Frisians regained control of Utrecht (before 695, 714–19), Willibrord retreated to the small monastery at Echternach (Luxembourg), given to him by Abbess Irmina, the mother-in-law of Pippin II. Between 704 and 706 he installed his own monastery there. A *scriptorium soon was in operation (see *Echternach Gospels). The Frisian mission succeeded definitively only after 733–4, when Charles Martel extended Frankish domination northwards. By then it was *Boniface, Willibrord's erstwhile collaborator, who was in control of christianization beyond the Rhine. Willibrord died in 739. Unlike Boniface, Willibrord did not leave a literary oeuvre. On palaeographical grounds it is highly unlikely that the (auto-)biographical annotation in the Echternach *Willibrord's Calendar* (Paris, BN lat. 10837, 39v) can be attributed to Willibrord's hand. The metrical and prose *Lives* were written between 785 and 797 by *Alcuin, a relative with sound knowledge of Echternach traditions.

The Calendar of St Willibrord, ed. H. A. Wilson, HBS 55 (London, 1918); *Willibrord, Apostel der Niederlande-Gründer der Abtei Echternach*, ed. G. Kiesel and J. Schröder (Luxembourg, 1989); *Willibrord, zijn wereld en zijn werk*, ed. P. Bange and A. G. Weiler (Nijmegen, 1990).

MARCO MOSTERT

WILLS. Much of our information about pre-Conquest forms of testamentary disposition is based upon a group of some sixty Anglo-Saxon vernacular *charters which date from the mid-ninth century onwards. These documents, conveniently known as wills, range in length from a few lines to several pages in their printed editions. Some record only the barest of details about bequests of land to the church, others describe at length the disposition of property, including that of personal effects, to family and friends. Testators include royalty, ecclesiastics (from a mass-priest to an archbishop), and laymen (including *reeves and *ealdormen). They range from the famous, like King *Alfred and King *Eadred, to men and *women whom we know only from these documents; bequests range from multiple estates to bed-clothes, from a thousand pounds of silver to a few pence, from a ship to a sheep. These texts provide us with unparalleled socio-historical detail, together with important information about land tenure and ecclesiastical holdings.

Wills survive in a variety of forms. Around a third are extant in single-sheet charters datable to before the end of the eleventh century. Some of these are preserved as portions of *chirographs. The rest are contained in post-Conquest cartularies and chronicles, alongside shorter Latin summaries of principal bequests to ecclesiastical foundations. Major archives include Christ Church, *Canterbury, *Bury St Edmunds, and the Old and New Minsters, *Winchester.

Few wills are likely to have constituted a complete disposition of the testator's entire property and possessions. It appears from narrative sources and from the written wills themselves that multi-gift donations of property and effects were often repeated and added to in front of different witness-groups on separate occasions. King Alfred alludes to the existence of several earlier versions of his will, and it is likely that many written records of multi-gift wills were only summaries of partial distributions of property and effects, to be added to during life by bequests to individual people and foundations, and finally rehearsed on the death-bed. It also seems that contractual elements in the wills could generally be revoked, at least in the event of the death of donees.

Although land left to the church in reversion ultimately belonged to it, the heirs of the testator seem to have enjoyed limited power of bequest over it dependent on the terms of the original arrangement, and could choose (in agreement with the church) who was next to succeed to the land as tenant. The right could be extended to outside the family. This type of bequest had advantages for both church and heirs. It constituted a charitable gift to the church in as much as the foundation received income from the estates in the shape of rents and dues. Additionally, it meant that the church would oversee the devolution of the property from generation to generation within a family in accordance with the wishes of the testator.

Pre-Conquest written dispositions of property are broadly divisible into two categories: the bequest (*post obitum* gift), and the multi-gift will, comprising a number of bequests, which often include the disposition of personal effects. Three forms of *post obitum* gift on the Continent have been identified, two of which are closely related.

The first type (*precaria oblata*) was completed in two transactions: in the first the donor gave the property to the donee, and then the property was re-acquired for one or more lives. In a variant of the type, the *precaria remuneratoria*, the donor paid rent to the donee as an acknowledgement of the donee's right to the property, and occasionally the use of a different estate was given. The third type of *post obitum* gift (*precaria data*) was a simpler transaction whereby the donor retained use of the bequeathed property until death without payment of rent or fee. All three types appear to have been employed in Anglo-Saxon England. However, although there appears to have been a role for the simplex *post obitum* form, it is likely that its use was less common than our records suggest, certainly in dealings with the church. An ecclesiastical beneficiary would surely have required some tangible assurance of the testator's intentions, either through payment of rent or through submission of the title-deed to the property. The latter may have been so general a custom that it was not recorded in the majority of charters. In many cases the apparent difference in form between the varieties of *post obitum* gift seems attributable not so much to differences in function as to the individual concerns and circumstances of the scribes and foundations responsible for their production and early copying. Preservation of detail, particularly in Latin versions of vernacular wills, often appears to have been born out of a necessity to guard against the possibility of future litigation over the property bequeathed by the testator. Complex arrangements described in these wills and bequests could be summarised, simplified or truncated once the details of such agreements ceased to be of relevance to the church. This treatment extended to documents preserved in the vernacular. Such changes, affecting our perception of the nature of the Anglo-Saxon will, are likely to have been made not so much by post- as pre-Conquest scribes, whose command of the language was sufficient to alter the structure of their exemplars. The alterations liable to have been made by later scribes to their copy-texts seem largely restricted to the omission of material of obvious unimportance to their foundations, such as the bequests of personal effects to family and friends, and the occasional substitution of familiar vocabulary for words considered archaic or obsolete.

Anglo-Saxon Wills, ed. D. Whitelock (Cambridge, 1930); M. M. Sheehan, *The Will in Medieval England*, Pontifical Institute of Mediaeval Studies: Studies and Texts 6 (Toronto, 1963); K. A. Lowe, 'The Nature and Effect of the Anglo-Saxon Vernacular Will', *Journal of Legal*

History 19 (1998), 23–61; idem, ' "As Fre as Thowt?" Some Medieval Copies and Translations of Old English Wills', *English Manuscript Studies, 1100–1700* 4 (1993), 1–23.

K. A. LOWE

WIMBORNE (Dorset) was one of the leading West Saxon royal *nunneries, founded before 718 for *Cuthburg, sister of King *Ine. Rudolf's *Life of Leofgyth* (Lioba), who was educated at Wimborne, describes it as a double house, the male and female communities strictly segregated by 'strong and lofty walls'. In the ninth century it was closely associated with the royal house: King Æthelred I was buried there in 871, and after *Alfred's death in 899 the claimant Æthelwold seized Wimborne and barricaded himself inside the residence (*hám*) there. *Domesday Book shows Wimborne as a small *town, with burgesses, at a royal estate centre. The street-plan reflects the development of the town from its ecclesiastical nucleus, which apparently comprised two concentric rectilinear enclosures. The church, in the central enclosure, stands on a Roman villa site and retains part of the late Anglo-Saxon crossing and *porticus*.

L. Keen, 'The Towns of Dorset', in Haslam, *Towns*, pp. 203–47; J. Blair, 'Wimborne Minster', *Archaeological Journal* 140 (1983), 37–8; Royal Commission on Historical Monuments, *Dorset: V: East Dorset* (London, 1975), pp. 77–85; P. Coulstock, *The Collegiate Church of Wimborne Minster* (Woodbridge, 1993).

JOHN BLAIR

WINCHCOMBE (Glos.) was a religious and territorial centre associated with the later Mercian kings, especially *Coenwulf. The aligned churches of St Mary (later the Abbey) and St Peter (now the parish church) probably existed by the early ninth century. Excavations show that the nucleus, containing the churches, was enclosed by a bank at some date before the late ninth century. Central-place functions within an early territory may underlie Winchcombe's status, until the 1010s, as the shire town of 'Winchcombeshire'. The cult of the boy-martyr Cynehelm (*'Kenelm'), supposedly a son of Coenwulf, probably developed there during the ninth century and was promoted from the late tenth. In the 960s St *Oswald reformed Winchcombe as a Benedictine abbey. It was one of the houses attacked by Ealdorman Ælfhere after 975 (its abbot, *Germanus, retreated to *Ramsey), and its history is obscure until abbots are recorded again from the 1040s. Winchcombe was a *mint from *Edgar's reign, and by *Domesday Book a small *town had developed around the monastic nucleus.

S. R. Bassett, 'A Probable Mercian Royal Mausoleum at Winchcombe, Gloucestershire', *AJ* 65 (1985), 82–100; P. Ellis, 'Excavations at Winchcombe', *Transactions of the Bristol and Gloucestershire Archaeological Society* 104 (1986), 95–138; R. C. Love, *Three Eleventh-Century Anglo-Latin Saints' Lives* (Oxford, 1996); *Oswald of Worcester*; J. Whybra, *A Lost English County: Winchcombeshire in the Tenth and Eleventh Centuries* (Woodbridge, 1990).

JOHN BLAIR

WINCHESTER, the Roman city of *Venta Belgarum*, established in the valley of the river Itchen below a late Iron Age settlement at the point where the river cuts through the Hampshire Downs, effectively came to an end in the early fifth century, having changed its character from a residential to an industrial centre in the later fourth century, and expanded in the process with an increasing presence of Germanic peoples. *Grave goods suggest two waves of settlement, in the mid-fourth and early fifth century: dates well before the traditional arrival of the Saxons in *Wessex. It is argued that, despite the collapse of urban life *c.*450, a nucleus of political power survived during the Dark Ages, with the possible continuation of an administrative centre on the site of the later royal palace, south of the Roman forum. A concentration of sixth- and seventh-century *cemeteries *around* the city again suggests a focus of interest within the walls. Furthermore, the excavations conducted by the Winchester Excavations Committee in the 1960s revealed evidence for small private estates of *thegn status within the walls from the late seventh century.

The theory that administrative power survived in Winchester finds support in the construction in 648 by Cenwalh, king of Wessex, of the church of SS. Peter and Paul later known as Old Minster. The church became a cathedral in the 660s, when the West Saxon bishopric was transferred thither from its original location at *Dorchester-on-Thames. Old Minster was constructed immediately east of the site where the Anglo-Saxon royal palace certainly stood by the late tenth century, and may initially have been intended as the palace church. The plan of Old Minster, predecessor of the present cathedral, was determined by excavation of its robber trenches in the 1960s; it was a modest, cruciform building, apparently little altered between 648 and 971.

The city owes its present form to an intense period of reconstruction in the late ninth century. By the end of the century the street plan had been totally redefined. The Roman plan had been completely obliterated, apart from the central east-

Fig. 20 The Old Minster, Winchester (reconstruction).

west axis of the High Street, which may have continued in use during the Dark Ages, and which, together with the Roman defensive wall, determined the orientation of the new street grid. The grid was the result of deliberate town planning under King *Alfred, intended to provide access to the walls for defensive purposes against the Danes. Winchester's first *mint appears to date from this period of renewal of urban life in the city.

The early tenth century was marked by two new ecclesiastical foundations in the south–eastern corner of the town, both planned by King Alfred but completed after his death by *Edward the Elder. By 901 New Minster had been founded immediately north of Old Minster; perhaps to serve the needs of the new population of the replanned city. It was also the burial place of the English royal house in the first half of the tenth century. Also dating from the early years of Edward's reign was Nunnaminster, later 'St Mary's Abbey', apparently established on an urban estate belonging to Ealhswith, Alfred's wife.

The tenth-century monastic reforms, which reached Winchester from continental centres such as *Fleury and Ghent, had considerable impact. Under Bishop *Æthelwold the secular canons of Old and New Minster were expelled in 964 and replaced by regular Benedictine monks. This involved the construction of new domestic buildings, and Æthelwold is remembered for the

creation of the monastic drainage system, the 'Lockburn', which served as Winchester's town drain until 1875 and still survives. In the 960s–70s King *Edgar enclosed the three religious foundations with a boundary, an action which involved the demolition of a number of secular buildings in this part of the town. In the same period the bishop's palace of Wolvesey was constructed in the south-western corner of the city, where Roman houses had been superseded by intramural fields. The three monastic foundations and the episcopal palace now occupied more than a quarter of the area of the Roman walled city.

The development of the cult of the ninth-century bishop, St *Swithun, was central to the reform of Old Minster, and at the time of his translations in 971 and ?974 the cathedral was greatly enlarged, first with the addition of a large west-work, dedicated in 980, over the site of his grave, which was formerly located *sub divo* in the atrium west of the church, and subsequently by extending the church eastwards. Perhaps to rival these works, a great western tower was added to New Minster.

The medieval names of Winchester's intramural streets indicate the growth of local industries since the refounding of the city under Alfred: Tanneres-tret, Goldestret, Sildwortenestret (silver-workers), Scowrtenestret (shoe-makers), etc. But the supreme artistic achievements were those pro-

481

duced by the three minsters, home of the artistic style known as the *Winchester School.

M. Biddle, '*Felix Urbs Winthonia*: Winchester in the Age of Monastic Reform', in *Tenth-Century Studies*, ed. D. Parsons (London, 1975), pp. 123–40; idem, 'Winchester: the Development of an Early Capital', in *Vor- und Früh-formen der europäischen Stadt im Mittelalter*, ed. H. Jankuhn, W. Schlesinger, and H. Steuer (Göttingen, 1973), pp. 229–61; idem, 'Excavations at Winchester, Interim Reports: 1964 (Third Report)', *AJ* 45 (1965), 230–64; 1966 (Fifth Report), *ibid.* 47 (1967), 251–79; 1967 (Sixth Report), *ibid.* 48 (1968), 250–84; 1968 (Seventh Report), *ibid.*, 49 (1969), 295–329; B.A.E. Yorke, 'The Foundation of the Old Minster and the Status of Winchester in the Seventh and Eighth Centuries', *Proceedings of the Hampshire Field Club* 38 (1982), 75–84; M. Biddle and D. Hill, 'Late Saxon Planned Towns', *AJ* 51 (1971), 70–85; M. Biddle and B. Kjølbye-Biddle, *The Anglo-Saxon Minsters of Winchester*, Winchester Studies 4.1 (Oxford, forthcoming); R. Quirk, 'Winchester New Minster and its Tenth-Century Tower', *JBAA* 3rd ser. 24 (1961), 16–54.

JOHN CROOK

'**WINCHESTER SCHOOL**' refers properly to artworks, principally manuscript illuminations, produced in or around *Winchester in the late Anglo-Saxon period. However, the term is sometimes loosely applied not only to any volumes illuminated in similar style, but also to all late Anglo-Saxon (as opposed to Anglo-Scandinavian) art.

The beginnings of the Winchester school proper are represented by the stole and maniple commissioned by Queen Ælfflæd for Bishop Frithestan of Winchester, demonstrating its intimate connection with the house of *Wessex. These golden *embroideries (datable to 909 × 916) are decorated with attenuated prophet figures and sprigs of foliage, reflecting Byzantine and Carolingian influence respectively. The touchstones for the mature Winchester style, the New Minster Charter and the *Benedictional of Æthelwold (BL, Cotton Vespasian A. viii and Add. 49598), dating from 966 and 971 × 984, are both key products of *Æthelwold's monastic reform. The frontispiece to the New Minster Charter, which shows King *Edgar presenting the volume to Christ, is surrounded by a rich border of trellis acanthus growing around parallel gold bars (pl. 22); the miniatures in the Benedictional are set within elaborate arch-shaped or rectangular frames, constructed from thick gold bars filled with panels of foliage, the corners and sides being articulated with foliage-adorned bosses. The artistic vocabulary of these borders, which are the hallmarks of the style, combines Franco-Saxon frame types,

panel 'acanthus' of Metz ancestry, and trellis foliage of the sort used in southern English art of the earlier tenth century. The figural compositions, which unite plasticity of form with glittering surface pattern, echo Carolingian exemplars in style and *iconography, with an undercurrent of Byzantine influence. Objects such as a triangular *ivory plaque decorated with two angels and a copper alloy mount, both excavated at Winchester, reveal the currency of these decorative and figural styles in other media; while an ivory Nativity now in Liverpool which is closely similar to the corresponding scene in the Benedictional of Æthelwold shows that iconographies were reduplicated from one medium to another. It is clear from late works such as the Tiberius Psalter (BL, Cotton Tiberius C. vi) that the style was still flourishing at Winchester at the time of the Conquest.

Decorated books were certainly 'exported' from Winchester – the Benedictional, Rouen, BM, Y. 7, which came to Jumièges is a case in point – and, reflecting the distribution of such models along with the connections between the various reformed monastic houses, foliate borders in similar style were rapidly adopted at other English *scriptoria. Eleventh-century examples are known from *Canterbury, Crowland, *Bury St Edmunds, *Exeter, and elsewhere. Related works in other media, such as the carved angels at *Bradford-upon-Avon and the painted ones at Nether Wallop (pl. 21), further attest to the distribution of the style in the south; while the late eleventh-century 'Winchester acanthus' capitals at Canterbury, *Worcester and Milborne Port demonstrate that it survived the Conquest in various locations.

The 'Winchester' style was also influential on the Continent, and similar foliate frames, reflecting English exemplars or personnel, appear in books produced at Saint-Bertin *c*.1000 and at various centres in *Normandy from the mid-eleventh century, as well as further afield, such as at Angers and Poiters in the late eleventh century, and at Weingarten in the twelfth century (the last reflecting the Anglo-Saxon *gospelbooks given to Weingarten Abbey by Judith of *Flanders). A late example in a remarkably pure style is the mid-twelfth century gospel book from Cysoing in northern France (Lille, Bibliothèque municipale, 479 (33)).

With its powerful royal and ecclesiastical patrons, Winchester was undoubtedly an important and innovative artistic centre in the late Anglo-Saxon period, and it appears to have been the epicentre of a very popular style of foliate

Pl. 22 'Winchester School decoration': the New Minster Charter (London, BL, Cotton Vespasian A.viii, 2v).

ornament. Whether it played a similarly important role in the development of all the southern figural art that is crudely labelled as 'Winchester School' work is doubtful. Furthermore, although the surviving evidence presents the 'Winchester School' as primarily ecclesiastical, with monastic works at the forefront of artistic development, this is probably a distortion resulting from the poor survival of non-religious art. The royal patronage of Frithestan's vestments, along with the fragments of contemporary *metalwork hint that it was as much a secular phenomenon; however, as most such work is lost, the implications of this are impossible to evaluate.

G. Zarnecki, 'The Winchester Acanthus in Romanesque Sculpture', repr. in his *Studies in Romanesque Sculpture* (London, 1979), ch. 2; *Golden Age of AS Art*; D. M. Wilson, *Anglo-Saxon Art* (London, 1984); R. G. Gameson, 'English Manuscript Art in the Mid-Eleventh Century', *AJ* 71 (1991), 64–122.

RICHARD GAMESON

WINDSOR (OLD) (Berks.), now a field called 'Kingsbury' beside the Thames, is the site of a royal palace recorded in the 1060s and abandoned after 1107. Excavations (still unpublished) revealed early Anglo-Saxon *settlement replaced, from the beginning of the ninth century, by a high-status complex including a stone building with glazed windows and a tiled roof. A massive triple-wheeled *mill on a large mill-leat was associated with these buildings by the excavator, though a date in the late seventh century has now been claimed on dendrochronological evidence. The complex was destroyed in the late ninth century; *timber buildings with sleeper-beams, and a simpler mill, occupied the site during the tenth and eleventh centuries. The now-isolated parish church stands on the north-east edge of the complex. Old Windsor is probably the strongest candidate so far for a ninth-century English royal palace, though it is important to remember the late date of the written evidence.

G. G. Astill, *Historic Towns in Berkshire: an Archaeological Appraisal* (Reading, 1978), pp. 69–73; Wilson, *Archaeology*, p. 433; J. Fletcher, 'Roman and Saxon Dendro Dates', *Current Archaeology* 76 (1981), 150–2.

JOHN BLAIR

WING (Bucks.) retains an important church, basically of the ninth century (pl. 23). The nave probably had single north and south *porticus* (the arcades which have prompted a basilican interpretation seem in fact to be later), and an irregular polygonal *crypt with niches, presumably for *relics, in its walls. The date of the polygonal apse with its external stripwork decoration, the most impressive surviving Anglo-Saxon east end, is controversial, but it may be contemporary with the crypt and must lie somewhere in the late ninth or tenth century. Perhaps in the tenth or eleventh century, an ambulatory was created inside the crypt by the insertion of large piers carrying vaults. The only hint that Wing was an important place comes from the *will of Ælfgifu (966 × 975), who leaves an estate there to King *Edgar; the status of the church has been forgotten, as have the saint or saints enshrined in its crypt.

Taylor and Taylor, *AS Arch*, ii. 665–72; H. M. Taylor, 'The Anglo-Saxon Church at Wing', *Archaeological Journal* 136 (1979), 43–52; Fernie, *Architecture*, pp. 69–70, 121; R. Gem, 'Architecture of the Anglo-Saxon Church, 735 to 870', *JBAA* 146 (1993), 29–66, at 53–4.

JOHN BLAIR

WISDOM LITERATURE is a term used by modern scholars to denote a wide range of Old English poems that have certain affinities with near-eastern wisdom texts best exemplified by the Old Testament books of Proverbs and Ecclesiastes. The term is not an exact one, and opinions differ as to whether particular poems belong to the genre, but a broad scholarly consensus identifies some fifteen to twenty extant Old English poems as wisdom literature. These poems share a common concern with the fundamentals of human existence and experience, with the articulation and communication of great and universal truths, and many adopt the fictive persona of a wise sage offering instruction to a younger disciple. Those that can be further classified as *gnomic poetry (*Maxims* I and II in particular) employ brief, tightly structured utterances made very distinctive by a characteristic use of the verbs *sculan* ('to be obliged', 'to have to') and *beon* ('to be'). Despite these common features, wisdom poetry varies widely in style and temper. *Maxims* I and II offer heterogeneous collections of folk wisdom, natural science, and religious counsel couched in terse, proverbial formulae. In *Precepts* an older narrating persona gives social and religious advice to a young listener. The *Rune Poem* presents a collection of more enigmatic proverbial matter, structured around the Anglo-Saxon *runes. Sharing with these poems the basic structural principle of the list or catalogue are the *Fortunes of Men and the *Gifts of Men, which enumerate the fates and the gifts that God bestows on human beings, but which also frame their lists in a more broadly developed moral and religious context. Other

Pl. 23 The church at Wing

wisdom poems take the form of extended meditations: in the *Order of the World* the poet-sage engages in rhapsodies on the glories of creation, while poems such as *Vainglory* and *Resignation* (the latter on the outside edge of what can be classified as wisdom poetry) explore the subjects of sinful pride and contrition respectively. The poetic *Solomon and Saturn* records a dialogue and a debate between two legendary sages of antiquity. Many Old English poems belonging to other genres have passages that exhibit the qualities of wisdom literature, certain *riddles, *elegies such as the *Wanderer* and the *Seafarer*, and long narrative poems such as *Beowulf* prominent among them.

N. D. Isaacs, *Structural Principles in Old English Poetry* (Knoxville, TN, 1968); T. A. Shippey, *Poems of Wisdom and Learning in Old English* (Totowa, NJ, and London, 1976); F. C. Robinson, 'Understanding an Old English Wisdom Verse: *Maxims* II, lines 10ff', in *The Wisdom of Poetry: Essays in Early English Literature in Honor of Morton W. Bloomfield*, ed. L. D. Benson and S. Wenzel (Kalamazoo, MI, 1982), pp. 1–11.

ROBERT DINAPOLI

WISTAN, ST (d. *c.*850), is known through a Life probably composed by Dominic of Evesham in the early twelfth century and preserved in three diverse fragments of thirteenth- and fourteenth-century date. It describes how Wistan, the grandson of Wiglaf, king of *Mercia (827–40), though having no desire to claim the throne for himself, was murdered by a rival, Brihtferth. A column of light from heaven confirmed that he was a martyr. Though late, this tale would seem to contain some truth, given the remarkable archaeological finds at *Repton, the principal centre of the saint's cult until his relics were translated to Evesham during the reign of King *Cnut (1016–35). They have shown that this church was built upon a royal mausoleum which had been converted within a decade or two of his alleged death into a crypt of a type used to facilitate the veneration of relics.

A. T. Thacker, 'Kings, Saints and Monasteries in Pre-Viking Mercia', *Midland History* 10 (1985), 1–25, at 12–14.

PAUL ANTONY HAYWARD

WITAN: *see* Council, King's

WOMEN. The status of women in Anglo-Saxon England has been the subject of considerable debate. Much of the evidence is contained in early *laws, which are often cryptically expressed and difficult to interpret. The same provisions have been taken to indicate on the one hand that women were subject to direct male control, and on the other that their legal standing equalled that of men. The latter view is supported by *wills and *charters showing women able to acquire and dispose of property on their own authority, by records of law-suits brought and defended by women, and by *place-names reflecting the prominence of women within society.

Many of the laws relating to women are concerned with marriage procedures and inheritance rights (cf. *marriage and divorce, *widow). Those dealing with criminal responsibility indicate that women were personally accountable under the law, and this is confirmed for instance by records of the forfeitures suffered by the widow Brihtwaru during the late tenth century as accessory after the fact to theft (S 1457), and by Æthelflæd during the early eleventh century for assisting her outlawed brother (S 926). Sexual assaults against women, whether *slave or free, were heavily penalised, and *Alfred's law-code specifies that for victims of ceorl rank and above, compensation was payable directly to the woman herself (ch. 11). Like men, women could also receive compensation for offences against people under their protection (Æthelberht 75, Ine 23). Perhaps most significantly, they were considered *oath-worthy. This is reflected not only in legislation allowing women to defend themselves on oath against false accusations (Ine 57, Alfred 11), but in recorded cases such as the tenth-century land dispute between Leofwine and Wynflæd, where the latter was allowed to prove her title by means of an oath supported by her friends of both sexes (S 1454). So too the ninth-century will of Æthelric, bequeathing estates to his mother Ceolburh, authorises her to defend her claim to the inheritance on oath (S 1187). In such instances women appear to be accorded the same rights under the law as men; and they also appear as grantors, grantees, and witnesses of charters.

Some of the major land-holders recorded in *Domesday Book are women; while toponyms preserving the names of female owners or lessees include Bamburgh, received by the Northumbrian queen Bebbe as her 'morning-gift' during the seventh century (cf. *marriage), Bibury, inherited by Beage during the eighth, and Wolverhampton, given to Wulfrun in 985. Surviving wills, of which more than a quarter are by female testatrices, also represent the land-holding classes, and provide substantial evidence of women's property rights. Among the items bequeathed and inherited by women are estates, slaves, livestock, household furnishings, *clothing, gold and jewels, and books.

In the absence of primogeniture, daughters could inherit equally with sons, and in general the testators show no marked preference for male as opposed to female heirs. The autonomy with which women could dispose of their own property is illustrated by a famous case from eleventh-century Herefordshire, where a mother whose son was attempting to deprive her of an estate disinherited him in favour of a female relative by means of a verbal declaration (S 1462).

Most documentary sources relate to women of aristocratic rank (cf. *Æthelflæd; *queens). Less information is available for women of the lower classes; but legal and testamentary texts show that female slaves were employed as corn-grinders, serving maids, wet-nurses, weavers and seamstresses, while other occupations pursued by women appear to have included baking and cheese-making. Women of ceorl class and above were responsible for the management of their own households, and it is possible that the key-shaped 'girdle-hangers' found in female graves from the early period symbolise the control of domestic economy (cf. *grave goods). The practice of fine *embroidery by ladies and members of their households is attested by a number of literary references and by surviving artifacts such as the St *Cuthbert stole and maniples, and the *Bayeux Tapestry.

With the foundation during the seventh and eighth centuries of the great double monasteries ruled by abbesses, the church offered significant opportunities for women to attain positions of authority. Again, the sources deal mainly with leading figures such as *Hild of Whitby, *Cuthburg of *Wimborne, and St *Æthelthryth of *Ely. Some female religious were women of great learning, as notably *Boniface's correspondents *Leobgyth, *Eadburg and Bugga, and it has been suggested that standards of *literacy may have been higher among women than among men. Among the earliest extant charters are grants of land to women in order to found religious communities, over whose financial assets they exercised full control; and it is not uncommon for abbesses and other powerful women to appear as principals in law-suits relating to these foundations. Instances include the litigation between Abbess Hrothwaru and her mother over the inheritance of a family minster during the early eighth century (S 1429), and the long-running disputes between Archbishop *Wulfred of Canterbury and Abbess Cwoenthryth, daughter of King *Coenwulf of *Mercia, during the early ninth (S 1434, 1436). The power of such abbesses did not survive the

*Viking invasions and the monastic reform movement, but women continued to play a major role in religious affairs during the later Anglo-Saxon period through the endowment and support of monastic communities, and through personal piety.

M. A. Meyer, 'Women and the Tenth Century English Monastic Reform', *RB* 87 (1977), 34–61; S. C. Dietrich, 'An Introduction to Women in Anglo-Saxon Society (*c*.600–1066)', *The Women of England From Anglo-Saxon Times to the Present*, ed. B. Kanner (London, 1980), pp. 32–56; M. A. Meyer, 'Land Charters and the Legal Position of Anglo-Saxon Women', ibid. pp. 57–82; A. L. Klinck, 'Anglo-Saxon Women and the Law', *JMH* 8 (1982), 107–21; C. Fell, C. Clark and E. Williams, *Women in Anglo-Saxon England and the Impact of 1066* (London, 1984); *New Readings on Women in Old English Literature*, ed. H. Damico and A. H. Olsen (Bloomington, IN, 1990); S. Hollis, *Anglo-Saxon Women and the Church* (Woodbridge, 1992); P. Halpin, 'Women Religious in Late Anglo-Saxon England', *HSJ* 6 (1994), 97–110; P. Stafford, 'Women and the Norman Conquest', *TRHS* 6th ser. 4 (1994), 221–49; C. Hough, 'Alfred, ch. 11, and the Language of Rape,' *MÆ* (forthcoming).

CAROLE HOUGH

WOODLAND covered roughly the same proportion of Anglo-Saxon England as it does of France today. The statistics of woods given in *Domesday Book at the end of the period add up to about 15 per cent of the land area. Woodland was very unevenly distributed. In some regions, such as the Weald and the Chiltern plateau, it predominated over non-woodland, although no point was more than five miles from some *settlement. In other areas, as in the Breckland, there was no woodland at all; many settlements were more than five miles from a wood.

Woodland is abundantly mentioned in *charters, usually in the context of boundaries. About one in four of these woods still exists. There were names both for individual wood-lots – many woods still have Old English names today – and for larger wooded areas. Woodland is also alluded to in *place-names, for example those ending in -*leah*, -*hyrst*, and Old Norse *þveit*. Charters and place-names also refer to hedges, hedgerow and isolated trees: these were more abundant in places which also had woodland.

Some Anglo-Saxon woods had been woodland since Mesolithic times; others had sprung up on farmland abandoned after the Roman period, for example where Stansted Airport is now. During the Anglo-Saxon period, woodland continued to increase in some places and decrease in others as people grubbed it out for farmland. There is

curiously little record of either change. With a rising population decreases were presumably commoner than increases, although there is no suggestion that the average Anglo-Saxon spent weeks every year digging up trees. Both charters and place-names indicate that the distribution of wooded and unwooded regions did not change radically during the period.

Some woods were valuable private property, and could give rise to lawsuits. Others were commonland. Wood boundaries were often defined by a structure called a *wyrtruma*, where there is now a bank and ditch. Other earthworks probably divided ownerships within a wood. Where a block of woodland was surrounded by a large woodless area, it was often divided into several lots belonging to places many miles away, as in Wychwood (Oxfordshire).

Anglo-Saxon woods were of many species of tree – hazel, ash, oak, hawthorn, lime, maple, service – corresponding to ancient woods today. (There were no conifers except for rare yew.) They varied in structure: coppice-woods, woods of timber trees, wood-pastures. The Old English words for woodland – *wudu*, *fyrhð*, *holt*, *scaga*, *bearu*, etc. – presumably refer to different structures, but their exact meanings are lost.

Anglo-Saxon England was very dependent on *timber for the carpentry of houses, *bridges, farm equipment, etc., and also on underwood (rods and poles) of various sizes for wattle construction, fencing, and fuel. Land grants sometimes include regular supplies of both. Coppicing – felling of woods at short intervals to produce underwood – was not yet the dominant form of woodmanship except in poorly-wooded areas. Woods without a more intensive use were used as pasture. This implies a sparse, savanna-like structure with grass between the trees, through which it was possible to ride a horse, as in the deer-hunt in which King *Edmund nearly broke his neck in *Cheddar Gorge. Trees may have been pollarded to produce successive crops of wood, and also leaves on which to feed livestock (pl. 24). Red and roe deer, though not confined to woodland, were a significant product of some woods. Woodland with enough oaks was used for fattening pigs in autumn in years in which there was an acorn crop; in the great wooded area of the Weald this was regarded, at least by record-keepers, as the principal use.

Woodland was a renewable resource. The Anglo-Saxons do not mention woodland conservation in their surviving writings, but it is implied in the trouble which they took to embank the

Pl. 24 Hatfield Forest, wood-pasture, showing pollard trees cut for the first time

edges of woods. They did not plant trees in woods: wherever a tree was felled, another would normally grow. However, where cattle, sheep, or deer could eat the young shoots, woodland may ultimately have turned into heath.

To gain an idea of what Anglo-Saxon woodland looked like, one should visit Hatfield Forest near Bishop's Stortford (National Trust) and the Bradfield Woods near Bury St Edmunds (Suffolk Wildlife Trust). The former is a complex of wood-pasture, coppice-woods, and young woodland, partly overlying Roman and earlier remains. The latter is a more intensively-managed coppice surrounded by great banks: occasional giant living stool-bases might even date back to Anglo-Saxon times.

G. Milne, *Timber Building Techniques in London c.900–1400* (London, 1992); O. Rackham, *Trees and Woodland in the British Landscape*, 2nd ed. (London, 1969); B. Schumer, *The Evolution of Wychwood to 1400: Pioneers, Frontiers and Forests* (Leicester, 1984); K. P. Witney, *The Jutish Forest* (London, 1976); D. Hooke, *The Landscape of Anglo-Saxon England* (Leicester, 1998).

OLIVER RACKHAM

WOOD-WORKING: *see* Timber Building

WORCESTER was the seat of a diocese founded by 680 (its foundation may have been projected as early as 675), when Archbishop *Theodore decided to increase the number of sees in the area under Mercian overlordship. The bishopric corresponded in area to the kingdom of the *Hwicce, and the rulers of this kingdom, already in the late seventh century subordinate to *Mercia, endowed it with, among other properties, a large block of land to either side of the Severn in Worcestershire, including the site of Worcester itself, a former Roman industrial town, which, since it was fortified and stood on a bluff overlooking the river, was appropriate for a major church. *Winchcombe and *Gloucester, sites more closely connected to the Hwiccian dynasty, had probably already been earmarked for the foundation of monasteries. Worcester probably already had at least one church, St Helen's, when the diocese was established, but the cathedral was built to the south of it and was dedicated to St Peter.

Since the Hwiccian rulers seem to have been connected with *Northumbria, it is not surprising to find that the first bishop to be appointed to Worcester, Tatwine, was from *Whitby (though he died before he could be consecrated). The background of his successor, Bosel, is unknown, but his assistant in his last years and successor, Oftfor, had also been trained at Whitby. Probably Oftfor encouraged a good standard of education among his *clergy. The cathedral community starts to make an appearance by the early eighth century, though we have to wait until *c*.800 to learn about its composition: about seventeen members, including nine priests. Probably the community consisted of clerks from the outset. During the latter part of the eighth and the ninth centuries the church of Worcester took over a large number of small private monasteries in the diocese whose endowments swelled its resources. Another source of economic growth was untapped at the turn of the ninth and tenth centuries when, in two separate agreements of the 890s and 904, the bishop and community leased land just outside the defences of Worcester to *Æthelred and *Æthelflæd of Mercia for urban development; the community also promised to pray for them in return for their friendship.

During this period the cathedral had maintained, to judge from its charters, a reasonable level of Latinity. *Alfred of Wessex made use of this by employing Bishop *Werferth (872–915) to improve educational standards at his court, and then rewarded his services by sending a copy of his OE translation of Gregory's *Pastoral Care* to Worcester. The tenth century was to see a gradual build-up of Worcester's *scriptorium and *library, but progress was slow until the early eleventh century.

The major force for change in tenth-century Worcester was *Oswald, of local family on his mother's side, highly connected with leading ecclesiastics on his father's, who became bishop of Worcester in 961. Oswald, who had been trained as a monk at *Fleury, set up a group of monks in his *parochia* at Westbury-on-Trym soon after his consecration, before moving them, perhaps in 965, to *Ramsey. Ramsey, in his father's homeland, was to be his flagship monastery, but he set up other monasteries in his diocese, including one in his cathedral precinct which he dedicated to St Mary, which he appears to have started to build in 966. Its appearance may be linked to a redefinition of the cathedral precinct on a smaller scale, but more strictly enclosed, in the tenth century. The building of St Mary's took a long time, as Oswald himself later commented; probably he had to face hostility from his cathedral clergy at St Peter's, which perhaps explains the absence of their names as witnesses to his charters in 964–5 and 970–6. Accounts of Oswald driving out his cathedral clergy in either 964 (according to the forged privilege of Edgar known as *Altitonantis*) or 969 (according to the probably forged synodal document of *Wulfstan II of 1092, and the *Chron-

icle of *John of Worcester), are later fabrications, created in the twelfth century to bring Worcester's past into line with Winchester's and to justify the status of the monks of Worcester, who by the early twelfth century were worried that non-monastic bishops might wish to replace them with secular canons.

Not until 977 is there secure evidence of monks in the cathedral community. By this time, however, the head of the community appears as a monk, and this practice continued under Oswald's successors. The rest of the community appears, however, to have been composed of a mixture of clerks and monks, for those who describe themselves as *clerici* in witness lists are not likely to have been monks, and Oswald's hagiographer says that both monks and clerks officiated at his funeral in 992. Probably the clerks continued to serve in St Peter's, which still housed the episcopal throne until at least the 990s, while the monks served St Mary's. The two churches co-existed until at least the mid-eleventh century, more probably until the 1080s when Bishop Wulfstan II (1062–95) started to build his new cathedral.

An event which gave the monks of St Mary's new impetus was the translation of St Oswald into their church in 1002. It may have been at this time that the episcopal throne was moved into St Mary's; it was certainly at about this time that *Byrhtferth of Ramsey composed his *Vita S. Oswaldi*, possibly at the request of the monks of Worcester (though Byrhtferth made sure that Oswald's foundation of Ramsey was the centrepiece of his work). Not long afterwards, probably before 1016, the monks of St Mary's compiled a cartulary (the first half of BL, Cotton Tiberius A.xiii), into which they entered, among many genuine charters, a number of forged and interpolated ones, several of which refer to the dedication of Worcester cathedral in the eighth and ninth centuries as St Mary's, and mention monastic life.

The strongest motive for the compilation of this cartulary, even more than the need to snub the clerical faction in the community, was the fact that the bishop between 1002 and 1016, *Wulfstan the Homilist, was simultaneously archbishop of *York, and, since he was also a senior adviser of *Æthelred the Unready, was absent for long periods. The idea of holding Worcester and York in plurality had begun under Oswald (archbishop of York from 971) and was to be re-attempted by Archbishop Ælfric of York in 1040–1 and by *Ealdred (bishop of Worcester 1046–61) between 1060 and 1061. In origin an attempt by *Edgar to ensure that the politically volatile see of York would be held by a loyal supporter, it became a useful means for the archbishops of York to increase their revenues. Wulfstan appropriated some of the property of the see and Ealdred, as a condition of his renunciation of the bishopric of Worcester, took even more. Nor were these the only losses in the first half of the eleventh century: under *Cnut and his successors the church of Worcester lost further lands to Danish royal followers. The losses were recorded at the end of the eleventh century by *Hemming, at the end of the pontificate of St Wulfstan, who had done much in his lifetime to make good the depredations by the archbishops of York.

Wulfstan of York (the Homilist), his nephew Brihtheah (bishop of Worcester 1033–8), and the younger Wulfstan (the future saint) were members of an influential local family. Young Wulfstan began his career as a clerk in the household of Brihtheah before deciding to become a monk. As prior and later, after 1062, as bishop, he enforced monastic discipline among his colleagues. The monks built up a large collection of manuscripts during the eleventh century, concentrating on homiletic literature, penitentials, law, and, increasingly, literature about the monastic life. The homilies were put into practical use, for the monks played an active part in pastoral care, preaching to the citizens of Worcester. Worcester preserved, under Wulfstan, a vigorous tradition of writing in Old English until the end of the eleventh century, and acted as a guardian of the Anglo-Saxon past.

By the tenth century there is archaeological evidence that Worcester was developing as a *town. Topographical analysis has recently suggested the existence of late Anglo-Saxon urban planning.

P. Sims-Williams, *Religion and Literature in Western England, 600–800*, CSASE 3 (Cambridge, 1990); S. R. Bassett, 'Churches in Worcester before and after the Conversion of the Anglo-Saxons', *AJ* 69 (1989), 225–56; *Oswald of Worcester*; E. Mason, *St Wulfstan of Worcester* (Oxford, 1990); J. Raine, ed., *Historians of the Church of York*, 3 vols., RS (London, 1879–94); T. Hearne, ed., *Hemingi Chartularium Ecclesiae Wigorniensis*, 2 vols. (Oxford, 1723); I. Atkins, 'The Church of Worcester from the Eighth to the Twelfth Century', *AJ* 17 (1937), 371–91; ibid. 20 (1940), 1–38; J. Barrow, 'How the Twelfth-Century Monks of Worcester Perceived their Past', in P. Magdalino, ed., *The Perception of the Past in Twelfth-Century Europe* (London and Rio Grande, OH, 1992); E. John, *Orbis Britanniae and Other Studies* (Leicester, 1966); J. Cross and J. Morrish, ed., *The Copenhagen Wulfstan Collection*, EEMF 25 (Copenhagen, 1993).

JULIA BARROW

WULF AND EADWACER. The most enigmatic of the Old English *elegies, the 19-line *Wulf and Eadwacer* in the *Exeter Book was long regarded as the first of the *riddles, which it immediately precedes in the manuscript. Disagreement about the poem persists, but it is acknowledged by most critics to be the impassioned lament of a woman separated from her lover. The 'Eadwacer' of the poem seems to be a tyrannical husband or guardian – unless he is the same person as the woman's lover, Wulf. The speaker also refers to 'the whelp of us two', that is, the child she has had with Wulf or Eadwacer, a child which Wulf (or 'a wolf') is carrying (or 'will carry') to the forest. Along with the *Wife's Lament, Wulf and Eadwacer* is an early example of medieval 'women's songs' or *Frauenlieder*.

ASPR iii. 179–80; P. S. Baker, 'The Ambiguity of *Wulf and Eadwacer*', *Studies in Philology* 78.5 (1981), 39–51 (repr. in *Old English Shorter Poems: Basic Readings*, ed. K. O'B. O'Keeffe (New York, 1994), pp. 393–407); P. A. Belanoff, 'Women's Songs, Women's Language: *Wulf and Eadwacer* and *The Wife's Lament*', in *New Readings on Women in Old English Literature*, ed. H. Damico and A. H. Olsen (Bloomington, IN, 1990), pp. 193–203; J. A. Tasioulas, 'The Mother's Lament: *Wulf and Eadwacer* Reconsidered', *MÆ* 65 (1996), 1–18.

ANNE L. KLINCK

WULFHERE, king of the Mercians (658–74). After the defeat of King *Penda, at the battle of the *Winwæd*, on 15 November 655, *Oswiu, king of the Northumbrians, ruled over the kingdom of the Mercians, 'as well as the rest of the southern kingdoms', for three years (*HE* iii.24). Oswiu entrusted the kingdom of the southern Mercians to Penda's elder son, Peada, who was murdered the following year. In 658 Immin, Eafa and Eadberht, described by *Bede as *'ealdormen of the people of the Mercians', rebelled against Oswiu, and set up Penda's younger son Wulfhere as king. Wulfhere soon established himself as overlord of other southern peoples; and, as in the case of Penda, this brought him into sustained conflict with *Northumbria. He gave land at Barrow, in *Lindsey, to Bishop *Chad, for the endowment of a monastery, and is said to have ruled over the kingdoms of the Mercians, the *Middle Angles, and *Lindsey (*HE* iv.3). He was in a position to sell the see of *London to Bishop Wine (*HE* iii.7); and the kings of the East Saxons were subject to him (*HE* iii.39). Frithuwold, ruler of Surrey, was regarded as a sub-king of Wulfhere (S 1165: *EHD* i, no. 54); and Wulfhere was able to put pressure on Æthelwealh, king of the South Saxons, to adopt Christianity, giving him the *prouinciae* of the Isle of Wight and of the *Meonware*, in *Wessex (*HE* iv.13). Yet the balance of power still lay between the peoples or confederacies established respectively north and south of the river Humber. In 674 Wulfhere roused 'all the southern peoples' against the Northumbians, in an attempt to subject them to him; in the event, however, he was defeated by Ecgfrith, king of the Northumbrians, who drove him out of the kingdom of Lindsey (*Stephen of Ripon, *Vita S. Wilfridi*, c. 20; *HE* iv.12). Wulfhere was succeeded by his brother Æthelred, king of the Mercians (675–704; d. 716), who fought 'a great battle' against King Ecgfrith in 679, somewhere near the river Trent; Archbishop *Theodore negotiated a settlement, and 'henceforth, for a long period, peace was maintained between these kings and their respective kingdoms' (*HE* iv.21). The Northumbrians appear to have been marginalised after this event, and the balance of effective political power began to shift southwards from the Humber estuary to the river Thames. The process had as much to do with the development of economic prosperity in the south, and with the consolidation of religious authority at *Canterbury (represented by the activities of Archbishop Theodore), as with the apparent 'decline' of *Northumbria itself (cf. *HE* iv.26); and if for some time the kingdoms of Wessex and *Kent held each other in check, and Mercia off, circumstances conspired *c.*725 in a way which allowed *Æthelbald, king of the Mercians, to come to the fore.

Stenton, *ASE*, pp. 84–5; P. H. Sawyer, *From Roman Britain to Norman England* (London, 1978), pp. 39–40; Yorke, *Kingdoms*, pp. 105–10; Kirby, *Kings*, pp. 113–17; M. Gelling, *The West Midlands in the Early Middle Ages* (Leicester, 1992), pp. 86, 94–5.

SIMON KEYNES

WULFRED, archbishop of *Canterbury (d. 832). Wulfred was an energetic archbishop, whose attempts to boost the position of the Canterbury primate and to curb secular interests in the English church led to a bitter clash with the Mercian King *Coenwulf. By birth he was probably a Mercian or Middle Saxon nobleman, and he was to use his personal fortune to acquire extensive estates for the archbishopric and the cathedral community at Canterbury. He was already a senior member of the community by 803, when he attended a synod in the entourage of Archbishop Æthelheard. Æthelheard died on 12 May 805; Wulfred was elected as his successor on 26 July and was conse-

crated towards the end of the same year. Almost certainly the election was approved by King Coenwulf, who was overlord of *Kent, ruling the province first through his brother Cuthred (d. 807) and later directly. But relations between king and archbishop deteriorated quickly and so seriously that in 808 their bitter disagreement was mentioned in correspondence between Pope Leo III and Charlemagne (*H&S*, iii. 563). What caused the breach is uncertain, and it would seem to have been papered over without too much delay. Between 809 and 815, under the auspices of the Mercian king, Wulfred occupied himself in a dazzling series of land-transactions, comprising straightforward purchases as well as complex exchanges with other land-owners, among them Coenwulf himself; an important underlying rationale seems to have been Wulfred's desire to rationalise his own property and the cathedral endowment into compact, manageable (and more profitable) blocks. These transactions left a 'paper trail' of *charters, which demonstrates that Wulfred was keenly aware of the importance of written evidence for land-holding. As well as using his financial expertise to build up the cathedral's resources, the archbishop also turned his attention to the reform and restructuring of the community at Christ Church. He drew up a new constitution for the brethren, whereby they agreed to carry out their proper liturgical duties and to share a common refectory and dormitory; in return they received some hereditary interest in the monastic housing, which they had personally helped to rebuild (S 1265). Wulfred's arrangements were perhaps influenced by the rule for canons drawn up by Chrodegang of Metz in *c.*755–6, but it remains unclear whether Christ Church was transformed under Wulfred into a community of regular canons or whether it retained some attributes of monastic life.

In 814–15 Wulfred travelled to *Rome, probably to seek the pope's approval for his plans to reform the English church. A synod of Southumbrian bishops convened at Chelsea under his presidency in July 816, and enacted a series of measures reinforcing episcopal authority, especially over the local monasteries and churches within the individual dioceses. These measures were contentious, to the extent that they diminished monastic independence and challenged long-established aristocratic and royal influence over minsters and their estates. King Coenwulf, who controlled a great hereditary network of monastic houses in Kent and elsewhere, was provoked by Wulfred's pretensions. The test-case was provided by Wulfred's bid for authority over two wealthy Kentish houses of *Minster-in-Thanet and *Reculver, then owned by the Mercian king. During the ensuing quarrel Wulfred was deprived of his office for several years (probably 817/18–821) and driven into exile, apparently with the pope's authority. Shortly before Coenwulf's death in 821 king and archbishop were reconciled and Wulfred was restored to office, after ignominiously surrendering a huge estate and paying a substantial fine (S 1436). After Coenwulf's death Wulfred revived his claims to Minster-in-Thanet and Reculver, now under the control of Coenwulf's daughter and heir, Cwoenthryth; but it was not until 826 that he was finally triumphant on the issue. Meanwhile, political conditions in Kent had changed, with the decline of Mercian power and an invasion by the West Saxon king *Ecgberht. The new rulers of Kent may not have regarded Wulfred with particular favour; they are not known to have made any grants to Canterbury in his lifetime, and indeed seem to have deprived Wulfred of at least one important estate on tendentious grounds (S 1438). Wulfred's loyalty may have remained with the now diminished Mercian rulers; the Mercian king Wiglaf certainly granted him land in Middlesex in 831 (S 188).

Wulfred died in 832, probably on 24 March. He bequeathed almost all his extensive estates to his kinsman, the priest Werhard, on condition that they be transferred to Christ Church on Werhard's death.

Brooks, *Canterbury*; C. Cubitt, *Anglo-Saxon Church Councils c.650–c.850* (London, 1995); B. Langefeld, 'Regula canonicorum or Regula monasterialis uitae? The Rule of Chrodegang and Archbishop Wulfred's Reforms at Canterbury', *ASE* 25 (1996), 21–36.

S. E. KELLY

WULFSIGE, bishop of *Sherborne (*c.*993–1002) was a native of London who became abbot of *Westminster shortly after its refoundation (*c.*959), and retained the abbacy until 997, in spite of his promotion to Sherborne *c.*993. At Sherborne he rebuilt the cathedral, and is known in the literary record as the recipient of a letter from the archbishop of Canterbury (unnamed) preserved in the 'Dunstan Pontifical' (now Paris, BN, lat. 943) as well as the addressee of *Ælfric's 'First Pastoral Letter' (993 × 995); another penitential letter, probably issued by Wulfsige, is preserved in the 'Dunstan Pontifical'. In the mid-eleventh century Wulfsige's remains were translated, and a *vita* of Wulfsige (*BHL* 8753) was composed by *Goscelin. Feast day: 8 January.

Sharpe, *Handlist*, 2227; Stubbs, *Memorials*, pp. 406–9; *Councils & Synods* i. 191–226 [Pastoral Letter I], 226–9 [letter from archbishop of Canterbury], 230–1 [penitential letter]; C. H. Talbot, 'The Life of St Wulsin of Sherborne by Goscelin', *RB* 69 (1951), 68–85 [with corrigenda by P. Grosjean in *AB* 78 (1951), 197–206]; J. H. P. Gibb, 'The Anglo-Saxon Cathedral at Sherborne', *Archaeological Journal* 132 (1975), 71–110; D. N. Dumville, *Liturgy and the Ecclesiastical History of Late Anglo-Saxon England* (Woodbridge, 1992), pp. 82–4.

MICHAEL LAPIDGE

WULFSTAN I, archbishop of York (931–56). Wulfstan was appointed archbishop of *York in 931, in succession to Hrothweard, and played a very significant part in the politics of the north for the next twenty-five years, until his death on 26 December 956. The course of his career, in respect of his relations with successive kings of the English, is suggested by the unfolding pattern of his attestations in royal *charters (reflecting his attendance or non-attendance at meetings of the king's councillors), supplemented by information derived ultimately from the set of northern *annals which lies behind the 'northern recension' of the *Anglo-Saxon Chronicle (*ASC*, MSS DE) and behind a part of the chronicle of *Simeon of Durham (*EHD* i, no. 3(c)). King *Æthelstan presumably sanctioned Wulfstan's appointment as one who could be relied upon to help ensure the loyalty of the notherners to his political cause; it would appear that the archbishop attested all of the king's charters issued between 931 and 935, and within this period he was the beneficiary of S 407, issued at Nottingham on 7 June 934. Curiously, Wulfstan was 'absent' in 936–41. It is not obvious precisely how to account for his non-appearance at court in the closing years of Æthelstan's reign (and so to judge whether he should be implicated in the campaign against Æthelstan which culminated at the *Battle of Brunanburh), but it seems likely enough that he was involved in the reception of Olaf Guthfrithsson at York in 939, and he is certainly found operating on Olaf's side in the initial struggle against King *Edmund in 939–40 (Simeon of Durham, s.a. 939; *ASC* MS D, s.a. 943). Wulfstan appeared at Edmund's court in 942 (when York was under the political control of Olaf's successors, Olaf Sihtricsson and Ragnald Guthfrithsson), but he was 'absent' in 943 (although Edmund seemingly remained on amicable terms with the Hiberno-Norse rulers), and then reappeared in 944 (in which year Edmund drove out Olaf Sihtricsson and Ragnald Guthfrithsson from York; interestingly, the chronicler *Æthelweard states that it was 'Bishop Wulfstan and the *ealdorman of the Mercians' who drove them out). Wulfstan attended meetings of Edmund's councillors regularly thereafter (though not invariably) until the king's death in May 946. He was among those who attended the coronation of King *Eadred, at *Kingston-upon-Thames, on 16 August 946 (S 520: *EHD* i, no. 105); but he was conspicuously 'absent' on at least one other occasion in that year. In 947 Eadred came to Tanshelf (on the river Humber), 'and there Archbishop Wulfstan and all the councillors of the Northumbrians pledged themselves to the king' (*ASC* MS D). Soon afterwards, however, the Northumbrians took *Eric Bloodaxe as their king; and it is interesting, in this connection, that Wulfstan was apparently 'absent' from meetings of King Eadred's councillors for what may have been an extended period in 947–8. In 948 Eadred invaded Northumbria; in the event, the Northumbrians 'deserted' Eric and apparently made terms with Eadred. It is appropriate, therefore, that Wulfstan and other northerners should have attended meetings of King Eadred's councillors for some while thereafter, from a point in 948 to a point in 950 (as suggested by *charters of standard type issued in 948 and 949, and as shown by charters of the 'alliterative' type issued in 949 and 950). Yet the Northumbrians were still not content with their lot. They seem to have taken Olaf Sihtricsson (again) in 950, exchanging him for Eric Bloodaxe (again) in 952 or 953 (*ASC* MS E, s.a. 949, 952). Wulfstan's complicity in the reception of Olaf is suggested by the fact that he was noticeably 'absent' from meetings of Eadred's councillors in 951. There are no surviving charters for 952; and it was in this year that King Eadred ordered (somehow) that Wulfstan be taken into the fortress at *Iudanbyrig* (sometimes identified as *Gothaburh* in the west country [? Castle Gotha, *Cornwall], which later functioned as a *mint), 'because accusations had often been made to the king against him' (*ASC* MS D, s.a. 952). It would appear, however, that Wulfstan was released from captivity (if that is what it was) in 953, if only to judge from the fact that he attested (as 'archbishop') one of the series of 'Dunstan B' charters issued in that year (S 560). In 954 the Northumbrians drove out Eric Bloodaxe, and Eadred resumed control of the north. There are no surviving charters for this year; and while Wulfstan was restored to episcopal office, it seems that he was obliged to exercise that office at Dorchester (*ASC* MS D, s.a. 954). Wulfstan attested charters in 955, as 'archbishop', and remained at court in the opening weeks of Eadwig's reign (S 582, 605); but he appears not

to have attended any of the later meetings in 956. It is possible that Wulfstan's sustained absence in 956 was in some way 'political', perhaps reflecting a reluctance in high places to let him loose in the north rather than a revival of dissent in the north; but of course it is also possible that Wulfstan was by then in failing health, and that his duties had for that reason been taken over by Osketel, bishop of Dorchester, who succeeded him as archbishop of York (cf. S 659, and *ASC* MSS BC, s.a. 971). Wulfstan died on 16 December 956 (*ASC* MSS DE), and was buried at Oundle (Northants.), in the diocese of Dorchester, where *Wilfrid of York had once founded a monastery and where he had died in 709 (*HE* v. 19).

A. Campbell, 'The End of the Kingdom of Northumbria', *EHR* 57 (1942), 91–7; D. Whitelock, 'The Dealings of the Kings of England with Northumbria in the Tenth and Eleventh Centuries' (1959), repr. in her *History*, art. III, pp. 70–88, at 71–5; C. R. Hart, *The Early Charters of Northern England and the North Midlands* (Leicester, 1975), pp. 376–7; A. P. Smyth, *Scandinavian York and Dublin*, 2 vols. (Dublin, 1975–9), ii.90–4, 155–90; C. E. Blunt, *et al.*, *Coinage in Tenth-Century England* (Oxford, 1989), pp. 209–34, 270–1; S. Keynes, *An Atlas of Attestations in Anglo-Saxon Charters c.680–1066* (1993; publication forthcoming); P. Sawyer, 'The Last Viking Kings of York', *NH* 31 (1995), 39–44; S. Keynes, 'The Vikings in England, c.790–1016', *The Oxford Illustrated History of the Vikings*, ed. P. Sawyer (Oxford, 1997), pp. 48–82, at 70–1.

SIMON KEYNES

WULFSTAN II, bishop of Worcester (1062–95), was born probably *c.*1008 into a family intimately connected with the church of *Worcester; he may well have been nephew to *Wulfstan the Homilist, bishop of Worcester and archbishop of *York (d. 1023). When young Wulfstan's half-brother Brihtheah became bishop of Worcester in 1033 he joined the latter's household; soon afterwards he decided to become a monk within the Worcester cathedral community. Under Bishop *Ealdred (1046–61), probably by 1055, he was appointed prior. In 1061 the see of Worcester became vacant when Ealdred was forced to renounce it on becoming archbishop of York, and in 1062 papal legates recommended Wulfstan, who had by then won renown for private prayer and for preaching to the laity, to *Edward the Confessor as the successor. At first Wulfstan was powerless to stop Ealdred from extracting revenues from Worcester; after the Norman Conquest, however, his loyalty to William I and, from 1070, to Lanfranc in the *Canterbury-*York primacy dispute enabled him to win back the lands which Ealdred had expropriated. As bishop, Wulfstan was stoutly litigious on Worcester's behalf and towards the end of his life commissioned the monk *Hemming to compile a new cathedral cartulary to record losses and gains. In cultural terms Wulfstan was keen both to import new ideas and to preserve old traditions: on the one hand he began to rebuild the cathedral at Worcester (St Mary's) in 1084 on a much larger scale and in a Romanesque manner, while on the other he encouraged his monks to keep the tradition of writing Old English, especially homiletic and monastic material, alive. The monk Coleman wrote Wulfstan's *vita* in Old English shortly after his death in 1095; the work survives only in the form of a Latin translation by *William of Malmesbury written after 1113.

The Vita Wulfstani of William of Malmesbury, ed. R. R. Darlington, Camden Society 3rd ser. 40 (London, 1928); *The Portiforium of Saint Wulstan*, ed. A. Hughes, 2 vols., HBS 89–90 (London, 1958–60); *Hemingi Chartularium Ecclesiae Wigorniensis*, ed. T. Hearne, 2 vols. (Oxford, 1723); *The Cartulary of Worcester Cathedral Priory*, ed. R. R. Darlington, Pipe Roll Society, new ser. 38 (London, 1968); E. Mason, *St Wulfstan of Worcester c.1008–1095* (Oxford, 1990); *Oswald of Worcester.*

JULIA BARROW

WULFSTAN CANTOR (fl. 996) was a monk, priest and precentor at the Old Minster, *Winchester, and one of the most prolific and skilled Anglo-Latin poets of the pre-Conquest period. Little is known of his life: he was apparently born *c.*960 and given as an oblate to the Old Minster, where he was a pupil of Bishop *Æthelwold, and where he eventually became priest and precentor (*cantor*). Most of his writings date from the 990s; many of them are concerned with commemorating Æthelwold. He may have left Winchester when his patron, *Ælfheah, bishop of Winchester (984–1005), was promoted to the archbishopric of *Canterbury. The year of Wulfstan's death is unknown, but his obit was recorded in a Winchester liturgical calendar (in *'Ælfwine's Prayerbook') against 22 July. Wulfstan's most substantial work – indeed it is the longest surviving pre-Conquest Anglo-Latin poem – is the *Narratio metrica de S. Swithuno*, a reworking in hexameters of *Lantfred's *Translatio et miracula S. Swithuni* (*c.*975); books i and ii follow the text of Lantfred closely, but are prefaced by an independent *Epistola specialis* dedicated to Bishop Ælfheah in which Wulfstan describes in elegiac verse the reconstruction and rededication of the Old Minster undertaken by Æthelwold and completed by Ælfheah. The poem was written during the years 992–4, but was apparently put into final form after

the translation of Bishop Æthelwold in 996. At approximately this time Wulfstan composed his prose *Vita S. Æthelwoldi*, the earliest Life to commemorate Æthelwold (the Life by *Ælfric is an abbreviation of Wulfstan's). He may also be suspected as the author of various mass-sets and hymns (in various metres) in honour of St Æthelwold, as well as various tropes and their melodies found in one of the 'Winchester Tropers', CCCC 473, a book datable on palaeographical grounds to *c.*1000 which may have belonged to Wulfstan himself. Wulfstan also composed a substantial poem in epanaleptic verse (in which the first words of each hexameter are repeated as the last words of the following pentameter) on the Feast of All Saints entitled *Breuiloquium de omnibus sanctis*; the opening lines of this poem have embedded in them the *acrostic legend VVLFSTANVS. Given his skill in composing verse in this demanding form, it is probable that a group of epanaleptic poems dedicated to the Winchester saints Æthelwold, *Birinus, and *Swithun, as well as one to All Saints (again) are also by Wulfstan. A work of Wulfstan entitled the *Breuiloquium super musicam* has not survived, except for a few sentences preserved in fifteenth-century musical commentaries.

Sharpe, *Handlist*, 2229; M. Lapidge and M. Winterbottom, *Wulfstan of Winchester: the Life of St Æthelwold* (OMT, 1991); P. Dronke, M. Lapidge and P. Stotz, 'Die unveröffentlichten Gedichte der Cambridger Liederhandschrift (CUL Gg.5.35)', *Mittellateinisches Jahrbuch* 17 (1982), 54–95, at 62–4 [epanaleptic poem on All Saints]; *Analecta Hymnica*, ed. C. Blume and G. M. Dreves (Leipzig, 1886–1922), xix.258–60 [poem on St Swithun]; xlviii.9–18 [Æthelwold, Birinus and Swithun]; F. Dolbeau, 'Le *Breuiloquium de omnibus sanctis*. Un poème inconnu de Wulfstan chantre de Winchester', *AB* 106 (1988), 35–98; *Frithegodi monachi Breuiloquium Vitae Beati Wilfredi et Wulfstani Cantoris Narratio metrica de sancto Swithuno*, ed. A. Campbell (Zurich, 1950), pp. 63–177.

MICHAEL LAPIDGE

WULFSTAN THE HOMILIST (Archbishop Wulfstan of *York) was one of the most distinctive and influential of all OE prose authors. Little is known for certain about Wulfstan's life before he became bishop of *London in 996, although some family connection with the fenlands of the East Midlands seems likely from the evidence of localised cults at Peterborough and at *Ely, where he is buried. In London he was already using the Latin pen-name Lupus ('wolf') that was later to characterise so many of his writings, most notably the *Sermo Lupi ad Anglos*, and a surviving letter written to him in the characteristically verbose contemporary Latin style commends him for the 'most sweet sagacity of [his] eloquence and the richness and simultaneous depth of [his] decorously set out prose'. The compliment underlines Wulfstan's position as a supreme and idiosyncratic stylist. In 1002 Wulfstan became bishop of *Worcester and archbishop of York, holding both sees in plurality until 1016, when he seems either to have resigned Worcester or established a suffragan to provide administration; he died on 28 May 1023.

In the most recent edition, twenty-six sermons are attributed to Wulfstan, of which twenty-two are in Old English and four in Latin, and recent research suggests that this is a conservative figure: certainly there seem to be fragments of genuine Wulfstan material embedded in several anonymous homilies and sermons clearly modelled on his work, the sheer extant number of which attests to his popularity. Much Wulfstan material is, moreover, attributed largely or even solely on the basis of his highly idiosyncratic prose style, in which strings of syntactically independent two-stress phrases are linked by complex patterns of *alliteration and other kinds of sound-play. Indeed, so idiosyncratic is Wulfstan's style that he is even ready to rewrite minutely works prepared for him by *Ælfric, the other great prose stylist of the late Anglo-Saxon period, substituting individual words and phrases, and adding the characteristic intensifying adverbs, doublets, and two-stress phrases that are the hallmark of his style.

In addition to his sermons, Wulfstan's style has also been detected in a number of *law-codes of both *Æthelred the Unready and *Cnut, as well as the prose sections of the so-called *Benedictine Office* found in a manuscript closely associated with his work. He was also the author of *The Institutes of Polity*, a detailed analysis of the roles of authorities in both church and state, and *The Canons of Edgar*, a text aimed primarily at the secular *clergy. Two further pieces, concerned with the management of a large estate, *Rectitudines* and *Gerefa*, seem to share much of Wulfstan's phraseology and characteristic rhythm, and likewise two alliterative prose passages in the D-version of the *Anglo-Saxon Chronicle* for the years 959 and 975 have been attributed to him. All these writings testify to Wulfstan's central role in both church and state, and demonstrate that he was interested in a wide range of secular affairs alongside the concerns for the national moral degeneration and warnings about the end of the world that so colour his *preaching.

Throughout the eleventh century Wulfstan's works were widely disseminated and imitated. His handwriting has been identified in no fewer than ten manuscripts, generally correcting or supplementing material, and it is clear that he was an assiduous reviser of his own texts: his best-known work, the *Sermo Lupi ad Anglos*, a dire warning about the moral decline of the English and the consequent *Viking depredations, exists in five manuscripts in three quite distinct versions, while another of his sermons is found in two versions in the same manuscript, copied by the same scribe. More recently aspects of *oral-formulaic theory have been applied to Wulfstan's sermons, suggesting that he was employing techniques of composition rather similar to those which had been used by Old English poets over many generations.

Sharpe, *Handlist*, 2228; *The Homilies of Wulfstan*, ed. D. Bethurum (Oxford, 1957); D. Bethurum, 'Wulfstan', in *Continuations and Beginnings: Studies in Old English Literature*, ed. E. G. Stanley (London, 1966), pp. 210–46; *The Copenhagen Wulfstan Collection: Copenhagen Kongelige Bibliotek Gl.kgl.sam. 1595*, ed. J. E. Cross and J. Morrish Tunberg, EEMF 25 (Copenhagen, 1993); M. McC. Gatch, *Preaching and Theology in Anglo-Saxon England: Ælfric and Wulfstan* (Toronto, 1977); K. Jost, *Wulfstanstudien* (Bern, 1950); *A Wulfstan Manuscript*, ed. H. R. Loyn, EEMF 17 (Copenhagen, 1971); A. McIntosh, 'Wulfstan's Prose', *PBA* 35 (1949), 109–42; A. Orchard, 'Crying Wolf: Oral Style and the *Sermones Lupi*', *ASE* 21 (1992), 239–64; D. Whitelock, 'Archbishop Wulfstan, Homilist and Statesman', *TRHS* 24 (1942), 25–45.

ANDY ORCHARD

WULFSTAN, VOYAGE OF *see* Ohthere

WYNNEBALD, abbot of Heidenheim (*c.*700–61), was from a Southumbrian (probably *Wessex) family, three of whom were at one time or another members of the mission of *Boniface in Thuringia: Wynnebald himself, his brother *Willibald (*c.*700–*c.*787), bishop of Eichstätt, and his sister *Walburg (d. 779), sometime abbess of Heidenheim. Wynnebald set out on *pilgrimage to *Rome with his brother Willibald in 720; after Willibald left Rome to travel to the Near East, Wynnebald remained there until 727, when he returned to England. He made a second lengthy trip to Rome (*c.*730–9), and was then coopted by Boniface for help with the Thuringian mission. Boniface consecrated him priest and entrusted him with the care of seven churches. He subsequently spent time at Mainz (747–51), and in 752 founded the double monastery of Heidenheim (near Eichstätt), becoming its first abbot. On his death in 761, his sister Walburg succeeded him as abbess. Willibald translated the remains of Wynne-bald in 777, and a few years later (782 × 785) an English nun of Heidenheim named *Hygeburg composed her Life of Wynnebald, the *Vita S. Wynnebaldi* (*BHL* 8996), from which most details of his life are known.

MGH, SS xv.106–17; W. Berschin, *Biographie und Epochenstil im lateinischen Mittelalter*, 3 vols. (Stuttgart, 1986–), iii. 18–26.

MICHAEL LAPIDGE

WYRD is a pre-Christian concept and, since all surviving texts exist within a Christian context, its primary meaning must be determined from etymology. The word is related to the verb *weorðan* 'become', and therefore it refers to that which inevitably must happen. Although often translated 'fate', it equates better with our 'destiny' since a link with the classical idea of an agency is misleading. Unlike the Greek Fates, it is not of itself a divine power. In *heroic poetry, *wyrd* is inescapable. But in Christian literature there develops the sense that God controls it. King *Alfred in his translation of Boethius uses *wyrd* in contrast to 'providence', the latter being divine intelligence, *wyrd* being God's will when it comes to pass.

B. J. Timmer, '*Wyrd* in Anglo-Saxon Prose and Poetry', *Neophilologus* 26 (1940–1), 24–33, 213–28 (repr. in *Essential Articles for the Study of Old English Poetry*, ed. J. B. Bessinger and S. J. Kahrl (Hamden, CT, 1968), pp. 124–58).

DONALD SCRAGG

Y

YEAVERING (Northumb.) is the site of the earliest known Anglo-Saxon royal residence. *Bede in the *Historia ecclesiastica* tells how *Paulinus travelled with King *Edwin in 626 to conduct a mass baptism *Ad Gefrin* in the kingdom of *Bernicia. In the 1950s an extraordinary excavation near the modern village of Yeavering uncovered what was almost certainly his hall: a magnificent residence, grand in scale, well constructed and carefully planned. The palace lay in a fertile valley beneath the northern edge of the Cheviot hills dominated by a Romano-British fort. A complicated sequence of buildings was found but there were few datable artifacts. Crude hand-made *pottery and only a few Germanic finds suggest that the site was in use during the late sixth and seventh centuries. A forged Merovingian *coin found in one of the latest structures has been dated *c.*630–40 AD, indicating that the site fell out of use around the middle of the seventh century. There are signs of decay in the final phase of the site and Bede states that the palace was eventually moved to Milfield.

The earliest feature was a massive palisaded enclosure, conjecturally a cattle corral where the herds could be periodically gathered. There is nothing to indicate when this was constructed, though it has affinities with Romano-British structures. The halls were located outside the enclosure, undefended by enclosing banks or walls. The first buildings were small, successively replaced by ever larger and stronger halls. The most massive of these measured nearly 25 m by 12 m and was constructed of enormous timbers set in foundations two metres deep. The halls would have made grand settings for royal feasts, plastered internally and externally and probably fitted with raised floors and balconies. In the centre of the site was a unique structure, probably an assembly place, with tiered seats and a small stage. To the north there were subsidiary buildings and to the south was an area of *metalworking and craft activity.

From the beginning, the palace incorporated prehistoric monuments, a round-barrow to the east and possibly a stone circle to the west. These monuments survived as visible features and became the foci for burials. The earliest medieval graves were associated with two halls on the western edge of the site. A heap of cattle skulls was stacked against the inside wall of one of these buildings and it is possible that this was a kitchen or butchering area. The only parallels for such finds come from late Iron Age religious contexts. The other *cemetery surrounded a hall-like structure that has been interpreted as a church, though, unusually, it has a doorway in the east wall.

One of the dominant features of the plan is a linear east-west arrangement of halls and posts. The conception can be compared with the alignment of groups of churches on a common axis such as at *Hexham and *Jarrow. A free-standing orthostat was erected on a barrow within the enclosure, precisely along the axis of the two largest halls; others were associated with the westerly halls and the assembly feature. The presence of these posts has never been satisfactorily explained; they may have been reference points for laying out the buildings, or had some totemic significance.

The absence of *settlement debris suggests that the site was never a permanent royal residence. Over a short period, perhaps no more than a century, Yeavering served as a centre for periodic royal assemblies. Whether the participants were Anglo-Saxon or British is uncertain. There are a few high-status burials in the vicinity and four people were buried at the palace with grave goods, indicative of the influence of Germanic ideas. Yeavering, with its grand halls and innovative design, testifies to the vigorous strength of an area ruled, but not peopled, by the Anglo-Saxons.

R. Bradley, 'Time Regained: The Creation of Continuity', *JBAA* 140–1 (1987–8), 1–17; R. Cramp, 'Anglo-Saxon Settlement', in *Settlement in North Britain 1000 BC–AD 1000* (Oxford, 1983), pp. 263–97; A. Harding, 'Excavations in the Prehistoric Ritual Complex near Milfield, Northumberland', *Proceedings of the Prehistoric Society* 47 (1981), 87–135; B. Hope-Taylor, *Yeavering: An Anglo-British Centre of Early Northumbria* (London 1977); C. Scull, 'Post-Roman Phase 1 at Yeavering: A Reconstruction', *MArch* 35 (1991), 51–63.

HELEN GITTOS

YORK, originating as the Romano-British for-

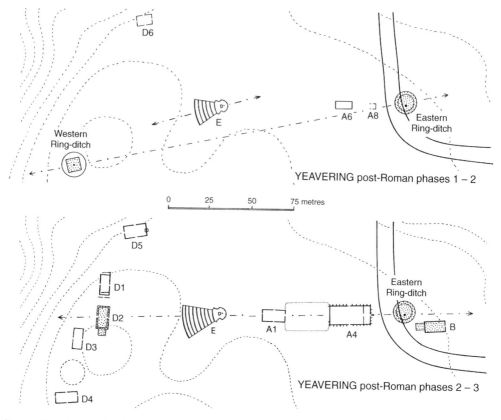

Fig. 21 Yeavering (Northumbria): the late sixth-and seventh-century ritual and assembly site and royal residence.

tress, provincial capital and bishopric of *Eburacum*, straddled the navigable river Ouse just upstream of its confluence with the tributary river Foss, 120 km from the Yorkshire coast. The latest Romano-British occupation is difficult to date, but need not extend much beyond *c*.400; the Romans' legacy was a regularly planned and well defended *settlement with imposing stone structures, the recognized regional seat of power.

The next datable archaeological remains are Anglo-Saxon cremation urns, probably of the sixth century, found in *cemeteries outside the Roman walls. Documentary sources record that in 627 the Anglo-Saxon King *Edwin of *Northumbria was baptized at York in a newly-built wooden church, presumably near the present cathedral, at the centre of the Roman fortress. His instructor was the papal *missionary *Paulinus, who was then designated bishop of the diocese, and it is bishops rather than royalty who predominate in seventh- and eighth-century documentary references to York. *Wilfrid refurbished the cathedral *c*.670; in 735 *Ecgberht became the first consecrated Anglo-

Saxon archbishop of York, and in 780 *Ælberht dedicated the church of Holy Wisdom. An associated *school achieved international renown as a focus of learning when Charlemagne head-hunted its former pupil and then master, *Alcuin, for his court.

Secular occupation in seventh- to ninth-century York has been archaeologically elusive. The only buildings yet recorded are downstream of the rivers' confluence at Fishergate, where associated objects include imported continental *pottery and evidence for crafts. Whether this settlement is part of the *wic* trading place commemorated in York's contemporary name, *Eoforwic*, remains unclear. A scatter of objects of seventh- to ninth-century date has also been found across much of the medieval walled area, but their significance is debatable.

In 866 an invading *Viking army captured York. Part of that army settled in Northumbria in 876 and the city, which became known as *Jorvik*, was the focus of Viking power in northern England. For just over half a century *Jorvik* remained independent under Scandinavian control; relatively little is known about internal events during most of this time, other than that an accommodation was reached with the church. In 927 *Æthelstan of *Wessex was recognized as king, but distance from Wessex, and the emergence of a hybrid Anglo-Scandinavian culture, encouraged a continuing local desire for independence. After Æthelstan's death in 939 there began a complex contest for the city and kingdom of *Jorvik*. The contenders were the West Saxons, Viking kings of Dublin, and the exiled Norwegian prince *Eric Bloodaxe. Only after Eric's expulsion in 954 was York brought finally into the new kingdom of England.

Archaeological excavations, albeit limited in number, have now proved that this century of political turmoil also saw the virtual refounding and growth of the city. South-east of the decayed Roman fortress, for example, in an area which had apparently been deserted since *c*.400, activity resumed just at about the time of the Vikings' takeover. More significantly, and with lasting impact, a new street and house plots were laid out *c*.900–35. The street's name, Coppergate, was an *Old Norse formation, like so many others in York. It indicates the sometime presence of wood-turners, and evidence for those craftsmen was found; but so too was debris from large-scale *metalworking, as well as from the working of bone/antler, amber and jet, *textile and *glass. One of *Jorvik*'s functions was, clearly, as a manufacturing centre. A wide range of goods was made, including everyday items and mass-produced minor luxuries such as cheap *jewellery. *Trade was another important aspect of *Jorvik*'s existence. There is evidence for contacts with Scandinavia, Scotland, Ireland, other regions of England, and north-west Europe. Goods from the East Mediterranean, the Arabian Gulf and Samarkand also reached *Jorvik*, presumably through the hands of many middlemen.

The city's industries, and the frequent rebuilding of the thatched, timber structures in which they were practised, required raw materials in abundance from the hinterland's farms and estates. Provisioning the city must also have been an enormous undertaking. *Byrhtferth's *Life of St Oswald* written 997 × 1002 refers to a population of 30,000, but this is probably two or three times too high; the more reliable *Domesday Book suggests that there were about 1,800 households in the city in 1066. However many there were, the people looked much like today's citizens, although on average a few centimetres shorter in height. Demographically, however, they were very different, with high infant mortality, half the adult women dying before the age of thirty-five, and few people living beyond the age of fifty.

Decorated stone *grave-markers prove not only that many of the city's churches existed by *c*.1000; their design, and the motifs on brooches and other metalwork, show that Scandinavian artistic influences flourished in York, alongside Anglo-Saxon styles. Unsurprisingly, *Swein Forkbeard of Denmark and his son *Cnut did not attack potentially pro-Scandinavian *Jorvik* during their early eleventh-century invasions and campaigns.

In 1066 the Northumbrian militia was defeated by Harald Hardrada of Norway at the battle of Fulford, a few kilometres outside the city, before *Harold Godwineson's sudden arrival and success at Stamford Bridge. When the Normans in turn finally subdued York in 1069, consolidating an initial takeover which had been overthrown by a massacre of their garrison in 1068, they gained control of the second city of England.

The Archaeology of York, ed. P. V. Addyman (York, in progress); *Alcuin. The Bishops, Kings and Saints of York*, ed. P. Godman (OMT, 1982); R. A. Hall, *Viking Age York* (London, 1994); J. T. Lang, CASSS III. *York and Eastern Yorkshire* (Oxford, 1991); R. Morris, 'Alcuin, York, and the *alma sophia*', in Butler and Morris, *AS Church*, pp. 80–9; D. Phillips and B. Heywood, *Excavations at York Minster* I. *From Roman Fortress to Norman Cathedral* (London, 1995).

R. A. HALL

APPENDIX
Rulers of the English, *c*.450–1066

Simon Keynes

The lists which follow present basic details of royal succession for all of the constituent kingdoms of Anglo-Saxon England. Some matters are inevitably concealed by the restrictions of the layout; and all manner of complications may lurk unsuspected beneath the surface of recorded events. The seven major kingdoms of the early Anglo-Saxon period are separately numbered, and lesser kingdoms or peoples are placed within this sequence where they seem most appropriate. The 'Jutish' kingdom of *Kent is followed by the 'Anglian' kingdoms of *Northumbria, *Mercia and *East Anglia, and by the 'Saxon' kingdoms of *Sussex, *Essex and *Wessex; the kingdom of Wessex leads via the kingdom 'of the Anglo-Saxons' to the 'kingdom of the English'. The lists are arranged in a way which is intended to convey some sense of the unfolding pattern of political development from the seventh century to the eleventh, and of the complications which sometimes interrupted, often impeded, and always enlivened the processes involved; the same pattern of development is represented by maps 9–12 on pp. 517–20.

The lists may provide a framework for approaching some basic historical issues, but they require much by way of animation. It is apparent, for example, that the principles of political organisation and royal succession differed from one kingdom to another, and that the varieties of practice may help to account for their respective political fortunes. Some kings were able to extend their power over other kings or peoples, and to establish an overlordship which might reach far outside the frontiers of their own kingdom; but the nature and configuration of one overlordship would differ from another, and to understand the manner in which they were put together is often to understand the circumstances in which they subsequently fell apart. Inter-dynastic marriages and other forms of personal association affected or helped to determine the dynamics of the relationships between the rulers of the various kingdoms; and for all the importance attached to the place at court of a *queen, and of *æthelings on the prowl, much could be said of sisters, aunts, and daughters. Attention may focus, however, on the process which led from the multiplicity of kingdoms in the sixth and seventh centuries to the emergence of a unified kingdom of the English in the tenth century. It may be that matters were driven by the desire of those in high places to transform *Bede's notion of a *gens Anglorum (derived via *Canterbury from Pope *Gregory the Great) from an airy ideal into a glorious reality; and it may be that from time to time the more ancient concept of 'Britain' was invoked as the ultimate political order subsuming all inhabitants of the island. It is also arguable that events were driven at the same time by a much darker combination of political, geographic, social, and economic forces, effectively beyond anyone's control, and perhaps favouring one kingdom or people as opposed to another; and it may be that unification, when it came, was a function of the determination of some to impose a semblance of social and political order, aided by the willingness of others to accept whatever was perceived to be in their own interests. Whatever the case, the kingdom of the English was far less the triumphant achievement of an original objective than it was the eventual outcome of an extended story.

Bede, writing in 731, stated that the royal families of many kingdoms traced their descent from Woden (*HE* i.15). *Genealogies extending back to Woden exist for the royal families of *Deira, *Bernicia, Mercia, *Lindsey, Kent, East Anglia, and Wessex; a genealogy extending back to Seaxnet exists for the royal family of Essex. *Regnal lists, indicating the succession of kings and assigning a number of years to each in turn, were constructed for Northumbria, Mercia, and Wessex, and are cited where appropriate below.

In certain cases, kings are known only or mainly from the *coinage issued in their names. In these cases, the king is placed in a kingdom, and assigned a necessarily approximate date in relation to other kings of the same kingdom, on the basis of the analysis of his coinage in relation to the coinage of other kings.

Sets of tabular genealogies of the main royal *dynasties are given in *The Anglo-Saxon Chronicle*, ed. Whitelock, *et al.*, pp. 205–23, and in *EHD* i. 934–47. Lists of the rulers of the constituent kingdoms of Anglo-Saxon England were published in the first edition of the *Handbook of British Chronology*, ed. F.

M. Powicke (1941). These lists were substantially revised and amplified by D. N. Dumville for the third edition of the *Handbook of British Chronology*, published in 1986; Professor Dumville's lists contain full details of the parentage, wives, consorts, and children of successive kings.

Abbreviations

ASC   *Anglo-Saxon Chronicle* (ed. Whitelock, *et al.*).
HE   Bede, *Historia ecclesiastica gentis Anglorum*.
HR   Simeon of Durham, *Historia regum* (in *EHD* i, ed. Whitelock).
S   Sawyer, *Anglo-Saxon Charters*, with number of charter.

Bibliography

Bassett, S., ed., *The Origins of Anglo-Saxon Kingdoms* (Leicester, 1989).
Campbell, J., 'Bede's *Reges* and *Principes*', in his *Essays in Anglo-Saxon History* (London, 1986), pp. 85–98.
Dumville, D. N., 'The Anglian Collection of Royal Genealogies and Regnal Lists', *ASE* 5 (1976), 23–50, repr. in his *Histories and Pseudo-Histories of the Insular Middle Ages* (Aldershot, 1990), no. V, with Addenda, pp. 4–5.
Dumville, D. N., 'The West Saxon Genealogical Regnal List and the Chronology of Early Wessex', *Peritia* 4 (1985), 21–66, repr. in his *Britons and Anglo-Saxons in the Early Middle Ages* (Aldershot, 1993), no. VIII.
Dumville, D. N., 'The West Saxon Genealogical Regnal List: Manuscripts and Texts', *Anglia* 104 (1986), 1–32.
Dumville, D. N., 'The Local Rulers of Anglo-Saxon England to AD 927' and 'Kings of England (1) 927–1066', *Handbook of British Chronology*, 3rd ed., ed. E. B. Fryde, D. E. Greenway, S. Porter and I. Roy, Royal Historical Society Guides and Handbooks 2 (London, 1986), pp. 1–25 and 25–9.
Finberg, H. P. R., *The Early Charters of the West Midlands*, 2nd ed. (Leicester, 1972), pp. 167–80 (the Hwicce) and 217–24 (the Magonsæte).
Grierson, P., and M. Blackburn, *Medieval European Coinage* I: *The Early Middle Ages (5th–10th Centuries)* (Cambridge, 1986), esp. pp. 267–325.
Kelly, S. E., ed., *Charters of St Augustine's Abbey, Canterbury*, Anglo-Saxon Charters 4 (Oxford, 1995), esp. 195–203.
Kelly, S. E., ed., *Charters of Selsey*, Anglo-Saxon Charters 6 (Oxford, 1998), esp. pp. lxxiii–lxxxiv.
Keynes, S., 'England, 700–900', *The New Cambridge Medieval History* II: *c.700–c.900*, ed. R. McKitterick (Cambridge, 1995), pp. 18–42.
Keynes, S., 'King Alfred and the Mercians', *Kings, Currency and Alliances: History and Coinage in Southern England in the Ninth Century*, ed. M. A. S. Blackburn and D. N. Dumville (Woodbridge, 1998), pp. 1–45.
Keynes, S., 'England, 900–1016', *The New Cambridge Medieval History* III. *c.900–1024*, ed. T. Reuter (Cambridge, 1999), pp. 456–84.
Kirby, D., *The Earliest English Kings* (London, 1991).
Pagan, H. E., 'Northumbrian Numismatic Chronology in the Ninth Century', *British Numismatic Journal* 38 (1969), 1–15.
Sawyer, P. H., *Anglo-Saxon Charters: an Annotated List and Bibliography*, Royal Historical Society Guides and Handbooks 8 (London, 1968; online at www.trin.cam.ac.uk/chartwww).
Sims-Williams, P., *Religion and Literature in Western England, 600–800*, CSASE 3 (Cambridge, 1990).
Smart, V., 'Table of Reigns and Types', *Cumulative Index of Volumes 1–20*, Sylloge of Coins of the British Isles 28 (London, 1981), pp. xxiii–xl, at xxix–xxxvii.
Yorke, B. A. E., 'The Kingdom of the East Saxons', *ASE* 14 (1985), 1–36.
Yorke, B. A. E., *Kings and Kingdoms in Early Anglo-Saxon England* (London, 1990).

I. Kings of Kent

'The people of Kent and the inhabitants of the Isle of Wight are of Jutish origin' (*HE* i.15). On the particular distinction of King *Æthelberht I, see *HE* ii.5. For different views of the succession of kings of Kent in the later seventh and eighth centuries, see Yorke, *Kings and Kingdoms*, pp. 25–44, and *Charters of St Augustine's*, ed. Kelly, pp. 195–203.

*HENGEST	acc. *c.455; d. ? 488
OERIC (Oisc)	acc. 488; d. ? 512
EORMENRIC	acc. ? 512, or later; d. *c.560, or later; it is possible that a king has been lost between Oeric and Æthelberht
*ÆTHELBERHT I	acc. 560 (*HE* ii.5: reigned 56 years), or *c.585 (described as the son of a king in Kent when he married Bertha, d. of Charibert, *c.580; perhaps aged 56 when he died); d. 24 Feb. 616 [3rd holder of *imperium* (Bede), or 3rd Bretwalda (*ASC*)]

EADBALD	acc. 616; d. 20 Jan. 640
EARCONBERHT	acc. 640 (after 20 Jan.); d. 14 July 664
ECGBERHT I	acc. 664 (after 14 July); d. 4 July 673
HLOTHHERE	acc. 673 (after 4 July); d. 6 Feb. 685 (from wounds received in battle against Eadric and the South Saxons)
EADRIC	acc. 685 (after 6 Feb.); d. ? Aug. 686

Following the death of King Eadric in 686, 'various usurpers or foreign kings' plundered the kingdom, until Wihtred 'freed the people from foreign invasion' (Bede, *HE* iv.26). Kings known to have been active in Kent during this period (686–90) include *Cædwalla and Mul (*ASC*, s.a. 686, 687), from Wessex, the usurper Oswine (S 12–14), and Swæfheard (S 10) and Swaberht (S 11), both from Essex.

WIHTRED	acc. 690; reigned initially with Swæfheard, but sole king by *c.*692; d. 23 April 725

After the death of King Wihtred in 725 (*HE* v.23), the kingdom of Kent appears to have been divided into its two component parts. Æthelberht, son of Wihtred, became king of east Kent (based at Canterbury), and Eadberht, son of Wihtred, became king of west Kent (based at *Rochester); a third son, Alric, makes no impression.

<table>
<tr><td colspan="2">KINGS OF WEST KENT</td><td colspan="2">KINGS OF EAST KENT</td></tr>
<tr><td colspan="2">EADBERHT I: acc. 725; d. 748 (ASC)</td><td colspan="2">ÆTHELBERHT II: acc. 725; d. 762 (ASC)</td></tr>
<tr><td colspan="2">EARDWULF: acc. ? 748; d. ? × 762</td><td colspan="2"></td></tr>
<tr><td colspan="2">SIGERED: acc. ? × 762; d. c.764</td><td colspan="2">EADBERHT II: acc. 762; d. c.764</td></tr>
<tr><td colspan="2">ECGBERHT II: acc. c.764</td><td colspan="2">EANMUND: acc. c.764; d. ?</td></tr>
<tr><td colspan="2"></td><td colspan="2">HEAHBERHT: acc. ? c.765; d. ?</td></tr>
</table>

During the second quarter of the eighth century, *Æthelbald, king of the Mercians (716–57), was able to extend his interests south-eastwards into Kent. In the mid-760s, following the death of King Æthelberht in 762, *Offa, king of the Mercians (757–96), brought the kingdom of Kent more firmly under his own control. In 776, at the battle of Otford, the men of Kent broke free from Mercian overlordship.

ECGBERHT II (cont'd)	k. of (? the whole of) Kent in the late 770s; d. 779 × ?
EALHMUND	k. of (? the whole of) Kent in 784 (*ASC*, MS. F); father of Ecgberht, king of the West Saxons (802–39)

King Offa asserted direct control of Kent in 784 or 785, and maintained it thereafter until his death in 796.

EADBERHT PRÆN	acc. 796; captured in 798, and taken into Mercia; d. ?

*Coenwulf, king of the Mercians (796–821), re-asserted Mercian control of Kent in 798, and immediately installed his brother CUTHRED as king of Kent. Cuthred died in 807, and thereafter Kent was under Coenwulf's direct control, until his death in 821.

BALDRED	acc. ? 821; driven from Kent by Ecgberht, king of the West Saxons, in *c.*825

From *c.*825, the people of Kent were ruled by the kings of the West Saxons (see further below).

II. Kings of the Northumbrians

The Northumbrians were originally divided between two kingdoms: Deira, reaching from the river Humber northwards to the Tyne (with a political centre at York), and Bernicia, reaching from the Tyne northwards to the Tweed and beyond (with a political centre at Bamburgh); see *HE* iii.1, iii.6. The kingdom of the Northumbrians came into existence during the central decades of the seventh century, as the combination of Deira and Bernicia. The Northumbrian overlords so much admired by Bede are listed below in bold type. A regnal list in the 'Moore Manuscript' of Bede's *Historia ecclesiastica* extends from Ida, in the mid-sixth century, to Ceolwulf, in the 730s. A list extending from Ida to Æthilred, at the end of the eighth century, was constructed in the ninth or early tenth century; see Dumville, 'The Anglian Collection', pp. 32, 35–6. For general discussion, see Yorke, *Kingdoms*, pp. 72–99.

KINGS OF DEIRA	KINGS OF BERNICIA

KINGS OF DEIRA

ÆLLE: acc. 560; d. 588 or 590

KINGS OF BERNICIA

IDA: acc. 547; d. 559 or 560

GLAPPA: acc. 559; d. 560

ADDA: acc. 560; d. 568

ÆTHELRIC: acc. 568; d. 572

THEODRIC: acc. 572; d. 579

FRITHUWALD: acc. 579; d. 585

HUSSA: acc. 585; d. 592

ÆTHELRIC: acc. 588; d. 593

Edwin, s. of Ælle, was in exile during the reign of King Æthelfrith, latterly at the court of Rædwald, king of the East Angles (*HE* ii.12).

ÆTHELFRITH: acc. 592; took control of Deira; defeated the 'Irish' at the battle of *Degsastan* 603 (*HE* i.34) and defeated the British at Chester (*HE* ii.2); d. 616 (killed by *Rædwald at the battle of the river Idle).

Oswald and Oswiu, sons of Æthelfrith, were in exile among the Irish or Picts during the reign of King Edwin.

*EDWIN: acc. 616; took control of Bernicia; d. 12 Oct. 633 (killed by Cadwallon and *Penda at the battle of Hatfield (*HE* ii.20); his body later removed from Hatfield to *Whitby (*Vita S. Gregorii*, cc. 18–19), and his head at *York (*HE* ii. 20) [5th holder of *imperium* (Bede), or 5th Bretwalda (*ASC*)]

OSRIC: acc. 633; reverted to paganism; d. 634 (killed at York, by Cadwallon, king of the Britons)

EANFRITH: acc. 633/4; reverted to paganism; d. 634 (killed by Cadwallon, king of the Britons)

In 633–4, following the deaths of Osric and Eanfrith, the two Northumbrian kingdoms were controlled by Cadwallon, king of the Britons; for which reason 'all those who compute the dates of kings have decided to abolish the memory of these perfidious kings and to assign this year to their successor Oswald' (*HE* iii.1; see also *HE* iii.9).

*OSWALD (of Bernicia) acc. 634; defeated Cadwallon at battle of Heavenfield (*HE* iii.1–2), and united Bernicia and Deira (*HE* iii.6); d. 5 Aug. 642 (killed by Penda at battle of Maserfelth) [6th holder of *imperium* (Bede), or 6th Bretwalda (*ASC*)]; buried at Bardney.

DEIRA

*OSWINE: acc. 642 (after 5 Aug.) or 643; d. 20 Aug. 651 (betrayed and killed at Gilling, on the orders of King Oswiu (*HE* iii.14))

OSWIU (of Bernicia)

BERNICIA

*OSWIU: acc. 642 (after 5 Aug.), but after 7 years proved unable to live at peace with Oswine, and presently made an end of him.

took control of Deira in 651; defeated Penda, king of the Mercians, at the battle of the *Winwæd*, in 655, and ruled kingdom of the Mercians 655–8; d. 15 Feb. 670 [7th holder of *imperium* (Bede), or 7th Bretwalda (*ASC*)]; buried at Whitby (*HE* iii. 24, iv.5).

DEIRA

Oethelwald, s. of Oswald: sub-king in Deira, *c*.651–5, but on Penda's side at *Winwæd*

Alhfrith, s. of Oswiu: sub-king in Deira, *c*.655–64

Ecgfrith, s. of Oswiu: ? sub-king in Deira, *c*.664–70

ECGFRITH (s. of Oswiu) acc. 670 (after 15 Feb.); sent an army to Ireland in 684; d. 20 May 685 (killed in battle against the *Picts, at *Nechtansmere* (*HE* iv.26))

DEIRA

Ælfwine, s. of Oswiu: ? sub-king in Deira, *c*.?670–79

In Bede's judgement, the death of King Ecgfrith in 685 marked a point after which 'the hopes and strength of the kingdom of the English began to ebb and fall away' (*HE* iv.26).

*ALDFRITH (s. of Oswiu) acc. 686 ('a man most learned in the Scriptures', who 'ably restored the shattered state of the kingdom although within narrower bounds' (*HE* iv.26)); d. 14 Dec. 705

EADWULF	reigned for 2 months in 705–6 (*Stephen's *Life of St Wilfrid*, c. 59); but not included in regnal list
OSRED I	acc. 706; d. 716
COENRED	acc. 716; d. 718
OSRIC	acc. 718; appointed Ceolwulf as his successor; d. 9 May 729 (*HE* v.23)
CEOLWULF	acc. 729; deposed and restored 731 (cf. Bede's remarks in *HE* v.23), yet also the king to whom Bede dedicated the *Historia ecclesiastica* (*HE* Pref.); resigned 737, in favour of Eadberht, and retired to Lindisfarne; d. *c*.764
EADBERHT	acc. 737; received a letter from Pope Paul I (*EHD* i, no. 184); resigned 758, in favour of his son Oswulf, and 'received the tonsure of St Peter' (*HE Cont.*, s.a. 758); d. at York 19/20 Aug. 768 (*HR*)
OSWULF	acc. 758; d. 24/25 July 759 (treacherously killed by his *thegns)
ÆTHELWALD MOLL	acc. 5 Aug. 759 (elected by his people); driven out 30 Oct. 765, at *Pincanheale*; d. ?
ALHRED	acc. 765; addressed a letter to Lul (*EHD* i, no. 187); exiled 774 (went first to Bamborough, then to the king of the Picts); d. ?
ÆTHELRED I	acc. 774; expelled 778 or 779, and driven into exile
ÆLFWALD I	acc. 778 or 779; a 'pious and just king' (*HR*); d. 23 Sept. 788, killed by the treachery of Sicga, and buried at Hexham (*HR*)
OSRED II	acc. 788; expelled 790, tonsured at York, and then driven into exile; d. 14 Sept. 792 (buried at Tynemouth)
ÆTHELRED I (again)	restored 790; married Ælfflæd, daughter of King Offa, at Catterick on 29 Sept. 792 (*HR*); received a letter from Alcuin (*EHD* i, no. 193); d. 18 Apr. 796 (killed near the Cover)
OSBALD	acc. 796; expelled 796 (reigned 27 days), and fled first to Lindisfarne and then to the king of the Picts; received a letter from Alcuin (*EHD* i, no. 200); d. 799 (*HR*)
EARDWULF	as an ealdorman, captured, brought to Ripon, and escaped 790; acc. 796; consecrated king at York, 26 May 796; received a letter from Alcuin (*EHD* i, no. 199); fought against Coenwulf, king of the Mercians, in 801 (*HR*); expelled ? 806
ÆLFWALD II	acc. ? 806: d. ? 808
EARDWULF (again)	restored ? 808 (with help from Charlemagne and Pope Leo III); d. ? 810
EANRED	acc. ? 810; submitted to Ecgberht, king of the West Saxons, in 829; d. 840 or 841
ÆTHELRED II	acc. 840 or 841; expelled 844
RÆDWULF	acc. 844; d. ?
ÆTHELRED II (again)	restored 844; d. ?848
OSBERHT	acc. 848 or 849; expelled 862 or 863, and replaced by Ælle, not of the royal line (*ASC*)
ÆLLE	acc. 862 or 863; d. 21 or 23 Mar. 867 (killed at York)
OSBERHT (again)	restored 867; d. 21 or 23 Mar. 867 (killed at York)

The 'Great Danish Army' which had arrived in England in 865 and which had attacked York in 867 indulged in various other activities before conquering the kingdom of the Northumbrians in 875.

SCANDINAVIAN KINGS OF YORK

HALFDAN I (brother of Ivar the Boneless): established as king of York in the mid-870s; driven out in 877

GUTHFRITH I: acc. 883; d. 24 Aug. ? 895

SIGFRITH: fl. *c*.895; coins in his name struck at York

CNUT: fl. *c*.895; coins in his name struck at York

RULERS OF THE NORTHUMBRIANS

Ecgberht I: acc. 867, appointed by the Danes; driven out 872; d. 873

Ricsige: acc. 873; d. 876

Ecgberht II: acc. 876; d. ? 878

Eadwulf of Bamburgh: acc. ? 878; d. 913

Æthelwold (s. of Æthelred, king of the West Saxons): gained recognition as king *c*.900; d. Dec. 902 (killed at battle of the Holme)

EOWILS and HALFDAN II, joint-rulers: d. 910 (killed at the battle of Tettenhall)

RAGNALD I (s. of Sihtric I, king of Dublin, s. of Ivar the Boneless): acc. 919; submitted to King Edward the Elder in 920; d. 920

Aldred: acc. 913; one of the sons of Eadwulf who submitted to Edward the Elder in 920, and to Æthelstan in 927; d. 927 × ?

SIHTRIC II Caech ('the One-Eyed') (s. of Sihtric I), king in Dublin: acc. 920/1; m. sister of King Æthelstan 926; d. 927

OLAF I Cuarán ('of the Sandal') (s. of Sihtric II): ? king in York 927

GUTHFRITH II (s. of Sihtric I), king in Dublin: acc. 927; driven out by King Æthelstan in 927; d. 934

King *Æthelstan 927–39

OLAF II (s. of Guthfrith II), king in Dublin: one of the confederates defeated by King Æthelstan at *Brunanburh* in 937; acc. 939; d. 941

OLAF I Cuarán ('of the Sandal') (s. of Sihtric II) (again): acc. 941; baptized 943; driven out by King Edmund in 944; became king in Dublin

RAGNALD II (s. of Guthfrith II): acc. 943; baptized 943; driven out by King Edmund in 944

King *Edmund 944–6, King *Eadred 946–7

*ERIC Bloodaxe: acc. 947; deserted by the Northumbrians in 948

Oswulf, high-reeve of Bamborough

King Eadred 948–50

OLAF I Cuarán ('of the Sandal') (s. of Sihtric II), king in Dublin (again): received back in 950; driven out by the Northumbrians in 952, and returned to Dublin

ERIC Bloodaxe (again): received back in 952; driven out by the Northumbrians in 954; d. 954 (killed at Stainmore, and soon afterwards welcomed into Valhalla)

King Eadred 954–5; King *Eadwig 955–7

The kingdom of the English was formally divided in 957 (see further below). The part north of the river Thames was assigned to King *Edgar; but on Eadwig's death, in 959, the kingdom of the English was re-unified.

III. Kings of the Mercians

The original heartland of the kingdom of the Mercians lay north and south of the upper Trent (*HE* iii.24); but successive kings of the Mercians were able to extend their rule over a number of other peoples, including the *Hwicce, the Magonsæte, the men of Lindsey, and the various peoples known collectively as the *Middle Angles. The political centre of the kingdom was at *Tamworth, Staffs., and the episcopal see was at Lichfield, also in Staffs. The five rulers of the Mercians credited with a degree of power or political influence which set them apart from their contemporaries are identified below in bold type. In the seventh century the main line of political tension was the river Humber, and East Anglia was effectively marginalised. In the early eighth century Northumbria was marginalised; and when the equilibrium between Wessex and Kent was broken, in 725–6, Æthelbald, king of the Mercians, came to

505

the fore. In effect, the line of tension moved southwards from the Humber to the river Thames, focussing attention on London and on control of interests in the kingdom of Kent. A Mercian regnal list, extending from Penda in the mid-seventh century to Berhtwulf in the mid-ninth century (ptd Dumville, 'The Anglian Collection', pp. 33, 36), was constructed in the ninth or early tenth century. Another Mercian regnal list, perhaps constructed in the eleventh century, is preserved in a Worcester cartulary (BL, Cotton Tiberius A. xiii, 114v). For general discussion, see Yorke, *Kings and Kingdoms*, pp. 100–27.

CEARL — reigning in the early seventh century (*HE* ii.14)

*PENDA — acc. ? 626 or 632; led an army comprising 30 'royal *ealdormen' into battle against King Oswiu (*HE* iii.24); d. 15 Nov. 655 (killed at the battle of the *Winwæd*, near Leeds)

Following the death of King Penda, the kingdom of the Mercians was ruled by Oswiu, king of the Northumbrians, for three years (655–8).

Peada — assigned a reign of one year, perhaps in his capacity as king of the southern Mercians under Oswiu's dispensation (*HE* iii.24)

In 658 Immin, Eafa and Eadberht, ealdormen of the Mercians, drove out the ealdormen of the Northumbrian king, and set up Penda's younger son Wulfhere as king (*HE* iii.24).

*WULFHERE — acc. 658; d. 675, or 674 (after 23 Sept.) = '675' (*HE* v. 24)

ÆTHELRED — acc. 674 or 675; resigned 704 and became a monk; d. ?716 (buried at Bardney)

COENRED — acc. 704; resigned and went to *Rome, *c*.709; d. *c*.709

CEOLRED — acc. 709; d. 716 (buried at Lichfield)

*ÆTHELBALD — acc. 716; by 731, ruler of all the peoples south of the river Humber (*HE* v.23); styled 'king of the south English', and 'king of Britain', in a charter dated 736 (S 89); d. 757 ('treacherously killed at night by his bodyguard in shocking fashion' (*HE Cont.*, s.a. 757), at Seckington) (buried at Repton)

BEORNRED — acc. 757 (though not included in regnal lists); driven out by Offa in 757; d. 769

*OFFA — acc. 757; d. 29 July 796 (buried at Bedford)

ECGFRITH — consecrated king of the Mercians in 787, during the lifetime of his father, King Offa; acc. 796 (after 29 July); d. 17 Dec. 796

*COENWULF — acc. 796 (after 17 Dec.); d. 821 (? at Basingwerk, Flintshire)

CEOLWULF I — acc. 821; deprived of his kingdom 823; d. ?

BEORNWULF — acc. 823; defeated by Ecgberht, king of the West Saxons, at the battle of *Ellendun* (825); d. 825 (killed by the East Angles)

LUDECA — acc. 825; d. 827 (killed, with his five ealdormen)

WIGLAF — acc. 827

In 829 Ecgberht, king of the West Saxons, 'conquered the kingdom of the Mercians and everything south of the Humber' (*ASC*), and was recognized as king of the Mercians for one year (829–30).

WIGLAF (again) — restored, under uncertain circumstances, in 830; d. 840

BERHTWULF — acc. 840; d. ? 852

BURGRED — acc. ? 852; driven out by the Danes in 873/4, and went to Rome, where he died (buried in the church of S. Maria in Sassia, in the English quarter)

CEOLWULF II — acc. 874 (appointed by the Danes); kingdom divided with the Danes in Aug. 877 (*ASC*)

WESTERN MERCIA	**EASTERN MERCIA**
CEOLWULF II (cont'd): retained control of 'western' Mercia [henceforth 'English' Mercia], apparently including regions dependent on *Oxford and *London; ? d. 879 (assigned 5 years in regnal list)	'Eastern' Mercia fell under the direct control of the Danish army

From *c*.880 until his death in 911, the people of 'English' Mercia were ruled by Ealdorman *Æthelred, based at *Gloucester. King *Alfred seems initially to have retained notional control of London, but in 886 he entrusted London to Ealdorman Æthelred. When Æthelred died, in 911, *Edward the Elder 'succeeded to London and Oxford and to all the lands which belonged to them' (*ASC*). From 911 until her death in 918, the people of 'English' Mercia were ruled by Æthelred's widow *Æthelflæd (daughter of King Alfred the Great). It is clear, however, that Æthelred and Æthelflæd operated all the while within a larger polity conceived as the kingdom 'of the Anglo-Saxons' (see further below). In 918 Ælfwynn, daughter of Æthelred and Æthelflæd, was deprived of her authority in Mercia, and taken into Wessex. For its part, 'Eastern' Mercia appears to have broken down, in the late ninth century, into several districts, controlled notionally by armies based at boroughs under the rule of 'earls'. The separate districts were brought under English control in the course of the military campaign orchestrated by Edward the Elder, which came to its climax in 917–18.

Rulers of other peoples absorbed within the Kingdom of Mercia

Rulers of the Hwicce

The kingdom of the Hwicce was roughly co-terminous with the medieval diocese of *Worcester; and the activities of its rulers are documented in charters preserved in the Worcester archive. For further discussion, see Finberg, 'Princes of the Hwicce', in his *Early Charters of the West Midlands*, pp. 167–80, and Sims-Williams, *Religion and Literature*, pp. 16–53.

The rulers of the Hwicce first leave their trace in the second half of the seventh century, and were clearly then under the control of Wulfhere, king of the Mercians (658–74), and of Æthelred, king of the Mercians (674–704).

EANHERE	brother of Eanfrith; see below
EANFRITH	brother of Eanhere, mentioned as joint rulers of the Hwicce in the 660s (*HE* iv.13)
OSRIC	active in the 670s and 680s; described with his brother Oswald as of noble family, and seemingly regarded by King Æthelred as one of his thegns (S 70)
OSHERE	active in the 690s (S 52–3; see also S 1429); d. before 716

Oshere was succeeded by his sons Æthelheard and Æthelweard, and later by his son Æthelric, operating under the control of Coenred, king of the Mercians (704–9), and of Æthelbald, king of the Mercians (716–57).

ÆTHELHEARD	acc. ? × 709; issued charter with Æthelweard (S 1177)
ÆTHELWEARD	acc. ? × 706; styled *subregulus*, 'son of Oshere former *rex* of the Hwicce' in 706 (S 54); issued charter with Æthelheard (S 1177); d. 716 × ?
ÆTHELRIC	acc. ? × 736; charter of King Æthelbald in favour of his *comes* Æthelric, 'son of Oshere, former *rex* of the Hwicce' (S 94); attested the Ismere charter of King Æthelbald (S 89), as *subregulus atque comes*; d. 736 × ?

The brothers Eanberht, Uhtred and Ealdred were active in the 750s, 760s, and 770s, but clearly operated under the control of Offa, king of the Mercians (757–96).

EANBERHT	acc. ? × 755; styled *regulus*; not recorded after 759
UHTRED	acc. ? × 755; styled *regulus*, issued a charter in 777 × 779, 'aliquod regimen propriae gentis Huicciorum tenens' (S 57)
EALDRED	acc. ? × 755; styled *regulus*, in 778 King Offa granted land to 'my *subregulus* Ealdred, namely *dux* of his own people of the Hwicce' (S 113)

Offa appears to have assumed direct control of the Hwicce in the 780s. Thereafter the kingdom was absorbed into the kingdom of the Mercians, though it retained its own ealdorman.

Rulers of the Magonsæte

The kingdom of the Magonsæte was roughly co-terminous with the medieval diocese of *Hereford. The people and their rulers make no respectable impression in the surviving corpus of *charters, but the absence of any substantial body of evidence from Hereford should perhaps prevent us from infering that they were necessarily any less visible in the seventh and eighth centuries than their Hwiccian counterparts. The people were presumably subject to the kings of the Mercians from the seventh century onwards; and their only attested rulers were seemingly of Mercian origin. For further discussion, see Finberg, 'St

Mildburg's Testament' and 'Princes of the Magonsæte', in his *Early Charters of the West Midlands*, pp. 197–216, 217–24, and Sims-Williams, *Religion and Literature*, pp. 16–53.

MEREWALH	said to be a son of Penda, king of the Mercians; married a Kentish princess called 'Domneva'; fl. *c*.650
MERCHELM	fl. *c*.675
MILFRITH	fl. *c*.675

Rulers of the Middle Angles

There is no reason to believe that the agglomeration of peoples known as the Middle Angles ever developed the sense of collective identity which might have found expression in the emergence of a single king as ruler of them all. When Penda, king of the Mercians, installed his son, Peada, as king of the Middle Angles, it was only for a short period (in the early 650s). Ecclesiastical organisation was similarly imposed from above; and in the late seventh century a see of the Middle Angles was established at *Leicester. The relative success enjoyed by the Middle Angles in preserving a sense of their separate identities is suggested by the document known as the *'Tribal Hidage'; and it seems likely that each people retained a ruler or rulers of its own, thereby contributing to the distinctive composition of the larger 'Mercian' regime. It is difficult, however, to identify these leaders on the ground. One would be Frithuric, styled *princeps* during the reign of Æthelred, king of the Mercians, and probably distinct from the person of the same name mentioned below, under Surrey.

Kings of Lindsey

A royal genealogy representing the kings of Lindsey is preserved in the so-called 'Anglian Collection'; and it is on this basis that a certain Aldfrith, son of Eata, is judged to have been king of Lindsey in the late eighth century. The attestation of an 'Ealfrid rex', which occurs in a Mercian confirmation of a South Saxon charter (S 1183), has been identified as Aldfrith of Lindsey; but the form, in this context, is more likely to be a scribal error for 'Ecgfrith rex', i.e. Ecgfrith, son of Offa.

Rulers of Surrey

In the early 670s Frithuwald, styled 'of the province of the men of Surrey, sub-king of Wulfhere, king of the Mercians', made arrangements for the endowment of a monastery at *Chertsey (S 1165); the charter was attested by Frithuwald and others, including a certain Frithuric and three other sub-kings, called Osric, Wigheard, and Æthelwold. The people of Surrey appear to have retained their separate identity under Mercian control, and Surrey was among the districts which fell under West Saxon control following the battle of *Ellendun* in 825 (*ASC*).

IV. Kings of the East Angles

The East Anglian royal dynasty, known as the Wuffingas, would appear to have originated in the second half of the sixth century, taking its name from Wuffa, grandfather of *Rædwald (*HE* ii.15). There was a royal estate at Rendelsham, in Suffolk (*HE* iii.22), not far from the royal burial ground at *Sutton Hoo. For general discussion, see Yorke, *Kings and Kingdoms*, pp. 58–71.

*RÆDWALD	acc. ? × 616; converted to Christianity in Kent (*HE* ii.15), but compromised his faith on his return; defeated Æthelfrith, king of Bernicia, at the battle of the river Idle 616 (*HE* ii.12); d. 616 × 627 [4th holder of *imperium* (Bede), or 4th Bretwalda (*ASC*)]
EARPWALD	acc. 616 × 627; persuaded to accept Christianity by Edwin, king of Deira (*HE* ii.15); d. 627 or 628 (killed by Ricberht)
Ricberht	a heathen, who may have been recognized as king (cf. *HE* ii.15)
SIGEBERHT	in exile in Gaul during the reign of Rædwald; acc. 630 or 631; joint-king with Ecgric; resigned and retired to a monastery; d. ? (killed in battle against Penda, king of the Mercians) (*HE* iii.18)
ECGRIC	acc. ?; joint-king with Sigeberht; d. ? (killed in battle against Penda, king of the Mercians)

ANNA	acc. ? early 640s; d. 654
ÆTHELHERE	acc. 654; d. ? (participated on Penda's side at the battle of the *Winwæd*, 15 Nov. 655, but it is not clear whether he was killed there)
ÆTHELWALD	acc. ?; d. ? 664
ALDWULF	acc. 663 or 664; d. 713
ÆLFWALD	acc. 713; d. 749
HUN, BEONNA, and ÆTHELBERHT I	joint-kings in 749 (*HR*); Beonna and Æthelberht are also known from coins

In the second half of the eighth century, the kingdom of the East Angles fell under the control of Offa, king of the Mercians (757–96).

*ÆTHELBERHT II	acc. ?; d. 794 (executed at the command of Offa, king of the Mercians); cult of St Æthelbert at Hereford
EADWALD	*c*.800 (known only from coins)

In the early ninth century, the kingdom of the East Angles fell under the control of Coenwulf, king of the Mercians (796–821); Mercian control was maintained thereafter by King Beornwulf (823–5) and King Ludeca (825–7).

ÆTHELSTAN	*c*.830 × 845 (known only from coins)
ÆTHELWEARD	*c*.845 × 855 (known only from coins)
*EDMUND	acc. 855; d. 20 Nov. 869 (killed by the Danes in the course of their invasion of the kingdom); cult of St Edmund at *Bury St Edmunds
ÆTHELRED	*c*.875 (known only from coins)
OSWALD	*c*.875 (known only from coins)

Scandinavian Kings of East Anglia (c.880–917)

*GUTHRUM (Æthelstan)	settled in East Anglia in 879/80; made a treaty with King Alfred; d. 890 (buried at Hadleigh, Suffolk)
EOHRIC	acc. ?; d. Dec. 902 (killed at the battle of the Holme)
Æthelwold (s. of Æthelred, king of the West Saxons)	chosen by the (Northumbrian and East Anglian) Danes as their king (*ASC*); d. Dec. 902 (killed at the battle of the Holme)

Little is known of political organisation within the Scandinavian kingdom of East Anglia after 902. Peace was made with the East Angles in 906; and the 'army of the district', with some 'Vikings whom they had enticed to their assistance', was seemingly defeated soon after laying siege to Maldon, Essex, in 917 (*ASC*). The people who had been under Danish rule in East Anglia, and 'all the army in East Anglia', were among those who submitted to Edward the Elder at Colchester in the autumn of 917.

V. Kings of the South Saxons

The kingdom of the South Saxons was conceived by Bede as stretching south and west from Kent, and was characterized by him as one of the last outposts of paganism (*HE* iv.13). Knowledge of the rulers of the South Saxons in the eighth century depends almost entirely on the evidence of charters; see *Charters of Selsey*, ed. Kelly, pp. lxxiii–lxxxiv. The lack of a royal genealogy for the South Saxons contributes to the difficulty of understanding the details of their political organisation. One would imagine that Oswald, Osmund and Oslac were members of the same family, and that Oswald, bishop of *Selsey, was another of their number; but it would be hazardous to resolve any of the other names into the same or into a different group.

ÆLLE	landed in Sussex '477'; king, still reigning in '491'; d. ? [1st holder of *imperium* (Bede), or 1st Bretwalda (*ASC*)]

Nothing is known of the rulers of the South Saxons in the sixth and first half of the seventh centuries.

ÆTHELWALH	king, acc. ? × 674; baptized in Mercia at the suggestion of King Wulfhere; d. *c*.682 (killed by Cædwalla, in exile from the kingdom of the West Saxons)

According to Bede (*HE* iv.15), Cædwalla was driven out, in the early 680s, by Berhthun and Andhun, described as 'royal ealdormen'. In 685 the South Saxons were interfering in Kent. Berhthun was later killed by Cædwalla, when king of the West Saxons (685 × 688).

NOTHHELM (Nunna)	king, acc. ? × 692; involved with his kinsman *Ine, king of the West Saxons, in attack on Geraint, 'king of the Britons' 710 (*ASC*); his charters attested by King Watt and King Æthelstan, and by 'Bruny', styled 'dux Suthsaxonum'; d. 714 × ? (buried at Selsey)
WATT	king, acc. ? × 692; attested charters of King Nothhelm and of 'Bruny', styled 'dux Suthsaxonum'; d. c.700 × ?
ÆTHELSTAN	king, acc. ? × 714; attested charters of King Nothhelm; d. 714 × ?
ÆTHELBERHT	king, acc. after 733; d. ? (a contemporary of Æthelbald, king of the Mercians)
OSWALD	conceivably reigned as a king in Sussex before 772, though not recorded as such; styled 'dux Suthsaxonum' in 772 (S 108); d. 772 × ?
OSMUND	king (presumably a contemporary of Oslac, Ealdwulf and Ælfwald), acc. ? × 758 or ?765; styled *dux* in 772 (in association with Oswald, Oslac, and Ælfwald); d. 772 × ?
OSLAC	? king (a contemporary of Ealdwulf and Ælfwald), probably in the 760s; styled *dux* in 772 (in association with Oswald, Osmund, and Ælfwald); styled 'dux Suthsaxonum' in 780; d. 780 × ?
EALDWULF	king (a contemporary of Oslac and Ælfwald), probably in the 760s; styled *dux* after 772 and 'dux Suthsaxonum' in the ? mid 780s and in ?791; d. c.790 × ?
ÆLFWALD	king (a contemporary of Oslac and Ealdwulf), probably in the 760s; styled *dux* in 772; d. 772 × ?

Offa, king of the Mercians (757–96), gained control of the kingdom of the South Saxons in the early 770s: in 771 he 'subdued the people of Hastings [east Sussex] by force of arms' (*HR*), and a charter of 772 (S 108) shows that under the Mercian dispensation the rulers who had previously been styled 'king' (*rex*) were henceforth reduced in status to 'ealdorman' (*dux*). Offa may not have been able to maintain control in the period 776–85 (cf. Kent), though he re-established his control thereafter. It would appear that one among the number of South Saxon ealdormen was designated the 'ealdorman of the South Saxons' (see above), perhaps with the implication that he took precedence over the others. The South Saxons appear to have retained their separate identity under Mercian control, and Sussex was among the districts which fell under West Saxon control following the battle of *Ellendun* in 825 (*ASC*).

VI. Kings of the East Saxons

According to Bede, the chief city of the kingdom of the East Saxons was *London, which he described as 'an emporium for many nations who come to it by land and sea' (*HE* ii.3). In the eighth century London itself seems to have been separated from the rest of the kingdom of the East Saxons, and became the centre of a 'Middle Saxon' territory under Mercian rule. A royal genealogy for the kings of the East Saxons, constructed in the ninth century, is preserved in BL Add. 23211, 1v; see Dumville, 'The West Saxon Genealogical Regnal List: Manuscripts and Texts', pp. 2–4 (with plate), 31–2 (text). For further discussion, see Yorke, 'The Kingdom of the East Saxons', and Yorke, *Kings and Kingdoms*, pp. 45–57.

SÆBERHT (Saba)	acc. ? × 604 (*HE* ii.3); said to be under the dominion of Æthelberht, king of Kent; d. 616 or 617, leaving three sons as heirs to his temporal kingdom (*HE* ii.5), as follows
SEAXRED, s. of Sæberht	acc. 616 or 617; d. c.617 (killed in battle against the *Gewisse*)
SÆWEARD, s. of Sæberht	acc. 616 or 617; d. c.617 (killed in battle against the *Gewisse*)
[a third brother]	acc. 616 or 617; d. c.617 (killed in battle against the *Gewisse*)
SIGEBERHT I 'the Small'	acc. c.617 × ?; d.?
SIGEBERHT II 'the Saint'	acc. ? × 653, in succession to Sigeberht the Small; a friend of Oswiu, king of the Northumbrians; d. 653 × 664 (murdered by two brothers who were his kinsmen) (*HE* iii.22)

SWITHHELM	[s. of Seaxbald] acc. 653 × 664, in succession to Sigeberht II; baptized at Rendelsham; d. *c*.664
SWITHFRITH	[? b. of Swithhelm] acc. ?; contributed to the endowment of *Barking abbey (S 1246); d. ?

<table>
<tr><th>PART OF ESSEX</th><th>PART OF ESSEX</th></tr>
<tr><td>SIGEHERE: succeeded Swithhelm, c.664, subject to Wulfhere, king of the Mercians; apostatized (HE iii.30); ? active in Kent in the 680s; d. ? c.690</td><td>SEBBI: succeeded Swithhelm, c.664, subject to Wulfhere, king of the Mercians; remained Christian (HE iii.30); lived in London, reigned for 30 years, resigned, and became a monk (HE iv.11); d. c.694</td></tr>
</table>

Oethelred	contributed to the endowment of Barking abbey in the late 680s (S 1171); a kinsman of Sebbi, though not himself a king

Swæfheard, son of Sebbi (S 10), and Swaberht (S 11), were among the 'foreign' kings active in Kent *c*.690.

SIGEHEARD	[s. of Sebbi] acc. *c*.694 (*HE* iv.11); d. *c*.705 × ?
SWÆFRED	[s. of Sebbi] acc. *c*.694 (*HE* iv.11); d. 704 × ?
OFFA	[s. of Sigehere] acc. *c*.694 × 709, though not certainly a full king; accompanied Coenred, king of the Mercians, to Rome in 709, and died there as a monk (*HE* v.9)
SWÆFBERHT	acc. ? *c*.709; d. 738 (*HR*)
SELERED	acc. ? *c*.738; d. 746 ('slain', *ASC*)
SWITHRED	acc. ? 746; d. ?
SIGERIC I	acc. ?; ? resigned, and went to Rome 798 (*ASC*, MS. F)
SIGERED	acc. ? 798; attested Mercian charters as *rex* and as *subregulus*; d. 823 × ?, possibly although not necessarily the Sigered *dux* who occurs in later Mercian charters
SIGERIC II	styled 'king of the East Saxons', and *minster* of Wiglaf, king of the Mercians, *c*.825 (S 1791)

Essex was among the districts which fell under West Saxon control following the battle of *Ellendun* in 825 (*ASC*). It was an integral part of the 'eastern' kingdom in the central decades of the ninth century, but thereafter fell under Danish control, and remained so when Alfred made his treaty with King Guthrum, *c*.880. In the early 890s, the Danes operated from bases at Benfleet and Shoebury, on the north shore of the Thames estuary, and also at Mersea island. A certain Beorhtwulf was styled 'ealdorman of Essex' in *ASC* 896. The process of the recovery of Essex by the English would appear to have begun, therefore, in the latter part of Alfred's reign; but it was not completed until submission was made to Edward the Elder at Colchester in 917.

VII. Kings of the West Saxons

The people known originally as the *Gewisse* (*HE* iii.7) came to be known as 'Saxons' in the seventh century and as 'West Saxons' in the late seventh and early eighth centuries, reflecting early stages in their political development. The *shires of Devon, Dorset, Somerset, Wiltshire, and Hampshire originated in the same process; and episcopal sees were established at *Winchester and at *Sherborne. A major commercial centre developed at *Southampton (*Hamwic*/*Hamtun*); but it was probably not until the late ninth century that Winchester emerged as the major political centre, and it was at about this time, in effect, that the kingdom was given its historical identity. The information on royal succession contained in regnal lists, and in the *Anglo-Saxon Chronicle*, was massaged by those who had a special interest in creating an impression of deep-rooted political order. For the text of the West Saxon regnal list (to Alfred), see Dumville, 'The West Saxon Genealogical Regnal List: Manuscripts and Texts', pp. 21–5; and for discussion of its historical value (or lack of it), see Dumville, 'The West Saxon Genealogical Regnal List and the Chronology of Early Wessex'. For general discussion, see Yorke, *Kings and Kingdoms*, pp. 128–56.

*CERDIC	acc. 519; d. 534

CYNRIC	ace. 534; d. 560
CEAWLIN	acc. 560; d. 593 [2nd holder of *imperium* (Bede), or 2nd Bretwalda (*ASC*)]
CEOL	acc. 591; d. ? 597
CEOLWULF	acc. 597; d. ? 611
CYNEGILS	acc. 611; d. ? 642

According to an entry in the *Anglo-Saxon Chronicle*, MS. E, Edwin, king of the Northumbrians, ravaged Wessex in 626, 'and destroyed there five kings'.

CENWEALH	acc. 642; driven out by *Penda, 645–8; d. 672

Following the death of King Cenwealh, 'sub-kings (*subreguli*) took upon themselves the government of the kingdom, dividing it up and ruling for about ten years' (Bede, *HE* iv.12).

SEAXBURH, queen	acc. 672; d. ? 674
ÆSCWINE	acc. 674; d. 676
CENTWINE	acc. 676; d. ? 685
*CÆDWALLA	removed the 'sub-kings'; acc. 685; resigned in 688, and went to Rome; d. 20 Apr. 689 (buried at Rome)
*INE	acc. 688; abdicated in 726, and went to Rome; d. ? 726 (buried at Rome)
ÆTHELHEARD	acc. 726; d. ? 740
CUTHRED	acc. 740; d. 756 ['he fought stoutly against King Æthelbald' (*ASC*)]
SIGEBERHT	acc. 756; deprived of his kingdom in 757, by Cynewulf and the councillors of the West Saxons (*ASC*); d. 757 × ? (stabbed to death by a swineherd avenging Ealdorman Cumbra)
CYNEWULF	acc. 757; d. 786 (ambushed by Cyneheard, Sigeberht's brother, and killed; buried at Winchester)
BEORHTRIC	acc. 786; d. 802 (accidentally poisoned by his wife; buried at Wareham)
*ECGBERHT	in exile in Francia, 789–92; acc. 802; defeated Mercians at *Ellendun* in 825

Kings of the Isle of Wight

The Isle of Wight was originally a Jutish kingdom, which extended across to the mainland opposite and which was associated with the kingdom of Kent (Bede, *HE* i.15). In the third quarter of the seventh century the island came under the control of Wulfhere, king of the Mercians, who gave it to Æthelwealh, king of the South Saxons (*HE* iv.13).

Arwald	'king of the island' in the mid 680s; his two brothers were among the first of the islanders to be converted to Christianity (*HE* iv.16)

The kingdom was integrated into the kingdom of the West Saxons during the reign of Cædwalla (685–8).

Kings of the West Saxons and of Other Peoples

Following the defeat of the Mercians at the battle of *Ellendun* (Wroughton, Wilts.), in 825, the people of Kent, Surrey, Sussex and Essex submitted to King Ecgberht, 'because they had been wrongfully forced away from his kinsmen' (*ASC*). In the same year the East Angles appealed to Ecgberht for peace and protection, 'because of their fear of the Mercians' (*ASC*). Ecgberht and his son *Æthelwulf secured the loyalty of the archbishop of Canterbury in a council convened at *Kingston-upon-Thames in 838. A form of sustained political alliance developed between the rulers of Wessex and Mercia. The alliance may have found its first expression *c.*830, with the restoration of Wiglaf, king of the Mercians. It found expression thereafter in 853 (a joint expedition against the Welsh; marriage of Æthelswith and Burgred), in 868 (a joint expedition against the Danes; marriage of Alfred and Ealhswith), and in 886 (restoration of London; ? marriage of Æthelflæd and Æthelred).

ECGBERHT (cont'd)	extended his rule over Kent and other eastern provinces in 825; conquered the kingdom of the Mercians, 'and everything south of the Humber', in 829 [8th Bretwalda (*ASC*)]; received the submission of the Northumbrians 829; d. 839 (? buried at Winchester)

*ÆTHELWULF	sub-king of Kent in the 830s, under Ecgberht; acc. 839; with his son Æthelbald defeated the Danes at Aclea in 851; sent his son Alfred to Rome in 853, and went to Rome himself, with Alfred, in 855–6
Æthelstan	appointed king of Kent, Essex, Surrey and Sussex, under Æthelwulf, in 839 (*ASC*); d. 851 × 855

When King Æthelwulf set off for Rome, in 855, he assigned control of the western kingdom to his son Æthelbald and of the eastern kingdom (Kent, with Surrey, Sussex and Essex) to his son Æthelberht:

WESTERN KINGDOM	EASTERN KINGDOM
ÆTHELBALD: put in control of the western part of the kingdom in 855; contrived to retain control of the 'more important' western kingdom when his father returned to England in 856 (Asser, c. 12)	ÆTHELBERHT: put in control of the eastern kingdom in 855; gave up the kingdom to his father in 856

ÆTHELWULF (cont'd)	married Judith, d. of Charles the Bald, in 856; confined to the eastern kingdom after his return to England in 856 (Asser, c. 12), though he retained the power to make arrangements for the division of the whole kingdom into two parts after his death (Asser, c. 16); d. 13 Jan. 858 (buried at *Steyning, Sussex; later re-buried at Winchester)

WESTERN KINGDOM	EASTERN KINGDOM
ÆTHELBALD (cont'd): acc. 858; married Judith, his step-mother; d. 860 (buried at Sherborne)	ÆTHELBERHT(again): acc. 858

ÆTHELBERHT (cont'd)	acc. 860 (to the kingdom as a whole, following the death of Æthelbald); d. 865 (buried at Sherborne)
ÆTHELRED I	may have served as a sub-king in Wessex during the early 860s; acc. 865; d. 871 (after 15 Apr.) (buried at Wimborne, Dorset)
*ALFRED the Great	journeyed to Rome twice as a child, in 853 and 855; acc. 871 (after 15 Apr.); received the submission of Æthelred, ealdorman of the Mercians, *c*.880

Kings of the Anglo-Saxons (*c*.880–927)

In the early or mid-880s, when or soon after Æthelred, ealdorman of the Mercians, submitted to Alfred, king of the West Saxons, a new polity came into existence, distinctively 'Alfredian' in its conception and symbolising his own political vision; it was this polity which endured until itself superseded in 927. See Keynes, 'King Alfred and the Mercians', pp. 34–9. In effect, the 'kingdom of the Anglo-Saxons' represented the combination for political purposes of the people of Wessex (and its eastern extensions) and the people of 'English' Mercia, and it could thus be formulated as subsuming all the English people who were not under subjection to the Danes. In certain contexts (notably his *law-code and his *will) Alfred chose to call himself 'king of the West Saxons'; but Asser, writing in 893, calls him 'king of the Anglo-Saxons' (clearly distinguished as such from his predecessors), and the same style is used in the king's charters. The new kingdom combined not only the 'Anglian' and 'Saxon' peoples, but also the land lying to the north and south of the river Thames; and if it was the Thames which served to unite its component parts, and to give it life and strength, it was only a matter of time before London would eclipse the political centres at Gloucester (for Mercia) and Winchester (for Wessex), and claim what was most naturally its own. It may be significant in this connection that the order of service for the king's coronation was apparently re-written as if for the new kingdom, and that the site chosen for the ceremonial from 900 to 979 was the royal estate at Kingston-upon-Thames. A continuation of the West Saxon regnal list includes lengths of reigns for Edward, Æthelstan, Edmund, Eadred, Eadwig and Edgar which appear to have been calculated from a date of coronation; see Dumville, 'The West Saxon Genealogical Regnal List: Manuscripts and Texts', pp. 29–30. The 'kingdom of the Anglo-Saxons' was extended in the early tenth century, eastwards to the coast and northwards towards the river Humber, in the course of Edward the Elder's campaign against the Danes of the southern Danelaw.

ALFRED the Great (cont'd)	acknowledged as ruler of the English, perhaps from *c*.880, and made treaty with Guthrum, king of the East Angles, at about the same time; recognized more formally, as 'king of the Anglo-Saxons', perhaps in connection with the general submission at London in 886; said (in retrospect) to have been consecrated king, at Rome, in 853; d. 26 Oct. 899 (buried at Winchester; re-buried at the New Minster, Winchester, *c*.901; removed to Hyde Abbey Winchester, in 1110)
*EDWARD the Elder	sub-king, perhaps of Kent, in the late 890s, under King Alfred; acc. 899 (after 26 Oct.); consecrated king at Kingston-upon-Thames, 8 June 900; extended his authority over the rulers and inhabitants of the southern Danelaw, 912–20; d. 17 July 924 (died at Farndon-on-Dee, Cheshire; buried at the New Minster, Winchester)

It is conceivable that Edward intended a division of the kingdom after his death, between Æthelstan (in Mercia) and Ælfweard (in Wessex). But it seems more likely that the political establishment in Wessex chose Ælfweard, and that the establishment in Mercia set up Æthelstan in opposition to him.

WESSEX	MERCIA
ÆLFWEARD: recognized as king, in Wessex, following the death of his father, Edward the Elder; d. 2 Aug. 924 (buried at the New Minster, Winchester)	*ÆTHELSTAN: recognized as king, in Mercia, following the death of his father, Edward the Elder

Ælfweard did not long survive his father, and sooner or later Æthelstan himself gained recognition as king 'of the Anglo-Saxons'.

ÆTHELSTAN (cont'd)	acc. 924 (after 2 Aug.), or 925, as 'king of the Anglo-Saxons and of the Danes' (S 1417); consecrated king at Kingston-upon-Thames, 4 Sept. 925

Kings of the English (927–1066)

In 927 King Æthelstan 'succeeded to the kingdom of the Northumbrians; and he brought under his rule all the kings who were in this island' (*ASC*); on 12 July, peace was established at Eamont, in north Derbyshire. Æthelstan and his successors were generally regarded as kings 'of the English', but for twenty years, from Æthelstan's death in Oct. 939 until Eadwig's death in Oct. 959, the unity of the kingdom of the English was far from secure.

ÆTHELSTAN (cont'd)	regarded as 'king of the English' from 927; defeated force of Norsemen and Scots at the battle of *Brunanburh* 937; d. 27 Oct. 939 (died at Gloucester; buried at *Malmesbury)
*EDMUND	acc. 939 (after 27 Oct.); consecrated king, probably at Kingston-upon-Thames, *c*.29 Nov. 939

Following the death of King Æthelstan, the Northumbrians accepted Olaf Guthfrithsson (from the Scandinavian kingdom of Dublin) as their king. In 939–40 Olaf extended his control further south, over the territory of the *Five Boroughs (Lincoln, Leicester, Nottingham, Stamford, and Derby), and came to terms with King Edmund at Leicester:

SOUTH OF WATLING STREET	NORTH OF WATLING STREET
EDMUND: king south of *Watling Street 940–2	OLAF II (s. of Guthfrith II): king of York, and of the territory of the Five Boroughs; d. 941

EDMUND (cont'd)	recovered control of the territory of the Five Boroughs in 942, and of Northumbria in 944; d. 26 May 946 (stabbed to death at Pucklechurch, Gloucs.; buried at *Glastonbury)
*EADRED the Weak-in-the-Feet	acc. 946 (after 26 May), and asserted control of Northumbria; consecrated king at Kingston-upon-Thames, 16 Aug. 946; lost control of Northumbria 947; recovered control of Northumbria 948; lost control of Northumbria *c*.950; recovered control of Northumbria 954; d. 23

Nov. 955 (buried at the Old Minster, Winchester, perhaps in defiance of his own intentions)

The draftsman of the series of 'alliterative' charters, issued in the 940s and 950s, employed royal styles of a kind which reflect his distinctive conception of a quadripartite kingdom, and which at the same time respect fluctuations in the king's political position. Edmund was styled 'king of the Anglo-Saxons' in the early 940s, when his rule was confined south of Watling Street. Eadred was 'king of the Anglo-Saxons, Northumbrians, pagans, and Britons' (*vel sim.*) in 946, and again in 949–50; but he was reduced (in this diplomatic parlance) to 'king of the English' in 951, and raised back to 'king of the Anglo-Saxons, Northumbrians, pagans, and Britons' in 954.

*EADWIG the All-Fair	acc. 955 (after 23 Nov.); consecrated king, probably at Kingston-upon-Thames, *c*.26 Jan. 956

In 957, some time after 9 May, the kingdom of the English was divided between Eadwig and his younger brother Edgar, apparently as the result of a formal political settlement:

SOUTH OF THE RIVER THAMES	NORTH OF THE RIVER THAMES
EADWIG: king 'of the English', from 957 (after 9 May); d. 1 Oct. 959 (buried at the New Minster, Winchester)	*EDGAR: acc. as king of the Mercians and Northumbrians, 957 (after 9 May)

EDGAR the Peacable	acc. as king of the English, 959 (after 1 Oct.); ? consecrated king, perhaps at Kingston-upon-Thames, *c*.960; if so, consecrated king for a second time, at *Bath, Pentecost (11 May) 973; d. 8 July 975 (buried at Glastonbury)
*EDWARD the Martyr	acc. 975 (after 8 July; ? 17 July); ? consecrated king at Kingston-upon-Thames, late summer 975; d. 18 Mar. 978 (murdered by supporters of his half-brother, Æthelred, at Corfe Castle, Dorset, and buried secretly nearby; body revealed and taken to *Wareham 13 Feb. 979; transl. from Wareham to *Shaftesbury 18 Feb. 979)
*ÆTHELRED II the Unready	acc. 978 (after 18 Mar.); consecrated king at Kingston-upon-Thames, 4 May 979; forced into exile in *Normandy in 1013, and remained there for the duration of the reign of Swein Forkbeard
*SWEIN Forkbeard	succeeded his father Harold Bluetooth as king of the Danes, *c*.987; active in England, 991–4, 1003–5, and 1013–14; acknowledged by the English as 'full king', 1013; d. 3 Feb. 1014, whereupon his son Cnut was acknowledged as king by the Danish fleet; his body was removed from England in 1014, and buried at Roskilde in Denmark
ÆTHELRED II the Unready (again)	returned to England, as king, in the spring of 1014; invasion of Cnut in 1015–16; d. 23 April 1016 (buried at St Paul's, London)
*EDMUND Ironside	acc. 1016 (after 23 Apr.), at London, and took control of Wessex

Edmund Ironside was defeated by King Cnut at the battle of Ashingdon, 18 Oct. 1016. The two kings came to terms at Olney (an island in the river Severn, near *Deerhurst, Gloucestershire):

SOUTH OF THE RIVER THAMES	NORTH OF THE RIVER THAMES
EDMUND: regarded after 18 Oct. 1016 as king 'of Wessex', with sovereignty; d. 30 Nov. 1016 (buried at Glastonbury)	*CNUT: regarded after 18 Oct. 1016 as king 'of Mercia'

CNUT	acc. 1016 (after 30 Nov.), as king of 'all the kingdom of England' (*ASC* 1017); king of Denmark from 1018, and extended rule over Norway and part of Sweden; journeyed to Rome in 1027; d. 12 Nov. 1035 (at Shaftesbury; buried at the Old Minster, Winchester)

Following the death of Cnut, on 12 Nov. 1035, there was 'an assembly of all the councillors at Oxford' (*ASC*). The outcome was apparently another division of the kingdom:

SOUTH OF THE RIVER THAMES	NORTH OF THE RIVER THAMES
*HARTHACNUT: chosen as king in the south (*in absentia*) in 1035; but deserted by his supporters in 1037	*HAROLD Harefoot: chosen as king in the north in 1035, with regency over all England; wished to be consecrated king, but failed to prevail over the archbishop; extended his rule south of the Thames in 1036–7

HAROLD Harefoot — acc. 1037, 'as king everywhere' (*ASC*); d. 17 Mar. 1040 (at Oxford; buried at Westminster; body exhumed by Harthacnut and thrown first into a fen and then into the river Thames; body recovered and buried in London)

HARTHACNUT — acc. 1040 (after 17 Mar.); d. 8 Jun. 1042 (suddenly, at Lambeth, while attending a wedding; buried at the Old Minster, Winchester)

*EDWARD the Confessor — in exile in Normandy 1016–41, and there regarded as king of the English; abortive return to England in 1036; 'sworn in as king' in 1041 (*ASC*), during the reign of Harthacnut; acc. 1042 (after 8 Jun.); consecrated king at Winchester, 3 Apr. 1043; d. 5 Jan. 1066 (buried at Westminster)

*HAROLD II, son of Earl Godwine — acc. 5 Jan. 1066; consecrated king at Westminster, 6 Jan. 1066; d. 14 Oct. 1066, at the battle of Hastings (buried at Waltham)

Following the death of King Harold, Archbishop *Ealdred (archbishop of York) and the citizens of London wanted to have Edgar the Ætheling, son of Edward the Exile and grandson of Edmund Ironside, as king, 'as was his proper due' (*ASC*); but in the event Ealdred, Edgar, and others, submitted to Duke William at Berkhamstead.

The Normans

WILLIAM I — defeated King Harold, 14 Oct. 1066; crowned at Westminster, 25 Dec. 1066; d. 9 Sept. 1087 (in Normandy; buried at St Stephen's, Caen)

WILLIAM II — acc. 26 Sept. 1087; d. 2 Aug. 1100

HENRY I — acc. 5 Aug. 1100; d. 1 Dec. 1135

STEPHEN — acc. 22 Dec. 1135; d. 25 Oct. 1154

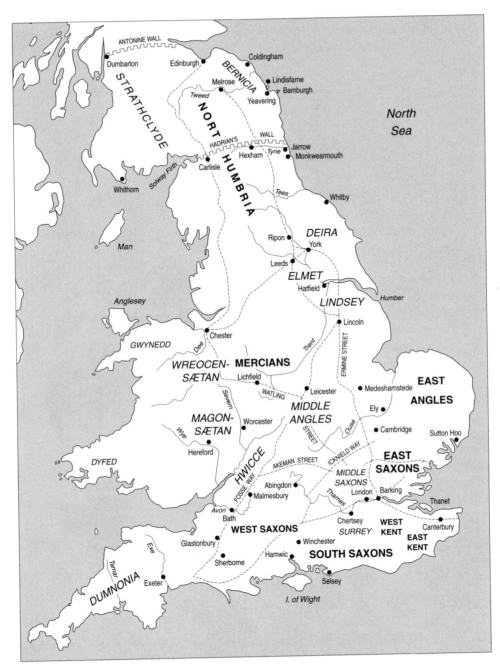

Map 9 The 'Heptarchy' (*c*.700).

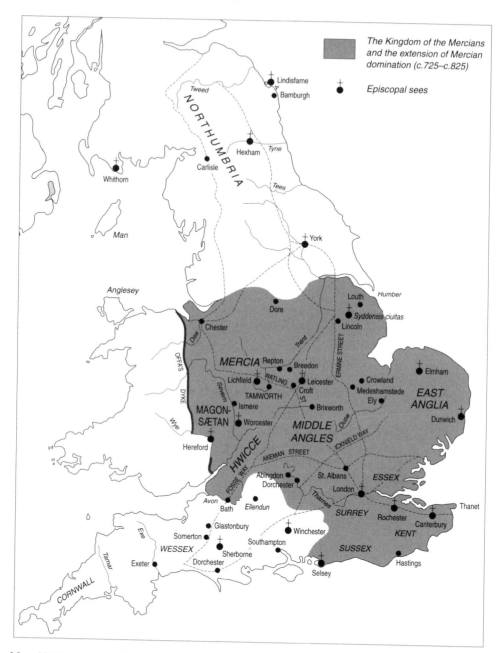

Map 10 The Mercian Supremacy (*c*.800).

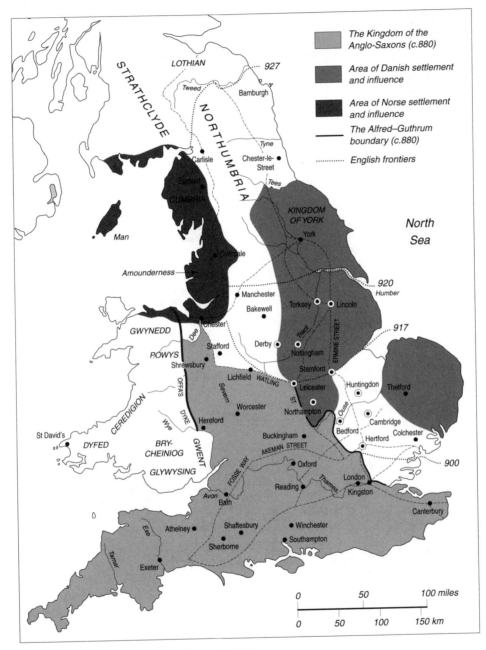

Map 11 The Kingdom of the Anglo-Saxons (*c.*900).

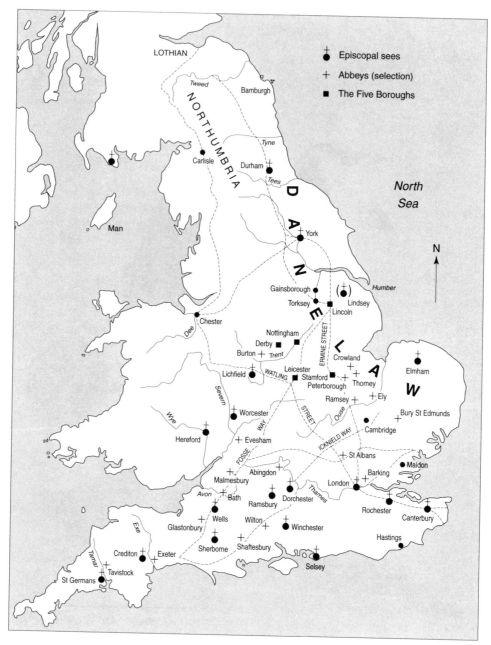

Map 12 The Kingdom of the English (*c.*1000).

INDEX OF CONTRIBUTORS

RICHARD ABELS
army; *here*; heriot; navy; *trinoda necessitas*

GRENVILLE ASTILL
trade

MARK ATHERTON
Bosworth, J.; dictionaries, modern; Sweet, Henry

RICHARD N. BAILEY
Bewcastle Cross; crosses, stone; Gosforth Cross; grave-markers; Hexham; hogbacks; Ripon; Sandbach; Scandinavian influence on art; sculpture, stone

PETER S. BAKER
computus; metrical calendars, OE; *Seasons for Fasting*

DEBBY BANHAM
food and drink; *Monasterialia indicia*

JULIA BARROW
cathedral clergy and canons; Worcester; Wulfstan II, b. of Worcester

MARTHA BAYLESS
entertainment

ALEX BAYLISS
bells and bellringing

PAUL BIBIRE
Germanic languages; Old Norse language

MARTIN BIDDLE
Repton

C. P. BIGGAM
colour

M. A. S. BLACKBURN
coinage; hoards; mints and minting; moneyers

JOHN BLAIR
Abingdon; Bakewell; Barking; Barton-upon-Humber; Bath; Bosham; Bradford-on-Avon; Brandon; Breamore; Breedon-on-the-Hill; bridges; Bury St Edmunds; canals; Carlisle; Chertsey; Cirencester; Coldingham; Cricklade; Diuma; Dorchester, Dorset; Dorchester-on-Thames; Earls Barton; Elmham, North; Escomb; Exeter; Eynsham; forts and fortifications; Gloucester; Goltho; Hartlepool; Hereford; Lastingham; Leicester; Lichfield; Lincoln; Lindisfarne; Lyminge; markets and fairs; Melrose; Minster-in-Sheppey; Minster-in-Thanet; monastic sites; Northampton; Norwich; Osgyth; Otley; Oxford; par-

STEPHANIE HOLLIS
Rhyming Poem; *Rune Poem*; *Theodulfi Capitula*

CAROLE HOUGH
kinship; marriage and divorce; wergild; widow; women

GILLIAN HUTCHINSON
ships

GEORGE JACK
Beowulf

ROHINI JAYATILAKA
Werferth

JOY JENKYNS
charter bounds

S. E. KELLY
Æthelberht, k.; Canterbury; Hengest and Horsa; Kent; Sussex; Wulfred

ALAN KENNEDY
crimes; feuds; jurisdiction

SIMON KEYNES
Adventus Saxonum; Ælfheah II; Æthelbald, k. of Mercia; Æthelred, lord of the Mercians; Æthelstan Ætheling; alms; *Anglo-Saxon Chronicle*; Anglo-Saxonism; Anglo-Saxons, kingdom of; Asser; *bretwalda*; Burghal Hidage; Ceolnoth; chancery, royal; charters and writs; Cnut; Coenwulf; County Hidage; Cynethryth; Eadric Streona; Edmund Ironside; Ely; *Encomium Emmae*; episcopal lists; Florence of Worcester; Giso; Harold Harefoot; Harthacnut; Hemming; heptarchy; *heregeld*; Hickes, George; Jænberht; Jews; Kemble, J. M.; Kingston-upon-Thames; Koenwald; Lindsey; liturgical commemoration; Mercia; Middle Angles; Nothhelm; Offa; papacy; Penda; Plegmund; shire; Swein Forkbeard; thegn; Vikings; Wanley, H.; Wulfhere; Wulfstan I of York

ANNE L. KLINCK
elegies; *Husband's Message*; *Ruin*; *Seafarer*; *Wanderer*; *Wife's Lament*; *Wulf and Eadwacer*

LUCIA KORNEXL
Regularis Concordia

MICHAEL LAPIDGE
Acca; acrostics; Adelard of Utrecht; Aediluulf; Ælberht of York; Ælfflæd of Whitby; Ælfheah I; Ælfhelm of Ely; Ælfric Bata; Ælfwine's Prayerbook; Æthelred and Æthelberht, SS; Æthelstan Psalter; Æthelwold; Æthilwald, b. of Lindisfarne; Albinus; Aldfrith, k.; Aldhelm; annals; Augustine of Canterbury; Benedict Biscop; Beornstan; Berhtwald; Boisil; Bosa; Burghard; Byrhtferth; Byzantium; canon law; clergy; colloquies; colophons; creeds; Cuthburg; Deusdedit; Dunstan; Ealdred of York; Eanflæd of Whitby; Earconwold; Eata; Ecgberht of York; Ecgwine; Eosterwine; Felix; Flanders; Frithegod; Fursa; Germanus; Germany; Gildas; Godeman; Grimbald of Saint-Bertin; Hadrian; Hæddi; Hewald; Hild; Hildelith; *Historia Brittonum*; Honorius; Hwætberht; Hygeburg; hymns, Latin; Indract; Ithamar; James the Deacon; John the Old Saxon; Lantfred; lapidaries; Laurentius; Leofric of Exeter; Leofwine (Lebuin); libraries; Liudger; Lull; Martyrology, OE; Mellitus; metrical calendar, Latin; Milred; monasticism; Oda; Oswald the Younger; Oswald of Worcester and York; pallium; Paulinus of York; poetic technique, Latin; pontifical ceremonies; prayer, private; Rome; schools; scriptorium; Stephen of Ripon; Swithun; *syllogae*; Talbot, R.; Tatwine; Theodore of Canterbury; *tituli*; 'Tremulous Hand'; visions; Wilfrid II; Willehad; Willibald; Wulfsige, b. of Sherborne; Wulfstan *Cantor*; Wynnebald

INDEX OF CONTRIBUTORS

VIVIEN LAW
grammar, Latin

GRAEME LAWSON
musical instruments; music

M. K. LAWSON
taxation

PATRIZIA LENDINARA
glossaries

R. M. LIUZZA
gospel translation

R. C. LOVE
Æthelthryth, St; Birinus, St; Botuulf, St; Chad, St; Eadgyth, St; Folcard of Saint-Bertin; Godiva; Goscelin; hagiography; Iwig, St; Judoc, St; Kenelm, St; Machutus, St; Mildburg, St; Mildrith, St; Neot, St; Pega, St; Rumwold, St; Sativola, St; Sexburg, St; Tancred, Torhtred and Tova, SS; Walburg, St; Waltheof, St

K. A. LOWE
chirograph; wills

PETER J. LUCAS
Daniel; *Exodus*; *Genesis*; Junius, F.

NIELS LUND
Ohthere, voyage of

ARTHUR MacGREGOR
bone-working

PATRICK McGURK
gospelbooks; pilgrimage

HELEN McKEE
script

K. MANCHESTER
diseases

RICHARD MARSDEN
Amiatinus, Codex; Bible; Ceolfrith

AUDREY MEANEY
amulets; charms; folklore; magic; paganism

SEAN MILLER
Ætheling; Æthelred the Unready; Æthelstan; Æthelstan Half-King; Æthelweard; Eadred; Eadwig; Edgar; Edmund; Edward the Elder; Edward the Martyr; Eric Bloodaxe; hostages; housecarls; hundreds; wapentakes

BRUCE MITCHELL
syntax

MARCO MOSTERT
Abbo of Fleury; Edmund, St; Fleury; Frisians; Willibrord

JANET NELSON
queens

MÁIRE NÍ MHAONAIGH
Celtic languages; Celts

WILLIAM NOEL
Harley Psalter; Utrecht Psalter

KATHERINE O'BRIEN O'KEEFFE
Cædmon; literacy; punctuation; *Solomon and Saturn*, poetic; *Solomon and Saturn*, prose

ÉAMONN Ó CARRAGÁIN
Ruthwell Cross

ANDY ORCHARD
Æthilwald, poet; alliteration; Beorhtgyth; Boniface; classical learning; Eadburg; *enigmata*; Leofgyth; *Liber monstrorum*; *Marvels of the East*; metre, Latin; octosyllables, Latin; oral-formulaic theory; preaching; prose style, Latin; Wulfstan the Homilist

GALE R. OWEN-CROCKER
clothing; tapestry

O. J. PADEL
Armes Prydein; Arthur; Cornwall; *Gododdin*; personal names, Celtic; place-names, Celtic

R. I. PAGE
Old English; personal names, OE; runes

DAVID PARK
wall-painting

DAVID PARSONS
Brixworth

SEBASTIAN PAYNE
animal husbandry

DAVID A. E. PELTERET
manumission; roads; slavery; transport and communication; Watling Street

RICHARD W. PFAFF
liturgical books; liturgy

KATHRYN POWELL
Alexander the Great, *Letter to Aristotle*; Apollonius of Tyre

DAVID PRATT
Fuller Brooch

PHILLIP PULSIANO
psalter glosses; Thorpe, B.

INDEX OF CONTRIBUTORS

OLIVER RACKHAM
woodland

PHILIP RAHTZ
cemeteries, unfurnished; Cheddar; Glastonbury; mills; royal sites

SUSAN RANKIN
chant; music

CHRISTINE RAUER
dragons

BARBARA C. RAW
Bible, illustrations; *Dream of the Rood*; iconography

ROGER E. RAY
Bede; exegesis

PAUL G. REMLEY
biblical translation, poems; Junius Manuscript

CHARLOTTE A. ROBERTS
malnutrition; parasites; surgery

JANE ROBERTS
Christ III; Cynewulf; Guthlac, St

DAVID ROLLASON
Northern Annals; ordeal; relics and relic cults; *Resting Places of the Saints*; Symeon of Durham

SUSAN ROSSER
Judith

DONALD SCRAGG
Advent Lyrics; alphabet; *Andreas*; Anglo-Norman; *Battle of Brunanburh*; *Battle of Maldon*; beasts of battle; Bede's *Death Song*; *Beowulf* Manuscript; *Christ and Satan*; *comitatus*; dating of vernacular texts; *Descent into Hell*; Elstob, E.; Exeter Book; homilies; prose style, OE; Rawlinson, R.; spelling and pronunciation; Sunday Letter; Thorkelin; Turner, S.; Vercelli Book; *wyrd*

RICHARD SHARPE
Adomnán; Aidan; Columba; Iona

ALICE SHEPPARD
Orosius, OE translation of

JEREMY J. SMITH
Grimm's Law; sound changes; Verner's Law

PAULINE STAFFORD
Ælfthryth; Eadgifu; Eadgyth, queen; ealdorman; Emma of Normandy; reeve

WESLEY M. STEVENS
astronomy; Easter controversy

INDEX OF CONTRIBUTORS

B. A. E. YORKE

Æthelwulf, k.; Alfred; Cædwalla; Cerdic; council, king's; dynasties, royal; Ecgberht, k.; Essex; *Gewisse*; Guthrum; *Hwicce*; Ine; Jutes; kings and kingship; Malmesbury; Middle Saxons; settlement, Anglo-Saxon; Wessex

S. M. YOUNGS

enamel; hanging-bowls; millefiori

CLASSIFIED INDEX OF HEAD-WORDS

Note: Cross-references are in square brackets.

PERSONS

Royalty (men)

East Anglia: Rædwald; St Æthelberht; St Edmund; Guthrum
Kent: Hengest and Horsa; Æthelberht; SS Æthelred and Æthelberht
Mercia: Penda; Wulfhere; Æthelbald; Offa; Coenwulf; St Kenelm; Æthelred, 'Lord of the Mercians'; [Æthelflæd, 'Lady of the Mercians']
Northumbria: Edwin; Oswald; Oswiu; Aldfrith; Eric Bloodaxe
Wessex, the Anglo-Saxons, and the English: Cerdic; Cædwalla; Ine; Ecgberht; Æthelwulf; Alfred; Edward the Elder; Æthelstan; Edmund; Eadred; Eadwig; Edgar; Edward the Martyr; Æthelred the Unready; Æthelstan ætheling; Swein Forkbeard; Edmund Ironside; Cnut; Harold Harefoot; Harthacnut; Edward the Confessor; Harold II
See also ætheling; dynasties, royal; genealogies, royal; kings and kingship; regnal lists; Appendix, 'Rulers of the English, c.450–1066'; *see also below, under* Kingdoms and peoples

Royalty (women)

Ælfthryth, queen; Æthelthryth of Ely; Cuthburg, queen; Cynethryth, queen, Eadgifu, queen; Eadgyth [Edith], queen; Eadgyth [Edith] of Wilton; Eanflæd of Whitby; [Edith]; Emma of Normandy, queen
See also queens

Bishops and archbishops

Province of Canterbury
Canterbury: Augustine; Laurentius; Mellitus; Justus; Honorius; Deusdedit; Theodore; Berhtwald; Tatwine; Nothhelm; Jænberht; Wulfred; Ceolnoth; Plegmund; Oda; Dunstan; Ælfheah
London: Mellitus; Earconwald; Dunstan; Wulfstan the Homilist
Rochester: Justus; Paulinus; Ithamar
Sherborne: Aldhelm; Asser; Wulfsige (III)
Winchester: Leuthere; Hæddi; Swithun; Beornstan; Ælfheah (I); Æthelwold (I); Ælfheah (II)
Worcester: Ecgwine; Milred; Werferth; [Cenwald]; Koenwald; Dunstan; Oswald; Wulfstan (I) the Homilist; Ealdred; Wulfstan II
Other sees: Birinus, bp of the West Saxons; Agilbert, bp of the West Saxons; Chad, bp of Lichfield; Diuma, bp of the Mercians and Middle Angles, Leofric, bp of Exeter; Giso, bp of Wells

Province of York
York: Paulinus; Wilfrid (I); Bosa; Wilfrid (II); Ecgberht; Ælberht; Wulfstan (I); Oswald; Wulfstan (II) the Homilist; Ealdred

Hexham: Eata; Cuthbert; Wilfrid; Acca
Lindisfarne: Aidan; Eata; Cuthbert; Æthilwald
See also cathedral clergy; episcopal lists

Abbesses

Ælfflæd of Whitby; Æthelthryth of Ely; Eadburg of Thanet; Eanflæd of Whitby; Hild of Whitby; Hildelith of Barking, Merewenna of Romsey; Mildburg of Much Wenlock; Mildrith of Minster-in-Thanet; Sexburg of Ely
Abbots, priests, etc.: Ælfric of Eynsham; Albinus; Benedict Biscop; Boisil; Botwulf; Ceolfrith; Eosterwine; Fursa; Germanus; Godeman; Guthlac; Hadrian; Hwætberht; James the Deacon
See also missionaries; *see also above, under* Bishops and archbishops

English missionaries on the Continent

Beorhtgyth; Boniface; Burghard; Hewald; Hygeburg; [Lebuin]; Leofgyth; Leofwine; Liudger; Lull; Walburg; Willehad; Willibald; Willibald of Mainz; Willibrord; Wynnebald
See also missionaries

Scholars

Ædiluulf; Ælberht, abp of York; Ælfhelm of Ely; Ælfric Bata; Ælfric of Eynsham; Æthelweard; Æthelwold, bp of Winchester; [Æthelwulf]; Æthilwald, poet; Alcuin of York; Aldhelm, bp of Sherborne; Aldred; Asser; [Bald]; Bede; Byrhtferth; Cædmon; [Eddius Stephanus]; Felix; Hadrian; Milred, bp of Worcester; Oswald the Younger; Stephen of Ripon; Tatwine; Theodore; Werferth; Wulfstan Cantor; Wulfstan the Homilist

Scholars of continental origin in Anglo-Saxon England
Abbo of Fleury; Adelard of Utrecht; Felix; Folcard of Saint-Bertin; Frithegod; Goscelin of Saint-Bertin; Grimbald of Saint-Bertin; Israel the Grammarian; John the Old Saxon; Lantfred

Other scholars (post-Conquest)
[Coleman]; Florence of Worcester; Hemming of Worcester; Henry of Huntingdon; John of Worcester; Symeon of Durham; William of Malmesbury
See also below, under Learning and literature

Other laymen and laywomen

Æthelstan Half-King; Æthelweard; Eadric Streona; Godiva; Godwine; Leofric; Ohthere; Waltheof
Other saints: [Cuthman]; Eadgyth [Edith] of Wilton; [Frithuswith]; Iwig; Neot; Osgyth; Pega; Rumwold; Sativola; Tancred, Torhtred and Tova; Waltheof; Werburg; Wistan

The Celtic world

Adomnán; Arthur; Asser; Columba; Fursa; Gildas; Indract; Judoc; Machutus; [Nennius]

Popes

Gregory the Great

Antiquaries and Anglo-Saxonists

John Bale; John Leland; Laurence Nowell; Matthew Parker; Robert Talbot; Sir Robert Cotton; Franciscus Junius; George Hickes; Humfrey Wanley; Elizabeth Elstob; Richard Rawlinson; Grimur Jonsson Thorkelin; Sharon Turner; J. M. Kemble; Benjamin Thorpe; Joseph Bosworth; Henry Sweet
See also Anglo-Saxonism; antiquaries

PEOPLES AND PLACES

Peoples

Celts; Franks; Frisians; Jews; Jutes; Picts; Vikings
Kingdoms and peoples: Anglo-Saxons; Bernicia; Deira; East Anglia; Elmet; English people; Essex; *Gewisse*; Hwicce; Kent; Lindsey; [*Magonsætan*]; Mercia; Middle Angles; Middle Saxons; Northumbria; Cornwall; Sussex; Wessex

Minsters, churches, towns, and other sites

England south of the Humber: Abingdon; Bakewell; Barking; Barton-upon-Humber; Bath; Bosham; Bradford-on-Avon; Brandon; Breamore; Breedon-on-the-Hill; Brixworth; Bury St Edmunds; Canterbury; Cheddar; Chertsey; Chester; Cirencester; *Clofesho*; Cricklade; Deerhurst; Dorchester; Dorchester-on-Thames; Earls Barton; Elmham, North; Ely abbey; Exeter; Eynsham; Glastonbury abbey; Gloucester; Goltho; [Greensted]; [*Hamwic*]; Hereford; Ipswich; Kingston-upon-Thames; Leicester; Lichfield; Lincoln; London; Lyminge; Malmesbury; Minster-in-Sheppey; Minster-in-Thanet; [minsters]; Mucking; Northampton; Norwich; Oxford; Ramsey; Raunds; Reculver; Repton; Rochester; St Albans; Sandbach; Selsey; Shaftesbury; Sherborne; Southampton; Stamford; Steyning; Sutton Hoo; Tamworth; Wallingford; Wareham; Wells; [Wenlock]; Westminster; Wimborne; Winchcombe; Winchester; Windsor (Old); Wing; Worcester
See also Five Boroughs; monastic sites; nunneries; Roman remains; parochial organisation; royal sites; towns
Northumbria and Scotland: Bewcastle; Carlisle; Coldingham; [Coppergate]; Escomb; Hartlepool; Hexham; Iona; [Jarrow]; Lastingham; Lindisfarne; Melrose; Monkwearmouth (or Wearmouth) and Jarrow; Otley; Ripon; [Wearmouth]; Whitby; Whithorn; Yeavering; York
See also monastic sites; nunneries; Roman remains; royal sites; towns

Places overseas

Byzantium; Flanders; Fleury; Germany; Normandy; Rome
See also papacy; pilgrimage

SUBJECTS

Archaeological or material evidence

cemeteries, furnished; cemeteries, unfurnished; [cremations]; [earthworks, defensive]; forts and fortifications; grave goods; grave-markers; mills; Mucking; Offa's Dyke; princely burials; Roman remains; settlement, Anglo-Saxon; settlement patterns; Sutton Hoo; Taplow burial; Wansdyke; Wat's Dyke
See also aerial reconnaissance; monastic sites; Roman remains; royal sites; towns; *see also above, under* Minsters, churches, towns, and other sites

Art, architecture, sculpture, etc.

Anglo-Saxon art, chronology; architectural stone sculpture; architecture, ecclesiastical; [architecture, secular]; Bible, illustrations; carpet-pages; [castles]; [cathedrals]; chi-rho; [churches]; colour; crosses, stone; crypts; embroidery; enamel; Gosforth Cross; [halls]; hogbacks; iconography (use of symbolism); illumination; [ornament]; Ruthwell Cross; Scandinavian influence on English art; sculpture, stone; sundials; tapestry; textiles; tiles; timber building; wall-painting; 'Winchester School'
See also below, under Artifacts; Manuscripts

Artifacts

Alfred Jewel; amulets; arms and armour; Bayeux Tapestry; bells and bellringing; bone and ivory carving; bone working; [brooches]; censers; [crown]; embroidery; Franks Casket; Fuller Brooch; Gandersheim Casket; glass; hanging-bowls; [harps]; [helmets]; inscriptions, non-runic; [inscriptions, runic]; [ivory]; jewellery; leather-work; metalworking; millefiori; musical instruments; Ormside Bowl; pottery; regalia; [rings]; runes; seals; [shields]; ships; [shoes]; shrines and reliquaries; Sutton Hoo; [swords]; tapestry; textiles; tiles; [weapons]; [wood-working]
See also above, under Art, architecture, sculpture, etc., *and below, under* Manuscripts

Miscellaneous subjects (historical, etc.)

Adventus Saxonum; ætheling; [*Angelcynn*]; army [borough]; Bretwalda; bridges; *comitatus*; conversion; coronation; council, king's; councils, church; [Danegeld]; Danelaw; [demesne, royal]; dynasties, royal; ealdorman; [earl]; English people; Five Boroughs; [fleet]; *foederati*; [fyrd]; [geld]; genealogies, royal; [*gens Anglorum*]; [*gesith*]; Hastings, battle of; Heptarchy; *here*; *heregeld*; *heriot*; hide; hostages; housecarls; hundreds; [invasions]; kings and kingship; land tenure; literacy; [lordship]; navy; Offa's Dyke; pilgrimage; queens; reeve; regalia; regnal lists; roads; royal sites; settlement, Anglo-Saxon; [sheriff]; shire; Sutton Hoo; taxation; thegn; [tithing];

Trinoda necessitas; Vikings; Wansdyke; wapentakes; Watling Street; Wat's Dyke; wergeld; [witan]; women

Charters, etc: [bookland]; chancery, royal; charter bounds; charters and writs; chirograph; [diploma]; [folkland]; land tenure; papacy; seals; *Trinoda necessitas*; wills; [writs]

Coins and coinage: coinage; hoards; mints and minting; moneyers; regalia; [*sceatta*]; [styca]

Law and legislation: courts; crimes; *Dunsæte*; frankpledge; hundreds; jurisdiction; jury; land tenure; laws; manumission; oaths; ordeal; parochial organisation; [sake and soke]; shire; wapentakes; wergeld; widow; wills

Other texts: *Anglo-Saxon Chronicle*; annals; Burghal Hidage; County Hidage; Domesday Book; *Encomium Emmae Reginae*; episcopal lists; genealogies, royal; northern annals; regnal lists; *Regularis Concordia*; Tribal Hidage

Miscellaneous subjects (social, economic, etc.)

aerial reconnaissance; agriculture; animal husbandry; astronomy; bells and bellringing; bridges; [building materials and techniques]; [burial]; canals; children; [churl (*ceorl*)]; clothing; colloquies; *comitatus*; conversion; [demography]; [diet]; diseases; ealdorman; [earl]; entertainment; estate management; [expectation of life]; [farming]; *feorm*; feuds; field systems; fishing; food and drink; [foodrent]; [forests]; [fowling]; [games]; [*gesith*]; hawking and wildfowling; *heriot*; hide; hunting; kinship; labour service; [landscape]; land tenure; literacy; [lordship]; magic; malnutrition; manors and manorial lordship; manumission; markets and fairs; marriage and divorce; mills; mining and quarrying; [nobility]; oaths; ordeal; paganism; parasites; peasants; [population]; prostitution; reeve; roads; royal sites; [sake and soke]; [sheriff]; shire; slavery; social class; [sokemen]; [status]; surgery; taxation; thegn; [tithing]; towns; trade; transport and communication; [villages]; Watling Street; wergeld; widow; wills; women; woodland

Language

[ablaut]; [Anglian dialect]; Anglo-Norman (in pre-Conquest texts); [breaking]; Celtic languages; colour; dialects; dictionaries, modern; Germanic languages; Grimm's Law; [Kentish dialect]; loan-translations; loan-words; [Mercian dialect]; Old English; Old Norse; runes; semantic change; sound change; spelling and pronunciation; [strong verb]; syntax; Verner's Law; West Saxon dialect

Personal names and place-names

by-names; habitation names; *-ingas, -inga* names; personal names, Celtic; personal names, Old English; personal names, Scandinavian; place-names, Celtic; place-names, OE; place-names, Scandinavian; river names; topographical names

Church, religious practices, liturgy, etc.

alms; [antiphonary]; [Benedictional]; [Benedictine reform]; Bible; canon law; [canons]; cathedral clergy; chant; clergy; *Clofesho*; [collectar]; colloquies; confession and penance; [confraternity book]; computus; conversion; coronation; councils, church; creeds; [customary]; Easter controversy; excommunication; exorcism; [gradual]; [homiliary]; homilies; [hymnal]; hymns;

[Kalendar]; [lectionary]; [litany of the saints]; liturgical books; liturgical commemoration; liturgy; [manual (ritual)]; [martyrologies]; *Monasterialia Indicia*; monasticism; monastic sites; music; nunneries; [oblature]; [office]; ordeal; [pallium]; papacy; parochial organisation; [pastoral care]; penitentials; [Peter's Pence]; pilgrimage; pontifical ceremonies; prayer, private; [prayer book]; preaching; [Proverbs]; [Psalter]; psalter glosses; punctuation; *Regularis Concordia*; relics and relic-cults; Resting-Places of Saints; [sacraments]; [saints' Lives]; schools; [sermons]; shrines and reliquaries; Sunday Letter; sundials; *syllogae*; [synod]; *Theodulfi Capitula*; [troper]; Virgin, cult of; [Whitby, synod of]

Learning and literature

acrostics; alliteration; beasts of battle; [bestiaries]; charms; classical learning; colloquies; *comitatus*; computus; [curriculum]; dating of vernacular texts; dragons; [Dryhthelm]; [education]; elegies; [elves]; *enigmata*; exegesis; folklore; [formulae]; glossaries; glosses; gnomic poetry; gospel translation; grammar, Latin; hagiography; herbals; heroic poetry; [homiliary]; homilies; [kenning]; lapidaries; letter collections; libraries; literacy; [*Maxims*]; medical literature and medicine; metre, Latin; metre, OE; metrical calendar, Latin; metrical calendar, OE; music; musical instruments; octosyllables, Latin; oral-formulaic theory; poetic technique, Latin; poetic technique, OE; prose style, Latin; prose style, OE; [Proverbs]; punctuation; riddles, OE; runes; [saints' Lives]; schools; [sermons]; *syllogae*; [versification]; visions; wyrd

Manuscripts and libraries

Ælberht, abp of York; Ælfwine, Prayerbook of; Æthelstan Psalter; Æthelwold, Benedictional of; alphabet; Amiatinus, Codex; Barberini Gospels; *Beowulf* manuscript; bookbindings; [book-production]; [Bosworth Psalter]; [Cædmon manuscript]; carpet-pages; Cerne, Book of; codicology; colophons; Durrow, Book of; Echternach Gospels; Exeter Book; gospelbooks; Harley Psalter; Junius Manuscript; [Lambeth Psalter]; Leofric; libraries; Lindisfarne Gospels; literacy; [manuscripts]; [palaeography]; [Paris Psalter]; psalter glosses; punctuation; [Rushforth Gospels]; St Augustine's gospels; [Salisbury Psalter]; [scribes]; script, Anglo-Saxon; scriptorium; Stonyhurst Gospel of St John; [Stowe Psalter]; 'Tremulous Hand'; Utrecht Psalter; Vercelli Book; Vespasian Psalter; 'Winchester School'

Poetry

Old English: Advent Lyrics; *Andreas*; [*Azarias*]; *Battle of Brunanburh*; *Battle of Finnsburh*; *Battle of Maldon*; Bede's Death Song; *Beowulf*; biblical translation; poems; Cædmon; [*Christ I, II*]; *Christ III*; *Christ and Satan*; Cynewulf; *Daniel*; *Deor*; *Descent into Hell*; *Dream of the Rood*; *Exhortation to Christian Living*; *Exodus*; *Fates of the Apostles*; *Finnsburh Fragment*; *Fortunes of Men*; *Genesis*; *Gifts of Men*; *Husband's Message*; *Judith*; *Juliana*; [*Maxims*]; [*Menologium*]; metre, OE; metrical calendar, OE; music; oral-formulaic theory; *Order of the World*; *Phoenix*; *Physiologus*; poetic technique, OE; [*Precepts*]; punctuation; *Resignation*; *Rhyming Poem*; riddles, OE; *Ruin*; *Rune Poem*; *Seafarer*; *Seasons for Fasting*; [Sievers' five types]; *Solomon and Saturn, poetic*; *Soul and Body*; [stress]; *Vainglory*; Vercelli Book; [versification]; *Waldere*; *Wanderer*; *Widsith*; *Wife's Lament*; Wisdom literature; *Wulf and Eadwacer*
Latin: Ædiluulf; [Æthelwulf]; Æthilwald, poet; Alcuin; Aldhelm; Bede; Frithegod; John the

Old Saxon; metre, Latin; metrical calendar, Latin; music; octosyllables, Latin; oral-formulaic theory; poetic technique, Latin; Milred; Oswald the Younger; punctuation; *syllogae*; *tituli*; [versification]; Wulfstan Cantor
See also above, under Learning and literature

Prose

Old English: [*Adrian and Ritheus*]; Ælfric of Eynsham; Æthelwold, bp of Winchester; *Alexander the Great, Letter to Aristotle*; Aldred; Alfredian texts; *Anglo-Saxon Chronicle*; apocrypha, biblical, OE; *Apollonius of Tyre*; [Bald]; Benedictine Rule, OE; [Blickling Homilies]; [Boethius]; Byrhtferth; [Canons of Edgar]; homilies; Martyrology, OE; *Marvels of the East*; medical literature and medicine; *Monasterialia Indicia*; Orosius, OE translation of; [Paul, St, Vision of]; prose style, OE; psalter glosses; punctuation; Resting-Places of Saints; *Solomon and Saturn*, prose; Sunday Letter; *Theodulfi Capitula*; Vercelli Book; Werferth; Wulfstan the Homilist; [Wulfstan, voyage of]
Latin: Abbo of Fleury; Ælfhelm of Ely; Ælfric Bata; Æthelweard; Æthelwold, bp of Winchester; Alcuin; Aldhelm; Asser; Bede; Byrhtferth; [Eddius Stephanus]; Felix; Hadrian; hagiography; Lantfred; *Liber monstrorum*; *Marvels of the East*; prose style, Latin; punctuation; Stephen of Ripon; Tatwine; Theodore; Wulfstan Cantor
See also above, under Learning and literature

The Celtic world

Armes Prydein; Celtic influences; Celtic languages; Celts; Cornwall; Elmet; *Gododdin*; *Historia Brittonum*; personal names, Celtic; place-names, Celtic; Picts